Fourth **4** Edition

Auditing

Fourth **4** Edition

Auditing

Dan M. Guy
Vice President, Professional Standards and Technical Services
AMERICAN INSTITUTE OF CERTIFIED PUBLIC ACCOUNTANTS

C. Wayne Alderman
Dean of the College of Business and Professor of Accountancy
AUBURN UNIVERSITY

Alan J. Winters
Director of the School of Accountancy and Legal Studies
CLEMSON UNIVERSITY

The Dryden Press
Harcourt Brace College Publishers
Fort Worth Philadelphia San Diego New York Austin Orlando San Antonio
Toronto Montreal London Sydney Tokyo

Executive Editor Mike Reynolds
Developmental Editor Van Strength
Project Editor Amy Schmidt
Art Director Bill Brammer
Production Manager Eddie Dawson
Art & Literary Rights Editor Adele Krause
Product Manager Craig Johnson
Marketing Coordinator Kelly Whidbee
Copy Editor Karen Carriere
Proofreader Carolyn Crabtree
Compositor Beacon Graphics Corporation
Text Type 10/12 Janson
Cover Image Mark Humphries

The views expressed herein by Dan M. Guy do not necessarily reflect the views of the American Institute of Certified Public Accountants. The official positions of the Institute are determined through specific committee procedure, due process, and deliberation.

Address for Orders
The Dryden Press
6277 Sea Harbor Drive
Orlando, FL 32887-6777
1-800-782-4479 or 1-800-433-0001 (in Florida)

Address for Editorial Correspondence
The Dryden Press
301 Commerce Street, Suite 3700
Fort Worth, TX 76102

ISBN: 0-03-011693-7

Library of Congress Catalog Card Number: 94-74812

Printed in the United States of America
5 6 7 8 9 0 1 2 3   048   9 8 7 6 5 4 3 2 1

The Dryden Press
Harcourt Brace College Publishers

Objectives of an Auditing Course

Auditing is the capstone course in an undergraduate education for an accounting career. It integrates accounting standards, accounting systems, internal control structures, and the dual auditing functions of obtaining and evaluating evidence and reporting—all within the context of the professional environment. In teaching the course and in writing this textbook, we use an approach designed to produce competence in auditing theory and practice and to enhance the student's ability to cope with and produce change. To that end, we have extensively revised this edition of the book and produced a shorter, more concise text.

Fourth Edition

The Fourth Edition of *Auditing* has been revised to incorporate all new Statements on Auditing Standards and Statements of Standards on Attestation Engagements. In addition, end of chapter materials have been strengthened. We have included an Auditing Issues Case at the end of each chapter as well as an Audit Judgment Case. The Auditing Issues Case covers the audit of Kelco Manufacturing Company, and the case is designed so that each chapter covers a different aspect of the audit engagement. By using this case, students are better able to integrate auditing issues covered in specific chapters to the overall framework of an audit engagement.

Teaching Approach

Each chapter is based on a set of clearly defined learning objectives. These are presented at the beginning of each chapter, integrated with the text material, and used in the assignment materials at the end of the chapters. The learning objectives provide direction to the instructor in planning classroom activities and in drafting relevant examinations.

Assignment Material

End-of-chapter assignment material is crucial to the learning process. Consequently, the assignment material in *Auditing* provides complete coverage of chapter learning objectives and is consistent with the learning strategies employed in the text. Each chapter's learning objectives are represented by basic review questions, objective questions, problems and cases, auditing judgment cases, and an auditing issues case.

v

Organization of the Text

The text contains six major parts: The Auditing Environment, Chapters 1–3; Auditing Concepts, Chapters 4–7; Auditing Tools and Techniques, Chapters 8–11; The Audit Engagement, Chapters 12–19; Reporting Responsibilities, Chapters 20–22; and Internal, Operational, and Governmental Audits, Chapters 23–24.

The Auditing Environment

The first part of *Auditing* defines and discusses the environmental influences bearing upon the audit function. These chapters deal with the social function of auditing, the structure of authoritative standards, professional ethics, and legal liability.

Auditing Concepts

The second part presents the conceptual structure underlying the audit process by establishing the link between the risk of a material misstatement of financial statement assertions and the evidence the auditor gathers to reduce audit risk to an acceptably low level. By understanding this logical conceptual structure, students can successfully apply that structure in subsequent procedural chapters. Those chapters present a conceptual framework that uses authoritative standards (particularly *SAS No. 31, Evidential Matter*, and *SAS No. 47, Audit Risk and Materiality in Conducting an Audit*) as a point of departure and one that is compatible with a logical approach to the audit engagement.

Auditing Tools and Techniques

The third part of the textbook clarifies the role of auditing tools and techniques such as the computer, audit sampling methods, and analytical procedures. This presentation is highlighted by a chapter (11) on analytical procedures and their application in audit engagements. This chapter fills a void in auditing education created when students do not clearly understand the nature and role of analytical procedures and do not fully appreciate their usefulness.

Chapters 9 and 10 focus on the judgments auditors make in selecting and using various audit sampling techniques. This material integrates both statistical and non-statistical sampling.

The Audit Engagement

The fourth part applies the conceptual structure and the audit methods developed in the second and third parts to an audit engagement from the planning process to the completion of the fieldwork. This section covers three major areas: Chapter 12, Planning the Engagement; Chapters 13–18, Understanding the Internal Control Structure, Assessing Control Risk, and Performing Substantive Tests; and Chapter 19, Completing the Engagement.

Chapters 13–18 cover four basic transaction cycles: revenue, expenditure, conversion, and financing and investing. For each cycle the understanding of the internal control structure, assessing control risk, and substantive tests are discussed in relation to the financial statement assertions pertaining to the relevant transactions and account balances. This presentation helps the student understand the relationship between the internal control structure, control risk, and substantive tests for financial statement assertions. It also permits the instructor to focus on selected transaction cycles in planning the topics to be covered.

Reporting Responsibilities

The fifth part of the textbook includes two chapters on reporting and one on compilation and review services. Chapter 20 covers the types of audit reports that can be issued in an audit of financial statements. Chapter 21 covers other reports that an auditor may issue (for example, special reports, reports on internal control structure, and prospective financial information). Chapter 22 discusses both the performance and reporting requirements for compilation and review services of nonpublic entities.

Special Features

Special features of the textbook include:

- Chapter opening vignettes
- Learning objectives
- Integration of the audit evidence model throughout the textbook, which relates audit risk to financial statement assertions and to audit objectives and procedures
- Integration of the most recent authoritative pronouncements
- Extensive use of flowcharts and illustrations
- "Real World of Auditing" boxes that represent current news in auditing
- "Professional Judgment" boxes that represent areas where auditors must exercise professional and personal skills to problem solve
- Lotus 1-2-3–based spreadsheet software
- An integrated auditing issues case (Kelco Manufacturing Co.) at the end of each chapter
- Audit judgment cases
- Full coverage of governmental, internal, and operational auditing (Chapters 23 and 24)
- Two chapters on the computer and its role in the audit process (Chapters 7 and 8)
- Coverage of audit sampling by presenting concepts (Chapter 9) and following with application of sampling methods (Chapter 10)
- Full coverage of analytical procedures (Chapter 11)
- In-depth discussion of understanding the internal control structure, assessing control risk, and performing substantive tests in relation to financial statement assertions (Chapters 13–18)
- Complete coverage of compilation and review engagements (Chapter 22)

Assignment of Chapters

Because the authors recognize the wide variety of teaching approaches in use, the textbook is designed to provide maximum flexibility in assigning chapters. The following suggestions may be helpful:

- Chapters 1–3 cover the auditing environment. However, some instructors prefer to cover professional ethics (Chapter 2) and legal liability (Chapter 3) later in the course. Internal and operational auditing (Chapter 24) can be integrated with Chapter 1.

- Chapters 4–7 cover auditing concepts and should generally be covered early in the course and in the sequence presented. Chapter 7 on computers and the internal control structure can be partially covered or eliminated, if necessary, as can the discussion of working papers in Chapter 5.

- Chapters 8–11 discuss the computer as an audit tool and cover audit sampling and analytical procedures. Instructors in institutions that offer a second auditing course may choose to reduce or omit coverage of these chapters in the first course.

- Chapters 12–19 concern the audit engagement. Chapter 12 on planning the engagement and Chapter 19 on completing the engagement should generally be covered. Chapters 13–18 discuss understanding the internal control structure, assessing control risk, and performing substantive tests for the four basic transaction cycles. Instructors who prefer a more conceptual approach or who are under time constraints may choose to give thorough coverage to only one or two of these cycles and to reduce or omit the others.

- Chapter 20 on audit reports can be covered after Chapter 1 if the instructor desires.

- Chapters 21–24 on reporting, compilation and review, compliance auditing, and internal and operational auditing can be partially covered or omitted from the first auditing course.

Supplementary Materials

The *Miller Comprehensive GAAS Guide: College Student Edition*, published every December, provides a comprehensive restatement of all current Statements on Auditing Standards and Statements of Standards on Attestation Engagements. The *GAAS Guide* is organized by topic and is fully cross-referenced to all original pronouncements.

The Dryden Press will provide complimentary ancillaries or ancillary packages to those *qualified* adopters under our adoption policy. Based on our adoption policy, please contact your sales representative if you would like to know if or how you may qualify. If the adopter or potential user does not use or will not be needing any of the materials received, please return materials to your sales representative or send them to:

> **ATTN:** *Returns Department*
> Troy Warehouse
> 465 South Lincoln Drive
> Troy, MO 63379

Acknowledgments

We acknowledge and thank the American Institute of Certified Public Accountants for its permission to quote extensively from the Code of Professional Conduct, Statements on Auditing Standards, other authoritative pronouncements, and the Uniform CPA Examination. These materials make a significant contribution to the text.

We also gratefully acknowledge the cooperation of the following organizations and people for granting permission to use their materials: The Institute of Internal Auditors, the Institute of Certified Management Accountants of the Institute of Management Accountants for the use of questions and unofficial answers from past CMA examinations, the American Accounting Association, Price Waterhouse & Co., Ernst & Young, Deloitte and Touche, Abraham D. Akresh and John E. Mitchell, Arnie Pahler of San Jose State University, and Fred Neumann of the University of Illinois.

We appreciate the contribution of those reviewers, including those from previous editions, who have so graciously helped us update the current edition: Mohammad J. Abdolmohammadi, Bentley College; Michael Akers, Marquette University; June Y. Aono, University of Hawaii at Manoa; Richard Asebrook, University of Massachusetts; S. Douglas Beets, Wake Forest University; Adrian Fitzsimons, St. John's University; Dan R. Hines, East Carolina University; Rita Hull, Virginia Commonwealth University; Raymond N. Johnson, Portland State University; Howard A. Kanter, DePaul University; David Kerr, Texas A&M University; Joyce C. Lambert, University of New Orleans; Arnold J. Pahler, San Jose State University; Alan Reinstein, Wayne State University; James H. Scheiner, Florida International University; and Ben S. Trotter, Texas Tech University.

We are especially indebted to the members of the book team at The Dryden Press: Mike Reynolds, Executive Editor; Van Strength, Developmental Editor; Amy Schmidt, Project Editor; Bill Brammer, Designer; and Eddie Dawson, Production Manager. Their ideas, guidance, encouragement, and patience contributed significantly to the book. We also appreciate the contributions of Walt Conn, KPMG Peat Marwick; Herbert Finklestein, AICPA; and Phil Cook, Michael Eanes, Mary Ann Hooper, and Cynthia Spinks all of Auburn University.

We wish to thank those who contributed to the ancillary package. We appreciate the contributions of Mark Beasley, Kent Finkle, and Sean Lanham, who each have enhanced the ancillary program.

Finally, the encouragement, support, and understanding of our families and friends was critical to the completion of this book and deeply appreciated.

Dan M. Guy
C. Wayne Alderman
Alan J. Winters

Dan M. Guy, Ph.D., CPA

Dan Guy is Vice President of Professional Standards and Technical Services at the American Institute of Certified Public Accountants (AICPA), which places him at the head of its Auditing Standards Division and its Accounting Standards Division. He is also the U.S. technical advisor to the International Federation of Accountants. Prior to his tenure with the AICPA, he was a member of the faculty at Texas Tech University for seven years and served as visiting professor at the University of Texas in 1978. He received his Ph.D. from the University of Alabama. His works have been published in a number of prestigious accounting journals, and he is the author of three books and over 50 articles.

C. Wayne Alderman, DBA, CPA

C. Wayne Alderman is Dean of the College of Business and Professor of Accountancy at Auburn University. He received his Bachelor of Science in Business and his Master of Business Administration degrees from Auburn University. In 1977 he earned a Doctor of Business Administration degree at the University of Tennessee and has since worked as teacher, author, administrator, and consultant. Throughout his career, Professor Alderman has received numerous teaching awards and has three times been recognized as "outstanding teacher" at Auburn University. As an author, Professor Alderman has written numerous continuing professional education courses, which he has also taught in over 20 states. He is a coauthor of college textbooks in the areas of auditing and accounting information systems. Professor Alderman has also been published in many academic journals. He serves as a consultant to several CPA firms.

Alan J. Winters, Ph.D., CPA

Alan J. Winters is Director of the School of Accountancy and Legal Studies at Clemson University, and was formerly Director of Auditing Research for the American Institute of CPAs. He holds the Ph.D. from Texas Tech University and was formerly Professor of Accounting at the University of South Carolina and Louisiana State University. He is a past member of the AICPA's Accounting and Review Services Committee. He also served as chairman of the task force that developed *SAS No. 55* and was the staff director responsible for the development of the AICPA's attestation standards. He has served as a consultant to various groups and accounting firms. He has published numerous articles in professional and academic journals, and is coauthor of two accounting and auditing handbooks. He has also developed many CPE courses for CPAs.

Brief Contents

Table of Contents

Fourth **4** Edition

Auditing

The Audit Function in Society

Learning Objectives

- Define auditing and identify the factors that generate a demand for it.

- Identify the three broad types of audits and the three types of auditors.

- Describe the important elements of the independent auditor's standard report, and identify the three other types of reports.

- List the organizations that affect auditing and describe their effect.

- Describe the requirements for becoming a CPA (certified public accountant).

- Discuss the organizational structure within a CPA firm and the services typically offered.

- Explain the relationship of auditing standards to auditing procedures.

- Describe the ten generally accepted auditing standards.

- Discuss quality control standards and quality review.

W ithout question, the independent audit function plays an important role in both business and society. Numerous third parties, including investors, creditors, and regulators, depend on the competence and professional integrity of independent auditors.

The 1989 failure of Lincoln Savings and Loan Association is an example of the dire consequences that can result from a breakdown in the audit function. Lincoln's collapse, which cost taxpayers at least $2.5 billion, was blamed in part on the thrift's auditors.

In making its case against the Big Six accounting firm, the government charged that the firm did not challenge the fictitious real estate sales that falsely inflated Lincoln's reported profits. Critics also questioned why auditors did not blow the whistle on Lincoln's burgeoning loan portfolio, which grew from $600 million to $6 billion in just five years.

As part of a settlement for the Lincoln case, and a number of other cases involving S&Ls it audited, the firm agreed to pay a fine of $400 million. Government officials hailed the settlement as a landmark victory and claimed it set a precedent for tightening standards of professional responsibility. ∎

Sources: "A Landmark Fine," *Time*, December 7, 1992, p. 28; "Bad Day at Jones Day," *Time*, April 3, 1993, p. 23; "Law and Disorder," *Canadian Business*, September 1993, p. 82.

Economic decisions are typically based upon the information available to the decision maker. To obtain the most benefit, users should have economic information that is both relevant and reliable. According to *Statement of Financial Accounting Concepts No. 1*, for information to be ***relevant*** it must "be capable of making a difference in a decision by helping users to form predictions about the outcomes of past, present and future events or to confirm or correct expectations." For information to be ***reliable*** it must "represent what it purports to represent."

This need for relevant and reliable financial information creates a demand for accounting and auditing services. Bankers and creditors need reliable information to make lending decisions, and investors need such information to make well-informed buy or sell decisions. Other users, for example, management and the government, also need reliable financial information to make decisions.

Role of Auditing

The demand for auditing results from four underlying factors: complexity, remoteness, bias and motives of the provider, and consequences.

Complexity

The volume of economic activity in business and other entities, along with the complexity of these economic exchanges, often makes it difficult to record properly transactions and allocations of costs and revenues. Difficult decisions regarding accounting treatments and disclosure require the services of professional accountants.

Remoteness

In today's environment, the decision maker is frequently separated from the organization. For example, a shareholder of a large corporation such as General Motors may never see the corporation or its facilities. In these cases the decision maker does not have firsthand knowledge of the organization and its activities and is separated from the organization's accounting records. Remoteness increases the likelihood both of intentional or unintentional misstatement and of demand for an independent party to examine the financial records.

Bias and Motives of the Provider

Whenever financial information is provided from a source that lacks independence, the user of that financial information may question the biases and motives of the provider. The provider of the financial information may have either an intentional or unintentional conflict of interest with the user of that financial information. For example, if management is naturally more optimistic about the future of the entity than others, it may lead to biased financial information in such areas as collectibility of accounts receivable. Biases and potential conflicts of interest create a demand for an independent party to lend credibility to the entity's financial information by auditing financial statements. Thus, auditor independence is necessary for users to believe that an audit is valuable.

Consequences

One characteristic of our society is the breadth and depth of participation by individuals, companies, and other entities in the marketplace. In today's economic environment, economic decisions often involve tremendous expenditures and affect many people. These important decisions require relevant and reliable financial information.

Auditing Defined

The American Accounting Association Committee on Basic Auditing Concepts has defined *auditing* as

a systematic process of objectively obtaining and evaluating evidence regarding assertions about economic actions and events to ascertain the degree of correspondence between those assertions and established criteria and communicating the results to interested users.

Figure 1–1 illustrates the important concepts underlying the term *auditing*.

Figure 1–1   **Definition of Auditing**

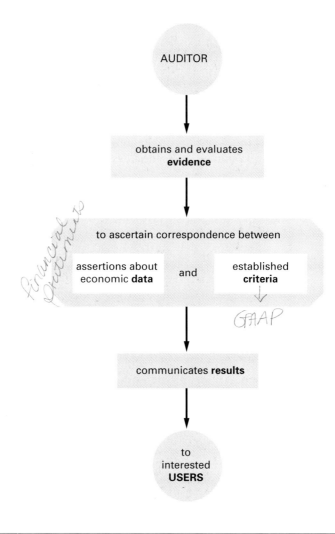

A Systematic Process

As a systematic process, auditing is a logical, purposeful, structured approach to decision making; it is not an unplanned, haphazard process.

Objectively Obtaining and Evaluating Evidence

Auditing involves the collection of evidence. Evidence represents information that will affect the auditor's decision process. Evidence may take a variety of forms, such as examination of documents, observations by the auditor, and confirmations of balances from third parties. Although the evidence itself may be more or less conclusive in nature, the process of collecting and evaluating evidence must be as objective as possible.

Assertions about Economic Actions and Events

A basic component of the auditing process is the collection of evidence regarding assertions about economic actions and events. These assertions relate to the financial statements. When conducting an audit, the auditor is given financial information and financial statements by the auditee. These financial statements represent the auditee's assertions about economic actions and events and include not only the financial statements themselves but also the accounting information system and the accounting process.

The Degree of Correspondence between Assertions and Established Criteria

While auditing financial statements, the auditor's objective is to determine whether the auditee's assertions correspond to the established criteria, which typically is referred to as generally accepted accounting principles or GAAP. In some circumstances, however, the auditor examines assertions other than those contained in financial statements. For example, a governmental auditor may be determining whether or not a contractor properly charged overhead in accordance with the governmental contract. Thus, the auditor examines the contractor's overhead to determine if it in fact complies with government criteria for overhead recognition.

Communicating Results to Interested Users

The audit serves little purpose if the auditor gathers evidence about economic actions and events and ascertains that these have been appropriately reflected in accordance with established criteria, but does not communicate the result to interested users. In the profession, the communication of the auditor's assurance on information is referred to as *attestation*, or the *attest function*.

Professional Judgment

Professional Standards

Even though professional standards exist to provide guidelines in performing an audit, the auditor's judgment in the design and application of specific audit procedures is an equally important aspect of the engagement. In 1977, the Securities and Exchange Commission (SEC) determined that the accounting firm of Lester Witte & Company failed to test adequately the controls related to accounts receivable of a particular client, J.B. Lippincott Company, and therefore exhibited a lack of judgment in the design of the related substantive tests.

Lippincott officials requested that 48 accounts not be confirmed. Because these accounts represented a small portion of the total number of accounts, the auditors decided not to apply appropriate alternative procedures to these particular receivable balances. The judgment of the auditors in failing to perform adequate testing demonstrates how client management should not be allowed to influence critical audit decisions. The lack of properly documenting any follow-up procedure that the accounting firm may have used can be construed as a violation of the third general standard, which requires auditors to exercise due professional care in the performance of an audit.

Source: N. R. Kleinfeld, "Harper's Headache with Lippincott," *New York Times*, August 9, 1979, pp. D1, D2.

Development of Auditing

Before the Industrial Revolution, auditing was not a formally recognized profession. However, historical documents indicate that even in ancient times, people used auditors to increase the credibility of financial information. For example, ancient Egyptian rulers used scribes working independently of each other to examine financial records. Likewise, the sixteenth-century trading companies that explored the New World employed auditors to verify financial records.

The Industrial Revolution was a primary impetus for the auditing profession. During the nineteenth century, companies expanded facilities, changed production methods, and created complex organizational structures. One result was that owners became less involved in directing their enterprises, assigning that function to professional managers. This separation of ownership from management increased the demand for auditing because the biases and motives of managers sometimes differed from those of the owners, who were the users of the financial statements. During the Industrial Revolution, the audit's primary purpose was to detect fraud and to assess the stewardship of the managers for the stockholders. A significant event for auditors was the passage of the Companies Act of 1862 in Great Britain, which required corporations or stock companies to have independent audits.

In the early 1900s, the emphasis of auditing shifted from the detection of fraud to the needs of the various users of financial statements. The growth of capital and credit markets (with their varied user constituents) further increased the demand for auditing. Changes in technology have also generated changes in audit methods during the latter half of the twentieth century. For example, the increasing complexity of computer data processing has created a demand for auditors to become more familiar with the information systems that generate transactions.

Relationship of Accounting and Auditing

People often assume that auditing is a branch or subdivision of accounting: auditing is typically taught as an accounting course, and auditors are generally known as accountants. However, there are significant differences between accounting and auditing.

Accounting is concerned with identifying, recording, and summarizing economic events. The end result of the accounting process is the financial statement. The overall objective of accounting is to provide financial information about economic entities that is useful in making economic decisions.

The primary purpose of *auditing* is to test accounting measurements for propriety. Whereas the accountant creates financial information in the form of financial statements, the auditor enhances the credibility of the financial statements by independent verification communicated through the audit report. The end result of the audit process is the audit opinion regarding the fairness of the financial statements in conformity with generally accepted accounting principles. Since auditors are testing records, they must naturally know accounting and generally accepted accounting principles. For this reason, auditors are also accountants.

Types of Audits

As previously defined, auditing is a process of gathering evidence regarding assertions about economic actions and events to ascertain the degree of correspondence between those assertions and established criteria for various users. There are several types of audits. The traditional type of audit is the audit of financial statements. However, auditors also may perform other attest engagements, including the traditional compliance audit and the operational audit.

Audits and Financial Statements

Audits of financial statements focus on whether financial statements conform to specified criteria. Auditors express an opinion as to whether the statements are fairly presented in conformity with generally accepted accounting principles. The primary characteristics of a financial audit are shown in Table 1–1.

Other Attest Engagements

Auditors are often requested to issue written reports regarding the reliability of assertions other than financial statements. Some of these audits are referred to as compliance audits in that they measure the compliance of an auditee with established criteria. For example, most companies have formal written policies and procedures. Auditors performing a compliance audit may be determining if employees have followed the policies and procedures established by management.

Audits that are concerned with the effectiveness and efficiency of the organization are known as operational audits. *Effectiveness* measures how successfully an organization achieves its goals and objectives. *Efficiency* measures how well an entity uses its resources to achieve its goals. For example, an auditor may examine a federal agency to determine if the agency is meeting its objectives as identified by Congress (effectiveness) and is using its financial resources wisely (efficiency).

Table 1-1	Important Characteristics of a Financial Statement Audit

- The objective of an audit is to add credibility to management's representations in financial statements.
- Auditors are independent of the entity's management, the preparers of financial statements. An auditor is not the representative of any particular group.
- Auditors form their opinions on the overall fairness, in conformity with GAAP, of the financial statements on the basis of selective testing. They rarely audit all of an individual item in the financial statements or all of the items in the financial statements.
- An audit is directed toward the discovery of *material* misstatements in the financial statements no matter what causes the misstatement.
- An audit provides reasonable assurance that the financial statements are free of material misstatement. Auditors are never absolutely certain about whether the financial statements are accurate.
- Auditors report on the financial statements as a *whole* and not on the individual items within the financial statements.
- An auditor is concerned with the financial presentation and *not* the financial quality of an entity, the wisdom of its management's decisions, or the risk of doing business with the entity.

Types of Auditors

Auditors are typically classified into three categories: independent auditors, internal auditors, and governmental auditors. Each may perform any of the three types of audits previously discussed.

Independent Auditors

Independent auditors, also known as external auditors, are certified public accountants (CPAs) who have their own independent practices and offer auditing and other services to clients. A company engages a CPA to perform an independent audit of the company's financial statements. The client pays the auditor's fee, but the auditor is generally considered to be independent of the client because the auditor serves numerous clients.

CPAs audit all of the publicly held companies and many nonpublic companies in the United States. Frequently, the terms *auditor* and *CPA* are used synonymously, even though other types of auditors exist.

CPAs may also perform compliance and operational audits. However, most CPAs primarily audit financial statements. The main emphasis of this book is on independent auditors and the performance of financial audits.

Responsibilities of the Independent Auditor

The auditor's responsibility is to audit the client's financial statements and gather sufficient competent evidential matter to render an opinion regarding the client's financial statements. The financial statements are the client's responsibility; that is, the client is responsible for recording, summarizing, and classifying economic transactions and allocations. The auditor is responsible for reporting whether the financial statements conform fairly with generally accepted accounting principles.

Types of Reports

The financial audit culminates when the auditor communicates the findings to users through an audit report that expresses the auditor's opinion on the client's financial statements. The audit report describes in broad terms what the auditor has done and what the auditor has found. A more detailed discussion of audit reports is presented in Chapter 20.

Unqualified Opinions The most common end-product of the financial audit is the auditor's standard report, or unqualified opinion. If, after gathering evidence, the auditor is satisfied that the financial statements are fairly presented in conformity with generally accepted accounting principles, the auditor then issues an unqualified opinion, that is, it has no qualifying phrases. An example of an unqualified opinion is shown in Figure 1–2.

Several distinct elements make up the standard report, including the following:

Title The audit report always has a title stating that it is an independent auditor's report.

Figure 1-2	**Example of an Auditor's Standard Report**

REPORT OF INDEPENDENT CERTIFIED PUBLIC ACCOUNTANTS

KPMG Peat Marwick

Certified Public Accountants

303 Peachtree Street, N.E.
Suite 2000
Atlanta, GA 30308

The Board of Directors and Shareholders
Total System Services, Inc.:

We have audited the accompanying consolidated balance sheets of Total System Services, Inc. and subsidiaries as of December 31, 1993 and 1992, and the related consolidated statements of income, shareholders' equity, and cash flows for each of the years in the three-year period ended December 31, 1993. These consolidated financial statements are the responsibility of the Company's management. Our responsibility is to express an opinion on these consolidated financial statements based on our audits.

We conducted our audits in accordance with generally accepted auditing standards. Those standards require that we plan and perform the audit to obtain reasonable assurance about whether the consolidated financial statements are free of material misstatement. An audit includes examining, on a test basis, evidence supporting the amounts and disclosures in the consolidated financial statements. An audit also includes assessing the accounting principles used and significant estimates made by management, as well as evaluating the overall financial statement presentation. We believe that our audits provide a reasonable basis for our opinion.

In our opinion, the consolidated financial statements referred to above present fairly, in all material respects, the financial position of Total System Services, Inc. and subsidiaries at December 31, 1993 and 1992, and the results of their operations and their cash flows for each of the years in the three-year period ended December 31, 1993 in conformity with generally accepted accounting principles.

KPMG Peat Marwick

February 25, 1994

Address   The audit report is addressed to the owners or to the stockholders and board of directors of a business enterprise rather than to management, because it is the owners or board of directors who hire the independent auditor.

Introductory Paragraph   The standard audit report is typically divided into three paragraphs: an introductory paragraph, a scope paragraph, and an opinion paragraph. The *introductory paragraph* identifies the financial statements being audited and differentiates between management's responsibilities for the financial statements and the auditor's role in expressing an opinion.

Scope Paragraph   The *scope paragraph* describes the nature of the audit. In this paragraph, the auditor makes a factual statement about the work performed, indicating that the audit was conducted in accordance with generally accepted auditing standards, which included any auditing procedures that the auditor deemed necessary in the circumstances.

Opinion Paragraph   In the *opinion paragraph*, the auditor identifies the basis of preparation of the financial statement (usually, generally accepted accounting principles) and gives the auditor's opinion using professional judgment as to the fairness of presentation of the financial statements.

Date of the Report The report is usually dated as of the last day of the auditor's field work—that is, the last day that the auditor performs any significant audit procedures. This date is important for legal reasons, as is discussed in Chapter 3. The auditor has certain responsibilities regarding any significant events that occur from the date of the balance sheet to the date of the audit report, events that may require either disclosure in or adjustment of the financial statements. These requirements are discussed in more detail in Chapter 19.

Signature The audit report should be signed by the CPA firm that has performed the audit. This indicates that the firm, rather than any one individual or partner, takes the responsibility for the audit.

Although the auditor and the client would generally prefer an unqualified opinion that the financial statements are fairly presented in accordance with generally accepted accounting principles, sometimes conditions exist that necessitate issuing one of three other types of reports: the qualified opinion, the adverse opinion, and the disclaimer of opinion.

Qualified Opinions In a qualified opinion, the auditor reports that the financial statements are fairly presented *except for* some material item(s). Qualified opinions are so categorized because the opinion sentence includes an *except for* qualifying phrase. For example, a CPA may state that the financial statements are fairly presented in conformity with generally accepted accounting principles except for inventories that the auditor was unable to observe.

Adverse Opinions In an adverse opinion, the auditor gives an opinion that the financial statements are *not* fairly presented in conformity with generally accepted accounting principles. Because the auditor is giving an opinion (although a negative one), sufficient evidence should exist to support this conclusion. Adverse opinions are infrequent because most entities strive for fair presentation of the financial statements.

Disclaimer of Opinion In a disclaimer of opinion, the auditor states that he or she is unable to give an opinion. For example, important accounting records may have been destroyed by a fire and the auditor may be precluded from gathering sufficient evidence to issue any type of opinion.

Conditions Resulting in a Departure from an Unqualified Opinion

Three types of conditions preclude an auditor from issuing an unqualified opinion. These conditions are summarized in Table 1–2 and discussed here:

Departure from Generally Accepted Accounting Principles If the client departs materially from generally accepted accounting principles, the auditor cannot render an unqualified opinion that the financial statements are presented fairly. For example, the client may have used replacement cost on property, plant, and equipment rather than historical cost. This departure, if material, would require modification of the unqualified opinion.

Scope *Scope* refers to the auditor's ability to perform the audit procedures deemed necessary. If unable to perform a procedure that is considered important, the auditor is precluded from issuing an unqualified opinion. Scope limitations can come

| Table 1-2 | Conditions That Preclude an Unqualified Opinion |

KNOW!! (handwritten)

	Type of Report			
Condition	Unqualified	Qualified	Disclaimer	Adverse
Departure from GAAP	If departure is immaterial	If departure is material	—	If departure is very material
Scope	If limitation is immaterial	If limitation is material	If limitation is very material	—
Lack of Independence	—	—	Only report that can be issued	—

Note: An item would be classified as very material if it would have an impact of great significance on the overall financial statements.

from one of two sources: client restrictions or restrictions caused by circumstances. For example, the client may instruct the auditor not to confirm certain accounts receivable. Restrictions caused by circumstances that restrict the scope of the auditor's work are typically beyond the client's or the auditor's control. For example, if the auditor is engaged after year-end to audit the financial statements, then it may be simply impossible to observe or otherwise support inventories as of year-end. Material scope restrictions require modification of the auditor's standard report.

Lack of Independence Independence is the cornerstone of the external audit. Financial statements users need assurance by an independent third party that the financial statements are fairly presented. Without independence, the auditor's opinion is of limited value. Consequently, the auditor who is not independent is precluded from issuing an opinion—and therefore must disclaim an opinion.

Internal Auditors

Internal auditors are hired as full-time employees of entities to conduct audits within the organization. Consequently, they are mainly concerned with determining whether or not organizational policies and procedures have been followed and with safeguarding the organization's assets. They may also be involved with reviewing the effectiveness and efficiency of operating procedures and with determining the reliability of information generated within the organization. Internal auditors primarily perform compliance audits and operational audits. Internal auditors may be certified as Certified Internal Auditors by the Institute of Internal Auditors.

Internal auditors typically report to the organization's board of directors, the primary users of the internal auditor's work. However, internal auditors affect a variety of other constituents too, including management, shareholders, and independent auditors. Internal auditing is discussed in detail in Chapter 24.

Government Auditors

A wide variety of federal, state, and local agencies use auditors to determine compliance with laws, statutes, policies, and procedures. For example, auditors for the Internal Revenue Service conduct compliance audits on tax returns to determine whether or not taxpayers have complied with tax laws. Department of Defense auditors often examine defense contractors whose contracts with the federal government include clauses regarding cost-plus or overhead agreements.

Perhaps the most common government audit activity is conducted by the General Accounting Office (GAO). The GAO, headed by the comptroller general, is an agency of Congress that audits the executive branch of government and reports directly to the legislative branch. In many ways its audit responsibilities resemble those of independent auditors. However, the GAO is also heavily involved in both compliance auditing and operational auditing. The GAO must determine whether or not government agencies have complied with federal statutes and regulations. Likewise, the GAO is concerned with evaluating the effectiveness and efficiency of various federal agencies and programs.

The GAO issues its reports to the Congress. The types of reports the GAO issues depend in large degree on the type of audit. The results of these audits are usually made available to the public and consequently are often used in the political arena.

Organizations That Affect Auditing

The auditing profession includes a variety of professional groups whose members either practice auditing or have a strong interest in auditing. These groups include the American Institute of Certified Public Accountants, the Institute of Internal Auditors, and the American Accounting Association. In addition, one federal agency, the Securities and Exchange Commission, has had a significant effect on the auditing profession.

American Institute of Certified Public Accountants

The American Institute of Certified Public Accountants (AICPA) is the national professional organization for CPAs. Originally founded in 1887 as the American Association of Public Accountants, the AICPA has a current membership of more than 310,000 CPAs in public practice, industry, government, and education. The AICPA has had an enormous effect on both accounting and auditing, and performs a variety of functions including setting auditing standards, upholding the profession's code of conduct, providing continuing education, and preparing and grading the Uniform CPA Examination.

Establishment of Standards

The AICPA has been instrumental in establishing standards in accounting and auditing. For example, the Accounting Principles Board (APB) was a committee of the AICPA that for many years promulgated authoritative pronouncements related to generally accepted accounting principles. Although the APB is no longer in existence, the AICPA continues to promote accounting standards. We will examine some of the most important standards at the end of the chapter.

Research and Publication

The AICPA has actively supported auditing and accounting research and the dissemination of the findings of research through its publications. AICPA publications include the *Journal of Accountancy*, *The Tax Advisor*, Accounting Research Studies, Auditing Research Monographs, Industry Audit and Accounting Guides, and *Accounting Trends and Techniques.*

Continuing Education

The AICPA actively supports continuing education through its sponsorship of a variety of seminars and other educational tools. It requires its members in public practice to have 120 hours of continuing professional education over a three-year period, with a minimum of 20 hours per year.

Institute of Internal Auditors

The Institute of Internal Auditors (IIA), an international voluntary professional organization, has been active in supporting the internal auditing branch of the profession and in establishing standards for internal auditing. The IIA has issued *Statements of Responsibilities of Internal Auditors* and *Standards for the Professional Practice of Internal Auditing*. It publishes a bimonthly journal, *The Internal Auditor*. The IIA also administers the Certified Internal Auditor examination, which is a professional certification program for internal auditors. This examination and the IIA are discussed in more detail in Chapter 24.

American Accounting Association / *Educators* .

The American Accounting Association (AAA) is the organization for accounting educators but its membership includes practitioners as well as academic accountants. The AAA encourages research in accounting and auditing, including its publication of *A Statement of Basic Auditing Concepts*, considered by many to be a leading source of auditing theory. The Auditing Section is composed of those members of the AAA whose primary area of interest is auditing.

Securities and Exchange Commission

The Securities and Exchange Commission (SEC) was established by Congress in 1934 to regulate the distribution of securities to the public and the interstate trading of securities in the securities exchanges. A primary concern of the SEC is that investors have appropriate financial information when they make investment decisions. The SEC has actively promoted generally accepted accounting principles and insisted upon auditing practice and reporting standards. The SEC's role in auditing is discussed further in Chapter 3.

Public Accounting

Independent or external auditors are typically certified public accountants. Although some states license public accountants, there is a distinction between the public accountant and the CPA. In most states only CPAs are allowed to perform audits and issue audit reports. Public accountants normally are allowed to perform only bookkeeping and tax services. The phrase *public accounting* generally refers to the practice of CPAs.

Requirements for Certification

Currently, no national licensing of CPAs exists: CPAs are licensed by the states, not the federal government. Most states have boards of accountancy that have the sole authority both to grant CPA certificates and to suspend or revoke such certificates. Generally, states will reciprocate with other states and allow CPAs from another state to practice as CPAs on a temporary basis.

To become a CPA, a candidate must meet the requirements of a particular state. In most states these requirements center upon three areas: education, experience, and the Uniform CPA Examination. In addition, most states and the AICPA now require continuing professional education once a person receives a CPA certificate.

Education

Most states require CPAs to have an undergraduate college degree. This often includes a requirement for a specific number of hours in accounting courses. Most states also now require that candidates have 150 semester hours (225 quarter hours) or a fifth year of education before they can become CPAs. The AICPA has established a requirement for AICPA membership of 150 semester hours of education, including a bachelor's degree, to be effective after the year 2000. All states have been encouraged to adopt the same requirement.

Experience

Some states require CPAs to meet certain experience requirements, usually one or two years of practical experience. Some states define practical experience as experience working with a CPA firm, whereas others also allow experience with governmental agencies, internal auditors, and managerial accounting to count as experience.

Examination

All states require that candidates pass the uniform national CPA examination. This examination is designed by the AICPA but is administered by each of the states. The examination is 2 days long and is offered twice a year, during the first week of May and November. It covers four areas: auditing, business law and professional responsibility, accounting and reporting (taxation, managerial, and governmental and non-profit organizations), and financial accounting and reporting (business enterprises). Approximately 10% of candidates taking the examination pass all parts at the first sitting. In most states candidates are allowed a conditional pass, which means at the next sitting the candidate does not have to take previously passed sections but only the remaining sections that need to be passed. At any given sitting of the CPA examination, approximately 30% of the candidates pass a given part.

Continuing Professional Education

Because of an ever-changing and expanding body of knowledge, most states require an average of 30 to 40 contact hours a year of continuing professional education for CPAs.

Types of Services

CPA firms offer five types of services: auditing, tax, consulting services, accounting and review services, and personal financial planning. A CPA firm may emphasize any one of these five areas, but most CPA firms offer all five types of services.

Auditing

In most states, only CPAs can conduct independent audits of financial statements. Auditing represents the primary service of many CPA firms both in terms of time spent and revenues earned.

Tax

Tax services represent an important component of the overall services provided by CPAs and are the primary service offered by some CPA firms.

CPAs engage in two broad categories of tax services: compliance work and tax planning. In performing compliance work, CPAs are engaged in the actual preparation of tax returns for corporations, individuals, estates and trusts, and others. In tax planning, the CPA anticipates the future consequences of taxation upon a client and determines how best to minimize future tax liabilities while at the same time meeting the client's requirements.

Consulting Services

Most CPAs provide a variety of services that allow their clients to operate more effectively and efficiently. These consulting services (also called management advisory or administrative services) may be rendered to an existing audit or tax client, or to a client for whom no other services are performed. Consulting services include computer systems analyses, installation of budgeting processes, accounting information systems, and any other activity for which the CPA has an expertise that will benefit the client.

Accounting and Review Services

CPA firms also offer bookkeeping (or write-up work) and accounting and review services for their clients. In these situations, the CPA may perform a variety of tasks, from actually recording transactions in the journal and making postings to the general ledger to drafting financial statements from the ledgers that the client has prepared. In performing these other services the CPA may issue either a compilation or a review report. *Compilation reports* provide no assurance by the CPA as to the fairness of the financial statements in conformity with generally accepted accounting principles, whereas *review reports* provide limited assurance as to the financial statements. Compilation and review reports are discussed in detail in Chapter 22.

Personal Financial Planning

CPA firms also advise clients on the planning and management of their personal finances. The AICPA offers the designation "Accredited Personal Financial Specialist" (APFS) to CPAs who meet certain requirements, including satisfying an experience requirement and passing a one-day AICPA examination on personal financial planning in such areas as income tax planning, risk management planning, investment planning, retirement planning, and estate planning. The APFS designation is the only specialist designation currently recognized by the AICPA.

Organization of the Profession

CPA firms may either be sole proprietorships, partnerships, professional corporations (PC), limited liability companies (LLC), or limited liability partnerships (LLP). Sole proprietors are individual CPAs in their own practice, while partnerships represent a group of CPAs in a practice. Professional corporations have the corporate advantage of limited liability to the owners but are taxed like a partnership. Severe legal limitations in the way PCs must function discourage most larger CPA firms from practicing as PCs. In recent years, many states have enacted laws authorizing LLCs and LLPs as additional forms of business organization.

In LLPs, partners remain personally liable for their own wrongful acts, the wrongful acts of staff under their supervision, and certain commercial debts incurred by the firm. The LLPs' assets, including the partners' capital investments, remain fully exposed to satisfying partnership obligations. However, a partner's personal assets are protected from seizure in settlement of claims and claims resulting from wrongful acts of another partner. Thus, LLPs allow CPA firms to practice as partnerships but remove the single greatest disadvantage to the traditional partnership today—the liability that each partner shoulders for the business debts and professional liabilities incurred by the firm. This potential liability, which has historically not been a major factor, has in recent years become very significant to many CPA firms because of the current malpractice environment in the United States. CPA firms are generally classified into four categories: Big Six firms, national firms, regional firms, and local firms.

Big Six Firms

The six largest public accounting firms in the United States, all of which operate internationally, are commonly referred to as the Big Six. These six firms audit most major corporations in the United States and all have annual revenues in the hundreds of millions of dollars. These firms include Arthur Andersen & Co., LLP; Coopers & Lybrand, LLP; Deloitte and Touche, LLP; Ernst & Young, LLP; KPMG Peat Marwick, LLP; and Price Waterhouse & Co., LLP. Because the Big Six firms have the largest companies in the United States as audit clients, and because a large percentage of CPAs work for Big Six firms, these firms are powerful forces with enormous exposure in the business community.

National Firms

Besides the Big Six firms, other national firms have offices in most major and many smaller cities within the country. Many of these firms also have international offices, and have hundreds of partners and thousands of CPAs on their staffs. These firms engage in substantial amounts of audit work for many of the largest companies and nonprofit organizations in the country.

Regional Firms

Regional firms have offices in several cities within a particular region. These firms are characterized by numerous partners and large professional staffs and often perform extensive audit work. Although these firms serve some very large audit clients, they also serve many medium-size and small entities.

Local Firms

Local firms generally operate in only one office or within a small geographical area. These firms are quite diverse and range from a sole proprietor to a partnership whose professional staff numbers in the hundreds. Local firms often service small entities and, as a general rule, perform more tax work and accounting and review services than do the larger firms.

Table 1–3 illustrates how different-sized CPA firms typically concentrate on different types of services. Of course, the information in Table 1–3 represents averages, and any given firm's sources of revenues by service may vary significantly.

The CPA Firm's Organizational Structure

Regardless of their size, most firms are set up with similar organizational structures consisting of staff accountants, senior accountants, managers, and partners.

Staff Accountant

When people first join a public accounting firm, they are typically classified as staff accountants (also called assistants or junior accountants). Staff accountants often perform the more detailed routine audit tasks, but because they have very limited experience, they must be closely supervised.

| Table 1-3 | **Percentage of Net Fees by Service for CPA Firms** |

Types of Services	Nonnational*				National**
	Individual	Small	Medium	Large	
Auditing	6.3	10.7	14.8	20.7	45.8
Tax services	48.9	47.2	44.8	41.1	37.8
Compilation and review	15.4	16.4	15.5	14.2	9.0
Management advisory services	6.2	5.0	5.5	8.6	5.0
Write up & data processing	17.5	15.6	14.4	10.5	2.0
Other	5.7	5.1	5.0	4.9	0.4
Totals	100.0	100.0	100.0	100.0	100.0

*Results of 1994 National MAP Survey, Texas Society of CPAs.
**Results of 1991 National MAP Survey, Texas Society of CPAs.

Senior Accountant

The senior accountant is in charge of audit fieldwork and typically has two to five years' experience in public accounting. The senior accountant conducts the audit engagement at the client's office while planning and supervising the work of the audit staff, and reviews working papers, maintains the time budget, and ensures that the audit progresses properly.

In some firms, the supervisor is a heavily experienced senior, typically with four to seven years of experience.

Manager

The manager in a CPA firm usually has at least five years of experience in public accounting. The manager generally is not at the client's office performing the audit on a day-to-day basis: this is the responsibility of the senior auditor. The manager helps the seniors plan their audit programs, reviews their working papers periodically, and provides other guidance to the seniors as necessary.

Partner

The partners are the owners of the CPA firm. They have overall responsibility for the operation of the firm and its practice, and also take the lead role in client development.

A partner typically has ten or more years of experience in public accounting. The partner has the overall and final responsibility for the conduct of an audit and therefore reviews the audit work of the staff, the seniors, and the manager. The partner is responsible for resolving audit problems with the client approving the form and content of the audit report. Because the partner has overall responsibility, the partner is the person who must make the final decisions involving complex judgments.

Professional Standards

In all professions, standards represent the minimum rules or principles that a profession's members have agreed to observe and that serve as a model for judging the quality of work performed. Auditing *standards* are broad conceptual guidelines that serve as a model for all auditors and should remain relatively stable over time. Auditing *procedures*, on the other hand, represent specific audit tasks to be performed; they are based on the auditor's professional judgment, given the broad auditing standards that apply. For example, to comply with an auditing standard that requires audits to be properly planned, the auditor may perform the specific audit procedure of holding a preliminary planning meeting with client personnel.

The Auditing Standards-Setting Process

The Auditing Standards Board of the AICPA is responsible for setting auditing standards and procedures to be observed by AICPA members. The board is always alert to opportunities for auditors to serve the public, both by assuming new responsibilities and by improving ways of meeting old ones. The AICPA then develops standards and procedures that enable auditors to assume those responsibilities.

Standards and procedures define the nature and extent of auditors' responsibilities and provide guidance for carrying out auditing duties. Where appropriate, the board makes special provisions to meet the needs of small enterprises. The board always takes into account the costs that the standards and procedures will impose on society in relation to the benefits expected to be derived from the audit function.

In addition, a separate committee of the AICPA sets standards for the services provided by accountants for unaudited financial statements of nonpublic companies. The Accounting and Review Services Committee is responsible for issuing the Statements on Standards for Accounting and Review Services (SSARS). This committee is discussed in more detail in Chapter 22.

The AICPA's Auditing Standards Division, which includes the board, subcommittees, and staff, issues the types of auditing and attest pronouncements shown in Table 1–4.

Board pronouncements typically progress through the following stages:

- *Identification*   The need for a pronouncement may be identified through litigation, regulatory pressure, or comments of practitioners. Whatever the source, the common element is a recognized need for more guidance in a particular area.
- *Research*   The shape of guidance needed is assessed through analysis of the issues, gathering of data on current practice, review of existing literature, and development of alternative approaches. This step is a combined effort of the AICPA staff and a small task force of practitioners, some or all of whom are members of the board.
- *Consideration*   The proposed pronouncement is deliberated by the board and alternatives are evaluated. The task force and staff submit a draft for discussion and revise it in response to the criticisms and suggestions of the board made in open meetings. Preliminary drafts normally are revised many times.
- *Exposure*   The proposed pronouncement must be approved for exposure by ten of the fifteen board members. Exposure drafts are distributed for comment to the offices of all CPA firms with AICPA members, regulators and similar interested parties, and anyone else who requests to receive them. Approximately 7,000 copies are distributed. At least ninety days are allowed for comments.

- *Issuance* All comments are reviewed by the board. Any matters raised in the comments that were not considered previously by the board are evaluated. However, the board does not normally change positions on matters thoroughly considered before exposure. The purpose of exposure is to identify matters that may have been overlooked or may not have been studied thoroughly. Exposure is not made to assess the popularity of proposed guidance. If approved by at least ten of the board members, a pronouncement is issued in the numbered series of Statements on Auditing Standards.
- *Implementation and Application* The final pronouncement usually results in policy statements by CPA firms on exactly how the standard is to be implemented in their practices. Application of the pronouncement in the field may raise new issues that result in an auditing interpretation or, in extreme cases, the identification of the need for a new pronouncement.

Table 1-4 **Audit Standards Division Pronouncements**

Type	Audience/Purpose
Statements on Auditing Standards (SASs)	Issued by the Auditing Standards Board to provide CPAs with guidance regarding application of generally accepted auditing standards. SASs are enforceable under the Code of Professional Conduct.
Auditing Interpretations	Provide CPAs with guidance regarding application of individual SASs in specific circumstances.
Audit and Accounting Guides	Provide CPAs with authoritative guidance regarding audits of entities in specialized industries or other specialized auditing areas.
Statements of Position of the Auditing Standards Division	Supplement or amend audit and accounting guides.
Auditing Research Monographs	Provide CPAs with background material and informed discussion to help them in reaching decisions on significant audit problems.
Auditing Procedures Studies	Inform practitioners of developments and advances in auditing procedures to provide practical assistance regarding auditing procedures.
Statements on Standards for Attestation Engagements	Issued by the Auditing Standards Board (but may also be issued by the Accounting and Review Services Committee and the Management Consulting Services Executive Committee) to provide guidance to CPAs engaged to perform attestation engagements. These statements are enforceable under the Code of Professional Conduct.
Attest Interpretations	Provide interpretive guidance for attest services.
Audit Risk Alerts	Provide auditors with an overview of recent economic, professional, and regulatory developments that may affect audits. Alerts are published annually and are nonauthoritative.

Generally Accepted Auditing Standards

Generally accepted auditing standards (GAAS), the authoritative standards that CPAs must comply with in performing an audit engagement, are the auditing profession's means of assuring the quality of audit performance. They do not address specific audit problems but rather represent an overall framework for the financial audit process.

To address specific issues, the Auditing Standards Board issues pronouncements entitled Statements on Auditing Standards (SASs). These interpretations of GAAS are authoritative guidelines for CPAs. *SAS No. 1* was issued in 1973 as a replacement and codification of all 54 previous authoritative auditing pronouncements, which were called Statements on Auditing Procedures (SAPs).

There are ten generally accepted auditing standards, divided into three categories: general standards, standards of fieldwork, and standards of reporting.

General Standards

According to *SAS No. 1, Generally Accepted Auditing Standards* (AU 150), three of the GAAS apply as general standards to every phase of the audit engagement. These include standards of technical training and proficiency, independence, and due professional care.

1. The audit is to be performed by a person or persons having adequate technical training and proficiency as an auditor.
2. In all matters relating to the assignment an independence in mental attitude is to be maintained by the auditor or auditors.
3. Due professional care is to be exercised in the performance of the audit and the preparation of the report.

Technical Training and Proficiency

The first general standard recognizes that however capable a person may be in other fields, one must nonetheless be properly trained and proficient in the field of auditing. A person trained in business and finance is not necessarily trained as an auditor. Consequently, auditors are expected to exhibit a high degree of understanding of both accounting and auditing matters. This standard places a responsibility upon the auditor to meet training and proficiency requirements through education and experience specifically in the field of auditing.

Technical training and proficiency include not only formal education but also the auditor's experiences in the profession. Just as auditors must have formal auditing education, so too must they acquire knowledge and proficiency in the field. In addition, the auditor should always be aware of new developments in accounting, auditing, and business, and apply new accounting and auditing authoritative pronouncements as they are issued. As previously noted, this need for continuing professional education has been formalized as a requirement in most states, and continued education is a requirement for membership in AICPA.

Independence

The second general standard requires that the auditor have independence in mental attitude during the engagement. Independence depends on two factors: the auditor's basic character and the public's perception of whether or not the auditor is independent. For example, an independent auditor may plan to audit a company in which the auditor has a direct financial interest (for instance, by owning common stock). The auditor may be so intellectually honest that he or she would never allow such a relationship to affect independence. Although in this case the auditor may in fact be independent, the public perception would probably be that the auditor is not independent. This reluctance on the part of the public to believe that the auditor is independent is why auditors must be independent not only in fact but also in appearance. The Code of Professional Conduct discussed in Chapter 2 provides further guidelines for the auditor on independence.

Due Professional Care

In almost every profession the concept of *due professional care* and the related concept of *the prudent practitioner* exist. The prudent practitioner concept represents a measure by which practitioners in any profession can be evaluated. Whenever a practitioner's quality of performance is questioned, the profession should evaluate that performance against the idea of a prudent practitioner; that is, what would a prudent practitioner have done in the same circumstances? The prudent practitioner, who is expected to exercise due professional care, establishes in most professions the boundaries of negligence.

Mautz and Sharaf have defined **the prudent practitioner** in auditing as one

> who is assumed to have a knowledge of the philosophy and practice of auditing, to have the degree of training, experience, and skill common to the average independent auditor, to have the ability to recognize indications of irregularities and to keep abreast of developments in the perpetration and detection of irregularities.[1]

The auditor must exercise due care from the planning stages of the audit through the performance of auditing procedures during fieldwork through the issuance of the report. An auditor who fails to complete all the important audit procedures or who accepts answers from management without critical analysis and investigation is not exercising due professional care. An auditor who issues a report that is not supported by the evidence or that fails to note the omission of important financial information likewise is not exercising due professional care.

Standards of Fieldwork → *Relates to audit itself.*

Three of the GAAS as identified in *SAS No. 1* (AU 150) are standards of fieldwork with which the auditor must comply in the actual performance of the independent financial audit. These standards address planning and supervision, the internal control structure, and sufficient competent evidential matter.

Planning and Supervision

To be effective in any endeavor, a person should institute appropriate planning. This is particularly true in auditing, where the performance of an audit is an enormous task often requiring many, many hours to complete. Planning includes such factors as determining how many auditors should be used and when audit procedures should be performed. Planning the auditing engagement is discussed in depth in Chapter 12.

---

[1]R. K. Mautz, and H. A. Sharaf, *The Philosophy of Auditing*, American Accounting Association, 1961, p. 14.

The new auditor, or one with limited experience, does not have the technical training and proficiency that a more experienced auditor has. To compensate for this lack of experience, the first standard of fieldwork requires that any assistant be properly supervised; the senior auditor is responsible for proper supervision of such an assistant.

Internal Control Structure

SAS No. 55, Consideration of the Internal Control Structure in a Financial Statement Audit (AU 319.06), defines ***internal control structure*** as "the policies and procedures established to provide reasonable assurance that specific entity objectives will be achieved."[2] Some of these policies and procedures are important in an audit because they represent the means by which an entity records, processes, summarizes, and reports financial data in a reliable manner. For example, a bookkeeper may reconcile the bank statement each month to provide assurance that all checks have been recorded.

The second standard of fieldwork requires the auditor to obtain a sufficient understanding of the internal control structure. A better internal control structure increases the probability that financial data are reliable and reduces the amount of evidence the auditor must collect through other audit tests. Conversely, a weaker internal control structure indicates a higher probability of less-reliable financial information and increases the amount of evidence the auditor must collect through other auditing procedures. The auditor's requirement to understand the internal control structure is discussed in detail in Chapter 6.

Sufficient Competent Evidential Matter

Most of the auditor's work in formulating an opinion as to the fairness of the financial statements consists of obtaining, examining, and evaluating evidential matter. An auditor must exercise professional judgment in determining the relevance of a specific piece of evidence, its objectivity, its timeliness, and its relationship to the conclusions as to the overall fairness of the financial statements.

The third standard of fieldwork requires the auditor to obtain sufficient competent evidential matter before expressing an opinion on the financial statements. ***Sufficiency*** relates to the quantity and quality of audit evidence obtained. In determining whether evidence is sufficient, the auditor must exercise professional judgment as to how much and what kind of audit evidence is needed, based on the nature of the item under examination, the materiality of possible errors and irregularities, the degree of risk involved, and the kinds and competence of evidential matter available. An experienced auditor seldom collects enough evidence to be convinced beyond all doubt as to the fairness of every aspect of the financial statements being audited. The auditor must decide, however, whether the evidential matter available is sufficient to support an opinion that the financial statements are fairly presented in conformity with generally accepted accounting principles.

For audit evidence to be ***competent*** it must meet two criteria: it must be valid and it must be relevant. The ***validity*** of audit evidence is determined by whether (1) the audit evidence was obtained from independent sources outside an enterprise, (2) the accounting data and financial statements were developed under satisfactory conditions of internal control, and (3) the audit evidence was gathered through direct personal knowledge of the auditor.

---

[2]An exposure draft to amend *SAS No. 55* has recently been issued. The draft would revise the definition and description of internal control structures to incorporate the concepts contained in *Internal Control Integrated Framework* published by the Committee of Sponsoring Organizations of the Trading Commission (COSO Report).

For evidence to be *relevant* it must apply to the audit objective and the assertion being tested. Thus, if attempting to gather evidence that accounts receivable are fairly stated, the auditor must gather evidence that applies to accounts receivable; for example, confirmations from customers, examination of the accounts receivable subsidiary ledger, and examination of sales documents.

II.

Standards of Reporting   ⟨ *memorize* ⟩

Four of the GAAS as identified in *SAS No. 1* (AU 150) are standards of reporting that provide guidelines for the auditor in the development of the audit report. These standards address generally accepted accounting principles, consistency, disclosure, and expression of an opinion.

Generally Accepted Accounting Principles

The first standard of reporting requires the auditor to express an opinion as to whether the financial statements conform with *generally accepted accounting principles* in the independent auditor's report. *Generally accepted accounting principles* are defined in *SAS No. 69, The Meaning of "Present Fairly in Conformity with GAAP"* (AU 411), as a "technical accounting term which encompasses the conventions, rules, and procedures necessary to define accepted accounting practice at a particular time." GAAP include not only authoritative pronouncements, such as Accounting Research Bulletins, Accounting Principles Board Opinions, and Financial Accounting Standards Board Statements, but also those methods and procedures that have general acceptance in accounting.

SAS No. 69 establishes two different hierarchies for GAAP: one for state and local government entities and one for other entities. FASB and GASB statements and interpretations represent the highest level on the GAAP hierarchy. The GAAP hierarchy is discussed in more detail in Chapter 20.

The auditor must exercise professional judgment in determining whether a particular accounting principle is generally accepted. At all times the auditor must recognize that an accounting principle should reflect the substance of a transaction rather than its form.

Consistency

The second standard of reporting requires that the auditor indicate those circumstances in which GAAP have not been applied consistently in the current period in relation to the preceding period. This standard ensures that the comparability of financial statements has not been affected by undisclosed changes in accounting principles. This does not preclude an entity from changing accounting principles; it does, however, require that such changes be noted in the auditor's report and be fully disclosed in the financial statements. The effect of changes in accounting principles on the auditor's report is discussed in detail in Chapter 20.

Disclosure

Informative disclosure

The third standard of reporting indicates to a reader of financial statements that all important relevant information has been disclosed unless noted otherwise by the auditor. In the absence of information to the contrary, the reader may assume that all disclosures required by GAAP have been made.

As indicated in *SAS No. 32, Adequacy of Disclosure in Financial Statements* (AU 431), disclosure includes not only the notes to the financial statements, but also such items as the terminology used in the financial statements; parenthetical comments in the financial statements; the form, arrangement, and content of the financial statements; and the classification of items in the statements. *SAS No. 32* further notes that verbosity should not be mistaken for adequate disclosure. That is, the auditor must exercise professional judgment in determining what items are necessary for adequate disclosure rather than simply disclosing all items without regard to relevance.

Expression of an Opinion

The fourth standard of reporting is probably the most complex of the ten GAAS. This standard requires that the auditor must either express an opinion on the financial statements taken as a whole, including the related notes, or disclaim an opinion on those financial statements.

The fourth standard gives the auditor the four options in reporting described previously: an unqualified opinion, a qualified opinion, an adverse opinion, or a disclaimer of opinion. These four options are discussed in more depth in Chapter 20. The fourth standard also requires, when an overall opinion (that is, an unqualified opinion) cannot be expressed, that the auditor state the reasons why.

In all cases, the auditor must indicate the character of the audit work and the degree of responsibility that the auditor is taking. The character of the work as described in the scope paragraph is the conduct of the audit in accordance with GAAS. However, if the audit is restricted in some way, this restriction must be stated in the scope paragraph. The degree of responsibility is indicated by the opinion that the auditor expresses.

[handwritten margin notes: Auditor Express fairly/unfairly form an opinion. Issue a disclaimer if you can't form an opinion]

The Real World of Auditing

CPAs Attest to More Than Just Financial Statements

After This, CPAs Take Over Instant-Replay Duties for Football

If you're hitting a few balls at the West Woods Golf Club range near Hartford, Conn., on Thursday, don't be surprised to see a certified public accountant pacing off some of the drives.

Accountants have broadened their audit services by attesting to the voting at the Academy Awards and the drawings of state lotteries. But now the Wilson Sporting Goods Co. unit of Finland's Amer Group Ltd. is using CPAs to prove that amateur golfers can hit Wilson's Ultra golf ball farther than they can hit competitors' golf balls. Wilson says the CPAs certify that Wilson's Ultra outdistances its competitors by an average of 5.7 yards per drive.

Competitors aren't impressed by Wilson's accountants. "I can walk off a golf ball's distance as well as any accountant," says Harry Groome, an account executive with Ayer Inc., ad agency for the Maxfli golf balls made by Dunlop Slazenger Corp.,

a unit of Britain's BTR PLC. "Using a CPA is an odd way to measure a golf drive." ...

Marlene Baddeloo, a manager for the Chicago office of Coopers & Lybrand, which oversees the golf-ball competitions sponsored by Wilson, agrees "that anyone could pace off a golf driving range to see how far a ball goes." But she says Coopers staffers check that Wilson employees haven't doctored the results at driving ranges. "We also make sure the amateurs participating aren't affiliated with Wilson or its competitors and haven't been paid to participate," she adds.

The use of accountants may upset Wilson's competitors, but it sure makes the accountants happy. "Our personnel love ... [to] wear shorts and spend the day out in the air," says Ms. Baddeloo. "I get a lot of volunteers."

Source: Lee Berton, "After This, CPAs May Take Over Instant-Replay Duties for Football," *Wall Street Journal*, March 9, 1991, B1.

Standards of Attestation

Attestation Engagement [handwritten annotation]

Standards Governing Audits [handwritten annotation]

Attest Function [handwritten annotation]

Audit vs Function [handwritten annotation]

The scope of practice by CPAs has enlarged significantly beyond the audits of historical financial statements that are the focus of the ten GAAS adopted in 1947. The marketplace has recognized that the CPA's attestation skill is a distinct service that is useful outside of its traditional application. Consequently, CPAs have been requested to provide, and have been providing, various forms of assurances on a wide variety of information.

In responding to these demands for nontraditional services, CPAs have been able to apply the basic concepts underlying GAAS to these new types of services. Of course, this process can be awkward because GAAS were developed for only one type of attest service—the audit of historical financial statements. Consequently, the Auditing Standards Board and the Accounting and Review Services Committee of the AICPA have developed a Statement on Standards for Attestation Engagements that presents 11 attestation standards, analogous to GAAS, that provide a general framework for all attest engagements. In 1994, the AICPA established a Special Committee on Assurance Services to analyze and report on the current state and future of the audit/attest function and the trends shaping the environment.

The Statement on Standards for Attestation Engagements defines an ***attest engagement*** as "one in which a practitioner is engaged to issue or does issue a written communication that expresses a conclusion with respect to the reliability of a written assertion that is the responsibility of another party." These attest functions are a natural extension of the auditor's traditional function.

The attestation standards do not supersede any of the previously mentioned Statements on Auditing Standards or the Statements on Standards for Accounting and Review Services that cover compilation and review engagements. Neither do the attestation standards supersede the Statement on Standards for Accountants' Services on Prospective Financial Information, discussed in Chapter 21. Rather, the attestation

---

Table 1–5   **Relationship of Types of Attest Services to Authoritative Guidelines**

Type of Service	Authoritative Guidance
■ Audits of Historical Financial Statements	■ Statements on Auditing Standards (SAS)
■ Unaudited Financial Statements of Publicly Held Companies	■ Statements on Auditing Standards (SAS)
■ Opinions on Internal Control Structure	■ Statement on Standards for Attestation Engagements
■ Unaudited Financial Statements of Nonpublic Companies	■ Statements on Standards for Accounting and Review Services (SSARS)
■ Reports on Prospective Financial Statements	■ Statement on Standards for Accountants' Services on Prospective Financial Information
■ All Other Attest Engagements	■ Statement on Standards for Attestation Engagements

standards cover other types of engagements, such as reports on descriptions of computer software, reports on investment performance statistics, and reports on compliance with various types of guidelines. A summary of the various types of attest services and the related authoritative guidelines is shown in Table 1–5. Tables 1–6, 1–7, and 1–8 present a comparison of the 11 attestation standards, with generally accepted auditing standards categorized by general standards, standards of fieldwork, and standards of reporting.

Quality Control

In any profession, the members should ensure that the services offered are of an acceptable level of quality. This is certainly true in public accounting. As a consequence, the AICPA has developed policies to ensure quality control among its members. These policies consist of a set of standards, a quality review program, and two voluntary programs for CPA firms to assist in the quality control process.

Table 1–6	Comparison between the General Standards for Attestation and Generally Accepted Auditing Standards
Attestation Standards	**Generally Accepted Auditing Standards**
1. The engagement shall be performed by a practitioner or practitioners having adequate technical training and proficiency in the attest function.	**1.** The audit is to be performed by a person or persons having adequate technical training and proficiency as an auditor.
2. The engagement shall be performed by a practitioner or practitioners having adequate knowledge in the subject matter of the assertion.	
3. The practitioner shall perform an engagement only if he or she has reason to believe that the following two conditions exist:	
■ The assertion is capable of evaluation against reasonable criteria that either have been established by a recognized body or are stated in the presentation of the assertion in a sufficiently clear and comprehensive manner for a knowledgeable reader to be able to understand them.	
■ The assertion is capable of reasonably consistent estimation or measurement using such criteria.	
4. In all matters relating to the engagement, an independence in mental attitude shall be maintained by the practitioner or practitioners.	**2.** In all matters relating to the assignment, an independence in mental attitude is to be maintained by the auditor or auditors.
5. Due professional care shall be exercised in the performance of the engagement.	**3.** Due professional care is to be exercised in the performance of the audit and the preparation of the report.

Table 1-7	Comparison between the Standards of Fieldwork for Attestation and Generally Accepted Auditing Standards

Attestation Standards	Generally Accepted Auditing Standards
1. The work shall be adequately planned and assistants, if any, shall be properly supervised. **2.** Sufficient evidence shall be obtained to provide a reasonable basis for the conclusion that is expressed in the report.	**1.** The work is to be adequately planned and assistants, if any, are to be properly supervised. **2.** The auditor should obtain a sufficient understanding of the internal control structure to plan the audit and to determine the nature, timing, and extent of tests to be performed. **3.** Sufficient competent evidential matter is to be obtained through inspection, observation, inquiries, and confirmations to afford a reasonable basis for an opinion regarding the financial statements under audit.

Standards

Auditing firms are required by *SAS No. 25, The Relationship of Generally Accepted Auditing Standards to Quality Control Standards* (AU 161), to establish quality control policies and procedures to provide reasonable assurance of conforming with GAAS. Guidance for these policies and procedures is provided through *Statement on Quality Control Standards No. 1,* issued in 1979. The nine elements of quality control are independence, assigning personnel to engagements, consultation, supervision, hiring, professional development, advancement, acceptance and continuance of clients, and inspection.

Independence

Statement on Quality Control Standards No. 1 identifies independence as the first element of quality control. The statement specifies that the firm should establish policies and procedures to provide reasonable assurance that persons at all organizational levels maintain independence to the extent required by the Code of Professional Conduct of the AICPA.

Assigning Personnel to Engagements

The firm should establish policies and procedures for assigning personnel to engagements to provide reasonable assurance that work will be performed by persons having the degree of technical training and proficiency required in the circumstances. In making assignments, the nature and extent of supervision to be provided should be taken into account. Generally, the more able and experienced the personnel assigned to a particular engagement, the less the need for direct supervision.

Consultation

The firm should establish policies and procedures for consultation to provide reasonable assurance that personnel will seek assistance, to the extent required, from persons having appropriate levels of knowledge, competence, judgment, and authority.

Table 1-8	Comparison between the Standards of Reporting for Attestation and Generally Accepted Auditing Standards	
	Attestation Standards	Generally Accepted Auditing Standards
	1. The report shall identify the assertion being reported on and state the character of the engagement. **2.** The report shall state the practitioner's conclusion about whether the assertion is presented in conformity with the established or stated criteria against which it was measured.	**1.** The report shall state whether the financial statements are presented in accordance with generally accepted accounting principles. **2.** The report shall identify those circumstances in which such principles have not been consistently observed in the current period in relation to the preceding period. **3.** Informative disclosures in the financial statements are to be regarded as reasonably adequate unless otherwise stated in the report.
	3. The report shall state all of the practitioner's significant reservations about the engagement and the presentation of the assertion.	**4.** The report shall either contain an expression of opinion regarding the financial statements, taken as a whole, or an assertion to the effect that an opinion cannot be expressed. When an overall opinion cannot be expressed, the reasons therefor should be stated. In all cases where an auditor's name is associated with financial statements, the report should contain a clear-cut indication of the character of the auditor's work and the degree of responsibility the auditor is taking.
	4. The report on an engagement to evaluate an assertion that has been prepared in conformity with agreed-upon criteria or on an engagement to apply agreed-upon procedures should contain a statement limiting its use to the parties who have agreed upon such criteria or procedures.	

The nature of the arrangements for consultation will depend on a number of factors, including the size of the firm and the levels of knowledge, competence, and judgment possessed by the persons performing the work. For example, within a firm an individual may be designated as an SEC expert or a governmental auditing expert.

Supervision

The firm should establish policies and procedures for the conduct and supervision of work at all organizational levels to provide reasonable assurance that the work performed meets the firm's standards of quality. The extent of supervision and review appropriate in a given instance depends on many factors, including the complexity of the subject matter, the qualifications of the person performing the work, and the extent of consultation available and used. The firm's responsibility for establishing procedures for supervision is distinct from an individual's responsibility to adequately plan and supervise the work on a particular engagement.

Hiring

The firm should establish policies and procedures for hiring to provide reasonable assurance that those employed possess the appropriate characteristics to perform competently. The quality of a firm's work ultimately depends on the integrity, competence, and motivation of personnel who perform and supervise the work. Thus, a firm's recruiting programs are factors in maintaining quality.

Professional Development

The firm should establish policies and procedures for professional development to provide reasonable assurance that personnel will have the knowledge required to fulfill responsibilities assigned. Continuing professional education and training activities enable a firm to provide personnel with the knowledge required to fulfill responsibilities assigned to them and to progress within the firm.

Advancement

The firm should establish policies and procedures for advancing personnel to provide reasonable assurance that those selected for advancement will have the qualifications necessary for fulfillment of the responsibilities they will be called on to assume. Practices in advancing personnel have important implications for the quality of a firm's work. Qualifications that personnel selected for advancement should possess include, but are not limited to, character, intelligence, judgment, and motivation.

Acceptance and Continuance of Clients

The firm should establish policies and procedures for deciding whether to accept or continue a client in order to minimize the likelihood of association with a client whose management lacks integrity. Suggesting that there should be procedures for this purpose does not imply that a firm vouches for the integrity or reliability of a client, nor does it imply that a firm has a duty to anyone but itself with respect to the acceptance, rejection, or retention of clients. However, prudence suggests that a firm be selective in determining its professional relationships.

Inspection

The firm should establish policies and procedures for inspection or review to provide reasonable assurance that the procedures relating to the other elements of quality control are being effectively applied. Procedures for inspection may be developed and performed by individuals acting on behalf of the firm's management. The type of inspection procedures used will depend on the controls established by the firm and the assignment of responsibilities within the firm to implement its quality control policies and procedures.

Quality Review

Quality review, or peer review, is a relatively recent development in the public accounting profession. A quality review (see Figure 1–3) is an examination of one CPA firm's accounting and auditing quality control procedures by another CPA firm or group of CPAs. The reviews, required for members of the AICPA who are in public practice and have financial reporting responsibilities, represent an important component of the profession's system of self-regulation. Quality review provides assurance to the public that not only is a high level of competence maintained but also that the profession is making an effort to eliminate substandard performance. The demand

---

Figure 1–3   **Example of a Quality Review Report**

November 1, 1990

To the Partners of
Price Waterhouse

We have reviewed the system of quality control for the accounting and
auditing practice of Price Waterhouse (the Firm), in effect for the year
ended June 30, 1990. Our review was conducted in conformity with
standards for peer reviews promulgated by the peer review committee of
the SEC Practice Section of the AICPA Division for CPA Firms (the Section).
We tested compliance with the Firm's quality control policies and
procedures at the Firm's National Office and at selected practice offices in
the United States and with the membership requirements of the Section to
the extent we considered appropriate. These tests included the application
of the Firm's policies and procedures on selected accounting and auditing
engagements. We tested the supervision and control of portions of
engagements performed outside the United States.

In performing our review, we have given consideration to the general
characteristics of a system of quality control as described in quality
control standards issued by the AICPA. Such a system should be
appropriately comprehensive and suitably designed in relation to a firm's
organizational structure, its policies and the nature of its practice.
Variance in individual performance can affect the degree of compliance
with a firm's prescribed quality control policies and procedures. Therefore,
adherence to all policies and procedures in every case may not be
possible.

In our opinion, the system of quality control for the accounting and
auditing practice of Price Waterhouse in effect for the year ended June 30,
1990, met the objectives of quality control standards established by the
AICPA and was being complied with during the year then ended to
provide the Firm with reasonable assurance of conforming with
professional standards. Also, in our opinion the Firm was in conformity
with the membership requirements of the Section in all material respects.

Signed
Deloitte & Touche

---

for quality reviews came out of discussions during the 1970s regarding the accounting profession's performance and its ability to regulate itself. Congressional hearings focused attention on the need for quality control, including self-regulation, in the accounting profession.

If the auditor's firm is a member of the AICPA's Division for CPA Firms (see below), he or she may participate in the division's quality review program. Other AICPA review programs are available for auditors whose firms do not belong to the division. The AICPA also requires that to become a member of the AICPA or to retain membership, applicants in the practice of public accounting must be associated with firms that participate in the quality review program.

The quality review examination is generally a three-phase process. First, a firm must have a system of quality control. The quality review team in this phase studies and evaluates the quality control system. Second, the firm must have procedures for ensuring compliance with the quality control system. In this area, the quality review committee reviews these procedures and selects working papers to determine that the procedures are followed. Third, the firm should have documentation that its procedures for ensuring compliance are being achieved. This documentation is examined by the quality review committee.

The objective of the quality review program is twofold: it is educational in the sense that firms are encouraged to develop and implement appropriate systems of quality control, and it is preventive in the sense that firms are notified during the quality review if their system of quality control does not meet professional standards so that the system can be improved.

Division for CPA Firms

In 1977, the AICPA established the Division for CPA Firms, with two sections: the SEC Practice Section (SECPS) and the Private Companies Practice Section (PCPS). As with the quality review program, this action was a response to critics of the profession and congressional committees that had charged that CPAs were not concerned with quality control or self-regulation. Each of the two current practice sections has membership requirements, quality review requirements, and a set of objectives. However, membership in each of the practice sections is optional. A CPA firm may belong to both sections, either section, or neither section.

Objectives

One of the objectives of the Division for CPA Firms is to improve the quality of practice by CPA firms by establishing practice requirements for member firms. It also seeks to establish and maintain an effective system of self-regulation of member firms by means of mandatory peer reviews, required maintenance of appropriate quality controls, and the imposition of sanctions for failure to meet membership requirements. Another objective is to provide a forum for making known views on professional matters and technical information.

Other Professional Standards

GAAS are the standards of CPAs when they are engaged in the performance of an independent audit engagement. Other standards, however, exist when the CPA performs different types of engagements. The AICPA has developed professional standards for performing management consulting services and tax engagements. Similarly, standards for the practice of audit engagements have been developed by organizations other than the AICPA.

Other AICPA Standards

The AICPA has established standards in the performance of management consulting services, tax engagements, forecasts and projections, and compilation and review services. These standards relate to the CPA's responsibilities in performing other engagements and apply to any CPA who is a member of the AICPA.

Management Advisory Services Standards

Management consulting services represent that portion of a CPA's practice in which the accountant serves as a business consultant to the client. Through its Management Consulting Services Executive Committee, the AICPA has issued standards for management consulting services. These standards require the accountant to have professional competency, exercise due professional care, adequately plan and supervise, and obtain sufficient relevant data to support conclusions reached in management consulting service engagements. These standards also require the CPA to serve the client interest while maintaining integrity and objectivity; establish an understanding with the client about the engagement; and inform the client about conflicts of interests that may occur, significant reservations about the engagement, and significant findings.

Responsibilities in Tax Practice

The Federal Taxation Executive Committee of the AICPA is responsible for issuing *Statements on Responsibilities in Tax Practice*, which applies to such items as the standards a CPA should follow in recommending tax return positions and in preparing or signing tax returns. It also covers the CPA's responsibilities regarding answering questions, examining or verifying supporting data for the tax return, recommending a position that departs from a treatment decided by Internal Revenue Service administrative proceedings of prior years, making estimates, taking action when he or she becomes aware of errors, and giving advice to clients.

Other Auditing Standards

The body of auditing standards for independent auditors is composed of GAAS. However, internal auditors through the Institute of Internal Auditors (IIA) and governmental auditors through the Governmental Accounting Office (GAO) have also developed sets of auditing standards. These standards in many ways are similar to GAAS because they require certain general standards, standards of fieldwork, and reporting standards. Standards for the practice of governmental auditing and internal auditing are discussed in Chapters 23 and 24, respectively.

International Standards on Auditing

In addition to U.S. auditing standards, the International Auditing Practices Committee of the International Federation of Accountants also issues professional pronouncements regarding standards for the practice of auditing, the *International Standards on Auditing*. The International Auditing Practices Committee is composed of representatives from 15 countries: Australia, Brazil, Canada, Egypt, France, Germany, India, Japan, Jordan, South Africa, Mexico, the Netherlands, a Scandinavian country, the United Kingdom and Ireland, and the United States.

International Auditing Guidelines can be used by countries as a basis for developing their own guidelines or they can be adopted by countries that decide not to develop their own guidelines. Most important, they help harmonize the practice of auditing throughout the world and, as a result, elevate the standards of the profession worldwide.

None of the guidelines issued by IFAC is obligatory. The International Federation of Accountants has no power to impose standards. Rather, the member bodies have committed themselves to work toward implementation to the extent practicable under local circumstances. In the United States, the international standards rarely exceed the requirements set forth in the SASs, Statements on Standards for Attestation Engagements, or the Statements on Standards for Accounting and Review Services.

Significant Terms

Accredited personal financial specialist A specialist designation for CPAs who pass a special examination on personal financial planning and meet other requirements designated by the AICPA.

Adverse opinion An auditor's report which concludes that the financial statements are not fairly presented in conformity with generally accepted accounting principles.

American Accounting Association (AAA) An organization composed primarily of accounting educators.

American Institute of Certified Public Accountants (AICPA) The national professional organization of CPAs.

Attest engagement An engagement in which a practitioner is hired to issue or does issue a written communication that expresses a conclusion about the reliability of a written assertion that is the responsibility of another party.

Attestation standards Eleven standards that provide a general framework and set reasonable boundaries around the attest function.

Audit of financial statements Examination of financial statements to determine that the statements are in conformity with specified criteria, usually generally accepted accounting principles.

Auditing A systematic process of objectively obtaining and evaluating evidence regarding assertions about economic actions and events to ascertain the degree of correspondence between those assertions and established criteria and communicating the results to interested users.

Big Six firms The six largest accounting firms in the United States: Arthur Andersen & Co.; Coopers & Lybrand; Deloitte and Touche; Ernst & Young; KPMG Peat Marwick; and Price Waterhouse & Co.

Certified public accountants (CPA) Accountants who are duly licensed by the state and have met the educational, examination, and experience requirements of the state.

Compliance audit An audit that attempts to measure the degree to which an auditee complies with some predetermined criteria.

Consulting services Professional services in which the CPA provides counsel to a client.

Disclaimer of opinion An auditor's report in which the auditor is unable to express an opinion as to the fairness of the financial statements in conformity with generally accepted accounting principles.

General standards The three broad standards of GAAS that apply to every phase of the audit engagement and include standards of technical training and proficiency, independence, and due professional care.

Generally accepted accounting principles (GAAP) A technical accounting term that encompasses the conventions, rules, and procedures necessary to define accepted accounting practice at a particular time.

Generally accepted auditing standards (GAAS) The ten authoritative standards with which the independent auditor must comply in performing an audit.

Government auditors Auditors employed by government entities.

Independent auditors (also called external auditors) Certified public accountants who have an independent practice and offer auditing services to the public.

Institute of Internal Auditors (IIA) The international professional organization for internal auditors.

Internal auditors Full-time employees of private organizations who conduct audits for the organization.

International Standards on Auditing Nonauthoritative pronouncements issued by the International Auditing Practices Committee of the International Federation of Accountants.

Limited Liability Partnership (LLP) A type of business organization where partners are personally liable for their own acts and the wrongful acts of staff under their supervision but are not personally liable for the acts of other partners.

Local firms CPA firms that have only one office or have several offices within a small geographic area.

Management consulting services The portion of a CPA's practice in which the accountant serves as a business consultant to the client.

National firms CPA firms that have offices in most major and often smaller cities in the country.

Operational audit An audit that measures the effectiveness and efficiency of an organization.

Partners The owners of a CPA firm who assume overall responsibility for the firm's operation. Partners usually have ten or more years of public accounting experience.

Prudent practitioner concept A measure by which practitioners can be evaluated based on what a prudent practitioner exercising due professional care would have done in the same or similar circumstances.

Qualified opinion An audit opinion with a qualifying phrase on the opinion. These are also referred to as *except for* opinions, in which the auditor believes the financial statements present fairly—in accordance with generally accepted accounting principles—the position of the entity except for a certain item or items.

Quality review The examination of a CPA firm's quality control procedures by another CPA firm or group of CPAs.

Regional firms CPA firms with offices in several major cities within a geographic region.

Securities and Exchange Commission (SEC) An agency established by Congress to regulate the distribution of securities to the public and the trading of securities on the securities exchanges via interstate commerce.

Senior accountant A person with two to five years' experience within a CPA firm. A senior accountant supervises audit fieldwork.

Staff accountant (also called assistant or junior accountant) Entry-level position in a public accounting firm. A staff accountant's work includes routine and detailed assignments and is heavily supervised.

Standards of fieldwork The three standards of GAAS that apply to the actual performance of audit work and include standards of planning and supervision, the internal control structure, and sufficient competent evidential matter.

Standards of reporting The four standards of GAAS that provide guidelines for the auditor in the development of the audit report and include standards of reference to GAAP, consistency, adequate disclosure, and expression of an opinion.

Unqualified opinion An auditor's report issued after the auditor is satisfied that the financial statements are fairly presented in conformity with generally accepted accounting principles.

Discussion Questions

1-1. What is the meaning of the terms *relevant* and *reliable* in financial reporting?

1-2. Identify and briefly discuss factors that have created the demand for auditing.

1-3. Define the term *auditing* and briefly discuss the key terms in the definition.

1-4. Why is the communication process important to the auditor?

1-5. What historical events have contributed to the development of auditing?

1-6. Discuss the relationship of *auditing* to *accounting*. Are the two terms synonymous? Why or why not?

1-7. What is the auditor's responsibility for the financial statements?

1-8. What are the important elements of the independent auditor's standard report?

1-9. What are the differences among the introductory, scope, and opinion paragraphs of the independent auditor's standard report?

1-10. Why is the date of the auditor's standard report important?

1-11. Briefly describe the three types of reports other than an unqualified opinion.

1-12. What are the two types of scope limitations on the independent auditor?

1-13. What types of audits do internal auditors typically perform?

1-14. What is the GAO and what are its responsibilities?

1-15. What are the three professional organizations that have had an effect on auditing?

1-16. What are the broad requirements in most states for receiving a CPA certificate?

1-17. Describe the types of services that could be offered by a CPA firm.

1-18. Identify the four general classifications of CPA firms and list the four basic positions within the organizational structure.

1-19. Briefly describe the process by which auditing standards are set.

1-20. What is the relationship between a SAS and GAAS?

1-21. What three categories are GAAS divided into?

1-22. What are the three general standards under GAAS?

1-23. What are the three standards of fieldwork?

1-24. What are the four standards of reporting?

1-25. What are the nine elements of quality control for a CPA firm?

1-26. What is a quality review? Why is it helpful?

1-27. What are the two practice sections established by the AICPA?

Objective Questions

*1-28. How does an independent audit aid in the communication of economic data?
   (1) It confirms the accuracy of management's financial representations.
   (2) It lends credibility to the financial statements.
   (3) It guarantees that financial data are fairly presented.
   (4) It assures the readers of financial statements that any fraudulent activity has been corrected.

*1-29. Which of the following criteria is unique to the auditor's attest function?
   (1) General competence.
   (2) Familiarity with the particular industry of which the client is a part.
   (3) Due professional care.
   (4) Independence.

---

*AICPA adapted.

*1-30.   The independent auditor of 1900 differs from the auditor of today in that in 1900 the auditor was more concerned with which of the following?
  (1) Validity of the balance sheet.
  (2) Determination of fair presentation of financial statements.
  (3) Improvement of accounting systems.
  (4) Detection of irregularities.

*1-31.   What is the essence of the external audit function?
  (1) To detect fraud.
  (2) To examine individual transactions so that the auditor may certify their validity.
  (3) To determine whether the client's financial statements are fairly stated.
  (4) To assure the consistent application of correct accounting procedures.

*1-32.   The securities of Ralph Corporation are listed on a regional stock exchange and are registered with the Securities and Exchange Commission. The management of Ralph engages a CPA to perform an independent audit of Ralph's financial statements. The primary objective of this audit is to provide assurance to which party?
  (1) Regional stock exchange.
  (2) Board of directors of Ralph Corporation.
  (3) Securities and Exchange Commission.
  (4) Investors in Ralph securities.

*1-33.   Operational audits generally have been conducted by internal auditors and government audit agencies but may be performed by CPAs. A primary purpose of an operational audit is to provide
  (1) a means of assurance that internal control structure is functioning as planned.
  (2) a measure of management performance in meeting organizational goals.
  (3) the results of internal audits of financial and accounting matters to a company's top-level management.
  (4) aid to the independent auditor who is conducting the audit of the financial statements.

*1-34.   Who is primarily responsible for adequate disclosure in the financial statements and footnotes?
  (1) CPA firm performing the audit.
  (2) Auditor in charge of fieldwork.
  (3) Staff person who drafts the statements and footnotes.
  (4) Client.

*1-35.   Which paragraphs of an auditor's standard report on financial statements should refer to generally accepted auditing standards (GAAS) and which paragraphs should apply to generally accepted accounting principles (GAAP)?

	GAAS	GAAP
(1)	Opening	Scope
(2)	Scope	Scope
(3)	Scope	Opinion
(4)	Opening	Opinion

*1-36.   Compared to the external auditor, what is more likely to concern an internal auditor?
  (1) Fairness of the financial statements.
  (2) Cost accounting procedures.
  (3) Management policies and procedures.
  (4) Generally accepted accounting principles.

*1-37.   Governmental auditing often extends beyond audits leading to the expression of opinion on the fairness of financial presentation and includes audits of efficiency, effectiveness, and
  (1) objectivity.
  (2) compliance with statutes and regulations.

---
*AICPA adapted.

(3) accuracy.

(4) reasonableness.

*1-38. Which of the following best describes what is meant by the term generally accepted auditing standards?

(1) Pronouncements issued by the Auditing Standards Board.

(2) Rules acknowledged by the accounting profession because of their universal application.

(3) Procedures to be used to gather evidence to support financial statements.

(4) Measures of the quality of the auditor's performance.

*1-39. The first general standard requires that an audit of financial statements is to be performed by a person or persons having which characteristic?

(1) Seasoned judgment with varying degrees of supervision and review.

(2) Adequate technical training and proficiency.

(3) Knowledge of the standards of fieldwork and reporting.

(4) Independence with respect to the financial statements and supplementary disclosures.

*1-40. Auditing standards differ from audit procedures in that procedures relate to

(1) measures of performance.

(2) audit principles.

(3) acts to be performed.

(4) audit judgments.

*1-41. What is the meaning of the *generally accepted auditing standard* that requires that an auditor be independent?

(1) The auditor must be without bias with respect to the client under audit.

(2) The auditor must adopt a critical attitude during the audit.

(3) The auditor's sole obligation is to third parties.

(4) The auditor may have a direct ownership interest in the client's business.

*1-42. What does the exercise of due professional care require an auditor to do?

(1) Examine all available corroborating evidence.

(2) Critically review the judgment exercised at every level of supervision.

(3) Reduce control risk below the maximum.

(4) Attain the proper balance of professional experience and formal education.

*1-43. What is the general character of the three generally accepted auditing standards classified as standards of fieldwork?

(1) The competence, independence, and professional care of persons performing the audit.

(2) The content of the auditor's report on financial statements and related footnote disclosures.

(3) Audit planning and supervision, the internal control structure, and evidence.

(4) The need to maintain independence in all matters relating to the audit.

*1-44. An opinion as to the fairness of financial statement presentation in accordance with generally accepted accounting principles is based on several judgments made by the auditor. One such judgment is whether the accounting principles used

(1) have general acceptance.

(2) are promulgated by the AICPA Auditing Standards Board.

(3) are the most conservative alternative.

(4) emphasize the legal form of transactions.

*1-45. Which of the following is the authoritative body designated to promulgate attestation standards?

(1) Auditing Standards Board.

(2) Governmental Accounting Standards Board.

(3) Financial Accounting Standards Board.

(4) General Accounting Office.

---

*AICPA adapted.

*1-46.   Janet Chen, a CPA firm's personnel partner, periodically studies the CPA firm's personnel advancement experience to ascertain whether individuals meeting stated criteria are assigned increased degrees of responsibility. This is evidence of the CPA firm's adherence to prescribed
  (1) standards of due professional care.
  (2) quality control standards.
  (3) supervision and review standards.
  (4) standards of fieldwork.

1-47.   The objective of quality control mandates that a public accounting firm should establish policies and procedures for professional development that provide reasonable assurance that all entry-level personnel
  (1) prepare working papers that are standardized in form and content.
  (2) have the knowledge required to enable them to fulfill responsibilities assigned.
  (3) will advance within the organization.
  (4) develop specialties in specific areas of public accounting.

*1-48.   A CPA firm evaluates its personnel advancement experience to ascertain whether individuals meeting stated criteria are assigned increased degrees of responsibility. This is evidence of the firm's adherence to which of the following prescribed standards?
  (1) Quality control.
  (2) Human resources.
  (3) Supervision and review.
  (4) Professional development.

*1-49.   A CPA establishes quality control policies and procedures for deciding whether to accept new clients and whether to continue to perform services for current clients. What is the primary purpose for establishing such policies and procedures?
  (1) To enable the auditor to attest to the integrity or reliability of a client.
  (2) To comply with the quality control standards established by regulatory bodies.
  (3) To minimize the likelihood of association with clients whose managements lack integrity.
  (4) To lessen the exposure to litigation resulting from failure to detect irregularities in client financial statements.

1-50.   Which of the following is an element of a CPA firm's quality control system that should be considered in establishing its quality control policies and procedures?
  (1) Complying with laws and regulations.
  (2) Using statistical sampling techniques.
  (3) Assigning personnel to engagements.
  (4) Considering audit risk and materiality.

Problems and Cases

1-51.   (Characteristics of Auditing) The following two statements are representative of attitudes and opinions sometimes encountered by CPAs in their professional practices.
  1. Today's audit consists of testing only selected transactions. This is dangerous because testing depends upon the auditor's judgment, which may be defective. An audit can be relied upon only if every transaction is verified.
  2. An audit by a CPA is essentially negative and contributes to neither the gross national product nor the general well-being of society. The auditor does not create but merely checks what someone else has done.
  REQUIRED
  Evaluate each of the above statements and indicate
  A. Areas of agreement with the statement, if any.

---

*AICPA adapted.

B. Areas of misconception, incompleteness, or fallacious reasoning included in the statement, if any.

Complete your discussion of each statement (both parts **A** and **B**) before going on to the next statement.

*1-52. (Purposes of an Audit) Jane Feiler, the sole owner of a small hardware business, has been told that the business should have financial statements reported on by an independent CPA. Feiler, having some bookkeeping experience, has personally prepared the company's financial statements and does not understand why such statements should be examined by a CPA. Feiler discussed the matter with Chuck Farber, a CPA, and asked Farber to explain why an audit is considered important.

REQUIRED

A. Describe the objectives of an independent audit.

B. Identify ten ways in which an independent audit may be beneficial to Feiler.

*1-53. (Auditor's Report) The complete opinion included in the annual report of The Modern Department Store for 19X4 is reproduced here:

Auditor's Opinion
Doe & Doe
New City, New State

To Whom It May Concern:

In our opinion, the accompanying balance sheet and statement of income and retained earnings present fairly the financial position of The Modern Department Store and the results of its operations. Our audit of these financial statements was made in accordance with generally accepted auditing standards and accordingly included such tests of the accounting records and such other auditing procedures as we considered necessary, except that we did not confirm accounts receivable, but instead accounted for subsequent collections on the accounts, and we did not observe the taking of the physical inventory because it was taken prior to our appointment as auditors.

REQUIRED

List and discuss the deficiencies of the auditor's report prepared by Doe & Doe.

1-54. (Types of Audit Reports) In an audit, a CPA may issue one of four types of reports:

1. unqualified opinion.

2. qualified opinion.

3. adverse opinion.

4. disclaimer of opinion.

Each of the following items represents material circumstances that the auditor could encounter in an audit situation.

A. A major lawsuit against the company remains unresolved.

B. The company changed from straight-line to accelerated depreciation.

C. The financial statements are not in conformity with GAAP.

D. The financial statements are in conformity with GAAP.

E. The auditor is unable to perform numerous important audit procedures.

REQUIRED

For each item identify the type of report the auditor should issue.

---

*AICPA adapted.

**1-55. (Roles of Internal and Independent Auditing) George Johnson, a local real estate broker, is a member of the board of directors of Pennset Corporation. At a recent board meeting, called to discuss financial plans, Johnson discovered two planned expenditures for auditing. In the controller's budget he found an estimate for internal audit activity, and in the treasurer's budget he found an estimate for the annual audit by a CPA firm.

Johnson could not understand the need for two different expenditures for auditing. Because the CPA fee for the annual audit was less than the cost of the internal audit activity, he proposed eliminating the internal audit function.

REQUIRED
A. Explain to Johnson the different purposes served by the two audit activities.
B. What benefits does the CPA firm performing an audit derive from the existence of an internal audit function?

*1-56. (Types of Audits and Auditors) Each of the following represents tasks that auditors frequently perform:
1. Evaluation of a company's computer system to determine whether the computer is being used <u>effectively</u>. *Int. – Operational.*
2. Examination of vacation records to determine whether employees followed company policy of two weeks' paid vacation annually. *I – Comp.*
3. Audit of a small college to determine that the college has followed requirements of a bond indenture agreement. *CPA – Comp.*
4. Audit of a government agency to determine if the agency has followed policies of Congress. *Gov. – Comp.*
5. Audit of annual financial statements to be filed with the SEC. *CPA→Fin*
6. Examination of a federal grant to a private company to determine whether it would have been feasible to accomplish the same objective at less cost elsewhere. *Gov. Operational*
7. Audit of Statement of Cash Receipts and Disbursements to be used by a creditor. *CPA FIN*
8. Audit of a federal department to determine that the department's financial statements are presented fairly. *Gov. Financial audit.*

REQUIRED
For each of the above, identify the most likely type of auditor (CPA, governmental, or internal) and the most likely type of audit (financial, compliance, or operational).

Compliance   Operational Audits

*1-57. (Accounting Organizations) The following groups have an important role in auditing:
1. AICPA.
2. IIA.
3. state boards of accountancy.
4. Financial Accounting Standards Board.
5. a CPA firm.
6. Securities and Exchange Commission.

REQUIRED
For each of the following activities, identify the group that would perform that activity.
A. Licenses individuals to practice as CPAs. *3*
B. Issues official pronouncements on GAAP. *4*
C. Conducts the certification program for internal auditors. *2*
D. Regulates reporting of companies whose securities are publicly traded. *6*
E. Designs the Uniform CPA Examination. *1*
F. Supports the Auditing Standards Board. *1*
G. May revoke the license of an individual to practice as a CPA. *3*
H. Conducts audits as part of a practice. *5*
I. Imposes mandatory continuing professional education requirements on individuals who wish to continue to practice as CPAs. *1 3*

*AICPA adapted.
**CMA adapted.

J. Develops and offers continuing education courses.

K. Issues disclosure requirements beyond generally accepted accounting principles for publicly held companies.

1-58. (Technical Training and Proficiency) Ron Anders, president of Chelsea Catfish Farms, has requested that your firm perform the audit of the company's financial statements. Your firm does not have any clients that conduct catfish farming operations, nor is any of your staff familiar with the business. You inquire with other CPA firms in your area but none has experience with this type of business.

REQUIRED

The first general standard of GAAS requires that the audit is to be performed by a person or persons having adequate technical training and proficiency as an auditor. If your firm performs the audit for Chelsea Catfish Farms, will this be a violation of the standard? Discuss.

1-59. (Quality Control) You have just been appointed to ensure that your firm is conforming to *SAS 25, The Relationship of Generally Accepted Auditing Standards to Quality Control Standards* (AU 161).

REQUIRED

A. Discuss each of the nine elements of quality control.

B. Why does the profession have quality control standards?

*1-60. (Standards of Fieldwork) You have accepted the engagement of auditing the financial statements of the Thorne Company, a small manufacturing firm that has been your client for several years. Because you were busy writing the report for another engagement, you sent an assistant accountant to begin the audit with the suggestion that she start with the accounts receivable. Using the prior year's working papers as a guide, the assistant prepared a trial balance of the accounts, aged them, prepared and mailed positive confirmation requests, examined underlying support for charges and credits, and performed such other work as she deemed necessary to obtain reasonable assurance about the validity and collectibility of the receivables. At the conclusion of her work you reviewed the working papers that she prepared and found that she had carefully followed the prior year's working papers.

REQUIRED

The opinion rendered by a CPA states that the audit was made in accordance with generally accepted auditing standards.

List the three generally accepted standards of fieldwork. Relate them to the above illustration by indicating how they were fulfilled or, if appropriate, how they were not fulfilled.

1-61. (Relating Procedures to GAAS) Below are statements that relate to generally accepted auditing standards.

1. The auditor prepares a listing of audit procedures to be performed.

2. The auditor reads a book on bank accounting to gain an understanding of unique banking practices.

3. The auditor discovers a suspicious expense charge and investigates further.

4. The auditor refuses an engagement because of a belief that he or she cannot be objective because the potential client is owned by a good friend.

5. The auditor verifies that the company is applying the last-in, first-out (LIFO) method in a manner similar to the prior year.

6. The auditor meets with a new auditor with no experience and reviews closely the procedures the new auditor is to perform.

7. The auditor determines that the financial statements meet the requirements of FASB Statements, APB Opinions, and other authoritative accounting pronouncements.

8. The auditor determines that an unusual transaction should be disclosed in the financial statements.

*AICPA adapted.

[handwritten: Internal Control]

9. The auditor studies the internal control structure.
10. The auditor determines that more invoices need to be examined so that a conclusion can be reached. *[handwritten: Sufficient Confident Evidence]*
11. The auditor expresses an opinion on the financial statements.

REQUIRED *[handwritten: 2]*

For each statement above, identify the specific generally accepted auditing standard to which the statement relates.

*1-62. (Violation of GAAS) Carole Ray, the owner of a small company, asked Greg Holmes, CPA, to conduct an audit of the company's records. Ray told Holmes that an audit is to be completed in time to submit audited financial statements to a bank as part of a loan application. Holmes immediately accepted the engagement and agreed to provide an auditor's report within three weeks. Ray agreed to pay Holmes a fixed fee plus a bonus if the loan was granted.

Holmes hired two accounting students to conduct the audit and spent several hours telling them exactly what to do. Holmes told the students not to spend time reviewing the control structure but instead to concentrate on proving the mathematical accuracy of the ledger accounts and on summarizing the data in the accounting records that support Ray's financial statements. The students followed Holmes's instructions and after two weeks gave Holmes the financial statements, which did not include footnotes. Holmes reviewed the statements and prepared the unqualified auditor's report. The report did not refer to GAAP nor to a circumstance in which an accounting principle had not been consistently observed.

REQUIRED

Briefly describe each of the generally accepted auditing standards and indicate how Holmes's action(s) resulted in a failure to comply with each standard. Organize your answer as follows:

A. Brief description of GAAS
B. Holmes's actions resulting in failure to comply with GAAS

1-63. (GAAP, GAAS, and Auditing Procedures) The auditor's standard report contains the phrases *generally accepted auditing standards* (GAAS), *generally accepted accounting principles* (GAAP), and *examining evidence*.

REQUIRED

A. Define each of the three phrases.
B. How do GAAS differ from GAAP?
C. How do GAAS differ from examining evidence?
D. GAAS appears in the second paragraph whereas GAAP appears in the third paragraph. What is the significance of this?

1-64. (Quality Control) The following questions are taken from the peer review manual for the Private Companies Practice Section.

1. Are criteria identified that will be considered in evaluating individual performance and expected proficiency (for example, technical knowledge, analytical and judgmental abilities, and communicative skills)?
2. Are the staffing requirements of specific engagements identified on a timely basis?
3. Does the firm provide for reporting inspection findings to the appropriate management levels and for monitoring actions taken or planned?
4. Is the effectiveness of the recruiting program monitored by reviewing hiring results periodically to determine whether goals and personnel needs are being achieved?
5. Is consideration given to the types of engagements that the firm would not accept or that would be accepted only under certain conditions?

---

*AICPA adapted.

6. Is background information developed or is information obtained from prior engagements reviewed and updated for changed circumstances?

7. Has the firm established responsibility for maintaining a reference library?

8. Does the firm require that personnel at all organizational levels adhere to the independence rules, regulations, interpretations, and rulings of the AICPA, state CPA society, state board of accountancy, state statute, and if applicable, the SEC and other regulatory agencies?

9. Are personnel encouraged to serve on professional committees, prepare articles, and participate in other professional activities?

REQUIRED

For each of the above questions, identify the applicable element of quality control.

Audit Judgment Cases

1-65. (Auditing Career) After another interesting day in their auditing class, four seniors are discussing their career plans. The first senior, Daniel Lindsey, says that he plans to go to work with a local CPA firm because of the diversity of their practice and the wide range of experience he can get. The second senior, Stephanie Allen, says that she wants to have a career with a national accounting firm so she can audit the largest companies in the country. She believes that this will be a great learning experience to learn about the most glamorous aspects of the business. The third senior, Mark Murphy, states that he would like to be employed as an internal auditor for a large corporation. He believes that by being a full-time employee he will gain more insights into business than by having many different companies as clients. Jeff Martin, the fourth senior, says that he plans to work for the GAO. He believes a career as a governmental auditor will be most interesting because he will do many kinds of audits, not just financial audits.

REQUIRED

For each of the four seniors, discuss the relative advantages of his or her career choice.

1-66. (Internal Auditors and an Audit Report) Dusty Pritchett, the CEO for Coop Products, Inc., has just been told by bank president Beth Crain that audited financial statements would be required in connection with the company's recent loan request. Pritchett replies, "No problem, I'll just have my internal audit staff perform the audit."

REQUIRED

Explain to Pritchett the following:

A. Why the internal audit staff cannot perform the audit.

B. The function of the internal audit staff.

1-67. (Violation of GAAS) Walter Harmon, the owner of a small appliance store, asked Ron Wilson, CPA, to conduct an audit of the company's records. Wilson's firm has more business than it can handle but due to his overwhelming desire to generate more fees, he accepts the engagement. Due to time constraints Wilson assigns two entry level staff to perform the fieldwork. Wilson told the two staff persons not to worry about the control structure because this company was a family run business. In the course of their work, the staff persons discovered that there were several large receivables from customers that appeared to be unusual for a small appliance store. The staff asked Wilson if they should send confirmation requests to the customers and his reply was, "We don't have time, we've got other engagements that are more important."

REQUIRED

Discuss the Generally Accepted Auditing Standards for fieldwork and indicate how Wilson has violated each.

1-68. (Establishing Auditing Standards) In 1978 the Metcalf Committee (the Senate Subcommittee on Reports, Accounting, and Management) recommended the following:

> The Federal Government should establish auditing standards used by independent auditors to certify the accuracy of corporate financial statements and supporting records. Again, participation by all segments of the public is necessary to develop auditing standards that will restore public confidence in the integrity of corporate reports. In view of the substantial record of previously unreported corporate wrong-doing which has been revealed during the past few years, a special review of present auditing standards should be undertaken to determine their adequacy prior to considering their adoption by the Federal Government. Auditing Standards could be established by the General Accounting Office, by the SEC, or by Federal statute.

REQUIRED
- **A.** How are auditing standards currently established?
- **B.** What are the advantages and disadvantages of establishing auditing standards through a federal agency such as the GAO?
- **C.** What are the advantages and disadvantages of establishing auditing standards through federal statutes?
- **D.** Discuss the appropriateness of establishing auditing standards in the public sector and accounting standards in the private sector.

1-69. (Establishing Auditing Standards) Brian Bates, CPA, stated that he felt frustrated by his lack of input into the establishment of auditing standards. In his opinion, auditing standards are issued "when a problem arises and the SEC and the Big Six firms get together and pass a new SAS through the Auditing Standards Board." According to Bates, no one else knows about these SASs until they arrive in the mail.

REQUIRED

Discuss the views held by Bates regarding the auditing standards-setting process.

Auditing Issues Cases

1-70. **KELCO MANUFACTURING COMPANY**

A specialty manufacturer of textiles, Kelco Manufacturing Company was started by its president and 75% shareholder, Steve Cook, in 19X4. Cook began his career as a textile engineer for a major textile manufacturer and left the company in 19X0 to start his own operation. He is known for his expertise as a textile engineer, but lacks sound business education and experience. He is a risk taker and has been very successful in the development of specialty textiles. The company has earned profits in all three years of operation, a record almost unheard of in the specialty textile business. Cook's personal style of living is extravagant. Living in a $600,000 home, driving a Jaguar convertible, and making trips to luxurious international resorts, his personal cash requirements are enormous.

Kelco wishes to make a major investment in state-of-the-art equipment that will increase the company's production of specialty textiles tenfold. To date, capital expenditures have been fully financed by the company. Cook hopes to finance the purchase with a substantial loan from the Florence National Bank. Because of substantial borrowing, the bank has asked Cook to provide audited financial statements of Kelco Manufacturing for the year ended December 31, 19X7.

Your firm has been providing Compilation and Tax services for Kelco since the company started operations. The Bank now wants audited financial statements.

You have just met with Cook. The dialogue of your conversation is as follows:

Cook:	The bank has requested audited financial statements of my company for the year ended December 31, 19X7. Would you send a copy of those statements to the bank?
Your Response:	Mr. Cook, the bank requires audited financial statements. To date, we have not performed an audit of your company's financial statements. In the past we have provided you with compilation services.
Cook:	Well, there could not be much of a difference. Ok, just go ahead and do whatever it takes to provide the bank with audited financial statements, and send them the bill for your services.
Your Response:	Mr. Cook, there is a big difference between an audit of financial statements and compilation services. The bank will not pay for the audit. You will have to pay for the audit.
Cook:	Why should I pay for the audit when the bank is going to use those financial statements?

— no assurance

REQUIRED

A. Explain to Cook how an audit differs from a compilation engagement.
B. Cook wants to know why he should pay for the audit. Provide him with an explanation.

1-71. KELCO MANUFACTURING COMPANY

You have just discussed with Steve Cook, president of Kelco Manufacturing Company, the nature of the audit process. Cook now understands the difference between the compilation services your firm provided in the past and the audit of financial statements. Cook has several concerns. Your conversation with Cook continues:

Cook:	I can see that more time would probably be required to conduct the audit. Can you give me an estimate of how much your fees for this type of engagement would be?
Your Response:	Fees for our services are based on the time required to complete the assignment plus out of pocket expenses.
Cook:	Does your firm have experience with specialty textile manufacturers?
Your Response:	Yes, we perform audits of financial statements for many manufacturers of specialty textiles.
Cook:	I assume your staff will perform the audit in an efficient manner. From talking to others I have gotten the impression that some CPA firms will assign inexperienced personnel to jobs of smaller clients. That will not be the case with my audit, will it?
Your Response:	No sir.
Cook:	Another concern of mine is confidentiality. I'm afraid that my competitors may hear of my plans for expansion. Will your personnel keep company information confidential?
Your Response:	No problem.
Cook:	On a final note, can you guarantee an audit report that will please the bank so that I will be granted the loan? If the company is not granted the loan, the company's expansion plans will be impossible.
Your Response:	No sir. No firm could provide such a guarantee without violating standards of my profession.

After quoting Cook a fee for the audit engagement, he replies, "That's outrageous, there's got to be an alternative." Cook pauses and then proposes that in exchange for audit services, he would sign over to your firm 100 shares in Kelco stock. He states that if you don't accept his proposal, he will ask his brother Phil, who is a CPA, to perform the audit. One of your firm's partners is a close friend of Phil Cook and happens to know that he has never performed an audit.

REQUIRED

1. Explain to Steve Cook why the audit is more expensive than the services your firm has provided in the past.
2. After your discussion of the fee for the audit engagement, Cook is satisfied with your explanation but insists that his offer of ownership in Kelco would be beneficial to both parties. Explain to Cook the following:
   a. Why such an arrangement is not possible due to professional standards.
   b. Why Phil Cook cannot perform the audit.
3. Address the issue raised by Cook concerning personnel assigned to the audit engagement.
4. Are the personnel required to keep all matters related to the engagement confidential? Discuss.

Professional Ethics

■ State the purpose of professional codes of ethics.

■ Identify the two parts of the AICPA Code of Professional Conduct.

■ Describe the six principles of ethical responsibilities for CPAs.

■ Discuss each of the rules of conduct of the AICPA.

■ Describe the crucial role of independence for auditors and indicate when independence would be impaired.

■ Explain the concept of confidentiality between the CPA and the client.

■ Describe the enforcement procedures for the Code of Professional Conduct.

W oolworth Corp. recently experienced the potentially catastrophic consequences of improperly reporting financial results. A breakdown in the company's internal controls apparently led to the overvaluing of goods and misrepresentation of profit margins on sale merchandise. The investigation into the possible accounting irregularities brought the integrity of the company's financial management into question and prompted the company's chief executive and chief financial officers to step down. Both, however, denied any wrongdoing.

A similar, if not worse, situation confronted women's apparel maker Leslie Fay in 1992. Independent auditors discovered that instead of profits of nearly $24 million, the company actually recorded losses of $13.7 million. Leslie Fay ultimately filed for Chapter 11 bankruptcy protection.

As these examples illustrate, ethical breaches in accounting can lead to devastating repercussions. This chapter examines the Code of Professional Conduct for AICPA members as well as the formal rulings that answer specific questions regarding proper ethical conduct. ■

Sources: Fairchild News Service, "Woolworth Hires Attorneys to Investigate Its Accounting," *Women's Wear Daily*, March 31, 1994, p. 7; "Woolworth Execs Step Down Pending Accounting Probe," *Discount Store News*, April 18, 1994, p. 4; "Who Played Dress-Up with the Books?" *Business Week*, March 15, 1993, p. 34.

Broadly defined, the term *ethics* represents the moral principles or rules of conduct recognized by an individual or group of individuals. Ethics apply when an individual has to make a decision from various alternatives regarding moral principles. All societies and individuals possess a sense of ethics in that they can identify what is "good" or "bad." As C. S. Lewis observed, "Human beings all over the earth have some sort of agreement as to what right and wrong are."[1]

Ethical conduct is determined by each individual. Each person uses moral reasoning to decide whether something is ethical or not. Ethics are a moral code of conduct that requires an obligation by us to consider not only ourselves but others.

There are numerous ways that individuals can receive ethical guidance in making moral decisions. Sources for ethical guidance include our family, friends, religion, and role models. Often such guidance is based on ethical theories or decision rules. These theories can be limited to certain simple ethical maxims such as:

The golden rule: Act in the way you would expect others to act toward you.

The utilitarian principle: Act in a way that results in the greatest good for the greatest number.

Kant's categorical: Act in such a way that the action taken under the circumstances could be a universal law or rule of behavior.

---

[1]C. S. Lewis, *Mere Christianity*, 1952, pp. 19–21.

Table 2-1	**Ethical Decision-Making Checklist Analysis**

Analysis

- What are the facts?
- Who is responsible to act?
- What are the consequences of action? (Benefits-Harm Analysis)
- What and whose rights are affected? (Rights-Principles Analysis)
- What is fair treatment in this case? (Social Justice Analysis)

Solution Development

- What solutions are available to me?
- Have I considered all of the creative solutions that might permit me to reduce harm, maximize benefits, respect more rights, or be fair to more parties?

Select the Optimum Solution

- What are the potential consequences of my solutions?
- Which of the options I have considered does the most to maximize benefits, reduce harm, respect rights, and increase fairness?
- Are all parties treated fairly in my proposed decision?

Implementation

- Who should be consulted and informed?
- What actions will ensure that my decision achieves the intended outcome?
- Implement the decision.

Follow-up

- Was the decision implemented correctly?
- Did the decision maximize benefits, reduce harm, respect rights, and treat all parties fairly?

Source: Adapted from Patrick E. Murphy, "Implementing Business Ethics," *Journal of Business Ethics*, December 1988, p. 913.

> The professional ethic: Take only actions which would be viewed as proper by a disinterested panel of professional colleagues.
>
> The TV test: A manager should always ask, "Would I feel comfortable explaining to a national TV audience why I took this action?"[2]

In making ethical decisions, individuals rely on such ethical theories. In applying these theories, the use of an ethical decision-making framework such as shown in Table 2–1 can be helpful. Ethics exist for individuals and for groups such as organizations and professions. Professional ethics differ from individual ethics because they emphasize the selective viewpoints and acceptable practices of the members of a profession, such as law or accounting.

---

[2]Gene R. Laezniak, "Framework for Analyzing Marketing Ethics," *Journal of Macromarketing* (Spring 1992), pp. 7–18.

Professional Ethics

According to one classic definition, a *profession* is

> a vocation of the highest standing: it calls on its members to serve (no doubt for re-
> ward) the public by offering to them highly technical and always confidential advice
> and services, which require a different standard of conduct from the tradesman. Its
> members stand in a different relationship altogether from the man doing ordinary
> business....
>
> The professional code must be different by the nature of its calling and the reliance
> placed on it by the public from those carrying on trade and commerce.
>
> Those seeking the advice of a professional man are entitled to expect of him the
> highest standards of ethical conduct.[3]

Consistent with this definition, most criteria for a profession include a requirement
for a professional code of conduct.

All professions have a primary responsibility to provide quality service to the
public. Because the body of knowledge in any given profession is quite complex, the
public often cannot evaluate the quality of a professional person's service. As Carey
and Doherty observe:

> When people need a doctor, or a lawyer, or a certified public accountant, they seek
> someone whom they can trust to do a good job—not for himself, but for them.
> They have to trust him, since they cannot appraise the quality of his service.
> They must take it on faith that he is competent, and that his primary motive is to
> help them....
>
> Professional men and women are accepted as persons highly skilled in some science
> or art, who desire to serve the public, and who place service ahead of personal gain.
> If they were not regarded in this light they would have no patients or clients. Who
> would engage a doctor, or a lawyer, or a certified public accountant who was known
> to put personal rewards ahead of service to his patient or client? How could anyone
> know whether to take his advice or not? If the practitioner were mainly interested
> in making money, he might be tempted to keep his patients sick, or keep his client
> in litigation, or extend his audit beyond the necessary scope.[4]

As Mautz and Sharaf note:

> Professional ethics are but a special application of general ethics. General ethics
> emphasize that there are certain guides by means of which an individual can gov-
> ern his conduct. Knowledge of the ultimate outcome of his actions on himself and
> others, awareness of the requirements of the society in which he lives, respect for
> divine law, acceptance of duty, obligation to act toward others as one would want
> all men to act at all times, and recognition of the norms of ethical conduct in the
> society in which one operates all aid the individual to attain a high degree of
> ethical conduct.[5]

---

[3]Lord Upjohn in *Pharmaceutical Society of Great Britain and Another* v. *Dickson* ([1968] 2 All E. R. 703).
[4]John L. Carey, and William O. Doherty, *Ethical Standards of the Accounting Profession*, AICPA, 1969, p. 4.
[5]R. K. Mautz, and Hussein A. Sharaf, *The Philosophy of Auditing*, American Accounting Association, 1961, p. 237.

By establishing rules of conduct, a profession assumes self-discipline beyond the requirements of law. Some people have criticized professional ethics as a means by which members of a profession set up restrictive practices to preserve their livelihood and protect their own interests. However, as Barradell notes:

> The observance of professional ethics often involves the individual practitioner in forbearance for the benefit of others. This is a fundamental distinction. No professional man is expected to be so altruistic as to disregard the material rewards of his services, but he will deservedly forfeit the respect of his fellow-practitioners and of the public at large if he allows these to take an absolute priority over the needs of his clients. The accountant would soon cease, for example, to be the "guide, philosopher and friend" to his clients if he were known to abuse their confidences for his own profit, to prolong work unnecessarily in expectation of an increased fee or to seek to attract work other than by merit.
>
> ...the distinctive mark of the professional man is his voluntary acceptance not only of the need for a high standard of skill (attested by long practical experience and searching examination) in the service of his clients, but also of obligations towards his clients, his fellow-practitioners and the community which transcend the strictest demands of the law.[6]

In auditing, users of financial statements cannot be expected always to understand generally accepted auditing standards, the auditing procedures performed, and the other complex areas of auditing knowledge. Through a code of professional ethics, auditors ensure that quality services have been provided.

This chapter discusses the ***AICPA Code of Professional Conduct***. The Code of Professional Ethics for the Institute of Internal Auditors is presented in Chapter 24.

The Code of Professional Conduct

Prior to 1973 the conduct of AICPA members in the practice of their profession was guided by a number of rules issued by the AICPA's governing body. In 1973, these rules were codified and adopted by the membership of AICPA. Since then, changes in the economic, legal, and regulatory aspects of American society, as well as changes in the nature, scope, and variety of services offered to the public by CPAs, have occurred. In recognition of these changes, in 1983 the AICPA appointed a special committee to study the relevance of the 1973 Code of Ethics to the economic and social environment. The committee was charged with evaluating the relevance of current ethical standards to professionalism, integrity, and commitment to both quality service and the public interest.

Based on the recommendation of the committee, a revised AICPA Code of Professional Conduct was approved by the membership of the AICPA in 1988. The code consists of two sections: principles and rules. The principles, which are goal oriented and aspirational, address six areas: (1) AICPA members' responsibilities, (2) the public interest, (3) integrity, (4) objectivity and independence, (5) due care, and (6) scope and nature of services. Although the principles are not enforceable against AICPA

---

[6]M. Barradell, *Ethics and the Accountant*, 1969, pp. 12–13.

members, they provide the moral reasoning, and thus a framework, for the rules governing the performance of services by CPAs. The rules are enforceable against AICPA members and are the minimum standards of the profession. Certainly any CPA or CPA firm may adopt more restrictive standards.

In addition to the principles and rules of the Code of Professional Conduct, the AICPA also issues interpretations and rulings. ***Interpretations***, which are not approved by the membership of the AICPA, represent guidelines for applying the rules of conduct. ***Rulings*** consist of formal rulings of the AICPA that answer specific questions regarding proper ethical conduct in a given circumstance.

Principles

The ***Principles of the Code of Professional Conduct*** represent the profession's recognition of its responsibilities to the public, to clients, and to colleagues. The principles form the basis of ethical and professional conduct and guide members in performing their professional responsibilities. As noted in the Code of Professional Conduct, "The principles call for an unswerving commitment to honorable behavior, even at the sacrifice of personal advantage." The six principles as stated in the Code of Professional Conduct are explained below:

CPAs' Responsibilities

In carrying out their responsibilities as professionals, CPAs should exercise sensitive professional and moral judgments in all their activities. As noted in Chapter 1, CPAs perform an essential role in society. They are responsible for cooperating with one another to improve methods of accounting and reporting, to maintain the public's confidence, and to carry out the profession's special responsibilities for self-governance.

The Public Interest

CPAs should accept the obligation to act in a way that will serve the public interest, honor the public trust, and demonstrate commitment to professionalism. A distinguishing mark of a profession is acceptance of its responsibility to the public. CPAs are relied upon by numerous elements of society including clients, creditors, governments, employers, investors, and the business and financial community. These groups rely on CPAs' objectivity and integrity to maintain the orderly functioning of commerce. When CPAs discharge their professional responsibilities they may sometimes encounter conflicting pressures from each of these groups. However, in every situation CPAs should act with integrity and with an understanding that when they fulfill their responsibility to the public, clients' and employers' interests are best served. As noted in the Code of Professional Conduct: "Those who rely on CPAs expect them to discharge their responsibilities with integrity, objectivity, due professional care, and a genuine interest in serving the public."

Integrity

To maintain and broaden public confidence, CPAs should perform all professional responsibilities with the highest sense of integrity. Another distinguishing characteristic of any profession is the recognition by its members of the need to possess integrity. For the public to trust any profession, that profession must act with integrity in making all decisions. Integrity requires CPAs to be honest and candid within the constraints of client confidentiality. Service and the public trust should not be subordinated to personal gain and advantage. Integrity can accommodate the inadvertent error and the honest difference of opinion; however, it cannot accommodate deceit or subordination of principle.

Objectivity and Independence

A CPA should maintain objectivity and be free of conflicts of interest in discharging professional responsibilities. A CPA in public practice should be independent in fact and appearance when providing auditing and other attestation services. The principle of objectivity requires a CPA to be impartial, intellectually honest, and free of conflict of interest. Independence precludes relationships that may impair a CPA's objectivity in rendering attestation services. For a CPA in public practice, the maintenance of objectivity and independence requires a continuing assessment of client relationships and public responsibility. In providing all other services, a CPA should maintain objectivity and avoid conflicts of interest. Although CPAs not in public practice cannot maintain the appearance of independence, they nevertheless have the responsibility to maintain objectivity in performing professional services. Regardless of the type of work performed, CPAs should protect the integrity of their work, maintain objectivity, and avoid any subordination of their judgment.

Due Care

A CPA should observe the profession's technical and ethical standards, strive continually to improve competence and the quality of service, and discharge professional responsibility to the best of his or her ability. The principle of due care requires CPAs to pursue excellence in providing professional services. In exercising due care, CPAs must discharge professional responsibilities with competence and diligence. CPAs obtain competence through both education and experience, beginning with a mastery of the common body of knowledge required for designation as a CPA. Competence also requires CPAs to continue to learn throughout their careers. All CPAs must assess their own competence and evaluate whether their education, experience, and judgment are adequate for the responsibilities they will assume. CPAs should also be diligent in fulfilling their responsibilities to clients, employers, and the public. Diligence imposes the responsibility to render services promptly and carefully, to be thorough, and to observe applicable technical and ethical standards. Due care requires CPAs to accept the responsibility to plan and supervise adequately any professional activity.

Scope and Nature of Services

A CPA in public practice should observe the principles of the Code of Professional Conduct in determining the scope and nature of services to be provided. In determining whether or not to perform specific services, members of the AICPA in public practice should consider whether such services are consistent with principles of professional conduct for CPAs. As noted previously, integrity requires that service and the public trust not be subordinated to personal gain and advantage. Likewise, objectivity and independence require that members be free from conflicts of interest in discharging professional responsibilities. Due care requires that services be provided with competence and diligence. CPAs should consider each of these principles in determining whether or not to provide specific services.

As noted in the Code of Professional Conduct, CPAs should

- practice in firms that have internal quality control procedures to insure that services are competently delivered and adequately supervised.
- determine whether the scope and nature of other services provided to an audit client would create a conflict of interest in the performance of the audit function for that client.
- assess whether an activity is consistent with their role as professionals (for example, is such an activity a reasonable extension or variation of existing services offered by the member or others in the profession?).

Table 2-2	**Scope of AICPA Rules of Conduct**

Rule 101   Independence
Rule 102   Integrity and Objectivity

Rule 201   General Standards
Rule 202   Compliance with Standards
Rule 203   Accounting Principles

Rule 301   Confidential Client Information
Rule 302   Contingent Fees

[There are currently no rules in the 400 series.]

Rule 501   Acts Discreditable
Rule 502   Advertising and Other Forms of Solicitation
Rule 503   Commissions and Referral Fees
Rule 505   Form of Organization and Name

Be familiar w/ the

Do not memorize for exam.

Rules

The bylaws of the AICPA require its members to adhere to the ***Rules of the Code of Professional Conduct***. AICPA members must be prepared to justify departure from these rules. In addition, AICPA members are held responsible for compliance with the rules by all persons associated with them in the practice of public accounting who are either under their supervision or are their partners or shareholders in the practice. Further, an AICPA member must not permit others to carry out on his or her behalf—either with or without compensation—acts that, if carried out by the CPA, would place him or her in violation of the rules.

As noted previously, the rules represent the minimum standards of the profession and rest upon the ethical concepts and behavioral guidelines found in the *Principles of the Code of Professional Conduct*. Although the *Rules of the Code of Professional Conduct* provide specific guidance regarding ethical behavior, the rules cannot and do not provide guidance to meet all conditions that might occur. CPAs must always look to the broad principles that underlie the Rules of Professional Conduct.

The AICPA's bylaws give authority to the Institute's Professional Ethics Executive Committee to interpret the rules and issue rulings. Both the interpretations and rulings are enforceable against AICPA members. Table 2–2 gives an overview of the Rules of the Code of Professional Conduct.

Independence

Rule 101 on independence states: "A CPA in public practice shall be independent in the performance of professional services as required by standards promulgated by bodies designated by council." As noted in Chapter 1, no matter how competent a CPA may be, the CPA's opinion on the financial statements is of little value to users unless the CPA maintains independence. Rule 101 requires independence for audits, review, and other attest engagements.

Interpretation 101-1 of Rule 101, issued by the AICPA, states:

Independence shall be considered to be impaired if, for example, a CPA had any of the following transactions, interests, or relationships:
A. During the period of a professional engagement or at the time of expressing an opinion, a CPA or a CPA's firm

any direct interest financial material indirect interest

1. Had or was committed to acquire any direct or material indirect financial interest in the enterprise.
2. Was a trustee of any trust or executor or administrator of any estate if such trust or estate had or was committed to acquire any direct or material indirect financial interest in the enterprise.
3. Had any joint, closely held business investment with the enterprise or with any officer, director, or principal stockholders thereof that was material in relation to the CPA's net worth or the net worth of the CPA's firm.
4. Had any loan to or from the enterprise or any officer, director, or principal stockholder of the enterprise except as specifically permitted in Interpretation 101-5.

B. During the period covered by the financial statements, during the period of the professional engagement, or at the time of expressing an opinion, a CPA or a CPA's firm
   1. Was connected with the enterprise as a promoter, underwriter or voting trustee, as a director or officer, or in any capacity equivalent to that of a member of management or of an employee.
   2. Was a trustee for any pension or profit-sharing trust of the enterprise.

The above examples are not intended to be all-inclusive.

✓ READ!

The Real World of Auditing

Supreme Court Strikes Down State Rule Prohibiting Solicitations

The U.S. Supreme Court struck down a Florida solicitation ban in ruling that states cannot prevent accountants from soliciting clients directly. The ban, enacted by the Florida State Board of Accountancy, prohibited CPAs from engaging in "direct, in-person, uninvited solicitation."

Scott Fane, the CPA who challenged the rule, argued that it presented him with serious obstacles to moving his practice from New Jersey to Florida. Fane sued the board in U.S. district court, alleging the antisolicitation rule violated the first and 14th amendments. The court ruled in his favor, as did the U.S. Court of Appeals for the 11th Circuit.

The U.S. Supreme Court upheld the decisions of both the lower court and the appellate court. By a vote of eight-to-one, the Supreme Court dismissed the board's argument that the ban was required to protect consumers from fraud and ensure CPAs' independence. Justice Anthony Kennedy said the board failed to show a substantial governmental interest that would justify the infringement on Fane's right to free speech.

The decision does not totally preempt states from limiting commercial speech in the area of CPAs' solicitation. Rather, what the decision does is point the way to how bans on solicitation can be upheld if credible evidence can be offered that justifies the ban. Supporters of the ban view uninvited solicitation as a manifestation of a trend away from professionalism, a force that compromises independence in mental attitude and a form of unfair competition. Opponents to the ban view the prohibition of in-person solicitation as a barrier to free competition, a deterrent to fair fees, and an impediment to an efficient market for accounting services.

Source: Terry Lantry, "Supreme Court Allows In-person Solicitation by CPAs," *CPA Journal*, October 1993, pp. 72–76; Wayne Baliga, "Supreme Court Ends CPA Solicitation Ban," *Journal of Accountancy*, September 1993, p. 28.

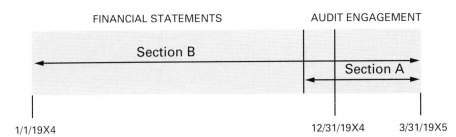

Figure 2-1

Rule 101 (Independence): Time Periods Covered

Rule 101–Section A: audit engagement; Section B: audit engagement + entire period covered by the financial statements

Each part of Interpretation 101-1 discusses a different type of relationship between CPA and client that may impair the CPA's independence. The first paragraph of the interpretation covers financial interest relationships a CPA may have with a client (Paragraph A). The second paragraph covers relationships a CPA may have with a client that involve the CPA in a management role with that client (Paragraph B). If the relationships specified in Paragraphs A and B exist during the time periods described in each of those paragraphs, the independence of the CPA and the firm of which he or she is a partner or shareholder would be considered to be impaired. Figure 2–1 provides an example of the periods involved for Paragraphs A and B.

For an audit, impairment of a CPA's independence would require that the CPA disclaim an opinion on the financial statements. Further, a CPA (or his or her firm) could not perform a review engagement if the independence of that CPA (or his or her partner or shareholder) is impaired; however, a compilation may be performed provided the CPA discusses a lack of independence in the compilation report.

Rule 101 and Interpretation 101-1 apply to a proprietor of and all partners and shareholders of a CPA firm. Thus, if a firm partner is not independent of an attest client, no other partner in that firm is considered independent of that client. Rule 101 and Interpretation 101-1 also apply to all full- and part-time professional employees participating in the attest engagement (whether these employees are audit, tax, or management advisory services personnel of the firm) and all full- and part-time managerial employees located in a firm office that participates in a significant portion of the attest engagement. Thus, for example, a nonmanagerial employee of a CPA firm who does not participate in an attest engagement may own a financial interest in the attest client.

Effects of Relatives on Independence   The independence rules apply not only to the CPA, but to the CPA's family as well. The CPA's spouse and persons financially dependent upon the CPA may impair the CPA's independence. However, there is one exception to the employment by an attest client of the CPA's spouse or financially dependent person. In such a situation, independence would only be impaired if that CPA's spouse or financially dependent person has a position with the attest client that allows significant influence over the client's operating, financial, or accounting policies; and, the CPA participates in the attest engagement, or is a proprietor, partner or shareholder of a firm and: (a) is located in an office participating in a significant portion of the attest engagement, or, (b) has the ability to exercise influence over the engagement; or, (c) has any involvement with the engagement (for example, consultation on accounting or auditing issues). Independence will also be impaired if the spouse or a person financially dependent on a CPA participating in the attest engagement has a position with the client involving activities that are audit sensitive even though the position is not one that allows significant influence, such as internal auditor, accounting supervisor, or purchasing agent.

Certain nondependent close relatives of the CPA who have a relationship with an attest client are also considered to impair independence under Rule 101 and Interpretation 101-1. These nondependent close relatives are the CPA's nondependent children, stepchildren, brothers, sisters, grandparents, parents, parents-in-law, and their respective spouses. Close relatives do not include the brothers and sisters of the CPA's spouse. Table 2–3 illustrates the effect of various relatives on a CPA's independence.

Ethics Interpretation 101-9 provides that a partner (or shareholder, or professional employee) of an accounting firm may impair his or her independence, as well as that of the firm, if that partner or employee participates in an attest engagement and has a *close relative* who (a) can exercise significant influence over the operating, financial, or accounting policies of the client, (b) is employed by the attest client in an audit sensitive position, or (c) has a material financial interest in the attest client that is known to the partner. Also, a partner of an accounting firm who is located in a firm office that participates in a significant portion of an attest engagement may impair the firm's independence if he or she has a close relative who can exercise significant influence over the operating, financial, or accounting policies of the attest client.

Financial Interests   As discussed earlier in this chapter, Paragraph A of Interpretation 101-1 covers financial interests, transactions, or relationships between a CPA and an attest client that impair a CPA's independence. A CPA owning or having a commitment to own a direct financial interest in or a material indirect interest in an attest client would impair independence. Note that any direct interest (even a

Table 2–3	Effects of a CPA's Relatives on Independence		
Type of Relative	**Examples**	**Effect on Independence**
Spouse and dependent relatives	Spouse, dependent children	Independence rules are the same as for the CPA.
Close relatives	Nondependent children, parents, grandparents, brothers, sisters	Would affect independence if close relative 1. can exercise significant influence over the client, 2. is employed by the client in an audit sensitive position, or 3. has a material direct financial interest in the client.
Remote relatives	Aunts, uncles, cousins	Ordinarily would not affect independence.

share of stock) is sufficient to cause an independence problem, but only a *material* indirect interest causes such a problem. Materiality is not defined in the independence rules, nor is the term "indirect financial interest."

Loans Section A-4 of Interpretation 101-1 provides that independence is considered to be impaired if a CPA had any loan to or from the enterprise or to its officers, directors, or principle stockholders, except as permitted by Interpretation 101-5. This interpretation makes an exception to the prohibition against loans to or from audit clients for financial institutions only. Specifically, the interpretation allows CPAs to obtain from financial institutions that are attest clients collateralized automobile loans or leases, loans on the cash surrender value of life insurance, loans fully collateralized by cash deposits, and credit-card and cash-advance balances that do not exceed $5,000 in the aggregate. Prior to 1992, CPAs could obtain home mortgage loans and other secured loans from financial institution clients under normal lending requirements. Although these existing loans have been grandfathered in, CPAs can no longer obtain home mortgages or other types of secured loans from financial institutions who are attest clients.

Honorary Directorships and Trusteeships Rule 101 provides that a CPA's independence will be impaired if the CPA is a director of his or her attest client. Frequently CPAs are asked to lend the prestige of their names to nonprofit civic, religious, or charitable entities. Organizations frequently do this by naming the CPA to that entity's board of directors. Ethics Interpretation 101-1 permits the CPA to accept such an appointment, without impairing independence, provided certain conditions are met. The primary conditions are that the director's position is honorary, that the position is identified as such in all of the organization's internally distributed materials (including letterheads), and that the CPA does not participate in management decisions.

CPAs and Employment Opportunities with Clients Another issue concerns a CPA participating in an audit engagement who seeks or is offered employment by the client. The independence rules require that the CPA in that situation remove himself or herself from the engagement until the employment offer is rejected or employment is no longer being sought. Should a CPA be aware that an individual participated in an engagement while employment was being considered or after it has been accepted, that CPA should consider what, if any, additional procedures may be necessary to ensure that all work had been performed with objectivity and integrity. Any additional procedures will depend on the nature of the engagement and may require re-performance of the work or other appropriate procedures.

Accounting and Bookkeeping Services CPAs often provide manual or automated bookkeeping or data-processing services as well as systems design and programming assistance to clients. Concerns may arise that if a CPA firm performs such services for audit clients, the CPA's independence is impaired. Such concerns result from the view that because they provided accounting services, the CPAs would be auditing their own work. According to Ethics Interpretation 101-3, a CPA performing accounting services for an audit client must meet certain requirements to retain the appearance that he or she is not, in substance, an employee of the client and therefore lacking in independence. These requirements are as follows:

1. The client must accept the responsibility for the financial statements as its own.
2. The CPA must not assume the role of an employee or of management of the attest client.

3. When financial statements are prepared from books and records which the CPA has maintained, the CPA must comply with applicable standards for audits, reviews, or compilations.

The Effect of Actual or Threatened Litigation on Independence

For a CPA to fulfill his or her obligation to issue an informed, objective opinion in an attest engagement, the CPA-client relationship must be one of candor and full disclosure; there must also be an absence of bias on the part of the CPA. When litigation is initiated or there is a threat to initiate litigation between the CPA and his or her client, the CPA-client relationship becomes adversarial and tainted with self-interest. The commencement of litigation by present client management alleging audit deficiencies against a CPA would impair independence. Independence would also be impaired if the CPA commenced litigation against present client management alleging fraud or deceit. If client management expresses an intent to commence litigation against the CPA alleging work deficiencies and the CPA concludes that it is probable that the lawsuit will be filed, independence is impaired. Actual or threatened litigation between CPA and client not related to an engagement usually will not be considered to impair independence if the amount involved in the lawsuit is immaterial to either the CPA's firm or the client.

Integrity and Objectivity

Rule 102 on integrity and objectivity states: "In the performance of any professional service, a CPA shall maintain objectivity and integrity, shall be free of conflicts of interest, and shall not knowingly misrepresent facts or subordinate his or her judgment to others."

Rule 102 requires all CPAs, not just those in public practice, to maintain objectivity and integrity in the performance of professional services as delineated in the Principles of the Code of Professional Conduct. Rule 102 also requires CPAs to be free of conflicts of interest and to not knowingly misrepresent facts or subordinate their judgment to others. Interpretation 102-2 says that a conflict of interest may occur if a CPA performs a professional service for a client or employer and the CPA has a significant relationship with another person, entity, product or service that could be viewed as impairing the CPA's objectivity. Examples of possible conflicts of interest are stated in the interpretation. The interpretation then suggests that if such a significant relationship is disclosed to and consent is obtained from such client, employer, or other appropriate parties, the conflict of interest would not operate to prohibit the performance of the professional service. However, see the discussion later in this chapter regarding confidential client information in terms of the disclosure requirement stated above. The interpretation points out that although conflicts of interest may be resolved by a process of disclosure and consent, independence impairments cannot. Interpretation 102-3 discusses the obligations of a CPA to his or her employer's external accountant. In an audit situation the CPA employed by the external accountant's (auditor's) audit client must be candid and not knowingly misrepresent facts or fail to disclose material facts to the auditor. Interpretation 102-4 provides guidance to a CPA who may be involved in a dispute with his or her supervisor that relates to financial statement preparation or transaction recording. It is designed to ensure that the situation does not constitute a subordination of judgment. Table 2-4 lists selected ethics rulings by the Ethics Division of the AICPA on independence, integrity, and objectivity. These rulings answer questions regarding the application of the Code of Professional Conduct to specific circumstances.

| Table 2-4 | Selected Ethics Rulings on Independence, Integrity, and Objectivity |

- If a CPA accepts more than a token gift from a client, independence may be impaired.

- If a CPA cosigns checks for a client even in an emergency situation, independence is lacking.

- A CPA may provide extensive advisory services to an audit client without losing independence as long as the CPA does not make management decisions.

- A CPA who is an elected legislator in a local government causes the CPA's firm not to be independent with respect to the governmental entity.

- A retired CPA has become an officer and director of several corporations audited by his former firm. If the retired CPA maintains an office, receives phone calls, and performs compensated services in and for the former firm, the firm is not independent.

- A CPA belongs to a country club in which members must own pro rata shares of equity or debt securities. The CPA's independence is not impaired with respect to the country club since the membership is essentially social.

- The spouse of a CPA has an uncle. Personal contacts are infrequent. The uncle owns one-third of a company and serves as one of its officers. The CPA in the absence of special circumstances is independent.

- The father of a CPA serves on a school board. The CPA is not independent.

- A CPA's daughter is a director of a savings and loan association. The CPA is not independent.

- A CPA purchased stock in a client public corporation and placed the stock in an educational trust for the CPA's minor son of which the CPA was a trustee. The interest is a direct financial interest; thus the CPA's independence is impaired.

- A CPA's spouse is a trustee of certain trusts. If the trust purchases stock in audit clients, the CPA will not be independent.

- A CPA who is a faculty member is asked to audit the financial statements of the Student Senate. These funds are processed through the university accounting system. The CPA is not independent since the CPA would be auditing functions performed by his or her employer.

- A CPA owns shares in a regulated mutual investment fund which holds shares of stock in clients of the CPA. The CPA has an indirect financial interest and, if it is not material, the CPA is independent even though the mutual fund owns client stock.

- A CPA owns a one-tenth interest in an investment club. If the investment club buys client shares the CPA is not independent, since the CPA has a direct financial interest.

- An employee of a CPA firm serves as treasurer of a charitable organization. The CPA firm is not independent.

- A CPA's client has been unable to pay the amounts due the CPA firm for the preceding year's audit. The CPA firm may not be independent.

- If a CPA recruits and hires a controller for an audit client, the CPA is not independent.

- A CPA owns a building and leases a portion of the space to a client. If this indirect financial interest is not material, the CPA is independent.

General Standards

Rule 201 on general standards states

A CPA shall comply with the following standards and with any interpretation thereof by bodies designated by (AICPA) council.

A. Professional Competence. Undertake only those professional services that the CPA or the CPA's firm can reasonably expect to be completed with professional competence. **B. Due Professional Care.** Exercise due professional care in the performance of professional services. **C. Planning and Supervision.** Adequately plan and supervise the performance of professional services. **D. Sufficient Relevant Data.** Obtain sufficient relevant data to afford a reasonable basis for conclusions or recommendations in relation to any professional services performed.

Rule 201 represents the comprehensive statement of the general standards that CPAs are expected to observe in all areas of professional service. This rule applies not only to auditing, but also to other types of services performed by CPAs in public practice and to professional services performed by CPAs not in public practice. Many of the elements in Rule 201 are similar to generally accepted auditing standards. Thus, in all areas of practice, CPAs are expected to be competent, exercise due care, perform proper planning and supervision, and gather sufficient relevant data.

Rule 201 does not prohibit a CPA from accepting an engagement for which the CPA does not currently have the needed expertise. Rather, Rule 201 prohibits the CPA from accepting any engagement for which the CPA cannot acquire the necessary knowledge through study and research. For a CPA to accept an engagement for which he or she has not acquired or would not be able to acquire the necessary expertise is unethical under Rule 201.

Compliance with Standards

Rule 202 on compliance with standards states: "A CPA who performs auditing, review, compilation, management advisory, tax, or other professional services shall comply with standards promulgated by bodies designated by council." Rule 202 covers *Statements on Auditing Standards*, *Statements on Accounting and Review Services*, *Attestation Standards*, *Standards on Forecasts and Projections*, and *Management Advisory Services Standards*. It also provides an enforcement mechanism through the Code of Professional Conduct to insure adherence to these authoritative pronouncements.

Accounting Principles

Rule 203 on accounting principles states the following:

A CPA shall not (1) express an opinion or state affirmatively that the financial statements or other financial data of any entity are presented in conformity with generally accepted accounting principles or (2) state that he or she is not aware of any material modifications that should be made to such statements or data in order for them to be in conformity with generally accepted accounting principles, if such statements or data contain any departure from an accounting principle promulgated by bodies designated by council to establish such principles that has a material effect on the statements or data taken as a whole. If, however, the statements or data contain such a departure and the member can demonstrate that due to unusual circumstances the financial statements or data would otherwise have been misleading, the CPA can comply with the rule by describing the departure, its approximate effects, if practicable, and the reasons why compliance with the principle would result in a misleading statement.

Rule 203 requires that all CPAs recognize as generally accepted accounting principles any statements promulgated by an authoritative body designated by the AICPA. The AICPA has designated the pronouncements of the Financial Accounting

Table 2–5	**Selected Ethics Rulings on General Standards, Compliance Standards, and Accounting Principles**

- A CPA performs accounting services for no charge as treasurer for a private club. The CPA may issue financial statements in the capacity as treasurer on the stationary of the club. If the CPA uses firm letterhead, then the CPA should comply with compilation standards.
- A CPA employed as a controller who audits the financial statements of a subsidiary corporation cannot express an independent opinion on those financial statements.
- A CPA in partnership with a non-CPA may not present the partnership as composed entirely of CPAs.
- A CPA wishes to add a systems analyst to the staff. Although it is not necessary for the CPA to be able to perform all the services that the analyst can perform, the CPA must be able to define the tasks and evaluate the end product of work done by the systems analyst.

Standards Board; its predecessor, the Accounting Principles Board; and the Governmental Accounting Standards Board as official pronouncements for the establishment of generally accepted accounting principles. Rule 203 places a burden on the CPA to justify any departure from promulgated accounting principles. Rule 203 does explicitly recognize, however, that unusual conditions may exist where compliance with promulgated accounting principles could create misleading financial statements. It thus requires adherence to promulgated accounting principles unless compliance would be misleading in what would be a rare situation. Chapter 20 discusses further the reporting requirements for a CPA who departs from a promulgated accounting principle to prevent misleading financial statements. Interpretation 203–204 discusses the responsibility of employees for the preparation of financial statements in conformity with generally accepted accounting principles. Table 2–5 lists selected ethics rulings on general standards, compliance with standards, promulgated accounting principles, and other technical standards.

Confidential Client Information

Rule 301 on confidential client information states:

A member in public practice shall not disclose any confidential client information without the specific consent of the client.

This rule shall not be construed (1) to relieve a member of his or her professional obligations under Rules 202 and 203, (2) to affect in any way the member's obligation to comply with a validly issued and enforceable subpoena or summons, or to prohibit a member's compliance with applicable laws and government regulations, (3) to prohibit review of a member's professional practice under AICPA or state CPA Society or Board of Accountancy authorization, or (4) to preclude a member from initiating a complaint with, or responding to any inquiry made by, the ethics division or trial board of the Institute or a duly constituted investigative or disciplinary body of a state CPA society or Board of Accountancy.

Members of any of the bodies identified in (4) above and members involved with professional practice reviews identified in (3) above shall not use to their own advantage or disclose any member's confidential client information that comes to their attention in carrying out those activities. This prohibition shall not restrict members' exchange of information in connection with the investigative or disciplinary proceedings described in (4) above, or the professional practice reviews described in (3) above.

Rule 301 establishes the concept of confidentiality as a vital ethical component of the CPA's obligation in public practice to the client. For the CPA to have the client in trust, the CPA must indicate to the client that matters discussed will be held in confidence. A client certainly would not want to discuss financial statements with the CPA if this information were disclosed to a competitor of the client. Rule 301 establishes confidentiality as an ethical rule, not a legal statute. However, some states have adopted various forms of CPA-client confidentiality in state statutes.

Confidentiality between a client and a CPA, a creation of ethical requirements, differs from privileged communications, a creation of law. Common law recognizes the need for protecting certain interests and relationships, such as attorney-client and husband-wife relationships. When privileged information is offered in a court, the holder of the privilege (for example, the client) can prevent its introduction as evidence in a trial.

Privileged communications resulting from common law do not exist for the CPA-client relationship because of the relatively recent emergence of accounting as a profession. Although the courts have been unwilling to recognize CPA-client privileged communication, 18 states have adopted statutes creating CPA-client privilege.[7] The purpose of CPA-client privileged communication is to insure an atmosphere in which the client can communicate all relevant information to the CPA without fear of subsequent disclosure in future litigation. CPA-client privileged communication is followed in these 18 states, and sometimes it is followed in federal courts involved with questions of state law when the plaintiff and defendant are in different states. The privilege may generally be waived voluntarily only by the client. However, CPA-client privileged communications have been held inapplicable to federal questions in federal courts.

Rule 301 has four important exceptions. The confidentiality rule does not apply when subpoenas or summonses enforceable by order of the court exist. Examinations of work papers as a part of an ethics division inquiry or a quality review are two other important exceptions to the confidentiality rule. However, in both of these situations, as noted in Rule 301, CPAs of a recognized investigative or disciplinary body and quality reviewers are required to maintain confidentiality. Rule 301 recognizes that even though the CPA may be disclosing confidential information in an ethics or quality review situation, the confidentiality of the client is still protected. In addition, Rule 301 allows disclosure when a member initiates a complaint with a recognized disciplinary body of the AICPA or state CPA society or state board of accountancy.

The fourth exception to Rule 301 holds that the confidentiality rule should not be construed "to relieve a CPA of his other professional obligations under Rules 202 and 203." Rules 202 and 203 establish generally accepted auditing standards and promulgated accounting principles as authoritative pronouncements. This exception to Rule 301 requires that the auditor follow generally accepted auditing standards and promulgated accounting principles even if these are in conflict with the confidentiality rule. For example, as will be noted in Chapter 3, *SAS No. 1, Subsequent Discovery of Facts Existing at the Date of the Auditor's Report* (AU 561), requires the CPA, when he or she discovers facts that existed at the date of the report but that were not

---

[7]These 18 states are Arizona, Colorado, Florida, Georgia, Illinois, Indiana, Iowa, Kentucky, Louisiana, Maryland, Michigan, Missouri, Montana, Nevada, New Mexico, Pennsylvania, Tennessee, and Texas. The Texas privilege is virtually nullified by its many exceptions. In addition, Puerto Rico also has adopted a CPA-client privileged communication statute.

Professional Judgment

CPA Should Apply Broad Principles in Making Ethical Decisions

Auditors must exercise judgment when making decisions on matters that involve moral principles. Although the AICPA Code of Professional Conduct provides the moral reasoning and framework for the rules governing the performance of services by CPAs, the CPA must use individual judgment to determine whether an action is ethical in a given situation. The first of the six principles outlined in the code states that "in carrying out their responsibilities as professionals, CPAs should exercise sensitive professional and moral judgments in all their activities."

Rulings answer questions regarding the application of the Code of Professional Conduct to specific circumstances; however, they cannot and do not provide guidance to meet all conditions that might occur. CPAs must always carefully analyze the broad principles that underlie the rules. When performing any professional service, a CPA should never subordinate his or her own judgment to others. A CPA who has doubts about the proper performance of an activity should consult both the state accountancy statutes and the AICPA Code of Professional Conduct. Then the CPA should use judgment in making the final decision.

appropriately disclosed, to disclose this information if the information would have an effect on the audit report and the financial statements and the client refuses to make such disclosure. Thus, *SAS No. 1* (AU 561) is an exception to Rule 301.

Contingent Fees

Rule 302 on contingent fees states that a CPA in public practice shall not:

(1) Perform for a contingent fee any professional services for, or receive such a fee from, a client for whom the CPA or the CPA's firm performs
   (a) an audit or review of a financial statement.
   (b) a compilation of a financial statement when the CPA expects, or reasonably might expect that a third party will use the financial statement and the CPA's compilation report does not disclose a lack of independence.
   (c) an examination of prospective financial information.
(2) Prepare an original or amended tax return or claim for a tax refund for a contingent fee for any client.

The prohibition applies during the period when a CPA is engaged to perform any of the listed services and the period covered by any historical financial statements involved in such services. Thus, CPAs may accept contingent fees from certain clients for whom the CPA does not perform audit, review, compilation, or examinations of prospective financial information. Note that contingent fees are permitted for compilation engagements if the financial statements and the CPA's compilation report are not expected to be used by third parties and the compilation report discloses a lack of independence. For example, a CPA could accept a fee contingent upon the return on an investment that the CPA recommended provided that the CPA has not performed such services as an audit for the client. Other examples of acceptable contingent fees include:

1. Representing a client in an examination of the client's federal or state income tax return by a revenue agent.

2. Filing an amended federal or state income tax return claiming a tax refund based on a tax issue that is either the subject of a test case (involving a different taxpayer), or with respect to which the taxing authority is developing a position.
3. Filing an amended federal or state income tax return (or refund claim) claiming a tax refund in an amount greater than the threshold for review by the Joint Committee on Internal Revenue Taxation ($1 million at March 1991) or state taxing authority.
4. Requesting a refund of either overpayment of interest or penalties charged to a client's account or deposits of taxes improperly accounted for by the federal or state taxing authority in circumstances where the taxing authority has established procedures for the substantive review of such refund requests.
5. Requesting, by means of "protest" or similar document, consideration by the state or local taxing authority of a reduction in the "assessed value" of property under an established taxing authority review process for hearing all taxpayer arguments relating to assessed value.
6. Representing a client in connection with obtaining a private letter ruling or influencing the drafting of a regulation or statute.

For example, a contingent fee would not be permitted if a CPA prepared an amended federal or state income tax return for a client claiming a refund of taxes because a deduction was inadvertently omitted from the return originally filed. There is no question as to the propriety of the deduction; rather the claim is filed to correct an omission. Note that Rule 302 may differ from rules adopted by state agencies that license CPAs.

Table 2–6 shows selected ethics rulings on confidential client information and contingent fees.

Acts Discreditable

Rule 501 on Acts Discreditable states: "A CPA shall not commit an act discreditable to the profession."

Rule 501 applies to all members of the AICPA regardless of whether or not they are in public accounting. Although the rules do not specify what acts would be considered discreditable, the AICPA's Ethics Committee has promulgated a number of interpretations of Rule 501 that define acts considered discreditable.

Interpretation 501-1 states that the retention of client records by a CPA after a demand is made for them is an act discreditable to the profession. Client records are any accounting or other records belonging to the client that were provided to the

---

Table 2–6 **Selected Ethics Rulings on Confidential Client Information and Contingent Fees**

- A CPA may use an outside service bureau to process tax returns for clients if the CPA takes precautions to ensure confidentiality.
- If a CPA withdraws from an engagement because the CPA discovers irregularities in the client's tax return, the CPA must obtain permission from the client to discuss the matter with a successor CPA.
- A CPA may use a record-retention agency to store client records and working papers.
- A CPA staff person submitting a resume to another firm may disclose the name of a client that the CPA has audited without the client's written consent unless disclosure of the client's name constitutes the release of confidential information.

CPA by, or on behalf of, the client. A CPA's working papers—including but not limited to analyses and schedules prepared by the client at the CPA's request—are the CPA's property, not client records, and need not be made available to the client. In some instances, a CPA's working papers contain information that is not reflected in the client books and records, which results in the client's financial information being incomplete. This information includes (1) adjusting, closing, combining, or consolidating journal entries and (2) information normally contained in books of original entry and general ledgers or subsidiary ledgers. When an engagement has been completed, such information should also be made available to the client upon request. However, the CPA may require that all fees due the member with respect to that completed engagement be paid before the information is provided. If an engagement is terminated prior to completion, the CPA is required to return only client records as defined above.

Interpretation 501-2 states that discrimination by CPAs in employment based upon race, color, religion, sex, or national origin is an act discreditable to the accounting profession.

Interpretation 501-3 covers engagements to audit government grants, governmental units, or other recipients of government monies. These audits usually require the CPA to follow not only generally accepted auditing standards but also auditing standards promulgated by the various government agencies that provide the grants. These standards are discussed in more detail in Chapter 23. The interpretation essentially provides that if a CPA accepts a government grant audit engagement and undertakes an obligation to perform that audit in accordance with the auditing standards of the particular government agency providing the grant funds, it is deemed an act discreditable to the profession for the CPA not to comply with those auditing standards unless the CPA discloses in the audit report the fact that such standards were not followed and the reasons therefor. Interpretation 501-4 that a CPA who, by virtue of negligence, makes or permits or directs another to make false or misleading entries in the financial statements or records of an entity has committed an act discreditable to the profession.

Advertising and Other Forms of Solicitation

Rule 502 on advertising and other forms of solicitation states: "A CPA in public practice shall not seek to obtain clients by advertising, or other forms of solicitation in a manner that is false, misleading or deceptive. Solicitation by the use of coercion, over-reaching, or harassing conduct is prohibited."

Until 1978, CPAs were prohibited from advertising by the Code of Professional Conduct. During the 1970s, in a case involving the legal profession, the U.S. Supreme Court decided that ethical prohibitions against advertising violated the constitutional right of free speech. Accordingly, the membership of the AICPA eliminated the old rule prohibiting advertising and adopted an ethical rule forbidding advertising or solicitation that is false, misleading, or deceptive. An advertisement is false, misleading, or deceptive if it

1. creates false or unjustified expectations of favorable results.
2. implies the ability to influence any court, tribunal, regulatory agency, or similar body or official.
3. contains a representation that specific professional services in current or future periods will be performed for a stated fee, estimated fee, or fee range when it was likely at the time of the representation that such fees would be substantially increased and the prospective client was not advised of that likelihood.
4. contains any other representations that would be likely to cause a reasonable person to misunderstand or be deceived.

For example, if a CPA advertised that he or she guaranteed an unqualified opinion for an audit, this would be considered a violation of Rule 502.

Commissions

(handwritten in margin: Contingent fees are prohibited (progressive billing))

Rule 503 on commissions states:

A. *Prohibited Commissions*
A member in public practice shall not for a commission recommend or refer to a client any product or service, or for a commission recommend or refer any product or service to be supplied by a client, or receive a commission, when the member or the member's firm also performs for that client.
(a) an audit or review of a financial statement; or
(b) a compilation of a financial statement when the member expects, or reasonably might expect, that a third party will use the financial statement and the member's compilation report does not disclose a lack of independence; or
(c) an examination of prospective financial information.
   This prohibition applies during the period in which the member is engaged to perform any of the services listed above and the period covered by any historical financial statements involved in such listed services.
B. *Disclosure of Permitted Commissions*
A member in public practice who is not prohibited by this rule from performing services for or receiving a commission and who is paid or expects to be paid a commission shall disclose that fact to any person or entity to whom the member recommends or refers a product or service to which the commission relates.
C. *Referral Fees*
Any member who accepts a referral fee for recommending or referring any service of a CPA to any person or entity or who pays a referral fee to obtain a client shall disclose such acceptance or payment to the client.

Rule 503 prohibits CPAs from recommending or referring for a commission any product or service to or receiving commissions from an attest client, and also prohibits CPAs from referring or recommending for a commission or receiving a commission with respect to any product or service to be supplied by a client. The logic here is the same as that for Rule 302 on contingent fees: to ensure objectivity for the CPA when performing an attestation service. Note that Rule 503 may differ from rules adopted by state agencies that license CPAs.

Form of Practice and Name

Rule 505 on form of practice and name states:

A member may practice public accounting only in the form of organization permitted by state law or regulation, or a professional corporation whose characteristics conform to resolutions of Council.
   A member shall not practice public accounting under a firm name that is misleading. Names of one or more past partners or shareholders may be included in the firm name of a successor partnership or corporation. The firm name should not indicate a partnership when it is a proprietorship.
   A firm may not designate itself as "Members of the American Institute of Certified Public Accountants" unless all of its partners or shareholders are members of the Institute.

Rule 505 permits a firm name that includes a fictitious name or that indicates specialization, provided that the firm name or specialization is not misleading. This is consistent with the rule on advertising and solicitation, which prohibits only statements or assertions that are false, misleading, or deceptive. Firms may advertise a specialty so long as they do not violate Rule 502 on advertising.

Table 2-7	**Selected Ethics Rulings on Acts Discreditable, Advertising and Other Forms of Solicitation, Commissions, and Form of Practice and Name**

- A CPA bank controller not in public practice may use the title "CPA" on bank stationery in paid bank advertisements.
- Providing actuarial services is not incompatible with the practice of public accounting.
- CPAs should not use a letterhead showing the names of two accountants when a partnership does not exist.
- A CPA may form a mixed partnership for the practice of public accounting with a public accountant provided the partnership does not represent itself as a partnership of CPAs. However, some state boards and CPA societies have rules prohibiting mixed partnerships.
- A CPA may permit his or her firm's name to be imprinted on a newsletter, tax booklet, or similar publication provided that the information contained therein is not false, misleading, or deceptive.

In addition, Rule 505 prohibits a firm from identifying itself as an AICPA member unless all of the owners are members of the institute. Rule 505 requires that all owners be CPAs. Council, the AICPA's governing body, has adopted a resolution permitting accounting firms to be owned by non-CPAs under certain circumstances. This resolution applies only to AICPA members. Most state regulatory bodies do not permit non-CPAs to own accounting firms.

Selected ethics rulings on acts discreditable, advertising and other forms of solicitation, commissions, and form of practice and name are shown in Table 2-7.

Enforcement Procedures

For the Code of Professional Conduct to be effective, enforcement procedures must be applied. Enforcement of ethics potentially involves four groups: state boards of accountancy, the Securities and Exchange Commission, the AICPA Professional Ethics Division, and the National Trial Board.

State Boards of Accountancy

CPAs are licensed to practice public accounting and receive their CPA certificates from boards of accountancy in the fifty states and four territorial jurisdictions that regulate CPAs in the United States.

The authority to license includes the authority to revoke or suspend that license for any infraction of the state or territory accountancy statutes. Boards of accountancy have the ultimate regulatory authority over CPAs. All CPAs, whether or not in public practice, should be thoroughly familiar with the accountancy statutes and regulations adopted by state boards of accountancy in the state or territory from which they received their license to practice and their certificate and in the state or territory where they work.

The regulations of most state boards of accountancy are similar in their provisions to the AICPA Code of Professional Conduct. However, in some states significant differences exist between state accountancy regulations and the AICPA's code. When a CPA doubts the proper performance of an activity, both the state accountancy statutes and the AICPA Code of Professional Conduct should be consulted.

A state board of accountancy may impose penalties against CPAs who perform services in a substandard manner, fail to meet continuing professional education requirements, or violate any other provision of an accountancy statute or board regulation. In general, these penalties are imposed after an investigation and due process hearing conducted by the board. The penalties may include suspension or revocation of a CPA's license and/or certificate or other penalties the board has authority to impose.

Securities and Exchange Commission

CPAs may perform services for clients whose securities are subject to regulation by the Securities and Exchange Commission (SEC), a federal agency discussed in more detail in Chapter 3. In this event, the CPA should be thoroughly familiar with SEC rules, regulations, and pronouncements, since the CPA is under the SEC's authority. As discussed in Chapter 3, SEC rules may differ in significant respects from those promulgated by the AICPA. For example, in a number of situations the SEC's independence rules differ from those of the AICPA. The SEC regulates CPAs practicing before it and may impose penalties against CPAs for violations of SEC rules and regulations.

AICPA Professional Ethics Division

The AICPA's *Professional Ethics Division* is comprised of an executive committee that sets division policy and three subcommittees: Independence and Behavioral Standards, Technical Standards, and Government Technical Standards. Under the AICPA bylaws, the Ethics Division is responsible for interpreting and enforcing the AICPA's Code of Professional Conduct. The division investigates complaints and other information that comes to its attention alleging potential violation of the AICPA's Code of Professional Conduct, rulings, and interpretations. The jurisdiction of the Ethics Division over AICPA members is derived from the members' agreement upon joining the AICPA to abide by its bylaws and Code of Professional Conduct. AICPA bylaws require that members cooperate with the Ethics Division in its investigations. After conducting an investigation in accordance with established procedures, the committees of the Ethics Division may find a violation of the Code of Professional Conduct (for example, an audit or review was conducted in a substandard manner). In such a case, depending upon the severity of the violation, a member may be required to take continuing professional education courses and to submit future work for division review. If after investigation a member is found to have violated the code in a sufficiently severe manner, the member will be referred to the Joint Trial Board. If a hearing panel finds a member guilty of violating the Code of Professional Conduct, the member's name and a brief description of violations and penalties are published in the *CPA Letter*. In all other respects Ethics Division investigations, conclusions, and penalties imposed are all confidential.

The enforcement activities of the AICPA's Ethics Division are performed in co-operation with the 50 state CPA societies under a program called the ***Joint Ethics Enforcement Program (JEEP)***. JEEP provides that a particular state society may perform an ethics investigation in situations in which a CPA is a member of both the state society and the AICPA. Upon concluding the investigation, the society will refer its investigation file to the AICPA for concurrence in the result and action to be taken. In this way, a member of both organizations is subject to only one investigation.

Joint Trial Board

The AICPA's ***Joint Trial Board*** conducts hearings of charges brought by the Ethics Division and/or state CPA societies against its joint members. The hearings are held under procedures adopted by the Trial Board. The rules of evidence that apply in courts do not apply to the Trial Board hearings, which are conducted informally. Decisions of the Trial Board are published in an AICPA publication called *The CPA Letter*, and transcripts of the hearing are made available to the state boards of accountancy on request. Members who appear before the Trial Board have a right to appeal a finding of guilt, which may carry with it such actions as expulsion or suspension from AICPA membership and peer review of the CPA firm.

Significant Terms

AICPA Code of Professional Conduct Set of rules and principles that address ethical responsibilities for members of the AICPA; used by CPAs as a means of assuring that quality services are provided.

Ethics The moral principles or rules of conduct recognized by an individual or a particular group of individuals.

Ethics rulings Formal published rulings made by the Executive Committee of the Professional Ethics Division of the AICPA that answer specific questions regarding proper CPA conduct.

Interpretations of the Rules of Conduct Published guidelines on the application and scope of the Rules of the Code of Professional Conduct.

Joint Ethics Enforcement Program (JEEP) Program consisting of the AICPA and state CPA societies that allows a particular state society to perform an ethics investigation in situations in which a CPA is a member of both the state society and the AICPA.

Joint Trial Board A board that disposes of ethics cases that are not resolved by the Professional Ethics Executive Committee or by state society ethics committees.

Principles of the Code of Professional Conduct A goal-oriented and aspirational framework for the rules governing the performance of services by CPAs.

Professional Ethics Division An executive committee of the AICPA that examines potential violation of professional standards.

Rules of the Code of Professional Conduct Enforceable rules approved by the membership of the AICPA that establish the minimum acceptable standards of conduct for CPAs and enforce such conduct on AICPA members.

Discussion Questions

2-1. Why have all professions established codes of ethics?

2-2. Identify and briefly describe the two parts of the AICPA Code of Professional Conduct.

2-3. Describe the six broad concepts of ethical responsibilities of the AICPA.

2-4. Why is independence such an important concept for CPAs?

2-5. Does Rule 101 on independence apply to CPAs conducting a tax engagement? An audit engagement?

2-6. According to Rule 101, when would a CPA be considered to lack independence?

2-7. What is the difference between a direct financial interest and an indirect financial interest?

2-8. What types of loans can a CPA obtain from a financial institution client? From other types of clients?

2-9. Can a CPA perform write-up or bookkeeping services for a client and also perform the audit? Why or why not?

2-10. Do the concepts of *due care* and *planning and supervision* apply only to CPAs performing an audit?

2-11. What does Rule 202 on compliance with standards state? Why is it important?

2-12. What effect do Rules 202 and 203 have on CPAs?

2-13. Describe the four exceptions to the confidentiality rule for CPAs.

2-14. What are contingent fees? Are CPAs always forbidden from accepting contingent fees? Why or why not?

2-15. How has Rule 501 regarding discreditable acts been enforced by the AICPA?

2-16. How is advertising prohibited for CPAs?

2-17. May a member of the AICPA ever accept a commission? Why or why not?

2-18. What are the purposes of Rule 505 on the form of practice and name for a CPA?

2-19. What is the Professional Ethics Division of the AICPA and what is its function?

Objective Questions

*2-20. Which of the following statements best describes why the CPA profession has deemed it essential to promulgate a code of ethics and to establish a mechanism for enforcing observance of the code?

(**1**) A distinguishing mark of a profession is its acceptance of responsibility to the public.

(**2**) A prerequisite for success is the establishment of an ethical code that stresses primarily the professional's responsibility to clients and colleagues.

(**3**) Most state laws require the profession to establish a code of ethics.

(**4**) An essential means of self-protection for the profession is the establishment of flexible ethical standards by the profession.

*2-21. A CPA purchased stock in a client corporation and placed it in a trust as an educational fund for the CPA's minor child. The CPA was a trustee of the trust. The trust securities were not material to the CPA but were material to the child's personal net worth. Would the independence of the CPA be considered to be impaired with respect to the client?

(**1**) Yes, because the stock would be considered a direct financial interest and, consequently, materiality is not a factor.

---

*AICPA adapted.

(2) Yes, because the stock would be considered an indirect financial interest that is material to the CPA's child.

(3) No, because the CPA would not be considered to have a direct financial interest in the client.

(4) No, because the CPA would not be considered to have a material indirect financial interest in the client.

*2-22. In which of the following circumstances would a CPA who audits XM Corporation lack independence?

(1) The CPA and XM's president are both on the board of directors of COD Corporation.

(2) The CPA and XM's president each own 25% of FOB Corporation, a closely held company.

(3) The CPA has a home mortgage from XM, which was obtained on January 15, 1991.

(4) The CPA reduced XM's usual audit fee by 40% because XM's financial condition was unfavorable.

*2-23. In which of the following instances would the independence of the CPA *not* be considered to be impaired? The CPA has been retained as the auditor of a brokerage firm

(1) that owes the CPA audit fees for more than one year.

(2) in which the CPA has obtained a car loan in the amount of $4,500.

(3) in which the CPA's brother is the controller.

(4) that owes the CPA audit fees for current-year services and has just filed a petition for bankruptcy.

*2-24. A CPA examines the financial statements of a local bank. According to the AICPA Code of Professional Conduct, the independence ordinarily would not be impaired if the CPA

(1) serves on the bank's committee that approves loans.

(2) owns several shares of the bank's common stock.

(3) obtains a short-term loan from the bank.

(4) uses the bank's time-sharing computer service to solve bank-related problems.

*2-25. Printers, Inc., an audit client of James Frank, CPA, is contemplating the installation of an electronic data-processing system. It would be inconsistent with Frank's independence as the auditor of Printers' financial statements for him to

(1) recommend accounting controls to be exercised over the computer.

(2) recommend particular hardware and software packages to be used in the new computer center.

(3) prepare a study of the feasibility of computer installation.

(4) supervise the operation of Printers' computer center on a part-time basis.

*2-26. In which of the following circumstances would a CPA be bound by the AICPA Code of Professional Conduct to refrain from disclosing any confidential information obtained during the course of a professional engagement?

(1) The CPA is issued a summons enforceable by a court order that requires the CPA to present confidential information.

(2) A major stockholder of a client company seeks accounting information from the CPA after management declined to disclose the requested information.

(3) Confidential client information is made available as part of a quality review of the CPA's practice by a review team authorized by the AICPA.

(4) An inquiry by a disciplinary body of a state CPA society requests confidential client information.

---

*AICPA adapted.

*2-27. Pat Clark, CPA, wishes to express an opinion that the financial statements of Smith Co. are presented in conformity with generally accepted accounting principles. However, the financial statements contain a departure from *FASB No. 5.*

(1) Under any circumstances, Clark would be in violation of the Code of Professional Conduct if he were to issue such an opinion.

(2) Clark should disclaim an opinion.

(3) Clark may issue the opinion if he can demonstrate that due to unusual circumstances the financial statements of Smith Co. would otherwise have been misleading.

(4) This specific situation is not covered by the rules established by the Code of Professional Conduct.

*2-28. The AICPA Code of Professional Conduct states that a CPA shall not disclose any confidential information obtained in the course of a professional engagement except with the consent of his or her client. In which one of the situations given below would disclosure by a CPA be in violation of the code?

(1) Disclosing confidential information in order to properly discharge the CPA's responsibilities in accordance with the profession's standards.

(2) Disclosing confidential information in compliance with a subpoena issued by a court.

(3) Disclosing confidential information to another accountant interested in purchasing the CPA's practice.

(4) Disclosing confidential information in a review of the CPA's professional practices by the AICPA Quality Review Committee.

*2-29. The CPA should not undertake an engagement if the fee is to be based upon which of the following?

(1) The findings of a tax authority.

(2) A percentage of audited net income.

(3) Per diem rates plus expenses.

(4) Rates set by a city ordinance.

*2-30. In determining estimates of fees, an auditor may take into account each of the following, *except* the

(1) value of the service to the client.

(2) degree of responsibility assumed by undertaking the engagement.

(3) skills required to perform the service.

(4) attainment of specific findings.

*2-31. Paula Godette, a non-CPA, has a law practice. Godette recommended one of her clients to Peter Doyle, CPA, and Doyle agreed to pay Godette 10% of the fee for services rendered by Doyle to Godette's client. Who, if anyone, is in violation of the Code of Professional Conduct?

(1) Both Godette and Doyle.

(2) Neither Godette nor Doyle.

(3) Only Godette.

(4) Only Doyle.

*2-32. A CPA's retention of client accounting records that were provided to the CPA on behalf of the client as a means of enforcing payment of an overdue audit fee is

(1) considered acceptable by the AICPA Code of Professional Conduct.

(2) ill advised, because it would impair the CPA's independence with respect to the client.

(3) considered discreditable to the profession.

(4) a violation of generally accepted auditing standards.

---

*AICPA adapted.

Problems and Cases

*2-33. (Independence) Auditors must not only appear to be independent; they must also be independent in fact.

REQUIRED

A. Explain the concept of *auditor's independence* as it applies to third-party reliance upon financial statements.

B. (1) What determines whether or not an auditor is independent in fact?

(2) What determines whether or not an auditor appears to be independent?

C. Explain how an auditor may be independent in fact but not appear to be independent.

D. Would a CPA be considered independent for an audit of the financial statements of a

(1) church for which the CPA is serving as treasurer without compensation? Explain.

(2) club for which the spouse is serving as treasurer-bookkeeper if the CPA is not to receive a fee for the audit? Explain.

*2-34. (Independence) An auditor's report was appended to the financial statements of Worthmore, Inc. The statements consisted of a balance sheet as of November 30, 19X4, and statements of income and retained earnings for the year then ending. The first three paragraphs of the report contained the wording of the standard unqualified report, and a fourth paragraph read as follows:

> **The wives of two partners of our firm owned a material investment in the outstanding common stock of Worthmore, Inc., during the fiscal year ending November 30, 19X4. The aforementioned individuals disposed of their holdings of Worthmore, Inc., on December 3, 19X4, in a transaction that did not result in a profit or a loss. This information is included in our report in order to comply with certain disclosure requirements of the Code of Professional Conduct of the American Institute of Certified Public Accountants.**
>
> **BELL & DAVIS**
> **Certified Public Accountants**

REQUIRED

A. Was the CPA firm of Bell & Davis independent with respect to the fiscal 19X4 audit of Worthmore, Inc.'s financial statements? Explain.

B. Do you find Bell & Davis's auditor's report satisfactory? Explain.

C. Assume that no members of Bell & Davis or any members of their families held any financial interests in Worthmore, Inc., during 19X4. For each of the following cases, indicate if independence would be lacking on behalf of Bell & Davis, assuming that Worthmore, Inc., is a profit-seeking enterprise. In each case, explain why independence would or would not be lacking.

---

*AICPA adapted.

(1) Two directors of Worthmore, Inc., became partners in the CPA firm of Bell & Davis on July 1, 19X4, resigning their directorships on that date.

(2) During 19X4, the former controller of Worthmore, now a Bell & Davis partner, was frequently called on for assistance by Worthmore. He made decisions for Worthmore's management regarding fixed asset acquisitions and the company's product marketing mix. In addition, he conducted a computer feasibility study for Worthmore.

*2-35. (Independence) The attribute of independence has been traditionally associated with the CPA's function of auditing and expressing opinions on financial statements.
REQUIRED
A. What is meant by *independence* as applied to the CPA's function of auditing and expressing opinions on financial statements? Discuss.
B. CPAs have imposed upon themselves certain rules of professional conduct that induce their members to retain independence and that strengthen public confidence in their independence. Which of the rules of professional conduct are concerned with the CPA's independence? Discuss.

*2-36. (Independence) The Rocky Hill Corporation was formed on October 1, 19X4, and its fiscal year will end on September 30, 19X5. You audited the corporation's opening balance sheet and rendered an unqualified opinion on it. A month after rendering your report you are offered the position of secretary of the company because of its need for a complete set of officers and for convenience in signing various documents. You will have no financial interest in the company through stock ownership or otherwise, will receive no salary, will not keep the books, and will not have any influence on its financial matters other than occasional advice on income tax matters and similar advice normally given a client by a CPA.
REQUIRED
A. Assume that you accept the offer but plan to resign the position prior to conducting your annual audit with the intention of again assuming the office after rendering an opinion on the statements. Can you render an independent opinion on the financial statements? Discuss.
B. Assume that you accept the offer on a temporary basis until the corporation has gotten under way and can employ a secretary. In any event you would permanently resign the position before conducting your annual audit. Can you render an independent opinion on the financial statements? Discuss.

*2-37. (Independence) Fred Browning, CPA, has audited the financial statements of Grimm Company for several years. Grimm's president has now asked Browning to install an inventory system for the company.
REQUIRED
What factors should Browning consider in determining whether to accept the engagement?

*2-38. (Independence and Management Advisory Services) Your audit client, Nuesel Corporation, requested that you conduct a feasibility study to advise management of the best way the corporation can utilize electronic data-processing equipment and to suggest which computer best meets the corporation's requirements. You are technically competent in this area and accept the engagement. Upon completion of your study, the corporation accepts your suggestions and installs the computer and related equipment that you recommend.
REQUIRED
A. Discuss the effect the acceptance of this management services engagement would have upon your independence in expressing an opinion on the financial statements of the Nuesel Corporation.

*AICPA adapted.

B. Instead of accepting the engagement, assume that you recommended Ike Mackey, of the CPA firm of Brown and Mackey, who is qualified in specialized services. Upon completion of the engagement, your client requests that Mackey's partner, John Brown, perform services in other areas. Should Brown accept the engagement? Discuss.

*2-39. (Possible Ethics Violations) Jack Gilbert and Will Bradley formed a corporation called Financial Services, Inc., each taking 50% of the authorized common stock. Gilbert is a CPA and a member of the AICPA. Bradley is a CPCU (chartered property casualty underwriter). The corporation performs auditing and tax services under Gilbert's direction and insurance services under Bradley's supervision. The opening of the corporation's office was announced by a three-inch, two-column "card" in the local newspaper.

One of the corporation's first audit clients was the Grandtime Company. Grandtime had total assets of $600,000 and total liabilities of $270,000. In the course of his examination, Gilbert found that Grandtime's building with a book value of $240,000 was pledged as security for a ten-year-term note in the amount of $200,000. The client's statement did not mention that the building was pledged as security for the note. However, as the failure to disclose the lien did not affect either the value of the assets or the amount of the liabilities, and his examination was satisfactory in all other respects, Gilbert rendered an unqualified opinion on Grandtime's financial statements. About two months after the date of his opinion, Gilbert learned that an insurance company was planning to loan Grandtime $150,000 in the form of a first-mortgage note on the building. Realizing that the insurance company was unaware of the existing lien on the building, Gilbert had Bradley notify the insurance company of the fact that Grandtime's building was pledged as security for the term note.

Shortly after the events described above, Gilbert was charged with a violation of the Code of Professional Conduct.

REQUIRED

Identify and discuss the ethical implications of those acts by Gilbert that were in violation of the AICPA Code of Professional Conduct.

2-40. (Working Papers) Susan Doyle, CPA, received a phone call from Purvis Corp., a client, requesting that Doyle provide Purvis with a copy of her consolidating worksheets used in preparing the consolidated financial statements. Doyle states that Purvis still owes half of the audit fee and upon payment of the fee she will provide a copy of the worksheet.

REQUIRED

Is Doyle's position appropriate? Would providing working papers violate the confidentiality rule of the Code of Conduct?

2-41. (Advertising) In 1978, the AICPA voted to eliminate the rule forbidding advertising, competitive bidding, offers of employment to employees of another firm, and encroachment on another firm's client.

REQUIRED

Discuss the purpose for these changes and what effect these changes have had.

2-42. (Possible Ethics Violations) For each of the following situations that involve a possible violation of the AICPA Code of Professional Conduct, state the applicable section of the rules of professional conduct and indicate whether the situation does in fact represent a violation.

A. In preparing Beth Hunt's tax return, Dale Geeslin, CPA, noted that the deduction for medical expenses was quite large. When he asked Hunt for further information on the deduction, she stated, "Don't ask me anything and I won't tell you any lies." Geeslin then proceeded to complete the return based on the information given.

---

*AICPA adapted.

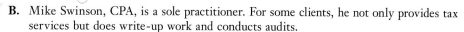

[handwritten margin note: OK, not in violation Rule 101]

[handwritten margin note: Be Careful! YES! Rule 101 OK]

[handwritten margin note: Client's Permission]

B. Mike Swinson, CPA, is a sole practitioner. For some clients, he not only provides tax services but does write-up work and conducts audits.

C. Laura Bailey, CPA, is an audit senior with Dalton and Company, CPAs, a regional CPA firm in the Southeast. She owns ten shares of stock in a client of Dalton and Company; however, she does not take part in the audit of this client nor is the amount of stock material to her total wealth.

D. Bill Weeks, CPA, recently set up his practice in a downtown office building. To encourage potential clients, he printed a poster stating, "Bill Weeks, CPA, income tax returns prepared here" for display in a window.   *NOT IN VIOLATION*

E. Paul Barber and Mark Jacobs, CPAs, recently formed a partnership to practice public accounting. To announce this fact, they ran an advertisement in the local newspaper stating that they had formed a partnership to practice public accounting in the city.   *NO VIOLATION*

F. Mark Beasley, CPA, recently sold his accounting practice to Steven Glasscock, CPA. After obtaining permission from all his audit clients, Beasley gave Glasscock all working papers for those clients.   *OK!*

2-43. (Possible Ethics Violations) For each of the following situations, indicate whether the CPA is in violation of the Code of Professional Conduct and what rule, if any, is violated.

A. Herb Lewis, CPA, discloses confidential information in a quality review of the firm's quality control procedures.

B. Cynthia Spinks, CPA, pays a commission to Abby Castellunas, an attorney, to obtain a client.

C. Ben Reeves, CPA, quotes an audit fee to a potential client on the basis of a standard hourly rate.

D. Steve Ostenson, CPA, incorporates and adopts the name Tax Refunds, Inc.

E. Macke Mauldin, CPA, and Joel Brown, CPA, open their own CPA firm, which they decide to name Cratchett & Co.

F. Barney Waters, CPA, was recently convicted of falsifying his own personal income tax returns and has received a five-year prison sentence.

2-44. (Possible Ethics Violations) For each of the following situations, indicate whether the CPA is in violation of the Code of Professional Conduct, and, if so, which rule is violated.

A. Stephen Kruse, CPA, has an automobile loan from Pontchartrain National Bank. Kruse also performs the audit engagement for this particular client.

B. Greg Henderson, CPA, has not received any accounting fees from Phigam, Inc., for the last four months. Consequently, Henderson has withheld the client's records that were provided to Henderson until the payment is received.

C. Rick Langreck, CPA, accepted an engagement to study the Nashville Hospital Supplies, Inc., data-processing system. Langreck has very limited computer experience and does not have the expertise to complete the engagement.

D. Jeff Sibley, CPA, recently obtained a collateralized automobile loan from Mount Hope Nurseries, Inc., a major audit client of Sibley.

E. Cole Portis, CPA, understands that he may be doing the audit of Toomer Supply, Inc., for the year ending December 31. As such, Portis sells his shares of stock in Toomer Supply, Inc., the prior November.

F. Dennis Scott, CPA, resigned his position as vice-president of finance of the Purple Pilgrim Co. effective March 31. He plans to accept the audit engagement for the Purple Pilgrim Co. for the year ending June 30.

2-45. (Possible Conflict of Interest) Rick Tabor, CPA, is auditing Knoxville Corporation, for whom he expects to express an unqualified opinion. Tabor has also just begun his audit of Martha, Inc., a major customer of Knoxville Corp. During the audit of Martha, Inc., Tabor discovers evidence that suggests that Martha, Inc., will be unable to pay Knoxville Corporation and thus the receivable should be written off.

REQUIRED
- **A.** Is it permissible for Tabor to share this information on Martha, Inc., with Knoxville Corporation?
- **B.** How should Tabor proceed?

2-46. (Possible Ethics Violations) For each of the following situations, indicate whether the CPA or his or her firm is in violation of the Code of Professional Conduct and what rule, if any, is violated.

- **A.** Jeff Leeper is a partner in Perry and Leeper, CPAs. Jeff's son owns 25% of a firm that Perry and Leeper audit.
- **B.** Susan Lumpkin, CPA, did the tax return for Guess Corp. in 1987. In 1988, Lumpkin found some information that was left out of the tax return. She has received the client's permission to inform the IRS.
- **C.** Steve Rice, CPA, is a sole practitioner. The sign outside his office says, "Steve Rice, CPA. Best Services in Town."
- **D.** Dan Schisler, Lisa Limbaugh, and Wes Hudson formed a CPA firm and designated themselves as "Members of the AICPA." However, Hudson's degree is in tax law and he is not a CPA.
- **E.** LouAnn Medlock, CPA, did some private consulting for the Ellis Company in 1988. Later, the Ellis Company asked Medlock to perform an audit.
- **F.** Becky McDaniel, CPA, was given an honorary director's position with the local chapter of the cancer society. All material distributed states that the position is honorary, and McDaniel does not participate in any management decisions. Her firm has been asked to perform an audit.

2-47. (Advertising) Bill Harmon, CPA, has started his accounting practice and is trying to decide how to inform the public of the availability of his services. Harmon placed an advertisement in the local newspaper to announce the opening of his practice. Included in the ad was the statement that he would be available to the public more than any other CPA in town. In fact, Harmon was the only CPA in town. Harmon also decided to place an advertisement in the yellow pages of the phone book. Included in the advertisement was the following statement:

"I will provide advice that could allow you to pay the minimum amount of taxes allowed by the law."

REQUIRED
Has Harmon violated the Code of Professional Conduct?

2-48. (Possible Ethics Violations) For each of the following situations, indicate whether the CPA is in violation of the Code of Professional Conduct, and if so, which rule is violated.

- **A.** Alley Timmons, CPA, has joined Cook, Lobeck & Almer CPAs as a senior staff accountant. Timmons has just obtained a home mortgage with First National Bank, which is an audit client of the firm.
- **B.** Tim Anthony, CPA, has a large brokerage account with the investment firm of Bankston and Wilbanks. Bankston and Wilbanks has hired Anthony to perform tax services.
- **C.** Mike Smith, CPA, has an outstanding loan with Tichenor National Bank. Smith has been informed that the bank is considering his firm for the audit of the current years' financial statements. Smith immediately refinances his loan with another bank.
- **D.** Terry Wilks, CPA, has a home equity line of credit with audit client First Bank of Wilson prior to changes in the Code of Professional Conduct that became effective January 1, 1992. Wilks still has the line of credit and intends to use it to purchase a new boat.
- **E.** Ginger Melvin, CPA, accepted a tax client under the condition that her fee for the engagement will be based on the final settlement obtained from the Internal Revenue Service. The services to be rendered are in connection with the filing of an amended return based on a tax issue with respect to which the Internal Revenue Service is developing a position.

Audit Judgment Case

2-49. (Confidentiality) The CPA firm, Pool, Gibbs, & Lee just accepted an audit engagement with the Sure Trust Savings & Loan Association. During the planning stage of the audit, Ron Wilson, CPA, was hired by the CPA firm as an audit staff person to replace Lisa Cook, who had taken an extended leave of absence. On his first day of employment, Wilson learned of the audit engagement with Sure Trust Savings & Loan. Wilson was one of the audit staff members hired to render an opinion on the financial statements of the S & L five years earlier with his preceding CPA firm. Wilson's firm had withdrawn from the engagement after reviewing the operations of the S & L and discovering several management deficiencies. Areas of concern were related party transactions with officers and directors of the S & L. Wilson feels that he has a moral obligation to reveal this information to the partners of his new employer but is concerned that he might violate Rule 301 of the Code of Professional Ethics related to confidential client information.
REQUIRED
Should Wilson inform the partners of Pool, Gibbs, & Lee? Discuss.

Auditing Issues Case

2-50. **KELCO MANUFACTURING COMPANY**

Kelco president Steve Cook has been working to obtain a large loan from the Florence National Bank to purchase the state-of-the-art equipment needed to increase the company's production of specialty textiles. Not only does Steve Cook sit on the board of directors, but his brother, James, is the bank's president. Your firm has been asked to perform the audit of Kelco's financial statements. When discussing this potential engagement with the partners and other key personnel, you learned that two of the partners have outstanding mortgages and three seniors have outstanding car loans with the Florence National Bank. One of the other partners also disclosed that he has had discussions with James Cook on behalf of the firm obtaining a loan to finance the firm's new office in Pensacola, Florida. You raised questions as to whether the firm could accept the engagement with Kelco due to ethical considerations and a possible conflict of interest. Jack Bryan, managing partner, asks for an explanation related to your concerns. The following is dialogue of the conversation:

You: I'm not so sure we should accept this engagement due to our personnel's dealings with the bank.

Bryan: What are you talking about? The engagement is with Kelco, not the bank.

You: Yes, but our firm could lack independence due to our relationship with the bank. I guess the loans of our partners and personnel were obtained before the recent AICPA changes related to obtaining loans from financial institutions who are audit clients.

Bryan: That is exactly my point. The Florence National Bank is not one of our audit clients.

You: Well, I'm just not comfortable due to our relationship with the Bank and the Bank's relationship with Kelco.

REQUIRED
Should the firm accept the engagement? Discuss.

Chapter 3

The Auditor's Legal Liability

Learning Objectives

- Define the important legal concepts (for example, privity, negligence, gross negligence, due diligence) needed to understand the auditor's legal liability.

- Identify the facts that must be established by a client or a third party in a suit against an auditor and the defenses available to the auditor.

- Explain the different theories of liability for negligence to third parties and under common law and identify the cases that developed these theories.

- Contrast liability to third parties under common law versus liability to third parties as established by the Securities Act of 1933 and the Securities Exchange Act of 1934.

- Identify the facts that must be established by a plaintiff in a suit under the 1933 Act and a suit under the Securities Exchange Act of 1934 and the defenses that an auditor may use under each of these acts.

- List the most important federal criminal statutes that may involve auditors.

- State the items in a criminal case that the plaintiff must establish and the defenses available to an auditor.

- Explain the auditor's responsibility for detecting material errors, irregularities, and illegal acts.

- Determine what course of action an auditor should take if he or she overlooks an important fact or omits an important audit procedure.

Expectations placed upon auditors have increased dramatically in the last ten years. The increased expectations are evidenced by a growing number of lawsuits where judgments have found auditors liable for areas seemingly beyond their control. This is especially disconcerting to auditors of large or international companies who rely upon the accuracy and veracity of the work performed by the individuals whose work they are auditing. Professional accounting and auditing organizations are working together with state chapters to define the perimeters of liability.

Consider how would you react if you conducted an audit of a major department store and you and your firm were later sued for misrepresentation of assets and inventory? No accounting firm is large enough to count every asset or inventory item of international department stores such as Neiman Marcus or Sears, for example. However, in some court cases, auditors were found negligent in these reporting areas. Worse, is the likelihood that you could be personally liable for the actions of a fellow partner in a branch office across the country.

Fortunately, auditors are afforded some protection by a number of federal and state laws designed to establish responsibilities of corporations and examiners. This chapter explores landmark cases and the scope of auditors' responsibilities for detecting errors and irregularities in financial reports. ∎

Sources: Shaun F. O'Malley, "Legal Liability Is Having a Chilling Effect on the Auditor's Role," *Accounting Horizons*, Vol. 7, No. 2, June 1993; and Kay O. Wilburn and Lowell S. Broom, "Liability Issues," *Journal of Accountancy*, Vol. 177, No. 3, March 1994.

We live in a litigious society. The auditor today can reasonably expect his or her every action—regardless of how right or wrong it may be—to be questioned in a court of law and possibly to result in substantial damages being awarded. Accountants once considered litigation a problem encountered only by slipshod practitioners. Today, however, even the most competent of practitioners may be involved in litigation as a defendant CPA.

Whenever an audited company goes into bankruptcy or experiences a financial reverse, disappointed investors, creditors, regulatory agencies, and trustees in bankruptcy consider who can be sued for the losses. Obviously, the bankrupt company cannot pay, so auditors, lawyers, and corporate directors provide tempting targets for lawsuits. Plaintiffs suing auditors today are finding it easier to get their claims before a jury. Cases are considerably more likely than ever before to result in large damage awards or negotiated settlements that are detrimental to the auditor. The cost to accounting firms from litigation is steadily increasing, while available insurance coverage has been shrinking rapidly and insurance premiums have been rising dramatically. Since 1984, aggregate premiums for the 11 largest accounting firms in the United States have multiplied by a factor of five, while available coverage has been cut in half. In fact, some insurers are withdrawing coverage altogether, and many small CPA firms can no longer afford insurance at all. According to a recent AICPA survey, 40 percent of CPA firms, other than the six largest, are not carrying liability insurance, largely because the insurance is simply too expensive.

Every person entering the public accounting profession today must be aware of the legal liability inherent in the practice of auditing. This chapter explains the auditor's liability to clients and others under both common and statutory law.[1] Most of the discussion is devoted to *civil liability* because this is the most frequent and severe legal problem facing the profession today. Statements on Auditing Standards that directly address significant legal risk areas, such as the auditor's responsibilities for fraud and illegal acts detection, are also discussed. The concluding section presents suggestions for minimizing the CPA's legal liability. Important legal duties established by or addressed in significant cases involving auditors are discussed throughout the chapter.

Definitions and Concepts

A number of legal concepts are important to the discussion in this chapter.

Privity of contract is a relationship between two or more parties that creates a contractual duty. In an auditing context, the CPA and the client have a privity or contractual relationship that is usually established by a contract called an engagement letter. Usually, however, third parties such as investors or creditors are not parties to the contract and are said to have a nonprivity or noncontractual relationship.

Due professional care as defined in Chapter 1 is the performance of, and reporting on, a professional engagement with the degree of care, competence, learning, and experience commonly possessed by other members of the accounting profession and required by professional standards.

Negligence is the failure of the CPA to perform or report on an engagement with the due professional care and competence of a prudent auditor. The CPA is negligent if he or she fails to do what the ordinary, reasonable, prudent auditor would do, or does what the prudent auditor would not do. Sometimes negligence may be referred to as simple or ordinary. Simple negligence, ordinary negligence, and negligence are synonymous terms.

Gross negligence (also called recklessness or constructive fraud) is a serious occurrence of negligence tantamount to a flagrant or a reckless departure from the standard of due care. These terms are frequently used interchangeably and are equivalent to sloppy auditing or lack of a reasonable basis for a belief. A plaintiff in establishing gross negligence must prove each of the following items:

1. The CPA made a representation about a material fact with lack of reasonable support.
2. The representation was intended to induce reliance by another (for example, a client or a third-party user of the financial statements).
3. The representation was relied on by the client or a third party.
4. The reliance caused damages to the client or third party.

Fraud occurs when a CPA issues an opinion on the financial statements knowing that the financial statements or the audit report thereon is false. Fraud differs from gross negligence in that the auditor does not merely lack reasonable support for belief, but has both knowledge of the falsity and intent to deceive a client or third party.

---

[1]An important case, *1136 Tenants' Corp.*, involving unaudited financial statements, is discussed in Chapter 22.

Figure 3-1	**Range of Misrepresentation**

INNOCENCE	ERROR OF JUDGMENT	NEGLIGENCE	GROSS NEGLIGENCE	FRAUD
Believed with adequate basis	Believed with debatable basis	Believed with inadequate basis	Without belief in the truth of a statement	Known to be false

Thus, fraud contains the following items: (1) false representation, (2) knowledge of a wrong and acting with the intent to deceive, (3) intent to induce reliance, (4) justifiable reliance, and (5) resulting damages.

Figure 3–1 illustrates the gradations of differences from innocent behavior to fraudulent behavior. In litigation, where a certain fact pattern falls on the range of misrepresentation is determined by the court. The distinction between (1) an error of judgment and negligence and (2) negligence and gross negligence is especially blurred and cannot be precisely defined.

Common Law versus Statutory Law

A plaintiff may bring suit against an auditor under common, statutory, or both common and statutory law. The difference between common law and statutory law is in the source of the legal standards that the courts apply. *Common law* refers to unwritten or case-made law that evolves from prior or precedent cases. When deciding a case not governed by written or statutory law, the court looks to the accumulated body of previously decided cases. If dealing with a legal issue identical to a case previously decided by the highest court of the state, the lower court is obligated to follow that precedent. However, the highest state court is not bound to follow its own precedents and occasionally will deliberately reject its own precedent in recognition of changing social needs.

Common law is state dependent. That is, the common law of Texas, for example, is not the same as the common law of New York or California. A court in one state may look to cases decided in another state but is not obligated to follow such cases. In a case without precedent, however, the court will usually borrow concepts from courts of other states.

Statutory law refers to written law as established by federal or state legislative bodies. In a case involving statutory law, such as the federal securities laws, the court is bound to apply the standards enacted by the legislature, unless the standards violate the federal or state constitution, whichever is relevant. Of course, if the statutes are unclear, the court will make its own interpretation.

Common Law Liability to Clients

Suits against the auditor brought by clients generally fall into two categories: (1) cases in which clients sustain a loss as a result of relying on audited financial statements that are materially misstated, and (2) cases in which the auditor fails to discover an embezzlement. For example, auditors have been successfully sued by clients for reporting an overstated profit that caused the client to pay dividends it otherwise would not have paid, and for failing to discover in timely fashion embezzlement by a bookkeeper.

In bringing suit against the auditor, the client may base the action on breach of contract, in tort,[2] or on both grounds. A *suit in contract* is based on the agreement between the auditor and the client (that is, a privity relationship) and on the auditor's alleged breach of that agreement. The agreement may be oral, but preferably it should be written in an engagement letter as discussed in Chapter 12. A *suit in tort* is based on negligence, gross negligence, or fraud.

Standard of Due Professional Care

The client is not justified in expecting infallibility from the CPA, but the client can expect reasonable care and competence. The client purchases services (for example, audits, reviews, or compilations) from the CPA, not insurance against all risks. The CPA is obligated to exercise reasonable ability and skill when compared to what other CPAs would exercise, given the same facts and circumstances. To illustrate, if an audit engagement calls for specialized skills to audit a complex financial transaction, the auditor should have or develop such skills or consult a specialist who has the needed expertise. The CPA is held to the same standard of reasonable care as lawyers, doctors, architects, and other professional people engaged in furnishing skilled services for compensation.

Although the common law standard of care requires the CPA to achieve the standard of reasonable care, the courts have consistently held that a CPA is not liable for mere errors of judgment (see Figure 3-1). The distinction between errors of judgment, which do not result in liability, and negligence, which can result in liability, is a matter of degree and evolves constantly as practice and social expectations change.

Cooley on Torts, a treatise that has stood the test of time, describes a professional's obligation for reasonable care as follows:

> Every man who offers his services to another and is employed, assumes the duty to exercise in the employment such skill as he possesses with reasonable care and diligence. In all these employments where peculiar skill is requisite, if one offers his service, he is understood as holding himself out to the public as possessing the degree of skill commonly possessed by others in the same employment, and if his pretensions are unfounded, he commits a species of fraud upon every man who employs him in reliance on his public profession. But no man, whether skilled or unskilled, undertakes that the task he assumes shall be performed successfully, and without fault or error; he undertakes for good faith and integrity, but not for infallibility, and he is liable to his employer for negligence, bad faith, or dishonesty, but not for losses consequent upon mere errors of judgment.[3]

---

[2]A *tort* is simply a civil wrong, other than breach of contract, for which the court will provide a remedy in the form of an action for damages.
[3]D. Haggard, *Cooley on Torts*, 4th ed., 1932, p. 472.

Burden of Proof and Defenses

The following points must be established by a client, the plaintiff, to succeed in a legal action, in tort or contract, against a CPA, the defendant:

1. The auditor has accepted a duty of care (for example, an obligation to audit certain financial statements).
2. The auditor has breached the duty of care (for example, a failure to deliver the audit report by an agreed-upon date).
3. The client suffered damages (for example, a purchaser of the client's business decides not to buy the business because of the lack of audited financial statements).
4. A close causal connection exists between the auditor's breach and the client's damages (for example, the client is forced to sell the business to another purchaser for $100,000 less than the first purchaser offered).

In defending against the client, the auditor may use one or more of the following defenses:

1. The audit was performed using reasonable care and skill and was performed in accordance with generally accepted auditing standards. (Note, however, that a CPA who violates generally accepted auditing standards is not necessarily liable under common law. For example, the client may be unable to prove that the violation caused damages.)
2. The client's own negligence was a contributing factor in the client's loss. The defense of contributory negligence cannot be used in an action for breach of contract, but it may be raised in a tort action in some states. The modern trend in most states is a defense of comparative or proportional negligence whereby the court allocates the total damages between the client and the CPA based on their relative fault.
3. No causal connection exists between the client's loss and the CPA's actions.

Rights of Subrogees

It is well grounded in law that the rights of the client may be assigned or subrogated (substituted) to a third party such as an insurance or bonding company, a receiver who takes over the client's insolvent business, or a trustee in bankruptcy. For example, an insurance company that reimburses a client for an employee's embezzlement has the same legal rights as the client to compensation. Therefore, if the client's financial statements were audited and the CPA did not detect the embezzlement because of negligence or breach of contract, the *subrogee* (insurance company) is entitled to recover any damages paid to the client by the CPA.

Dantzler Lumber and Export Co. v. *Columbia Casualty Co.* (Florida, 1934) illustrates the rights of a subrogee. Dantzler engaged a CPA firm to perform audits, including the examination of all cash transactions. The audit reports indicated that this had been done. Later, it was determined that Dantzler's bookkeeper had embezzled approximately $40,000 over a four-year period. Had the CPA firm performed proper examinations, they would have uncovered the embezzlements. Columbia Casualty reimbursed Dantzler under a surety bond for $10,000. The court stated that Columbia Casualty was entitled to sue the CPA firm under the theory of subrogation. That is, any claim Dantzler could have asserted against the CPA firm could be asserted by Columbia Casualty. The court also concluded that the CPA firm negligently and fraudulently misrepresented their audit findings for each of the four years, and it held the firm liable for the embezzlements that occurred after the first audit.

exam

Liability to Third Parties (Nonclients) under Common Law

The most frequent common-law actions brought by third parties against auditors involve situations when the third party makes a loan or invests in a business based on the CPA's audit report, only to find out afterwards that the audited financial statements overstated the client's financial position. The third party then claims that the CPA was negligent, grossly negligent, or fraudulent in conducting the audit.

A third party that is not a subrogee can sue a CPA only in a tort action, not for breach of contract. In a tort action, the third party must prove the same elements that a client must prove in an action against the CPA. The basic elements again are a duty of care, breach of that duty, damages suffered, and causal connection between the CPA's breach and the third party's damages.

If the third party can prove the elements of gross negligence or fraud *in any state*, it can recover proven damages or losses suffered. However, the ability of the third party to recover by proving negligence is more complex and varies among the states. Until the late 1960s, CPAs were liable under common law only to their clients for negligence. This was an application of an old English common-law rule that a person who was not a party to a contract—that is, who had a nonprivity relationship— had no right of recovery for negligent performance.

Ultramares Rule

most favorable to CPAS

Third parties have to be specifically known as beneficiaries.

Hardest one for 3rd parties to prove. and actually have to be beneficiary.

The most famous common-law case for negligence to third parties is *Ultramares Corp.* v. *Touche, Niven & Co.*, decided by New York's highest court in 1931. The CPA's client borrowed money from Ultramares, who relied on the CPA's audit report on the client's financial statements. Ultramares, the third party, alleged that the client's records were false and that Touche, Niven & Co., CPAs, were negligent in failing to discover the deception. The court noted that the audit report had not been prepared for the expressed benefit of Ultramares. Considering the question of whether Ultramares could sue for negligence, the court ruled in favor of the auditor and the judge stated:

> If liability for negligence exists, a thoughtless slip or blunder, the failure to detect a theft or forgery beneath the cover of deceptive entries, *may expose accountants to a liability in an indeterminate amount for an indeterminate time to an indeterminate class* [emphasis added]. The hazards of a business conducted on these terms are so extreme as to enkindle doubt whether a flaw may not exist in the implication of a duty that exposes to these consequences.

The *Ultramares* rule may be summarized as follows: if the CPA's conduct is more serious than a mere error of judgment, but not gross negligence or fraud, a third party who is assigned the client's rights as subrogee or who qualifies as a third-party beneficiary[4] may recover, but other third parties may *not* recover.

Ultramares does not apply nationwide, but it is a landmark case and some states have embraced it: for example, Alabama (*Colonial Bank of Alabama* v. *Ridley & Schweigert*, 1989), Colorado (*Stephens Indus., Inc.* v. *Haskins & Sells*, 1971), Idaho (*Idaho*

---

[4]Third-party beneficiaries are persons who are recognized as having enforceable rights created in them by a contract to which they are not parties and for which they gave no consideration.

Bank & Trust Co. v. *KMG Main Hurdman*, 1989), Indiana (*Toro Co.* v. *Krouse Kern & Co.*, 1987), and Nebraska (*Citizens National Bank* v. *Kennedy and Coe*, 1989). *Ultramares* was reconfirmed (in the same court that handed down the original ruling) in *Credit Alliance Corporation* v. *Arthur Andersen & Co.* (New York, 1985). The court stated that before CPAs may be held liable in negligence to nonprivity parties who rely to their detriment on inaccurate financial reports, certain prerequisites must be satisfied:

1. The CPA knew that the financial statements would be used for a particular purpose.
2. The CPA knew that the financial statements were to be used by a particular third party for the particular purpose in prerequisite 1, above.
3. Some conduct on the part of the CPA must exist that links the CPA to the third party.

Because these prerequisites were not met, the court ruled that the action should be dismissed. In other words, the third party cannot be considered a beneficiary unless prerequisites 1, 2, and 3 are met. Thus, if the above prerequisites are not established, the third party must prove gross negligence or fraud to recover from the CPA; simple negligence is insufficient to establish liability to the third party.

In states where the *Ultramares* or privity rule has been established it is usually created by case law. However, Arkansas, Kansas, Illinois, and Utah have established the privity rule, drawn principally from the *Credit Alliance* decision, by statutory law.

Restatement of Torts Rule

Although *Ultramares* may still be a popular view, the trend has been to create a duty of care for negligence toward certain third parties. The cases that have made inroads on the *Ultramares* doctrine categorize third parties into (1) members of an actually foreseen and limited class—the *Restatement of Torts* rule—or (2) reasonably foreseeable parties who rely on the auditor's report—the *Rosenblum* rule.

The *Restatement of Torts* rule provides that an auditor's liability for negligence extends to third parties who are members of a limited class of known or intended beneficiaries of audited financial statements. The *Restatement* is not a binding legal document; it is merely the opinion of legal scholars as to what the common law should be in each state. The rule, in part, states,

1. One who, in the course of his business, profession or employment, or in any other transaction in which he has a pecuniary interest, supplies false information for the guidance of others in their business transactions, is subject to liability for pecuniary loss caused to them by their justifiable reliance upon the information, if he fails to exercise reasonable care or competence in obtaining or communicating the information.
2. ...the liability stated in Subsection (1) is limited to loss suffered
   (a) by the person or one of a limited group of persons for whose benefit and guidance he intends to supply the information or knows that the recipient intends to supply it; and
   (b) through reliance upon it in a transaction that he intends the information to influence or knows that the recipient so intends or in a substantially similar transaction.

A leading case applying the *Restatement* rule is *Rusch Factors, Inc.* v. *Levin* (Rhode Island, 1968). In *Rusch Factors,* a corporation sought financing from the plaintiff who, in turn, requested delivery of audited financial statements to ascertain the credit status of the corporation. The CPA was aware of the general purpose for which the financial statements were to be used but not the name of the specific lender. Although the financial statements showed the corporation to be solvent it was, in fact, insolvent. In reliance on the financial statements, Rusch Factors extended credit to the corporation. Subsequently, the corporation went into receivership and the plaintiff could recover only a fraction of the amount loaned. The court held against the CPA's plea that the absence of privity provides a complete defense and held that the CPA should be liable for negligence to actually foreseen and limited classes of persons. The court concluded,

> Why should an innocent reliant party be forced to carry the weighty burden of an accountant's professional malpractice? Isn't the risk of loss more easily distributed and fairly spread by imposing it on the accounting profession, which can pass the cost of insuring risk on to its customers, who can in turn pass the cost on to the entire consuming public?

The *Restatement* and *Rusch Factors* have been followed in a number of other states: for example, California (*Robert R. Biley* v. *Arthur Young & Company*, 1992), Florida (*First Florida Bank, N.A.* v. *Max Mitchell & Co.*, 1990), Georgia (*Badische Corp.* v. *Caylor*, 1987), Iowa (*Ryan* v. *Kanne*, 1969), Kentucky (*Ingram Industries, Inc.* v. *Nowicki*, 1981), Louisiana (*Monco Agency, Inc.* v. *Arthur Young & Co.*, 1990), Massachusetts (*Massachusetts Fleet National Bank* v. *The Gloucester Co.*, 1994), Michigan (*Law Offices of Lawrence J. Stockler, P.C.* v. *Rose*, 1989), Minnesota (*Bonhiver* v. *Graff*, 1976), Missouri (*Aluma Craft Mfg. Co.* v. *Elmer Fox & Co.*, 1973), Montana (*Thayer* v. *Hicks*, 1990), New Hampshire (*Spherex, Inc.* v. *Alexander Grant & Company*, 1982), North Carolina (*Raritan River Steel Co.* v. *Cherry, Bekaert & Holland*, 1988), North Dakota (*Bunge* v. *Eide*, 1974), Ohio (*Haddon View Investments Co.* v. *Coopers & Lybrand*, 1982), Tennessee (*Bethlehem Steel Corp.* v. *Ernst & Whinney*, 1991), Texas (*Shatterproof Glass Corp.* v. *James*, 1971), and West Virginia (*First National Bank of Bluefield* v. *Crawford*, 1989).

The generalities of "members of an actually foreseen and limited class of persons" may be difficult to understand. The following illustrations, adapted from *Restatement (Second) of Torts*, should help to clarify the CPA's liability for negligence to third parties not in privity.

1. A is negotiating with X Bank for a credit of $50,000. The Bank requires an audit. A employs CPA to make the audit, telling him or her the purpose of the audit is to meet the requirements of X Bank in connection with a credit of $50,000. CPA agrees to make the audit, with the expressed understanding that it is for transmission to X Bank only. X Bank fails, and A, without any further communication with CPA, submits its financial statements accompanied by CPA's opinion to Y Bank, which in reliance upon it extends a credit of $50,000 to A. The audit is so carelessly made as to result in an unqualified favorable opinion on financial statements that materially misstates the financial position of A, and in consequence Y Bank suffers pecuniary loss through its extension of credit. CPA is *not* liable to Y Bank for negligence because of the expressed agreement that the audit report was for X Bank only.

2. The same facts as in Illustration 1, except that nothing is said about supplying the information for the guidance of X Bank only, and A merely informs CPA that he expects to negotiate a bank loan for $50,000, requires the audit for the purpose of the loan, and has X Bank in mind. CPA is liable to Y Bank for negligence. Y Bank is a member of a limited class of known users, bank creditors.

3. The same facts as in Illustration 2, except that A informs CPA that he expects to negotiate a bank loan but does not mention the name of any bank. CPA is liable to Y Bank. Again, Y Bank or any other bank is a member of a limited class of known users.

4. CPA is retained by A to conduct an annual audit of the customary scope for the corporation and to furnish his or her opinion on the corporation's financial statements. CPA is not informed of any intended use of the financial statements, but CPA knows that the financial statements, accompanied by an auditor's opinion, are customarily used in a wide variety of financial transactions by the corporation and that they may be relied upon by lenders, investors, shareholders, creditors, purchasers, and the like in numerous possible kinds of transactions. In fact, A uses the financial statements and accompanying auditor's opinion to obtain a loan from X Bank. Because of negligence, CPA issues an unqualified favorable opinion upon a balance sheet that materially misstates the financial position of A, and through reliance upon it X Bank suffers pecuniary loss. CPA is *not* liable to X Bank. X Bank is not a member of a limited class of known users.

Rosenblum Rule

In a New Jersey case, *Rosenblum, Inc.* v. *Adler* (1983), the liability of the auditor for negligence was extended beyond the *Restatement of Torts* rule to cover all those whom the auditor should reasonably foresee as recipients of the audited financial statements. *Rosenblum* was followed by decisions in Wisconsin (*Citizens State Bank* v. *Timm, Schmidt & Co.*, 1983), California (*International Mortgage Co.* v. *John P. Butler Accounting Corp.*, 1986[5]), and Mississippi (*Touche Ross & Co.* v. *Commercial Union Insurance Co.*, 1987) that followed the same logic. That is, reasonably foreseeable third parties who receive negligently audited financial statements from a company for a proper business purpose and who rely on those financial statements and thereby suffer a loss may bring an action against the CPA to recover damages.

The facts in *Rosenblum* illustrate the concept of **reasonably foreseeable third parties**. Giant Stores Corp. acquired the plaintiff company, H. Rosenblum, Inc., by exchanging Giant stock in an amount determined by Giant's audited financial statements. Giant's financial statements were accompanied by an unqualified opinion, but after completing the exchange, it was discovered that the financial statements were false due to fraud on the part of Giant's management. The auditors had negligently failed to discover the fraud, and, as a consequence, the securities received by Rosenblum were worthless.

The New Jersey Supreme Court ruled in favor of Rosenblum. The court noted that it is common knowledge that companies submit audited financial statements to banks and other lending institutions that might advance funds and to suppliers of services and goods that might advance credit. Such third-party users of financial statements are foreseeable, the court reasoned; thus, auditors may be held liable for negligence to such third parties.[6]

Observations on Third-Party Liability

Some states follow the *Ultramares* rule making it difficult for a third party not in privity to recover damages from the auditor for negligence. In interpreting *Ultra-*

---

[5]Subsequently overturned by *Robert R. Biley* v. *Arthur Young & Company*, 1992, making California a *Restatement of Torts* state.
[6]According to the May 1995 *CPA Letter*, the New Jersey legislature has passed a statute that adopts a strict privity standard for lawsuits involving CPAs. Under a strict privity standard, a negligence suit against an accountant may only be brought by the client or by those third parties with whom the accountant has a relationship approaching that of an accountant-client relationship.

mares, however, the *Credit Alliance* decision establishes that if the auditor knows the third party by name and by explicit action indicates an awareness of the third party's use of the financial statements for a particular purpose, the third party—even if it is not in privity—may sue the auditor for negligence.

Other states follow the *Restatement of Torts* rule and have held that, if the third party is not in privity but is a member of a foreseen class of users, the auditor may be held liable for negligence. A ***foreseen class of users*** is defined as a particular defined group, of any size, sometimes very large, specifically identified to the auditor by class, though not necessarily known to him or her individually. However, it should be noted that courts adopting the *Restatements of Torts* rule have reached differing results on the scope of the rule. Some courts have interpreted the rule narrowly, requiring the plaintiff to prove that the CPA had actual knowledge of the particular plaintiff. Other courts have adopted a broader interpretation of the rule, holding that liability is not limited to suits brought by those who were actually known to the CPA; instead, liability may extend to those persons that the CPA, at the time the audit report is issued, should reasonably expect to receive and rely on the information.

Finally, a recent development in some states is to follow the *Rosenblum* rule and hold the auditor liable to foreseeable third parties that use the audited financial statements in the ordinary course of business. In these states, the third party may be a member of a foreseen class or a member of a wider foreseeable class. A ***foreseeable class of users*** may potentially be a very large number of persons, not identified as specific persons or a specific class in a specific transaction.

The Real World of Auditing

Tennessee Rules on Privity

The Tennessee Supreme Court ruled an accountant may be liable both to known parties and to parties the accountant should reasonably expect to receive and rely on the audit report.

Bethlehem Steel Corporation extended credit to W. L. Jackson Manufacturing Company. After Jackson defaulted on the loan, Bethlehem sued Ernst & Whinney (now Ernst & Young), alleging the firm negligently prepared the audit report Bethlehem relied on in extending credit to Jackson. Had it known Jackson's true financial condition, Bethlehem alleged, it would not have extended the loan.

The Tennessee Supreme Court weighed various approaches adopted by other states in defining an accountant's duty to nonclients. It rejected the strict privity approach, which holds an accountant may be liable only to those who are in privity of contract or near privity of contract with him or her.

The court reasoned that the accountants' significant role in business and commerce mandated a greater duty to nonclients.

Conversely, the court also rejected the more liberal interpretation, adopted in a few states, that an accountant owes a duty to all parties that might reasonably be foreseen to rely on the audit. The court reasoned this standard creates an environment of potentially uncontrolled risk for accountants.

In adopting a middle ground, an accountant's liability was limited to parties that the accountant intended to rely on his or her report or to parties an accountant knew the client intended to influence with his or her report. (*Bethlehem Steel Corporation* v. *Ernst & Whinney*, 822 S.W. 2d 592)

_____

Source: Wayne Baliga, ed., "News," *Journal of Accountancy*, October 1992. Copyright © 1992, *Journal of Accountancy*. Reprinted with permission by AICPA.

Until the *Credit Alliance* decision, it was clear that the common law was tending away from *Ultramares*. But at present, the trend of law is in flux because of *Credit Alliance*, and it is difficult to predict what the law might be in a given state, especially in states that have not ruled on a case involving auditor negligence to third parties.

Liability to Third Parties under the Federal Securities Acts

The Securities Act of 1933 (1933 Act) and the Securities Exchange Act of 1934 (1934 Act) substantially increased the CPA's liability to third parties beyond the bounds of common law. These acts are administered by the Securities and Exchange Commission (SEC), an agency of the federal government. The acts are intended to make available to investors full and fair disclosure of the financial position and earnings of all corporations whose securities are publicly held. Companies offering new securities for sale in interstate commerce and companies whose securities are listed or traded on a national securities exchange or on over-the-counter markets are required to register with the SEC. At registration and annually thereafter, these companies (*registrants*) are required to file with the SEC audited financial statements. The SEC does not, however, warrant or assume responsibility for the fairness of the filed financial statements. That responsibility rests with the registrant and the independent accountant who audits the financial statements. The SEC does not pass on the merits of a security, and the federal securities laws do not prohibit the sale or trading of highly speculative securities, provided their speculative risks are disclosed. Table 3–1 highlights important SEC publications and report forms.

SEC Independence and Opinion Requirements

As discussed in Chapter 2, the AICPA has promulgated independence rules and extensive interpretations on independence. The SEC does not, however, rely on those rules. Instead it has adopted its own independence rules and interpretations. The SEC's rules are substantially the same as the AICPA's except for differences in the following four areas. The SEC

1. prohibits performance of bookkeeping and related professional services for audit clients.
2. has more stringent requirements regarding business relationships between close relatives of the accountant and the client.
3. prohibits business relationships with an accountant's client and the officers, directors, and principal stockholders thereof.
4. has more stringent requirements pertaining to the activities of retired partners.

Another SEC uniqueness concerns the type of acceptable audit opinion. The SEC ordinarily will not accept an auditor's opinion that is qualified (i.e., because of limitations on the scope of the audit or exceptions caused by a departure from generally accepted accounting principles), adverse opinion, or disclaimer of opinion.

The 1933 Act (Section 11)

The Securities Act of 1933 regulates the initial offering and sale of securities through the mails and other forms of interstate commerce. The primary purpose of the 1933 Act is to promote full and fair disclosure and to prohibit fraudulent

Table 3–1	**SEC Publications and Reporting Forms**

Regulation S-X Identifies the specific financial statements that must be filed with the SEC and the basic rules to be followed in the preparation and certification of those financial statements.

Regulation S-K Identifies requirements for nonfinancial statement disclosures that are required in registration statements, annual reports, and other required reports. For example, Regulation S-K requires the registrant to discuss and analyze its financial condition and results of operations with an emphasis on trends or events expected to have a material future effect on liquidity, resources, or operations (referred to as management's discussion and analysis or MD&A).

Regulation A A simplified registration form for public offerings of securities that do not exceed $1.5 million in one year.

Financial Reporting Releases (FRRs) Releases issued by the SEC to announce new or revised rules or its views on general accounting and auditing matters.

Accounting and Auditing Enforcement Releases (AAERs) Announcements concerning accounting and auditing matters that relate to the SEC's enforcement activities.

Staff Accounting Bulletins (SABs) Published interpretations from the SEC's Office of the Chief Accountant and the Division of Corporation Finance. SABs are not official rules of the SEC, but departures from them must be justified.

Form S-1 The most comprehensive form used for registration of an initial public offering of securities, used by issuers who are not eligible to use abbreviated registration forms.

Form S-2 A 1933 Act filing form used by companies that have been subject to periodic reporting to the SEC for at least three years but that are not as widely followed by financial analysts as Form S-3 companies.

Form S-3 A 1933 Act abbreviated filing form used by large public companies.

Form 10-K The required SEC annual report used to update the information provided in a company's initial registration. The 10-K must be filed within 90 days following the registrant's year-end.

Form 10-Q The required SEC quarterly report, which must be filed within 45 days of the end of the quarter for the first three quarters of a registrant's fiscal year.

Form 8-K A current SEC report that must be filed within 15 days of the occurrence of certain specified events. The events that trigger the need to file an 8-K are changes in control of registrant, acquisition or disposition of assets, bankruptcy or receivership, changes in auditors or directors (8-K must be filed within 5 days), and other events deemed important.

Rule 2(e) Covers the SEC's disciplinary power over auditors and other professionals. The Commission may disqualify auditors permanently or for a specified time from practicing before it for a variety of reasons, including lack of the requisite qualifications, character, or integrity; engaging in violations of the securities laws; or engaging in unethical or improper conduct. The Commission may also bar auditors from accepting new publicly owned companies as clients for a stipulated period of time, require auditors to submit to peer review, or even recommend criminal proceedings against auditors.

misrepresentation. The 1933 Act requires a company to file a registration statement, including prospectus, with the SEC before making a primary sale of securities in interstate commerce, unless the sale qualifies for exemption. The sale has to be by the issuing company. The 1933 Act does not apply to sales by one shareholder to another. Certain security offerings are exempt from registration under the 1933 Act. For example, offerings of governmental units; securities issued by religious, educational, and charitable organizations; offerings sold intrastate; and private offerings to a limited number of sophisticated investors are exempt. Section 11(a) of the 1933 Act makes accountants liable for purchases of securities containing material misstatements in those portions of the registration statement for which the CPA is responsible. The registration statement must include audited financial statements.

Any purchaser of a security may sue the CPA under Section 11(a). The purchaser must, however, prove that the security was part of the offering of shares covered by the registration statement and that the registration statement was false or misleading or omitted material information that should have been included. The plaintiff or purchaser does not have the burden of proving that the CPA was negligent or fraudulent or that the financial statements were the proximate causes of any loss. In other words, the CPA must prove that he or she was not negligent or fraudulent or that the cause of the purchaser's loss was something other than the untrue financial statements.

Defenses Available   Section 11(a) is the most severe liability clause in the United States concerning accountants because it puts the burden of proof (beyond proving material misstatement or omission) on the CPA, the defendant, rather than on the plaintiff. Section 11(a), however, provides that the CPA may defend against a suit brought under the section by proving ***due diligence***. Section 11 states that the CPA is not liable if

> he had, after reasonable investigation, reasonable ground to believe and did believe, at the time such part of the registration statement became effective, that the statements therein were true and that there was no omission to state a material fact required to be stated therein or necessary to make the statements therein not misleading.

If the CPA raises the defense of due diligence, he or she has the burden of proving due diligence. This is the opposite of common-law cases, in which the plaintiff has to prove that the CPA was negligent. In other words, the CPA has to prove that he or she was not negligent.

In addition to due diligence, there are other defenses available to the CPA under Section 11. The CPA may prove that

1. the financial statements are not false, misleading, or incomplete.
2. a misstatement or omission is not material.
3. the plaintiff knew, at the time of purchase, that the statements were false, misleading, or incomplete.
4. the plaintiff's loss was not caused by false, misleading, or incomplete financial statements.
5. the statute of limitations has expired; the suit is untimely. (Section 11 requires actions to be brought within one year from the discovery of the untruth or omission, but in any event within three years from the effective date of the registration statement.)
6. the plaintiff purchased the securities after the issuance of an earnings statement covering twelve months following the effective date of the registration statement and did not rely on the registration statement.

Responsibility for Subsequent Events

Window — Looking for subsequent event.

The CPA's responsibility for events after the balance sheet date is more extensive in a registration statement than in any other audit. For financial statements filed in a registration statement, the CPA's responsibility for subsequent events extends beyond the date of the audit report to the effective date of the registration statement. *SAS No. 37, Filings under Federal Securities Statutes* (AU 711) sets forth additional procedures for subsequent events. These additional procedures must be performed in order to sustain the due diligence defense. The CPA should therefore

1. read the entire prospectus and other pertinent portions of the registration statement.
2. inquire of and obtain written representations from financial and accounting officers and executives about subsequent events that should be disclosed in order to keep audited financial statements in the prospectus from being misleading.

Comfort Letters

In addition to the requirement for additional subsequent events procedures contained in the Statements on Auditing Standards, the CPA usually performs certain agreed-upon procedures for subsequent events and other items on behalf of the securities underwriter (that is, the brokerage firm that assumes responsibility for selling the securities). To fulfill this responsibility, the CPA usually furnishes a letter to the underwriter, commonly called a ***comfort letter***. Such a letter is regarded by the underwriter as one means of learning promptly of any subsequent event that may require disclosure. The comfort letter is usually addressed to the registrant, underwriter, or both and is dated on or shortly before the closing date on which the securities are delivered to the underwriter in exchange for the proceeds from their sale. When issuing a comfort letter, the CPA is governed by *SAS No. 72, Letters for Underwriters* (AU 634).

The comfort letter normally begins with a paragraph identifying the financial statements contained in the registration statement and a statement regarding the CPA's independence according to SEC rules. Later paragraphs address unaudited interim financial statements, pro forma financial information, changes in specified financial statement items subsequent to the latest financial information in the offering document, tables, statistics, and other financial information in the registration statement that the underwriter has requested the accountant to consider by the application of agreed-upon procedures.

Comfort letters are not required by the 1933 Act and are not filed with the SEC. They are prepared solely to enable the registrant to comply with the terms of the underwriting agreement. Accordingly, the letter concludes with a paragraph that restricts the distribution of the letter to the parties to the underwriting agreement.

The BarChris Decision

The landmark decision on the question of the CPA's liability under Section 11 of the 1933 Act is *Escott* v. *BarChris Construction Corp.* (Federal District Court, New York, 1968). The accounting firm's audit and subsequent events review program in the case conformed to the standards of the profession and would have been sufficient to sustain a due diligence defense if the auditors actually performing the procedures had properly followed the firm's program. The court found, however, that the work conducted was inadequate, because "glib answers" received in response to certain questions should have elicited further questions and made further investigation mandatory. The court also found that the CPA firm's senior accountant was inexperienced in auditing the construction of bowling centers, including bar and restaurant facilities, which were the primary businesses conducted by BarChris.

The CPA firm had also issued a comfort letter to the underwriter, containing the customary assurance that they had no reason to doubt the financial statements, including the unaudited interim financial statements. The underwriter filed suit against the CPA firm, but that claim was settled out of court.

The 1934 Act—(Section 10(b)

The Securities Exchange Act of 1934 deals primarily with trading in previously issued securities. All securities sold on a national securities exchange or issued by companies having assets in excess of $5 million and 500 or more stockholders come under the continuous disclosure provisions of the act (for example, these companies are required to file forms 10-K, 10-Q, and 8-K as discussed in Table 3-1). Section 10(b) and Rule 10b-5 promulgated under the 1934 Act have been the most fertile source of litigation under the federal securities acts. Section 10(b) makes it unlawful for any person in interstate commerce

> to use or employ, in connection with the purchase or sale of any security registered on a national exchange or any security not so registered, any manipulative or deceptive device or contrivance in contravention of such rules and regulations as the [Securities and Exchange] Commission may prescribe as necessary or appropriate in the public interest or for the protection of investors.

Note that 10(b) applies to the purchase or sale of securities. Rule 10b-5 describes in more detail the prohibited types of conduct. It makes it unlawful for any person to

1. employ any device, scheme, or artifice to defraud,
2. make any untrue statement of a material fact or to omit to state a material fact necessary in order to make the statements made, in the light of the circumstances under which they were made, not misleading, or
3. engage in any act, practice, or course of business which operates or would operate as a fraud or deceit on any person, in connection with the purchase or sale of any security.

Although neither Section 10(b) nor Rule 10b-5 expressly subjects CPAs to liability for accounting or auditing deficiencies, the statute and the rule are sufficiently broad to create an implied liability for accountants.

In bringing a case under Section 10(b) or Rule 10b-5, the plaintiff must prove (1) the materiality of the alleged false, misleading, or omitted statement; (2) the CPA's knowledge of the statement; (3) reliance on the statements; and (4) actual damages sustained as a result of such reliance.

The most famous Rule 10b-5 case is *Ernst & Ernst* v. *Hochfelder*. In the 1976 *Hochfelder* decision, the U.S. Supreme Court made it clear that more than mere negligence must be proven by the plaintiff to impose liability on the CPA. The main issue decided by *Hochfelder* was the standard of care to which the defendant CPA should be held. There was a conflict among decisions in the federal courts. Some courts had permitted recovery under Rule 10b-5 for negligence. Other courts had required plaintiffs to prove scienter (pronounced "sigh enter"), which is something more than negligence. The Supreme Court, in *Hochfelder*, ruled that the plaintiff must prove scienter. The court defined **scienter** as "a mental state embracing intent to deceive, manipulate, or defraud."

Defenses available to the CPA under Rule 10b-5 are as follows:

1. The CPA's conduct does not include scienter.
2. The plaintiff's loss was not due to reliance on the statements, or any misstatements or omissions are immaterial.
3. The statute of limitations has expired.

Section 10(b) of the 1934 Act does not include a provision regarding the time within which suit must be brought. Recently, however, the Supreme Court ruled that a plaintiff must bring suit one year from the date he or she knew or should have known of the 10b-5 violation and in no event later than three years after the violation.

Criminal Liability

In recent years many accountants have been shocked to realize that they could be criminally prosecuted, fined, and even imprisoned for charges arising from a professional engagement. *Criminal liability* is a means of both punishing and deterring behavior that society, acting through the legislature, has deemed unacceptable. Auditors are subject to a number of federal and state criminal statutes. The most important of these is the securities fraud and false filing statute under the Securities Exchange Act of 1934. Section 32(a) of the 1934 Act prohibits willful violation of any provision of the 1934 Act or of SEC rules under it. It also prohibits the willful and knowing making of a false or misleading statement of any material fact in any document required to be filed with the SEC or a securities exchange under the act. Most criminal cases brought against independent auditors involve Section 32(a).

Other statutes under which an auditor may be criminally prosecuted are as follows:

1. The mail fraud statute, prohibiting use of the U.S. mail, and the wire fraud statute, prohibiting the use of wire, radio, or television in any scheme to defraud or to obtain money or property by false or fraudulent means.
2. Section 24 of the Securities Act of 1933, which prohibits willful violation of any provision of the 1933 Act or the SEC rules under it and the willful making of a material misstatement or omission in a registration statement.
3. The general false statement statute, which prohibits willfully and knowingly making a false statement or representation to governmental personnel in any matter within the jurisdiction of any department or agency of the United States.
4. The Uniform Securities Act, which has been enacted in more than two-thirds of the 54 U.S. jurisdictions. Section 404 of that act is generally similar to the federal false filing and false statement provisions in the 1933 and 1934 Acts discussed above.
5. State criminal fraud statutes. Arizona has a reckless auditing statute that applies to CPAs holding a permit to practice in that state. The statute defines a felony of fraudulent auditing as a situation in which the permit holder recklessly "prepares, issues, delivers or files with any public agency an audit report or certificate on any financial statement which is false or fraudulent or which fails to fairly present the financial condition... reported on."

In a criminal action against an auditor, the U.S. Justice Department or the state attorney general files the suit as the plaintiff. It is not necessary for the plaintiff to prove damages; violation of a criminal statute must, however, be established. The plaintiff must also establish beyond a reasonable doubt that the auditor knew he or she was participating in a crime and therefore was acting willfully. Typically, these cases involve clients who are guilty of egregious falsification of the financial statements to hide illegal acts. Usually, the auditor has not been personally enriched beyond receipt of the engagement fee. The government, federal or state, establishes its case by showing that the auditor either deliberately failed to see facts he or she had a duty to see and disclose or recklessly stated as facts things of which he or she was ignorant.

The primary defense that the CPA has in a criminal action is good faith. That is, the CPA must establish that he or she complied with generally accepted accounting principles and auditing standards, did not act willfully or with knowledge of the false statement or omission, and, by complying with applicable professional standards (see "AICPA Standards Are Not Absolute"), was not reckless.

A guilty verdict in a criminal case, besides resulting in a fine or imprisonment, almost always leads to a revocation of the CPA's certificate and license to practice. Two of the best-known criminal cases against CPAs are Continental Vending and Equity Funding. Both of those cases resulted in criminal convictions.

Continental Vending

In *United States* v. *Simon* (1969), a footnote to the audited financial statements of a subsequently bankrupt Continental Vending Machine Corporation failed to disclose that certain accounts and notes receivable from an affiliate were virtually worthless. In receiving monies from Continental, the affiliate had loaned approximately the same amount to the dominant officer of both companies. The officer was unable to repay the affiliate, which in turn was unable to repay Continental. In addition, the stock collateralizing the loan was largely stock in Continental. In effect, the officer was looting Continental through its affiliate and diverting corporate funds for private benefit. According to the decision, the footnote to the financial statements was presented in an obscure manner and did not disclose the known dishonesty of the officer. The court convicted two audit partners and an audit manager and fined them for conspiring to violate the federal securities and false statement statutes, and for mail fraud. The auditors were fined and placed on probation. In 1972 President Richard Nixon pardoned them.

A central issue in *United States* v. *Simon* was whether the auditors could successfully defend themselves by demonstrating compliance with generally accepted auditing standards. The court held that even if the defendants proved that their audit conformed to accepted standards, this was not necessarily a complete defense to the criminal charge of willfully and knowingly making a false statement. The decision clearly illustrates that the auditor must make sure that the financial statements adequately disclose known and material management irregularities.

Equity Funding

In *United States* v. *Weiner* (1978), the court affirmed the criminal conviction of Equity Funding Corporation of America's audit partner and two audit managers. The Equity Funding case involved massive overstatement of net income and assets (over $100 million in fictitious assets) of a life insurance–mutual fund sales and financing company. The financial statements were manipulated by recording fictitious commission income, borrowing funds without recording the corresponding liability, and creating fictitious life insurance policies.

The Equity Funding debacle is frequently referred to as a computer fraud. However, a special AICPA committee found that "the fraud was not based on a sophisticated application of data processing technology." According to the committee, the fraud consisted of the manual preparation and recording of fictitious entries, although the computer was useful in creating a mass of supporting detail designed to conceal the fraud. The committee concluded "that customary audit procedures properly applied would have provided a reasonable degree of assurance that the existence of fraud at Equity Funding would be detected."

In addressing the above point, the bankruptcy trustee stated that the fraud

> was relatively unsophisticated in both design and execution. It was neither comprehensively planned nor systematically developed. Rather, [it was] helter-skelter, hand-to-mouth.... Moreover, ... the fraud was not the brainchild of computer-age financial wizards. It was to a great extent simply a pencil fraud.... That the fraud persisted undetected for so long is attributable to the audacity and luck of its perpetrators and, just as importantly, to the glaring failure of the Company's auditors to perform properly the obligations which they had undertaken.

In finding against the auditors, the court found the evidence largely circumstantial and even believed that the auditors were at first victims of the fraud. But, given the sheer magnitude ($62 million adjustment) of the fraud, the length of time over which the auditors were involved, the persistence of erroneously recorded transactions, the absence of backup papers or supporting schedules for entries, and numerous mathematical errors that were readily detectable in the auditors' workpapers, the court decided the auditors must have come to a point where they knew of the fraud and performed acts in furtherance of the fraud. Equity Funding is an important case because it illustrates the criminal risk that auditors accept when they perform sloppy work. The case also emphasizes that the best defense to a potential criminal charge is simply to have performed a thorough audit.

The Real World of Auditing

AICPA Standards Are Not Absolute

An Oregon appellate court has held that the standards promulgated by the American Institute of Certified Public Accountants (AICPA) may be considered as evidence of the standard of care in a malpractice action against an accountant, but they are not controlling.

A client sued an accounting firm that audited its financial statements, alleging that the accounting firm negligently failed to detect fraudulent conduct. A jury found the accountant partially responsible for the client's damages. In an appeal brought by both parties, the accountant argued that it was incorrect for the trial court to refuse to give an instruction that stated, in effect, that an auditor is not liable for failing to detect fraud unless the auditor failed to comply with generally accepted auditing standards. The appellate court rejected this argument. The appellate court held that the AICPA standards may be considered by a jury in determining the standard of care for an auditor, but they are not controlling. Rather, the amount of care, skill and diligence required of an auditor is a question of fact, just as it is in fields involving other professionals. The court reasoned that the AICPA embodied principles and procedures developed by the accounting profession rather than by the courts or the legislature.

Source: *Maduff Mortgage Corp.* v. *Deloitte Haskins & Sells* (1989).

Fraud[7] and Illegal Acts

Recently, public interest in the auditor's responsibility for client fraud and illegal acts has increased. The news media have focused attention on recent business failures and questionable accounting practices by businesses that involved alleged fraud or illegal acts. These well-publicized instances attracted the attention of Congress and inevitably raised the questions: Where were the auditors? Did the auditors fulfill their responsibilities? These questions highlight the need to understand the auditor's existing responsibilities and liabilities for fraud and illegal acts.

The auditor's responsibility to detect and report fraud, irregularities, or illegal acts is set out in *SAS No. 53, The Auditor's Responsibility to Detect and Report Errors and Irregularities* (AU 316)[8] and *SAS No. 54, Illegal Acts by Clients* (AU 317). The standards were developed in response to criticisms by members of Congress, financial writers, judges, and some large CPA firms. Many criticisms were voiced in a series of hearings by the U.S. House of Representatives on the accounting profession and the SEC's oversight of the profession. In addition, the National Commission on Fraudulent Financial Reporting was formed in 1985 to study the causes of fraud and to make recommendations on ways to eliminate or significantly reduce its occurrence. The commission's final report was released in October 1987. Among its recommendations was a call for auditors to detect fraud and spell out in auditing standards an affirmative obligation to detect fraud in clear and nondefensive language.

SAS No. 53 (AU 316.02–.03) makes a distinction between errors and irregularities. *Errors* are defined as unintentional misstatements in financial statements, including

1. mistakes in gathering or processing accounting data,
2. incorrect accounting estimates arising from oversight or misinterpretation of facts, and
3. mistakes in the application of accounting principles relating to amount, classification, manner of presentation, or disclosure.

Irregularities are defined as intentional distortions of financial statements (sometimes called *management fraud*) or misappropriation of assets (sometimes called *defalcation*). Irregularities may include

1. manipulation, falsification, or alteration of accounting records or supporting documents,
2. misrepresentation or intentional omission of events or transactions, and
3. intentional misapplication of accounting principles.

SAS No. 53 (AU 316.05) establishes affirmative requirements for auditors: the auditor is required (1) to assess the risk that errors and irregularities may cause the financial statements to contain a material misstatement and (2) to design the audit to provide reasonable assurance that errors and irregularities material to the financial statements will be detected. To achieve this assurance, the auditor must exercise due care in planning, performing, and evaluating the results of audit procedures. Furthermore, he or she must exercise the proper degree of professional skepticism; that is, the auditor makes no assumptions about management's honesty or dishonesty.

---

[7]The term *fraud* is used interchangeably with *irregularities.*
[8]In 1993 the ASB created the Fraud Task Force, which was intended to clarify the auditor's responsibility for the detection of fraud as described in *SAS No. 53.* In addition, the task force is considering revising factors that may indicate increased risk of management and employee fraud. A final standard is not expected before late 1996.

The auditor's report explicitly indicates his or her belief that the financial statements are free of material misstatements resulting from errors or irregularities.

SAS No. 53 (AU 316.08) also recognizes that the auditor's opinion is based on the concept of reasonable assurance; therefore, the auditor is not an insurer and the audit report does not constitute a guarantee. The subsequent discovery that a material misstatement exists in the financial statements does not necessarily indicate inadequate auditor performance. Specifically, *SAS No. 53* (AU 316.07) states the following:

> Because of the characteristics of irregularities, particularly those involving forgery and collusion, a properly designed and executed audit may not detect a material irregularity. For example, generally accepted auditing standards do not require that an auditor authenticate documents, nor is the auditor trained to do so. Also, audit procedures that are effective for detecting a misstatement that is unintentional may be ineffective for a misstatement that is intentional and is concealed through collusion between client personnel and third parties or among management or employees of the client.

SAS No. 54 (AU 317.02) defines ***illegal acts*** as violations of laws or governmental regulations. The auditor's responsibility for illegal acts is less distinct than the responsibility for irregularities as defined in *SAS No. 53* and as discussed above. It simply is not feasible to design an audit to provide reasonable assurance of detecting *all* illegal acts that could have a material effect on the financial statements. U.S. businesses and other entities are subject to a host of laws and regulations that, if violated, lead to material consequences in their financial statements, including laws governing securities trading, occupational safety and health, food and drug administration, environmental protection, equal employment, and price fixing and other antitrust violations. Auditors usually are not trained to identify violations of such laws and regulations, and as a practical matter they have little, if any, chance of detecting them unless informed of them by clients or clients' attorneys, or unless there is evidence of a government investigation or enforcement proceeding in the corporate minutes or correspondence made available to the auditor. For these reasons, the auditor does not include audit procedures specifically designed to detect illegal acts. However, auditors are obligated to be aware that some matters may come to their attention during the audit that suggest illegal acts. The auditor who suspects that such acts might have occurred must apply audit procedures specifically designed to detect illegal acts.

There is one very important exception to the generalization that the auditor does not design the audit to detect illegal acts: when illegal acts have both a *direct* and a *material* effect on financial statement line-item amounts, auditors have exactly the same responsibility as the one they have for detecting material errors and irregularities. For example, assume a client obtains a government contract requiring compliance with certain specified laws and regulations in order for revenue to be earned. Also assume that the amount of revenue earned is material. The auditor then needs to test compliance with the laws and regulations on which the revenue stream is dependent.

Violation of other laws and regulations also might cause the government to suspend the contract. These laws and regulations have an indirect effect on the financial statements, and this indirect contingency may need to be disclosed. Nevertheless, the need to disclose this contingency does not make auditors responsible for designing the audit to detect violations of laws and regulations that could have a material

effect. If the auditor discovers an irregularity or an illegal act, unless it is clearly inconsequential, he or she is required to make sure that the audit committee of the board of directors or others with equivalent authority know about it. The auditor is also required to assess its effect on the financial statements and, if the effect is material, to insist on adjustment or additional disclosures in the financial statements or to qualify the audit report.

Subsequent Discovery of Facts and Omitted Procedures

An auditor may be held liable in civil or criminal suits for (1) not disaffirming an opinion if he or she becomes aware of facts demonstrating that the financial statements and audit report are incorrect or (2) not doing additional work to support a previously issued audit report if he or she becomes aware of the omission of an important audit procedure. If appropriate actions are not taken in these situations, the auditor may be guilty of *deceit*, fraud, or gross negligence.

Discovery of Facts Existing at the Audit Report Date

In a 1967 case, *Fischer* v. *Kletz* (commonly known as the *Yale Express* case), the auditor did not promptly disclose material errors in audited financial statements that were subsequently discovered during a management consulting engagement performed by the auditor's firm. In response to the case, the Auditing Standards Board (at that time known as the Auditing Standards Executive Committee) issued an authoritative statement (see AU 561) to give guidelines to auditors who discover facts after issuing a report on the financial statements. The guidance is applicable when

1. certain facts existed at the date of the audit report
2. that were *not* known by the auditor at the date of the report, but
3. would have required the auditor to change the report had he or she been aware of them.

If the discovered information is reliable, the auditor should advise the client to disclose the newly discovered facts and their effect on the financial statements to persons known to be currently relying on or who are likely to rely on the financial statements. If the client refuses to make the needed disclosures, the auditor is obligated to notify each member of the board of directors of the refusal. The auditor should also communicate to the board of directors that he or she plans to notify regulatory agencies having jurisdiction over the client and others relying on the financial statements that the audit report should no longer be relied on. Experience has shown that in most cases the client will make the necessary announcement of revision of its financial statements. Figure 3–2 details the decisions that must be considered by the auditor when facts are discovered after the report date.

Omitted Procedures after the Report Date

Sometimes an auditor discovers that an important audit procedure was not applied in an engagement. For example, a peer reviewer may determine that the auditor did not make enough inventory test counts to support the opinion on the financial statements. *SAS No. 46, Consideration of Omitted Procedures after the Report Date*

Figure 3-2

Subsequent Discovery of Facts Existing at the Date of the Auditor's Report

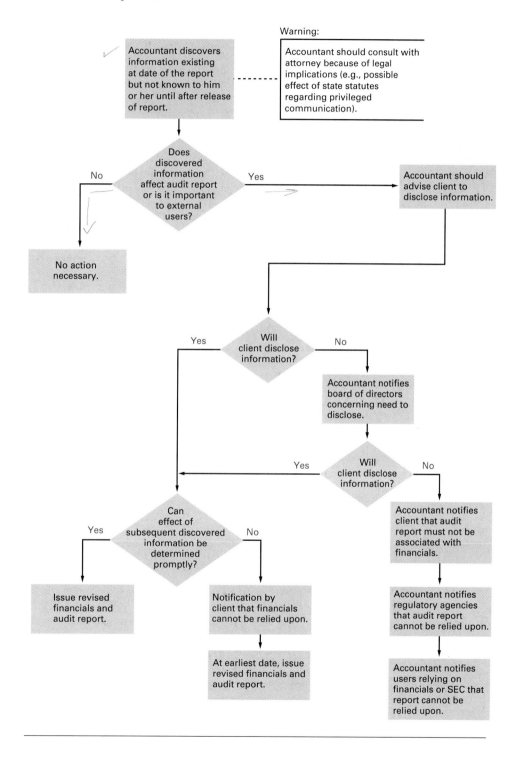

(AU 390) may require the auditor to do additional work. For instance, the auditor may have to perform additional test counts on inventory. If additional work is not done, the auditor may not be able to support the opinion and, if sued, could be found guilty of violating criminal statutes. *SAS No. 46* was issued because of the AICPA's peer review program. No legal cases to date have dealt with this matter.

Minimizing Legal Liability

A number of practices or safeguards are available that a prudent auditor can follow to reduce the likelihood of being sued and that, if the auditor is sued, will increase the likelihood of a successful defense. The following suggestions are based primarily on lessons learned from litigation:

- The prudent auditor will candidly assess the firm's competence to perform work before accepting an engagement. CPAs should not accept an engagement for which they are not qualified.
- The prudent auditor will thoroughly investigate potential clients before accepting them and will use an engagement letter upon acceptance to document the contractual agreement.
- The prudent auditor will give special attention to significant risks whose existence might be suggested by previous audit experience (the auditor's own or that of others), the history of the entity being audited, or the industry in which it operates.
- The prudent auditor will consider any unusual circumstances or relationships in planning and performing the audit. Examples of unusual circumstances (red flags) are as follows:
  - Serious weaknesses in internal control structure.
  - Difficulties in obtaining information or documentation.
  - Unauthorized or unsupported transactions.
  - Material transactions not recorded in the usual manner.
  - Highly irregular or unexplained conduct by management or other client personnel.
  - Confusing or suspicious confirmation replies.
  - Extensive dealings with related parties.
  - Guarded, incomplete, or seemingly glib responses by the client.
  - Apparent obstruction of audit procedures or unexplained lack of client cooperation.
  - Extremely complex revenue transactions conducted at year-end.
  - Client financial deterioration.
- The prudent auditor must recognize unfamiliar situations and take such precautionary measures as are warranted by the circumstances.
- The prudent auditor will avoid undue reliance on management, the client's attorney, or client employees.
- The prudent auditor must take all appropriate steps to remove any doubtful impressions or unanswered questions concerning matters material to the engagement.
- The prudent auditor will recognize the necessity for review of the work of assistants and will perform such review with full understanding of its importance.

- The prudent auditor recognizes that he or she is in a more defensible position when a problem has been spotted, resolved, and documented in the working papers than when the problem is overlooked or glossed over without documentation.

- The prudent auditor will keep abreast of developments in accounting and auditing; he or she will seek knowledge of methods of perpetrating, concealing, and detecting irregularities and illegal acts.

- The prudent auditor will comply with, if not exceed, the standards for professional ethics and conduct.

- The prudent auditor will maintain high standards of quality control and will participate in an acceptable peer review program.

In addition to the suggestions made above, the prudent auditor should follow two other practices to avoid legal liability problems: (1) do not sue a client for unpaid fees and (2) carry adequate liability insurance.

Filing a lawsuit against a client for unpaid fees may be a hazardous course to follow. In *Ryan* v. *Kanne* (Iowa, 1969), the CPA firm had unpaid fees of $4435 and brought suit to receive its fees. The court awarded the fee to the CPA firm, but it also awarded a counterclaim to the defendant for $23,043 because of deficiencies in the work done. A better course would have been to collect periodic payment from the client as the work is performed.

Sometimes, despite auditors' best efforts, it is impossible to avoid litigation. Therefore, it is prudent of auditors to insulate themselves from the monetary costs of legal defenses and adverse judgments by carrying malpractice insurance obtained under programs of the AICPA or state societies of CPAs, or from private carriers. Finally, prudent auditors should consider the legal structure of their firms in order to protect the personal assets of partners and shareholders. Increasingly, CPA firms are organized as limited liability partnerships or limited liability corporations.

Significant Terms

Civil liability A means of compensating one individual for the damages inflicted on him or her by another.

Comfort letter A letter addressed to an underwriter, based on certain agreed-to procedures that a CPA has performed for the underwriter.

Common law Unwritten, case-made law that evolves from prior cases.

Constructive fraud *See* Gross negligence.

Criminal liability A means of punishing and deterring behavior that society, acting through a state or federal legislature, has deemed unacceptable.

Deceit A type of fraud that has been construed to include the failure of an auditor to disaffirm an erroneous opinion on which others are relying.

Due diligence A defense available to a CPA under Section 11(a) of the 1933 Securities Act that requires a reasonable investigation and reasonable grounds for the belief that the financial statements in a registration statement are true and not misleading.

Due professional care A legal concept that requires the exercise of reasonable ability and skill in carrying out a professional engagement.

Errors Unintentional misstatements in financial statements.

Foreseeable class of users Third-party users who use audited financial statements in the ordinary course of business.

Foreseen class of users A defined group of third-party users specifically identified to the auditor by class.

Fraud A knowing intent to deceive.

Gross negligence Flagrant negligence that is tantamount to a reckless departure from the standard of due care.

Illegal acts Bribes and other violations of laws and governmental regulations.

Irregularities Intentional distortions of financial statements (sometimes called *management fraud*) or misappropriation of assets (sometimes called *defalcation*).

Negligence The failure to perform or report on an audit with due care and competence.

Omitted procedure The failure to apply an important audit procedure needed to support the opinion on the financial statements.

Privity A contractual relationship.

Recklessness *See* Gross negligence.

Registrant A company that is required to file audited financial statements with the SEC.

Scienter An intent to deceive, manipulate, or defraud.

Statute of limitations A period of time within which a lawsuit must be filed.

Statutory law Written law established by federal or state legislative bodies.

Subrogee A third party, such as an insurance or bonding company, that is assigned the rights of a client.

Tort A civil wrong, other than breach of contract.

Discussion Questions

3-1. What does *privity* mean?

3-2. *Due professional care* basically means that a CPA must exercise reasonable ability and skill when compared with other CPAs. Do you agree?

3-3. What is the primary difference between *negligence* and *gross negligence*? Between *gross negligence* and *fraud*?

3-4. In an engagement in which the CPA issues an unqualified opinion on financial statements that are to be used to obtain a loan when he or she knows that statements are misstated, is the CPA fraudulent or constructively fraudulent? Could he or she be held liable to a bank that extends a loan and subsequently suffers a loss, or must the bank have a privity relationship to successfully sue the CPA?

3-5. When a client brings a suit against a CPA for substandard auditing, what facts must be proved by the client?

3-6. What is a *subrogee*? If a subrogee sues an auditor, what facts must be established by the subrogee?

3-7. What standards of care do courts establish as the minimum level of care for auditors? What is the conceptual difference between an error in professional judgment and negligence?

3-8. What various defenses may an auditor use in defending against a suit brought by a client or a subrogee?

3-9. In order for a third party, such as a bank, to be successful in suing a CPA for negligence, what must the third party establish or prove?

3-10. Does *Ultramares Corp.* v. *Touche, Niven & Co.* prevent a third party from bringing a successful negligence claim against a CPA?

3-11. What was the court's primary rationale in the *Ultramares* decision for not holding the CPA liable for negligence?

3-12. *Credit Alliance Corporation* v. *Arthur Andersen & Co.* builds on and adds to *Ultramares*. What was the legal theory established in *Credit Alliance* that could permit a third party to be successful in suing a CPA for negligence?

3-13. Contrast the *Ultramares* doctrine with the *Restatement of Torts* rule and the *Rosenblum* rule. Also, distinguish between a foreseen person and a foreseeable person.

3-14. *Rusch Factors, Inc.* v. *Levin* makes substantial inroads on *Ultramares*. In what way? Under *Rusch Factors* or the *Restatement of Torts* rule, is it necessary for the third party to be identified by name?

3-15. Assume that a client requests a CPA to audit its financial statements for the expressed purpose of using the financial statements to obtain bank credit. If the CPA is negligent, will the third party bank be able to recover damages under *Ultramares*? Under *Rusch Factors*? Under *Rosenblum*?

3-16. Using the facts in Question 3-15, would the CPA be liable under *Rusch Factors* if, instead of obtaining bank credit, the client used the financial statements to sell a $20,000 equity interest in the company to a private investor?

3-17. According to *Rosenblum, Inc.*, v. *Adler*, the CPA is basically liable to all third parties that rely on the financial statements in making decisions. Do you agree?

3-18. Before 1983, auditors generally could not be subject to liability for negligence to most third parties who were neither actually foreseen users of the audited financial statements nor in privity with the auditor. Is this correct? If so, why?

3-19. What is the primary purpose of the federal securities acts?

3-20. The SEC has some unique rules relating to independence of accountants and type of acceptable auditor's opinion. What are these?

3-21. In order to bring an action under Section 11 of the 1933 Securities Act, what must the plaintiff prove?

3-22. Contrast the burden of proof for negligence under common law with the burden of proof under Section 11(a) of the 1933 Act.

3-23. What defenses are available to the accountant under Section 11(a)?

3-24. How does the CPA's responsibility for subsequent events in a registration statement differ from his or her responsibility for subsequent events in the usual audit engagement?

3-25. What is a comfort letter? Is it filed with the SEC?

3-26. What was the main defense in *Escott* v. *BarChris Construction Corp.*? Why did it fail?

3-27. What is the primary difference between the 1933 Securities Act and the 1934 Securities Exchange Act?

3-28. What items must a plaintiff establish in a Rule 10b-5 case against an accountant?

3-29. What was the main question before the Supreme Court in *Ernst & Ernst* v. *Hochfelder*? How was the question decided?

3-30. Define *scienter*. Is it equivalent to recklessness or gross negligence?

3-31. What defenses are available to a defendant CPA in a Rule 10b-5 case?

3-32. Section 32(a) of the Securities Exchange Act of 1934 is the most important criminal statute that is of concern to auditors. What acts are prohibited by Section 32(a)?

3-33. What are other criminal statutes under which auditors may be criminally prosecuted?

3-34. In a criminal action against an auditor, who is the plaintiff? What must the plaintiff prove? What defenses are available to the auditor?

3-35. What is the primary lesson to be learned by the accounting profession in the Continental Vending case?

3-36. The Equity Funding case is frequently referred to as a computer fraud. Is this a correct classification?

3-37. Contrast the auditor's responsibility for irregularities with his or her responsibility for illegal acts.

3-38. What is the primary difference between an *error* and an *irregularity*? (Give examples of each in your response.)

3-39. What action should an auditor take if an irregularity or an illegal act is discovered while performing an audit procedure?

3-40. Does the subsequent discovery of a material misstatement indicate inadequate auditor performance?

3-41. What is the auditor's obligation when he or she discovers that an important fact was overlooked during the audit that significantly changes the client's financial statements? Would the auditor's course of action differ depending on how the auditor becomes aware of the overlooked fact?

3-42. What are *omitted procedures*? What responsibility does the auditor have when he or she determines that an important audit procedure has been omitted?

3-43. Why is suing for unpaid fees hazardous?

Objective Questions

*3-44. DMO Enterprises, Inc., engaged the accounting firm of Martin, Seals & Anderson to perform its annual audit. The firm performed the audit in a competent, nonnegligent manner and billed DMO for $16,000, the agreed fee. Shortly after delivery of the audited financial statements, Gerald Hightower, the assistant controller, disappeared, taking with him $28,000 of DMO's funds. The company then discovered that Hightower had been engaged in a highly sophisticated, novel defalcation scheme during the past year. He had previously embezzled $35,000 of DMO funds. DMO has refused to pay the accounting firm's fee and is seeking to recover the $63,000 that was stolen by Hightower. Which of the following is correct?
  (1) The accountants *cannot* recover their fee and are liable for $63,000.
  (2) The accountants are entitled to collect their fee and are *not* liable for $63,000.
  (3) DMO is entitled to rescind the audit contract and thus is *not* liable for the $16,000.
  (4) DMO is entitled to recover the $28,000 defalcation and is *not* liable for the $16,000 fee.

*3-45. Major, Major & Sharpe, CPAs, are the auditors of MacLain Industries. In connection with the public offering of $10 million of MacLain securities, Major expressed an unqualified opinion on the financial statements. Subsequent to the offering, certain misstatements and omissions were revealed. Major has been sued by the purchasers of the stock offered pursuant to the registration statement, which included the financial statements audited by Major. In the ensuing lawsuit by the MacLain investors, which of the following arguments will allow Major to avoid liability?
  (1) The errors and omissions were caused primarily by MacLain.
  (2) Major can show that at least some of the investors did *not* actually read the audited financial statements.
  (3) Major can prove that due diligence was exercised in the audit of the financial statements of MacLain.
  (4) MacLain had expressly assumed any liability in connection with the public offering.

*3-46. Donalds & Company, CPAs, audited the financial statements included in the annual report submitted by Markum Securities, Inc., to the Securities and Exchange Commission. The audit was improper in several respects. Markum is now insolvent and unable to satisfy the claims of its customers. The customers have instituted legal action against Donalds based upon Section 10(b) and Rule 10b-5 of the Securities Exchange Act of 1934. Which of the following is likely to be Donalds' best defense?
  (1) It did *not* intentionally certify false financial statements.
  (2) Section 10(b) does *not* apply to it.
  (3) It was *not* in privity of contract with the creditors.
  (4) Its engagement letter specifically disclaimed any liability, to any party, that resulted from Markum's fraudulent conduct.

---

*AICPA adapted.

*3-47. **Parts I and II** are based on the following information:
If a CPA firm is being sued for common-law fraud by a third party based upon false financial statements, which of the following is the best defense the accountants could assert?
Part I
(1) Lack of privity.
(2) Lack of reliance.
(3) A disclaimer contained in the engagement letter.
(4) Contributory negligence on the part of the client.
Part II
(1) The CPA did not financially benefit from the alleged fraud.
(2) The contributory negligence of the client.
(3) The third party lacks privity.
(4) The false statements were immaterial.

*3-48. Joan Locke, CPA, was engaged by Hall, Inc., to audit Willow Company. Hall purchased Willow after receiving Willow's audited financial statements, which included Locke's unqualified auditor's opinion. Locke was negligent in the performance of the Willow audit engagement, and as a result, Hall suffered damages of $75,000. Hall appears to have grounds to sue Locke for

	Breach of Contract	Negligence
(1)	Yes	Yes
(2)	Yes	No
(3)	No	Yes
(4)	No	No

*3-49. Lewis & Clark, CPAs, rendered an unqualified opinion on the financial statements of a company that sold common stock in a public offering subject to the Securities Act of 1933. Based on a false statement in the financial statements, Lewis & Clark are being sued by an investor who purchased shares of this public offering. Which of the following represents a viable defense?
(1) The investor has *not* met the burden of proving fraud or negligence by Lewis & Clark.
(2) The investor did *not* actually rely upon the false statement.
(3) Detection of the false statement by Lewis & Clark occurred after their examination date.
(4) The false statement is immaterial in the overall context of the financial statements.

*3-50. The Apex Surety Company wrote a general fidelity bond covering defalcations by the employees of Watson, Inc. Thereafter, Edward Grand, an employee of Watson, embezzled $18,900 of company funds. When Grand's activities were discovered, Apex paid Watson the full amount in accordance with the terms of the fidelity bond and then sought recovery against Watson's auditors, Kane & Dobbs, CPAs. Which of the following would be Kane & Dobbs's best defense?
(1) Apex is not in privity of contract.
(2) The shortages were the result of clever forgeries and collusive fraud that would not be detected by an audit made in accordance with generally accepted auditing standards.
(3) Kane & Dobbs were not guilty either of gross negligence or fraud.
(4) Kane & Dobbs were not aware of the Apex–Watson surety relationship.

---

*AICPA adapted.

*3-51. A CPA is subject to criminal liability if he or she
   (1) refuses to turn over the working papers to the client.
   (2) performs an audit in a negligent manner.
   (3) willfully omits a material fact required to be stated in the registration statement.
   (4) willfully breaches the contract with the client.

*3-52. Gaspard & Devlin, a medium-size CPA firm, employed Mary Marshall as a staff accountant. Marshall was negligent in auditing several of the firm's clients. Under these circumstances, which of the following statements is true?
   (1) Gaspard & Devlin is not liable for Marshall's negligence because CPAs are generally considered to be independent contractors.
   (2) Gaspard & Devlin would not be liable for Marshall's negligence if Marshall disobeyed specific instructions in the performance of the audits.
   (3) Gaspard & Devlin can recover against its insurer on its malpractice policy even if one of the partners were also negligent in reviewing Marshall's work.
   (4) Marshall would have no personal liability for negligence.

*3-53. Winslow Manufacturing, Inc., sought a $200,000 loan from National Lending Corporation. National insisted that audited financial statements be submitted before it would extend credit. Winslow agreed to this and also agreed to pay the audit fee. An audit was performed by an independent CPA who submitted the audit report to Winslow to be used solely for the purpose of negotiating a loan from National. National, upon reviewing the audited financial statements, decided in good faith not to extend the credit desired. Certain ratios, which as a matter of policy were used by National in reaching its decision, were deemed too low. Winslow used copies of the audited financial statements to obtain credit elsewhere. It was subsequently learned that the CPA, despite the exercise of reasonable care, had failed to discover a sophisticated embezzlement scheme by Winslow's chief accountant. Under these circumstances, what liability does the CPA have?
   (1) The CPA is liable to third parties who extended credit to Winslow based upon the audited financial statements.
   (2) The CPA is liable to Winslow to repay the audit fee because credit was not extended by National.
   (3) The CPA is liable to Winslow for any losses Winslow suffered as a result of failure to discover the embezzlement.
   (4) The CPA is not liable to any of the parties.

*3-54. Arthur Martinson is a duly licensed CPA. One of his clients is suing him for negligence, alleging that he failed to meet generally accepted auditing standards in the current year's audit, thereby failing to discover large thefts of inventory. Which of the following applies under the circumstances?
   (1) Martinson is not bound by generally accepted auditing standards unless he is a member of the AICPA.
   (2) Martinson's failure to meet generally accepted auditing standards would result in liability.
   (3) Generally accepted auditing standards do not currently cover the procedures that must be used in verifying inventory for balance sheet purposes.
   (4) If Martinson failed to meet generally accepted auditing standards, he would undoubtedly be found to have committed the tort of fraud.

*3-55. Hall purchased Eon Corp. bonds in a public offering subject to the Securities Act of 1933. Kosson and Co., CPAs, rendered an unqualified opinion on Eon's financial statements, which were included in Eon's registration statement. Kosson is being sued by Hall based upon misstatements contained in the financial statements. In order to be successful, Hall must prove:

---

*AICPA adapted.

	Damages	Materiality of the Misstatement	Kosson's Scienter
(1)	Yes	Yes	Yes
(2)	Yes	Yes	No
(3)	Yes	No	No
(4)	No	Yes	Yes

*3-56.   **Parts I and II** are based on the following information:
West & Co., CPAs, rendered an unqualified opinion on the financial statements of Pride Corp., which were included in Pride's registration statement filed with the SEC. Subsequently, Hex purchased 500 shares of Pride's preferred stock, which were acquired as part of a public offering subject to the Securities Act of 1933. Hex has commenced an action against West based on the Securities Act of 1933 for losses resulting from misstatements of facts in the financial statements included in the registration statement.
Part I.   Which of the following elements must Hex prove to hold West liable?
(1) West rendered its opinion with knowledge of material misstatements.
(2) West performed the audit negligently.
(3) Hex relied on the financial statements included in the registration statement.
(4) The misstatements were material.
Part II.   Which of the following defenses would be *least* helpful to West in avoiding liability to Hex?
(1) West was *not* in privity of contract with Hex.
(2) West conducted the audit in accordance with GAAS.
(3) Hex's losses were caused by factors other than the misstatements.
(4) Hex knew of the misstatements when Hex acquired the preferred stock.

*3-57.   **Parts I and II** are based on the following information:
Mead Corp. orally engaged Dex & Co., CPAs, to audit its financial statements. The management of Mead informed Dex that it suspected that the accounts receivable were materially overstated. Although the financial statements audited by Dex did, in fact, include a materially overstated accounts receivable balance, Dex issued an unqualified opinion. Mead relied on the financial statements in deciding to obtain a loan from City Bank to expand its operations. City relied on the financial statements in making the loan to Mead. As a result of the overstated accounts receivable balance, Mead has defaulted on the loan and has incurred a substantial loss.
Part I.   If Mead sues Dex for negligence in failing to discover the overstatement, Dex's best defense would be that
(1) no engagement letter had been signed by Dex.
(2) the audit was performed by Dex in accordance with generally accepted auditing standards.
(3) Dex was *not* in privity of contract with Mead.
(4) Dex did *not* perform the audit recklessly or with an intent to deceive.
Part II.   If City sues Dex for fraud, Dex would most likely avoid liability if it could prove that
(1) Dex was *not* in privity of contract with City.
(2) Dex did *not* perform the audit recklessly or with an intent to deceive.
(3) Mead should have provided more specific information concerning its suspicions.
(4) Mead was contributorily negligent.

---

*AICPA adapted.

*3-58. **Parts I and II** are based on the following information:

Brown & Co., CPAs, issued an unqualified opinion on the financial statements of its client, King Corp. Based on the strength of King's financial statements, Safe Bank loaned King $500,000. Brown was unaware that Safe would receive a copy of the financial statements or that they would be used in obtaining a loan by King. King defaulted on the loan.

Part I. If Safe commences an action for negligence against Brown, and Brown is able to prove that it conducted the audit in conformity with GAAS, Brown will

(1) be liable to Safe because Safe relied on the financial statements.

(2) be liable to Safe because the statute of frauds has been satisfied.

(3) not be liable to Safe because there is a conclusive presumption that following GAAS is the equivalent of acting reasonably and with due care.

(4) not be liable to Safe because there was a lack of privity of contract.

Part II. If Safe commences an action for common law fraud against Brown, then to be successful, Safe must prove in addition to other elements that it

(1) was in privity of contract with Brown.

(2) was *not* contributorily negligent.

(3) was in privity of contract with King.

(4) justifiably relied on the financial statements.

*3-59. An auditor concludes that the omission of a substantive procedure considered necessary at the time of the examination may impair the auditor's present ability to support the previously expressed opinion. The auditor need not apply the omitted procedure if

(1) the risk of adverse publicity or litigation is low.

(2) the results of other procedures that were applied tend to compensate for the procedure omitted.

(3) the auditor's opinion was qualified because of a departure from generally accepted accounting principles.

(4) the results of the subsequent period's tests of controls make the omitted procedure less important.

*3-60. Which of the following statements best describes an auditor's responsibility to detect errors and irregularities?

(1) The auditor should assess the client's internal control structure, and design the audit to provide reasonable assurance of detecting all errors and irregularities.

(2) The auditor should assess the risk that errors and irregularities may cause the financial statements to contain material misstatements, and determine whether the necessary internal control procedures are prescribed and are being followed satisfactorily.

(3) The auditor should consider the types of errors and irregularities that could occur, and determine whether the necessary internal control procedures are prescribed and are being followed.

(4) The auditor should assess the risk that errors and irregularities may cause the financial statements to contain material misstatements, and design the audit to provide reasonable assurance of detecting material errors and irregularities.

*3-61. Which of the following statements concerning illegal acts by clients is correct?

(1) An auditor's responsibility to detect illegal acts that have a direct and material effect on the financial statements is the same as that for errors and irregularities.

(2) An audit in accordance with generally accepted auditing standards normally includes audit procedures specifically designed to detect illegal acts that have an indirect but material effect on the financial statements.

(3) An auditor considers illegal acts from the perspective of the reliability of management's representations rather than their relation to audit objectives derived from financial statement assertions.

(4) An auditor has no responsibility to detect illegal acts by clients that have an indirect effect on the financial statements.

---

*AICPA adapted.

Problems and Cases

3-62. (Important Cases) Match the following cases with the appropriate legal concept or doctrine. There is only one match per case.

Cases

_____ A. *Rosenblum, Inc.* v. *Adler*
_____ B. *Escott* v. *BarChris Construction Corp.*
_____ C. *Ultramares Corp.* v. *Touche, Niven & Co.*
_____ D. *Ernst & Ernst* v. *Hochfelder*
_____ E. *United States* v. *Simon*
_____ F. *Dantzler Lumber and Export Co.* v. *Columbia Casualty Co.*
_____ G. *Credit Alliance Corporation* v. *Arthur Andersen & Co.*
_____ H. *United States* v. *Weiner*
_____ I. *Rusch Factors, Inc.* v. *Levin*

Legal Concepts or Doctrines

1. A Supreme Court decision that established the standard of culpability in Rule 10b-5 actions as scienter or fraudulent conduct, not negligence.
2. The rights of a client may be subrogated to a third party.
3. A landmark case decided under Section 11(a) of the 1933 Securities Act.
4. A criminal case that is frequently incorrectly identified as a computer fraud case.
5. The most famous case with respect to common-law liability for negligence to third parties.
6. A criminal case that clearly established that the auditor must make sure that the financial statements adequately disclose known and material management fraud.
7. A recent New York case that reconfirmed *Ultramares*.
8. A leading case that ruled that an auditor can be held liable to a third party for negligence when that third party is foreseen.
9. An important common-law case that indicates that an auditor may be held liable to foreseeable third parties for negligence.
10. A civil case demonstrating that it is risky for a CPA to sue for unpaid fees.

*3-63. (Privity and Liability to Third Parties) Marcall is a limited partner of Guarcross, a limited partnership, and is suing a CPA firm that was retained by the limited partnership to perform auditing and tax return preparation services. Guarcross was formed for the purpose of investing in a diversified portfolio of risk capital securities. The partnership agreement included the following provisions:

> The initial capital contribution of each limited partner shall not be less than $250,000; no partner may withdraw any part of an interest in the partnership, except at the end of any fiscal year upon giving written notice of such intention not less than 30 days prior to the end of such year; the books and records of the partnership shall be audited as of the end of the fiscal year by a certified public accountant designated by the general partners; and proper and complete books of account shall be kept and shall be open to inspection by any of the partners or his or her accredited representative.

---

*AICPA adapted.

Marcall's claim of malpractice against the CPA firm centers on the firm's alleged failure to comment, in its audit report, on the withdrawal by the general partners of $2,000,000 of their $2,600,000 capital investment based on back-dated notices, and the lumping together of the $2,000,000 withdrawals with $49,000 in withdrawals by limited partners so that a reader of the financial statement would not be likely to realize that the two general partners had withdrawn a major portion of their investments.

The CPA firm's contention is that its contract was made with the limited partnership, not its partners. It further contends that because the CPA firm had no privity of contract with the third-party limited partners, the limited partners have no right of action for negligence.

REQUIRED

Discuss the various theories Marcall would rely upon in order to prevail in a lawsuit against the CPA firm.

3-64. (Third-Party Liability) Watts and Williams, a firm of certified public accountants, audited the balance sheet of Red Raider Incorporated, a corporation that imports and deals in fine furs. Upon completion of the audit, the auditors supplied Red Raider with 20 copies of the audited balance sheet. The firm knew in a general way that Red Raider wanted that number of copies of the auditor's report to furnish to banks and other potential lenders.

The balance sheet in question was in error by approximately $800,000. Instead of having a $600,000 net worth, the corporation was insolvent. The management of Red Raider had "altered" the books to avoid bankruptcy. The assets were overstated by $500,000 of fictitious and nonexisting accounts receivable and $300,000 of nonexisting furs listed as inventory when in fact there were only empty boxes. The audit failed to detect these fraudulent entries. Raul Martinson, relying on the audited balance sheet, loaned Red Raider $200,000. He seeks to recover his loss from Watts and Williams.

REQUIRED

Indicate whether each of the following statements is true or false.

(1) If Martinson alleges and proves negligence on the part of Watts and Williams, he would be able to recover his loss in a state that follows the *Restatement of Torts*.

(2) If Martinson alleges and proves constructive fraud, that is, gross negligence on the part of Watts and Williams, he would be able to recover his loss in any state.

(3) Martinson is not in privity of contract with Watts and Williams.

(4) Unless actual fraud on the part of Watts and Williams could be shown, Martinson could not recover.

(5) Martinson is a foreseeable third party.

*3-65. (Third-Party Liability) Pelham & James, CPAs, were retained by Tom Stone, sole proprietor of Stone Housebuilders, to compile Stone's financial statements. Stone advised Pelham & James that the financial statements would be used in connection with a possible incorporation of the business and sale of stock to friends. Prior to undertaking the engagement, Pelham & James were also advised to pay particular attention to the trade accounts payable. They agreed to use every reasonable means to determine the correct amount.

At the time Pelham & James were engaged, the books and records were in total disarray. Pelham & James proceeded with the engagement, applying all applicable procedures for compiling financial statements. They failed, however, to detect and disclose in the financial statements Stone's liability for certain unpaid bills. Documentation concerning those bills was available for Pelham & James's inspection had they looked. This omission led to a material understatement ($60,000) of the trade accounts payable.

Pelham & James delivered the compiled financial statements to Tom Stone with their compilation report that indicated that they did not express an opinion or any other

---

*AICPA adapted.

assurance regarding the financial statements. Tom Stone met with two prospective investors, Ellen Dickerson and Harold Nichols. At the meeting, Pelham & James stated that they were confident that the trade accounts payable balance was accurate to within $8000.

Stone Housebuilders was incorporated. Dickerson and Nichols, relying on the financial statements, became stockholders along with Tom Stone. Shortly thereafter, the understatement of trade accounts payable was detected. As a result, Dickerson and Nichols discovered that they had paid substantially more for the stock than it was worth at the time of purchase.

REQUIRED

Answer the following, setting forth reasons for any conclusions stated.

Will Pelham & James be found liable to Dickerson and Nichols in a common-law action for their damages?

3-66. (1933 Securities Act) Dandy Container Corporation engaged the accounting firm of Adams and Adams to audit financial statements to be used in connection with a public offering of securities. Adams and Adams completed the audit and expressed an unqualified opinion on the financial statements that were submitted to the Securities and Exchange Commission along with the registration statement. Dandy Container offered two hundred thousand shares of common stock to the public at $11 a share. Eight months later the stock fell to $2 a share when it was disclosed that several large loans to two "paper" corporations owned by one of the directors were worthless. The loans were secured by the stock of the borrowing corporation that was owned by the director. These facts were not disclosed in the financial statements. The director involved and the two corporations are insolvent.

REQUIRED

Indicate whether each of the following statements is true or false.

(1) The Securities Act of 1933 applies to the above-described public offering of securities in interstate commerce.

(2) The accounting firm has potential liability to any person who acquired stock described in the registration statement.

(3) An investor who bought shares in Dandy Container would make a prima facie case if he or she alleged that the failure to explain the nature of the loans in question constituted a false statement or misleading omission in the financial statements.

(4) The accountants could avoid liability if they could show they were neither negligent nor fraudulent.

(5) The accountants could not avoid or reduce the damages asserted against them even if they could establish that the drop in price was due in whole or in part to other causes.

(6) It would appear that the accountants were negligent with respect to the handling of the secured loans in question—if they discovered the facts regarding the loans in the "paper" corporations and failed to disclose them in the financial statements.

(7) The Securities and Exchange Commission would defend any action brought against the accountants in that the SEC examined and approved the registration statement.

*3-67. (1933 Securities Act) Francine Jackson is a sophisticated investor. As such, she was initially a member of a small group that was going to participate in a private placement of $1 million of common stock of Clarion Corporation. Numerous meetings were held between management and the investor group. The participants were supplied with detailed financial and other information. Upon the eve of completion, the placement was aborted when one major investor withdrew. Clarion then decided to offer $2.5 million of Clarion common stock to the public pursuant to the registration requirements of the Securities Act of 1933. Jackson subscribed to $300,000 of the Clarion public stock offering. Nine months later, Clarion's earnings dropped significantly and as a result the stock dropped 20% beneath the offering price. In addition, the Dow Jones Industrial Average was down 10% from the time of the offering.

---

*AICPA adapted.

Jackson has sold her shares at a loss of $60,000 and seeks to hold all parties liable who participated in the public offering, including Allen, Dunn, and Rose, Clarion's CPA firm. Although the audit was performed in conformity with generally accepted auditing standards, there were some relatively minor irregularities. The financial statements of Clarion Corporation, which are part of the registration statement, contained minor misleading facts. Clarion and Allen, Dunn, and Rose believe that Jackson's asserted claim is without merit.

REQUIRED

Answer the following, setting forth reasons for any conclusions.

A. Assuming Jackson sues under the Securities Act of 1933, what will be the basis of her claim?

B. What are the probable defenses that might be asserted by Allen, Dunn, and Rose in light of these facts?

*3-68. (1933 Securities Act and Common-Law Third Party Liability) The common stock of Wilson, Inc., is owned by 20 stockholders who live in several states. Wilson's financial statements as of December 31, 19X4, were audited by Doe & Co., CPAs, who rendered an unqualified opinion on the financial statements.

In reliance on Wilson's financial statements, which showed a net income for 19X4 of $1,500,000, Russell Peters on April 10, 19X5, purchased 10,000 shares of Wilson stock for $200,000. The purchase was from a shareholder who lived in another state. Wilson's financial statements contained material misstatements. Because Doe did not carefully follow GAAS it did not discover that the statements failed to reflect unrecorded expenses that reduced Wilson's actual net income to $800,000. After disclosure of the corrected financial statements, Peters sold his shares for $100,000, which was the highest price he could obtain.

Peters has brought an action against Doe under federal securities law and state common law.

REQUIRED

Answer the following, setting forth reasons for any conclusions stated.

A. Will Peters prevail on his federal securities law claims?

B. Will Peters prevail on his state common-law claims?

*3-69. Under Section 11 of the Securities Act of 1933 and Section 10(b), Rule 10b-5, of the Securities Exchange Act of 1934, a CPA may be sued by a purchaser of registered securities.

REQUIRED

Items 1 through 6 relate to what a plaintiff who purchased securities must prove in a civil liability suit against a CPA. For each item, determine whether the statement must be proven under Section 11 of the Securities Act of 1933, under Section 10(b), Rule 10b-5, of the Securities Exchange Act of 1934, both Acts, or neither Act.

■ If the item must be proven *only* under Section 11 of the Securities Act of 1933, select Ⓐ as your answer.

■ If the item must be proven *only* under Section 10(b), Rule 10b-5, of the Securities Exchange Act of 1934, select Ⓑ as your answer.

■ If the item must be proven under *both* Acts, select Ⓒ as your answer.

■ If the item must be proven under *neither* of the Acts, select Ⓓ as your answer.

*AICPA adapted.

Only Section 11	Only Section 10(b)	Both	Neither
Ⓐ	Ⓑ	Ⓒ	Ⓓ

The plaintiff security purchaser must allege or prove
(1) material misstatements were included in a filed document.
(2) a monetary loss occurred.
(3) lack of due diligence by the CPA. *D*
(4) privity with the CPA. *D*
(5) reliance on the document. *B*
(6) the CPA had scienter. *B*

*3-70. (1934 Securities Exchange Act and Common Law) Whitlow & Company is a brokerage firm registered under the Securities Exchange Act of 1934. The act requires such a brokerage firm to file audited financial statements with the SEC annually. Mitchell & Moss, Whitlow's CPAs, performed the annual audit for the year ended December 31, 19X4, and rendered an unqualified opinion, which was filed with the SEC along with Whitlow's financial statements. During 19X4 Charles, the president of Whitlow & Company, engaged in a huge embezzlement scheme that eventually bankrupted the firm. As a result, customers and shareholders of Whitlow & Company suffered substantial losses, including Roger Thaxton, who had recently purchased several shares of stock of Whitlow & Company after reviewing the company's 19X4 audit report. Mitchell & Moss's audit was deficient; if the firm had complied with generally accepted auditing standards, the embezzlement would have been discovered. However, Mitchell & Moss had no knowledge of the embezzlement nor could its conduct be categorized as reckless.
REQUIRED
Answer the following, setting forth reasons for any conclusions stated.
A. What liability to Thaxton, if any, does Mitchell & Moss have under the Securities Exchange Act of 1934?
B. What theory or theories of liability, if any, are available to Whitlow & Company's customers and shareholders under the common law?

*3-71. (Criminal Liability) **Parts I and II** are based on the following information: James Danforth, CPA, audited the financial statements of the Blair Corporation for the year ended December 31, 19X4. Danforth rendered an unqualified opinion on February 6, 19X5. The financial statements were incorporated into Form 10-K and filed with the Securities and Exchange Commission. Blair's financial statements included as an asset a previously sold certificate of deposit (CD) in the amount of $250,000. Blair had purchased the CD on December 29, 19X4, and sold it on December 30, 19X4, to a third party who paid Blair that day. Blair did not deliver the CD to the buyer until January 8, 19X5. Blair deliberately recorded the sale as an increase in cash and other revenue, thereby significantly overstating working capital, stockholders' equity, and net income. Danforth confirmed Blair's purchase of the CD with the seller and physically observed the CD on January 5, 19X5.
Part I.   Assume that on January 18, 19X5, while auditing other revenue, Danforth discovered that the CD had been sold. Further assume that Danforth agreed that, in exchange for an additional audit fee of $20,000, he would render an unqualified opinion on Blair's financial statements (including the previously sold CD).

---

*AICPA adapted.

REQUIRED

Answer the following, setting forth reasons for any conclusions stated.

A. The SEC charges Danforth with criminal violations of the Securities Exchange Act of 1934. Will the SEC prevail? Include in your discussion what the SEC must establish in this action.

B. Assume the SEC discovers and makes immediate public disclosure of Blair's action with the result that no one relies to his or her detriment upon the audit report and financial statements. Under these circumstances, will the SEC prevail in its criminal action against Danforth?

Part II.   Assume that Danforth performed his audit in accordance with generally accepted auditing standards and exercised due professional care, but did not discover Blair's sale of the CD. Two weeks after issuing the unqualified opinion, Danforth discovered that the CD had been sold. The day following this discovery, at Blair's request, Danforth delivered a copy of the audit report, along with the financial statements, to a bank that in relying on it made a loan to Blair that ultimately proved uncollectible. Danforth did not advise the bank of his discovery.

REQUIRED

Answer the following, setting forth reasons for any conclusions stated.

If the bank sues Danforth for the losses it sustains in connection with the loan, will it prevail?

*3-72. (Responsibility for Fraud) Arm Watchband Company manufactures a full line of expansion watchbands, including platinum, gold, and a medium-priced silver. With the skyrocketing prices of precious metal and booming sales, Arm is bursting at the seams with cash and extremely valuable inventory. Jack Dutch, the controller of Arm, noted some irregularities that aroused his suspicion that there might be some embezzlement of company funds. He instituted a full-fledged internal audit of the company's books and records, examined all accounting procedures, and took other appropriate steps necessary to assure himself that nothing was amiss. The only thing unearthed by this was a $300 discrepancy in petty cash that had apparently been stolen.

Dutch talked to Joseph Wheeler, the president of Arm, and told him his fears. He also suggested that, in addition to the regular annual audit performed by Rice & Campbell, CPAs, they be engaged to perform a full-fledged defalcation audit. This was authorized by Wheeler, and the engagement letter for the audit in question clearly reflected this understanding.

Rice & Campbell performed the normal annual audit in its usual competent, nonnegligent manner. The special defalcation audit revealed additional shortages in petty cash. The method was determined and the culprit was exposed and dismissed. Nothing else was revealed despite the fact that the customary procedures for such an audit were followed. Ten months later, Schultz, the warehouse supervisor, was caught by another employee substituting inexpensive copies of the watchbands for the genuine Arm items. The copies were remarkably similar to the originals in appearance. In fact, it would take a precious metals expert to tell the difference based upon a careful visual examination. The packaging was the same because Schultz had access to the packaging materials, including the seals that were used in an attempt to provide greater security and detect theft. Schultz always placed the boxes of the copies at the bottom of the inventory supplies. Despite this fact one such carton had been shipped to a leading department store several months ago, but the substitution of copies for the originals had not been detected.

REQUIRED

Answer the following, setting forth reasons for any conclusions stated.

Would Rice & Campbell be liable for failure to detect the defalcation scheme in question?

---

*AICPA adapted.

*3-73. (Responsibility for Fraud) The CPA firm of Martinson, Brinks & Sutherland, a partnership, was the auditor for Masco Corporation, a medium-size wholesaler. Masco leased warehouse facilities and sought financing for leasehold improvements to these facilities. Masco assured its bank that the leasehold improvements would result in a more efficient and profitable operation. Based on these assurances, the bank granted Masco a line of credit.

The loan agreement required annual audited financial statements. Masco submitted to the bank its 19X3 audited financial statements that showed an operating profit of $75,000, leasehold improvements of $250,000, and net worth of $350,000. In reliance thereon, the bank loaned Masco $200,000. The audit report that accompanied the financial statements disclaimed an opinion because the cost of the leasehold improvements could not be determined from the company's records. The part of the audit report dealing with leasehold improvements reads as follows:

> Additions to fixed assets in 19X3 were found to include principally warehouse improvements. Practically all of this work was done by company employees and the costs of materials and overhead were paid by Masco. Unfortunately, fully completed, detailed cost records were not kept of these leasehold improvements and no exact determination could be made as to the actual cost of said improvements. The total amount capitalized is set forth in Note 4.

In late 19X4 Masco went out of business, at which time it was learned that the claimed leasehold improvements were totally fictitious. The labor expenses charged as leasehold improvements proved to be operating expenses. No item of building material cost had been recorded. No independent investigation of the existence of the leasehold improvements was made by the auditors.

If the $250,000 had not been capitalized, the income statement would have reflected a substantial loss from operations and the net worth would have been correspondingly decreased.

The bank has sustained a loss on its loan to Masco of $200,000 and now seeks to recover damages from the CPA firm, alleging that the accountants negligently audited the financial statements.

REQUIRED

Answer the following, setting forth reasons for any conclusions stated.

A. Will the disclaimer of opinion absolve the CPA firm from responsibility for not detecting the irregularity?

B. Are the individual partners of Martinson, Brinks & Sutherland, who did not take part in the audit, liable?

*3-74. (Responsibility for Errors, Irregularities, and Illegal Acts) Reed, CPA, accepted an engagement to audit the financial statements of Smith Company. Reed's discussions with Smith's new management and the predecessor auditor indicated the possibility that Smith's financial statements may be misstated due to the possible occurrence of errors, irregularities, and illegal acts.

*AICPA adapted.

REQUIRED
A. Identify and describe Reed's responsibilities to detect Smith's errors and irregularities. Do not identify specific audit procedures.
B. Identify and describe Reed's responsibilities to report Smith's errors and irregularities.
C. Describe Reed's responsibilities to detect Smith's material illegal acts. Do not identify specific audit procedures.

3-75. (Illegal Acts) Rip Snort, CPA, has concluded that a transaction entered into by the Shady Corporation constitutes an illegal act. When confronted with the situation, the management of Shady Corporation informs Snort that corrective action regarding the act has been put into motion. The corporation has admitted its part in the act and has agreed with the appropriate authorities to pay certain penalties and to refrain from such dealings in the future. Snort has verified the facts as expressed by management and is convinced that the information is reliable. When he approaches management regarding financial statement disclosure of the situation, management objects. Management reasons as follows: "We have admitted our guilt and have corrected the situation with the appropriate authorities. Because we were unsure of the legality of the transaction when it was entered into, and based upon our commitment not to enter into such transactions in the future, we feel that disclosing the situation would serve no useful purpose."

REQUIRED
How should Rip Snort respond?

3-76. (Omitted Procedures) Nancy Fox, CPA, as a result of information discovered during an internal quality control review, has admitted that she failed to apply an important audit procedure in the audit of Parmir, Inc. Furthermore, she cannot perform the omitted procedure or apply alternative procedures because Parmir, Inc., has recently changed auditors. Upon presenting the situation to her firm's attorney, the attorney concludes, "Let sleeping dogs lie"; that is, take no action at this time. Fox is really worried and believes that she should at least notify Parmir's board of directors. Do you agree?

Audit Judgment Case

3-77. For several years, a New York mortgage company retained Walt Conn, CPA, to audit the company's financial statements. Conn provided multiple copies of the audit reports to the mortgage company, but did not provide copies to anyone else. As part of the auditing procedure, he asked XYZ Bank, which was one of the mortgage company's creditors, to complete certain standard financial institution confirmation inquiries. The mortgage company furnished XYZ Bank with a copy of each of the annual audit reports. XYZ Bank made substantial loans to the mortgage company.

After the mortgage company defaulted on the loans, XYZ Bank sued Conn for negligence, wantonness, fraud, and breach of contract based on the theory that the bank was a third-party beneficiary of the contracts between the mortgage company and Conn. The claims were based on the contention that it was reasonably foreseeable that the mortgage company would use the audits to influence the bank.

REQUIRED
A. Would Conn be successful using a privity defense in
    (1) a *Credit Alliance* state?
    (2) a *Restatement of Torts* state?
    (3) a *Rosenblum* state?
B. Given that the case occurred in a *Credit Alliance* state (New York State), did Conn meet the prerequisites that must be established by a third party to overcome the privity defense?

[handwritten margin notes: "3rd party" "not a generally" "possibly a foreseen party" "NO"]

C. Does the fact that Conn used the standard financial institutions confirmation form to confirm certain loans with XYZ Bank establish one of the *Credit Alliance* prerequisites?

D. What is a third-party beneficiary? Is XYZ a third-party beneficiary?

E. Assuming that Conn was negligent, how would you rule in the case *XYZ Bank* v. *Conn* (provide supporting rationale)? *[handwritten: Ultramare State CPA was found not Guilty]*

Auditing Issues Case

3-78.   KELCO MANUFACTURING COMPANY

During the course of Kelco's 19X7 audit, you discovered a material misstatement in financial statements that your firm had rendered a compilation report on for the year ended December 31, 19X6. The misstatement was related to leases that should have been capitalized but were erroneously treated as operating leases. Such treatment of the leases resulted in an understatement of net income in the amount of $114,000. Kelco president Steve Cook has requested comparative financial statements be presented with the December 31, 19X7 audit report.

REQUIRED

Upon discovering the error, what action should you take?

[handwritten: Should be address to Client and revise X7 Report notify to reviewer/users. Correct the compilation report.]

Part Two

Auditing Concepts

An understanding of auditing concepts is necessary to design properly a logical approach to an audit engagement.

Chapter 4 discusses the audit evidence process. This includes identifying assertions in the financial statements and applying concepts of audit risk and materiality to determine audit objectives.

Chapter 5 illustrates how the auditor designs specific audit techniques by applying the audit risk and materiality concepts presented in Chapter 4 to financial statement assertions. The chapter also discusses the documentation of audit evidence in working papers.

Chapter 6 presents the basic elements of internal control structure and describes the auditor's assessment of control risk.

Chapter 7 describes the effect of a computer on internal control structure and the effect on the auditor's assessment of control risk.

The Audit Evidence Process

Learning   Objectives

- List and explain assertions in the financial statements.

- Define audit risk and explain its relationship to the audit evidence decision.

- Identify the three components of audit risk and describe their interrelationships.

- Define materiality and describe its application to auditing.

- Translate financial statement assertions into specific audit objectives for accounts in the financial statements.

- Identify and explain the characteristics of audit evidence.

Shareholders and other interested parties rely on auditors to provide certain assurances about management-generated financial information. They want to be sure that the financial statements are fairly presented and that the company is not engaged in fraud and mismanagement. But a disparity exists between what investors expect and what auditors can verify absolutely. This is known as the expectation gap.

A recent survey of investors published in the *Journal of Accountancy* found that nearly 50% of respondents expected an absolute assurance that financial statements are free of unintentional misstatements due to errors. More surprising, almost three in four investors expected *absolute* assurance that auditors would detect material misstatements attributable to fraud.

This chapter examines the evidence that auditors must gather and analyze as they strive to meet this high-level expectation. ■

Source: Marc J. Epstein and Marshall A. Geiger, "Investor Views of Audit Assurance: Recent Evidence of The Expectation Gap," *Journal of Accountancy*, January 1994, pp. 60–64.

The overall objective of an audit of financial statements is to render an opinion as to the fairness of the financial statements in conformity with generally accepted accounting principles. Before rendering an opinion, however, the auditor must first gather and evaluate evidence. The third standard of fieldwork states that

> sufficient competent evidential matter is to be obtained through inspection, observation, inquiries, and confirmations to afford a reasonable basis for an opinion regarding the financial statements under audit.

Chapters 4 and 5 examine the conceptual framework by which auditors comply with the third standard of fieldwork. Chapter 4 discusses the assertions embodied in financial statements and how the auditor obtains reasonable assurance regarding financial statements by considering audit risk and materiality. Chapter 5 discusses how the auditor designs audit procedures to gather *sufficient competent evidential matter* and documents the evidence obtained in working papers.

The Audit Logic Process

The audit logic process is shown in Figure 4–1. By following these steps, the auditor is able to form an opinion on the financial statements.

The steps in the audit logic process are as follows:

1. Identify the client's assertions regarding each material component of the financial statements.
2. Consider the risk of material misstatement.
3. Establish specific audit objectives relating to the assertions in the financial statements considering the risk of material misstatement.

| Figure 4–1 | **The Audit Logic Process** |

1
Identify client's assertions regarding each material component of the financial statements.

2
Consider the risk of material misstatement.

3
Establish audit objectives.

4 Determine the specific audit procedures to be performed (nature).

audit program

5
Determine when to perform the procedure (timing).

Interim Testing vs. Year-End, After Year End   → *(timing).*

6
Determine how many items the procedure should be applied to (extent).

more on. Audit Sampling Chapter

4. Determine the audit procedures to be performed to accomplish the audit objectives (the nature of the tests).
5. Determine when to perform the audit procedures (the timing of the tests).
6. Determine how many items to apply procedures to (the extent of the tests).

Steps 1, 2, and 3 are discussed in this chapter. Step 4 is discussed in Chapter 5. Step 5 (timing of audit tests) is discussed in Chapter 12, and step 6 (extent of audit tests) is discussed in Chapters 9 and 10.

Client's Assertions → *are being made by Management*

The first step in the audit logic process is to identify client assertions. *Client assertions* are explicit or implicit representations by management that are embodied in the financial statements. *understate / leave out liab.*

In effect, assertions are propositions that pertain to every account in the financial statements. Auditors must test these propositions by gathering evidence to support or refute them. *SAS No. 31, Evidential Matter* (AU 326), classifies financial statement assertions into five categories.

- Existence or occurrence
- Completeness
- Rights and obligations
- Valuation or allocation
- Presentation and disclosure

[handwritten: Memorize and know]

[handwritten: Embodied in F/S]

As an example of the application of these assertions, consider the following account appearing in a financial statement.

Inventory (at lower of cost or market) $1,253,000

In including this account in its financial statements, management makes several representations or assertions about inventory:

1. The inventory exists as of the balance sheet date (existence or occurrence).
2. All of the inventory that should be included in the inventory account has been included (completeness).
3. The inventory is owned by the client (rights and obligations).
4. The proper value for the inventory in accordance with generally accepted accounting principles is $1,253,000 (valuation or allocation).
5. Items included in inventory are current assets held for sale in the normal course of business and all disclosures necessary to an adequate understanding of the inventory account have been included in the financial statements (presentation and disclosure).

Each financial statement account can be broken down into these five assertions just as inventory has been.

Existence or Occurrence

The *existence or occurrence assertion* is management's representation that the assets and liabilities recorded in the financial statements actually exist at the balance sheet date and that the transactions recorded in the financial statements occurred during the period covered by the financial statements. Audit programs should contain procedures designed to test the existence or occurrence assertion for material elements of the financial statements.

The existence of inventory may be tested through the auditor's observation of inventory items. Accounts receivable may be tested for existence by corresponding with the client's customers. Certain income statement transactions such as sales or expenses may be tested for occurrence by examining the invoices and cancelled checks supporting them.

Completeness

The *completeness assertion* may be viewed as the converse of the existence assertion. *Completeness* means that all transactions and accounts that should have been recorded in the financial statements have been recorded. *Existence*, on the other hand, means that the accounts and transactions that have been recorded in the financial statements are those that should have been recorded. If the existence assertion is not true, the account would be overstated, whereas if the completeness assertion is not true, the account would be understated.

Completeness relates to whether all items have been included in the financial statements. That is, the completeness assertion is violated if a transaction or account is not included in the financial statements at all. A violation of the completeness assertion would occur, for example, if management failed to record a shipment of merchandise as a sale or failed to record all of the liabilities it owed at year-end. The audit program should include procedures to test the completeness assertion for each material element of the financial statements.

If a transaction was recorded in the wrong account but nevertheless was included in the financial statements, the completeness assertion would not be violated. The account would be incorrect because of a misclassification error—that is, a violation of the presentation and disclosure assertion—but not because of a completeness error.

Auditors test the completeness assertion in various ways, depending on the specific account being tested. Testing for completeness of inventory, for example, might involve gathering evidence that all of the inventory was counted during the physical inventory. Completeness of accounts payable, on the other hand, is usually tested by correspondence with creditors and by tracing payments to creditors made after year-end to proper initial recording of the debt. Specific tests for the completeness objective for the various financial statement components are discussed in Chapters 13–18.

For many accounts, the completeness assertion is the most difficult to test. The difficulty arises because the auditor must gather evidence about potential unrecorded items. Sources of audit evidence regarding unrecorded items often are not readily available.

Rights and Obligations

Auditors must be concerned with whether recorded assets are actually rights of the client and whether recorded liabilities are actually owed by the entity. Some assets, for example, even though they exist and are in the client's possession, may not be owned by the client. Inventories held on consignment are not the property of the client and should not be included in the balance sheet. A similar situation may exist regarding liabilities. Although liabilities exist, they may not be owed by the entity being audited. For example, an amount may be owed to a third party, but the debt may have been incurred by the owner for personal reasons. Thus, although the debt exists, it is not the obligation of the company.

The ***rights and obligations assertion*** takes on added emphasis in audits of small businesses where there is a potential for commingling the personal transactions of the owner with those of the business. In these situations the client's financial statements may contain the personal assets or liabilities of its owners or officers.

Evidence regarding rights and obligations varies with the nature of the asset and liability account being audited. For plant and equipment, auditors seek evidence of ownership from titles, deeds, or lease agreements. For inventory, auditors inquire about consignment agreements and remain alert for inventory transactions that may indicate consignment activity. The rights and obligations assertion for liabilities can be tested by examining the debt instrument giving rise to the liability.

Valuation or Allocation

The *valuation or allocation assertion* is concerned with whether the assets, liabilities, revenues, and expenses are included in the financial statements at the appropriate amounts. Proper valuation of financial statement items is specified by generally accepted accounting principles. For example, inventory may be valued using FIFO, LIFO, or the weighted average method. Inventory should also be valued at cost or market, whichever is lower, considering the principles of net realizable value (ceiling) and net realizable value less a normal profit (floor). The auditor's objective is to obtain evidence to support proper valuation of the financial statement elements.

Allocation is a part of proper valuation for many financial statement items. Inventory acquisitions during the year must be allocated between cost of goods sold and ending inventory, the costs of plant and equipment must be allocated between depreciation expense and the undepreciated balance, and revenue must be allocated to the accounting period in which it was earned.

Auditors use a variety of procedures to test valuation or allocation. The valuation of cash may be tested simply by counting it. The valuation of inventory or marketable securities at the lower of cost or market may be tested by first gathering evidence to support the market value at the balance sheet date and then comparing that value with cost.

Presentation and Disclosure

The *presentation and disclosure assertion* is a representation by management that the financial statement components are properly classified, described, and disclosed in conformity with generally accepted accounting principles. Classification requirements include the presentation of some assets as current and others as noncurrent. Proper description is illustrated by principles requiring the use of specific account

---

Professional Judgment

Auditing Requires Use of Professional Judgment

Auditors must use professional judgment when forming an opinion on the fairness of financial statements. But they also must use judgment in analyzing the risk that they will incorrectly give an unqualified opinion on financial statements that are materially misstated, as well as the risk that they could suffer a loss from litigation stemming from an audit. The auditor can limit risk by carefully analyzing which areas of the financial statement are most likely to contain a material misstatement and planning the audit program accordingly. Although quantitative tools can assess the various risk components, the final assessment involves a complex judgment.

Experience and judgment also are required in considering materiality. An auditor must make a preliminary judgment about materiality before beginning detailed audit planning and conclude the audit by evaluating whether known and likely misstatements will materially misstate the financial statements taken as a whole. The amount of competent evidence necessary to provide a basis for an opinion depends largely on the auditor's professional judgment.

titles such as "retained earnings" rather than "earned surplus." Disclosure relates to whether information in the financial statements, including the related notes, clearly explains matters that may affect their use. For example, material assets pledged as collateral for debt should be disclosed in the statements.

The audit program should include procedures designed to gather evidence about the proper presentation and disclosure for each material financial statement component. This evidence may come from many different sources. Evidence about the proper classification of debt may be obtained by examining the note for maturity and terms of repayment, and evidence concerning assets pledged as collateral may be obtained from correspondence with the lender. Proper classification of repairs and maintenance as an expense rather than as a capitalized asset may be evidenced by examining documentation supporting expenditures recorded in that account.

Assessing Risk of Material Misstatement

The auditor's work in forming an opinion on financial statements consists mainly of obtaining and evaluating evidential matter about financial statement assertions. The auditor's objective is to gather sufficient competent evidential matter to afford a reasonable basis for an opinion regarding the financial statements.

The scope paragraph in the auditor's report states that "our audit provides a reasonable basis for our opinion." The opinion paragraph states, "In our opinion, the financial statements present...fairly, in all material respects,...in conformity with generally accepted accounting principles...." With this wording, the auditor explicitly recognizes the concept of risk and materiality.

Audit risk is the risk that the auditor will incorrectly give an unqualified opinion on financial statements that are materially misstated. *Business risk* is the risk that the auditor will suffer loss or injury to his or her professional practice due to litigation or adverse publicity in connection with an audit. Exposure to business risk is always present whether or not an auditor conducts the audit in accordance with generally accepted auditing standards. For example, an auditor may conduct a proper audit and yet be sued by a disgruntled owner. In this case, the auditor may win the lawsuit but suffer a damaged professional reputation. Business risk differs from audit risk; however, the auditor may very well decide to gather more evidence as a result of increased business risk. *Under generally accepted auditing standards, the auditor cannot decide to gather less evidence as a result of auditing a client with minimal business risk.*

Users of the financial statements represent a primary element of business risk. In determining the necessary level of assurance, the auditor must first identify the potential users of the financial statements. A larger number of financial statement users increases business risk and may increase the auditor's desired level of assurance.

In evaluating the degree to which external users rely upon the financial statements, the auditor should consider a variety of factors. If the client is a publicly held company registered with the Securities and Exchange Commission, there are a greater number of potential users in the form of shareholders than for a nonpublic company. In the case of a client with large liabilities, there could be more potential users in the form of creditors who rely upon the financial statements. In potential bankruptcies or mergers by the client, a dramatic change in ownership increases the importance of the financial statements to the users of those statements. For example, if a client is acquired by another company, the acquiring company probably placed a high degree of reliance upon the financial statements and the auditor's opinion. Similarly, in a bankruptcy, creditors and shareholders probably have emphasized the financial statements issued immediately prior to bankruptcy. These situations entail a greater chance that the users will question the audit results. Where the likelihood of bankruptcy exists, increased business risk also exists for the auditor. As a result the auditor often desires a higher level of assurance and thus more evidence.

The auditor should assess which financial statement areas are more likely to have a material misstatement and should plan the audit program accordingly. For example, in auditing accounts payable, a material misstatement is most likely to occur as an understatement of accounts payable. Thus, the auditor recognizes the greater audit risk of potential understatement of the account and therefore gathers more evidence on accounts payable.

Risk Components

SAS No. 47, Audit Risk and Materiality in Conducting an Audit (AU 312.20), states that audit risk consists of three components:

1. *Inherent Risk* is the susceptibility of an assertion to a material misstatement, assuming there were no related internal control structure policies or procedures. The risk of such misstatement is greater for some financial statement assertions and related balances or classes than for others. For example, there is a greater risk of material misstatement of the financial presentation and disclosure assertion for complex transactions than for simple ones. Likewise, the risk of a material misstatement of the existence assertion is more likely for cash than for an inventory of coal, because of their relative susceptibility to theft. The valuation assertion for accounts consisting of amounts derived from accounting estimates poses greater risks than does an assertion for accounts consisting of relatively routine, factual data. External factors also influence inherent risk. For example, technical developments might make a particular product obsolete, thereby causing a material misstatement in the valuation assertion.
2. *Control Risk* is the risk that a material misstatement could occur in an assertion for an account balance or class of transactions, and would not be prevented or detected on a timely basis by the internal control policies and procedures. This risk is a function of the effectiveness of the design and operation of the entity's internal control structure policies and procedures relevant to an audit of the entity's financial statements. Some control risk will always exist because of the inherent limitations of any internal control structure.
3. *Detection Risk* is the risk that an auditor will not detect a material misstatement in an assertion. This risk is a function of the effectiveness of an auditing procedure and of its application by the auditor. It arises partly from uncertainties that exist when the auditor does not examine all of an account balance or class of transactions to gather evidence on a particular assertion. Other uncertainties might arise because an auditor might select an inappropriate auditing procedure, misapply an appropriate procedure, or misinterpret the audit results. These other uncertainties can be reduced to a negligible level through adequate planning, supervision, and conduct of a firm's audit practices in accordance with appropriate quality standards.

Illustration of Risk

The components of audit risk mentioned above are illustrated in Figure 4–2. An audit may contain financial statement assertions with material misstatements as represented by the spigot in Figure 4–2. The sieves represent the means by which the client and

Figure 4-2	**Components of Audit Risk**

[handwritten annotations: "occuring issuing materially Overall risk of mistatements are issued audit report"]

The possibility of material misstatement in a financial statement assertion is *inherent risk*. The possibility that misstatements will evade the internal control structure (upper sieve) is *control risk*. *Detection risk* is the possibility that audit procedures (lower sieve) will fail to detect material misstatements. *Audit risk* is the possibility that financial statements will include material misstatements.

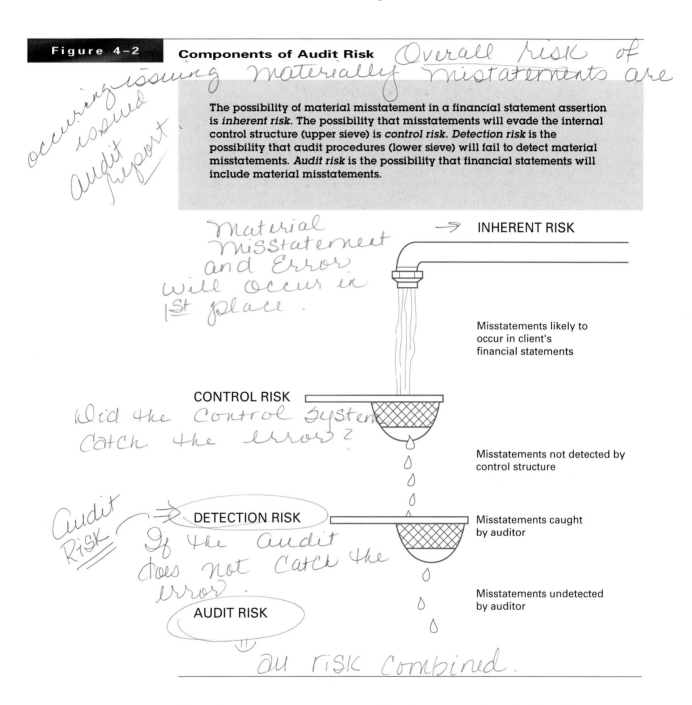

INHERENT RISK

[handwritten: "Material misstatement and Error will occur in 1st place."]

Misstatements likely to occur in client's financial statements

CONTROL RISK

[handwritten: "Did the Control System catch the error?"]

Misstatements not detected by control structure

DETECTION RISK

[handwritten: "Audit Risk — If the audit does not catch the error."]

Misstatements caught by auditor

Misstatements undetected by auditor

AUDIT RISK

[handwritten: "all risk combined."]

the auditor attempt to remove material misstatements from the financial statements. The auditor has no way of knowing how many misstatements exist. In fact, there may be no material misstatements for any of the financial statement assertions.

The client may install certain internal control structure policies or procedures to detect material misstatements. In Figure 4–2, the first sieve represents the client's internal control structure. Ideally, the control structure should detect any material misstatements before they enter the financial statements. However, there is some risk that misstatements will pass undetected through the control structure. For example, a weakness or breakdown in the client's structure may allow misstatements to continue through the first sieve. These material misstatements would be processed through the control structure.

If the client's internal control structure does not detect and remove any misstatements, the misstatements will be included in the financial statements. The auditor's responsibility is to design audit procedures that will provide reasonable assurance that any material misstatements will be detected and removed from the financial statements. In Figure 4–2, the auditor's procedures are represented by the final sieve. Of course, the auditor cannot have absolute assurance that all material misstatements have been detected in the financial statements. In other words, some detection risk will always be present.

Because of the potential that (1) a material misstatement will exist, (2) it will not be detected by the client's internal control structure, (3) it will not be detected by the auditor, and (4) it will affect the financial statements, there will always be some audit risk (represented in Figure 4–2 by misstatements that have flowed through both sieves). The auditor's responsibility is to reduce the possibility of audit risk to a low level.

Inherent risk and control risk differ from detection risk in that they are not under the control of the auditor. Detection risk on the other hand relates to the auditor's procedures, which can be changed at the auditor's discretion.

Risk Assessment and Planning

During engagement planning, the auditor should assess the inherent and control risks that material misstatements could reach the financial statements by considering information obtained about the client, its industry, its operations, the control environment, the accounting system, and control procedures. Based on this assessment, the auditor determines an audit strategy. Planning is discussed in greater detail in Chapter 12.

The auditor should assess inherent and control risks to determine how much detection risk can be accepted and still restrict audit risk to an acceptably low level. The auditor may make either separate or combined assessments of inherent and control risks. If the auditor assesses inherent and control risks as low, the acceptable level of detection risk is correspondingly higher. If the auditor considers either inherent risk or control risk to be less than the maximum (100%), the auditor should have an appropriate basis for making such an assessment. This basis may include, but is not limited to, the use of questionnaires or checklists and the testing of controls. Ordinarily, the assessed levels of inherent and control risks would not be sufficiently low to eliminate the need to perform substantive tests for relevant assertions of material account balances or transaction classes.

One must recognize that the assessment of risk may sometimes vary among auditors in any given audit situation. Ideally, these variations should not occur. However, the determination of risk is a subjective, professional judgment and is difficult to measure. In the exercise of judgment, auditors sometimes will come to different conclusions. Furthermore, some auditors are simply not willing to accept as much risk as others.

Components of Inherent Risk

Many factors can affect the auditor's determination of inherent risk, including whether the audit is an initial or a repeat engagement, the results of prior audits, the integrity of management, client motivation, and accounting estimates and complex

Figure 4–3

Overview of Audit Evidence Decision, Considering Inherent, Control, and Detection Risk

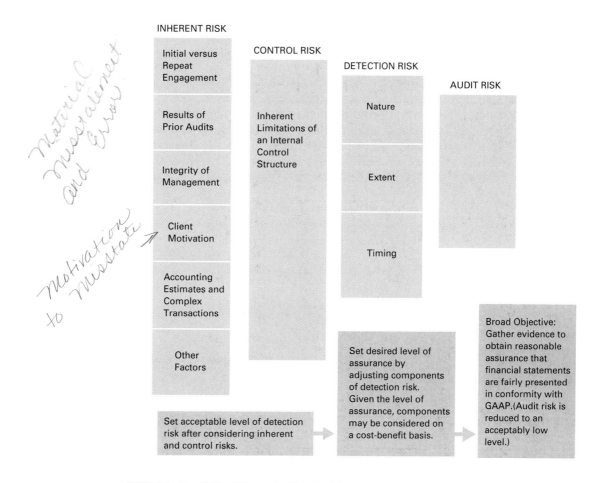

transactions. Figure 4–3 illustrates these components of inherent risk. It also shows the effect of inherent and control risks on detection risk and on the auditor's evidence decision. Factors affecting inherent risk may also affect control risk.

Initial versus Repeat Engagement One factor affecting the audit engagement is whether or not this is the first time an audit has been performed. Financial statements are always for a given time period. Even though the balance sheet or statement of financial position is as of a point in time, the income statement and the statement of cash flows are for a period of time. Furthermore, the accounts on the balance sheet must start out as a beginning balance and then be increased or decreased by activity during the year. Because previous audit engagements will have collected much pertinent information, it is easier to obtain evidence in a repeat rather than an initial engagement.

Another factor that aids in a repeat engagement is simply the auditor's familiarity with the client. With prior knowledge about the client's operations, the auditor is able to plan and perform the engagement more efficiently. In addition, results of prior audits may be useful to the auditor in assessing control risk. Alternatively, an initial audit may indicate a higher level of inherent and control risk because of such factors as a lack of familiarity with the client's motivations or a lack of familiarity with complex and unusual transactions.

Results of Prior Audits   Prior audits provide knowledge of the client's business and provide evidence of the client's ability to record reliable financial information. If previous audits indicate that unreliable financial information is being generated, the auditor will be more concerned about the sufficiency and competence of evidence and will assess inherent risk at a higher level. Knowledge of the client's business includes information about the nature of the client's business and industry, the client's organization and personnel, and the client's operating characteristics.

Integrity of Management   Integrity of management is one factor that the CPA must recognize in assessing inherent risk. Clearly, if management lacks integrity the possibility of a material misstatement of the financial statements increases and, in fact, the client's financial statements may not be auditable. An increase in this possibility and thus in inherent risk requires an increase in the amount of evidence collected or perhaps withdrawing from the engagement. The effect of the integrity of management on the planning process is discussed in more detail in Chapter 12.

Client Motivation   A client may have particular motivations to misstate the financial statements. For example, the company may have liquidity problems and management may be motivated to misstate the financial statements to obtain loans for working capital. Likewise, in the case of a publicly held company, management may feel pressure to present increased earnings to the shareholders each year. Once again, an increased likelihood of a material misstatement establishes the need for additional audit evidence.

Accounting Estimates and Complex Transactions   The auditor should be alert for those situations that require the client to make accounting estimates regarding unusually complex accounting matters or transactions. The client may make an erroneous estimate in applying generally accepted accounting principles. Such a misstatement, although perhaps unintentional, often results from the client's inexperience or from a somewhat unusual accounting situation. For example, the client may erroneously determine that the loss is extraordinary when the loss does not meet the two criteria of being both unusual and infrequent as set forth in *APB Opinion No. 30, Reporting the Results of Operations.* Similarly, the client may incorrectly estimate an appropriate amount for the allowance for doubtful accounts. Such misstatements involving accounting estimates or the application of complex accounting rules, of course, increase the probability that the financial statements are materially misstated.

Other Factors   Other environmental factors can increase inherent risk and the likelihood of a material misstatement of the financial statements. For example, technological development may cause a particular inventory item of the client to be obsolete. The characteristics of the client's assets represent another factor that may affect inherent risk. For example, an inventory of diamonds is more susceptible to theft than an inventory of soybeans. Regardless of the factors, the auditor should assess inherent risk.

Control Risk Assessment

Items related to internal system control (handwritten annotation)

The auditor must also make an assessment of control risk for financial statement assertions as required by *SAS No. 55, Consideration of the Internal Control Structure in a Financial Statement Audit* (AU 319). To assess control risk, the auditor must first obtain an understanding of the internal control structure of the entity. This includes an understanding of items such as management's philosophy and operating style, the organizational structure of the entity, whether the company has an internal audit function in place, the records, documents and accounts used in the processing and reporting of transactions, and specific control procedures such as proper authorization, separation of duties, and prenumbered documents.[1]

The higher the level of control risk, the less likely the internal control structure will prevent or detect a material misstatement in a specific assertion. Because a higher level of control risk increases the likelihood of a material misstatement of an assertion, the auditor must gather more audit evidence to provide reasonable assurance that material misstatements will be detected and removed from the financial statements. The assessment of control risk is discussed in more detail in Chapter 6.

Detection Risk Assessment

Solving for what kind of test being done (handwritten annotation)

Some limitation (handwritten annotation)

The auditor's assessments regarding audit risk and its components of inherent risk, control risk, and detection risk are determined by his or her professional judgment. Although the auditor may use quantitative tools in assessing the risk components, the ultimate assessment of audit risk is a complex judgment.

After assessing inherent and control risks for a given assertion, the auditor decides what level of detection risk will bring audit risk to a sufficiently low level. The auditor then decides what mix of audit evidence will be necessary to reduce detection risk (and thus, audit risk) to an acceptably low level.

The audit evidence mix decision has three components: the nature, extent, and timing of audit testing. By changing any one of these three factors, the auditor affects the reliability of audit evidence and thus changes detection risk. In evaluating these three evidence components, the auditor also considers the cost-benefit relationships. For example, the auditor may find it possible to reduce detection risk to an acceptable level by increasing either the nature or the extent of audit testing. If these two options yield similar results, the auditor would select the less costly option. In this situation, the less costly audit would be just as effective and more efficient than the more expensive procedure. A brief discussion of the nature, extent, and timing of audit evidence follows.

Nature: What Procedure to Use   The auditor has a variety of audit procedures from which to choose. In determining that inventory physically exists (the existence assertion), the auditor may, for example, either physically inspect the inventory or examine invoices and cancelled checks that document purchases. The auditor must decide which audit procedures to use; that is, he or she must determine the *nature* of the audit test. The nature of an audit test depends upon the degree to which

---

[1]The auditor should also recognize that any internal control structure has inherent limitations. These are discussed in more detail in Chapter 6.

its procedures produce competent evidence, that is, evidence that is relevant, free from bias, and objective. In determining the nature of an audit test, the auditor should, as discussed previously, take into account costs and benefits.

Extent: How Many Items to Test After deciding to perform a specific audit procedure, the auditor must decide how many items to test, that is, the *extent* of the audit test. For example, to confirm accounts receivable, the auditor must decide whether to confirm all customer accounts or only a sample of customer accounts. If the latter, the auditor must decide how many items to sample. The fourth characteristic of audit evidence, persuasiveness, is affected by the sample size—the more items the auditor samples, the more persuasive the evidence.

After determining the specific audit procedure and the appropriate sample size, the auditor still must identify the particular items to be tested. For example, if 100 of the total population of accounts receivable should be confirmed, the auditor must decide *which* 100 items will be selected. In general, the auditor should select items that are expected to be representative of the population. This topic is discussed further in Chapter 9.

Timing: When to Use the Procedure Even after having determined the nature and extent of the audit test, the auditor must make one more decision: When should the procedure be performed? Often, audit procedures are performed some time after year-end; however, in certain instances they may be performed during the year under review. Timing is discussed in detail in Chapter 12. Generally, the reliability of audit evidence increases as the date of the audit test approaches year-end.

The Audit Evidence Mix As noted previously, the auditor may adjust the nature, extent, and timing of audit tests to reduce both detection risk and audit risk to acceptable levels and to achieve the desired level of assurance. Figure 4–4 illustrates how the auditor may vary these three components to achieve the same level of assurance in a given audit situation. For example, Auditor A relies on timing, that is, on a variety of audit tests with an appropriate number of items at an appropriate time. In contrast, Auditor B relies less on timing (for example, performing certain procedures before year-end) and more on the nature and extent of audit tests. Although Auditor B has reduced the reliability of audit evidence through timing, the auditor has also increased the reliability of audit evidence by improving the nature and extent of audit tests. Overall, Auditor B has achieved the same level of assurance as Auditor A.

Materiality

According to *SAS No. 47* (AU 312.08), "the auditor should consider audit risk and materiality both in (a) planning the audit and designing auditing procedures and (b) evaluating whether the financial statements taken as a whole are presented fairly in conformity with generally accepted accounting principles." As noted in *FASB Statement of Financial Accounting Concepts No. 2 (SFAC No. 2)*, **materiality** is "the magnitude of an omission or misstatement of accounting information that, in the light of surrounding circumstances, makes it probable that the judgment of a reasonable person relying on the information would have been changed or influenced by the omission or misstatement."

Figure 4-4   **Adjusting the Nature, Extent, and Timing of Audit Tests to Achieve the Desired Level of Assurance**

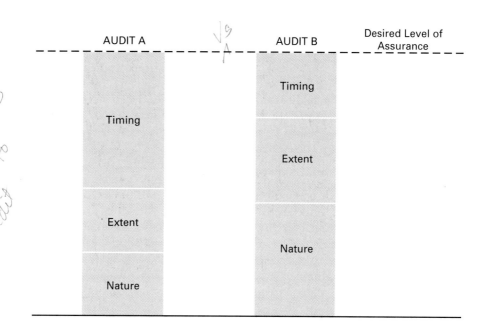

In audit planning the auditor should consider a preliminary judgment about materiality for the financial statements taken as a whole to plan appropriately the nature, timing, and extent of audit procedures. At the conclusion of the audit, the auditor evaluates whether known and likely misstatements will materially misstate the financial statements taken as a whole.

Materiality in Audit Planning

An auditor needs to make a preliminary judgment about materiality before detailed audit program planning. Materiality should be viewed in audit planning as an allowance for likely and potential undetected misstatements. In other words, materiality represents a cushion that the auditor allows for the necessary imprecision in applying auditing procedures to detect misstatement of the financial statements.

SAS No. 47 (AU 312) does not require that materiality be quantified in the planning stages of the audit. However, in determining the nature, timing, and extent of audit procedures to be applied to a specific account balance or class of transactions, the auditor should design procedures to detect misstatements that the auditor believes, based on preliminary judgment about materiality, could be material to the financial statements as a whole when aggregated with misstatements in other balances or classes.

A variety of factors may enter into the decision about materiality in audit planning. The most common consideration in audit planning has to do with the size of the item in question. An item of very large dollar amount that is omitted from the financial statements is generally material. The omission of a large dollar amount could definitely affect the user's decision-making process. Size is generally measured in relative terms, for example, as a percentage of a relative base. A misstatement of $10,000 may be trivial for a very large company but devastating for a small company.

The measuring of materiality in percentages is probably the most common application by auditors of the materiality concept in planning. In this type of analysis, the auditor may consider the items' percentage of effect not only on the financial statements (for example, income before income taxes) but also on the trend of the financial statements (for example, the change in income before income taxes from the prior period). For example, an item may be immaterial to current income before income taxes but may represent a material portion of the increase in income before income taxes for the year.

To apply a percentage guideline, the auditor must determine what base to use. Generally, the auditor should select a stable and predictable base in planning the audit. Common bases include income before income taxes, total revenues, and total assets. If income before income taxes fluctuates greatly from year to year, total revenues or total assets are a more useful base. For example, one would not expect audit costs to double because income is cut in half in a particularly difficult year. Likewise, if past experience indicates a reasonable expectation of significant audit adjustments, a preliminary amount based on income would not be useful. For these reasons, a more stable amount such as total revenue or total assets is often preferable.

The use of total revenues or total assets as a base also allows for the effects of industry characteristics. Financial institutions, such as banks and savings and loans, are usually asset intensive. However, governmental organizations usually have modest assets but large revenues. Thus, this approach automatically incorporates an adjustment for industry characteristics. When total revenues or total assets are used as a base, the scope of the audit is determined more by the size of the company than by the operating results in a particular period. However, the choice of a base for planning purposes does not predetermine what will be relevant in evaluating known and likely misstatements at the conclusion of the audit.

SAS No. 47 (AU 312.12) states that "the auditor ordinarily considers materiality for planning purposes in terms of the smallest aggregate level of misstatements that could be considered material to any one of the financial statements." Misstatements normally become material to the income statement before they become material to the balance sheet. However, this does not mean that the materiality base for planning must be an income statement amount. The planning materiality amount should be suitably small relative to the income statement. Nevertheless, the base may be chosen on the basis of relative stability, predictability, and representativeness of entity size. As noted previously, the larger of total assets or revenue ordinarily provides a sound base.

In planning, the auditor generally selects a single base for determining materiality. Different materiality levels may be used for different financial statements when evaluating misstatements at the audit's conclusion. However, in planning, the auditor does not know in advance whether the misstatements that a particular audit procedure will detect will affect the balance sheet only, the income statement only, or both statements. Thus, use of several levels of materiality is impractical in planning.

No authoritative standards for percentage guidelines on materiality exist. One common guideline used for planning materiality is 5% to 10% of income before income taxes or 1% of the larger total assets or total revenues.

After the auditor selects a suitable base and determines materiality for planning purposes, materiality must be related to account balances and classes of transactions. *SAS No. 47* (AU 312.18) does not require an apportionment of dollar amounts to specific accounts and transactions. However, some consideration of the relationship between the preliminary judgment of materiality and individual accounts is needed in planning. For example, in applying audit procedures to prepaid expense, it is not efficient to regard 10% of the amount as material if the total amount of prepaid expense is immaterial to the financial statements. For some accounts and transactions, consideration of the relationship to the preliminary judgment is unnecessary because the nature of the item and cost of possible audit procedures is such that the account can be audited to very close tolerances. For example, long-term debt, property, plant, and equipment can usually be examined to close tolerances. In making planning decisions for other accounts, such as receivables and inventory, the auditor should consider the relationship between his or her preliminary judgment about materiality and the amount that would be material to the account balance. An auditor, for example, might use this judgment in deciding (1) what items in a balance to examine 100%, (2) whether it is necessary to sample the remaining items, or (3) whether to apply analytical procedures instead of more detailed substantive tests.

Materiality in Audit Evaluation

According to *SAS No. 47* (AU 312.27), "in evaluating whether the financial statements are presented fairly in conformity with generally accepted accounting principles, the auditor should aggregate misstatements that the entity has not corrected, in a way that enables him to consider whether, in relation to individual amounts, subtotals, or totals in the financial statements, they materially misstate the financial statements taken as a whole."

Materiality in planning often differs from materiality in the evaluation at the conclusion of the audit. If materiality is significantly lowered at the audit's conclusion, the auditor should reevaluate the auditing procedures that were performed based on planning materiality to ensure that they were indeed sufficient to detect material misstatement.

In aggregating misstatements at the conclusion of the audit, the auditor should include both *known* misstatements (the amount of misstatements specifically identified) and *likely* misstatements (the auditor's best estimate of total misstatements in the account balances or class of transactions). For example, if the auditor sampled 10% of the items in a population and found total misstatements of $1,000 (the known misstatements), the auditor could project this misstatement to the account balance as $10,000 (the likely misstatements).

Even though the likely misstatements do not cause the financial statements to be materially misstated, the auditor should recognize that the statements might still be materially misstated due to further, undetected misstatement. As the total of the likely misstatements increases, the risk that the financial statements are materially misstated also increases, and the auditor should reduce audit risk to an acceptable level by modifying the nature, extent, and timing of audit procedures.

Nature of the Item In evaluating materiality, the auditor typically examines an item by a relevant base. The auditor cannot quantify the materiality decision in all cases; certain items may have significance even though the dollar amount may not be quite as large as the auditor typically would assume to be material. For example, a political bribe by a client, even though immaterial in size relative to total assets or income before income taxes, may nonetheless be of such a sensitive nature and have such an effect on the company that users would need to know about it. In this situation, the nature of the item—its qualitative characteristic—makes it material even though quantitatively it may be classified as immaterial. Of course, in the long run these qualitative characteristics can be quantified, because they will ultimately have a quantifiable effect on cash flow.

Cumulative Effect In addition to evaluating each potential item for materiality, the auditor must also recognize the cumulative materiality effect: a group of misstatements that are immaterial individually may be material when examined collectively. For example, in evaluating whether to record certain expenses, the auditor may decide that each item is separately immaterial but that, when aggregated, the items have a total effect on net income that *is* material. The auditor must not only determine materiality for individual items but must also record all such immaterial items to determine if the total effect is material. Likewise, the auditor should consider likely misstatements that the entity did not correct in prior periods because the misstatements did not cause the financial statements for those periods to be materially misstated. These misstatements might also affect the current period's financial statements.

Establishing Audit Objectives

A misrepresentation of any of the five financial statement assertions could cause a material misstatement in the financial statements. As noted in Figure 4–1, the auditor should consider the risk of material misstatement for each assertion in the financial statements and obtain evidence to support the financial statement assertions to reduce the risk of material misstatement to an acceptably low level. To determine what type of evidence to obtain, the auditor develops specific audit objectives related to each assertion. Because audit objectives and assertions are closely related, auditors often use the terms interchangeably.

In determining audit objectives, the auditor should evaluate each of the five assertions as they relate to the specific account balance or class of transactions being examined. For example, if the auditor is attempting to gather evidence on the assertions of existence of inventory, the auditor's objective would be to gather evidence that the inventory included in the balance sheet physically existed at the date of the balance sheet. An example of the relationship between financial statement assertions and audit objectives for inventory is shown in Table 4–1.

Concept of Evidence

Once the auditor has established the audit objectives as shown in step 3 of Figure 4–1, the auditor must then collect sufficient competent evidential matter as required by the third standard of fieldwork to afford a reasonable basis for the opinion on the fairness of the financial statements in conformity with GAAP. Evidence may include the underlying accounting data (for example, journals, ledgers, or worksheets) or corroborating information (for example, checks, invoices, and information obtained by inquiry, observation, and inspection).

Table 4-1	Relationship of Assertions and Objectives for Inventory

Financial Statement Assertion	Illustrative Audit Objectives
Existence or occurrence	Inventories included in the balance sheet physically exist.
Completeness	Inventory quantities include all products, materials, and supplies on hand.
	Inventory quantities include all products, materials, and supplies owned by the client that are in transit or stored at outside locations.
	Inventory listings are accurately compiled and the totals are properly included in the inventory accounts.
Rights and obligations	The entity has legal title or similar rights of ownership to the inventory.
Valuation or allocation	Inventories are properly stated at cost (except when market is lower).
Presentation and disclosure	Inventories are properly classified in the balance sheet as current assets.

[handwritten margin notes: "Compare w/ Audit Program on Ch. 12 Pg. 423"; "Everything that should be there"; "i.e. Obsolete or damaged inv. are properly written off."]

The Real World of Auditing

Real Audit Evidence to Audit Risk

Facts: An accounting firm was engaged to conduct several annual audits of a client's chain of banks. The manager of one of these banks embezzled over $250,000. The accounting firm, although performing the audits during the periods of the defalcations, failed to detect the embezzlement. The embezzlement was ultimately discovered internally by the bank. Upon review of the accounting firm's work, it was discovered that the accounting firm had detected some evidence of an ongoing defalcation but had failed to extend audit procedures in order to confirm or deny their suspicions. The owner of the chain of banks sued the accounting firm for $350,000.

Issues: The client claimed that the accounting firm was negligent in performing the audit because even though the firm suspected something wrong, it failed to investigate further.

Resolution: Liability was clear and the expense and settlement payments to resolve this case were in excess of $200,000.

Commentary: The accounting firm's failure to confirm or disaffirm evidence of embezzlement was the major cause of the audit failure in this case. The accounting firm did not meet the standard of care for this engagement and, therefore, was wholly liable for the damages when the embezzlement was discovered.

Source: G. Spellmire, W. Baliga, D. Winiarski, *Accountants Legal Liability Guide*, Harcourt Brace Jovanovich, 1990, p. 335.

For evidence to be useful to the auditor it must have the following four characteristics: (1) persuasiveness, (2) relevance, (3) freedom from bias, and (4) objectivity. The third standard of fieldwork requires the auditor to collect sufficient, competent evidence. The characteristic of persuasiveness relates to the sufficiency of evidence, whereas the characteristics of relevance, freedom from bias, and objectivity relate to the competence of evidence.

Persuasiveness

Evidence is *persuasive* if it is sufficient in quantity and quality to allow the auditor to reach a conclusion. Persuasiveness should stand the test of evaluation by other auditors; that is, other auditors should also agree that the amount of evidence is persuasive.

The amount of competent evidence necessary to provide a basis for an opinion depends largely on the exercise of professional judgment. The following guidelines are helpful:

1. Usually the auditor relies on evidence that is persuasive rather than convincing; an auditor is seldom convinced beyond all doubt with respect to all aspects of the financial statements being examined.
2. A rational relationship exists between the cost and usefulness of evidence, but the difficulty and expense of a test is not a valid reason for omitting it.
3. If the auditor remains in substantial doubt about any material assertion, the auditor must continue until enough evidence has been obtained to remove the doubt, or the auditor should express a qualified opinion or disclaim an opinion.

Relevance

For evidence to be *relevant* it must support the objective or assertion being tested. If evidence is irrelevant, it is of no value to the auditor. The auditor should always remember the objective of a particular audit test and obtain evidence that is relevant to the objective. For example, if the auditor is trying to determine that an inventory physically exists, physical observation of the inventory would be relevant evidence. On the other hand, physically observing the inventory does not necessarily establish that the client owns the inventory.

Freedom from Bias

In collecting audit evidence, the auditor should attempt to gather evidence that is *free from bias*, that is, evidence that does not unduly influence one alternative over another. Bias may come from either the characteristics of the evidence being examined or the auditor's selection of items for examination. For example, an opinion from the sales manager regarding collectibility of accounts receivable provides evidence that may be objective but may not be free from bias. In this situation, the evidence is relevant, because the inquiry of the sales manager relates to the assertion being tested, but the evidence is not free from bias, because the sales manager may have a vested interest in accounts receivable appearing to be collectible. Alternatively, evidence regarding collectibility of receivables that was obtained from an independent credit bureau would be free from bias.

The auditor sometimes cannot eliminate bias in the collection of evidence. Nonetheless, the auditor should be aware of this characteristic and its effect on the quality of audit evidence. For example, evidence from sources independent of the client is more reliable than evidence secured solely from within the company.

Objectivity

readily measured

Objectivity is the ability of different auditors to reach a similar conclusion based on an examination of evidence. If the evaluation of the evidence varies widely among auditors, the evidence lacks objectivity. For example, when the auditor documents valuation by examining purchase invoices and prices, the evidence is generally objective: other auditors would reach a similar valuation of the inventory by using that evidence. Alternatively, if the auditor determines the value of the inventory by soliciting opinions of client employees, that evidence is not as objective: different auditors would solicit different opinions of the valuation of the inventory—or would evaluate the same opinions differently—and so would calculate the value of the inventory differently.

For evidence to be useful to the auditor, it must possess to some degree the four characteristics just discussed. Clearly all audit evidence does not possess all four characteristics to the same degree. For example, some evidence may be particularly relevant, but not very objective. Other evidence may be very objective but not be free from bias. In collecting audit evidence, the auditor must gather evidence that, on the whole, has these four characteristics. Any one item of evidence, however, may possess some characteristics more clearly than others.

As a consequence, auditors often gather a variety of types of evidence to support a given audit objective or assertion. In selecting what particular audit evidence to gather, the auditor should consider the audit objective, the characteristics of the evidence to be obtained, and how this particular piece of evidence ties into other audit evidence obtained. The specific types of audit evidence are discussed in the following chapter.

Significant Terms

Audit risk The risk that the auditor may unknowingly fail to modify appropriately an opinion on financial statements that are materially misstated.

Business risk The risk that an auditor will suffer loss or injury to his or her professional practice due to litigation or adverse publicity in connection with an audit.

Client assertions Explicit or implicit representations by management that are embodied in the financial statements. These include five representations:

- Completeness
- Existence or occurrence
- Presentation and disclosure
- Rights and obligations
- Valuation or allocation

Completeness assertion Representation by management that all transactions and accounts that should have been recorded in the financial statements have been recorded.

Detection risk The risk that an auditor will not detect a material misstatement in a financial statement assertion.

Existence or occurrence assertion Representation by management that the assets and liabilities recorded in the financial statements actually exist at the balance sheet date and that the transactions recorded in the financial statements occurred during the period covered by the financial statements.

Inherent risk The susceptibility of a financial statement assertion to a material misstatement, assuming there were no related internal control structure policies or procedures.

Materiality The magnitude of an omission or misstatement in the financial statements that would result in a difference in the user's decision-making process.

Objectivity The ability of two or more auditors to reach a similar conclusion based on an examination of evidence.

Persuasiveness A characteristic of evidence that makes it sufficient in terms of quality and quantity to allow the auditor to reach a conclusion.

Presentation and disclosure assertion Representation by management that the financial statement components are properly classified, described, and disclosed in conformity with generally accepted accounting principles.

Rights and obligations assertion Representation by management that recorded assets are actually rights of the client and recorded liabilities are actually owed by the client.

Valuation or allocation assertion Representation by management that the assets, liabilities, revenues, and expenses have been included in the financial statements at the appropriate amounts.

Discussion Questions

4-1. Summarize the third standard of fieldwork. What is its purpose?

4-2. Describe the steps an auditor follows to determine which specific audit procedures to include in the financial statements.

4-3. What are assertions and what are the five classifications of assertions?

4-4. What is the objective of the existence or occurrence assertion?

4-5. What is the difference between the existence assertion and the completeness assertion?

4-6. Why is the completeness assertion often the most difficult to test?

4-7. What is meant by the rights and obligations assertion?

4-8. What does the valuation or allocation assertion refer to?

4-9. What does the presentation and disclosure assertion refer to? Why is it important?

4-10. Why does risk affect the decision regarding audit evidence?

4-11. Identify and describe the components of inherent risk.

4-12. Define *materiality.*

4-13. Identify the factors that affect materiality.

4-14. What is the difference between materiality in audit planning and in evaluation?

4-15. What is the purpose of developing audit objectives? How does the auditor develop these objectives?

4-16. Define objectivity. Why is it an important characteristic of evidence?

4-17. Briefly describe the characteristics of audit evidence.

4-18. Give an example of audit evidence that would be irrelevant to prove a specific audit objective.

Objective Questions

*4-19. What is the major reason that an independent auditor gathers evidence?
(1) To form an opinion on the financial statements.
(2) To detect fraud.
(3) To evaluate management.
(4) To assess control risk.

*4-20. When is evidential matter generally considered sufficient?
(1) When it is competent.
(2) When enough of it is present to afford a reasonable basis for an opinion on the financial statements.
(3) When it has the qualities of being relevant, objective, and free from unknown bias.
(4) When the auditor uses professional judgment in its selection.

*4-21. Evidential matter supporting the financial statements consists of the underlying accounting data and all corroborating information available to the auditor. Which of the following is an example of corroborating information?
(1) Minutes of meetings.
(2) General ledgers.
(3) Accounting manuals.
(4) Worksheets supporting consolidated financial statements.

*4-22. An auditor selected items for test counts while observing a client's physical inventory. The auditor then traced the test counts to the client's inventory listing. This procedure most likely obtained evidence concerning management's assertion of which of the following?
(1) Rights and obligations.
(2) Completeness.
(3) Existence or occurrence.
(4) Valuation.

*4-23. Audit risk, against which the auditor requires reasonable protection, is a combination of the risk that a material misstatement will occur in the accounting process by which the financial statements are developed, and that
(1) a company's internal control structure is not adequate to detect errors and irregularities.
(2) those errors that occur will not be detected in the audit.
(3) management may lack integrity.
(4) evidential matter is not competent enough for the auditor to form an opinion based on reasonable assurance.

*4-24. The risk that an auditor's procedures will lead to the conclusion that a material misstatement does *not* exist in an account balance when, in fact, such error does exist is referred to as
(1) audit risk.
(2) inherent risk.
(3) control risk.
(4) detection risk.

*4-25. Which of the following elements ultimately determines the specific auditing procedures that are necessary in the circumstances to afford a reasonable basis for an opinion?
(1) Auditor judgment.
(2) Materiality.
(3) Relative risk.
(4) Reasonable assurance.

*4-26. When is evidential matter generally considered competent?
(1) When it has the qualities of being relevant, objective, and free from known bias.
(2) When enough of it is present to afford a reasonable basis for an opinion on the financial statements.
(3) When it has been obtained by random selection.
(4) When it consists of written statements made by managers of the enterprise under audit.

---

*AICPA adapted.

*4-27. Which of the following statements relating to the competence of evidential matter is always true?

(1) Evidential matter gathered by an auditor from outside an enterprise is reliable.

(2) Accounting data developed under satisfactory conditions of an internal control structure are more relevant than data developed under an unsatisfactory internal control structure.

(3) Oral representations made by management are *not* valid evidence.

(4) Evidence gathered by auditors must be both valid and relevant to be considered competent.

*4-28. Which of the following audit risk components may be assessed in nonquantitative terms?

	Inherent Risk	Control Risk	Detection Risk
a.	Yes	Yes	No
b.	Yes	No	Yes
c.	No	Yes	Yes
d.	Yes	Yes	Yes

*4-29. The concept of materiality would be least important to an auditor when considering the

a. effects of a direct financial interest in the client upon the CPA's independence.

b. decision whether to use positive or negative confirmations of accounts receivable.

c. adequacy of disclosure of a client's illegal act.

d. discovery of weaknesses in a client's internal control structure.

*4-30. When an auditor increases the assessed level of control risk because certain control procedures were determined to be ineffective, the auditor would most likely increase which of the following?

(1) Extent of tests of controls.

(2) Level of detection risk.

(3) Extent of tests of details.

(4) Level of inherent risk.

*4-31. Which of the following circumstances is most likely to cause an auditor to consider whether a material misstatement exists?

a. Transactions selected for testing are not supported by proper documentation.

b. The turnover of senior accounting personnel is exceptionally low.

c. Management places little emphasis on meeting earnings projections.

d. Operating and financing decisions are dominated by several persons.

Problems and Cases

4-32. (Relating Assertions to Audit Objectives) The following audit objectives apply to the audit of property, plant, and equipment and management assertions:

Audit Objectives	Management Assertions
a. Determine whether interest costs have been capitalized in conformity with GAAP.	1. Existence or occurrence 2. Completeness
b. Review whether miscellaneous income has credits representing proceeds from fixed asset sales for fixed assets still on the books.	3. Rights and obligations 4. Valuation 5. Presentation and disclosure
c. For fixed asset additions, vouch additions to invoices and canceled checks to determine if recorded fixed assets are bona fide.	

---

*AICPA adapted.

4   **d.** Examine documentation supporting the cost of assets acquired by exchanging non-cash assets and determine whether they have been properly accounted for.   *# amt.*

4   **e.** Test individual computations of depreciation in fixed asset records.

3   **f.** For fixed asset additions, trace serial numbers to titles and insurance records to determine if fixed assets belong to the client.

5   **g.** Review large amounts recorded in repairs and maintenance expense and determine if items should have been capitalized.

5   **h.** Review operating leases to determine if leases should have been capitalized.

Answer key says 2   Prof. says 5.

REQUIRED

Identify the most appropriate assertion for each specific audit objective.

4-33. (Audit Risk) Consider the following risk matrix. Identify whether **1** and **2**, or only **1**, or only **2** is covered by *SAS No. 47, Audit Risk and Materiality in Conducting an Audit.*

| | Client's Financial Statements Are ||
Audit Evidence Indicates	Fairly Stated	Materially Misstated
Accept (unqualified opinion)	Good Decision	1 *concern for auditor*
Reject (qualified or adverse opinion)	2 *not addressed in SAS 47*	Good Decision

REQUIRED

ignore

A. Describe the audit risks for each client.

B. Identify the differences and similarities in audit risks.

C. Describe how these risks affect the audit planning for each client. Assume that each company's economic situation is expected to last for at least another year.

4-34. (Types of Risk) For each of the following factors, indicate whether they affect primarily (A) business risk, (B) inherent risk, or (C) control risk.

1. Management integrity. *B*
2. Possibility of litigation against the auditor. *a*
3. Internal control structure. *C*
4. Motivation of management to misstate the financial statements. *B*
5. Accounting knowledge of client's controller. *B? / C*
6. Quality of the internal audit function. *C*
7. Users' understanding of auditor responsibilities. *a*
8. Complex accounting transaction on leases. *(b) c*
9. Sophistication of the accounting system. *C*
10. Client understanding of the auditor's responsibilities. *a*

4-35. (Materiality) An illegal payment of an otherwise immaterial amount could be material if a reasonable possibility exists that it could lead to a material contingent liability or a material loss of revenue. Therefore, the auditor should plan the audit and design the procedures to detect illegal payments.

REQUIRED

Do you agree?

4-36. (Materiality) Kelly Bullock, CPA, was discussing her difficulties in making a materiality judgment for one of her clients, Stone Mountain Engineering, Inc., with Pamela Davis, CPA. Bullock stated her belief that *SAS No. 47, Audit Risk and Materiality in Conducting an Audit*, should have given the auditor a specific rule-of-thumb for determining materiality.

REQUIRED

Do you agree or disagree with Bullock? Why or why not?

***4-37.** (Concept of Evidence) The third generally accepted auditing standard of fieldwork requires that the auditor obtain sufficient competent evidential matter to afford a reasonable basis for an opinion regarding the financial statements under examination. In considering what constitutes sufficient competent evidential matter, a distinction should be made between underlying accounting data and all corroborating information available to the auditor.

REQUIRED

Discuss the nature of evidential matter to be considered by the auditor in terms of the underlying accounting data, all corroborating information available to the auditor, and the methods by which the auditor tests or gathers competent evidential matter.

****4-38.** (Materiality) Mary Williams, CPA, is performing the annual audit of Crestline Corporation. Crestline has a general ledger net income of $350,000 for 19X5. The income tax rate is 30%. Williams proposed the following journal entries as of 12/31/X5 to correct errors relating to the accounts payable cutoff as of the physical inventory count date of 12/31/X5 and to record unrecorded legal fees:

(1) Cost of goods sold	40,000	
Accounts payable		40,000
(2) Administrative expenses	10,000	
Accrued liabilities		10,000

REQUIRED

A. What amount of net income should Crestline report for 19X5?

B. If Crestline should decide not to book Williams' proposed journal entries, by what percent would net income be misstated?

****4-39.** (Materiality) Assume that in problem 4-38 Williams had proposed the following journal entries at the end of 19X4, and that Crestline did not book them, the purpose of the entries being to correct sales cutoff errors at 12/31/X4, and to record depreciation on assets acquired in January 19X4 ($100,000 cost to be depreciated over four years on a straight-line basis).

(1) Inventory	30,000	
Cost of goods sold		30,000
(2) Depreciation expense	25,000	
Accumulated depreciation		25,000

REQUIRED

A. Considering the cumulative effect of the adjusting entries for 19X4 and 19X5, what amount of net income should Crestline report for 19X5?

B. If Crestline should decide not to book the journal entries Williams proposed at 12/31/X5, by what percent would net income be misstated?

C. What amount of net income should be reported assuming that the $30,000 proposed entry at 12/31/X4 had the debit and credit reversed?

D. Using the assumption in requirement C and assuming that Crestline decides not to book Williams' proposed entries at 12/31/X5, by what percent would net income be misstated?

---

*AICPA adapted.

**Arnold J. Pahler, San Jose State University.

Audit Judgment Cases

4-40. (Assessing Materiality) Gene Hall, CPA, in performing the audit of Wright Manufacturing Corporation, has waived the following proposed entries:

Salaries expense	30,000	
Accrued salaries		30,000
Interest expense	15,000	
Accrued interest		15,000
Accounts receivable	20,000	
Sales		20,000

Net income before taxes for the year was $320,000. Total assets were $3,000,000.

REQUIRED

A. What materiality guidelines would you suggest?

B. Should Hall apply materiality guidelines to each proposed adjustment or to adjustments taken as a whole?

*4-41. (Audit Risk) You are in charge of the audits of two unrelated automobile dealerships. Both have exclusive franchises for a given area. Although unrelated, the accounting systems are similar. Each dealership

- sends monthly financial statements to the manufacturer,
- has a computerized parts control system, and
- has good inventory controls.

Although similar in many ways, the current economic situation of one company differs sharply from that of the other.

Japanese Imported Auto (JIA) sells two different automobiles. The top-of-the-line sports car, the Itsopeachi 6, has a speedometer calibrated to 150 miles per hour, and it's easy to run the needle up to the redline. The car goes from zero to 60 in 4.8 seconds, and gets 40 miles per gallon in the city and 55 on the highway. It is simple to service, and there are plenty of service facilities. There is a waiting list of customers. The dealership is currently getting a premium of about $1,000 over sticker price.

JIA's other model is the Itibitti 4. This stripped compact holds only 10 gallons of gas, but it does not need a gas gauge; just run it until it's empty and it will go another 15 miles on the fumes alone. It's equipped with two bucket seats advertised as accommodating two large men. This might be true in Japan, but in the United States the Itibitti will comfortably seat a medium-size woman and a large cat. Nevertheless, the fact that it needs an oil change only once every 50,000 miles, plus its incredible fuel economy, makes it the most popular car sold in America. Here, too, JIA has a waiting list and charges a premium.

Things are somewhat different across town at the plush display room of the Behemoth Motors dealer (BM). This dealership sells the fanciest (and most expensive) automobile made in the United States, the Juggernaut 8. Beautifully appointed and instrumented, the car has power steering, brakes, windows, headlamps, and window-washers. BM's engineering is the most precise in the land; Juggernauts self-destruct within 24 hours after the warranty expires. Standard equipment includes a 50-gallon gas tank; this assures the proud owner of at least 200 miles between fuel stops. BM runs a high-powered advertising program for the Juggernaut. On TV, it features a lovely lady singing a lilting tune: "The people stood in line and fought, for a chance to drive a Juggernaut."

In the interest of accuracy, note that the singing commercial is written in the past tense. No one is standing in line at the BM dealership these days. There is no waiting list.

---

*Adapted from Laventhol and Horwath (A. D. Akresh, CPA, and J. E. Mitchell, CPA).

The sticker price is simply the opening bid. Management offers bargains, the salespeople offer discounts, and BM pays a cash rebate. If the potential customer offers $100 more than dealer cost, a deal has been struck.

Both JIA and BM are run by an owner/manager. Each offers a full line of services: new and used cars, warranty service, and other repairs and maintenance. Mechanical labor is flat rated; mechanics can increase their pay substantially by working faster than the flat rate for the job.

The inventory and service philosophy of each dealer is different, however. JIA maintains a minimal inventory of new cars, realizing that people will wait for the car they want. Similarly, JIA's parts department inventories only the fast-moving items; customers will wait for parts, too. BM, on the other hand, maintains an extensive inventory of new cars. Its parts department carries almost every part for the last six model years.

The monthly financial statements prepared for the manufacturers report most of the items that would show on audited financial statements but in somewhat greater detail. The manufacturers are primarily concerned with inventories, sales, and liquidity. New car inventories are carried at cost, as required by the manufacturers (and also by the lending institutions that finance the autos).

This is only the third year of JIA's existence. It broke even the first year, made a decent profit last year and is projecting an enormous profit for this year. The BM dealership, on the other hand, has been established for 20 years. Always profitable in the past, the dealership broke even last year and is projecting a major loss for this year.

REQUIRED

A. Describe the audit risks for each client.

B. Identify the differences and similarities in audit risks.

C. Describe how these risks affect the audit planning for each client. Assume that each company's economic situation is expected to last for at least another year.

Auting Issues Case

4-42. KELCO MANUFACTURING COMPANY

You are in the planning stage of the audit for Kelco's financial statements for the year ended December 31, 19X5. While considering materiality, you examined the following account balances:

	19X4	19X5
Total revenues	18,000,000	33,561,000
Net income before taxes	3,000,000	750,000
Total assets	20,000,000	32,525,000

One common guideline used for planning materiality is 10% of income before income taxes or 1% of the larger of total assets or total revenues. Applying these guidelines would provide the following results:

	19X4	19X5
10% Net income before taxes	300,000	75,000
1% of larger of total assets or revenues	200,000	335,610
Materiality (smaller of two)	200,000	75,000

The decrease in net income is due to the write-off of obsolete equipment in the amount of $800,000.

REQUIRED

1. Do you follow the normal guidelines for assessing materiality?

2. If not, what do you propose to use?

3. How would you justify and document your assessment of materiality?

Chapter *5*

Obtaining and Documenting Audit Evidence

Learning Objectives

- Define the types of audit evidence and describe the characteristics of each.

- Describe the purposes of working papers and their format and arrangement.

- Define and explain the difference and interrelationship between tests of controls and substantive tests.

- Describe and explain the purpose of the four major audit tests: (1) analytical tests, (2) observation and inquiry, (3) tests of transactions, and (4) tests of balances.

- List, describe, and explain the objectives of the fundamental audit techniques.

- Explain the relationships among assertions, objectives, evidence, techniques, and procedures.

- Describe an audit program and explain the basic approach to audit program development.

Auditors have always relied on physical evidence such as canceled checks, purchase orders, and deposit slips when investigating financial statements. In recent years, auditors have begun to rely on electronic records, such as electronic check requests and wire transfers. Ironically, the same technology that simplified the daily tasks of bookkeeping personnel has led to increased fraud, complicating matters for auditors.

Criminals have used check paper and magnetic ink to produce forged checks. A number of factors, including government regulations designed to protect the consumer, require most checks to clear within five days. Consequently, money is often withdrawn before financial institutions and corporations discover the violations. Because advanced electronic equipment has made it easier to produce counterfeit checks and receipts, auditors must be cautious in performing tests of transactions, physical examination, and confirmation. These and other types of audit evidence are discussed in this chapter. ■

Source: Amy Barrett, *Business Week* (May 23, 1994), p. 109.

The overall objective of an audit is to express an opinion on whether or not the financial statements are fairly presented in conformity with generally accepted accounting principles. To express this opinion, the auditor must reduce to an acceptably low level the risk that the financial statements contain a material misstatement. In performing this task, the auditor is concerned with whether the data representing economic activity (that is, accounting information) correspond with established criteria (generally accepted accounting principles).

As discussed in Chapter 4, the auditor first identifies assertions for each material component of the financial statements and considers the risk of a material misstatement for each assertion. The auditor then establishes audit objectives related to those assertions.

Once audit objectives are established, the auditor designs specific audit procedures that will generate sufficient competent evidential matter to allow the auditor to form an opinion on the financial statements. These procedures are steps or activities designed to collect specific types of audit evidence. As the auditor performs these procedures, he or she must also document or make a record of the work performed and the findings. Chapter 5 examines the design of audit procedures and how they are documented in working papers.

Audit Programs

An *audit program* is a set of procedures that an auditor believes are necessary to perform to express an opinion. The procedures in an audit program outline the evidence-gathering steps the auditor plans to use. The programs vary in form and detail from audit to audit, and the specifics of each program should be in written form. Audit programs are usually prepared for each major account balance or transaction cycle. They

- provide a basis for coordinating and supervising the audit work and controlling the time spent on the audit.
- aid in guiding the assistants in the work to be done.
- provide evidence of proper planning and a record of the work done during the audit.

An example of an audit program for cash is shown in Figure 5–1.

Types of Audit Evidence

The audit program lists the evidence-gathering steps to be used in the audit. As noted in the preceding chapter, for evidence to be useful to the auditor it must possess to some degree each of four characteristics: relevance, freedom from bias, objectivity, and persuasiveness. Six types of audit evidence are available to the auditor to support a given audit objective:

- Physical evidence
- Representations by third parties
- Mathematical evidence
- Documentation
- Representations by client personnel
- Data interrelationships

These six types all possess to varying degrees the four characteristics of evidence and thus have different strengths. The auditor should select the type of evidence that meets the audit objective at the lowest cost.

Physical Evidence

Physical evidence is evidence the auditor can actually see. Physical evidence is of two kinds: examination of assets and observation of client activities. For example, in determining that inventory exists, the auditor may gather evidence by examining the inventory. Or, the auditor may wish to gather evidence about an activity. For example, the auditor may want to determine whether or not a clerk stamps all invoices as paid when a check is written. In this case the auditor could gather physical evidence by observing the activity of a clerk performing a certain function.

Physical evidence represents a primary type of evidence used by auditors. It is particularly competent and is often used to verify the existence of physical assets: for example, cash, inventories, and equipment. Though physical evidence typically provides good evidence of the existence of assets or activities, it provides only limited evidence of other audit objectives. For example, even though the auditor may physically examine the inventory and thus gather particularly relevant evidence that the inventory exists, such examination provides little evidence that the inventory is properly valued.

Figure 5–1	**Audit Program for Cash**

Item No. Auditing Procedure	Done By	Date

AUDIT OBJECTIVES: **1.** Determine whether cash balances represent cash and cash items on hand, in transit, or on deposit.
2. Determine whether the amounts shown on the balance sheet are properly classified and adequately described as to any commitments or restrictions on withdrawal.

CASH ON DEPOSIT

1. Obtain bank reconciliations for all bank accounts existing at the verification date and proceed as follows:
  a. Test the clerical accuracy, including the list of outstanding checks.
  b. Compare the book balances to the general ledger balances.
  c. Determine whether other reconciling items have been properly accounted for.
  d. Trace cash cut-off information to the bank reconciliation, bank statement, and cash books.
  e. Compare the bank confirmations to the bank balances.
2. Obtain an analysis of transfers between bank accounts, including transfers between branches, divisions, and subsidiaries, for a reasonable period prior and subsequent to the reconciliation date and proceed as follows:
  a. Test the completeness of the analysis.
  b. Compare with and record the dates of receipts recorded in the books and those reflected on the bank statement.
  c. Compare with and record the dates of disbursements recorded in the book and those reflected on the bank statement.
  d. Cross-reference deposits in transit and outstanding checks to the bank reconciliations.
  e. Determine that transfers are accounted for in the proper period.

CASH ON HAND

3. Inquire into the nature and purpose of the cash on hand accounts and review related accounting policies and procedures to determine whether such accounts are effectively controlled.
4. Select the cash funds to be counted, especially those that are an integral part of the operations and procedures as follows:
  a. Identify the cash funds to be counted.
  b. Count cash and other cash items in the presence of the custodian, and, where appropriate, maintain control over all the cash counted at the selected locations until the count is completed.
  c. List date, source, and amount of deposited receipts.
  d. List date, payee, and amount of unreimbursed expenditures.
  e. Reconcile amounts to appropriate records and obtain explanations for unusual items, differences and exceptions.
  f. Obtain the signature of fund custodian attesting to the accuracy of the count and the return of the fund.

CONCLUDING PROCEDURES

5. Determine whether matters for disclosure in the financial statements have been identified and cross-referenced to footnote data at index 1650.

Representations by Third Parties

reliable

Representations by third parties are evidence obtained by the auditor through direct correspondence with individuals or entities other than the client. Most accounting transactions involve the client and an outside third party. In obtaining representations directly from these third parties, the auditor gathers evidence regarding the third party's view of the transaction. Obviously, the value of such a representation depends upon the third party's qualifications and willingness to cooperate.

Auditors often obtain representations from the following third parties:

- Customers—to confirm accounts receivable balances
- Vendors—to confirm accounts payable balances
- Banks—to confirm checking account balances, note balances, and other information
- Attorneys—to confirm contingent liabilities
- Inventory agents—to confirm inventory items on consignment or in public warehouses

The most common audit procedure for gathering evidence of representations from a third party is the confirmation request. *SAS No. 67, The Confirmation Process* (AU 330), addresses the auditor's responsibility for obtaining evidence through the confirmation process and requires the auditor to tailor the confirmation request to the audit objective and the assertion being addressed. To ensure the reliability of evidence gathered by confirmation, the auditor should select the items to be confirmed, control the mailing of confirmation requests, and receive third-party responses directly. Of course, management must be involved in the process, because the financial statements are ultimately management's responsibility. For example, the balance to be confirmed is generated by the client. Likewise, for most third parties, the client must authorize the release of such information to the auditor. For example, a bank will not tell the auditor the balance in a client's checking account without the client's authorization. Consequently, confirmations are generally signed by the client but are controlled and mailed by, and responses returned directly to, the auditor.

Confirmation requests typically are positive or negative. A *positive confirmation request*, as shown in Figure 5–2, indicates to the third party that (1) the auditor is performing an engagement and (2) the third party needs to respond to the confirmation request by providing certain information. In a positive confirmation request the auditor asks the third party to respond whether or not the balance is correct.

In a *negative confirmation request*, as shown in Figure 5–3, the auditor asks the third party to respond only if the information is incorrect. Thus, the negative confirmation implicitly assumes that the information is correct unless the third party responds. Of course, a third party may not respond to a negative confirmation for many reasons when, in fact, the balance is incorrect. For example, the third party may not understand the confirmation and simply discard it. The assumption that a negative confirmation is correct unless the third party responds may be questionable. For this reason, positive confirmations provide more reliable audit evidence than negative confirmations. To use negative confirmations, *SAS No. 67* requires that there be no reason to believe that the recipients of the confirmation requests are unlikely to give them consideration, that the combined assessed level of inherent and control risk is low, and that there is a large number of small balances.

| Figure 5–2 | **Positive Confirmation Request** |

Crim Company
1861 Lee Blvd.
New Orleans, LA 70101
January 14, 19X5

RC Enterprises
1865 Arcadia Street
Lafayette, LA 71012

Gentlemen:

Our auditors, K. A. Kruse & Co., CPAs, are currently auditing our financial statements. To facilitate this audit, please confirm the balance due us as of December 31, 19X4, which is shown on our records as $2,322.00.

Indicate in the space below if this amount is in agreement with your records. If there are exceptions, please provide any information that will assist the auditors in reconciling the difference.

Please mail your reply directly to K. A. Kruse & Co., 1 Canal Street, New Orleans, LA 70101. A stamped, self-addressed envelope is enclosed for your convenience.

Very truly yours,

Kim Overstreet
Crim Company
Vice-President

K. A. Kruse & Company:

The amount shown above of $2,322.00 is correct as of December 31, 19X4, with the following exceptions (if any):

_____

_____

Signed _____

By _____

Representations from third parties exemplify very good audit evidence. They typically are free from any bias and generally are relevant to the assertion being tested. Such representations are regularly used by auditors in many aspects of the audit engagement.

Figure 5-3	**Negative Confirmation Request**

June 15, 19X4

Smith T Building Supply
Dozier, Illinois 61001

Gentlemen:

Our auditors, <u>Richard Hare & Co.</u>, are now engaged in an examination of our financial statements. In connection therewith, they desire to verify the balance in your account at <u>May 31, 19X4</u>, which was shown on our records (and the enclosed statement) as <u>$2117.00</u>.

If this information is NOT correct, please note any exceptions below, and sign and return this form in the enclosed envelope. If this information is correct, please disregard this confirmation.

Very truly yours,

St. James Corporation

The above balance is INCORRECT.
The current balance is $_____ .

Signed _____

By _____

Date _____

Mathematical Evidence

Mathematical evidence involves recalculations of the client's computations by the auditor to verify the mathematical accuracy of the client's records. The auditor, for example, may foot (add) a listing of inventory items to determine that total inventory agrees with the detailed listing.

Mathematical evidence is generally a necessary part of the audit engagement. Even though the client may have a reliable accounting system and individual items may be properly stated, if the totals are incorrect the financial statements could be materially misstated. Of course, mathematical evidence alone is not sufficient competent evidential matter. The numbers being recalculated are no better than the underlying accounting data from which they are drawn. For example, inventory may be correctly added but may not be properly stated: the numbers themselves may be added correctly, but that does not prove that the inventory physically exists or is properly valued.

Documentation

Documentation is the auditor's examination of documents to support a given accounting transaction. For example, to determine that an expense is appropriate, the auditor may go back to the client's files and examine the vendor's invoice for the expense. The auditor may also want to examine cancelled checks and purchase orders for the transaction.

Documentation may come from either internal or external documents. *Internal documents* are prepared within the company. They may flow from the client to a third party and return to the client (for example, deposit slips and cancelled checks), or they may remain at the client's location and never flow to a third party (for example, trial balance, receiving reports, and bank reconciliations). Often, the auditor will intercept (with the client's permission) internal documents that have flowed to a third party before they are returned to the client. By intercepting these documents the auditor may improve the reliability of the evidence obtained.

External documents are prepared by an outside third party but are on file within the client's offices. For example, a vendor will send the client an invoice requesting payment for goods or services. The client will keep the invoice on file. External documents are considered more reliable evidence than internal documents because they are from an independent third party and are less likely than internal documents to be biased. However, because external documents have entered the client's information system they are not as reliable as direct evidence from representations by third parties.

Representations by Client Personnel

Auditors generally must obtain some evidence directly from the client. For example, the auditor may inquire of the client whether any obsolete or damaged goods in inventory exist. Likewise, the auditor may ask what the minimum dollar amount is for capitalization of a fixed asset. *Representations by client personnel* are statements in response to queries by the auditor.

Representations by client personnel are often used by the auditor in the early planning stages of the audit to provide evidence of specific client policies and information regarding the general environment. Because these representations are made by the client, they have very limited usefulness. Clearly, representations by client personnel lack one of the four essential characteristics of evidence: freedom from bias. However, certain client representations are required in an audit; these are discussed in Chapter 19.

Data Interrelationships

Data interrelationships involve the examination and comparison of relationships among data. Such data, which may be nonfinancial (for example, number of customers, direct labor hours) or financial (for example, prior year financial information, industry financial information), may be examined to determine trends and relationships. Evidence regarding data interrelationships can be obtained through analytical procedures.

SAS No. 56, *Analytical Procedures* (AU 329), notes that analytical procedures must be used during the planning phases and at the conclusion of the audit. Analytical procedures are discussed in detail in Chapter 11.

The Nature of Audit Tests

The audit procedures used to obtain evidence are usually referred to as *audit tests.* Various terms are often used in the professional literature and during an audit to describe specific audit tests. Auditing students should be able to distinguish among the different terms by understanding the purpose and interrelationships of each test. One useful approach to obtaining this understanding is to classify audit tests by (1) overall test objectives, (2) major types of tests, and (3) specific audit techniques.

Overall Test Objectives

An audit program is composed of audit tests designed to accomplish one or both of two primary objectives.

- *Tests of controls* determine the effectiveness of the design and operation of control structure policies and procedures.
- *Substantive tests* determine if material dollar or disclosure misstatements exist in the financial statements.

As Figure 5–4 shows, the quality of the client's internal control structure affects the quality of the financial statements the client prepares and therefore affects the nature, timing, and extent of the auditor's substantive tests. *SAS No. 47, Audit Risk and Materiality in Conducting an Audit* (AU 312), recognizes this relationship in the audit risk model with the concept of control risk (discussed in Chapter 4). If the internal control structure is strong (that is, control risk is low), the financial statements are less likely to contain material misstatements than if the internal control structure is weak (that is, control risk is high).

If the client has established a good internal control structure, the auditor may decide to restrict substantive testing because the client's internal control structure is likely to prevent or detect material misstatements. This relationship is logical and simply means that if the financial statements are less likely to contain material

---

Figure 5–4   **The Relationship of the Internal Control Structure to the Auditor's Substantive Testing**

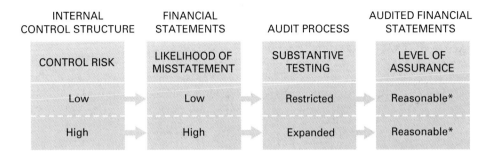

INTERNAL CONTROL STRUCTURE	FINANCIAL STATEMENTS	AUDIT PROCESS	AUDITED FINANCIAL STATEMENTS
CONTROL RISK	LIKELIHOOD OF MISSTATEMENT	SUBSTANTIVE TESTING	LEVEL OF ASSURANCE
Low	Low	Restricted	Reasonable*
High	High	Expanded	Reasonable*

---

*The basis for an auditor's opinion must be a reasonable level of assurance that the financial statements do not contain material misstatements.

misstatements, the auditor may properly do less substantive audit work than if the financial statements are likely to contain material misstatements. A more detailed discussion of the effect of the internal control structure on the audit program is presented in Chapter 6.

Major Types of Tests

Auditors achieve the tests of control and substantive tests objectives by performing tests that may be divided into four major categories:

- Analytical tests
- Observation and inquiry
- Tests of transactions
- Tests of balances

Analytical Tests

Analytical tests of financial information are made by the study and comparison of the relationships among data. They focus on the reasonableness of these relationships and the identification of unusual fluctuations in such data. Although analytical tests are discussed in detail in Chapter 11, some examples are given here:

Test	Example
Comparison of financial information for comparable prior periods	Compare fourth quarter sales for the audit year with fourth quarter sales of the preceding year.
Comparison of financial information with anticipated results	Compare actual ending inventory with budgeted ending inventory.
Study of relationships of elements of financial information that would be expected to conform to a predictable pattern	Determine that there is an appropriate increase in bad debt expense associated with an increase in sales volume.
Comparison of financial information with similar information regarding the industry in which the entity operates	Compare the entity's current ratio with the industry average.
Study of relationships between financial information and relevant nonfinancial information	Relate the number of units sold to recorded sales.

These tests can alert the auditor to potential material dollar misstatements in the financial statements. For example, a significant increase in the gross margin percentage from the previous year to the current year could be caused by an overcounting or overpricing of ending inventory.

Observation and Inquiry

Observation and inquiry are used to test controls that leave no audit trail of documentary evidence. Auditors make inquiries of various individuals and conduct observation tests to determine who performs a particular activity or how or when the activity is done. For example, the auditor may ask different individuals who posts to the receivables ledger, may observe who prepares the bank reconciliation, or may observe which employees enter data into the computer.

Inquiry can also be used as a substantive test. For example, inquiries regarding subsequent events would be a substantive test because they provide evidence regarding the adequacy of disclosures in the financial statements.

Tests of Transactions

A *test of transactions* is the auditor's examination of the documents and accounting records involved in the processing of a specific type of transaction. These tests can serve either test of controls or substantive objectives.

Tests of transactions accomplish a control objective when the purpose of the auditor's examination is to determine if internal control structure policies and procedures have been followed. For example, an auditor may examine sales invoices for the initials of a clerk responsible for checking their mathematical accuracy. If the initials are present, that is an indication the control procedure has functioned properly. If no initials are present, the auditor may conclude that the control procedure was not performed.

Tests of transactions accomplish a substantive objective when the purpose of the auditor's examination is to determine if dollar errors have occurred during the processing of the transaction. An auditor may select a sample of sales invoices to determine if they were correctly recorded in the sales journal and posted to the general ledger. If this testing reveals invoices that were not recorded, the auditor has discovered a monetary error.

If a test simultaneously accomplishes tests of controls and substantive objectives, it is a *dual purpose test.* For example, an auditor might select a sample of sales invoices and (1) examine the invoices for the clerk's initials indicating control performance and (2) determine that the sales invoices were posted to the sales journal correctly. The former is a test of controls, because the auditor is assessing whether a control was applied, and the latter is a substantive test, because the auditor is testing for dollar errors.

Tests of Balances

Audit tests performed directly on the ending balance in an account are termed *tests of balances*. These are substantive tests designed to identify misstatements by a direct test of the ending balance rather than by a test of the transactions that make up that balance. As an example, when auditors confirm accounts receivable they are testing the ending balance directly.

Substantive tests of transactions and tests of balances are interrelated in that each class of transactions affects a related account balance. Because financial statement amounts are the accumulation of transactions, an auditor may test the transactions that enter the account, the account balance itself, or both.

The auditor's overall objective is to obtain sufficient competent evidence regarding the ending balance in accounts receivable. One means of obtaining this evidence is to test the transactions entering the account, that is, the debits and credits. The auditor may select a sample of the sales and cash receipt transactions affecting accounts receivable and examine the supporting documentation for these transactions.

Another means of obtaining evidence is to confirm a sample of accounts receivable subsidiary balances. This test involves a direct examination of the ending balance without reference to the individual transactions that accumulated to the balance. In most audits the auditor will employ both types of tests, selecting the appropriate test on the basis of the quality of evidence it provides, the cost of performing the procedure, and the applicability of the procedure in the circumstances. Some accounts in the financial statements are not susceptible to tests of balances. For example, income statement accounts are of such a nature that their ending balances cannot be tested

Figure 5-5 **Matrix of Audit Tests by Type and Purpose**

according to Standards to be considered

		Purpose of Test	
		Substantive test	Test of controls
Type of Test	Analytical procedures	Yes (Example A)	Not applicable
	Observation and inquiry	Yes (Example B)	Yes (Examples C,D)
	Tests of transactions	Yes (Example E)	Yes (Examples F,G)
	Tests of balances	Yes (Example H)	Not applicable

Examples:

A– Compare this year's expenses with last year's expenses, and investigate unusual fluctuations.

B– Inquire about subsequent events.

C– Observe that cash is deposited daily by a specific clerk.

D– Inquire about who deposits cash and how often.

E– Examine invoices to support additions (specific transactions) to fixed assets account during year.

F– Examine sales invoices to see if initials of credit manager are there to indicate a credit file and credit approval (inspection test).

G– Vouch from sales invoices to credit files to see if customer has a credit file and has been approved for credit (reperformance test).

H– Confirm year-end balances in accounts receivable.

directly. For these accounts, the auditor relies on tests of transactions or tests of balances on balance sheet accounts that affect a related income statement account.

Figure 5–5 shows the relationship between audit tests classified by overall objective and audit tests classified by type.

Specific Audit Techniques

(handwritten margin note)

Audit techniques are the methods auditors use to gather evidence. These methods may be classified into ten fundamental techniques that form the basis for audit program design:

- Physical examination
- Confirmation →
- Vouching
- Tracing
- Reperformance
- Observation
- Reconciliation
- Inquiry
- Inspection
- Analytical procedures

**Physical
Examination**

Physical examination is the activity of gathering physical evidence. It is a substantive test involving the counting or inspection of assets that have a tangible existence, such as cash, inventory, and plant and equipment. When the auditor counts cash or inventory or inspects a new machine, the physical examination technique is being applied. This technique is not applicable to assets whose existence is evidenced primarily by documentation, such as accounts receivable, investments, or prepaid expenses. In addition, this technique does not apply to liabilities, revenues, or expenses.

The primary audit assertion tested by physical examination is existence. However, the technique also provides evidence about valuation, because quantities are directly involved in determining the value of most assets. In addition, an auditor can sometimes obtain evidence about the quality or condition of assets through physical examination, and that too affects valuation. The rights and obligations assertion is tested through physical examination only to the extent that possession supports ownership of an asset. The completeness assertion may also be tested through physical examination in that items omitted from the financial statements may be discovered. For example, during inventory test counts the auditor may discover that the client failed to include some items in the inventory count.

Although physical examination usually provides the most reliable form of evidence about the existence of an asset, alternative forms of evidence may be acceptable in some situations. When an asset does not have tangible existence, physical examination is inappropriate and other forms of evidence such as invoices or confirmations may be used. In addition, the desirability of an asset, the ease with which it can be converted to cash, and its susceptibility to manipulation affect the need for physical examination. Physical examination of material amounts of cash on hand would be quite important, while physical examination of plant and equipment is sometimes omitted or restricted to examination of additions during the period being audited.

Whether an auditor will physically examine assets held by third parties depends on the nature of the asset and its importance to the financial statements, the reputation and independence of the third party, the authority delegated to the third party, and the client's control over that party. Thus, if inventory held by a third party, such as a public warehouse, is a material portion of current or total assets, the auditor might consider physical examination of that inventory to be essential.

The reliability of evidence produced by physical examination depends on the skill and expertise of the auditor performing the examination. If an auditor makes counts carelessly or is unfamiliar with the client's procedures for determining volumes, weights, or dimensions, the evidence obtained by physical examination might be misleading. In addition, if the auditor lacks the expertise to judge the type or quality of inventory, such as in the audit of a jewelry store, then the auditor should obtain expert assistance from an independent party regarding the asset being examined.

Confirmation

When using the *confirmation* technique, the auditor requests a written response from a specific third party about a particular item affecting the financial statements. Auditors use confirmation evidence extensively. Thus, the specific third party from whom the confirmation is requested will depend on the particular account being audited.

The primary assertions tested by confirmation are existence and rights and obligations. This technique can also provide evidence about the valuation or allocation, completeness, and presentation and disclosure assertions. Both the existence or occurrence and the rights and obligations assertions for cash and accounts receivable are often tested by confirmation. Note that confirmation of current customers' accounts receivable could not be expected to provide reliable evidence about completeness, because customers might not be inclined to report understatement errors in their accounts and because the auditor typically selects the accounts with a higher recorded balance to be confirmed. The valuation or allocation assertion for accounts receivable is partially tested through confirmation, although valuation of that account would require audit of the allowance of doubtful accounts as well. When an auditor confirms cash with the bank, the confirmation form also requests information regarding pledged collateral for loans. Thus, the confirmation technique may also provide evidence about presentation and disclosure.

Vouching

Vouching is the examination of documents that support a recorded transaction or amount. Because the purpose of the vouching technique is to obtain evidence about a recorded item in the accounting records, the direction of the search for the supporting documents is crucial. In vouching, the direction of testing is from the recorded item to supporting documentation.

For example, to gather evidence to determine if a recorded sale actually occurred, the auditor could vouch the sale back to supporting documentation such as a shipping report. Vouching is also frequently used to obtain evidence about recorded additions to plant and equipment during the year. By vouching recorded purchases of plant and equipment to supporting documents such as vendor invoices, the auditor can obtain evidence about whether the purchase occurred (existence or occurrence), whether the recorded amount is correct (valuation or allocation), whether the asset belongs to the client (rights and obligations), and whether the item purchased is properly classified as a fixed asset (presentation and disclosure).

The completeness assertion is more difficult to test through vouching because testing for completeness requires the auditor to search for evidence of unrecorded items. Vouching begins with recorded items and generally cannot identify unrecorded transactions or accounts. However, the auditor can use vouching in some circumstances to test for completeness. For example, an auditor may select sales recorded after year-end and vouch these items to the sales invoices to determine whether these were sales that should have been recorded prior to year-end (that is, completeness).

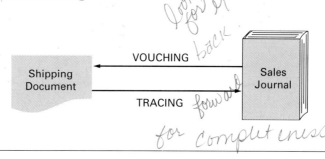

Figure 5-6   **Vouching and Tracing**

[handwritten: looking for existence]

VOUCHING *[handwritten: back]*

Shipping Document ←——— Sales Journal

TRACING *[handwritten: forward]*

[handwritten: for completeness.]

Generally, tests of documents for unrecorded items are made by use of another audit technique—tracing.

Tracing

[handwritten: from invoice to records]

[handwritten: Ving for completeness]

Tracing is the following of source documents to their recording in the accounting records. An auditor performs this procedure by selecting source documents, such as sales invoices or shipping reports, and tracing them through the accounting system to their ultimate recording in the accounting records, such as journals and ledgers. The direction of testing in tracing is the opposite of that in vouching. Therefore, auditors often use tracing to test the completeness assertion. Figure 5–6 illustrates the difference between the tracing and vouching techniques.

Completeness can be tested by tracing because the auditor begins with a source document that should result in a recorded transaction or amount in the accounting records. By following the source document to the accounting records, the auditor obtains evidence as to whether or not the item was recorded. Source documents not recorded represent misstatements in the completeness assertion.

The valuation or allocation and the presentation and disclosure assertions may also be tested by tracing. Because the auditor will not only determine that the item was recorded but that it was recorded at the proper amount, the valuation or allocation assertion is examined. In addition, if the auditor discovers that the item was recorded, but in the wrong account, then he or she has identified a misstatement in presentation and disclosure.

Reperformance

[handwritten: re-do some steps.]

A common technique auditors use to obtain evidence is the *reperformance* of client activities involved in the accounting process. In effect, the auditor obtains evidence about client activities by repeating these activities and comparing the result with the client's result. Because the technique involves repeating something the client has already done, it can be used as both a test of controls and a substantive test.

Reperformance serves as a test of controls when the auditor reperforms control procedures to determine if the original performance was effective. For example, if the auditor refoots a sample of invoices footed and initialed by a client clerk and finds an error, it indicates the control did not function properly.

Examples of the reperformance technique in substantive testing are numerous. Auditors often recalculate depreciation expense or earnings per share for the period and compare their results with those of the client. Auditors may also test the mathematical accuracy of inventory by reperforming the extending and footing of inventory items. These recalculations address valuation or allocation.

Reperformance also applies to the clerical bookkeeping functions performed by the client. To obtain evidence about proper posting and the clerical accuracy of journals, ledger accounts, and trial balances, the auditor may reperform these clerical functions. Thus the auditor may repost a sample of journal entries to test the accuracy of posting or refoot journals and ledger accounts to test their mathematical accuracy.

Misstatements the auditor discovers when performing these tests may represent violations of the existence or occurrence, completeness, or presentation and disclosure assertions. For example, if in refooting a ledger account the auditor discovers that some items have been double counted, the existence or occurrence assertion has been violated. If the auditor finds that some items have been omitted, the completeness assertion has been violated. When reposting, the auditor may find presentation and disclosure misstatements if journal entries have been posted to the wrong accounts.

Observation

In *observation* the auditor witnesses the physical activities of the client. For example, the auditor may observe the client's inventory taking to assess the degree of care exercised. In addition, some internal control structure policies and procedures can only be verified by observation because their performance leaves no documentary evidence. Examples of these controls include proper segregation of duties and competence of personnel.

Observation differs from physical examination. Physical examination involves an auditor's counting or inspection of a specific asset, such as cash, inventory, or plant and equipment. Observation focuses on client activities to understand who does them or how and when they are done.

Reconciliation

Reconciliation is the process of matching two independent sets of records. In an audit, one set of records is usually the client's and the other set is the third party's. The preparation of a bank reconciliation is a common example of this technique. When using the reconciliation technique, the auditor will examine the client's verification of the cash records against the bank's records. By considering outstanding checks, deposits in transit, and other reconciling items, the auditor attempts to account for all items causing a difference between client and bank records.

Reconciliation primarily serves the assertions of completeness and existence or occurrence. In reconciling two sets of records, the auditor may discover items that were not recorded on the client's records. For example, in a bank reconciliation the auditor may identify a cash disbursement recorded by the bank that was not recorded by the client, that is, a completeness misstatement. Or, the auditor may find that a cash disbursement in the client's accounting records was also recorded as a disbursement by the bank. This evidence supports the occurrence of the cash disbursement transaction recorded on the client's books.

Inquiry

The *inquiry* technique (asking questions) is used extensively in an audit. The responses to these questions may be oral or in writing. Because management and employees of the client are quite knowledgeable of the operations and the control structure, even the most experienced auditor will benefit from inquiry.

Although the responses to written or oral inquiries are usually of limited reliability, they do provide a starting point for the performance of other auditing techniques. The responses to inquiries generally are substantiated through performance of other techniques. However, the auditor is usually more efficient when corroborating responses to inquiries than when finding answers independently through an undirected examination of detailed evidence.

Because the inquiry technique is so broad, it applies to both tests of controls and substantive testing and is useful in testing all of the financial statement assertions. Auditors may use inquiry to learn what control structure policies and procedures have been established, what accounting principles have been used, and how certain transactions are processed, or to obtain an explanation from management of the results of a specific audit test.

Inspection

Inspection is the examination of documents in other than the vouching or tracing techniques. It is the critical reading of a document comparing the information therein with other information known to the auditor or recorded in the accounts. This technique may be applied to many different documents such as leases, contracts, minutes of meetings, formal debt instruments, and insurance policies.

Scanning is a type of inspection by which the auditor reviews a document for unusual items. For example, an auditor may scan the accounts receivable ledger to determine the existence of any customers with large credit balances that should be reclassified as liabilities.

Inspection may also provide the auditor with information on which to base a particular audit test, such as inspection of a debt instrument to determine interest rates to be used in testing interest expense. Inspection may also serve to corroborate information recorded in the accounting records, such as determining approval for acquisition of plant and equipment by inspecting the minutes of the board of directors meeting. Because of the variety of documents that auditors may inspect, the inspection technique addresses all of the financial statement assertions.

Analytical Procedures

The technique of ***analytical procedures*** encompasses a number of specific procedures the auditor may elect to perform. Earlier in this chapter some common types of analytical tests that analyze the relationships among data were discussed. Auditors employ this technique to assess the reasonableness of data. For example, the computation of certain ratios or trends from financial statement information may indicate unusual conditions that prompt the auditor to seek further evidence about a particular item in the financial statements. Because unusual relationships among data can occur for a number of reasons, analytical procedures serve all five financial statement assertions.

Matching Audit Techniques with Audit Evidence

Auditors use these ten audit techniques to gather the six types of evidence discussed earlier in this chapter. The relationships between the various types of audit evidence and audit techniques are illustrated in Table 5–1. Table 5–2 gives an example of how the auditor may match audit evidence with audit techniques.

More than one technique may be needed to satisfy a particular audit objective. Alternatively, a specific audit technique may satisfy more than one audit objective. Furthermore, in performing an audit technique for a particular account, the auditor also gathers evidence on other financial statement accounts as a result of the dual nature of the double entry bookkeeping system. For example, when the auditor tests a customer's receivable account for validity (existence), the auditor is also gathering evidence on the validity of sales.

Table 5–1	**Relating Audit Evidence to Audit Techniques**

Types of Evidence	Related Audit Techniques	Type of Test
Physical evidence	Physical examination Observation	Test of balances Observation and inquiry
Representations by third parties	Confirmation	Test of balances Test of transactions
Mathematical evidence	Reperformance	Test of balances Test of transactions
Documentation	Reperformance	Test of balances Test of transactions
	Vouching	Test of balances Test of transactions
	Tracing	Test of balances Test of transactions
	Inspection	Test of balances Test of transactions
	Reconciliation	Test of balances Test of transactions
Representations by client personnel	Inquiry	Observation and inquiry
Data interrelationships	Analytical procedures	Analytical tests

Table 5–2	**Matching Audit Evidence with Audit Techniques**

Objective: Is equipment balance fairly stated?
Assertion: Existence (Does equipment actually exist?)

Options	Audit Procedure	Audit Evidence	Audit Technique	Type of Test
1.	Beginning balance was audited last year; support additions for this year by vouching to invoices.	Documentation	Vouching	Test of Transactions
2.	Physically examine equipment listed in ending balance.	Physical evidence	Physical Examination	Test of balances
3.	Compare balance this year with balance last year.	Data interrelationships	Analytical Procedures	Analytical tests
4.	Inquire of client regarding any changes.	Representations by client personnel	Inquiry	Observation and inquiry
5.	Obtain listing of changes in equipment and compare to insurance documents.	Documentation	Inspection	Test of balances

Note: All five of these options provide evidence of existence for equipment. The auditor decides which option(s) to use in the context of the cost of the option versus its benefits (of reducing audit risk).

Finalizing the Audit Program

At the beginning of this chapter the process of developing an audit program was outlined as a sequence of steps that links audit assertions to audit objectives to audit evidence to audit techniques to audit procedures. When an auditor selects a particular audit technique (such as tracing) to obtain a specific type of evidence (such as documentation in the form of a sales invoice) to achieve an audit objective (such as determining if all sales invoices prepared during the period were recorded as sales) that was developed from an audit assertion (such as completeness), the result is an audit procedure. Thus, an audit procedure is simply an instruction on how to obtain evidence to satisfy a specific audit objective derived from an audit assertion. An illustration of how these steps are linked in preparing an inventory audit program is shown in Table 5–3.

Table 5–3

Assertions, Objectives, Evidence, Techniques, and Procedures for Inventory

Financial Statement Assertion	Illustrative Audit Objectives	Related Audit Evidence	Audit Techniques	Audit Procedures
Existence or occurrence	Inventories included in the balance sheet physically exist.	Physical evidence	Physical examination	Make test counts of inventory.
Completeness	Inventory quantities include all products, materials, and supplies on hand.	Documentation	Tracing	Trace receiving reports prepared just before year-end to inventory records.
Rights and obligations	The entity has legal title or similar rights of ownership to the inventory.	Documentation	Inspection	Inspect consignment agreements to identify consignment customers or vendor.
Valuation or allocation	Inventories are properly stated at cost (except when market is lower).	Documentation	Vouching	Vouch recorded inventory costs to vendor invoices.
Presentation and disclosure	Inventories are properly classified in the balance sheet as current assets.	Documentation	Inspection	Inspect drafts of the financial statements.

Obtaining and Documenting Evidence

Representations by client personnel are a common form of evidence obtained on every audit. This evidence is documented by means of a memo or other type of work paper. The auditor must be familiar with the client's business in order to make appropriate judgments about the sufficiency and competence of the evidence. In almost all situations regarding client representations, the auditor will eventually be tempted to believe the client unconditionally or to do what is easy.

For example, in the audit of inventory, a primary concern is valuation. An auditor should be aware of, and search for, any indications of obsoles-cence. Simple signs, such as the excessive collection of dust or evidence of rusting, should signal to the auditor that the client's inventory may not be salable or may have to be sold at a significant discount. Auditors must be cognizant of the unique issues regarding their particular client's inventory. In many cases, an expert may be called upon to assist the auditors in properly determining whether obsoles-cence is a problem, such as in a high-technology industry.

Management's explanations on the material findings of an audit are to be considered as evidence, but not necessarily as competent evidence. Judgment, therefore, plays an important role in determining the adequacy of audit evidence.

Documentation

The third standard of fieldwork requires the auditor to collect sufficient competent evidential matter. The auditor must collect evidence and also document the collection process. Documentation is achieved through the use of *working papers*. *SAS No. 41, Working Papers* (AU 339), requires that the auditor prepare and maintain working papers to support the audit report.

Although the purpose of working papers remains the same regardless of the auditor, the mechanical aspects of working papers, such as files, formats, and arrangements, sometimes differ. Nonetheless, certain characteristics are common in all audit engagements. *SAS No. 41* (AU 339.01) states that the form and content of working papers should be designed to meet the circumstances of the particular engagement.

Purposes

Working papers have two primary functions: (1) they provide the principal record that the audit has conformed to generally accepted auditing standards, and (2) they aid the auditor in the conduct and supervision of the audit.

Record of Evidence

A primary purpose of audit working papers is to serve as a record of the auditor's evidence and as a basis of support for the audit report. The auditor is required to collect sufficient competent evidential matter to render an opinion. The collection of evidence is documented through the use of working papers. Working papers represent all of the trial balances, checklists, programs, confirmations, schedule analyses, and other documentation of the auditor. Working papers are primary evidence that the auditor has performed the audit in conformity with generally accepted auditing standards, including the standards of fieldwork, and has reached an appropriate conclusion.

Planning

Working papers also allow the auditor to plan the audit properly, as required by the first standard of fieldwork. During the audit the auditor must determine which procedures should be and have been performed, assess the current status of the audit, and note matters that need to be resolved before the audit is completed. Working papers both facilitate such planning and document that planning has been performed.

Review

The first standard of fieldwork also requires that assistants be properly supervised. One important aspect of such supervision is the review of the assistants' work by appropriate, high-level personnel. Each member of the audit team prepares working papers. The senior auditor, by examining the working papers, can review the work performed by members of the audit team and thereby evaluate the entire audit process.

Files

As noted previously, the details of audit working papers usually vary among auditors and auditing firms. However, working papers have several common characteristics and are typically categorized into two types of files: permanent and current.

Permanent File *Permanent files* contain information that is of continuing relevance to the auditor in performing recurring engagements on an audit client. Permanent files include copies of such documents as the articles of incorporation, the bylaws of the company, chart of accounts, organization charts, contracts, bond indenture agreements, pension plans, and lease agreements. Figure 5–7 illustrates the arrangement of a typical set of working papers.

Current File The *current* working paper or analysis file contains information relevant to a given audit client for a particular audit year. Although the client will have only one permanent file, there will be a current file for each year's audit. Current files include a variety of information that is often separated into individual folders or divisions. Working papers in the current file include the audit program, the working trial balance, lead schedules, and detail schedules.

Figure 5–7	**Arrangement of a Set of Working Papers**

Audit Program The initial *audit program* represents the detailed listing of all audit procedures to be performed during the engagement. As each audit procedure is performed, the auditor initials or signs off by the audit step to indicate that the audit procedure has in fact been performed. Audit programs are discussed in detail in Chapter 12.

Working Trial Balance The *working trial balance*, or trial balance worksheet, is a listing of all the accounts and balances from the general ledger. The auditor is, of course, auditing financial statements that are composed of the accounts from the general ledger. These accounts as listed in the working trial balance represent the primary focus of the audit. In performing an audit, the auditor typically obtains a working trial balance as early as possible.

The working trial balance usually includes columns for the auditor's proposed adjusting entries. When the auditor identifies material errors in the financial statements, the material errors are corrected through proposed adjusting entries. For example, the auditor may discover that a significant purchase at year-end for goods in transit was not appropriately recorded. In this case the auditor will propose a debit to the inventory account and a credit to accounts payable. The working trial balance also includes a column for adjusted balances after posting adjusting entries to the initial trial balance column. A portion of a working trial balance is shown in Figure 5–8.

Lead Schedules The working trial balance includes numerous general ledger accounts. These accounts are often grouped into major categories on the financial statements. For example, all of the accounts representing fixed assets may be grouped into one account called property, plant, and equipment. A *lead schedule* details each individual account comprised within a major account category. An example of a lead schedule for accrued liabilities is shown in Figure 5–9.

Detailed Schedules *Detailed schedules* indicate specific audit procedures performed for a given account. These detailed schedules should support the lead schedule in a given financial statement area. In turn, the lead schedule should tie into the financial statements under audit. For example, the auditor may prepare a detailed schedule analyzing all additions to the particular asset account of automobiles. This represents a detailed audit schedule that will support the lead schedule of property, plant, and equipment. Detailed schedules display a variety of formats, including the following:

- *Analysis* An *analysis schedule* examines the activity in an account. An analysis schedule takes a beginning balance for the current year, as indicated in the prior year's audit, and then it supports increases and decreases in the account. This procedure results in support for the ending balance. For example, in examining the fixed asset account of automobiles, the auditor may prepare an analysis schedule to show the beginning balance, additions and deletions with supporting evidence, and the computed ending balance. Analysis schedules are normally prepared for balance sheet accounts for which there is either very little or quite significant activity, such as long-term debt, during the year.

- *Listings* A *listing schedule* is a simple listing of all the detailed items that make up a total, usually an ending balance. For example, a listing of accounts receivable would include a detail of each customer's account balance, along with the total of all the accounts. In this case, the listing would be used to support the accounts receivable control account.

Figure 5-8   **Working Trial Balance**

War Eagle Printing Service
Working Trial Balance
For Year Ended Dec. 31, 19X4

	Initials	Date
Prepared By	A-1	
Approved By	MKA	2-4-x5

	Working Paper Reference	Account Title	Trial Balance Dr.	Trial Balance Cr.	Adjustments Dr.	Adjustments Cr.	Income Statement Dr.	Income Statement Cr.	Balance Sheet Dr.	Balance Sheet Cr.
1	A	Cash	10625						10625	
2	B	Accounts Receivable	21775						21775	
3	C	Supplies	25650			(a) 18250			7400	
4	D	Prepaid Insurance	1200			(b) 600			600	
5	F	Printing Equipment	27250						27250	
6	Q	Accounts Payable		8725						8725
7	R	Unearned Revenue		1725	(e) 725					1000
8	S	Barney Waters, Capital		34750						34750
9	W	Barney Waters, Drawing	14000						14000	
10	AA	Sales		64250		(e) 725		64975		
11	EE	Salary Expense	7200		(d) 750		7950			
12	GG	Miscellaneous Expense	1750				1750			
13			109450	109450						
14										
15		Supplies Expense			(a) 18250		18250			
16		Insurance Expense			(b) 600		600			
17		Depreciation Expense			(c) 2725		2725			
18		Accumulated Depreciation				(c) 2725				2725
19		Salaries Payable				(d) 750				750
20					23050	23050	31275	64975	81650	47950
21		Net Income					33700			33700
22							64975	64975	81650	81650

■ *Reconciliation* In a **reconciliation schedule**, the auditor supports a specific account by matching the working trial balance total to some other type of record. For example, a bank reconciliation ties in the client's general ledger account on cash with the checking account records from the bank.

Figure 5-9   **Lead Schedule**

Summary Schedule show accounts are grouped

		Initials	Date
Prepared By	R-1		
Approved By	MKA	2-8-X6	

Merritt Mfg. Co.
Accrued Liabilities
12-31-19X5

	Working Paper Reference		Final 12-31-X4	Per Books 12-31-X5	Adjustments	Final 12-31-X5				
1	R-1-1	Payroll	7250(4)	8500 -	(15)<175>	8325 -				
2	R-1-2	Commissions	102750(4)	110250	-	110250 -				
3	R-1-3	Interest	68450(4)	71675	-	71675 -				
4		Royalties	16500 -	-	-					
5			194950 -	190425 -	<175>	190250 -				
6			A-3	A-3	A-3	A-3				
7										
8										
9				(4) per last year's working papers						

■ *Reasonableness Tests* **Reasonableness tests** are working papers that show the
auditor's computation determining whether or not an account balance appears
reasonable. For example, Allowance for Doubtful Accounts is often evaluated as
a percentage of total accounts receivable or past history of collections.

- *Memorandum* A ***memorandum*** is a type of audit schedule frequently used by auditors to give a written description or analysis of a situation. For example, the auditor may write a memorandum describing the client's internal control environment. Alternatively, the auditor may write a memorandum formally documenting tests that have been performed or results that have been obtained in a test.

- *Outside Documentation* The auditor often collects ***outside documentation*** during the audit. For example, the auditor may obtain confirmation replies from customers or may copy client information, such as an invoice. This documentation, although not usually part of formal working papers, nonetheless represents evidence to the auditor and would be included in the current file.

Format

The auditor should use a working paper format that enhances the effective communication of the evidence obtained. Although the mechanics of the format may differ among auditors and auditing firms, nonetheless similar characteristics may be found among auditors' working papers.

Headings

All working papers should have a proper heading. Each page of the working papers should include a title describing what purpose the working paper serves, along with the name of the audit client and the date of the financial statements being audited. Unless headings are used, the reviewer of the work papers may not understand the particular audit to which the working paper applies.

Indexing

Many auditors use an indexing system for working papers. Indexing often allows better control over the working papers during the audit, provides for a logical order in the arrangement of the working papers that aids in review, requires less time in assembling working papers in the index files, and may provide quicker access to specific working papers after they are filed.

Not all auditors use indexing. Nonetheless, although indexing may not be formally used, auditors still arrange their working papers into various standard general categories (such as planning and administration, internal control structure, and account balances) and employ a rational or logical approach to organizing working papers.

In indexing working papers, the auditor typically uses some predetermined code for indexing by using letters or numbers. For example, the auditor may assign each important financial statement area a letter of the alphabet. Thus, fixed assets, or property, plant, and equipment, may be assigned the letter F. The lead schedules may then be assigned a number behind the letter and detailed analyses supporting the lead schedule may *then* be assigned a second number. For example, the lead schedule for property, plant, and equipment may be F-1, and a detailed analysis supporting automobiles may be F-1-1. Other detailed schedules that support the primary detailed schedule could then be assigned a third number. An example of indexing is shown in Figure 5–10.

Tick Marks

A ***tick mark*** is a symbol keyed to a footnote that explains some item. For example, the auditor may use a tick mark beside an addition to the automobile account. That tick mark, or symbol, can be found at the bottom of the page of the working paper with an explanation that the auditor has examined an invoice. Because tick marks

Figure 5-10	**Standard Working Paper Index**

Pending matters point sheet
Draft copy of financial statement
Working trial balance
Adjusting, closing, reversing, and reclassification entries
General matters:

Disclosure checklist	G/M-1
Engagement letter	G/M-2
Client representation letter	G/M-3
Attorney letter	G/M-4
Time budget	G/M-5
Cash	A
Receivables	B
Inventories	C
Prepaid expenses	D
Securities and investments	T
Property, plant, and equipment including capital leases	F
Other assets	M
Notes payable and long-term debt including capitalized lease obligations	P
Accounts payable	Q
Accrued expenses	R
Income taxes	S
Equity	W
Sales/revenue	AA
Cost of sales	BB
General selling and administrative expense	GG
Other income/expense	KK
Assessment of control risk	I/C

serve as explanations, the auditor should make sure that all tick marks are clearly explained on the working paper. Tick marks should be simple so that they communicate information clearly to the reviewer of the working paper. Common examples of tick marks include a simple check mark (✔), a check mark with a slash (✔), and a double check mark (✔✔). An example of a working paper with tick marks is shown in Figure 5–11.

Although the concept of tick marks may seem quite simple, differences exist among auditors about the appropriate use of tick marks. For example, some auditing firms have a standard set of tick marks used for all audit engagements. In these cases, the auditors believe that standard tick marks aid in the preparation of working papers and in their review. Other auditors believe that standardized tick marks are inappropriate, because they reduce the auditor's flexibility. Some auditors believe that tick marks should be in different colors on the working paper so that they can be easily distinguished. Other auditors, however, believe that it is a waste of time to use different colors for tick marks. Policies regarding tick marks depend upon the CPA firm.

Figure 5–11 | **Working Paper with Tick Marks**

Correct footle *auditor Reviewer*

Tiger Manufacturing Inc.
Trade Accounts Receivable Aging   B-2

	Initials	Date
Prepared By	PFS	2-2-x9
Approved By	CWA	2-10-x9

Customers	Balance per Books 12-31-x8		Current	30-60	60-90	90-over	Subsequent Collections 2-12-x9	
1 Lochapoka Construction	4255 –	W	1775 –	1653 –	827 –			
2 Waters Plumbing Co.	681 –	ⓧ		681 –				
3 Greg's Concrete	1914 –	W	1250 –			64 –		
4 Interfax Inc.	2313 –	W	1750 –	188 –	375 –			
5 Dye Welding	1478 –	E	1478 –					
6 Thompson Foundries Inc.	619 –	ⓧ	500 –	119 –				
7 King's Hardware	6482 –	✓	615 –	2000 –	1750 –	2117 –	5867 –	✓
8 Williams Dry Goods	128 –	E	128 –				128 –	✓
9 Sanford Machinery	918 –	✓				918 –	918 –	✓
10 Walls and Sons	473 –	E	273 –	105 –	95 –			
11 Huiton & Huiton	65 –	W			65 –		65 –	✓
12 Turner Construction	3727 –	ⓧ	3175 –	552 –				
13	23053 –		10944 –	5298 –	3112 –	3699 –	6978 –	
14	B-1 F		F	F	F	F	F	

W   Confirmations received, no exception
E   Confirmation returned with exception
       See W/P B-3
F   Footed
ⓧ   Second request mailed 2-10-x9
✓   Traced to cash receipt journal, no exceptions

Confirmations are located at W/P B-6

CF = Cross footing

Sign-off   Working papers should include an indication of the auditor who prepared the working paper and the date the working paper was prepared.

General Considerations

The auditor should include many general considerations in determining the content, format, and arrangement of working papers. As noted in the AICPA *Audit and Accounting Manual* (AAM 6300.02), general considerations include the following:

- Working papers should be sufficiently intelligible, clear, and neat so that another auditor, who has had no previous association with the audit, can review the papers and determine the nature and extent of the work done and how the conclusions were reached that support the auditor's resulting report.
- The content of an individual working paper or group of related papers should include identification of (1) the source of the information presented (e.g., fixed assets ledger, cash disbursements journal), (2) the nature and extent of the work done and conclusions reached (by symbols and legend narrative, or a combination of both), and (3) appropriate cross-references to other working papers.
- Before completion of the audit, all questions or exceptions in the working papers should be resolved. If for some reason the auditor must leave the assignment without resolving all items, he or she should provide an open-items listing on a separate temporary paper for the in-charge auditor's attention. An unresolved exception or incomplete explanation in the working papers may be construed by some as indication of an inadequate audit.
- Information and comments in the working papers generally represent statements of fact and professional conclusions. Accordingly, language should be clear and free from such vague judgmental adjectives as *good* or *bad*. Conclusions should be supported by documented facts, especially if they concern the adequacy of the client's records.
- Working papers should be viewed as an integrated presentation of information. The auditor should cross-reference working papers to call attention to interaccount relationships and to reference a paper to other working papers summarizing or detailing related information.
- The preparer should view the working papers as if he or she were the in-charge auditor. All inferences and conclusions should be supported in the working papers and no misleading or irrelevant statements should be made.
- It is preferable to indicate negative figures in working papers by parentheses instead of red figures to preserve their identity if the papers are photocopied or microfilmed.

The AICPA *Audit and Accounting Manual* (6300.03) also notes a number of ways to save time and avoid unnecessary detail in working paper preparation. The following examples may be helpful.

- Whenever possible, have the client's employees prepare schedules and analyses.
- Use of a detailed audit program may eliminate the need for lengthy comments in the working papers on the scope of audit procedures. (However, some believe that such comments are still necessary when a detailed program is used; this is a matter of individual firm judgment.)
- Analyze asset (or liability) accounts and their related expenses or income accounts on the same working paper. Examples include property, plant, and equipment, accumulated depreciation, and related depreciation expense; notes receivable, accrued interest receivable, and interest income; notes payable, accrued or prepaid interest, and interest expense; and accrued taxes and related provisions for tax expense.

- Avoid unnecessary computations. For example, if only the totals are meaningful and they can be tested by a single independent computation, verify the total and avoid unnecessarily checking details.
- Consider using carryforward analyses for accounts that tend to remain constant each year or vary only in accordance with a constant predetermined formula. Examples may include long-term assets and related depreciation or amortization such as plant, equipment, and intangibles; long-term debt with predetermined payment schedules; and capital stock.
- Consider using adding machine tapes instead of writing separate lists. Enter names or explanations on the tapes, when appropriate.

Storage

From a practical standpoint, the bulkiness of working papers often makes storing them quite expensive and inconvenient. However, the auditor must maintain working papers on file to support the audit conclusions. Working papers involving present

---

The Real World of Auditing

Management Assertion and Audit Evidence

Facts: An accounting firm was engaged to perform an audit for an auto parts retailer. At the beginning of the audit, a 50 percent shareholder informed the accounting firm that the company had $1 million worth of inventory stored off-premises in a warehouse owned by a company unrelated to the retailer or the shareholder. Confirmation forms were sent to the company that owned the warehouse to verify this inventory and were completed and returned. However, the accounting firm was unable to complete its audit report for six months, due to the poor condition of the client's records.

The day after the accounting firm issued the financial statements, the shareholder confessed that the inventory confirmations were fraudulent and that the inventory had never existed. He admitted this inventory manipulation was concocted to disguise a scheme to inflate the retailer's stock price. The accounting firm immediately demanded return of the statements and informed users of the financial statements that the statements were not reliable.

The retailing company's other shareholders filed suit against the accounting firm, claiming $500,000 in damages.

Issues: The shareholders alleged that the accounting firm was negligent in that it did not detect the overvalued inventory and thus did not discover the stock price inflating scheme. The accounting firm contended that its audit was performed in accordance with GAAS and that the withdrawal and disclaiming of the statements prevented any damage that would have resulted from the stock price fraud.

Resolution: This case was settled for $80,000. The settlement reflected the probable high cost of defending this case to conclusion.

Commentary: This case presented serious exposure to the accounting firm, but correct and timely actions taken by the firm prevented even greater exposure. By immediately withdrawing the statements and informing potential financial statement users of the unreliability of the statements, the accounting firm limited its liability exposure.

Source: G. Spellmire, W. Baliga, D. Winiarski, *Accountants Legal Liability Guide*, Harcourt Brace Jovanovich, 1990, pp. 3.52–3.53.

clients are, in general, retained permanently. Many auditing firms store working papers on computer disks or microfilm working papers after some period of time, say three years. There is substantial variation in the retention periods used from firm to firm. Working papers should be kept for as long as a potential legal liability exists regarding the audit; thus, before adopting a retention policy, the firm should consult with its legal counsel.

Ownership

Working papers are the auditor's property, not the client's. Working papers are the auditor's evidence of the procedures performed and thus belong ethically to the auditor and are necessary for the auditor to support any legal questions regarding the quality of work performed. Although working papers often may be useful to the client, they are not a part of, nor are they a substitute for, the client's accounting records.

As noted in Chapter 2, Rule 301 of the Code of Professional Conduct requires the auditor to maintain the confidentiality of working papers. Thus, ordinarily the auditor may not reveal information compiled in the working papers without the client's express consent. However, as also noted in Chapter 2, the ethical rule regarding confidentiality of the working papers does not preclude the auditor from responding to a subpoena, a quality review, or an ethics inquiry. Unless declared privileged by statute, communications between the auditor and the client are not privileged.

Significant Terms

Analysis schedule A schedule that examines the activity in an account for a period of time.

Analytical procedures Evaluation of financial information made by a study of plausible relationships among both financial and nonfinancial data.

Audit program A detailed list of all procedures to be performed during an audit.

Confirmation A technique in which the auditor requests a written response from a specific third party about a particular item affecting the financial statements.

Current file The working paper file that includes information relevant to an audit client for a particular year.

Data interrelationships A type of evidence in which the auditor examines and compares relationships among financial or nonfinancial data.

Detailed schedules Schedules that indicate specific audit procedures that have been performed for a given account.

Documentation A type of audit evidence whereby the auditor examines documents to support an accounting transaction.

Inquiry A technique of asking questions to gather audit evidence.

Inspection A technique of gathering evidence by reading a document and comparing the information therein with other information known to the auditor or recorded in the accounts.

Lead schedule A schedule that details each account making up a major asset grouping.

Listing schedule A single list of all detailed items that make up a total, usually an ending balance.

Mathematical evidence Evidence obtained through the auditor's recalculations of the client's arithmetic computations.

Memorandum An audit schedule in which the auditor gives a written description of a situation or analyzes a situation and presents a conclusion.

Negative confirmation request A confirmation request in which the auditor asks the third party to respond only if the information is incorrect.

Observation A technique in which the auditor witnesses the activities of the client in order to gather evidence.

Outside documentation Documentation from outside parties such as confirmation replies that represent audit evidence.

Permanent file The working paper file that includes information of continuing relevance in performing recurring engagements for an audit client.

Physical evidence A type of evidence that the auditor can actually see.

Physical examination A technique of gathering physical evidence involving counting or inspecting assets that have a tangible existence.

Positive confirmation request A confirmation request in which the auditor asks the third party to respond whether or not the balance is correct.

Reasonableness tests Working papers that show the auditor's computations in determining whether or not an account balance appears to be reasonable.

Reconciliation A technique of gathering evidence by bringing two independent sets of records into agreement.

Reconciliation schedule A schedule that supports a specific account by matching the working trial balance total to another source.

Reperformance A technique of gathering evidence about the client's activities by redoing client activities involved in the accounting process and comparing the result with the client's result.

Representations by client personnel A type of evidence obtained by the auditor through inquiries of client personnel.

Representations by third parties A type of evidence obtained by the auditor through direct correspondence with individuals or entities other than the client.

Substantive tests Tests performed to determine if material dollar or disclosure misstatements exist in the financial statements.

Tests of balances Substantive audit tests performed directly on the ending balance in an account.

Tests of controls Tests directed toward the design or operation of an internal control structure policy or procedure to assess its effectiveness in preventing or detecting material misstatements in a financial statement assertion.

Tests of transactions Substantive tests or tests of controls that involve the auditor's examination of the documents and accounting records of the processing of a specific transaction.

Tick mark A symbol the auditor uses in the working papers to indicate that a specific procedure was performed.

Tracing A technique of gathering evidence by following the source documents to their recording in the accounting records.

Vouching A technique of gathering evidence about an item recorded in the accounting records by testing from the recorded item to supporting documentation.

Working papers The trial balances, checklists, programs, and other documentation that compose evidence that the auditor has performed the audit in conformity with generally accepted auditing standards.

Working trial balance A working paper that lists all accounts and balances from the general ledger.

Discussion Questions

5-1. What is the overall objective of an audit and how does an auditor go about meeting this overall objective?

5-2. What is the overall purpose of an audit program?

5-3. What are the primary objectives an audit program is designed to accomplish?

5-4. Identify and define the sources and types of audit evidence.

5-5. Why would observation be used by the auditor?

5-6. Why should confirmations be controlled by the auditor?

5-7. What is the difference between a positive and negative confirmation? Which is more reliable and why?

5-8. What is the primary limitation of evidence gathered by using mathematical evidence?

5-9. What is the primary limitation of evidence gathered by inquiries?

5-10. List and define the four major categories of tests of controls and substantive testing.

5-11. What are the ten fundamental techniques used to form the basis of the audit program?

5-12. What is the difference between observation and physical examination?

5-13. What is the main purpose of audit techniques?

5-14. What is an *audit procedure*?

5-15. Why would an auditor need to obtain an expert opinion on the physical examination of assets?

5-16. Explain why vouching is not a good test for the completeness assertion but tracing is.

Objective Questions

*5-17. Which of the following best describes the primary purpose of audit program procedures?
(1) To detect errors or irregularities.
(2) To comply with generally accepted accounting principles.
(3) To gather corroborative evidence.
(4) To verify the accuracy of account balances.

*5-18. Which of the following is ordinarily designed to detect possible material dollar misstatements on the financial statements?
(1) Tests of controls.
(2) Analytical procedures.
(3) Computer controls.
(4) Working paper review.

*5-19. Which of the following types of documentary evidence should the auditor consider to be the most reliable?
(1) A sales invoice issued by the client and supported by a delivery receipt from an outside trucker.
(2) Confirmation of an account payable balance mailed by and returned directly to the auditor.
(3) A check issued by the company and bearing the payee's endorsement, which is included with the bank statements mailed directly to the auditor.
(4) A working paper prepared by the client's controller and reviewed by the client's treasurer.

*5-20. How does the extent of substantive tests required to constitute sufficient evidential matter vary with the auditor's assessed level of control risk?
(1) Randomly.
(2) Disproportionately.
(3) Directly.
(4) Inversely.

---
*AICPA adapted.

*5-21. Which of the following is a substantive test that an auditor most likely would perform to verify the existence and valuation of recorded accounts payable?
  (1) Investigating the open purchase order file to ascertain that prenumbered purchase orders are used and accounted for.
  (2) Receiving the client's mail, unopened, for a reasonable period of time after the year-end to search for unrecorded vendor's invoices.
  (3) Vouching selected entries in the accounts payable subsidiary ledger to purchase orders and receiving reports.
  (4) Confirming accounts payable balances with known suppliers who have zero balances.

*5-22. In the context of an audit of financial statements, substantive tests are audit procedures that
  (1) may be eliminated under certain conditions. *(Wrong)*
  (2) are designed to discover significant subsequent events.
  (3) may be either tests of transactions, direct tests of financial balances, or analytical tests. *(Wrong)*
  (4) will increase proportionately with the auditor's assessed level of control risk.

*5-23. The third standard of fieldwork states that sufficient competent evidential matter may in part be obtained through inspection, observation, inquiries, and confirmations to afford a reasonable basis for an opinion regarding the financial statements. The evidential matter required by this standard may in part be obtained through
  (1) auditor working papers.
  (2) proper planning of the audit engagement.
  (3) analytical procedures.
  (4) tests of controls.

*5-24. Each of the following might, in itself, form a valid basis for an auditor to decide to omit a test *except* the
  (1) relative risk involved.
  (2) relationship between the cost of obtaining evidence and its usefulness.
  (3) difficulty and expense involved in testing a particular item.
  (4) assessed level of control risk.

*5-25. The following statements were made in a discussion of audit evidence between two CPAs. Which statement is not valid concerning evidential matter?
  (1) "I am seldom convinced beyond all doubt with respect to all aspects of the statement being examined."
  (2) "I would not undertake that procedure because at best the results would only be persuasive and I'm looking for convincing evidence."
  (3) "I evaluate the degree of risk involved in deciding the kind of evidence I will gather."
  (4) "I evaluate the usefulness of the evidence I can obtain against the cost to obtain it."

*5-26. The strongest criticism of the reliability of audit evidence that the auditor physically observes is that
  (1) the client may conceal items from the auditor.
  (2) the auditor may not be qualified to evaluate the items observed.
  (3) such evidence is too costly in relation to its reliability.
  (4) the observation must occur at a specific time, which is often difficult to arrange.

*5-27. Audit working papers are used to record the results of the auditor's evidence-gathering procedures. What should the auditor remember when preparing working papers?
  (1) Working papers should be kept on the client's premises so that the client can have access to them for reference purposes.
  (2) Working papers should be the primary support for the financial statements being audited.
  (3) Working papers should be considered a substitute for the client's accounting records.
  (4) Working papers should be designed to meet the circumstances and the auditor's needs on each audit.

---

*AICPA adapted.

*5-28. Although the quantity, type, and content of working papers will vary with the circumstances, the working papers generally would include which of the following?
(1) Copies of those client records examined by the auditor during the course of the audit.
(2) Evaluation of the efficiency and competence of the audit staff assistants by the partner responsible for the audit.
(3) Auditor's comments concerning the efficiency and competence of client management personnel.
(4) The auditing procedures followed and the testing performed in obtaining evidential matter.

*5-29. Which of the following eliminates voluminous details from the auditor's working trial balance by classifying and summarizing similar or related items?
(1) Account analyses.
(2) Supporting schedules.
(3) Control accounts.
(4) Lead schedules.

*5-30. The permanent (continuing) file of an auditor's working papers most likely would include copies of which of the following?
(1) Bank statements.
(2) Debt agreements.
(3) Lead schedules.
(4) Attorney's letters.

*5-31. With regard to the third general auditing standard requiring that due professional care be exercised in the performance of the audit and preparation of the report, due care in the matter of working papers requires that working paper
(1) format be neat and orderly and include both a permanent file and a general file.
(2) content be sufficient to provide support for the auditor's report, including the auditor's representation as to compliance with auditing standards.
(3) ownership be determined by the legal statutes of the state in which the auditor practices.
(4) preparation be the responsibility of assistant accountants whose work is reviewed by senior accountants, managers, and partners.

*5-32. Audit evidence can come in different forms with different degrees of persuasiveness. Which of the following is the *least* persuasive type of evidence?
(1) Documents mailed by third parties to the auditor.
(2) Correspondence between auditor and vendors.
(3) Sales invoices inspected by the auditor.
(4) Computations made by the auditor.

*5-33. Which of the following factors will *least* affect the independent auditor's judgment as to the quantity, type, and content of working papers desirable for a particular audit?
(1) Nature of the auditor's report.
(2) Nature of the financial statements, schedules, or other information upon which the auditor is reporting.
(3) Need for supervision and review.
(4) Number of personnel assigned to the audit.

*5-34. Audit evidence can come in different forms with different degrees of persuasiveness. Which of the following is the *least* persuasive type of evidence?
(1) Vendor's invoice.
(2) Bank statement obtained from the client.
(3) Calculations made by the auditor.
(4) Prenumbered client invoices.

---

*AICPA adapted.

*5-35. For what minimum period should audit working papers be retained by the independent CPA?
  (1) For the period during which the entity remains a client of the independent CPA.
  (2) For the period during which an auditor-client relationship exists, but not more than seven years.
  (3) For the statutory period within which legal action may be brought against the independent CPA.
  (4) For as long as the CPA is in public practice.

*5-36. During an audit, pertinent data are compiled and included in the audit working papers. The working papers primarily are considered to be
  (1) a client-owned record of conclusions reached by the auditors who performed the audit.
  (2) evidence supporting financial statements.
  (3) support for the auditor's representations as to compliance with generally accepted auditing standards.
  (4) a record to be used as a basis for the following year's audit.

*5-37. Which of the following statements is true regarding an auditor's working papers?
  (1) They should not be permitted to serve as a reference source for the client.
  (2) They should not contain critical comments concerning management.
  (3) They should show that the accounting records agree or reconcile with the financial statements.
  (4) They should be considered the primary support for the financial statements being audited.

*5-38. In general, which of the following statements is correct with respect to ownership, possession, or access to work papers prepared by a CPA firm in connection with an audit?
  (1) The work papers may be obtained by third parties when they appear to be relevant to issues raised in litigation.
  (2) The work papers are subject to the privileged communication rule which, in a majority of jurisdictions, prevents third-party access to the work papers.
  (3) The work papers are the property of the client after the client pays the fee.
  (4) The work papers must be retained by the CPA firm for a period of ten years.

Problems and Cases

*5-39. (Audit Program) The first generally accepted auditing standard of fieldwork requires, in part, that "the work be adequately planned." An effective tool that aids the auditor in adequately planning the work is an audit program.
  REQUIRED
  What is an audit program, and what purpose does it serve?

5-40. (Audit Program) Jonathan Doyle, CPA, thinks that he does not need to use an audit program because he has quite a bit of experience in conducting an audit. He feels that audit programs are only useful for auditors without much experience. However, his partner, Pat Adams, CPA, believes that every auditor should use an audit program.
  REQUIRED
  A. Who is right about the use of an audit program?
  B. List the reasons for your answer and provide appropriate citations to relevant authoritative literature.

*AICPA adapted.

*5-41. (Concept of Evidence) In the audit of financial statements, the auditor is concerned with the examination and accumulation of accounting evidence.

REQUIRED

A. What is the objective of the auditor's examination and accumulation of accounting evidence during the course of the audit?

B. The source of the accounting evidence is of primary importance in the auditor's evaluation of its quality. Accounting evidence may be classified according to source. For example, one class originates within the client's organization, passes through the hands of third parties, and returns to the client, where it may be examined by the auditor. List the classifications of accounting evidence according to source, briefly discussing the effect of the source on the reliability of the evidence.

5-42. (Types of Evidence) Listed below are a variety of audit procedures:

1. Counted cash on hand.
2. Scanned accounts receivable subsidiary ledger for credit balances.
3. Asked the client questions about the internal control structure.
4. Received letter from client's attorney stating that the attorney was not aware of any lawsuits.
5. Computed gross margin and compared to prior years.
6. Examined sales document to support sales journal entry.
7. Reviewed next year's invoices to see if any invoices that related to current year expenses were paid but not recorded.
8. Watched client count ending inventory.
9. Verified the client's computation of inventory by multiplying quantity times price.
10. Took beginning balance in equipment account, added debits and subtracted credits to verify ending balance.
11. Stood beside mailroom clerk to determine whether clerk made listing of all cash receipts in incoming mail.
12. Supported repairs expense by examining invoices.
13. Compared utilities expense to utilities expense for prior years.
14. Received letter from a public warehouse verifying that company had goods stored in the warehouse.
15. Examined equipment purchased during the year.
16. Compared bad debts expense to credit sales.
17. Added sales journal column to see if totals were correct.
18. Obtained written reply from a customer stating that he owed company for goods purchased.
19. Examined minutes of board of directors to support payment of dividends.
20. Discussed with credit manager collectibility of accounts receivable.

REQUIRED

For each audit procedure above, clarify each item as one of the following sources or types of evidence.

A. Physical evidence.
B. Representations by third parties.
C. Mathematical evidence.
D. Documentation.
E. Representations by client personnel.
F. Data interrelationships.

5-43. (Types of Evidence) Listed below are several types of documentation examined by the auditor.

1. Canceled checks.
2. Lease agreements.
3. Sales invoices.
4. Receiving reports.

---

5. Minutes of the board of directors.
6. Notes receivable.
7. Bank statements.
8. Payroll time cards.
9. General ledger.
10. Remittance advices.
11. Purchase orders.
12. Accounts receivable subsidiary ledger.

REQUIRED

A. Classify each document above as either internal or external.

B. Why is external documentation considered more reliable than internal documentation?

*5-44. (Confirmation) An auditor accumulates various kinds of evidence on which to base an opinion on the financial statements. Among this evidence are confirmations from third parties.

REQUIRED

A. What is an audit confirmation?

B. What characteristics should an audit confirmation possess if an auditor is to consider it as valid evidence?

*5-45. (Confirmation) You are the auditor of Star Manufacturing Company. You have obtained the following data:

■ A trial balance taken from the books of Star one month prior to year-end follows:

	Dr.	(Cr.)
Cash in bank	$ 87,000	
Trade accounts receivable	345,000	
Notes receivable	125,000	
Inventories	317,000	
Land	66,000	
Buildings, net	350,000	
Furniture, fixtures, and equipment, net	325,000	
Trade accounts payable		(235,000)
Deferred income taxes payable		(84,000)
Mortgages payable		(400,000)
Capital stock		(300,000)
Retained earnings		(510,000)
Sales		(3,130,000)
Cost of sales	2,300,000	
General and administrative expenses	622,000	
Legal and professional fees	3,000	
Interest expense	35,000	

■ No inventories are consigned either in or out.

■ All notes receivable are due from outsiders and held by Star.

REQUIRED

Which accounts should be confirmed with outside sources? Briefly describe by whom they should be confirmed and the information that should be confirmed. Organize your answer in the following format:

Account Name   From Whom Confirmed   Information to Be Confirmed

*AICPA adapted.

5-46. (Audit Procedures) The following are examples of audit procedures:

1. Reviewing the procedures for receiving and depositing cash receipts with the cashier.
2. Counting the inventory and recording this amount in the auditor's working papers.
3. Obtaining a letter from each of the client's banks stating the amount the client has on deposit and any amounts owed by the client to the bank.
4. Determining that recorded sales are supported by a sales invoice.
5. Obtaining a letter from the client's insurance company stating the amount of insurance coverage the client has with the company.
6. Examining a representative sample of inventory receiving reports to determine that they are properly recorded.
7. Comparing the actual repairs and maintenance expense with the budgeted amount.
8. Watching the client's personnel count inventory to determine if the client's control procedures are being followed.
9. Calculating the depreciation expense to determine if the client correctly calculated it for the financial statements.
10. Reading a lease agreement to ascertain that the client has properly recorded it as a capital lease.

REQUIRED

Classify each of the above procedures according to the following types of audit techniques: (1) physical examination, (2) confirmation, (3) vouching, (4) tracing, (5) reperformance, (6) observation, (7) reconciliation, (8) inquiry, (9) inspection, and (10) analytical procedure.

*5-47. (Audit Evidence) In their audit of financial statements, auditors must judge the validity of the audit evidence they obtain.

REQUIRED

A. In the course of their audit, auditors ask many questions of client officers and employees.
   (1) Describe the factors that auditors should consider in evaluating oral evidence provided by client officers and employees.
   (2) Discuss the validity and limitations of oral evidence.
B. An auditor may include computation of various balance sheet and operating ratios for comparison to prior years and industry averages. Discuss the validity and limitations of ratio analysis.
C. In connection with an audit of the financial statements of a manufacturing company, an auditor is observing the physical inventory of finished goods, which consists of expensive, highly complex electronic equipment. Discuss the validity and limitations of the audit evidence provided by this procedure.

*5-48. (Audit Objectives for Securities) Cate Kent, CPA, who is engaged in the audit of the financial statements of Bass Corporation for the year ended December 31, 19X5, is about to commence an audit of the noncurrent investment securities. Bass's records indicate that the company owns various bearer bonds, as well as 25% of the outstanding common stock of Commercial Industrial Inc. The various securities are at two locations as follows:

- Recently acquired securities are in the company's safe in the custody of the treasurer.
- All other securities are in the company's bank safe deposit box.

All of the securities in Bass's portfolio are actively traded in a broad market.

REQUIRED

A. What are the objectives of the examination of these noncurrent investment securities?
B. What audit procedures should be undertaken by Kent with respect to the examination of Bass's noncurrent investment securities?

5-49. (Audit Techniques) One major area of an audit is the examination of accounts receivable.

REQUIRED

List some of the audit techniques described in this chapter that could be applied to the examination of accounts receivable.

5-50. (Relating Assertions to Audit Objectives) The following audit objectives apply to the audit of accounts receivable and management assertions:

Audit Objectives	Management Assertions
a. No unrecorded receivables exist.	1. Existence or occurrence
b. Receivables have not been sold, discounted, or otherwise factored.	2. Completeness
c. An adequate provision exists for uncollectible accounts.	3. Rights and obligations
d. Receivables that are uncollectible have been written off.	4. Valuation
e. Sales cutoff prior to year-end is proper.	5. Presentation and disclosure
f. All accounts are expected to be collected within one year.	
g. All accounts arose from the normal course of business.	
h. Any agreement or condition that restricts the nature of trade receivables is known and disclosed.	
i. Sales cutoff after year-end is proper.	

(handwritten annotations: confidentiality; cut-off procedures; a. 2; b. 3 (ownership); c. 4; d. 4; e. 2 → completely recorded; f. 5 (noncurrent vs current); g. 5; h. 5; i. 1 → Sales Revenue complete? did it really occur?)

REQUIRED

Identify the most appropriate assertion for each specific audit objective.

5-51. (Classifying Audit Techniques) Listed below are a series of specific audit techniques or procedures performed during an audit.

1. Trace shipping documents to sales invoices and sales journal to determine that sales have been recorded.
2. Physically observe physical count of inventory.
3. Confirm customers' accounts receivable.
4. Examine sales invoices to see if initials of credit manager are present to indicate a credit file and credit approval.
5. Ask client if any liens exist on fixed assets.
6. Trace shipping documents to sales invoices to see if sales invoices were matched with shipping documents before being recorded in sales journal by clerk.
7. Verify pricing of items in inventory by checking against invoices.
8. Verify additions to fixed assets by checking against invoices and canceled checks.
9. Review charges to repairs and maintenance expense to determine if charges should have been capitalized by examining invoices.
10. Observe that responsibilities for custody of cash and accounting for cash are done by separate people.
11. For an audit of an electrical utility, obtain number of kilowatt hours used and multiply by authorized rates to determine that all revenues were recorded.

REQUIRED

For each of these audit techniques, complete the following:

Technique	Assertion	Type of Evidence	Purpose of Test	Type of Test

If a particular column is not applicable, write N/A.

*5-52. (Working Papers) The preparation of working papers is an integral part of an audit of financial statements. On a recurring audit, the auditor plans the current audit while reviewing audit programs and working papers from prior audits to determine their usefulness for the current audit.

---

*AICPA adapted.

REQUIRED

A. What are the purposes or functions of audit working papers?

B. What records may be included in audit working papers?

C. What factors affect the CPA's judgment of the type and content of the working papers for a particular audit?

5-53. (Preparation of Working Papers) An important part of every audit of financial statements is the preparation of audit working papers.

REQUIRED

A. Discuss the relationship of audit working papers to each of the standards of fieldwork.

B. You are instructing an inexperienced staff member, Lee Colquitt, on his first auditing assignment. He is to examine an account. An analysis of the account has been prepared by the client for inclusion in the audit working papers. Prepare a list of the comments, commentaries, and notations that Colquitt should make or have made on the account analysis to provide an adequate working paper as evidence of the audit. (Do not include a description of auditing procedures applicable to the account.)

5-54. (Working Paper Deficiencies) Examine the working paper for Toomers Corporation, shown in Figure 5–12, and state any deficiencies.

5-55. (Review of Working Papers) Auditors are in disagreement over whether or not the review notes made by a supervisor in performing a review of the working papers should be kept as a part of those working papers. Some auditors argue that keeping such review notes, which represent their supervisor's questions concerning audit procedures, is dangerous from the point of view of legal liability.

REQUIRED

In your opinion, should review notes be kept in the working papers or be destroyed?

*5-56. (Ownership of Working Papers) James Garold, CPA, was engaged for several years by the Bond Corporation to make annual audits. As a result of a change in ownership, the corporation discontinued the engagement of Garold and retained another firm of accountants. The Bond Corporation thereupon demanded that Garold surrender all working papers prepared by the accounting firm in making audits for the corporation. Garold refused on the grounds that the working papers were his property. The corporation brought legal action to recover the working papers.

REQUIRED

State briefly what the law is, in general, as to ownership of accountants' working papers.

5-57. (Working Papers and Accountant-Client Privilege) Ralph Sharp, CPA, has audited the Fargo Corporation for the past ten years. It was recently discovered that Fargo's top management has been engaged in some questionable financial activities since the last audited financial statements were issued.

Subsequently, Fargo was sued in state court by its major competitor, Nuggett, Inc. In addition, the SEC commenced an investigation against Fargo for possible violations of the federal securities laws. Both Nuggett and the SEC have subpoenaed all of Sharp's working papers relating to his audits of Fargo for the past ten years. There is no evidence either that Sharp did anything improper or that any questionable financial activities by Fargo occurred prior to this year.

Sharp estimates that the cost for his photocopying of all the work papers would be $25,000 (approximately one year's audit fee). Fargo has instructed Sharp not to turn over the working papers to anyone.

REQUIRED

Answer the following, setting forth reasons for any conclusions stated. You may want to refer to Chapter 2, Professional Ethics, before answering these questions.

---

*AICPA adapted.

Figure 5-12   **Working Paper for Toomers Corporation**

Analysis of Fixed Assets
Toomers Corp.
December 31, 19X7

	Beginning Balance 1-1-X7	Additions	Deletions	Ending Balance 12-31-X7
Balance 1-1-X7	12100			
Additions:				
19X6 Ford Pickup		9200 ✓		
Forklift - Serial No. X1721672		16305 Ⓐ		
19X4 Oldsmobile		14108 ✓		
Deletions:				
Forklift - Serial No. A1471716			14000 Ⓐ	
19X3 Chevy Pickup				
Sold for scrap			7100 ч	
Ending Balance 12-31-X7	12100	39613	21100	30613

Conclusion: "Account appears reasonable."

RDS
2/2/X8

✓ Examined
X Calculation tested
ч Traced cost to property ledger

Ⓐ Represents trade in:
   Net Book Value of
      old equipment   11100 -
   Cash Paid   5205 -
   Book Value- New Equipment 16305 -

A. If Sharp practices in a state that has a statutory accountant-client privilege, may the state's accountant-client privilege be successfully asserted to avoid turning over the working papers to the SEC?

B. Other than asserting an accountant-client privilege, what major defenses might Sharp raise against the SEC and Nuggett in order to resist turning over the subpoenaed working papers?

Audit Judgment Case

5-58. (Assertion and Audit Risk) Audit supervisor Benny Cranford has just met with the senior auditor on the Dyeco company engagement, Rick Tabor. Tabor was concerned that accounts payable had decreased significantly over last year's ending balance. Tabor asserted that the amount of accounts payable confirmation requests sent out should be increased significantly due to the material decrease. Tabor is concerned that all accounts payable are not recorded and that additional tests of the account are necessary. Cranford, under pressure to finish the engagement, makes the following statements to Tabor:

> Rick, we performed the same tests that were applied last year. The risk associated with the account is essentially the same and the balance is less material. In addition, we performed the same amount of work on controls this year as we did last year.

REQUIRED

You are consulted as partner in charge of the engagement. What action do you suggest? Explain.

Auditing Issues Case

5-59. KELCO MANUFACTURING CORPORATION

You are considering the audit work to be performed related to Kelco's accounts payable. A quick glance at the comparative balance sheet reveals a significant decrease in accounts payable from the previous year's balance. Kelco does business with more than 500 suppliers located throughout the United States. Kelco president Steve Cook has returned to you the following Internal Control questionnaire related to accounts payable:

Internal Control Questionnaire
Accounts Payable

	YES	NO	COMMENTS
1. Does the company maintain a voucher system?	✓		
2. Are vouchers approved by someone who maintains a supervisory position?	✓		
3. Are all purchases recorded in the voucher register before disbursement?		✓	*Sometimes*
4. Does the company maintain an accounts payable subsidiary ledger?	✓		
5. Is the accounts payable subsidiary ledger reconciled to the accounts payable control ledger?		✓	*Sometimes*
6. Are vendors monthly statements reconciled to the accounts payable subsidiary ledger?		✓	*Sometimes*
7. Are all vendor's invoices checked for proper pricing, extensions, footings and terms?		✓	*Sometimes*
8. Are all unmatched invoices, receiving reports, and purchase orders reviewed periodically?		✓	
9. Are supporting documents reviewed by signers of the check?	✓		
10. Are supporting documents marked canceled?	✓		*The controller cancels them*
11. Are checks mailed directly by person signing the check?		✓	*mailed by purchasing agent who maintains cash disbursements journal and Accounts Payable Documents*

REQUIRED

1. What assertions would you be primarily concerned with related to accounts payable?
2. What types of audit procedures might you use to reduce the risk of a material misstatement in accounts payable to an acceptable low level?

Chapter *6*

Consideration of the Internal Control Structure

Learning Objectives

- Describe the internal control structure and its effect on the audit.

- Explain the requirements for an auditor's consideration of the internal control structure in an audit.

- Define tests of controls and explain how an auditor uses them to assess control risk.

- Explain the requirements for the auditor's communication of reportable conditions in the internal control structure.

For the last eight years, internal control has been a subject of widespread interest and vigorous debate. External and internal auditors, financial statement preparers, professional associations, and legislative and regulatory bodies have been intensely interested in several aspects of internal control: (1) what constitutes effective internal control, (2) the relationship of internal control to reliable financial reporting, and (3) the role of internal control in an effective financial statement audit strategy.

Although a summary of the events of the last eight years concerning internal control is well beyond the scope of this chapter, a brief discussion of two important documents will provide the necessary perspective about internal control for the remainder of the textbook.

In 1988, the AICPA issued *SAS No. 55, Consideration of the Internal Control Structure in a Financial Statement Audit* (AU 319). That standard defined and described the elements of an effective internal control structure for purposes of a financial statement audit and explained how independent CPAs considered that structure when they audited financial statements.

In 1992, The Committee of Sponsoring Organizations of the Treadway Commission (COSO) issued its report, *Internal Control—Integrated Framework*. This report provided a common internal control framework designed to satisfy the needs of all groups concerned with internal control: entity managements, external and internal auditors, chief financial officers, management accountants, and legislators and regulators. It also established standards or criteria against which internal control can be evaluated.

The COSO report has received widespread acceptance among the groups previously mentioned. Managements and internal audit departments of numerous profit and nonprofit entities are using it to implement and evaluate internal control. Legislative and regulatory bodies have cited the COSO report and in laws and regulations. External auditors have adopted the COSO report in their professional standards by recently revising *SAS No. 55* to incorporate the COSO criteria. Because *SAS No. 55* is the primary professional standard interpreting the second standard of fieldwork, the COSO report has had a prominent effect on auditing standards. ■

Sources: Thomas P. Kelley, "The COSO Report: Challenge and Counterchallenge," *Journal of Accountancy*, February 1993, pp. 10–18; AICPA Professional Standards: AU 319, Consideration of the Internal Control Structure in a Financial Statement Audit.

The second standard of fieldwork states that

> A sufficient understanding of the internal control structure is to be obtained to plan the audit and to determine the nature, timing, and extent of tests to be performed.

SAS No. 55 defines **internal control structure** as a process, effected by an entity's board of directors, management, and other personnel, designed to provide reasonable assurance regarding the achievement of objectives in the following categories: (1) reliability of financial reporting, (2) compliance with applicable laws and regulations, and (3) effectiveness and efficiency of operations.

The internal control structure consists of policies and procedures established to provide reasonable assurance of achieving each of the three objectives listed. These policies and procedures are means of controlling the entity's activities to help ensure that they accomplish the desired objectives.

An internal control structure may include a wide variety of specific objectives and related policies and procedures. For example, a manufacturing company may establish certain policies and procedures to control the quality of its products, to acquire raw materials at the lowest possible prices, to motivate its employees, to participate in the social development of the community in which it operates, or to avoid making credit sales to customers who are unlikely to pay. Although the internal control structure usually pertains to numerous different entity objectives, many of its policies and procedures are often relevant to an audit of an entity's financial statements.

An entity's internal control structure policies and procedures can be relevant to an audit in two ways. First, they may pertain to the entity's objective of preparing financial statements for external purposes that are fairly presented in conformity with generally accepted accounting principles. For example, an entity may establish a specific policy to help ensure that all goods shipped to customers are recorded as sales. Such a policy addresses the completeness assertion for revenue. Second, they may pertain to data the auditor uses to apply auditing procedures. For example, an internal control structure policy may help ensure that nonfinancial data, such as accurate production statistics, are generated. An auditor, in turn, may use these production statistics as data in an analytical procedure.

In this chapter, the components of an internal control structure are examined and the auditor's responsibility to consider the internal control structure under the second standard of fieldwork is explained (see Figure 6–1). Chapter 7 discusses the effect of a computer environment on the internal control structure and the auditing process. The application of the auditor's consideration of the internal control structure to an audit engagement is discussed in Chapters 13 through 18.

Components of an Internal Control Structure

An entity's internal control structure consists of five components:

- The control environment
- Risk assessment
- Control activities
- Information processing and communication
- Monitoring

Figure 6-1

Consideration of the Internal Control Structure in a Financial Statement Audit

Why & How Auditors

What makes up Internal Control.

↓ Components

Management's responsibility.
Overall Environment.

Centralized vs. decentralized.

Obtain sufficient understanding to plan the audit, recognizing it necessary
(a) to identify the types of potential material misstatements,
(b) to consider factors that affect the risk of material misstatement, and
(c) to design effective substantive tests.

Obtain understanding of the design of relevant policies and procedures and whether they have been placed in operation for the

- Control Environment

- Risk Assessment

How do they assess? Actual procedures they follow

Control Acivities

- Information and Communication

- Monitoring

Document the understanding of the internal control structure obtained to plan the audit.

The form and extent of documentation is influenced by entity's size and complexity and nature of internal control structure.

For some assertions, the auditor may assess control risk at the maximum level because it may be more effective or efficient to do so.

Assess the contol risk.

For the other assertions, the auditor may desire an assessed level of control risk that is less than the maximum. For these asserstions,

(A)

(1) consider policies and procedures relevant to specific assertions.
(2) consider results of any test of controls to evaluate the effectiveness of design and operation of policies and procedures in preventing or detecting material misstatements in assertions.

Results of procedures performed to obtain understanding may be considered tests of controls if they provide sufficient evidential matter about effectiveness of design and operation.

The results of the procedures performed may support an assessed level of control risk that is less than maximum for these assertions.

Figure 6–1   *continued*

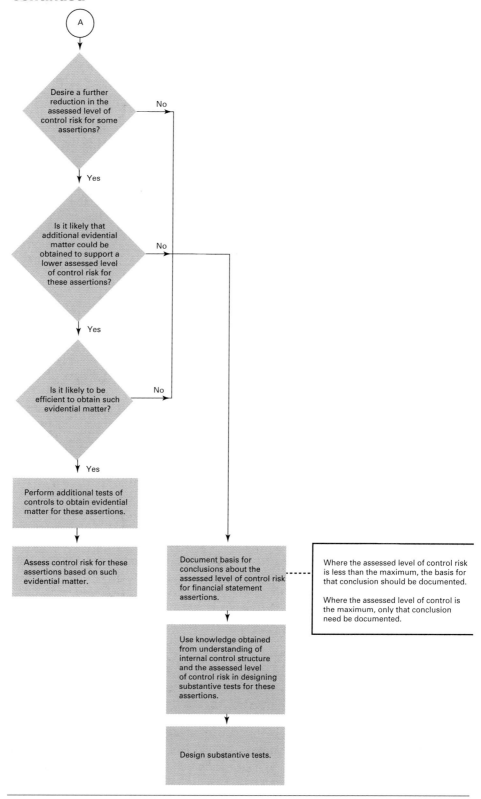

The policies and procedures that an entity establishes within these five components can have a significant direct effect on how the auditor plans and performs the audit.

- First, they provide an important source of information about the types and risks of potential material misstatements—including management misrepresentations—that could occur in financial statement assertions.
- Second, they are a primary source of information about the specific processes, methods, records, and reports the entity uses to prepare its financial statements.

Both types of information are important to auditors in determining the specific auditing procedures to perform. Although the five classifications may be somewhat arbitrary, they are helpful in discussing the nature of an internal control structure and how it is considered in an audit. The auditor's primary concern, however, is whether an internal control structure policy or procedure pertains to a financial statement assertion, not how it is classified.

Control Environment

The *control environment* sets an organization's tone by influencing the control consciousness of its people. As such, it reflects the overall attitude, awareness, and actions of the board of directors, management, employees, and others concerning the importance of control and the emphasis it is given in the entity. It is the foundation that provides the discipline and structure for all other internal control structure components.

The control environment consists of seven factors: (1) integrity and ethical values, (2) commitment to competence, (3) the board of directors or audit committee, (4) management's philosophy and operating style, (5) organizational structure, (6) assignment of authority and responsibility, and (7) human resource policies and practices.

Integrity and Ethical Values

Integrity and ethical values are management's value judgments, preferences, and management styles. They form the set of moral and behavioral standards that management adheres to. The effectiveness of an entity's internal control structure policies cannot rise above the integrity and ethical values of the management who creates, administers, and monitors them. Integrity and ethical behavior are the product of the entity's moral and behavioral standards, how they are communicated, and how they are reinforced in practice. They include management's actions to remove or reduce incentives and temptations that might prompt personnel to engage in dishonest, illegal, or unethical acts. They also include the communication of entity values and behavioral standards to personnel through policy statements, codes of conduct, and by example.

Auditors recognize that management's integrity and ethical values have a substantial effect on their ability to audit an entity. If an auditor believes that management lacks integrity and is unethical, the auditor would potentially need to question the authenticity of all records and documents obtained from the client and would require conclusive rather than persuasive evidence to corroborate all management representations. An audit conducted under such circumstances would be unreasonably costly and impractical.

Commitment to Competence

Competence is the knowledge and skills necessary to accomplish tasks that define an individual's job. Commitment to competence requires management to consider the competence levels necessary for particular jobs and to use employees with the appropriate skills and knowledge for that job.

The Board of Directors and Its Committees

The board of directors and its committees generally guide and oversee an entity. They may be responsible for monitoring the entity's operations and progress, for authorizing certain activities, for providing advice to management, and for overseeing the internal control structure and financial reporting. However, boards have different responsibilities and levels of involvement in various entities. Consequently, auditors are interested in knowing what responsibilities a board of directors has and how actively and effectively it operates. Factors that affect the effectiveness of the entity's board of directors or audit committee include its independence from management, the experience and stature of its members, the extent of its involvement and scrutiny of activities, the appropriateness of its actions, the degree to which difficult questions are raised and pursued with management, and its interaction with internal and external auditors.

audit committee / not employees of the co.

The audit committee of the board of directors plays a particularly significant role in overseeing an entity's accounting and financial reporting policies and practices. Although audit committees in different entities have differing responsibilities, in many cases they review the financial statements and the results of independent and internal audits, review management's selection of accounting policies, review external and internal auditors' recommendations concerning the internal control structure, and communicate financial and audit matters to the board of directors. An active and involved audit committee can significantly enhance the quality of an entity's financial reporting.

Management's Philosophy and Operating Style

Management's philosophy and operating style is simply its general approach to running the entity. One aspect of this factor is management's methods for taking and monitoring business risks. For example, management may be conservative or aggressive in taking business risks, and it may be careful or cavalier in evaluating the potential outcome of such risks and in monitoring the entity's progress after deciding on a specific action. Another aspect of philosophy and operating style involves how much emphasis management places on meeting budgetary, profit, and other financial and operating goals. In addition, management's attitude about financial reporting, such as the importance it places on presenting proper financial statements, is part of its philosophy and operating style.

Analyzing management's philosophy and operating style requires the auditor's careful judgment. A management's tendency to be aggressive in taking business risks or to emphasize the achievement of goals is not in itself a negative factor. In fact, many successful managements have this characteristic. However, a tendency to take risks recklessly, place undue emphasis on achieving goals, or not demonstrate concern for proper financial reporting are negative factors. Such conditions should heighten an auditor's concern about the possibility that management overrides its own internal control structure policies or procedures, or about its selection and application of generally accepted accounting principles, its judgments about accounting estimates, or its decisions about disclosures in the financial statements.

Management Philosophy and Operating Style

...Yet interviews with current and former executives, employees, competitors, suppliers and industry analysts depict a corporation run amok. Mr. Wiles's unrealistic sales targets and abusive management style created a pressure cooker that drove managers to cook the books or perish. And they did—booking shipments as sales, manipulating reserves and simply fabricating figures—to maintain the illusion of unbounded growth even after the industry was hit by a severe slump.

Mr. Wiles also turned up the heat under his lieutenants. Four times a year, he would summon as many as a hundred MiniScribe employees to Palm Springs for several days of intense "dash meetings" at which participants were force-fed his idiosyncratic management philosophy. At one of the first such meetings he attended, says a former division manager, Mr. Wiles demanded that two controllers stand, "and then he fired them on the spot, saying to everyone, 'That's just to show everyone I'm in control of the company.'"

Source: "Cooking the Books: How Pressure to Raise Sales Led MiniScribe to Falsify Numbers," *The Wall Street Journal,* September 11, 1989.

Organizational Structure

An entity's organizational structure is the form and nature of its subunits and the management functions and reporting relationships related to those subunits. It affects how authority and responsibility are assigned within the entity. In a centralized organizational structure, decision-making authority is concentrated in one or a few upper-level subunits. In a decentralized organizational structure, this authority is dispersed among many subunits. An entity may be organized in many different ways, no one of which is necessarily more appropriate than another. Auditors need an understanding of the entity's organizational structure, however, to give adequate consideration to the potential causes of misstatements in the entity's financial statements.

Assignment of Authority and Responsibility

The entity's personnel should have a clear understanding of the entity's objectives, how their individual actions interrelate and contribute to those objectives, and how and for what they will be held accountable. Management may use a variety of methods to promote this understanding, including assigning authority and responsibility for specific activities, establishing reporting relationships and authorization procedures, specifying and communicating appropriate business practices, and providing resources for carrying out duties. A well-defined and clearly understood assignment of authority and responsibility in an entity may diminish the auditor's concern about the likelihood of material misstatements in financial statements.

Human Resource Policies and Practices

An entity's ability to employ sufficient, competent personnel to accomplish its objectives is an important consideration in an audit. The personnel policies and practices an entity establishes bear significantly on this ability. Such policies and practices concern hiring, training, evaluating, promoting, and compensating employees, and giving them the resources necessary to perform their tasks. Auditors recognize that many of these policies and practices often affect the likelihood of misstatements in an entity's financial statements.

Risk Assessment

All entities—large or small, profit or nonprofit, service or manufacturing—encounter risks. Many of these risks, if not addressed, can cause misstatements in the entity's financial statements. Risk assessment, therefore, is an important component of the internal control structure. Risk assessment is an entity's identification, analysis, and management of risk relevant to the preparation of financial statements that are fairly presented in conformity with generally accepted accounting principles. An entity's risk assessment process considers external and internal events and circumstances that may adversely affect its ability to record, process, and report financial data consistent with management's assertions in the financial statements. Examples of such risks are new or revamped information systems, new technology, new product lines or activities, and new foreign operations.

Once risks are identified, management considers their significance, the likelihood of their occurrence, and how they should be managed. Auditors recognize that management's risk assessment process and their response to identified risks can significantly affect the likelihood of material misstatements occurring in financial statements.

Control Activities

Control activities are the policies and procedures that management establishes to address those risks that might prevent the entity from achieving its objectives. Control activities have various objectives and are applied at various organizational and functional levels within the entity. Although control activities may be performed either manually or by computer, with today's widespread use of computers, computerized controls are almost always used to some extent. (Chapter 7 discusses computer controls.)

Generally, control activities fall into the following categories:

■ *Performance Reviews* These reviews take a variety of forms and may be applied to diverse activities. Actual performance may be compared with budgets, forecasts, and prior periods, and various types of data—financial or nonfinancial—may be related to one another, such as in ratio analysis. Functional or activity performance also may be reviewed. For example, a bank's consumer loan manager may review reports by branch, region, and loan type for appropriate approvals and collections.

■ *Information Processing* These control activities are used to check the authorization, accuracy, and completeness of transactions. Because even the smallest entities generally use some form of computer information processing, these control activities are often performed by computer. For example, a computer program may check the validity of account numbers entered from invoices before accepting them for processing and account for the numerical sequence of the invoices. A customer's order may be accepted only after it has been referenced to an approved customer file and credit limit. A credit manager may review an aged trial balance of accounts receivable produced by computer analysis. The computer may be programmed to compare the total dollar value of products shipped to a customer with the total dollar amount billed to that customer.

■ *Physical Controls* These activities encompass the physical security of assets, including adequate safeguards over access to assets and records such as secured facilities, authorization for access to computer programs and data files, and the periodic counting of assets and comparison with amounts shown on control records.

■ *Segregation of Duties* Duties should be divided to reduce the possibility of any person both perpetrating and concealing errors or irregularities in the normal course of his or her duties. Management can segregate duties by assigning different people the responsibilities of authorizing transactions, recording transactions, and maintaining custody of assets. For example, an employee who receives cash should not authorize or record cash transactions. Figure 6-2 illustrates the three ways these responsibilities could be segregated.

Although control activities are classified as a separate component of the internal control structure, they are often integrated and embedded in the other four components (control environment, risk assessment, information and communication, and monitoring). In fact, effective and efficient design and operation of the internal control structure often require such integration. For example, the processing methods in the information system may require that certain control activities, such as recalculations or bank reconciliations, be recorded at specific points. Consequently, the practical design and application of an internal control structure will contain an overlap of control procedures with the other four components.

Information and Communication

This component encompasses both the information system used to produce financial information and the communication of that information. The information system relevant to financial reporting objectives, which includes the accounting system, consists of the methods and records established to identify, assemble, analyze, classify, record, and report entity transactions (as well as events and conditions) and to

| **Figure 6-2** | **Overview of Segregation of Duties** |

maintain accountability for the related assets and liabilities. For example, an entity may use a sales journal, an accounts receivable subsidiary ledger, customer invoices, prenumbered checks, and receiving reports as part of the records in its information system. In addition, it may specify methods of processing these documents, of making entries in the sales journal, and of posting to the subsidiary ledger as part of its information system.

The financial reporting information system records and files may be created and maintained either manually or by computer. For example, in some entities, the computer prepares sales invoices and automatically creates a sales journal computer file. In other entities, sales invoices and the sales journal may be prepared manually.

The financial reporting information system processing methods may also be computerized or manual. A wide variety of software is available for virtually all accounting applications, such as sales and accounts receivable, inventories, and payroll. Because computers have become more affordable over the last decade, most entities use computers for at least some of the accounting functions in their information systems.

An effective financial reporting information system attempts to establish methods and records that will accomplish the following objectives:

- *Identify and record all valid transactions.* This objective concerns the financial statement assertions of existence or occurrence and completeness.

- *Describe on a timely basis the transactions in sufficient detail to permit proper classification of transactions for financial reporting.* This objective concerns the financial statement assertion of presentation and disclosure.

- *Measure the value of transactions in a manner that permits recording their proper monetary value in the financial statements.* This objective concerns the financial statement assertion of valuation or allocation.

- *Determine the time period in which transactions occurred to permit recording of transactions in the proper accounting period.* This objective concerns the financial statement assertions of existence or occurrence and completeness.

- *Present properly the transactions and related disclosures in the financial statements.* This objective concerns the financial statement assertions of rights and obligations and presentation and disclosure.

Communication involves providing the information generated by the financial reporting information system to the appropriate parties in the entity on a timely basis. Communication, however, embraces the broader goal of providing a clear understanding of individual roles and responsibilities pertaining to the internal control structure over financial reporting. It includes the extent to which personnel understand how their activities in the financial reporting information system relate to the work of others and the means of reporting exceptions to an appropriate higher level within the entity.

Monitoring

An internal control structure can change over time. These changes can occur for various reasons. Entities may expand or contract their operations, new personnel may join the entity, or the effectiveness of training and supervision may vary. Management, therefore, needs to determine whether the internal control structure continues to be effective. Management does this by monitoring—the process of assessing the quality of the internal control structure's performance over time.

Monitoring can be done through ongoing activities or separate evaluations. Ongoing monitoring procedures are built into the normal recurring activities of an entity and include regular management and supervisory activities. For example, in some entities, internal auditors regularly provide information about the functioning of the internal control structure, focusing considerable attention on evaluating the design and operation of internal control.

Separate evaluations are periodic assessments of all or a portion of the internal control structure. They may be done by internal personnel or by an outside party, such as an independent CPA firm.

Management's Responsibility for the Internal Control Structure

An entity's management is responsible for establishing and maintaining an internal control structure. However, the specific internal control structure policies and procedures are influenced by the size of the entity, its organization and ownership characteristics, the nature of its business, the diversity and complexity of its operations, its methods of processing data, and the legal and regulatory requirements that apply to it.

Internal control structure policies and procedures that are important for one entity may not be important or even applicable for another. For example, an organizational structure that provides for formal delegation of authority may be significant to the control environment of a large entity. However, a small entity with effective owner/manager involvement may not need a formal organizational structure. Similarly, such an entity may not need extensive accounting procedures, sophisticated accounting records, or formal control procedures, such as a formal credit policy.

In establishing an internal control structure, management's goal is to provide reasonable assurance that an entity's objectives will be achieved. The concept of reasonable assurance involves two considerations. First, the cost of an entity's internal control structure should not exceed the expected benefits. Consequently, management may decide it is not reasonable to establish specific policies or procedures because their cost outweighs potential losses from not having established them.

Second, limitations exist in any internal control structure. Although the structure may be well designed, mistakes will still occur as a result of such factors as carelessness, faulty judgment, and communications breakdowns. In addition, internal control structure policies and procedures can be circumvented by collusion among persons inside and outside the company, including management. In many companies, especially smaller firms dominated by the owner/manager, management may override the control decisions of others. For example, management may dictate that selected expense transactions be recorded next year to improve current-period earnings.

Auditor's Understanding of the Internal Control Structure

The second standard of fieldwork requires an auditor to have a sufficient understanding of the five internal control structure components to plan the audit. This responsibility is indicated as the first step in the flowchart in Figure 6–1.

In the broad sense, an auditor's understanding must be sufficient to enable him or her to accomplish the following planning objectives:

1. Identify types of potential material misstatements that could occur in the financial statements.
2. Consider factors that affect the risk that such misstatements will occur.
3. Design substantive tests.   *How to design.*

This understanding includes knowledge of the design of relevant internal control structure policies and procedures and of whether they have been placed in operation by the entity. The term ***placed in operation*** means that the entity is using (or has installed) a specific policy or procedure—that is, it does not exist only in theory or on paper but is actually being used. *Placed in operation*, however, does not refer to the operating effectiveness of the policy or procedure. Operating effectiveness refers to whether the policy or procedure is applied in the appropriate manner, by the appropriate personnel, and at the appropriate time. Auditors are not required to evaluate ***operating effectiveness*** as part of their understanding.

Knowledge about Components of the Internal Control Structure

To accomplish the three planning objectives listed above, the auditor must have a sufficient ***understanding of the internal control structure***. Such an understanding is influenced by a number of factors. A primary factor is the knowledge requirement that *SAS No. 55* (AU 319) establishes for each of the five elements of the control structure. These requirements are summarized in the five boxes under the first step in Figure 6–1 and are discussed in the following sections.

Knowledge Needed about the Control Environment

The auditor should obtain sufficient knowledge of the control environment to understand the attitude, awareness, and actions of management and the board of directors concerning the seven control environment factors discussed earlier in this chapter. Obtaining this knowledge requires that the auditor gather information about each of the relevant control environment factors and then analyze that information to reach an understanding of management's consciousness of and concern for those factors and the specific actions management has taken in consideration of them.

For example, to gain an understanding of the organizational structure, the auditor could inquire about the entity's organization, observe how it is organized, and inspect documents pertaining to organizational structure. The auditor would use this information to form an understanding of how management has organized the entity and the emphasis it places on an effective organizational structure. Similarly, to understand an entity's human resource policies and practices, an auditor could inquire about the specific policies and procedures used, observe their application, and inspect documents pertaining to these methods.

Knowledge Needed about Risk Assessment

The auditor should obtain sufficient knowledge about the entity's risk assessment process to understand how management considers risks relevant to financial reporting objectives, estimates their significance, assesses the likelihood of their occurrence, and determines actions to address those risks.

Knowledge Needed about the Control Activities

Auditors generally need to obtain knowledge about the same control environment factors, risk assessment features, financial reporting information system and communication components, and monitoring activities for all audit clients. The control activities an auditor must know about to plan the audit, however, are likely to vary more from client to client and may require more judgment. As a result, auditing standards are not as specific in prescribing the knowledge to be obtained about control activities as they are for the other four internal control structure components.

In discussing the necessary understanding of control activities, *SAS No. 55* (AU 319.22) recognizes that as auditors obtain an understanding of the other four components, they are also likely to gain knowledge about some control activities. For example, in understanding the cash accounting system, auditors usually become aware of whether bank accounts are reconciled.

In some audits, the knowledge of the control activities acquired in understanding the other four components will be sufficient to meet the three planning objectives. In others, the auditor, for either of two reasons, must devote more attention to control activities to plan the audit. One reason is to plan effective substantive tests for specific assertions. For example, when auditing a nonprofit entity with significant cash donations, the auditor may not be able to design effective substantive tests for the completeness assertion without understanding the control activities related to cash receipts.

The second reason is to avoid planning an unreasonably costly audit. For example, the auditor typically will want to understand an entity's control activities for taking the physical inventory because it would be unreasonably costly to plan the audit without that understanding. Usually, however, the auditor will not need to know about control activities related to each account balance or transaction class component in the financial statements or to every assertion relevant to those components.

Knowledge Needed about the Financial Reporting Information System and Communication

SAS No. 55 (AU 319.21) requires the auditor to obtain sufficient knowledge of an entity's financial reporting information system to understand the following matters:

- *The classes of transactions in an entity's operations that are significant to its financial statements.* For example, the auditor would need to know the entity's major revenue sources and its major types of expenditures.

- *How an entity's transactions are initiated.* The auditor would want to know what action triggers the beginning of a transaction within the entity and who takes that action.

- *The accounting records, supporting documents, computer databases and files, and specific accounts in the financial statements involved in processing and reporting an entity's transactions.* Auditors need to know what accounts are affected by transactions and what source documents, journals, ledgers, and other records the entity uses to capture and preserve these transactions. For example, to plan an audit the auditor generally needs to know the specific source documents used, such as invoices, checks, and shipping reports; whether the documents are converted to computer files and the nature of any accounting-data computer files; the specific accounts used in both the general and subsidiary ledgers; and other relevant accounting reports, journals, and ledgers.

- *The accounting processing involved from the initiation of a transaction to its inclusion in the financial statements, including how the computer is used to process data.* This process concerns knowledge about the flow of documents and use of computer files that affect financial statement accounts and notes and the steps taken and computer programs used to process these documents and files. For example, an order is received by the sales department, where a customer order document is prepared and entered in the computer. The computer performs a credit check and prints a shipping document that the stockroom uses to release the goods; the document is then forwarded to shipping for delivery of goods; then the computer prepares an invoice to bill the customer and posts the transaction to the accounts receivable, revenue, inventory, and cost of goods sold accounts in the financial statements.

- *The financial reporting process used to prepare the entity's financial statements.* This process concerns how the financial statements are prepared. The auditor should understand such matters as the entity's adjusting entries; how it develops significant accruals, such as income tax accruals; and how it develops significant accounting estimates, such as depreciation and the allowance for uncollectible credit sales.

In addition, the auditor should obtain sufficient knowledge of the means the entity uses to communicate financial reporting roles and responsibilities and significant matters relating to financial reporting. These means may take many forms, such as policy manuals, accounting and financial reporting manuals, and memoranda, as well as orally and through the actions of management.

Monitoring

The auditor should obtain sufficient knowledge of the major types of activities the entity uses to monitor the internal control structure over financial reporting, including how those activities are used to initiate corrective actions. These activities may be embedded in the normal management and supervisory activities, performed by internal auditors, or done by parties outside the entity.

Other Factors Affecting Knowledge of the Internal Control Structure

In addition to the specific knowledge requirements set forth in *SAS No. 55* (AU 319), auditors are also guided by other factors in determining the level of understanding of the internal control structure necessary to plan the audit. Auditors consider their assessments of inherent risk, judgments about materiality, and the complexity and sophistication of the entity's operations and systems. As inherent risk increases, as amounts the auditor considers material become smaller, or as an entity's operations and systems become more complex, it becomes necessary to obtain additional knowledge of each element of the internal control structure to gain a sufficient understanding to plan the audit. For example, when auditing a large entity with a complex computerized financial reporting information system, the auditor ordinarily would devote more effort to understanding that system and control activities than when auditing a smaller company with a simple system.

Another factor influencing the level of understanding of the internal control structure needed to plan the audit is the knowledge about planning matters that the auditor has obtained or will obtain from other sources. An understanding of the entity's specific internal control structure is usually not the only source of knowledge about the types and risks of potential misstatements and about the design of substantive tests. This knowledge is also based on prior audits and on an understanding of the client's business and industry. Consequently, the level of understanding of the internal control structure will vary with the planning knowledge obtained from other sources.

Procedures to Obtain an Understanding of the Internal Control Structure

The knowledge that provides the auditor with an understanding of the internal control structure sufficient to plan the audit comes from several sources. The auditor's prior experience with the client may provide some of this knowledge. For example, based on prior audits, the auditor may have knowledge of the client's organizational structure, its major classes of transactions, and the control activities the client uses to safeguard physical access to its inventory.

Auditors also use a variety of procedures during the audit to obtain and update knowledge about the design of internal control structure policies and procedures and whether they have been placed in operation. One procedure is making inquiries of appropriate management, supervisory, and staff personnel within the client entity. For example, the auditor may ask about personnel policies and practices, the types of accounting documents and records used to process sales transactions, and what control activities exist for authorizing a credit sale.

Observing client activities and operations and inspecting documents and records are also commonly used procedures. An auditor may observe personnel performing certain functions to understand the organizational structure, accounting processing steps, or segregation of duties. An auditor may also inspect documentation describing the client's methods of assigning authority and responsibility, accounting system processing steps, or use of computer programs and data files. Both observation of activities and inspection of documentation can provide knowledge about the design of policies and procedures and whether they have been placed in operation.

Documentation of the Understanding

As noted in the second step in the flowchart in Figure 6–1, auditors are required to document in their work papers their understanding of the entity's internal control structure components obtained to plan the audit. The form and extent of this documentation is influenced by the size and complexity of the entity, as well as the nature of the entity's internal control structure. Consequently, auditors may use different means of documentation to satisfy this requirement. The most common methods are *narrative descriptions, flowcharts,* and *questionnaires.*

Narrative

A *narrative* is a written description or memorandum of the auditor's understanding of an internal control structure element. Such a narrative generally identifies the specific policies and procedures the auditor considered and describes how they are designed and used by the client. Narratives are often appropriate for documenting all or part of the internal control structure of a small, relatively simple entity, but they tend to become cumbersome as the size and sophistication of the client increases. An example of a portion of a narrative for the accounting system pertaining to sales transactions is shown in Figure 6–3.

Figure 6–3   **Partial Narrative of a Sales Accounting System**

SMR 11-5-X8

Columbia Products Co.
Description of Sales Transaction Accounting System

Sales Department

Customer order forms are prepared by sales representatives after obtaining an order from a customer. The customer order forms are assigned to sales representatives in prenumbered batches, prepared in numerical order, and the sequence is independently checked. For all new customers, a credit application is obtained. The customer order form and, if applicable, the credit application is routed to the credit department for approval.

Credit Department

The credit department reviews the customer's current credit status or credit application. For new customers a credit check is performed and the credit applications are filed alphabetically by customer in the customer credit file. If credit cannot be approved, the customer is notified of the reasons. If credit is approved, the approved customer order is sent to the order department.

Order Department

After receiving an approved customer order, the order department prepares a three-part sales order form. Sales order forms are prenumbered, prepared in numerical order, and checked independently for sequence. One copy of the sales order is sent to the customer to acknowledge receipt and approval of the order. Another copy of the sales order form is filed alphabetically by customer in the order department. The third copy of the sales order, along with the customer order, is forwarded to the shipping department.

Shipping Department

Upon receipt of the sales order and customer order, the shipping department obtains the merchandise from the stockroom and prepares a four-part bill of lading. Bills of lading are prenumbered, prepared in numerical order, and checked independently for sequence. One copy of the bill of lading is used as a packing slip and included with the merchandise shipped to the customer, and another copy is given to the carrier. The third copy of the bill of lading is filed numerically in the shipping department. The fourth copy of the bill of lading, along with a copy of the customer order and sales order, is sent to the accounts receivable department to use for customer billing.

Flowchart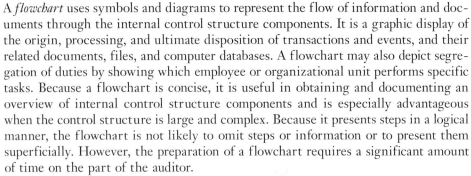

A *flowchart* uses symbols and diagrams to represent the flow of information and documents through the internal control structure components. It is a graphic display of the origin, processing, and ultimate disposition of transactions and events, and their related documents, files, and computer databases. A flowchart may also depict segregation of duties by showing which employee or organizational unit performs specific tasks. Because a flowchart is concise, it is useful in obtaining and documenting an overview of internal control structure components and is especially advantageous when the control structure is large and complex. Because it presents steps in a logical manner, the flowchart is not likely to omit steps or information or to present them superficially. However, the preparation of a flowchart requires a significant amount of time on the part of the auditor.

In an auditor's flowchart, the organizational unit or individual performing a function is typically shown in columns across the top of the chart, and the flow of documents is from left to right. The flowchart of the accounting system for sales transactions shown in Figure 6–4 illustrates the processing of a customer sales order through the sales department, order department, credit department, and shipping department. Although auditors are not required to use standard symbols, most auditors use symbols derived from the American National Standards Institute. The symbols that auditors most commonly use are shown in Figure 6–5.

Questionnaire

A *questionnaire* lists a series of questions about a specific internal control structure component that result in a "yes," "no," or "not applicable" response. The questions are usually grouped by category (for example, the internal audit function, cash receipts, or inventory) and help identify the existence and use of specific internal control structure policies and procedures. The questions are answered either through interviewing appropriate personnel, such as the controller, department heads, or other employees responsible for specific duties, or through observation of client activities or inspection of documents or records. An example of a questionnaire is shown in Figure 6–6.

Questionnaires can be an efficient and effective approach to documenting the auditor's understanding of the internal control structure. They provide a structured, organized, and comprehensive approach to documentation. Questionnaires are generally preprinted and are designed to meet the needs of a CPA firm in a variety of engagements. On the other hand, when using a questionnaire, the auditor should understand the meaning of each question, be aware of circumstances in which questions may not be appropriate, and realize that clients may provide expected ("yes") but incorrect answers rather than answers that may be unexpected but correct.

In many audits, auditors use a combination of narratives, flowcharts, and questionnaires to document their understanding of the internal control structure. For example, an auditor may use a narrative to document the understanding of management's philosophy and operating style, a flowchart to document the understanding of the payroll accounting system, and a questionnaire to document the understanding of control activities for the taking of the annual physical inventory.

Assessing Control Risk

SAS No. 47, Audit Risk and Materiality in Conducting an Audit (AU 312.20), requires the auditor to assess control risk. The auditor assesses this risk after obtaining an understanding of the internal control structure. Stated simply, ***control risk*** is the likelihood that a material misstatement will get through the internal control structure and into the financial statements (see Chapter 4).

As noted in Figure 6–1, *SAS No. 55* (AU 319.29) requires the auditor to assess control risk for financial statement assertions. This assessment is referred to as the ***assessed level of control risk***. The assessed level of control risk for an assertion may be anywhere along a range from maximum risk to minimum risk. It may be expressed in quantitative terms, such as percentages, or in nonquantitative terms, such as "maximum," "substantial," "moderate," or "low." Both means of expressing a control risk level involve considerable judgment by the auditor. Because of the variety and subjective nature of the factors involved in assessing this risk, precise, statistically valid quantitative measures are not possible.

The term ***maximum level of control risk*** means the greatest probability that the internal control structure will not prevent or detect a material misstatement in a financial statement assertion. Stated in quantitative terms, maximum level means a 100% likelihood that the internal control structure will not prevent or detect a material misstatement in a specific assertion.

As noted in the discussion of the audit risk model in Chapter 4, the assessed level of control risk has a significant effect on the auditor's design of substantive tests. As the assessed level of control risk for an assertion increases, the likelihood of a material misstatement in that assertion increases. The higher this likelihood, the more evidence the auditor needs from substantive tests to provide reasonable assurance that material misstatements will be detected and removed from the financial statements. Consequently, as the assessed level of control risk increases, the auditor may modify substantive tests in one or more of the following ways:

- Change the nature of substantive tests from a less effective to a more effective procedure, such as using tests directed toward independent parties outside the entity rather than tests directed toward parties or documentation within the entity.
- Change the timing of substantive tests, such as performing them at year-end rather than at an interim date.
- Change the extent of substantive tests, such as applying them to a larger number of items.

Determining the Assessed Level of Control Risk

The assessed level of control risk will be different for some assertions than for others. Assessing control risk at below the maximum level for an assertion involves two steps. First, the auditor must identify policies or procedures in one or more components of the internal control structure that affect a financial statement assertion. Second, the auditor must evaluate how effective those policies and procedures are in preventing or detecting material misstatements in that assertion.

① max not need to document

need to document its less than max to do the Test of control.

① design of control ② Operating Effectiveness of control → faster and cheaper.

reliable = Clean System

Figure 6-4 **Flowchart of Sales Transactions**

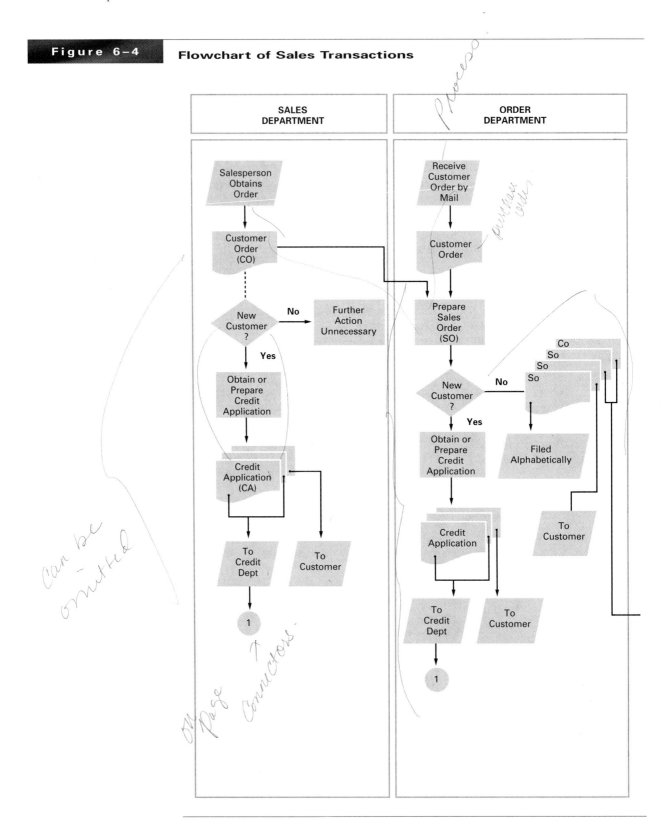

Figure 6–4   *continued*

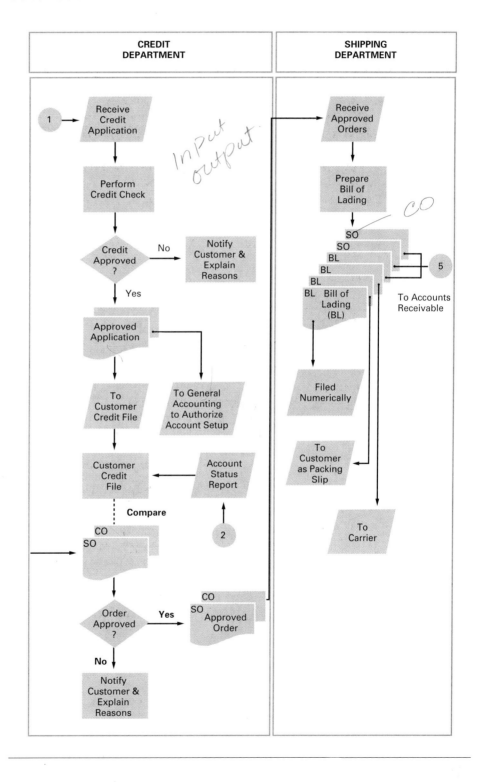

Figure 6-5   **Key to Flowchart Symbols**

Process   The performing of a primary operation that changes data from one form or location to another.

Input/Output   Indication of information entering or leaving the system.

Document   A printed document or report.

Offline File   Manually stored and retrieved information.

Decision   Indication of decision requiring different processes for "yes" and "no" answers.

Information Flow   Indication of direction of flow of information.

Connector   Indication of information exiting one part of chart but reentering at another point. Tied together by entering the same number or letter in both connectors.

Terminal   The entry or exit of accounting documents or information into or from the system.

Magnetic Tape   A file stored on magnetic tape.

Figure 6-6	**Internal Control Structure Questionnaire**

Accountant	C. Joseph
Date	10/16/X4

Company ___La Grange Electronics, Inc.___ Period ended ___Dec. 31, 19X4___

Branch, division, or subsidiary_____

		Answer		
Question	Yes	No	Remarks	
A - 1. Are internal auditors reasonably independent of the individuals or departments subject to audit?	N/A		Company has no internal auditing department. (M/L)	
2. Is the scope of internal audit work reasonably comprehensive?	N/A			
3. Do the internal auditors work from written programs?	N/A			
4. Are written reports issued by internal auditors on all work undertaken?	N/A			
5. Does the company follow the practice of accruing all income and expense through receivable or liability accounts so that the contra to a cash entry is always a balance sheet account?	✓		Unusual items are entered by the controller, via journal entry.	
6. Is it company policy for all employees to take annual vacations?	✓			
7. Is the work of persons on vacation performed by someone else during their absence?		✓	The plant and office close for two weeks. Jobs are not rotated. (M/L)	
8. Does the company have appropriate fidelity bond coverage?	✓			
9. Are all journal entries adequately explained and, in addition, approved by a responsible official?	✓			
			L	

*Note: In the case of a "No" answer, the "Remarks" column should (1) cross-reference either to the audit program step (or steps) that recognizes the deficiency or to the supporting permanent file memorandum on internal control structure policies and procedures that explains the mitigating circumstances or lack of importance of the item, and (2) indicate whether or not the item is to be included in the draft of the letter to management on reportable conditions.

Table 6-1	Relating the Internal Control Structure to Assertions for Accounts Receivable		

Internal Control Structure Policy or Procedure	Entity's Objective	Assertion
Credit manager approves credit for customer orders over $5,000.	Reduce losses from uncollectible credit sales.	Valuation
Credit manager follows up on customer complaints on monthly statements.	Identify erroneous amounts or transactions charged to customers.	Existence Valuation Completeness
Quantities shipped are reconciled to quantities billed.	Ensure that all goods shipped are billed and all goods billed are shipped.	Completeness Existence
Owner-manager reviews aged customer trial balance each quarter.	Identify potential collection problems and review makeup of receivables.	Valuation Presentation and Disclosure Rights and Obligations
Approved price lists are used for billing.	Ensure that customers are charged the correct price.	Valuation

Identifying Policies and Procedures Relevant to an Assertion

An internal control structure policy or procedure can be relevant to an assertion either because it has a pervasive effect on many assertions or because it has a specific effect on an individual assertion. Most of the policies and procedures in the control environment, risk assessment, and many of those in the financial reporting information system and monitoring have a widespread effect on many account balances and transaction classes, and therefore often affect many assertions. Many control activities, on the other hand, often have a specific effect on an individual assertion in a particular account balance or transaction class. Table 6–1 illustrates some internal control structure policies and procedures relevant to assertions for the accounts receivable account balance.

The relevance of an internal control structure policy or activity is also affected by whether it is directly or indirectly related to an assertion. The more directly related an internal control structure policy or activity is to an assertion, the more effective it tends to be in preventing or detecting material misstatements in that assertion. For example, a control activity that requires shipping documents to be matched with customer invoices is intended to ensure that all merchandise shipped to a customer is also billed to that customer. Consequently, it is directly related to the completeness assertion for revenue.

Some internal control structure policies or activities may not be intended to address directly a particular assertion but may, nevertheless, be related to it. For example, an entity may require a sales manager to review a summary of sales activity for specific stores by region for the primary purpose of monitoring sales performance. However, the procedure may also identify unrecorded sales and therefore have an indirect relationship to the completeness assertion for revenue.

Evaluating the Effectiveness of Policies and Procedures

After a policy or procedure affecting an assertion has been identified, the auditor must evaluate its effectiveness to be able to assess control risk at below the maximum level. To evaluate effectiveness, the auditor obtains evidence about two characteristics of the policy or procedure: (1) how the policy or procedure is *designed*, and (2) how it *operates*. Auditing procedures used to obtain such evidence are referred to as ***tests of controls***.

Tests of Controls for Design Effectiveness

Tests of controls to evaluate design effectiveness are concerned with whether the policy or procedure is suitably designed to prevent or detect material misstatements in specific financial statement assertions. To evaluate design, an auditor generally needs evidence about what action the policy or procedure requires, when it is to be done, and who is to do it. For example, the client may have established a procedure to ensure that all recorded sales actually occurred (the existence or occurrence assertion for revenue). To evaluate the design of that procedure, the auditor needs to know what actions and what entity personnel are involved in the procedure—for example, that the procedure requires (1) using prenumbered sales orders and shipping documents, (2) accounting for the numerical sequence of both types of documents once per month by an employee with no authorization or recording responsibilities, and (3) matching the recorded sales transactions with the related sales orders and shipping documents.

Tests of Controls for Operating Effectiveness

A well-designed internal control structure policy or procedure is not, by itself, sufficient to reduce control risk; it must also operate effectively. Therefore, to assess control risk at below the maximum level, the auditor must evaluate the operating effectiveness of internal control structure policies and procedures. To evaluate operating effectiveness, the auditor needs evidence about how the policy or procedure is actually applied, the consistency with which it is applied, and who applies it.

Procedures Used as Tests of Controls

Various audit procedures discussed in Chapter 5 can be used as tests of controls to evaluate either design effectiveness or operating effectiveness. These procedures include making inquiries of appropriate entity personnel, inspecting documents and records pertaining to the design or application of the policy or procedure, and observing the application of the policy or procedure. Another procedure used as a test of controls for operating effectiveness is reperformance of the application of the policy or procedure by the auditor.

Inquiries An auditor may obtain evidence about either design or operating effectiveness by making inquiries of appropriate entity personnel. For example, an auditor may ask about the organizational structure or the accounting system for purchases to obtain evidence about their design. An auditor may also ask who performs the bank reconciliation to obtain evidence about how the segregation of duties affects the operating effectiveness of that control procedure.

Inspecting Documents and Records Documents and records may provide evidence about design effectiveness by describing how a policy or procedure is intended to work. For example, the entity's accounting manuals may discuss in some detail the design of its accounting system, or its personnel manual may describe its personnel policies and practices. Inspecting documents and records can also provide evidence about operating effectiveness. An auditor may inspect sales orders for evidence that a credit approval procedure is operating, such as stamps or initials, or the auditor may inspect computer-generated exception reports pertaining to the processing of inventory transactions as evidence that the computer control procedure is operating.

Observing Entity Activities *Observation* is often used as a test of controls for design effectiveness. For example, an auditor may observe the processing of cash receipts to obtain evidence about how effectively the accounting system for cash receipts is designed. Observing the application of a policy or procedure also provides evidence about its operating effectiveness. For example, the auditor may observe who prepares the bank reconciliation to evaluate the effectiveness of segregation of duties or may observe client personnel taking a physical inventory to evaluate whether prescribed procedures are actually being followed.

Reperformance *Reperformance* occurs when the auditor redoes a policy or procedure to obtain evidence about whether it operated effectively. For example, if a control activity requires a clerk to check the calculations on sales invoices, the auditor may recompute those calculations to determine if the clerk effectively performed the control procedure.

Selecting Tests of Controls

No one specific test of controls is always necessary, applicable, or equally effective in every circumstance. For some internal control structure policies or procedures, a specific test of controls may address the effectiveness of both design and operation. For others, however, a combination of tests of controls may be necessary to evaluate the effectiveness of design and operation. A number of considerations affect the auditor's selection of the nature, timing, and extent of the tests of controls used to obtain evidence about design and operating effectiveness. These considerations include (1) type of evidence, (2) source of evidence, (3) timeliness of evidence, and (4) interrelationship of evidence.

Type of Evidence When documentation of design or operation is available for internal control structure policies and procedures, the auditor may decide to inspect it. This documentation may take such diverse forms as organization manuals, written codes of corporate conduct, accounting manuals or flowcharts of the accounting system, and documents that indicate that specific control procedures—for example, initialed invoices, receiving reports, and shipping documents and computer printouts of control exceptions detected by a computer program—were performed. On the other hand, documentation may not be available for or relevant to some policies or procedures. For example, documentation of design or operation may not exist for some factors in the control environment, such as assignment of authority and responsibility, or for some types of control activities, such as segregation of duties. In these circumstances an auditor may decide to use observation or reperformance tests of controls.

Source of Evidence   Tests of controls that allow the auditor to obtain evidence directly, such as observation, are generally more persuasive than tests of controls that provide evidence indirectly, such as inquiry. For example, evidence about the segregation of duties obtained by an auditor's observation of who performs a policy or procedure is generally more persuasive than evidence obtained by asking entity personnel who performs the policy or procedure. However, the presence of the auditor when making the observation may influence the way the policy or procedure is applied. It might not be performed the same way when the auditor is not present.

Timeliness of Evidence   Evidence provided by some tests of controls, such as observation, pertains only to the point in time at which the test was applied. Consequently, these tests may be insufficient to evaluate the effectiveness of design or operation for periods not subjected to observation. In these circumstances, the auditor may supplement these tests with other tests of controls capable of providing evidence pertaining to the entire audit period.

Auditors also consider evidence provided by tests of controls performed in prior audits or in an interim period when assessing control risk in the current audit. In determining how much weight to give such evidence, the auditor considers several factors, such as the significance of the assertion involved, the specific policy or procedure evaluated in the prior audits or interim period, the results of the tests of controls used to make those evaluations, and the length of time since those tests of controls were performed.

Interrelationship of Evidence   The nature, timing, and extent of tests of controls are influenced by the combined effect of the five components of an entity's internal control structure on specific assertions. For example, the auditor may conclude that the control environment is effective and thus may reduce the number of locations at which to observe inventory. If, however, the auditor evaluates specific control activities and concludes they are ineffective, he or she may question whether the control environment really is effective. Consequently, the auditor may reevaluate the conclusion about the control environment and decide to observe inventory at additional locations.

Sources of Evidence about Control Risk

Evidence about the effectiveness of the design and operation of an internal control structure policy or procedure may come from three sources during the audit: (1) the understanding of the internal control structure obtained to plan the audit, (2) any planned tests of controls the auditor performed while obtaining the understanding, and (3) any additional tests of controls performed after the understanding has been obtained.

Understanding of the Internal Control Structure

The knowledge obtained from the understanding of the internal control structure generally provides information the auditor can use in two ways in assessing control risk. First, for some assertions, the understanding may cause the auditor to conclude that policies or procedures are unlikely to pertain to an assertion or that they are unlikely to be effective. Even when potentially effective policies or procedures exist, the auditor may decide that it would be inefficient to evaluate their effectiveness. For these assertions, the auditor would assess control risk at the maximum level.

Second, for other assertions, the auditor's understanding of the internal control structure may result in an assessed level of control risk below the maximum level. Such an assessment can result, however, only if the understanding provides a basis for evaluating the effectiveness of the design and operation of a policy or procedure.

As discussed earlier in this chapter, the auditor is not required to evaluate the effectiveness of policies and procedures as part of an understanding of the internal control structure. He or she is only required to understand their design and determine that they have been placed in operation. However, in most audits, obtaining an understanding involves substantial audit effort. That audit effort often unintentionally provides considerable knowledge about the design and operating effectiveness of some policies and procedures in each of the five internal control structure components. Stated differently, many of the procedures the auditor performs to obtain the understanding qualify as tests of controls even though the auditor did not intentionally plan them as such.

For example, in obtaining an understanding of the control environment, the auditor may inquire about management's use of budgets and may inspect reports about the investigation of variances between budgeted and actual amounts. The auditor performs these procedures specifically to understand the design of budgeting policies and procedures and to determine whether they have been placed in operation. However, these same procedures also provide evidence about how effective the budgeting policies and procedures are in preventing or detecting material misstatements in the classification of expenses (the presentation and disclosure assertion for expenses). This evidence may be sufficient to support an assessed level of control risk below the maximum level for that assertion.

Planned Tests of Controls

When beginning an audit, the auditor usually has a preliminary audit strategy or audit approach that incorporates a **planned assessed level of control risk** for relevant assertions. The planned level of control risk is the anticipated level of control risk that the auditor plans to use in auditing a particular assertion. This level may be the maximum or some lower level and, of course, will vary among assertions.

The planned assessed level of control risk has a direct effect on the nature, timing, and extent of the tests of controls the auditor plans to perform. In most audit approaches, auditors expect to be able to obtain the evidence necessary to support an assessment of control risk at below the maximum level for at least some assertions, even though they plan to assess control risk at maximum for other assertions. Consequently, for audit efficiency reasons, the auditor may plan to perform specific tests of controls for assertions with a planned assessed level of control risk below maximum at the same time he or she obtains the understanding of the control structure. Stated differently, because the auditor knows that evidence will be necessary to support a below-maximum assessment of control risk for certain assertions, he or she performs tests of controls to obtain that evidence while obtaining the understanding of the control structure.

Further Reduction in Assessed Level of Control Risk

As shown in Figure 6–1, after using the evidence obtained from these two sources to assess control risk, the auditor may believe that a further reduction in control risk for some assertions could be supported by obtaining additional evidence. In deciding whether to obtain additional evidence, the auditor evaluates two factors. First, the auditor considers whether additional evidence is likely to be available—that is, whether additional tests of controls would provide additional evidence. Second, the auditor considers whether it would be efficient to perform these additional tests of controls. For those assertions for which the auditor performs additional tests of controls, he or she determines the assessed level of control risk that the results of the tests support. The auditor uses this assessed level of control risk in determining the nature, timing, and extent of substantive tests for those assertions. When the auditor concludes it is inefficient to perform additional tests of controls for specific assertions, he or she uses the assessed level of control risk based on the understanding of the internal control structure and any tests of controls performed concurrently with obtaining the understanding.

Forming a Conclusion about the Assessed Level of Control Risk

As discussed earlier in this chapter, each of the five internal control structure components can affect control risk for an assertion. The auditor's evaluation of the combined effect of these components on the level of control risk for a specific assertion is a subjective decision that requires the use of seasoned professional judgment.

Considering the Five Internal Control Structure Components

Many of the policies and procedures in the financial reporting information system and control activities components are often applied to specific transactions and account balances. As a result, they have an effect on the control risk for specific assertions that the auditor can evaluate in a fairly objective manner. For example, a computer program may match shipping documents with sales invoices to help ensure that all shipments are recorded as sales (the completeness assertion). By performing a test of controls to assess how frequently the computer matches these documents and to determine that exceptions are properly acted upon, the auditor can evaluate the procedure's effectiveness.

The policies and procedures in the control environment, risk assessment, and monitoring components, on the other hand, generally are not applied to specific assertions or to individual transactions or account balances. Instead, they often affect the assertions for many transactions classes and account balances. For several reasons, however, policies and procedures in these three components can reduce control risk for specific assertions.

First, control environment, risk assessment, and monitoring policies and procedures often act as checks on the effectiveness of the policies and procedures in the other two components of the internal control structure applied to the processing of individual transactions. For example, the internal audit department's monitoring of specific control activities for credit sales may reveal weaknesses caused by additions of customers or product lines. Actions may then be taken to modify the control activity and make it effective once again.

Second, control environment, risk assessment, and monitoring policies and procedures can decrease the types of potential misstatements that specific policies in the other two components are designed to prevent or detect. For example, hiring and training competent personnel; informing employees of their duties, authority, and responsibility; developing codes of conduct; and establishing an internal audit function all reduce the likelihood of material misstatements.

Third, the control environment, risk assessment, and monitoring components enhance the effectiveness of policies and procedures in the other two components. For example, careful attention to organizational structure can enhance the quality of segregation of duties; communication and assigning authority and responsibility can enhance the effectiveness of control activities pertaining to changes in computer programs or databases; and an audit committee review of the application of accounting principles, development of accounting estimates, and preparation of financial statement disclosures can enhance the effectiveness of control activities over financial reporting.

The quality of an entity's control environment, risk assessment, and monitoring components may influence the way in which an auditor considers the other two components in assessing control risk. When the control environment, risk assessment, and monitoring components are not considered to be particularly strong, the auditor's tests of controls are likely to concentrate heavily on the other two components—although he or she will have performed some tests of controls to evaluate the effectiveness of the control environment, risk assessment, and monitoring components.

Conversely, when the auditor believes the control, risk assessment, and monitoring components to be particularly effective, he or she may concentrate heavily on tests of controls for those components and restrict tests of controls for the other two components of the internal control structure in one or more of the following ways:

1. Not performing tests of controls at all of the entity's locations. Those with greater audit significance will be visited, but others will be selected on a representative basis.
2. Limiting tests of controls to only the policies and procedures in the financial reporting information system and control activities components that apply to significant transactions and accounts.
3. Performing most tests of the financial reporting information system and control activities at an interim date rather than at year-end.
4. Performing most tests of controls of policies and procedures that apply directly to individual transaction processing primarily to obtain evidence to support the effectiveness of the control environment, risk assessment, and monitoring components, rather than to assess their direct effect on a specific assertion.

Evaluating Operating Effectiveness

The operating effectiveness of a policy or procedure is generally gauged by the number of deviations from the policy or procedure that the auditor identifies through the tests of controls and the significance of those deviations. Although auditors ordinarily do not expect policies or procedures to operate perfectly—that is, without any deviations—they do form judgments about the number and significance of deviations that are acceptable for a specific assessed level of control risk. They compare the actual deviations identified by tests of controls with their judgment about acceptable deviations in forming a conclusion about the assessed level of control risk.

For example, if the auditor's inspection of evidence about the client's matching of sales invoices and shipping documents (test of controls) reveals many instances in which matching did not occur (deviations), the auditor is likely to assess control risk at the maximum or high level. On the other hand, if the auditor's tests of controls identify only a few deviations in this matching procedure, the auditor is likely to assess control risk at a low level. Similarly, if management only occasionally follows up on significant budget variances or customer complaints about monthly statements or does so in a cursory and perfunctory manner, the auditor will conclude that those policies or procedures do not operate effectively enough to reduce the assessed level of control risk below maximum for the related assertions.

An auditor may use an audit sampling application for some tests of controls. In these applications, the auditor uses the deviation rate in the sample to estimate the deviation rate in the population. The auditor then uses the estimated population deviation rate in forming a conclusion about the assessed level of control risk. Audit sampling applications for tests of controls are discussed in detail in Chapters 9 and 10.

Documenting the Assessed Level of Control Risk

SAS No. 55 (AU 319.39) requires the auditor to document the assessment of control risk. The specific matters to be documented depend on whether the assessed level of control risk for an assertion is at the maximum level or is below it. For those assertions for which the assessed level of control risk is below the maximum level, the auditor is required to document the basis for the conclusion that the effectiveness of the design and operation of the internal control structure policy or procedure supports that assessed level. The specific nature and extent of this documentation is not prescribed. However, documentation in the working papers describing the tests of controls the auditor performed, their results, and the auditor's evaluation of the effectiveness of the policies and procedures would be sufficient. *SAS No. 55* (AU 319.39) does not require the documentation to state what the specific assessed level of control risk is for assertions when it is below the maximum level. Furthermore, the SAS does not require the auditor to explain how the design of substantive tests was affected by the assessed level of control risk. However, some auditors use qualitative expressions of the assessed level of control risk (high, moderate, low) and describe its effect on substantive tests to facilitate the supervision and review of the audit.

For those assertions in which the control risk is assessed at the maximum level, the auditor is required only to document that the assessed level of control risk is the maximum level, not the reasons that conclusion was reached. Figure 6–7 illustrates one approach to documenting control risk assessments. However, many other alternatives could also be used.

Transaction Cycle Approach   *omit for now.*

Many auditors use a transaction cycle approach to obtaining an understanding of the internal control structure and assessing control risk. A ***transaction cycle*** is a grouping of related transactions by major areas of business activity within an entity. The specific cycles may vary from entity to entity. However, the classification of cycles shown in Table 6–2 is quite common. The relationship of these cycles to various transactions and to each other is shown in Figure 6–8.

Figure 6-7 **Documentation of Control Risk Assessments**

> | | |
> |---|---|
> | Accountant | |
> | Date | |
>
> **CONTROL RISK ASSESSMENTS**
>
> Client _____ Period ended _____
>
> We have assessed control risk at the maximum level for all financial statement assertions except those noted below. The basis for our conclusions that control risk is below maximum for the assertions noted is summarized below and detailed in related workpapers. Our substantive audit tests have been designed in consideration of the assessed level of control risk for the relevant assertions.
>
> | Financial Statement
Account | Working
Paper
Ref. |
> |---|---|
> | _____ Cash | |
> | _____ Marketable Securities | |
> | _____ Accounts Receivable | |
> | __X__ Inventory | E-6 |
>
> Control risk for the existence and valuation assertions is assessed at below maximum based on our tests of controls concerning the client's physical inventory counts and materials pricing.

A transaction cycle approach helps auditors understand the internal control structure and assess control risk. This approach allows the auditor to break down an entity's transactions and account balances into distinct categories called cycles. The auditor can then obtain an understanding of how the internal control structure relates to a specific cycle and can assess control risk for the assertions related to the transaction classes and account balances in that cycle. For example, to plan the audit of the revenue cycle, the auditor would obtain an understanding of the policies and procedures in the control environment, accounting system, and control procedures that relate to transactions involving the exchange of goods and services with customers and the collection of revenue in cash. The auditor would also assess control risk for the assertions related to the transactions and account balances in the revenue cycle, such as sales and accounts receivable.

Table 6-2	Classification of Transaction Cycles		
Transaction		**Cycle**	**Accounts**
1. Capital is received from investors and creditors and is invested.		Financing/investing cycle	Cash (balances) Property, plant, and equipment Investments Long-term debt Capital
2. Materials and labor are acquired and the resulting obligations are paid.		Expenditure cycle	Purchases Accounts payable Cash (disbursements)
3. Resources are held or converted into other products.		Conversion cycle	Inventory Payroll
4. Goods and services are sold to customers and payments are received.		Revenue cycle	Sales Accounts receivable Cash (receipts)

Figure 6-8   **Transaction Cycle Approach**

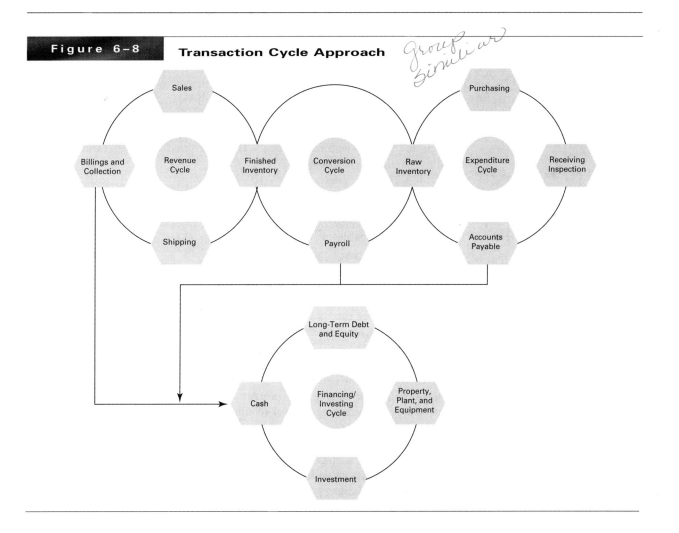

The transaction cycles shown in Table 6–2 will be used in Chapters 13–18 to discuss the auditor's consideration of the internal control structure for each cycle and the design of substantive tests for the related account balances.

Effect of an Internal Audit Function

As discussed in Chapter 1, internal auditors perform a variety of activities for an entity, including studying and evaluating internal control structure policies and procedures, auditing compliance with managerial policies, and reviewing operating practices to promote effectiveness. Usually, some of these activities are relevant to an audit of an entity's financial statements. *SAS No. 65, The Auditor's Consideration of the Internal Audit Function in an Audit of Financial Statements* (AU 322), establishes the auditor's responsibility to consider the internal audit function.

Because the internal audit function is part of monitoring, the independent auditor should obtain an understanding of that function sufficient to identify those internal audit activities that are relevant to audit planning. One type of relevant activity provides evidence about the design or effectiveness of internal control structure policies or procedures applicable to financial statement assertions. An internal audit activity may also be relevant if it provides direct evidence about potential misstatements in financial statement assertions, such as accounts receivable confirmation responses obtained by the internal audit function.

For some entities, the auditor may conclude that the internal audit function is not relevant to the audit or that it would be inefficient to give the internal audit function any additional consideration beyond the understanding phase. For other entities, however, the auditor may decide to give additional consideration to how the internal auditors' work might affect audit procedures.

Internal audit activities may influence the nature, timing, and extent of three major audit procedures categories:

1. The procedures needed by the independent auditor to obtain the understanding of the entity's internal control structure.
2. The tests of controls needed by the auditor to support the assessed level of control risk.
3. The substantive tests needed by the auditor to restrict detection risk to an acceptable level.

When the independent auditor concludes that the internal auditors' work may affect the audit in one or more of the above areas, he or she should assess the competence and objectivity of the internal audit function. Assessing competence includes considering factors such as the following:

- Internal auditors' education level, professional experience and certification, and continuing education.
- Internal audit policies; programs; procedures; and practices for assigning, supervising, and reviewing internal auditors' activities.
- Quality of internal audit working-paper documentation, reports, and recommendations, and the evaluation of internal auditors' performance.

Assessing objectivity includes considering factors such as (1) the organizational status of the internal auditor who is responsible for the internal audit function and

(2) the policies established to maintain internal auditors' objectivity ab[...] audited.

If, after assessing competence and objectivity, the independent auditor inte[...] use the internal auditors' work, the quality and effectiveness of that work shoul[...] evaluated. The independent auditor's evaluation should consider such factors as (1) th[...] scope of the internal auditors' work, (2) the adequacy of their audit programs and working papers, and (3) the appropriateness of their conclusions.

In making the evaluation, the independent auditor should test some of the internal auditors' work. *SAS No. 65* (AU 322) states that these tests can be accomplished by either (1) examining some of the controls, transactions, or balances that the internal auditors examined, or (2) examining similar controls, transactions, or balances not actually examined by the internal auditors.

The independent auditor may use the direct assistance of internal auditors in obtaining an understanding of the internal control structure or in performing tests of controls or substantive tests. For example, the independent auditor may ask the internal auditors to perform specific tests of controls or substantive tests. In such circumstances, *SAS No. 65* (AU 322) requires the independent auditor to not only consider the internal auditors' competence and objectivity, but also to supervise, review, evaluate, and test the internal auditors' work.

Finally, *SAS No. 65* (AU 322) offers an important warning to independent auditors who use internal auditors' work. The responsibility to report on the financial statements rests solely with the independent auditor. This responsibility cannot be shared with internal auditors. Because the auditor has the ultimate responsibility to express an opinion on the financial statements, judgments about assessments of inherent and control risks, the materiality of misstatements, the sufficiency of tests performed, the evaluation of significant accounting estimates, and other matters affecting the independent auditor's report should always be those of the independent auditor. Figure 6–9 presents a flowchart of *SAS No. 65* (AU 322).

Communication of Internal Control Structure Related Matters

Establishing and maintaining an internal control structure is an important management responsibility. However, the auditor may be able to assist the client by reporting significant deficiencies in the internal control structure identified during the audit and by making suggestions for corrective action.

Reportable Conditions

SAS No. 60, Communication of Internal Control Structure Related Matters Noted in an Audit (AU 325.02), defines a **reportable condition** as a matter coming to the auditor's attention that, in the auditor's judgment, must be communicated to the audit committee (or its equivalent) because it represents a significant deficiency in the design or operation of the internal control structure that could adversely affect the organization's ability to record, process, summarize, and report financial data consistent with the assertions of management in the financial statements.

vchart of *SAS No. 65* (AU 322)

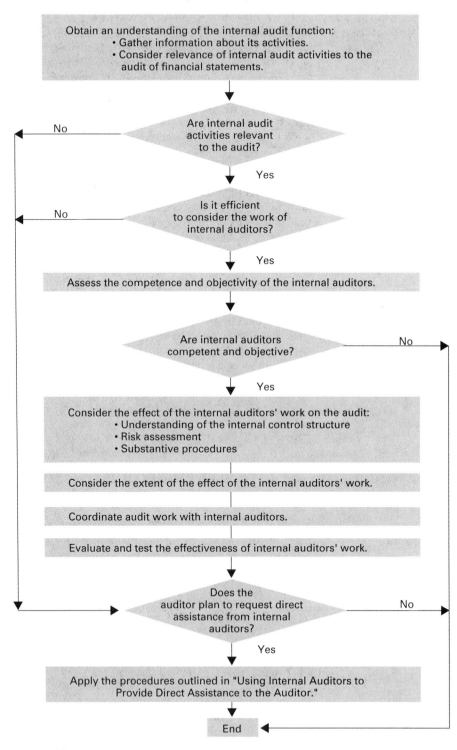

[handwritten margin note: don't have to id & material weaknesses.]

A reportable condition may involve any of the five internal control structure components. The following are examples of reportable conditions:

- Inadequate procedures for appropriately assessing and applying accounting principles.
- Evidence of failure to safeguard assets from loss, damage, or misappropriation.
- Evidence of the intentional override of the internal control structure by those in authority to the detriment of the overall objectives of the organization.
- Absence of a sufficient level of control consciousness within the organization.

Requirements for Communicating Reportable Conditions

SAS No. 60 (AU 325.02) requires the auditor to report to the audit committee or its equivalent reportable conditions that come to the auditor's attention during the audit. The equivalent of an audit committee in organizations that do not have one is an individual or group with equivalent authority and responsibility, such as the board of directors, the board of trustees, an owner in an owner-managed enterprise, or others who may have engaged the auditor. However, *SAS No. 60* acknowledges that management may already know of some reportable conditions and may have made a conscious decision to accept such deficiencies based on cost or other considerations. If the audit committee has acknowledged its understanding and consideration of these reportable conditions and the associated risks, the auditor may decide that the matter need not be reported.

Some reportable conditions may be of such magnitude as to be considered a material weakness. *SAS No. 60* (AU 325.15) defines a ***material weakness*** as a reportable condition in which the design or operation of the specific internal control structure elements does not reduce to a relatively low level the risk that errors or irregularities in amounts that would be material in relation to the financial statements being audited may occur and not be detected within a timely period by employees in the normal course of performing their assigned functions. Auditors are not required to identify separately and communicate material weaknesses. However, they may choose to do so or their client may ask them to do so.

The auditor may also report other matters concerning the internal control structure that are not reportable conditions, but he or she is not required to do so. In communicating reportable conditions, the auditor may choose, but is not required, to suggest corrective action for the client's consideration. The auditor may decide to do so to better serve the client.

An auditor is not required to perform audit procedures to search for reportable conditions. However, the auditor may become aware of reportable conditions while obtaining an understanding of the internal control structure, performing tests of controls, or performing substantive tests.

Communication Guidelines

An auditor may communicate reportable conditions either orally or in writing. Oral communication must be documented in the auditor's working papers. There is no specific guidance on the type and extent of documentation the working papers should include, but either a memorandum or notation on a control structure questionnaire indicating the reportable conditions communicated to the audit committee would be sufficient. In addition, the documentation should include the date of the communication and should indicate to whom the reportable conditions were communicated.

When communicating reportable conditions in writing, the report should include the following items:

- An indication that the purpose of the audit was to report on the financial statements and not to provide assurance on the internal control structure.
- A definition of reportable conditions.
- A statement that the report is intended solely for the information of the audit committee, management, others within the organization, and, when applicable, specific regulatory agencies that have requested copies of the report.
- A description of the reportable conditions noted.

The auditor may also wish to include additional statements regarding the inherent limitations of the internal control structure, the specific nature and extent of the consideration of the internal control structure during the audit, or other matters regarding the basis for the comments made. However, such statements are optional.

Because of the potential for a reader to misinterpret the limited assurance associated with such a statement, an auditor is prohibited from issuing a written report stating that no reportable conditions were noted. The auditor may, however, include a statement in a written report that no material weaknesses were identified during the audit.

The auditor may communicate reportable conditions during the course of the audit or after the audit is concluded. The decision when to communicate is affected by the relative significance of the conditions identified and the urgency of corrective follow-up action.

An example of a communication of reportable conditions is presented in Figure 6–10.

Foreign Corrupt Practices Act

One development that focused much attention on the internal control structure was the enactment of the Foreign Corrupt Practices Act (FCPA). The FCPA evolved from investigations and a public scandal in the early 1970s that revealed that nearly 450 American businesses had secretly made kickbacks, bribes, or other questionable payments to foreign officials to obtain or maintain business connections. In response to those investigations, Congress passed the Foreign Corrupt Practices Act of 1977. The two significant aspects of this act are its illegal foreign payments provisions and its accounting provisions.

Illegal Foreign Payments

The FCPA makes it a criminal offense for any American business to pay, promise to pay, or authorize payment of anything of value to foreign officials to obtain or maintain business relationships. A business enterprise violating these provisions may be fined up to $1 million, and individuals acting as representatives of the business may be fined up to $10,000, imprisoned for up to five years, or both. Many businesses have established written codes of conduct to address issues covered by the FCPA.

| Figure 6–10 | **Communication of Reportable Conditions Related to the Internal Control Structure** |

To the Audit Committee of Maplewood Products Corporation

In planning and performing our audit of the financial statements of Maplewood Products Corporation for the year ended December 31, 19X4, we considered its internal control structure in order to determine our auditing procedures for the purpose of expressing our opinion on the financial statements and not to provide assurance on the internal control structure. However, we noted certain matters involving the internal control structure and its operation that we consider to be reportable conditions under standards established by the American Institute of Certified Public Accountants. Reportable conditions involve matters coming to our attention relating to significant deficiencies in the design or operation of the internal control structure that, in our judgment, could adversely affect the organization's ability to record, process, summarize, and report financial data consistent with the assertions of management in the financial statements.

An inadequate segregation of duties exists for cash transactions that could adversely affect Maplewood Products Corporation's ability to record, process, summarize, and report cash sales, collections of accounts receivable, and cash disbursements. We also noted that reports comparing budgeted revenue and expenses with actual amounts are not used to follow up on and seek the reasons for significant variations between budgeted and actual amounts.

This report is intended solely for the information and use of the audit committee, management, and others within the organization.

Sincerely,

James Buffet

James Buffet
Seger & Buffet, CPAs

Accounting Provisions

Although the illegal payments provisions apply to essentially every American business, the accounting provisions apply only to registrants that file reports with the SEC as required by the Securities Exchange Act of 1934. For 1934 Act companies, however, all transactions are covered, not only transactions related to illegal foreign payments. Failure by publicly held companies to meet the accounting provisions of the FCPA violates the Securities Exchange Act of 1934.

Two major requirements are mandated by the accounting provisions of the FCPA. First, the FCPA requires registrants to establish and maintain books, records, and accounts that accurately reflect the transactions of the registrant. Second, it requires registrants to establish a system of internal accounting controls (a subset of the internal control structure) sufficient to meet the following four objectives:

- Transactions are executed in accordance with management's general or specific authorization.
- Transactions are recorded as necessary (1) to permit preparation of financial statements in conformity with generally accepted accounting principles or any other criteria applicable to such statements, and (2) to maintain accountability for assets.
- Access to assets is permitted only in accordance with management's authorization.
- The recorded accountability for assets is compared with the existing assets at reasonable intervals and appropriate action is taken with respect to any differences.

The accounting provisions of the FCPA amend the Securities Exchange Act of 1934 and are subject to SEC enforcement. An entity's management is responsible for compliance with the FCPA. No direct responsibilities are imposed on auditors.

Significant Terms

Assessed level of control risk The level of control risk the auditor uses in determining the detection risk to accept for a financial statement assertion and, accordingly, in determining the nature, timing, and extent of substantive tests. This level may vary along a range from maximum to minimum as long as the auditor has obtained evidential matter (performed tests of controls) to support any assessment below maximum.

Assessing control risk The process of evaluating the effectiveness of the design and operation of an entity's internal control structure policies and procedures in preventing or detecting misstatements in financial statement assertions.

Control activities The policies and procedures that management has established to help ensure that necessary actions are taken to address those risks that might prevent the entity from achieving its objectives.

Control environment The atmosphere that sets the tone of an organization by influencing the control consciousness of its people.

Financial reporting information system The methods and records established to identify, assemble, analyze, classify, record, and report an entity's transactions and to maintain accountability for the related assets and liabilities.

Internal control structure A process, effected by an entity's board of directors, management, and other personnel, designed to reasonably assure the achievement of objectives in the following categories: (1) reliability of financial reporting, (2) compliance with applicable laws and regulations, and (3) effectiveness and efficiency of operations.

Internal control structure policies and procedures relevant to an audit The policies and procedures in an entity's internal control structure that pertain to the entity's ability to record, process, summarize, and report financial data consistent with management's assertions embodied in the financial statements or that pertain to data the auditor uses to apply auditing procedures to financial statement assertions.

Material weakness in the internal control structure A reportable condition in which the design or operation of the specific internal control structure components does not reduce to a relatively low level the risk that errors or irregularities in amounts that would be material in relation to the financial statements being audited may occur and not be detected within a timely period by employees in the normal course of performing their assigned functions.

Maximum level of control risk The greatest probability that a material misstatement in a financial statement assertion will not be prevented or detected on a timely basis by an entity's internal control structure.

Monitoring The process of assessing the quality of the internal control structure's performance over time.

Operating effectiveness How an internal control structure policy or procedure was applied, the consistency with which it was applied, and by whom.

Placed in operation An entity is using an internal control structure policy or procedure.

Planned assessed level of control risk The anticipated level of control risk that the auditor plans to use in auditing a particular financial statement assertion. The auditor believes sufficient evidence can be obtained to support this level.

Reportable conditions Matters coming to the auditor's attention that, in his or her judgment, should be communicated to the audit committee because they represent significant deficiencies in the design or operation of the internal control structure that could adversely affect the organization's ability to record, process, summarize, and report financial data consistent with management's assertions in the financial statements.

Risk assessment An entity's identification, analysis, and management of risk relevant to the preparation of financial statements that are fairly presented in conformity with generally accepted accounting principles.

Tests of controls Tests directed toward the design or operation of an internal control structure policy or procedure to assess its effectiveness in preventing or detecting material misstatements in a financial statement assertion.

Transaction cycle Grouping of related transactions based upon the type of activity. One common classification of cycles includes the revenue, conversion, expenditure, and financing/investing cycles.

Understanding of the internal control structure The knowledge of the control environment, accounting system, and control procedures that the auditor believes is necessary to plan the audit.

Discussion Questions

6-1. What is an *internal control structure?*

6-2. What is the difference between management's and the auditor's responsibility for the internal control structure?

6-3. Describe the concept of *reasonable assurance* as it relates to the internal control structure. Give an example.

6-4. What are the five objectives of an accounting system?

6-5. What are the reasons that all entities would not have the same internal control structure policies and procedures?

6-6. Describe the two ways in which an internal control structure policy or procedure can be relevant to an audit of an entity's financial statements. Give an example of a specific policy or procedure for each way.

6-7. Describe some ways that duties can be segregated in an internal control structure. If duties are not segregated in these ways, what types of misstatements can occur in the entity's financial statements?

6-8. What are the minimum requirements for an auditor's consideration of the internal control structure in an audit?

6-9. What are the documentation requirements for the auditor's understanding of the internal control structure?

6-10. Describe the three basic methods of documenting the understanding of the internal control structure. Identify the advantages and disadvantages of each method.

6-11. What is the difference between *placed in operation* and *operating effectiveness?*

6-12. Describe the two major steps involved in assessing control risk.

6-13. What is *assessed level of control risk?* What is meant by the maximum level of control risk?

6-14. What is the relationship between the assessed level of control risk, detection risk, and the nature, timing, and extent of substantive tests?

6-15. What is the difference between the pervasive effect and the specific effect of an internal control structure policy or procedure on an assertion?

6-16. What is the objective of tests of controls? Give an example of such a test.

6-17. Identify and explain the four types of tests of controls. Are any of these tests required?

6-18. What are the limitations of each of the following procedures when used as a test of controls: inquiry, observation, inspection of documents, and reperformance?

6-19. How might a procedure performed to obtain an understanding of the internal control structure also be used as a test of controls?

6-20. What are the documentation requirements for the assessed level of control risk?

6-21. What are *reportable conditions* and what are the requirements for communicating them in an audit? Must an auditor design auditing procedures to identify reportable conditions? Why or why not?

6-22. How might the independent auditor use an entity's internal audit function to (1) assess control risk and (2) perform substantive tests? Give a specific example for each situation.

Objective Questions

6-23. An auditor assesses control risk to do which of the following?
   (1) Determine the tests of controls to perform.
   (2) Determine the nature, timing, and extent of substantive tests to perform.
   (3) Ascertain whether reportable conditions exist.
   (4) Ascertain whether there is an appropriate segregation of duties among employees.

6-24. Which of the following auditing procedures would not be considered a test of controls?
   (1) Observing preparation of the bank reconciliation.
   (2) Inquiring about the entity's organizational structure.
   (3) Inspecting customer order forms for the signature of the credit manager.
   (4) Confirming with the customer the amount owed to the client.

6-25. One of the company's internal control structure procedures requires that shipping documents be matched with customer invoices. To which of the following is that procedure relevant?
   (1) The completeness assertion for revenue.
   (2) The existence assertion for inventory.
   (3) The occurrence assertion for purchases.
   (4) The presentation and disclosure assertion for accounts receivable.

6-26. Tests of controls are primarily concerned with all but which of the following questions?
   (1) How were policies or procedures performed?

(2) Were the policies or procedures performed?

(3) How were the policies or procedures designed?

(4) Do policies or procedures exist?

6-27. Which of the following is not a reason an auditor should obtain an understanding of the elements of an entity's internal control structure when planning an audit?

(1) To identify types of potential misstatements that can occur.

(2) To design substantive tests.

(3) To consider the operating effectiveness of the internal control structure.

(4) To consider factors that affect the risk of material misstatements.

6-28. Which of the following audit techniques would most likely provide an auditor with the most assurance about the effectiveness of an internal control structure?

(1) Inquiry of client personnel.

(2) Recomputation of account balance amounts.

(3) Observations of client personnel.

(4) Confirmation with outside parties.

6-29. The sequence of steps in the auditor's consideration of the internal control structure is as follows:

(1) Obtain an understanding, design substantive tests, perform tests of controls, determine assessed level of control risk.

(2) Design substantive tests, obtain an understanding, perform tests of controls, determine assessed level of control risk.

(3) Obtain an understanding, perform tests of controls, determine assessed level of control risk, design substantive tests.

(4) Perform tests of controls, obtain an understanding, determine assessed level of control risk, design substantive tests.

6-30. Carolina Sales Corporation maintains a large, full-time internal audit staff that reports directly to the company president. Audit reports prepared by the internal auditors indicate that the internal control structure is suitably designed and operating effectively. The independent auditor will probably

(1) eliminate tests of controls.

(2) avoid duplicating work performed by the internal audit staff.

(3) use the work performed by the internal audit staff in assessing control risk.

(4) perform more substantive tests.

6-31. When control risk is assessed at the maximum level for all financial statement assertions, an auditor should document the auditor's

	Understanding of the entity's internal control structure elements	Conclusion that control risk is at the maximum level	Basis for concluding that control risk is at the maximum level
(1)	Yes	No	No
(2)	Yes	Yes	No
(3)	No	Yes	Yes
(4)	Yes	Yes	Yes

6-32. Which of the following statements is correct concerning an auditor's communication of internal control structure related matters (reportable conditions) noted in an audit?

(1) The auditor may issue a written report to the audit committee stating that no reportable conditions were noted during the audit.

(2) Reportable conditions should be recommunicated each year even if the audit committee has acknowledged its understanding of such deficiencies.

(3) Reportable conditions may not be communicated in a document that contains suggestions regarding activities that concern other topics, such as business strategies or administrative efficiencies.

(4) The auditor may choose to communicate significant internal control structure related matters either during the course of the audit or after the audit is concluded.

6-33. In a written report communicating reportable conditions an auditor should not

(1) state that no reportable conditions were noted.

(2) state that the purpose of the audit was to report on the financial statements and not to provide assurance on the internal control structure.

(3) define reportable conditions.

(4) state that no material weaknesses were noted.

6-34. When documenting the assessed level of control risk, the auditor should

(1) express the assessed level of control risk in either quantitative or qualitative terms for all assertions.

(2) state the basis for the conclusion when the assessed level of control risk is at the maximum level for an assertion.

(3) state the basis for the conclusion when the assessed level of control risk is below the maximum level for an assertion.

(4) describe how the planned substantive tests have been affected by the assessed level of control risk.

6-35. In determining the assessed level of control risk, which of the following statements is correct?

(1) The knowledge obtained from the understanding of the internal control structure cannot be used.

(2) The knowledge obtained about the internal control structure from prior audits can be used.

(3) The auditor evaluates the design of a policy and whether it has been placed in operation.

(4) Observation provides more persuasive evidence about the operating effectiveness of a policy or procedure than inspecting documentation.

6-36. The higher the assessed level of control risk for an assertion,

(1) the greater the likelihood that material misstatements will be in that assertion.

(2) the greater the acceptable detection risk will be for that assertion.

(3) the less evidence the auditor will need from substantive tests of that assertion.

(4) the less likely that reportable conditions will be identified for that assertion.

Problems and Cases

6-37. (Understanding the Internal Control Structure) Ernie Blanco, CPA, has been engaged to audit the financial statements of Somerset Company and is about to begin obtaining an understanding of Somerset's internal control structure.

REQUIRED

A. What are the reasons for obtaining an understanding of the internal control structure in an audit?

B. What sources of knowledge might Blanco use to obtain an understanding of Somerset's internal control structure?

6-38. (Understanding the Internal Control Structure) Generally accepted auditing standards require auditors to document their understanding of the internal control structure.

REQUIRED

A. Explain why this documentation requirement exists.

B. Give two advantages and two disadvantages of each of the following methods of documentation.

(1) Narrative.

(2) Questionnaire.

(3) Flowchart.

6-39. (Segregation of Duties) Listed below are some common responsibilities in an accounting system.
1. Receive cash from customers.
2. Deposit cash receipts in bank.
3. Authorize purchase orders.
4. Post cash receipts to accounts receivable ledger.
5. Perform bank reconciliations.
6. Sign payroll checks.
7. Prepare payroll journal.
8. Receive goods shipped to company.

REQUIRED

Assign each of the above responsibilities to one of four personnel to obtain the best segregation of duties possible. No person may be assigned more than two responsibilities.

6-40. (Understanding the Internal Control Structure) Rich White, CPA, has been assigned to make a presentation to the audit staff in his firm about obtaining an understanding of control activities in an audit. To prepare for his presentation, he has come to you with the following questions.

REQUIRED

Answer the following questions for White.

A. Do generally accepted auditing standards require the auditor to obtain an understanding of control activities in every audit? Explain your answer.

B. How does an auditor decide how much, if any, audit effort to devote to obtaining an understanding of control activities in an audit?

6-41. (Assessing Control Risk) Generally accepted auditing standards require an auditor to assess control risk in every audit.

REQUIRED

A. What is meant by "assessing control risk"?

B. Why is it necessary for the auditor to assess control risk?

C. Explain how the assessed level of control risk is related to (1) audit effectiveness and (2) audit efficiency.

6-42. (Assessing Control Risk) To assess control risk, an auditor performs tests of controls.

REQUIRED

A. What is the objective of tests of controls?

B. How do tests of controls differ from substantive tests?

C. Give three specific examples of tests of controls.

6-43. (Assessing Control Risk) Peg Fagan, CPA, is explaining to Mark Beasley, a new audit staff member, how to document the assessed level of control risk for financial statement assertions. Beasley is confused about the different documentation requirements for maximum and below maximum assessed levels of control risk.

REQUIRED

A. Explain the documentation requirements when the assessed level of control risk is at the maximum for an assertion.

B. Explain the documentation requirements when the assessed level of control risk is below the maximum for an assertion.

C. Must the auditor's work papers state the assessed level of control risk for each financial statement assertion in the client's financial statements? Explain your answer.

D. Why do generally accepted auditing standards establish documentation requirements for the assessed level of control risk?

6-44. (Communication of Reportable Conditions) *SAS No. 60, Communication of Internal Control Structure Related Matters Noted in an Audit*, requires the auditor to communicate to the audit committee or its equivalent reportable conditions noted in an audit.

REQUIRED

A. Does *SAS No. 60* require the auditor to design the audit specifically to search for reportable conditions?

[handwritten margin note: obtain understanding but done sometimes]

B. How does an auditor become aware of reportable conditions in the internal control structure?

C. Does *SAS No. 60* require the auditor to communicate reportable conditions in a specific form? *[handwritten: No, orally or writing]*

D. Does *SAS No. 60* require the auditor to identify which reportable conditions are material weaknesses in the internal control structure? *[handwritten: No]*

E. Does *SAS No. 60* require the auditor to submit suggestions for corrective action in the communication of reportable conditions? *[handwritten: No]*

F. What documentation, if any, are auditors required to make for the communication of reportable conditions? *[handwritten: Doc. work papers how they were communicated if verbally or copy of a letter.]*

Audit Judgment Case

6-45. AcquaGlass manufactures fiberglass sport and fishing boats. It has been operating for seven years and, after a sluggish start, has shown a modest profit for the last two years. Your CPA firm, Lake, Waters & Stream, has audited the company for the last five years and is planning the next year's audit (19X8). This year the entity will apply for a substantial bank loan to maintain its working capital. You have been assigned to evaluate the entity's control environment as it affects control risk and make recommendations about how the control environment should affect your audit. You and other staff members have collected the following information:

- AcquaGlass's senior management consists of four company officers: Buck Bass, president; Shirley Shore, vice-president of marketing; Taylor Tide, vice-president of Manufacturing; and Rubin Shore, vice-president of finance and controller. These four people, all in their early thirties, have been with the company since its inception. They were college classmates and formed the company a few years after graduation. Shirley and Rubin Shore are married to each other. They sold the business during the year, but all four have five-year contracts to remain as the management team. The purchase agreement sets an annual salary for each officer and also provides for a substantial bonus if the company achieves operating profits that exceed a stipulated amount. The new owners have no expertise in the pleasure boat industry, but do meet semiannually with the officers to discuss operations and performance.

- The four executives meet monthly to discuss the company's progress and analyze problems currently facing the company. Buck Bass makes the key management decisions after consulting with the other three officers. Financial information is frequently used at these meetings and Bass strongly believes that accurate and timely financial information is a key to successful management. They have asked your firm to sit in on one meeting each quarter to provide both financial and operating suggestions.

- During the last year, AcquaGlass began manufacturing and marketing a new boat it had been developing over the past three years. It has a unique hull design that allows quick acceleration and high speed—a perfect boat for waterskiing. Several of the company's competitors began developing a similar boat a year or so before AcquaGlass began its development project. However, the competitors abandoned their efforts and AcquaGlass's management believed it was in a strong market position as the sole source of this boat design. Orders have not yet met expectations, but management believes that there has not been sufficient time for marketing strategies to pay off. A substantial portion of the bank loan will be used to support the continued production and marketing of this new boat.

- The new owners have asked the officers to form a board of directors to oversee operations and financial reporting. The officers, however, believe that forming a board now would require substantial management attention, which is currently needed to successfully complete the new boat design. The owners and officers agreed to postpone forming such a board for two years.

- There is one other level of management below the four officers. This level consists of supervisors in the three major areas: marketing, manufacturing, and finance and accounting. These supervisors report to the respective vice-presidents. Mr. Bass sets budget goals and compares actual with budget each quarter. Variations from budget are investigated quarterly, but management does not have the time to document the results of these investigations.

- The chief accountant, Connie Wave, who reports to Rubin Shore, has been with AcquaGlass for 15 months. She is responsible for the entire accounting function, including preparation of financial statements, and is also responsible for establishing control over the finance function. Shore hired Wave immediately after her graduation from Waterford University and has delegated virtually all accounting responsibilities to her. This allows Shore time to manage the company's capital and negotiate bank loans.

- In past audits, both Buck Bass and Rubin Shore have been receptive to audit adjustment suggestions your firm has made, except for several accounting estimates, where they have maintained that their judgment and knowledge about the business qualifies them to make the final decisions about those matters. They have also been receptive to your firm's suggestions about improving internal control, although their priorities are in other areas. Generally, the accounting system has functioned satisfactorily, although the accounting staff seems to always be working long hours to get everything done.

- The officers have stated that they recognize the need to begin developing more written business policies and guidelines. However, the new boat effort does not currently permit them to devote time to that project.

- Employees in all major areas are hired after completing a job application form, taking an aptitude test, and undergoing a brief interview with the area supervisor. No formal training programs have been established, but supervisors and other employees do conduct on-the-job training. In the accounting area, four of the five accounting clerk positions have been filled three times each within the last two years. The most common reason for this turnover was employees leaving for jobs with better pay or with better employee benefits. Because some positions were vacant for as much as six months, Rubin Shore purchased an accounting software package eight months ago and three microcomputers to speed up the processing of accounting information and preparation of financial statements.

- Because boat sales are seasonal, the company has been exploring new uses for its fiberglass compounds. Shirley Shore is an avid snow skier and has suggested that the company manufacture skis. The addition of this product would provide sales virtually year-round. In addition, it would help retain members of the sales force, several of whom have left the company because they had difficulty earning adequate commissions during the winter months. Taylor Tide, VP of manufacturing, has held initial discussions with two companies who manufacture snow ski equipment to explore the possibility of merging with or buying out one of the companies. Buck Bass likes the idea, but has told Shore and Tide that the snow ski business is not within his expertise and he will leave the negotiating and ultimate decision about product line expansion up to them.

REQUIRED

Read and analyze the above information, then

A. describe the major conditions in each of the seven control environment elements for AcquaGlass.

B. identify at least five specific financial statement assertions, including the financial statement accounts they pertain to, and describe the effect that AcquaGlass's control environment has on control risk for those assertions.

Auditing Issues Case

6-46. KELCO MANUFACTURING COMPANY

You are about to obtain an understanding of the internal control structure of Kelco. You want to be very careful because this is your first audit engagement with Kelco. A particular area of concern relates to disbursements. You have just interviewed Steve Cook, president of Kelco, regarding the disbursement function. The following is a summary of your findings:

> The company has two departments, accounting (includes all administrative functions) and production. Request for purchases and purchase orders are prepared within each department of the company. One copy of the purchase order is retained within the department making the request, and one copy is sent to the vendor. Upon receipt of goods purchased, a receiving report is prepared by either the department head or his or her assistant. The receiving report is sent to the department requesting the goods or services. It is then filed. Purchase invoices are approved by the department heads. The production department sends approved purchase invoices to accounting. The accountants prepare checks and send them to Cook. He signs the checks and sends them back to the department heads. If Cook is unavailable to sign the checks, that is not a problem because the head of the accounting department is also authorized to sign on the company's operating account. The department heads then mail the checks to the vendors.

REQUIRED

1. List the reportable conditions in Kelco's internal control structure.
2. What recommendations do you have for the company?
3. Prepare a flowchart of Kelco's system which incorporates your recommendations.

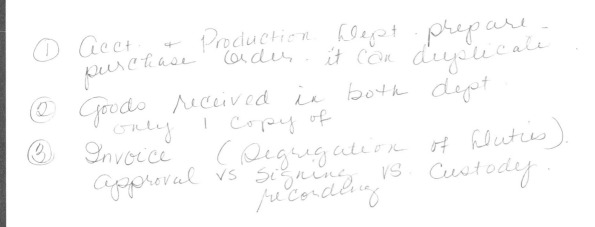

Weaknesses

④

① Acct. + Production Dept. prepare purchase order. it can duplicate.

② Goods received in both dept only 1 copy of

③ Invoice (Segregation of duties).
approval vs signing vs. custody.
recording

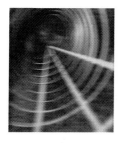

Chapter 7

The Computer Environment and the Internal Control Structure

Learning Objectives

- Identify characteristics of a computerized system that differ from a manual system.

- Describe the various types of computerized systems.

- Define the term *general controls* and give examples of these types of controls in a computerized environment.

- Define the term *application controls* and give examples of these types of controls in a computerized environment.

- Discuss the auditor's understanding of the internal control structure in a computerized environment.

- Describe four approaches an auditor can use to assess control risk in a computerized environment.

A study published in *The Journal of Accountancy* questioned the safety of data transmissions and reported some alarming results about the degree of involvement by auditors in assessing the internal audit role in data processing. Fifty percent of respondents stated that internal auditing was heavily involved in auditing the data processing function. However, only 16 percent of respondents cited heavy involvement in auditing the telecommunications of data.

Clearly, many auditors do not have an understanding of the methods of data transmission and their risks. Since 1990, computer hackers have been convicted of infiltrating numerous large multinational companies and accessing confidential financial information. Many companies have not properly equipped networks with safety devices or educated employees about the confidentiality of on-line files. The following are four recommendations designed to reduce the risk of transmission error and tampering:

- Install network monitoring software designed to detect transmission errors.
- Install private phone lines.
- Install procedures and other protocol controls to verify transmitted data.
- Use passwords or encryption techniques.

One of the best ways to reduce the likelihood of data transmittal errors is to understand data transmission techniques and implement safeguards. Understanding changing technology, computer systems, and networks is critical to reducing susceptibility to computer viruses, sabotage, and transmission errors. ■

Source: Sid R. Ewer, Harold E. Wills, and Richard L. Nichols, "How Safe Are Your Data Transmission?" *Journal of Accountancy*, September 1993, pp. 66–70.

With increasing frequency, entities are using computers for accounting applications. Auditors should consider the methods of data processing, including the use of computers, in essentially the same way and at the same time that they consider other significant factors that may affect the audit of the financial statements. Although the presence of a computer may change the specific audit procedures to be used, it does not necessitate a change in auditing logic and standards. Consequently, the auditor's obligation to understand the internal control structure is the same whether accounting information is processed manually or by using a computer.

According to *SAS No. 48, The Effects of Computer Processing on the Examination of Financial Statements* (AU 311.09):

> The auditor should consider the methods the entity uses to process accounting information in planning the audit because such methods influence the design of the internal control structure. The extent to which computer processing is used in significant accounting applications, as well as the complexity of that processing, may also influence the nature, timing, and extent of audit procedures.

Onut. 257

Computer Auditors Take a Fresh Look at Books

A new report which is likely to set global standards for the audit and security of IT systems was launched in the UK this week.

Systems Auditability and Control (SAC), published by the Institute of Internal Auditors, is the first study for 15 years to present auditors with a comprehensive analysis of risks and best practices in the control of IT.

Its predecessor in 1977 became the standard reference work for computer auditors. The 1992 version, launched at Compacs, the IIA's annual conference, is designed to be of wider appeal reflecting a trend for auditors to cover both IT and non-IT aspects.

SAC has a trenchant message for managers. Some 40 percent of IT systems fail to meet business requirements, it says, while only 11 percent of organisations operate effective controls during systems development. Many new systems are late, overrun their budget or are abandoned before completion.

"This is not the auditor's responsibility—it's top management's," says David Bentley, chief internal auditor at Leeds Permanent Building Society, and chairman of Compacs.

Specific IT risks identified by SAC include poor controls in end-user systems, the openness of systems to intruders, impaired accuracy and integrity of data, and interruption of business due to system or network failure.

SAC also details the use of IT in auditing. "There's no way we can audit a mass of networks and computer systems using traditional techniques," says Charles Le Grand, director of research at the IIA.

SAC is based on a survey of 400 companies worldwide including Rolls Royce, Lloyds Bank and British Petroleum in the UK. It was launched in the U.S. last May and is being translated into French, Japanese and German.

—Ian Holdsworth

This chapter examines the effect of a computer environment on the internal control structure and the auditing process. It discusses first the characteristics of computer systems and, second, the effects of a computer environment on the internal control structure. Finally, the chapter discusses the auditor's understanding of the internal control structure and assessment of control risk in a computer environment.

Characteristics of Computer Systems

Computerized accounting systems differ from manual systems. Certain characteristics common to computerized systems are not found in manual systems. In addition, differences exist among the various types of computerized accounting systems.

Characteristics That Differ from Manual Systems

SAS No. 55, Consideration of the Internal Control Structure in a Financial Statement Audit (AU 319.08), notes that "the five components of the internal control structure are applicable to every entity, but the way the components are applied should be considered in the context of the entity's methods of processing data." Characteristics that distinguish computer processing from manual processing include

- transaction trails
- uniform processing of transactions
- segregation of duties
- potential for errors or irregularities
- potential for increased management supervision
- initiation or subsequent execution of transactions by computer
- dependence of other controls on controls over computer processing

Transaction Trails

Transaction trails represent the chain of evidence from the original transactions and calculations to the account balances and other summary results. In other words, a transaction trail begins with a transaction that is subsequently recorded and posted to a journal, then enters the ledger, and finally appears in a financial report.

In a manual system, the transaction trail is generally characterized by source documents, journals, ledgers, and reports. This traditional trail typically provides for accessible records, identifiable activities, and detailed supporting documents. However, in a computer system the transaction trail often differs from this standard manual model. Frequently, transaction trails in a computer system exist for only a limited period of time and only in machine-language form. A *machine language* is an original set of instructions (source program) translated (compiled) into a language that is understood by a computer. In addition, source documents may not be available when the computer system directly captures transactions at their points of initiation. For example, when a clerk records a sale directly on a computer terminal, the company may not keep a sales ticket. However, a transaction trail in a computerized system can be beneficial to the auditor if it summarizes related data and incorporates cross-references not typically found in manual systems.

Uniform Processing of Transactions

A computerized system uniformly subjects all transactions to the same processing. Random errors occur with a very low probability in computerized recording of transactions. Typically, data entry errors are the primary source of random errors in a computerized system. The low probability of random errors often affects the auditor's decision regarding the design of audit tests and sampling. Alternatively, errors that do occur in a computerized system are generally systematic, in that the errors occur consistently over time. Thus, the effect of systematic errors can be greater than random errors. Of course, once systematic errors are discovered, they may be easier to evaluate, because their pattern is predictable.

Segregation of Duties

A computerized system may concentrate many of the recording, processing, and control procedures that would be performed by separate individuals in a manual system. A computerized system may perform functions that would be incompatible if performed by a single individual in a manual system. In addition, many individuals may have access to the computer and its records. Thus, segregation of duties in a computerized environment must be evaluated in a different manner than in manual systems. Adequate segregation of duties can, however, be achieved in a computer environment.

The factors to be considered in obtaining adequate segregation of duties are discussed later in this chapter.

Potential for Errors and Irregularities

The potential for individuals to have unauthorized access to assets or related accounting records or to alter data without visible evidence may increase when an accounting system is computerized. These changes often result from a lack of visible evidence regarding who has had access to the computer, a reduced potential for detection resulting from decreased human involvement in handling transactions, and the ability of computer-processing errors to remain undetected for long periods of time because no manual verification of processing occurs. For example, an employee may alter records that are only computer-readable without any visible evidence of the unauthorized change.

Potential for Increased Management Supervision

Computer systems offer many types of information that management can use to review and supervise transaction processing. With this information, management can perform a strong supervisory function and thus strengthen the internal control structure. For example, the computer may be programmed to process only sales to customers who are on a management-approved master credit file.

Initiation of Transactions by Computer

Transactions can be automatically initiated and the procedures required to execute a transaction can be automatically performed by a computerized system. Automatic initiation of transactions, of course, cannot occur in a manual accounting system, but must be triggered by an individual. For example, a computer accounts payable system may automatically generate checks for payment to vendors based on due dates.

Dependence of Other Controls on Controls over Computer Processing

A computer system often generates reports and other output used elsewhere as a part of manual controls. Thus, the effectiveness of these manual controls is dependent upon controls over the computer processing of these reports and outputs. For example, in processing payroll, the computer may print out an exception report for all employees who worked an unusually large number of hours. An internal auditor uses the exception report to investigate these unusual items. The manual control (the investigation by the internal auditor) therefore depends on a reliable exception report.

Types of Computerized Systems

Computerized systems differ from each other according to the characteristics they possess. A particular computerized system may incorporate one or more of the following elements:

- Batch systems
- On-line systems
- Database systems
- Distributed processing systems
- Microprocessing
- Service organizations

Batch Systems

When input data in a computerized system are grouped and processed periodically, the system is referred to as a ***batch system***, or as a periodic or a discontinuous system. In other words, due to time breaks in the flow of transactions, data are processed in batches. Batch systems can be classified as either *selective* (or scheduled) or *random* (or unscheduled or periodic batch) systems depending on whether information is processed at regular or irregular intervals. For example, payroll is generally processed using a selective batch system: payroll is processed at predetermined intervals (for example, monthly). On the other hand, the process of updating inventory from the receiving department may be random, depending upon the amount and frequency of goods received. In this situation, the processing of a group of inventory data may be performed hourly, daily, or weekly, depending on the circumstances. However, both random and selective systems are classified as batch systems because information is grouped and processed periodically.

On-Line Systems

The alternative to batch processing is an ***on-line system***, the only other basic type of data processing. On-line processing requires no preliminary data preparation, batching, or sorting. It collects input data directly from originators. Some on-line systems are known as ***real-time systems***. These systems are able to process information immediately and update the accounting records so that the user can control the activity being monitored (such as the systems used by air-traffic controllers in large airports). On-line systems can be advantageous because data can be entered into the system directly from various types of terminals and the output is sent directly to the user without passing through other processes or people. Because fewer people handle the data, an on-line system may reduce human error, increase security, and eliminate duplication. Table 7–1 compares the characteristics of the two basic types of data processing: batch and on-line.

Database Systems

Database systems store a collection of related data, or a database, which is used by one or more transaction-processing systems. Two of the basic characteristics of a database system are centralized data and multiple users. For example, a bank may maintain a database system for customers' savings accounts that includes the customers' names, addresses, account numbers, and the activity in and balances of the savings accounts. From this database, a variety of users can extract information. Tellers can use the database to determine whether or not a customer has sufficient funds for a withdrawal. Accountants can use the database to compute interest payments. Marketing personnel can use the database to gather names and addresses for a marketing survey.

An entity that uses a database may employ a database administrator function made up of one or more individuals who are responsible for database administration. Database administrators usually have the following responsibilities:

- Defining data elements and designing the database
- Maintaining data integrity, security, accuracy, and completeness
- Coordinating computer operations
- Monitoring and improving systems performance
- Providing administrative support

Both batch and on-line systems can use a database system by employing generalized database management systems (DBMS) programs, software products that facilitate the use of a database system.

Table 7-1 **Characteristics of Batch and On-Line Systems**

	Batch Systems	On-Line Systems
Transaction Trails	Batch systems originate with a source document and normally are followed by output report of transactions processed in the batch.	On-line computer systems may maintain extensive records of processing activity for recovery purposes rather than for management or audit purposes. The need for processing efficiency, especially when immediate updating of accounting records is performed, may result in complex transaction trails that require extensive processing to interpret. Transaction trails may only reflect changes to data stored by the system and therefore may require reconstruction of previous processing activity to be usable by the auditor. Input data are collected directly from the originator, so source documents independent of the computer system often are not prepared or, if prepared, may not be readily available for review.
Uniform Processing of Transactions	Because input data are processed in groups, a misstatement in one transaction may cause rejection of other transactions in the batch.	Input data can alter or affect the processing of subsequent transactions.
Segregation of Duties	A group responsible for input/output control or conversion may be involved in the flow of transactions between preparers of input and the batch computer system. This group may assist in preventing or detecting errors and irregularities by applying independent control procedures over the input submitted by preparers.	On-line computer systems provide users with direct access to transaction-processing functions. Users may perform incompatible duties as a result of using the on-line computer system unless adequate restrictions are placed on the processing functions available to each user. On-line computer systems with proper access restrictions (such as passwords) can facilitate segregation by enforcing authorization controls over individuals' access to transaction-processing functions. Proper access restrictions may also facilitate segregation of functions among data processing personnel (such as between programming and operations).

(continued)

Table 7–1   *continued*

	Batch Systems	On-Line Systems
Potential for Errors and Irregularities	Misstatements in a batch computer system caused by incorrect programs or data can remain undetected for a long period because of time delays in the processing of transactions.	Originators of input data directly interact with on-line computer systems, so the identification and correction of misstatements in input data are typically performed as part of the data-collection process.
Potential for Increased Management Supervision	Assurance that transactions processed by a computer system are initiated according to explicit management authorization requires that the identity of input preparers be preserved as input batches are collected and processed. The method used to collect input data in batch systems does not often allow the identity of the preparer to be determined or verified by the system, thereby requiring that such procedures be performed manually by a group responsible for input control.	The computer system interacts directly with the user, so procedures can be performed such as verifying the identity of the user and reporting attempts to enter unauthorized transactions. Such procedures enhance management supervision of the transaction-processing functions of the system.
Initiation or Subsequent Execution of Transactions by Computer	Batch computer systems can automatically initiate transactions in response to events such as the passage of time that are not directly initiated by or reported to an individual.	On-line computer systems can provide users with easy-to-use facilities for altering the specific authorizations contained within the system. Obtaining reasonable assurance that transactions initiated by the computer system are authorized should include an evaluation of processing functions available to users, as well as consideration of procedures to control changes to the programs and data that provide authorization.
Dependence of Other Controls on Controls over Computer Processing	Batch computer systems typically produce reports used in manual control procedures.	On-line computer systems often provide approval indications or codes that are a critical step in manual transaction-processing procedures. Manual-processing control procedures may therefore depend upon controls over the computer system used for inquiry or approval.

Distributed Processing Systems

Distributed processing systems are networks of computers that process data independently but that communicate with each other and share databases. Distributed processing systems are decentralized to serve remote locations, diverse operations, and real-time applications. Because a distributed processing system locates computer system components throughout the organization, inputs and processing can occur at the local level. However, each local system must be able to interface with the higher level and provide data that the higher level demands.

An example of a distributed processing system can be found in a bank holding company that owns individual banks throughout a geographic region. Each individual bank may develop its own computer system and its own databases. Personnel in each bank have access through the computer system to such items as checking account balances, savings account balances, and loan activity. However, management of the holding company may also want reports on checking accounts, savings accounts, and loans. Thus, each bank's computer system must interface with the computer system at the higher level of the holding company in order to generate the appropriate management reports.

Microprocessing Systems

Microprocessing systems are smaller computer systems (for example, an IBM personal computer) operated and controlled directly by users. These systems can incorporate any of the types of computer systems previously mentioned but may not be subject to the same level of controls that would exist in a larger computerized environment. For example, in microprocessing, segregation of duties may be inadequate because the computer system is operated and controlled by users. Microprocessing systems use microcomputers, which are economical yet powerful, self-contained, general-purpose computers consisting typically of a processor, memory, video display unit, data storage unit, keyboard, and connections for a printer and communications. Programs and data are stored on removable storage media (diskettes) or hard disks. Microcomputers are often referred to as *personal computers* or *PCs.*

Microcomputers can be used to process accounting transactions and to produce reports that are essential to the preparation of financial statements. They also can be used by entities for strategic planning, budgeting, and decision-making.

Service Organizations

Service organizations are computer systems and facilities operated by an organization other than the entity whose information is being processed. Service organizations perform a variety of services for customers, including recording transactions and related data-processing services such as programming and data entry. For example, a service organization may process a client's biweekly payroll on the computer. Divisions of control between the service organization and clients vary depending on circumstances. An auditor may consider control procedures performed at the service organization as well as control procedures performed at the client's location. A service organization can use any of the types of computer systems previously described. The independence of service organizations from the customer can facilitate segregation of duties. Reliability of service organization operations, however, must be established. Service organizations are discussed in more detail in Chapter 8.

Control Activities in a Computer Environment

The characteristics of a computerized financial reporting information system can affect the types of control activities an entity establishes but should not affect the control activity objectives. For example, in a manual system, management may indicate its approval by providing a signature on a source document, whereas in a computer system, approval may be indicated by an authorized password entered into the system before a transaction can be processed. In this situation, although the control objective is identical for both the manual and computerized systems, the control activities used to achieve the objective and the evidence that the activities were performed would differ significantly. Consequently, the differences in the characteristics of control activities in manual systems and computerized systems can have a considerable effect on how tests of controls are performed.

Control activities in a computer environment can be classified into one of two types: general control procedures pertain to many or all of the aspects of a computerized accounting system, whereas application control procedures pertain to the use (application) of the computer to perform a specific accounting task, such as to process payroll or accounts receivable.

General Control Procedures

As mentioned above, *general control procedures* pertain to many or all computer applications. They tend to have a pervasive effect and include control procedures for

- development of new programs and systems
- changes to existing programs and systems
- computer operations
- access to programs and data

Development of New Programs and Systems

Program and system development control procedures are intended to ensure that new applications are properly authorized, designed, and tested prior to being put into use. These control procedures typically include the following:

- Written requests from users for development of a new application to achieve specific objectives.
- Evaluation and authorization of the application by electronic data processing (EDP) management and personnel.
- Design of the application by EDP personnel with participation and approval of users, EDP management, and internal auditors. Design includes designating the input data, programmed control procedures, file specifications, and report formats.
- Programming the application and developing program documentation with approval by EDP management.
- Testing the application by processing test data and comparing achieved results with predetermined results with participation of users, EDP management, and internal auditors.
- Implementing the application, including training EDP personnel and users and developing or converting data files for the new application.

Changes to Existing Programs and Systems

Program and systems change control procedures are intended to ensure that authorized modifications of existing applications are analyzed, designed, and tested so that applications will continue to function properly. Requests for application changes frequently come from users and may involve minor modifications, such as changing a report title, or major changes, such as incorporating new tax withholding tables into the payroll application program. EDP personnel may also request modifications to accommodate new file layouts or improve operating efficiency.

Control procedures for modifying existing applications are generally the same as those for developing new applications. Requests for changes are reviewed and approved by EDP management and users. The effect of the modification on other applications is evaluated, and the change is designed, programmed, tested, and implemented. As with the development of new applications, participation and approval by the users, EDP management, and internal auditors at each stage of the modification process is important.

Computer Operations

Computer operations control procedures are intended to ensure that application programs are used properly to meet the entity's needs and that only the proper data files are used during processing. One important operations control procedure is scheduling daily computer processing. Job scheduling helps assure that applications are authorized for processing, are actually processed, are processed in the proper sequence, and are processed on time.

Scheduling may be done manually, or computer programs may be used to control processing. Either approach should produce a record of which application programs and data files were used and when and for how long they were used. These records can then be compared to the planned job schedules, and significant deviations can be identified and investigated.

In addition to scheduling processing, the receipt of input and distribution of output should also be scheduled. Computer operations should know who is authorized to submit input and when and in what form it is to be submitted. Computer operations should also know what documents, reports, and files are produced, when they are produced, and who is authorized to receive them.

Other computer operations control procedures include checking file labels. File labels generally contain the file name, volume number, date created, and version number. File labels may be attached to the outside of the file and read by the computer operator (*external label*) or contained in the tape or disk itself and read by the operating program (*internal label*). Such labels help to assure that the proper file is used.

Professional Judgment

Computer Reliance Can Alter Accounting Processes

Businesses of today increasingly rely on computers, and computerized accounting systems are now also in widespread use. Computers change the accounting process. Auditors must use professional judgment in deciding how a computer system may affect control and what adjustments are appropriate with regard to audit tests. Very likely, some aspects of the accounting process will be improved, while others will be diminished. But one thing is certain: The auditor who is lulled into a false sense of security by technologically sophisticated accounting software will very shortly live to regret the lapse. In fact, the potential for introducing errors is greater since data can be lost and/or altered when transferred from a company's software package to that of the auditing firm's. Professional judgment is at least as critical now as when accounting, and the world, moved a bit more slowly.

Access to Programs and Data

Control procedures over access to programs and data are intended to prevent or detect unauthorized changes to programs and data files. ***Access control procedures*** pertain to both physical access and access through the computer. Access is usually controlled by a variety of control procedures.

One common significant control activity pertaining to access is proper segregation of duties within the computer department and among the computer department and user departments. Because many individuals in an entity may have access to the computer, proper segregation of duties requires an analysis of each person's opportunity for affecting computer processing procedures. Proper segregation of duties is subject to the following considerations:

- *Independence of control procedures* Computerized control procedures designed to prevent or detect errors or irregularities perpetrated by an individual are considered to be performed independently only if that individual cannot, in the normal course of his or her duties, alter the program or data associated with the control procedure.

- *Opportunities for concealment* Individuals who enter transactions or have access to assets have incompatible functions if they can, in the normal course of their duties, also alter programs or data to conceal misstatements.

- *Access to incompatible transaction processing functions* Data-processing personnel may perform incompatible functions if they can perform functions through the computer that would be considered incompatible if performed manually. This would normally depend on their access to the computer and their ability to change computer programs or data.

Instead of separating duties by accounting function (for example, accounts receivable versus cash receipts), in a computer system duties are typically separated by management function. For good organization controls in a computer environment, clear-cut lines of authority and responsibility within the computer department are needed. A computer environment with typical proper organization controls within the computer department is illustrated in Figure 7–1. This organizational structure provides for the following segregation of duties:

EDP Manager The ***EDP manager*** supervises the operation of the computer department. The EDP manager should have considerable autonomy from the major user departments and should report to someone who is not regularly involved in authorizing transactions for computer processing. The EDP manager should exercise control over the department, develop short-term and long-term plans for the department, and approve new systems.

Systems Analyst *Systems analysts* are responsible for designing computer systems. They evaluate existing systems design, determine and outline what systems are needed, prepare the specifications for the programmer, design and supervise tests of the system, and prepare systems and user documentation.

Programmer Guided by the specifications provided by the systems analyst, the ***programmer*** designs flowcharts for computer programs required by the system. From these flowcharts the programmer develops the document program in a computer language and then debugs these programs. The programmer also prepares the computer operator instructions.

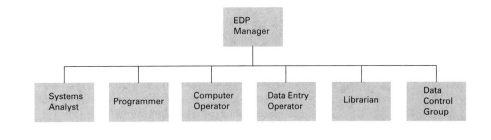

Figure 7–1 **Organizational Structure of a Computer Department**

Computer Operator   The *computer operator* manages the computer hardware and executes programs according to operating instructions developed by the programmer. The separation of the computer operator from programming is important in achieving good internal control. An employee performing both functions would have the opportunity to make unauthorized changes in computer programs or to manipulate data in the system.

Data Entry Operator   The *data entry operator* prepares data for processing by recording it in machine-readable format. For example, a keypunch operator who keys data onto a magnetic disk would be a data entry operator.

Librarian   The *librarian* maintains custody of systems documentation, programs, and files. The librarian's purpose is to protect files and records from loss, damage, and unauthorized use or alteration. The librarian should maintain a formal checkout system.

Data Control Group   The *data control group* reviews and tests procedures, monitors computer processing, handles the reprocessing of errors detected by the computer, and reviews and distributes computer output. The data control group acts as a liaison with user departments, reviews the console log of interventions during computer processing, and reviews the library log of program uses.

Another effective control feature over access to programs and data is access control software. This software requires users to identify themselves by entering a unique *password*. When the software validates the password it knows who the user is, what programs and data files that user is authorized to access, and what operations that user is allowed to perform. Most access control software can restrict a user's access to only a portion of a file (for example, a specific user can access customer names and addresses but not their account balances) and can limit the functions a specific user can perform (such as reading data only or entering input data only). In addition, most access control software will block a user from the system after a certain number of invalid passwords are entered. These software packages produce reports of access violations and program and data file usage. To obtain the maximum benefit from access control software, management should review and follow up on these reports.

In on-line computer systems, *terminal access controls* prevent unauthorized access to programs and data. These controls include placing terminals in secured locations, requiring passwords for access to terminals, limiting the activities that can be performed and the data that can be accessed from a particular terminal, and management review and follow-up of terminal use reports.

Physical access control procedures are also important for protecting against unauthorized use or modification of programs and data files. Physical access to the computer operations area, programs, and data files should be restricted to authorized personnel. A variety of techniques, including key systems, combination locks, and magnetic cards are used to restrict access. In addition, many entities assign a librarian to control the storage and issuance of programs and data files and to maintain a log of their use. Management reviews these logs periodically and identifies and investigates indications of unauthorized access.

 ## Application Control Procedures

Application control procedures pertain to the use of the computer to perform a particular accounting task. They may be performed either manually or by computer software (programmed control). Application controls are broadly divided into three areas: input controls, processing controls, and output controls.

Input Controls

Input controls are designed to ensure that data received for processing represent properly authorized transactions and are accurate and complete when read by the computer. These controls are crucial in a computerized system because most misstatements occur at this point. Input controls are designed to provide reasonable assurance that data received for processing have been properly authorized, converted into machine-readable form, and subsequently accounted for.

Authorization   Transactions should be properly authorized and approved in accordance with management's general or specific authorization. This authorization may come in the form of individually approved documentation or approval of batches of documents. As noted previously, the computer may also perform the authorization function.

Conversion into Machine-Readable Form   Conversions of data into machine-readable form are often a major source of misstatement. Common mistakes include data entry errors and losing records. Controls include the following:

- *Record counts* The transactions to be converted are counted. After conversion the new records are counted, with the second count compared to the original count. For example, the number of cash receipts from customers' collections to be processed would be a **record count**.
- *Batch totals* The items to be processed are summed. After processing, the total for each batch is reconciled to the original batch total. For example, the sum of the cash receipts from customers' collections would be a **batch total**.
- *Hash totals* A total of information being entered. **Hash totals** are similar to batch totals except a hash total has no value other than its use as a control. The sum of a batch total represents a value of and by itself. For example, the total of net payroll for all employees would be a batch total because that number gives the total payroll liability. Alternatively, the total of all employees' social security numbers would be a hash total because this total is only used for

control purposes and has no meaning other than its use as a control. An illustration of record counts, batch totals, and hash totals is shown in Figure 7–2.

■ *Computer editing* The computer, if properly programmed, can provide a wide range of edit tests of input records, including tests of reasonableness, checks between files to verify relationships, and tests for nonnumeric data in numeric fields.

■ *Verification* Data conversion is performed on a dual basis, and after conversion, results between the two sets of data are compared. ***Verification*** is often used in the keying of data for batch operations. For example, data that have been prepared for entry may be reentered a second time on a machine that compares the reentered data to the data initially prepared and determines whether discrepancies exist.

Subsequent Accountability   Controls are needed to determine that input data have not been lost, duplicated, added, or otherwise changed en route between processing steps or departments. Transmittal controls, routing slips, and control totals are methods often used to account for data.

Processing Controls

Processing controls are designed to ensure the reliability and accuracy of data processing. These controls provide reasonable assurance that data processing has been

---

Figure 7–2   **Illustration of Record Count, Hash Total, and Batch Total for Customer Receipts**

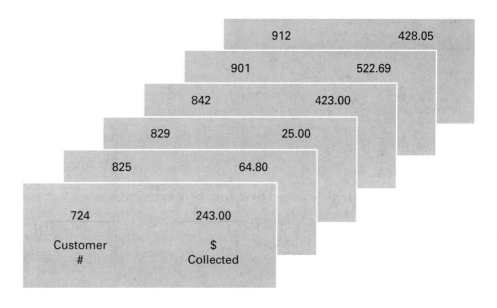

	912		428.05
	901		522.69
	842		423.00
	829		25.00
	825		64.80
724		243.00	
Customer #		$ Collected	

Record Count	Batch Total	Hash total
6	$1,706.54	5,033
	($ collected)	(total of customer's #'s)

performed as intended for the particular application; that is, all transactions are processed as authorized, no authorized transactions are omitted, and no unauthorized transactions are added. Processing controls can take a variety of forms. Common processing controls include the following:

- *Control total* A total of information being processed. For example, the total of sales for a batch of sales orders would be a **control total**. Having the computer program include a requirement to accumulate control totals facilitates the balancing of input control totals with processing control totals. Control totals include batch totals, hash totals, and record counts.

- *Hash total* A sum of information being processed. The sum has no value or meaning other than its use as a control.

- *Record count* A count or tally of the number of items or transactions processed in a given batch.

- *Validity check test* A comparison of items being processed with a master file to test for authenticity. For example, during payroll processing, a **validity check test** could determine whether the social security number contained nine characters and whether all these characters were numbers.

- *Limit test* **Limit tests** verify the reasonableness of data being processed by comparing the data to predetermined upper and lower limits. For example, the computer may determine that weekly payroll hours do not exceed 60 hours for any employee.

- *Self-checking digit* An additional digit or digits added to a number that is determined from a mathematical calculation of the original number being processed. The additional digit provides a means to check for accuracy after the original number has been transmitted from one device to another. An example of a **self-checking digit** is shown in Figure 7–3.

Output Controls

Output controls are designed to ensure the reliability of computer output and to determine that outputs are distributed only to authorized personnel. One common output control is the reconciliation of output control totals generated by the computer with input and processing control totals. This reconciliation is typically performed by either the data control group or the user departments. Another output control is a comparison of output data to details of source documents. Other output controls include reviews by user departments, reviews by the computer department, and recording and investigating error listings.

Control Procedures in an On-Line System

In addition to the foregoing control procedures, on-line systems use additional safeguards because of the increased vulnerability created by the use of terminals and remote operational centers. Common control procedures in an on-line system pertain to the accurate transmission of data from user locations to the central processing unit, user identification codes so that access to files can be restricted to authorized personnel, and the use of passwords to control terminal accessibility.

Control Procedures in a Database System

The basic control objectives in a database environment are not different from those in a nondatabase environment. However, because of the centralized data and the

| Figure 7–3 | **Illustrative Self-Checking Digit** |

1. Original account number = 629
2. Multiply every other digit by 2:
   $6 \times 2 = 12$, $9 \times 2 = 18$
3. Sum the digits in the resulting numbers and the digits not multiplied in the original number:
   $1 + 2 + 2 + 1 + 8 = 14$
4. Subtract the sum from the next highest multiple of 10:
   $20 - 14 = 6$
5. Add the check digit to the end of the original number to form an account number with a self-checking digit:
   6296
6. Assume that during subsequent processing, the account number is transposed:
   6926
7. The check digit would be calculated as follows:
   $6 \times 2 = 12$, $2 \times 2 = 4$
   $1 + 2 + 9 + 4 = 16$
   $20 - 16 = 4$
8. The check digit that was entered with the input was a 6. The calculated check digit was 4. Because the two numbers do not match, the account number would be flagged as an error.

sharing of data among diverse users in a database environment, specific control procedures may differ from those in a nondatabase environment in three areas:

- Control procedures should exist to ensure that a user has access to and can update only those data elements for which he or she has been authorized access.
- Database systems allow the sharing of data by diverse users; therefore the coordination of user activities must be controlled. However, shared use does not imply that controls should be equal for every user. For example, inventory users who have only retrieval access do not need the same degree of control as do users who are allowed to update and change inventory files. The requirements of the most critical items in a file should be of primary concern in the design of the control features.
- The sharing of data files means that multiple users rely on the continued availability of particular files. Thus, controls are especially important to prevent loss of and unauthorized changes in files. The files also require sufficient computer personnel to service the database system for users.

Planning the Audit in a Computer Environment

Several of the ten generally accepted auditing standards are related to audit planning. The first general standard requires the auditor to have adequate technical training and proficiency. The first standard of fieldwork requires the auditor to properly plan and supervise the engagement, and the second standard of fieldwork requires the auditor to obtain a sufficient understanding of the internal control structure to plan the audit. These standards apply when auditing in either a manual or a computerized environment.

Adequate Technical Training

Generally, adequate technical training for an auditor in a computer environment would include a basic knowledge of computer systems; a general knowledge of computer languages; the ability to design, analyze, and flowchart basic systems; an understanding of computer controls; and the ability to audit by using a computer.

The auditor's required knowledge of computers varies with the complexity of the processing system. For example, an audit of an entity with a small, batch-oriented data-processing installation requires less proficiency in computers than an audit of an entity having a large, complex, on-line computer system. In addition, the availability of human-readable audit evidence that can be tested by the auditor affects the auditor's required knowledge of computers.

Planning

Planning involves developing an overall strategy for the expected conduct and scope of the examination. According to *SAS No. 48* (AU 311.10), in planning an audit in a computer environment the auditor should consider

1. the extent to which a computer is used in each significant accounting application
2. the complexity of the entity's computer operations
3. the organizational structures of the computer processing activities
4. the availability of data
5. the use of computer-assisted audit techniques to increase the efficiency of performing audit procedures
6. the need for specialized skills.

Supervision

Supervision involves directing the efforts of assistants and determining whether the audit objectives have been met. The extent of supervision depends upon the complexity of the subject matter and the qualifications of the persons performing the work.

A person who possesses specialized, computer-related skills and who participates in the audit should be considered as a member of the audit team, whether the individual is employed by the auditor's firm or is a consultant. Thus, a computer specialist must be supervised as a member of the audit team and the requirements of *SAS No. 22, Planning and Supervision* (AU 311), apply.

Understanding the Internal Control Structure

As discussed in Chapter 6, in every audit the auditor must obtain an understanding of the internal control structure sufficient to plan the audit. This requirement exists whether the client has a manual or computerized accounting system. When a client has computer applications that process accounting data that can materially affect the financial statements, the auditor must consider how the computer affects the understanding of each of the five internal control structure components needed to plan the audit properly.

The Control Environment, Risk Assessment, and Monitoring

When *significant accounting applications* are processed by a computer, the auditor should understand management's attitude, awareness, and actions concerning computer processing, risk assessment, and monitoring. This understanding normally includes determining

- to whom the head of data processing reports in senior management.
- the general organizational structure of the data-processing function (for example, centralized or decentralized).
- senior management's involvement in establishing overall policies and procedures that assign authority and responsibility for computer operations, and management's involvement in monitoring such activities as access to computer equipment, programs, and files; authorizing system development and changes; and operating the computer.
- internal auditor involvement in reviewing computer-processing activities.
- personnel policies and procedures for hiring, training, evaluating, promoting, and compensating data-processing employees and giving them the resources necessary to perform their assigned tasks.

The Financial Reporting Information System

The understanding of a computerized financial reporting information system closely parallels that of a manual system. The auditor should obtain sufficient knowledge to understand

- how computer-processed transactions are initiated, for example, whether they are approved by a specific individual or are initiated automatically by the computer.
- how the transactions are processed by the computer. This understanding includes knowledge about the specific accounting processing procedures that the computer software performs, such as multiplying quantity times unit price or calculating payroll withholding taxes.
- the key files that the computer accesses or updates. For example, in a computerized billing function, the computer may access a standard price list file and customer file, and it may update the accounts receivable master file and the inventory master file.
- the types of reports produced by the computer application, such as a payroll register, accounts receivable aging schedule, or a list of shipping documents that have not been matched with sales invoices.
- how the amounts produced by computer processing are entered in the financial statement accounts. For example, the auditor would determine what computer-produced amounts are posted to the financial statement accounts and whether the computer posts them directly or they are posted manually from a computer-generated report.

Control Activities

As in a manual system, as the auditor obtains an understanding of the other four internal control structure components, he or she will unavoidably learn about some control activities. In a computerized system this knowledge is likely to include an understanding of the design of both some general controls and some application controls and whether they have been placed in operation. For example, while obtaining knowledge about the accounting processing procedures performed by the computer, the auditor is also likely to learn about some control activities performed by the computer software.

After considering the knowledge of control activities obtained as a byproduct of the understanding of the other four components, the auditor will determine whether additional knowledge of control activities is necessary to plan the audit. As computerized accounting systems become more complex, additional knowledge of control activities may be necessary to plan the audit. In addition, the auditor's decision about whether to obtain additional knowledge about general and application control activities is influenced by the audit strategy the auditor plans to use in assessing control risk.

Assessing Control Risk in a Computer Environment

Computer applications often generate data that directly affect an assertion related to an account balance or transaction class. For example, a computer application may process sales to customers and update the sales revenue, accounts receivable, and inventory account balances. In addition, computer applications sometimes generate data that auditors use in performing substantive audit procedures, such as listings of the dollar amount of additions; retirements; and balances for property, plant, and equipment that are used in performing analytical procedures to test depreciation expense. In either circumstance, the auditor assesses the control risk related to the computer-generated data.

The process used to assess control risk when computer applications are involved is essentially the same as the general process discussed in the previous chapter. The auditor considers the five internal control structure components related to a computer application in assessing control risk for the financial statement assertions relevant to that application (or for data used in substantive tests). In other words, the auditor assesses the risk that the computer application will produce data that can cause a material misstatement in an assertion. An auditor may use several approaches to assess this risk.

Approaches to Assessing Control Risk

The auditor's approach to assessing control risk is influenced by the number and significance of computer applications the client uses, the types of user controls the client has, and the relationship between general control procedures and application control procedures. Although four basic approaches are discussed below and summarized in Table 7–2, a combination of these approaches is often used on many audits.

Table 7–2	**Approaches to Assessing Control Risk in an EDP Environment**	
Approach	Description	When Used
Auditing Around the Computer	■ Auditor uses input data to reperform the accounting processing and compares results with amounts recorded in the financial statement accounts	■ Few significant computer accounting applications ■ No computer processed data necessary to reperform accounting processing

| Table 7-2 | *continued* |

Approach	Description	When Used
	■ No tests of controls applied to either general controls or application controls	
	■ Control risk assessed at maximum level	
Testing User Reperformance Controls	■ Auditor applies tests of controls only to user reperformance application controls	■ Client requires users of computer-generated data to reperform computer processing on a test basis and follow up on exceptions
	■ No tests of controls applied to other application controls or to general controls	
	■ Tests of user reperformance controls may support an assessed level of control risk below the maximum	
Testing Programmed Application and Follow-up Controls	■ Auditor applies tests of controls to the accounting processing procedures and control procedures built into the computer application software (often by using test data)	■ Client uses one or more significant computer accounting applications
	■ Auditor also applies tests of controls to follow-up controls client performs on computer output data	■ Application software contains programmed control procedures
	■ No tests of controls applied to general controls	■ Client has established follow-up procedures for computer-produced exception reports resulting from programmed application controls
	■ Tests of both types of application controls may support an assessed level of control risk below the maximum	■ Auditor can efficiently establish that application program is one client uses regularly
Testing General Controls and Follow-up Controls	■ Auditor applies tests of controls to general control procedures to obtain support that application programs are approved, designed, tested, implemented, and operated properly	■ Client uses one or more significant computer accounting applications
	■ Auditor also applies tests of controls to follow-up controls client performs on computer output data	■ Client has established general control procedures that are likely to be effective
	■ Tests of general controls and client follow-up controls may support an assessed level of control risk below the maximum	■ Client has established follow-up procedures for computer-produced exception reports resulting from programmed application controls

Auditing Around the Computer   When a client has only a few computer applications or the applications are not very significant, the auditor may choose to assess control risk at the maximum level and design substantive tests that reperform the accounting processing that the computer application is designed to do. For example, the auditor may test the data submitted for computer processing (input) and compare the results of these tests with the amounts recorded in the financial statement accounts (output). In this approach the auditor does not apply tests of controls to either the general or application control procedures.

This approach is often referred to as *auditing around the computer* and is discussed more fully in the next chapter. Although the term *auditing around the computer* may imply that the computer can be ignored, the auditor must still obtain an understanding of the internal control structure relevant to computer applications, discussed earlier in this chapter. In addition, the substantive procedures used to reperform the accounting processing cannot involve the use of any computer-processed data. Moreover, these procedures must also test the completeness of the input data. For these reasons, this approach is often inefficient (and sometimes impossible) to use.

Testing User Reperformance Controls   In some computer applications, users of computer-generated data reperform computer processing on a test basis. For example, an accounting clerk might test the results of a computer payroll calculation for a selected number of employees each pay period. Although this type of application control procedure is not frequently used, when it does exist, the auditor may perform tests of controls to evaluate its operating effectiveness. If these controls are effective, the auditor may assess control risk at below the maximum level and modify the nature, timing, or extent of substantive tests applied to the computer-generated data. In this approach, it is unnecessary for the auditor to consider general control procedures.

Testing Programmed Application and Follow-up Controls   A third approach to assessing control risk involves testing two different types of application control procedures. First, the auditor tests the accounting processing procedures and the control procedures built into the computer software. Auditors commonly use test data that they develop themselves to perform these tests of controls. Test data (discussed more fully in Chapter 8) are processed through the client's computer application to evaluate whether the programmed accounting processing procedures and control procedures function effectively.

After the auditor has determined that the programmed accounting and control procedures function effectively and produce accurate data and exception reports, he or she must test the effectiveness of follow-up control procedures concerning these reports. These follow-up control procedures may be performed by the user of the computer output or by a data control group. For example, the computer may produce an input edit report identifying misstatements in input data. If these misstatements are not investigated and resolved, the programmed control procedure is useless. The results of the auditor's tests of these controls may support an assessed level of control risk below the maximum. As with the two previous approaches, the auditor does not consider general control procedures. However, as discussed in the next chapter, this approach is often inefficient because the auditor must also establish that the computer program tested is the one the client uses regularly.

Testing General Controls and Follow-up Controls   A fourth approach to assessing control risk in a computer environment is to test the general control procedures and the follow-up application control procedures. This approach is based on the relationship between general control procedures and application control procedures. As discussed earlier in this chapter, general control procedures are intended to help assure (1) that computer applications are properly authorized, designed, tested, and implemented and (2) that they continue to operate properly. The more effective the general control procedures are, the more likely it is that the individual applications will consistently achieve their intended objectives.

For example, effective general controls provide a high degree of assurance that a computer application for billing customers has been properly authorized, designed, tested, and implemented through the participation and review of EDP management and personnel, users of the application, and internal auditors. This means that the accounting processing procedures and control procedures designed into the application are likely to produce accurate and complete billings, and properly stated sales and accounts receivable balances. Moreover, effective general controls provide a high degree of assurance that any changes made to the billing application are authorized, designed, tested, and implemented properly so that they will continue to produce properly stated account balances.

In this approach, the auditor applies tests of controls to evaluate whether these control procedures are designed and operating effectively. If the results of these tests provide evidence that the general controls are effective, the auditor may conclude that there is a low risk that an individual computer application did not function as intended throughout the audit period. In such circumstances the auditor would then apply tests of controls to the follow-up application control procedures to obtain evidence that any computer-generated exception reports are being investigated and resolved properly.

The auditor may decide not to perform any direct tests of the programmed accounting or control procedures in the computer application. Evidence showing that these procedures are designed and operating effectively is provided by the tests of controls applied to the general control procedures and the follow-up application controls. Some auditors, however, follow a policy of always directly testing the programmed processing procedures and control procedures in a computer application at least once, even when effective general controls exist.

Assessing Control Risk for Minicomputer or Microcomputer Applications

Many small entities use minicomputers or microcomputers to process accounting data, and often these applications are significant. Minicomputer and microcomputer applications share several common characteristics that affect the auditor's assessment of control risk.

- One or a few individuals have responsibility for programming, operating, and controlling the application.
- Personnel responsible for computer activities have little data-processing knowledge.
- Personnel in user departments often initiate and authorize source documents, enter data into the application, operate the computer, use the computer output, and have access to assets.
- Access controls to computer equipment, programs, and data files are limited.
- The software is purchased from outside vendors and does not permit much user customization and control.

Because of these characteristics, auditors often assess control risk at the maximum level for assertions relevant to the computer application, and they design substantive tests to obtain evidence about those assertions (i.e., they audit around the computer).

In other circumstances, manual application control procedures that do not depend on computer-generated data may exist. The auditor's tests of controls of those procedures may support an assessed level of control risk below the maximum.

In some mini- or microcomputer applications, however, general control procedures may be fairly effective. For example, in an entity that uses purchased software and employs computer operators who do not have the knowledge of or access to codes necessary to modify these programs, the likelihood of unauthorized or inaccurate changes to programs may be minimal. In addition, some small entities establish effective access controls by using passwords, locking computers or the areas in which computers are kept, and keeping the data files, such as tapes or floppy disks, in secured storage areas. When these general controls exist, the auditor may assess control risk at below the maximum by using the fourth approach to assessing control risk discussed earlier in the chapter (that is, testing general controls and follow-up controls).

Significant Terms

Access control procedures Controls designed to prevent the unauthorized use of computer equipment, files, and programs.

Application control procedures The broad category of control procedures that relate to specific computer applications or areas (for example, specific payroll controls).

Batch system System in which input data are periodically grouped and processed in the computerized system.

Batch total A total or sum of a set of items (a batch) to be processed.

Computer operations control procedures Controls over daily computer operations to minimize the likelihood of errors and to ensure that operations could continue in the event of a physical disaster or other computer failure.

Computer operator The person who manages the computer hardware and executes programs according to operating instructions developed by the programmer.

Control total A total or sum of information being processed. Control totals include batch totals, hash totals, and record counts.

Database systems Systems that store a collection of related data shared and used by a number of different users for different purposes.

Data control group A group that reviews and tests procedures, monitors computer processing, handles the reprocessing of errors detected by the computer, and reviews and distributes computer output.

Data entry operator The person who prepares data for processing by recording it in machine-readable format.

Distributed processing systems Networks of computers that process data independently but that are also interactive communications facilities with centralized, shared data files.

EDP manager The person who supervises the operation of the computer department.

External label A label containing the file name, volume number, date created, and version number that is attached to the outside of the file and read by the computer operator.

General control procedures The broad category of control procedures that relate to all computer activities.

Hash totals A sum or total of information being processed that has no meaning other than as a control sum.

Input controls Application control to ensure that data received for processing represent properly authorized transactions and are accurate and complete when read by the computers.

Internal label A label containing the file name, volume number, date created, and version number that is contained within the magnetic disk or tape itself and is read by the operating program.

Librarian The person who maintains custody of systems documentations, programs, and files.

Limit tests A control that verifies the reasonableness of data being processed.

Machine language Original set of instructions (source program) translated (compiled) into a language that is understood by the computer.

Microprocessing systems Smaller computer systems operated and controlled directly by users.

On-line system A system that processes data by collecting input data directly from originators and sends output directly to originators without passing through other processes or people.

Output controls Application controls designed to ensure the reliability of computer output and to determine that outputs are distributed only to authorized personnel.

Passwords An identification technique that controls access to on-line systems, programs, and data.

Processing controls Application controls designed to ensure the reliability and accuracy of data processing.

Program and systems change control procedures Control procedures intended to ensure that authorized modifications of existing computer applications are analyzed, designed, and tested so that applications will continue to function properly.

Program and systems development control procedures Control procedures intended to ensure that new computer applications are properly authorized, designed, and tested prior to being put into use.

Programmer The person who designs flowcharts, develops the computer programs, and prepares necessary documentation.

Real-time system An on-line system that processes transactions as soon as they are entered by the user so that he or she is provided with an immediate response.

Record count A count or tally of the number of items to be processed.

Self-checking digit An additional digit or digits added to a number to verify the correctness of the original number.

Service centers Computer systems and facilities operated by an organization other than the entity whose information is being processed.

Significant accounting applications Those computer applications that relate to the data processing of accounting information that can materially affect the financial statements the auditor is examining.

Systems analyst A person responsible for designing computer systems.

Trailer label A record that follows a group of records on a file, containing summary information related to those records.

Transaction trails The chain of evidence from the original transactions and calculations to the accounts balances and other summary results.

Utility program   Computer programs that perform common data processing tasks, many of which are termed housekeeping tasks, such as sorting or merging files.

Validity check test   A control that compares items being processed with a master file to check for authenticity.

Verification   An input control in which data conversion is performed on a dual basis and results between the two sets of data, after conversion, are compared.

Discussion Questions

7-1.   Which characteristics distinguish computer processing from manual processing? Briefly explain each.

7-2.   What is the difference between a transaction trail in a manual system and one in a computer system?

7-3.   What is the difference between a batch system and an on-line system?

7-4.   What is a database system? Give an example of such a system.

7-5.   Define *distributed processing system* and give an example.

7-6.   What are the objectives of a computerized accounting system?

7-7.   What is the difference between general controls and application controls?

7-8.   What are the four types of general controls? Briefly define each.

7-9.   How is the proper segregation of duties in a computer environment maintained?

7-10.   Briefly discuss common controls over the development of new programs and systems.

7-11.   What are the requirements for the auditor's understanding of the internal control structure in a computer environment?

7-12.   What items should the auditor consider in planning an audit in a computer environment?

7-13.   What is the relationship between general control procedures and application control procedures?

7-14.   What are the basic control environment factors an auditor should consider in obtaining an understanding of the internal control structure in a computer environment?

7-15.   What are the four basic approaches to assessing control risk related to computer applications?

7-16.   How does the relationship between general control procedures and application control procedures influence the auditor's approach to assessing control risk for computer applications?

7-17.   Why are user follow-up application control procedures important in the auditor's assessment of control risk?

7-18.   How might an entity's use of a microcomputer increase or decrease control risk related to a computer application?

Objective Questions

*7-19.   Which of the following would lessen the effectiveness of the internal control structure in an electronic data-processing system?

(1)   The computer librarian maintains custody of computer program instructions and detailed program listings.

(2)   Computer operators have access to operator instructions and detailed program listings.

(3)   The control group maintains sole custody of all computer output.

(4)   Computer programmers write and debug programs that perform routines designed by the systems analyst.

*7-20.   In updating a computerized accounts receivable file, which of the following would be used as a batch control to verify the accuracy of the posting of cash receipts remittances?

(1)   The sum of the cash deposits plus the discounts, less the sales returns.

(2)   The sum of the cash deposits.

---

*AICPA adapted.

(3) The sum of the cash deposits less the discounts taken by customers.

(4) The sum of the cash deposits plus the discounts taken by customers.

*7-21. When an on-line, real-time electronic data-processing system is in use, which of the following could strengthen the internal control structure?

(1) Providing for the separation of duties between keypunching and error-listing operators.

(2) Attaching plastic file protection rings to reels of magnetic tape before new data can be entered on the file.

(3) Making a validity check of an identification number before a user can obtain access to the computer files.

(4) Preparing batch totals to insure that file updates are made for the entire input.

*7-22. When erroneous data are detected by computer program controls, such data may be excluded from processing and printed on an error report. Who should most probably review and follow up on the error report?

(1) The supervisor of computer operations.

(2) The systems analyst.

(3) The EDP control group.

(4) The computer programmer.

7-23. In a client's EDP system, the auditor will encounter general controls and application controls. Which of the following is an application control?

(1) Password.

(2) Hash total.

(3) Systems flowchart.

(4) Control over program changes.

*7-24. Control procedures within the EDP activity may leave no visible evidence indicating that the procedures were performed. In such instances, the auditor should test these accounting controls by

(1) making corroborative inquiries.

(2) observing the separation of personnel duties.

(3) reviewing transactions submitted for processing and comparing them to related output.

(4) reviewing the run manual.

7-25. Which of the following is likely to be least important to an auditor who is obtaining an understanding of the internal control structure surrounding the automated data-processing function?

(1) Disposition of source documents.

(2) Operator competence.

(3) Bit storage capacity.

(4) Segregation of duties.

7-26. After obtaining an understanding of a client's internal control structure, an auditor may decide not to perform tests of controls related to the control procedures within the EDP portion of the client's control structure. Which of the following would *not* be a valid reason for choosing to omit tests of controls?

(1) The controls appear adequate.

(2) The controls duplicate controls existing elsewhere in the system.

(3) Major weaknesses appear to exist that would preclude an assessment of control risk at below the maximum.

(4) The time and dollar costs of testing exceed the time and dollar savings in substantive testing if the tests of controls show the controls to be operative.

*7-27. Which of the following constitutes a weakness in the internal control structure of an EDP system?

(1) One generation of back-up files is stored outside the premises.

(2) Machine operators distribute error messages to the control group.

---

*AICPA adapted.

(3) Machine operators do not have access to the complete systems manual.

(4) Machine operators are supervised by the programmer.   *does not*

7-28. The internal control structure procedure of segregation of duties exists when computer department personnel do which of the following?

(1) Participate in making decisions about acquiring computer software.

(2) Design documentation for computer applications.

(3) Initiate changes in master files.

(4) Provide physical security for program files.

Problems and Cases

*7-29. (General and Application Controls) When auditing an EDP system, the independent auditor should have a general familiarity with the effects of the use of EDP on the internal control structure. The independent auditor must be aware of those control procedures that are commonly referred to as general and application controls. *General controls* relate to all EDP activities and *application controls* relate to specific accounting tasks.

REQUIRED

A. What are the general controls that should exist in EDP-based accounting systems?

B. What are the purposes of each of the following categories of application controls?

(1) Input controls.

(2) Processing controls.

(3) Output controls.

**7-30. (General Controls) Emily Johnson, CPA, was engaged to audit the financial statements of Horizon Incorporated, which has its own computer installation. Johnson found that Horizon lacked proper segregation of the programming and operating functions but determined that the existing compensating general controls provided reasonable assurance that control risk was low.

REQUIRED

A. In a properly functioning EDP environment, how is the separation of the programming and operating functions achieved?

B. What are the compensating general controls that Johnson most likely found? Do not discuss application controls.

*7-31. (General Controls) The Lakesedge Utility District is installing an EDP system. The CPA who conducts the annual audit of the district's financial statements has been asked to recommend control structure policies and procedures for the new system.

REQUIRED

Discuss the recommended policies and procedures for each of the following:

A. Program documentation.

B. Program testing.

C. EDP equipment.

D. Tape files and software.

7-32. (Application Controls) Greg Heston, CPA, has been asked by his client, Atlanta Manufacturing, to explain the purpose of application controls in an EDP system because the client is considering installing a computerized system.

REQUIRED

A. Explain the differences among input, processing, and output controls.

B. Give examples of each type of control.

7-33. (Identifying Types of Controls) Various types of control structure policies and procedures are appropriate for prevention, detection, or correction of misstatements.

---

*AICPA adapted.

**CMA adapted.

REQUIRED

For each of the following situations, identify a policy or procedure that would have prevented, detected, or corrected the situation.

Back-up Computerize

A. A computer malfunction caused the system to be down for three days at the end of the month. As a result, payroll was late, end-of-month posting could not be made, and several reports were not on time. During this period the company could not find compatible equipment on which the critical activities could be processed.

B. A computer department employee was given two weeks' notice before he was terminated. During this time he removed the external labels from all the files in the library.

C. Late one night an employee was smoking in the data file library and carelessly dropped ashes in a waste paper container. The resulting fire destroyed several reels of tape on which the only master file of inventory and payroll was stored. The files had to be manually reconstructed.

D. During a street riot, several people forced their way into the computer center, which was on the main level of the office building. Several gunshots were fired into the computer and other minor destruction was incurred. The system was inoperable for several days.

E. A night operator knew more about the system than anyone else. During a period of several weeks, she accessed the master payroll program, which was stored on-line, and increased her tax withholding so that she would get a large refund when she filed her tax return.

F. A customer payment was entered by the keypunch operator as $147.22 instead of $14,722.00.

G. An employee using a direct-access terminal entered the wrong account number for a customer. The charges were entered on the account of another customer, who was very irritated when he received the bill for goods not ordered.

H. The accounts payable printout was not verified, and a double payment was made to a vendor. The vendor notified the company.

7-34. (Controls in an On-Line System) An on-line, real-time system is immediately updated when valid transactions are entered into the system. Various types of controls are used to insure that data are entered and processed correctly.

REQUIRED

Briefly comment on each of the following areas and discuss which control structure policies and procedures the auditor would be interested in to insure that the system is protected and functioning properly. The on-line system is in a retail store.

A. Terminals.

B. Data Access.

C. Processing Controls.

7-35. (Internal Control Considerations in a Microcomputer Environment) The second standard of fieldwork requires the auditor to obtain an understanding of the internal control structure sufficient to plan the audit.

Given the increasing use of microcomputers by many businesses today, the auditor must be cognizant of the potential internal control structure weaknesses that may be inherent in a microcomputer environment. Such knowledge is crucial if the auditor is to make a proper assessment of control risk and plan an effective and efficient audit approach.

In the following case study, assume you are participating in the audit of XYZ Company and the following background information has been obtained during the planning phase.

XYZ Company is a wholesale distributor of electric appliances. The company's sales in each of the past two years have been approximately $40,000,000. All accounting applications are handled at the company's corporate office.

The data-processing operations have historically centered around an onsite minicomputer. The computer applications include accounts payable, cash disbursements, payroll, inventory, and general ledger. Accounts receivable and fixed asset records have been prepared manually in the past. Control procedures in all areas have been considered strong in the last few years.

During the past year, financial management decided to automate processing of sales, accounts receivable, fixed asset transactions, and accounting. Management also concluded that purchasing a microcomputer and related available software was more cost-effective than increasing the minicomputer capacity and hiring a second computer operator. The controller and accounting clerks have been encouraged to find additional uses for the microcomputer and to experiment with it when they are not too busy.

The accounts receivable clerk is enthusiastic about the microcomputer, but the fixed asset clerk seems somewhat apprehensive about it because of a lack of experience with computers. The accounts receivable clerk explained that the controller had purchased a "very easy to use" accounts receivable software application program for the microcomputer that enables her to input quickly the daily information regarding billings and payments received. The controller has added to the software some programming of his own to give it better report-writing features.

During a recent demonstration, the accounts receivable clerk explained that the program requires her only to input the customer's name and invoice amount in the case of billings, or the customer's name and check amount in the case of payments. The microcomputer then automatically updates the respective customer's account balance. At the end of every month, the accounts receivable trial balance is printed and reconciled by the clerk to the general ledger balance. The reconciliation is reviewed by the controller.

The fixed asset program was also purchased from an outside vendor. The controller indicated that the software package had just recently been put on the market and that it was programmed to compute tax depreciation based on recent changes in the federal tax laws. He also stated that because of the fixed asset clerk's reluctance to use the microcomputer, he had input all the information from the fixed asset manual records. He indicated, however, that the fixed asset clerk would be responsible for the future processing related to the fixed asset files and for generating the month-end and year-end reports used to prepare the related accounting entries.

The various accounts receivable and fixed asset diskettes are all adequately labeled as to the type of program or data file and are arranged in an organized manner in a diskette holder located near the microcomputer.

REQUIRED

What are the potential effects on control risk that have been introduced by the micro-computer applications and how do those effects alter the audit plan for the current year?

7-36. (Controls in a Financial Institution) The Lee County Savings and Loan Association has the following organizational structure in its data processing department. The company employs three keypunch operators, two computer operators, one programmer, and a department head who assists with systems analysis and design. The programmer and the department head assist the operators when the workload is heavy, and on occasion the department head has done some programming. The programmer is primarily responsible for maintaining the existing system and for making infrequent changes. When no programming is necessary, she helps user departments interpret output information.

REQUIRED

How would you evaluate this situation, given the importance of controls in a financial institution? What changes would you recommend?

7-37. (Understanding the Internal Control Structure) Auditors are obligated to obtain an understanding of the internal control structure. That is, without regard to the method of processing—manual or EDP—the auditor has to obtain an understanding of the control structure sufficient to plan the audit.

REQUIRED

Does this require the auditor always to understand and document the general EDP controls?

7-38. (Internal Auditing and EDP) David Shaffer is the director of internal auditing at Azel College. Recently Shaffer met with Katherine Cater, EDP manager, and expressed the desire to establish a more effective cooperation between the two departments.

Subsequently, Cater requested Shaffer's views and help on a new computerized accounts payable system being developed. Cater recommended that internal auditing assume line responsibility for auditing suppliers' invoices prior to payment. Cater also requested that internal auditing make suggestions during development of the system, assist in its installation, and approve the completed system after making a final review.

REQUIRED

State how Shaffer should respond to the EDP manager, giving the reason why Shaffer should accept or reject each of the following:

A. The recommendation that the internal auditing department be responsible for the preaudit of suppliers' invoices. *(Reject)*

B. The request that internal auditing make suggestions during development of the system.

C. The request that internal auditing assist in the installation of the system and approve the system after making a final review.

Audit Judgment Case

7-39. You have audited Conn, Inc., for the last five years. During that time, Conn has grown to a size where it can no longer justify the inefficient manual accounting system it has used since its inception. As a result, it has purchased five minicomputers to use in the following aspects of its accounting system:

- Payroll processing
- Billing and accounts receivable processing
- Perpetual inventory record maintenance
- Accounts payable processing
- Fixed asset accounting

Conn has sent its two junior accountants as well as its accounting manager to an intensive two-week training course specializing in the hardware and accounting software it has purchased. In addition, each member of the accounting department has been assisted in installing and using the hardware and software by a vendor representative working on site for the first month of computer operations.

REQUIRED

Develop an internal control checklist to be used to both obtain an understanding of Conn's internal control structure for all of the above areas and to assess control risk for billing and accounts receivable and accounts payable. Your checklist should be in the form of specific questions to be asked to obtain the necessary information for the understanding and control risk assessments.

Auditing Issues Case

7-40. **KELCO MANUFACTURING COMPANY**

Kelco president, Steve Cook, has just been informed that the auditors believe that control procedures related to computer operations are sometimes weak. They have suggested the development of new programs and systems and also changes to existing programs and systems.

REQUIRED

1. What procedures and controls should Kelco use in developing new programs and systems?
2. What procedures and controls should Kelco use when making changes to existing programs and systems?
3. What are the disadvantages of adding controls after a system is operational?
4. What is the best way to add new procedures and controls?

Part Three

Auditing Tools and Techniques

Three tools and techniques available to the auditor in performing an audit engagement are computers, audit sampling, and analytical review procedures.

Chapter 8 discusses auditing in a computer environment and focuses on computer-assisted audit techniques.

Chapter 9 presents the underlying concepts of audit sampling and their effect on audit judgment.

Chapter 10 describes audit sampling applications, including both nonstatistical and statistical techniques.

Chapter 11 discusses the use of analytical procedures in an audit.

Auditing with Computers

Learning   Objectives

- Describe auditing around the computer.

- Identify the basic approaches for using computer-assisted audit techniques.

- Compare and contrast test data, parallel simulation, and an integrated test facility.

- Define *purpose-written programs* and describe their use by the auditor.

- Define *generalized audit software programs* and describe their use by the auditor.

- Identify the factors the auditor should consider when using a computer-assisted audit technique.

- Describe the effect of a computer service organization on the internal control structure and the audit.

As you begin to plan the audit of Best Client, Inc., you are called to a meeting with the audit partner to discuss the audit. Yesterday the audit partner and the client discussed ways of improving the audit—decreasing the audit costs, and obtaining more value from the audit. The audit partner believes that this can be accomplished by auditing more efficiently and by the increased use of technology. The audit partner and the client have both noticed that a significant amount of time is spent by the audit staff keying client accounting data into a microcomputer in order to perform certain audit tests using Lotus 1-2-3 and Paradox. This data is available in the client's large mainframe computer and two minicomputers.

The audit partner wants to know why this information cannot be transferred from the client's computers automatically into the audit staff's microcomputer. The audit partner believes that this would be more efficient and would like you to explain why you cannot implement this automatic transferral of data.

After some research, you determine that data can be transferred from a mainframe computer or a minicomputer into a microcomputer, by a process called downloading. ■

Source: J. Christopher Reimel, "Using Downloading as an Audit Tool," *AICPA InfoTech Update*, Spring 1994, p. 3. Reprinted with permission from *InfoTech Update*, Spring 1994. Copyright © 1994 by AICPA.

In planning, as noted in the preceding chapter, the auditor should consider the methods an entity uses to process its accounting information. Most accounting systems today, of course, use a computer to process accounting information. Thus, the auditor should consider the effects of computer applications on the entity's financial statements and then design auditing procedures accordingly.

The preceding chapter discussed the characteristics of a computer system and presented a computer's effect on the internal control structure. This chapter describes the auditor's responsibilities when auditing in such a computer environment by discussing the two basic approaches: auditing around the computer and computer-assisted audit techniques. When *auditing around the computer*, the auditor examines inputs and outputs of the computer but does not use the computer to test controls or to extract and analyze data for substantive testing. In other words, the auditor's procedures are designed as if the client did not have a computer, and the auditor does not use microcomputer-aided auditing. Alternatively, *computer-assisted audit techniques* are the tools and techniques that include the computer as an integral part of the audit procedures performed.

Auditing Around the Computer

Normally, as a part of the audit process, the auditor examines various documents used as inputs into the accounting system, such as sales invoices, purchases invoices, or employee time cards. These documents are typically tested for accuracy and compared to journals and ledgers. Testing of these inputs is the basis for substantiation of such outputs as financial statements or listings of accounts receivable. If a client uses a computer to help process information, prepare journals and ledgers, and provide various statements and schedules, much of the information and output may be stored in the computer and may not be available to the auditor except in a computer file. In these situations, the audit trail may not be visible.

When auditing around the computer, the auditor examines inputs and outputs of the computer system but does not use the computer to perform tests of controls or substantive tests. If portions of the audit trail are stored in the computer, auditing around the computer requires that various documents, journals, ledgers, and statements be printed. The auditor performs the audit similarly to any other audit in which documents, journals, and ledgers are available as an audit trail. The printouts can be costly and may be time-consuming for the client to print.

Auditing around the computer may be acceptable if the auditor has confidence that the printouts are genuine replicas of the documents and records, and that the cost of performing the audit procedure is less than one using computer-assisted audit techniques. However, auditing around the computer still requires the auditor to sufficiently understand the internal control structure, including computer processing, to design an appropriate audit program.

Computer-Assisted Audit Techniques

When a client uses a computer for significant accounting applications, the auditor may use computer-assisted audit techniques (CAATs) to aid in performing a more efficient and effective audit.[1] However, before deciding to use CAATs, the auditor must satisfactorily answer the following questions:

1. Will the audit objectives be accomplished with CAATs? In short, will the audit be effective?
2. Is it practical for the auditor to perform audit tests manually? Due to the nature of computer processing, the auditor cannot always carry out tests using conventional methods. Many computerized accounting systems perform tasks for which no visible evidence is available. For example, input documents may not exist for sales in an on-line system. Also, no visible evidence of internal control structure policies and procedures may exist when customer credit limits are checked using a computer.
3. Will the client cooperate with requests for assistance? The client is interested foremost in processing data on the computer to facilitate daily operations. The client must be willing to cooperate by allowing use of the computer, providing assistance by computer department personnel, and allowing access to data and computer programs. The auditor will need to schedule use of any of these items around the client's schedule. Assistance by the client improves the efficiency and reduces the cost of the audit.
4. What is the cost of developing CAATs? Does each audit require a different CAAT, or can CAATs be easily modified for use in audits of other clients?

Questions 1 and 2 relate to the *effectiveness* of the audit, whereas Questions 3 and 4 relate to the *efficiency* of the audit. With answers to the above questions the auditor can decide whether to use CAATs, and which CAAT to use. Table 8–1 compares auditing around the computer to using CAATs.

---

[1] Some auditors use the terms *auditing through the computer* and *auditing with the computer* for various CAATs.

Table 8-1	Comparison of Auditing Around the Computer to Using Computer-Assisted Audit Techniques

Auditing Around the Computer

Advantages	Disadvantages
Requires very little knowledge of computers. May be less costly. May be quicker and easier. Entails no risk of tampering with live client data.	May require printouts, which can be costly. May use printouts that are not genuine replicas of documents. May not be possible because there is no audit trail. May result in an unreadable printout. Is usually not adequate or efficient for most computer systems.

Computer-Assisted Audit Techniques

Advantages	Disadvantages
Increases extent of tests. Achieves greater confidence of data processing. May obtain greater reliance on outputs. Can verify rejection of incorrect inputs by the computer into the system. May reduce or eliminate printouts. May eliminate certain audit procedures. May allow better timing of audit procedures. May re-sort various data files for additional or different audit tests. Can evaluate on-line systems.	Requires more extensive knowledge of computers. May be more costly. May encounter problems with scheduling use of client's computer and personnel.

[Handwritten marginal notes: "Substantive based audit 10-15-94" and "All substantive. Data expensive and more time consuming"]

Types of CAATs

Numerous types of CAATs are available to auditors. These CAATs use diverse approaches and require varying levels of computer expertise. Commonly used CAATs include

- test data
- integrated test facility
- parallel simulation
- review of program logic
- purpose-written programs
- generalized audit software programs
- utility programs
- artificial intelligence and expert systems

The test data, integrated test facility, parallel simulation, and review of program logic techniques are generally used in mainframe (large) computer environments for purposes of testing computer-based controls. Purpose-written, generalized audit software, and utility programs are used primarily for substantive test applications in mainframe, minicomputer, and microcomputer environments.

Test Data

In a *test data* approach, the auditor develops different types of transactions that are subsequently processed using the client's computer system. The audit objective is to determine whether the client's computer system can correctly identify and process valid transactions and reject invalid transactions. The auditor traces the sample transactions through the client's system to their final disposition. When using test data, the auditor knows what the input is, how these transactions should be processed, and what output should result.

Test data should include all types of transactions, including exceptions and errors. For example, an auditor normally would want to include in the test data missing transactions, erroneous transactions, out-of-balance batches, and out-of-sequence records. The auditor may either create test data or select them from actual client data. To increase efficiency, the auditor may use test data generator software to develop test data.

Test data are usually used on a surprise basis so that client personnel will not be able to modify computer programs in anticipation of the auditor's application of the test data. Because the auditor knows what processing errors should be identified, test data allow the auditor to check the error listings against input.

Advantages of test data include the ability to provide for an objective assessment of computer programs, the ability to test on a surprise basis, and a method that provides a good opportunity to review the overall system and its controls. However, using test data does have limitations. It is often difficult to establish that the program being tested is the one that the client uses regularly. The auditor also assumes that the system processing the test data is the same system that has been in effect through the time period under audit. In addition, test data require that the auditor have a great deal of expertise and are not conclusive because of the difficulty of testing all combinations and conditions. Figure 8–1 illustrates a test data approach.

Integrated Test Facility (ITF)

In an *integrated test facility (ITF)*, a fictitious entity is established (for example, a customer, department, division, or employee) in the database of the system. Unknown to the systems personnel, fictitious data are used to test transactions during processing of regular transactions. This approach integrates test data into the system and permits the auditor to monitor the performance of the system continuously. The ITF requires the auditor to verify the output of dummy transactions against the results expected by the auditor. ITF is similar to a test data approach but, with ITF, dummy transactions and real transactions are processed together while the client personnel are unaware of the testing process. Figure 8–2 illustrates an ITF.

Parallel Simulation

An alternative to the test data approach is to use parallel simulation. In *parallel simulation*, the auditor processes client input data using a controlled duplicate program that is under the auditor's control. The programs used in parallel simulation may be purpose-written, generalized audit software, or utility programs, which will be discussed later in this chapter. Otherwise, in parallel simulation the auditor will use a controlled client program (that is, a copy of a client program maintained by the auditor that has not been affected by any subsequent unauthorized changes in the client

Providing Auditor Prepared data and client data processing

Testing Client's Program

Figure 8–1	**Test Data Approach**

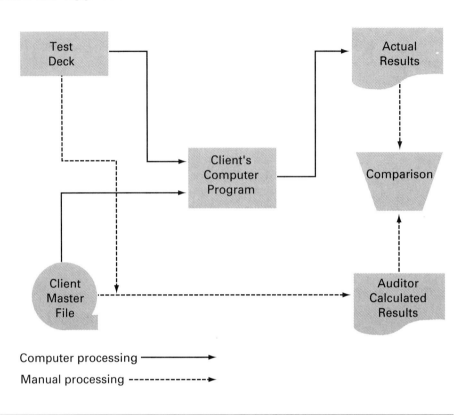

Computer processing ──────▶

Manual processing ------------▶

program). The auditor can compare the output from this audited run to the client's original output. Parallel simulation is advantageous because it allows the auditor to test genuine input against a controlled program, thus eliminating the need to prepare test data. Figure 8–3 illustrates parallel simulation using a generalized audit software program (GASP) discussed later in this chapter.

Review of Program Logic

Reviewing programming

Review of program logic is a technique used to enhance the auditor's understanding of a client's particular computer program or a critical processing element of a program (for example, interest calculations in a financial institution). The review would normally include gathering the available documentation for the program or application and reviewing the documentation to develop a sufficient understanding of the program or application to meet the auditor's objective.

Rather than review the program logic, the auditor could obtain an understanding of the client's program both by reviewing system descriptions, flowcharts, and file layouts, and by questioning data processing personnel and users. However, a review of program logic is useful when documentation and client personnel do not provide the auditor with an adequate understanding of the system or when possible errors or fraud come to the auditor's attention and the auditor wishes to investigate the

Figure 8-2

Integrated Test Facility (ITF)

Secretive

Fictitious entity is invented.

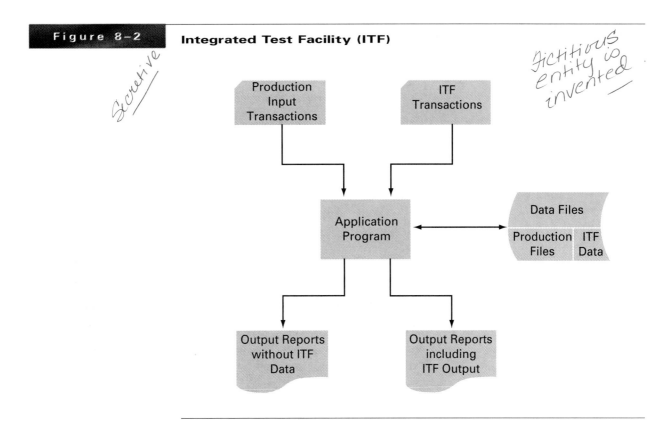

application in detail. To perform a review of program logic, the auditor should have sufficient knowledge of the computer language in which the program is written. Sometimes the auditor may use flowcharting software to produce flowcharts of program logic. Finally, the auditor must establish that the program reviewed is, in fact, the program that the client uses.

Purpose-Written Programs

The auditor may want to use computer programs to process data of audit significance from the client's accounting system. The auditor may use any of four types of computer programs: purpose-written programs, generalized audit software programs, utility programs, and artificial intelligence and expert systems. *Purpose-written programs* are computer programs designed to perform audit tasks in specific circumstances. These programs may be prepared by the auditor, by the client, or by an outside programmer engaged by the auditor and may be run on the client's computer or the auditor's microcomputer.

If programs written by the client are readily available, they may be adapted to the auditor's use. The client may also be willing to reduce the cost of the audit by writing new programs specifically for the auditor. The auditor must still verify and test these client-written programs, however, and must be satisfied that they do not circumvent the auditor's objectives. For example, does a program that provides a listing of the accounts receivable and a total fail to list certain accounts but nevertheless add the amounts for these accounts into the total?

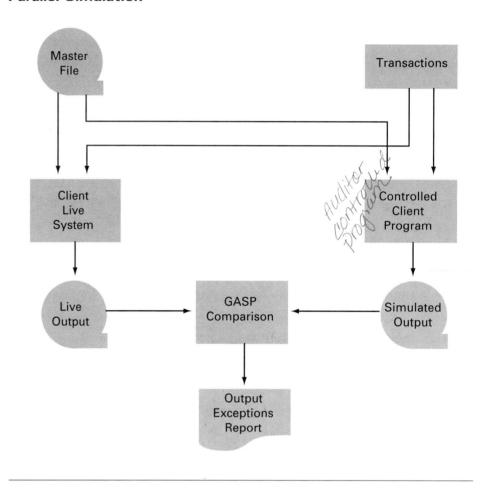

Figure 8-3   **Parallel Simulation**

To avoid the possibility that errors or irregularities exist in programs written by the client, auditors may choose to write their own programs. This process requires that the auditor have a thorough knowledge of computer programming, write the program, and test and debug the program. This type of purpose-written program provides greater assurance but requires extensive time by the auditor, possibly increases the audit costs, and may apply only to a particular client.

Generalized Audit Software Programs (GASP)

To alleviate many of the potential problems associated with purpose-written programs, *generalized audit software programs (GASPs)* have been developed for mainframes, minicomputers, and microcomputers. These are computer programs written in programming languages to perform routine audit procedures such as reading computer files, selecting information, performing calculations, and printing reports. Their primary purpose is to reduce the programming effort and technical knowledge required by the auditor. A CPA firm may develop its own GASP or use

Table 8-2	**Advantages and Disadvantages of Generalized Audit Software Programs**	
	Advantages	Disadvantages
	Reduces auditor reliance on client computer personnel.	Disregarding efficiency, written for ease of implementation.
	Eliminates the need to learn a programming language.	Functions only on certain computers, thus it may require that data be downloaded or processed elsewhere.
	Requires a short time to learn.	Is usually limited to testing data files.
	Reduces required level of computer expertise.	
	Accesses a wide variety of client records interchangeably without special programming.	
	Allows auditor to control program execution.	
	Facilitates review of entire data files or selected data and performs calculations and other useful audit tasks.	
	Produces audit work papers.	

° Testing for mathematical correctness.

one developed by another organization. GASPs are the most widely used computer-assisted audit technique, and are readily available from software vendors. They are primarily used to assist with substantive testing.

A major advantage of GASPs is that members of the audit staff who are not computer experts can easily be trained to use a GASP. These programs have already been tested, and user manuals and training programs are readily available. A disadvantage is that a particular GASP may not be compatible with the client's computer facility. However, in those cases the auditor may be able to process the client's file at another location or download data from the client's mainframe or minicomputer to the auditor's microcomputer. Advantages and disadvantages of GASPs are shown in Table 8–2.

Performance and Audit Procedures

By using GASPs, many audit procedures can be performed by the computer to make the audit more efficient. For example:

1. *Change in Extent of Testing* The prior audit procedure might have required the auditor to test and review the aging of the accounts receivable, manually verify the totals of the ages and listing of accounts receivable, manually select the accounts to be confirmed, and observe the preparation of the confirmation requests. With the use of a computer, the prior audit procedure can be made more extensive. The computer can age all of the accounts, total the ages and listing of the accounts receivable, and select the accounts to be confirmed statistically. The confirmation requests can also be printed by the computer.

2. *Change in Nature of Testing* Under the old procedure, the auditor observed the inventory at the inventory date and made a list of selected items. After the client prepared and

completed the final inventory listing, which might be several weeks later, the auditor traced the items from the list of selected items into the final inventory listing. Under the new procedure, the auditor could observe the inventory, verify that a computer inventory card was prepared for each inventory item, and maintain control of the inventory cards until a listing of the computer inventory cards was run on the computer by the client. The entire procedure could be completed the same day. The auditor, therefore, would not have to trace the items from the list of selected items into the final inventory listing several weeks later.

3. *Change in Timing of Testing* Under the old procedure, the auditor manually selected the accounts receivable to be confirmed from the client's accounts receivable schedule. This schedule typically would not have been prepared and completed until several days after year-end. If the accounts receivable schedule is prepared by the computer, the auditor could statistically select the accounts to be confirmed by the computer and have the computer print the confirmation requests all on the same day.

Numerous audit functions can be performed with GASPs. In general, they are used to accomplish six basic kinds of tasks. These are as follows:

1. *Examining records based on criteria specified by the auditor.* Because the records in a manual system are visible, the auditor can scan for inconsistencies or inaccuracies without difficulty. For records on computer data files, the auditor can specify GASPs instructions to scan the records for propriety in terms of specified criteria and print records that are exceptions to the criteria, so that follow-up action can be taken. Examples of this type of procedure are

   - reviewing accounts receivable balances for amounts over credit limit.

   - reviewing inventory quantities for negative and unreasonably large balances.

   - identifying transactions with related parties.

2. *Testing calculations and making computations.* The auditor can use GASPs to test the accuracy of computations and to perform quantitative analyses to evaluate the reasonableness of client representations. Examples are

   - recalculating the extensions of inventory items.

   - recalculating depreciation amounts.

   - recalculating interest.

   - determining the accuracy of employee net pay computations.

3. *Comparing data on separate (different) files.* When records on separate files should contain compatible (comparable) information, GASPs may be able to compare the files to determine if the information agrees. Examples are

   - comparing payroll details with personnel records.

   - comparing current and prior period inventory files to assist in reviewing for obsolete or slow-moving items.

4. *Selecting and printing audit samples.* Many GASPs have the capability to select samples using random or other sampling methods. Multiple criteria may be used for selection—for example, a judgment sample of high-dollar and old items and a representative sample of all other items. Selected items can be printed in the auditor's working paper format or on special confirmation forms. Examples are

   - accounts receivable balances for confirmations.

   - inventory items for observation.

   - plant asset additions for vouching.

5. *Summarizing or resequencing data and performing analyses.* GASPs can reformat and aggregate data in a variety of ways. This allows the auditor to prepare analyses and to simulate the client's data processing systems to determine the reasonableness of the client's results. Examples are

   - totaling transactions on account files.
   - preparing general ledger trial balances.
   - testing accounts receivable aging.
   - summarizing inventory turnover statistics for obsolescence analysis.
   - resequencing inventory items by location to facilitate physical observations.

6. *Comparing data obtained through other audit procedures with client records.* Audit evidence generated manually can be converted to machine-readable form (that is, keyed as input) and compared to other machine-readable data. An example is

   - comparing inventory tests counts with perpetual records.

Use of GASPs with Microcomputers

As noted in Chapter 7, many clients use microcomputers both to process data and to aid in conducting the daily affairs of the entity more quickly and in a less costly manner. Auditors also use microcomputers in their offices and sometimes carry portable microcomputers to the client's office.

Many microcomputer GASP products are useful for auditing. Some of these are specifically designed to perform audit tasks, such as audit sampling or assessing control risk. Other GASPs are intended to perform general functions and may be used to perform audit tasks. Common types of GASPs include electronic spreadsheets, word processing, database management, text database software, communications software, graphics software, and practice management software.

Electronic Spreadsheet Software   One of the primary uses of the microcomputer is the preparation of an electronic spreadsheet by using a software program. Spreadsheets are computerized columnar pads and can be adjusted easily to handle numerous types of problems and calculations. The number of rows and columns can vary; the information can be rearranged in different sequences, such as in alphabetical instead of numerical order; and errors can be corrected or changes made by as little as a single keystroke. Any audit task that requires a pencil, worksheet, and calculator can be performed using an electronic spreadsheet.

Word Processing Software   Word-processing programs increase the speed and ease with which documents can be prepared and edited. They combine the capabilities of the typewriter with those of the microcomputer so that copy can be changed, deleted, or moved, and text inserted without retyping the entire document. Most word-processing products also have spelling and dictionary features to improve the accuracy of documents. Word-processing software is particularly useful when documents are subject to frequent revisions or when a number of documents contain similar wording. Audit applications of word processing include preparation of engagement letters, representation letters, attorney letters, system narratives, audit programs, audit reports, and financial statements.

Database Management Software   Database management software manages the storing, processing, and retrieving of information. Data such as accounts receivable are organized in the form of predefined records, and the database software is used to select, update, sort, display, or print these records. Procedures for preparing and controlling confirmation of accounts receivable are common audit applications of this software.

Text Database Software These software packages allow the auditor to view any text that is available in an electronic format. The software programs allow the auditor to browse through text much like reading a book, only faster. The auditor can search the text based upon specified criteria. For example, the auditor can key in the words "statistical sampling" and within seconds see every location in the SASs where "statistical sampling" appears.

Communications Software These packages enable a microcomputer user to transmit or receive data directly to or from another computer. This software requires a device called a *modem*, which permits data transmission over telephone lines. These programs are used in audits to communicate with word-processing equipment, the client's computers, and commercial database services, as well as with members of the engagement team in other locations.

Graphics Software Graphics software takes numerical data and displays it in the form of graphic representations such as lines, bars, and pie charts. Some graphics software can produce three-dimensional, multicolor, or text-supplemented graphics. Applications of graphics software include engagement proposals, financial reports, and analytical procedures. Special printers may be needed to take advantage of the software's graphics capabilities.

Practice Management Software In many CPA firms, the use of an automated practice management program permits more timely and accurate client billing. If time worked for various clients is entered into the system daily, these programs allow bills to be generated upon job completion. Many packages also enable the CPA firm to generate management reports to control allocation and use of staff resources.

Microcomputer Applications

Prior to arriving at the client's office, the auditor may have used the microcomputer to prepare audit working papers that might include the following:

Audit Programs Microcomputers can be used to prepare and update audit programs through the use of word-processing software. These programs can be saved from one year to the next to facilitate updates and changes. Special use programs allow for more sophisticated microcomputer use in developing audit programs. By helping the auditor think through the planning consideration of the audit and selecting the appropriate procedures from a database of audit procedures, an audit program is formed.

Internal Control Structure Checklists Microcomputers can be used to document the understanding of the internal control structure with either a narrative description or an internal control structure questionnaire.

Working Trial Balances The microcomputer is easily used to develop working trial balances. As adjusting journal entries are made, they can be posted electronically and an updated version of the trial balance will be immediately available. Upon completion of the audit work, the final trial balance accounts can be aggregated for drafting the financial statements.

Engagement Time Schedules   Electronic spreadsheets are extremely useful for preparing time budgets and monitoring time spent in relation to budget.

Lead Schedules   Microcomputers can be used to develop lead and related detailed schedules for the various financial statement accounts. As with the working trial balances, adjusting journal entries electronically update the lead schedules. This updated information is immediately available.

Prior Year Financial Statements   With the use of the microcomputer, prior year financial statements are easily saved and retrieved for comparisons.

Besides performing audit procedures and tests, microcomputers can also be used for the following tasks:

1. Preparing the tax-return supporting schedules as well as the tax return.
2. Generating information for consulting services for the client such as
   a. What will be the effect on the financial statements if the client leases or buys an asset?
   b. What will be the effect on the financial statements if the client acquires another company?
   c. What effects will issuing stocks or bonds have on earnings per share?
3. Developing compilation or review checklists and generating the related accountant's reports.

Utility Programs

Utility programs are computer programs typically provided by the computer manufacturer that perform such common data processing functions as

- changing the media of a file (for example, from tape to disk).
- modifying the data by changing or deleting records within a file.
- creating, deleting, or erasing a file.
- changing the name or password of a file.
- printing the file so that it may be visually inspected.
- resequencing the file by sorting.

These functions may be useful to the auditor in performing tests of controls and substantive tests and in understanding the control structure. Auditors can use utility programs in a variety of ways, including the following:

- To sort a file into a specific sequence before using it as input.
- To copy a representative sample of records from a file, to be used as a test file.
- To print a portion or all of the records on a specific file so that they can be visually inspected.
- To copy a disk file so that it can be processed at another installation.

Utility programs often duplicate many of the capabilities of a GASP and may be available when GASPs are not. However, utility programs are usually written for use by operators and programmers, and the auditor may find them more difficult to use than a GASP. When utility programs are used, the auditor should properly control their application.

Artificial Intelligence and Expert Systems

A recent development in auditing is the application of artificial intelligence software products. Artificial intelligence represents computer applications in which the computer, through programming, is given human-like abilities to reason and to learn. Artificial intelligence includes three branches: expert systems, natural language communicating, and robotics. Of most interest to auditors are *expert systems*, which are computer programs that emulate the thought processes of human experts in solving problems. Expert systems can be used by auditors in a variety of areas such as planning, assessing control risk, and quality review. For example, the auditor may use an expert system in audit planning by entering financial statement balances in the computer and then allowing the expert system to suggest specific audit procedures to be performed.

Considerations in Using Computer-Assisted Audit Techniques

In using CAATs, the following factors should be considered:

- Planning
- Impracticality of manual tests
- Effectiveness and efficiency
- Timing of tests
- Controlling the application

Planning

Technical information must be gathered to meet the requirements of the CAATs being used. A description of the computer facilities and the systems documentation, including flowcharts, is needed. A knowledge of the client's files, the various input documents, how each type of transaction is processed, and the various outputs must also be obtained. The client's assistance is necessary to confirm the accuracy and completeness of the information and to minimize costs. In addition, the auditor must have sufficient knowledge and experience to use the particular CAAT selected.

Specific audit objectives must be defined, such as to test the mathematical accuracy of extensions and footings on sales invoices or to verify that a shipping document number is noted for all sales invoices. Arrangements should be made for client personnel to be available for assistance and for needed forms and computer tapes or files to be supplied.

The auditor should also determine that suitable computer facilities are available. If the auditor plans to use the client's computer, a schedule should be developed for use of computer facilities and a target date established for completing the work. Frequently, the auditor will use the entity's facilities, but other facilities, or the auditor's microcomputer, may be used when the entity's computer is uneconomical or impractical (for example, when a GASP is not compatible with the entity's computer).

Are you able to plan and take advantage of the CAATs

Impracticality of Manual Tests

In some situations, performing audit tests manually is impractical. This is often the case when a computer performs tasks for which no visible evidence is available. The lack of visible evidence may occur at different stages of the accounting process, including the following:

- Input documents may be nonexistent when, for example, sales orders are entered on-line. In addition, accounting transactions, such as discounts and interest calculations, may be generated by computer programs with no visible authorization of individual transactions.

- The system may not produce a visible audit trail of transactions processed through the computer. Receiving reports and supplier's invoices may be matched by a computer program. In addition, programmed control procedures, such as checking customer credit limits, may provide visible evidence only on an exception basis. In such cases, there may be no visible evidence that all transactions have been processed.

- Output reports may not be produced by the system. In addition, a printed report may only contain summary totals while supporting details are retained in computer files.

Effectiveness and Efficiency

In many situations, the effectiveness and efficiency of auditing procedures may be improved by using CAATs. For example, the computer may be better able to perform routine calculations, such as totaling the accounts receivable subsidiary ledger. Similarly, analytical procedures can often be performed effectively and efficiently by using the computer. The development and initial use of a CAAT may be expensive; however, the continued use of the CAAT over time may make the CAAT an effective and efficient audit approach.

Timing of Tests

The auditor should consider whether the entity's computer files are available and for what period of time. For example, some computer files are retained for a short time and then are destroyed. In this situation, the auditor should make arrangements either to have the files retained or to perform the audit procedures during the time the data are available.

**Controlling the
Application**

When using a CAAT, the auditor should determine that its application has been properly controlled. This would include having reasonable assurance that the audit objectives and detailed specifications of the CAAT have been met and that the CAAT has not been improperly manipulated by the entity personnel.

In controlling the application, the auditor should review the entity's general computer controls that may contribute to the integrity of the CAAT — for example, controls over program changes and access to computer files. When such controls cannot be relied upon to ensure the integrity of the CAAT, the auditor may consider processing the CAAT application at another computer facility or using microcomputer software.

When the CAAT that the auditor has selected is a purpose-written program, a GASP, or a utility program, numerous control procedures are available. The specific control procedures necessary, of course, depend upon the circumstances. Procedures that may be considered by the auditor include the following:

- Participating in the design and testing of the computer programs.
- Checking the coding of the program to ensure that it conforms with the detailed program specifications.
- Running the audit software on small test files before running it on the main data files.
- Ensuring that the correct files were used — for example, by checking with external evidence, such as control totals maintained by the user.
- Obtaining evidence that the audit software functioned as planned — for example, reviewing output and control information.
- Establishing appropriate security measures to safeguard against manipulation of the entity's data files.

Computer Service Organizations

Many entities use another organization to execute transactions and maintain accountability for the related asset. For example, a bank trust department may invest and hold investment assets for an employee benefit trust. Further, some entities choose not to have their own data processing system for certain systems because of such factors as expense, the additional employees that might be required, and lack of technical knowledge by anyone in the company. In these varied situations, entities will often elect to use the services of a computer service organization.

As described in Chapter 7, a computer *service organization* processes the client's input data and provides the output to the client. Some service organizations provide the physical computer facility, while users of the service organization provide their own programs, data entry services, and computer operators. Other service organizations provide not only the computer equipment but programming services, data entry services, input–output control functions, and report distribution services as well. Service organizations typically provide computer operators and computer programs for use in processing user data.

Many similarities exist between a computer service organization's system and a computerized data processing system that an entity might have. For example, programs must be written, tested, and debugged. In addition, controls over inputs, processing, and outputs must be developed and implemented.

Effect on Internal Control Structure

When an entity uses a service organization to process significant financial data, its internal control structure is generally affected. Although the computer processing performed at a service organization may result in account records similar to those of a client, differences typically exist between the way a service organization is operated and the way a client would use its own accounting system.

A client that uses a service organization may also use control policies and procedures at the service organization as well as control policies and procedures at the client location. In fact, most clients use a combination of control policies and procedures performed by both the service organization and client personnel.

Responsibilities of service organizations to users vary. Typically, user personnel are responsible for providing accurate data on a timely basis, maintaining controls to detect inaccurate data entry, and making corrections in data as necessary.

Effect on the Auditor's Understanding and Assessment of Control

When an entity uses a service organization to process accounting data, transactions that affect the entity's financial statements flow through an internal control structure that is partially separate from the client. As discussed in Chapter 6, the client's auditor is required to obtain an understanding of the internal control structure sufficient to plan the audit. The auditor considers the information available about the service organization's control environment, accounting system, and control procedures, including information in the client's possession such as user manuals, systems overview, technical manuals, and service organization audit reports on control structure. The service organization's auditor reports, if available, will at a minimum, provide an opinion on the service organization's systems description and its design (type A report). That opinion is useful in helping the client's auditor gain the required understanding of internal control structure.

Input–Output Controls

As *SAS No. 70, Reports on the Processing of Transactions by Service Organizations* (AU 324), observes, the entity's auditor may be able to reduce the assessed level of control risk by testing input and output controls without considering the control policies and procedures of the service organization relating to processing. For example, an entity may use a service center to process payroll transactions. The entity may establish controls over the payroll data that are sent to the service organization (for example, a review of employee time reports by supervisory personnel) and over the payroll data returned by the service organization (for example, an employee may reperform payroll calculations on a test basis).

Controls of the Service Organization

In other circumstances, however, the auditor may find that in order to do an effective audit it is necessary to assess controls located at the service organization. The auditor may sometimes also decide to assess controls at the service organization to do an efficient audit. If the auditor plans to assess control risk below the maximum, he or she should consider the controls located at the service organization.

Two methods are used by auditors to assess control risk of controls at service organizations: direct testing by the auditor and use of the service organization auditor.

Direct Testing by the Auditor   The auditor may use the same criteria to assess the service organization's internal control structure as is used to assess the client's internal control structure. The auditor may use a variety of techniques, including test data, parallel simulation, and integrated test facilities. He or she should identify the control procedures located at the client's facility and at the service organization. Certain controls, such as input controls, may be used by the client to verify correct processing of the data by the service organization. Other controls, such as processing controls, could be located at the service organization. Once having identified the controls and their location, the auditor may perform tests of controls to reduce the assessed level of control risk.

Use of the Service Organization Auditor   Because service organizations often process data for many entities, it may be more efficient to have one auditor test controls for the service organization rather than to have the auditor of each customer test the controls separately. To avoid inefficiency and to provide assurances of the effectiveness of the internal control structure, service organizations often have external auditors issue a report (type B report) on the service organization that includes (a) an opinion on the description of the service organization's system and its design and (b) an opinion on the system's operating effectiveness based on tests of controls. The detailed tests of controls, appended to the service organization auditor's report, may be used by the client's auditor to assess control risk below the maximum for certain assertions. *SAS No. 70* (AU 324.1.22–.58) provides guidelines to service organization auditors for issuing reports on the design and effectiveness of service organization controls.

Significant Terms

Auditing around the computer   An audit approach whereby the auditor tests inputs and outputs of the computer but does not use the computer to perform tests of controls or substantive tests.

Computer-assisted audit techniques (CAATs)   The tools and techniques, such as audit software and test data, used by the auditor with the computer to aid in the effective and efficient performance of an audit.

Expert systems   Computer programs that emulate the thinking processes of human experts to attain a performance level comparable to those experts in carrying out a specific task.

Generalized audit software programs (GASPs)   Readily available computer programs that read the client's data, process the data, perform the indicated audit procedures, and require little programming effort and technical knowledge by the auditor.

Integrated test facility (ITF)   A computer-assisted audit technique that uses fictitious data and processes it with real data to test computer controls while the client's personnel are unaware of the testing process.

Parallel simulation   A computer-assisted audit technique that uses client input data and processes it on a duplicate or controlled program to test controls in the computer system without having to develop test data.

Purpose-written programs   Audit programs designed to perform audit tasks in specific client circumstances.

Review of program logic   A computer-assisted audit technique in which the auditor, to develop an understanding of a computer program, gathers documentation of the program and then reviews that documentation.

Service organization An independent organization that provides computer services to other entities.

Test data Data developed by the auditor that are subsequently processed using the client's computer system to determine whether the system can correctly identify and process valid transactions and reject invalid transactions.

Utility programs Computer programs that perform common data processing functions, such as sorting, creating, and printing files.

Discussion Questions

8-1. What is the difference between auditing around the computer and computer-assisted audit techniques (CAATs)?

8-2. What are the requirements for auditing around the computer?

8-3. What questions should the auditor consider before deciding to use computer-assisted audit techniques?

8-4. Identify and describe types of computer-assisted audit techniques.

8-5. Compare and contrast the test data and parallel simulation approaches.

8-6. Give examples of types of test data that could be used when the auditor is testing a client's payroll system.

8-7. How does an integrated test facility use test data?

8-8. What advantages does an integrated test facility have over a test data approach?

8-9. If the auditor decides to use a purpose-written program written by the client, what responsibilities does the auditor have?

8-10. What are the advantages and disadvantages of generalized audit software programs?

8-11. Describe types of outputs for which extensions and footings can be verified using a generalized audit software program (GASP).

8-12. In what ways might data be listed and summarized in a different manner for the auditor using a GASP? For example, sales may be summarized by sales personnel rather than by types of product.

8-13. List three documents or audit working papers that could be prepared by the auditor with a microcomputer before the auditor arrives at the client's office.

8-14. In what ways could the auditor use the microcomputer both during and after the audit?

8-15. A client may ask the auditor, "What will be the effects if we change from...to...?" In what situations could the auditor use the microcomputer to determine the effects?

8-16. What are some examples of how an auditor may use a utility program?

8-17. What factors should the auditor consider in using a CAAT?

8-18. How should the auditor control the use of a CAAT?

8-19. What control procedures does an auditor turn to when using a GASP?

8-20. What types of services does a computer service organization provide?

8-21. What effects does a computer service organization have on a client's internal control structure?

8-22. What effects does a computer service organization have on the auditor's understanding of internal control structure and assessment of control risk?

8-23. How might an auditor of a user entity use the auditor of a computer service organization?

Objective Questions

8-24. Which of the following is true of generalized audit software programs?

(1) They can be used only in auditing on-line computer systems.

(2) They can be used on any computer without modification.

(3) Each has its own characteristics that the auditor must carefully consider before using it in a given audit situation.

(4) They cannot be used on microcomputers.

8-25. Smith T Enterprises has changed from a manual to a computerized payroll clock card system. Factory employees now record time in and out with magnetic cards and the computer system automatically updates all payroll records. Because of this change,

    (1) the auditor must use a computer-assisted audit technique.

    (2) the internal control structure has improved.

    (3) part of the audit trail has been lost.

    (4) the potential for payroll-related fraud has been diminished.

*8-26. When testing a computerized accounting system, which of the following is *not* true of the test data approach?

    (1) Test data are processed by the client's computer program under the auditor's control.

    (2) The test data must consist of all possible valid and invalid conditions.

    (3) The test data need consist only of those valid and invalid conditions in which the auditor is interested.

    (4) Only one transaction of each type need be tested.

*8-27. A primary advantage of using GASPs in the audit of an advanced computer system is that they enable the auditor to

    (1) substantiate the accuracy of data through self-checking digits and hash totals.

    (2) use the speed and accuracy of the computer.

    (3) verify the performance of machine operations that leave visible evidence of occurrence.

    (4) gather and store large quantities of supportive evidential matter in machine-readable form.

8-28. Which of the following is true of tests of controls for a computer system?

    (1) They can only be performed using actual transactions because testing of simulated transactions is of no consequence.

    (2) They can be performed using actual transactions or simulated transactions.

    (3) They are impractical because many procedures within the computer activity leave no visible evidence of having been performed.

    (4) They are inadvisable because they may distort the evidence in master files.

*8-29. What does the flowchart below depict?

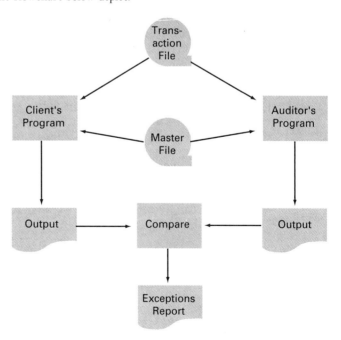

---

(1) Program code checking.
(2) Parallel simulation.
(3) Integrated test facility.
(4) Controlled reprocessing.
*8-30. Which of the following computer-assisted auditing techniques allows fictitious and real transactions to be processed together without client operating personnel being aware of the testing process?
(1) Parallel simulation.
(2) Generalized audit software programming.
(3) Integrated test facility.
(4) Test data approach.

Problems and Cases

*8-31. (Using the Computer) In the past, the records to be evaluated in an audit have been printed reports, listings, documents, and written papers, all of which are visible output. However, in fully computerized systems that employ daily updating of transaction files, output and files are frequently in machine-readable forms such as tapes or disks. Thus, they often present the auditor with an opportunity to use the computer in performing an audit.
REQUIRED
Discuss how the client's computer can be used to aid the auditor in auditing accounts receivable in such a fully computerized system. Include the following areas:
A. Testing extensions and footings.
B. Confirmation requests.
C. Summarizing data and performing analyses.
D. Selecting and printing audit samples.
E. Comparing data.
F. Checking to see if customers have exceeded credit limits.

8-32. (Test Data Approach) Test data are used to see if data are processed correctly and if improper data are rejected.
REQUIRED
Listed below are several ways test data can be used to detect improper data. Briefly explain each and give an example of its use.
A. Validity check.
B. Limit and reasonableness check.
C. Invalid character checks.
D. Excessive character checks.
E. Improperly authorized transactions.
F. Improper sign (negative).

8-33. (Test Data Approach) Anja Watson, CPA, would like to test the aging schedule of the client's accounts receivable software. The client has 1,000 customers, and it ages the accounts based on the month of the sale. A December sale would be 0–30 days old; a November sale, 31–60 days old; an October sale, 61–90 days old; July, August, and September sales, 91–120 days old; and all others, more than 120 days old. Most of the balances range from about $120 to $900; however, some of the accounts have balances up to $5,000, some have credit balances (which are considered 0–30 days old), and about 20% of the accounts have zero balances.
REQUIRED
A. Describe the audit objectives of the test data approach.
B. What are the limitations of the test data approach?
C. What types of data might the auditor include in the test data?
D. What printouts would the auditor likely find beneficial?

---

*AICPA adapted.

8-34. (Use of Test Data) James Deitrick, CPA, is auditing Grove City Golf Supply Corporation. Deitrick plans to use test data in the audit of the payroll account.

The data elements of payroll are defined as follows:

Element Number	Description of Contents
1	Employee Number
2	Employee Name
3	Employee Address
4	Social Security Number
5	Sex
6	Marital Status
7	Job Classification
8	Date Employed
9	Hourly Rate of Pay
10	Salaried Rate of Pay
11	Year-to-Date Gross Pay
12	Year-to-Date Federal Withholding
13	Year-to-Date FICA Withholding
14	Last Transaction Date
15	Employee Status

REQUIRED

Identify six types of test data Deitrick could use to audit payroll.

8-35. (Integrated Test Facility Approach) Carolyn Mason, CPA, wishes to test the payroll system of Courtney Corporation by using an integrated test facility approach. Time cards are assigned to employees and include their name, employee number, and hours worked during the pay period. The time cards are processed through the system and payroll checks are issued. Mason has created several fictitious employees in the database and plans to test the processing of time cards for these fictitious employees along with the regular transactions.

REQUIRED

For each of the following areas, indicate how Mason would check the inputs, processing, outputs, and what she is looking for. Letter **A.** is given as a partial example:

A. Employees. Time cards with fictitious numbers would be processed to see if the payroll information for those fictitious employees created by the auditor is located in the database. What additional test would the auditor be interested in at this point?

B. Hours worked.

C. Gross pay.

D. Federal and state income taxes.

E. Social Security deductions.

F. Other deductions—both weekly and monthly.

G. Net pay.

H. Payroll checks.

I. Earnings records.

*8-36. (Use of Computer-Assisted Audit Techniques) After determining that computer controls are valid, Howard Hastings, CPA, is reviewing the sales system of Rosco Corporation to determine how a computerized audit program may be used to assist in performing tests of Rosco's sales records.

---

*AICPA adapted.

Rosco sells crude oil from one central location. All orders are received by mail and indicate the preassigned customer identification number, desired quantity, proposed delivery date, method of payment, and shipping terms. Because prices fluctuate daily, orders do not indicate a price. Price sheets are printed daily and details are stored in a permanent disk file. The details of orders are also maintained in a permanent disk file.

Each morning the shipping clerk receives a computer printout that indicates details of customers' orders to be shipped that day. After the orders have been shipped, the shipping details are entered in the computer, which simultaneously updates the sales journal, perpetual inventory records, accounts receivable, and sales accounts.

The details of all transactions, as well as daily updates, are maintained on disks available for use by Hastings in the performance of the audit.

REQUIRED

How may Hastings use a computerized audit program to perform substantive tests of Rosco's sales records in their machine-readable form? (Do not discuss accounts receivable or inventory.)

*8-37. (Generalized Audit Software Package) An auditor is conducting an audit of the financial statements of a wholesale cosmetics distributor with an inventory consisting of thousands of individual items. The distributor keeps its inventory in its own distribution center and in two public warehouses. An inventory computer file is maintained on a computer disk and at the end of each business day the file is updated. Each record of the inventory file contains the following data:

- Item number
- Location of item
- Description of item
- Quantity on hand
- Cost per item
- Date of last purchase
- Date of last sale
- Quantity sold during year

The auditor is planning to observe the distributor's physical count of inventories as of a given date. The auditor will have available a computer tape of the data on the inventory file on the date of the physical count and a general-purpose computer software package.

REQUIRED

The auditor is planning to perform basic inventory auditing procedures. Identify these procedures and describe how the use of the generalized audit software package and the tape of the inventory file data might be helpful to the auditor in performing such auditing procedures.

Organize your answer as follows:

Basic inventory auditing procedure	How general-purpose computer software package and tape of the inventory file data might be helpful
1. Observe the physical count, making and recording test counts where applicable.	Determining which items are to be test-counted by selecting a random sample of a representative number of items from the inventory files as of the date of the physical count.

---

*8-38. (Generalized Audit Software Programs) A CPA's client, Boos & Baumkirchner, Inc., is a medium-size manufacturer of products for the leisure-time activities market (for example, camping equipment, scuba gear, and bows and arrows). During the last year, the client installed a computer system, and inventory records of finished goods and parts were converted to computer processing. The inventory master file is maintained on a disk. Each record of the file contains the following information:

- Item or part number
- Description
- Size
- Unit of measure code
- Quantity on hand
- Cost per unit

- Total value of inventory on hand at cost
- Date of last sale or usage
- Quantity used or sold this year
- Economic order quantity
- Code number of major vendor
- Code number of secondary vendor

In preparation for year-end inventory, the client has two identical sets of preprinted inventory count cards. One set is for the client's inventory counts and the other is for the CPA's use in making audit test counts. The following information has been keypunched into the cards and interpreted on their face:

- Item or part number
- Description
- Size
- Unit of measure code

In taking the year-end inventory, the client's personnel will write the actual counted quantity on the face of each card. When all counts are complete, the counted quantity will be keypunched into the cards. The cards will be processed against the disk file, and quantity-on-hand figures will be adjusted to reflect the actual count. A computer listing will be prepared to show any missing inventory count cards and all quantity adjustments of more than $100 in value. These items will be investigated by client personnel, and all required adjustments will be made. When adjustments have been completed, the final year-end balances will be computed and posted to the general ledger.

The CPA has available a program that will run on the client's computer and can process both card and disk files.

REQUIRED

A. In general, and without regard to the facts above, discuss the nature of generalized audit software programs and list the various types and uses of such programs.

B. List and describe at least five ways generalized audit software programs can be used to assist in all aspects of the audit of the inventory of Boos & Baumkirchner, Inc. (For example, the program can be used to read the disk inventory master file and list items and parts with a high unit cost or total value. Such items can be included in the test counts to increase the dollar coverage of the audit verification.)

8-39. (Audit Procedures Are Changed) Audit procedures may be affected in several ways if the computer is used. The nature, timing, and extent of the procedures can be changed.

REQUIRED

For each of the following areas, indicate what changes may occur in the audit procedures if the client uses a computer and the auditor plans to use the client's computer or a microcomputer.

A. A manufacturing company uses a job-order cost system. In the previous audit procedures, the auditor selected certain job orders and footed and extended the information to verify the totals. A test was made on each job selected to determine if direct materials, direct labor, and overhead appeared reasonable.

---

*AICPA adapted.

B. The client sells to customers throughout the United States. In the past the auditor has tested the aging of the accounts receivable and calculated the allowance for doubtful accounts as 1% for accounts 0–30 days old, 2% for accounts 31–60 days old, 5% for accounts 61–90 days old, and 20% for all accounts over 90 days old. A number of the customers are having financial difficulties because of the economy; however, those customers having economic problems seem to be located in certain geographic areas.

C. The client has a new system for taking inventory. The client prepares a computer card for each inventory item, and the inventory counters need only write the quantity on the card and initial it. In the past, the counters used a listing of all the inventory items and entered the quantity on the listing. The auditor would take the listing for a particular area after the inventory was counted and select certain items to verify that the quantity was recorded correctly. The auditor would then prepare a listing of certain items and verify that the items on the listing eventually appeared correctly in the final inventory calculation.

8-40. Match the following items with the blanks in the statements below.

A.	Downloading	**E.**	Electronic spreadsheet
B.	Modem	**F.**	Text database software
C.	Expert systems	**G.**	Microcomputer-aided auditing
D.	Flowcharting software	**H.**	Service organization

1. _____G_____ are the tools and techniques that use the client's computer or the auditor's microcomputer in performing audit tasks.

2. If a link between the client's computer and the auditor's computer is made via telephone lines, a _____B_____ must be used.

3. _____G_____ does not obviate the need for the auditor to understand the internal control structure sufficient to plan the audit.

4. _____A_____ is a process whereby the auditor transfers a data file (or part of a data file) from the client's mainframe computer to the auditor's microcomputer.

5. _____F_____ is the process of using a computer to prepare an engagement letter, audit report, or other document.

6. _____G_____ are the most widely used computer-assisted audit techniques.

7. _____F_____ allows the auditor to view technical literature that is available in electronic format.

8. A(n) _____E_____ is a table of rows and columns into which numbers can be inserted and various mathematical operations can be performed on the numbers.

Audit Judgment Case

8-41. Plainsmen Industries is a small manufacturing company with approximately twenty manufacturing employees and four office employees. The company's payroll is processed biweekly by Dye Service Center, Inc.

Every other Wednesday, Mary Sue Samford, an office employee, sends Dye Service Center the time cards for all manufacturing and office employees. She maintains a record of regular and overtime hours worked from each time card.

Dye Service Center processes these time cards on its computer system and generates payroll checks and a payroll register for delivery to Plainsmen on Mondays. When the payroll checks are received, Plainsmen writes a check to deposit to the imprest payroll account to cover the payroll. Pat Sullivan, owner of Plainsmen Industries, reviews the payroll register and distributes checks. Sullivan is heavily involved with the company and maintains tight controls. For example, Sullivan is quite familiar with his employees and their wage rates. He also has a good knowledge of the hours they work in any given period.

Changes in payroll (for example, addition or deletion of employees, changes in wage rate) are approved by Sullivan and then sent to Dye Service Center. Although no formal check of these changes is made by Plainsmen Industries, Sullivan, as usual, maintains close tabs on these items when the payroll register and checks are received.

REQUIRED

A. Is this a situation in which Dye Service Center controls interact with those of the entity, Plainsmen Industries?

B. Could the entity's auditor adequately assess control risk without a study of Dye Service Center controls?

C. If the entity's auditor determines that control risk can be reduced below the maximum, must the auditor still obtain a service auditor's report?

D. If the owner did not review the payroll register or distribute checks, would your answer to Question B be different?

E. If the auditor determined that control risk cannot be reduced below the maximum without a study of service center controls, what options would the auditor then have?

[handwritten margin notes: B/C Good controls no int. @ Plainsmen; Det others report]
[handwritten: Yes ; No ; Possibly]

Auditing Issues Case

8-42. KELCO MANUFACTURING COMPANY

You have decided to use CAATs (Computer-Assisted Audit Techniques) in your audit of Kelco. Lisa Moon, one of the audit staff, believes the use of CAATs would disrupt Kelco's daily operations, and that auditing around the computer is a more appropriate approach. You explain to Moon that using the computer to perform various tasks such as testing accounts receivable aging, preparing general ledger trial balances, and comparing payroll details with personnel records, has proved to be very effective for other client engagements.

REQUIRED

1. Discuss the conclusion that you made (to use CAATs) after obtaining an understanding of the control structure.
2. Discuss Moon's approach to audit around the computer.
3. Which approach should be applied for the Kelco engagement?

[handwritten notes at bottom of page:]
① CAATs - B/C of Efficiency and Effectiveness
② Not efficient or effective re a simple environment still not efficient
③ CAATs. First Audit takes more time Audit through the computer

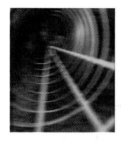

Chapter 9

Audit Sampling Concepts

Learning Objectives

- Define *audit sampling*.
- Explain the difference between statistical and nonstatistical sampling and identify the advantages and disadvantages of each approach.
- Define *audit risk, sampling risk*, and *nonsampling risk*.
- Distinguish among attribute, variable, discovery, and probability-proportionate-to-size approaches to statistical sampling.
- Determine when dollar value estimation versus hypothesis testing should be used.
- Define *representative sample, population*, and *sampling frame*.
- Explain the differences among random sampling, systematic selection, block sampling, and haphazard sample selection.
- Select a representative sample.
- Define *tolerable rate, estimated deviation rate, tolerable misstatement*, and *projected misstatement*.
- Illustrate and define the tests of controls sampling risks of assessing control risk too high and assessing control risk too low.
- Illustrate and define the substantive testing risks of incorrect acceptance and incorrect rejection.
- Present in general terms the steps involved in sampling in tests of controls and in substantive tests.

n 1992, the Audit Sampling and Analytical Techniques Committee of the New York State Society of CPAs conducted a survey of New York accounting firms. The committee's objective was to obtain information regarding the use of audit sampling under *SAS No. 39, Audit Sampling*. Of particular interest was the use of audit sampling by local accounting firms.

Audit sampling is a commonly used testing procedure. Statistical sampling, however, is not widely used by the smaller firms that were the subject of this survey. Nevertheless, those firms that do employ audit sampling generally also use selection methods that have been explicitly sanctioned by *SAS No. 39* as satisfying the representativeness requirement. Since many firms use probability sampling methods, practice can be viewed as moving toward more objective, measurable procedures, even if statistical measurement is not performed.

Yet, many of these firms also ignore (or are unaware of) the tolerable error, risk, and projection requirements of *SAS No. 39*, especially for nonstatistical sampling. Whatever the proponents of *SAS No. 39* may have had in mind, its effect on the smaller audit practice has been muted. ■

Source: Neal B. Hitzig, "Audit Sampling: A Survey of Current Practice," *The CPA Journal*, July 1995, p. 54–57. Reprinted with permission of *The CPA Journal*, July 1995, copyright © 1995.

To develop an audit program, an auditor has to make many decisions about the nature, timing, and extent of testing. As discussed in Chapter 4, *nature* concerns what audit procedure should be applied to bring evidence to bear on a given audit objective or financial statement assertion. *Timing* governs when the procedure is applied. *Extent* determines the number of items to which the procedure is applied. For example, to determine whether the individual accounts making up an accounts receivable balance actually exist, the auditor may decide to confirm selected accounts with customers. In confirming accounts receivable, the auditor has to determine how many accounts should be confirmed. That is, what is the extent of testing, and, given the extent of testing, which individual accounts should be selected for testing? This chapter and the next are designed to help answer those two questions. This chapter discusses the concepts inherent in audit sampling. The discussion pertains to both statistical and nonstatistical approaches to sampling, except when otherwise indicated. The next chapter explains the various statistical sampling methods used to calculate sample size and to evaluate sample results.

Definition of Audit Sampling

Auditors frequently use sampling, usually in combination with other auditing procedures, to examine account balances or classes of transactions. ***Audit sampling*** is the application of an audit procedure to less than 100% of the items within an account balance or class of transactions for the purpose of evaluating some characteristic of the balance or class. According to *SAS No. 39, Audit Sampling* (AU 350), three conditions must be met to constitute audit sampling. First, less than 100% of the population must be examined. Second, the sample results must be projected as population characteristics. Third, the projected sample results must be compared to an existing client-determined account balance to determine whether to accept or reject the client's balance, or the projected sample results must be used to assess control risk. For example, to determine whether inventory quantities are appropriately recorded, an auditor may complete an internal control structure questionnaire on inventory and also may select some items for independent count. Completing the questionnaire is a nonsampling procedure, whereas making independent counts is a sampling procedure if the auditor projects the sample findings to evaluate the accuracy of the client's inventory count.

Numerous situations exist in an audit when an auditor does not use audit sampling. For example, sometimes an auditor may perform a 100% examination of an account or transaction balance because he or she is not willing to accept any sampling risk for the balance. Alternatively, the auditor may select a transaction for purposes of following it through the client's accounting system (a walk-through) to gain an understanding of how transactions are processed. In those situations, the auditor is not sampling. Likewise, the auditor may examine a small number of large-dollar items in an account balance, like property, plant, and equipment, and thereby account for a high percentage of the total account balance. If the remaining portion of the account balance is immaterial, the auditor may decide not to apply detailed tests to the untested portion. In such cases, the auditor has not engaged in sampling but, in effect, has limited the population to material items and has audited the entire population of material items.

Statistical Sampling versus Nonstatistical Sampling

Two general overall approaches to audit sampling exist: *statistical* and *nonstatistical* sampling. Either approach, when properly applied, can provide sufficient competent evidential matter. In fact, even those auditors who are proponents of statistical sampling usually combine the two approaches in their engagements.

Prior to the publication of *SAS No. 39* (AU 350) in 1981, auditors typically referred to nonstatistical sampling as ***judgment sampling***. *SAS No. 39* (AU 350) does not define nonstatistical sampling as judgment sampling, because both statistical and nonstatistical sampling require the use of auditor judgment. To illustrate, without regard to whether statistical or nonstatistical sampling is used, an auditor uses judgment to identify items of special interest (for example, large-dollar, unusual, or high-risk items) and to design and implement an appropriate sampling plan. An auditor also uses judgment to decide whether to use statistical or nonstatistical sampling or whether to sample at all.

Statistical sampling does not eliminate the need for professional judgment. In applying statistical sampling, judgment must be exercised and quantified in numerous areas. For example, the auditor must define the population in terms of its size, select the characteristics of significance to the audit, and decide what constitutes a misstatement. This requires judgment and audit experience.

Statistical Sampling

Statistical sampling is the use of a sampling plan in such a way that the laws of probability can be used to make statements or generalizations about a population. A statistical sampling approach must meet both of the following conditions:

1. The sample, which is projected as a population characteristic, must have a known probability of selection (that is, the sample must be expected to be representative).
2. The sample results must be quantitatively or mathematically evaluated.

Nonstatistical Sampling

In contrast, *nonstatistical sampling* is the determination of sample size *or* the selection of the sampled items using judgmental reasoning rather than probability concepts. If a sample that is projected to the population or generalized as a population characteristic does not meet both of the requirements for statistical sampling, it is, by definition, a nonstatistical sample. In many audit situations, nonstatistical sampling is more appropriate than statistical sampling. Thus, one should not conclude that nonstatistical sampling is a less desirable approach to audit sampling.

Uncertainty and Audit Sampling

When an auditor renders an opinion on a client's financial statements, he or she expresses reasonable assurance, rather than absolute certainty, as to the reliability of the financial statements. The justification for being reasonably sure, but not certain, is based on the third standard of fieldwork: "Sufficient competent evidential matter is to be obtained . . . to afford a *reasonable* basis for an opinion." If the auditor could not justify accepting some risks, the audit cost would be prohibitive because a much larger number of transactions would have to be examined. Sampling would not be permitted without the concept of reasonable assurance.

Audit Risk

As noted in Chapter 4, *audit risk* is actually a combination of three risks:

1. A material misstatement occurs in the financial statements (inherent risk).
2. The internal control structure fails to detect and correct the misstatement (control risk).
3. The auditor fails to detect the misstatement (detection risk).

Given all of the foregoing, audit risk can be expressed as

$$\text{Audit Risk} = (\text{Probability of Material Misstatement})$$
$$\times (\text{Probability of Internal Control Structure Failure})$$
$$\times (\text{Probability of Auditor Failure})$$

In practice, the probability that material misstatement occurs is difficult to quantify; thus, it is sometimes conservatively assumed to equal one, or a combined assessment of inherent and control risk is made to determine the probability. Audit risk thus becomes the probability of internal control structure failure times the probability of auditor failure. Audit risk includes uncertainties due to sampling, called *sampling risk*, and uncertainties due to factors other than sampling, called *nonsampling risk*.

Sampling Risk

Sampling risk arises whenever the auditor samples. ***Sampling risk*** is the risk that the auditor's conclusion based on a sample may differ from the conclusion he or she would reach if the test were applied in the same way to the entire population. In other words, it is the risk that there will be sampling error, that is, that the projected sample results and the true condition will differ. For example, an auditor selecting a sample of sales invoices processed during 19X4 may project that a maximum of 5% of the total sales invoices were not properly stamped with "credit approved." If the auditor were to examine all credit sales for 19X4, he or she might find that the true deviation rate (unstamped credit approvals) is actually 8%. The difference between the projected sample rate of 5% and the true deviation rate of 8% is the sampling error.

Nonsampling Risk

Nonsampling risk is caused by human error, whereas sampling risk is due entirely to chance. Nonsampling risk may occur because the auditor uses an audit procedure that is not appropriate for the specific audit objective or uses appropriate procedures but fails to recognize deviations or misstatements in sampled items. Examples of nonsampling risk include the following:

■ Inadequate planning or deviation/misstatement definition causes the auditor to overlook an obvious deviation or misstatement.

■ A customer returns an accounts receivable confirmation stating that the balance is correct when it is actually understated by $1,000.

■ A staff auditor omits an important procedure in an audit program because of time budget pressures.

If sampling risk is subtracted from audit risk, the balance or remainder is equal to nonsampling risk:

$$\text{Audit Risk} - \text{Sampling Risk} = \text{Nonsampling Risk}$$

According to *SAS No. 39* (AU 350.11), nonsampling risk can be reduced to a negligible level through such factors as adequate planning and supervision and a sound system of quality control in the CPA firm.

Advantages and Disadvantages of Statistical Sampling

Three major advantages of statistical sampling are that it helps the auditor (1) design an efficient sample, (2) measure the sufficiency of evidence (that is, the adequacy of sample size), and (3) evaluate the sample results.

Statistical sampling permits the auditor to optimize the sample size given the acceptable sampling risk. As a result, if the sampling application is properly designed, executed, and evaluated, sample size is neither too large (that is, it is efficient) nor too small (that is, it is sufficient). By using statistical sampling, sample findings can be objectively projected to the population by using accepted probability concepts.

Statistical sampling also permits the auditor to calculate and control the risk of reliance on a sample. In other words, statistical sampling makes it easier to calculate sampling risk. Conceptually, this is the most important distinction between statistical sampling and nonstatistical sampling.

Three major disadvantages of statistical sampling are that it (1) involves additional costs of training in the CPA firm, (2) sometimes requires additional sample design costs, and (3) sometimes requires more costly sample selection.

Auditors generally agree that statistical sampling is useful in many, but not all, situations. As we have already stated, nonstatistical sampling is more appropriate than statistical sampling for numerous situations in an audit engagement. In fact, a major part of most audit tests is often performed using nonstatistical sampling or by not sampling at all. This includes audit procedures such as confirming cash balances, footing various journals, reviewing records, searching for unusual entries, and obtaining representations from client personnel and attorneys. In many audit areas, the cost of statistical sampling may exceed the benefit. For example, a given account balance may be more efficiently audited by using analytical procedures. The auditor chooses between statistical and nonstatistical sampling after considering their relative cost and effectiveness in the circumstances. A decision to use, or not use, statistical or nonstatistical sampling depends primarily on auditor judgment.

Types of Statistical Sampling Models

Three broad categories of statistical sampling exist: attribute, variable, and probability-proportionate-to-size sampling. Attribute sampling is used primarily for tests of controls. (Discovery sampling, another sampling method discussed here, is classified as an attribute sampling method.) Variable sampling, in contrast, is most frequently used to test the monetary value of account balances or transactions. Finally, probability-proportionate-to-size sampling (or dollar-unit sampling), which is a modified form of attribute sampling, is used for both tests of controls and substantive tests.

Attribute Sampling

Attribute sampling is a statistical sampling method used to estimate the rate (percentage) of occurrence of a specific quality (attribute) in a population. The method is designed to answer the question, "How many?" For example, attribute sampling may be used to estimate the percentage of total shipments that were not billed. For this application, the auditor may conclude: "I am 95% confident that not more than 2% of the shipping reports are not supported by a sales invoice."

In using attribute sampling to test internal control structure policies and procedures, the auditor tests to determine if an item was processed correctly or incorrectly. There are no degrees of error: the response will be yes or no. Sampled items are processed as prescribed or not processed as prescribed. In an attribute sampling application, each occurrence (or deviation) is given equal treatment in the auditor's statistical evaluation regardless of the dollar amount of the item on which the deviation occurred; thus, a $10,000 shipping report not billed is equivalent to a $1,000 shipping report not billed—both represent deviations from prescribed policies or procedures.

Discovery Sampling

Discovery sampling is a special type of attribute sampling. Discovery sampling is typically used when the auditor expects very few or near zero occurrences (or deviations). It is often applied when the audit objective is to seek out expected fraud, serious evasion of internal control structure (for example, fictitious employees on a payroll), deliberate circumvention of regulations, or other severe irregularities. Auditors also sometimes use discovery sampling for substantive testing in situations when few misstatements are expected (for example, in the audit of a bank's demand deposits). *Looking for any*

Variable Sampling

Variable sampling is applied when the auditor desires to reach a dollar or quantitative conclusion about a population. Variable sampling applications are designed to answer the question, "How much?" For example, if a student wanted to use a sample to estimate the total dollar amount of money held by students in an auditing class for a given day, variable sampling would be used; however, if the student wanted to estimate the percentage of people in a large class who are six feet tall or taller, attribute sampling is the appropriate model to use.

As one might expect, auditors primarily use variable sampling for substantive testing. As a statistical technique to estimate the dollar amount of an account balance, or some other quantity, it is generally viewed by auditors as a useful measurement device because results are presented in monetary amounts rather than frequency percentages.

Probability-Proportionate-to-Size Sampling

Attribute, discovery, and variable sampling models are sometimes referred to as classical statistical sampling methods. In contrast, *probability-proportionate-to-size sampling* (PPS) is a modified form of attribute sampling. PPS sampling enables the auditor to make dollar conclusions about the total dollar amount of misstatement in a population. Unlike classical sampling techniques, which focus on physical units of the population, such as sales invoices or disbursement vouchers, PPS sampling focuses on the dollar units of a population; that is, instead of an auditor viewing a $100,000 accounts receivable population as containing 500 individual customer balances, the auditor considers the population as 100,000 individual dollar units from which to draw a sample. Classical approaches consider a $500 account equivalent to a $1,000 account; they each constitute a sampling unit. In PPS sampling, each dollar is a sampling unit. Thus, individual accounts with larger balances have a proportionally higher chance of being selected in a sample because they contain more sampling units, hence the name probability-proportionate-to-size sampling.

PPS sampling is frequently referred to as *dollar-unit sampling*. It was first applied in an auditing context by Deloitte, Haskins & Sells (now Deloitte and Touche) and is referred to by them as *cumulative monetary amount sampling*. PPS applications are designed to produce conclusions similar to the following: "Based on the sample evidence, I am X% confident that the dollar amount of misstatement in the account does not exceed Y (where Y depends on the sampling results)."

Dollar Value Estimation versus Audit Hypothesis Testing

In using variable sampling, an auditor must decide whether the objective is to (1) make an estimate of an account balance, such as LIFO inventory, independent of the client's account balance, or (2) test the reasonableness of a client's account balance, such as the dollar balance in accounts receivable or inventory. In other words, once the auditor decides to use variable sampling, he or she must next determine if a dollar value estimation approach or a hypothesis testing approach is needed.

A *dollar value estimation* approach should be used when the client does not present an account balance that purports to be correct (for example, improper accounting principles have been used or numerous errors are known to exist in the accounting records) or when an account balance is to be determined by variable sampling. In situations involving an incorrect account balance, the auditor generally intends to propose an adjustment to bring the balance into agreement with the statistical estimate. Likewise, if an account balance does not exist, the statistical estimate is recorded as the account balance.

In contrast to dollar value estimation, **audit hypothesis testing** is used when an auditor desires to accept a client's account balance without adjustment if it is not materially misstated. In this situation, the auditor is testing an already existing client account balance that is believed to be fairly stated; thus, the auditor would propose an adjustment only if it is probable that the client's account balance is materially understated or overstated. The audit hypothesis approach statistically discriminates between the hypothesis that the account balance as presented is correctly stated and the alternative hypothesis that the account balance is materially misstated.

According to *SAS No. 39* (AU 350.01),

> Audit sampling is the application of an audit procedure to less than 100 percent of the items within an account balance or class of transactions for purposes of *evaluating* some characteristic of the balance or class [emphasis added].

This definition clearly includes audit hypothesis testing, but does not include dollar value estimation. Therefore, in an audit hypothesis test application when the auditor is evaluating (or testing) an existing client account balance, the auditor must follow *SAS No. 39*. But if the auditor is using dollar value estimation to determine an account balance, *SAS No. 39* does not apply; the objective is to estimate, not to evaluate, an account balance or class of transactions.

The main distinction between the two approaches is that dollar value estimation should *not* be used if the client has an existing account balance that an auditor is sampling from to decide whether to accept or reject. If this type of decision is to be made, the audit hypothesis approach is used. Auditors typically use hypothesis testing because they are concerned with evaluating a client-generated amount. The two approaches are illustrated in the next chapter.

Selecting a Sample

Because of the high cost of testing 100% of a population in relation to benefits, an auditor is often willing to accept some sampling risk. Having made a decision to sample, the auditor then faces the question of which items from the population should be selected as sample items.

Population, Sampling Frame, and Representative Sample

The *population* is the universe about which the auditor desires certain information. The population must be defined in advance. The auditor should adhere to two conditions when defining a population:

1. The population should be relevant to the audit objectives.
2. The population definition should enable another auditor to determine whether an item belongs or does not belong to the population.

To illustrate, if the population is defined as "all customer accounts as of year-end," then accounts with zero balances, debit balances, and credit balances are part of the population. If the population is defined as "all accounts receivable appearing in the year-end trial balance," debit and credit balances are included but not zero balances.

In addition to very carefully defining the population, the sampling frame must be precisely defined in advance. The *sampling frame* is a listing or other physical representation of the individual items in the population that is used to select a sample. For example, a sampling frame for accounts receivable may be a printout of all customer accounts receivable as of a given date. In testing physical inventory, a sampling frame may be an inventory listing, the perpetual inventory records, or the physical items of inventory. The sampling frame is actually the physical representation of the population. Because the sampling frame is what the auditor samples from, it affects any projection of the sample. If the sampling frame and the population are not the same, the auditor's projection may be incorrect.

If the auditor wishes to measure sampling risk when less than 100% of a population is examined, a sample that is expected to be representative must be used. A *representative sample* is a sample that exhibits approximately the same characteristics as the population from which it is drawn. For example, if a population contains a high percentage of deviations or misstatements, the sample should contain a high percentage of deviations or misstatements. Otherwise, the sample is nonrepresentative. To be representative, a sample should be selected in such a way that every item or dollar in the population has an opportunity to be selected.

Stratification

Stratification is the process of dividing a population into subpopulations that have similar characteristics (often monetary value). The strata must be explicitly defined so that each sampling unit can belong to only one stratum. This procedure reduces the variability of the items within each stratum and enables the auditor to concentrate effort on the items most likely to contain the greater monetary misstatement. Stratification may improve the efficiency of the sample by enabling the auditor to reduce the extent of sampling procedures. For example, the auditor might direct attention to larger value items for accounts receivable when he or she is primarily concerned with overstatement misstatements. After a population is stratified and the auditor desires to sample from one or more strata, the sample should be selected by using random number, systematic, or haphazard selection.

Random Number Selection

A random selection offers the best chance that a sample will be representative. A **random sample** is a sample selected in such a way that every item in the sampled population has an equal chance of being selected. It also is sometimes called a *probability sample*. A random number table is one technique for selecting a representative sample. Such a table is composed of randomly generated digits 0 through 9. Each digit appears in the table approximately the same number of times, and the order in which each digit appears is random. Columns in a random number table are designed to make the table easier to use; otherwise, they are meaningless.

To use a random number table, the auditor must follow three steps:

1. *Define correspondence.* **Correspondence** defines the relationship between the sampling frame and the random number table. To establish correspondence, each population item must have a unique number in the table. By reading from the table, the auditor can determine the exact item to draw from the population. For example, if examining a population of inventory items numbered from 1 to 950, the auditor could use a three-digit numbering scheme to establish correspondence.
2. *Determine the selection route.* The auditor may go up or down the table columns—left or right. Any route can be used as long as it is consistently followed. In determining a selection route, an important consideration is that it be documented in the working papers so that another auditor reviewing the selection could reproduce the exact sample combination.
3. *Select a starting point.* A random number table consists of many pages. To select a starting point, the table or book should be opened at random and the random stab method used to define row, column, and digit starting position.

Table 9–1 is an illustrative page from a random number table. Note that the illustrative page contains 7 columns and 45 rows. Assume that the auditor uses the random stab method to select three digits corresponding to a sales invoice population numbered from 1 to 750. The auditor's random stab lands on column 5, row 14, digit 4. The column 5, row 14 number is 48237. To select a three-digit number, begin with digit 4 (which is a 3) and continue reading to the right. The first number selected is thus 375. (The 5 comes from the first digit of column 6—remember, columns are arbitrary and simply enhance table readability.) The second number selected (reading down the column, under number 375) is 331. The third is 521, followed by 681, 730, 161, 980, and so on. Note that the seventh number selected exceeds the upper limit of the population, 750; thus, 980 is discarded and an additional number in the sequence is selected to replace it.

A more efficient way to generate random numbers is to use a computer. Random numbers may be generated by time-sharing programs, audit software, or personal computers. The advantages of computer-generated random numbers are that (1) discards are eliminated and (2) working papers are automatically produced. Perhaps the

Table 9-1	Illustrative Page from a Random Number Table						
	(1)	(2)	(3)	(4)	(5)	(6)	(7)
1	10480	15011	01536	02011	81647	91646	69179
2	22368	46573	25595	85393	30995	89198	27982
3	24130	48360	22527	97265	76393	64809	15179
4	42167	93093	06243	61680	07856	16376	39440
5	37570	39975	81837	16656	06121	91782	60468
6	77921	06907	11008	42751	27756	53498	18602
7	99562	72905	56420	69994	98872	31016	71194
8	96301	91977	05463	07972	18876	20922	94595
9	89579	14342	63661	10281	17453	18103	57740
10	85475	36857	53342	53988	53060	59533	38867
11	28918	69578	88231	33276	70997	79936	56865
12	63553	40961	48235	03427	49626	69445	18663
13	09429	93969	52636	92737	88974	33488	36320
14	10365	61129	87529	85689	48237	52267	67689
15	07119	97336	71048	08178	77233	13916	47564
16	51085	12765	51821	51259	77452	16308	60756
17	02368	21382	52404	60268	89368	19885	55322
18	01011	54092	33362	94904	31273	04146	18594
19	52162	53916	46369	58586	23216	14513	83149
20	07056	97628	33787	09998	42698	06691	76988
21	48663	91245	85828	14346	09172	30168	90229
22	54164	58492	22421	74103	47070	25306	76468
23	32639	32363	05597	24200	13363	38005	94342
24	29334	27001	87637	87308	58731	00256	45834
25	02488	33062	28834	07351	19731	92420	60952
26	81525	72295	04839	96423	24878	82551	66566
27	29676	20591	68086	26432	46901	20849	89768
28	00742	57392	39064	66432	84673	40027	32832
29	05366	04213	25669	26122	44407	44048	37937
30	91921	26418	64117	94305	26766	25940	39972
31	00582	04711	87917	77341	42206	35126	74087
32	00725	69884	62797	56170	86324	88072	76222
33	69011	65795	95876	55293	18988	27354	26575
34	25976	57948	29888	88604	67917	48708	18912
35	09763	83473	73577	12908	30883	18317	28290
36	91567	42595	27958	30134	04024	86385	29880
37	17955	56349	90999	49127	20044	59931	06115
38	46503	18584	18845	49618	02304	51038	20655
39	92157	89634	94824	78171	84610	82834	09922
40	14577	62765	35605	81263	39667	47358	56873
41	98427	07523	33362	64270	01638	92477	66969
42	34914	63976	88720	82765	34476	17032	87589
43	70060	28277	39475	46473	23219	53416	94970
44	53976	54914	06990	67245	68350	82948	11398
45	76072	29515	40980	07591	58745	25774	22987

most significant advantage, however, is the reduction of human error (nonsampling risk) in the sample selection process.

Systematic Sampling

In *systematic sampling*, the auditor calculates a sampling interval by dividing the number of items in the population by the sample size. For example, if the population size N contains 1,052 items, and the sample size desired n is 100, the uniform sampling interval is 10 (always rounded down to insure that the desired sample size is selected). A random start between 1 and 10 is selected as the first sample item. Afterward, every tenth item is selected.

Because systematic selection uses a random number for the first item selected, every item in the population initially has an equal chance of being selected. However, after the first sample item is selected, every combination of the sample size does not have an equal chance of selection. Thus, systematic selection differs from random number selection.

The primary advantage of systematic selection is its ease of use. The auditor, however, must guard against a biased selection. To reduce the chances of selecting a nonrepresentative sample, the auditor should be satisfied that the population is in random order. Also, the auditor should consider using more than one random start. For example, a conservative policy to follow is to use five random starts as a minimum number of starts whenever systematic selection is applied. In using multiple starts, the sampling interval is multiplied by the desired number of random starts to arrive at an adjusted interval. For example, in the illustration above, for five random starts, the sampling interval of 10 becomes an interval of 50. Five random numbers between 1 and 50 are selected, and then every 50th item from each of the five random numbers is selected. If proper precautions against biases are taken, systematic selection, like random number selection, produces a representative sample (that is, a sample expected to be representative) that can be used for statistical or nonstatistical sampling.

Haphazard Selection

A *haphazard sample* is selected by the auditor without any special reason for including or excluding a given item from the sample. For example, an auditor may select disbursement vouchers from a file cabinet, without regard to their size or location, as a haphazard sample. A haphazard selected sample may be representative of population characteristics, but it is not selected based on defined probability concepts. Consequently, haphazard samples cannot be used in statistical sampling. Haphazard selection is, however, useful in nonstatistical sampling and is permitted if the auditor expects it to be representative.

Block Selection

A *block sample* consists of contiguous transactions selected from the population. For example, a sample of all checks issued for the months of March and August in examining cash disbursements for the year is a block sample. Because checks from other months had no opportunity to be selected, the block sample may not be representative; therefore, a block sample cannot be statistically projected to the population. Block selection must be used with caution and generally should be avoided.

Unexamined Sample Items

A frequently encountered problem in tests of controls and substantive tests is what to do about selected sample items that are missing. A fundamental sampling tenet is that auditing procedures appropriate to a particular audit objective should be applied to each sample item, but the auditor may not be able to apply a planned audit procedure to selected sample items because, for example, supporting documentation may be missing.

What should the auditor do when items cannot be located? The auditor's action depends on the effect of the missing item on the evaluation of the sample. That is, if the auditor's conclusion based on the sample would not change by considering the item a deviation or misstatement, it is not necessary to attempt to locate the missing item. But, if the inability to examine the item leads to a conclusion that an account balance is *materially* misstated, the auditor will have to consider applying alternative procedures. Alternative procedures should generate sufficient evidence to permit the auditor to determine whether the account balance is acceptable.

To illustrate, suppose an auditor does not obtain a response to an account receivable confirmation. The auditor has two options: (1) if the conclusion based on the projected sample results does not change by treating a nonresponse as a misstatement, the auditor need not apply alternative procedures, or (2) if the conclusion would change, the auditor can apply alternative procedures (for example, review of subsequent payment of the receivable).

The decision process for unexamined items is less complex in testing controls. Usually, if the auditor is not able to apply a planned test of controls to an individual item because of a missing document, the item is considered a deviation from the prescribed control policy or procedure. This decision is likely to increase the auditor's assessed level of control risk and thereby increase substantive testing, but it does not require the performance of alternative tests of controls. In such a situation, the auditor simply shifts from tests of controls to substantive procedures to obtain a low audit risk.

Sampling with or without Replacement

Sampling with replacement permits a selected sample item to be returned to the population and reselected. In other words, the same item may be included in the sample more than once. This may occur if a random number table produces the same number more than once. In contrast, *sampling without replacement* removes an item from the population once it is selected. An item can be included only once in a sample selection. If a random number table produces a duplicate number, the number is discarded after its initial selection. Because of logic and efficiency, sampling without replacement is typically used in accounting and auditing.

Sampling in Tests of Controls

Sampling risk arises from the possibility that the auditor's conclusions based on a sample may differ from the conclusion he or she would reach if the entire population were subjected to the audit procedure. In performing tests of controls, sampling risk consists of two aspects, as illustrated in Figure 9–1.

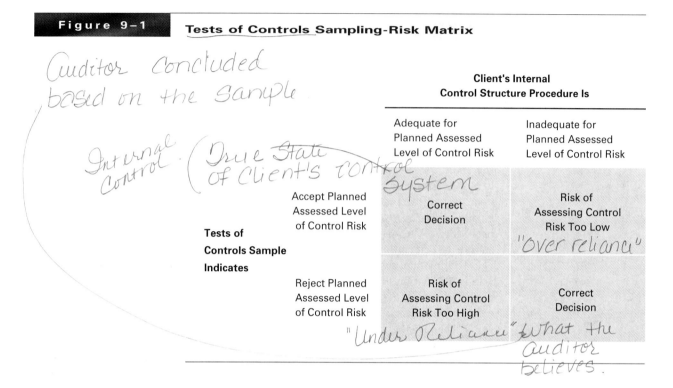

Figure 9–1 **Tests of Controls Sampling-Risk Matrix**

[Handwritten annotations: "Auditor concluded based on the sample", "Internal Control (True State of Client's Control System)", "over reliance", "Under Reliance" what the auditor believes.]

		Client's Internal Control Structure Procedure Is	
		Adequate for Planned Assessed Level of Control Risk	Inadequate for Planned Assessed Level of Control Risk
Tests of Controls Sample Indicates	Accept Planned Assessed Level of Control Risk	Correct Decision	Risk of Assessing Control Risk Too Low
	Reject Planned Assessed Level of Control Risk	Risk of Assessing Control Risk Too High	Correct Decision

The ***risk of assessing control risk too low*** is the risk that the assessed level of control risk based on the sample is less than the true operating effectiveness of the control structure policy or procedure.[1] For example, the auditor's sample may lead to a conclusion that the assessed level of control risk is low because the deviation rate does not exceed 5%; however, if a 100% test of controls were performed, the true deviation rate of 8.5% would cause the auditor to assess the level of control risk as high.

The ***risk of assessing control risk too high*** is the risk that the assessed level of control risk based on the sample is greater than the true operating effectiveness of the control structure policy or procedure.[2] For example, the auditor's sample may lead to a conclusion that the assessed level of control risk is high because the deviation rate exceeds, say, 5%, when the true deviation rate may be 3%.

When the auditor assesses control risk too high, the consequence is that substantive tests are unnecessarily large. For example, if the auditor's evaluation of a sample leads him or her to increase unnecessarily the assessed level of control risk, he or she would ordinarily increase the scope of substantive tests to compensate for the perceived higher control risk. Although the audit may be less efficient in these circumstances because more costly or extensive substantive tests are applied, the audit is, nevertheless, effective, because the audit objective is achieved.

---

[1]*SAS No. 39* uses the term *risk of assessing control risk too low* instead of ***beta risk***, which is a statistical term that has not been consistently used by auditors. This risk is also sometimes referred to as the *risk of overreliance*.

[2]*SAS No. 39* uses the term *risk of assessing control risk too high* instead of ***alpha risk***. Like beta risk, alpha risk is a statistical term that has not been consistently applied by auditors. This risk is also sometimes referred to as the *risk of underreliance*.

In an audit engagement, the more serious error is to assess control risk too low. This risk relates to an audit's effectiveness and may result in inadequate substantive testing. In the next chapter, we focus on controlling the risk of assessing control risk too low.

Planning Test of Controls Samples

When planning a specific sample for a test of controls, the auditor should consider

1. the relationship of the sample to the objective of the test of controls.
2. the planned assessed level of control risk for the prescribed internal control structure procedure or policy being tested.
3. the maximum rate of deviation from the prescribed control procedure or policy that would support the planned assessed level of control risk.
4. the auditor's allowable risk of assessing control risk too low.
5. the likely or expected rate of deviations in the population.
6. the degree of assurance desired from the sample evidence relative to nonsampling tests of controls.

Table 9–2 depicts the effect of each of these factors on tests of controls sample sizes, given that the other factors remain the same. Table 9–2 also indicates that population size generally has no effect on sample size.

For many tests of controls, sampling does not apply. Procedures performed to obtain an understanding of the internal control structure (as required by the second standard of fieldwork) generally do not involve audit sampling. Sampling generally is not applicable to tests of controls that depend on appropriate segregation of duties or that provide no documentary evidence of performance. For example, segregation of duties, an important feature of the internal control structure, cannot usually be tested by sampling but rather is normally tested by observation. An auditor ordinarily structures the specific test of controls in terms of deviations from pertinent control structure policies or procedures. *Pertinent control structure policies or procedures* are ones whose absence from the internal control structure would cause the auditor to increase the assessed level of control risk.

After identifying the control policy or procedure to be tested and determining if an audit trail exists, the auditor determines the maximum rate of deviations from the prescribed control policy or procedure that he or she would accept without altering the planned assessed level of control risk. *SAS No. 39* (AU 350.34) defines this concept as the ***tolerable rate***.[3] Deviations in excess of the tolerable rate would cause the auditor to increase the assessed level of control risk, perhaps to the maximum. Experienced auditors usually determine tolerable rates based on CPA firm policy guidelines. For example, if the auditor plans to assess control risk at a low level, and he or she desires a high degree of assurance from the evidence provided by the sample tests of controls, a tolerable rate of 5% or less would be used. If the auditor, in contrast, either plans to assess control risk at a higher level or obtains substantial evidence from nonsampling tests of controls (for example, evidence from inquiries or observation), a tolerable rate of 10% would be used. Thus, to determine the tolerable rate, the

---

[3]*SAS No. 39* uses the term *tolerable rate* instead of *upper precision limit.*

| Table 9–2 | Factors Influencing Tests of Controls Sample Sizes | | | |

| | | Conditions Leading to | | |
| | | --- | --- | |
Factor	Smaller Sample Size	Larger Sample Size	Relationship to Sample Size
Planned assessed level of control risk	Higher planned assessed level of control risk	Lower planned assessed level of control risk	Inverse
Maximum rate of deviations (tolerable rate)	Higher rate (e.g., 10%) of deviations	Lower rate (e.g., 5%) of deviations	Inverse
Risk of assessing control risk too low	Higher risk of assessing control risk too low is acceptable	Lower risk of assessing control risk too low is necessary	Inverse
Likely rate of population deviations	Lower expected rate of deviations in population	Higher expected rate of deviations in population	Direct
Degree of assurance desired from sample evidence	Lower degree of assurance from sample test of controls (nonsample tests of controls provide substantial evidence about control effectiveness)	Higher degree of assurance from sample test of controls (nonsample tests of controls are minimal)	Direct
Number of items in population	No effect on sample size unless population is small (that is, under 500)		

auditor considers (1) the planned assessed level of control risk and (2) the degree of assurance desired by the sample evidence.

In setting tolerable rates, auditors recognize that control deviations do not necessarily produce monetary misstatements in the financial statements. For example, an unapproved disbursement voucher (that should have been approved) may nevertheless be a valid transaction that was properly authorized and recorded. Control deviations increase the risk of material monetary misstatements, but not in a one-to-one ratio.

Selecting the Tests of Controls Sample

Paragraph 39 of *SAS No. 39* (AU 350.39) states: "Ideally, the auditor should use a selection method that has the potential for selecting items from the entire period under audit." In practice, auditors often apply sampling tests of controls for a portion of a year at an interim date (for example, the first nine months of the year). Thus, at year-end, the auditor has to determine what additional tests of controls are needed.

The following factors should be considered when sample tests of controls are selected from transactions representing less than the complete period under audit:

- The significance of the assertion involved.
- The results of the interim tests of controls.
- The length of the remaining period.
- Client responses to inquiry tests of controls concerning the remaining period.
- Evidence provided by substantive tests of control effectiveness within the remaining period.
- Other evidence about the nature and extent of any significant changes in the internal control structure, including its policies, procedures, and personnel, that occur subsequent to the interim period.

After considering these factors, the auditor may decide that additional sampling tests of controls are not needed and may determine that inquiries, observation, and other nonsampling tests of controls provide sufficient competent evidence to support the planned assessed level of control risk.

Evaluating Test of Control Sample Results

Assuming that the auditor has selected a test of control sample that is expected to be representative and has considered unexamined items, if any, as deviations from pre-scribed control policies or procedures, the next task is to project the sample findings to the population. The auditor uses the deviation rate in the sample as a best estimate of the deviation rate in the population. Thus, if a sample of 75 items produces three deviations, the deviation rate is 4% (that is, 3 ÷ 75). The auditor compares the *estimated deviation rate* with the tolerable rate and considers the risk that the true deviation rate might exceed the estimated deviation rate. In doing this in a nonstatistical sampling application, the auditor judgmentally compares the projected deviation rate of 4% (from the example above) to the tolerable rate of, say, 10%. Because the 4% projected deviation rate is substantially less than the 10% tolerable rate, the auditor will probably judgmentally conclude that there is an acceptably low sampling risk that the true rate exceeds the tolerable rate. If, however, the projected deviation rate equaled 9%, the auditor would assess the sampling risk as being too high and would probably assess the level of control risk as high or at the maximum for this assertion. (The next chapter examines the statistical sampling approach to tests of controls.)

Sampling in Substantive Tests

Just as there are two aspects of sampling risk in a test of controls sample, there also are two aspects of sampling risk in a substantive test sample. The two aspects of substantive testing risk are (1) the risk of incorrect acceptance and (2) the risk of incorrect rejection.

As depicted in Figure 9–2, the risk of incorrect acceptance and the risk of incorrect rejection occur whenever an auditor samples without regard to whether statistical or nonstatistical sampling is used. The *risk of incorrect acceptance* is the risk that the sample supports the conclusion that the recorded account balance is not materially misstated when in fact it really is materially misstated. The *risk of incorrect*

| Figure 9-2 | Substantive Test Sampling Risk Matrix |

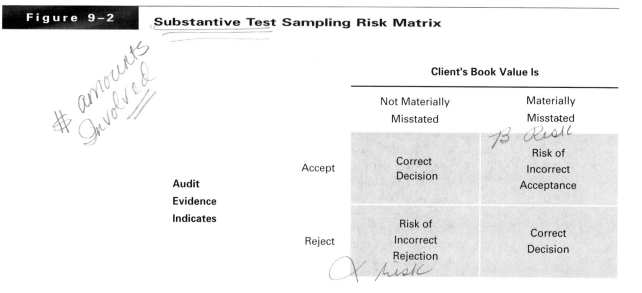

rejection is the risk that the sample supports the conclusion that the recorded account balance is materially misstated when in fact it is not materially misstated.[4]

Given these two risks, the auditor's primary concern is controlling the risk of incorrect acceptance. A simple illustration explains why. If an auditor rejects the client's recorded receivable balance when it is not materially misstated (i.e., fairly stated), the client will generally insist on (1) an increase in sample size or (2) a search for additional evidence that the receivable balance is materially misstated. The combined evidence available afterward will likely lead to the correct decision. Because of the need to perform additional audit procedures, the risk of incorrect rejection affects audit efficiency, not audit effectiveness; that is, the auditor generally reaches the correct conclusion by incurring additional costs.

Conversely, if the auditor accepts the client's recorded receivable balance when it is materially misstated (risk of incorrect acceptance), the client will not demand an increase in sample size or a search for additional evidence. The risk in this situation comes from bankers and other external financial statement users who have relied on an erroneous audit opinion. The auditor may be sued and possibly could lose the right to practice. The risk of incorrect acceptance relates to audit effectiveness and is, therefore, the more crucial of the two substantive test sampling risks.

Planning Substantive Samples

The auditor should consider the following factors when planning a substantive test sample:

1. The relationship of the sample to the relevant audit objective (as discussed in Chapter 4).
2. Preliminary judgments about materiality levels (as discussed in Chapter 4).

---

[4]*SAS No. 39* uses the term *risk of incorrect acceptance* rather than *beta risk*, and *risk of incorrect rejection* rather than *alpha risk*.

3. The auditor's allowable risk of incorrect acceptance.
4. Characteristics of the population.

In planning a substantive sample, the auditor considers how much monetary misstatement in an account balance or class of transactions could exist without causing the financial statements to be materially misstated. This maximum monetary misstatement is called ***tolerable misstatement***. Tolerable misstatement, a planning concept, is related to the auditor's overall estimate of materiality for the financial statements taken as a whole. Based on judgment, the auditor determines materiality and relates it to balances or classes that are sampled. Materiality at the balance or class level is tolerable misstatement. The auditor does not need to determine tolerable misstatement for populations audited 100% because no sampling risk is involved.

As discussed in Chapter 4 and earlier in this chapter, audit risk consists of three components. Algebraically, this may be written as

$$AR = IR \times CR \times DR$$

where AR is the allowable audit risk that monetary misstatement equal to tolerable misstatement might remain undetected for the account balance or class of transactions after the auditor has completed all audit procedures deemed necessary; IR, the auditor's assessment of the susceptibility of an account balance or class of transactions to misstatement that is material, assuming that no related internal control structure policies and procedures (inherent risk) were in use; CR, the auditor's assessment of the risk that, given that misstatements equal to tolerable misstatement occur, the client's control structure policies and procedures fail to detect them, whether because of poorly designed controls or deviations from prescribed controls (control risk); DR, the auditor's assessment of the risk that, given that misstatements equal to tolerable misstatement occur and the client's internal control structure does not detect them, the auditor's substantive test procedures fail to detect them (detection risk).

If the auditor assesses inherent risk at its maximum of 100%, the equation becomes

$$AR = CR \times DR$$

Detection risk consists of the auditor's (1) substantive tests of details and (2) analytical procedures and other substantive tests applied to the population. Thus, substituting these two factors for DR, the formula becomes

$$AR = CR \times AP \times TD$$

where AP is the auditor's assessment of the risk that analytical procedures and other relevant substantive tests would fail to detect misstatements equal to tolerable misstatement, given that they occurred and were not detected by the internal control structure; and TD is the allowable risk of incorrect acceptance for the substantive tests of details, given material misstatement occurrence, internal control structure failure, and other substantive test failure.

An auditor using this model for statistical or nonstatistical sampling may rearrange it as

$$TD = \frac{AR}{CR \times AP}$$

This equation clearly shows that the lower the assessed level of control risk (CR is smaller) or the greater the assurance obtained from other substantive tests directed

Table 9-3			

Factors Influencing Substantive Test Sampling Sizes

	Conditions Leading to		
Factor	Smaller Sample Size	Larger Sample Size	Relationship to Sample Size
Assessment of inherent risk	Low assessed level of inherent risk	High assessed level of inherent risk	Direct
Assessment of control risk	Low assessed level of control risk	High assessed level of control risk	Direct
Assessment of risk for other substantive tests related to same assertion for account balance or class of transactions	High assurance provided by other substantive tests	Low assurance provided by other substantive tests	Direct
Measure of tolerable misstatement for a specific account	Larger measure of tolerable misstatement	Smaller measure of tolerable misstatement	Inverse
Expected size and frequency of misstatements	Smaller misstatements or lower frequency	Larger misstatements or higher frequency	Direct
Population total	Smaller monetary significance to the financial statements	Larger monetary significance to the financial statements	Direct
Variation in audit risk	Higher audit risk	Lower audit risk	Inverse

attribute Sampling

toward the same audit objective (AP is smaller), the greater the allowable audit risk (AR) of incorrect acceptance for the substantive test of details (TD) and, thus, the smaller the required sample size. Conversely, if the auditor assesses control risk as high and decides not to use analytical procedures or other substantive tests for a given audit objective, he or she should allow for a low risk of incorrect acceptance. Thus, the substantive test sample for the test of details is larger. Table 9–3 illustrates the relationship of sample size to the variation in substantive planning factors when other factors are held constant. The substantive planning factors are illustrated quantitatively in the next chapter.

Selecting and Evaluating the Substantive Sample

A substantive test sample should be expected to be representative; therefore, all items or dollars in the population should have an opportunity to be selected. After the sample is selected using one of the techniques discussed in this chapter, the auditor should project the sample results to the population. A nonstatistical way of doing this is to divide the net dollar misstatements by the sample size and multiply the result by the population size. For example, for overstatements of $3,000 in a sample of

The Real World of Auditing

Excerpt from Peer Review Letter—Audit Sampling Deficiencies

Finding—Our review disclosed several instances where the firm failed to document its consideration of objectives of sampling applications, tolerable deviation rates, risk of incorrect acceptance and characteristics of the population being tested. Our review also disclosed several instances where errors noted in sampling applications were not projected to the population and were not otherwise evaluated to determine if the objectives of the sampling application were achieved.

Recommendation for Improvement—The procedure manual purchased and used by the firm contains forms for documenting sample design and error evaluation considerations; however, the firm has prescribed that use of such forms is optional. The firm should either mandate use of such forms or prescribe that alternative equivalent documentation be prepared for all audit sampling applications.

50 items, the auditor could project total overstatement for a population of 1,000 items of $60,000 (that is, [$3,000 ÷ 50] × 1,000). The $60,000 *projected misstatement* is added to any misstatements discovered in any items examined 100% that were excluded from the 1,000-item count. The total projected misstatement is compared with the tolerable misstatement, and an assessment of the potential sampling risk is made. If the total projected misstatement is less than the tolerable misstatement and the sampling size is adequate, the auditor judgmentally concludes that the amount is not misstated. For example, if the tolerable misstatement in an account balance of $1 million is $50,000 and the total projected misstatement is $10,000, the auditor may be reasonably assured that sampling risk is low. On the other hand, if total projected misstatement is close to tolerable misstatement, the auditor may decide that additional procedures should be performed. (In the next chapter, statistical approaches to substantive testing are discussed.)

Summary of Important Sampling Requirements

SAS No. 39 (AU 350) requirements apply to both statistical and nonstatistical audit sampling applications and are presented below in summary form.

- The concept that some items exist for which, in the auditor's judgment, acceptance of some sampling risk is not justified and which therefore should be examined 100%. This simply reminds the auditor that some items may individually be so significant or may have such a high likelihood of being misstated that they should not be sampled.

- A requirement that the auditor consider the maximum rate of deviations from a prescribed internal control structure policy and procedure that he or she would be willing to accept without altering the planned assessed level of control risk, and a substantive testing requirement to consider how much monetary misstatement may exist without causing the financial statements to be materially misstated.

- A requirement that the auditor select a sample that he or she believes is representative of the items composing the pertinent account balance or class of transactions when performing tests of controls or substantive tests. Probability selection (that is, using a random number table), systematic selection, and haphazard selection are all permitted under *SAS No. 39* (AU 350).
- A requirement that the auditor consider unexamined items to determine their effect on the evaluation of the sample.
- A requirement that the auditor project the evaluation of the sample to the account balance or class of transactions from which the sample was selected. Because the sample is expected to be representative of the population, deviations or misstatements found are also expected to be representative of the population.
- A requirement that the auditor consider, in the aggregate, projected misstatement results for all audit sampling applications and all known misstatements from nonsampling applications when the financial statements are evaluated to determine if they are materially misstated.

Significant Terms

Alpha risk *See* Risk of incorrect rejection; Risk of assessing control risk too high.

Attribute sampling A statistical method used to estimate whether the rate of deviation (for example, a deviation from a prescribed control policy or procedure) in a population exceeds a tolerable rate.

Audit hypothesis testing A statistical decision approach used to test the reasonableness of an existing client account balance or class of transactions.

Audit risk A combination of the risk that material misstatements will occur in the accounting process used to develop the financial statements and the risk that any material misstatements that occur will not be detected by the auditor.

Audit sampling The application of an audit procedure to less than 100% of the items within an account balance or class of transactions for the purpose of evaluating some characteristics of the balance or class.

Beta risk *See* Risk of incorrect acceptance; Risk of assessing control risk too low.

Block sample A sample consisting of contiguous transactions; for example, selecting 50 checks in sequence for testing.

Correspondence The relationship between the sampling frame and a random number table.

Discovery sampling A special case of attribute sampling that is used to determine a specified probability of finding at least one example of an occurrence (attribute) in a population.

Dollar-unit sampling *See* Probability-proportionate-to-size sampling.

Dollar value estimation A statistical approach used to estimate independently the value of an account balance or class of transactions.

Estimated deviation rate The deviation rate in a test of controls sample that is used as the auditor's best estimate of the population deviation rate.

Haphazard sample A sample selected by the auditor without any special reason for including or excluding particular items.

Judgment sampling *See* Nonstatistical sampling.

Nonsampling risk All aspects of audit risk not due to sampling risk.

Nonstatistical sampling A sampling technique in which the auditor does not use statistical theory to measure sampling risk.

Population An account balance or class of transactions or a portion thereof.

Probability-proportionate-to-size sampling A statistical method that uses attribute sampling theory to express dollar conclusions.

Projected misstatement An estimate of the monetary misstatement in the population based on a substantive test sample.

Random sample A selection technique used to generate a probability sample that can be used in statistical evaluations.

Representative sample A sample that is expected to exhibit approximately the same characteristics as the population from which it is drawn. A representative sample may be selected using probability concepts (for example, random number selection) or using haphazard selection.

Risk of assessing control risk too high The risk that the assessed level of control risk based on the sample is greater than the true operating effectiveness of the control structure policy or procedure.

Risk of assessing control risk too low The risk that the assessed level of control risk based on the sample is less than the true operating effectiveness of the control structure policy or procedure.

Risk of incorrect acceptance The risk that the sample supports the conclusion that the recorded account balance is not materially misstated when it is in fact materially misstated.

Risk of incorrect rejection The risk that the sample supports the conclusion that the recorded account balance is materially misstated when it is not materially misstated.

Sampling frame A listing or physical representation of a sampling unit. For example, for a test of cash disbursements, the individual check number could be a sampling frame.

Sampling risk The risk that the auditor's conclusion based on a sample may be different from the conclusion he or she would reach if the test were applied to an entire population.

Sampling with replacement A sampling technique that permits a selected item to be returned to the population and reselected.

Sampling without replacement A sampling technique in which an item, once included in a sample, cannot be reselected.

Statistical sampling Audit sampling that uses the laws of probability for selecting and evaluating a sample.

Stratification The process of dividing a population into subpopulations that have similar characteristics.

Systematic selection A method of drawing a sample in which every nth item is drawn from one or more random starts.

Tolerable misstatement An estimate of the maximum monetary misstatement that may exist in an account balance or class of transactions without causing financial statements to be materially misstated.

Tolerable rate The maximum rate of deviations from a prescribed control structure policy or procedure that the auditor would tolerate without altering the planned assessed level of control risk.

Variable sampling A statistical model that produces an independent dollar estimate of an account balance or is used to test an existing account balance.

Discussion Questions

9-1. Is *SAS No. 39, Audit Sampling*, used to help the auditor determine the nature, timing, or extent of testing?

9-2. What three conditions must be met to satisfy the *SAS No. 39* definition of sampling?

9-3. What are the two general approaches to audit sampling?

9-4. Does the AICPA require the use of statistical sampling?

9-5. It is a misnomer to refer to *nonstatistical sampling* as *judgment sampling*. Do you agree?

9-6. What is the definition of *statistical sampling*? *Nonstatistical sampling*?

9-7. Define *audit risk, sampling risk*, and *nonsampling risk*. Also, illustrate their interrelationship.

9-8. Sampling risk can be reduced to a negligible level. Do you agree?

9-9. What are the major advantages of statistical sampling?

9-10. What are the major disadvantages of statistical sampling?

9-11. What are the three major types of statistical sampling?

9-12. A primary distinction between classical variable or attribute sampling and probability-proportionate-to-size sampling is the way in which a sampling unit is defined. What does this mean?

9-13. How do dollar value estimation and audit hypothesis testing differ?

9-14. Does *SAS No. 39* apply to a dollar value estimation application?

9-15. How does a representative sample differ from a nonrepresentative sample?

9-16. What is a sampling frame? How does it relate to the population?

9-17. List three items that must be predefined to use a random number table.

9-18. In using systematic sampling, an auditor should guard against bias. What steps should an auditor take to reduce the chance of a biased selection?

9-19. Systematic selection and haphazard selection can only be used in nonstatistical sampling applications. Do you agree?

9-20. How should an auditor evaluate a voucher that was selected for substantive testing from a random number table when the voucher is missing?

9-21. How do *sampling with replacement* and *sampling without replacement* differ?

9-22. Tests of controls sampling risks consist of two aspects. What are they? Which is more important? Why?

9-23. What is *tolerable rate*?

9-24. In evaluating the results of a test of control sample, if the tolerable rate is close to the estimated deviation rate, would the auditor conclude that sampling risk is low or high?

9-25. How does the risk of incorrect acceptance differ from the risk of incorrect rejection?

9-26. Why is the risk of incorrect acceptance more important to an auditor than the risk of incorrect rejection?

9-27. Define the concept of *tolerable misstatement* for a substantive test.

9-28. What is the equation for audit risk?

9-29. A decrease in assessed control risk and an increase in use of analytical procedures permit a (higher/lower) risk of incorrect acceptance and a (larger/smaller) sample size of substantive test of details. Why?

9-30. Under what conditions would an auditor generally allow for a low risk of incorrect acceptance?

9-31. If an auditor discovers $4,000 of understatement errors and $6,000 of overstatement errors in a sample of 100 from a population of 2,583 items, what is the projected misstatement?

Objective Questions

*9-32. An auditor may find many kinds of statistical estimates useful, but basically every accounting estimate is either of a quantity or of a deviation rate. Which of these statistical terms roughly correspond to *quantities* and *deviation rate?*

---

*AICPA adapted.

     (1) Attributes and variables.

     (2) Variables and attributes.

     (3) Constants and attributes.

     (4) Constants and variables.

*9-33. Which of the following is an advantage of systematic sampling over random number sampling?

     (1) It provides a stronger basis for statistical conclusions.

     (2) It enables the auditor to use the more efficient "sampling with replacement" tables.

     (3) There may be correlation among the location of items in the population, the feature of sampling interest, and the sampling interval.

     (4) It does not require the auditor to establish correspondence between random numbers and items in the population.

*9-34. An example of sampling for attributes would be estimating the

     (1) quantity of specific inventory items.

     (2) probability of losing a patent infringement case.

     (3) percentage of overdue accounts receivable.

     (4) dollar value of accounts receivable.

9-35. Tests of controls are intended to provide reasonable assurance that the internal control structure procedures are being applied as prescribed. Which sampling method is most useful when testing controls?

     (1) Haphazard sampling.

     (2) Attribute sampling.

     (3) Sampling with replacement.

     (4) Stratified random sampling.

*9-36. Which of the following best describes what the auditor means by the rate of deviation in an attribute sampling plan?

     (1) The number of deviations that can reasonably be expected to be found in a population.

     (2) The frequency with which a certain characteristic occurs within a population.

     (3) The degree of confidence that the sample is representative of the population.

     (4) The dollar range within which the true population total can be expected to fall.

*9-37. Which of the following best describes the distinguishing feature of statistical sampling?

     (1) It provides for measuring mathematically the degree of uncertainty that results from examining only a part of the data.

     (2) It allows the auditor to have the same degree of confidence as with judgment sampling but with substantially less work.

     (3) It allows the auditor to substitute sampling techniques for audit judgment.

     (4) It provides for measuring the actual misstatements in financial statements in terms of reliability and precision.

*9-38. If an auditor, planning to use statistical sampling, is concerned with the number of client's sales invoices that contain mathematical misstatements, which method would the auditor most likely use?

     (1) Random sampling with replacement.

     (2) Sampling for attributes.

     (3) Sampling for variables.

     (4) Stratified random sampling.

9-39. Which of the following sampling plans is designed to produce a numerical measurement, such as a dollar value?

     (1) Sampling without replacement.

     (2) Discovery sampling.

     (3) Sampling for attributes.

     (4) Sampling for variables.

---

*AICPA adapted.

9-40. Rachel Jones, CPA, believes the expected deviation rate of client billing errors is 3% and has established a tolerable deviation rate of 5%. In the review of client invoices, which method should Jones use?
   (1) Discovery sampling.
   (2) Attribute sampling.
   (3) Stratified sampling.
   (4) Variable sampling.

*9-41. The risk of incorrect acceptance and the risk of assessing control risk too low relate to the
   (1) preliminary estimates of materiality levels.
   (2) allowable risk of tolerable misstatement.
   (3) efficiency of the audit.
   (4) effectiveness of the audit.

*9-42. The diagram below depicts the auditor's estimated deviation rate compared with tolerable rate and the true population deviation rate compared with the tolerable rate.

		True State of Population	
		Deviation Rate Exceeds Tolerable Rate	Deviation Rate Is Less than Tolerable Rate
Auditor's Estimate Based on Sample Results	Deviation Rate Exceeds Tolerable Rate	I.	III.
	Deviation Rate Is Less than Tolerable Rate	II.	IV.

As a result of the sampling test of controls, the auditor assesses control risk too high and thereby increases substantive testing. This is illustrated by
   (1) I.
   (2) II.
   (3) III.
   (4) IV.

*9-43. Which of the following combinations results in a decrease in sample size in a sample for attributes?

	Risk of Assessing Control Risk Too Low	Tolerable Rate	Expected Population Deviation Rate
(1)	Increase	Decrease	Increase
(2)	Decrease	Increase	Decrease
(3)	Increase	Increase	Decrease
(4)	Increase	Increase	Increase

Problems and Cases

9-44. (Audit Sampling Overview) Bart Ward, CPA, has been assigned responsibility as a discussion leader in his firm for a continuing education course on "Audit Sampling

---

Applications." In developing course material, Ward's firm indicated that he should assume that the audit staff is familiar with audit sampling concepts. He should, in other words, develop material to illustrate how statistical and nonstatistical sampling are applied in a typical audit engagement. Ward has developed the following true–false questions to assess the staff's knowledge of sampling concepts.

REQUIRED

Indicate whether each of the following statements is true or false.

A. Audit risk includes both uncertainties due to sampling and uncertainties due to factors other than sampling.

B. If the auditor is using nonstatistical sampling, it is generally appropriate to select only high dollar sales invoices in testing controls.

C. A properly designed nonstatistical sampling application can provide results that are as effective as a properly designed statistical sampling application.

D. A sampling approach that does not use random number selection is a nonstatistical sampling procedure.

E. Nonstatistical sample sizes are logically smaller than the size of a well-designed statistical sampling application.

F. If an auditor wishes to measure the dollar amount of transactions containing deviations from an internal control structure procedure, the auditor could use variable sampling.

G. Audit sampling for tests of controls is generally used only where a trail of documentary evidence exists.

H. If a population is arranged randomly, systematic selection is essentially the same as random number selection.

I. A properly selected haphazard sample can be used for statistical sampling.

J. A major advantage of statistical sampling is that it allows an auditor to project errors.

9-45. (Definition of Audit Sampling) Jane Meryl, CPA, is examining fixed asset additions in the audit of Wallach's Manufacturing. The fixed asset additions total $2 million. She is primarily concerned with overstatements. In analyzing the additions, she determines that five additions pertain to a plant expansion program. They total $1.6 million. She also notes that 400 smaller additions account for the remaining $400,000 book value. Meryl decides that the five large additions are individually significant and need to be examined 100%. Assume that she has applied the following audit strategies to the remaining 400 items.

Strategy 1

Meryl has performed other procedures related to fixed asset additions, including
1. assessing control risk for fixed assets assertions, which supported a low assessed control risk.
2. a review of entries to the fixed asset ledger, which revealed no unusual items, and
3. an analytical procedure that suggests that the $400,000 book value of the 400 smaller additions is consistent with the trend from prior years.

Strategy 2

Meryl has not performed any procedures related to the remaining 400 items, but she has decided that any misstatements in those items would be immaterial.

Strategy 3

Meryl has performed some or all of the same procedures in Strategy 1, but she concludes that she should obtain some additional evidence regarding the 400 small additions by selecting a sample of them.

Strategy 4

Meryl and Wallach's have agreed that the fixed asset additions contain numerous errors; therefore, Meryl takes a sample of the 400 smaller additions to estimate the total. Wallach's has indicated that they will record her estimate plus the total of the five large additions as their book value.

REQUIRED

Discuss each of the above strategies in terms of whether *SAS No. 39, Audit Sampling,* governs the application.

9-46. (Dollar Value Estimation versus Audit Hypothesis Testing) Bernie Nayman, CPA, has had numerous situations in audit engagements during the past year where statistical sampling could be effectively used. For example, he encountered the following client situations, all involving material account balances.

Client A

Client A has an accounts receivable balance of $289,486. The controls over credit sales are very good and Nayman has proposed no adjustments to accounts receivable in the last three audits.

Client B

Client B has an inventory consisting of 5,000 items. The inventory is valued on FIFO; the client wants to switch to LIFO.

Client C

Client C has an allowance for uncollectibles of $155,000. During the audit of receivables, Nayman noticed that credits were being applied to the wrong accounts and some accounts were exceptionally old. Also, several customers appear to have financial problems. Client C admits to Nayman that the allowance account is significantly understated.

Client D

Client D has not taken a physical inventory for the current year. Nayman suggests that Client D consider using a statistical method to estimate this year's inventory and avoid the expense of a complete count of the 6,500 inventory items.

REQUIRED

Indicate in each of the above client situations whether dollar value estimation or audit hypothesis testing is appropriate. Also, identify whether *SAS No. 39, Audit Sampling*, applies to the client situation.

9-47. (Using a Random Number Table) In every audit sampling application involving a projection of sample characteristics to the population, the auditor should select a sample that he or she expects to be representative. For the situations described in **A** and **B** below, identify an acceptable sample selection approach.

A. Identify an effective and efficient method to select a random sample by using a random number table. Also, identify the discard range and the first six random numbers selected for each situation. Use the random number table in Table 9–1. The starting point is row 3, column 4, digit starting position 3. The route is down the table reading from left to right.

    (1) Sales invoices numbered from 252 to 5,689.

    (2) Disbursement vouchers numbered from 5,006 to 14,500.

    (3) Voucher register having 43 pages, each page with a maximum of 32 lines per page.

B. Design an efficient method (minimum discards) to select a random sample of sales invoices by using a random number table (see Table 9–1) for the following client situation. Sales invoices are identified by month and the number within the month. Each month starts over with number 1. The sales invoices are listed in a sales journal that has a total of 95 pages for the year. Each sales journal page has 70 lines. No month has more than 15 sales invoice pages.

9-48. (Sample Selection) In the audit of Zuber Corporation for the year ended December 31, 19X7, Ray Clay, CPA, decides to select one representative three-week period during 19X7. Clay tested all sales invoices issued during the three-week period. He also resolved all deviations to his satisfaction and assessed the internal control structure as very effective. In fact, he plans to reduce his confirmation of accounts receivable sample size by 25% because of his assessed level of control risk.

REQUIRED

A. Is the sample selection approach that Clay has used appropriate under *SAS No. 39, Audit Sampling*?

B. Is this a block sample?

C. Can block samples be evaluated statistically?

[handwritten: Random no. pareer] *[handwritten: Random Sample selection]*

[handwritten: Depends] **D.** How would you recommend that Clay select sales invoices for examination? *[handwritten: Selection]*
E. Is it appropriate for Clay to perform interim tests of controls for the period January 1 through October 15 and not perform additional testing at year-end? *[handwritten: Possibly.]*

9-49. (Sample Design and Interim Testing) The audit team assigned to Roll Tide, Inc. is planning interim work for 19X7. Roll Tide has a December 31 year end. The audit team will start work in early November. One of the populations that they want to perform tests of controls on is in the sales/receivable area. Roll Tide issued sales invoices numbered 1 to 10,000 for the first ten months of the year.

REQUIRED

A. What factors should the audit team consider in deciding if the remaining period (November and December) sales invoices should be sampled?

B. The audit team estimated that 2,500 additional sales invoices will be generated in November and December. They identified sample items for selection from the population 1 to 12,500. However, only 2,000 sales invoices were generated during November and December. How should the auditors handle the identified sample items from 12,001 to 12,500 when they return to perform year-end work?

C. Assume that the audit team underestimated the November and December sales invoices. Instead of 2,500, November and December produced 3,200 sales invoices; therefore, no sample items were identified for sales invoices numbered 12,501 through 13,200. What audit options should be considered for the sales invoice population number 12,501 through 13,200?

9-50. (Attribute and Variable Sampling) The following are examples of tests an auditor might perform in an audit of financial statements. For each test listed, identify whether the procedure usually involves sampling. If it does, state whether attribute or variable sampling would typically be used.

[handwritten left margin: dual Either Attribute or variable / attribute / DUAL PURP.]

A. Tests of recording of shipments. *[handwritten: Yes. Sampling # attribute]*
B. Comparison of financial information with budgeted information. *[handwritten: NO! Analytical Proced]*
C. Tests of controls over payroll and related personnel policy systems. *[handwritten: Yes.]*
D. Obtaining written representations from management. *[handwritten: NO!]*
E. Inspecting land and buildings. *[handwritten: NO! / YES!]*
F. Completing an internal control structure questionnaire. *[handwritten: NO!]*
G. Tests of controls over inventory pricing. *[handwritten: YES! ATTRIBUTE]*
H. Tests of recorded payroll expense. *[handwritten: YES! VARIABLE]*
I. Observing cash-handling procedures. *[handwritten: YES! ATTRIBUTE NO!]*
J. Tests of the amount of transactions that are not supported by proper approval. *[handwritten: VARIABLE.]*
K. Selecting one transaction to obtain an understanding of the entity's internal control structure. *[handwritten: NO!]*

Organize your answer as follows:

Procedure	Involves Sampling? (Yes or No)	Attribute/Variable/Not Applicable

9-51. (Projecting Sample Results) Alfred Jones of Jones & Co., CPAs, designed a nonstatistical sample to test the December 31, 19X4, accounts receivable of Short Circuit, Inc. Short Circuit, an electrical supply company, is a new client of Jones & Co. For the year ended December 31, 19X4, Short Circuit had sales of approximately $25 million. At December 31, the company had 1,100 accounts receivable, with debit balances aggregating $4 million. These balances ranged from $10 to $140,000. In auditing the account, Jones decided that a misstatement of $130,000 might result in a material misstatement of the financial statements. Jones separated the population into three strata, based on the book value of the items. The first group contained 5 balances that totaled $500,000. The second group consisted of the 250 balances equal to, or greater than, $3,000, and the third group consisted of the remaining balances with book values less than $3,000. Jones mailed confirmations to each of the five big accounts, to 73 accounts from the $3,000 and over group and to 37 accounts from the under-$3,000 group. In all, 90 of the 115 confirmations were returned to him. Jones was able to obtain reasonable assurance through alternative procedures that the 25 customer balances that were not confirmed were bona fide receivables and were not misstated. Of the 90 responses, only 3 indicated that the balance was overstated. Jones summarized his sample as follows:

Stratum	Book Value of Stratum	Book Value of Sample	Audit Value of Sample	Amount of Overstatement
100% examination	$ 500,000	$500,000	$499,000	$ 1,000
Over $3,000	2,250,000	739,000	727,500	11,500
Under $3,000	1,250,000	62,500	61,000	1,500
	$4,000,000			

REQUIRED

A. Calculate Jones's total projected misstatement.

B. What should Jones conclude based on his sample?

C. Assuming that Jones's projected misstatement was $129,000, would his conclusion change?

D. Assuming that the above test was a test of controls instead of a substantive test, what would be Jones's projected deviation rate?

9-52. (Risk of Incorrect Acceptance) Calculate the auditor's allowable risk of incorrect acceptance (TD) for each of the following independent situations.   *50%*

Substantive Test of Detail

	Control Risk (%)	Risk of Analytical Procedure and Other Substantive Test Failure (%)	Audit Risk (%)
A.	10 *50%*	100	5
B.	30 *33%*	50	5
C.	50 *200%*	10 *Not Rely on*	10 *TD*
D.	100 *33%*	30	10
E.	100 *10%*	100 *RELY ON TD 10*	

*9-53. (Comprehensive Attribute Sampling) Sampling for attributes is often used to allow an auditor to reach a conclusion concerning a rate of occurrence in a population. A common use in auditing is to test the rate of deviation from a prescribed internal control procedure to determine whether planned reliance on that control is appropriate.

REQUIRED

A. When an auditor samples for attributes, identify the factors that should influence the auditor's judgment concerning the determination of
   (1) acceptable level of risk of overreliance,
   (2) tolerable deviation rate, and
   (3) expected population deviation rate.

---

*AICPA adapted.

B. State the effect on sample size of an increase in each of the following factors, assuming all other factors are held constant:
    (1) acceptable level of risk of assessing control risk too low,
    (2) tolerable deviation rate, and
    (3) expected population deviation rate.

C. Evaluate the sample results of a test for attributes if authorizations are found to be missing on 7 check requests out of a sample of 100 tested. The population consists of 2,500 check requests, the tolerable deviation rate is 8%, and the acceptable level of risk of overreliance is low.

D. How may the use of statistical sampling assist the auditor in evaluating the sample results described in part C above?

Audit Judgment Case

9-54. (Substantive Sampling under *SAS No. 39*) The senior audit partner of your firm, Donald Dale, is concerned about whether the firm is complying with *SAS No. 39, Audit Sampling*. Dale is especially concerned about the use of nonstatistical sampling for substantive testing. Because most of the firm's clients are small businesses that are owner/manager dominated and have limited segregation of duties, your firm rarely performs extensive tests of controls. According to Dale, "In our kind of client, it is not efficient to perform extended tests of controls, beyond the tests of controls performed to obtain the necessary knowledge of the internal control structure, to reduce substantive testing. Besides," he adds, "it's risky to test controls in our clients. I feel better doing primarily substantive testing."

Dale has taken a two-day continuing professional education course on attribute sampling; however, because the firm does not do a lot of sampling tests of controls on the firm's commercial clients, the materials from the course are not used very much. Basically, Dale's knowledge of sampling is limited to attribute sampling and nonstatistical substantive sampling.

Dale has been worrying about *SAS No. 39*. To determine if it is being appropriately applied, he selected a sampling application in the accounts receivable area for review. Here is the situation. The receivables contained 2,610 customer accounts with a book value total of $1,260,000. The accounts were stratified for audit purposes as follows:

Account Balance Range ($)	Number of Accounts	Book Value ($)
5,000–65,000	10	460,000
250–4,999	400	450,000
1–249	2,200	350,000
	2,610	1,260,000

Joe Bob Sinclair, the senior in charge of the engagement, confirmed all 10 of the largest accounts, 70 of the second group of accounts, and 50 of the third group of accounts. He found a $2,000 overstatement error from the first group of 10 confirmations. From the second batch of confirmations and alternative procedures, he found no errors or misstatements. And in the last group from the 50 confirmations, he found net overstatements of $200.

Because the errors were corrected and not material, Sinclair concluded that the account balance was fairly stated. He, of course, included details on the confirmations and alternative procedures applied in his working papers to support his conclusion.

REQUIRED

A. The auditor should determine that the population drawn from the sample is appropriate for the specific audit objective. What do you think was Sinclair's audit objective?

[handwritten margin note: 5 to 10% of total A/R]

[handwritten margin note: Stratifying Homogeneous Sub Pop]

[handwritten margin note: Systematic Selection — Every nth item]

[handwritten margin note: Representative Sample RECEIP]

[handwritten margin note: Same as 9-50]

B. When planning a sample for a substantive test of details, the auditor should consider how much monetary misstatement in the related account balance or class of transactions may exist without causing the financial statements to be materially misstated. Although Sinclair did not make a preliminary estimate of materiality last year, what would you recommend as materiality or tolerable misstatement?

C. When planning a sample for a substantive test of details, the auditor uses his or her judgment to determine which items, if any, in an account balance or class of transactions should be individually examined and which items, if any, should be subject to sampling. The auditor should examine those items for which, in his or her judgment, acceptance of some sampling risk is not justified. Did Sinclair properly identify the key account balances for 100% confirmation? What happens to sampling risk for the 100% examined balances? *[handwritten: Sampling risk = 0]*

D. The auditor may be able to reduce the required sample size by separating items subject to sampling into relatively homogeneous groups on the basis of some characteristic related to the specific audit objectives. Did Sinclair properly stratify the receivable balance? *[handwritten: YES!]*

E. Sample items should be selected in such a way that the sample can be expected to be representative of the population; therefore, all items in the population should have an opportunity to be selected. How would you suggest that Sinclair select a representative sample? *[handwritten: Random / Systematic]*

F. If Sinclair does not obtain a response to a positive confirmation of a given receivable balance, is it appropriate to rely on alternative procedures such as review of subsequent payment and review of internal evidence? *[handwritten: YES!]*

G. The auditor should project the misstatement results of the sample to the items from which the sample was selected. What is the total projected overstatement? How should Sinclair control sampling risk? Was Sinclair's conclusion, that the receivable book value was fairly stated, correct? *[handwritten: $2,000 ② -0- ③ $200 Sample Projection $4 Error $10,800 Total accept]*

H. Did Sinclair give adequate consideration to qualitative evaluation?

Auditing Issues Case

9-55. KELCO MANUFACTURING COMPANY

The following list contains examples of tests an auditor might perform when examining Kelco's financial statements. For each test listed, identify whether the procedure usually involves sampling, and if it does, state whether attribute or variable sampling would be typically used.

A. Tests of recording shipments.

B. Comparison of financial information with budgeted information.

C. Tests of controls over payroll and related personnel policy systems.

D. Obtaining written representations from management.

E. Inspecting land and buildings.

F. Completing an internal control questionnaire.

G. Test of controls over inventory pricing.

H. Tests of recorded payroll expense.

I. Tests of the amount of transactions that are not supported by proper approval.

J. Selecting one transaction to obtain an understanding of Kelco's internal control structure.

Organize your answer as follows:

Procedure	Involves Sampling (Yes or No)	Attribute/Variable/Not Applicable

Chapter 10

Audit Sampling Applications

- Differentiate between a statistical and a nonstatistical test of controls.

- Calculate sample sizes and evaluate test of controls sample results using attribute sampling.

- Use a discovery sampling table to determine sample sizes.

- Apply dollar value estimation to estimate account balances using the mean per unit or difference estimation.

- Calculate substantive test sizes and evaluate sample results using classical variables sampling and probability-proportionate-to-size sampling.

This chapter illustrates the statistical approach to using attribute, discovery, classical variables, and probability-proportionate-to-size sampling. The sampling concepts presented in Chapter 9 are applied in this chapter to practical audit situations. Dollar value estimation, an accounting tool, as opposed to an auditing tool, is reviewed as appropriate background for understanding classical variables sampling in audit hypothesis testing. This chapter emphasizes the statistical calculation of sample size and the statistical evaluation of sample results. As an introduction to statistical sampling in auditing, this chapter is designed to serve as a starting point for additional readings and applications. ■

Attribute Sampling

Chapter 9 discusses the factors that the auditor needs to consider when planning, selecting, and evaluating a sample for a test of controls. In a statistical test of controls, the auditor has to specify explicitly (1) the allowable risk of assessing control risk too low, (2) the tolerable rate, and (3) the expected population deviation rate.

Table 10–1 delineates the steps in a test of controls using either a statistical or a nonstatistical sampling application. In this chapter we illustrate how to use attribute sampling to determine sample size (Step 4 in Table 10–1) and to evaluate quantitatively the sample results (Step 8).

Attribute sampling is easy to use. Consequently, some auditors have a policy of using only statistical (rather than nonstatistical) test of controls sampling. In other words, whenever they perform a test of controls under *SAS No. 39, Audit Sampling* (AU 350), they use attribute sampling to determine sample size and to evaluate sample results.

Determining the Sample Size

The allowable risk of assessing control risk too low, the tolerable rate, and the expected population deviation rate are the major determinants of sample size in an attribute application. In contrast, the population size has little or no effect on sample size. For populations with more than 5,000 sampling units, the population size has no effect on sample size. A population size greater than or equal to 5,000 is assumed in this chapter.[1]

---

[1] Tables 10–2 and 10–3 are based on a large population. For a small population, especially when the sample size is more than 10% of the population, the following adjustment, called the *finite correction factor*, should be applied.

$$n = \frac{n'}{1 + \left(\dfrac{n'}{N}\right)}$$

where
n' = Sample size before considering the effect of population size.
n = Revised sample size.
N = Population size.
For example, if $n' = 100$ and population size = 500, we calculate the revised sample size as follows:

$$n = \frac{100}{1 + \dfrac{100}{500}} = 84.$$

| Table 10-1 | **Steps in Performing Tests of Controls Sampling: Statistical or Nonstatistical** |

KNOW ! (handwritten)

Step	Explanation
1. Determine the objective of the test.	The objective is to provide evidence about whether an internal control structure policy or procedure is operating effectively.
2. Define the deviation condition.	A deviation is a departure from a prescribed internal control structure policy or procedure.
3. Define the population.	The population should be appropriate for the specific audit objective. The auditor should determine the period covered and the sampling frame (for example, a document, an entry, a line item).
4. Determine the sample size.	The sample size is dependent on the allowable risk of assessing control risk too low, the tolerable rate, and the expected population deviation rate.
5. Determine the sample selection method.	Sample items should be selected in such a way that the sample can be expected to be representative of the population.
6. Select the sample.	Random number or systematic selection should be used. Haphazard selection may be used for nonstatistical test of controls. Unexamined items should be considered deviations from the prescribed policy or procedure.
7. Audit the sample.	Selected items should be examined to determine if they deviate from the prescribed policy or procedure.
8. Evaluate the sample results.	The sample should be evaluated quantitatively (use appropriate table) and qualitatively. The effect on nature, timing, and extent of substantive audit testing should be determined.
9. Use sample results in making conclusion on assessed level of control risk.	If the sample results, along with other relevant evidential matter, support the planned assessed level of control risk, the auditor generally does not need to modify planned substantive tests.

The following table illustrates the limited effect of population size on attribute sample size. The table assumes a risk of assessing control risk too low of 5%, an expected population deviation rate of 1%, and a tolerable rate of 5%.

Population Size	Sample Size
50	45
100	64
500	87
1,000	90
2,000	92
5,000	93
100,000	93

Assessing Control Risk Too Low

In Chapter 9, the risk of assessing control risk too low was defined as the risk that the assessed level of control risk based on the sample is less than the true operating effectiveness of the control structure policy or procedure. The risk of assessing control risk too low refers to the probability of assessing control risk low or moderate when the control structure policy or procedure is not operating effectively. For example, if an auditor selects a 10% risk of assessing control risk too low, he or she has a 10% chance of assessing the level of control risk as low or moderate when control is ineffective given a certain tolerable rate. Conversely, a 10% risk of assessing control risk too low means that the auditor has a 90% reliability level, or probability of being right.

According to audit sampling policy guidelines in many CPA firms, the maximum risk of assessing control risk as too low should be 10%. In other words, whenever control risk is assessed at less than the maximum for any assertion, at least a 90% reliability level should be used. A 5% risk of assessing control risk too low (95% reliability) should be used when the planned assessed level of control risk is low and a high degree of assurance is desired from the sample test of controls.

Tolerable Rate

An auditor using attribute sampling for a test of controls has to predefine the maximum rate of deviation that is acceptable without altering the planned assessed level of control risk. A high probability of deviations in excess of tolerable rate would cause the auditor to assess control risk as high, or at the maximum (that is, 100%). According to some auditors, tolerable rate may vary as follows:

Planned Assessed Level of Control Risk	Assurance Desired from Sample Test of Controls	Risk of Assessing Control Risk Too Low	Tolerable Rate
Lower level	High or substantial	5%	2–5%
Moderate level	Low or moderate	10%	6–10%
Slightly below the maximum	Low	10%	11–20%
Maximum	None	N/A	Omit test

Some CPA firms have a policy of (1) using a 5% risk of assessing control risk too low and a tolerable rate of 5% when the planned assessed level of control risk is low and a high degree of assurance is desired from the sample test of controls, or (2) using a 10% risk of assessing control risk too low and a tolerable rate of 10% when the planned assessed level of control risk is higher and a lower degree of assurance is desired from the sample test of controls.

Expected Population Deviation Rate

In an attribute sampling application, the auditor also must predefine the *expected population deviation rate*. The rate may be estimated based on the auditor's judgment or prior knowledge (for example, results of the prior year's test of controls).

Figure 10–1	**Sample Size Determination for 10% Risk of Assessing Control Risk Too Low**

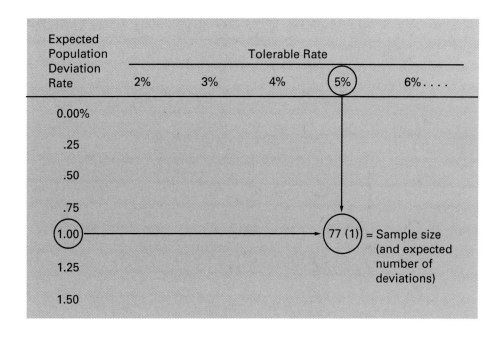

In situations in which the auditor does not know the expected population deviation rate, some auditors select a ***pilot sample*** of 50 or 60 items to estimate the occurrence rate. To illustrate, if a sample of 50 is randomly selected and 2 deviations are discovered for a given attribute, the estimated population deviation rate is 4% (2 ÷ 50).

Sample Size Tables[2]

Tables 10–2 and 10–3 are used to determine sample sizes for attribute applications. Table 10–2 is used for 5% risk of assessing control risk too low and Table 10–3 for 10% risk of assessing control risk too low.

To use the tables, the auditor first selects the table based on the desired risk of assessing control risk too low. He or she then reads down the expected population deviation rate column to find the appropriate rate. Next, he or she locates the column corresponding to the tolerable rate. The sample size is shown in the box where the expected population deviation rate and the tolerable rate intersect. Figure 10–1 shows a sample size of 77 for an expected population deviation rate of 1%, a tolerable rate of 5%, and a risk of assessing control risk too low of 10%. The parenthetical number is the expected number of deviations. It is calculated as the sample size (77) multiplied by the expected population deviation rate (1%).

---

[2] The sample size tables are based on the cumulative binomial distribution. Auditors seldom use the binomial equation to calculate sample sizes because a wide range of values have been put in table form.

| Table 10-2 | **Statistical Sample Sizes for Tests of Controls—5% Risk of Assessing Control Risk Too Low (with Number of Expected Deviations in Parentheses)** |

(handwritten margin note: 5% Risk of Overreliance)

Expected Population Deviation Rate	Tolerable Rate				
	2%	3%	4%	5%	6%
0.00%	149(0)	99(0)	74(0)	59(0)	49(0)
.25	236(1)	157(1)	117(1)	93(1)	78(1)
.50	*	157(1)	117(1)	93(1)	78(1)
.75	*	208(2)	117(1)	93(1)	78(1)
1.00	*	*	156(2)	93(1)	78(1)
1.25	*	*	156(2)	124(2)	78(1)
1.50	*	*	192(3)	124(2)	103(2)
1.75	*	*	227(4)	153(3)	103(2)
2.00	*	*	*	181(4)	127(3)
2.25	*	*	*	208(5)	127(3)
2.50	*	*	*	*	150(4)
2.75	*	*	*	*	173(5)
3.00	*	*	*	*	195(6)
3.25	*	*	*	*	*
3.50	*	*	*	*	*
3.75	*	*	*	*	*
4.00	*	*	*	*	*
5.00	*	*	*	*	*
6.00	*	*	*	*	*
7.00	*	*	*	*	*

*Sample size is too large to be cost-effective for most audit applications.
Used with permission of the AICPA.

Sample Evaluation Tables

Tables 10–2 and 10–3 can also be used to evaluate sample results. If the auditor finds that the number of deviations found in the audited sample does not exceed the parenthetical number, he or she can conclude that the maximum population deviation rate is not more than the tolerable rate. In other words, in the example in Figure 10–1, if no more than one deviation is found in the sample, the auditor may conclude that he or she has 90% reliability (or a 10% risk of assessing control risk too low) that the population deviation rate does not exceed 5%.

Instead of using Tables 10–2 and 10–3 for evaluating the sample results, the auditor may use Tables 10–4 and 10–5. Table 10–4 or 10–5 must be used if the actual number of deviations exceeds the parenthetical number in Table 10–2 or 10–3 and the auditor wants to assess the *maximum population deviation rate*.

Figure 10–2 illustrates how to use Tables 10–4 and 10–5. To use Table 10–4 or 10–5, the auditor first selects the appropriate table based on the acceptable level of risk of assessing control risk too low. As illustrated in Figure 10–2, he or she then reads down the sample size column to find the appropriate sample size. (If the sample

		Tolerable Rate			
7%	8%	9%	10%	15%	20%
42(0)	36(0)	32(0)	29(0)	19(0)	14(0)
66(1)	58(1)	51(1)	46(1)	30(1)	22(1)
66(1)	58(1)	51(1)	46(1)	30(1)	22(1)
66(1)	58(1)	51(1)	46(1)	30(1)	22(1)
66(1)	58(1)	51(1)	46(1)	30(1)	22(1)
66(1)	58(1)	51(1)	46(1)	30(1)	22(1)
66(1)	58(1)	51(1)	46(1)	30(1)	22(1)
88(2)	77(2)	51(1)	46(1)	30(1)	22(1)
88(2)	77(2)	68(2)	46(1)	30(1)	22(1)
88(2)	77(2)	68(2)	61(2)	30(1)	22(1)
109(3)	77(2)	68(2)	61(2)	30(1)	22(1)
109(3)	95(3)	68(2)	61(2)	30(1)	22(1)
129(4)	95(3)	84(3)	61(2)	30(1)	22(1)
148(5)	112(4)	84(3)	61(2)	30(1)	22(1)
167(6)	112(4)	84(3)	76(3)	40(2)	22(1)
185(7)	129(5)	100(4)	76(3)	40(2)	22(1)
*	146(6)	100(4)	89(4)	40(2)	22(1)
*	*	158(8)	116(6)	40(2)	30(2)
*	*	*	179(11)	50(3)	30(2)
*	*	*	*	68(5)	37(3)

size is not shown, the auditor may interpolate.) Next, the auditor locates the column for the actual number of deviations found. The intersection of the sample size row with the actual number of deviations column gives the projection of the sample results to the population plus an ***allowance for sampling risk*** (that is, maximum population deviation rate). If the maximum population deviation rate is less than or equal to the tolerable rate, the test supports the auditor's planned assessed level of control risk *from a strict quantitative perspective.*

Figure 10–2 shows that the maximum population deviation rate is 12.1% for a sample size of 50 having 2 deviations at a 5% risk of assessing control risk too low. Assuming that Table 10–2 was used to determine the sample size of 50 (based on an expected population deviation rate of 6% and a tolerable rate of 15%), the sample deviation rate is 4% (2 ÷ 50) and the allowance for sampling risk is 8.1% (12.1 − 4.0).

Test of Controls Sample Evaluation

Statistical tests of controls may be a primary source of support for the auditor's assessment that the level of control risk is below maximum. However, it is naive to

| Table 10-3 | Statistical Sample Sizes for Tests of Controls—10% Risk of Assessing Control Risk Too Low (with Number of Expected Deviations in Parentheses) |

10% RISK OF OVER COMPLIANCE (handwritten annotation)

Expected Population Deviation Rate	Tolerable Rate				
	2%	3%	4%	5%	6%
0.00%	114(0)	76(0)	57(0)	45(0)	38(0)
.25	194(1)	129(1)	96(1)	77(1)	64(1)
.50	194(1)	129(1)	96(1)	77(1)	64(1)
.75	265(2)	129(1)	96(1)	77(1)	64(1)
1.00	*	176(2)	96(1)	77(1)	64(1)
1.25	*	221(3)	132(2)	77(1)	64(1)
1.50	*	*	132(2)	105(2)	64(1)
1.75	*	*	166(3)	105(2)	88(2)
2.00	*	*	198(4)	132(3)	88(2)
2.25	*	*	*	132(3)	88(2)
2.50	*	*	*	158(4)	110(3)
2.75	*	*	*	209(6)	132(4)
3.00	*	*	*	*	132(4)
3.25	*	*	*	*	153(5)
3.50	*	*	*	*	194(7)
3.75	*	*	*	*	*
4.00	*	*	*	*	*
4.50	*	*	*	*	*
5.00	*	*	*	*	*
5.50	*	*	*	*	*
6.00	*	*	*	*	*
7.00	*	*	*	*	*
7.50	*	*	*	*	*
8.00	*	*	*	*	*
8.50	*	*	*	*	*

*Sample size is too large to be cost-effective for most audit applications.
Used with permission of the AICPA.

believe that sample results indicating that the estimated deviation rate is no greater than 5 to 10% (with the risk of assessing control risk too low equal to 5 or 10%) are sufficient to justify a low assessed level of control risk.

Auditors should understand the true significance of sample deviation rates. Consider the two frequently used sample sizes of 59 (for 5% risk of assessing control risk too low and a tolerable rate of 5%) and 22 (for 10% risk of assessing control risk too low and a tolerable rate of 10%). If no deviations are found in the samples, the auditor may conclude that the deviation rate in the population being tested does not exceed 5% (with a 5% risk of assessing control risk too low) or 10% (with a 10% risk of assessing control risk too low). The true deviation rate could be anywhere between zero and 5% or zero and 10%. If all other audit evidence indicates that controls will permit few, if any, deviations to pass undetected and the sample results above are

		Tolerable Rate			
7%	8%	9%	10%	15%	20%
32(0)	28(0)	25(0)	22(0)	15(0)	11(0)
55(1)	48(1)	42(1)	38(1)	25(1)	18(1)
55(1)	48(1)	42(1)	38(1)	25(1)	18(1)
55(1)	48(1)	42(1)	38(1)	25(1)	18(1)
55(1)	48(1)	42(1)	38(1)	25(1)	18(1)
55(1)	48(1)	42(1)	38(1)	25(1)	18(1)
55(1)	48(1)	42(1)	38(1)	25(1)	18(1)
55(1)	48(1)	42(1)	38(1)	25(1)	18(1)
75(2)	48(1)	42(1)	38(1)	25(1)	18(1)
75(2)	65(2)	42(1)	38(1)	25(1)	18(1)
75(2)	65(2)	58(2)	38(1)	25(1)	18(1)
94(3)	65(2)	58(2)	52(2)	25(1)	18(1)
94(3)	65(2)	58(2)	52(2)	25(1)	18(1)
113(4)	82(3)	58(2)	52(2)	25(1)	18(1)
113(4)	82(3)	73(3)	52(2)	25(1)	18(1)
131(5)	98(4)	73(3)	52(2)	25(1)	18(1)
149(6)	98(4)	73(3)	65(3)	25(1)	18(1)
218(10)	130(6)	87(4)	65(3)	34(2)	18(1)
*	160(8)	115(6)	78(4)	34(2)	18(1)
*	*	142(8)	103(6)	34(2)	18(1)
*	*	182(11)	116(7)	45(3)	25(2)
*	*	*	199(14)	52(4)	25(2)
*	*	*	*	52(4)	25(2)
*	*	*	*	60(5)	25(2)
*	*	*	*	68(6)	32(3)

achieved, an auditor may confidently conclude that the deviation rate is probably low and the control risk may be assessed as low or moderate. If, on the other hand, evidence from other tests of controls (for example, inquiries of entity personnel, inspection of documents and records, and observation of the application of control policies or procedures) indicates deviations from control structure policy and procedures—to the extent of, say, 3 to 4%—and the above results are achieved (that is, zero errors in samples of 59 or 22), a low or moderate level of assessed control risk may not be justified. A statistical test is simply one piece of evidence that, together with other evidence from other tests of controls, supports the auditor's assessed level of control risk as low, moderate, high, or at the maximum.

Auditors sometimes test key internal control structure attributes by selecting 5, 10, or 15 sample items. As Table 10–3 shows, these sample sizes are generally too

Actual No. of Deviation found from Previous CHART

Table 10–4

Statistical Sample Results Evaluation Table for Tests of Controls—5% Risk of Assessing Control Risk Too Low

	Actual Number of Deviations Found				
Sample Size	0	1	2	3	4
25	11.3	17.6	*	*	*
30	9.5	14.9	19.5	*	*
35	8.2	12.9	16.9	*	*
40	7.2	11.3	14.9	18.3	*
45	6.4	10.1	13.3	16.3	19.2
50	5.8	9.1	12.1	14.8	17.4
55	5.3	8.3	11.0	13.5	15.9
60	4.9	7.7	10.1	12.4	14.6
65	4.5	7.1	9.4	11.5	13.5
70	4.2	6.6	8.7	10.7	12.6
75	3.9	6.2	8.2	10.0	11.8
80	3.7	5.8	7.7	9.4	11.1
90	3.3	5.2	6.8	8.4	9.9
100	3.0	4.7	6.2	7.6	8.9
125	2.4	3.7	4.9	6.1	7.2
150	2.0	3.1	4.1	5.1	6.0
200	1.5	2.3	3.1	3.8	4.5

*Over 20%.
Note: This table presents upper limits as percentages.
Used with permission of the AICPA.

small, even when they result in zero deviations, to produce acceptable tolerable rates. In fact, a sample of 15 items enables the auditor to conclude only that the maximum population deviation rate is 15%. A small sample may generate sufficient evidence to reduce the assessed level of control slightly below the maximum. However, sample sizes less than 15 should be considered walk-through tests used to understand the internal control structure, not sampling tests of controls.

Discovery Sampling

Discovery sampling is primarily used for special studies (for example, fraud investigations) and occasionally is used to determine a substantive test sample size. It is not used to calculate sample sizes for typical test of controls applications. Two conditions usually exist before discovery sampling is used:

1. A very low error or population occurrence rate is expected (for example, zero or near zero).
2. The auditor is evaluating a critical population characteristic that, if discovered, might indicate manipulation of records supporting the financial statements.

		Actual Number of Deviations Found			
5	6	7	8	9	10
*	*	*	*	*	*
*	*	*	*	*	*
*	*	*	*	*	*
*	*	*	*	*	*
*	*	*	*	*	*
19.9	*	*	*	*	*
18.1	*	*	*	*	*
16.7	18.8	*	*	*	*
15.5	17.4	19.3	*	*	*
14.4	16.2	18.0	19.7	*	*
13.5	15.2	16.9	18.4	20.0	*
12.7	14.3	15.8	17.3	18.8	*
11.3	12.7	14.1	15.5	16.8	18.1
10.2	11.5	12.7	14.0	15.2	16.4
8.2	9.3	10.3	11.3	12.2	13.2
6.9	7.7	8.6	9.4	10.2	11.0
5.2	5.8	6.5	7.1	7.7	8.3

Discovery sampling applications are designed to determine a sample size that will produce an example of an occurrence if the occurrence rate exceeds a certain percentage. In a discovery sampling application, the auditor has to determine (1) the population size, (2) the maximum tolerable occurrence rate (or tolerable rate), (3) the desired reliability, and (4) the population characteristic to be evaluated. To obtain discovery sample sizes, auditors usually use tables. The appropriate table to use depends on the population size. Tables exist for population sizes 2,000 to 5,000, 5,000 to 10,000, and over 10,000. This chapter uses the over 10,000 population size table to illustrate how sample sizes are determined (see Table 10–6).

Discovery sampling tables contain reliability percentages instead of risk percentages. However, the complement of a reliability percentage gives the risk of assessing control risk too low. Thus, if an auditor specifies a reliability of 95%, this is equivalent to a 5% risk.

Table 10–6 illustrates how discovery sampling tables are used. Assume that the auditor is examining a population of 14,500 payroll checks as part of a special study to detect fictitious employees on a payroll. The auditor desires to see an example of payroll padding at a 95% reliability level if 1% or more of the checks are not payable to bona fide employees. To determine sample size, the auditor goes down the 1% critical rate of occurrence column until the desired reliability of 95% (or the next

Table 10–5	Statistical Sampling Results Evaluation Table for Tests of Controls—10% Risk of Assessing Control Risk Too Low

	Actual Number of Deviations Found				
Sample Size	0	1	2	3	4
20	10.9	18.1	*	*	*
25	8.8	14.7	19.9	*	*
30	7.4	12.4	16.8	*	*
35	6.4	10.7	14.5	18.1	*
40	5.6	9.4	12.8	15.9	19.0
45	5.0	8.4	11.4	14.2	17.0
50	4.5	7.6	10.3	12.9	15.4
55	4.1	6.9	9.4	11.7	14.0
60	3.8	6.3	8.6	10.8	12.9
70	3.2	5.4	7.4	9.3	11.1
80	2.8	4.8	6.5	8.3	9.7
90	2.5	4.3	5.8	7.3	8.7
100	2.3	3.8	5.2	6.6	7.8
120	1.9	3.2	4.4	5.5	6.6
160	1.4	2.4	3.3	4.1	4.9
200	1.1	1.9	2.6	3.3	4.0

*Over 20%.
Note: This table presents upper limits as percentages.
Used with permission of the AICPA.

higher reliability if the one desired is not in the table) is located. The sample size in this case is 300.

After determining sample size, the auditor selects a representative sample of 300 from the payroll check population of 14,500. If no irregularities are discovered in the sample examined, the auditor can state that he or she is 95% certain that the maximum tolerable occurrence rate does not exceed 1%. However, if the auditor locates one or more irregularities (including missing items), the statistical statement above cannot be made. No statistical conclusion is usually made. Extended procedures may be applied. One course of action may be to have client employees, under the auditor's supervision, examine all remaining payroll checks.

Dollar Value Estimation

Chapter 9 distinguished between a sampling application used to *estimate* an amount and a sampling application used to *test* an existing amount. The first application is referred to as dollar value estimation, whereas the second is called audit hypothesis testing.

An auditor's approach to a dollar value estimation application significantly differs from an audit hypothesis test. Recall that the latter approach is governed by *SAS*

Actual Number of Deviations Found					
5	6	7	8	9	10
*	*	*	*	*	*
*	*	*	*	*	*
*	*	*	*	*	*
*	*	*	*	*	*
*	*	*	*	*	*
19.6	*	*	*	*	*
17.8	*	*	*	*	*
16.2	18.4	*	*	*	*
14.9	16.9	18.8	*	*	*
12.8	14.6	16.2	17.9	19.5	*
11.3	12.8	14.3	15.7	17.2	18.6
10.1	11.4	12.7	14.0	15.3	16.6
9.1	10.3	11.5	12.7	13.8	15.0
7.6	8.6	9.6	10.6	11.6	12.5
5.7	6.5	7.2	8.0	8.7	9.5
4.6	5.2	5.8	6.4	7.0	7.6

Figure 10–2   **Sample Size Evaluation for 5% Risk of Assessing Control Risk Too Low**

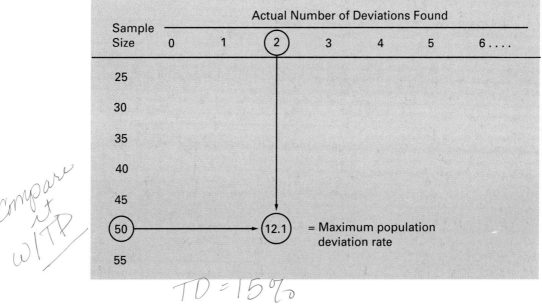

| Table 10-6 | Discovery Sampling Tables: Probability of Including at Least One Occurrence in a Sample (for Populations over 10,000) |

Upper Precision Limit: Critical Rate of Occurrence

Sample Size	.01%	.05%	.1%	.2%	.3%	.5%	1%	2%
50		2%	5%	9%	14%	22%	39%	64%
60	1%	3	6	11	16	26	45	70
70	1	3	7	13	19	30	51	76
80	1	4	8	15	21	33	55	80
90	1	4	9	16	24	36	60	84
100	1	5	10	18	26	39	63	87
120	1	6	11	21	30	45	70	91
140	1	7	13	24	34	50	76	94
160	2	8	15	27	38	55	80	96
200	2	10	18	33	45	63	87	98
240	2	11	21	38	51	70	91	99
300	3	14	26	45	59	78	95	99+
340	3	16	29	49	64	82	97	99+
400	4	18	33	55	70	87	98	99+
460	5	21	37	60	75	90	99	99+
500	5	22	39	63	78	92	99	99+
600	6	26	45	70	84	95	99+	99+
700	7	30	50	75	88	97	99+	99+
800	8	33	55	80	91	98	99+	99+
900	9	36	59	83	93	99	99+	99+
1,000	10	39	63	86	95	99	99+	99+
1,500	14	53	78	95	99	99+	99+	99+
2,000	18	63	86	98	99+	99+	99+	99+
2,500	22	71	92	99	99+	99+	99+	99+
3,000	26	78	95	99+	99+	99+	99+	99+

Used with permission of the AICPA.

No. 39, Audit Sampling (AU 350). The auditor's responsibility for a dollar value estimation application is discussed in *SAS No. 1, Inventories* (AU 331.11), where it is couched in terms of an inventory example. However, that audit approach applies to all dollar value estimation applications. AU 331.11 states:

> In recent years, some companies have developed inventory controls or methods of determining inventories, including statistical sampling, which are highly effective in determining inventory quantities and which are sufficiently reliable to make unnecessary an annual physical count of each item of inventory. In such circumstances, the independent auditor must satisfy himself that the client's procedures or methods are sufficiently reliable to produce results substantially the same as those which would be obtained by a count of all items each year.... If statistical sampling methods are used by the client in the taking of the physical inventory, the auditor must be satisfied that the sampling plan has statistical validity, that it has been properly applied, and that the resulting precision and reliability, as defined statistically, are reasonable in the circumstances.

Precision, as used in AU 331.11, is a dollar range within which the true value is expected to fall. ***Reliability*** expresses the probability that the dollar range contains the true value. Statistically, the reliability percentage expresses the proportion of sampling applications that would contain the true value if the same estimating procedures were employed a large number of times.

The mean per unit method and the difference estimation method are used here to illustrate dollar value estimation. A review of dollar value estimation facilitates the understanding of classical sampling for audit hypothesis testing.

Mean per Unit

In a ***mean per unit*** (MPU) application, the objective is to calculate a sample mean to project a population total. Of course, the dollar value projection (that is, the sample mean times the population size) will not correspond exactly to the true, but unknown, population total. But the dollar value projection plus and minus precision (an allowance for sampling risk) should contain the true population total at a defined reliability percentage.

To determine the sample size for an MPU application, four factors are predefined:

1. Reliability.
2. Standard deviation.[3]
3. Population size.
4. Tolerable misstatement or desired precision.

---

[3] The standard deviation is a statistic widely used to measure the extent to which the values of the items are spread about the mean. A shortcut way to calculate standard deviation is by using the equation

$$\text{SD} = \sqrt{\frac{\Sigma x^2 - n\bar{x}^2}{n - 1}}$$

where n is the sample size, x the value of each item, and $\bar{x}$ the mean value of the items. For example:

x	x^2	
10	100	Sample Mean:
18	324	$\bar{x} = \dfrac{\Sigma x}{n} = \dfrac{200}{10} = 20$
15	225	
20	400	Standard Deviation:
24	576	$\text{SD} = \sqrt{\dfrac{4252 - 10(20)^2}{10 - 1}}$
26	676	
26	676	
17	289	
25	625	$= \sqrt{\dfrac{252}{9}} = 5.29$
19	361	
200	4252	

The standard deviation of 5.29 for this example measures the variability of this distribution. In a normal distribution, 68% of all items fall within ±1 standard deviation, 95% within ±1.96 standard deviations, and 99% within ±2.58 standard deviations.

The reliability is based on the amount of sampling risk that can be tolerated. Usually a high reliability is selected in dollar value estimation applications. Otherwise, the probability is higher that the projected amount plus and minus precision will not contain the true population total.

The standard deviation is estimated by a pilot sample or by prior knowledge. A pilot sample of 30 usually is sufficient to estimate the standard deviation. The population is determined by the sampling objective and depends on the part of the population that will be sampled. The total population may be divided into a sampled group (smaller items) and a 100%-examined group (larger items).

Having predefined reliability, standard deviation, and population size, and having determined the precision needed, the auditor calculates sample size as

$$n = \left(\frac{U_R \times SD_E \times N}{P}\right)^2$$

where n is sample size (with replacement), U_R the reliability factor, SD_E the estimated standard deviation, N the population size, and P the precision (or desired precision).[4]

Steps in Applying Mean per Unit

The detailed steps involved in an MPU application are as follows:

1. Define reliability (generally a high reliability should be used, for example, 95%).
2. Convert reliability into a reliability factor (U_R) according to the following table:

Reliability	U_R
.99	2.58
.95	1.96
.90	1.65

3. Determine (or estimate) precision (P).

---

[4] The sample size equation can be derived from the mathematical definition of precision (see step 9). Mathematically, precision (P) is

$$P = U_R \times SD_E \times N$$

$$P = U_R \times \frac{SD}{\sqrt{n}} \times N$$

$$\sqrt{n} \times P = U_R \times SD \times N$$

$$\sqrt{n} = \frac{U_R \times SD \times N}{P}$$

$$n = \left(\frac{U_R \times SD \times N}{P}\right)^2$$

4. Calculate sample size according to the following equation:

$$n = \left(\frac{U_R \times SD_E \times N}{P}\right)^2$$

If SD_E is known from prior sampling work, use that as an estimate or use a pilot sample of 30 to calculate an estimate of SD_E.

5. Select a representative sample equal to n.
6. Examine the items selected (for example, count inventory).
7. Calculate the calculated standard deviation (SD_c) based on the sample size in step 4.
8. Calculate the standard error (SE) of the estimate using the following equation:

$$SE = \frac{SD_c}{\sqrt{n}}$$

9. Calculate *achieved precision* (P') or allowance for sampling risk based on the following equation. Use SE from step 8.

$$P' = U_R \times SE \times N$$

10. Is $P' \leq P$ in step 3? If yes, go to step 12; if no, go to step 11.
11. Increase the sample size by substituting SD_c from step 7 for SD_E in the sample size formula at step 4. (Note: This will be the case when the estimated standard deviation at step 4 was understated.) Reperform steps 5–10.
12. Calculate the mean ($\bar{x}$) of the total sample.

$$\bar{x} = \frac{\text{sum of examined sample}}{n}$$

13. Calculate the dollar value estimate (DVE)

$$DVE = \bar{x} \times N$$

and conclude that you are certain, at the reliability percentage specified in step 1, that the true value is within DVE $\pm$ P'. Record DVE as the book value.[5]

Difference Estimation

 *# Value Estimation Method.*

Avg Diff of BV vs. AV

Sometimes it may be appropriate and more efficient (that is, a smaller sample size may be used) to use ***difference estimation*** in a dollar value estimation application. Difference estimation may be advantageous when (1) each population item has a book value and (2) the total book value is known and is equal to the sum of all individual book values. A situation in which these conditions are usually met occurs in inventory accounting. Frequently, businesses maintain FIFO inventory records that are converted to LIFO at year-end. Difference estimation is useful in making this conversion.

Instead of computing the mean value and the standard deviation of the sample values, as in MPU, difference estimation uses the mean value and standard deviation of the individual *differences* between each sample item's audited value (for example,

---

[5] Problem 10-62 requires application of the steps in applying mean per unit. To maximize your understanding of the process, you may want to work problem 10-62 at this point.

LIFO value) and its book value (for example, FIFO value). A difference is defined as the audited value minus book value and will be zero if these quantities are equal.

Before the standard deviation of differences can be safely estimated, a minimum number of nonzero differences must be observed. Experts disagree about what the minimum number should be. The required minimum number of differences has been described as from 20 to 50. One recognized author recommends 15 or 20 as a guideline.[6]

The approach to a difference estimation application is essentially the same as that used in MPU. The primary differences are that the mean of differences, $\bar{d}$, and the standard deviation of differences, SD_d, are calculated instead of $\bar{x}$ and SD_E. The mean of differences is calculated as

$$\bar{d} = \frac{\Sigma\, d_i}{n}$$

where $\bar{d}$ is the mean of the differences and $\Sigma\, d_i$ is the sum of observed differences considering signs ($+$ or $-$).

The equation for the standard deviation of differences is

$$SD_d = \sqrt{\frac{\Sigma\, d_i^2 - n\bar{d}^2}{n - 1}}$$

The equation clearly shows why some differences have to be observed before difference estimation can be applied. If no differences are observed, SD_d would be zero. This would lead to the erroneous conclusion that no sampling risk exists when less than 100% of the population has been sampled. The sample size equation for differences shown below also demonstrates that the size of the pilot sample, used to estimate SD_d, must be large enough to contain several differences. Otherwise, n could not be computed.

$$n = \left(\frac{U_R \times SD_d \times N}{P}\right)^2$$

The sample size equation also shows why difference estimation is more efficient than MPU. SD_d tends to be smaller than SD_E, causing sample sizes to be smaller and more efficient.

Given $\bar{d}$, the estimated population difference is calculated as

$$\hat{D} = N\bar{d}$$

where $\hat{D}$ is the estimated population difference.

The dollar value estimate of the population total is calculated as

$$DVE = \text{book value} + \hat{D} \text{ (if net differences are positive)},$$
$$\text{or} - \hat{D} \text{ (if net differences are negative)}.$$

---

[6] Donald M. Roberts, *Statistical Auditing* (New York: American Institute of Certified Public Accountants, 1978), p. 74.

Audit Hypothesis Testing: Classical Variables Sampling

To calculate sample sizes by using classical variables sampling to test existing client account balances is more complex than dollar value estimation. The sample size in a classical variables hypothesis test depends on the auditor's determination of the risk of incorrect acceptance and an estimation of the standard deviation.

Calculating the Risk of Incorrect Acceptance

The equation for TD (the allowable risk of incorrect acceptance for the substantive test of details, given that misstatements equal to tolerable misstatement occur and are not detected by the internal control structure or analytical procedures and other relevant substantive tests) as presented in Chapter 9 was

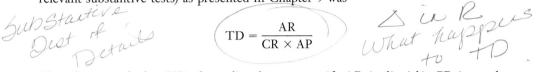

Substantive Dist of Details

$$TD = \frac{AR}{CR \times AP}$$

△ in R What happens to TD

Therefore, to calculate TD, the auditor has to quantify AR (audit risk), CR (control risk), and AP (risk of analytical and supplementary procedures failure).

Quantifying Audit Risk

In practice, the acceptable level of AR is predefined. *SAS No. 39* (AU 350.19) illustrates an AR of 5%. Many auditors believe that AR should usually be 5% and never greater than 10%. Variations up to 10% might be justified, for example, because the client is a nonpublic entity and the financial statements will not be used by a large number of external users (for example, stockholders).

Quantifying Control Risk

The assessment of CR is also judgmentally determined in practice. CR must be separately determined at the assertion level for each transaction cycle (or account balance), because strengths in one assertion do not offset weaknesses in another. CR is assessed based on the auditor's inquiries, observations, inspections, and reperformance of a policy or procedure that pertains to an assertion.

Some auditors permit CR to vary from 100% down to 10%. The 10% lower limit assumes that even the best control structure has inherent limitations. The following table shows possible CR ranges.

Auditor's Subjective Assessed Level of Control Risk	CR Risk Percentage
Excellent	10
Good	30
Fair	50
Poor	70
No control (or high potential for management override)	100

The CR percentage may be interpreted to mean that even for an excellent control structure there is a 10% chance that deviations could occur on enough accounts or to such a degree that their total effect would materially misstate the client's financial statements.

Quantifying Supplemental Procedure Risk

Quantifying AP is difficult. Any substantive audit procedure that is not part of the variables sampling statistical test is a supplemental procedure. For example, an auditor may decide to use variables sampling to select accounts receivable for confirmation (the existence assertion). He or she may also review collections of accounts receivable subsequent to the balance sheet date and perform certain analytical tests of accounts receivable. All the tests but the confirmation work are by definition supplementary procedures.

Some CPA firms estimate AP very conservatively and do not permit it to go below 50%. Research to date is inadequate to devise precise methods for quantifying AP or CR. In this chapter, we will permit AP to vary from 100 to 50% and CR to vary from 100 to 10%.

Allowable Risk of Incorrect Acceptance

Given that all the variables needed to calculate TD are quantified, the auditor can determine the risk of incorrect acceptance for the statistical test. Once TD is calculated, the auditor uses it to adjust tolerable misstatement. The adjusted tolerable misstatement is introduced into the sample size equation as desired precision. In other words, in a classical variables sampling application, the auditor controls the risk of incorrect acceptance by varying tolerable misstatement.

Determining Sample Sizes

The MPU sample size equation for a classical variables sampling application is

$$n = \left(\frac{U_R \times SD_E \times N}{P} \right)^2$$

where P is the desired precision. For difference estimation, the auditor would simply substitute SD_d for SD_E.

To determine sample size, the auditor must quantify U_R, SD_E, N, and P. U_R is based on the auditor's risk of incorrect rejection. In practice, auditors use either 90% (U_R of 1.65) or 95% (U_R of 1.96), which gives a risk of incorrect rejection of either 10% (1.00 − .90) or 5% (1.00 − .95). Recall from Chapter 9 that if an auditor rejects a correct account balance that is not materially misstated, he or she may be inefficient (that is, have to increase sample size) but usually not ineffective (that is, reach the wrong conclusion).

SD_E (or SD_d) is calculated based on a pilot sample or is estimated using prior knowledge. Likewise, N is easy to determine because it represents the population size.

Desired precision (P) depends on TD, the risk of incorrect rejection, and tolerable misstatement. Table 10–7 is used to determine a percentage to multiply tolerable misstatement by to arrive at P. To illustrate, if tolerable misstatement is $10,000 and risk of incorrect acceptance (TD) is 10%, and the auditor wants a 5% risk of incorrect rejection, desired precision is $6,050 ($10,000 × .605). Note that if the auditor set P equal to tolerable misstatement, the risk of incorrect acceptance would be 50%. This is illustrated in Figure 10–3.

Table 10-7	**Tolerable Misstatement Adjustments**[7]	

	Multiplication Factor	
Risk of Incorrect Acceptance %*	5% Risk of Incorrect Rejection	10% Risk of Incorrect Rejection
1	.457	.413
2.5	.500	.456
5	.543	.500
7.5	.576	.532
10	.605	.561
15	.653	.612
20	.700	.661
25	.742	.708
30	.787	.756
35	.834	.808
40	.883	.863
45	.937	.926
50	1.000	1.000

*The allowable risk of incorrect acceptance (TD) is calculated as follows:

$$TD = \frac{AR}{CR \times AP}$$

Executing and Evaluating Sample Applications

Having determined the appropriate sample size, the auditor is now ready to execute the application. At this stage, he or she selects a representative sample, applies audit procedures to the selected items, and analyzes detected misstatements. Then, the auditor is ready to calculate a dollar value estimate for the audited balance and to calculate achieved precision. For an MPU application, the DVE is determined by multiplying $\bar{x}$ times N. Achieved precision is $P' = U_R \times SE \times N$.

To evaluate the client's balance, the auditor determines if (1) P' (achieved precision) is equal to or less than tolerable misstatement (TM) and (2) the client's book value falls with DVE $\pm$ P'. If both conditions are met, the auditor concludes that the

[7]Table 10–7 is derived from the following equation:

$$Multiplication\ factor = \frac{U_R}{U_R + Z_{beta}}$$

The normal curve area table is used to determine the beta risk coefficient (Z_{beta}). Z_{beta} is the normal curve value that includes an area of .5 minus beta. For example, the Z_{beta} coefficient for a 1% beta risk is 2.33 (.5 minus .01 equals .4900, which from the normal curve area table corresponds to 2.33). Thus, for a 5% risk of incorrect rejection and a 1% beta risk, the multiplication factor is

$$.457 = \left(\frac{1.96}{1.96 + 2.33}\right)$$

Figure 10-3

Risk of Incorrect Acceptance When Precision Is Set Equal to Tolerable Misstatement

Facts: Book value (BV) is overstated by tolerable misstatement. Precision (P) equals tolerable misstatement (TM). T equals true value.

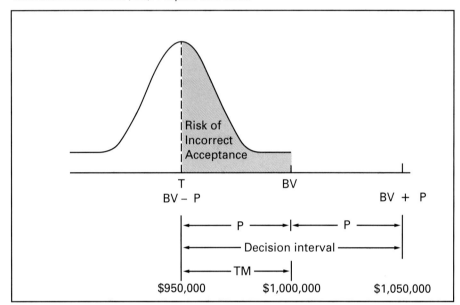

EXPLANATION: If repeat samples of the same size were selected, according to the central limit theorem, the distribution of sample means ($\bar{x}$) would approximate a normal curve with a center at true value. Given that the book value is overstated by $50,000, an unacceptable amount, the best sample would be one that rejects book value. However, 50 samples out of 100 would result (as shown by the portion of the normal distribution that overlaps the decision range) in accepting an overstated book value. Sample means projections falling below true value would lead to a rejection decision.

client's book value is not materially misstated according to the statistical test. However, if the book value does not fall within the precision interval (DVE ± P′), and if achieved precision (P′) is less than precision (P), book value may still not be materially misstated. In this situation, the auditor should use the following decision rule: if the acceptable level for the risk of incorrect rejection is not larger than twice the risk of incorrect acceptance, and if the difference between the client's book value and the far end of the range is less than tolerable misstatement, the sample would support the recorded book value.

To illustrate, assume the auditor has calculated a sample size based on a 5% risk of incorrect acceptance and a 10% risk of incorrect rejection. The auditor has assessed tolerable misstatement at $10,000 for a population with a book value of $150,000 and has set a desired precision of $5,000. In evaluating the sample, the auditor determined that DVE is $145,000 with a $3,000 achieved precision. Although the book value is outside the range estimate ($145,000 ± $3,000), the auditor will still find that the sample supports the book value because the 10% risk of incorrect rejection is not larger than twice the 5% risk of incorrect acceptance, and the difference between the book value and the far end of the range ($150,000 minus $142,000) is less than tolerable misstatement.

Achieved *Precision*	DVE	*Achieved* *Precision*	BV
$142,000	$145,000	$148,000	$150,000

$8,000 = maximum overstatement

Steps in Applying Classical Variables Sampling

The sequential logic involved in an MPU or difference estimation audit hypothesis test is as follows:

1. Assess control risk. Set CR from 10% to 100%.
2. Evaluate risk of failure of analytical procedures and other substantive tests. Set AP from 50% to 100%.
3. Set risk of incorrect rejection at 10% or 5%. If 10%, U_R is 1.65. If 5%, U_R is 1.96.
4. Set audit risk (AR) at 10% or 5%.
5. Calculate risk of incorrect acceptance.

$$TD = \frac{AR}{CR \times AP}$$

6. Determine tolerable misstatement for the account balance.
7. Calculate desired precision, P, based on tolerable misstatement, TD, and risk of incorrect rejection. Use Table 10–7.
8. Calculate required sample size (n).
   A. For mean per unit

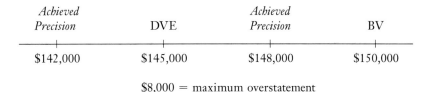

   B. For difference estimate, substitute SD_d for SD_E.
9. Select a representative sample of size n.
10. Perform audit procedures on the selected items.
11. Analyze misstatements found in the sample to determine their cause and nature. Reconsider CR if control risk is higher than planned at step 1.

12. Calculate achieved precision (P′), or allowance for sampling risk.
   A. For mean per unit

$$P' = U_R \times SE \times N$$

   where

$$SE = \frac{SD_c}{\sqrt{n}}$$

   B. For difference estimation

$$P' = U_R \times SE_d \times N$$

   where

$$SE_d = \frac{SD_d}{\sqrt{n}}$$

13. Calculate the dollar value estimate.
   A. For mean per unit

$$DVE = \bar{x} \times N$$

   B. For difference estimation

$$DVE = BV + \text{(plus) if net positive differences}$$
$$\text{or} - \text{(minus) if net negative differences}$$
$$(\bar{d} \times N).$$

14. Determine if P′ (step 12) is equal to or less than tolerable misstatement (step 6) and if client's book value (BV) falls within DVE ± P′. If no, go to step 15. If yes, stop and conclude that statistical test supports BV.
15. Determine if the risk of incorrect rejection (10% or 5% at step 3) is not larger than twice the risk of incorrect acceptance (at step 5) and if the difference between BV and the far end of DVE ± P′ range is less than tolerable misstatement (at step 6). If yes, stop and conclude that statistical test supports BV.
16. If statistical evidence does not support book value, consider whether extended sample is needed or request client to perform investigation of account balance detail. If client makes an adjustment to BV after investigation, statistical evidence should support that account balance is not materially misstated.

Audit Hypothesis Testing: Probability-Proportionate-to-Size Sampling

As discussed in Chapter 9, probability-proportionate-to-size (PPS) sampling is a modified form of attribute sampling that enables the auditor to make conclusions about the total dollar amount of misstatement in a population. Unlike classical attribute and variables sampling, which focus on physical units (for instance, invoices and vouchers) of the population, PPS sampling focuses on dollar units of the population.

Before the auditor decides to use PPS sampling, he or she should determine whether the assumptions of the approach are valid for the population being tested. Two important assumptions underlie PPS sampling:

1. The expected misstatement rate in the population should be small (less than 10%) and the population should contain 2,000 or more items.

2. The amount of misstatement in any physical unit in the population cannot be more than the reported book value of the item. That is, if the book value of a customer balance is $1,000, the amount of misstatement in the balance cannot exceed $1,000.

Because the dollar is defined as the sampling unit in a PPS application, each individual dollar in the population has an equal chance of selection. Thus, physical units having more dollars have a higher probability of selection. For example, a customer account with a $1,000 balance would have a ten times better chance of being selected than a customer account with a $100 balance. In contrast, in a classical sampling application, the above two account balances would have an equal chance of being selected unless stratified selection were used.

Advantages and Disadvantages of Using PPS Sampling

PPS sampling has several attractive features in addition to the general advantages inherent in using statistical sampling instead of nonstatistical sampling. PPS sampling

1. is generally easier to use than classical variables sampling. The calculations in a classical variables application are more tedious.
2. does not require calculation of the standard deviation to determine sample size or evaluate sample results.
3. automatically stratifies the population. Sample items are selected in proportion to their dollar values. Thus, a physical unit with more dollars in it has a higher probability of being selected relative to a physical unit with fewer dollars in it. Physical units equal to or in excess of tolerable misstatement are automatically included in the selected sample. Because PPS tends to choose large-dollar-value items, more total dollars of a population are tested than under classical variables sampling of the same sample size.
4. will usually result in a smaller sample size relative to classical variables sampling, if no or few misstatements are expected.
5. permits sample selection to begin prior to the availability for the entire population.

Some of the disadvantages of PPS sampling are that

1. as the number of misstatements increases, sample size increases, and sample size may be larger than the sample size computed under a classical variables application.
2. it may overstate the allowance for sampling risk when misstatements are found and cause the auditor to reject a fairly stated client book value.
3. it cannot be applied to accounts or physical units with zero or negative balances. Also, understated physical units have a lower probability of being selected. PPS sampling is easier to use when the small number of expected misstatements will be overstatements.

Determining the PPS Sample Size

To calculate sample size in a PPS application, the auditor predefines (1) book value, (2) a reliability factor for the risk of incorrect acceptance, (3) tolerable misstatement, (4) expected misstatement, and (5) an expansion factor. The book value is the recorded amount of the population. Tolerable misstatement is the maximum dollar misstatement that may exist in the population without causing the financial statements to be materially misstated. Expected misstatement is the auditor's estimate of the dollar amount of error in the population. It is estimated based on prior experience and knowledge of the client. The reliability factor for the risk of misstatement is

| Table 10–8 | **Probability-Proportionate-to-Size Sampling Table (for Overstatements)** |

Number of Over-statement Errors				Risk of Incorrect Acceptance					
	1%	5%	10%	15%	20%	25%	30%	37%	50%
0	4.61	3.00	2.31	1.90	1.61	1.39	1.21	1.00	.70
1	6.64	4.75	3.89	3.38	3.00	2.70	2.44	2.14	1.68
2	8.41	6.30	5.33	4.72	4.28	3.93	3.62	3.25	2.68
3	10.05	7.76	6.69	6.02	5.52	5.11	4.77	4.34	3.68
4	11.61	9.16	8.00	7.27	6.73	6.28	5.90	5.43	4.68
5	13.11	10.52	9.28	8.50	7.91	7.43	7.01	6.49	5.68
6	14.57	11.85	10.54	9.71	9.08	8.56	8.12	7.56	6.67
7	16.00	13.15	11.78	10.90	10.24	9.69	9.21	8.63	7.67
8	17.41	14.44	13.00	12.08	11.38	10.81	10.31	9.68	8.67
9	18.79	15.71	14.21	13.25	12.52	11.92	11.39	10.74	9.67
10	20.15	16.97	15.41	14.42	13.66	13.02	12.47	11.79	10.67

Used with permission of the AICPA.

always determined from the "zero errors" row of Table 10–8. If a 10% risk of incorrect acceptance is desired, the auditor uses a reliability factor of 2.31 from Table 10–8. The expansion factor comes from Table 10–9. For a 20% risk of incorrect acceptance, the expansion factor is 1.3.

The equation for sample size is

$$n = \frac{\text{Book Value} \times \text{Reliability Factor}}{\text{Tolerable Misstatement} - (\text{Expected Misstatement} \times \text{Expansion Factor})}$$

The auditor determines the risk of incorrect acceptance based on the extent of evidence required from the sample—the same approach that is used for classical sampling. The risk of incorrect rejection is indirectly controlled by the auditor's estimate of expected misstatement. If the auditor underestimates expected misstatement, the sample size will be too small and additional testing will be necessary.

If book value is $500,000, the risk of incorrect acceptance is 5%, tolerable misstatement is $25,000, and expected misstatement is $6,250, sample size is

$$n = \frac{\$500,000 \times 3.00}{\$25,000 - (6,250 \times 1.6)}$$

$$= 100$$

Selecting the PPS Sample

One choice the auditor has is to use a random number table to determine which dollars are selected. For the example above, the auditor would select 100 numbers from a

Table 10-9	Expansion Factors for Expected Misstatement

				Risk of Incorrect Acceptance					
	1%	5%	10%	15%	20%	25%	30%	37%	50%
Factor	1.9	1.6	1.5	1.4	1.3	1.25	1.2	1.15	1.0

Used with permission of the AICPA.

random number table by using six digits for the selection procedure. Six digits are used because the population contains 500,000 dollars or sampling units.

When an individual dollar is selected for examination, the dollar unit is not verified by itself. Instead, it acts as a hook and drags a whole physical or logical unit (for example, account balance) with it. To find the physical unit associated with the particular dollar unit being sampled, the auditor must progressively add through the population.

To illustrate, assume that the following numbers were selected from a random number table based on the 500,000 total dollar units: 000020, 001890, 002010, and 003502. A partial listing of the $500,000 accounts receivable appears below.

Customer Account	Book Value	Cumulative Total	Associated Dollar Units
1	$ 150	$ 150	$ 1–150
2	600	750	151–750
3	250	1,000	751–1,000
4	1,210	2,210	1,001–2,210
5	489	2,699	2,211–2,699
6	895	3,594	2,700–3,594
.	.	.	.
.	.	.	.
.	.	.	.
2000	$ 650	$500,000	$499,350–500,000

The four illustrative sample units correspond to customer account numbers as follows:

Dollar Selected	Corresponding Customer Balance
$ 20	1
1,890	4
2,010	4
3,502	6

Note that customer account balance 4 was selected twice. The auditor should ignore the repeat selection and consider the account balance only once when the sample results are evaluated. Because sampling units may cause physical units to be selected more than once, the actual number of customer accounts examined may be less than the computed sample size (100 in this illustration).

A more widely used method of selecting a PPS sample is systematic sampling, as discussed in Chapter 9. To apply systematic sampling, the auditor determines a dollar sampling interval. The dollar sampling interval is calculated by dividing the book value of the population by the sample size. To begin the selection of the sample, the auditor chooses a number between one and the dollar sampling interval as the first unit in the sample.

PPS Sample Evaluation

If no misstatements are found in the sample, the auditor's misstatement projection is zero and the allowance for sampling risk is equal to the reliability factor times the sampling interval (300 × 5,000). Thus, in the example above, the auditor could conclude the following: 3.00×5.000

> Based on the sample evidence, I am 95% confident (or I have 5% risk of incorrect acceptance) that the dollar amount of misstatement in the $500,000 accounts receivable balance does not exceed $15,000 (tolerable misstatement).

If misstatements are found in the sample, the physical unit is said to be tainted. *Tainting* is the amount of misstatement divided by the reported book value of the unit.

$$\text{Tainting} = \frac{\text{Amount of Misstatement}}{\text{Book Value of Physical Unit}}$$

To project misstatements when taintings occur, the auditor determines the percentage of misstatement in the physical unit and multiplies this percentage by the sampling interval (book value ÷ sample size). For example, if a $100 account receivable has an audited amount of $50, tainting equals 50%. If the sampling interval is $1,000, projected misstatement is $1,000 times 50%, which equals $500. The auditor should calculate a tainting percentage for all physical units *except for those that have book values equal to or greater than the sampling interval*. For physical units that have this characteristic, projected misstatement is equal to actual misstatement. For example, if a sampling interval of $1,000 is used and a $1,500 account receivable having an audited amount of $1,200 is selected, projected misstatement and actual misstatement are the same: $300.

To calculate the **upper limit on misstatements** when overstatement misstatements occur, the auditor uses Table 10–8. To illustrate, assume that the auditor specifies a 5% risk of incorrect acceptance and a tolerable misstatement of $3,000, uses a $1,000 sampling interval, expects no errors, but finds four misstatements in the total sample.

Misstatement #	Book Value	Audited Amount	Amount of Overstatement	Tainting Percent
1	$ 500	$ 250	$250	50%
2	100	25	75	75%
3	50	0	50	100%
4	2,000	1,900	100	N/A (exceeds sampling interval)

Actual or known misstatements total $475, and projected misstatement is calculated as follows:

Misstatement #	Tainting Percent	Sampling Interval	Projected Misstatement
1	50%	$1,000	$ 500
2	75	1,000	750
3	100	1,000	1,000
4	N/A	N/A	100 (actual misstatement)
		Total Projected Misstatement	$2,350

In order to calculate the upper limit on misstatements, the auditor should rank the projected misstatement by percentage tainting (from highest to lowest) and multiply the projected misstatements by the incremental changes in reliability factors derived from Table 10–8.

Ranked Misstatement #	Projected Misstatement	Incremental Change in Reliability Factors (Table 10–8)	Increment for Upper Limit on Misstatement
3	$1,000	1.75 (4.75 − 3.00)	$1,750.00
2	750	1.55 (6.30 − 4.75)	1,162.50
1	500	1.46 (7.76 − 6.30)	730.00
		Total	$3,642.50
		Less: Projected Misstatement	2,350.00
		Incremental Allowance	$1,292.50

The auditor calculates upper limit on misstatement as follows:

1. Projected misstatement	$2,350.00
2. Basic precision (reliability factor × sampling interval) 3.0 × $1,000	3,000.00
3. Incremental allowance upper limit on misstatement	1,292.50
	$6,642.50

Components 2 and 3 above when added together in a PPS application represent the allowance for sampling risk.

Because there is a 5% risk that the book value is overstated by more than $6,642.50, which exceeds tolerable misstatement ($3,000), the auditor faces a number of choices. The auditor might select an additional representative sample or perform other substantive tests directed toward the audit objective. The latter could allow the auditor to accept a greater risk of incorrect acceptance than originally planned. If unanticipated misstatements had not been found (that is, zero errors were detected instead of the four misstatements identified above), projected misstatement and incremental allowance would have been zero. The auditor would have concluded that there is a 5% risk of the book value being overstated by $3,000—an acceptable result.

Significant Terms

Achieved precision A calculated amount determined by multiplying reliability (U_R) times the standard error (SE) times the population size (N).

Allowance for sampling risk A test of controls sampling term for the difference between the sample deviation rate (sample errors ÷ sample size) and the maximum population deviation rate, or in a variable sampling application, a concept that is labeled "achieved precision."

Difference estimation A statistical model used to estimate the total differences between audited and book values based on differences identified from sample observations.

Expected population deviation rate The anticipated rate of deviations in a population based on prior knowledge of the population or a pilot sample.

Maximum population deviation rate A rate determined by adding an allowance for sampling risk to a compliance sample deviation rate. The maximum population deviation rate is compared to the tolerable rate to determine if the sample results support the auditor's planned assessed level of control risk.

Mean per unit (MPU) A statistical model whereby a sample mean is calculated and projected as an estimated total.

Pilot sample A preliminary sample used to estimate the population deviation rate in test of controls statistical sampling or the standard deviation in classical substantive statistical sampling.

Precision A measure of closeness of a sample estimate to the corresponding population characteristic, or a range of values around an estimate within which the true population value is expected to fall.

Reliability As used in attribute sampling, the probability of being correct in placing reliance on an effective internal control structure procedure. As used in variables sampling, the probability of a sample estimate plus and minus achieved precision containing the true population value.

Tainting The ratio of the amount of a misstatement to the size of the physical unit (for example, an account receivable) containing the misstatement.

Upper limit on misstatements An amount in a probability-proportionate-to-size application equal to the projected misstatements found in the sample, plus an allowance for sampling risk.

Discussion Questions

10-1. What factors must be predefined to use a statistical test of controls sample size table?

10-2. What are the primary differences between a statistical test of controls application and a nonstatistical test of controls application?

10-3. If an auditor plans to assess control risk as low for a control attribute to limit substantive testing, should the risk of assessing control risk too low be 5% or 10%? Should the tolerable rate be 5% or 10%?

10-4. Before using an attribute sample size table, the auditor must predefine the expected population deviation rate. How does the expected population deviation rate affect sample size? How is it determined?

10-5. How are Tables 10–2 and 10–3 used to evaluate sample results?

10-6. How are Tables 10-4 and 10-5 used to evaluate sample results?

10-7. Determine sample sizes for each of the following situations.

	A	B	C	D	E	F
Risk of assessing control risk too low	5%	10%	5%	10%	5%	10%
Population deviation rate	1.25%	1.50%	2.00%	2.00%	0	0
Tolerable rate	4%	5%	5%	10%	5%	10%
Sample size	____	____	____	____	____	____

10-8. What is the sample size for a statistical test of controls if the risk of assessing control risk too low is 5%, the population deviation rate is estimated to be 2%, the tolerable rate is 5%, and the population size is 5,500? What if the population size is 100,000?

10-9. Calculate the maximum deviation rate, the sample size deviation rate, and the allowance for sampling risk for the following sample results.

	A	B	C	D	E	F
Risk of assessing control risk too low	5%	10%	5%	10%	5%	10%
Sample size	60	40	100	30	75	25
Actual number of deviations	0	1	4	3	3	0
Maximum deviation rate	____	____	____	____	____	____
Sample deviation rate	____	____	____	____	____	____
Allowance for sampling risk	____	____	____	____	____	____

10-10. How does an auditor determine whether the results from a statistical test of controls application support the planned assessed level of control risk?

10-11. The auditor uses judgments in evaluating the results and reaching an overall conclusion, whether the test of controls sample is statistical or nonstatistical. Do you agree?

10-12. Generally, the risk of assessing control risk too low should not be greater than ____ % if moderate assurance is to be placed on the sample. And, if substantial assurance is to be placed on the sample, the risk of assessing control risk too low should be ____ % or less.

10-13. Generally, the tolerable rate should not exceed ____ % if moderate assurance is to be placed on the sample. And, if substantial assurance is to be placed on the sample, the tolerable rate should be ____ % or less.

10-14. What is discovery sampling? When is it typically used?

10-15. What is the minimum sample size that should be used for a test of controls?

10-16. Determine the discovery sample sizes for each of the following situations (assume that the population size is over 10,000 items).

	A	B	C
Maximum tolerable occurrence rate	1%	.2%	.5%
Desired reliability	90%	95%	90%
Sample size	——	——	——

10-17. If the auditor observes one or more deviations in a discovery sampling application, what action should the auditor pursue? What statistical conclusion could be expressed?

10-18. If an auditor examines 340 items from a population of 13,489 items in a discovery sampling application and finds no deviations, what statistical conclusion(s) could be expressed?

10-19. Is it permissible for an auditor to allow a client to use statistical sampling instead of requiring the client to take a 100% physical inventory?

10-20. What is the statistical meaning of reliability? Precision?

10-21. What factors must be predefined in a mean per unit dollar value estimation application?

10-22. Why is a high reliability percentage typically used in a dollar value estimation application?

10-23. What is the sample size equation for a mean per unit application? A difference estimation application?

10-24. Calculate the standard deviation of the following items: 225, 819, 405, 699, 582, 648, 842, 506, 235, 436, and 450.

10-25. What are the equations for the standard error of the estimate and achieved precision?

10-26. Calculate the mean of differences for the following items:

Audited Value	Book Value
25	20
15	18
32	32
48	49
12	8
18	20

10-27. What is the standard deviation of differences for the items presented in Question 10-26 above?

10-28. You cannot calculate an estimate of the standard deviation of differences unless some differences are observed. Do you agree?

10-29. What two conditions must be met before difference estimation can be used?

10-30. Difference estimation is usually more efficient than mean per unit. Why?

10-31. If a population of size N is footed and totals $10,000, and the mean of the differences is +$50, what is the estimated population difference if $N = 125$?

10-32. If the estimated population difference ($\hat{D}$) is +$500, what is the estimated audited value if the recorded book value totals to $10,000?

10-33. In the equation for TD (the allowable risk of incorrect acceptance), how does the auditor quantify AR, CR, and AP?

10-34. Is it permissible to set CR (control risk) as 1 minus the risk of assessing control risk too low that was used in an attribute sampling application?

10-35. In a classical variables sampling application, how does the auditor control the risk of incorrect acceptance?

10-36. If tolerable misstatement (based on materiality) is $25,000, TD is 5%, and the auditor wants a 10% risk of incorrect rejection, what is the desired precision?

10-37. Under what circumstances in a variable sampling application would an auditor conclude that the client's book value is fairly stated when BV falls outside DVE $\pm$ P'?

10-38. In the MPU sample size equation, $n = (U_R \times SD_E \times N/P)^2$, how does the auditor determine U_R, SD_E, N, and P?

10-39. How should the auditor determine the risk of incorrect acceptance in a probability-proportionate-to-size (PPS) sampling application?

10-40. What are the primary assumptions underlying PPS sampling?

10-41. What are the advantages and disadvantages of PPS sampling.

10-42. What is the equation for calculating a PPS sample size?

10-43. What general form of conclusion is generated by a PPS sampling application?

10-44. What is tainting and how is it calculated in a PPS sampling application?

10-45. Calculate tainting and total projected misstatements for the following:

Book Value	Audit Amount	Tainting	Sampling Interval	Projected Misstatement
$ 100	$ 25	———	$5,000	———
1,000	950	———	5,000	———
500	250	———	5,000	———
50	0	———	5,000	———
10	9	———	5,000	———
10,000	9,000	———	5,000	———

10-46. How does the auditor calculate the upper limit on misstatements in a PPS sampling application when overstatement errors are found?

Objective Questions

*10-47. An auditor selects a preliminary sample of 100 items out of a population of 1,000 items. The sample statistics generate an arithmetic mean of $120, a standard deviation of $12, and a standard error of the mean of $1.20. If the sample was adequate for the auditor's purposes

---

*AICPA adapted.

and the auditor's tolerable misstatement was plus or minus $2,000, what would be the minimum acceptable dollar value of the population?

(1) $122,000.
(2) $120,000.
(3) $118,000.
(4) $117,600.

10-48. In which of the following cases would the auditor be most likely to conclude that all of the items in an account under consideration should be examined rather than tested on a sample basis?

	The Measure of Tolerable Misstatement Is	Misstatements Are Expected to Be
(1)	Large	Low
(2)	Small	High
(3)	Large	High
(4)	Small	Low

*10-49. Items **A** and **B** are based on the following information:

The diagram below depicts the auditor's estimated deviation rate compared with the tolerable rate, and it also depicts the true population deviation rate compared with the tolerable rate.

Auditor's Estimate Based On Sample Results	True State of Population	
	Deviation Rate Exceeds Tolerable Rate	Deviation Rate Is Less Than Tolerable Rate
Deviation Rate Exceeds Tolerable Rate	I.	II.
Deviation Rate Is Less Than Tolerable Rate	III.	IV.

A. In which of the situations would the auditor have properly assessed the level of control risk?
(1) I.

(2) II.

(3) III.

(4) IV.

B. As a result of testing controls, the auditor assesses control risk too high and thereby increases substantive testing. Which situation illustrates this result?

(1) I.

(2) II.

(3) III.

(4) IV.

*10-50. If all other factors specified in an attribute sampling plan remain constant, changing the tolerable rate from 6% to 10% and changing the specified reliability from 97% to 93% (changing the risk of assessing control risk too low from 3% to 7%) would cause the required sample size to

(1) increase.

(2) remain the same.

(3) decrease.

(4) change by 4%.

*10-51. In estimation sampling for variables, which of the following must be known in order to estimate the appropriate sample size required to meet the auditor's needs in a given situation?

(1) The total amount of the population

(2) The desired standard deviation

(3) The desired confidence level *= Reliability.*

(4) The estimated rate of misstatement in the population

*10-52. If statistical sampling methods are used by a client in the taking of its physical inventory, the CPA must

(1) insist that the client take a complete physical inventory at least once each year and observe the inventory count if it is reasonable and practicable to do so.

(2) observe such test counts as he or she deems necessary to obtain satisfaction that the sampling plan has statistical validity, that it was properly applied, and that the resulting precision and reliability are reasonable in the circumstances.

(3) either observe a complete inventory count sometime during the year to obtain satisfaction that the statistical procedures are valid or qualify or disclaim an opinion on the financial statements taken as a whole.

(4) either observe a statistical inventory count each year to qualify or disclaim an opinion on the financial statements taken as a whole.

10-53. The estimated deviation rate obtained from attribute sampling is most useful in satisfying the auditing standard that states

(1) the work is to be adequately planned, and assistants, if any, are to be properly supervised.

(2) sufficient competent evidential matter is to be obtained through inspection, observation, inquiries, and confirmations to afford a reasonable basis for an opinion.

(3) the audit is to be performed by a person or persons having adequate technical training and proficiency as an auditor.

(4) a sufficient understanding of the internal control structure is to be obtained to plan the audit and to determine the nature, timing, and extent of tests to be performed.

*10-54. Which of the following models expresses the general relationship of risks associated with the auditor's assessment of control risk (CR), analytical procedures and other relevant

---

*AICPA adapted.

substantive tests (AP), and audit risk (AR) that would lead the auditor to conclude that additional substantive tests of details of an account balance are not necessary?

	AP	CR	AR
(1)	20%	40%	10%
(2)	20%	60%	5%
(3)	10%	70%	4½%
(4)	30%	40%	5½%

*10-55. Anthony Hill has decided to use PPS sampling, sometimes called dollar-unit sampling, in the audit of a client's accounts receivable balances. Hill plans to use the following PPS sampling table:

Reliability Factors for Errors of Overstatement

Number of Over-statement Errors	Risk of Incorrect Acceptance				
	1%	**5%**	**10%**	**15%**	**20%**
0	4.61	3.00	2.31	1.90	1.61
1	6.64	4.75	3.89	3.38	3.00
2	8.41	6.30	5.33	4.72	4.28
3	10.05	7.76	6.69	6.02	5.52
4	11.61	9.16	8.00	7.27	6.73

Additional Information

Tolerable misstatement
(net of effect of expected misstatement) .... $ 24,000
Risk of incorrect acceptance... 20%
Number of errors allowed.. 1
Recorded amount of accounts receivable $240,000
Number of accounts.. 360

What sample size should Hill use?
(1) 120
(2) 108
(3) 60
(4) 30

*10-56. In a probability-proportional-to-size sample with a sampling interval of $10,000, an auditor discovered that a selected account receivable with a recorded amount of $5,000 had an audit amount of $2,000. What was the projected error of this sample?
(1) $3,000
(2) $4,000
(3) $6,000
(4) $8,000

Problems and Cases

10-57. (Attribute Sample Size Determination) Calculate the test of controls sample size using the appropriate attribute sampling table for each of the following levels of sampling risk. Use a tolerable rate of 5% and an expected population deviation rate of 1%. Why does sample size increase as risk of assessing control risk too low decreases?

Risk of Assessing Control Risk Too Low	Sample Size
10%	_____
5%	_____

10-58. (Attribute Sample Size Determination) Calculate the test of controls sample size using the appropriate attribute sampling table for each of the following tolerable rates. Use a risk of assessing control risk too low of 5% and an expected population deviation rate of zero. As tolerable rate increases, sample size decreases. Why?

Tolerable Rate	Sample Size
2%	_____
4%	_____
6%	_____
8%	_____
10%	_____

10-59. (Attribute Sample Size Determination) Calculate the test of controls sample size using the appropriate attribute sampling table for each of the following expected population deviation rates. Use a tolerable rate of 5% and a risk of assessing control risk too low of 5%. Why does sample size increase as the expected population deviation rate increases.

Expected Population Deviation Rate	Sample Size
0.0%	_____
1.0%	_____
1.5%	_____
2.0%	_____
2.5%	_____
3.0%	_____

10-60. (Attribute Sample Evaluation) Fred Hancock, a senior accountant with Louis & Dent, CPAs, has just completed a continuing professional education course on attribute sampling. He has decided to apply attribute sampling to a current assignment.

He believed it would be appropriate to apply attribute sampling in a test of purchase transactions. He decided that a 5% tolerable rate with a 10% risk of assessing control risk too low would be appropriate. His expected deviation rate was 2%, so he took a sample of 100 items.

Because Hancock felt that the larger items deserved more attention than the smaller ones, he included in the sample 60 items with a value of $5,000 or more each; the remainder of the 100 items was valued at less than $5,000 each. He was very careful to take a representative sample of his test month for each of these two types of items.

When testing the sample for the various attributes, he found only five deviations. One deviation was a missing vendor's invoice, so he sent a confirmation to the vendor to make certain that it was a valid invoice. The confirmation indicated no errors. Another deviation was simply a missing approval by the authorized official. Hancock went to the official who agreed he had failed to sign the invoice and stated it was valid and correct. The client official also signed the invoice as required by prescribed procedure.

A third deviation was simply a missing purchase order. However, the amount of the transaction was small. Hancock decided it was too small to define as an error or deviation.

Other deviations both involved dollar amounts. One was an error in the extension of the invoice in the amount of $50 and the other a misclassification error of $850. Hancock was not particularly concerned about the $50 error because it was not material, but the $850 was fairly large. Fortunately, it was a misclassification between expenses and did not affect net income.

He decided to call the last two deviations actual errors and concluded that the maximum deviation rate was 3.8% at a 10% risk of assessing control risk too low. Thus, he concluded that purchases for the year were almost certain to contain fewer deviations than the 5% tolerable rate. As a result, he accepted the population and decided to reduce the test of year-end accounts payable based on a low assessed level of control risk.

Hancock was pleased with the use of attribute sampling because he had objective results. The reviewing partner, who could not attend the course because she was talking to a prospective client that day, also liked it because it reduced their exposure to legal liability and reduced the time budget to complete the engagement.

REQUIRED

Identify each weakness in the attribute sampling application and state why it is a weakness.

10-61. (Attribute Sample Size Determination and Sample Evaluation) In the audit of the cash disbursements cycle of the Carmichael Company, the auditor identified the following attributes for tests of controls. The statistical parameters for each attribute and the number of deviations found in the sample are also specified.

Attribute	Risk of Assessing Control Risk Too Low	Tolerable Rate	Expected Population Deviation Rate	Number of Sample Deviations
1. Examine vouchers for supporting documents.	5%	3%	0%	1
2. Examine supporting documents for evidence of cancellation (marked "paid").	5%	5%	1%	1
3. Ascertain whether cash discounts were taken.	10%	15%	5%	4
4. Review voucher for clerical accuracy.	10%	5%	1%	2
5. Agree purchase order price to invoice.	10%	6%	2%	1

REQUIRED

A. Determine the sample size for each attribute.

B. Determine the maximum population deviation rate for each attribute. (Indicate whether you used Table 10–2, 10–3, 10–4, or 10–5 to determine the maximum population rate.)

C. For attributes 1 and 2 in the table, calculate the allowance for sampling risk. What is the allowance for sampling risk?   *Sample Dev. Rate*

D. Based on the quantitative evaluation, identify the controls that can be used to lower the assessed level of control risk.

Max. Acceptable Reject Rate
Max. Pop. Rate

10-62. (Dollar Value Estimation) Red Raider, Inc., is using sampling to estimate the total dollars in inventory for one of its subsidiaries. The subsidiary does not have perpetual records or a book total for inventory. Red Raider decides that a material misstatement for inventory would be $60,000. They desire 95% reliability. To estimate the standard deviation of the inventory population, a pilot sample of thirty items from the total population of 2,000 items was selected. The pilot sample produced a mean of $4,000 and a standard deviation of $150.

REQUIRED

A. What sample size is needed to achieve the above objectives?

B. Assuming that the standard deviation of the sample size determined in **A** is $136, what is the achieved precision?

C. What statistical conclusion can be made concerning the subsidiary's inventory balance?

D. If you were the auditor of Red Raider's subsidiary, could you permit them to take a sample for purposes of estimating inventory? If so, what audit responsibilities would you have? What authoritative auditing literature applies?

10-63. (Difference Estimation) Fairmont Company has examined 100 items from a population of 1,000 inventory items for purposes of converting its year-end inventory from FIFO to LIFO. The total FIFO inventory per books is $1,040,000. The accountant compares the FIFO value with the LIFO calculated value for each of the 100 sampling units and accumulates the differences between the FIFO values ($208,000) and the LIFO values ($196,000).

REQUIRED

A. Calculate $\bar{d}$.

B. Calculate $\hat{D}$.

C. Calculate the dollar value estimate of the LIFO inventory.

D. Explain how precision would be calculated and how the accountant could express the results in a statistical statement.

10-64. (Audit Hypothesis Testing) Eileen Cooper, CPA, is auditing Axline Corporation's inventory. The inventory is recorded on Axline's balance sheet at $1,000,000. It consists of 12,500 kinds of items of approximately equal value. No identifiable dollar value strata exist. Axline does not use perpetual inventory unit records but does have a well-planned inventory-taking and counting operation. Axline uses two count teams with the supervision of counting in each department performed by a member of the internal audit department. Axline shuts down plant operations for inventory-taking purposes. Based on (1) test counting, (2) observation to ascertain that inventory-taking instructions are followed, and (3) evaluation of the competence and carefulness of client personnel taking inventory, Cooper decides that control risk (CR) should be assessed at 20%.

Cooper concludes that the inventory valuation of $1,000,000 will be acceptable if she can be 95% confident that the actual inventory is within $50,000 of the valuation. The statistical test will consist of recounting, repricing, and extending each sample item selected. Other audit procedures (AP) consist of inventory turnover calculations, comparison with prior years, and cutoff tests to insure that purchases and sales are reflected in inventory in the proper accounting period. Cooper's best guess is that these other procedures have an 80% risk. (Remember that AP represents the auditor's judgment concerning the risk that such procedures would fail to detect a material monetary misstatement if it existed in the account.)

Having completed the control risk assessment and evaluation of Axline's inventory-taking procedures, Cooper begins her substantive test planning. To estimate the standard deviation, she takes a pilot sample of 30 inventory lines. The standard deviation that results from the pilot sample is $25.

REQUIRED

A. What is the risk of incorrect rejection?
B. What is the risk of incorrect acceptance (assume that audit risk is 5%)?
C. What is the amount of tolerable misstatement?
D. Calculate desired precision.
E. Calculate sample size.
F. Assuming that a sample size of 256 is used and that the standard deviation of the 256 sampled items is $28, calculate the standard error of the mean.
G. Calculate achieved precision.
H. If the mean of the 256 sampled items is $81, calculate the dollar value estimate of the total inventory.
I. Does the statistical test support Axline's inventory valuation?
J. If the statistical test did not support the inventory valuation, what actions should Cooper take?

*10-65. (Audit Hypothesis Testing) Fill in the following blanks assuming sampling *without* replacement:

Book value (believed to be correct)	$2,820,000
Tolerable misstatement	$ 60,000
Estimate of standard deviation	$ 150
Population elements	$ 1,000
Desired risk of incorrect rejection	5%
Desired risk of incorrect acceptance	5%
Sample standard deviation	$ 140
Sample mean	$ 2,800

Risk of incorrect rejection coefficient	___
Tolerable misstatement adjustment factor	___
Desired precision	___
Sample size	___
Dollar value estimate of population total	___
Achieved precision	___
What is the maximum potential overstatement?	___
What is the maximum potential understatement?	___

Assuming the following book values and achieved precisions, should you accept or reject the book value? ___

	Book Value	Achieved Precision	
1.	$2,820,000	$15,000	___
2.	2,820,000	35,000	___
3.	2,820,000	45,000	___
4.	2,840,000	15,000	___
5.	2,840,000	25,000	___

10-66. (Probability-Proportionate-to-Size Sampling) Determine the PPS sample size for the audit of an accounts receivable balance of $168,000 consisting of 2,000 accounts. Tolerable misstatement is equal to $5,000 and the auditor has assessed control risk at 50% and

*Adapted from Arnold J. Pahler, San Jose State University.

supplemental test risk at 50%. The auditor desires a 5% audit risk. The receivable balance contains $5,000 of credit balance dollars. If no misstatements are found, what conclusion can the auditor reach? Under classical sampling, what selection chance does an account balance of $16,800 have? Under PPS sampling, what selection chance does an account balance of $16,800 have?

*10-67. (Probability-Proportionate-to-Size Sampling) An auditor employs PPS sampling in testing the valuation of inventory. The book value of inventory is $500,000 and represents the cumulative value of 2,000 vouchers. The maximum tolerable misstatement is determined to be $25,000 and the auditor decides on a 5% risk of incorrect acceptance. This completes the auditor's design specifications for the sample.

REQUIRED
A. What sample size should be used by the auditor?
B. How might the sample be selected using a random number table and systematic (sampling interval) sampling?
C. What are the advantages of using PPS sampling?
D. What are the disadvantages of using PPS sampling?

10-68. (Probability-Proportionate-to-Size Sample Selection) Fairview Publishing Company has an inventory of unsold books for its eighty titles as follows:

Title Number	Book Value	Title Number	Book Value	Title Number	Book Value	Title Number	Book Value
1	$2,030	21	$2,075	41	$1,831	61	$ 419
2	1,979	22	201	42	1,132	62	1,726
3	219	23	32	43	580	63	448
4	985	24	697	44	1,477	64	1,365
5	679	25	168	45	1,704	65	2,403
6	2,233	26	984	46	1,498	66	1,752
7	1,760	27	1,317	47	1,238	67	1,797
8	1,657	28	633	48	1,154	68	750
9	340	29	1,438	49	2,041	69	1,156
10	426	30	1,794	50	2,411	70	1,005
11	872	31	425	51	577	71	2,409
12	1,362	32	2,081	52	1,291	72	2,063
13	1,256	33	520	53	1,915	73	881
14	1,558	34	1,485	54	1,489	74	907
15	1,001	35	1,912	55	828	75	972
16	2,083	36	369	56	2,080	76	1,531
17	1,778	37	1,435	57	855	77	1,359
18	1,523	38	1,538	58	1,475	78	1,544
19	1,293	39	1,961	59	2,147	79	1,885
20	2,116	40	1,449	60	1,369	80	818
							$105,946

REQUIRED
A. Use Table 9–1 to select a dollar unit sample that produces ten inventory titles for recount and repricing. (Identify the dollar selected and the related inventory title.) Start the random dollar selection at Column 3, Row 10, of Table 9–1.

---

*IIA Adapted.

B. Instead of using a random number table to select a dollar unit sample, identify the dollar selected and the related inventory title using systematic sampling. Select ten inventory titles.

C. Which sample selection is easiest to use in this case?

D. Identify the inventory titles selected, using the same starting point in **A** above, based on physical unit selection. Select ten inventory titles.

E. What are the advantages of dollar unit selection over physical unit selection?

 *10-69. (Probability-Proportionate-to-Size Sampling) Mike Edwards has decided to use PPS sampling, sometimes called dollar-unit sampling, in the audit of a client's accounts receivable balance. He expects few, if any, misstatements of account balance overstatement.

Edwards plans to use the following PPS sampling table:

Reliability Factors for Errors of Overstatement

Number of Over-statement Errors	Risk of Incorrect Acceptance				
	1%	**5%**	**10%**	**15%**	**20%**
0	4.61	3.00	2.31	1.90	1.61
1	6.64	4.75	3.89	3.38	3.00
2	8.41	6.30	5.33	4.72	4.28
3	10.05	7.76	6.69	6.02	5.52
4	11.61	9.16	8.00	7.27	6.73

REQUIRED

A. What are the advantages of PPS sampling over classical variables sampling?

B. Calculate the sampling interval and the sample size Edwards should use given the following information:

Tolerable misstatement $15,000
Risk of incorrect acceptance 5%
Number of misstatements allowed... 0
Recorded amount of accounts receivable $300,000

Note: Requirements **B** and **C** are *not* related.

C. Calculate the total projected misstatement if the following three errors were discovered in a PPS sample:

	Recorded Amount	Audit Amount	Sampling Interval
1st error	$ 400	$ 320	$5,000
2nd error	500	0	5,000
3rd error	3,000	2,500	5,000

D. If no misstatements were found, what could the auditor conclude?

*AICPA adapted, except requirements D–F.

E. Calculate the upper limit on misstatements based on the results in **C**, above, assuming that the specifications in **B** apply.

F. Calculate **B** and **C**, above, assuming that a 15% risk of incorrect acceptance was appropriate.

Audit Judgment Case

10-70. (Probability-Proportionate-to-Size Sampling) Andrews of Andrews, Baxter & Co. is the auditor for the EZ Credit Bank. Andrews designed a sampling application to test EZ Credit's commercial loans receivable balance as of September 30, 19X7. The balance of commercial loans receivable was $5 million. Andrews expected little, if any, misstatement to exist in the commercial loans receivable balance because of the bank's effective internal control structure policies and procedures over loan transactions. If any misstatements did exist, Andrews believed that they would be overstatements. As a result, Andrews decided that probability-proportional-to-size sampling would be an appropriate sampling approach to use.

Andrews decided to confirm selected commercial loans receivable with the bank's customers. He decided that a misstatement of $55,000 or more in the commercial loans receivable balance, when combined with misstatements in other accounts, might result in the financial statements being materially misstated. As a result, tolerable misstatement for the sampling application was $55,000. In addition, because Andrews decided to assess control risk at the maximum and because the sampling application was the primary test of existence of the commercial loans receivable, Andrews decided that a 10% risk of incorrect acceptance was appropriate.

Because Andrews had only a very limited period of time to complete his examination, he decided to expect some misstatement in the account balance when he determined the appropriate sample size. Therefore, based on his professional judgment, he decided to use an expected misstatement of $10,000 in designing his sampling application. Although this would result in a somewhat larger sample size, providing for some misstatement when determining the sample size would reduce the possibility that he would have to extend the sampling application.

Andrews mailed confirmation requests to each of the customers whose commercial loan balances had been selected, and 200 of the confirmation requests were returned to him. Andrews was able to obtain reasonable assurance through alternative procedures that the remaining balances were bona-fide receivables and were not misstated. Of the 200 responses, only 2 indicated that the recorded balances were overstated as follows:

Recorded Amount	Audit Amount
$9,000	8,100
500	480

REQUIRED

A. Calculate sample size.

B. Calculate the appropriate sampling interval.

C. Calculate projected misstatement for the 2 overstated balances.

D. Calculate the allowance for sampling risk (i.e., basic precision and the incremental allowance).

E. What can Andrews conclude based on the sampling findings?

Auditing Issues Case

10-71. KELCO MANUFACTURING COMPANY

Kelco president, Steve Cook, is concerned about the accuracy of the company's chemicals and dye inventory balance for the year ended December 31. The inventory was counted without internal audit supervision. Katie Wilks has been hired independently to recount the inventory. Wilks wants to design a PPS sampling application that will give her 5% risk that inventory misstatements do not exceed 25,000. Kelco's final chemical and dye inventory shows a balance of $1,000,000. Because she expects few misstatements in her recount work, Wilks sets the tolerable misstatements for sample size determination at 25,000. The expected misstatement is 6,250.

REQUIRED

A. What is the need sample size?

B. Calculate the upper limit on misstatement given that Wilks used a 5,000 sampling interval and observed the following errors.

Misstatement #	Book Value	Audited Amount
1	2,000	500
2	1,000	750
3	8,000	7,500

C. Given the results in part B, what can Wilks conclude?

D. Given the conclusion derived in part C, what are Wilks' options?

Analytical Procedures

[handwritten marginal notes:] looking to see if #s. look like meeting the expectations → amt. budgeted → vs. actual → industrial averages

L e a r n i n g   **O b j e c t i v e s**

■ Define analytical procedures.

■ Identify and describe the nature of analytical procedures: trend analysis, ratio analysis, and reasonableness tests.

■ Describe how analytical procedures are used in audit planning, fieldwork, and final review.

■ Explain the effectiveness and efficiency of analytical procedures as substantive tests.

■ Explain the relationship of analytical procedures to other substantive audit tests.

Analytical procedures are classified in *SAS No. 56* (AU 329) as: "evaluations of financial information made by a study of plausible relationships among financial and nonfinancial data which involves comparing recorded amounts to expectations developed by the auditor." The auditor has an important role in deciding and developing the expectations. An auditor needs to understand the dynamics of an industry in order to understand the financial information that pertains to it. Numerous publications such as *Standard & Poor's* and *Dun and Bradstreet* provide insights on research and development, insurance, operating expenses, and other costs within industry sectors. Senior managers and partners participate in developing expectations and criteria for evaluating financial and nonfinancial data because they are familiar with examining internal or client data and external data. The reasons for this are that they may have work history in that business field or have audited that field for several years and are aware of the professional judgments an auditor must make that are industry specific. ■

Analytical procedures are evaluations of financial information made by a study of plausible relationships among financial and nonfinancial data. Understanding such relationships is essential to the audit process. A basic premise underlying the application of analytical procedures is that plausible relationships among data may reasonably be expected to exist and continue in the absence of known conditions to the contrary.

Analytical procedures are used in an audit for the following purposes:

1. To assist the auditor in *planning* the nature, timing, and extent of other auditing procedures.
2. As a *substantive test* to obtain evidence about particular assertions.
3. As an overall review of the financial information in the *final review* stages of an audit.

SAS No. 56, Analytical Procedures (AU 329.04) mandates that analytical procedures be applied at stages 1 and 3 above for all audits of financial statements. In addition, *SAS No. 56* recognizes that, in some cases, analytical procedures may be more effective than tests of details for achieving some substantive test audit objectives.

For certain nonaudit engagements (specifically, reviews of interim financial statements and reviews of financial statements of nonpublic companies), where risk is required to be reduced to only a moderate level (rather than to a low level), analytical procedures are also required. These two types of engagements are discussed in Chapters 21 and 22.

Analytical procedures involve comparisons of recorded amounts or ratios to expected amounts, developed by the auditor. The comparisons are developed by using plausible relationships that are reasonably expected to exist, based on the auditor's understanding of the entity and of the industry in which the entity operates. Expected amounts are developed from a variety of sources, including the following:

1. Financial information for comparable prior period(s).
2. Anticipated results, such as budgets or forecasts.
3. Relationships of elements of financial information within the period.
4. Similar information regarding the industry in which the entity operates. (Because of the difficulties in comparing a particular client's data to industrywide averages—difficulties due to specific industry definition; geographic separation; differences in ownership, age, and productivity of assets; customer mix; and other factors—industry data should be used with caution.)
5. Relationships of financial information with operating data or other relevant nonfinancial information.

Examples of how these sources are used to develop expected amounts are shown in Table 11–1.

Nature of Analytical Procedures

Analytical procedures analyze the relationships among data to provide evidence of a material misstatement of the financial statements. Three common types of analytical procedures (Table 11–2) are used:

- *Trend analysis* The analysis of the change of an account balance over time.
- *Ratio analysis* A comparison of relationships among financial statement accounts.
- *Reasonableness tests* Computations usually involving nonfinancial data used to estimate an account balance.

Table 11–1   **Examples of Expected Amounts**

Source of Expected Amount	Example
Financial information for comparable prior period(s).	Develop expected current-year sales based on prior-year sales.
Anticipated results, such as budgets or forecasts.	Develop expected current-year sales based on current budget.
Relationships of elements of financial information within the period.	Develop expected accounts receivable based on accounts receivable turnover ratio.
Similar information regarding the industry in which the entity operates.	Develop expected wage expense based on industry averages of percentage of wage expense to total sales.
Relationships of financial information with operating data or other relevant nonfinancial information.	Develop expected revenues for a hotel based on number of rooms, standard room charges, and occupancy rates.

Table 11–2	**Examples of Common Analytical Review Procedures**

Type	Example
Trend analysis	Compare sales revenue for 19X8 with sales revenues for 19X4–19X7.
Ratio analysis	Compute accounts receivable turnover (credit sales divided by average net receivables) and compare to the industry average.
Reasonableness tests	Estimate payroll expenses by multiplying the number of employees by the time worked and average wage rates.

Trend Analysis

Trend analysis is the most commonly used analytical procedure. By analyzing changes in an account balance over past accounting periods, the auditor can develop an expected result for the current period. This approach to trend analysis, referred to as the *causal approach*, requires the auditor to develop an explicit expected result. An alternative approach to trend analysis is to use a *diagnostic approach*, in which the auditor simply compares the current amount to the trend to see if the current amount appears to be acceptable. In applying the diagnostic approach, the auditor does not develop an explicit prediction; rather the auditor assumes that no problem exists if an account balance does not appear out of line. However, from an auditing perspective, an item that appears to be properly stated may be materially misstated. Thus, auditors should consider using the causal approach by developing an understanding of what factors cause the account to change and then using those factors to compute an expected amount for comparison to the actual amount. Because it requires more effort, the causal approach is more costly. Thus, the auditor should consider the costs and benefits of the two approaches in determining which one to use. However, when using analytical procedures as a *substantive test*, the causal approach is generally preferable under *SAS No. 56, Analytical Procedures* (AU 329.20). Figure 11–1 shows an example of a working paper using the causal approach.

Simple Trend Analysis

A *simple trend analysis* determines an expected amount based on the account balance in prior periods. For example, a company may have an average annual increase in sales revenue of 10%. The auditor could expect that sales revenues would increase by 10% during the current year. If sales did not increase by 10%, this could be explained by such factors as increased competition or an economic recession but it might also indicate that all sales have not been recorded (completeness assertion).

Regression Analysis

Of course, sales revenues are affected by a variety of factors, including economic conditions, marketing, and product lives. More complex types of trend analysis that incorporate other variables are also available to auditors in performing trend analysis. *Regression analysis* is a commonly used technique that is more precise than a simple trend analysis.

Figure 11-1 **Trend Analysis Causal Approach**

11—6B of B

			Initials	Date
Prepared By				
Approved By				

		19X4	Expected 19X5	19X5 General Ledger	Change	% Change
	Expectation: Sales and sale related expense accounts					
	will increase 10% in comparison to prior year accounts.					
	(1) Sales	1000000	1100000	1115000	15000	1.40
	(2) Cost of goods sold	700000	770000	772000	2000	0.30
	(3) Sales commissions	50000	55000	66000	11000	20.00
	(4) Advertising	8000	8800	8320	(480)	(5.50)
	Explanation					
	(1) Client opened a new store in November.					
	(2) The mix of goods sold changed to higher					
	gross margin goods.					
	(3) Increased the rate of sales commissions					
	from 4% to approximately 5%					
	in 19x5.					
	(4) Advertising budget was frozen from					
	the prior year.					

Regression analysis is a statistical method for finding the best-fitting line for an equation in the form $y = a + bx$ through a given set of data points. The variable y is the dependent variable, x the independent variable, b the coefficient of the independent variable, and a the intercept. By using regression analysis, the auditor develops a

Figure 11-2 **Regression Estimate**

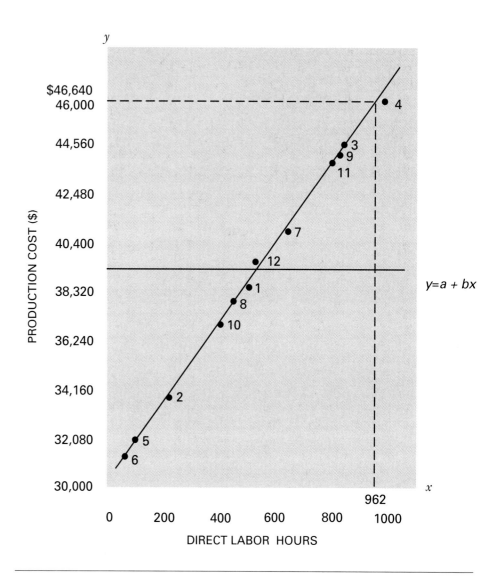

mathematical equation ($y = a + bx$) that uses one item (x) to predict another item (y). In the equation, a represents a constant term and b measures the change in y for each unit change in x.

For example, an auditor may want to determine whether the total production cost for a particular job or project is reasonable. The relationship between direct labor hours and production cost could be determined by using the activity for the past 12 months to develop a regression equation. This relationship is portrayed in Figure 11–2. Assume Job No. 876 has 962 direct labor hours and a production cost of

$42,000. As Figure 11–2 indicates, a regression equation in the form of $y = a + bx$ can be determined and production cost estimated. In this particular example, the equation would be $y = 30,000 + 16.64x$. In other words, production costs would include a constant amount of $30,000 (probably fixed costs) and then $16.64 for each direct labor hour used. Thus, for Job No. 876, the auditor would expect production costs to be approximately $46,000 — that is, production costs = $30,000 + $16.64(962). Because Job No. 876 has a production cost of only $42,000, additional inquiries and audit procedures may be necessary to determine if the difference is reasonable or if perhaps an error or irregularity has occurred.

Ratio Analysis

A second common type of analytical procedure is *ratio analysis*, which compares relationships among account balances. Trend analysis focuses on a single balance and does not incorporate knowledge about the relationships among account balances; ratio analysis uses the auditor's knowledge of relationships among accounts.

Ratio analysis is useful for examining both the income statement and the balance sheet, whereas trend analysis has only limited usefulness in the examination of balance sheet accounts. Income statement accounts measure flows that are generally more predictable than balance sheet accounts, which represent amounts at a point in time that are the net effect of several flows. Because trend analysis focuses on the change in account balances from prior periods, it is not as useful with balance sheet accounts, which are relatively unpredictable.

Ratio analysis is very effective for income statement accounts because it typically captures the variations in operating activity (for example, sales) that influence account balances (for example, cost of sales). Although balance sheet accounts are more difficult to predict, ratio analysis is nevertheless often a useful analytical procedure because it measures relationships among balance sheet accounts, which, although they may not be predictable individually, often have predictable relationships.

Approaches to Ratio Analysis

Ratio analysis allows the auditor to compare an entity's current performance with prior performance because these relationships often remain stable over time. In addition, ratio analysis can be used to compare an entity's financial position with that of other entities, since these relationships also do not usually vary significantly. Thus, a major benefit of ratio analysis is its ability to identify both stable relationships within an entity over time and common relationships among entities within a given industry.

Accordingly, two approaches to ratio analysis are *time-series analysis*, in which ratios for a given firm are compared over time, and *cross-sectional analysis*, in which ratios among firms at a given point in time are compared. Figure 11–3 illustrates the differences between these two approaches.

Methods of Ratio Analysis

Auditors use two common methods to apply ratio analysis: financial ratios, based on ratios between financial statement accounts, and common-size financial statements, in which account balances are shown as a percentage of an aggregate amount.

Figure 11-3	Two Approaches to Ratio Analysis: Time-Series Analysis and Cross-Sectional Analysis

Accounts Receivable Turnover

	Firm A	Firm B	Firm C	Firm D	Industry Average
19X4	3.5	3.0	3.8	3.5	3.5
19X5	3.4	2.9	3.9	3.6	3.4
19X6	3.2	2.9	3.9	3.6	3.4
19X7	3.2	3.0	3.6	3.5	3.3
19X8	3.3	3.2	3.5	3.4	3.2
19X9	3.2	3.3	3.7	3.5	3.3
19X0	3.2	3.2	3.7	3.6	3.5
19X1	3.1	3.1	3.8	3.8	3.6

Cross-Sectional Analysis

Time-Series Analysis

Financial Ratios   Financial ratios analyze relationships among account balances that the auditor expects either to remain stable over time (a time-series analysis) or to be common across firms (a cross-sectional analysis). Table 11–3 shows examples of commonly used financial ratios and how they are computed.

By using the financial ratios shown in Table 11–3, the auditor can perform time-series or cross-sectional analyses of financial statement accounts. For example, the accounts receivable turnover ratio shown in Figure 11–3 is a good indicator of a company's credit policy. In this particular case, the 19X8 ratio for Firm A is lower than in prior years and lower than the industry average. This may indicate that Firm A has problems with the collectibility of its receivables (for example, valuation), that fictitious credit sales exist, or that there was an improper cutoff of sales at year-end. In this situation, the auditor should investigate further by perhaps analyzing the aging of accounts receivable in more detail; increasing sales cutoff testing or examining the sales to cost of sales ratio; or by reviewing further the adequacy of the allowance account.

Common-Size Statements   In preparing common-size financial statements, the auditor converts the dollar amount of each account balance to a percentage of some relevant aggregate amount, such as total assets, total sales, or total expenses. *Common-size statements* can be prepared in either time-series or cross-sectional formats, although the time-series format is more common. Figure 11–4 shows an example of common-size statements using a time-series approach.

Although common-size statements are often prepared for the balance sheet, common-size income statements are generally more useful. Most revenue and expense accounts have a clear relationship to total sales. For example, the ratio of cost of goods sold to sales is among the most common analytical procedures used by auditors. For most entities, this ratio has a stable and predictable pattern useful for comparison across time or with similar firms.

Use of Industry Ratios

When performing a cross-sectional analysis, the auditor may use industry ratios. Two particular sources of information on industry ratios are commonly used:

- *Dun and Bradstreet* Provides industry norms and 14 key business ratios for 840 different classifications in industries such as retail trade, wholesale trade, agriculture, mining, construction, finance other than banks, real estate, and services. *Dun and Bradstreet* also publishes five-year summaries. The data are presented in three ranges: lower quartile, median, and upper quartile.

- *Robert Morris Associates* Provides financial and operating ratios for more than 360 lines of business (including manufacturers, wholesalers, retailers, services, and contractors) based on information obtained from member banks of RMA. Data are broken down by company size.

Table 11–3   Common Ratios

Ratios	Formula	Purpose
Liquidity ratios—Measure the entity's ability to meet its short-term obligations, and provide an indication of the company's solvency.		
Current ratio	$= \dfrac{\text{Current assets}}{\text{Current liabilities}}$	Indicates whether claims of short-term creditors can be met with current assets.
Quick ratio or acid test	$= \dfrac{\text{Current assets} - \text{Inventory}}{\text{Current liabilities}}$	Measures the entity's ability to pay off short-term creditors without relying on the sale of inventories.
Leverage ratios—Measure the extent to which the entity is financed by debt and provide a measure of the risk of the entity borne by the creditors.		
Debt ratio	$= \dfrac{\text{Total debt}}{\text{Total assets}}$	Indicates percentage of total funds provided by creditors; high ratios when economy is in downturn indicate more risk for creditors.
Times interest earned	$= \dfrac{\text{Earnings before interest and taxes}}{\text{Interest charges}}$	Measures extent to which earnings can decline and still provide entity with ability to meet annual interest costs; failure to meet this obligation may result in legal action by creditors, possibly resulting in bankruptcy.
Long-term debt to equity	$= \dfrac{\text{Long-term debt}}{\text{Stockholders' equity}}$	Indicates the proportion of the entity financed through long-term debt versus owners' equity.

(continued)

Table 11–3	*continued*

Ratios	Formula	Purpose

Activity ratios—Measure how effectively an entity employs its resources.

Inventory turnover $= \dfrac{\text{Cost of goods sold}}{\text{Average inventory}}$

Estimates how many times a year inventory is sold.

Age of inventory $= \dfrac{360 \text{ days}}{\text{Inventory turnover}}$

Indicates number of days of inventory on hand at year-end.

Accounts receivable turnover $= \dfrac{\text{Net credit sales}}{\text{Average accounts receivable}}$

Estimates how many times a year accounts receivable are collected.

Age of accounts receivable $= \dfrac{360 \text{ days}}{\text{Accounts receivable turnover}}$

Indicates the age of accounts receivable or number of days sales not collected.

Total asset turnover $= \dfrac{\text{Net sales}}{\text{Total assets}}$

Estimates volume of sales based on total assets.

Profitability ratios—Measure how effectively the entity is being managed.

Sales to total assets $= \dfrac{\text{Net sales}}{\text{Total assets}}$

Indicates the ability of an entity to use its assets to generate sales.

Gross margin $= \dfrac{\text{Gross margin}}{\text{Net sales}}$

Provides a percentage relationship based on sales.

Profit margin on sales $= \dfrac{\text{Net income}}{\text{Net sales}}$

Indicates the return a company receives on sales.

Net operating margin $= \dfrac{\text{Operating income}}{\text{Net sales}}$

Indicates management's effectiveness at using entity's assets to generate operating income.

Return on total assets $= \dfrac{\text{Net income} + \text{Interest expense}}{\text{Total assets}}$

Indicates the return a company receives for its assets.

Return on common stockholders' equity $= \dfrac{\text{Net income} - \text{Preferred dividends}}{\text{Average stockholders' equity}}$

Indicates return on investment to common stockholders.

Figure 11-4	**Common-Size Financial Statements Using a Time-Series Approach**

Colbert Company

Common-Size Balance Sheet

	19X4	19X5	19X6	19X7
Assets				
Cash	5.0	5.2	4.9	4.5
Accounts receivable	16.1	17.2	14.1	15.0
Marketable securities	15.0	14.7	15.1	15.7
Inventories	20.1	21.1	19.3	19.0
Investments and other				
noncurrent assets	15.1	14.4	17.1	16.6
Plant and equipment	28.7	27.4	29.5	29.2
	100.0	100.0	100.0	100.0
Liabilities and equity				
Accounts payable	21.1	22.6	23.1	21.8
Other current liabilities	9.9	9.7	8.8	8.9
Long-term debt	30.7	31.8	31.3	32.0
Deferred tax	5.0	4.9	4.9	5.1
Stockholders' equity	33.3	31.0	31.9	32.2
	100.0	100.0	100.0	100.0

Common-Size Income Statement

	19X4	19X5	19X6	19X7
Revenues				
Sales	102.0	102.9	104.0	103.1
Sales returns	2.0	2.9	4.0	3.1
Net sales	100.0	100.0	100.0	100.0
Expenses				
Cost of goods sold	41.1	40.8	39.9	40.4
General selling and				
administrative expenses	21.3	22.4	23.4	23.3
Interest expense	18.1	18.8	19.4	20.0
Other expenses	5.2	4.6	3.8	1.8
Tax expense	5.4	5.3	5.1	5.4
Income after tax	8.9	8.1	8.4	9.1
	100.0	100.0	100.0	100.0

Limitations

In using ratio analysis, the auditor should recognize its inherent limitations. For example, different accounting principles can make financial ratios noncomparable (for example, LIFO versus FIFO for inventory valuation). Likewise, ratios may differ among entities depending upon such differences as geographic location, production technologies, capacity utilization, and financial leverage. Thus, the auditor should exercise caution when comparing client ratios with industry ratios. In addition, ratios are not calculated in a standard manner. For example, in computing inventory turnovers, some industry sources divide cost of sales by inventory, whereas other industry sources divide net sales by inventory.

Reasonableness Tests

Reasonableness tests are computations that calculate an expected amount by using operating data as independent variables. For example, the number of passengers, passenger miles, and average revenue per passenger mile can be used to determine an estimate of passenger revenue for an airline or bus company. The percentage of occupancy of the rooms for a hotel or motel can be used to predict total room revenue. A study of the number of employees could provide support for various payroll costs, such as total salaries, payroll taxes, accrued vacation pay, and employee medical insurance costs. To perform a reasonableness test, the auditor develops a model that explains changes in a dependent variable (for example, payroll expense) by analyzing changes in independent variables (for example, number of employees, average wages, and average hours worked).

Reasonableness tests differ from both trend analysis and ratio analysis. Trend analysis involves a time-series model, whereas reasonableness tests involve a one-period model. Ratio analysis involves comparisons of relationships among financial data, whereas reasonableness tests use operating data (that is, nonfinancial data) to predict financial data. Thus, examining the relationship of sales commissions expense to sales is classified as ratio analysis, whereas examining sales commission expense based upon number of sales personnel is classified as a reasonableness test. Because reasonableness tests involve operating data, which typically measure flows, they are more applicable to income statement accounts than to balance sheet accounts.

Reasonableness tests can sometimes be excellent tests for the completion assertion, an assertion that is often difficult to test otherwise. For example, computing expected revenues for an electrical utility based on kilowatt hours used and standard charges provides an effective way to test that all revenues have been recorded.

Timing of Analytical Procedures

As previously indicated, analytical procedures are performed during three phases of an audit: planning, fieldwork, and final review. Although the procedure itself may remain the same, the purpose of the analytical procedure depends upon the phase of the audit.

Planning

During the planning phase of the audit, the auditor is required to use analytical procedures to draw attention to audit areas with significant potential for misstatements.

For example, an accounts receivable turnover calculation during the planning phase can signal potential valuation problems. The planning phase analytical procedures are also used to enhance the auditor's understanding of the client's operations and the transactions and events that have occurred since the last audit date.

Analytical procedures used in planning the audit generally use data aggregated at a high level. The sophistication, extent, and timing of the procedures vary widely depending on the size and complexity of the client. For example, for a small business the procedures may consist entirely of reviewing changes in account balances from the prior year using the general ledger or an unadjusted trial balance. For a larger public client, the procedures might involve an extensive analysis of quarterly financial statements or monthly financial information.

Analytical procedures are also useful in the planning stages to assist the auditor in assessing risk at the financial statement level. For example, a trend analysis of earnings, liquidity ratios, and profitability ratios could aid the auditor in assessing inherent risk at less than 100% for certain financial statement assertions.

Fieldwork

As noted in Chapter 5, substantive testing provides evidence as to the fairness of financial statement balances and consists of tests of details of transactions and balances and analytical procedures.

The auditor's reliance on substantive tests to achieve a particular audit objective derives from tests of details of transactions and balances, from analytical procedures, or from a combination of both, depending upon the expected effectiveness and efficiency of each type of procedure. In applying tests of details, the auditor uses evidence obtained from the details tested to form conclusions about the aggregate. For example, the auditor may examine a sample of individual accounts receivable balances to draw a conclusion about the total balance in accounts receivable. In applying analytical procedures, on the other hand, the auditor infers conclusions about details from evidence concerning the aggregate. For example, the auditor may compute a ratio for accounts receivable to draw a conclusion that certain assertions for individual accounts receivable balances are fairly stated.

Although not required, analytical procedures may be used during audit fieldwork as audit evidence. Unlike the objective of attracting attention to potential problem areas in the planning phase, in the fieldwork phase analytical procedures are used as audit evidence to reduce the scope of other substantive tests.

Final Review

As previously stated, *SAS No. 56* (AU 329.04) requires that analytical procedures always be performed during the final review phase of an audit. Analytical procedures used in the overall or final review stage of the audit help the auditor to assess the adequacy of the substantive tests performed, the sufficiency of the evidential matter obtained, and the validity of the conclusions reached, including the opinion on the financial statements taken as a whole.

The application of analytical procedures during the final review should be performed by someone having in-depth knowledge of the entity and extensive knowledge and experience in auditing. Usually, the engagement partner or the senior manager on an engagement performs this review.

The Real World of Auditing

Case History—Using Analytical Procedures during Final Review

The Client—A small manufacturer of toys and games.

The Problem—The question of valuation of excess inventories, which was not raised until the final review by the firm's report reviewer.

Observations by Report Reviewer—The problem surfaced about two minutes into the final review. The final review began with what the reviewing partner considered to be one of the most important analytical procedures—a close reading of the financial statements. That reading yields a good sense of the overall financial statement presentation and key areas before continuing with the rest of the review.

Initial comparisons showed that sales were down while inventory increased substantially. A quick calculation indicated well over a year's supply of inventory at year-end. The client's past experience and readily available industry data suggested that a three or four month supply would be more typical.

The inventory work papers were extensive and indicated a significant amount of audit work relating to

existence, completeness, rights and obligations (pledged and consigned inventory), and even valuation as it related to the company's method of pricing inventory; but there was no analysis of excess inventory and no consideration of that aspect of the valuation assertion. In essence, a two-minute analysis in the final review identified a significant audit issue that simple analytical procedures could have identified in the planning stage and which also was not identified by all of the substantive tests of details performed during the course of the audit.

Epilogue—Fortunately, the valuation problem was corrected before the report was issued—but not without certain costs. Those costs included performing additional procedures that could have been completed more efficiently earlier in the audit. More importantly, the CPA firm could have avoided the delays in issuing the report, aggravation to the client, and embarrassment from raising such a key issue so late in the audit.

Source: Adapted from Patrick S. Callahan, Henry R. Jaenicke, and Donald L. Neebes, "Increasing Audit Effectiveness," *Journal of Accountancy* (October 1988), p. 58.

In performing the final review, the auditor should read the financial statements and

1. focus on critical audit areas, by means of a review of trends and important ratios. In using or reviewing trends and ratios in a final review, the auditor should determine that the trend and ratio calculations reflect any audit adjustments or reclassifications.
2. review unusual or unexpected audit findings to determine if there is an area of audit concern not previously identified and addressed during the audit.
3. reassess client integrity based on findings during the audit that would lead the auditor to question management's intentions.
4. reconsider whether there is substantial doubt about the client's ability to continue as a going concern.

Results of the application of analytical procedures during the final review phase will indicate that procedures were sufficient or that additional procedures may need to be performed in order for the auditor to issue a report on the financial statements. Figure 11–5 presents a case history that demonstrates the benefit of performing final review analytical procedures.

Figure 11–5

Case History—Using Analytical Procedures during the Final Review

The Client—A furrier

The Problem—The question of increased accounts receivables.

Observations by the senior auditor—Analysis showed 116% increase in accounts receivable. A comparison of the doubtful accounts as of 19X4 and 19X5 shows a decline in the percentage of doubtful accounts:

	December 31	
	19X4	19X5
Accounts receivable (A)	120,000	260,000
Allowance for doubtful accounts (B)	2,400	4,940
Percent (B/A)	2%	1.9%

Further analysis of accounts receivable showed that a larger percent of the receivables were outstanding for longer periods of time. The aged accounts receivable schedule is presented below:

	Aged Accounts Receivable				
	less than 30	31–60	61–90	over 90	Total
12-31-19X4	40,000	60,000	15,000	5,000	120,000
12-31-19X5	20,000	40,000	80,000	120,000	260,000

Inquiries related to the overall increase in accounts receivable and the larger account balances in the 61–90 and over 90 days outstanding categories of the aging schedule. The auditor's primary concern was the collectibility of the accounts. The client's response was that the company had started focusing on direct sales as opposed to sales through retailers. Most sales were made through the company's lay-away plan. When the company made a lay-away sale, the following entries were made:

Accounts receivable	xxx	
Sales		xxx
Cost of goods sold	xxx	
Inventory		xxx

The company would keep the coat as collateral until fully paid. As customers paid, the following entries would be made:

Cash	xxx	
Accounts receivable		xxx

This explanation satisfied the senior auditor as to collectibility of accounts receivable.

Observations by parties reviewing working papers—Applying analytical procedures and then receiving the client's response raised two more issues related to revenue recognition and inventories. In order for the sale to be complete, there must be a transfer of goods to the customer. Thus until the customer receives the furs, revenue should not be recognized. Secondly, if the fur coats had been recorded as a sale, they should not be counted in inventory.

Epilogue—In this case the analytical procedures used identified problems in accounts receivable. Client gave satisfactory response explaining the changes in accounts receivable and changes in the aging schedule. However, the client's response raised two more issues. Analytical procedures may identify a problem but the auditor must always be sure to consider interrelationships of GAAP and GAAS issues.

Analytical Procedures as a Component of Substantive Testing

Analytical procedures are an important type of substantive audit test. Some audit objectives may be difficult or impossible to achieve without relying to some extent on analytical procedures because the procedures may be more effective than tests of details. Specifically, these procedures may be more effective than tests of details in testing the completeness assertion for income statement accounts.

Alternatively, some audit objectives may be difficult or impossible to achieve by relying solely on analytical procedures. For example, analytical procedures may not be effective in testing an account balance that is highly subject to management discretion or that does not show a predictable relationship with other financial or operating data. Accounts such as cash and investments usually cannot be audited using analytical procedures.

Aids in Designing Effective and Efficient Analytical Procedures

Designing effective and efficient analytical procedures involves the following considerations: (1) reliability of the data used to develop the expectation, (2) the precision of the expectation, and (3) the basis for assurance that differences from the expectation are not caused by errors or irregularities.

Reliability of Data Used to Develop Expectations

In evaluating the reliability of data being used to develop an expectation, the auditor considers knowledge obtained during previous audits, the assessed level of control risk, and the results of tests of details of transactions and balances.

Data used to develop an expectation are more likely to be free of misstatement if they are

- data obtained from independent sources outside the entity.
- internally generated data from records maintained by people not in a position to manipulate relevant accounting records. Information generated outside the accounting department, such as production and shipment records, often meet this criterion. In many computer systems, however, the same data generate accounting and nonaccounting records. Likewise, data maintained by people outside the accounting department may also be subject to manipulation. For example, certain production statistics may be important evaluation criteria for production managers.
- internally generated data derived from an adequate internal control structure.
- data that were subjected to audit testing in the current or prior year.
- data developed from a variety of sources.

Accuracy and Precision of the Expectation

As noted previously, in performing an analytical procedure the auditor should develop an expected result. The precision of the expected result depends on how thoroughly the auditor considers the factors that may affect the amount of audit interest, the level of detail of the data used to develop the expected result, and the method used to convert the data into an expected result.

As the intended reliance on analytical procedures increases, more careful consideration of factors that affect the amount is needed to reduce the possibility that offsetting factors could obscure misstatements. For example, last year's comparable amounts might be adjusted for known price and volume changes or for changes in product mix. A simple comparison to last year's data may be adequate if the auditor expects no changes or if a low level of reliance is being placed on the analytical procedure.

Expectations developed at a more detailed level give the auditor a greater chance of detecting misstatements. According to *SAS No. 56* (AU 329.19), monthly amounts will generally be more precise than annual amounts, and comparisons by location or line of business will usually be more precise than entity-wide comparisons. The appropriate level of detail depends on the nature of the entity, its size and complexity, and the level of detail available in the client's records. Generally, the likelihood that material misstatements could be obscured by offsetting factors increases as an entity's operations become more complex and more diversified. An increased level of detail reduces this risk.

The method used to develop an expectation can vary from a simple comparison to more complex statistical techniques. The method used depends on the auditor's judgment, using a cost–benefit analysis. For example, if there are only a few known changes in the circumstances of the entity that can be readily quantified, a simple trend analysis may be the best method. Alternatively, if several of the factors involved are difficult to quantify precisely, a more sophisticated technique, such as regression analysis, may be useful.

Basis for Assurance on Differences from Expectations

The auditor investigates significant differences from expected results by considering plausible reasons for the differences, considering information obtained from performing other audit procedures, considering inquiries of management, and extending audit procedures, if necessary. (Management responses, however, must be corroborated with other evidence.)

As the reliance on analytical procedures increases, so does the need for assurance that significant differences from the expectation do not represent errors or irregularities. This greater assurance is obtained by a careful investigation of differences.

For example, at a low level of planned reliance, the auditor's knowledge of the client and other information obtained in the conduct of the examination may be sufficient to corroborate the explanation for the difference. At a higher level of planned reliance, however, the auditor may need to examine additional evidence to corroborate the explanation, even though the explanation is consistent with the auditor's other knowledge.

The determination of how much difference from the expectation can be accepted without investigation is influenced primarily by materiality. Figure 11–6 is a working paper that documents an investigation of a significant account balance fluctuation.

Cost of Analytical Procedures

As with many other business and nonbusiness relationships, the costs of analytical procedures should be compared to the benefits expected. The auditor works within economic limits, and auditing procedures must be performed within a reasonable length of time and cost.

Figure 11-6	Working-Paper Investigation of Increased Sales Commissions

	19X5	19X4	Increase (Decrease)
Sales commissions expense per trial balance	42 100	5 175	36 925
Sales salaries	-0-	31 200	(31 200)

Sales commissions increased substantially from 19X4 to 19X5. The increase was discussed with Mary Ann Haquod, sales manager.

She stated that in 19X4 the two salespeople were paid $300 per week plus 0.5% commission on net sales. In 19X5 the company initiated a new commission policy of 4% on net sales but with no guaranteed weekly salary. The following amounts were obtained from the trial balance for 19X5 and 19X4:

	19X5	19X4
Sales	1,078 200	1,056 420
Sales returns and allowances	25 350	20 870
Sales salaries	-0-	31 200 *
Sales commissions	42 100	5 175

* $300 x 52 weeks x 2 employees = 31,200

	19X5	19X4
Net sales from above	1,052 850	1,035 550
Commission rate	4%	.5%

	19X5	19X4
Sales commissions	42 114	5 177.75
Per above	42 100	5 175
Differences— not material	14	2.75

The explanation provided by the sales manager and the computations above explain satisfactorily the fluctuations in both the sales commissions expense and sales salaries accounts. NHG 6—15—X6.

Planning, substantive, and final review analytical procedures are relatively easy to perform and usually require very little time. Some procedures are as simple and easy as comparing two numbers or dividing one number by another. Others may be more complex but could be performed very easily and quickly on a microcomputer with a generalized audit software program. Substantive test analytical procedures are often much less costly than tests of details.

Significant Terms

Analytical procedures Evaluation of financial information made by a study of plausible relationships among financial and nonfinancial data.

Common-size statements A type of ratio analysis in which account balances are shown as a percentage of an aggregate amount, usually total assets or total sales.

Cross-sectional analysis An approach to ratio analysis whereby ratios for a given firm are compared to ratios of other firms at the same point in time.

Ratio analysis A comparison of relationships among financial statement accounts.

Reasonableness tests Computations, usually involving nonfinancial data, used to estimate an account balance.

Regression analysis A type of trend analysis in which a dependent variable (y) is predicted based upon an independent variable (x), using a statistical method of finding the best-fitting line for an equation in the form of $y = a + bx$.

Time-series analysis An approach to ratio analysis whereby ratios for a given firm are compared over time.

Trend analysis The analysis of the change of an account balance over time.

Discussion Questions

11-1. What are analytical procedures and why are they performed?

11-2. List four sources that can provide the expected amounts for use in analytical comparisons.

11-3. List, explain, and give an example of each of three types of analytical procedures.

11-4. What is the difference in trend analysis between a causal approach and a diagnostic approach?

11-5. What is the regression analysis equation? What does each variable represent?

11-6. Why is ratio analysis, as opposed to trend analysis, more effective for balance sheet accounts?

11-7. What are the benefits of ratio analysis?

11-8. What are common-size financial statements?

11-9. Give two sources of information on industry ratios.

11-10. What are the limitations involved in using ratio analysis?

11-11. What is the difference between trend analysis and reasonableness tests?

11-12. Why does *SAS No. 56, Analytical Procedures* require the use of analytical procedures during the planning phase of an audit?

11-13. What is the purpose of performing analytical procedures during audit fieldwork?

11-14. When using analytical procedures during fieldwork, what factors should the auditor consider?

11-15. What is the objective of analytical procedures during the final review stage?

11-16. Who should perform analytical procedures during the final review stage?

11-17. Are analytical procedures required during the final review stage? The fieldwork stage?

11-18. What is the role of analytical procedures as a component of the auditor's substantive tests?

11-19. What does the precision of the expected result of an analytical procedure depend on?

11-20. How should the auditor investigate significant differences from expected results?

11-21. Explain the cost–benefit decision relating to analytical procedures.

Objective Questions

11-22. What are analytical procedures?
  (1) Substantive tests designed to assess control risk.
  (2) Tests of controls designed to evaluate the validity of management's representation letter.
  (3) Audit tests designed to evaluate the plausibility of financial and nonfinancial information.
  (4) Tests of controls designed to evaluate the reasonableness of financial information.

11-23. In the context of an audit of financial statements, substantive tests are audit procedures that
  (1) may be eliminated for an account balance under certain conditions.
  (2) are designed to discover significant subsequent events.
  (3) may be either tests of transactions, direct tests of financial balances, or analytical tests.
  (4) will increase proportionately when the auditor decreases the assessed level of control risk.

*11-24. Auditors sometimes use comparison of ratios as audit evidence. For example, an unexplained decrease in the ratio of gross profit to sales may suggest which of the following possibilities?
  (1) Unrecorded purchases.
  (2) Unrecorded sales.
  (3) Merchandise purchases being charged to selling and general expense.
  (4) Fictitious sales.

*11-25. What should analytical procedures used in planning an audit focus on identifying?
  (1) Material weaknesses in the internal control structure.
  (2) The predictability of financial data from individual transactions.
  (3) The various assertions that are embodied in the financial statements.
  (4) Areas that may represent specific risks relevant to the audit.

*11-26. The auditor notices significant fluctuations in key elements of the company's financial statements. If management is unable to provide an acceptable explanation, what should the auditor do?
  (1) Consider the matter a scope limitation.
  (2) Perform additional audit procedures to investigate the matter further.
  (3) Intensify the audit, expecting to detect management fraud.
  (4) Withdraw from the engagement.

*11-27. To help plan the nature, timing, and extent of substantive auditing procedures, what should be the focus of preliminary analytical procedures?
  (1) Enhancing the auditor's understanding of the client's business and events that have occurred since the last audit date.
  (2) Developing plausible relationships that corroborate anticipated results with a measurable amount of precision.
  (3) Applying ratio analysis to externally generated data such as published industry statistics or price indices.
  (4) Comparing recorded financial information to the results of other tests of transactions and balances.

*11-28. What is the primary objective of analytical procedures used in the final review stage of an audit?
  (1) To obtain evidence from details tested to corroborate particular assertions.
  (2) To identify areas that represent specific risks relevant to the audit.

---

*AICPA adapted.

(3) To assist the auditor in assessing the validity of the conclusions reached.

(4) To satisfy doubts when questions arise about a client's ability to continue in existence.

*11-29. Which of the following is *not* a typical analytical procedure?

(1) Study of relationships of financial information with relevant nonfinancial information.

(2) Comparison of financial information with similar information regarding the industry in which the entity operates.

(3) Comparison of recorded amounts of major disbursements with appropriate invoices.

(4) Comparison of recorded amounts of major disbursements with budgeted amounts.

*11-30. Of the following, which is the *most* efficient audit procedure for verification of interest earned on bond investments?

(1) Tracing interest declarations to an independent record book.

(2) Recomputing interest earned.

(3) Confirming interest rate with the issuer of the bonds.

(4) Vouching the receipt and deposit of interest checks.

*11-31. Which of the following would be *least* likely to be comparable between similar corporations in the same industry?

(1) Earnings per share.

(2) Return on total assets before interest and taxes.

(3) Accounts receivable turnover.

(4) Operating cycle.

*11-32. After using analytical procedures and determining that accounts receivable had increased due to slow collections in a "tight money" environment, what is the CPA likely to do?

(1) Increase the balance in the allowance for bad debts account.

(2) Review the going concern ramifications.

(3) Review the credit and collection policy.

(4) Expand tests of collectibility.

*11-33. An auditor testing long-term investments would ordinarily use analytical procedures as the primary audit procedures to ascertain the reasonableness of the

(1) valuation of marketable equity securities.

(2) classification of gains and losses on the disposal of securities.

(3) completeness of recorded investment income.

(4) existence and ownership of investments.

*11-34. What basic premise underlies analytical review procedures?

(1) These procedures **cannot** replace tests of balances and transactions.

(2) Statistical tests of financial information may lead to the discovery of material errors in the financial statements.

(3) The study of financial ratios is an acceptable alternative to the investigation of unusual fluctuations.

(4) Relationships among data may reasonably be expected to exist and continue in the absence of known conditions to the contrary.

*11-35. The third standard of fieldwork states that sufficient competent evidential matter is to be obtained through inspection, observation, inquiries, and confirmations to afford a reasonable basis for an opinion regarding the financial statements under audit. The substantive evidential matter required by this standard may be obtained, in part, through which of the following?

(1) Flowcharting the internal control structure.

(2) Proper planning of the audit engagement.

(3) Analytical procedures.

(4) Auditor working papers.

---

*AICPA adapted.

*11-36. For all audits of financial statements made in accordance with generally accepted auditing standards, the use of analytical procedures is required to some extent

	In the Planning Stage	As a Substantive Test	In the Review Stage
(1)	Yes	No	Yes
(2)	No	Yes	No
(3)	No	Yes	Yes
(4)	Yes	No	No

Problems and Cases

11-37. (Explaining Fluctuations) Rick Hempstead, CPA, has completed the audit of Huffman Corp. and has made comparisons with data from the prior year. Hempstead is interested in possible explanations for various unexpected changes.
REQUIRED
For each of the following separate situations, list several possible explanations.
A. Sales have decreased but accounts receivable have increased.
B. Gross margin has increased but cost of sales amount has also increased.
C. Total wages expense has remained the same but total payroll taxes have declined.

11-38. (Explaining Fluctuations) Bill Widhelm, CPA, has compared data from the client with industry averages and has found several deviations.
REQUIRED
A. Suggest several explanations for the deviations.
B. Why would earnings per share for the client be different from the industry average but the price/earnings ratio be the same?
C. Would earnings-per-share comparison be considered a useful analytical procedure?
D. Industry analysis should be used with caution and may not be useful in an audit. Do you agree?

11-39. (Analytical Procedures in Planning) Analytical procedures are extremely useful in the initial audit planning stage and as substantive tests during the fieldwork stage.
REQUIRED
A. Explain why analytical procedures are considered substantive tests when applied during the fieldwork stage.
B. Explain how analytical procedures may be useful in the initial audit planning stage.
C. Identify the analytical procedures that one might expect a CPA to use during an audit performed in accordance with generally accepted auditing standards.

11-40. (Timing) Jan Colbert, CPA, and John Stein, CPA, are discussing the timing of analytical procedures. Colbert states that the auditor may perform the analytical procedures at different times during the audit. Stein, on the other hand, believes that analytical procedures should only be performed at the conclusion of the audit.
REQUIRED
A. Discuss the timing of the analytical procedures.
B. How does the auditor's objective vary in relation to the timing of analytical procedures?

11-41. (True/False Questions) For each of the following statements, indicate whether the statement is true or false.
A. An auditor should not rely exclusively on analytical procedures when audit risk and materiality are high for a given account balance.

---
*AICPA adapted.

B. Industry comparisons are among the most widely used and most reliable analytical procedures.

C. When there is high audit risk of a material misstatement, the objective of an analytical procedure is usually to draw attention to potential errors.

D. Analytical procedures should not be used to assess inherent risk.

E. Trend analysis is the most commonly used analytical procedure.

F. Ratio analysis incorporates knowledge about the relationships among account balances, whereas trend analysis focuses on a single balance.

G. Ratio analysis is more useful in examining balance sheet accounts than is trend analysis.

H. Trend analysis involves a time-series model, whereas reasonableness tests involve a one-period model.

I. In determining the use of analytical review procedures and the potential reduction of other audit tests, the auditor should consider precision and reliability.

J. The audit reviewer should always perform analytical review procedures during the final review process.

11-42. (Ratio Analysis) The following balance sheets and income statements are for the Wittenburg Theses Company for 19X4 and 19X5.

Balance Sheets

	December 31,	
	19X5	**19X4**
Assets	(in thousands)	
Current Assets		
Cash	$ 50	$ 60
Accounts receivable	400	375
Inventory	600	500
Other current assets	20	25
Total current assets	$1,070	$ 960
Plant and equipment	2,100	1,950
Total assets	$3,170	$2,910

Liabilities and Stockholders' Equity

	19X5	**19X4**
Current liabilities		
Accounts payable	$ 175	$ 153
Notes payable	318	296
Income taxes payable	45	37
Other liabilities	15	22
Total current liabilities	$ 553	$ 508
Long-term liabilities	870	795
Total liabilities	$1,423	$1,303
Stockholders' equity		
6% Preferred stock, $100 par (2000 shares)	$ 200	$ 200
Common stock, $10 par (30,000 shares)	300	300
Retained earnings	1,247	1,107
Total stockholders' equity	$1,747	$1,607
Total liabilities and capital	$3,170	$2,910

	Year Ended December 31,	
	19X5	19X4

Income Statements

	19X5	19X4
Sales	$2,700	$2,520
Cost of goods sold	1,510	1,480
Gross margin	$1,190	$1,040
Selling, general and administrative expenses	410	377
Operating income	$ 780	$ 663
Interest expense	130	111
Net income before taxes	$ 650	$ 552
Federal income taxes	290	220
Net income	$ 360	$ 332
Preferred dividends paid	$ 12	$ 12
Common dividends paid	$ 208	$ 180

REQUIRED

A. Compute the following ratios for 19X5 and 19X4, if applicable.

  (1) Current ratios.
  (2) Quick ratios.
  (3) Debt ratios.
  (4) Times interest earned.
  (5) Inventory turnover.
  (6) Age of inventory.
  (7) Accounts receivable turnover.
  (8) Age of accounts receivable.
  (9) Total asset turnover.
  (10) Gross margin.
  (11) Profit margin on sales.
  (12) Net operating margin.
  (13) Return on common stockholders' equity.

B. What fluctuations would you investigate further and what are some possible explanations for the fluctuations?

11-43. (Reasonableness Tests) Marshall Crim, CPA, is interested in determining the reasonableness of delivery revenue and delivery expenses for Monroeville Corp. The client has four delivery trucks and four drivers who normally drive the same truck all the time. Trucks A, B, and C are used almost exclusively for delivery purposes to produce revenue, but Truck D is used about 40% of the time for non-revenue-producing activities of Monroeville Corp. The trucks were all purchased at the same time. In assessing control risk, Crim concluded that Monroeville Corp. had a good internal control structure and it was working effectively. The client provided the following yearly information.

		Truck A	Truck B	Truck C	Truck D
Miles driven	(A)	60,000	39,000	57,000	66,000
Revenue	(B)	$30,000	$19,200	$29,800	$21,100
Expenses					
Depreciation		$ 5,000	$ 5,000	$ 5,000	$ 5,000
Insurance		1,000	1,000	1,000	1,000
Taxes and licenses		400	400	400	400
Gas and oil		17,600	12,100	16,500	19,200
Repairs and maintenance		800	400	700	900
Damages not covered by insurance			2,000		
Total expenses	(C)	24,800	20,900	23,600	26,500
Net income (loss)		$ 5,200	$(1,700)	$ 6,200	$(5,400)

The results of the procedures are

	Truck A	Truck B	Truck C	Truck D
Revenue per mile (B ÷ A)	$ .500	$ .492	$ .523	$ .320
Costs per mile (C ÷ A)	.413	.536	.414	.402
Net income (loss) per mile	$ .087	$ (.044)	$ .109	$ (.082)

Crim's evaluation of the results is that delivery revenue and delivery expenses are not reasonable, especially for Trucks B and D. He recommended that additional substantive testing be done.

REQUIRED

A. Discuss the use of nonfinancial data by Crim in performing analytical procedures.

B. Comment on the procedures, conclusions, and recommendations by Crim. (Do not prepare any additional statistics.)

C. If you do not agree with Crim's procedures, conclusions, and recommendations, prepare your own analysis and evaluation.

11-44. (Ratios during Planning Phase) You have been appointed as the new auditor for James Company for 19X6. The company is listed on a national stock exchange and has been audited regularly in the past by other auditors. You have not audited a company in this industry before. You are in the planning phase of the audit and have obtained the following information from the predecessor auditor and from the client's current year's information.

	19X4	19X5	19X6
Current ratio	2.0 to 1	1.9 to 1	1.8 to 1
Debt ratio	.40	.50	.60
Accounts receivable turnover	13.1	12.0	10.9
Times interest earned	2.0	1.7	1.5
Inventory turnover	7.0	6.4	6.1

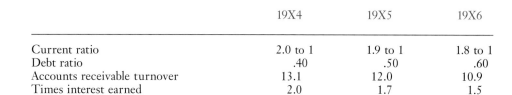

Credit terms are net thirty days.

A debt restriction requires James Company to maintain a current ratio of at least 1.8:1 and a debt ratio of 50% or less.

The industry average for inventory turnover is 6.3.

REQUIRED

A. Briefly discuss the purpose of analytical procedures the auditor would perform in the planning phase of the audit.

B. Comment on any trends the information indicates and possible reasons for these trends.

C. Based on the time-series analysis of the above ratios, what areas should the auditor identify as having high risk?

11-45. (Analytical Procedures for Sales) Jennifer Wynn, CPA, audits the Florida Squeeze Company, a manufacturer of three sizes of plastic containers that are sold to ten regular customers. The manufacturing equipment the company uses has very specific operating capabilities as described in the maintenance contract covering the equipment. The company operates 24 hours a day and maintains detailed records of any shutdowns due to maintenance or other problems. The inventory is physically counted monthly, and the general ledger is adjusted accordingly.

REQUIRED

A. How can Wynn effectively use analytical procedures to test sales?

B. The Florida Squeeze Company uses only two main raw materials in the manufacturing process for its containers. These two materials are mixed evenly and then a molding process is applied. The manufacturing process requires a relatively small amount of labor. About 70% of the final cost is represented by materials. The company maintains its cost of sales segregated by raw materials, labor, and overhead. How can Wynn apply analytical procedures to obtain evidence about cost of sales?

*11-46. (Financial Ratios) Ratio analysis often is employed to gain insight into the financial character of a firm. The calculation of ratios can lead to a better understanding of a firm's financial position and performance. A specific ratio or a number of selected ratios can be calculated and used to measure or evaluate a specific financial or operating characteristic of a firm.

REQUIRED

A. Identify and explain what financial characteristic of a firm would be measured by an analysis in which the following four ratios were calculated:

(1) Current.

(2) Quick.

(3) Accounts receivable turnover.

(4) Inventory turnover.

Do these ratios provide adequate information to measure this characteristic or are additional data needed? If other data are needed, list two types.

B. Identify and explain which specific characteristic regarding a firm's operations would be measured by an analysis in which the following three ratios were calculated:

(1) Gross margin.

(2) Net operating margin.

(3) Profit margin on sales.

Do these ratios provide adequate information to measure this characteristic or are additional data needed? If other data are needed, list two types.

11-47. (Common-Size Statements) The following information represents the financial statements of Tidwell Company.

---

*AICPA adapted.

Tidwell Company
Balance Sheet
December 31, 19X5 and 19X4

	19X5	19X4
Assets		
Current Assets		
Cash	$ 3,600,000	$ 3,700,000
Marketable securities, at cost that approximates market	12,000,000	12,000,000
Accounts receivable net of allowance for doubtful accounts	104,000,000	90,000,000
Inventories, lower of cost or market	125,000,000	155,000,000
Prepaid expenses	2,400,000	2,500,000
Total current assets	247,000,000	263,200,000
Noncurrent Assets		
Property, plant, and equipment, net of accumulated depreciation	315,000,000	312,000,000
Investments, at equity	2,500,000	3,500,000
Long-term receivables	15,000,000	17,000,000
Goodwill and patents, net of accumulated amortization	7,000,000	7,500,000
Other assets	7,500,000	9,000,000
Total assets	$594,000,000	$612,200,000
Liabilities and Stockholders' Equity		
Current Liabilities		
Notes payable	$ 4,000,000	$ 14,000,000
Accounts payable	35,000,000	45,000,000
Accrued expenses	23,500,000	26,000,000
Income taxes payable	1,000,000	1,000,000
Payments due within one year on long-term debt	6,250,000	7,250,000
Total current liabilities	69,750,000	93,250,000
Noncurrent Liabilities		
Long-term debt	174,250,000	189,950,000
Deferred income taxes	74,000,000	67,000,000
Other liabilities	9,000,000	8,000,000
Total liabilities	327,000,000	358,200,000
Stockholders' Equity		
Common stock, par value $1 per share; authorized 20,000,000 shares; issued and outstanding 10,000,000 shares	10,000,000	10,000,000
5% cumulative preferred stock par value $100 per share; $100 liquidating value; authorized 50,000 shares; issued and outstanding 40,000 shares	4,000,000	4,000,000
Additional paid-in capital	107,000,000	107,000,000
Retained earnings	146,000,000	133,000,000
Total stockholders' equity	267,000,000	254,000,000
Total liabilities and stockholders' equity	$594,000,000	$612,200,000

Tidwell Company
Statements of Income and Retained Earnings
For the years ended December 31, 19X5 and 19X4

	19X5	19X4
Net sales	$604,000,000	$450,000,000
Cost and expenses		
Cost of goods sold	490,000,000	350,000,000
Selling, general, and administrative expenses	66,000,000	60,000,000
Other, net	7,000,000	6,000,000
Total costs and expenses	563,000,000	416,000,000
Income before income taxes	41,000,000	34,000,000
Income taxes	18,450,000	15,800,000
Net income	22,550,000	18,200,000
Retained earnings at beginning of period	133,000,000	125,000,000
Dividends on common stock	9,350,000	10,000,000
Dividends on preferred stock	200,000	200,000
Retained earnings at the end of period	$146,000,000	$133,000,000

REQUIRED

A. Prepare a common-size balance sheet and income statement for Tidwell Company.

B. What items may require further investigation?

Audit Judgment Case

11-48. (Comparisons with Nonfinancial Data) Arco Cable Company's auditors have just completed the following revenue analysis:

Arco Cable Company
12 Months activity ended 12-31-19X4

Location	1	2	3	4	5	6	7
CATV revenue	258361	70986	36207	74810	74598	84483	24181
Miscellaneous revenue	12341	2913	1407	2433	2931	4933	1739
Total	270702	73899	37614	77243	77529	89416	25920
6 months activity 19X4	135351	36950	18807	38622	38765	44708	12960

6 Months activity ended 6-30-19X5

	1	2	3	4	5	6	7
CATV revenue	140513	40023	16648	36656	45474	45690	11875
Miscellaneous revenue	10907	2800	811	2124	2869	3857	224
Total	151420	42823	17459	38780	48343	49547	12099
PY vs. CY variance	16069	5873	−1348	158	9578	4839	−861
Subscribers							
June 19X5	1052	339	125	237	271	306	48
December 19X4	1011	347	127	199	264	328	45
Average monthly revenue per subscriber	24.5	21.24	24.45	28.98	29.95	26.99	42.01

Some have ↗ vs.
and

REQUIRED
1. After applying analytical procedures, what information would the auditor question?
2. What are some possible client explanations for the differences or variances?
3. How would you respond to those client explanations?

Auditing Issues Case

11-49. KELCO MANUFACTURING COMPANY

Kelco president Steve Cook has provided you with the following analysis for 19X7 and the first six months of 19X8.

Sales $000's
12 months ended 12-31-X7

	Jan	Feb	Mar	Apr	May	June	July	Aug	Sept	Oct	Nov	Dec	Total
Product A	1750	1800	1790	1900	1925	2000	1950	2100	2450	2500	2560	2600	25325
Product B	825	850	800	700	650	625	620	600	590	595	681	700	8236
Total	2575	2650	2590	2600	2575	2625	2570	2700	3040	3095	3241	3300	33561
Cost of goods sold	1200	1300	1260	1280	1270	1290	1275	1400	1700	1750	1840	1850	17415
Gross profit	1375	1350	1330	1320	1305	1335	1295	1300	1340	1345	1401	1450	16146

6 months ended 6-30-X8

							Total
Product A	2750	2780	2825	3010	3150	3300	17915
Product B	800	860	815	740	645	615	4475
Total	3550	3640	3640	3750	3795	3915	22390
Cost of goods sold	2350	2430	2425	2510	2530	2550	14975
Gross profit	1200	1210	1215	1240	1265	1365	7595

Unit Production of Product A

	19X4	19X5
January	100000	174050
February	103000	175394
March	99500	178778
April	108500	180456
May	108146	189076
June	114285	200000
July	114705	
August	123529	
September	140000	
October	149254	
November	157539	
December	160991	

Upon your review of the previous analysis, you have the following concerns:
1. Sales of product A increased from $1,750,000 in January 19X7 to $2,600,000 in December of the same year.
2. Sales of product A increased dramatically from $2,600,000 in December 19X7 to $3,300,000 in June 19X8.
3. Total sales for the first six months of 19X8 were up dramatically, yet gross profit has decreased.
REQUIRED
Using analytical procedures, provide possible explanations for the changes above.

Part Four

The Audit Engagement

Chapters 12–19 apply the auditing concepts, tools, and techniques already discussed for the audit engagement. The chapters are a guide through the various phases of the audit engagement: audit planning, the understanding of internal control structure and substantive testing by cycle, and the completion of the audit.

Chapter 12 describes the planning phase of the audit engagement.

Chapter 13 discusses the understanding of the internal control structure and the assessment of control risk for the revenue cycle.

Chapter 14 discusses the performance of substantive tests for the revenue cycle.

Chapter 15 discusses the understanding of the internal control structure, the assessment of control risk, and the performance of substantive tests for the expenditure cycle.

Chapter 16 discusses the understanding of the internal control structure and the assessment of control risk for the conversion cycle.

Chapter 17 discusses the performance of substantive tests for the conversion cycle.

Chapter 18 discusses the understanding of the internal control structure, the assessment of control risk, and the performance of substantive tests for the financing/investing cycle.

Chapter 19 discusses the completion of the audit engagement.

Chapter *12*

Planning the Engagement

Learning Objectives

- Present an overview of the planning process in an audit.
- Explain the process the auditor uses in determining whether to accept a client.
- Describe the purpose and content of an engagement letter.
- Identify the methods by which an auditor obtains knowledge of the client's industry and business.
- Define *related party* and explain its importance to the auditor.
- Explain the purpose of an audit program and identify considerations in audit program design.
- Describe the timing, staffing, and budgeting factors in planning an audit.
- Describe the responsibilities of the auditor when using the work of a specialist.
- Explain the process of auditing accounting estimates.

The first standard of fieldwork states that the audit is to be adequately planned and assistants, if any, are to be properly supervised. This standard relates to an old proverb that states, "proper planning prevents poor performance." In the planning phase of an engagement, it is important for auditors to "check out" properly their client's operations and to identify all potential red flags in the financial statements.

A landmark case that highlights the importance of adequate planning involved Four Seasons Nursing Centers of America, Inc., and the company's auditors. Federal prosecutors alleged that material misstatements in the financial statements were the result of incorrect application of the percentage-of-completion method of accounting for profits on long-term construction contracts and the inclusion of intercompany sales and profits in the company's income statement.

Proper planning for this engagement could have made the auditors aware that the percentage-of-completion method is one of the most abused and misused of all accounting methods. In addition, a number of red flags were evident, which should have signaled to the auditors that there was a higher than normal risk of management fraud, including new products which promised an extraordinary rate of return, client executives who lacked a strong background in the industry, and extensive transactions with affiliated companies.

In today's business environment, the planning phase of the engagement has become a critical part of the determination and documentation of assessed risk. ■

Source: M.C. Knapp, "Four Seasons Nursing Centers of America, Inc.," *Contemporary Auditing Issues and Cases*, West Publishing Company, 1993.

Chapter 12 is the first of eight chapters in Part IV, "The Audit Engagement." In these chapters, auditing concepts, tools, and techniques discussed in the prior chapters are applied to audit engagements. Logically, any audit engagement begins with the planning process. Thus, Chapter 12 describes the audit planning process, including the client acceptance decision, the sending of an engagement letter, the general planning phase of the audit, and the continuous planning of audit procedures, timing, and staffing that occurs throughout the engagement. An overview of planning the engagement is shown in Figure 12–1.

Client Contact and Acceptance

The audit process begins when the auditor obtains an audit client. Obtaining a client is a two-step process. First, there must be an initial contact in which the potential client requests an audit. Second, once a request is made, the auditor must evaluate whether or not to accept the engagement.

| **Figure 12–1** | **Overview of Planning the Engagement** |

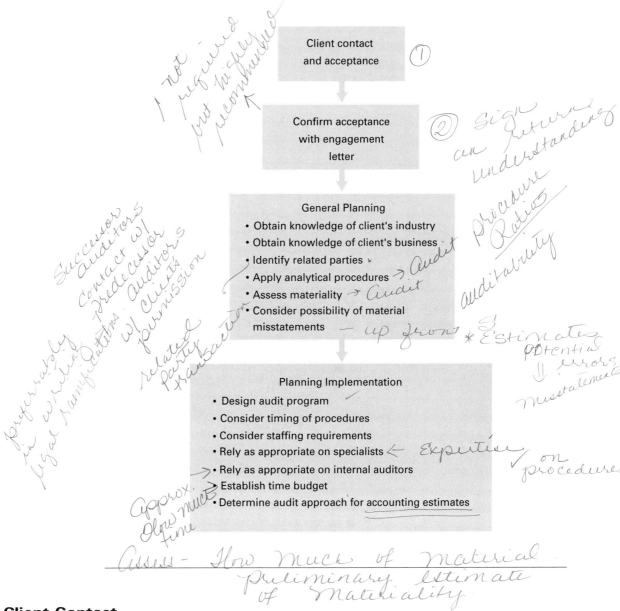

(Handwritten annotations on figure)

① not required but is helpful / recommended

② Sign Return an understanding Procedure Ratios / Auditability

Successor Auditors Contact w/ Predecessor Auditors w/ Clients permission

related party transaction

preferably in writing / legal ramifications

Audit Procedure / Ratios

*Estimates Potential ↓ errors misstatements

— up front

Expertise on procedures

Approx. How much time

Assess — How much of material / Preliminary Estimate of Materiality

(Figure flowchart text)

Client contact and acceptance ①

Confirm acceptance with engagement letter

General Planning
- Obtain knowledge of client's industry
- Obtain knowledge of client's business
- Identify related parties
- Apply analytical procedures → Audit
- Assess materiality → Audit
- Consider possibility of material misstatements

Planning Implementation
- Design audit program
- Consider timing of procedures
- Consider staffing requirements
- Rely as appropriate on specialists ← Expertise
- Rely as appropriate on internal auditors
- Establish time budget
- Determine audit approach for accounting estimates

Initial Client Contact

The audit process begins when a potential client contacts an accounting firm regarding the performance of an audit. The method by which a client selects an accounting firm is no different from the method used by individuals and companies to select the services of other professionals, such as doctors or attorneys. Generally, entities examine the reputation of the accounting firm and the costs and benefits of the services that they provide. Reputations are built through the performance of quality work and recognition by clients, bankers, creditors, attorneys, financial advisors, and others in influential business positions. Although the reputation of accounting firms may not generally be known to the public at large, such reputations are widely shared by the business community.

Often a potential client will request a proposal letter from the auditor. A *proposal letter* generally includes a variety of information about the auditing firm (such as size, office locations, and areas of specialization and expertise), the audit proposal, and audit fees. An example of a proposal letter is shown in Figure 12–2. Proposal letters vary significantly and can be much more detailed than the example in Figure 12–2.

Figure 12–2 | **Sample Proposal Letter for an Audit Engagement**

David King & Company
Certified Public Accountants

April 20, 19X5

Board of Directors
Sports Theme Restaurants, Inc.
1510 Beltway Blvd.
Washington, D.C. 20014

Ladies and Gentlemen:

As you requested, we present the following information about our firm and our proposed approach to your audit requirements. You have indicated that Sports Theme Restaurants, Inc., and its related entities are considering retaining a public accounting firm to audit the company's combined financial statements at December 31, 19X5.

Our objective would be to audit the combined balance sheet of Sports Theme Restaurants, Inc., and its related entities at December 31, 19X5, and the related combined statements of income, retained earnings, and cash flows for the year then ended, and to report to the Board of Directors.

Our audit would be made in accordance with generally accepted auditing standards. Those standards require that we plan and perform the audit to obtain reasonable assurance about whether the financial statements are free of material misstatement. An audit includes examining, on a test basis, evidence supporting the amounts and disclosures in the financial statements. An audit also includes assessing the accounting principles used and significant estimates made by management, as well as evaluating the overall financial statement presentation.

We understand that the proposed engagement will not require us to prepare federal and state tax returns, although we are prepared to act in a consulting capacity if the need arises.

Figure 12–2   *continued*

David King & Company traces its origin to 1915 and is a national firm of accountants, auditors, and consultants with seven offices. Our East Coast offices are located in Washington, D.C., and Philadelphia.

In addition to traditional accounting and auditing functions, our broad-based and diversified practice also offers tax and management advisory services. Our personnel include experts in many technical and business fields. We are especially proud of our capabilities in the food and hospitality fields where our publications and pronouncements are quoted by *The Wall Street Journal, Business Week,* and *Institution* as authoritative material. As you requested, several of these publications are enclosed.

We are represented in many organizations concerned with restaurant operations. Our personnel regularly conduct continuing professional education classes in all aspects of restaurant activities. Many firm members are officers, directors, and committee members in local, state, and national professional organizations.

Fees for our services are based on the time required to complete our assignment plus out-of-pocket expenses. Every effort will be made to keep our services to the minimum consistent with the requirements of the engagement. We estimate that our fee for the initial audit for the year ended December 31, 19X5, will range between $17,000 and $22,000.

Thank you for allowing us the opportunity to submit this proposal.

Sincerely,
David King & Company

Client Acceptance

Although most auditors want to obtain new clients, care must be exercised before accepting clients. Auditing firms have no obligation to accept every potential client. The auditor should evaluate whether accepting a potential client will increase the auditor's business risk or otherwise harm the firm's reputation and image.

Quality Control Considerations

As discussed in Chapter 1, *Statement on Quality Control Standards No. 1, System of Quality Control for a CPA Firm,* identifies the quality control considerations for auditors. One of the nine elements of quality control identified in this standard is the establishment of policies and procedures regarding the acceptability and continuance of clients. Paragraph 7(h) of the standard states:

> Policies and procedures should be established for deciding whether to accept or continue a client in order to minimize the likelihood of association with a client whose management lacks integrity. Suggesting that there should be procedures for this purpose does not imply that a firm vouches for the integrity or reliability of a client, nor does it imply that a firm has a duty to anyone but itself with respect to the acceptance, rejection, or retention of clients. However, prudence suggests that a firm be selective in determining its professional relationships.

To document their compliance with quality control standards regarding the acceptance of new clients, many firms complete client acceptance reports. An example of a new client report is shown in Figure 12–3. In addition, many auditors find that an annual client continuance evaluation program provides an effective framework for considering client continuance.

Management Integrity

The auditor's primary responsibility is to render an opinion on the fairness of the financial statements in accordance with generally accepted accounting principles. As discussed in Chapter 3 and noted in *SAS No. 53, The Auditor's Responsibility to Detect and Report Errors and Irregularities* (AU 316.08), "The auditor should exercise (a) due care in planning, performing, and evaluating the results of audit procedures, and (b) the proper degree of professional skepticism to achieve reasonable assurance that material errors or irregularities will be detected." However, the detection of management fraud or misrepresentations is often very difficult and may not be discovered even though the auditor exercises due care and complies with professional standards. Rather, auditors are expected to detect only those management frauds or misrepresentations that could be uncovered while performing an audit in accordance with generally accepted auditing standards.

Auditors are, however, required to plan and perform an audit with an attitude of professional skepticism. The auditor neither assumes that management is dishonest nor assumes unquestioned honesty. As noted in *SAS No. 53* (AU 316.17), when approaching assertions that are difficult to substantiate, the auditor should recognize the increased importance of factors that bear on management integrity. A presumption of management dishonesty, however, is contrary to the accumulated experience of auditors. Moreover, if dishonesty were presumed, the auditor would potentially need to question the authenticity of all records and documents obtained from the client and would require conclusive rather than persuasive evidence to corroborate all management representations. Audits conducted on these terms would be unreasonably costly and impractical. However, the auditor should remember that management integrity is crucial to the audit process since management can misrecord transactions or conceal information in a manner that materially misstates the financial statements.

Communication with Predecessor Auditors

In evaluating a potential client that has been audited previously by another CPA firm, a primary source of information is the potential client's **predecessor auditor**. *SAS No. 7, Communications between Predecessor and Successor Auditors* (AU 315), recognizes this and requires the **successor auditor** to communicate with the predecessor auditor.

Figure 12-3   **Sample New Client Form**

Office _____ Huntsville
Date _____ 11/4/X5

Client's name ___ Grissom Company ___ Fiscal Year __ 12/31/X5
Address __ 2322 Shades Crest Drive _____
Phone _870-1716_ Major contact at client ___ Brian McNew ___
Title _President_ Nature of business _____ Space Helmets ___
S.I.C. code number* _6811_

Sales _____ 142,000,000 _____ Net Income _____ 17,163,020 _____
Form of Organization:
_____ Individual _____ Partnership _X___ Corporation
Other: (indicate) _____
Publicly held: _X_ no _____ yes (indicate) _____
Source of client: _____ acquaintance of partner or staff;
_____ Client; _____ Attorney; _X_ Bank;
_____ Another office, new client; _____ Other _____
Name of Source _____ SpaceCity Bank _____

Name of partner or staff member responsible for source contact
Erin Colquitt
Acknowledgement to source by _Lewis Gayden_
Partner in charge _Jeff Martin_ Client code number ___ 1730 ___

Nature of assignment and assignment code number:
_X_ Audit _____   ___ Tax Returns ___ MAS
___ Compilation   ___ Special tax ___ Review

Estimated fees:
a) Annual _$42,000_
b) Nonrecurring or special _____
    Previous auditors _Adam & Cheatham, CPAs_
    Reason for change (if known) _lack of timely service_
    Attorney and law firm _H.B. Lee of Amber, Lance, Chaser,&Co._
    Federal identification no. _63-8323222_
    Related clients, parent, or affiliates _Jetson Corp. (affiliate)_

Source: Adapted from AICPA *Audit and Accounting Manual*, 1984.

SAS No. 7 places the initiative for the communication on the successor auditor and requires the successor auditor to make inquiries regarding the integrity of management, disagreements with management as to accounting principles or auditing procedures, and the predecessor's understanding as to the reasons for the change in auditors. Because of the confidentiality rule in the Code of Professional Conduct, the successor auditor must request that the potential client authorize the predecessor auditor to respond to these inquiries. Failure of the potential client to grant such permission should be considered by the auditor in evaluating whether or not to accept the engagement.

Planning the Engagement

The planning phase of any audit engagement relies heavily on the use of professional judgment in determining the risk and related audit strategies for various account balances. Analytical procedures are required in the planning phase of an engagement and are used to help identify the high-risk financial statement line items, which may require additional investigation. Trend analyses and common-size statements are often used as analytic techniques during audit planning. These analytical procedures, though, are only as useful as the judgment of the auditor in determining the appropriate audit strategy.

In the case of United States Surgical Corporation, its auditors, Ernst & Whinney (now Ernst & Young) failed to detect an unusual trend that could

have led to a more thorough investigation of certain accounts. Specifically, accrued expenses is a typically high-risk account because of the ease with which it can be manipulated. The balance in this account was fairly stable at United States Surgical between 1979 and 1981, even though the company was growing at a staggering rate. By using a common-size statement, the auditor could determine that the balance, as a percentage of total assets, decreased more than 60 percent from the end of 1979 to the end of 1981. This unusual trend should have been a signal to the auditors to expand their substantive testing by performing a more extensive search for unrecorded liabilities.

_____

Source: N. R. Kleinfeld, "U.S. Surgical's Checkered History," *New York Times*, May 13, 1984, p. F4.

The predecessor auditor is required under *SAS No.* 7 (AU 315.07) to respond fully and promptly to the successor auditor. If legal problems or other unusual circumstances exist, the predecessor auditor may provide a limited response while noting the limitation. In this situation, the successor auditor should seriously consider the implications of a limited response in deciding whether or not to accept the engagement. The form of communication with the predecessor auditor may be oral or written. Further communications with the predecessor auditor after client acceptance are not required but are generally undertaken as a matter of audit efficiency. Figure 12–4 presents a flowchart of *SAS No.* 7.

Fee Arrangements   Another consideration in evaluating a potential client is the fee arrangements between the client and the CPA firm. Most CPA firms prefer to bill their clients on a per diem basis (that is, on an hourly or daily standard rate). Because an audit involves professional judgments, it is usually not possible to set a fair charge for an engagement until the audit has been completed. However, clients, of course, need to know what to expect in regard to audit fees. Thus, CPAs often give the client an estimate of the final fee, which is subject to change as the audit progresses.

Auditability   A final but most important consideration by the auditor in evaluating whether to accept a client is the determination of whether or not the client is *auditable*. Although the potential client and users of the financial statements may want an audit, certain factors might preclude the auditor from auditing the client and expressing an opinion. For example, a fire loss may have destroyed accounting records needed by the

Figure 12-4

Flowchart of Communications between Predecessor and Successor Auditors

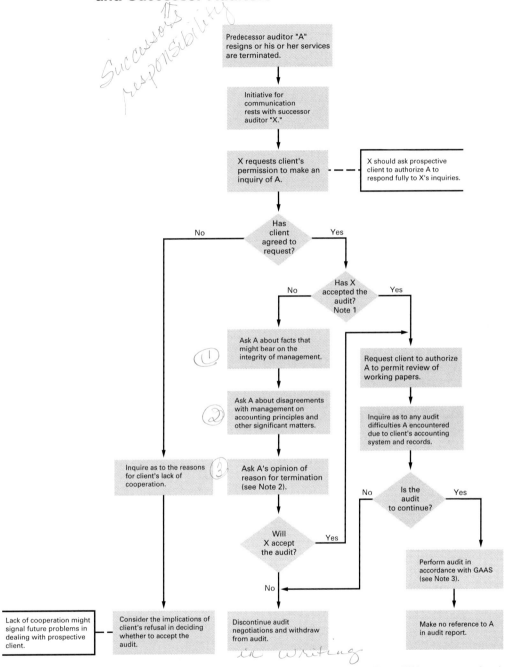

Note 1: The inquiries noted to the left of the decision (a "no" response) are to be attempted prior to acceptance of the audit. The inquiries to the right of the decision (a "yes" response) may be performed either before or after acceptance. However, it is recommended that these latter two inquiries be made after acceptance to avoid placing an unreasonable burden on auditor A.

Note 2: Auditor A should respond promptly and fully, on the basis of facts known to him or her, to X's reasonable inquiries. Should A not respond fully to the inquiries, he or she should indicate that the response is limited.

Note 3: If X becomes aware of needed revision in financial statements audited by A, X should request client to arrange a meeting of A, X, and client to resolve problem. See AU 315.10-.11.

auditor. Although authoritative guidance on assessing auditability is limited, due professional care requires that the following items be considered by the auditor:

Management Integrity and Control Consciousness Management integrity is essential to the ability to perform any audit. If management lacks integrity, the auditor would not be able to rely on any representations made by management or the accounting records. In addition, management should take the lead in creating an atmosphere of control consciousness. Concerns about management integrity may be so serious that the auditor concludes that the audit cannot be conducted.

Adequate Accounting System The client's accounting system must provide sufficient evidence to support the transactions that have occurred. The accounting system should also insure that all transactions that should be recorded have, in fact, been recorded. Concerns about the accounting system may cause the auditor to conclude that it is unlikely that sufficient competent evidence will be available to support an opinion on the financial statements. However, a client need not have a sophisticated accounting system to be auditable.

The Real World of Auditing

Accepting an Engagement and Communicating with a Predecessor Auditor

Facts: An accounting firm was engaged to audit the financial statements of a mortgage company for two years. During the screening process, the accounting firm was informed of several problems that the predecessor accounting firm had encountered with the client that had resulted in the firm's dismissal. The predecessor accounting firm had discovered possible misappropriations of funds by officers of the mortgage company and had refused to issue an unqualified opinion.

Despite discussing these problems with the predecessor accounting firm and reviewing its working papers, the successor accounting firm accepted the engagement and issued an unqualified opinion for both audit years.

The mortgage company began to experience financial problems soon after the successor accounting firm had issued its second unqualified opinion on the financial statements. A subsequent investigation revealed that the client had engaged in undisclosed related-party transactions and illegal acts in order to distort the company's true financial position.

The company was forced into bankruptcy, and the shareholders filed suit against the successor accounting firm, claiming $2 million in damages.

Issues: The shareholders claimed that the successor accounting firm was negligent in performing its audits because of the undetected financial problems.

Resolution: Liability of the successor firm in this case was clear and ended in a $1 million settlement. The predecessor accounting firm was exonerated from any liability and did not contribute to the settlement.

Commentary: The accounting firm should not have ignored the information supplied by the predecessor accounting firm, especially when it was of such a serious nature. Before accepting the engagement, the firm should have discussed these issues with the prospective client. The successor firm should not have accepted the engagement without first resolving potential problems with this engagement.

Source: G. Spellmire, W. Baliga, D. Winiarski, *Accountants Legal Liability Guide*, Harcourt Brace Jovanovich, 1990, pp. 3.05–3.06.

Engagement Letters

Having decided to accept a client, the first step the auditor should take is to send the client an ***engagement letter*** to set forth the terms of the engagement to be performed and to identify any understandings between the auditor and client. By returning a signed copy of the letter, the client agrees to cooperate, render assistance, and compensate the auditor. Although engagement letters are not required in professional standards, most CPA firms require them as a part of their practices. Many CPA firms send engagement letters not only to new clients but also to continuing clients for each engagement, whether the services performed are for audit, tax, compilation, review, or some other special engagement. The engagement letter serves as the agreement or contract between the two parties regarding the conduct of the audit and any related services that are to be performed. The *1136 Tenants' Corporation* case (discussed in Chapter 22) illustrates the legal liability of a CPA when an engagement letter is not prepared and misunderstandings subsequently arise between the client and the CPA. The accountant in *1136 Tenants' Corporation* was found liable for $237,000, although the annual fee for the engagement was $600. The primary question in the case was whether the accountant had agreed to perform an audit. The case would probably never have been litigated if the accountant had used an engagement letter.

The engagement letter should achieve the following objectives:

1. Document the contractual duties agreed to by the auditor and the client.
2. Explain the auditor's and client's responsibilities. An engagement letter should explain in nontechnical language the nature of the services to be rendered and establish that the financial statements are the responsibility of the client.
3. Protect the auditor from legal liability.
4. Provide audit staff with an understanding of the nature of the engagement.

Normally, audit engagement letters are addressed to the board of directors, the audit committee, or the chief executive officer. Engagement letters generally include statements about

- the objective of the audit of the financial statements.
- management's responsibility for the financial statements.
- the scope of the audit, including reference to generally accepted auditing standards.
- the form of any reports or other communication of results of the engagement.
- the fact that, because of the test nature and other inherent limitations of an audit, together with the inherent limitations of any internal control structure, there is an unavoidable risk that some material misstatement may remain undiscovered.
- the expectation of receiving from management written confirmation concerning representations made in connection with the audit.
- a request for the client to confirm the terms of the audit by acknowledging receipt of the engagement letter.
- a description of any other letters or reports the auditor expects to issue to the client.
- the basis on which fees are computed and billing arrangements.

An example of an engagement letter is shown in Figure 12–5.

Figure 12–5   **Sample Engagement Letter**

Auditor's Letterhead

Johnson, Cox, and Barnes
Certified Public Accountants

December 7, 19X5

Addressed to Client

Brock Warner
Plainsmen, Inc.
2320 Tiger Blvd.
Lancaster, Pennsylvania 19701

To the Board of Directors:

This letter will confirm our understanding of the arrangements covering our audit of the financial statements of Plainsmen, Inc. for the year ending December 31, 19X5.

Scope of Engagement

We will audit the company's balance sheet as of December 31, 19X5, and the related statements of income, retained earnings, and cash flow for the year then ended. Our audit will be made in accordance with generally accepted auditing standards and will include such tests of the accounting records and such other auditing procedures as we consider necessary in the circumstances. The objective of our audit is to express an unqualified opinion on the financial statements, although it is possible that facts or circumstances encountered may require us to express a less than unqualified opinion.

Objective of Engagement and Form of Report

Our procedures will include tests of documentary evidence supporting the transactions recorded in the accounts, tests of the physical existence of inventories, and direct confirmation of receivables and certain other assets and liabilities by correspondence with selected customers, creditors, legal counsel, and banks. At the conclusion of our audit, we will request certain written representations from you about the financial statements and related matters.

Client's Representations

Client's Responsibilities

The fair presentation of financial position and results of operations in conformity with generally accepted accounting principles is management's responsibility. Management is responsible for the development, implementation, and maintenance of an adequate internal control structure and for the accuracy of the financial statements. Although we may advise you about appropriate accounting principles and their application, the selection and method of application are responsibilities solely of management.

Detection of Fraud

Our engagement is subject to the risk that material errors or irregularities, including fraud or defalcations, if they exist, will not be detected. However, we will inform you of any such matters that come to our attention.

What's included

Figure 12–5   *continued*

Fees

Fees for our services are based on our regular per diem rates, plus travel and other out-of-pocket expenses. Invoices will be rendered every two weeks and are payable upon presentation. We estimate that our fee for this audit will be between $11,000 and $13,000. Should any situation arise that would materially increase this estimate, we will, of course, advise you.

Use of Client Personnel

Whenever possible, we will attempt to use your company's personnel. This effort could substantially reduce our time requirements and help you hold down audit fees.

Other Work

We will also prepare federal and state tax returns for the year ended December 31, 19X5. The fee for tax return preparation should be approximately $1000.

Communications about Internal Control Structure

During the course of our audit we may observe opportunities for economy in, or improved controls over, your operations. We will bring such matters to the attention of the appropriate level of management, either orally or in writing.

Please indicate your agreement to these arrangements by signing the attached copy of this letter and returning it to us.

We appreciate your confidence in retaining us as your certified public accountants and look forward to working with you and your staff.

Sincerely,

Carol Cox

Signed by CPA

Johnson, Cox, and Barnes

Signed by Client and Returned to CPA

Approved

By _Broch Warner_

Title _President_

Plainsmen, Inc.

Date _12/14/X5_

General Planning

After accepting an audit engagement, the auditor begins the general planning of the audit. In the general planning phase, as identified in *SAS No. 22, Planning and Supervision* (AU 311), the auditor obtains a knowledge of the client's industry, the client's business, and related parties. Obtaining this understanding early in the audit is necessary so that the auditor may properly plan the audit. Also in this phase, the auditor considers the possibility of material misstatements, makes a preliminary assessment of materiality, and performs analytical procedures as discussed in Chapter 11.

Knowledge of the Client's Industry

SAS No. 22 (AU 311.07) requires the auditor to obtain an understanding of the industry in which the client operates. This understanding is essential if the auditor is to perform the audit with due professional care. Many industries have unique accounting practices. A regulated industry like a bank has certain practices regarding the establishment of loan loss reserves, and government units use fund accounting; each has certain unique accounting principles. Furthermore, accounting principles vary in their importance depending upon the industry. For example, revenue recognition criteria are quite complex in the construction industry, inventory measurement is crucial in the retail industry, and cost accounting is vital in manufacturing. To understand the client, the auditor must first understand the industry in which the client operates.

The auditor can draw this understanding from many sources. The approach probably used most often is to discuss the industry with auditors who have audited either the client in prior years or other clients who are in the same industry. Likewise, discussions with appropriate client personnel are helpful.

Auditors may also be able to use numerous published sources. The AICPA publishes accounting and auditing guides for a variety of industries such as airlines, banks, brokers and dealers in securities, state and local governments, and colleges and universities. Many industries have trade journals and technical publications that can be quite helpful. In fact, some CPAs who have a concentration of clients in a particular industry subscribe to specialized industry journals. In addition, the AICPA and state societies of CPAs offer numerous continuing professional education courses for specific industries.

Knowledge of the Client's Business

Understanding the client's industry is important for understanding the client's business. However, the auditor must understand not just the industry but also the many unique aspects of a particular entity. To perform the audit properly, the auditor must have knowledge about such factors as organizational structure, product lines and services, capital structure, locations, production and distribution methods, valuation procedures for inventory, and compensation methods. The auditor should obtain enough knowledge about the client's business to understand the events, transactions, and practices that may have an effect on the financial statements.

Review of Results of Previous Audits

Knowledge of the client's business is generally obtained through experience with the client and discussions with other auditors or client personnel. Prior-year working papers usually contain a wealth of information regarding the client and its business, organizational structure, and other operating characteristics.

Review the Permanent File

As discussed in Chapter 5, many auditing firms maintain a permanent file for each client. The auditor often will find the review of permanent files extremely helpful in obtaining a knowledge of the client's business. Because the permanent file includes copies of such items as the corporate charter and bylaws, mortgages and notes, lease agreements, credit policies, and statements of accounting policies, the auditor is often able to gather valuable information regarding capital structure, debt and leasing information, and the accounting principles used.

Tour of Facilities

A tour of the client's facilities gives the auditor firsthand knowledge of the client's production or merchandising process. The tour also allows the auditor to meet many of the key personnel in the entity and gives the auditor a broad overview of the client's business.

Identification of Related Parties

During the planning phase of the audit the auditor should identify any of the client's related parties. In general terms related parties are entities or individuals in a position to influence the entity. *FASB No. 57, Related Party Disclosures,* defines ***related parties*** as

Affiliates of the enterprise.[1]

Entities for which investments are accounted for by the equity method by the enterprise.

Trusts for the benefit of employees, such as pension and profit-sharing trusts that are managed by or under the trusteeship of management.

Principal owners of the enterprise.

Management.

Members of the immediate families of principal owners of the enterprise and its management.

Other parties with which the enterprise may deal if one party controls or can significantly influence the management or operating policies of the other to an extent that one of the transacting parties might be prevented from fully pursuing its own separate interests. Another party is also a related party if it can significantly influence the management or operating policies of the transacting parties, or if it has an ownership interest in one of the transacting parties and can significantly influence the other to an extent that one or more of the transacting parties might be prevented from fully pursuing its own separate interests.

The auditor has two possible concerns regarding the existence of related parties: (1) that all material related-party transactions are adequately disclosed and (2) that all related-party transactions are recorded so as to reflect economic substance rather than form.

---

[1] A party that, directly or indirectly through one or more intermediaries, controls, is controlled by, or is under common control with an enterprise.

Related-party transactions, per se, are not inherently bad. The auditor's concern is that these transactions are properly accounted for and disclosed. Disclosure of material related-party transactions includes descriptions of the transactions, relationships, and amounts due (including financing terms) to or from related parties. In addition, if the client does include an assertion in the financial statements that related-party transactions are equivalent to arms-length transactions, the auditor must examine the substantiation of the assertion.

Analytical Procedures

As discussed in Chapter 11, analytical procedures are required in audit planning to assist in planning the nature, timing, and extent of auditing procedures that will be used to obtain evidential matter. Typically, analytical procedures used in planning the audit focus on two objectives: (1) enhancing the auditor's understanding of the client's business and the transactions and events that have occurred since the last audit date, and (2) identifying areas that may represent specific risks relevant to the audit. By performing analytical procedures during the planning stages, the auditor is often able to identify basic issues regarding the financial statements early in the audit. The performance of analytical procedures in planning vary widely depending on the size and complexity of the client. For some entities, analytical procedures may consist of reviewing changes in account balances from the prior to the current year using the general ledger or the auditor's preliminary or unadjusted working trial balance. In contrast, for more sophisticated entities, the procedures might also include an extensive analysis of quarterly financial statements.

Assessment of Materiality

In audit planning, the auditor must make a preliminary assessment of the materiality level. According to *SAS No. 47, Audit Risk and Materiality in Conducting an Audit* (AU 312), in planning the audit, the auditor should make a preliminary judgment about audit risk and materiality so as to make a reasonable evaluation about whether or not the financial statements are materially misstated. As noted in Chapter 4, audit risk and materiality must be considered in the planning stages of the audit so that the auditor can determine the nature, timing, and extent of audit tests. During the planning phase, the auditor determines the more important account balances and classes of transactions and the areas for audit emphasis. In making these planning decisions, the auditor takes into account materiality. For example, in planning the auditor may note that accounts receivable increased materially during the year. As a result, the auditor might emphasize accounts receivable, sales, the allowance account, and bad debt expense during the audit.

Consideration of the Possibility of Material Misstatements in Audit Planning

In planning, the auditor should assess the risk of material misstatements. Understanding the internal control structure will allow the auditor to assess control risk and thus affect the auditor's assessment of the risk of material misstatements.

Table 12-1	**Risk Factors to Be Considered in Assessing Audit Risk**

Management Characteristics

- Management operating and financing decisions are dominated by a single person.
- Management's attitude toward financial reporting is unduly aggressive.
- Management (particularly senior accounting personnel) turnover is high.
- Management places undue emphasis on meeting earnings projections.
- Management's reputation in the business community is poor.

Operating and Industry Characteristics

- Profitability of entity relative to its industry is inadequate or inconsistent.
- Sensitivity of operating results to economic factors (inflation, interest rates, unemployment, etc.) is high.
- Rate of change in entity's industry is rapid.
- Direction of change in entity's industry is declining with many business failures.
- Organization is decentralized without adequate monitoring.
- Internal or external matters that raise substantial doubt about the entity's ability to continue as a going concern are present. (See *SAS No. 59, The Auditor's Consideration of an Entity's Ability to Continue as a Going Concern*.)

Engagement Characteristics

- Many contentious or difficult accounting issues are present.
- Significant difficult-to-audit transactions or balances are present.
- Significant and unusual related-party transactions not in the ordinary course of business are present.
- Nature, cause (if known), or amount of known and likely misstatements detected in the audit of prior period's financial statements is significant.
- It is a new client with no prior audit history, or sufficient information is not available from the predecessor auditor.

In addition to the considerations of internal control structure, the auditor should consider the following risk factors in planning: *management characteristics, operating and industry characteristics,* and *engagement characteristics.* Examples of each of these characteristics from *SAS No. 53* (AU 316.10) are shown in Table 12–1.

In reviewing risk factors and the internal control structure, the auditor should assess the risk of management misrepresentation. According to *SAS No. 53* (AU 316.12), in making this assessment the auditor should consider the following issues:

- Are there known circumstances that may indicate a management predisposition to distort financial statements, such as frequent disputes about aggressive application of accounting principles that increase earnings, evasive responses to audit inquiries, or excessive emphasis on requiring the meeting of quantified targets to receive substantial management compensation?

- Are there indications that management has failed to establish policies and procedures that provide reasonable assurance of reliable accounting estimates, such as personnel who develop estimates appearing to lack necessary knowledge and experience or supervisors of these personnel appearing careless or inexperienced? Is there a history of unreliable or unreasonable estimates?

- Are there conditions that indicate lack of control of activities, such as constant crisis conditions in operating or accounting areas, disorganized work areas, frequent or excessive back orders, shortages, delays, or lack of documentation for major transactions?

- Are there indications of a lack of control over computer processing, such as a lack of controls over access to applications that initiate or control the movement of assets (for example, a demand deposit application in a bank), high levels of processing errors, or unusual delays in providing processing results and reports?

- Are there indications that management has not developed or communicated adequate policies and procedures for security of data or assets, such as not investigating employees in key positions before hiring, or allowing unauthorized personnel to have ready access to data or assets?

Planning Implementation

After gathering the background information on the client, developing a working knowledge of the client's business, and making a preliminary assessment of risk and materiality, the auditor must begin the implementation stage of the audit. In this stage the auditor determines preliminary answers to the questions of what, who, and when in the audit. Specifically, the auditor determines what audit procedures should be performed, who should perform them, and when they should be done.

Audit Program Design

The *audit program* lists the procedures to be performed during the engagement. (Figure 12–6 presents an illustrative audit program for marketable securities.) A list of planned procedures should be developed early in the audit to provide the following:

1. The appropriate planning for the audit, including documentation that proper planning was performed.
2. Guidance to less-experienced staff as to which specific audit procedures are to be performed.
3. A means of controlling the engagement by determining which audit steps have been performed and which other audit steps need to be performed.
4. Evidence that audit procedures have been completed. After completing an audit procedure, the auditor signs or initials the audit program next to the audit procedure that has been completed.

In designing an audit program, the auditor must consider a variety of factors to determine what audit procedures are to be performed. Such factors as the client's industry, related parties, anticipated assessment of control risk, and potential problem areas must be considered in determining the nature, timing, and extent of audit procedures performed. The key to designing an appropriate audit program is to assess

Figure 12–6	**Audit Program for Marketable Securities**

Item No.	Auditing Procedure	Done By	Date
	AUDIT OBJECTIVE — Existence, completeness, and ownership.		
1.	Obtain and check arithmetical accuracy of a detail schedule of securities, including transactions for the year, classified as to (1) short-term investments, (2) long-term investments, (3) affiliated companies, and (4) other, and reconcile with general ledger. Identify separately marketable equity securities.	____	____
2.	Inspect securities on hand. This inspection should preferably be made on the balance sheet date. Reconcile the information obtained during inspection to the detail schedule of securities.	____	____
3.	Obtain confirmation from holders of securities not on hand or inspect such securities at the custodian's premises.	____	____
4.	Determine whether any securities are pledged as collateral on borrowings.	____	____
	AUDIT OBJECTIVE — Proper valuation and classification.		
5.	Determine that valuation and classification of securities are in conformity with generally accepted accounting principles.	____	____
6.	Examine supporting documents for purchases during the period. Determine that broker fees, other acquisition costs, premiums, and discounts have been accounted for properly.	____	____
7.	Obtain market values as of balance sheet date and determine whether any adjustments to carrying values are necessary.	____	____
	AUDIT OBJECTIVE — Proper recognition of dividend, interest and other income, and gains and losses.		
8.	Check income (both realized and accrued) from securities, including interest, dividends, amortization of premium, and discounts. Such checks could include recomputation, reference to published rates, etc.	____	____
9.	Examine supporting documentation for securities sold during year and check the computation of gain or loss.	____	____
10.	Determine that unrealized gain or loss on marketable equity securities is properly recorded.	____	____
	CONCLUSION		
11.	After performing the audit procedures, state your conclusion with respect to the work performed. If the auditor performing the procedures does not believe that they attained the audit objectives, the auditor should immediately inform the in-charge accountant and appropriate action should be taken.	____	____

the risk of material misstatements for the financial statement assertions and then to link properly these assertions and related audit objectives to the specific audit procedures delineated in the audit program. The concepts of audit risk and materiality were discussed in Chapter 4, and the linkage of assertions and audit objectives to audit procedures was discussed in Chapter 5.

All audit programs should be designed so that audit evidence supports audit conclusions. For example, the objective of the CPA may be to give an opinion as to the fairness of the financial statements in accordance with generally accepted accounting principles, whereas the objective of the internal auditor may be to report on adherence to management's policies. In each case, the auditor should design the audit program to suit the audit objectives.

The initial audit program is designed early in the audit and may need to be altered as conditions change. Modifications of the initial audit program are not unusual, because it is often difficult to anticipate all conditions. For example, if anticipating that control risk will be low, the auditor may include an audit step to confirm a few accounts receivable. However, after assessing control risk, the auditor may determine that control risk is higher than anticipated and increase substantive audit testing. In this case, the auditor may, for example, change the audit program to increase the number of accounts receivable confirmations.

Timing Considerations

In planning the audit, the auditor must not only decide what procedures should be performed (nature) and how many items should be examined (extent) but also when procedures should be performed (timing). Well-planned timing allows auditors to better schedule their time and the time of their assistants and promotes audit efficiency.

In performing an audit of the financial statements, the auditor generally is auditing a time frame of one year (for example, the Income Statement for 19X4). Theoretically, the audit could begin on the first day of the year and continue until the end of the year. In fact, the audit must continue after year-end because the amounts in balance sheet accounts are not usually known until after year-end. These balance sheet numbers cannot be completely audited until they are known. For example, under a periodic inventory system, ending inventory is not known until it is counted and tallied at year-end.

Audit tests are classified by their timing into work performed (1) before year-end (*interim work*) and (2) on or after year-end (*year-end work*). A significant portion of audit work for some clients can be done as interim work. By performing some audit tasks before year-end, the auditor can shift some work from year-end to earlier in the year. This becomes especially important when the auditor has numerous clients with the same year-end (for example, December 31), which would produce an extremely heavy workload unless some audit tasks are shifted to an earlier date. Likewise, if the deadline for the audited financial statements is shortly after year-end, the auditor as a practical matter would perform more interim tests. Most interim work occurs nine to ten months into a client's year (Figure 12–7).

Interim Tests of Controls

The assessment of control risk is often performed as interim work. When this occurs, the auditor assesses control risk for the period reviewed and determines what additional evidence needs to be obtained for the remaining period. In making this determination the auditor should consider the significance of the assertion involved, the specific internal control structure policies and procedures that were evaluated, the degree to which the effective design and operation of these policies and procedures were evaluated, the results of tests of controls used to make the evaluation, the time period remaining, and the evidential matter about design or operation that may

Figure 12-7   **Timing of a Typical Audit Engagement**

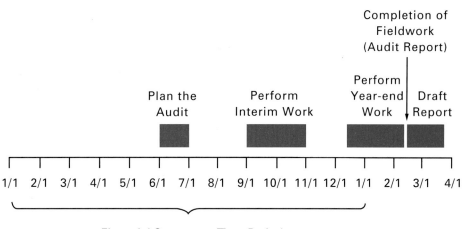

result from the substantive tests performed for the remaining period. In addition, the auditor should obtain evidential matter about the nature and extent of any significant changes in the internal control structure that occur subsequent to the interim period.

Interim Substantive Testing

Sometimes when the auditor finds that the assessment of control risk is low at an interim date, he or she may also perform certain substantive tests, such as confirming receivables, as of the interim date. By assessing control risk as low, the auditor is able to reduce substantive testing. In this case, the auditor has reduced the strength of the substantive test (confirming receivables) by changing the timing of the test rather than by changing the nature or extent of the test.

Although most auditors emphasize assessing control risk rather than substantive testing when performing interim work, the auditor may perform substantive testing at an interim date regardless of the assessed level of control risk. In practice, interim substantive testing typically occurs for the following types of substantive tests:

1. Tests of transactions on balance sheet accounts such as property, investments, debt, and equity (for example, to support the ending equipment balance, auditors typically vouch additions and retirements).
2. Tests of transactions on revenue and expense accounts (for example, vouching all expense charges over a certain dollar amount).
3. Some analytical procedures (for example, computing monthly gross profit percentages).

The auditor can perform these substantive tests even if the planned level of control risk assessment is high. Further, performance of these tests at an interim date is often both efficient and effective. For example, if performing the tests of transactions for equipment, the auditor must vouch additions for the early part of the year anyway.

Staffing

Once the auditor has obtained an understanding of the client and its business and has designed the audit program, he or she is in a position to determine how the engagement should be staffed. At this point, the auditor selects the ***audit team***. The audit team should be selected based on the number of people needed, the experience levels desired, and the technical expertise required. Usually the audit team consists of one or more staff accountants, a senior, a manager, and a partner. Their responsibilities were described in Chapter 1.

One important element of planning is to make sure that the audit team includes personnel who can adequately supervise inexperienced members on the audit, as required by the first standard of fieldwork. New staff accountants often are unsure of themselves when performing audit work because they lack experience and do not completely understand what procedure they are performing, why they are doing the audit procedure, or how the results should be evaluated. Sometimes, staff accountants may mechanically perform audit procedures based on the audit program and the prior-year work papers. Although the audit program and prior-year work papers are certainly good guides, they should not be mechanically followed. The auditor in charge should communicate to each staff accountant that such uneasiness and lack of confidence are only natural for the inexperienced auditor. The important point is that the senior or in-charge auditor should properly communicate with and supervise the inexperienced auditor.

SAS No. 22 (AU 311) places a heavy responsibility on the in-charge auditor for supervision. These supervisory responsibilities should be anticipated during the planning stages of the audit and provided for in the time budget. *SAS No. 22* identifies several elements of supervision, including instructing assistants, keeping informed of significant problems encountered, reviewing the work performed, and dealing with differences of opinion among firm personnel. *SAS No. 22* requires the auditor to inform assistants what their responsibilities are and what the objectives of any audit test to be performed are, and to encourage assistants to ask the in-charge auditor any accounting or auditing questions they might have. When differences of opinion concerning accounting or auditing issues surface among audit-firm personnel, assistants should be allowed to document disagreements. The basis for the final resolution of the disagreements should also be documented. An auditing interpretation that explains the responsibility of assistants when disagreements arise is presented in Table 12–2.

Often, the in-charge auditor will schedule a pre-audit conference with the audit team. A pre-audit conference allows the in-charge auditor to give guidance to the staff regarding both the technical and human-relations aspects of the audit, to establish good communications among the audit team, and to answer the staff's questions.

Using the Work of a Specialist

The auditor may find that no one on the audit staff has the expertise, or would be able to develop such expertise, to perform certain necessary audit procedures. An auditor's education and experience provide an appropriate background for most accounting and auditing issues. However, the auditor may not have expertise in the valuation of certain types of inventories, such as works of art, precious jewels, or mineral reserves. Likewise, the auditor may not have the appropriate background to

Table 12-2	**Responsibility of Assistants for the Resolution of Accounting and Auditing Issues**

Question—*SAS No. 22, Planning and Supervision* (AU 311.14), states "The auditor with final responsibility for the audit and assistants should be aware of the procedures to be followed when differences of opinion concerning accounting and auditing issues exist among firm personnel involved in the audit." What are the responsibilities of assistants when there are disagreements or concerns with respect to accounting and auditing issues of significance to the financial statements or auditor's report?

Response—Rule 201 of the Code of Professional Conduct states that "a member shall exercise due professional care in the performance of an engagement." The discussion of the third general standard states that "due care imposes a responsibility upon each person within an independent auditor's organization to observe the standards of field work and reporting." The first general standard requires assistants to meet the responsibility attached to the work assigned to them.

Accordingly, each assistant has a professional responsibility to bring to the attention of appropriate individuals in the firm, disagreements or concerns the assistant might have with respect to accounting and auditing issues that he or she believes are of significance to the financial statements or auditor's report, however those disagreements or concerns may have arisen. In addition, assistants should have a right to document their disagreement if they believe it is necessary to disassociate themselves from the resolution of the matter.

Source: *Auditing Interpretation: Responsibility of Assistants for the Resolution of Accounting and Auditing Issues* (AU 9311.35–.37), AICPA, 1986.

evaluate certain types of contracts or legal documents. In these cases, if no one on the audit staff has such expertise, the auditor may decide to use an outside specialist.

SAS No. 73, Using the Work of a Specialist (AU 336), provides guidance to auditors when they need to use the work of an outside specialist. When using a specialist, an auditor must evaluate the specialist's professional qualifications, understand the objectives and scope of the specialist's work and the appropriateness of using a specialist's work for the intended purpose, and examine the form and content of the specialist's findings. The auditor should consider a specialist's relationship to the client, including circumstances that might impair the specialist's objectivity.

In using a specialist's work, the auditor has to understand the methods and assumptions used, perform appropriate tests of data provided to the specialist, and evaluate whether the specialist's findings support related financial statement assertions. The specialist's work should not be referred to in the auditor's report unless such a reference would help report users understand the need for an explanatory paragraph or a departure from an unmodified opinion.

Time Budgets

Another element of planning used by auditors is the ***time budget***, which simply establishes guidelines in numbers of hours for each section of the audit.

Time budgets, when properly used, can have numerous benefits. They provide an efficient method to schedule staff, provide guidelines about the relative importance of the various audit areas, give incentive to audit staff for efficient performance, and serve as a tool in setting audit fees. However, improperly used time budgets can be disadvantageous. Time budgets represent guidelines, not absolutes. Just as the auditor may deviate from the audit program due to changes in conditions, the auditor may likewise be forced to deviate from the time budget. Blind adherence to the time budget as an end in itself is not appropriate. The primary objective of the audit is to render an opinion in accordance with generally accepted auditing standards, not to meet the time budget.

Auditing Accounting Estimates

In developing financial statements, entities typically develop *accounting estimates*. For example, accounting estimates are needed for net realizable values of inventory, assessing collectibility of accounts receivable, property and casualty insurance loss reserves, revenues from contracts accounted for by the percentage-of-completion method, and pension and warranty expenses.

Of course, management is responsible for making the accounting estimates included in the financial statements. The auditor, however, is responsible for evaluating the reasonableness of accounting estimates made by management. In planning, the auditor should recognize that in the evaluation of management's estimates the auditor must obtain evidence indicating that

1. all material accounting estimates have been developed.
2. such estimates are reasonable in the circumstances.
3. the estimates are presented and disclosed in conformity with applicable accounting principles.

To evaluate reasonableness, the auditor must acquire an understanding of how management developed the estimate. Based on that understanding, the auditor uses one or a combination of the following approaches to assess reasonableness:

- Review and test the process used by management to develop the estimate.
- Develop an independent expectation of the estimate to corroborate management's estimate.
- Review subsequent events or transactions occurring prior to completion of fieldwork.

Significant Terms

Accounting estimates The judgments management makes concerning the account balances for such items as net realizable values of inventory, accounts receivable, pension expenses, and warranty expenses.

Audit program A detailed listing of the specific audit procedures to be performed during an audit. This listing of planned procedures, required by *SAS No. 22, Planning and Supervision*, should be designed for each audit.

Audit team The audit personnel assigned to a particular audit.

Auditability The determination by the auditor of whether or not factors exist, such as lack of client integrity or an inadequate accounting system, that would preclude the auditor from performing an audit and expressing an opinion.

Engagement letter A letter sent by the auditor to the client that sets forth the terms of the audit and identifies the understandings between the auditor and the client.

Interim work Audit procedures to be performed prior to the client's year-end balance sheet date.

Predecessor auditor The auditing firm that previously served as auditor to the client and has either resigned from the audit or has been terminated by the client.

Proposal letter A letter from the auditor to a potential client that presents information about the audit firm and the firm's ability to perform audit and other services for the potential client.

Related party An individual, group, or company that has the ability to significantly influence the client or its operating policies.

Specialist A person (or firm) possessing special skill or knowledge in a particular field other than accounting or auditing.

Successor auditor The auditing firm that succeeds a predecessor auditor on an auditing engagement.

Time budget A schedule showing the estimated time for each section of the audit program.

Year-end work Audit steps to be performed on or after the client's year-end balance sheet date.

Discussion Questions

12-1. What is a proposal letter?

12-2. Why should an auditor exercise care before accepting an audit client?

12-3. How does management integrity affect the auditor's decision regarding client acceptance?

12-4. What requirements does *SAS No. 7, Communications between Predecessor and Successor Auditors,* place on the successor auditor to communicate with the predecessor auditor?

12-5. What requirements does *SAS No. 7* place on the predecessor auditor to communicate with the successor auditor?

12-6. How do auditors typically handle fee arrangements with clients?

12-7. What is an engagement letter?

12-8. Why are engagement letters important to the auditor?

12-9. Identify the factors that an auditor should consider in assessing auditability.

12-10. How does the auditor obtain a general understanding of the industry in which a client operates?

12-11. Identify three ways an auditor may obtain knowledge of a client's business.

12-12. What is a related party?

12-13. Why should the auditor be concerned with related parties?

12-14. What is the purpose of performing analytical procedures in the planning phase of the audit?

12-15. Identify the three types of risk factors that the auditor should consider in planning. Give two examples of each type of risk factor.

12-16. Why is materiality important in audit planning?
12-17. What is an audit program?
12-18. What purposes does an audit program serve?
12-19. What are the two time frames in which an auditor may perform audit work?
12-20. What types of audit procedures may be done as interim work?
12-21. What factors should an auditor consider in selecting an audit team?
12-22. Why is supervision important in an audit?
12-23. What elements of supervision are stated in *SAS No. 22, Planning and Supervision*?
12-24. Give three examples of when an auditor might need to use the work of a specialist.
12-25. What are the responsibilities of the auditor when using the work of a specialist?
12-26. What effect would a specialist's work have on an audit performed by an independent auditor?
12-27. What is a time budget?
12-28. List four advantages of using time budgets.
12-29. What evidence should the auditor obtain when auditing accounting estimates?

Objective Questions

12-30. What information should a successor auditor obtain during the inquiry of the predecessor auditor prior to acceptance of the audit?
I. Facts that bear on the integrity of management.
II. Disagreements with management concerning auditing procedures.
III. Whether statistical or nonstatistical sampling was used to gather evidence.
IV. The effect of the client's internal audit function on the scope of the independent auditor's examination.
  (1) I and II.
  (2) III and IV.
  (3) I and IV.
  (4) II and III.

12-31. Prior to accepting an audit, a successor auditor should inquire of the predecessor auditor whether
  (1) there had been disagreements with management concerning accounting principles.
  (2) analytical procedures used by the predecessor had been effective.
  (3) substantive tests prior to the balance sheet date had been performed each year.
  (4) other auditors who report on the subsidiaries of the client have always issued unqualified opinions.

12-32. Prior to accepting an audit, what should a successor auditor obtain during the inquiry of the predecessor auditor?
  (1) The predecessor's understanding about the reason for the change.
  (2) A copy of the predecessor's prior year engagement letter.
  (3) The predecessor's knowledge of other auditors who are being considered as successor auditor.
  (4) An estimate of the predecessor's preliminary judgment about the current year's materiality levels.

12-33. After a client has authorized its predecessor auditor to fully respond to the successor auditor's inquiries concerning information that may help the successor decide whether to accept the audit, the predecessor's response is usually limited to which of the following?
  (1) An acknowledgment that the predecessor had been the auditor and the predecessor's understanding about the reason for the change.

(2) A listing of disagreements with management concerning accounting principles and auditing procedures.

(3) Supplying the successor with the prior year's working papers which the successor may review or copy.

(4) Any significant information that may be of assistance to the successor in determining whether to accept the audit.

*12-34. In an audit, communication between successor and predecessor auditors should be
(1) authorized in an engagement letter.
(2) acknowledged in a representation letter.
(3) either written or oral.
(4) written and included in the working papers.

12-35. The audit engagement letter should generally include a reference to each of the following except
(1) the expectation of receiving a written management representation letter.
(2) a description of the auditor's method of sample selection.
(3) the risk that material misstatements may remain undiscovered.
(4) a request for the client to confirm the terms of the engagement.

12-36. The objective of the audit and the estimated completion date are among the items that are generally included in which of the following?
(1) A letter of audit inquiry.
(2) A management representation letter.
(3) An engagement letter.
(4) A comfort letter.

12-37. An engagement letter drafted by the auditor and acknowledged by the client is one method of assuring that the auditor will have which of the following?
(1) Access to whatever records and documents are needed for the audit.
(2) Cooperation of the client's attorney concerning the letter of audit inquiry.
(3) Verification that the financial statements adhere to generally accepted accounting principles.
(4) Enough competent evidential matter to render an opinion.

12-38. The use of an audit engagement letter is the best method of documenting
I. the required communication of significant deficiencies in internal control structure.
II. significantly lower materiality levels than those used in the prior audit.
III. the description of any letters or reports that the auditor expects to issue.
IV. notification of any changes in the original arrangements of the audit.
(1) I and II.
(2) I and IV.
(3) II and III.
(4) III and IV.

*12-39. Engagement letters are widely used in practice for professional engagements of all types. What is the primary purpose of the engagement letter?
(1) To remind management that the primary responsibility for the financial statements rests with management.
(2) To satisfy the requirements of the CPA's liability insurance policy.
(3) To provide a starting point for the auditor's preparation of the preliminary audit program.
(4) To provide a written record of the agreement with the client as to the services to be provided.

---

*AICPA adapted.

*12-40. After preliminary audit arrangements have been made, an engagement letter should be sent to the client. The letter usually would not include which of the following?

(1) A reference to the auditor's responsibility for the detection of errors or irregularities.

(2) An estimate of the time to be spent on the audit work by audit staff and management.

(3) A statement that management advisory services would be made available upon request.

(4) A statement that a management letter will be issued outlining comments and suggestions as to any procedures requiring the client's attention.

*12-41. The first standard of fieldwork, which states that the work is to be adequately planned, and assistants, if any, are to be properly supervised, recognizes that

(1) early appointment of the auditor is advantageous to the auditor and the client.

(2) acceptance of an audit engagement after the close of the client's fiscal year is generally not permissible.

(3) appointment of the auditor subsequent to the physical count of inventories requires a disclaimer of opinion.

(4) performance of substantial parts of the audit is necessary at interim dates.

*12-42. The first standard of fieldwork recognizes that early appointment of the independent auditor has many advantages to the auditor and the client. Which of the following advantages is least likely to occur as a result of early appointment of the auditor?

(1) The auditor will be able to plan the audit work so that it may be done expeditiously.

(2) The auditor will be able to complete the audit work in less time.

(3) The auditor will be able to plan better for the observation of the physical inventories.

(4) The auditor will be able to perform the audit more efficiently and will be finished at an early date after the year-end.

*12-43. An auditor who accepts an audit but does not possess the industry expertise of the business entity should

(1) engage financial experts familiar with the nature of the business entity.

(2) obtain a knowledge of matters that relate to the nature of the entity's business.

(3) refer a substantial portion of the audit to another CPA who will act as the principal auditor.

(4) first inform management that an unqualified opinion cannot be issued.

*12-44. Which of the following is an example of a related-party transaction?

(1) An action is taken by the directors of company A to provide additional compensation for vice-presidents in charge of the principal business function of company A.

(2) A long-term agreement is made by company A to provide merchandise or services to company B, a long-time, friendly competitor.

(3) A short-term loan is granted to company A by a bank that has a depositor who is a member of the board of directors of company A.

(4) A nonmonetary exchange occurs whereby company A exchanges property for similar property owned by company B, an unconsolidated subsidiary of company A.

*12-45. For a reporting entity that has participated in related-party transactions that are material, disclosure in the financial statements should include which of the following?

(1) The nature of the relationship involved and a description of transactions.

(2) Details of the history of all related-party relationships.

(3) A statement to the effect that a transaction was consummated on terms no different than those that would have been obtained if the transaction had been with an unrelated party.

(4) A reference to deficiencies in the entity's internal control structure.

*12-46. Which of the following would *not* necessarily be a related-party transaction?

(1) Sales to another corporation with a similar name.

(2) Purchases from another corporation that is controlled by the corporation's chief stockholder.

---

*AICPA adapted.

        (3) Loan from the corporation to a major stockholder.

        (4) Sale of land to the corporation by the spouse of a director.

*12-47. Which of the following auditing procedures most likely would assist an auditor in identifying related-party transactions?

        (1) Retesting ineffective internal control procedures previously reported to the audit committee.

        (2) Sending second requests for unanswered positive confirmations of accounts receivable.

        (3) Reviewing accounting records for nonrecurring transactions recognized near the balance sheet date.

        (4) Inspecting communications with law firms for evidence of unreported contingent liabilities.

*12-48. What would an audit program prove?

        (1) Sufficient competent evidential matter was obtained.

        (2) The work was adequately planned.

        (3) There was compliance with generally accepted standards of reporting.

        (4) There was a proper assessment of control risk.

*12-49. Which of the following *best* describes how the detailed audit program of the CPA who is engaged to audit the financial statements of a large publicly held company compares with the audit client's comprehensive internal audit program?

        (1) The comprehensive internal audit program is more detailed and covers areas that would normally *not* be reviewed by the CPA.

        (2) The comprehensive internal audit program is more detailed although it covers fewer areas than would normally be covered by the CPA.

        (3) The comprehensive internal audit program is substantially identical to the audit program used by the CPA because both review substantially identical areas.

        (4) The comprehensive internal audit program is less detailed and covers fewer areas than would normally be reviewed by the CPA.

*12-50. What are those procedures specifically outlined in an audit program primarily designed to do?

        (1) Prevent litigation.

        (2) Detect errors or irregularities.

        (3) Assess control risk.

        (4) Gather evidence.

*12-51. Audit programs generally include procedures necessary to test actual transactions and resulting balances. What are these procedures primarily designed to do?

        (1) Detect irregularities that result in misstated financial statements.

        (2) Assess control risk.

        (3) Gather corroborative evidence.

        (4) Obtain information for informative disclosures.

*12-52. With respect to the auditor's planning of an audit, which of the following statements is always true?

        (1) An engagement should *not* be accepted after fiscal year-end.

        (2) An inventory count must be observed at the balance sheet date.

        (3) The client's audit committee should *not* be told of the specific audit procedures that will be performed.

        (4) It is an acceptable practice to carry out substantial parts of the audit at interim dates.

*12-53. When scheduling the work to be performed on an audit, the auditor should consider confirming accounts receivable balances at an interim date if which of the following situations exist?

        (1) Subsequent collections are to be reviewed.

---

(2) Internal control structure over receivables is good.

(3) Negative confirmations are to be used.

(4) There is a simultaneous audit of cash and accounts receivable.

*12-54. Emily Fox, CPA, is succeeding Walter Tyrone, CPA, on the audit of Genesis Corporation. Fox plans to consult Tyrone and to review Tyrone's prior-year working papers. Under what circumstances will Fox be allowed to do this?

(1) Tyrone and Genesis both consent.

(2) Tyrone consents.

(3) Genesis consents.

(4) Tyrone and Fox consent.

*12-55. In which of the following instances would an auditor be *least* likely to require the assistance of a specialist?

(1) Assessing the valuation of inventories of artworks.

(2) Determining the quantities of materials stored in piles on the ground.

(3) Determining the value of unlisted securities.

(4) Ascertaining the assessed valuation of fixed assets.

*12-56. May a CPA hire for the CPA's public accounting firm a non-CPA systems analyst who specializes in developing computer systems?

(1) Yes, provided the CPA is qualified to perform each of the specialist's tasks.

(2) Yes, provided the CPA is able to supervise the specialist and evaluate the specialist's end product.

(3) No, because non-CPA professionals are *not* permitted to be associated with CPA firms in public practice.

(4) No, because the development of computer systems is *not* recognized as a service performed by public accountants.

*12-57. Which of the following situations would *most* likely require special audit planning by the auditor?

(1) Some items of factory and office equipment do *not* bear identification numbers.

(2) Depreciation methods used on the client's tax return differ from those used on the books.

(3) Assets costing less than $500 are expensed even though the expected life exceeds one year.

(4) Inventory comprises precious stones.

*12-58. The scope and nature of an auditor's contractual obligation to a client ordinarily is set forth in which of the following documents?

(1) Management letter.

(2) Scope paragraph of the auditor's report.

(3) Engagement letter.

(4) Introductory paragraph of the auditor's report.

*12-59. Which of the following procedures would an auditor most likely include in the initial planning of an examination of financial statements?

(1) Discussing the examination with firm personnel responsible for non-audit services to the client.

(2) Inquiring of the client's attorney as to any claims probable of assertion.

(3) Obtaining a written representation letter from management of the client.

(4) Determining whether necessary internal accounting control procedures are being applied as prescribed.

---

*AICPA adapted.

Problems and Cases

12-60. (Client Acceptance) Hopson Nance, CPA, was contacted early in December by Clarksdale Enterprises about performing an audit for the year ending December 31. Nance knows that Clarksdale Enterprises is a closely held company and that the company is well respected in the business community. Nance is somewhat surprised that he has been contacted about doing the audit since the company has been an audit client of another CPA firm for more than 20 years.

REQUIRED

Discuss what factors Nance should consider in determining whether to accept this engagement.

*12-61. (Acceptance of Engagement) Johnson, Inc., a closely held company, wishes to engage Mary Perritt, CPA, to audit its annual financial statements. Johnson was generally pleased with the services provided by its prior CPA, Daughtry Bennett, but thought the audit work performed was too detailed and interfered excessively with Johnson's normal office routines. Perritt asked Johnson to inform Bennett of the decision to change auditors, but Johnson did not wish to do so.

REQUIRED

List and discuss the steps Perritt should follow before accepting the audit.

12-62. (Communication with Predecessor Auditor) Morris Glassgow, CPA, was approached by Tiger Company to take over its account. Tiger was previously served by Rob Mann, CPA, who performed a monthly compilation and an annual audit of Tiger's financial statements for the past two years. In discussions with Tiger's management, Glassgow is informed that Mann was terminated because he "spent more time on the audit than Tiger thought reasonable—resulting in high fees and a significant delay in generating timely financial statements." Glassgow immediately requested and received permission from Tiger to communicate with Mann. Glassgow then called Mann and received the following answers to his inquiries.

1. *Integrity of Management:* "The management personnel are reluctant to divulge financial information without considerable prodding. They always viewed me as an outsider, a sort of necessary evil. Because of their attitude I never felt comfortable with the financial statements—I always thought they might be hiding something."

2. *Disagreements with Management:* "Once I was able to secure the information, they normally agreed with the manner in which it was accounted for and reported. But they constantly questioned the extent of my inquiry and analytical procedures during the audit. They couldn't understand why a person who prepared the financial statements each month spent so much time auditing the same information at year-end."

3. *Cooperation of Management:* "As I have already indicated, getting information from these people was like pulling teeth. For example, during my first audit of the financial statements I concluded that the allowance for uncollectible accounts was far too low given the economic condition of their customers and the industry statistics. When I asked for certain accounts receivable information to expand my procedures in this area, I was told that the data I wanted were confidential. I worked around this situation by using other available data, but it resulted in at least a one-week delay in issuing the audit report."

4. *Reason for the Change:* "I assume they thought I was too conscientious—maybe they would characterize it as being too slow. They're perhaps the most frustrating client I've ever had. In fact, I had already decided to resign this audit when I was informed of the termination."

---

*AICPA adapted.

REQUIRED

do quickly

A. Was Glasgow's decision to communicate a bit hasty?

B. Is this a potentially viable audit or would any accountant experience the same frustration as Mann?

12-63. (Successor Auditor) Ann Bennett, CPA, is auditing Fuzzy Company, Inc., for the current year. However, she did not perform the audit of the previous years.

REQUIRED

What responsibility does Bennett have with respect to communicating with the predecessor auditor regarding her new client?

12-64. (Auditability) Coleman Huffham was recently asked to audit Barnes Electric Contractors. He has had several meetings with selected employees, has talked to their banker, and has decided that no integrity problems exist that would prevent him from accepting Barnes Electric as a client. Huffham notifies the president, Mary Beth Farris, that he would be delighted to perform the audit and Farris signs one of Huffham's standard audit engagement letters.

REQUIRED

A. What specific factors regarding auditability should Huffham have considered before accepting the audit?

B. Assume that Huffham has considered the above factors and his inquiries lead him to believe that the company is auditable; however, after accepting the client, his initial review of the internal control structure indicates there is a good chance that the company may not be auditable and that a qualified opinion or a disclaimer of opinion may be necessary. What steps should Huffham take?

*12-65. (Engagement Letter) A CPA has been asked to audit the financial statements of a publicly held company for the first time. All preliminary verbal discussions and inquiries have been completed among the CPA, the company, the predecessor auditor, and all other necessary parties. The CPA is now preparing an engagement letter.

REQUIRED

A. List the items that should be included in the typical engagement letter in these circumstances.

B. Describe the benefits derived from preparing an engagement letter.

12-66. (Knowledge of Client and Industry) Steve Barranco, CPA, has recently accepted Hare Enterprises, Inc., as an audit client. Hare Enterprises is in the retail restaurant business and Barranco has had very limited exposure to this industry.

REQUIRED

Suggest ways that Barranco may acquire a knowledge of this client and its industry.

12-67. (Related Parties) The following situations all relate to Mockingbird Corp.

1. Sale of equipment to a subsidiary. *YES — same co.*
2. Sale of old typewriter to accounts receivable clerk. *NO*
3. Loan to spouse of major stockholder. *YES*
4. Installment loan on sale of product to insignificant stockholder. *NO*
5. IOU accepted from inventory clerk for $20 paid out of petty cash fund. *NO*
6. Purchase of land from another company in which there is an investment of 28% in common stock (accounted for under equity method). *YES*
7. Purchase of major equipment from a supplier who has agreed to sell the company land next to the plant that is badly needed for expansion. *YES*

REQUIRED

For each of the above situations, state whether or not a related party is involved.

12-68. (Related Parties) Shelli Holt, CPA, is the auditor for Montgomery Building Supply, Inc., a closely held company controlled by Brent Hicks and his family. During 19X1, Montgomery Building Supply purchased 50 acres of prime industrial land from Bob Porter, the son-in-law of Brent Hicks. In exchange for the land, Montgomery Building Supply issued 100 shares of common stock to Porter and signed a note, with interest payable in two years, for $100,000. Until this issuance, 1,000 shares of common stock (par value of $10 per share) were outstanding.

Monique Key, controller of the company, received an appraisal from Wayne Rector stating that the land was worth $300,000. Key made the following journal entry:

Land	300,000	
Common stock		1,000
Premium on common stock		199,000
Note payable		100,000

REQUIRED

What procedures should Holt perform in regard to this transaction?

*12-69. (Materiality) During the course of an audit, an independent auditor gives serious consideration to the concept of materiality. This concept is inherent in the work of the independent auditor and is important for planning, preparing, and modifying audit programs. It underlies the application of all the generally accepted auditing standards, particularly the standards of fieldwork and reporting.

REQUIRED

A. Briefly describe what is meant by the independent auditor's concept of materiality.

B. What are some common relationships and other considerations used by the auditor in judging materiality?

C. Identify how the planning and execution of an audit program might be affected by the independent auditor's concept of materiality.

*12-70. (Audit Planning) In late spring of 19X5 you are advised of a new assignment as in-charge accountant of your CPA firm's recurring annual audit of a major client, the Lancer Company. You are given the engagement letter for the audit covering the calendar year December 31, 19X5, and a list of personnel assigned to this audit. It is your responsibility to plan and supervise the fieldwork for the audit.

REQUIRED

Discuss the necessary preparation and planning for the Lancer Company annual audit prior to beginning fieldwork at the client's office. In your discussion include the sources you should consult, the type of information you should seek, the preliminary plans and preparation you should make for the fieldwork, and any actions you should take relative to the staff assigned to the engagement. Do not write an audit program.

12-71. (Time Allocation in an Audit) Pete Doyle graduated from college this past year and has worked with the CPA firm of Washington & Lee for six months. He has worked on three different audits with different seniors and has been assigned a variety of work. In his first audit, he audited cash and spent an enormous amount of time on cash disbursements and cash transfers among the client's checking accounts. In his second audit, he also performed the cash work, but the time involved was significantly less because the audit program did not call for such extensive tests. He also sent out receivables confirmations in this audit.

*AICPA adapted.

In his third audit, he worked exclusively on receivables and confirmed many more receivables than on the second audit. Given his variety of experiences, Doyle is confused about how much audit work should be done in any situation and has concluded that this is totally dependent upon the senior.

REQUIRED

A. What are some factors (other than the preferences of the senior auditor) that could explain the differences in time spent?

B. What could the seniors have done to prevent Doyle from drawing this erroneous conclusion?

12-72. (Disagreement on Audit Team) Pauline Small is a new staff accountant in her first year with the public accounting firm of Foot, Tick and Tie. Small is currently engaged in the audit of Raider Manufacturing Company. The audit is being supervised by Bill Big, an audit senior with five years' experience. During the course of the audit, Small takes exception to the client's justification for a change in the method of computing depreciation. Big, on the other hand, sees no problem with the client's justification and indicates to Small that further discussion of the matter would damage the good client relations he has worked so hard to develop over the past few years. Small points out the fact that *APB Opinion No. 20, Accounting Changes*, discusses the justification for a change in accounting principle. Big states that he is fully aware of the requirements of *APB Opinion No. 20* and wants the matter dropped immediately. Small agrees to drop the matter, but she continues to have reservations about the justification for the change.

REQUIRED

How should disagreements such as this be resolved and what documentation should be provided about their existence and their resolution?

12-73. (Use of a Specialist) For each of the following situations, state what procedures the auditor should perform so that the work of the specialist may be used.

A. Use of an art appraiser to evaluate works of art.

B. Use of a geologist to evaluate quantity of mineral reserves.

C. Use of an actuary in assessing potential pension liability.

12-74. (Time Budgets) Tammy Dunaway is the senior in charge of the audit of Capilouto Manufacturing Corp. At the conclusion of the audit she completed the time budget and had the following significant variations.

Audit Area	Hours Budgeted	Actual	Level of Auditor Performing Procedures
Cash	20	28	Staff
Inventory	42	61	Senior
Receivables	35	27	Senior

REQUIRED

What are some possible reasons for these variations?

12-75. (Developing Accounting Estimates) Pamela Stanford, CPA, performs audits for several small businesses for which she also develops accounting estimates as part of her accounting services.

REQUIRED

How does the performance of accounting services alter her responsibilities under *SAS No. 57, Auditing Accounting Estimates?*

Audit Judgment Case

12-76. (Acceptance of Engagement) Criminoles, Inc., a high-tech security system company, has requested Gene Hall, CPA to perform the annual audit of its financial statements. Having only been in practice for two years, Hall is careful in accepting new audit clients because firm reputation and image is very important in developing his practice. Hall requested the company president, Bobby Falwell, to authorize the predecessor auditor, Susan Burns, CPA to respond to his inquiries related to integrity of management, disagreements with management as to accounting principles or auditing procedures, and her understanding as to the reason for the change in auditors. Falwell was hesitant and evasive but agreed to contact Burns the next morning.

During a discussion with Burns, Hall discovered that the company was in the process of being audited by the Internal Revenue Service and was being represented by the local firm Find, Fool, & Forget. Burns showed Hall the following letter:

FIND, FOOL & FORGET, P.C.
ATTORNEYS AT LAW
2165 CAPITAL BLVD.
Omaha, Nebraska 71204

October 31, 19X5

Ms. Susan Burns, CPA
Post Office Drawer 777
Omaha, Nebraska 71204

Re: Criminoles, Inc.

Ms. Burns:

This firm has been representing Criminoles, Inc., in an audit by the Internal Revenue Service. As of this time, the audit continues and it appears that there will be some additional tax and interest owed with regard thereto. At this point, we have no idea what these amounts may be and I would not try to estimate those figures.

The audit will most likely continue for some time. At the conclusion of the audit, in all probability, we will litigate some of the issues involved.

At the present time no amounts are due us from Criminoles, Inc.

Yours very truly,

Im A. Fool
For the Firm

REQUIRED
1. Should Hall accept the engagement? Discuss. *No / reasons for concern about the management integrity*
2. If he does accept the engagement, what impact would the letter have on the audit? *Significant Uncertainty Contingent Liab. Should be noted on audit report*

Auditing Issues Case

12-77. **KELCO MANUFACTURING COMPANY**

Being the partner in charge, you are in the planning stage of the audit of Kelco's financial statements and are about to select the audit team. You decide to staff the engagement with your newest hire, Joe Moxly, a recent college graduate, Mark Madison who was just appointed to senior, and JoAnn Almer who was recently promoted to manager. Almer, who has worked on several engagements similar to Kelco, has received favorable reviews on all of her assignments but has never assumed complete responsibility for an engagement. Because this is the firm's first audit engagement with Kelco and Almer's first engagement as manager in charge, you suggest that she call a meeting of the audit team next Friday to discuss the engagement. You also suggest that she review the audit programs of other similar clients before the meeting.

REQUIRED
1. List the major points that Almer should discuss at the Friday meeting.
2. Is an audit program required in order to be in compliance with GAAS?
3. What purpose does the audit program serve?
4. How would you design the audit program?
5. Describe Almer's responsibilities as in-charge auditor.

Understanding the Internal Control Structure and Assessing Control Risk: The Revenue Cycle

Learning Objectives

- Describe the major categories of revenue cycle transactions.
- Explain how an entity's control environment relates to the revenue cycle.
- Describe the key elements of the revenue cycle accounting system.
- Identify and explain common internal control structure policies and procedures relevant to sales and cash collection transaction assertions.
- Describe the typical tests of controls for policies and procedures relevant to key revenue cycle assertions and explain how they are applied.

When Deloitte & Touche signed on as outside accountants for Cambridge Bio-tech, the Big Six firm was in for some surprises. Several of Cambridge's European sales looked phony. A couple of sales to a European company—the total was $816,000 in gross revenues—seemed particularly dubious in origin. Auditors immediately suspected the transaction was designed solely to pump up revenues and window-dress the company's statement. Another transfer was worse; the $800,000 exchange appeared to be a Pandora's box of improprieties. Auditors not only suspected it to be in violation of U.S. import/export laws, but a calculated attempt to get around regulatory requirements as well. Cambridge appointed a special counsel to investigate its records, but Deloitte & Touche withdrew from the audit anyway, no doubt with an even firmer conviction that it is incumbent upon outside accountants to carefully verify all company provided information. ■

Source: "Deloitte Questions Legality of Client Dealings," *Accounting Today*, May 2, 1994, p. 15.

Chapter 6 explained that auditors are required to (1) obtain an understanding of an entity's internal control structure sufficient to plan the audit and (2) assess control risk for financial statement assertions. That chapter also noted that auditors typically use a transaction cycle approach to meet these requirements. A transaction cycle is a grouping of related transactions by major area of business activity within the entity.

In using the transaction cycle approach, the auditor obtains an understanding of how the internal control structure relates to a specific cycle and assesses control risk for the assertions related to the transaction classes and account balances in that cycle. The auditor uses the information from the understanding and assessment to design substantive tests for the transaction cycle. This textbook uses the following common transaction cycles identified in Chapter 6: revenue cycle, expenditure cycle, conversion cycle, and financing/investing cycle.

Chapters 13–18 cover the internal control structure and substantive tests for each major cycle. This chapter discusses the understanding of the internal control structure and assessing control risk for the revenue cycle. Chapter 14 addresses the design and performance of substantive tests for that cycle. Chapter 15 explains both the internal control structure and substantive tests for the expenditure cycle. Chapter 16 discusses the internal control structure for the conversion cycle, and Chapter 17 addresses substantive tests for this cycle. Chapter 18 discusses both the internal control structure and substantive tests for the financing/investing cycle.

Understanding the Internal Control Structure for the Revenue Cycle

The *revenue cycle* is the exchange of an entity's goods and services for cash. Revenue cycle transactions can be classified into three broad categories: (1) sales transactions, (2) sales adjustment transactions, and (3) cash collection transactions. The specific major activities in each category are shown in Table 13–1. To understand the internal control structure for the revenue cycle, the auditor must consider the client's control environment, accounting system, and control procedures as they relate to these activities.

Control Environment, Risk Assessment, Communication, and Monitoring

An entity's control environment, risk assessment process, communication system, and monitoring program, as discussed in Chapter 6, are usually broad components of the internal control structure and pertain to all transaction cycles. These components, unlike accounting systems and control activities, do not exist for individual cycles. Consequently, the auditor does not obtain a separate understanding of each of these components for each transaction cycle. Rather, the auditor obtains an understanding of the overall control environment, risk assessment process, communication system, and monitoring program and then relates that understanding to each of the individual transaction cycles.

Chapter 6 discusses how the auditor obtains an understanding of these broad components. This chapter later explains how the auditor takes these components into consideration in assessing control risk for the revenue cycle assertions.

Accounting System

The term "accounting system" is used throughout this book when discussing the information and communication component of the internal control structure for individual transaction cycles. The authors believe that this term is more relevant and understandable in the context of both financial statement transaction cycles and financial reporting. Using the term "accounting system," however, in no way changes the nature or propriety of the discussion.

Table 13–1 **Revenue Cycle Activities**

Sales Transactions

- Accepting and processing customer orders
- Granting credit
- Shipping customer orders
- Billing customers

Sales Adjustments

- Approving returns and allowances
- Determining uncollectible accounts

Cash Collections

- Collecting cash sales
- Receiving payment for credit sales
- Granting cash discounts
- Depositing cash

The revenue cycle accounting system consists of the methods and records an entity uses to identify, assemble, classify, record, and report revenue-related transactions and to account for the related assets and liabilities. To understand the revenue cycle accounting system, the auditor must know about how revenue cycle transactions are initiated; about the accounts, journals, ledgers, and documents used to account for these transactions; and about the methods or steps taken to process them and report them in the financial statements. Table 13–2 describes the common accounts, accounting records, documents, and files associated with the revenue cycle accounting system.

The specific types of accounting records, documents, and processing steps in a revenue cycle accounting system vary from entity to entity. The following two sections describe the fundamental elements of a revenue cycle accounting system common to many entities.

Sales Transactions

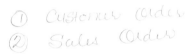

Sales transactions are initiated by a *customer order*, which may be taken in person by sales personnel or be received by mail or telephone. (A credit application should also be processed for an order from a new customer.) The customer order provides the basis for preparing a *sales order*. Typically, when the sales order is prepared, one copy is sent to the credit department for approval and one copy is sent to the customer. This notifies the customer that his or her order has been received and is being processed, and allows the customer to check for discrepancies between the sales order and the original customer order.

In a computerized accounting system, the customer order may be entered into the computer database. The computer may be programmed to compare the order against established credit limits, determine whether the item ordered is in stock, and produce a sales order.

When the sales order is approved for credit, copies of the approved order are sent to the warehouse for filling and to the shipping department for shipping. In entities that use computers to process customer orders, the computer may automatically print a *shipping document* or, for many entities, a bill of lading, instructing the stockroom to forward the goods to shipping. A *bill of lading* details the items shipped, gives instructions to the freight carrier, and serves as acknowledgment that the carrier has received the goods.

The shipping department verifies that the goods received from the stockroom agree with the customer order and the sales order. One copy of the shipping document is filed in the shipping department, and another is often packed with the order as a packing slip. One or more copies are given to the carrier, and copies are sent to accounts receivable to initiate the billing and recording processes.

When accounts receivable personnel receive copies of a matched sales order and shipping document, they have evidence that a sale has been made and goods have been shipped. They then prepare a *sales invoice* and post the transaction to the customer's account in the *accounts receivable subsidiary ledger.* Alternatively, the computer may automatically generate a sales invoice and post the transaction. A copy of the invoice is then sent to the customer and another copy is filed, along with the matched sales order and shipping document, in the accounts receivable department. A *daily sales summary* is prepared, and the total is posted to the *sales journal*. If the company manually maintains a perpetual inventory system, a copy of the invoice or shipping document is sent to inventory accounting to update the perpetual inventory records. In a computerized system, inventory records may be automatically updated when the computer generates the shipping document.

| Table 13-2 | Key Accounts, Documents, and Files of the Revenue Cycle |

Accounts (may be maintained on computer media or hard copy)

- Sales
- Sales Returns and Allowances
- Trade Accounts Receivable
- Allowance for Uncollectible Accounts
- Bad Debts Expense
- Cash in Bank
- Cash Discounts Granted

Documents (may be prepared by a computer or manually)

Customer order   A customer's request for merchandise, frequently in the form of a purchase order prepared by the customer's purchasing department.

Daily cash summary   An internal report that summarizes cash collections from customers on account and from cash register sales.

Daily sales summary   An internal report that summarizes sales on account and cash sales.

Monthly statement   A document sent to customers each month showing the opening balance; transactions for sales, sales adjustments, and cash collections during the month; and closing balance.

Remittance advice   A description of the items paid by check, often attached to the check by a perforated line for easy removal prior to depositing the check.

Sales invoice   A document used to bill customers for merchandise, specifying the description, quantity, and price of goods sold and the date and terms of sale.

Sales order   An internally prepared document that specifies the goods requested in the customer order.

Shipping document (bill of lading)   A document that specifies the date, description, and quantity of goods shipped to customers.

Accounting Records (may be prepared or maintained by a computer or manually)

Sales journal   A book of original entry for recording sales transactions.

Accounts receivable subsidiary ledger   A record of sales and cash collection transactions and the resulting balance owed for individual customers.

Files (may be maintained by a computer or manually)

Approved customer list   A list of customers in good standing. In many companies, orders from customers on this list can be accepted without special approval.

Customer order file   A file of unfilled customer orders.

Standard price list   A list or catalog showing approved prices for merchandise. Departures from this list usually require special approval.

Professional Judgment

Determining Control Risks Alleviates Misstatements

The quality of an entity's internal control structure over revenue cycle transactions significantly affects the propriety of recorded revenue transactions. Auditors must use their judgment to determine where control risks are such that material misstatements could occur in revenue accounts. This means that auditors must understand how the entities process revenue transactions from start to finish, including what accounting principles must be used to determine revenue recognition and how their internal control structures help ensure that recognition occurs at the proper time. In addition, the auditor must evaluate the control policies and procedures pertaining to granting credit in order to determine whether a proper allowance for uncollectible accounts is provided.

Cash Collections

Cash is received from many sources, including cash sales, collections of accounts receivable, issuance of debt, sale of equity stock, and sales of assets held for investments. This chapter focuses on cash collections arising from the sale of goods and services. This type of cash receipt includes both cash sales and collections from accounts receivable.

Payments from customers are usually received by the mail clerk, who endorses the checks "for deposit only" and prepares a duplicate listing of payments received. The clerk then sends one copy of the listing to general accounting and another, along with the checks, to the cashier. The cashier prepares a deposit slip and a *daily cash summary*, which includes the checks received by mail from customers and cash received from other sources such as cash register sales. Copies of this cash receipts summary are sent to general accounting for posting to the general ledger and to accounts receivable for posting to the individual customers' accounts. These records may be posted manually or by computer.

Occasionally, sales adjustments are made for items such as returned goods, damaged goods, and volume rebates. Sales adjustments should be approved by responsible personnel and then posted to the general ledger accounts and the customer's subsidiary ledger account.

Flowcharts of the sales and cash collection accounting system, such as that shown in Figure 13–1, can help the auditor to understand the accounting system. Although specific revenue cycle activities vary from entity to entity, the flowchart depicts a revenue cycle accounting system common to many entities. It shows how the key accounts, documents, and files in Table 13–1 are used to process sales and cash collection transactions and the processing steps involved in the flow of those transactions.

Control Activities

As stated in Chapter 6, the auditor must obtain an understanding of control activities sufficient to plan the audit. The nature and extent of control activities pertaining to the revenue cycle vary from entity to entity. Some of the typical control activities in the revenue cycle are discussed in the following subsections according to the control activities classification outlined in Chapter 6. The relationship of these procedures to sales, sales adjustments, and cash collections assertions is discussed in the section on assessing control risk.

Performance Reviews

Performance review control activities in the revenue cycle often include the comparison of actual revenues with budgets, forecasts, and prior periods. These comparisons may be done for the overall entity, or by division, function, or even individual. For example, a district sales manager may review sales reports by region or by salesperson. In addition, nonfinancial information, such as the number of passenger miles for an airline or the percentage of occupancy for a hotel, can be used to estimate revenues.

Information Processing

A variety of control activities may be performed to check the authorization, accuracy, and completeness of revenue cycle transactions.

Authorization often is required for (1) accepting customer orders, (2) granting credit, (3) filling and shipping customer orders, and (4) billing customers. Authorization procedures generally designate the department or individual responsible for authorizing these activities and specify how authorizations are to be documented.

Using and *accounting for the serial continuity of prenumbered documents* is a common control procedure. For example, many entities use prenumbered sales orders, sales invoices, shipping documents, and checks, and they periodically account for the numerical sequence of these documents. Further, documents should be designed to capture all of the information necessary to properly process and record revenue cycle transactions.

An entity may use numerous internal checks on performance and valuation. These checks may be performed either manually or by using computer programs designed to execute such checks by independent personnel within the entity. Common examples of independent checks include (1) matching customer orders, sales orders, shipping documents, and sales invoices for consistency; (2) recomputing the extensions (quantity times unit price) and footings (totals) on sales invoices for accuracy; (3) reviewing authorizations for credit, shipment, and billing; (4) reviewing an aged trial balance of accounts receivable to evaluate whether customers continue to be creditworthy; and (5) mailing monthly statements to customers to allow them to review transactions recorded in their account during the month.

The audit effort devoted to obtaining an understanding of control procedures for revenue cycle transactions varies from one client to another and is a matter of auditing judgment. However, as can be seen from the description of the accounting system in the preceding section and Figure 13–1, the auditor is likely to become aware of a number of control procedures when he or she obtains an understanding of the accounting system. For example, the auditor is likely to know whether documents such as sales orders, sales invoices, and shipping documents are prenumbered and accounted for; whether shipping documents are matched with sales invoices; whether standard price lists are used to bill customers; and whether the client mails monthly statements to customers.

After the auditor considers the knowledge of control procedures obtained from an understanding of the control environment and accounting system, he or she will decide whether effective audit planning requires additional audit effort to understand control procedures.

Figure 13–1 **Flowchart of Sales Transactions and Cash Collection Activities**

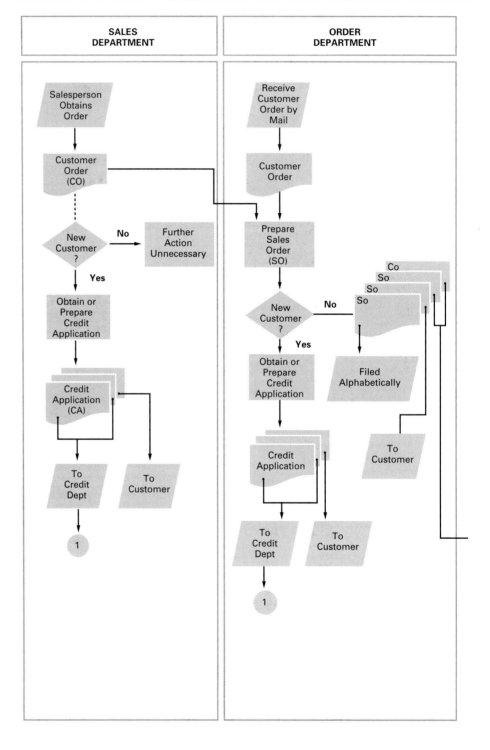

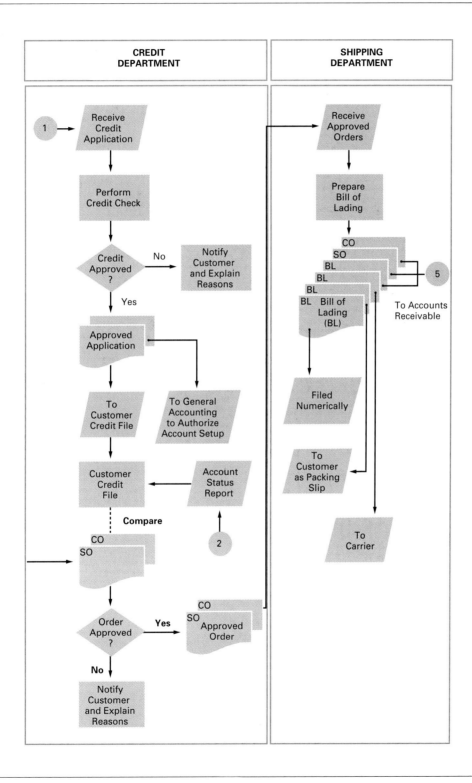

(*continued*)

Figure 13-1 *continued*

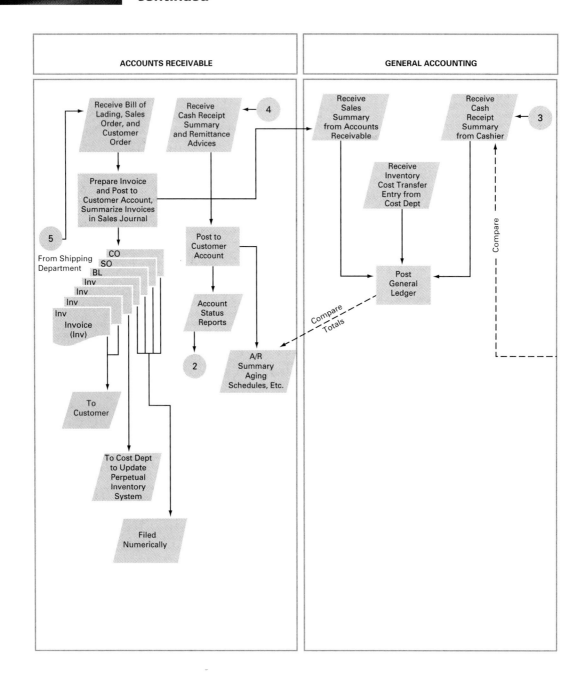

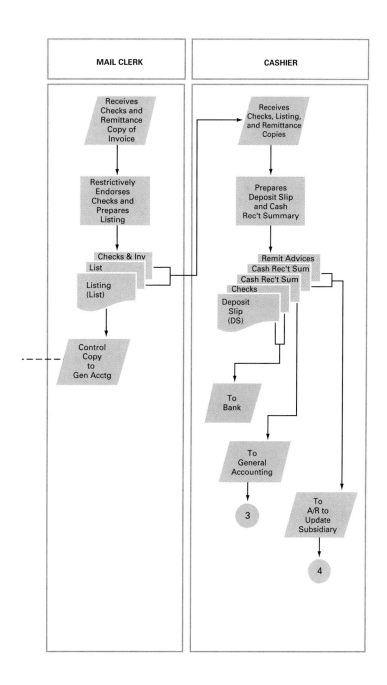

Physical Controls

Entities often restrict access to cash, goods in the warehouse, or goods awaiting shipment to designated individuals. Establishing secure locations for storing inventory and cash on hand is also a common practice. In addition, accounting records and documents, such as sales invoices, shipping documents, and computer data files, are often maintained in protected locations to safeguard them from unauthorized access and use.

Proper Segregation of Duties

Segregation of duties for sales transactions is accomplished by assigning different departments or people the responsibilities for authorizing sales transactions, recording sales, and maintaining custody of goods in the warehouse or awaiting shipment. For cash collection transactions, different departments or personnel should be assigned the duties of recording cash collections and maintaining custody of cash. Effective segregation of duties requires that duties be segregated not only among major departments but also within the departments. For example, in the accounting department, personnel responsible for posting cash collections to the individual customer's account should not post to the general ledger cash account.

Assessing Control Risk for the Revenue Cycle

Once the auditor understands the internal control structure policies and procedures needed to plan the audit of the revenue cycle, he or she assesses control risk for the financial statement assertions related to the revenue cycle transactions and account balances. As explained in Chapter 6, when assessing control risk the auditor evaluates the likelihood that material misstatements will get through the internal control structure elements pertaining to the revenue cycle and into the assertions related to the revenue cycle transactions and accounts. For example, the completeness assertion for sales transactions means that all sales that should have been recorded have been recorded. The auditor uses his or her knowledge of the internal control structure policies and procedures pertaining to this assertion to evaluate the likelihood that the client might not have recorded material amounts of sales.

The knowledge of the internal control structure that the auditor uses to assess control risk for revenue cycle assertions comes from three major sources: (1) prior audits, (2) the understanding of the internal control structure obtained to plan the current audit of the revenue cycle, and (3) specific planned tests of controls performed to assess control risk for certain revenue cycle assertions.

Prior audits and the understanding of the internal control structure obtained in the current audit are usually significant sources of evidence for assessing control risk for many assertions, not only for the revenue cycle but for the other transaction cycles as well. As discussed earlier in this chapter and in Chapter 6, a proper understanding of the internal control structure includes knowledge about the design of internal control structure policies and procedures relevant to planning the revenue cycle audit and about whether they have been placed in operation. In certain cases, this understanding also provides sufficient knowledge about the operating effectiveness of policies and procedures to support an assessed level of control risk below the maximum level for certain revenue cycle assertions.

In addition to using knowledge provided by prior audits and by the understanding obtained in the current audit, the auditor may perform other specific tests of controls on particular policies or procedures relevant to revenue cycle assertions. These tests may be performed while the auditor is obtaining an understanding of the internal control structure or after the understanding has been obtained. An auditor usually performs these tests if he or she believes that the additional evidence they provide about the effectiveness of the design and operation of a policy or procedure will lower the assessed level of control risk for an assertion. As discussed in Chapter 6, a lower assessed level of control risk allows the auditor to devote less effort to substantive testing and results in a more efficient audit.

Tables 13–3, 13–4, and 13–5 relate assertions to internal control structure policies and procedures for sales transactions, sales adjustment transactions, and cash collection transactions respectively. Each table lists some common major policies and procedures from each of the five internal control structure components that may reduce the risk of material misstatements in each of the five financial statement assertions in each revenue transaction category. Each table also explains why those policies and procedures are relevant to the assertions and gives examples of related tests of controls. The next three sections discuss in greater detail (1) how the internal control structure policies and procedures in Tables 13–3, 13–4, and 13–5 affect control risk for the assertions in each major revenue transaction category, and (2) how the auditor performs the tests of controls related to those policies and procedures.

Because the control environment, risk assessment, communication, and monitoring can significantly affect control risk for specific assertions, the auditor carefully considers these components in assessing this risk. For example, management's philosophy and operating style may influence the likelihood that aggressive accounting principles are used to record sales prematurely—the existence or occurrence assertion for sales. An entity's organizational structure, methods of assigning authority and responsibility, and human resource policies and practices all may affect the likelihood that revenue transactions are recorded at the proper amounts—the valuation assertion for sales. Management's analysis of and response to the risks of rapid expansion can affect the entity's ability to properly process and record all of its sales—the completeness assertion for revenue. When an internal audit function exists, it may monitor the receipt, deposit, and custody of cash collections and thus affect the chance that cash is misappropriated—the existence assertion for cash collections.

Sales Transactions

Although a wide variety of internal control structure policies and procedures can affect sales transaction assertions, Table 13–3 focuses on the major ones found in many entities. Some of these policies and procedures may be relevant to more than one assertion; in such cases, they are discussed in detail for only one assertion to avoid repetition. However, their applicability will be indicated in the discussion of other assertions.

Existence or Occurrence Assertion

The *existence or occurrence assertion* for sales transactions means that the recorded sales transactions actually occurred and that the related accounts receivable balance actually exists. An entity might erroneously record sales transactions when goods have not been shipped (or services provided), or it might intentionally record invalid sales. In either case, income and assets will be overstated.

Table 13-3

**Overview of Internal Control Structure Policies and Procedures
and Tests of Controls for Sales Transaction Assertions**

Assertion	Relevant Internal Control Structure Policy or Procedure
Existence or Occurrence	■ Compare budgeted with actual sales and analyze significant variances.
	■ Use prenumbered sales invoices and account for continuity of numerical sequence.*
	■ Independently match sales invoices with evidence of shipment.*
	■ Mail monthly statements to customers.
Completeness	■ Compare budgeted with actual sales and analyze significant variances.
	■ Use prenumbered shipping documents and account for continuity of numerical sequence.*
	■ Independently match shipping documents with sales invoices.*
	■ Mail monthly statements to customers.
Rights and Obligations	Generally not a significant assertion for sales transactions
Valuation or Allocation	■ Use authorized price lists.*

*This policy or procedure may be performed either manually or by a computer programmed to compare information relevant to the control and produce a report of exceptions.

Why Policy or Procedure Is Relevant to Assertion	Common Tests of Controls for Policy or Procedure
■ Significant variances of actual sales over budget may be due to recording sales that did not occur.	■ Inquire about use of budgets and inspect reports on follow-up of variances.
■ Using formal, controlled sales invoices as basis for recording sales helps ensure that only sales transactions that actually occurred are recorded.	■ Inquire about and observe use of prenumbered invoices and inspect evidence of accounting for sequence. For example, examine computer generated exception report of nonsequential document use.
■ Ability to support sales invoice with evidence that goods were shipped helps substantiate that sale actually occurred before it is recorded.	■ Inspect evidence that sales invoice matched with shipping document. For example, examine computer generated exception report of unmatched documents.
■ Customers are likely to report sales charged to their accounts that did not occur.	■ Inquire about and observe mailing of monthly statements and inspect customer correspondence files and follow-up records.
■ Significant variances of actual sales under budget may be due to failure to record sales.	■ Inquire about use of budgets and inspect reports on follow-up of variances.
■ Establishes a formal, controlled record that a shipment has occurred and should be recorded as a sale.	■ Inquire about and observe use of prenumbered shipping documents and inspect evidence of accounting for sequence. For example, examine computer generated exception report of nonsequential document use.
■ Ability to support shipping document with evidence that sale was invoiced helps substantiate that sale was recorded.	■ Inspect evidence that shipping documents matched with sales invoices. For example, examine computer generated exception report of unmatched documents.
■ Customers may report sales that have not been recorded in their accounts.	■ Inquire about and observe mailing of monthly statements and inspect customer correspondence files and follow-up records.
■ Provides billing personnel with a predetermined approved price to charge customers.	■ Inquire about use and updating of price lists, observe use of price lists, and compare invoiced price with price list. For example, examine computer generated exception report of differences between product prices on invoices and approved price list.

(continued)

Table 13-3 *continued*

Assertion	Relevant Internal Control Structure Policy or Procedure
Valuation or Allocation	■ Independently review sales invoices for price list used and price charged.
	■ Independently recompute sales invoice extensions and footings.
	■ Compare budgeted with actual sales and analyze significant variances.
	■ Mail monthly statements to customers.
	■ Conduct credit check or review payment performance to approve credit.*
Presentation and Disclosure	■ Use chart of accounts with adequate detail.
	■ Independently review account codings on sales documents.
	■ Compare budgeted with actual sales and analyze significant variances.
	■ Mail monthly statements to customers.
	■ Use disclosure checklists.
	■ Independently review disclosures.

*This policy or procedure may be performed either manually or by a computer programmed to compare customer's current account balance and sales transaction amount with approved credit limit and produce a report of exceptions.

Why Policy or Procedure Is Relevant to Assertion	Common Tests of Controls for Policy or Procedure
■ Helps identify incorrect prices on invoices before billed to customers.	■ Inspect evidence that sales invoice pricing has been reviewed.
■ Helps identify incorrect extensions or footings on invoices before customer billed.	■ Inspect evidence that extensions and footings have been recomputed.
■ Significant variances of actual sales over or under budget may be due to incorrect sales valuation.	■ Inquire about use of budgets and inspect reports on follow-up of variances.
■ Customers may report incorrect amounts charged to their accounts because of incorrect sales valuation.	■ Inquire about and observe mailing of monthly statements and inspect customer correspondence and follow-up records.
■ Helps ensure that customers can pay for credit sales and, thus, accounts receivable are properly valued.	■ Inquire about credit policies and inspect records of credit checks and account monitoring. For example, examine computer generated exception report of sales that exceed credit limit.
■ Helps identify specific accounts in which sales should be classified when recorded.	■ Inquire about, inspect, and observe use of chart of accounts.
■ Helps identify incorrect account classifications before sale recorded.	■ Inspect evidence that account codings were reviewed.
■ Significant variances of actual sales over or under budget may be due to incorrect transaction classification.	■ Inquire about use of budgets and inspect reports on follow-up of variances.
■ Customers may report errors in their accounts caused by incorrect sales classification.	■ Inquire about and observe mailing of monthly statements and inspect customer correspondence files and follow-up records.
■ Helps ensure that all necessary disclosures have been made and that adequate information has been disclosed.	■ Inspect checklists and evidence that they are used.
■ Helps ensure that disclosures are complete and accurate.	■ Inspect evidence that disclosures have been reviewed.

Several internal control structure policies and procedures are commonly used to prevent or detect such misstatements. Management may budget sales and compare that budget with actual sales. In order to explain an excess of actual over budgeted sales, management may identify nonexistent sales and accounts receivable. The tests of controls that auditors commonly use to evaluate the effectiveness of the design and operation of this procedure are inquiring about the use of budgets, inspecting reports concerning the investigation of significant variances of actual from budgeted sales, and following up on those variances.

The client's accounting system may also require sales invoices to document the occurrence of a sale. Prenumbering these invoices, authorizing their preparation, and periodically accounting for the serial continuity of invoice numbers creates a formal, controlled document that serves as the basis for recording each sale. Such documents help to ensure that only sales that actually occur are recorded. In addition, a computer program or an independent individual within the entity may match sales invoices with evidence of the shipment of goods or provision of services. Such a procedure aids in authenticating that a sale occurred. In the typical tests of controls for these policies and procedures, the auditor inquires about and observes the use of sales invoices, inspects evidence that the numerical sequence of invoices is accounted for, and inspects evidence that invoices and shipping documents are matched by appropriate entity personnel or by the computer. Such evidence often consists of the exception reports identifying unmatched invoices and describing follow-up actions.

Entities often mail monthly statements to their customers. In addition to informing customers of their outstanding balance, monthly statements help the entity to reconcile the accounts receivable records with the customer's accounts payable records. Discrepancies in the two sets of records may be caused by sales that were billed but did not take place. Proper follow-up of customer complaints about monthly statement amounts may identify misstatements in the existence assertion for sales and accounts receivable. The typical tests of controls that auditors use for this procedure are observation of the mailing of monthly statements and inspection of customer correspondence files and follow-up records.

Completeness Assertion

The *completeness assertion* for sales transactions means that all of the sales transactions and related accounts receivable balances that should have been recorded have been recorded. An entity may erroneously fail to record the shipment of goods (or provision of services) or may intentionally not record certain sales transactions and receivables. In either case, income and assets will be understated.

Management's use of budgets to compare planned sales with actual sales can identify misstatements in the completeness assertion for sales and accounts receivable. When actual sales are significantly below planned sales, the cause may be unrecorded sales transactions and receivables. The tests of controls for this procedure are the same as those discussed in the preceding section for the existence assertion.

The accounting system for most entities requires prenumbered shipping documents, with the authorization to ship goods noted on the document. In addition, the continuity of the numerical sequence of these documents is accounted for. These procedures provide a formal, controlled document for each shipment of goods that helps to ensure that sales transactions will be recorded. In addition, an independent individual within the entity may match shipping documents with sales invoices. Such a procedure greatly reduces the risk that shipments can be made but not recorded. The tests of controls for these procedures are similar to the tests of controls for prenumbered sales invoices. The auditor inquires about and observes the use of prenumbered shipping documents, inspects evidence of the accounting for their numerical sequence, and inspects evidence that shipping documents are matched with sales invoices by appropriate entity personnel.

Clients with computer capabilities may develop a computer program to reconcile shipping documents with recorded sales. For example, the computer may determine that every prenumbered shipping document appears in the sales journal within an established period of time. Tests of controls for computer programs are discussed in detail in Chapter 7. However, as an example of one such test, the auditor might inspect documentation related to the computer program and inspect the computer-generated reports of shipping documents not recorded in the sales journal within the specified time period.

The client's monthly statements may identify unrecorded sales and accounts receivable in the same manner as it identifies improperly recorded sales. Customers may notify the client if a sale is not reflected in the statement balance. However, monthly statements are not as effective for the completeness assertion as for the existence assertion. Customers may be less likely to complain about unrecorded sales (understatements in their accounts) than about invalid sales (overstatements in their accounts).

Rights and Obligations Assertion

The *rights and obligations assertion* is generally not relevant to sales transactions and accounts receivable. However, for entities that *factor* (sell) their accounts receivable to obtain financing, the auditor may want to consider whether the client has established policies and procedures to prevent factored receivables from being shown as assets in its financial statements.

Valuation or Allocation Assertion

The *valuation or allocation assertion* for sales transactions and related accounts receivable means that the amounts recorded for valid sales and receivables are correct. Sales and receivable amounts may be recorded incorrectly for a number of reasons. An incorrect price may be charged to the customer on the sales invoice, erroneous footings or extensions may cause the invoiced sales amount to be misstated, or credit sales may have been made to customers who are unlikely to pay. Misstatements in the valuation of sales and receivables can result in either overstatement or understatement of income and assets.

To help ensure that customers are charged the right price, entities often use authorized price lists. Billing personnel refer to these lists to determine the appropriate price. In some cases, different customers are charged different prices. For example, a manufacturer who sells to both wholesalers and retailers is likely to charge them different prices. Exceptions to the authorized price list amount for a customer should be approved by an employee authorized to do so. Also, because prices change from time to time, billing personnel must be sure to use the most recent price list.

An independent individual within the entity may verify that billing personnel used the correct price from the most current price list and may recompute the extensions and footing of sales invoices. To test controls for these policies and procedures, the auditor may inquire about the use and updating of price lists and observe their use; inspect authorizations for departures from standard prices; inspect evidence that the independent individual has verified the prices, extensions, and footings on sales invoices; compare prices on sales invoices to the appropriate price lists; and recompute extensions and footings.

In entities using computers, the computer may determine prices from the inventory database according to product codes and customer identification numbers and may compute the extensions and footings. Because computers perform these tasks consistently, they reduce the risk of mathematical mistakes associated with performing them manually. The auditor's test of controls for this type of computer function involves inspecting evidence that the computer performs these tasks.

Where material misstatements in sales pricing have occurred, management's analysis of variances between budgeted and actual sales may identify them. In addition, customer complaints about their monthly statements may reveal incorrect pricing.

Because credit sales to poor credit risks can cause misstatements in the valuation or allocation assertion for sales and accounts receivable, entities often evaluate a customer's creditworthiness before making a credit sale. Such evaluations usually include a credit check of the customer, credit approval by an authorized entity employee, and periodic review of payment performance and credit limits. As tests of controls over an entity's credit policies, auditors usually inquire about the entity's credit-granting procedures, inspect records of credit checks and approvals, and inspect records of payment performance evaluations and of management's monitoring of overdue accounts receivable.

Presentation and Disclosure Assertion

The *presentation and disclosure assertion* for sales transactions and related accounts receivable means that sales and receivables are classified in the appropriate accounts and that notes to the financial statements contain the disclosures about those accounts required by generally accepted accounting principles. Although misclassifications in the sales and receivables accounts are not usually a major concern in most entities, they do sometimes occur. Credit sales may be classified as cash sales or vice versa. The proceeds from sales of investments or property, plant, and equipment may be classified as product or service sales. In addition, in some entities required disclosures about the accounting principles used to recognize sales revenue can be quite complex and require careful management attention.

An accounting system that includes a detailed ***chart of accounts*** helps ensure that sales and receivables are properly classified. Many entities require ***account coding***, a procedure in which sales invoices are coded with the number of the account in which the sale is to be recorded. These codings may be reviewed by independent entity personnel before recording the transactions to increase the likelihood that they will be recorded in the proper account. The typical tests of controls for these procedures include inspecting the chart of accounts, observing the coding of sales invoices, inspecting sales invoices for correct coding, and inspecting evidence that an independent individual checks the coding prior to recording.

Misclassifications of sales and receivables may also be detected when management follows up on significant variances between planned and actual sales or when customers complain about monthly statements.

To reduce the likelihood of inadequate or erroneous disclosures about sales and accounts receivable, entity accounting personnel may use checklists, and knowledgeable independent entity personnel may review the financial statement disclosures before their final preparation. Tests of controls concerning disclosures for sales and receivables usually include auditor inquiries about which entity personnel prepare disclosures and whether checklists are used and disclosures are reviewed. Also typically included is inspection of completed checklists and evidence of disclosure review by independent entity personnel.

Sales Adjustment Transactions

Adjustments to sales may include the following:

- Cash discounts
- Returned goods
- Allowances or concessions
- Volume rebates
- Write-offs of uncollectible accounts
- Corrections of billing and processing errors

In many situations, sales adjustments are infrequent in number or relatively small in amount, so that tests of controls may not be cost-effective and the auditor may examine sales adjustments by performing substantive tests.

Table 13–4 lists some major internal control structure policies and procedures relevant to sales adjustment assertions. These policies and procedures are similar to those relevant to sales transactions. Because these policies and procedures and related tests of controls were discussed in detail in the preceding sections concerning sales transactions, only their general application to sales adjustment transactions is discussed in this section.

Existence or Occurrence Assertion

The major concern of management and the auditor for sales adjustment transactions is ensuring that recorded sales adjustments actually occurred. Invalid sales adjustments can be recorded for many reasons. For instance, credits for returned goods, cash discounts, or price adjustments might be recorded when they should not be, or accounts receivable might be written off as uncollectible when they could be collected. Whether such misstatements are unintentional or intentional, they cause income and assets to be understated.

To help ensure that only legitimate sales adjustments are recorded, entities generally establish specific policies for granting cash discounts, for returns and allowances, and for determining uncollectible accounts. In addition, entities often use prenumbered sales adjustment forms (such as credit memos), account for the numerical sequence of these forms, require approval of sales adjustments to be recorded on the forms, and have the forms and the approvals checked by an independent individual within the entity. The tests of controls for these policies and procedures are applied in the manner discussed in the sections concerning sales transactions.

Completeness and Valuation or Allocation Assertions

The completeness assertion means that all sales adjustment transactions that should have been recorded were recorded. The valuation or allocation assertion means that the sales adjustments were recorded at the proper amounts. Generally, the policies and procedures discussed earlier for the existence assertion also apply to the completeness assertion. For example, using prenumbered sales adjustment forms and accounting for their numerical sequence helps ensure that all sales adjustments are recorded. In addition, mailing monthly statements allows customers to identify instances in which sales adjustments have not been recorded in their accounts. Monthly statements are also relevant to the valuation or allocation assertion because customers may detect incorrect sales adjustment amounts. Independent review of sales adjustment amounts is another procedure directed toward recording correct amounts.

Table 13-4	Overview of Internal Control Structure Policies and Procedures and Tests of Controls for Sales Adjustment Transaction Assertions

Assertion	Relevant Internal Control Structure Policy or Procedure
Existence or Occurrence	■ Follow established policies for granting cash discounts, returns, and allowances and for determining uncollectible accounts.
	■ Use prenumbered sales adjustment forms, account for continuity of numerical sequence, and require approval for adjustment be recorded on form.*
	■ Independently review sales adjustment approval.
Completeness	■ Use prenumbered sales adjustment forms and account for continuity of numerical sequence.*
	■ Mail monthly statements to customers.
Rights and Obligations	Generally not a significant assertion for sales adjustment transactions
Valuation or Allocation	■ Mail monthly statements to customers.
	■ Independently review sales adjustments.
Presentation and Disclosure	Generally not a significant assertion for sales adjustment transactions

*This policy or procedure may be performed either manually or by a computer programmed to compare information relevant to the control and produce a report of exceptions.

	Why Policy or Procedure Is Relevant to Assertion	Common Tests of Controls for Policy or Procedure
	■ Helps ensure that only legitimate sales adjustments are recorded.	■ Inquire about policies and observe their application.
	■ Using formal, controlled sales adjustment forms as basis for recording sales adjustment transactions helps ensure that only sales adjustments that actually occurred are recorded.	■ Inquire about and observe use of prenumbered adjustment forms and inspect evidence of accounting for sequence. For example, examine computer generated exception report of nonsequential document use.
	■ Helps ensure that a legitimate sales adjustment occurred.	■ Inspect evidence that sales adjustments forms and approvals have been reviewed.
	■ Establishes a formal, controlled record that a sales adjustment has occurred and should be recorded.	■ Inquire about and observe use of prenumbered adjustment forms and inspect evidence of the accounting for sequence. For example, examine computer generated exception report of nonsequential document use.
	■ Customers may report sales adjustments that have not been recorded in their accounts.	■ Inquire about and observe mailing of monthly statements and inspect customer correspondence files and follow-up records.
	■ Customers may report incorrect amounts recorded in their accounts because of incorrect sales adjustment valuation.	■ Inquire about and observe mailing of monthly statements and inspect customer correspondence files and follow-up records.
	■ May identify incorrect valuation of sales adjustments.	■ Inspect evidence that sales adjustment forms and approvals have been reviewed.

ZZZZ Best's Internal Control

During Z Best's fiscal year 1986, it had material weaknesses in its internal controls, including but not limited to:

(1) excessive use of cashier's checks and checks made out to cash, which rendered it virtually impossible to trace to whom payments were made or what they were for;

(2) the control of cash receipts by Minkow (Z Best's CEO); and

(3) Minkow's overriding of existing internal controls.

Greenspan [the auditor] knew of each of these material weaknesses.

When the auditor considers the internal control systems to be weak, the auditor must perform substantive tests of transactions and balances. Greenspan failed to obtain sufficient competent evidential matter and failed to perform necessary substantive tests, notwithstanding Z Best's material weaknesses in internal controls and his knowledge thereof.

Securities and Exchange Commission
Accounting and Auditing Enforcement
Release No. 312, August 21, 1991.

The rights and obligations and presentation and disclosure assertions usually are not significant for sales adjustment transactions. Consequently, we will not discuss them here.

Cash Collections

In many entities *cash collection transactions* occur more frequently and involve larger amounts than other transaction classes. In addition, cash is the most liquid asset. Therefore, cash collection transactions may be more susceptible to errors and irregularities, and most entities establish comprehensive internal control structure policies and procedures for cash collections. Table 13–5 lists typical internal control structure policies and procedures and related tests of controls relevant to cash collections assertions.

Existence or Occurrence Assertion

The existence or occurrence assertion for cash collections means that recorded cash collections actually occurred and that the resulting cash balances in the financial statements actually exist. Although some fraud schemes may involve attempts to record fictitious cash collections, the risk that recorded cash collections are bogus is typically not high. As discussed in the following section, the greatest risk is usually associated with the failure to record valid cash collections—the completeness assertion. Unrecorded cash collections usually cause cash balances to be understated—the existence assertion for cash balances. Because of the relationship between the completeness assertion for cash collections and the existence assertion for cash balances, many of the policies and procedures discussed for the completeness assertion are also relevant to existence and occurrence.

Monthly bank reconciliations are often prepared to ensure that the client's cash accounting records agree with the bank statement. This internal control structure procedure is relevant to the existence assertion for cash balances because it can identify cash recorded in the accounting records that has not been deposited in the bank. The typical test of controls for bank reconciliations is auditor observation or inspection of such reconciliations.

Safeguards over access to cash are also relevant to the existence assertion. Because cash is very susceptible to theft, most entities store it in secure locations. Tests of controls for these procedures include auditor inquiry about these policies and observation of cash handling and storage procedures.

Completeness Assertion

The completeness assertion for cash collections means that all cash collected has been recorded. A major control procedure for ensuring that cash collections are recorded in the accounting records is documenting cash collections at the time of receipt. Prenumbered remittance advices and cash receipt lists are frequently used to document cash received through the mail. Cash registers are a common means of documenting cash sales collections. Copies of these documents are used later to make independent comparisons of the cash collections recorded and deposited in the bank. For example, someone in general accounting may compare a copy of the listing of cash received by mail from customers with the daily cash summary and a validated deposit slip. The duties of receiving cash and preparing the initial documentation should, of course, be segregated from the duties of making entries in a journal, posting the cash collections, and depositing them in the bank. In addition, checks should be endorsed "for deposit only" immediately upon receipt.

An auditor's tests of controls for the above policies and procedures usually involve inquiring about the entity's cash collections policies, observing the cash collection and recording process, accounting for the numerical sequence of prenumbered remittance advices, and inspecting evidence of the independent comparison of the initial record of cash collections with the recording and depositing of cash.

Bank reconciliations comprise another common internal control structure procedure relevant to the completeness assertion for cash collections. Cash collections deposited but not recorded in the accounting records can be identified when the bank statement and cash accounting records are reconciled.

Mailing monthly statements to customers can also help ensure that cash collections are recorded. The customer will likely question any failure to record a cash payment. In addition, management's follow-up on significant variances in cash budgets may disclose unrecorded cash collections.

Valuation or Allocation Assertion, Rights and Obligations Assertion, and Presentation and Disclosure Assertion

The valuation of cash is usually not a significant assertion unless foreign exchange is involved. The rights and obligation assertion and presentation and disclosure assertion also are not generally significant, because the ownership of cash balances and their classification are usually straightforward. However, when an entity has obtained a bank loan and made a commitment to keep a compensating balance, these assertions may be affected.

Determining the Assessed Level of Control Risk

The auditor determines the assessed level of control risk for revenue cycle assertions based on evidence obtained about the effectiveness of the design and operation of the internal control structure policies and procedures relevant to those assertions. The more effective the design and operation of these policies and procedures, the lower the assessed level of control risk will be.

Table 13-5

Overview of Internal Control Structure Policies and Procedures and Related Tests of Controls for Cash Collection Transaction Assertions

Assertion	Relevant Internal Control Structure Policy or Procedure
Existence or Occurrence	■ Use prenumbered remittance advices or prepare cash receipt lists.
	■ Prepare monthly bank reconciliations.
	■ Store cash in secure locations.
Completeness	■ Use prenumbered remittance advices or prepare cash receipt lists.
	■ Use cash registers for cash sales.
	■ Endorse checks restrictively.
	■ Prepare monthly bank reconciliations.
	■ Mail monthly statements to customers.
	■ Compare budgeted with actual cash collections and analyze significant variances.
Rights and Obligations	Generally not a significant assertion for cash collections
Valuation or Allocation	Generally not a significant assertion for cash collections
Presentation and Disclosure	Generally not a significant assertion for cash collections

Why Policy or Procedure Is Relevant to Assertion	Common Tests of Controls for Policy or Procedure
■ Using formal, controlled records as basis for recording cash collection transactions helps ensure that only cash collections that occurred are recorded.	■ Inquire about and observe use of prenumbered remittance advices or cash receipt lists and inspect evidence of accounting for sequence.
■ May identify cash collections recorded in the accounting records but not deposited in the bank because they did not actually occur.	■ Inquire about and observe preparation of bank reconciliations or inspect reconciliations.
■ Restricts access to cash on hand to authorized individuals and helps prevent misappropriation.	■ Inquire about cash access and storage policies.
■ Establishes a formal, controlled record of cash collections received in the mail that should be recorded.	■ Inquire about use of prenumbered remittance advices or cash receipt lists and inspect evidence of accounting for sequence.
■ Establishes a formal, controlled record of collections from cash sales that should be recorded.	■ Inquire about and observe use of cash registers and tapes.
■ Requires that checks be deposited only to company account, which helps ensure they will be recorded in accounting records.	■ Inquire about, observe, and inspect use of restrictive endorsements.
■ May identify cash collections deposited in bank but not recorded in the accounting records.	■ Inquire about and observe preparation of bank reconciliations or inspect reconciliations.
■ Customers may report cash paid to client but not recorded in their account.	■ Inquire about and observe mailing of monthly statements and inspect customer correspondence files and follow-up records.
■ Significant variances of cash collections under budget may be due to failure to record cash collections.	■ Inquire about use of budgets and inspect reports on follow-up of variances.

Evidence about the effectiveness of design and operation is obtained from tests of controls performed in prior audits, such tests performed while obtaining an understanding of the internal control structure, and any additional tests of controls performed after obtaining the understanding. The assessed level of control risk for a specific sales, sales adjustment, or cash collection assertion is used in determining the substantive tests to apply to that assertion. Substantive tests of transactions and account balances for the revenue cycle, as well as the effects of control risk on those tests, are discussed in the next chapter.

Significant Terms

Account coding An indication of the account number(s) in which a specific transaction should be recorded. Coding is usually accomplished by writing the account number(s) from the chart of accounts directly on the relevant source document, such as writing the account number for credit sales on the sales invoice.

Accounting for serial continuity of prenumbered documents Determining that prenumbered documents are used sequentially and that the use of each prenumbered document in a series can be accounted for.

Cash collection transactions Cash received by the entity from cash sales, collection of accounts receivable, issuance of debt, sale of equity stock, sale of investments, and sale of assets held for use in the business.

Chart of accounts A list of all account titles and numbers used in an entity's accounting system.

Restrictive endorsement Endorsing a check so that it can only be deposited in the entity's bank account. Such endorsements are often styled "for deposit only to account of XYZ Company."

Revenue cycle The exchange of an entity's goods and services for cash.

Sales adjustment transactions Changes made to original sales transactions to recognize transactions or events occurring after the sale. Usually such adjustments are made for returned goods, damaged goods, discounts for prompt payment, corrections of billing errors, and write-offs of uncollectible accounts.

Sales transactions Exchanges of an entity's goods or services for cash or the promise to pay for cash.

Discussion Questions

13-1. Why are checks received in the mail usually endorsed "for deposit only"?

13-2. What four important duties should be segregated in the revenue cycle and why should they be segregated?

13-3. What are the significant activities in the revenue cycle for which authorization is important?

13-4. Describe three internal control structure policies or procedures relevant to preventing or detecting material misstatements in the existence or occurrence assertion for sales transactions. Briefly explain how each one can prevent or detect such misstatements.

13-5. Explain why sales orders, shipping documents, and checks should be prenumbered.

13-6. What does the completeness assertion for cash collection transactions mean? Describe two internal control structure policies or procedures that can reduce control risk for that assertion.

13-7. Describe the tests of controls an auditor might perform for the following internal control structure policies and procedures: (1) a client mails monthly statements to its customers and (2) a clerk independently checks the pricing, extensions, and footings on sales invoices.

13-8. How can management's comparison of actual and budgeted sales and follow-up on significant variances help prevent or detect material misstatements in the completeness assertion for sales transactions?

13-9. What tests of controls might an auditor use to evaluate the effectiveness of management's use of budgets to prevent or detect material misstatements in the completeness assertion for sales transactions?

13-10. How do monthly bank reconciliations reduce control risk for the completeness assertion for cash collections?

13-11. What major types of sales adjustment transactions are commonly found in most entities? Which of the five financial statement assertions is usually most significant for sales adjustment transactions? Explain why.

13-12. How does the auditor determine the assessed level of control risk for a specific assertion?

13-13. What does the term *deviation rate* mean for tests of controls? What is the significance of the deviation rate found in applying tests of controls?

Objective Questions

13-14. Which of the following additional duties would cause an inappropriate segregation of duties if the cashier prepares the daily bank deposit?
(1) The cashier receives daily cash mail receipts from the mailroom.
(2) The cashier posts cash receipts to the accounts receivable subsidiary ledger.
(3) The cashier endorses the checks.
(4) The cashier deposits the cash daily in the bank.

13-15. Which of the following internal control structure policies and procedures is most likely to reduce control risk for the existence or occurrence assertion for sales transactions?
(1) All sales invoices are traced to supporting shipping documents.
(2) The credit department must authorize all credit sales over $1,000.
(3) Prenumbered remittance advices are prepared for cash received through the mail.
(4) All shipping documents are traced to supporting sales invoices.

13-16. The controller of RM Aviators, Inc. reviews an aged trial balance of accounts receivable each month. This internal control structure policy is most directly related to the
(1) existence or occurrence assertion for cash collections.
(2) existence or occurrence assertion for accounts receivable.
(3) valuation or allocation assertion for accounts receivable.
(4) completeness assertion for cash collections.

13-17. The use of prenumbered sales invoices is an internal control structure policy that most directly relates to the
(1) completeness assertion for sales transactions.
(2) existence or occurrence assertion for sales transactions.
(3) completeness assertion for cash collections.
(4) valuation or allocation assertion for cash collections.

13-18. Mailing monthly statements to customers is an internal control structure policy that is ordinarily *not* related to the
(1) valuation or allocation assertion for sales transactions.
(2) completeness assertion for cash collections.
(3) rights and obligations assertion for sales adjustments transactions.
(4) completeness assertion for sales adjustments transactions.

13-19. To achieve an appropriate segregation of duties, the billing function should report to the
(1) sales manager.
(2) credit manager.
(3) customer service manager.
(4) controller.

13-20. Which of the following errors would cause a misstatement in the existence or occurrence assertion for sales transactions?

(1) A sales invoice is incorrectly extended for $500 instead of $5,000.

(2) The credit manager mistakenly approved a credit sale to a customer who is bankrupt.

(3) A sale of company land was erroneously recorded as a sale of merchandise.

(4) A shipment of goods in July was billed to the customer in July and billed again in August.

Questions 13-21 through 13-24 are based on the following information:

The following sales procedures were encountered during the annual audit of Marvel Wholesale Distributing Company.

Customer orders are received by the sales order department. A clerk computes the dollar amount of the order and sends it to the credit department for approval. Credit approval is stamped on the order and it is returned to the sales order department. An invoice is prepared in two copies, and the order is filed in the "customer order" file.

The "customer copy" of the invoice is sent to the billing department and held in the "pending" file awaiting notification that the order was shipped.

The "shipping copy" of the invoice is routed through the warehouse and the shipping department as authority for the respective departments to release and ship the merchandise. Shipping department personnel pack the order and prepare a three-copy bill of lading: the original copy is mailed to the customer, the second copy is sent with the shipment, and the third copy is filed in sequence in the "bill of lading" file. The invoice "shipping copy" is sent to the billing department.

The billing clerk matches the received "shipping copy" with the customer copy from the "pending" file. Both copies of the invoice are priced, extended, and footed. The customer copy is then mailed directly to the customer, and the "shipping copy" is sent to the accounts receivable clerk.

The accounts receivable clerk enters the invoice data in a sales accounts receivable journal, posts the customer's account in the "subsidiary customers' accounts ledger," and files the "shipping copy" in the "sales invoice" file. The invoices are numbered and filed in sequence.

13-21. In order to gather audit evidence concerning the proper credit approval of sales, the auditor would select a sample of transaction documents from the population represented by the

(1) "customer order" file.

(2) "bill of lading" file.

(3) "subsidiary customers' accounts ledger."

(4) "sales invoice" file.

13-22. In order to determine whether the internal control structure operated effectively to minimize errors of failure to post invoices to the customers' accounts ledger, the auditor would select a sample of transactions from the population represented by the

(1) "customer order" file.

(2) "bill of lading" file.

(3) "subsidiary customers' accounts ledger."

(4) "sales invoice" file.

13-23. In order to determine whether the internal control structure operated effectively to minimize errors of failure to invoice a shipment, the auditor would select a sample of transactions from the population represented by the

(1) "customer order" file.

(2) "bill of lading" file.

(3) "subsidiary customers' accounts ledger."

(4) "sales invoice" file.

13-24. In order to gather audit evidence that uncollected items in customers' accounts represented valid trade receivables, the auditor would select a sample of items from the population represented by the

(1) "customer order" file.

(2) "bill of lading" file.

(3) "subsidiary customers' accounts ledger."

(4) "sales invoice" file.

Problems and Cases

*13-25.   (Tests of Controls for Billings and Cash Receipts) Your audit of the financial statements of General Department Store, Inc., disclosed the following:

1. The store has 30,000 retail accounts that are billed monthly on a cycle basis. There are 20 billing-cycle divisions of the subsidiary accounts receivable ledger, and accounts are apportioned alphabetically to the divisions.
2. All credit sales tickets, which are prenumbered, are microfilmed in batches for each day's sales. These sales tickets are then sorted into their respective cycle divisions, and adding-machine tapes are prepared to arrive at the total daily sales for each division. The daily totals for the divisions are then combined for comparison with the grand daily total credit sales determined from cash register readings. After the totals are balanced, the daily sales tickets are filed behind the related customer account cards in the respective cycle divisions.
3. Cycle control accounts for each division are maintained by postings of the tapes of daily sales.
4. At the cycle billing date, the customers' transactions (sales, remittances, returns, and other adjustments) are posted to the accounts in the individual cycle. The billing machine automatically accumulates six separate totals: previous balances, purchases, payments, returns, new balances, and overdue balances. After posting, the documents and the customers' statements are microfilmed and then mailed to the customer.
5. Within each division, a trial balance of the accounts in the cycle, obtained as a by-product of the posting operation, is compared with the cycle control account.
6. Credit terms for regular accounts require payment within ten days of receipt of the statement. A credit limit of $300 is set for all accounts.
7. Before the statements are mailed, they are reviewed to determine which are past due. Accounts are considered past due if the full balance of the prior month has not been paid. Past due accounts are noted for subsequent collection effort by the credit department.
8. Receipts on account and customer account adjustments are accumulated and posted in a similar manner.

REQUIRED

List the audit procedures that you would apply as a test of controls for the transactions of one billing-cycle division. Confine your audit procedures to the sales tickets and charges to the accounts. Do not discuss the audit of cash receipts or customer account adjustments.

13-26.   (Identifying Cash Receipts Control Structure Policies or Procedures) Each of the following items describes an error or irregularity for cash receipts.

1. Theft of checks in the mailroom.
2. Granting an unjustified cash discount.
3. Theft of checks by the cashier.
4. Theft of cash from cash sales by retail clerks.
5. Lack of posting cash receipts to the accounts receivable subsidiary ledger.
6. A cash receipt shortage concealed by the cashier who also prepares the monthly bank reconciliation.

REQUIRED

For each of the above situations, describe a cash receipts internal control structure policy or procedure that, if implemented, would prevent or detect the situation. Consider each situation independently.

---

*AICPA adapted.

*13-27. (Internal Control Structure for Cash Receipts) The United Charities organization in your town has engaged you to audit its statement of receipts and disbursements. United Charities solicits contributions from local donors and then apportions the contributions among local charitable organizations.

The officers and directors are local bankers, business professionals, and other leaders of the community. A cashier and a clerk are the only full-time salaried employees. The only records maintained by the organization are a cashbook and a checkbook. The directors prefer not to have a system of pledges.

Contributions are solicited by a number of volunteer workers. The workers are not restricted as to the area of their solicitation and may work among their friends, neighbors, coworkers, and so forth, as convenient for them. To assure blanket coverage of the town, new volunteer workers are welcomed.

Contributions are in the form of cash or checks. United Charities receives the donations from the solicitors, who personally deliver the contributions they have collected, or directly from the donors by mail or personal delivery.

The solicitors complete official receipts that they give to the donors when they receive contributions. These official receipts have attached stubs that the solicitors fill in with the names of the donors and the amounts of the contributions. The solicitors turn in the stubs with the contributions to the cashier. No control is maintained over the number of blank receipts given to the solicitors or the number of receipt stubs turned in with the contributions.

REQUIRED

Discuss the internal control structure policies or procedures you would recommend for greater assurance that all contributions received by the solicitors are turned over to the organization. (Do not discuss the control of the funds in the organization's office.)

*13-28. (Internal Control Structure for Cash Receipts) The town of Oaks Park operates a private parking lot near the railroad station for the benefit of town residents. The guard on duty issues annual prenumbered parking stickers to residents who submit an application form and show evidence of residency. The sticker is affixed to the auto and allows the resident to park anywhere in the lot for 12 hours if four quarters are placed in the parking meter. Applications are maintained in the guard office at the lot. The guard checks to see that only residents are using the lot and that no resident has parked without paying the required meter fee.

Once a week the guard on duty, who has a master key for all meters, places the coins from the meters in a locked steel box. The guard delivers the box to the town storage building where it is opened, and the coins are manually counted by a storage department clerk who records the total cash counted on a "weekly cash report." This report is sent to the town accounting department. The storage department clerk puts the cash in a safe, and on the following day the town's treasurer picks up the cash, recounts it manually, prepares the bank deposit slip, and delivers the deposit to the bank. The deposit slip, authenticated by the bank teller, is sent to the accounting department where it is filed with the "weekly cash report."

REQUIRED

Describe reportable conditions in the existing structure and recommend one or more improvements for each of the conditions to strengthen the internal control structure for parking lot cash receipts. Organize your answer sheet in two columns, headed "Reportable Conditions" and "Recommended Improvement," respectively.

*13-29. (Internal Control Structure for Cash Receipts) The board of trustees of a local church has asked you to review its internal control structure. As a part of this review, you have prepared the following comments relating to the collections made at weekly services and recordkeeping for members' pledges and contributions:

The church's board of trustees has delegated responsibility for financial management and audit of the financial records to the finance committee. This group prepares the annual budget and approves major disbursements but is not involved in collections or recordkeeping. No audit has been considered necessary in recent years because the same trusted employee has kept church records and has served as financial secretary for 15 years.

The collection at the weekly service is taken by a team of ushers. The head usher counts the collection in the church office following each service. He then places the collection and a notation of the amount counted in the church safe. The next morning, the financial secretary opens the safe and recounts the collection. She withholds about $100 to meet cash expenditures during the coming week and deposits the remainder of the collection intact. In order to facilitate the deposit, members who contribute by check are asked to draw their checks to "cash."

At their request, a few members are furnished prenumbered, predated envelopes in which to insert their weekly contributions. The head usher removes the cash from the envelopes to be counted with the loose cash included in the collection and discards the envelopes. No record is maintained of issuance or return of the envelopes, and the envelope system is not encouraged.

Each member is asked to prepare a contribution pledge card annually. The pledge is regarded as a moral commitment by the member to contribute a stated weekly amount. Based upon the amounts shown on the pledge cards, the financial secretary furnishes a letter to members that supports the tax deductibility of their contributions.

REQUIRED

Describe the reportable conditions and recommended improvements in procedures for
A. collections made at weekly services.
B. recordkeeping for members' pledges and contributions.

Organize your answer sheet in two columns, headed "Weakness" and "Recommended Improvement," respectively.

13-30. (Preparing a Flowchart for Shipping) When a shipment is made, the shipping department of BAP Company prepares a shipping order form in three copies. The first copy is sent out with the goods to the customer as a packing slip. The second copy is forwarded to the billing department, and the third copy is sent to the accountant. When the billing department receives the second copy of the shipping order, it uses the information on the order to prepare a two-part sales invoice. The second copy of the shipping order is then filed in the billing department. The first copy of the sales invoice is sent to the customer. The second copy of the sales invoice is forwarded to the accountant. Periodically the accountant matches the copy of the shipping order with the copy of the sales invoice and files them alphabetically by customer name. Before doing so, however, she uses her copy of the sales invoice to post the sales entry in the subsidiary accounts receivable ledger.

REQUIRED

A. For use in appraising the internal control structure for shipping, prepare a flowchart covering the flow of documents reflected in the above situation.
B. List those deficiencies and/or omissions revealed by the flowchart that would lead you to question the internal control structure.

13-31. (Internal Control Structure for Accounts Receivable) Tidy Tiger Company maintains a manual general ledger system with subsidiary ledgers for accounts receivable, property, and accounts payable. As credit sales are made, the sale is entered in the sales journal along with the customer name and number. At the end of each week, a duplicate copy of the sales journal is forwarded to the accounts receivable clerk for posting to the accounts receivable subsidiary ledger.

Cash receipts for credit sales come into the mailroom, where a remittance listing is prepared detailing the customer name, customer number, and amount. The remittance listing is forwarded to the accounts receivable subsidiary ledger. Remittances consisting of cash and checks are forwarded to the cashier, who enters the total amount in the cash receipts journal daily.

At the end of each week, the sales clerk writes a journal voucher for total credit sales and forwards the voucher to the general ledger. Likewise, the cashier prepares a weekly journal voucher for cash receipts and forwards the voucher to the general ledger personnel. All vouchers received by the general ledger system are manually entered in the general ledger upon receipt. Because of a lack of personnel, the accounts receivable control is not compared to the total per the accounts receivable subsidiary ledger.

REQUIRED

A. Cite reportable conditions in the company's general ledger system as it relates to accounts receivable.

B. How might these conditions hurt the company?

C. What improvements would you suggest?

13-32. (Internal Control Structure for Shipping and Accounts Receivable) Steve Rutledge, CPA, is auditing the financial statements of the Opelika Sales Corporation, which recently installed an online computer system. The following comments have been extracted from Rutledge's notes on computer operations and the processing and control of shipping notices and customer invoices:

To minimize inconvenience, Opelika converted, without change, its existing data-processing system, which utilized tabulating equipment. The computer company supervised the conversion and has provided training to all computer department employees (except keypunch operators) in systems design, operations, and programming.

Each computer run is assigned to a specific employee, who is responsible for making program changes, running the program, and answering questions. This procedure has the advantage of eliminating the need for records of computer operations because each employee is responsible for his or her own computer runs.

At least one computer department employee remains in the computer room during office hours, and only computer department employees have keys to the computer room.

System documentation consists of those materials furnished by the computer company—a set of record formats and program listings. These and the tape library are kept in a corner of the computer department.

The company considered the desirability of programmed controls but decided to retain the manual controls from its existing system.

Company products are shipped directly from public warehouses, from which shipping notices are forwarded to general accounting. There a billing clerk enters the price of the item and accounts for the numerical sequence of shipping notices from each warehouse. The billing clerk also prepares daily adding-machine tapes ("control tapes") of the units shipped and the unit prices.

Shipping notices and control tapes are forwarded to the computer department for keypunching and processing. Extensions are made on the computer. Output consists of invoices (in six copies) and a daily sales register. The daily sales register shows the aggregate totals of units shipped and unit prices, which the computer operator compares with the control tapes.

All copies of the invoice are returned to the billing clerk. The clerk mails three copies to the customer, forwards one copy to the warehouse, maintains one copy in a numerical file, and retains one copy in an open-invoice file that serves as a detailed accounts receivable record.

REQUIRED

Describe reportable conditions in the internal control structure for information and data flows and the procedures for processing shipping notices and customer invoices. Recommend improvement in the control structure. Organize your answer sheet in two columns, headed "Reportable Condition" and "Recommended Improvement," respectively.

Audit Judgment Case

13-33. (Labeling Flowchart of Sales and Cash Receipts) Charting, Inc., a new audit client of yours, processes its sales and cash receipts documents in the following manner.

Payment on account The mail is opened each morning by a mail clerk in the sales department. The mail clerk prepares a remittance advice (showing customer and amount paid) if one is not received. The checks and remittance advices are then forwarded to the sales department supervisor, who reviews each check and forwards the checks and remittance advices to the accounting department supervisor.

The accounting department supervisor, who also functions as credit manager in approving new credit and all credit limits, reviews all checks for payments on past due accounts and then forwards the checks and remittance advices to the accounts receivable clerk, who arranges the advices in alphabetical order. The remittance advices are posted directly to the accounts receivable ledger cards. The checks are endorsed by stamp and totaled. The total is posted to the cash receipts journal. The remittance advices are filed chronologically.

After receiving the cash from the previous day's cash sales, the accounts receivable clerk prepares the daily deposit slip in triplicate. The third copy of the deposit slip is filed by date, and the second copy and the original accompany the bank deposit.

Sales Sales clerks prepare sales invoices in triplicate. The original and second copy are presented to the cashier. The third copy is retained by the sales clerk in the sales book. When the sale is for cash, the customer pays the sales clerk, who presents the money to the cashier with the invoice copies.

A credit sale is approved by the cashier from an approved credit list after the sales clerk prepares the three-part invoice. After receiving the cash or approving the invoice, the cashier validates the original copy of the sales invoice and gives it to the customer. At the end of each day, the cashier recaps the sales and cash received and forwards the cash and the second copy of all sales invoices to the accounts receivable clerk.

The accounts receivable clerk balances the cash received with cash sales invoices and prepares a daily sales summary. The credit sales invoices are posted to the accounts receivable ledger and then all invoices are sent to the inventory control clerk in the sales department for posting to the inventory control cards. After posting, the inventory control clerk files all invoices numerically. The accounts receivable clerk posts the daily sales summary to the cash receipts journal and sales journal and files the sales summaries by date.

The cash from cash sales is combined with the cash received on account to make up the daily bank deposit.

Bank deposits The bank validates the deposit slip and returns the second copy to the accounting department, where it is filed by date by the accounts receivable clerk.

Monthly bank statements are reconciled promptly by the accounting department supervisor and filed by date.

REQUIRED

You recognize significant deficiencies in the existing internal control structure described above and believe a flowchart of information and document flows would help you assess control risk for the relevant financial statement assertions as you prepare your audit.

A. Complete the flowchart (Figure 13–2) for sales and cash receipts of Charting, Inc., by labeling the appropriate symbols and indicating information flows. The chart is complete as to symbols and document flows.

Figure 13-2   **Sales and Cash Receipts for Charting, Inc.**

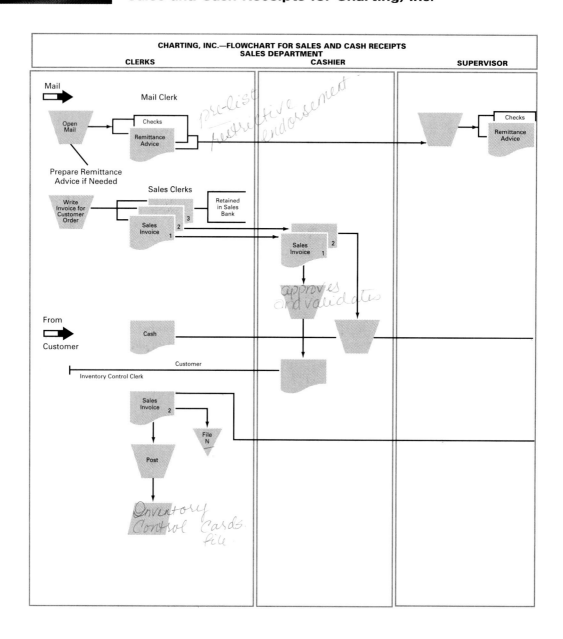

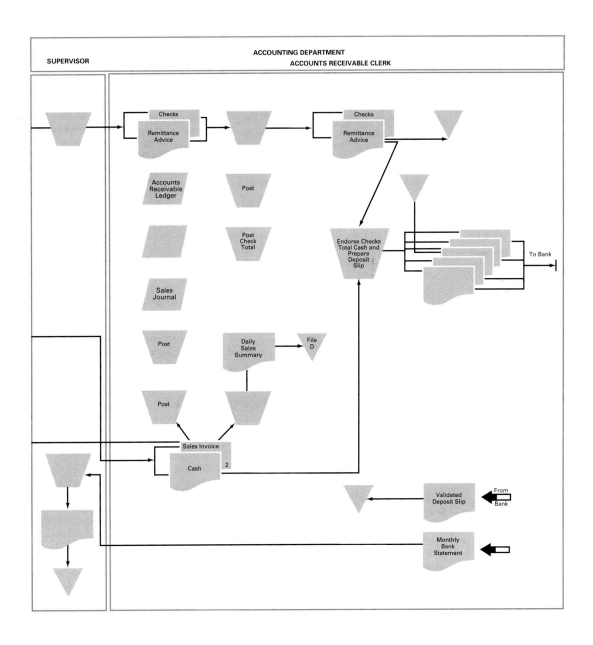

B. Make an assessment of control risk for each of the five basic financial statement assertions for both the cash account and the revenue account. Use a qualitative assessment measure by assigning each assertion one of the following risk levels: maximum, high, moderate, low. For each assessment, discuss why you assigned that particular level of control risk. Your response to Part B should be organized as follows.

	Assessed Level of Control Risk (place check in appropriate column)			
Account/Assertion	Maximum	High	Moderate	Low
Cash				
Existence				
Completeness				
Valuation				
Rights and Obligations				
Presentation and Disclosure				
Revenue				
✓Existence				
Completeness				
Valuation				
Rights and Obligations				
Presentation and Disclosure ✓				

Foreign Exchange (handwritten note)

Auditing Issues Case

13-34. KELCO MANUFACTURING COMPANY

Kelco currently sells its products to large retailers. In an effort to increase sales, Kelco opened four factory outlet stores during the second quarter of 19X8. Because Kelco's president Steve Cook wants to minimize the possibility of theft by employees, he has asked you to recommend procedures that should be implemented related to the cash sales of the outlet stores. Additionally, Cook requests that you make recommendations for a new billing and collection system related to retailer sales.

REQUIRED
1. Set up an internal control structure for cash sales of the factory outlets.
2. Set up a collection system for sales to retailers.

Chapter *14*

Substantive Tests of Cash Balances and the Revenue Cycle

Learning Objectives

- Describe common substantive audit tests for cash.
- State the audit objectives and procedures for cash counts.
- Identify the audit procedures for a bank reconciliation and the cutoff bank statements.
- Define *kiting* and its relationship to a bank transfer schedule.
- Discuss the purpose of a proof of cash.
- Identify common substantive audit tests for sales.
- Describe common substantive audit tests for accounts receivable.
- Identify the audit requirements for confirmation of receivables.
- Discuss how the auditor can vary the nature, timing, and extent of receivable confirmations.

L ike a lot of newfangled office equipment, the fax machine has made doing business easier and more convenient. But for auditors who used to lament having to use courier services or the U.S. Postal Service, fax machines have also led to problems that can turn into major headaches. For example, faxed audit confirmations have become commonplace. And though it may sound like spy technology, fax machines can be preprogrammed to mistransmit numbers. It's also easy to erase some types of fax paper, and many varieties fade quickly. Fortunately, there are available remedies. Fax contents can be confirmed by phone or with receiving machines that actually "pull" faxes instead of simply accepting transmissions. Also, instituting an office policy where everyone—from secretaries to members of the board—immediately makes copies of faxes can help. But the difficulty with faxes highlights a bedrock auditing fundamental: Never rely on a single source for an audit confirmation without conducting other corroborating procedures. ∎

Source: Donald J. Cockburn, "FAX Magic" *Ca Magazine*, May 1993, pp. 57, 58.

The preceding chapter addressed the internal control structure and examined how to assess control risk for the ***revenue cycle***. This chapter discusses the design and performance of substantive tests for that cycle. Substantive tests, as explained in Chapter 5, are auditing procedures performed to detect material dollar or disclosure misstatements in the financial statements. Both substantive tests and tests of controls are directed toward financial statement assertions. Substantive tests differ from tests of controls in that tests of controls are used to *evaluate the likelihood* that material dollar or disclosure misstatements will occur in financial statement assertions. Substantive tests are used to *detect* material misstatements that have occurred.

The third standard of fieldwork requires the auditor to gather sufficient competent evidential matter to reduce to an acceptably low level the risk of a material misstatement in the financial statement assertions. To accomplish this, the auditor generally applies the following process:

1. Assess the inherent risk and control risk for a specific financial statement assertion.
2. Select the audit technique(s), as discussed in Chapter 5, that will most effectively and efficiently provide evidence about those assertions.
3. Design the substantive audit procedures using the designated audit techniques.

Audit of Cash Balances

Cash balances include cash on hand, cash in bank accounts, petty cash funds, and other imprest accounts such as payroll. Cash, of course, is critical to the operation of any business and is typically the focal point of an entity's operations. Cash flows into the company through sales and collections of receivables; it flows out through purchases and payments of expenses and accounts payable. Not only is the cash account affected by a large amount of activity, it also is an asset very susceptible to embezzlement. Although cash generally is a small percentage of total assets, it is a high-risk asset because of its liquidity, its desirability, and the high activity in cash accounts. As a consequence, the auditor generally spends more time on the audit of cash balances than on other assets that may have larger dollar balances. However, auditors often overaudit cash, because of tradition or client expectations, by searching for immaterial misstatements beyond their responsibilities under professional standards.

Objectives of the Audit of Cash

The overall objective of the audit of cash is to determine that cash is fairly presented in conformity with generally accepted accounting principles. In most audits, the primary assertions that generate audit risk for cash are existence or occurrence, completeness, rights and obligations, and presentation and disclosure. Valuation is generally not a major concern in the audit of cash because the financial statements are presented in monetary units; valuation of cash is typically a problem only if conversion to or from foreign currencies is involved.

Substantive Audit Tests

Numerous substantive audit tests provide a fair presentation of cash balances. Of course, the nature, timing, and extent of these tests depend upon the overall risk level of the client (as discussed in Chapter 4) and the assessed levels of control risk (as discussed in Chapters 6 and 13). If the assessed levels of control risk are relatively low, the nature, timing, and extent of the substantive audit tests can be modified.

The most common substantive audit tests for cash balances include cash counts, footing of cash journals and tracing of postings to the general ledger, bank confirmations and cutoff bank statements, bank transfer schedules, and proofs of cash. Table 14–1 summarizes these substantive audit tests.

Table 14–1   **Common Substantive Audit Tests for Cash**

Common Audit Tests	Technique	Type of Test	Assertions
Perform counts of cash on hand	Physical examination	Test of balances	Existence or occurrence Rights and obligations Completeness
Foot cash journals and trace to posting in ledger	Reperformance	Test of transactions	Existence or occurrence Completeness
Obtain bank confirmation and cutoff bank statement	Confirmation Reconciliation	Test of balances	Existence or occurrence Rights and obligations Completeness Presentation and disclosure
Prepare bank transfer schedule	Reconciliation	Test of transactions	Existence or occurrence Completeness
Prepare proof of cash	Reconciliation	Test of transactions	Existence or occurrence Completeness Rights and obligations

Cash Counts

Counts of cash on hand generally include undeposited cash receipts, petty cash funds, and change funds. In performing a cash count, the auditor must ascertain that all cash on hand is controlled until the cash count is finished. This procedure prevents the client from shifting cash from one location to another so that cash would be erroneously counted more than once by the auditor. To prevent this from happening, auditors often control cash by sealing cash boxes until all cash is counted, and they often require other auditors to go simultaneously to all locations where cash is on hand.

Whenever performing a cash count, the auditor should insist that the cash custodian be present throughout the count to preclude the client from blaming any cash shortage on the auditor. At the conclusion of the cash count, the auditor should require the custodian to sign an acknowledgment that all funds were returned intact to the custodian.

During a cash count, the auditor should also establish control over all negotiable assets, such as securities, investments, and notes receivable. Without control, these negotiable assets may be used as collateral to generate cash funds to cover up cash shortages.

In addition to undeposited cash receipts, many companies maintain cash on hand by using imprest funds, including petty cash funds and change funds. Imprest funds are set up with a specific balance and one individual is responsible for the fund. These funds generally are separated from other cash sources. For example, a custodian controls the petty cash fund. At any given time, the cash in the petty cash fund plus receipts for payments from the fund should equal the imprest total. When the cash balance in petty cash becomes small, the custodian receives a reimbursement from the general cash account.

Petty cash funds are frequently counted on a surprise basis, often before the balance sheet date. As with other cash counts, the auditor should maintain control of the count, insist that the custodian be present throughout the count, and obtain a signed receipt upon completion of the count. Unreimbursed expenses that are included as part of the petty cash balance should be evaluated because they represent unrecorded disbursements.

From an audit efficiency viewpoint, cash counts may be unnecessary. In fact, in many audits cash is not counted. Cash generally is counted only when the cash on hand is material. Examples of entities with material cash on hand include banks, credit unions, and casinos.

Footing Cash Journals and Tracing to Postings in General Ledger

One common audit test for cash is to foot the cash receipts journal and cash disbursements journal and trace these totals to the posting in the cash account in the general ledger. Monthly totals of the columns of each journal should be traced to the appropriate general ledger accounts. For example, monthly totals of the cash receipts journal should be traced both to the posting in the cash account and to the posting in the accounts receivable control account.

This test is classified as a test of transactions and may be either a substantive audit test or a test of controls, depending upon the purpose of the test. This test provides evidence that cash transactions, both disbursements and receipts, have been recorded properly throughout the year. Of course, if the ending balances in the cash accounts have been adequately supported, this test may be unnecessary, because misstatements in posting of cash receipts and cash disbursements would be reflected as a misstatement in the ending cash balance.

Auditing Revenue

ZZZZ Best Co. filed financial statements with the Securities and Exchange Commission in October and November 1986. These financial statements contained numerous misrepresentations, including one that Z Best received $5 million for the first quarter of 1986, 45% of which was from insurance restoration contracts. In addition, Z Best reported $5 million of revenue for the first quarter of 1987, 86% of which was from insurance restoration contracts. As it turned out, Z Best's insurance restoration business was almost entirely fictitious.

Representatives of Z Best posed as agents of those granting the restoration contracts and guided the auditor on a tour of a building which had purportedly just had $7 million of insurance restoration work completed by Z Best. In fact, no restoration work had been performed. The building was actually a new structure under construction and the Z Best representatives bribed the security personnel to allow them to show the building to the auditor on a weekend.

The following excerpts relate to the Z Best case.

ZZZZ BEST CO. GETS CONTRACT

Reseda, Calif.—ZZZZ Best Co. said it received a $13.8 million restoration contract for carpeting and related work from Assured Property Management, Sacramento, Calif., and Interstate Appraisal Services, Inc., Culver City, Calif.

> Wall Street Journal
> May 19, 1987

"The ZZZZ Best prospectus told the public that revenues and earnings from insurance restoration contracts were skyrocketing but did not reveal that the contracts were completely fictitious. Where were the independent auditors and the others that are paid to alert the public to fraud and deceit?"

> Representative John D. Dingell
> Chairman, U.S. Committee on
> Energy and Commerce, House of
> Representatives, U.S.
> Government Printing Office,
> Washington, D.C., 1988
> (As quoted in Failure of ZZZZ
> Best Co. Hearings of the
> Subcommittee on Oversight)

Financial Institution Confirmations and Related Tests

Probably the most common substantive audit tests for cash involve the bank reconciliation as of year-end. Most entities reconcile their bank accounts with the cash ledger balances monthly. Numerous procedures may be performed on a client's bank reconciliation. Frequently these procedures include confirming various arrangements with banks and other financial institutions and obtaining a cutoff bank statement.

Financial Institution Confirmations   In many audits, the auditor confirms the client's deposit and loan balances in most financial institutions with which the client has done business during the financial statement period. In addition, because financial institutions now offer a wide array of arrangements ranging from compensating balances and lines of credit to futures contracts, the auditor may also confirm these other arrangements. Figure 14–1 lists some of the financial arrangements clients may make with financial institutions, which auditors may wish to confirm.

The auditor confirms deposit and loan balances by using a standard confirmation form. That form, illustrated in Figure 14–2, has been approved by the American Bankers Association, the AICPA, and the Bank Administration Institute. As with other confirmations, the request must be signed by the client; however, the confirmation should be mailed and controlled by the auditor and returned directly to

Figure 14–1	**Examples of Client Arrangements Auditors May Confirm with Financial Institutions**

- Compensating balances
- Automatic investment services
- Bankers' acceptances
- Cash management services
- Commitments to purchase foreign currencies and U.S. dollar exchange
- Cutoff account statements
- Futures and forward contracts

- Import or export letters of credit
- Listing of authorized signers
- Loan agreements and related covenants
- Securities and other items held in safekeeping on behalf of the client
- Standby contracts, letters of credit, and similar arrangements

the auditor. The form is generally prepared in duplicate so that the financial institution can retain the copy and return the original to the auditor. If the financial institution does not respond to a confirmation request, the auditor will generally send a second request and perhaps have the client telephone the bank to ask that the confirmation be completed.

Auditors decide whether to send standard confirmation requests to financial institutions based on their assessments of the inherent and control risks for the existence, completeness, rights and obligations, and presentation and disclosure assertions for cash. If these risks are low, auditors often decide not to send confirmation requests. When these risks are moderate or high, auditors usually send such requests.

As shown in Figure 14–2, the standard confirmation request includes two major components. Item 1 concerns cash balances (deposits) and provides evidence of cash accounts per the financial institution's records and interest rates on interest-bearing accounts. Item 2 represents confirmation of loan amounts, accrued interest, due dates, and the existence of collateral. This information is useful in examining notes payable.

The auditor frequently includes account names and numbers under items 1 and 2 when testing the existence assertion. However, if the auditor has assigned a high degree of risk to the completeness assertion for either cash or loan balances, including that information could be inappropriate because it may lead the financial institution to omit information on accounts and activities not listed in the confirmation request.

Even though the standard form is not designed to seek information not appearing on the request, it does ask financial institution employees to indicate any other deposits or loans that come to their attention while completing the form. However, because the employee is not asked to perform a comprehensive search, the auditor cannot rely on the response to provide all evidence about the completeness assertion for cash and loans. In addition, the standard confirmation form is frequently completed by employees using a database that provides the dollar amount of deposit and loan balances but that does not contain information about other arrangements a client has with the institution. Employees responsible for completing these forms are often unaware of these other financial relationships and thus cannot provide adequate information for other than deposit and loan balances.

Figure 14-2   **Standard Financial Institution Confirmation Request**

STANDARD FORM TO CONFIRM ACCOUNT
BALANCE INFORMATION WITH FINANCIAL INSTITUTIONS

ORIGINAL
To be mailed to accountant

CUSTOMER NAME

We have provided to our accountants the following information as of

the close of business on _____ , 19 ____ ,
regarding our deposit and loan balances. Please confirm the accuracy
of the information, noting any exceptions to the information provided.
If the balances have been left blank, please complete this from by
furnishing the balance in the appropriate space below." Although we
do not request nor expect you to conduct a comprehensive, detailed
search of your records, if during the process of completing this confirmation additional information about other deposit and loan accounts
we may have with you comes to your attention, please include such
information below. Please use the enclosed envelope to return the
form directly to our accountants.

Financial
Institution's
Name and
Address

[ ]

[ ]

1. At the close of business on the date listed above, our records indicated the following deposit balance(s):

ACCOUNT NAME	ACCOUNT NO.	INTEREST RATE	BALANCE

2. We were directly liable to the financial institution for loans at the close of business on the date listed above as follows:

ACCOUNT NO./ DESCRIPTION	BALANCE*	DATE DUE	INTEREST RATE	DATE THROUGH WHICH INTEREST IS PAID	DESCRIPTION OF COLLATERAL

_____   _____
(Customer's Authorized Signature)   (Date)

The information presented above by the customer is in agreement with our records. Although we have not conducted a
comprehensive, detailed search of our records, no other deposit or loan accounts have come to our attention except as noted below.

_____   _____
(Financial Institution Authorized Signature)   (Date)

_____
(Title)

EXCEPTIONS AND/OR COMMENTS

Please return this form directly to our accountants: [   ]

* Ordinarily, balances are intentionally left blank if they are not
available at the time the form is prepared.   [   ]

Approved 1990 by American Bankers Association, American Institute of Certified Public Accountants, and Bank Administration
Institute. Additional forms available from: AICPA - Order Department, P.O. Box 1003, NY, NY. 10108-1003   D451 5951

When the auditor believes additional evidence is needed about other client arrangements with financial institutions, the auditor should send a separate confirmation letter to the institution. For example, the auditor might want to confirm
arrangements such as compensating balances, lines of credit, or contingent liabilities.
Auditors decide whether to send separate confirmation letters based on their understanding of the types of arrangements that exist between the client and financial
institutions and their assessment of the inherent and control risks for material accounts, transactions, or agreements related to these arrangements.

| Figure 14-3 | Illustrative Letter for Confirmation of Contingent Liabilities |

Audit Client, Inc.
123 Three Bears Road
Primetown, USA 12345

February 28, 19X5

Ms. Beth B. Banker
First Standard Bank
Anytown, USA 00000

Dear Ms. Banker:

In connection with an audit of the financial statements of Audit Client, Inc., as of December 31, 19X4, and for the year then ended, we have advised our independent auditors of the information listed below, which we believe is a complete and accurate description of our contingent liabilities, including oral and written guarantees, with your financial institution. Although we do not request nor expect you to conduct a comprehensive, detailed search of your records, if during the process of completing this confirmation additional information about other contingent liabilities, including oral and written guarantees, between Audit Client, Inc., and your financial institution comes to your attention, please include such information below.

Name of Maker	Date of Note	Due Date	Current Balance
Oak Brook Products	6-30-W3	7-1-X6	$325,000

Interest Rate	Date Through Which Interest Is Paid	Description of Collateral	Description of Purpose of Note
9.80%	12-31-X4	Title to Oak Brook's plant and equipment	To finance plant addition

When the auditor sends a separate confirmation letter, it should be signed by the client and addressed to the financial institution official who is responsible for the client's relationship with that institution or who is knowledgeable about the specific transactions or arrangements. The letter in Figure 14–3 illustrates requests for information about contingent liabilities. This letter can also be used as a model for letters confirming the other types of financial arrangements shown in Figure 14–1.

Obtaining Bank Reconciliations and Performing Audit Procedures Most entities prepare a bank reconciliation monthly. This reconciliation

| Figure 14-3 | *continued* |

Information related to oral and written guarantees is as follows:

No additional contingent liabilities, including oral and written guarantees, exist between Audit Credit, Inc. and First Standard Bank.

Please confirm whether the information about contingent liabilities presented above is correct by signing below and returning this letter directly to our independent auditors, Wright & True, CPAs, 321 Fair Lane, Anytown, USA 00000.

Sincerely,

Audit Client, Inc.

By: _____
    I. M. Ballance

Dear Wright & True, CPAs:

The above information listing contingent liabilities, including oral and written guarantees, agrees with the records of this financial institution. Although we have not conducted a comprehensive, detailed search of our records, no information about other contingent liabilities, including oral and written guarantees, came to our attention. (Note exceptions below or in an attached letter.)

First Standard Bank

By: _____   _____
    (Officer and Title)   (Date)

verifies the cash balance per the general ledger with the balance per the bank statement. In most audit engagements, the auditor obtains a copy of the year-end bank reconciliation and reviews the reconciliation to determine that it has been properly prepared. Common audit procedures performed by the auditor on a bank reconciliation include the following:

■ Verifying the reconciliation's arithmetic accuracy.
■ Tracing bank balances to the bank statement and the bank confirmation response.

- Tracing the balance per the books to the general ledger account.
- Examining documents (as appropriate) in support of the reconciliation.
- Scanning the bank statement for changes or erasures.

The objective in reviewing a bank reconciliation is for the auditor to support all significant items included on the reconciliation. If the auditor can reconcile the balance per the books to the balance per the bank, then the auditor has gathered excellent evidence that the cash both exists and belongs to the client. As a consequence, support for reconciling items becomes very important in auditing the bank reconciliation. For this reason, auditors often obtain and use a bank cutoff statement. Figure 14–4 is an example of a working paper on a bank reconciliation prepared by the client.

Cutoff Bank Statements   A *cutoff bank statement* is a bank statement for a period of time usually from year-end to some date subsequent to year-end, generally 7 to 14 days. For example, a bank cutoff statement for a calendar-year entity may run from January 1 to January 14.

A cutoff statement yields relevant information to support reconciling items. Most reconciling items clear shortly after year-end. The client should request the cutoff bank statement and then mail it directly to the auditor.

Having received the bank cutoff statement, the auditor may use the statement to verify a variety of reconciling items. Common audit procedures performed with the cutoff bank statement include the following:

- Tracing deposits in transit from the bank reconciliation to the cutoff statement to determine that amounts agree and that no unusual time delays exist between the date recorded per books and the date recorded per bank.
- Tracing all cleared, prior-year checks listed in the cutoff statement to the year-end outstanding check list.
- Examining the cutoff statement and enclosed data for unusual items (for example, large checks payable to cash).
- Determining that checks dated after year-end are recorded in the subsequent-year's cash disbursements and are not listed as outstanding checks at year-end.

Once the auditor finishes with the cutoff bank statement, the statement should be given to the client, because it is part of the client's records.

Tracing checks received with the cutoff bank statement to the bank reconciliation serves two purposes: to identify any checks that cleared and should have been listed as outstanding but were not, and to identify checks listed as outstanding but that have still not cleared the bank. Both of these are matters of concern and should be investigated. Of course, a check listed as outstanding that has not cleared may simply mean that the payee has been slow in depositing the check or that perhaps the check has been lost in the mail. In these situations, the auditor frequently traces the check to the cash disbursements journals and examines supporting documentation. The auditor may also ask the client about these items. If the checks that have not cleared the bank are material, a second cutoff bank statement may be needed.

When a significant number of checks have not cleared the bank, the client may have written checks and recorded them in the cash disbursements journals but held the checks for mailing until year-end. A client may do this to reduce the current liabilities shown on the balance sheet and thereby improve the current ratio.

Figure 14–4	**Audit Working Paper on a Bank Reconciliation Prepared by the Client**

Plainsman Co.
Bank Reconciliation
12/31/X4

A-2

	Initials	Date
Prepared By	LG	1/10/X5
Approved By	WA	1/18/X5

Acct. 101 – General account, Second National Bank

Balance per Bank			110819 –	A-2/1
Add:				
Deposits in transit ①				
12/30		10213		
12/31		11100	21313	
Deduct:				
Outstanding Checks				
#8321	12/16	2123		
8368	12/21	7821		
8397	12/24	4960		
8400	12/26	11039		
8403	12/28	1672		
8404	12/29	13000	<40615>	
Other reconciling items: Bank error				
Deposits to Payroll accounts credited				
to general account by bank in error			<15700>	A-3
Balance per bank adjusted			75817	T/B
Balance per books before adjustments			76807	A-1
Adjustments:				
Nonsufficient funds check				
returned by bank, not collectible				
from customer		978		A-3
Service Charge		12	<990>	C-3/1
Balance per books adjusted			75817	A-1

① Cutoff bank statement procedures completed by L.G. 1/10/X5

② Cutoff bank statement enclosure returned to
client, acknowledged by R. Delaney   1/2/X5

If the auditor finds any checks that are dated prior to year-end and that have cleared the bank according to the cutoff statement, but that are not on the outstanding check list, this is an indication that the cash balances as of year-end were overstated: that is, cash balances per the books did not exist.

Bank Transfer Schedules

Another common substantive audit procedure for cash is the preparation of a *bank transfer schedule*, a test of transactions that provides evidence as to existence or occurrence and completeness. Many entities maintain more than one bank account. For example, an entity may maintain a general account and a payroll account. If more than one bank account exists, a bank transfer schedule is an appropriate procedure.

With more than one bank account, the entity will typically transfer funds between accounts. For example, a common payroll procedure is to transfer an amount equal to the net payroll from the general account to the payroll account to cover payroll checks. In this situation, the general bank account will have an outstanding check until the check clears, whereas the payroll account will have a deposit in transit until the receiving bank records the deposit. Thus, at least four sets of records are involved in any bank transfer: the two general ledger cash accounts (in this example, the payroll account and the general account) and the two bank accounts (the payroll and the general account per the bank's records).

The primary purpose for performing a bank transfer test is to make sure that the same deposit is not shown in two accounts at the same time. An intentional overstatement is an irregularity known as *kiting*—a means of overstating bank balances either to conceal a cash shortage or to increase the cash reported on the balance sheet. For example, an employee may embezzle funds from recorded cash receipts. These cash receipts will never be recorded as a deposit at the bank. As a consequence, a bank reconciliation could be out of balance, because the cash receipts recorded on the general ledger account are greater than the cash received by the bank. To cover this shortage, the employee may draw a check from another bank account and deposit that check in the account with the cash shortage. This would eliminate the shortage as a reconciling item on the bank reconciliation. At the same time, because the check has been drawn on another account and has not cleared the other bank, the money can be included as a deposit at one bank and not listed as an outstanding check at the other bank.

Kiting generally occurs under a weak internal control structure, typically when one individual can both issue checks and record them, or when there is collusion among employees, that is, when there is a breakdown of the segregation of duties. To detect kiting and gather evidence that cash has been properly recorded, a bank transfer schedule is usually prepared. As illustrated in Figure 14–5, a bank transfer schedule lists all bank transfers for a few days before and after the balance sheet date as recorded in the cash receipts and cash disbursements journals.

The bank transfer schedule includes four dates. For example, consider Check No. 2354. The check was written on the Orlando cash account on December 24 and recorded as a disbursement. The Atlanta cash account treated that check as a receipt on December 31. Once it was recorded as a receipt, the check was deposited in the Atlanta account at the bank. The bank recorded the deposit on January 4 and the check finally cleared the bank of the Orlando account on January 5. In this case, the bank transfer should be listed both as a deposit in transit in the Atlanta account and as an outstanding check in the Orlando account. Once the bank transfer schedule is prepared, each transfer should be analyzed to determine the appropriate treatment on the individual bank reconciliations (that is, as an outstanding check or deposit in

Figure 14-5 **Bank Transfer Schedule**

Plainsman Co.
Schedule of Bank Transfers
December 31, 19X4

A-3

LG 1/20/X5
WA 2/4/X5

Bank Accounts From	To	Check No.	Amount	Disbursement Date Per Books	Per Bank	Receipt Per Books	Date Per Bank
Dayton	Atlanta	1432	5400	12-23-X4 √	12-31-X4 √	12-30-X4 √	12-30-X4 ↲
General	Payroll	675	4650	12-27-X4 √	12-31-X4	12-31-X4 √	12-31-X4 ↲
Orlando	Atlanta	2354	10275	12-24-X4 √	1-5-X5 √	12-31-X4 √√	1-4-X5 ↲
Atlanta	Seattle	8672	9867	1-3-X5 √	1-6-X5 √	1-4-X5 √	1-4-X5 ↲
Birmingham	Atlanta	1125	3210	1-5-X5 √	1-13-X5 √	1-10-X5 √	1-11-X5 ↲

√   per cash disbursement record
√   per cash receipts book
↲   agreed to Orlando outstanding check list, A-2
√   agreed to Atlanta General account deposit-in-transit, A-2
√   agreed to cancelled check
√   agreed to deposit slip and bank statement

transit). Each item determined to be a reconciling item should then be traced to that reconciliation. Dates per the bank are obtained from the bank cutoff statements or the client's regular bank statements.

Proof of Cash

A *proof of cash*, often referred to as a comprehensive bank reconciliation or a four-column bank reconciliation, is a substantive audit test of transactions. An auditor usually performs a proof of cash for one month for clients with a weak internal control structure. When control risk is high, the auditor may need to gather evidence that transactions have been properly recorded during the year. One way to gather this evidence is by performing a proof of cash.

A proof of cash is really four different reconciliations:

■ A reconciliation of the balance per the bank with the balance per the books at the beginning of the month.

■ A reconciliation of cash receipts as recorded per the bank (deposits) with cash receipts as recorded per the books (that is, debits to the cash account).

■ A reconciliation of cash disbursements as recorded by the bank (for example, canceled checks, service charges) with cash disbursements as recorded per the books (that is, credits to the general ledger account).

■ A reconciliation of the balance per the bank with the balance per the books at the end of the month.

Figure 14-6 presents an example of a proof of cash.

Figure 14-6   **Proof of Cash**

Plainsman Co.   A-5
Proof of Cash
12-31-X4

Initials	Date
Prepared By	LG	1/18/X5
Approved By	WA	2/4/X5

	Beg. Bal. Nov. 30	Receipts	Disburs.	End Bal. Dec. 31	
1 Balance per Bank St.	5353	12455	10918	6890	
2 Deposits in transit					
3 November 30	410	(410)			
4 December 31		644		644	
5 Checks outstanding					
6 November 30	(1385)		(1385)		
7 December 31			1505	(1505)	
8 True cash balance	4387	12689	11038	6029	
9					

	Beg. Bal. Nov. 30	Receipts	Disburs.	End Bal. Dec. 31	
10					
11					
12 Bal. per client books	802	12668	11044	2426	
13 Bank service chg.					
14 November	(36)		(36)		
15 December			30	(30)	
16 Bank charges for					
17 NSF checks		(412)		(412)	
18 Collections by bank	3612	(3612)			
19 Collections by bank		4045		4045	
20 True cash balance	4378	12689	11038	6029	
21					
22					

	Relevant Data			11-30-X4	12-31-X4
23					
24 Bank service charge for month					
25 not shown on company books				36	30
26 Bank debit memos for NSF checks not					
27 shown on company books					412
28 Collection of note by bank not					
29 shown on company books				3612	4045
30					

As with tests of the year-end bank reconciliation, the auditor should support all significant items in a proof of cash. Thus, all balances per bank are generally traced to the bank statement. Outstanding checks, deposits in transit, and other reconciling items should also be supported. These are typically supported in a manner similar to that used in the test of a regular bank reconciliation. For example, a deposit in transit at the beginning of the month should be recorded as a cash receipt on the bank's records shortly thereafter. Likewise, outstanding checks should clear the bank during the next time period.

A proof of cash provides excellent evidence that all recorded cash transactions during the month have been accounted for in the cash account, because the proof of cash connects recorded cash receipts and recorded cash disbursements per the books to an outside source—the bank. Of course, the auditor should recognize that proof of cash is by definition an examination of recorded cash receipts and disbursements. It will not reveal unrecorded and undeposited receipts; however, it will reveal unrecorded disbursements that have cleared the bank. Thus, the proof of cash does not provide conclusive evidence about completeness of all cash transactions. Its primary purpose is to provide evidence about existence and rights. For example, a proof of cash provides evidence that a cash receipt existed and that a cash receipt was deposited at the bank, providing the client with the rights to withdraw the deposit.

Audit of Sales

The overall objective of the audit of sales is to determine that sales as reported on the income statement are fairly presented in conformity with generally accepted accounting principles. In other words, the auditor needs to gather evidence that no material misstatements exist in the financial statements for sales. The audit of sales emphasizes tests of transactions rather than tests of balances, because the balance in the sales account represents the cumulative total of individual sales transactions throughout the year.

The sales account is closely tied to cash receipts and accounts receivable. Because of the double-entry bookkeeping system, evidence supporting cash and accounts receivable tends to support sales. For example, having determined that an account receivable is valid (the debit side of an accounting entry), the auditor has thereby also supported the validity of the sale (the credit side of the accounting entry).

In many entities, internal control structure policies and procedures for sales are effective. This allows the auditor to support sales primarily through tests of controls

---

Professional Judgment

Auditors Must Watch for Excessive Revenue Transactions

Some people tend to exaggerate when it comes to talking about their incomes. Many companies are exactly the same way. That's why revenue transactions are often misstated on financial statements. An auditor's judgment is critical in assessing the terms, timing, and characteristics of revenue transactions to determine if they meet both the letter and the spirit of GAAP. For example, a spate of year-end transactions should be scrutinized, especially if it includes generous return provisions. Bill and hold sales should also sound alarm bells and be carefully checked.

Auditors must use sound judgment in substantiating and valuing accounts receivable. Several factors can play a significant role in this process. Both the duration of the company's relationship with the customer and the type of business they are in are important. The physical scope of the business as well as the particular industry and the regulations that affect it and its customers should also be carefully examined. Again, like individuals, the promise to pay is only as good as the individual who issues it.

Table 14-2	**Common Substantive Audit Tests for Sales**			
	Common Audit Tests	Technique	Type of Test	Assertions
	Agree sales journal entries to shipping documents	Vouching	Tests of transactions	Existence or occurrence
	Trace shipping documents to sales invoices and entries in sales journal	Tracing	Tests of transactions	Completeness
	Perform cutoff tests for sales and shipping	Vouching Tracing	Tests of transactions	Existence or occurrence Completeness
	Recompute information on sales invoice	Reperformance	Tests of transactions	Valuation
	Scan sales journal for large or unusual items	Inspection	Tests of transactions	Presentation and disclosure
	Apply analytical procedures	Analytical	Analytical procedures	All

rather than through substantive testing. The relationship of sales to receivables and cash in the double-entry bookkeeping system and the low assessed levels of control risk for sales assertions enable the auditor to limit substantive audit tests of sales. Table 14–2 shows the more common substantive audit tests for sales.

Agree Sales to Shipping

A common substantive audit test for sales is to agree sales journal entries to shipping documents. This test of transactions is designed to support the existence of recorded sales. If a sale did occur, a shipping document or other transmittal document should exist for the sale.

Tracing Shipping Documents to the Sales Journal

Tracing information from the shipping document to the sales invoice and the sales journal entry is a common substantive test of transactions. This audit test is the reverse of the preceding test, where the auditor agreed sales journal entries to shipping documents. In tracing from shipping documents to sales invoices, the auditor tests for completeness rather than for existence/occurrence. The assumption here is that if shipping documents or other related transmittal documents have been prepared, a sale has been made and a sales invoice and journal entry should exist. In performing this type of test, the auditor often selects a representative sample of shipping documents from throughout the year and agrees the shipping document information to the sales invoice.

Sales Cutoff Tests

A *sales cutoff test* is designed to determine that recorded sales during the year occurred in that accounting period (existence) and that sales recorded after year-end are sales in the next accounting period (completeness). A sales cutoff involves examining documents prepared immediately before and after the balance sheet date. The auditor (1) examines sales invoices to determine that shipments have been made properly, (2) examines shipping documents to determine that sales have been recorded properly and that the shipping terms support the sale recognition, and (3) agrees shipping documents to sales invoices and inventory records to determine that items were recorded in the correct accounting period.

In performing a sales cutoff test, the auditor must be aware of the shipping terms (for example, F.O.B. shipping point or F.O.B. destination), because the shipping terms dictate when title passes and may influence when the sale should be recorded as revenue. The sales cutoff test is discussed in more detail in Chapter 17.

Recomputing Information on Sales Invoices

Another potential substantive audit test of transactions for sales is to recalculate the information on the sales invoice. In this procedure, the auditor multiplies the quantity per the sales invoice by the price to see if the customer has been billed for the proper amount. The auditor may also trace the invoice price to a price list and may foot the sales invoice to determine that the totals have been correctly added. Because most clients have controls over sales, this test is most commonly performed as a test of controls, as discussed in Chapter 13. However, the test can be a substantive test if the purpose of the test is to support the valuation of sales and determine that dollar amounts have been correctly recorded.

Scanning Sales Journal

Another common substantive audit test over sales is to scan the sales journal for large or unusual transactions. In performing this test, the auditor looks for items that may indicate questions about accounting propriety or that require further investigation by the auditor.

Analytical Procedures

As discussed in Chapter 11, analytical procedures can often be used to test the sales account. For example, comparison of sales to prior-year sales and budgeted sales can provide audit evidence of the reasonableness of sales revenues. An excellent analytical procedure for sales is to relate sales revenue to an operating statistic or to other data that are independent of the accounting system (for example, unit production, unit sales, number of patient-days for a hospital). By using available operating statistics, the auditor can obtain support for the reasonableness of sales revenues. This particular analytical procedure is especially useful in gathering evidence on the completeness assertion.

Audit of Accounts Receivable

Accounts receivable represent the entity's claims against customers that have arisen from the sale of goods or services in the normal course of business. An account receivable is recorded when a sale on account is made and is reduced when the entity receives cash from a customer in payment of the account.

The overall objective of the audit of accounts receivable is to gather sufficient evidence regarding fair presentation of the account in conformity with generally accepted accounting principles. As with all other accounts, this objective can be accomplished by assessing the risk of a material misstatement for the five assertions identified in Chapter 4. The primary emphasis on accounts receivable is on testing the assertions of existence or occurrence, valuation, and rights and obligations. In addition, the auditor should have reasonable assurance of adequate disclosure of related-party, employee, pledged, discounted, and assigned receivables.

Common Substantive Audit Tests

Table 14–3 shows the more common substantive audit tests for accounts receivable. By far the most common audit procedure for accounts receivable is confirmation. Other common procedures include footing the subsidiary ledger and verifying its total against the general ledger, obtaining and evaluating an aging schedule of receivables, and applying analytical procedures.

Footing Subsidiary Ledger and Verifying Total against General Ledger
An important audit test performed on accounts receivable is to foot the subsidiary ledger that details each customer's receivable balance and to compare this total with the general ledger control account for accounts receivable. Footing the subsidiary ledger helps determine that the detail listing of the individual accounts agrees with the control total. Although the balance sheet will show only total accounts receivable, this balance consists of a detail listing of individual accounts. If the total of the detail listing does not agree with the control total balance, a question exists as

---

Table 14–3   **Common Substantive Audit Tests for Accounts Receivable**

Common Audit Tests	Technique	Type of Test	Assertions
Foot subsidiary ledger and agree total to general ledger	Reperformance	Test of balances	Completeness Existence or occurrence
Obtain and evaluate aging schedule	Analytical	Analytical procedure	Valuation
Obtain confirmations	Confirmation	Test of balances	Existence or occurrence Valuation Rights and obligations
Apply analytical procedures	Analytical	Analytical procedures	All

to whether accounts receivable is fairly stated. Frequently, this test is performed on the aging schedule, because the aging schedule often serves as a surrogate for the subsidiary ledger.

Obtaining and Evaluating Aging Schedule

An *aging schedule*, or aged trial balance of accounts receivable, is a breakdown of each individual customer's account showing how long each account or its components have been outstanding. The aging schedule, as shown in Figure 14–7, is often prepared by the client for the auditor. The auditor who receives an aging schedule may foot this schedule rather than the subsidiary ledger. The aging schedule not only shows the auditor the composition of the individual accounts but also how long each account has been outstanding (for example, 0–30 days, 31–60 days, 61–90 days, and more than 90 days, as shown in Figure 14–7). The age of a receivable is measured from the date of the sale to the balance sheet date. Thus, a sale on account that was made in September and that is still uncollected as of December 31 would be more than 90 days old. This type of information helps the auditor determine the proper valuation of accounts receivable. Ordinarily, the older accounts (for example, those more than 90 days old) are less likely to be collectible than the more recent accounts.

After receiving the client's aged trial balance of receivables, the auditor should verify the accuracy of the aging schedule. This should be done by recalculating and footing the totals in the schedule, tracing a sample of customer balances in the aging schedule to the subsidiary ledger, and verifying the aging itself by tracing some items to the dates of sales invoices.

By footing the subsidiary ledger or aging schedule, the auditor gathers some limited evidence as to completeness. Gathering evidence on completeness or understatement for accounts receivable is difficult. The primary audit test for understatement of receivables is the substantive audit test of tracing shipments to sales documents as previously discussed in the audit of sales.

The purpose of the aging schedule is to gather evidence on valuation. Along with other analytical tests, the aging schedule gives a strong indication of the client's ability to collect its receivables. Generally, auditors use the aging schedule to calculate certain ratios and to discuss delinquent accounts with the client in determining the probability of collection.

Confirmations

The auditing standards board issued *SAS No. 67, The Confirmation Process* (AU 330), to provide expanded guidance for confirmations in general, as discussed in Chapter 5, including accounts receivable confirmations. *SAS No. 67* states that "confirmation of accounts receivable is a generally accepted auditing procedure." That statement requires auditors to confirm accounts receivable unless they meet one of three conditions: (1) accounts receivable are immaterial to the financial statements, (2) the use of confirmations would not be effective, or (3) confirmations are not necessary to reduce audit risk to an acceptably low level for the assertions relevant to accounts receivable.

Condition 2 recognizes that for some types of audit clients inadequate response rates or inattentive consideration of confirmations by third parties may make them an insufficient or unreliable source of audit evidence. Consequently, the auditor may decide to forgo their use and obtain audit evidence from other sources.

Figure 14-7 **Aging Schedule**

Plainsman Co.
Aged Trial Balance
12/31/X4

Acct #140 Account Name				Past Due More Than 90 days	More Than 60 days	More Than 30 days
Applied Devices						3261 75
Burrell Industries					4721 50	514 62
CWA Corp.				< 4603 13 >	10257 13	1347 21
Deloney Electronics					2305 16	795 64
Eastern Electronics						2458 67
Glisson Manufacturing						
Instrumentation Corp.				1374 26	732 45	
National Products				874 57	543 26	
R & L Enterprises						
RG Mfg. Corp.					879 21	723 00
Schuster Inc.				1092 82	957 24	2175 63
Vice Radio					514 00	212 81
Miscellaneous						121 00
				< 1261 48 >	20909 95	12663 59

Ⓔ To record credit memo issued 1 x 12 x 2 AJE ⑦ See EE6
    Dr. Sales Returns   689 14
    Cr. Accounts Receivable   689 14
C Confirmed
ℵ Traced to subledger – verified aging
✓ Footed
Ⓞ Traced to cash receipts journal and examined remittance advices
Ⓤ Unable to confirm
Ⓞ Correction of error in aging schedule

Condition 3 acknowledges that a low risk of material misstatement in accounts receivable assertions coupled with evidence from substantive tests other than confirmations may sometimes cause confirmations to be unnecessary. For example, the auditor may assess a low level of inherent risk and control risk for the relevant accounts receivable assertions. That assessment combined with evidence obtained from analytical procedures applied to those assertions may, in some cases, be sufficient to reduce audit risk to an acceptably low level. In such a circumstance, the auditor would not need to obtain confirmations because audit risk is already sufficiently low.

Although an auditor may decide not to use accounts receivable confirmations for one of the above reasons, *SAS No. 67* requires that auditors document in their workpapers how they reached that decision.

Figure 14-7   *continued*

8	9	10		11	12	13	14
Current (0-30 days)	Conf #	Balance Per Books 12/31/x4		Adjustments	Balance Per Audit 12/31/x4	Cash Received 1/1/x5 1/31/x5	
102416	1	C	428591 n√		428591	320000	0
62542			586154 n√		586154	367500	0
231200	2	C	931321 n√		931321	691721	
132667			442747 n√		442747	145547	0
			245867 n√		245867	100000	
432916	3	C	432916 n√		432916		
64819	4	C	307902 n√		307902	244502	0
98747		(E)	313444 n√	(68914)(7)	244530	140030	
218894 0		U	218894 n√		218894	200000	0
96536			256757 n√		256757	87921	
187863	5	C	610432 n√		610432	267432	0
34876	6	C	107557 n√		107557	68857	
15713			27813 n√		27813		
1679189			4910395		4841481	2633510	

Nature of the Test   As discussed in Chapter 5, when the auditor decides to send confirmation requests, he or she chooses to send either a positive or negative confirmation request. A *positive confirmation request* is addressed to the customer asking the customer to respond directly to the auditor and to indicate whether the information shown on the request is correct. In a positive confirmation request, the auditor wants the customer to respond regardless of whether the balance shown on the confirmation is correct. A positive confirmation request was shown in Figure 5–2.

Alternatively, in a *negative confirmation request*, the auditor wants the customer to respond only if the information shown on the confirmation is incorrect. The presumption with the negative request form is that if the customer does not respond, the information is correct. Often, negative confirmations are in the form of a sticker or a rubber stamp placed on a customer's statement. A negative confirmation request was shown in Figure 5–3.

Negative confirmations provide less reliable evidence than positive confirmations. Auditors recognize that a failure to reply to a negative confirmation request does not necessarily mean that the customer has concluded that the information in the confirmation is correct. Sometimes customers ignore negative requests. Thus, if the customer does not respond, the auditor is uncertain whether the information is correct or the customer simply disregarded the confirmation.

Because negative confirmations produce less reliable evidence, they should be used only when all three of the following conditions exist:

- The combined assessed level of inherent risk and control risk is low.
- A large number of small individual balances is involved.
- The auditor has no reason to believe that the confirmation recipients are unlikely to give them consideration.

For example, the auditor may decide to use negative requests when examining demand deposit accounts in a savings and loan institution if the combined inherent risk and control risk assessment is low and the auditor has no reason to believe that the S & L's customers will ignore the requests.

Negative confirmations are more likely to produce responses that indicate misstatements when a large number of requests are sent and misstatements are widespread. The auditor should investigate all relevant information on returned negative requests and, if widespread misstatements are indicated, the auditor should reconsider the combined assessment of inherent and control risk and whether planned audit procedures should be revised.

Positive requests provide evidence only when recipients respond. The reliability of those responses, however, is not absolute. Some customers may not actually verify the information in the request, but may simply sign and return the form. To mitigate this risk, auditors may use blank positive confirmations where the customer is asked to supply the relevant information, such as the account balance. Although blank confirmations may increase their reliability, they may decrease the response rates because of the additional effort required of the recipient. Thus, the auditor may have to perform additional audit procedures to offset the unreturned requests.

Nature of Information Confirmed   The type of information the auditor chooses to confirm directly affects both the competence of the evidence obtained and the confirmation response rate. To ensure that confirmations provide competent evidence, the auditor should decide whether to confirm information other than amounts. To make this decision, the auditor should thoroughly understand the substance of the terms of the client's transactions and agreements with its customers. When unusual or complex transactions or agreements exist, the auditor may decide to confirm their terms with the customers. For example, unusual and substantial year-end sales to customers, uncommon payment terms, or liberal rights of product return may cause the auditor to confirm the terms of such agreements and whether any oral modifications have been made, as well as the amounts involved.

The information confirmed should also be that which customers will be readily able to confirm. Some customers (for whom the receivables are accounts payable), may maintain their accounts payable system on a voucher basis (for example, government agencies). In these situations, the customer records accounts payable by voucher number and individual transaction rather than by the total due to a particular vendor. Thus, customers using the voucher system may not know the total amount they owe an auditor's client but will know the amount they owe for individual invoices. In this situation, the auditor can ask the customer to confirm individual transactions rather than balances. In addition, respondents may not be able to confirm the balances of their installment loans, but they may be able to confirm the payment amount, the key loan terms, and whether their accounts are up-to-date.

Timing of the Test   The auditor must also make a decision as to the timing of the confirmation request. In determining the timing of the confirmation, the auditor must decide the date for which accounts receivable will be confirmed. Confirmations most often are sent as of the balance sheet date. This represents the most reliable audit evidence (given that the nature and extent of testing are constant), because the receivables shown on the financial statements are as of the balance sheet date. However, as discussed in Chapter 12, the timing of audit tests may vary. For example, when control risk is low, auditors will sometimes confirm receivables as of a month or two before the balance sheet date. Of course, the auditor must perform limited procedures from the confirmation date to the balance sheet date to give evidence that receivables are still fairly stated as of year-end.

Extent of the Test   The auditor must also decide how many confirmations to send and to which customers. This is primarily a sampling question, as discussed in Chapters 9 and 10. The auditor may determine the extent of confirmations by using statistical analyses or by judgmentally determining the sample size. To increase the reliability of the audit test, the auditor may increase the extent of testing. In examining a client with large accounts receivable or with unusual risks, the auditor should increase the reliability of the evidence. This could be accomplished by increasing the extent of confirmation testing. Alternatively, the nature or timing of the test could also be varied.

The auditor must also determine which individual receivables balances to select for confirmation. The auditor may select items to confirm judgmentally or may use some type of random or systematic sample selection.

Maintaining Control   For confirmation procedures to be effective, the auditor must maintain control of the confirmations from the time they are prepared and mailed until they are returned by the customer. Maintaining control means establishing direct communication between the customer and the auditor to minimize the possibility of interception or alteration of the confirmation requests or responses. The auditor may get assistance from the client in preparing the confirmation in areas such as typing the confirmation requests, inserting confirmations in envelopes, and stamping the envelopes. However, the auditor must closely supervise the process and should mail the confirmations directly. Likewise, all confirmations should be returned directly to the auditor rather than to the client. Accordingly, auditors generally include a postage-paid, self-addressed return envelope with the confirmation request. These steps ensure that confirmation requests are an independent communication between the auditor and the customer. The auditor should be careful when a confirmation request cannot be delivered and is returned by the post office.

Although this situation may indicate that a customer has moved, it may also indicate that this is a fictitious customer and the receivable is not valid. Likewise it may indicate that although the receivable is valid, the collectibility of the receivable is questionable.

Some customers may respond to a confirmation other than in a written response mailed to the auditor, such as a facsimile (fax) response or an oral confirmation. Such responses often require additional evidence to support their validity. For example, the risk associated with a fax response is the inherent uncertainty about its actual source. To address this risk and treat the confirmation as valid evidence, auditors often verify the source and contents of the fax response in a telephone call to the purported sender. Auditors may also request the purported sender to mail the original confirmation directly to them.

When the auditor obtains oral confirmations, they should be documented in the workpapers. If the information in the oral confirmation is significant, the auditor should ask the customer for a written confirmation.

Disposition of Responses Confirmation responses from customers sometimes contain exceptions that the customer has noted. The auditor must maintain control over all exceptions and clear them satisfactorily. The auditor may have the client investigate the exceptions; however, the auditor should maintain control and obtain support for the client's responses. Frequently, exceptions between the customer and the client's records result from items in transit. For example, the customer may have written a check on December 31, whereas the client will not receive the payment until after year-end. Sometimes, however, exceptions will result from items in dispute, errors, or irregularities. Regardless of the exception, the auditor should determine the reason for any differences, investigate them appropriately, and draw a conclusion as to their significance.

Nonresponses Because nonresponses to negative confirmations are presumed to mean the customer agrees with the information, auditors do not take further action. However, for positive requests, the auditor asks the customer to respond. Once an account is selected for positive confirmation, the account must usually be supported. If a customer fails to respond to the first request, the auditor generally sends a second or third request or asks the client to call the customer to request that the confirmation be returned. For those customers who do not respond to additional requests, the auditor usually applies alternative procedures to obtain support for the account balance. Common alternative procedures include examining subsequent cash collections and reviewing documentation supporting transactions in the customer's account.

Examining subsequent cash collections For accounts receivable, the auditor may examine cash receipts subsequent to the confirmation date to determine if the receivable has, in fact, been collected. Often, receivables will be collected within a month or so after the balance sheet date. Sometimes a customer does not respond to a positive confirmation but the auditor can verify that the customer has sent in payment on the receivable. This verification, along with shipping documents to indicate that the receivable was owed prior to year-end, provides good evidence that the receivable does exist. Subsequent collection also supports collectibility and the valuation of receivables, and it is often used to support valuation in cases of nonresponse on positive confirmations. Of course, sometimes the auditor cannot relate the specific collections from a customer with the receivable balance. For example, the customer may make a lump sum payment that does not fully pay off the receivable.

Reviewing documentation Another alternative procedure for supporting a receivables balance is to review the documentation for the receivable. For example, a sales invoice should be issued on the date that the receivable was created and there should also be shipping documents related to the sale. By reviewing this documentation, the auditor gathers evidence about existence. Because review of subsequent cash collections involves an examination of evidence outside the entity (that is, a cash receipt from a customer), it is usually considered to provide more reliable audit evidence than a review of documentation.

In some circumstances, it may be acceptable to omit alternative procedures. For example, the auditor may decide to treat the entire balance in a nonresponse as a misstatement instead of performing alternative procedures to support it. However, these assumed misstatements must be projected to the population of accounts receivable, added to the sum of all other unadjusted differences, and not cause the auditor to conclude that the financial statements are materially misstated.

The auditor may also decide to omit alternative procedures when he or she has not identified any unusual qualitative factors or systematic characteristics related to the nonresponses. If such factors or characteristics do exist, such as all nonresponses pertain to year-end sales transactions, then the auditor should perform additional procedures to resolve any concerns about these items.

Evaluating Confirmation Procedure Results Both returned confirmation requests and any alternative procedures performed provide evidence about accounts receivable. The auditor must evaluate this evidence and decide whether it is sufficient for all of the assertions applicable to accounts receivable. To make this evaluation, the auditor considers the following factors:

- The reliability of the confirmations and alternative procedures
- The nature of any exceptions, including both quantitative and qualitative implications
- Evidence provided by other audit procedures related to accounts receivable assertions
- Whether additional evidence is needed

If the auditor concludes the combined evidence is not sufficient, he or she should request additional confirmations or extend other tests, such as tests of details or analytical procedures.

Analytical Procedures

Accounts receivable is an area in which computation of ratios and related comparisons are frequently performed by auditors. As discussed in Chapter 11, these analytical procedures provide evidence as to the overall fairness of the accounts receivable balances in conformity with generally accepted accounting principles.

Numerous relationships exist between receivables and other balances, such as the allowance account, bad debt expense, and net sales. The following analytical procedures are typically performed for accounts receivable:

- Age of accounts receivable.
- Accounts receivable turnover.
- Bad debts as a percentage of sales.
- Aging categories as a percentage of receivables.
- Allowance account as a percentage of receivables.
- Comparison of bad debts with anticipated write-offs.

These analytical procedures provide evidence as to the fairness of receivables. As with any other analytical procedure, any unusual fluctuations or questionable items should be investigated further.

Lapping

One common type of fraud involving accounts receivable is ***lapping***: to cover a cash theft, an employee defers recording cash receipts from one customer and covers the shortage with receipts from another customer. Lapping typically occurs when one employee records cash in both the cash receipts journal and the accounts receivable subsidiary ledger. Lapping generally will be revealed by unsupported discrepancies found while confirming accounts receivable balances. It may be substantiated by comparing information on remittance advices and deposit slips (for example, names and amounts) to the cash receipts journal. However, because lapping usually involves immaterial amounts, specific audit procedures (other than confirmation) to detect lapping are seldom performed.

Significant Terms

Aging schedule A listing of each individual customer's account with a breakdown of how long each account, or its components, has been outstanding.

Bank transfer schedule A schedule that lists all bank transfers for a few days before and after the balance sheet date as recorded in the cash receipts and cash disbursements journals.

Cutoff bank statement A bank statement for a period from year-end to some date subsequent to year-end, usually 7 to 14 days.

Kiting A means of overstating bank balances either to conceal a cash shortage or to increase the cash reported on the balance sheet by transferring cash between bank accounts.

Lapping A fraud involving abstracting cash from a customer and covering the resulting shortage with subsequent cash collections from another customer.

Negative confirmation A statement of balances due that is addressed to the customer with the request that the customer respond directly to the auditor only if the amount shown is incorrect.

Positive confirmation A statement of balances due that is addressed to the customer with the request that the customer respond directly to the auditor regardless of whether the balance is correct or incorrect.

Proof of cash A substantive test of transactions in which the auditor reconciles cash receipts and disbursements per the books with the bank's records.

Revenue cycle The segment of a business operation in which goods or services are exchanged for cash.

Discussion Questions

14-1. If the auditor determines that the client's internal control structure for the revenue cycle is excellent, can the auditor omit all substantive testing for sales and accounts receivable assertions and use tests of controls alone?

14-2. What are five common audit tests for cash?

14-3. Are cash counts normally a necessary audit procedure? Why or why not?

14-4. What is a cutoff bank statement and what is its purpose?

14-5. What is a bank transfer schedule and what is its purpose?

14-6. What are the common substantive audit tests for sales?

14-7. What is the difference between vouching sales journal entries to shipping documents and tracing shipping documents to sales journal entries?

14-8. How can analytical procedures be used in the audit of sales?

14-9. What are the common substantive audit tests for accounts receivable?

14-10. How does the auditor use an aging schedule?

14-11. Are confirmations of receivables required?

14-12. What is the difference between a positive and a negative confirmation? Which is more reliable?

14-13. What should the auditor do when a customer takes exception to an accounts receivable confirmation?

14-14. If an auditor cannot obtain a reply to a positive confirmation request, what alternative procedures should he or she consider?

14-15. Is an auditor always required to confirm at least some of the client's bank accounts and accounts receivable? Explain why or why not.

Objective Questions

*14-16. Which of the following is one of the better auditing techniques that an auditor can use to detect kiting?
(1) Review composition of deposit slips stamped by the bank.
(2) Review subsequent bank statements and canceled checks received directly from the bank.
(3) Prepare a schedule of bank transfers from the client's books.
(4) Prepare year-end bank reconciliations.

*14-17. An auditor is testing sales transactions. One step is to trace a sample of debit entries from the accounts receivable subsidiary ledger back to the supporting sales invoices. What would the auditor intend to establish by this step?
(1) Sales invoices represent bona fide sales.
(2) All sales have been recorded.
(3) All sales invoices have been properly posted to customer accounts.
(4) Debit entries in the accounts receivable subsidiary ledger are properly supported by sales invoices.

*14-18. The auditor obtains corroborating evidential matter for accounts receivable by using positive or negative confirmation requests. Under which of the following circumstances might the negative form of the accounts receivable confirmation be useful?
(1) A substantial number of accounts are in dispute.
(2) Control risk for accounts receivable is high.
(3) Client records include a large number of relatively small balances.
(4) The auditor believes that recipients of the requests are unlikely to give them consideration.

---

*AICPA adapted.

*14-19. In determining the adequacy of the allowance for uncollectible accounts, the *least* reliance should be placed upon which of the following?
(1) The credit manager's opinion.
(2) An aging schedule of past due accounts.
(3) Collection experience of the client's collection agency.
(4) Ratios calculated showing the past relationship of the valuation allowance to net credit sales.

*14-20. Which of the following procedures would ordinarily be expected to best reveal unrecorded sales at the balance sheet date?
(1) Compare shipping documents with sales records.
(2) Apply gross margin rates to inventory disposed of during the period.
(3) Trace payments received subsequent to the balance sheet date.
(4) Send accounts receivable confirmation requests.

*14-21. Customers having substantial year-end past due balances fail to reply after second request forms have been mailed directly to them. Which of the following is the most appropriate audit procedure?
(1) Examine shipping documents.
(2) Review collections during the year being examined.
(3) Extend tests of controls for assertions related to receivables.
(4) Increase the balance in the accounts receivable allowance (contra) account.

*14-22. To verify that all sales transactions have been recorded, a test of transactions should be completed on a representative sample drawn from which of the following?
(1) Entries in the sales journal.
(2) The billing clerk's file of sales orders.
(3) A file of duplicate copies of sales invoices for which all prenumbered forms in the series have been accounted for.
(4) The shipping clerk's file of duplicate copies of bills of lading.

*14-23. During the process of confirming receivables as of December 31, 19X5, a positive confirmation was returned indicating the "balance owed as of December 31 was paid on January 9, 19X6." The auditor would most likely
(1) determine whether there were any changes in the account between January 1 and January 9, 19X6.
(2) determine whether a customary trade discount was taken by the customer.
(3) reconfirm the zero balance as of January 10, 19X6.
(4) verify that the amount was received.

*14-24. Which of the following is the best argument against the use of negative accounts receivable confirmations?
(1) The cost-per-response is excessively high.
(2) There is no way of knowing if the intended recipients received them.
(3) Recipients are likely to feel that in reality the confirmation is a subtle request for payment.
(4) The inference drawn from receiving no reply may *not* be correct.

*14-25. If accounts receivable turned over 8.4 times in 19X4 as compared to only 6.6 times in 19X5, it is possible that there were
(1) unrecorded credit sales in 19X5.
(2) unrecorded cash receipts in 19X4.
(3) more thorough credit investigations made by the company late in 19X4.
(4) fictitious sales in 19X5.

*14-26. An auditor will be *least* likely to use a negative accounts receivable confirmation form when
(1) control risk for accounts receivable is low.
(2) a large number of small balances are involved.

*AICPA adapted.

(3) the number of requests mailed will be minimal.

(4) customers are unlikely to confirm the information.

*14-27. Which of the following is not a primary objective of the auditor in the audit of accounts receivable?

(1) To determine the approximate realizable value.

(2) To establish existence of the receivables.

(3) To determine the approximate time of collectibility of the receivables.

(4) To determine that receivables are from trade customers, not officers or employees.

14-28. An aged trial balance of accounts receivable is usually used by the auditor to

(1) verify the existence of recorded receivables.

(2) ensure that all customer payments are properly posted.

(3) evaluate the results of tests of controls.

(4) evaluate the collectibility of accounts receivable.

*14-29. Cindy Smith is auditing a cable television firm that services a rural community. All receivable balances are small, customers are billed monthly, and control risk is low. How would Smith most likely determine the existence of accounts receivable balances at the balance sheet date?

(1) Send positive confirmation requests.

(2) Send negative confirmation requests.

(3) Examine evidence of subsequent cash receipts instead of sending confirmation requests.

(4) Use statistical sampling instead of sending confirmation requests.

*14-30. In the confirmation of accounts receivable the auditor would most likely

(1) request confirmation of a sample of the inactive accounts.

(2) seek to obtain positive confirmation for at least 50% of the total dollar amount of receivables.

(3) require confirmation of all receivables from agencies of the federal government.

(4) require that confirmation requests be sent within one month of the fiscal year-end.

14-31. Jane Beverly, CPA, is auditing the financial statements of a small rural municipality. The receivable balances represent residents' delinquent real estate taxes. The assessed level of control risk for all accounts receivable assertions is high to maximum. How would Beverly most likely obtain sufficient competent evidence about the existence of receivables at the balance sheet date?

(1) Send positive confirmation requests.

(2) Send negative confirmation requests.

(3) Examine evidence of subsequent cash receipts instead of sending any confirmation requests.

(4) Inspect internal municipality records such as copies of property tax assessment bases and the tax bills mailed to residents instead of sending any confirmation requests.

14-32. Bruce Hadlock, CPA, is examining Low Country Industries' accounts receivable. He is trying to decide whether to send confirmations to some of Low Country's customers. Under which one of the following conditions would Hadlock be most likely to send confirmations?

(1) Combined assessments of inherent and control risks for the accounts receivable existence assertion is low.

(2) All of Low Country's customers use a voucher system and cannot confirm balances owed to Low Country.

(3) Accounts receivable are immaterial to the financial statements taken as a whole.

(4) In past audits, properly designed confirmation requests have resulted in extremely low response rates.

---

*AICPA adapted.

Problems and Cases

14-33.   (Audit of Cash) Melissa Emily, CPA, is performing the audit of Toto Corporation for the year ending December 31, 19X4. While testing cash balances, she performs the following procedures:

1. Traces deposits in transit on the bank reconciliation to the cutoff bank statement and the cash receipts journal for the current year.
2. Obtains bank confirmations from each bank with which Toto does business.
3. Compares the balance on the bank reconciliation obtained from the client with the bank confirmation.
4. Prepares a proof of cash.
5. Reviews minutes of the meetings of the board of directors, bank confirmations, and loan agreements for restrictions on cash withdrawals, interest-bearing deposits, and compensating balance agreements.
6. Compares the bank cancellation date with the date on the canceled check for checks dated on or shortly before the balance sheet date.
7. Compares the checks returned along with the cutoff bank statement with the checks listed as outstanding on the bank reconciliation.
8. Prepares a list of all material checks not returned with the cutoff bank statement. Lists the check number, payee, and amount.
9. Prepares a bank transfer schedule for transactions from December 20, 19X4, through January 10, 19X5.
10. Counts all cash on hand.
11. Foots cash journals and traces the posting to the ledger.

REQUIRED

For **1–11** above, state the objective of the procedure.

14-34.   (Linking Audit Objectives to Assertions for Cash) The following list illustrates audit objectives for cash.

1. Cash exists and is owned by the client.
2. Cash balances reflect a proper cutoff of receipts and disbursements.
3. Cash balances as presented in the balance sheet properly reflect all cash and cash items on hand, in transit, or on deposit with third parties.
4. Cash balances are properly classified in the financial statements, and adequate disclosure is made of restricted or committed funds and of cash not subject to immediate withdrawal (time deposits, long-term maturity certificates of deposit, and so on).

REQUIRED

For each objective, identify the relevant client assertion(s).

*14-35.   (Audit of Cash) When you arrive at your client's office on January 11, 19X7, to begin the December 31, 19X6, audit, you discover that the client had been drawing checks as creditors' invoices became due but not necessarily mailing them. Because of a working capital shortage, some checks may have been held for two or three weeks.

The client informs you that unmailed checks totaling $27,600 were on hand at December 31, 19X6. He states that these December-dated checks had been entered in the cash disbursements book and charged to the respective creditors' accounts in December because the checks were prenumbered. Heavy collections permitted him to mail the checks before your arrival.

The client wants to adjust the cash balance and accounts payable at December 31 by $27,600 because the cash account had a credit balance. He objects to submitting to his bank your audit report showing an overdraft of cash.

---

*AICPA adapted.

REQUIRED

A. Prepare an audit program indicating the procedures you would use to satisfy yourself of the accuracy of the cash balance on the client's statements.

B. Discuss the acceptability of reversing the indicated amount of outstanding checks.

*14-36. (Bank Reconciliation) In connection with your audit of the Lanier Company at December 31, 19X7, a company employee gives you a bank reconciliation that shows the following:

Balance per bank	$15,267
Deposits in transit	18,928
	$34,195
Checks outstanding	21,378
Balance per books	$12,817

As part of your verification, you obtain the bank statement and canceled checks from the bank on January 15, 19X8. Checks issued from January 1 to January 15, 19X8, per the books were $11,241. Checks returned by the bank on January 15 amounted to $29,219. Of the checks outstanding December 31, $4,800 were not returned by the bank with the January 15 statement, and of those issued per the books in January 19X8, $3,600 were not returned.

REQUIRED

A. Prepare a schedule showing the foregoing data in proper form.

B. Suggest four possible explanations for the condition existing here and state what your action would be in each case, including any necessary journal entries.

*14-37. (Bank Reconciliation) In connection with an audit, you were given the following worksheet:

Bank Reconciliation

December 31, 19X7

Balance per ledger 12-31-X7	$17,174.86
Add:	
Collections received on the last day of December and charged to "cash in bank" on books but not deposited	2,662.25
Debit memo for customer's check returned unpaid (check is on hand but no entry has been made on the books)	200.00
Debit memo for bank service charge for December	5.50
	$20,142.61

(continued)

Deduct:

Checks drawn but not paid by bank (see detailed list below)	$2,267.75	
Credit memo for proceeds of a note receivable that had been left at the bank for collection but that has not been recorded as collected	400.00	
Check for an account payable entered on books as $240.90 but drawn and paid by bank as $419.00	178.10	2,945.85
Computed balance...		$17,196.76
Unlocated difference		200.00
Balance per bank (checked to confirmation)		$16,996.76

Checks Drawn but Not Paid by Bank

No.	Amount
573	$ 67.27
724	9.90
903	456.67
907	305.50
911	482.75
913	550.00
914	366.76
916	10.00
917	218.90
	$2,267.75

REQUIRED

A. Prepare a corrected reconciliation.

B. Prepare journal entries for items that should be adjusted prior to closing the books.

14-38. (Client Holding Checks) Myrtle Doyle, CPA, is performing the 19X5 audit of Stardust Tours, Inc. During the audit of cash, Doyle notes a lengthy list of checks in numerical sequence, all dated December 31, 19X5.

REQUIRED

What procedure(s) might Doyle perform to determine if there are any checks dated December 31, 19X5, but not released until 19X6?

14-39. (Bank Transfers) Southeastern Mills Corporation is a large branch that maintains its own bank account. Cash is periodically transferred to the central account in Atlanta. On the branch account's records, bank transfers are recorded as a debit to the home office clearing account and as a credit to the branch bank account. The home office account is recorded as a debit to the central bank account and a credit to the branch office clearing account.

Robert Cole is the chief bookkeeper for both offices. As the auditor, you are concerned because he also reconciles the bank account. A staff auditor prepared a schedule of bank transfers for December 23, 19X4, through January 9, 19X5. The list follows:

Amount of Transfer	Date Recorded in Branch Office Cash Disbursements Journal	Date Recorded in the Home Office Cash Receipts Journal	Date Deposited in the Home Office Bank Account	Date Cleared the Branch Bank Account
$39,000	1-7-X5	1-3-X5	1-2-X5	1-6-X5
26,000	1-6-X5	1-9-X5	12-27-X4	1-4-X5
31,000	1-4-X5	1-4-X5	12-26-X4	12-31-X4
10,000	12-28-X4	12-25-X4	12-23-X4	12-24-X4
23,000	1-2-X5	12-29-X4	12-29-X4	12-30-X4
16,000	12-30-X4	1-3-X5	12-27-X4	12-28-X4
12,000	12-25-X4	12-25-X4	12-27-X4	1-4-X5

REQUIRED

A. State the audit procedures to be performed in verifying each bank transfer.
B. Prepare adjusting entries for the home office records.
C. Prepare adjusting entries for the branch bank records.
D. How should each bank transfer be included in the 12-31-X4 bank reconciliation for the home office before the adjustments made in **B**?
E. How should each bank transfer be included in the 12-31-X4 bank reconciliation of the branch bank account before your adjustments in **C**?

*14-40. (Audit of Sales) Your client is the Quaker Valley Shopping Center, Inc., a shopping center with 30 store tenants. All leases with the store tenants provide for a fixed rent plus a percentage of sales, net of sales taxes, in excess of a fixed dollar amount computed on an annual basis. Each lease also provides that the landlord may engage a CPA to audit all records of the tenant for assurance that sales are being properly reported to the landlord.

Your client has requested that you audit the records of the Bali Pearl Restaurant to determine that the sales totaling $390,000 for the year ended December 31, 19X7, have been properly reported to the landlord. The restaurant and the shopping center entered into a five-year lease in January, 19X7. The Bali Pearl Restaurant offers only table service. No liquor is served. During mealtimes there are four or five waitresses in attendance who prepare handwritten prenumbered restaurant checks for the customers. Payment is made at a cash register, operated by the proprietor, as the customer leaves. All sales are for cash. The proprietor is also the bookkeeper. Complete files are kept of restaurant checks and cash register tapes. A daily sales book and general ledger are also maintained.

REQUIRED

A. For purposes of this audit, which audit objectives are you primarily concerned with?
B. List the auditing procedures you would employ to verify the total annual sales of the Bali Pearl Restaurant. (Disregard vending machine sales and counter sales of chewing gum and candy.)

*14-41. (Sales Cutoff) Your client took a complete physical inventory under your observation as of December 15 and adjusted the inventory control account (perpetual inventory method) to agree with the physical inventory. You have decided to accept the balance of the control account as of December 31, after reflecting transactions recorded therein from December 16 to December 31, in connection with your examination of financial statements for the year ended December 31.

right before and right after year end

---

*AICPA adapted.

Your examination of the sales cutoff as of December 15 and December 31 disclosed the following items not previously considered.

| | | | Date | |
Cost	Sales Price	Shipped	Billed	Credited to Inventory Control
$2,840	$3,690	12-14	12-16	12-16
3,910	5,020	12-10	12-19	12-10
1,890	2,130	1-2	12-31	12-31

REQUIRED

What adjusting journal entries, if any, would you make for each of these items?

*14-42. (Audit of Revenue) You are engaged in your first audit of the Licitra Pest Control Company for the year ended December 31, 19X8. The company began doing business in January 19X8 and provides pest control services for industrial enterprises.

Additional information:

1. The office staff consists of a bookkeeper, a typist, and the president, Tony Licitra. In addition, the company employs 20 service personnel on an hourly basis who are assigned to individual territories to make both monthly and emergency visits to customers' premises. The service people submit weekly time reports, which include the customer's name and the time devoted to each customer. Time charges for emergency visits are shown separately from regular monthly visits on the report.

2. Customers are required to sign annual contracts that are prenumbered and prepared in duplicate. The original is filed in numerical order by contract anniversary date, and the copy is given to the customer. The contract entitles the customer to pest control services once each month. Emergency visits are billed separately.

3. Fees for monthly services are payable in advance—quarterly, semiannually, or annually—and are recorded on the books as "income from services" when the cash is received. All payments are by checks received by mail.

4. Prenumbered invoices for contract renewals are prepared in triplicate from information in the contract file. The original invoice is sent to the customer 20 days prior to the payment due date, the duplicate copy is filed chronologically by due date, and the triplicate copy is filed alphabetically by customer. If payment is not received by 15 days after the due date, a cancellation notice is sent to the customer and a copy of the notice is attached to the customer's contract. The bookkeeper notifies the service people of all contract cancellations and reinstatements and requires written acknowledgment of receipt of such notices. Licitra approves all cancellations and contract reinstatements.

5. Prenumbered invoices for emergency services are prepared weekly from information shown on the time reports of the service people. The customer is billed at 20% of the service people's hourly rate. These invoices, prepared in triplicate and distributed as shown above, are recorded on the books as "income from services" at the billing date. Payment is due 30 days after the invoice date.

6. All remittances are received by the typist, who prepares a daily list of collections and stamps a restrictive endorsement on the checks. A copy of the list is forwarded to the bookkeeper, who posts the date and amount received on the copies of the invoice in both the alphabetical and chronological files. After posting, the copy of the invoice is

---

transferred from the chronological file to the daily cash receipts binder, which serves as a subsidiary record for the cash receipts book. The bookkeeper totals the amounts of all remittances received, posts this total to the cash receipts book, and attaches the daily remittance tapes to the paid invoices in the daily cash receipts binder.

7. The typist prepares a daily bank deposit slip and compares the total with the total amount shown on the daily remittance tapes. All remittances are deposited in the bank the day they are received. (Cash receipts from sources other than services need not be considered.)

REQUIRED

List the audit procedures you would employ in the audit of the "income from services" account for 19X8. In developing the procedures, consider the strengths and weaknesses in the internal control structure.

14-43. (Linking Audit Objectives to Assertions for Accounts Receivable) The following list illustrates audit objectives for accounts receivable.

1. Accounts receivable are authentic obligations owed to the company at the balance sheet date.
2. Accounts receivable include all amounts owed to the company as of the balance sheet date.
3. The allowance for doubtful accounts is adequate but not excessive.
4. Pledged, discounted, or assigned accounts receivable are properly disclosed. Related party and employee receivables are properly disclosed.
5. Accounts receivable are properly classified in the balance sheet.
6. For a company using the direct write-off method, all significant doubtful accounts have been written off and the bad debt exposure in the remaining accounts is insignificant.

REQUIRED

For each objective, identify the relevant client assertion(s).

*14-44. (Confirmation of Receivables) You are considering using the services of a reputable outside mailing service for the confirmation of accounts receivable balances. The service would prepare and mail the confirmation requests and remove the returned confirmations from the envelopes and give them directly to you.

REQUIRED

What reliance, if any, could you place upon the services of the outside mailing service? State and discuss the reasons for your answer.

14-45. (Confirmation of Receivables) You have been engaged to perform the 19X4 audit of Southern Hardware Company. You have tested the trial balance and are selecting accounts receivable for confirmation. As you begin to select these, you are interrupted by the controller, who has a list of several accounts she would like to omit from confirmation:

Company	Balance
Royal Motors, Inc.	$ (155.00)
Jordan Supply	-0-
Hare Furniture Mfg.	$ 20.00
Dye Industrial Mfg. Co.	$2,500.00

The controller feels that a confirmation would upset these companies and might prompt Royal Motors to request a refund of its credit balance. Some of the companies, she feels, will withdraw their business if Southern becomes a nuisance.

She compiles a list of fifteen other accounts she would like for you to confirm. These typically are slow-paying customers and she feels that this will prompt them to pay off their accounts.

REQUIRED

A. Is it appropriate for the controller to review the list of accounts the auditor plans to confirm?

B. Should the auditor send the fifteen additional confirmations? If so, what effect would it have on the auditor's report?

*14-46. (Confirmation Requests) Billie Dodge, CPA, is auditing the financial statements of a manufacturing company with a significant amount of trade accounts receivable. Dodge is satisfied that the accounts are properly summarized and classified and that allocations, reclassifications, and valuations are made in accordance with generally accepted accounting principles. She is planning to use accounts receivable confirmation requests to satisfy the third standard of fieldwork as to trade accounts receivable.

REQUIRED

A. Identify and describe the two forms of accounts receivable confirmation requests and indicate what factors Dodge will consider in determining when to use each.

B. Assume that Dodge has received a satisfactory response to the confirmation requests. Describe how Dodge could evaluate collectibility of the trade accounts receivable.

*14-47. (Nonreply to Confirmation Requests) Maria Nolan, CPA, in auditing the financial statements of the Quinn Helicopter Corporation for the year ended September 30, 19X7, found a material amount of receivables from the federal government. The government agencies replied neither to the first nor to the second confirmation requests, nor to a third request made by telephone.

REQUIRED

A. How could Nolan satisfy herself as to the fairness of the receivables as of the balance at September 30, 19X7?

B. Assuming she was able to satisfy herself, what is the effect on the auditor's report?

*14-48. (Exceptions to Confirmation Requests) You have been assigned to the first audit of the accounts of the Chicago Company for the year ending March 31, 19X8. The accounts receivable were confirmed at December 31, 19X7, and at that date the receivables consisted of approximately 200 accounts with balances totaling $956,750. Seventy-five of these accounts with balances totaling $650,725 were selected for confirmation. All but 20 of the confirmation requests have been returned; 30 were signed without comments and 14 had minor differences that have been cleared satisfactorily, whereas 11 confirmations had the following comments:

1. We are sorry but we cannot answer your request for confirmation of our account as the JKA Company uses an accounts payable voucher system.
2. The balance of $1,050 was paid on December 23, 19X7.
3. The balance of $7,750 was paid on January 5, 19X8.
4. The balance noted above has been paid.
5. We do not owe you anything at December 31, 19X7, as the goods represented by your invoice dated December 30, 19X7, number 25050, in the amount of $11,550, were received on January 5, 19X8, on F.O.B. destination terms.
6. An advance payment of $2,500 made by us in November 19X7 should cover the two invoices totaling $1,350 shown on the statement attached.
7. We never received these goods.
8. We are contesting the propriety of this $12,525 charge. We think the charge is excessive.
9. Amount okay. As the goods have been shipped to us on consignment, we will remit payment upon selling the goods.

---

*AICPA adapted.

10. The $10,000, representing a deposit under a lease, will be applied against the rent due to us during 19X9, the last year of the lease.

11. Your credit memo dated December 5, 19X7, in the amount of $440, cancels the balance above.

REQUIRED

What steps would you take to clear satisfactorily each of the above 11 comments?

14-49. (Overstatement of Accounts Receivable) In recent years your audit client, Landscapes International, has experienced a decrease in income due to competition from a number of new landscaping firms. Most recently, Landscapes incurred a severe loss and realized the need to make changes in operations. While discussing this year's audit, Anita Baker, the controller, mentions that she has criticisms of your firm and the accounting profession as a whole. She feels that your audit approach concerns itself excessively with the overstatement of assets and the understatement of liabilities. To illustrate, she points to an incident in which a customer said nothing about the understatement of his account while customers whose accounts were overstated responded promptly. She feels that even the accounts selected for tests emphasize overstatement, because large balances are most frequently confirmed. At one point, she even threatens to change firms to someone who is more concerned with a balance of overstatements and understatements.

REQUIRED

As the auditor, you feel that you should respond to her arguments and you decide to expound on her accounts receivable example. How would you respond?

*14-50. (Accounts Receivable Confirmation) The CPA firm of Wright & Co. is in the process of auditing William Corporation's 19X5 financial statements. The following open matters must be resolved before the audit can be completed:

1. No audit work has been performed on nonresponses to customer accounts receivable confirmation requests. Both positive and negative confirmations were used. A second request was sent to debtors who did not respond to the initial positive request.

2. William's management has not completed and signed the client representation letter. Wright has started to outline the content of the representation letter and believes the following matters should be included: Management should acknowledge whether or not

- all material transactions have been properly reflected in the financial statements.

- it is aware of irregularities that could have a material effect on the financial statements or that involve management or employees.

- events have occurred subsequent to the balance sheet date that would require adjustment to, or disclosure in, the financial statement.

- there are any communications from regulatory agencies concerning noncompliance with, or deficiencies in, financial reporting practices.

- the company has complied with all aspects of contractual agreements that would have a material effect on the financial statements in the event of noncompliance.

- there are any plans or intentions that may materially affect the carrying value or classification of assets or liabilities.

- there are any losses from sales commitments.

- there are any losses from purchase commitments for inventory quantities in excess of requirements or at prices in excess of market.

- there are any agreements to repurchase assets previously sold.

---

*AICPA adapted.

- there are any violations or possible violations of laws or regulations whose effects should be considered for disclosure in the financial statements or as a basis for recording a loss contingency.

- there are any capital stock repurchase options or agreements or capital stock reserved for options, warrants, conversions, or other requirements.

REQUIRED

A. What alternative audit procedures should Wright consider performing on the nonresponses to customer accounts receivable confirmation requests?

B. Identify the other matters that Wright would expect to be included in William's management representation letter.

Audit Judgment Case

14-51. You have been asked to serve as an expert witness for an auditor in a lawsuit charging the auditor with negligent conduct of the audit. The plaintiff claims that the auditor failed to perform adequate tests of revenue and, as a result, the entity's revenue for 19X4 was overstated by $30,000,000 and net income for that year was overstated by $10,000,000. Both amounts are conceded to be material.

You have just finished your initial meeting with the auditor's legal counsel and obtained the information summarized below. The attorney has asked you to identify the areas in which the auditor's work conforms with generally accepted auditing standards and could be presented as a defense against the negligence charge. The attorney, however, also wants to be informed of any areas where you believe the auditor's work might be vulnerable to the negligence claim.

- The overstatements occurred because the sales were recorded in the last ten days of the client's fiscal year but were not actually shipped until the first two weeks of the next year (19X5).

- Total sales and net income (including the effect of the premature revenue recognition) were, respectively, $120,000,000 and $50,000,000.

- Large shipments close to year-end are not unusual for this client or for other companies in this industry. Pressure to meet budget causes companies in the industry to "work like crazy" to get products out of the door during the last week or two of the fiscal year. In addition, the auditor had not found material overstatements of either the number or dollar amount of shipments during the previous ten years he had audited this client. However, the dollar amount of shipments in the last week of 19X4 was 20% higher than any of the prior ten years.

- The auditor sent positive accounts receivable confirmation requests to 55 of the client's 197 customers. These confirmations represented $32,000,000, or 80%, of the client's $40,000,000 total accounts receivable.

- A total of 38 of the responses were returned. Of those, 12 responses contained similar comments to the effect that the merchandise did not arrive until after the date of the account balance being confirmed. The senior auditor on the engagement followed up on those comments with the controller. He provided customer purchase orders, sales invoices, and bills of lading for 10 of those responses showing that the merchandise was ordered, shipped, and billed in 19X4. After the lawsuit was filed, the controller disclosed that the shipment dates on 4 of the bills of lading had been altered by client personnel to show 19X4 shipment instead of the actual 19X5 shipment date. For 6 of the other comment responses, the controller revealed that client personnel prepared fictitious bills of lading using blank forms stolen from the trucking company. For the remaining 2 responses with comments, the auditor treated the accounts as if the entire balance was in error because the total of those 2 accounts did not result in a material missstatement of the financial statements.

■ For the 17 nonresponses, the auditor took the following steps:

8 responses—sent second requests and received 2 fax replies and 1 oral confirmation. Two customers replied that they were unable to confirm balances because they used the voucher system and the auditor took no further action. The 3 remaining second requests were still outstanding when the audit report was issued.

7 responses—examined subsequent cash payments by the customers and observed that they paid the amount shown in the confirmation request no later than February 28, 19X5.

2 responses—discussed the balances in telephone conversations with the customers' controllers and was told that they had purchased the merchandise but were returning it under the right of return provisions of the sales agreements.

■ The dollar amounts related to the above confirmation request categories were as follows:

26 responses received without comment	$11,000,000
12 responses received with comments	13,000,000
17 nonresponses	8,000,000

■ The auditor had assessed control risk as moderate for both the existence assertion for accounts receivable and the occurrence assertion for revenue.

REQUIRED
After reading the information above, prepare a list of what you perceive to be the positive and negative aspects of the auditor's procedures and evaluations.

Auditing Issues Case

14-52. KELCO MANUFACTURING COMPANY

Kelco has three bank accounts: an operations account, a payroll account, and an administrative account. Both Cook, the company's president, and Hill, the head of the accounting department, are authorized to sign on the accounts. The company also maintains a $1,000 petty cash account for which Hill was responsible. Hill was having a bit of financial hard luck. On May 15, hard pressed for cash, she wrote a check for $5,000 payable to cash, endorsed the back of the check, and cashed it. Having committed the crime, Hill devised a way to conceal the embezzlement until she could make restitution to the company.

The $5,000 check was written out of the operating account. Hill did not record the transaction on the company books. The bank statement for the month ended May 31 showed a balance of $17,523. The outstanding checks were #1011 for $1,525, #1013 for $1,415, #1016 for $1,500, #1017 for $2,245, #1018 for $3,000, #1019 for $1,649, #1020 for $3,145, #1021 for $575, #1022 for $1,886, and #1023 for $560. The bank reconciliation prepared by Hill is presented below:

Kelco Manufacturing Company
Bank Reconciliation—Operating Account
For the Month ended May 31, 199X

Cash per books		$ 9,040
Add: interest earned..		58
		$ 9,098
Less: Bank service charge	$ 15	
Check printing charge	60	75
Adjusted cash balance		$ 9,023
Cash per bank statement		$17,523
Add: deposit in transit..		4,500
Less: outstanding checks		
#1017..	$2,245	
#1018..	3,000	
#1019	1,649	
#1020	3,145	
#1021	575	
#1022	1,886	$12,500
Adjusted cash balance..		$ 9,023

On the last day of the following month, June 30, Hill wrote check #585 from the administrative account in the amount of $5,000 and deposited it in the operating account thus covering the check she had written in connection with her embezzlement of company funds. She did not record the check on the company books. On the last day of July, Hill again in an effort to cover her theft wrote check #1254 on the operating account in the amount of $5,000 and deposited it in the administrative account.

REQUIRED
1. What techniques did Hill employ to cover the theft of funds?
2. What procedure could you as the auditor use to discover the theft?
3. What recommendations would you make to Cook that could prevent this from occurring in the future?

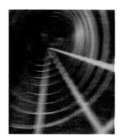

Understanding the Internal Control Structure, Assessing Control Risk, and Performing Substantive Tests: The Expenditure Cycle

Learning Objectives

- Identify the common internal control structure policies and procedures for the significant assertions related to the expenditure cycle.

- Explain the accounting system for purchases and cash payments.

- Describe the typical tests of controls for significant expenditure cycle assertions.

- Describe and explain the common substantive tests for significant purchases assertions.

- Describe and explain the substantive tests for significant accounts payable assertions, including the search for unrecorded liabilities.

Many companies like Bethlehem Steel Corporation now make substantial purchases on a time and material basis. Contractors multiply worker hours by a set rate and charge a preset profit margin on materials used. This billing method solves several problems for contractors, who in the past have often padded fixed job bids in anticipation of future unforeseen problems. The method is also beneficial when the estimation of a job's duration is nearly impossible.

Contractors may be enthusiastic about time and material purchasing, but the method leaves companies like Bethlehem vulnerable. For example, there is no way for accountants to tell if an invoice is accurate simply by looking at it, and most contractors have no incentive to pinch pennies on labor or materials. So, to protect the company, accountants from Bethlehem conduct periodic compliance audits to ensure that company suppliers and contractors are maintaining an accurate handle on billings. These auditors must remain alert because there are a host of different contract arrangements: Some wage rates are set, and others are based on the market; some suppliers work with established materials pricing, while others utilize a mark-up factor. The number of potential variations is limitless, and because of that fact, one thing is certain. Accountants must first get a firm grasp of an agreement before they can hope to conduct a useful and meaningful audit. ∎

Source: Paul R. Hubling, "Auditing Time and Material Contractors at Bethlehem Steel," *Management Accounting*, September, 1994, pp. 53–55.

The *expenditure cycle*, the second transaction cycle discussed in this textbook, includes the purchase of goods and services from parties outside the entity and the disbursement of cash to pay for those purchases. Expenditure cycle transactions can be classified into two major categories: (1) purchase transactions and (2) cash payment transactions. The specific major activities in each category are shown in Table 15–1.

The expenditure cycle does not include the acquisition and payment of employees' services (payroll transactions). These are part of the conversion cycle and are discussed in Chapters 16 and 17. Neither does the expenditure cycle include the acquisition and payment of capital such as debt or stockholder's equity, which are part of the financing and investing cycle discussed in Chapter 18.

The first part of this chapter discusses the five internal control structure elements for purchase and cash payment transactions and the related account balances. The second part discusses assessing control risk for the assertions pertaining to those transactions and balances. Part three discusses substantive tests for the assertions related to expenditure cycle transactions and account balances.

Understanding the Internal Control Structure for the Expenditure Cycle

For most merchandising and manufacturing entities, the purchase and payment of goods and services are major transaction categories. The assets acquired, the liabili-

Table 15–1	**Expenditure Cycle Activities**	
	Purchase Transactions	Cash Payment Transactions
	■ Requisitioning goods or services ■ Ordering goods or services ■ Receiving goods or services ■ Storing goods	■ Paying for goods and services

ties incurred, and the cash disbursed are often material in amount, and a sound internal control structure is necessary to ensure the proper matching of revenues and expenses.

Control Environment, Risk Assessment, Communication, and Monitoring

An entity's control environment, risk assessment process, communication system, and monitoring program, as discussed in Chapter 6, are usually broad components of the internal control structure and pertain to all transaction cycles. These components, unlike accounting systems and control activities, do not exist for individual cycles. Consequently, the auditor does not obtain a separate understanding of each of these components for each transaction cycle. Rather, the auditor obtains an understanding of the overall control environment, risk assessment process, communication system, and monitoring program and then relates that understanding to each of the individual transaction cycles.

Chapter 6 discusses how the auditor obtains an understanding of these broad components. This chapter later explains the auditor's consideration of these components in assessing control risk for the expenditure cycle assertions.

Accounting System

The expenditure cycle accounting system consists of the methods and records an entity uses to identify, assemble, classify, record, and report purchase and cash payment transactions and to account for the related assets and liabilities. To understand the expenditure cycle accounting system, the auditor learns about how purchase and cash payment transactions are initiated; the accounts, ledgers, journals, and documents used to account for those transactions; and the methods or steps taken to process them and report them in the financial statements. Table 15–2 describes the common accounts, documents, and files associated with the expenditure cycle accounting system. The flowchart in Figure 15–1 shows how these key accounts, documents, and files are used in a common expenditure cycle accounting system and the typical processing steps that occur in the transaction flow. The flowchart also indicates how duties are segregated among major functions of the expenditure cycle.

Table 15–2	Key Accounts, Documents, and Files of the Expenditure Cycle*

Accounts	Documents
■ Purchases ■ Purchases Returns and Allowances ■ Accounts Payable ■ Cash in Bank ■ Selling Expenses (various) ■ Manufacturing Expenses (various) ■ Administrative Expenses (various)	*Check* A document that authorizes the transfer of cash from the entity's bank account to another party. *Purchase Order* A written notice to a vendor to indicate that the entity desires to purchase specific goods or services. The purchase order usually describes the type of goods or services, the quantity, price, and terms of shipment and payment. *Purchase Requisition* A written request by an authorized employee to purchase specific goods or services. *Receiving Report* A written report of goods received from suppliers. It usually records the description, quantity, condition, vendor name, and date of receipt. *Vendor Invoice* A document used by the vendor to bill its customers. It usually includes a description of the goods or services, quantity, price, and date and terms of sale. *Vendor Statement* A document sent to the vendor's customers each month showing the customer's opening balance; customer's transactions for purchases, purchase adjustments, and cash payments during the month; and closing balance. *Voucher* A document used to establish a formal, controlled record of purchases. It serves as the basis for recording purchase and accounts payable transactions and for making cash payments.

*The documents, journals, ledgers, and files may be prepared and maintained either manually or with a computer.

Purchase and Cash Payment Transactions

Purchase transactions are typically initiated by preparing a *purchase requisition form* either manually or by computer. Preparing requisition forms is usually the responsibility of central stores or a warehouse. When the requisition form is prepared and approved, one copy is filed in central stores and another is sent to the purchasing department.

The purchasing department uses the requisition form to prepare the *purchase order*. When the department finds a vendor who will supply the goods on favorable terms, it mails a copy of the purchase order to the vendor. One copy of the purchase order is filed numerically in the purchasing department and other copies are sent to the receiving department, vouchers payable department, and central stores. The copy sent to receiving alerts the receiving clerk that goods have been ordered and serves

Journals and Ledgers	Files
Accounts Payable Subsidiary Ledger A ledger used to record individual purchases, cash payments, and accounts payable balances for each vendor. Companies that do not use an accounts payable subsidiary ledger generally pay vendors by individual vouchers. The total of accounts payable at any given time is the total of unpaid vouchers.	*Approved Vendor File* A list of authorized vendors with whom orders may be placed.
	Paid Voucher File Contains vouchers that have been paid.
	Receiving Report File Contains copies of completed receiving reports.
	Unfilled Purchase Order File Contains purchase orders for which goods have not been received.
Cash Payments Journal A journal (book of original entry) used to record cash payments made by check. It contains columns for the credit to cash, the debit to accounts payable, and for recording any purchase discounts or other adjustments.	*Unfilled Purchase Requisition File* Contains copies of purchase requisitions sent to purchasing for which goods have not been received.
	Unpaid Voucher File Contains vouchers authorized for payment filed by payment due date.
Voucher Register An accounting journal (book of original entry) used to record individual vouchers or batches of vouchers. Generally a voucher register includes columns for recording the type of purchase (inventory or various expenses) and accounts payable.	

as a means of comparing goods ordered with goods received. The copy sent to vouchers payable is used to compare goods ordered with the vendor's invoice. The copy returned to central stores is compared to the copy of the original requisition so that the stores can notify purchasing of any discrepancies.

When goods are received, the receiving clerk matches their description with the accompanying shipping document and the purchase order and then prepares a *receiving report*. The receiving report usually includes the vendor name, item description, quantity, date received, and comments about the condition of the goods. One copy of the receiving report is typically filed numerically in receiving, one copy accompanies the goods to central stores, and other copies are forwarded to vouchers payable.

Figure 15-1   **Flowchart of Purchases and Cash Payments**

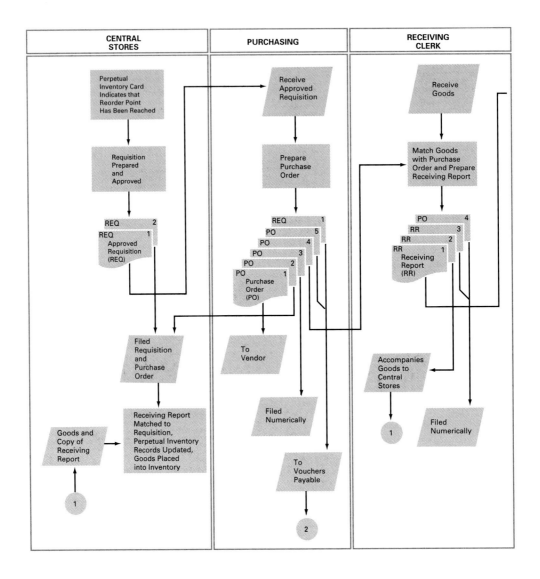

The vouchers payable department matches copies of the purchase order and receiving report with the *vendor's invoice* and prepares a *voucher*, a document used to summarize and record a purchase transaction and approve payment. A copy of the voucher is sent to general accounting for recording and posting to the *accounts payable subsidiary ledger*. The voucher is then filed in an *unpaid voucher file*. Near the payment due date, copies of the voucher and all supporting documents are sent to the treasurer for payment.

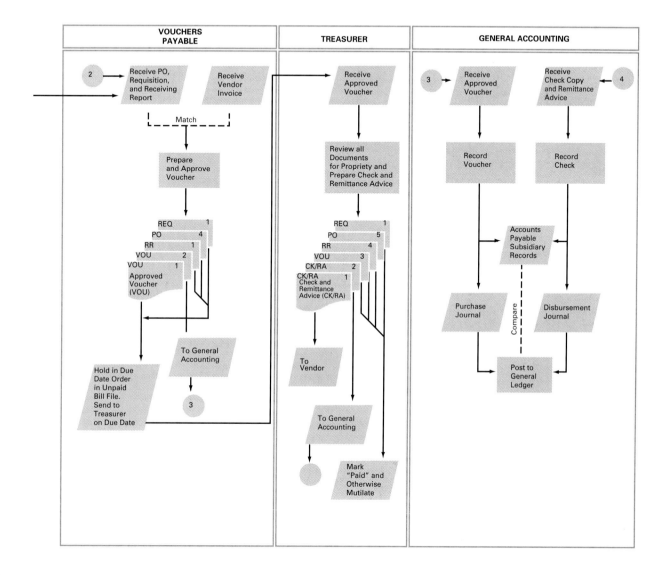

The treasurer reviews the approved voucher and supporting documents for proper authorization and approval. The treasurer's office then prepares a check and remittance advice and mails them to the vendor. The voucher and the vendor's invoice are marked "PAID" and the voucher is filed numerically in a *paid voucher file.* A copy of the check or paid voucher is then sent to general accounting for journalizing and posting to the accounts payable subsidiary ledger.

Control Activities

The type and extent of control activities pertaining to the expenditure cycle will vary from entity to entity. A number of the common control activities in this cycle are discussed below according to the control activities classification outlined in Chapter 6. The relationship of these control procedures to the purchases and cash payments assertions is discussed later in the section on assessing control risk.

Performance Reviews

Performance review control activities in the expenditure cycle often include comparing actual expenditures for inventory purchases, manufacturing, selling, and administrative expenses with budgets, forecasts, and prior periods. These comparisons may be done for the overall entity, or by division, function, or even individual. For example, a purchasing manager may review inventory acquisition reports for specific products with the budget and follow up on significant variances. In addition, nonfinancial information, such as the number of units manufactured or the number of sales calls made can be used to determine the reasonableness of manufacturing costs or selling expenditures.

Information Processing

A variety of control activities may be performed to check the authorization, accuracy, and completeness of expenditure cycle transactions.

Authorization often is required for (1) requisitioning goods, (2) placing the purchase order, (3) receiving goods, (4) storing or using goods, and (5) paying the vendor. These authorizations help the entity to avoid over- or under-stocking inventory or supplies, to obtain the best purchase prices, to protect the goods on hand, and to avoid improper cash payments.

Using and accounting for prenumbered forms designed to capture all information necessary to process properly a purchase or cash payment transaction are common control procedures. Requisitions, purchase orders, receiving reports, vouchers, and checks are examples of forms for which these procedures may be used. These forms are generally imprinted with the entity name and often contain other information to help ensure proper accounting for purchase and cash payment transactions. For example, purchase orders may be preprinted with the receiving location and may instruct vendors to deliver only to that location.

Requisitions, purchase orders, receiving reports, and vendor invoices may be compared for consistency, and the amounts on vendor invoices may be recomputed for proper extensions and footings. These comparisons and recomputations may be done manually or by computer. The approval of requisitions, purchase orders, and vouchers may be reviewed by independent entity personnel. Bank accounts are usually reconciled with accounting records.

The auditor is likely to become aware of a number of these control procedures when obtaining an understanding of the accounting system. As can be seen from the preceding description of the accounting system and from the flowchart in Figure 15–1, the auditor is likely to learn whether requisition forms, purchase orders, receiving reports, vouchers, and checks are prenumbered and accounted for; whether requisitions, purchase orders, and receiving reports are matched with vendors' invoices prior to preparing and paying a voucher; and whether vouchers are approved prior to payment and canceled after they have been paid. The auditor is also likely to become aware of control procedures over the physical handling of goods, such as whether they are inspected and counted and whether they are stored in secure locations from the point of receipt to placement in the warehouse or stockroom. Furthermore, the auditor will probably learn something about the segregation of duties among the personnel and departments that process purchasing and cash payment transactions.

The auditor decides whether the knowledge of control procedures obtained from an understanding of the control environment and the accounting system is sufficient to plan the audit. If the auditor believes additional knowledge of control procedures is necessary, he or she will perform additional inquiry, observation, and inspection procedures to obtain sufficient knowledge.

Physical Controls

Using secured locations and designating individuals allowed access to purchased goods protect against unauthorized access to goods received. In addition, storing accounting records and documents, such as the vouchers payable file, purchase orders, and checks, in secure areas protects them from unauthorized access and use.

Proper Segregation of Duties

No one involved in purchase and cash payment activities should be in a position both to perpetrate and to conceal errors or irregularities. In larger organizations, separate departments are responsible for the major expenditure cycle activities. For example, a stores department may be responsible for requisitions, a purchasing department may be responsible for issuing and following up on purchase orders, and a receiving department may be responsible for accepting goods from vendors. Vouchers are usually prepared by the vouchers payable department, and checks are issued by the treasurer. Within these departments, and in smaller companies in which such departments are not feasible, individuals are assigned these duties in such a manner that no one person is responsible for authorizing purchase or cash payment transactions, recording those transactions, and maintaining custody of goods or cash.

Assessing Control Risk for the Expenditure Cycle

After obtaining the understanding of the internal control structure necessary to plan the expenditure cycle audit, the auditor assesses control risk for the financial statement assertions related to the transactions and account balances in that cycle. Tables 15–3 and 15–4 relate assertions to internal control structure policies and procedures for purchase transactions and cash payment transactions. Each table lists some key policies and procedures in the five internal control structure components that can reduce the risk of material misstatements in each of the five assertions for each expenditure cycle transaction category. Each table also explains why a policy or procedure is relevant to a specific assertion and describes the related tests of controls.

Although the control environment, risk assessment, communication, and monitoring have a general effect on all transaction cycles, a number of specific factors in these components may directly affect control risk for the financial statement assertions related to expenditure cycle transactions. For example, the methods an entity uses to assign and communicate authority and responsibility may define acceptable business practices and conflicts of interests in the purchase of goods and services. Such policies may cover "kickbacks" and purchases from vendors where a purchasing agent has a vested interest. The policies may reduce the likelihood that invalid purchase or cash payment transactions will be recorded—the existence or occurrence assertion.

Table 15-3	Overview of Internal Control Structure Policies and Procedures and Tests of Controls for Purchase Transactions Assertions

Assertion	Relevant Internal Control Structure Policy or Procedure
Existence or Occurrence	■ Use prenumbered purchase requisitions, purchase orders, and receiving reports, and account for their numerical sequence.*
	■ Independently review authorizations of purchase requisitions and purchase orders and independently match vendor invoice with those documents and with related receiving report.*
	■ Cancel purchase transaction documents immediately after processing.
	■ Reconcile vendors' statements with accounts payable records.
	■ Compare budgeted with actual purchases and analyze significant variances.
Completeness	■ Use prenumbered purchase requisitions, purchase orders, and receiving reports, and account for their numerical sequence.*
	■ Reconcile vendors' statements with accounts payable records.
	■ Use checklists or budgets to determine whether all purchased services have been recorded.

*This policy or procedure may be performed either manually or by a computer programmed to compare information relevant to the control and produce a report of exceptions.

An entity's assessment and response to the risks associated with adding new product lines may help avoid the failure to record certain inventory purchases—the completeness assertion—or to misclassify those purchases as noninventory items—the presentation and disclosure assertion.

Why Policy or Procedure Is Relevant to Assertion	Common Tests of Controls for Policy or Procedure
■ Establishes formal, controlled records documenting that a purchase occurred.	■ Inquire about and observe use of these prenumbered documents and accounting for sequence. For example, examine computer generated exception reports of nonsequential document use.
■ Ability to support vendor invoice with authorized requisition, order, and receiving report helps substantiate that a purchase occurred.	■ Inspect evidence that documents were authorized and matched with vendor invoice. For example, examine computer generated exception reports of unmatched documents.
■ Cancellation prevents documents from being reused to support another transaction.	■ Inquire about, observe, and inspect document cancellations.
■ Accounts payable records may contain purchase transactions that are not on vendor statements because they did not occur.	■ Inquire about and observe reconciliation and inspect vendor correspondence files and follow-up records.
■ Significant variances of actual purchases over budget may be due to recording purchases that did not occur.	■ Inquire about use of budgets and inspect reports that follow up on variances.
■ Establishes formal, controlled records that an order and receipt have occurred and should be recorded as a purchase.	■ Inquire about and observe use of these prenumbered documents and accounting for sequence. For example, examine computer generated exception reports of nonsequential document use.
■ Vendor statements may identify purchases that have not been recorded in accounts payable records but should be.	■ Inquire about and observe reconciliation and inspect vendor correspondence files and follow-up records.
■ Checklists and budget analysis help identify services received that should be recorded as purchases.	■ Inquire about, observe, and inspect use of checklists and budgets.

(continued)

Purchase Transactions

Table 15–3 contains a number of fundamental internal control structure policies and procedures found in many entities that pertain to purchase transaction assertions.

Table 15-3	*continued*

Assertion	Relevant Internal Control Structure Policy or Procedure
Rights and Obligations	■ Require that documentation for consignment orders and receipts clearly specifies a consignment transaction.
	■ Require that goods received on consignment are tagged or physically separated from purchased goods.
Valuation or Allocation	■ Independently compare item description, quantities, and prices on vendor invoices with related data on purchase requisitions, orders, and receiving reports.*
	■ Independently recompute extensions and footings on vendor invoices.*
	■ Reconcile vendors' statements with accounts payable records.
	■ Compare budgeted with actual purchases and analyze significant variances.
Presentation and Disclosure	■ Use chart of accounts with adequate detail.
	■ Independently review account codings on purchase requisitions, orders, or vendor invoices.
	■ Compare budgeted with actual purchases and analyze significant variances.
	■ Use disclosure checklists.
	■ Independently review disclosures.

*This policy or procedure may be performed either manually or by a computer programmed to compare information relevant to the control and produce a report of exceptions.

Why Policy or Procedure Is Relevant to Assertion	Common Tests of Controls for Policy or Procedure
■ Helps prevent consignment transactions from being recorded as purchases.	■ Inquire about documentation policies for consignment transactions and inspect such documentation for proper codings.
■ Helps prevent consigned goods from being recorded as purchases.	■ Inquire about tagging or separation policies for consigned goods and observe tagging or separation of such goods.
■ Helps identify incorrect items, quantities, and prices on vendor invoices before recorded as purchases.	■ Inspect evidence that vendor invoices matched with requisitions, orders, and receiving reports. For example, examine computer generated exception report of unmatched documents.
■ Helps identify incorrect extensions or footings on vendor invoices before recorded as purchases.	■ Inspect evidence that extensions and footings recomputed. For example, examine computer generated exception reports of erroneous extensions and footings.
■ Incorrect valuation of purchases recorded in accounts payable may be identified by comparison with vendor statements.	■ Inquire about and observe reconciliation, and inspect vendor correspondence files and follow-up records.
■ Significant variances of actual purchases over or under budget may be due to incorrect purchases valuation.	■ Inquire about use of budgets and inspect reports that follow up on variances.
■ Helps identify specific accounts in which purchases should be classified when recorded.	■ Inquire about, inspect, and observe use of chart of accounts.
■ Helps identify incorrect account classifications before purchase recorded.	■ Inspect evidence that account codings were reviewed.
■ Significant variances of actual purchases over or under budget may be due to incorrect transaction classification.	■ Inquire about use of budgets and inspect reports that follow up on variances.
■ Helps ensure that all disclosures have been made and that adequate information has been disclosed.	■ Inspect checklists and evidence that they are used.
■ Helps ensure that disclosures are complete and accurate.	■ Inspect evidence that disclosures have been reviewed.

Although some of these policies and procedures are relevant to more than one assertion, to avoid repetition they are discussed in detail for only one assertion. Their applicability, however, will be indicated in the discussion of other assertions.

Existence or Occurrence Assertion

The existence or occurrence assertion for purchase transactions means that the recorded purchase transactions actually occurred and that the related accounts payable balance actually exists. An entity might erroneously record purchase transactions when goods or services have not been received or might intentionally record purchases that did not occur. In either case, assets, expenses, and liabilities will be overstated.

Several internal control structure policies and procedures are frequently used to prevent or detect such misstatements. The entity's accounting system may require that it prepare purchase requisitions, purchase orders, and receiving reports. Prenumbering these documents, requiring their authorization, and accounting for their serial continuity creates formal, controlled documents that serve as the basis for recording a purchase. Such documents help to ensure that only purchases that actually occurred are recorded. In addition, an independent entity employee may review the authorizations on these documents and match them with the vendor's invoice before a journal entry is made. This review and matching aids in authenticating that a purchase occurred and that an account payable exists before the transaction is recorded in the accounting records. The auditor's typical tests of controls for these policies and procedures are inquiring about and observing the use of these documents, inspecting evidence that their numerical sequence is accounted for, and inspecting evidence that the authorization review and document matching have been done by appropriate entity personnel.

Receiving reports are particularly important in documenting both that goods were received and the date of their receipt. Typically, the purchase order copy sent to the receiving department has the quantities blocked out to help ensure that receiving department personnel count the incoming goods. Receiving personnel should also determine that the item received is the item ordered, inspect its condition, and record the receipt date. Without receiving reports, misstatements may occur in the existence or occurrence assertion for purchases and the related accounts payable balances because the entity may record a purchase for goods it did not receive. This assertion is usually more susceptible to misstatement around year-end, when the cutoff of these transactions between the current year and subsequent year becomes particularly important.

The auditor's tests of control for receiving reports include inquiring about how they are used and observing their preparation. The auditor may also compare the data on receiving reports with related documents such as purchase orders and vendor invoices on a test basis.

Immediately after documents supporting a vendor invoice are used to record a purchase transaction, they should be canceled. Cancelation prevents the intentional or unintentional reuse of these documents to record a duplicate (nonexistent) purchase. As tests of controls for this control procedure, auditors usually inquire about document cancelation procedures, observe cancelations, and inspect supporting documents to determine that they have been canceled.

The Real World of Auditing

Cash Fraud Techniques and Frequency of Use

Fraud Techniques	Percentage of Frauds Involving This Method
Cash taken from receipts using	
Unrecorded sales	30%
Collections of recorded receivables with	
Concealment by customer adjustments	18%
Concealment by lapping	17%
No attempt to conceal	14%
Other concealment	5%
Collections of unrecorded receivables for insurance claims, refunds due employer and written off	
accounts receivable	8%
Other receipts	1%
*Cash taken from disbursements using	
Fictitious payables or customer refunds	24%
Unauthorized loans	10%
Petty cash disbursements	6%
Payroll and involving	
Overstated earnings for self	7%
Overstated earnings for others	3%
Other payroll	3%
Fictitious employees	2%
Other disbursements	6%

Note: The percentages add to more than 100% because many of the cases involved the use of more than one fraud method.
*Emphasis added.

"... it was very surprising that the largest frauds were associated with non-financial areas. Purchasing had the largest frauds with an average of $349,750.

Other fraud methods could be very difficult for management to prevent or detect with ordinary procedures. For example, a scheme involving payments of fictitious payables combined with collusion among employees or with outsiders could be conducted for a long time. It might continue until it was divulged by informants or became so large that it was obvious."[1]

_____

[1]John P. Guercio, E. Barry Rice, and Martin F. Sherman, "Old Fashion Fraud by Employees Is Alive and Well: Results of a Survey of Practicing CPAs," *The CPA Journal*, September 1988.

Monthly vendor statements also provide an entity with a means of detecting purchase transactions that did not occur. Reconciling these statements with the entity's accounts payable subsidiary ledger may identify purchases and related payables recorded on the books that do not appear in the vendor's statement because they never occurred. The usual tests of controls for this procedure are auditor inquiry about and observation of whether it is used and inspection of the client's vendor correspondence and follow-up files to assess how effectively the procedure is operating.

An entity's budget of purchases may also help identify recorded purchase transactions that did not occur. In seeking an explanation of the excess of actual purchases over budget, management may identify improperly recorded purchases and accounts payable. Tests of controls that auditors commonly use to evaluate the effectiveness of the design and operation of this procedure are inquiring about the use of budgets and inspecting reports concerning the investigation of those instances in which the actual purchases significantly varied from the budget. The auditor is usually particularly concerned with how conscientiously management investigates and follows up on the causes of budget variances.

Completeness Assertion

The completeness assertion for purchases means that all of the purchase transactions and related accounts payable that should have been recorded were recorded. An entity may erroneously fail to record the receipt of goods or services or may intentionally not record certain purchase transactions and accounts payable. In either case, assets, expenses, and liabilities will be understated.

As indicated in the discussion of the existence or occurrence assertion above, the accounting system for most entities calls for the use of prenumbered purchase requisitions, purchase orders, and receiving reports and includes accounting for the numerical sequence of these documents. This procedure provides formal, controlled documents indicating that a purchase transaction was initiated and that goods were received. When the entity accounts for the numerical sequence of these documents and periodically traces them to the formal accounting records, the risk that purchase transactions and related payables will not be recorded is greatly reduced. The tests of controls for this procedure involve auditor inquiry about and observation of the use of these prenumbered documents and inspection of evidence that entity personnel have accounted for their numerical sequence and traced them to the accounting records.

In entities with computerized accounting systems, on-line terminals are sometimes used to compare simultaneously goods received to goods ordered and to update accounts payable and purchase files. This procedure helps ensure that each purchase transaction is valid (the existence or occurrence assertion) and that it is recorded in the accounting records (the completeness assertion).

The client's reconciliation of vendor statements with its accounts payable subsidiary ledger may identify unrecorded purchases and accounts payable. A purchase shown on the vendor's statement but not recorded in accounts payable may result from a failure to record a purchase that should have been recorded. The tests of controls for this procedure are the same as that discussed for the existence assertion.

Purchases of services, as opposed to goods, sometimes pose special problems regarding the completeness assertion. Typically, entities do not prepare receiving reports for the receipt of services, such as consulting services, even though these service purchases may require purchase requisitions and purchase orders. Moreover, for some services, such as utilities, entities do not prepare purchase requisitions, purchase orders, or receiving reports. Ideally, an entity should require that other types of documentation be prepared when major services are purchased. The lack of documentation of the purchase and receipt of such services may increase the risk of not recording such transactions unless compensating policies or procedures are established.

Commonly used compensating policies and procedures include using checklists and budgets of standard purchased services to help identify purchases that should be recorded. For example, a checklist or budget may include services for utilities, taxes, leases, consultants, and advertising. The typical tests of controls for this control procedure are auditor inquiry about and inspection of the use of checklists or budgets. The auditor should be particularly concerned that the checklist or budget is not used in a perfunctory manner. Employees responsible for using these instruments should know which entity personnel to consult to determine whether specific services have been purchased.

Rights and Obligations Assertion

The rights and obligations assertion for purchases means that the recorded purchases and related accounts payable are actually purchases and liabilities of the client. Although this assertion is not significant to all entities, it can be important in small businesses where there is a danger of commingling the owner's personal transactions with those of the entity. It may also be significant when an entity acquires a material amount of goods on consignment. If a client records a purchase and account payable for goods received on consignment, assets and liabilities will be overstated—a misstatement in the rights and obligations assertion.

To avoid recording a purchase and payable for goods received on consignment, entities often mark consignment purchase requisitions, purchase orders, and receiving reports to indicate a consignment transaction. The tests of controls for this procedure are auditor inquiry about consignment documentation practices and inspection of such documentation to determine that it is properly identified. Some entities also physically segregate or tag goods held on consignment to help prevent improper accounting for such goods. As a test of this control procedure, auditors normally inquire about its application and observe the tags or segregation.

Valuation or Allocation Assertion

The valuation or allocation assertion for purchase transactions and related accounts payable means that amounts recorded for purchases and payables are correct. Purchase and payable amounts may be recorded incorrectly for a number of reasons. An incorrect price may be charged on the vendor invoice, or erroneous extensions or footings may cause the vendor invoice to be misstated. In addition, the wrong item, defective items, or incorrect quantities may be accepted. Such mistakes can affect the valuation or allocation assertion because they may result in damaged, slow-moving, or obsolete goods.

To help ensure that vendors only accept items of the correct type, quality, and quantity, entities usually designate personnel to inspect and count goods received and to prepare receiving reports to document these data. In addition, personnel compare receiving reports with purchase requisitions, purchase orders, and vendor invoices, and check the mathematical accuracy of vendor invoices before purchases are recorded. These control procedures help identify vendor mistakes that can cause improper valuation of purchases.

The common tests of controls for these procedures involve auditor inquiry about and observation of the preparation, use, comparison, and recalculation of these documents. In addition, the auditor inspects evidence that appropriate entity personnel compared the documents and made the recalculations. In some circumstances, the auditor may reperform the mathematical checks of vendor invoices on a test basis.

Client reconciliation of vendor statements with accounts payable records may also identify improper purchase valuations. Discrepancies between amounts in a vendor's statement and in the payable records may be caused by incorrect valuation of a purchase transaction. In addition, where material misstatements in the valuation of purchase transactions have occurred, management's analysis of variances between budgeted and actual purchases may identify them. The tests of controls for these control procedures were discussed earlier in this chapter.

Presentation and Disclosure Assertion

The presentation and disclosure assertion for purchase transactions and related accounts payable means that purchases and payables are classified in the appropriate accounts and that notes to the financial statements contain the disclosures about those accounts that are required by generally accepted accounting principles. Misclassifications of purchase transactions can occur when a purchased asset is classified as an expense or vice versa. In addition, a misclassification in payables can result when a trade account payable is improperly recorded as a nontrade payable—for example, when the liability for an inventory purchase is erroneously recorded as a lease liability.

An accounting system that includes a detailed chart of accounts can help ensure that purchases and accounts payable are properly classified. Many entities require that purchase requisitions, purchase orders, vendor invoices, and related vouchers be coded with the number of the account in which the purchase is to be recorded. These codings may be reviewed by independent entity personnel or by a computer prior to recording the transaction to increase the likelihood that they will be recorded in the proper account. The auditor's typical tests of controls for these procedures include inspecting the chart of accounts, observing and inspecting the coding of purchase transaction documents, and inspecting evidence that independent personnel or the computer checks the coding prior to recording.

Purchase and payable misclassification may also be detected when management follows up on significant variances between budgeted and actual purchases or when monthly vendor statements are reviewed. Such variances may be caused by recording purchase transactions in the wrong accounts.

Although disclosures about purchases of goods and services and the related accounts payable are usually not complex, they may become so when transactions involve related parties or foreign countries. Entity accounting personnel may use checklists to reduce the likelihood of inadequate or erroneous disclosures about purchases and payables, and knowledgeable entity personnel may review the financial statement disclosures prior to the statements' final preparation. Tests of controls concerning disclosures for purchases and payables usually include auditor inquiry about which entity personnel prepare disclosures and whether checklists are used and disclosures are reviewed, and inspection of completed checklists and evidence of disclosure review by appropriate entity personnel.

Purchase Return and Allowance Transactions

Purchase returns and allowances result from adjustments made for various reasons to purchase transactions. For example, purchase adjustments may be necessary because the vendor shipped more goods than ordered, some goods were damaged, or not all ordered goods were shipped. In addition, a vendor may grant price adjustments to correct mistakes in pricing.

Although purchase returns and allowance transactions are common in most entities, this chapter does not discuss them in detail, since the internal control structure policies and procedures for the assertions related to these transactions are basically the same as for purchase transactions. Generally they include the use of prenumbered, authorized documents to record purchase adjustment transactions. These documents, such as debit memos or claim forms, document that a purchase adjustment transaction occurred (existence or occurrence assertion) and help ensure that all such transactions are recorded (completeness assertion) at the proper amount (valuation or allocation assertion) and in the proper account (presentation and disclosure assertion). The documents are processed in virtually the same manner as purchase transactions.

Cash Payments

Table 15–4 lists typical internal control structure policies and procedures and the related tests of controls relevant to cash payments assertions.

Existence or Occurrence Assertion

The existence or occurrence assertion for cash payments means that recorded cash payments actually occurred. Although some fraud schemes may involve attempts to record fictitious cash payments, the risk that recorded payments are bogus is ordinarily not high. As discussed in the following section, the greatest risk is usually associated with the failure to record cash payments—the completeness assertion.

Virtually all cash accounting systems include the use of prenumbered checks imprinted with the entity's name. In addition, specific entity personnel are authorized to sign checks. Consequently, a properly authorized, numbered entity check provides a formal, controlled record of a cash payment. The typical tests of controls for these control procedures include inquiring about and observing the use and authorization of prenumbered checks, inspecting signatures on canceled checks, and inspecting evidence that the sequence of checks is periodically accounted for.

Monthly bank reconciliations may also help identify cash payments recorded in the accounting records that did not actually occur. A recorded cash payment that cannot be reconciled to the bank statement may be invalid.

Completeness Assertion

The completeness assertion for cash payments means that all cash disbursed has been recorded. A major control procedure for ensuring that cash payments are recorded is documenting cash payments at the time of disbursement. Using prenumbered checks,

Table 15–4	Overview of Internal Control Structure Policies and Procedures and Tests of Controls for Cash Payment Transactions

Assertion	Relevant Internal Control Structure Policy or Procedure
Existence or Occurrence	■ Use prenumbered checks and account for continuity of numerical sequence.*
	■ Authorize specific individual(s) to sign checks.
	■ Prepare monthly bank reconciliation.
Completeness	■ Use prenumbered checks and account for their numerical sequence.*
	■ Periodically compare issued checks with cash disbursements journal.*
	■ Prepare monthly bank reconciliation.
Rights and Obligations	Generally not a significant assertion for cash payments
Valuation or Allocation	Generally not a significant assertion for cash payments
Presentation and Disclosure	Generally not a significant assertion for cash payments

*This policy or procedure may be performed either manually or by a computer programmed to compare information relevant to the control and produce a report of exceptions.

designating authorized check signers, and periodically accounting for the numerical sequence of the checks are common means of establishing this documentation. These checks provide a formal, controlled record of cash payments that should be recorded. Periodically comparing issued checks with the cash payments journal helps ensure that all cash payments are recorded. As tests of controls for this procedure, the audi-

Why Policy or Procedure Is Relevant to Assertion	Common Tests of Controls for Policy or Procedure
■ Establishes a formal, controlled record documenting that a cash payment occurred.	■ Inquire about and observe use of prenumbered checks and the accounting for sequence. For example, examine computer generated exception reports of nonsequential document use.
■ Confines authority for issuing checks, thus reducing likelihood that invalid cash payments will be recorded.	■ Inquire about authorized check signer(s) and inspect check signatures.
■ May identify cash payments recorded in the accounting records but not recorded in the bank statement because they did not occur.	■ Inquire about and observe preparation of bank reconciliations or inspect reconciliations.
■ Establishes a formal, controlled record of cash payments made that should be recorded.	■ Inquire about and observe use of prenumbered checks and the accounting for sequence. For example, examine computer generated exception reports of nonsequential document use.
■ May identify checks issued but not recorded in the accounting records.	■ Inspect evidence that periodic comparison has been made. For example, examine computer generated exception report of unmatched checks and follow-up.
■ May identify cash payments recorded in the bank statement that were not recorded in the accounting records.	■ Inquire about and observe preparation of bank reconciliations or inspect reconciliations.

tor inquires about which employee makes this comparison and observes the comparison or inspects evidence that it has been made.

Monthly bank reconciliations also help identify unrecorded cash payments. The reconciliation should reveal checks that have cleared the bank but were not recorded in the accounting records.

Rights and Obligations Assertion, Valuation or Allocation Assertion, and Presentation and Disclosure Assertion

The rights and obligations assertion, valuation or allocation assertion, and presentation and disclosure assertion are ordinarily not significant for cash payments per se. As a result of the double entry bookkeeping effect, the potential for misstatements in these assertions is addressed by internal control structure policies and procedures for purchase transactions and related accounts payable. That is, internal control structure policies and procedures pertaining to the debit side of the entry (purchases) also affect the credit side (cash payments). For example, policies and procedures designed to help ensure that purchases and payables are properly valued also help ensure that the resulting cash payment is properly valued. Similarly, policies and procedures designed to promote proper classification of purchases and payables also promote correct classification of the resulting cash payment.

Determining the Assessed Level of Control Risk

The auditor determines the assessed level of control risk for purchase and cash payments assertions based on the evidence obtained about the effectiveness of the design and operation of the internal control structure policies and procedures relevant to those assertions. The more effective the design and operation of these policies and procedures, the lower the assessed level of control risk will be.

Evidence about the effectiveness of design and operation is obtained from tests of controls performed in prior audits, those performed while obtaining an understanding of the internal control structure, and any additional tests of controls performed after obtaining the understanding. The assessed level of control risk for a specific purchase or cash payment assertion is used in determining what substantive tests to apply to that assertion.

Substantive Tests of Balances and Transactions for the Expenditure Cycle

As shown in Table 15–2, expenditure cycle transactions affect several account balances. For most entities, the more significant of these accounts are usually accounts payable and purchases.

Accounts Payable

Accounts payable typically represents the client's primary current liability. Current liabilities often are very significant to a company and to the users of the financial statements. Along with current assets, current liabilities represent one of the primary means by which creditors evaluate the liquidity of a company.

Because of the importance of current liabilities to working capital, a primary measure of liquidity and solvency, clients may be motivated to understate current liabilities and thus improve the reported working capital of the company. Because of this factor, auditors generally are concerned with the understatement of liabilities and the overstatement of assets. Consequently, auditors typically emphasize the completeness assertion (understatement) for liabilities and the existence assertion (overstatement) for assets. The assertions of rights and obligations and valuation typically do not present problems in liabilities unless related parties exist. Valuation of most liabilities is the dollar amount required to discharge the debt, assuming the debt reflects a market rate of interest at the date of issuance.

Table 15-5 **Common Substantive Audit Tests for Accounts Payable**

Common Audit Tests	Technique	Type of Test	Assertions
Foot and vouch accounts payable listing	Reperformance Vouching	Test of balances	Completeness Existence
Confirm accounts payable or requests for statements	Confirmation	Test of balances	Completeness Existence
Search for unrecorded liabilities	Vouching	Test of transactions	Completeness

Companies maintain receivable records by customer because they must encourage customers to pay. No such burden exists for accounts payable, and many companies therefore do not maintain accounts payable records by customer. Rather, they record accounts payable by voucher number, purchase order number, or due date. For example, companies may record accounts payable by due date so that they can take advantage of cash discounts by paying these accounts payable as they become due. Some companies do not record accounts payable at all but, instead, simply record the transaction when the cash disbursement is made.

The more common substantive audit tests for accounts payable are shown in Table 15–5. These include footing and vouching the accounts payable listing, confirming accounts payable, and performing a search for unrecorded liabilities. Accounts payable is closely tied to the audit of cash disbursements, purchasing, receiving, and inventory.

Foot and Vouch Accounts Payable Listing

One of the first audit tests generally performed on accounts payable is to obtain a listing from the client of accounts payable amounts owed to creditors. Of course, this procedure cannot be performed if the client does not record accounts payable but only cash disbursements. The auditor should verify this list by refooting the schedule either manually or by using computer software and making sure the total agrees with the balance in the general ledger. Further, the auditor may vouch from the listing to the appropriate purchase orders and invoices as a test of existence. The auditor should scan the listing to determine that no material debit balances exist that should be reclassified as receivables.

Confirm Accounts Payable or Requests for Creditor Statements

Confirmation, or requests for creditor statements, is one of the primary audit tests for accounts payable. Two principal types of accounts payable confirmation requests are used: (1) a request that the creditor confirm the balance per the client's records (similar to a positive accounts receivable confirmation request) and (2) a request that the creditor send a copy of its statement to the auditor. A *request for statement of account* is the more common request because it usually generates a higher response rate by vendors and provides more detail to assist the auditor in reconciling the vendor's receivable and the client's payable. Figure 15–2 illustrates a request for statement of account.

Figure 15–2	**Request for Statement of Account**

> **Plainsman Company**
> **P.O. Box 2322**
> **Grand Rapids, Michigan 48101**
>
> **January 10, 19X5**
>
> **Propst Corporation**
> **3520 West Paces Ferry Rd.**
> **Potsdam, New York 13676**
>
> **Gentlemen:**
>
> **Will you please send directly to our auditors, Matt Oaks & Co., Certified Public Accountants, an itemized statement of our account at December 31, 19X4? In addition to the statement, would you please include the following information:**
> **1) Amount of purchase commitments**
> **2) Collateral held**
> **3) Amounts past due**
>
> **Enclosed is a business reply envelope addressed to our auditors. A prompt reply is requested.**
>
> **Sincerely yours,**
>
> *Ben Palmer*
> **Ben Palmer**
> **Controller**
> **Plainsman Company**
>
> **BP/hp**

Confirmation of accounts payable may provide evidence on either completeness or existence. The assertion addressed (completeness or existence) depends upon how the auditor designs the test. The auditor generally emphasizes *completeness* for accounts payable because liabilities are more likely to be understated. Confirmation of accounts payable will provide evidence of completeness if the auditor includes confirmations of balances that are small (for example, a common supplier with a zero balance) but that have the potential to be quite large. To gather evidence as to completeness, the auditor sends confirmations on accounts payable to the client's principal vendors and suppliers regardless of the balances in those accounts at the balance sheet date. This differs from the procedure used for accounts receivable, in which the auditor emphasizes existence and confirms large account balances while confirming only a few, if any, small account balances.

To gather evidence on completeness for accounts payable, the auditor often confirms zero balances. The auditor's objective is to obtain evidence for accounts payable that may possibly have large balances that have not been recorded. Depending on the audit objective, the auditor will select for confirmation those accounts payable that have a variety of characteristics, such as the following:

- Small or zero balance creditors.
- Vendors used in prior periods.
- New vendors used subsequent to year-end.
- High-value individual accounts.
- High-volume vendors.

Confirmations of accounts payable will not always allow the auditor to discover unrecorded liabilities because no record of the creditor may exist.

If attempting to gather evidence of the *existence* (overstatement) of accounts payable, the auditor would choose a quite different sample selection. In this case, the auditor would tend to select for confirmation accounts payable with large balances. As is the case with other confirmations, the auditor should maintain control over the preparation, mailing, and receipt of accounts payable confirmations. Likewise, the auditor must reconcile all differences between the client's records and the accounts payable confirmations received from vendors. Differences frequently result from payments or shipments in transit, but they sometimes may be the result of clerical errors, disputed items, or unrecorded payables.

As with accounts receivable confirmations, accounts payable confirmations that are not returned may require alternative procedures. The auditor must follow the requirements of *SAS No. 39, Audit Sampling* (AU 350) when selecting a sample of accounts payable for confirmation. *SAS No. 39* requires the auditor either to perform alternative procedures or to consider the nonresponses as a misstatement. A nonresponse to an accounts payable confirmation (especially a request for statement of account) probably indicates that the client has a zero balance. Because the accounts payable confirmation test is usually designed to test completeness (that is, is there an unrecorded item?), a nonresponse is generally not serious. The auditor may appropriately conclude that the accounts payable balance is not understated. However, if the auditor is testing for existence, the implication that the client probably does not owe anything is much more serious. In testing for existence, the auditor is concerned about balances that are shown to exist in the financial records but that, in fact, do not exist. Thus, in cases of nonresponse alternative procedures may need to be performed.

Search for Unrecorded Liabilities

As noted previously, the completeness assertion generally receives more attention in the audit of accounts payable because there is motivation to understate liabilities. Another important substantive audit test usually performed on accounts payable is a **search for unrecorded liabilities**. In practice, this test is often performed along with confirmation of accounts payable. This test provides evidence as to completeness and some evidence as to valuation.

In a search for unrecorded liabilities, the auditor reviews disbursements made by the client for a period after the balance sheet date, sometimes to the date of completion of fieldwork. Even though a client may not record an accounts payable at year-end, vendors will probably pressure the client to pay the accounts payable within a reasonable period of time. Because of this pressure, most unrecorded accounts payable are paid within a reasonable time after the balance sheet date. By reviewing cash disbursements subsequent to the balance sheet date, the auditor gains a good idea of the potential population of unrecorded accounts payable.

The search for unrecorded liabilities generally begins with a review of the cash disbursements journal for a period after the balance sheet date. From this review, the auditor selects items (generally those over a minimum amount) for testing. The auditor then vouches the sample to the invoices to determine whether the purchase relates to the period before year-end or after year-end. For example, the auditor, in examining January disbursements, may find that an electric utility bill was paid. By taking this cash disbursement and vouching it to the invoice from the utility company, the auditor may determine that the bill relates to the period of December, prior to year-end. This would result in an unrecorded liability that the auditor would propose as an adjusting entry, if material.

The search for unrecorded liabilities supplies good evidence for completeness because it provides a greater range of coverage than confirmations. Of course, there is the implicit assumption in a review of cash disbursements after year-end that accounts payable have been paid when, in fact, accounts payable due at year-end may not be paid until a month or more following year-end. In this situation the account would not be included in the population from which the auditor reviews cash disbursements. Confirmations or requests for statements may reveal this type of situation, however, so auditors may perform both a search for unrecorded liabilities and a confirmation of accounts payable.

Other potential substantive audit tests for unrecorded accounts payable (completeness) include the following:

- For an appropriate period before and after the balance sheet date, check vendor invoices to and from receiving records and determine that any liability was recorded in the proper period.

- Review bank confirmations.

- Reconcile vendor monthly statements with client records.

- Compare the balance of accounts payable to purchases or gross margin and compare to previous periods.

- Compare current-year expense account balance with that of the prior year and consider whether large decreases could represent unrecorded debt.

Accounts Payable Substantive Tests and Control Risk

The assessed level of control risk for each of the significant assertions related to accounts payable affects the nature, timing, and extent of substantive tests the auditor performs. To illustrate, when the assessed levels of control risk for the completeness and valuation assertions are low, the auditor may decide not to confirm accounts payable (or request creditor statements) or may confirm fewer creditor accounts and confirm payables as of an interim date rather than at year-end. In addition, the auditor may review fewer cash disbursement transactions in the period after the balance sheet date, increase the minimum amount of such transactions, or shorten the length of the review period. The auditor is also likely to use more analytical procedures. Furthermore, the auditor may omit or reduce reconciling vendor monthly statements with client records. As the assessed levels of control risk for these assertions increase, however, the auditor will modify these substantive tests in the opposite manner.

Purchases

As with the audit of sales, audit procedures for purchases are primarily tests of transactions rather than a test of balances, because the balance in purchases is a summation of the individual purchases made throughout the year. Whether the audit of purchases is performed primarily by tests of controls or substantive tests, the procedures are typically tests of transactions.

If control risk for purchases is low, substantive testing of purchases may be limited. Alternatively, if control risk is high, the auditor must perform more extensive substantive tests of purchases. In performing audit tests on accounts payable, cash, and cash disbursements, the auditor has already indirectly gathered evidence on purchases. For this reason, substantive audit tests over purchases generally are limited. Table 15–6 lists the more common substantive audit tests for purchases.

Scanning the Purchases Journal

The auditor will often review or scan the purchases journal for the year to determine if any unusual or large amounts exist. This audit test provides evidence of valuation and presentation and disclosure because large items are identified and then investigated further.

Vouch Cash Disbursements

Another common substantive test of purchases is vouching cash disbursements. In this test of transactions, the auditor selects a sample of cash disbursements and vouches them by examining the underlying documentation for reasonableness and authenticity. The primary purpose of vouching cash disbursements is to gather evidence on occurrence, presentation and disclosure, and valuation. Having selected a sample of cash disbursements from the cash disbursements journal, the auditor should then examine such documents as purchase orders, receiving reports, vendors' invoices, and canceled checks. The auditor should verify that the quantities are correct, the descriptions are consistent, and the amount of purchase equals the amount received and the amount billed. This type of audit test provides evidence that all recorded purchases are for goods and services received and are appropriately classified.

| Table 15-6 | Common Substantive Audit Tests for Purchases |

Common Audit Tests	Technique	Type of Test	Assertions
Scan purchases journal	Inspection	Test of transactions	Valuation Presentation and disclosure
Vouch cash disbursements	Vouching	Test of transactions	Existence or occurrence Valuation Presentation and disclosure
Trace from receiving reports to purchases journal and cash disbursements journal	Tracing	Test of transactions	Completeness

Tracing

Another common substantive audit test for purchases is tracing from purchase orders and receiving reports to the purchases journal and cash disbursements journal. This test, of course, goes in the opposite direction of vouching cash disbursements. In tracing, the auditor starts at the beginning of the transactions—the purchase orders. For selected purchase orders, the auditor examines receiving reports and the purchases journal entry to determine that purchases were properly recorded. As with vouching, the auditor should examine quantities, descriptions, and computations. In performing the tracing procedure, the auditor is concerned that all purchases have been recorded. Thus, this audit test is primarily related to completeness.

Other Tests

Numerous other audit tests exist for purchases, some of which have been discussed in connection with the audit of other accounts. For example, a proof of cash as discussed in the preceding chapter represents good evidence not only for cash receipts but also for cash disbursements and purchases. The proof of cash is a substantive test of transactions.

In performing the vouching procedure, the auditor should verify that cash disbursements are for goods and services actually received by examining canceled checks and by determining that the payees are the same as those entered into the purchases journal. Another common audit test previously discussed is the purchase cutoff procedure performed in connection with inventory. The purchase cutoff test also provides evidence of the completeness and existence of purchases.

Accruals and Deferrals

Because accruals and deferrals do not generally represent large dollar balances, the audit time and effort expended on accruals and deferrals typically is small. Many accruals and deferrals are supported by examining other accounts in the financial statements. For example, in examining bonds payable, the auditor often tests accrued interest payable on the bonds. Likewise, in the audit of payroll, the auditor determines if any accrual needs to be made not only for wages payable but for other items such as sick leave and payroll taxes. Thus, the primary audit tests for accruals and deferrals frequently come from the audit of other financial statement accounts.

A common audit test for both accruals and deferrals is recalculation. For example, if the client has accrued warranty claims payable, the auditor typically gathers evidence to support the assumptions underlying the accrual and makes a recalculation to determine that it is properly computed. Another example relates to prepaid insurance, a deferred account. In this situation, the auditor might obtain a schedule of prepaid insurance from the client and test the client's computations to determine how much of the prepaid insurance has expired during the year. Once again, these procedures are generally quite limited because these accounts are typically immaterial. Analytical procedures such as reasonableness tests also represent common audit tests for accruals and deferrals. Comparison of accrued balances of this year with those of last year and comparisons of accruals and deferrals with budgets also produce evidence that accruals and deferrals are fairly stated in conformity with generally accepted accounting principles.

Significant Terms

Expenditure cycle The purchase of goods and services from parties outside the entity and the disbursement of cash to pay for those purchases.

Request for statement of account A request from the client that a vendor provide a statement to the auditor of the balance owed by the client. The procedure is used to determine the existence, completeness, and valuation of a client's accounts payable.

Search for unrecorded liabilities A substantive audit test designed to detect understatement (completeness assertion) of a client's liabilities.

Tests of controls for purchases and cash payments Tests that evaluate the effectiveness of the design and operation of the internal control structure policies and procedures for purchases and cash payments.

Discussion Questions

15-1. What is the purpose of and relationship among the following expenditure cycle documents? (1) purchase requisition, (2) purchase order, (3) receiving report, (4) voucher.

15-2. Briefly describe the flow of documents for the purchase and cash payments transactions.

15-3. How might management's use of budgets reduce the likelihood of a material misstatement in the completeness assertion for purchases?

15-4. What two specific mistakes that can occur in processing purchase transactions would result in the failure to record accounts payable? Briefly explain why the mistakes would result in unrecorded payables.

15-5. What three important duties should be segregated in the expenditure cycle? Why should they be segregated?

15-6. How is the reconciliation of vendor statements with the accounts payable subsidiary ledger relevant to the completeness assertion for purchases?

15-7. To which assertion or assertions in the expenditure cycle does the control procedure of monthly bank reconciliations relate? Why does this relationship exist?

15-8. Generally, receiving reports are not prepared for purchased services. What are two internal control structure policies or procedures that an entity might use to help ensure that the purchase and related liability for services are recorded in the accounting records?

15-9. If an entity orders goods on a consignment basis, what financial statement assertion would be misstated if the consigned goods were erroneously recorded as a purchase? Explain why.

15-10. Five internal control structure policies and procedures relevant to expenditure cycle assertions are listed below. For each policy or procedure, identify the assertion or assertions to which it relates and describe for it a test of controls.
1. Cancel purchase transactions documents after processing.
2. Clearly mark documentation for consignment orders and receipts as consignment transactions.
3. Use chart of accounts to determine appropriate account in which to record a purchase.
4. Prepare monthly bank reconciliation.
5. Periodically compare issued checks with the cash disbursements journal.

15-11. Why is the auditor particularly concerned about the potential understatement of liabilities?

15-12. When confirming accounts payable, what class of vendors would the auditor most likely confirm and why? How does an account payable confirmation differ from a request for statement of account?

15-13. In searching for unrecorded liabilities, the auditor will review disbursements made by the client after the balance sheet date. Why?

Objective Questions

15-14. Which of the following sets of duties would be considered an improper segregation of duties in the expenditure cycle?

(1) Receiving, counting, and inspecting goods, and also preparing the receiving report.

(2) Preparing, approving, and issuing purchase orders, and also following up on unfilled orders.

(3) Approving vouchers for payment and also preparing and signing checks.

(4) Comparing vendor invoices with purchase orders, requisitions, and receiving reports, and also approving vouchers for payment.

15-15. Control risk for the completeness assertion for purchase transactions can be reduced by all of the following internal control structure policies or procedures except

(1) cancelling purchase transaction documents immediately after processing them.

(2) reconciling vendors' statements with the accounts payable subsidiary ledger.

(3) reviewing checklists of services ordinarily purchased by the entity.

(4) comparing budgeted with actual purchases.

15-16. Which of the following internal control structure policies or procedures would help reduce control risk for the completeness assertion for cash payments?

(1) A check signing machine is used.

(2) Voided checks are destroyed immediately.

(3) Vouchers are prepared by individuals responsible for signing checks.

(4) Each month, bank statements are reconciled with the entity's cash accounting records.

15-17. Fagan Products, Inc., requires that an approved receiving report be prepared before an entry is made in the voucher register to record a purchase and related account payable. To test the effectiveness of this control procedure, the auditor compares the date on the receiving report with the date of the entry in the voucher register. The auditor would be most likely to question the effectiveness of this control procedure when the test of controls reveals that

(1) voucher register entries are dated on or after the corresponding receiving report dates.

(2) receiving reports are dated on or before the corresponding voucher register entry dates.

(3) receiving reports are dated after the corresponding voucher register entry dates.

(4) voucher register entries are dated after the corresponding receiving report dates.

15-18. A clerk in Blanco Enterprises is assigned to reconcile monthly vendor statements with the company's accounts payable subsidiary ledger. This internal control structure procedure is least likely to reduce control risk for the

(1) completeness assertion for accounts payable.

(2) presentation and disclosure assertion for purchases.

(3) existence or occurrence assertion for cash payments.

(4) valuation or allocation assertion for purchases.

15-19. Which of the following internal control structure policies or procedures would least likely prevent or detect a misstatement in the existence or occurrence assertion for cash payments caused by the duplicate payment of a voucher?

(1) Cancelling documentation supporting the voucher immediately after the voucher is paid.

(2) Reconciling monthly vendor statements with the accounts payable subsidiary ledger.

(3) Individuals responsible for signing checks also preparing and approving vouchers.

(4) Attaching a check copy to the voucher immediately after the voucher is paid.

15-20. Sultan Products ordered a six months' supply of part X29. A receiving clerk erroneously accepts the shipment of 2,000 units of part X29, even though only 20 units were ordered.

The terms of sale are such that the vendor will not accept returned goods once they have been accepted. This error is most likely to result in a misstatement in which of the following expenditure cycle assertions?
(1) The valuation or allocation assertion for purchases.
(2) The completeness assertion for purchases.
(3) The existence or occurrence assertion for purchases.
(4) The presentation and disclosure assertion for purchases.

15-21. Sauter Enterprises receives substantial quantities of goods on consignment from Mancino, Inc. These goods are not recorded in Sauter's accounting records until they are sold to customers. To help prevent recording consigned goods in inventory, Sauter uses receiving reports for such goods that are of a different color than receiving reports for purchased inventory. This accounting procedure is intended to help prevent a misstatement in which one of the following assertions?
(1) The valuation or allocation assertion for purchases.
(2) The completeness assertion for cash payments.
(3) The rights and obligations assertion for purchases.
(4) The existence or occurrence assertion for purchases.

15-22. In comparing the confirmation of accounts payable with suppliers and confirmation of accounts receivable with debtors, which of the following statements is true?
(1) Confirmation of accounts payable with suppliers is a more widely accepted auditing procedure than is confirmation of accounts receivable with debtors.
(2) Statistical sampling techniques are more widely accepted in the confirmation of accounts payable than in the confirmation of accounts receivable.
(3) As compared with the confirmation of accounts payable, the confirmation of accounts receivable will tend to emphasize accounts with zero balances at the balance sheet date.
(4) It is less likely that the confirmation request sent to the supplier will show the amount owed the supplier than that the request sent to the debtor will show the amount due from the debtor.

15-23. Why do the audit procedures used to verify accrued liabilities differ from those employed for the verification of accounts payable?
(1) Accrued liabilities usually pertain to services of a continuing nature, whereas accounts payable are the result of completed transactions.
(2) Accrued liability balances are less material than accounts payable balances.
(3) Evidence supporting accrued liabilities is nonexistent, whereas evidence supporting accounts payable is readily available.
(4) Accrued liabilities at year-end will become accounts payable during the following year.

15-24. Under which of the following circumstances would it be advisable for the auditor to confirm accounts payable with creditors?
(1) Internal control structure policies and procedures for accounts payable are adequate and sufficient evidence is on hand to minimize the risk of a material misstatement.
(2) Confirmation response is expected to be favorable and accounts payable balances are of immaterial amounts.
(3) Creditor statements are not available and internal accounting control over accounts payable is unsatisfactory.
(4) The majority of accounts payable balances are with associated companies.

15-25. Which of the following audit procedures is least likely to detect an unrecorded liability?
(1) Analysis and recomputation of interest expense.
(2) Analysis and recomputation of depreciation expense.
(3) Mailing of standard bank confirmation form.
(4) Reading of the minutes of meetings of the board of directors.

Problems and Cases

*15-26. (Raw Materials and Purchases Deficiencies) You were engaged by the management of Alden, Inc., to review its internal control structure policies and procedures over the purchase, receipt, storage, and issue of raw materials. You have prepared the following comments that describe Alden's procedures.

> Raw materials, which consist mainly of high-cost electronic components, are kept in a locked storeroom. Storeroom personnel include a supervisor and four clerks. All are well trained, competent, and adequately bonded. Raw materials are removed from the storeroom only upon written or oral authorization of one of the production foremen.
>
> There are no perpetual-inventory records; hence, the storeroom clerks do not keep records of goods received or issued. To compensate for the lack of perpetual records, a physical-inventory count is taken monthly by the storeroom clerks, who are well supervised. Appropriate procedures are followed in making the inventory count.
>
> After the physical count, the storeroom supervisor matches quantities counted against predetermined reorder levels. If the count for a given part is below the reorder level, the supervisor enters the part number on a materials-requisition list and sends this list to the accounts-payable clerk. The accounts-payable clerk prepares a purchase order for a predetermined reorder quantity for each part and mails the purchase order to the vendor from whom the part was last purchased.
>
> When ordered materials arrive at Alden, they are received by the storeroom clerks. The clerks count the merchandise and verify the counts against the shipper's bill of lading. All vendors' bills of lading are initialed, dated, and filed in the storeroom to serve as receiving reports.

REQUIRED

Describe the deficiencies in the internal control structure and recommend improvements of Alden's procedures for the purchase, receipt, storage, and issue of raw materials. Organize your answer sheet as follows:

Deficiencies	Recommended Improvements

*15-27. (Controls over Purchases) Lyle Anthony, CPA, prepared the flowchart in Figure 15–3, which portrays the raw-materials purchasing function of one of Anthony's clients, a medium-size manufacturing company, from the preparation of initial documents through the vouching of invoices for payment in accounts payable. The flowchart was a portion of the work performed on the audit engagement to understand the internal control structure and assess control risk.

REQUIRED

Identify and explain the deficiencies evident from Figure 15–3. Include the internal control structure deficiencies resulting from activities performed or not performed. All documents are prenumbered.

*15-28. (Control Deficiencies in Purchases) You have completed an audit of activities within the purchasing department of your company. The department employs 30 buyers, 7 supervisors, a manager, and clerical personnel. Purchases total about $500 million a year. Your audit disclosed the following conditions:

1. The company has no formal rules on conflicts of interest. Your analysis produced evidence that one of the 30 buyers in the department owns a substantial interest in a major supplier and that he procures supplies averaging $50,000 a year from that supplier. The prices charged by the supplier are competitive.

2. Buyers select proposed sources without submitting the lists of bidders for review. Your tests disclosed no evidence that the department incurred higher costs as a result of that practice.

3. Buyers who originate written requests for quotations from suppliers receive the suppliers' bids directly from the mailroom. In your test of 100 purchases based on competitive bids, you found that the low bidders were awarded the purchase orders in 75 of the cases.

4. Requests to purchase (requisitions) received in the purchasing department from other departments in the company must be signed by persons authorized to do so. Your examination of 200 such requests disclosed that 3, all for small amounts, were not properly signed. The buyer who had issued all 3 orders honored the requests because he misunderstood the applicable procedure. The clerical personnel charged with reviewing such requests had given them to the buyer in error.

REQUIRED

For each of the four conditions, state

A. the risk, if any, that is incurred if each condition described above is permitted to continue.

B. the control, if any, you would recommend to prevent continuation of the condition described.

15-29. (Controls over Purchases) The Blue Chip Company frequently experienced the need to acquire small, high-value items both for its production operations and for certain "ceremonial" occasions. Such purchases were often made on a short lead-time basis. The company produced a highly technical product under government contract and followed the public relations practice of giving expensive miniature replicas of its product to visiting senators and high-ranking military personnel.

Frank Allgood, an experienced buyer, usually handled such purchases for the company. Allgood knew company procurement policy and procedures like the palm of his hand. The particular procedure he used to make such special purchases specified that delivery should be made to a designated company representative whose signature constituted official acceptance, which was then used to support the issuance of a receiving document.

A request to purchase 30 such items valued at $10,000 came to Allgood's desk marked "Rush."

Allgood followed the standard procedure of obtaining several competitive bids for the order, adding a new twist that he had been planning for some time—he had decided to become a bidder himself! He had set up a fictitious company with a legitimate-sounding name using a post office box address in a nearby large city. Being in a position to review

---

Figure 15-3

**Flowchart of a Raw-Materials Purchasing Function in a
Medium-Size Manufacturing Company**

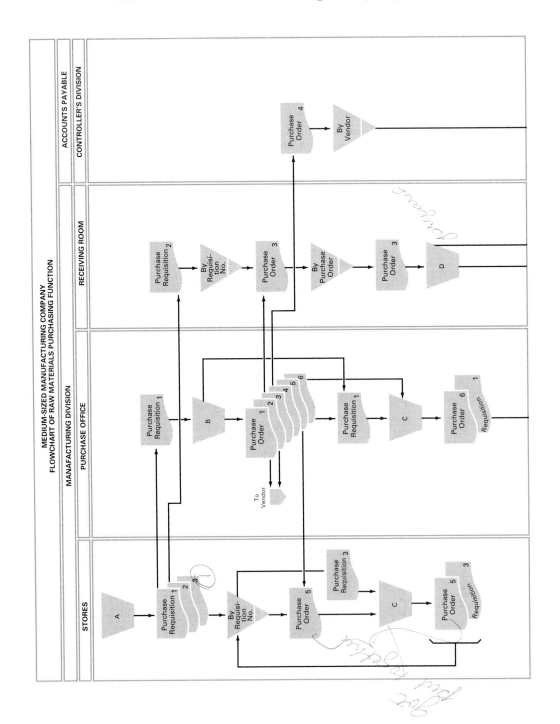

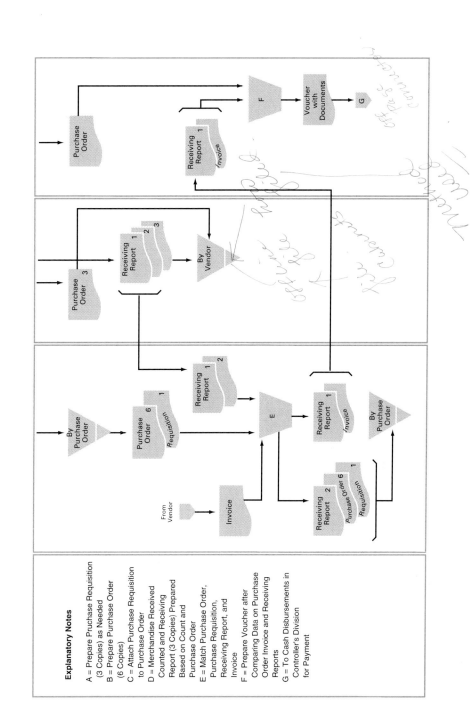

Explanatory Notes

A = Prepare Pruchase Requisition (3 Copies) as Needed

B = Prepare Purchase Order (6 Copies)

C = Attach Purchase Requisition to Purchase Order

D = Merchandise Received Counted and Receiving Report (3 Copies) Prepared Based on Count and Purchase Order

E = Match Purchase Order, Purchase Requisition, Receiving Report, and Invoice

F = Prepare Voucher after Comparing Data on Purchase Order Invoice and Receiving Reports

G = To Cash Disbursements in Controller's Division for Payment

all bids, Allgood had no difficulty ensuring that his bid was the lowest. Because company procedure required no formal review of bids of $10,000 or less, he naturally awarded the contract to himself (his "company"). An official purchase order was issued and subsequently acknowledged.

In due time, Allgood shipped a box containing filler materials of approximately the same weight and size as the real merchandise, specifying on the packing list that the shipment was to be picked up at the dock, unopened, by Allgood. Delivery was accomplished without incident, and an official receiving report was issued and distributed. Shortly thereafter, Allgood dispatched his invoice—an impressive document especially printed for his purpose by a friend in the printing business, bearing attractive discount terms of 2/10, n/30.

In the meantime, the accounts payable department was routinely assembling all the documents supporting the "transaction." Desiring to earn the $200 cash discount, the obligation was paid promptly on the due date. Account distribution was made to the expense account specified on the purchase order, and the completed transaction was put to rest in permanent record storage.

The accounting firm that audited the company's affairs discovered the fraud through its sample testing techniques. Much of the money was recovered from Allgood and his accomplice, who had falsified the purchase request resulting in the rush order.

REQUIRED

A. Point out as many internal control structure deficiencies as you can that might have allowed this fraud to happen.

B. What procedural changes would you recommend to preclude a recurrence of this kind of activity?

*15-30. (Controls over Receiving) Dunbar Camera Manufacturing, Inc., manufactures high-price precision motion-picture cameras in which the specifications of component parts are vital to the manufacturing process. Dunbar buys valuable camera lenses and large quantities of sheetmetal and screws. Screws and lenses are ordered by Dunbar and are billed by the vendors on a unit basis. Sheetmetal is ordered by Dunbar and is billed by the vendors on the basis of weight. The receiving clerk is responsible for documenting the quality and quantity of merchandise received.

The auditor's understanding of the internal control structure indicates that the following procedures are being followed:

> *Receiving Report* Properly approved purchase orders, which are prenumbered, are filed numerically. The copy sent to the receiving clerk is an exact duplicate of the copy sent to the vendor. Receipts of merchandise are recorded on the duplicate copy by the receiving clerk.
>
> *Sheetmetal* The company receives sheetmetal by railroad. The railroad independently weighs the sheetmetal and reports the weight and date of receipt on a bill of lading (waybill), which accompanies all deliveries. The receiving clerk checks only the weight on the waybill against the purchase order.
>
> *Screws* The receiving clerk opens cartons containing screws, then inspects and weighs the contents. The weight is converted to number of units by means of conversion charts. The receiving clerk then checks the computed quantity against the purchase order.
>
> *Camera Lenses* Each camera lens is delivered in a separate corrugated carton. The receiving clerk counts cartons as they are received and checks the number of cartons against purchase orders.

---

*AICPA adapted.

REQUIRED

A. Explain why the internal control structure policies and procedures as they apply individually to receiving reports and the receipt of sheetmetal, screws, and camera lenses are adequate or inadequate. Do not discuss recommendations for improvements.

B. What financial statement distortions may arise because of the inadequacies in Dunbar's internal control structure and how may they occur?

15-31. (Controls over Cash Disbursements) Describe a cash disbursements control feature that, if implemented, would prevent or detect each of the following situations. Consider each situation independently.

A. Payment of an invoice twice.

B. Payment for goods not received.

C. Payment of an invoice with prices higher than the purchase order and sales acknowledgment.

D. Payment of an invoice with errors in the extensions on the invoice.

E. Payment to an employee who has set up a fictitious company.

F. Writing of checks by an employee who does not record the cash disbursement.

*15-32. (Audit of Accounts Payable) Your firm has been engaged to audit the financial statements of Brown Appliances, Inc., for the year ended December 31. The company manufactures major appliances sold to the general public through dealers and distributors. Significant financial information of the company, as of December 31, is as follows:

Trade receivables	$12,000,000
Inventories	14,000,000
Property—net	6,000,000
Other assets	3,000,000
Total assets	$35,000,000
Trade accounts payable	$ 4,000,000
Other liabilities	6,000,000
Stockholders' equity	25,000,000
Total liabilities and equity	$35,000,000
Net sales for the year	$74,000,000
Net income for the year	3,000,000

You are to audit the trade accounts payable of a division of Brown Appliances. The trade accounts payable aggregate $2,500,000. Excerpts from the internal control structure memorandum follow:

Invoices from suppliers are received in the purchasing department, where they are matched with receiving reports and checked to the applicable purchase order for quantities and pricing. Invoices and receiving reports are then forwarded to the accounting department for clerical checking and final approval for payment.

On the payment date, invoices with attached receiving reports are separated into two groups, one group representing items owed for the prior month, and the other group representing items owed for the current month. The check register is then prepared, with each group having a separate total and check number sequence. The accounts payable for monthly financial statement purposes is the total of the check register for invoices representing items owed for the prior month. A voucher register is not maintained.

*Used with permission of Ernst & Young.

The purchasing department holds unmatched receiving reports and unmatched invoices.

Cutoff procedures as established by the company appear adequate; however, the company makes it a practice not to record inventory in transit.

Vendors' statements received by the company are forwarded to a clerk in the accounting department. The clerk does not check all charges appearing on the vendors' statements, but does reconcile all old outstanding charges appearing thereon.

The company has prepared an accounts payable listing for the auditors. As explained above, this listing was prepared from the check register of December charges paid in January, and shows vendor, check number, invoice date, date paid, and amount. A quick review of the listing reveals the following:

January-dated invoices amounting to $200,000 appear on the listing payable to Talley and Parks Advertising Agency, for advertising to appear in *Better Homes and Gardens* magazine in February and March. This was included in the year-end accounts payable listing at the request of the vice-president of advertising because she wanted to match more closely the advertising department's budgeted expense with actual expenditures for the year. The distribution was made to advertising expense.

Amounts appear on the listing as payments for payrolls, payroll taxes, other taxes, profit-sharing plans, and so on.

No amounts appear on the listing for legal or accounting services.

REQUIRED

Discuss the problems and procedures involved in auditing this company's accounts payable. Specifically discuss the auditing procedures you recommend be used in your audit and the adjustments you recommend be made to the accounts payable listing.

15-33. (Audit of Accounts Payable) Alan Barnes, CPA, is performing the audit of Huntsville, Inc., whose policy is to record purchases at the date legal title passes. While auditing the accounts payable balance, Barnes found the following:

1. Items purchased from Magnolia Corp. were returned and Huntsville received a credit memo for $2,089.00. However, the liability was still on Huntsville books.
2. Accounts payable balances for several major suppliers were unusually low. Actual balances for these accounts were understated by $10,000.
3. Merchandise shipped F.O.B. shipping point was received on January 2. It had been shipped on December 30 and was not recorded as a liability.
4. Accounts payable amounts were extended incorrectly in the accounts payable ledger.
5. Payments were made on January 24 to Plainsman Corporation. There is no longer an account for Plainsman Corporation.
6. Huntsville ordered from McDonald Company Part A2320, which Huntsville decided to keep, and Part A2322, which Huntsville returned on December 30. Part A2320 costs $250; Part A2322 costs $150. The balance of the McDonald account is still carried at $400.
7. Items ordered from Thomas Co. were paid for on January 15. The invoice date was December 20 and terms were 2/10 net 30. Barnes had recorded the account payable net of the discount. Accounts payable were therefore understated by $100.

REQUIRED

A. Identify an audit procedure that should enable the auditor to detect each item listed.
B. For each procedure, identify the assertion addressed.

*15-34. (Accounts Payable Confirmation) The following are situations or questions pertaining to the audit of accounts payable:

A. With regard to statements requested from vendors, the auditor's memo states, "We requested statements from all vendors with balances of more than $2,000 as shown by the trial balance." Do you believe this procedure is satisfactory? Give reasons for your answer.

---

*Used with permission of Ernst & Young.

B. Why should an auditor be particularly careful to investigate past due accounts payable?

C. Discuss some of the sources from which the auditor can prepare a list of vendors from whom statements should be requested.

D. All vendors' statements on hand and received by the auditor have been reconciled by the company at the auditor's request. How much checking of the reconciliations should be done?

E. In connection with the year-end audit of trade accounts payable, the following are noted. Describe briefly what each could indicate and what procedures you would follow in the circumstances.

(1) Several long-standing credit balances.

(2) A number of debit balances included in accounts payable.

(3) A substantial dollar amount of purchase commitments in a situation of declining market prices.

15-35. (Reconciling Accounts Payable Confirmations) Skid Logan, CPA, was engaged to perform the 12/31/X4 audit of CCC Manufacturing Company. To confirm accounts payable, Logan sent requests for statements to 34 vendors. Of the 27 statements returned, 6 showed balances that differed from the balances shown in CCC's accounts payable subsidiary ledger. Logan asked Marilyn Davis, CCC's accountant, to reconcile the differences. Later, Davis returned the six statements to Logan, along with the following information:

Statement No. 1	Balance per vendor's statement	$10,629.03
	Payment by CCC 12/17/X4	(1,500.00)
	Invoices not received by CCC	(2,372.97)
	Balance per subsidiary ledger	$ 6,756.06
Statement No. 2	Balance per vendor's statement	$ 5,392.73
	Balance per subsidiary ledger	3,974.67
	Unable to locate difference because vendor did not provide details of what composes the account balance	$ 1,418.06
Statement No. 3	Balance per vendor's statement	$ 9,724.00
	Payment by CCC 12/31/X4	(3,265.00)
	Balance per subsidiary ledger	$ 6,459.00
Statement No. 4	Balance per vendor's statement	$ 157.78
	Balance per subsidiary ledger	0
	Unlocated difference is immaterial	$ 157.78
Statement No. 5	Balance per vendor's statement	$ 7,364.42
	Credit memo issued on 12/14/X4	2,516.03
	Balance per subsidiary ledger	$ 9,880.45
Statement No. 6	Balance per vendor's statement	$ 8,216.19
	Payment by CCC 12/5/X4	(2,500.00)
	Balance per subsidiary ledger	$ 5,716.19

REQUIRED
A. Discuss Logan's decision to have Davis reconcile these statements. (Assume that Logan does plan to test these items additionally.)
B. List audit procedures Logan might use for nonresponses to these requests.
C. Describe additional tests Logan should perform for each of the 6 statements returned by Davis.

Audit Judgment Case

*15-36. The King Company manufactures and distributes duplicating machines and related supplies. The company has grown rapidly since its formation by the merger of two smaller manufacturing companies in 19X4. Sales last year reached $80 million. This growth has been particularly attributable to a management policy emphasizing high product quality and fast, responsive customer service.

Initially, the duplicating machines were manufactured entirely in King Company factories. The rapid growth in machine sales, however, has forced the company to buy an increasing number of subassemblies rather than produce and assemble all the parts itself. All duplicating supplies, however, are purchased from outside vendors.

King's 4 manufacturing plants and 13 warehouses located in the midwestern and western states are managed from corporate headquarters in Des Moines, Iowa. Sales are made through local sales agents who place orders with the nearest warehouse.

To provide greater flexibility in meeting local needs, purchases of parts, subassemblies, materials, and supplies are made by the individual plants and warehouses. Each manufacturing plant purchases the raw materials and subassemblies for its own production requirements. Warehouses order machines from the factories and purchase duplicating supplies from the best local vendors. Corporate headquarters does not interfere with this decentralized purchasing function unless a plant or warehouse is not providing an adequate return on investment or shows other signs of difficulty. All cash disbursements for purchases, however, are centralized in the headquarters at Des Moines.

Processing at Purchase Location Purchases by manufacturing plants and warehouses are made with prenumbered purchase orders issued by a separate purchasing section. One copy of each purchase order goes to accounting, which also gets and date-stamps a copy of each receiving report and all copies of the vendors' invoices. The accounting department accounts for purchase order numbers and matches their details to the receiving reports and vendors' invoices. The latter are also checked for clerical accuracy.

When all the detail is in agreement, the accounting department prepares a prenumbered disbursement voucher summarizing the detailed information of each purchase. These disbursement vouchers, together with supporting documents, are reviewed and approved for payment by plant controllers or warehouse office managers. The vouchers, together with the supporting documents, are then turned over to the approver's secretary, who holds the former and cancels and returns the latter to accounting for filing. Periodically, the secretary batches the approved disbursement vouchers, attaches a transmittal slip indicating the number of vouchers in the batch, and forwards them to Des Moines for payment.

The corporate office at Des Moines distributes to each plant and warehouse a report listing the checks prepared that week, cross-referenced to the disbursement vouchers submitted. At the 4 manufacturing plants, the controller's office compares

---
*DeLoitte & Touche.

the checks listed to a retained copy of each disbursement voucher. The warehouse accounting offices are severely understaffed and do not perform this reconciliation. Vendor statements and inquiries about unpaid bills are replied to by the purchase location if invoices have not yet been forwarded for payment. Otherwise, they are sent to Des Moines for a response.

Cash Disbursement Processing Corporate headquarters in Des Moines processes each disbursement voucher using the combination of manual and computer data-processing activities flowcharted in Figure 15–4 and listed in the following table.

Group	Activity Performed
Input	Open the mail containing approved disbursement vouchers and transmittal slips from the manufacturing plants and warehouses. Make test counts of disbursement vouchers against transmittal slips and forward both for further processing.
Vendor Code	File transmittal slips. Sort disbursement vouchers alphabetically by vendor. Scan vouchers for completeness and check vendor code, name, address, and terms against vendor master file. Initiate changes or additions to vendor master file if warranted. Forward acceptable vouchers for further processing.
Batching	Scan vouchers for missing data and check calculations. Group acceptable vouchers by type, in batches of approximately 50. Create batch control totals on dollars and hash totals on quantities. Forward batches and control totals for processing.
Control Desk	Scan batches for missing data and recalculate control totals. Assign control numbers to batches. Log them in with their control totals. Forward batches with control numbers and totals for further processing.
Data Entry	Key and verify data. Send batched documents to control desk for cancellation and return to accounting for filing. Create tape transfer status report and convert input to tape. Forward tape with control and summary for processing.
Data Center	Perform program edits for completeness and reasonableness as well as appropriate limit and validity checks. Process acceptable data against vendor master file and transaction history file. Mechanically sign resulting prenumbered checks. Forward signed checks, reports, and unresolved rejects to control desk.
Control Desk	Log and reconcile data center totals. Distribute data center output as appropriate. Foot, balance, and mail checks. Correct errors and otherwise resolve rejects.

REQUIRED

A. Determine the assessed level of control risk you would assign to the existence/occurrence, completeness, and valuation assertions for (1) cash disbursements and (2) purchases. Use the following scale to select your assessed risk level: maximum, high, moderate, low.

B. For each assessed level of control risk below maximum, identify the specific internal control structure policies or procedures in King Company's system that support your assessment.

C. For each assessed level of control risk other than low, identify the internal control structure improvements (i.e., additional policies or procedures or changes therein) that would allow you to reduce your assessment at least one level.

Figure 15–4

Flowchart of Manual and Computer Processing of Cash Disbursements, King Company

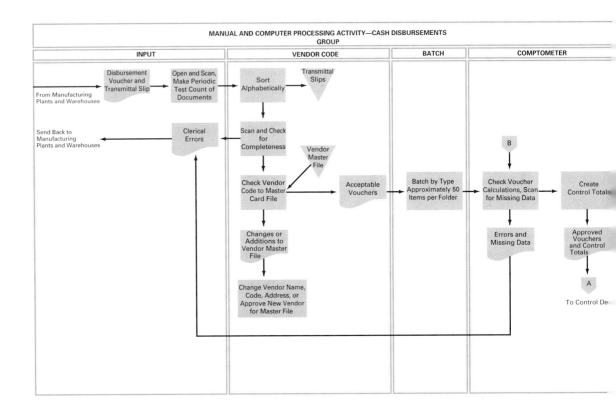

MANUAL AND COMPUTER PROCESSING ACTIVITY—CASH DISBURSEMENTS
GROUP

| INPUT | VENDOR CODE | BATCH | COMPTOMETER |

Auditing Issues Case

15-37.   KELCO MANUFACTURING COMPANY

Kelco's president is very concerned that certain employees within the company might be accepting kickbacks from one of the company's goods and services suppliers and has requested a review of internal control as part of the December 31, 19X7, examination of financial statements. Cook is very suspicious of Jerry Glenn, a purchasing agent who joined the company last year. Glenn has been living a lifestyle that apparently exceeds what others within the company, who have had a long-time association with the purchasing agent, thought he was accustomed to living. The findings of the review were somewhat alarming:

All purchase orders for supplies and services were initiated out of Glenn's office. Purchase invoices for those supplies and services were approved for payment by Glenn. Receiving reports were prepared and initialed by Glenn or his assistant and brother-in-law, Jack Castellion.

One of the largest suppliers has a post office box in the Cayman Islands.

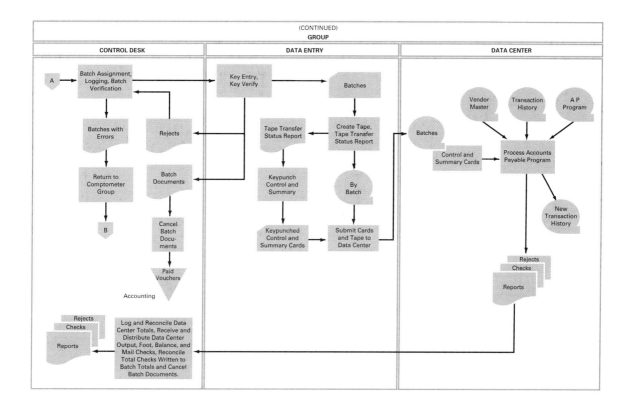

REQUIRED
1. List the audit procedures you applied to company records that resulted in the findings above.
2. What recommendations do you have for Cook?

Chapter *16*

Understanding the Internal Control Structure and Assessing Control Risk: The Conversion Cycle

Learning Objectives

- Explain the major functions in the conversion cycle.

- Describe the documents, accounting records, files, and flow of transactions in a typical conversion cycle accounting system.

- Explain the primary documents and the flow of transactions in a payroll accounting system.

- Describe the common internal control structure policies and procedures relevant to the significant assertions for production and payroll transactions in the conversion cycle.

- Identify and explain the common tests of controls for production and payroll.

Today, businesses operate in highly competitive environments where product quality, fast service, and low prices are top priorities. These changes in business have led to changes in accounting cost systems. For example, managers require in-depth information to effect the lowest product cost and to implement competitive strategies and innovative technologies. Traditional cost systems before 1980 concentrated on short-term planning and control, decision-making, and product costing. The succeeding generation of systems recognized a business need for information about actual processes as well as costs. Generation III ABC systems provided an aggregate view of not only a business unit but also its relationship with other entities inside the company and within the industry as a whole. Today's systems attempt to link business unit functions, and, as a result, product information about entire companies.

Despite the change in focus, some aspects of cost systems remain constant. They must still strike a balance between meeting the internal needs of management while fulfilling the requirements of GAAP and regulatory agencies. In the near future, cost systems will undoubtedly evolve to fulfill the strategic needs of management without being hindered by a company's external demands. ∎

Source: Charles D. Mecimore and Alice T. Bell, "Are We Ready for Fourth Generation ABC?" *Management Accounting,* January 1995, pp. 22–26.

Chapters 13–15 discussed the internal control structure and substantive tests for the revenue cycle and the expenditure cycle. This chapter addresses understanding the internal control structure and assessing control risk for the conversion cycle. Chapter 17 discusses the substantive tests for conversion cycle transactions and account balances.

The conversion cycle involves using raw materials, labor, and overhead to produce finished goods. The major functions in this cycle are (1) issuing raw materials to production, (2) producing finished goods, and (3) storing these goods. Table 16–1 shows the key activities for each of these functions. As noted in Figure 6–7 in Chapter 6, the expenditure cycle is connected to the conversion cycle because the expenditure cycle concerns the acquisition of goods and services used in production. The revenue cycle is linked to the conversion cycle because the former concerns the sale of finished inventory. Unlike the expenditure cycle and revenue cycle, most of the transactions in the conversion cycle do not involve parties outside the entity. Two exceptions are payroll transactions and storing finished inventory in a public warehouse.

Understanding the Internal Control Structure for the Conversion Cycle

The conversion cycle is normally associated with the inventories of a manufacturing entity. Other types of entities, however, often also maintain material amounts of inventory. For example, certain service entities, such as hospitals, carry large inventories that are used in the sale of services, and retail and wholesale businesses stock

Table 16-1	**Conversion Cycle Activities**

Raw Materials Issuance Transactions

- Requisitioning raw materials
- Authorizing issuance of raw materials
- Recording issuance of raw materials
- Issuing raw materials

Production Transactions

- Authorizing production
- Recording quantities and costs of
  - raw materials
  - labor (payroll)
  - overhead
- Controlling movement of work in process

Storing Finished Goods

- Transferring finished goods to storage
- Recording finished goods inventory
- Safeguarding access to finished inventory

---

inventory for resale without undertaking any production effort. Although this chapter is written from the perspective of a manufacturing entity, much of the discussion is applicable to inventories in a variety of entities.

Control Environment, Risk Assessment, Communication, and Monitoring

Chapter 6 discussed the control environment, risk assessment, communication, and monitoring components that auditors usually consider, and it explained how auditors obtain an understanding of these components. Because these components do not exist separately for individual transaction cycles, no separate understanding of them is necessary for the conversion cycle. The auditor relates his or her overall understanding of these components to the conversion cycle in planning the audit.

However, specific policies and procedures exist within each of these components that may affect control risk for assertions related to the conversion cycle. These policies and procedures are discussed later in this chapter in the section on how the auditor assesses control risk for conversion cycle assertions.

Accounting System

Accounting systems for the conversion cycle vary significantly among entities. One reason for this variation is the many different types of inventories that entities produce. For example, an entity that produces breakfast cereals will have markedly different accounting records and procedures than an entity that manufactures microchips for specific customer applications. Another reason for the variation is the nature and sophistication of the cost accounting methods an entity uses. Some entities use ***standard cost systems***, have both job cost and process cost applications, and maintain perpetual inventory records, while others do not.

Because conversion cycle accounting systems can vary widely, this chapter will describe the basic elements of an accounting system and give examples of common accounting records and procedures. Table 16–2 shows the common accounts, documents, and files associated with many conversion cycle accounting systems.

Transactions Involving Raw Materials Issuance

Once the production of goods has been authorized the stockroom issues raw materials to production. Typically some type of document, such as a *materials requisition*, *production order*, or *bill of materials*, is used to authorize and account for the release of raw materials. This document is ordinarily used to update *perpetual inventory records* when they are employed. In some entities, raw material issues may be initiated and recorded by computer, and the computer may update the perpetual inventory file. Raw materials are usually issued only to designated individuals, such as a production supervisor, who signs the requisition document to acknowledge receipt of the goods.

Production Transactions

The production process usually begins with an authorization to manufacture goods. These authorizations can occur in a variety of ways. Some entities produce goods only upon receipt of a customer order, at which time a production order is usually approved and issued. Other entities keep finished inventory on hand to meet customer orders immediately upon receipt. These entities often use sales forecasts or predetermined inventory levels to determine when to initiate a production order. In some entities, the computer monitors inventory levels and initiates production orders.

Once production is initiated, the accounting system normally accounts for the physical movement of goods and their related costs. The raw materials requisition establishes accountability for the quantity and cost of the raw materials and their movement into the production process.

The production process uses labor and overhead to convert raw materials into finished inventory. A *routing sheet* accompanies a job or production run through the production process. This sheet specifies the sequence of labor operations and machine requirements, and it provides the basis for controlling the movement of work in process among departments or work areas. In computerized production operations, a computer record of each job or production run may be established to monitor the movement of goods through the production process.

The overhead used to convert raw materials into finished inventory includes a variety of costs—for example, supplies, utilities, maintenance, and rent. The internal control structure and audit approach for these costs were discussed in Chapter 15 on the expenditure cycle. Once overhead costs are accumulated in the expenditure cycle, they are charged to job orders, production runs, or cost centers. These charges are generally made on the basis of an activity measure such as direct labor hours or machine hours, which are recorded on some type of document. For example, in a job order cost system, a *time ticket* or *job cost sheet* is used to record labor or machine hours. In some entities, labor and overhead costs may be entered in computer records to accumulate costs for jobs or production runs.

Labor costs are accounted for through the processing of payroll transactions. This textbook treats payroll transactions as part of the conversion cycle because a substantial part of payroll is usually charged to product costs in a manufacturing

Table 16-2	**Key Accounts, Documents, Records, and Files of the Conversion Cycle**

Accounts (may be maintained on computer media or hard copy)

- Raw Materials Inventory
- Work in Process Inventory
- Finished Goods Inventory
- Cost of Sales
- Direct Labor
- Manufacturing Overhead

Documents (may be prepared and/or maintained manually or by a computer)

Bill of Materials   A document scheduling the type and quantity of raw materials for a particular job or production run.

Inspection Record   A document used to record the results of final inspection of completed production units. It often serves to document the transfer of completed production to finished inventory.

Job Cost Sheet   A document designed to accumulate the materials, labor, and overhead assigned to a job.

Labor Cost Distribution   A schedule of the distribution of labor costs to specific cost centers or departments.

Materials Requisition   A document that authorizes the release of materials and parts from inventory.

Payroll Summary   A report for a specific pay period that shows total gross earnings, deductions, and net pay for all employees.

Production Order   A document that authorizes the commencement of the production process. It authorizes a particular job or run.

Rate and Deduction Authorization Forms   Forms that specify the pay rate and payroll deductions authorized for a specific employee.

Routing Sheet   A schedule that specifies, in sequential order, the labor and machine operations required for a particular job. This sheet accompanies the job through the production process.

Sales Forecast   A forecast of sales volume in units for each product.

Time Card   A document showing the time worked each day by a specific employee.

Time Ticket   A form used to record time worked by an employee on a specific job order or production run.

Accounting Records (may be prepared and/or maintained manually or by a computer)

Payroll Check Register   A record of the payroll checks issued to employees each pay period.

Perpetual Inventory Records   Contains the quantity and price of inventory additions and withdrawals by date of occurrence and the current quantity in stock.

Files (may be maintained manually or by a computer)

Employee Earnings Record   A record of an employee's gross wages, deductions, and net pay by pay period during the year.

Employee Personnel Record   An employment history for each employee. It generally contains the employment application form, evaluation forms, vacation and sick days, and a record of any disciplinary actions.

firm. The discussion of payroll, however, is also applicable to retail, wholesale, and service entities.

Figure 16–1 is an example of a flowchart of a payroll accounting system. Although the detailed payroll records and procedures vary from entity to entity, this flowchart covers the basic activities in different departments. It also shows key documents and records—such as personnel files, time cards, payroll summaries, payroll checks, and the payroll register—that are used in a typical payroll accounting system. A brief review of the flowchart follows.

A payroll transaction begins when an employee is hired. An *employee personnel file* is established, containing the employment application, letters of reference, and *rate and deduction authorization forms.* The rate and deduction authorization forms are sent to the payroll department, and an *employee earnings record* is established.

For hourly-paid employees, *time cards* and time clocks ordinarily are used to maintain a record of hours worked. The supervisor totals and approves the time cards and sends them to the timekeeping department for review and comparison with the *labor-cost distribution;* the timekeeping department then forwards the time cards to the payroll department.

Using the earnings record and time cards, the payroll department prepares checks for each employee, updates the earnings records, and prepares a *payroll summary* and a *payroll register.* Payroll then sends a copy of the payroll summary and labor-cost distribution to general accounting and cost accounting and files a copy of the payroll summary by date. The payroll checks and the payroll register are sent to the treasurer.

The treasurer reviews the payroll register and signs the checks. The checks are then distributed to the employees, and the payroll register is sent to general accounting for posting.

In computerized payroll systems, computer files may be established for the employee earnings records that contain pay rates and deduction authorizations. Time cards may be entered through the computer to update the earnings records, prepare the paychecks, and produce the payroll summary and payroll register.

Storing Finished Goods

Before goods are transferred to finished inventory, they are usually inspected to ensure that they meet established quality standards. After inspection, the specific form used to document the transfer to finished inventory varies from entity to entity. It may be an approved *inspection record*, a copy of the production order, a router sheet copy, or some other document.

The physical transfer of goods to the finished inventory stockroom is usually acknowledged by stamping, signing, or initialing the transfer form. This form may also be used to update perpetual inventory records, either manually or by computer, when they are maintained. To safeguard finished inventory, the stockroom normally is established in a secured area or structure and access to the stockroom is limited to designated personnel.

Control Activities

The nature and extent of control activities over the conversion cycle vary from entity to entity. A number of common control activities in the conversion cycle are discussed in the following sections according to the control activities classification outlined in Chapter 6. The relationship of control activities to the conversion cycle assertions are discussed later in the section on assessing control risk.

Performance Reviews

Performance reviews in the conversion cycle encompass a number of techniques. Because many manufacturing entities use standard cost systems, calculation and analysis of variances between the actual costs of materials, labor, and overhead with their standard costs provides an overall control of these costs. This variance analysis can detect problems related to the valuation assertion for inventory. In addition, production managers may reconcile the goods placed in production, completed production, and finished goods additions to provide an overall test of inventory existence and completeness.

Management may also use sales forecasts or economic production runs to help avoid producing or ordering excess goods. As a result, inventory valuation problems resulting from obsolete or slow-moving inventory are less likely.

Information Processing

A variety of control activities may be performed to check the authorization, accuracy, and completeness of conversion cycle transactions.

Authorization is usually required for (1) initiating production, (2) issuing raw materials, (3) paying employees and charging payroll costs to production, (4) charging overhead to production, and (5) transferring completed goods to finished inventory. These authorizations help to avoid overstocking of inventory, improper use of raw materials, invalid payments to employees, improper product costing and recording, and loss of inventory.

The documents used in the conversion cycle accounting system provide added control when they are properly designed and accounted for. Production orders, requisition forms, job cost sheets, routers, time cards, cost distribution reports, and inspection reports should be designed to record all information necessary to process production transactions. For example, they should provide accurate and complete product and raw material descriptions and quantities, accurate dates of activity and transfers, accurate labor and machine times, and appropriate approvals. In addition, these documents should be prenumbered and the numerical sequence periodically accounted for.

Entity personnel or computer programs may independently compare for consistency the descriptions, quantities, monetary amounts, and dates on materials requisitions, production orders, job cost sheets, router sheets, payroll time cards, and labor and overhead distribution reports. Labor and overhead charges to jobs or production runs may be recomputed either manually or by computer. In addition, the approval of production orders, requisitions, payroll records and checks, job cost sheets, and finished inventory transfer documents may be reviewed by independent entity personnel. Units placed in production are often reconciled with units transferred to finished inventory, and payroll bank accounts are ordinarily reconciled with payroll accounting records.

As discussed in Chapter 6, the knowledge of specific control procedures needed to plan the audit of the conversion cycle will vary from entity to entity. The understanding of the control structure and the conversion cycle accounting system is likely to provide the auditor with knowledge of many of the control procedures over the conversion cycle.

Physical Controls

Access to raw materials, work in process, and finished goods inventories is usually limited to authorized personnel. Inventories may be physically segregated in separate warehouses or storage areas and released only upon proper authorization. Access to payroll records, perpetual inventory records, and other conversion cycle accounting

Figure 16-1 **Flowchart of Payroll Activities**

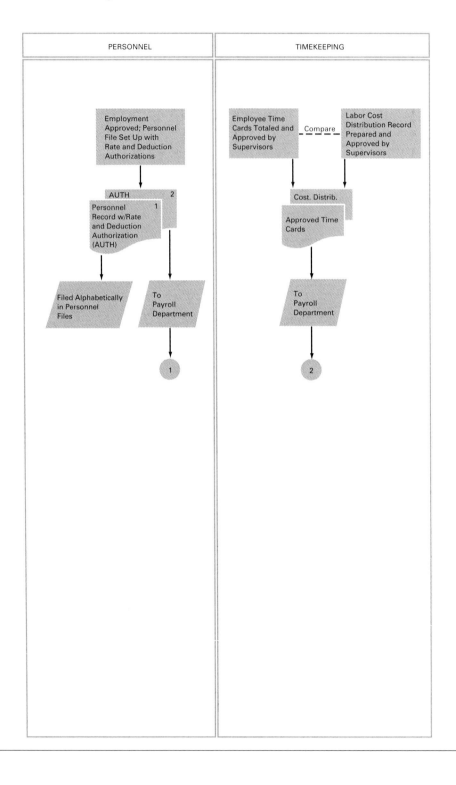

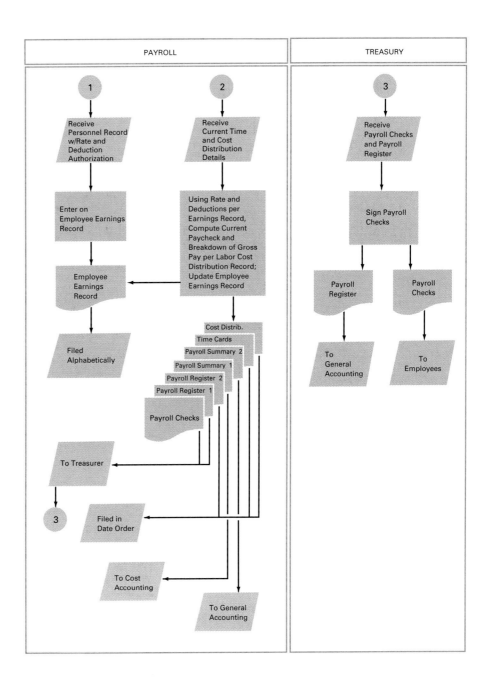

records should be restricted to designated personnel with an appropriate segregation of duties, and physical safeguards should be provided for storing these records.

Proper Segregation of Duties

The responsibility for authorizing production, issuing raw materials, charging labor and overhead to production, and transferring goods to finished inventory should ordinarily be assigned to separate individuals or departments. These individuals or departments should not maintain or have access to accounting records for inventories, labor, or overhead. Similarly, individuals or departments maintaining accounting records should not have access to inventories.

Assessing Control Risk for the Conversion Cycle

After obtaining the understanding of the internal control structure necessary to plan the conversion cycle audit, the auditor assesses control risk for the financial statement assertions related to the transactions and accounts in that cycle. Table 16–3 relates assertions to internal control structure policies and procedures for payroll transactions. Because payroll transactions are often significant in both manufacturing and nonmanufacturing entities, control structure policies and procedures related to the assertions for those transactions are considered separately. Table 16–4 relates assertions to internal control structure policies and procedures for all production transactions other than payroll. As in previous chapters on transaction cycles, each table explains why a policy or procedure is relevant to a specific assertion and describes related tests of controls.

Payroll Transactions

Table 16–3 contains a number of common internal control structure policies and procedures that pertain to payroll transactions. Although some of these policies and procedures are relevant to more than one assertion, to avoid repetition they are discussed in detail for only one assertion. Their applicability, however, will be noted in the discussion of other assertions.

Existence or Occurrence Assertion

The existence or occurrence assertion for payroll transactions means that the recorded payroll transactions actually occurred and that the related payroll expense and liability accounts actually exist. An entity might intentionally or unintentionally record payroll transactions when employees have not provided services. In either case, payroll expense, payroll liability, and inventory or other assets will be overstated.

A number of common internal control structure policies and procedures relate to the existence or occurrence assertion for payroll transactions. Entities usually maintain approved, up-to-date records of when employees are hired or terminated to establish accurate records of which employees are entitled to be paid for a specific payroll period. In addition, independent entity personnel may be assigned to compare employee status records with the payroll records to show that the recorded payroll transactions actually occurred. An entity may maintain employee status records and compare them with payroll records either manually or by computer.

The auditor's tests of controls for these policies and procedures usually include inquiring about and inspecting the entity's hiring and termination records to determine what information they contain, who updates and approves them, and how frequently they are updated. The auditor also inspects evidence that employee status records are independently compared with payroll records. When employee status records and payroll records are maintained on computer files, the auditor will inquire about how these files are updated and how access to them is protected. In addition, the auditor will examine evidence, often by inspecting computer-generated exception reports, that the computer has compared employee status files with payroll records and that exceptions have been resolved.

Many entities use time clocks and time cards to record the time worked by each employee. Each pay period, a supervisor reviews and approves the time cards. Because the approved time cards are used to prepare payroll checks, they help ensure that payroll transactions are recorded only when employee services have been provided—that is, when a payroll transaction has actually occurred. To further reduce the risk of recording payroll transactions that did not occur, an entity may require an independent comparison of the approved time cards with payroll records. A computer may perform this comparison when time records and payroll records are maintained on computer files.

Auditors usually test these controls by inquiring about how time clocks and time cards are used, observing their use, and inspecting the time cards for accuracy and approval. The auditor will also examine evidence of the independent comparison of the time cards with the payroll records, such as exception reports of differences and their reconciliation. For entities that do not make internal comparisons of time cards and payroll records, auditors may perform these comparisons themselves on a test basis.

When an entity uses a standard cost accounting system, variances between standard and actual labor may arise. A significant variance of actual over standard may be the result of recording payroll transactions that did not occur. Management's thorough and careful follow-up on such variances may identify such misstatements. Auditors commonly test this control by inquiring about how the standard cost system operates, such as how frequently standard costs are revised, what cost elements are considered, and how labor and overhead bases are established. The auditor also inspects reports documenting the follow-up on and appropriate resolution of significant labor variances.

Segregating payroll-related functions is also a typical control procedure for the existence or occurrence assertion. The functions of maintaining and approving personnel records, timekeeping, and disbursing payroll should be separated to reduce the risk that payroll transactions will be recorded for nonexistent employees. The tests of controls for this control procedure are auditor inquiry about and observation of how these functions are segregated.

Completeness Assertion

The completeness assertion for payroll means that all payroll transactions that occurred are recorded. If an entity intentionally or unintentionally fails to record a payment for employee services, then payroll expense and liabilities, as well as inventory and other assets, will be understated.

Using prenumbered payroll checks provides a formal, controlled document indicating that a payroll transaction should be recorded. Periodically accounting for the numerical sequence of these checks and comparing them with payroll records can identify unrecorded payroll transactions. To test this control, the auditor inquires about and observes the use of prenumbered checks and inspects evidence that their sequence is accounted for and that the checks have been compared with the payroll records.

Table 16-3

Overview of Internal Control Structure Policies and Procedures and Tests of Controls for Payroll Transaction Assertions

Assertion	Relevant Internal Control Structure Policy or Procedure
Existence or Occurrence	▪ Use authorized hiring and termination documents and independently compare them with payroll.*
	▪ Use time clocks and time cards, and require supervisory approval of time cards.
	▪ Independently compare approved time cards with payroll.*
	▪ Analyze and follow up on labor variances.
	▪ Segregate functions of personnel, timekeeping, and payroll disbursement.
Completeness	▪ Use prenumbered payroll checks and account for their numerical sequence.*
	▪ Perform independent payroll bank reconciliation.*
	▪ Analyze and follow up on labor variances.
	▪ Segregate functions of payroll preparation, check signing and disbursement, and recording of payroll.

*This policy or procedure may be performed either manually or by a computer programmed to compare information relevant to the control and produce a report of exceptions.

Input → Process → Output

One of the Output should be an exception report

Why Policy or Procedure Is Relevant to Assertion	Common Tests of Controls for Policy or Procedure
■ Establishing that legitimate employees exist helps substantiate that recorded payroll transactions actually occurred.	■ Inquire about use and authorization of hiring and termination records, and inspect evidence of their independent comparison with payroll. For example, examine computer generated exception report of unmatched payroll records.
■ Using authorized record of time worked as a basis for recording payroll transactions helps ensure that only payroll transactions that actually occurred are recorded.	■ Inquire about, inspect, and observe use of time clocks, time cards, and time card approval.
■ Independent verification of authorized record of time worked helps substantiate that recorded payroll transactions actually occurred.	■ Inspect evidence that independent comparison was made. For example, examine computer generated exception report of unmatched payroll time cards.
■ Excess of actual over standard labor may be due to recording payroll transactions that did not occur.	■ Inquire about use of standard cost system and inspect reports on follow up on labor variances.
■ Helps prevent recording payroll transactions for nonexistent employees.	■ Inquire about and observe segregation of these duties.
■ Establishes formal, controlled record of payroll disbursements that should be recorded.	■ Inquire about and observe use of prenumbered payroll checks, and inspect evidence of accounting for their numerical sequence. For example, examine computer generated exception report of nonsequential document use.
■ May identify payroll disbursements recorded in payroll account bank statement that were not recorded in accounting records.	■ Inquire about and observe preparation of payroll account bank reconciliations or inspect reconciliations. For example, examine computer generated exception report of bank reconciliations.
■ Excess of standard over actual labor may be due to payroll transactions that occurred but were not recorded.	■ Inquire about use of standard cost system and inspect reports that follow up on labor variances.
■ Segregation of these functions reduces the opportunity to approve and make payroll disbursements and intentionally or unintentionally fail to record them.	■ Inquire about and observe segregation of these duties.

(*continued*)

Table 16–3	*continued*	

Assertion	Relevant Internal Control Structure Policy or Procedure
Rights and Obligations	Generally not a significant assertion for payroll transactions
Valuation or Allocation	■ Independently compare approved pay rates, deductions, and time cards with payroll computations.*
	■ Independently recompute gross wages, deductions, and net pay.
	■ Analyze and follow up on labor variances.
Presentation and Disclosure	■ Use chart of accounts with adequate detail.
	■ Independently review account codings for payroll transactions.*
	■ Analyze and follow up on labor variances.

*This policy or procedure may be performed either manually or by a computer programmed to compare information relevant to the control and produce a report of exceptions.

When payroll amounts are large, many entities establish separate payroll checking accounts. Generally, the entity transfers the amount of the net payroll to the payroll checking account just prior to distributing the checks. This ***imprest system*** provides a separate payroll account bank statement. Periodically reconciling this statement with the payroll records can identify checks paid by the bank that were not recorded in the accounting records. The auditor's tests of controls for this procedure are the same as for the general account bank reconciliation: inquire about and observe or inspect the reconciliations.

Management's analysis of and follow-up on the excess of standard labor costs over actual may also identify misstatements in the completeness assertion. Standard may exceed actual because some payroll transactions were not recorded. The tests of controls for this policy are the same as those discussed for the existence or occurrence assertion.

Why Policy or Procedure Is Relevant to Assertion	Common Tests of Controls for Policy or Procedure
■ Helps ensure that accurate pay rates, deductions, and time worked are used to make and record payroll computations.	■ Inspect evidence that independent comparison was made. For example, compare computer generated exception report of comparison of pay rates, deductions, and time cards with payroll computations.
■ May detect errors in payroll calculations prior to recording payroll.	■ Inspect evidence of independent recomputation.
■ Significant variances of actual and standard labor may be due to incorrect payroll valuation.	■ Inquire about use of standard cost system and inspect reports on follow-up on labor variances.
■ Helps identify specific accounts in which payroll transactions should be classified when recorded.	■ Inquire about, observe, and inspect use of chart of accounts.
■ Helps identify incorrect account classifications before payroll transactions are recorded.	■ Inspect evidence that account codings were reviewed. For example, examine computer generated exception report of incorrect account codings.
■ Significant variances of actual and standard labor may be due to incorrect payroll classification.	■ Inquire about use of standard cost system and inspect reports that follow up on labor variations.

Management can also help ensure that all payroll transactions are recorded by segregating the functions of (1) payroll preparation, (2) check signing and disbursement, and (3) payroll recording. Separating these functions allows each to act as a check on the other and greatly reduces the risk that payroll checks can be prepared and distributed without being recorded. This control procedure is tested by inquiring about and observing how these duties are separated.

The completeness assertion is also significant to the recognition and payment of payroll tax expenses and liabilities. Penalties and interest charges may result if payroll tax returns and related payments are not filed on time. Several different control structure policies and procedures may be used to help ensure that payroll tax transactions are recorded. Clearly documented tax filing procedures, schedules or checklists of monthly and quarterly return forms and dates, and standard journal entries for payroll taxes are commonly used. The tests of controls for these policies and procedures include auditor inquiry about the specific control procedures the entity uses, and observation and inspection of evidence indicating that the policies have been followed.

Rights and Obligations Assertion

The rights and obligations assertion is ordinarily not significant for payroll transactions.

Valuation or Allocation Assertion

The valuation or allocation assertion for payroll transactions and related account balances means that the amounts recorded for valid payroll transactions are correct. Payroll transaction amounts may be recorded incorrectly for several reasons. An incorrect pay rate, amount of time worked, or payroll deduction may be used, or the payroll amount may be computed incorrectly. Misstatements in the valuation or allocation assertion for payroll transactions may result in either overstatement or understatement of payroll expenses and liabilities, and of inventory or other assets.

To reduce the risk that incorrect pay rates, amount of time worked, and deductions are used, entities often require that an independent employee compare these items as documented in approved personnel records with the payroll computations. The computer may also make this comparison when the appropriate data are maintained in computer files. In addition, computer programs can check the reasonableness of pay rates, amount of time worked, and deductions by performing reasonableness checks as the payroll calculations are made. Auditors test these controls by inquiring about the use of the control procedure and inspecting evidence that a manual or computer comparison was performed and that exceptions were resolved. For entities that do not make internal comparisons of the personnel records with payroll computations, the auditor may perform such comparisons for a sample of payroll transactions.

Manual payroll systems are particularly susceptible to mistakes in payroll computations. To help ensure that payroll amounts are calculated correctly, an independent employee often recomputes payroll calculations. An independent recalculation can identify such mistakes before the payroll is recorded. To test this control procedure, the auditor inquires about who performs the recomputation and how it is done. The auditor also inspects evidence that the procedure was performed, often by inspecting initials or exception reports. In some circumstances, the auditor may reperform some of the calculations.

Significant variances between actual and standard labor costs may also be the result of material misstatements in payroll valuation or allocation. Management analysis of and follow-up on these variances can help identify these misstatements.

The valuation or allocation assertion for *payroll tax returns* and related payments is also usually significant. To help reduce the risk of misstatements in payroll tax computations and payments, entities usually assign personnel to perform an independent review of payroll tax computations and forms. The auditor's tests of controls usually involve inquiring about who does the review and when it is done and inspecting evidence that the review was performed.

Presentation and Disclosure Assertion

The presentation and disclosure assertion for payroll transactions and related accounts means that payroll expenses and liabilities are properly classified in the appropriate accounts. Direct labor payroll expenses may be misclassified as indirect labor, administrative expense, or selling expense, or vice versa. Such misclassifications can cause overstatements or understatements in expenses, and in inventory and other assets.

An accounting system that includes a detailed chart of accounts can help ensure that payroll expenses and liabilities are properly classified. Payroll transactions can be coded with the number of the account in which the expense and liability are to be recorded. These codes may be reviewed by independent entity personnel prior to recording the transactions to further reduce the risk of misclassification. In computerized systems, computer programs can compare an employee's identification number with the specific account in which the payroll expense should be recorded. For example, the computer could identify instances in which direct labor employees' wages are charged to administrative expense. The typical tests of controls for these procedures include auditor inspection of the chart of accounts, observation or inspection of payroll document coding, and examination of evidence that manual or computer reviews of codes were made.

Production Transactions

Table 16–4 identifies common internal control structure policies and procedures for production transactions. Although some of these policies and procedures are relevant to more than one assertion, they are discussed in detail only for one assertion. Their applicability, however, is noted in the discussion of other assertions.

Existence or Occurrence Assertion

The existence or occurrence assertion for production transactions means that all recorded production transactions, such as production material, labor, and overhead, actually occurred and that the related inventory balances actually exist. This assertion also means that the recorded transfers of inventory from raw material, work in process, and finished goods actually occurred. If these transactions are recorded when they did not occur, inventory and net income will be misstated.

To prevent recording of production transactions that did not occur, many entities use prenumbered and authorized requisition forms, production orders, job cost sheets, and inspection reports, and periodically account for their numerical sequence. These formal, controlled production documents are used to record production transactions. Consequently, they help ensure that only transactions that actually occur are recorded. As with other types of prenumbered documents, the auditor's tests of controls include inquiring about and observing their use and inspecting evidence that their numerical sequence has been accounted for. The auditor also usually inspects a sample of these documents to determine that they are properly authorized.

An entity may also require that these production documents be independently compared with each other to determine that the data they contain are consistent. For example, the item description, quantity, monetary amounts, and dates may be compared either manually or by computer. Matching the data on these documents for consistency helps substantiate that a production transaction actually occurred before it is recorded. In a batch-processing computer system, the computer can balance production document batch totals with the totals of computer-processed transactions to help identify invalid transactions before they are recorded. In an on-line system, the computer can compare key production information at various stages of the production process. For example, the computer can compare part numbers, quantities, and monetary amounts at each major transfer point in the production process.

Table 16–4

Overview of Internal Control Structure Policies and Procedures and Tests of Controls for Production Transaction Assertions

Assertion	Relevant Internal Control Structure Policy or Procedure
Existence or Occurrence	■ Use prenumbered and authorized requisitions, production orders, job cost sheets, and inspection reports, and account for their numerical sequence.*
	■ Independently compare requisitions, production orders, job cost sheets, and inspection reports for consistency.*
	■ Reconcile production labor costs and overhead on job orders with payroll records and overhead incurred.*
	■ Analyze and follow up on materials and overhead variances.
	■ Reconcile goods placed in production, completed production, and finished goods additions.*
	■ Use perpetual inventory records and periodically compare with physical inventory count.
	■ Use secured inventory storage areas and security personnel and systems.
Completeness	■ Use prenumbered requisitions, production orders, job cost sheets, and inspection reports, and account for their numerical sequence.*

*This policy or procedure may be performed either manually or by a computer programmed to compare information relevant to the control and produce a report of exceptions.

Why Policy or Procedure Is Relevant to Assertion	Common Tests of Controls for Policy or Procedure
■ Using authorized, controlled production documents as a basis for recording production transactions helps ensure that only production transactions that actually occurred are recorded.	■ Inquire about and observe use of prenumbered production documents and inspect evidence of the accounting for their numerical sequence. For example, examine computer generated exception report of nonsequential document use.
■ Ability to support production transaction with consistent production documents helps substantiate that transaction actually occurred before it is recorded.	■ Inspect evidence that independent comparison was made. For example, examine computer generated exception report of comparison of related production documents.
■ Inability to reconcile labor or overhead costs charged to job orders with payroll or overhead records may be due to recording charges that did not occur.	■ Inquire about reconciliation of job orders with payroll and overhead records, and observe or inspect reconciliations. For example, examine computer generated exception report of unreconciled labor or overhead costs.
■ Excess of actual over standard material, labor, or overhead cost may be due to recording transactions that did not occur.	■ Inquire about use of standard cost system and inspect reports on follow up on variances.
■ Inability to reconcile goods placed in production, completed, or added with finished goods may be due to recording production transactions that did not occur.	■ Inquire about reconciliation of these items and observe or inspect reconciliations. For example, examine computer generated exception report of unreconciled inventory transfers.
■ Perpetual records document the occurrence of inventory transactions, and periodic comparisons with physical inventory may identify recorded inventory transactions that did not occur.	■ Inquire about use of perpetual records and physical inventory, vouch and trace production documents to records, and inspect evidence of reconciliation with physical inventory.
■ Helps ensure that inventory exists by protecting against unintentional removal of inventory.	■ Inquire about and observe use of secured storage areas and security personnel and systems.
■ Using formal, controlled records to document production transactions helps ensure that production transactions will be recorded.	■ Inquire about and observe use of prenumbered production documents and inspect evidence of accounting for their numerical sequence. For example, examine computer generated exception report of nonsequential document use.

(continued)

581

Table 16-4

continued

Assertion	Relevant Internal Control Structure Policy or Procedure
Completeness *(continued)*	■ Independently compare requisitions, production orders, job cost sheets, and inspection reports for consistency and reconciliation with accounting records.*
	■ Analyze and follow up on materials and overhead variances.
	■ Reconcile goods placed in production, completed production, and finished goods additions.*
	■ Use perpetual inventory records and periodically compare with physical inventory count.
Rights and Obligations	Generally not a significant assertion for production transactions
Valuation or Allocation	■ Independently compare raw materials quantities and prices on requisitions, production orders, and job orders for consistency.*
	■ Independently compare raw materials prices on requisitions to vendor invoices or perpetual inventory records.*
	■ Independently review departmental overhead rates used on job orders and recompute overhead charged to jobs.*

*This policy or procedure may be performed either manually or by a computer programmed to compare information relevant to the control and produce a report of exceptions.

Why Policy or Procedure Is Relevant to Assertion	Common Tests of Controls for Policy or Procedure
■ Comparison of production documents for consistency and tracing them to accounting records may identify unrecorded production transactions.	■ Inquire about and inspect evidence that production records are matched with each other and traced to accounting records. For example, examine computer generated exception report that compares related production documents.
■ Excess of standard over actual material, labor, or overhead cost may be due to failure to record production transactions.	■ Inquire about use of standard cost system and inspect reports that follow up on variances.
■ Inability to reconcile goods placed in production, completed, or added with finished goods may be due to failure to record production transactions.	■ Inquire about reconciliation of these items and observe or inspect reconciliations. For example, examine computer generated exception report of unreconciled inventory transfers.
■ Perpetual records document the recording of inventory transactions, and periodic comparisons with physical inventory may identify inventory transactions that should have been recorded but were not.	■ Inquire about use of perpetual records and physical inventory, vouch and trace production documents to records, and inspect evidence of reconciliation with physical inventory.
■ Helps identify errors in recording quantities and prices on production documents as inventory moves through the production process.	■ Inspect evidence that independent comparison was made. For example, examine computer generated exception report of unmatched quantities and prices on production documents.
■ Helps identify inaccurate raw material prices before they are used to value inventory.	■ Inspect evidence that independent comparison was made. For example, examine computer generated exception report of unmatched prices on requisitions, invoices, and inventory records.
■ Helps identify incorrect overhead rates or overhead computations on job orders before they are used to value inventory.	■ Inspect evidence of independent review and recomputation. For example, examine computer generated exception report of incorrect overhead rates and computations.
■ Helps identify inaccurate extensions and footings in production documents before they are used to value inventory.	■ Inspect evidence of independent recomputation of extensions and footings. For example, examine computer generated exception report of incorrect extensions and footings.

(continued)

Table 16-4	*continued*

Assertion	Relevant Internal Control Structure Policy or Procedure
Valuation or Allocation *(continued)*	■ Analyze and follow up on material, labor, and overhead variances.
	■ Use perpetual inventory records.
	■ Use sales forecasts or economic production run models.
	■ Establish effective product specifications and inspections.
Presentation and Disclosure	■ Use chart of accounts with adequate detail.
	■ Independently review account codings for materials, labor, and overhead costs.*
	■ Reconcile production labor and overhead costs on job cost sheets with payroll and overhead accounting records.*
	■ Use disclosure checklists.
	■ Independently review disclosures.

*This policy or procedure may be performed either manually or by a computer programmed to compare information relevant to the control and produce a report of exceptions.

Why Policy or Procedure Is Relevant to Assertion	Common Tests of Controls for Policy or Procedure
■ Excess of standard over actual material, labor, or overhead cost may be due to incorrect valuation of materials, labor, or overhead.	■ Inquire about use of standard cost system and inspect reports on follow up on variances.
■ Provides a record of inventory usage and quantities on hand that helps prevent excess production or ordering of goods, which results in slow-moving or obsolete inventory.	■ Inquire about use of perpetual inventory records in determining production or order quantities, and inspect evidence of their consideration.
■ Helps avoid production or ordering of excess goods, which results in slow-moving or obsolete inventory.	■ Inquire about use of sales forecasts or economic production run models, and inspect evidence of their use.
■ Helps avoid production of defective or unsalable goods and resulting overvaluation of inventory.	■ Inquire about and observe product specification and inspection policies and procedures, and inspect evidence of their performance.
■ Helps identify specific accounts in which production transactions should be classified when recorded.	■ Inquire about, observe, and inspect use of chart of accounts.
■ Helps identify incorrect account classifications in materials, labor, and overhead before production transactions are recorded.	■ Inspect evidence that account codings were reviewed. For example, examine computer generated exception report of incorrect account codings.
■ Inability to reconcile labor or overhead costs charged to job orders with payroll or overhead records may be due to misclassification of such costs.	■ Inquire about reconciliation of job orders with payroll and overhead records, and observe or inspect reconciliations. For example, examine computer generated exception report of unreconciled job cost sheets and accounting records.
■ Serves as a reminder of the disclosures that should be made and of the information the disclosures should contain.	■ Inquire about use of checklists and observe or inspect evidence of their use.
■ Helps identify incomplete or inaccurate disclosures.	■ Inquire about and inspect evidence of independent review.

To test these control procedures, the auditor usually inquires about how and when these comparisons are made and inspects evidence indicating that they were performed and followed up on. Such evidence usually consists of exception or error reports prepared either manually or by the computer. If the entity does not require an independent comparison, the auditor may select a sample of production documents and inspect them for consistency to help evaluate the effectiveness of the production transaction accounting system.

Reconciling the labor and overhead costs charged to job orders with the payroll and overhead accounting records may also identify recorded transactions that did not occur. Costs recorded on job orders that cannot be reconciled with the payroll and overhead accounting records may be the result of recording nonexistent transactions. The auditor will inquire about the client's use of the reconciliation procedure and observe or inspect the reconciliations.

Management's analysis of and follow-up on an excess of actual materials and overhead costs over standard may also be relevant to the existence or occurrence assertion. Variances of actual over standard may be due to recording materials or overhead transactions that did not occur.

Reconciling goods placed in production, completed production, and additions to finished inventory helps substantiate the transfer of goods during the production process. Discrepancies among these three categories may be due to recording production transfers that did not occur. These reconciliations may be performed manually or by computer. Auditors usually test these reconciliations by inquiring about how and when they are done and who does them, by observing or inspecting the reconciliations or reports of discrepancies, and by inspecting evidence that appropriate follow-up action is taken.

Perpetual inventory records document increases and decreases in individual raw materials and finished goods inventory. An entity may verify these changes by ***vouching*** them to supporting production documents. This vouching can be done manually or by computer. In addition, a physical inventory on either a cycle or annual basis may identify differences between the perpetual records and the physical quantities caused by recording production transactions that did not occur. The auditor's tests of controls for these policies and procedures usually include inquiring about the entity's procedures for maintaining perpetual records, inspecting those records, inspecting evidence that entries in those records were vouched to supporting production documents, and inspecting evidence that the physical inventory was reconciled with the perpetual records. In some circumstances, the auditor may select a sample of entries in the perpetual records and vouch them to supporting production documents.

Entities usually address the physical existence of inventory units by providing secured storage locations, such as separate stockrooms or warehouses; by restricting access to those locations to authorized personnel; and by using security guards and systems. The tests of controls for these procedures involve inquiring about and observing how and where inventory is stored, who is authorized access to inventory, and what other security measures the entity has established.

Completeness Assertion

The completeness assertion for production transactions means that all materials, labor, and overhead that should be recorded as product costs have been recorded. This assertion also means that all transfers of goods from raw materials, work in process, and finished goods inventory have been recorded and that the inventory balances include all inventory that should be included. The failure to record these costs, transfers, or inventory items usually results in an understatement of inventory and net income.

Prenumbered production documents are commonly used to help ensure that all production transactions are recorded. These documents provide a formal, controlled record indicating that a transaction has taken place and should be recorded. Accounting for the sequence of these documents helps ensure that each document will be considered in recording production transactions. The tests of controls for these policies and procedures were discussed previously in conjunction with the existence or occurrence assertion.

Comparing the data on different production documents for consistency and tracing those documents to the accounting records also allow an entity to identify unrecorded transactions. Differences may exist in the data on various production documents because certain production transactions were not recorded at some stage of production. *Tracing* production documents to the accounting records helps identify documents that were not recorded. An entity may compare production documents and trace them to the accounting records either manually or by computer. To test these control procedures, the auditor usually inquires about the comparison and tracing of production documents and inspects evidence that the comparison and tracing have been done and that exceptions have been resolved. In some circumstances, the auditor may reperform the comparison and tracing. For entities that do not compare and trace production documents internally, auditors may select a sample of those documents and perform the comparison and tracing themselves.

Significant variances of standard costs for material, labor, and overhead over actual costs may result from failing to record production transactions. Management's analysis of and follow-up on these variances may reveal these omissions.

Discrepancies between goods placed in production, completed production, and finished inventory additions may also result from not recording certain production transactions. Requiring a periodic reconciliation of these three items can disclose these unrecorded transactions. Such reconciliations may be provided automatically when computerized production files are maintained.

Using perpetual inventory records to document increases and decreases in raw materials and finished goods and periodically comparing these records to a physical inventory also addresses the completeness assertion. Differences between the perpetual records and the physical count may be caused by not recording certain inventory transactions.

Rights and Obligations Assertion

The rights and obligations assertion is generally not significant for production transactions and the resulting finished inventory account balance. In some entities, however, customers may supply some or all of their own components for use in the production process. Because the client does not own these goods they should not be included in raw materials, work in process, or finished goods inventory. The internal control structure policies and procedures concerning these types of transactions are virtually identical to those for goods held on consignment, discussed in detail in Chapter 15 in relation to the rights and obligations assertion for purchase transactions in the expenditure cycle.

Valuation or Allocation Assertion

The valuation or allocation assertion for production transactions and related inventory balances means that production transactions and inventories are recorded at the correct amounts. Production and inventory amounts may be recorded incorrectly for a number of reasons. An incorrect quantity or incorrect material price may be charged to production. The wrong labor or overhead rate may be used in a department or cost center, or inaccurate labor or machine hours may be recorded. Errors in extensions and footings can also cause valuation or allocation misstatements.

Inventory balances can be overstated or understated as a result of the errors just discussed. In addition, incorrect application of inventory accounting principles, such as LIFO or FIFO, can cause inventory values to be misstated. The quality of inventory in stock and the demand for those goods also affects inventory value. Slow-moving or obsolete inventory needs to be considered in inventory valuation.

Several policies or procedures are commonly used to help ensure that production transactions are properly valued and allocated to the appropriate inventory balance. Independent entity personnel can compare the raw material quantities and prices on requisitions, production orders, and job orders to reduce the risk of using incorrect quantities and prices to value production transactions. In addition, raw material prices on requisitions may be independently compared with vendor invoices or perpetual inventory records to help prevent errors in pricing materials. These comparisons may either be performed manually or, when the information is stored in computer files, by computer.

To test these control procedures, the auditor usually inquires about how the comparisons are performed and inspects evidence that the comparisons are made and exceptions corrected. In some cases, the auditor may reperform some of the comparisons. When the entity does not make such comparisons, auditors may select a sample of production documents and perform the comparisons themselves.

Many entities also address valuation misstatements by requiring an independent review of departmental overhead rates used to cost production and an independent recomputation of the overhead charged to specific production jobs or batches. In addition, independent recomputation of the extensions and footings on production documents helps identify and correct errors that can result in misstatement of inventory values. A computer can be programmed to check the overhead rates and calculations for accuracy and recompute extensions and footings. The tests of controls for these procedures involve inquiring about how the review and recomputations are performed and observing them or inspecting evidence that they have been performed. The auditor may also reperform extensions and footings for a sample of production documents in some audits.

Significant variances between standard and actual costs may be caused by mistakes in valuing production transactions or inventory balances. Management's analysis of and follow-up on these variances can help identify these misstatements.

Perpetual inventory records serve as a formal, controlled document of quantities and prices for individual inventory items. Their use helps improve the clerical accuracy of processing inventory transactions by reducing the risk of using incorrect quantities and prices. In addition, perpetual records show the activity and quantities on hand for individual inventory items. Management can use this information to identify slow-moving or obsolete inventory or to avoid producing or ordering excess inventory.

The auditor's tests of controls usually include inquiring about how perpetual records are maintained, inspecting those records, and obtaining evidence that the perpetual records are properly maintained. This evidence is usually obtained from tracing to the perpetual inventory records the documents used to record increases and decreases in those records and vouching changes in perpetual records to supporting documents.

Auditors generally perform these tests of controls as part of the audit of the revenue cycle, expenditure cycle, and conversion cycle. The quantities and prices for additions to the raw materials perpetual records are tested by tracing and vouching receiving reports and vendor invoices to those records when auditing the expenditure cycle. The quantities and prices for reductions in the raw materials perpetual records are tested during the conversion cycle audit by tracing and vouching materials requisitions to those records. Similarly, increases in the finished inventory perpetual records are tested by tracing and vouching production reports with those records as part of the conversion cycle audit. The auditor tests decreases in finished goods perpetual records as part of the revenue cycle audit by tracing and vouching shipping documents and customer invoices to those records.

Management's use of sales forecasts or economic production runs helps avoid producing or ordering excess goods. As a result, inventory valuation problems resulting from obsolete or slow-moving goods are less likely. The auditor's test of controls generally is to inquire about the entity's forecasting or production run techniques and to inspect evidence that these techniques are used to plan and schedule production.

Poor quality goods can also cause misstatements in inventory valuation. Entities that carefully establish product specifications and that require inspection of completed production reduce the risk of producing defective goods that will ultimately result in inventory write-downs. To test these policies, auditors inquire about and read the product specification and inspection policies. They also observe quality inspection or obtain evidence that those inspections are being performed. For example, auditors may inspect reports of defective items detected through quality control.

Presentation and Disclosure

The presentation and disclosure assertion for production transactions and related inventory balances means that production transactions and inventories are classified in the appropriate accounts. This assertion also means that notes to the financial statements contain the disclosures about those accounts that are required by generally accepted accounting principles. Misclassifications arise when raw material, work in process, or finished goods transactions are recorded in an incorrect inventory account. For example, work in process may be classified as finished goods before it is completed. Incorrect classification can also occur when inventory production costs are not classified as current assets, such as when direct labor or overhead costs are incorrectly charged to expense or property, plant, or equipment accounts.

Disclosure misstatements arise when inadequate or incorrect information about the basis of inventory valuation is presented in the financial statements. For example, such misstatements may occur if the entity does not follow the requirements of generally accepted accounting principles to disclose the basis upon which inventory classifications are stated (such as lower of cost or market) and the method of determining costs (such as first-in, first-out). In addition, in some industries, such as construction, items that might appear to be inventories receive special accounting treatment and are not presented in the financial statements as inventories. For example, costs in excess of billings on construction contracts in progress should not be shown as inventory.

Using a detailed chart of accounts can help an entity to classify properly production transactions and inventories. In addition, many entities require that production transaction documents be coded with the number of the account in which the transaction is to be recorded. These codes may be reviewed by independent entity personnel or by the computer to reduce the risk of misclassification. The auditor's tests of controls for these procedures include inspecting the chart of accounts, observing the coding of certain production transactions, and inspecting evidence that these codes are independently reviewed.

Misclassified labor or overhead costs may be identified by reconciling the payroll and overhead accounting records with the labor and overhead charges recorded on the job cost sheets. Where payroll and overhead records and job records are maintained on computer files, the computer may be used to perform the reconciliation. Costs that cannot be traced from the accounting records to the job cost records may indicate costs that have been misclassified in the accounting records. For example, direct labor may be misclassified as maintenance expense. The auditor's tests of controls for this reconciliation procedure involve inquiring about how the reconciliation is done and observing or inspecting the reconciliation report.

To reduce the risk of inadequate or erroneous disclosures about production transactions and inventories, entity accounting personnel may use disclosure checklists and independent entity personnel may review the financial statement disclosures prior to their final preparation. Tests of controls over an entity's disclosure procedures generally include auditor inquiries about which entity personnel prepare disclosures and whether checklists are used and disclosures are reviewed, and inspection of completed checklists and evidence that independent entity personnel review disclosures.

Determining the Assessed Level of Control Risk

The auditor determines the assessed level of control risk for conversion cycle assertions based on evidence obtained about the effectiveness of the design and operation of the internal control structure policies and procedures relevant to those assertions. The more effective the design and operation of these policies and procedures, the lower the assessed level of control risk will be. Evidence about the effectiveness of design and operation is obtained from tests of controls performed in prior audits, those performed while obtaining an understanding of the internal control structure, and any additional tests of controls performed after obtaining the understanding. The assessed level of control risk for a specific conversion cycle assertion is used in determining the substantive tests to apply to that assertion. Substantive tests of transactions and account balances for the conversion cycle are discussed in Chapter 17.

Significant Terms

Economic production run A predetermined quantity of goods to be produced that achieves the best balance between production costs, storage costs, and sales demand.

Imprest system A system in which a fund (account) is maintained at a fixed amount. The sum of unexpended cash in the fund and disbursements from the fund should always equal the fixed amount of the fund.

Payroll tax returns Forms for determining and documenting the calculation of various employer payroll taxes and employee taxes withheld, such as FICA and unemployment taxes.

Standard cost system A system whereby the costs that should be incurred for materials, labor, and overhead are determined after considering normal efficiency and usage factors. Standard costs are often developed through engineering studies of the production process.

Tracing to perpetual inventory records Following source documents for inventory transactions to the perpetual records to determine whether they have been recorded properly.

Vouching perpetual inventory records Supporting recorded entries in the perpetual inventory records by examining the source documents for those entries.

Discussion Questions

16-1. Describe the relationship of the conversion cycle to the expenditure cycle and the revenue cycle.

16-2. Describe the purpose and relationship among the following conversion cycle documents: (1) production order, (2) raw materials requisition form, (3) bill of materials, and (4) job cost sheet.

16-3. What assertions for production transactions might be misstated if management does not adequately follow up on significant differences between standard and actual overhead costs? Why?

16-4. Why is it important to control both the costs and physical movement of inventory during the production process? Describe two internal control structure policies or procedures that can provide this control.

16-5. What four independent comparisons are performed for production transactions, either manually or by the computer? For each comparison, identify one assertion for which control risk may be reduced if that comparison is done effectively.

16-6. How does obsolete or slow-moving inventory affect the valuation or allocation assertion for inventory? What three internal control structure policies or procedures can reduce the risk of misstatements in that assertion caused by obsolete or slow-moving inventory?

16-7. What types of mistakes in processing production transactions can result in misstatements in the valuation or allocation assertion for work-in-process inventory? Describe three internal control structure policies that can reduce the risk of such mistakes.

16-8. Describe the flow of transactions in a typical payroll accounting system.

16-9. What three internal control structure policies or procedures can reduce the risk of recording payroll transactions that did not occur? How does each of them help reduce this risk?

16-10. What four mistakes in processing payroll can result in misstatements in the valuation or allocation assertion for payroll transactions? List one specific internal control structure policy or procedure that can reduce control risk for each mistake.

Objective Questions

16-11. A proper segregation of duties for payroll transactions would permit the payroll accounting department to perform which of the following functions?
   (1) Sign payroll checks.
   (2) Prepare payroll checks.
   (3) Distribute payroll checks.
   (4) Approve employee time cards.

16-12. Which of the following internal control structure policies and procedures would be most effective in reducing control risk for the existence or occurrence assertion for payroll transactions?

(1) Using prenumbered payroll checks and accounting for their numerical sequence.

(2) Using a chart of accounts with adequate detail.

(3) Using time clocks and time cards and requiring that time cards be approved by a supervisor.

(4) Requiring an independent employee to recalculate net pay for a sample of employees each pay period.

16-13. The use of prenumbered payroll checks is a control procedure that is primarily related to the

(1) completeness assertion for payroll transactions.

(2) valuation or allocation assertion for payroll transactions.

(3) rights and obligations assertion for payroll transactions.

(4) presentation and disclosure assertion for payroll transactions.

16-14. Janix Co. requires that an independent accounting clerk recompute the gross wages, payroll deductions, and net pay for a sample of employees each pay period. This control procedure is designed to reduce control risk for which of the following payroll transaction assertions?

(1) Existence or occurrence.

(2) Completeness.

(3) Rights and obligations.

(4) Valuation or allocation.

16-15. Which of the following internal control structure policies and procedures would be least effective in preventing the accumulation of obsolete or slow-moving inventory?

(1) Using perpetual inventory records.

(2) Using secured storage areas for inventory.

(3) Using sales forecasts.

(4) Using authorized production orders.

16-16. Each month Emerson Enterprises reconciles labor and overhead costs charged to job cost sheets with the payroll and overhead accounting records. One month the reconciliation revealed that a material amount of direct labor payroll costs were erroneously charged to maintenance expense instead of the appropriate job cost sheets. If the reconciliation had not detected this error, then

(1) the existence or occurrence assertion for work in process would be misstated.

(2) the completeness assertion for work in process would be misstated.

(3) the valuation or allocation assertion for work in process would be misstated.

(4) the presentation and disclosure assertion for work in process would be misstated.

16-17. Which of the following tests of controls is primarily related to the completeness assertion for production transactions?

(1) The auditor inspects a sample of materials requisition forms for the proper approval signature.

(2) The auditor vouches entries in the perpetual inventory records to inspection forms authorizing the transfer and recording of finished goods inventory.

(3) The auditor inspects the exception report prepared by the computer based on the computer's recomputation of the extensions and footings of materials and labor charges on job order cost sheets.

(4) The auditor traces a sample of materials requisition forms to job-order cost sheets.

16-18. Lutel Manufacturing Corporation mass-produces 12 different products. The controller who is interested in strengthening internal control structure policies and procedures for the existence assertion for finished inventory would be most likely to implement which of the following?

(1) A separation of duties among production personnel.

(2) The use of sales forecasts.

(3) A job-order cost accounting system.

(4) A perpetual inventory system.

16-19. Holly, Inc., uses time clocks and time cards to help ensure that employee work time is accurately recorded. Which internal control structure policy or procedure would be most effective in determining whether production employees are properly recording their time on the payroll time cards at a time clock station?

(1) The production supervisor should approve daily time charged to job orders and compare that time with hours recorded on the time cards.

(2) Payroll checks should be distributed by the internal auditing department.

(3) Hours recorded on the time cards should be compared to payroll computations by an independent employee.

(4) The duties of hiring, payroll computation, and paying employees should be segregated.

Problems and Cases

16-20. (Understanding the Control Structure) Kay Tatum, CPA, is participating in the conversion cycle audit of Wainwright Products. Tatum is a new audit staff member and this is her first audit of a manufacturing entity. She was assigned to obtain an understanding of the conversion cycle accounting system and has determined that the company uses several documents and procedures, listed below, with which she is unfamiliar.

1. An authorized, prenumbered production order for each job.

2. A router sheet for each production order.

3. A bill of materials for each production order.

4. Employee time cards approved by a production supervisor.

5. Signed inspection reports for completed products.

REQUIRED

A. Briefly explain the purpose or function of each document or procedure.

B. Identify the assertion or assertions for which control risk may be reduced because of each document or procedure.

C. Describe one test of controls for each document or procedure.

*16-21. (Controls for Inventory) The Jameson Company produces a variety of chemical products for use by plastics manufacturers. The plant works on two shifts, five days per week, with maintenance work performed on the third shift and on other days as required.

An audit conducted by the staff of the new corporate internal audit department has recently been completed and the comments on inventory control were not favorable. Audit comments were particularly directed to the control of raw material ingredients and maintenance materials.

Raw material ingredients are received at the back of the plant, signed for by one of the employees of the batching department, and stored near the location of the initial batching process. Receiving tallies are given to the supervisor during the day, and he forwards the tallies to the inventory control department at the end of the day. The inventory control department calculates ingredient usage by using weekly reports of actual production and standard formulas. Physical inventories are taken quarterly. The inventory control department prepares purchase requisitions and rush orders are frequent. In spite of the need for rush orders, the production superintendent regularly gets memos from the controller stating that there must be excess inventory because the ingredient inventory dollar value is too high.

Maintenance parts and supplies are received and stored in a storeroom. There is a storeroom clerk on each of the operating shifts. Storeroom requisitions are to be filled out for everything taken from the storeroom; however, this practice is not always followed.

*CMA adapted.

The storeroom is not locked when the clerk is out because of the need to get parts quickly. The storeroom is also open during the third shift for the maintenance crews to get parts as needed. The storeroom clerk prepares the purchase requisitions, and physical inventory is taken on a cycle count basis. Rush orders are frequent.

REQUIRED

A. (1) Identify the deficiencies in Jameson Company's internal control structure policies and procedures for

- ingredients inventory.
- maintenance material and supplies inventory.

(2) Recommend improvements for each of these areas.

B. What procedures would the internal auditors use to identify the deficiencies in Jameson Company's inventory control?

*16-22. (Control Deficiencies in Payroll) A CPA's audit working papers contain a narrative description of a segment of the Croyden Factory, Inc., payroll system and an accompanying flowchart as follows:

> The internal control structure policies and procedures with respect to the personnel department function effectively and are not included in the flowchart [Figure 16–2].
>
> At the beginning of each work week, payroll clerk No. 1 reviews the payroll department files to determine the employment status of factory employees and then prepares time cards and distributes them as each individual arrives at work. This payroll clerk, who is also responsible for custody of the signature stamp machine, verifies the identity of each payee before delivering signed checks to the foreman.
>
> At the end of each work week, the foreman distributes payroll checks for the preceding work week. Concurrent with this activity, the foreman reviews the current week's employee time cards, notes the regular and overtime hours worked on a summary form, and initials the aforementioned time cards. The foreman then delivers all time cards and unclaimed payroll checks to payroll clerk No. 2.

REQUIRED

A. Based upon the narrative and accompanying flowchart (Figure 16–2), what are the deficiencies in the internal control structure?

B. Based upon the narrative and accompanying flowchart, what inquiries should be made to clarify the existence of possible additional deficiencies in the internal control structure? Do not discuss the internal control structure for the personnel department.

16-23. (EDP Control Deficiencies in Payroll) The Vane Corporation is a manufacturing concern that has been in business for the past 18 years. During this period, the company has grown from a very small, family-owned operation to a medium-size manufacturing concern with several departments. Despite this growth, a substantial number of the procedures that Vane Corporation employs have been in effect since the business was started. Just recently Vane Corporation computerized its payroll function.

---

*AICPA adapted.

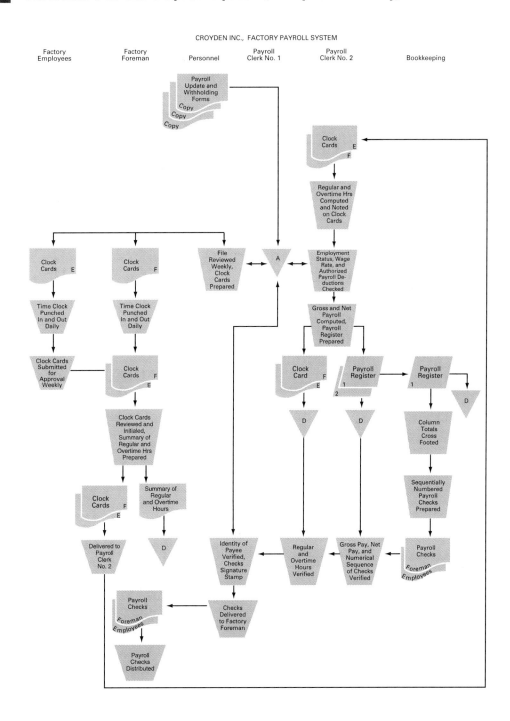

Figure 16–2   **Flowchart of the Payroll System, Croyden Factory, Inc.**

The payroll function operates in the following manner: Each worker picks up a weekly time card near the factory entrance on Monday morning and writes in his or her name and identification number. The workers write on the time card the time of their daily arrival and departure. On the following Monday the factory foremen collect the completed time cards for the previous week and send them to data processing.

In data processing the time cards are used to prepare the weekly time file. This file is processed with the master payroll file, which is maintained on magnetic tape according to worker identification number. The checks are written by the computer on the regular checking account and imprinted with the treasurer's signature. After the payroll file is updated and the checks are prepared, the checks are sent to the factory foremen, who distribute them to the workers or hold them for the workers to pick up later if they are absent.

The foremen notify data processing of new employees and terminations. Changes in hourly pay rate or any other changes affecting payroll are usually communicated to data processing by the foremen.

The workers also complete a job time ticket for each individual job they work on each day. The job time tickets are collected daily and sent to cost accounting where they are used to prepare a cost distribution analysis.

Further analysis of the payroll function reveals the following:
1. A worker's gross wages never exceed $300 per week.
2. Raises never exceed 55 cents per hour for the factory workers.
3. No more than 20 overtime hours are allowed each week.
4. The factory employs 150 workers in ten departments.

The payroll function has not been operating smoothly for some time, but even more problems have surfaced since the payroll was computerized. The foremen have indicated that they would like a weekly report indicating worker tardiness, absenteeism, and idle time so they can determine the amount of productive time lost and the reason for the lost time. The following errors and inconsistencies have been encountered during the past few pay periods.

1. A worker's paycheck was not processed properly, because he had transposed two numbers in his identification number when he filled out his time card.
2. A worker was issued a check for $1,531.80 when it should have been $153.18.
3. One worker's paycheck was not written, and this error was not detected until the paychecks for that department were distributed by the foreman.
4. Part of the master payroll file was destroyed when the tape reel was inadvertently mounted on the wrong tape drive and used as a scratch tape. Data processing attempted to reestablish the destroyed portion from original source documents and other records.
5. One worker received a paycheck for an amount considerably larger than she should have. Further investigation revealed that 84 had been punched instead of 48 for hours worked.
6. Several records on the master payroll file were skipped and not included on the updated master payroll file. This was not detected for several pay periods.
7. In processing nonroutine changes, a computer operator included a pay rate increase for one of his friends in the factory. This was discovered by chance by another employee.

REQUIRED
Identify the control structure deficiencies in the payroll procedure and in the computer processing as it is now conducted by the Vane Corporation. Recommend the changes necessary to correct the system. Arrange your answer in two columns, headed "Control Deficiencies" and "Recommendations," respectively.

*16-24. (Audit of Payroll) You are auditing the financial statements of Henry Brown, a large independent contractor. All employees are paid in cash because Brown believes this arrangement reduces clerical expenses and is preferred by his employees.

---

*AICPA adapted.

During the audit you find in the petty cash fund approximately $200, of which $185 is stated to be unclaimed wages. Further investigation reveals that Brown has installed the procedure of putting any unclaimed wages in the petty cash fund so that the cash can be used for disbursements. When the claimant to the wages appears, he is paid from the petty cash fund. Brown contends that this procedure reduces the number of checks drawn to replenish the petty cash fund and centers the responsibility for all cash on hand in one person inasmuch as the petty cash custodian distributes the pay envelopes.

REQUIRED
A. Does Brown's internal control structure provide proper procedures for unclaimed wages? Explain fully.
B. Because Brown insists on paying salaries in cash, what procedures would you recommend to provide better control over unclaimed wages?

Audit Judgment Case

*16-25. (Controls over Inventory and Purchases) Peabock Company is a wholesaler of soft goods whose inventory is composed of approximately 3,500 different items. The company employs a computerized batch processing system to maintain its perpetual inventory records. The system is run each weekend so that the inventory reports are available on Monday morning for management use. The system has been functioning satisfactorily for the past 15 months, providing the company with accurate records and timely reports.

Purchase order preparation has been an automatic part of the inventory system to ensure that the company will maintain enough inventory to meet customer demand. When an inventory item falls below a predetermined level, a record of the item is written. This record is used in conjunction with the vendor file to prepare the purchase orders.

Exception reports are prepared during inventory update and purchase order preparation. These reports disclose any errors or exceptions identified during processing. In addition, the system provides for management approval of all purchase orders exceeding a specified amount. Any exceptions or items requiring management approval are handled by supplemental runs on Monday morning and are combined with the weekend results.

A system flowchart of Peabock Company's inventory and purchase order procedure is shown in Figure 16–3.

REQUIRED
A. The illustrated system flowchart of Peabock Company's inventory and purchase order system (Figure 16–3) was prepared before the system was fully operational. Several steps that are important to the successful operations of the system were inadvertently omitted from the chart. Now that the system is operating effectively, management wants the system documentation complete and would like the flowchart corrected. Describe the steps that have been omitted and indicate where the omissions have occurred. You need not redraw the flowchart.
B. In order for Peabock's inventory/purchase order system to function properly, control procedures would be included in the system. Describe the type of control procedures Peabock should use in its system to ensure proper functioning and indicate where these procedures would be placed in the system.

---

*AICPA adapted.

Figure 16-3 **Peabock Company's Inventory and Purchase Order Procedure**

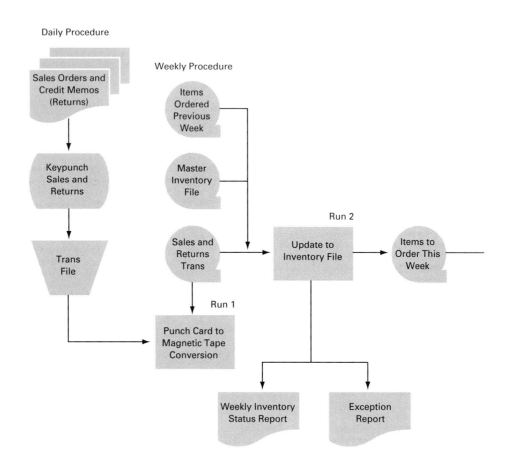

Auditing Issues Case

*16-26. KELCO MANUFACTURING COMPANY

Your review of the internal control structure of Kelco's payroll system revealed the following:

Kelco president, Steve Cook, interviews all applicants. When hired, Cook's secretary, Maxine Adams, prepares an employee personnel file that contains the employment

*AICPA adapted.

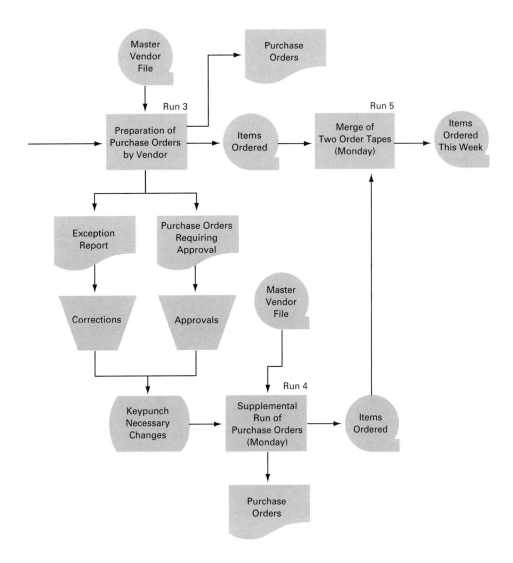

application and letters of reference. Cook telephones the accounting department when new employees are hired.

Two accounting clerks perform the payroll functions. Together the clerks keep the payroll records; record employee time; compute gross pay, deductions, and net pay; write payroll checks; and prepare federal and state payroll tax returns.

Factory employees obtain time cards from the factory foreman each week. At the end of the week, the employees write in the number of hours worked and return the time cards to the accounting clerks. When the employees turn in their time cards, they receive their weekly payroll check from one of the clerks.

There is no evidence that Kelco uses preprinted forms.

REQUIRED
1. Discuss the control structure weaknesses in Kelco's payroll system.
2. You have just made Cook aware of the payroll system's weaknesses. Cook is very concerned. Due to increased demand for Kelco products, he plans to hire an additional 50 employees in the coming months. Provide Cook with recommendations to correct the control structure weaknesses in Kelco's payroll system.

Substantive Tests of the Conversion Cycle Balances and Transactions

Learning Objectives

- Describe the common substantive tests for inventory and explain their relationship to financial statement assertions.

- Explain the major audit considerations in the client's inventory count procedures.

- Describe the major elements in the auditor's observation of inventory.

- Explain and illustrate the primary substantive tests related to inventory cutoff.

- Describe the complexities of and apply substantive tests to inventory pricing.

- Explain the effect of the assessed levels of control risk for inventory assertions on the nature, timing, and extent of common substantive tests for inventory.

- Describe the typical substantive tests of payroll.

I nventories, particularly those of manufacturers or distributors, are material to financial statements and can represent substantial amounts of capital. There are a number of options confronting auditors trying to accurately assess vast inventory stockpiles. The audit must be completed in a timely, cost-effective manner, which generally means that only a portion of the inventory may be tested. This can be risky, especially if management has demonstrated any past predisposition toward financial statement fraud or misstatement. Inventories can also be quite complex, meaning great attention to detail is required. Coupling inventories' vast sizes with a complex number and range of components is another source of potential auditing errors. ■

Source: Auditing Inventories—Physical Observations," *AICPA Practice Alert*, Professional Practice Issues Task Force, July 1994, p. 1.

This chapter examines the audit of account balances in the conversion cycle. As discussed in Chapter 16, the accounts in the conversion, or production, cycle depend on the type of entity. For example, for a retail company no conversion takes place; the goods that are purchased in the expenditure cycle become the merchandise inventory. Unlike a retail concern, a manufacturing company must purchase raw materials and convert them into finished products through the conversion cycle. Thus, a manufacturing company will have not only finished goods inventory but also raw materials, work-in-process, and overhead accounts.

Audit of Balances in the Conversion Cycle

The common and material account balance in the conversion cycle is inventory. For many entities inventory and the related cost of sales are the most important accounts within the financial statements. Not only does inventory represent a current asset and thus affect liquidity, it also directly affects the cost of goods sold. Inventory is crucial to determining current assets, total assets, gross margin, and net income. The significance of inventory for the financial statements and the complexities involved in accounting for inventories mean that considerable audit time is spent on inventory in most audit engagements.

Significant complexities exist in accounting for inventory. A common element of accounting for inventories is the determination of cost. All entities must make a cost-flow assumption and determine which assumption is appropriate in the circumstances: for example, LIFO, FIFO, and weighted average. Further, in applying the lower of cost or market technique, the accountant must also determine market prices, including the complexities of applying ceiling and floor market prices. Obsolete inventory, excess inventory, and drastic changes in market price can all affect the appropriate accounting for inventories.

Numerous audit procedures are applied to test the assertion that inventories are fairly stated in conformity with generally accepted accounting principles. A summary of these tests is shown in Table 17–1. In most audits, the primary risk of a material misstatement of inventory relates to the existence and valuation assertions.

Table 17–1	Common Substantive Audit Tests for Inventory		

Common Audit Tests	Technique	Type of Test	Assertions
Inventory observation	Physical examination	Test of balances	Existence Completeness Rights and obligations Valuation
Inventory cutoff	Vouching Tracing	Test of transactions	Existence Completeness
Confirmation of inventories in public warehouse	Confirmation	Test of balances	Existence Rights and obligations Completeness Presentation and disclosure
Inventory price tests	Vouching	Test of balances	Valuation
Apply analytical procedures	Analytical	Analytical procedure	All (limited evidence about existence and rights and obligations)

Inventory Observation

One of the most common audit procedures is the auditor's observation of the physical inventory count. This procedure has been a generally accepted auditing procedure since 1939 when a major fraud involving the McKesson & Robbins Co. led the AICPA to require inventory observations. In the **McKesson & Robbins scandal**, fictitious inventories amounted to approximately $10 million. The auditors, following generally accepted auditing procedures of the time, did not observe the inventory but rather supported the existence of the inventory through a written representation. Prior to the McKesson & Robbins investigation, auditors avoided taking responsibility for inventory quantities and physical existence, arguing that they were not qualified to identify and measure the great variety of their clients' inventories. As noted in Chapter 14, in the McKesson & Robbins investigation, receivables were also found to be fraudulently overstated by approximately $9 million. As a result of the SEC investigation, two audit procedures became generally accepted: *inventory observation* and *confirmation of receivables.*

According to *SAS No. 1, Receivables and Inventories* (AU 331), confirmation of receivables and observation of inventories are generally accepted auditing procedures. Auditors who issue an opinion when they have not employed these procedures must bear the burden of justifying the opinion expressed. Consequently, inventory observation is required whenever inventories are material and such observation is practicable.

SAS No. 1 (AU 331) requires the auditor to *observe* the client's inventory count. However, the inventory is actually counted by the client. This is an important distinction because the client is responsible for the counting, supervising, and recording of inventory as well as for the preparation of the financial statements. The auditor's responsibility is to be satisfied that the client's inventory count is proper.

Some auditors believe that inventory observation is a test of controls. They state that the primary purpose of the auditor's inventory observation is to evaluate the reliability of the client's inventory count procedures. Thus, the auditor is primarily gathering evidence about the client's use of appropriate inventory counting procedures and the effectiveness of those procedures. If the inventory observation is viewed as a test of controls, the auditor performs audit tests to determine that the client's instructions are actually followed.

Other auditors state that the inventory observation is a substantive test because the auditor is testing physical existence of quantities recorded in the inventory account. Both views have merit: the inventory observation is typically *both* a test of controls and a substantive test, that is, a dual-purpose test. In this chapter, inventory observation is presented as a substantive test, which is the traditional view of the purpose of inventory observation. However, even though classified as a substantive test, inventory observation also has significant test of controls objectives. In fact, when no test of controls objective is served and the auditor is concerned solely with substantive objectives, observation of the counting process may not be necessary. In that case, the auditor will do extensive test counting.

In performing an inventory observation, the auditor should address several issues. These include examining the inventory instructions, determining the timing of testing, performing the inventory observation, and using specialists.

Review of Inventory-Taking Instructions

Before observing inventory, the auditor should review the client's inventory taking instructions. The review should include an analysis of the planned procedures to determine that those procedures will produce a complete and accurate inventory count. For example, the auditor should note items such as the names of the personnel responsible for supervising the inventory count; the locations and dates of the counts; the detailed instructions on how the inventory counts are to be made (for example, one person will count and another person will record); whether inventory tags are to be used and how these tags are to be controlled; and how cutoff procedures are to be handled (for example, how the client plans to handle the receiving and shipment of goods during the inventory count). This review of inventory taking instructions is important because it allows the auditor to suggest any changes in the inventory count procedure prior to the count. Table 17–2 highlights **client inventory count** procedures that promote completeness and accuracy.

Timing of Testing

The timing of the inventory observation depends on when the client counts the inventory. For many companies with a *periodic* inventory system, the inventory count occurs at the close of business on the last day of the fiscal year. However, some entities (often, larger entities) with *perpetual* inventory systems perform cycle inventory counts. In a *cycle inventory count*, different parts of inventory are counted periodically. For example, each week a different type of inventory is counted (perhaps in Week 1 Item A is counted, in Week 2 Item B is counted, in Week 3 Item C is counted, and so on). In this way, inventory is taken throughout the year and is compared to perpetual records, and any necessary adjustments are made. When a client relies on a cycle count, internal control structure policies and procedures over inventory should be strong. However, for clients who are on a periodic inventory count system, the presence or absence of controls *throughout the year* should have very little

---

Table 17-2 **Client Inventory Count Procedures**

1. *Competence of count personnel* The inventory should be identified and counted by persons familiar with the items. Preferably, a person who does not ordinarily have access to the inventory should also be involved in the count. This is often achieved by using two-member count teams — composed of one counter and one recorder—in which one person is familiar with the goods and the other is independent. In small businesses where this is not possible, a single employee could perform the function, as long as another individual, perhaps the owner/manager, test-checks the counts.

2. *Inventory identification procedures* Procedures should be adequate for subsequent pricing of the items. These procedures include identification of the stage of work in process, condition of goods (damaged or obsolete), and quality of goods, as, for example, in the case of lumber grading and steel.

3. *Procedures to reduce the potential for double-counting or missing items* A good method is the use of duplicate prenumbered inventory tags or some similar system or procedure that provides the same controls. In many situations, items are tagged before the count by persons familiar with the inventory. One copy of the tag remains with each lot of goods counted, and another is retained by the counters and returned to the supervisor. A separate control of tag numbers issued and returned is maintained by the supervisor.

4. *Inventory organization* Stock should be organized and laid out in an orderly fashion to facilitate the count.

5. *Identification and segregation of consignment or other customer stock* Consignment or other customer stock should be identified and segregated so that such stock is not included as part of the client's inventory.

6. *Procedures to check counts* Procedures to check counts may include having a second, independent count team checking and initialing the original counts or, if perpetual inventory records are used, having a second team investigate significant fluctuations. In a small entity, such procedures might be performed by two individuals who can check each other's counts.

7. *Procedures to control the movement of goods* Ideally, there should be no movement of goods during the inventory count. On occasion, however, it may be necessary for the client to continue production, receiving, or shipping operations during the count. In such circumstances, it is essential that the client have procedures adequate for identifying and recording such goods in the appropriate period. There should be cutoff procedures to identify goods received and shipped before and after inventory count and goods in transit between departments.

Source: Adapted from *Auditing Procedures Study: Audit of Inventories,* AICPA, 1986. Used with permission of the AICPA.

effect on the auditor's inventory observation at year-end because those controls do not affect the physical count.

If the client, however, desires to take the physical inventory prior to the balance sheet date, the auditor will carefully consider whether effective substantive tests can be performed to cover the remaining period (the period between the date of the physical inventory and the balance sheet date). The auditor's assessed level of control risk for the existence assertion is an important factor in this consideration. The lower the assessed level of control risk, the more likely it will be that substantive tests for the remaining period will be effective.

Of course, a client may use a perpetual inventory system that does not include a cycle system. Even in a perpetual system, physical counts should periodically be made and compared to perpetual records. Verification of perpetual records through periodic counts allows both client and auditor to conclude that the perpetual system is working properly with no material misstatements.

Even though many clients have periodic systems with inventory counts taken at year-end, the inventory count procedures can be quite varied. Regardless of the count procedures used, the auditor's primary objective is to substantiate an opinion that inventories are fairly stated in conformity with generally accepted accounting principles.

Physical Observation

After reviewing the client's inventory taking instructions and properly planning the observation, the auditor can observe the inventory count. The auditor will perform many procedures during the count.

Test Counts   One of the most important procedures the auditor performs during the physical observation is *test counts*. The auditor should test count (recount) some items that the client's employees have already counted and recorded. By comparing these counts with the client's counts, the auditor gathers evidence that client personnel are properly counting inventory in accordance with instructions. The

The Real World of Auditing

Slick Inventory

"I had been getting mysterious telephone calls... I think my secretary first spoke with the voice and then I had several conversations with him. The voice said his name was Taylor and I think he said he worked on the night shift at Allied (Crude Vegetable Oil). And he said the biggest hoax that was ever pulled was being pulled on American Express Company because there was in fact water in the tanks, and we were counting it as oil...he said that there had been built into the tank a metal chamber of some kind which went from the top to the bottom of the tank. It was under the hole where you would normally drop a bomb (sampling device) to determine the quality of the content of the tank. Whenever we went to take inventory at that tank, he said, we would be dropping the bomb down this metal chamber which was filled with soybean oil but that the balance of the tank had water in it."...more than three years later, after Allied went bankrupt, inspectors opened a big faucet on Tank 6006, which was supposed to hold $3,575,000 worth of soybean oil, and salt water poured out for twelve days.

The tank's floating roof sank and sank and sank until finally the false chamber welded to the underside of the roof, which held a few hundred pounds of soybean oil, came to rest on the bottom of the tank.

The inspectors knew, too, that all the tanks at Allied were interconnected by a spaghetti-like tangle of pipes above and below the ground....As the inspection slowly proceeded over the course of a week, it would have been simple for (employees) to jitney oil from tank to tank. So it's likely the inspectors were counting the oil over and over.

Somehow, the financiers didn't notice that for their money they were accepting papers for a truly astounding quantity of salad oil—more, in fact, than the Government counted in its monthly reports of all the salad oil stocks in the country.

Source: Norman C. Miller, *The Great Salad Oil Swindle.* Baltimore, MD: Penguin Books, 1965, pp. 79–82.

number of test counts the auditor makes is generally a matter of professional judgment. In determining the number of test counts the auditor should consider such factors as the significance of the items, considered either individually or when grouped; the use of second, independent count teams; and the involvement of internal auditors.

In selecting the specific items to test count, the auditor often stratifies the test count selection by emphasizing inventory items with high dollar values. Likewise, an auditor may wish to stratify test counts by turnover. For example, the auditor will often select more high-turnover items than low-turnover items for test counts. Similarly, an auditor will often select those items of raw materials (with high turnover and large supplies on hand) that are included in a variety of finished goods inventory items.

The auditor should record the counts tested and a sample of remaining client counts for subsequent use when the final inventory listing is prepared. This procedure ensures that the client's counts accurately appear on the final inventory listing and are recorded in the financial statements. Correctly counting inventory does not guarantee that the counts will actually be recorded as inventory and recorded correctly in the general ledger. The recording of test counts allows the auditor to verify later that the counts do in fact appear in the accounting records and that the inventory count tags have not been changed. Tracing test counts to the inventory records provides good evidence of completeness (that is, are the goods on hand actually included in the accounting records?).

Inventory Tags Because inventory tags are generally the method by which the client controls the inventory count, the auditor should also gather evidence that inventory tags are controlled (usually by being prenumbered and accounted for properly). If inventory tags are not properly controlled, the client could insert fictitious quantities, double count inventories, or omit items that have been counted. In performing test counts, the auditor should record not only physical quantities but also tag numbers. The auditor should also verify that tag numbers are properly used and controlled.

During the observation, the auditor should determine that all tags have been either used, unused, or voided. For example, the auditor will generally record the tag numbers used and tag numbers not used during the inventory observation. Later, after receiving the final inventory listing, the auditor can determine that unused tags do not appear on the inventory sheets. The auditor also should select some items on the listing and vouch them back to the inventory tags. This test provides evidence of existence and is primarily a test of overstatement. The auditor should also test the compilation sheets that summarize inventory data from the observation.

Observations Auditors should also be alert for obsolete, slow-moving, and damaged items during the observation. For example, if the auditor observes that inventory tags are being placed on items that appear damaged, the auditor should make an inquiry because these items may have to be valued at a lower price. Likewise, if the auditor observes that a large quantity of inventory items appear to be slow-moving (for example, a large amount of dust covers the items or the items are stored in an inaccessible place), he or she should make an inquiry. The auditor should always be alert for the general condition of inventory items that are being observed. Further, in performing the inventory count the auditor should be alert for empty containers and hollow squares (empty spaces) that may exist when inventory items are stacked.

Figure 17–1 **Inventory Test Count Sheet**

Plainsman Co.
Raw Materials Test Counts
12/31/X4

					1-2	Initials	Date
					Prepared By	LG	12/31/X4
					Approved By	WA	1/10/X5

	TAG NO.	INVENTORY SHEET NO.	INVENTORY NUMBER	DESCRIPTION	COUNT CLIENT	AUDIT	DIFFERENCE
1	6432	16	1-35-002	Copper Plate	145 ✓	145	
3	8610	19	1-84-016	Pinewood	93 ✓	93	
5	1537	25	2-12-008	Single wire	1423 yds ✓	1425 yds	2 yds
7	4422	27	2-26-797	Copper Tubing	323 ft ✓	323	
9	3678	50	4-28-204	Steel Plate	84 ✓	90	6
11	8231	66	7-47-312	Steel Aluminum	96 ✓	96	
13	8945	70	7-89-467	1/2" Copper Wire	503 ft ✓	503 ft	
15	6327	94	3-48-260	3/8" Copper Wire	529 ft ✓	529 ft	

Each difference was corrected by the client. The net
effect of the correction was to increase inventory
by $453. Total inventory values for which
test counts were made and traced to inventory
summaries were $27,460 or 22% of the total. Total
projected error would be $453 / 22% or $2,060. In
my opinion, errors were immaterial.

✓ = Traced to client inventory summary
sheets (F-6). No differences noted.

In summary, the auditor should record test counts and include a description of the items, any relevant identification numbers, the quantities counted, and inventory tag numbers. This information is necessary for the auditor to use later when tracing this information to the inventory records. The auditor should investigate any differences. An example of inventory test count sheets is shown in Figure 17–1.

Inventory Observation Memorandum   After completing the inventory observation, the auditor generally prepares an *inventory observation memorandum.* This memorandum describes the client's inventory count procedures, the auditor's observation of those procedures, the nature and extent of testing during the observation, the auditor's opinion as to the overall condition of the inventory, and the auditor's conclusions. Figure 17–2 shows an example of an inventory observation

---

Figure 17-2   **Inventory Observation Memo**

Plainsman Co.

Inventory Observation Memorandum

Prepared by: K.L.M. 1/4/X5

Reviewed by: H.F.J. 1/6/X5

Two members of our audit staff arrived at the Manufacturing Plant on the morning of 1/1/X5. We met with the controller, Terri Sinclair, to obtain and discuss with her the inventory instructions. Manufacturing operations had been shut down for the day. After our meeting with Sinclair, we began our audit procedures:

1. Observation of inventory taking. We observed the client's inventory taking in different parts of the plant. We checked to make sure that there was proper control over the inventory count tags. We believe that the instructions were being carried out properly.

2. Test counts. We made test counts of approximately 19% of the inventory. In each case, the accuracy of the client's count was confirmed with one exception. The Finished Goods area had one miscount by the client. I informed the count team, who recounted the item and agreed to our number. Subsequent test counts showed that the recount was accurate. Our test counts are recorded in our work papers (see E-4).

3. Inquiry of client. We inquired of the client as to obsolete, damaged, or slow-moving goods. We observed no obsolete or slow-moving items. We found one case of damaged goods. These items were taken out of our inventory balance (see E-6).

4. Observation of cutoff. We observed that receiving reports were prepared on all goods that had been received through year-end. We also observed the shipping documents and found that shipping documents had been prepared for all items shipped through year-end. No goods were received or shipped on 1/1/X5. We recorded the first unused shipping report number and receiving report number for subsequent use. Based upon the procedures outlined above, it is my opinion that the inventory count of goods on hand at year-end was carried out according to the inventory taking instructions and that all observed damaged or obsolete goods were identified and adjustments were correctly made.

K. Murray

memorandum. The inventory observation memo documents information regarding the inventory observation that has not been documented elsewhere in the working papers. The memo describes the procedures the auditor performed during the entire inventory observation and provides the auditor's conclusions.

Use of Specialists

In some cases, the auditor must observe inventory where determination of quantities or physical condition necessitates the use of a specialist. For example, inventory in the electronics industry is often so complex that the auditor may not have the expertise necessary to distinguish among the various electronic components. Similarly, in the audit of a jewelry company, the auditor may not have the expertise needed to evaluate properly precious jewels or stones. In these cases the auditor may need to use a specialist, as discussed in Chapter 12.

Special Problems

Special problems can arise in the inventory observation of certain industries. Examples of these industries and inventory types, their special count procedures, and related possible audit procedures are shown in Table 17–3.

Inventory Cutoff

During the inventory observation, the auditor performs ***inventory cutoff*** tests to determine that shipments and receipts near year-end were recorded in the proper period. The auditor's primary objectives with the inventory cutoff are existence and completeness. The inventory cutoff tests provide evidence that all goods owned by the client are counted and included in the inventory and that no other goods are included in the inventory.

Professional Judgment

Liquid and Dry Weights Are One Complicator to Measuring Inventory

Auditing inventories can present unique challenges and requires a range of professional judgment calls. Today's business managers have become more specialized in managing inventories; agreements with suppliers are now typically more explicit, and just-in-time inventory delivery systems have minimized the amount of capital tied up in inventory stores. Nonetheless, there are two primary reasons why innovative judgment is required on the part of the auditor when assessing inventories. No matter how efficient businesses become in managing inventory, certain levels must always be on hand in order to meet customers' demands. And inventories will almost always contain a wide and varying nature of assets. Inventory products such as coal, petroleum products, or beer present different valuation problems than do individual cars, appliances, or clothing items. But, as is the case when assessing the assets of any firm, auditors should gain as much insight as possible into the workings of the business. Becoming familiar with products, as well as obtaining a working knowledge of computer processing applications and relevant control systems are essential. The auditor should also apply professional judgment in evaluating a company's physical counting procedures, inventory summarization, pricing, and cutoff procedures before actually beginning a physical count.

Table 17-3	**Industries Using Other Count Methods**	

Inventory Type	Count Procedures and Potential Problems	Possible Audit Procedures
Lumber, steel coils, tubes	Usually not tagged, but marked or chalked when counted	Check for marking
	Possible problems in identifying quality or grade of items	Possibly use specialist or experienced client personnel
Pile inventories (for example, sugar, coal, scrap steel)	Usually not tagged or marked	Possibly use engineering estimates, geometric computation, aerial surveys, and reliance on detailed inventory records
	Quantity estimation problems	Physically count when pile is low or eliminated through the use of pile rotation
Items weighed on scales	Quantity estimation problems	Check scales for accuracy before and during counts and watch movement of scales and rebalancing procedures
		Use a combination of inspection and reweighing procedures
		Check conversion factors
Bulk materials (for example, storage tanks, grains, liquids)	Usually not identified as counted	Use tank counts or prenumbered lists for identification
	Quantity estimation problems	Use dipping, measuring sticks, engineering reports, and perpetual inventory records
	Quality determination problems	Select samples for assay or analysis, or use specialists
Precious metals, stones, works of art, collectibles	Potential identification and quality determination problems	Select samples for assay or analysis or use specialists
Pulp wood, livestock	Identification and quantity estimation problems	Use aerial photographs for existence and comparison purposes and rely on perpetual inventories
	Movement may not be controllable	

Source: Adapted from *Auditing Procedures Study: Audit of Inventory*, AICPA, 1986. Used with permission of the AICPA.

The auditor's primary concern with inventory cutoff tests is to determine that physical counts of items and their cost have been treated systematically. For example, if an item is counted in inventory, any liability associated with the item should also be recorded. Similarly, if an inventory item is counted in inventory, a sale should not be recorded. The purpose of inventory cutoff tests is twofold: (1) a *sales cutoff* determines consistency in recording the credit side of inventory (that is, a debit to accounts receivable and cost of sales and a credit to sales and inventory), and (2) a *purchase cutoff* determines consistency in recording the debit side of the inventory (that is, a debit to inventory and a credit to a payable).

Inventory cutoff misstatements have an important effect upon the financial statements. Purchase cutoff misstatements have special significance because they result in an erroneous book-to-physical-count inventory adjustment, with a resultant misstatement of cost of goods sold, net income, and accounts payable. Likewise, sales cutoff misstatements can result in a misstatement of revenues, net income, and accounts receivable. The auditor should thus be careful to determine that the client has a proper inventory cutoff.

As noted in Chapter 14, to test the sales cutoff, the auditor reviews shipments from the entity for several days before and after the inventory observation date. By documenting the shipping document number, description, quantity, and date from the shipping department records, the auditor can subsequently trace this information and determine that the sale has been properly accounted for. Figure 17–3 is an example of a sales cutoff schedule.

Figure 17–3 **Sales Cutoff Schedule**

Plainsman Co.
Sales Cutoff
12-31-x4

S-2

	Initials	Date
Prepared By	LG	1/21/x5
Approved By	WA	2/8/x5

		Description	Shipping Number	Quantity	Date Shipped	Date Included in Sales
1		Baseballs	B-31	125	12-30-X4	12-30-X4 √
2		Golf Balls - Grade A	B-32	70	12-31-X4	12-31-X4 √
3		Golf Balls - Grade B	B-33	1235	12-31-X4	12-31-X4 √
4		Basketballs	B-34	175	12-30-X4	1-2-X5 √
5		Golf Balls - Grade B	B-35	980	12-30-X4	12-30-X4 √
6		Basketballs	B-36	25	12-30-X4	12-31-X4 √
7		Baseballs	B-37	200	12-31-X4	12-31-X4 √
8		Footballs	B-38	35	1-2-X5	1-2-X5 √
9		Frisbees	B-39	21	1-2-X5	1-3-X5 √
10						
11						
12	√	Per sales journal				
13						
14						
15						

Figure 17-4   **Purchase Cutoff Schedule**

Plainsman Co.
Purchases Cutoff   P-2
12/31/x4

	Initials	Date
Prepared By	LG	2/1/x5
Approved By	WA	2/14/x5

	Description - Part #	Receiving Report #		Date Received		Date included in Purchases		
1	# A 1257	855		12-30-x4		12-30-x4 √		
2	# A 2379	856		12-30-x4		12-31-x4 √		
3	# C 25937	857		12-31-x4		12-31-x4 √		
4	# C 201	858		12-31-x4		1-1-x5 √		ɴ
5	# C 500	859		12-31-x4		1-1-x5 √		ɴ
6	# D 862	860		12-31-x4		12-31-x4 √		
7	# D 862	861		1-1-x5		1-1-x5 √		ɴ
8	# A 1257	862		1-1-x5		1-1-x5 √		ɴ
9								
10								
11								
12								
13	√ Per purchases journal							
14								
15	ɴ Cutoff error by client. Net effect was to increase purchases by $302.75							
16	See adjusting journal entry #2, working paper E-7.							
17								
18								
19								
20								

For the purchase cutoff, the auditor reviews the receiving reports for several days before and after the inventory observation date and lists document numbers, quantities, dates, and descriptions of the items. In performing a purchase cutoff test, the auditor may trace the receiving reports to the accounts payable listing and vendors' invoices to determine that accounts payable have also been recorded properly. For both the purchase and sales cutoff tests, the auditor typically gathers the needed information (receiving report and shipping document numbers) during the inventory observation. If this information is not obtained at or near the inventory observation date, the auditor may have difficulty in verifying the information at a later date. Figure 17–4 is an example of a purchase cutoff schedule.

The period of time and number and size of transactions included in both sales and purchases cutoff tests is influenced by the assessed levels of control risk for the existence/occurrence and completeness assertions for both types of transactions. For example, when control risk is low, the auditor may shorten the cutoff period and reduce the number and size of transactions tested.

Goods in transit present a special situation in performing inventory cutoff tests. Legal title to goods, which is determined by the shipping terms, is often used to set accounting policy regarding goods in transit. Thus, incoming goods (purchases) shipped *F.O.B.* (free on board) ***shipping point*** would be included in inventory once they are shipped. Alternatively, goods shipped to the client ***F.O.B. destination*** would not be included in inventory until the goods arrive. Outgoing goods (sales) that are in transit and that have been shipped F.O.B. destination would be counted in inventory because the client still holds the legal title. If the goods are in transit and have been shipped F.O.B. shipping point, title has passed and the goods would not be included in inventory. In practice, many entities ignore the F.O.B. legality and use shipping and receiving dates to decide when to record sales and purchases, respectively.

Confirming Inventories in Public Warehouses

Clients sometimes store inventories in ***public warehouses***, that is, warehouses operated by third parties who lease space to different entities to store their inventories. If the client uses a public warehouse, the auditor should obtain evidence that these inventories exist. The auditor frequently gathers this evidence by sending a confirmation request to the custodian of the warehouse. However, if the inventory in the public warehouse represents a significant portion of the inventory, the auditor should consider obtaining additional evidence beyond the confirmation. The gathering of additional evidence may include physical observation of the inventory, confirmations with lenders when the inventory has been pledged as collateral, and an evaluation of the control procedures at the warehouse (for example, a request for a report on controls from the warehouse's auditor). *SAS No. 1, Public Warehouses—Controls and Auditing Procedures for Goods Held* (AU 901), provides guidance to the independent auditor with respect to a client who uses a public warehouse.

Price Tests

The observation of inventory focuses on the quantity of inventory. However, it is not inventory quantity but a dollar amount of inventory that is reported in the financial statements. This dollar amount is calculated by multiplying quantities of inventory times their prices and then summing those computations. Although the auditor's inventory observation may support the quantity of inventory, the auditor must also test the prices and related computations to address the valuation assertion.

Accounting Method
To test the prices that a client uses in compiling inventory, the auditor must first determine the accounting method the client uses (for example, LIFO or FIFO). The auditor should also determine that the pricing method used is consistent with the method used in prior years, because a change in pricing method represents a change in accounting principle.

The price test the auditor uses will largely depend upon the client's policies, procedures, and inventory pricing system. For example, if the client uses LIFO, the auditor must be concerned not only with prices but also with LIFO layers, LIFO liquidations, and compliance with tax regulations. Likewise, if the client is a manufacturer, the auditor must know whether the client uses job-order costing or process costing.

Support of Prices
For goods purchased, inventory pricing is generally not complex. The auditor may test these items by vouching costs to vendor invoices. For example, for a client that

uses FIFO inventory, the auditor will trace the quantities back to the latest invoice purchases made during the year. The extent of vouching depends on the assessed level of control risk for the valuation assertion for purchases.

Price tests become more complex for a client that manufactures inventory, because the auditor not only must verify materials cost by examining invoices but also must gather sufficient evidence that direct labor charges are appropriate, and that factory overhead has been correctly applied. The auditor should also review the cost accounting system to determine that the system is appropriate and has been consistently applied. Generally, tests of materials and labor are fairly routine; however, overhead costs can sometimes be quite complex. Of course, if labor and overhead are not significant, they may not be tested. The examination of the cost accounting system would include an analysis of all variances and their accounting treatment. It is sometimes more efficient to test elements of the cost system by analytical procedures than by detailed testing.

Support of Compilation

Once the auditor has performed price tests for individual items of inventory and has observed the physical counts, he or she is ready to determine that the compilation for overall inventory is correct. At this point the auditor is satisfied that inventory quantities and prices are correct but still must gather evidence that the multiplications of prices times quantities and the summations of those multiplications are correct. Conceivably, inventory quantities and prices could be correct and the multiplications could be correct but the additions for the final inventory figure could be incorrect. Thus, the auditor must be satisfied not only as to quantities and prices but also as to the extensions (multiplications) and the footings (additions) of inventory. Generally, the auditor tests that the client has properly computed the extension of price times quantity by recomputing certain extensions selected for testing. The auditor should also foot the inventory listing to determine that the total of inventory (the only inventory item that appears in the financial statements) is correct.

The auditor often scans the entire inventory listing for unusual items. For example, in scanning the inventory the auditor may observe that one particular item is listed on page after page or that enormous quantities of a particular item exist, raising the question as to whether the item is slow moving and should be written down to net realizable value. The computations involved in checking multiplication and footings may be made by using generalized audit software if the client has maintained inventory records on the computer.

Analytical Procedures

As noted in Chapter 11, auditors frequently perform analytical procedures to gather evidence for many audit areas, including inventory. As with analytical procedures in other areas, these procedures for inventory represent substantive audit evidence. Common analytical procedures for inventory include comparisons of

- gross profit.
- inventory (including raw materials) turnover.
- age of inventory.
- inventory amounts with budgets and prior years.
- shrinkage ratio (the ratio of inventory written down to total inventory).

These procedures are often computed by product line or location.

The computation of the gross profit percentage is one of the most common audit tests performed. For most companies, gross profit percentages remain fairly constant from one year to the next. Because the gross profit relationship is often predictable, the auditor frequently uses the gross profit test to gather evidence that inventories are fairly stated.

Other Tests

An auditor may perform numerous audit tests on inventory other than the ones discussed here. The selection of specific tests depends upon the client's inventory characteristics, the risks posed by the client, and the auditor's cost–benefit analysis. For example, if the client maintains goods on consignment, the auditor may need to determine whether the client is the consignee or the consignor, make inquiries of management, examine consignment agreements, and confirm goods held by selected customers on account.

Another example involves audit clients who have purchase commitments. If the client has committed to make purchases, the auditor should make appropriate inquiries and determine that the proper accounting treatment and disclosures are made in conformity with generally accepted accounting principles. For example, a loss on a noncancellable purchase commitment should be recorded in the financial statements.

In addition, special problems arise regarding beginning inventory when an auditor is engaged to perform an audit for the first time. Beginning inventory is an integral component of the income statement and is ordinarily supported by a continuing auditor by observing the ending inventory of the prior year. However, an auditor who is performing an audit for the first time is typically engaged after the beginning inventory date (last-year's ending inventory) and thus cannot support beginning inventory by observation. In this case, *SAS No. 1* (AU 331.13) permits the auditor to test beginning inventory by other procedures. For example, the auditor may become satisfied as to the beginning inventory by tests of prior transactions, reviews of the records of prior counts, and the application of gross profit tests—provided that the auditor is satisfied with ending inventory. In addition, if the client has been audited by other auditors for the prior year, the auditor may become satisfied as to the beginning inventory by reviewing the predecessor auditor's report and/or working papers.

Most of the common audit tests discussed here relate primarily to the audit objectives of existence, valuation, and presentation and disclosure. The auditor should also gather evidence on rights and obligations and completeness. Generally this evidence is obtained when the auditor is supporting cash disbursements and determining that purchases and subsequent payments have been properly recorded. Gross profit percentage and analytical procedures provide additional evidence as to rights and obligations and completeness.

Management Fraud Related to Inventory

During the past several years, inventory frauds have resulted in material misstatements in financial statements. The manner in which an entity's management has allegedly circumvented auditors with these frauds varies. However, inventory is a common and effective area for financial statement manipulation. In planning and performing inventory procedures, auditors should be aware of the types of manipulations used.

A frequent manipulative practice is to record nonexistent items as inventory. This practice is easier to achieve if client employees know which inventory items or locations the auditor plans to test count. In some cases, goods shipped between two sites within a company have been recorded as inventory at both locations, scrap materials have been substituted for genuine inventory, and entity personnel have created fictitious inventory count sheets to overstate inventory. In other cases, goods that have been sold, and recorded as sales, have been included in inventory.

These examples emphasize the need for the auditor to plan and control the inventory audit carefully and to use analytical procedures to supplement the transactions tests performed.

Payroll

The nature, timing, and extent of payroll substantive tests depends on (1) the materiality of labor costs to the entity's financial statements and (2) the effectiveness of internal control structure policies and procedures for payroll transactions. In an entity in which labor cost is material to the financial statements and in which the assessed levels of control risk for payroll assertions are relatively high, the auditor may perform extensive substantive tests for payroll. For example, the auditor may (1) recompute the hours worked from employee time cards for an extensive number of employees, (2) determine the pay rates from personnel records, (3) recompute gross and net pay, and (4) trace labor costs to job cost sheets or production run cost records to determine that these labor costs are recorded as inventory costs (presentation and disclosure) and that they are properly calculated (valuation or allocation). The auditor may also vouch all material labor costs charged to maintenance or capitalized in fixed asset accounts. In addition, the auditor will probably recompute the accrued payroll liability.

When payroll is not a significant inventory cost or when the assessed levels of control risk for payroll assertions are relatively low, auditors often limit substantive payroll tests to analytical procedures. For example, the auditor may (1) compare direct labor costs as a percentage of sales or production volume with prior years or compare direct labor costs with the number of production employees for prior years, (2) compare payroll costs with budgets, or (3) compare labor variances with incurred payroll expenses. To test the reasonableness of the accrued payroll liability, auditors often approximate the portion of the payroll for the first pay period subsequent to year-end that pertains to the audit period. For example, if payroll is paid every ten working days and the first pay period subsequent to year-end includes three working days for the audit period, then approximately 30% of the payroll should represent the accrued liability.

Significant Terms

Cycle inventory counting A method of inventory counting in which different portions of inventory are counted periodically throughout the year.

F.O.B. destination Sales terms that provide that the legal title of goods transfers when the goods reach their destination.

F.O.B. shipping point Sales terms that provide that the legal title of goods transfers at the goods' origin (shipping point).

Inventory cutoff An audit procedure designed to gather evidence that the client has included in inventory all goods owned (completeness) and only those goods (existence and rights and obligations).

McKesson & Robbins case A 1930s fraud case that had a major effect on the auditing profession. The case resulted in the requirements that auditors observe inventory and confirm receivables.

Price tests Vouching of prices used in compiling inventory to support proper inventory valuation.

Public warehouses Warehouses operated by third parties in which different entities store their inventories.

Test counts Counts of inventory items on a test basis made by the auditor after the client has taken a physical inventory to determine whether the client has correctly counted the items.

Discussion Questions

17-1. Why is the inventory account significant for most entities?

17-2. Identify the issues of the McKesson & Robbins case and the audit procedures that are required as a result.

17-3. Discuss the requirements of auditing procedures for inventories as identified in *SAS No. 1, Receivables and Inventories* (AU 331).

17-4. The review of inventory instructions is important to the auditor. What types of information should the auditor gather in this review?

17-5. Briefly describe the test count procedure.

17-6. What is the importance of inventory tags that are prenumbered and properly accounted for?

17-7. Give an example of an inventory situation in which the auditor would use a specialist.

17-8. Discuss how an auditor would typically gather evidence to support inventory pricing. Why is this important?

Objective Questions

*17-9. Purchase cutoff procedures should be designed to test whether merchandise is included in the inventory of the client company, if the company
   (1) has paid for the merchandise.
   (2) has physical possession of the merchandise.
   (3) holds legal title to the merchandise.
   (4) holds the shipping documents for the merchandise issued in the company's name.

*17-10. An auditor has accounted for a sequence of inventory tags and is now going to trace information on a representative number of tags to the physical inventory sheets. The purpose of this procedure is to obtain assurance that
   (1) the final inventory is valued at cost.
   (2) all inventory represented by an inventory tag is listed on the inventory sheets.
   (3) all inventory represented by an inventory tag is bona fide.
   (4) inventory sheets do not include untagged inventory items.

---

*AICPA adapted.

*17-11. The physical count of inventory of a retailer was higher than shown by the perpetual records. Which of the following could explain the difference?
    (1) Inventory items had been counted but the tags placed on the items had not been taken off the items and added to the inventory accumulation sheets.
    (2) Credit memos for several items returned by customers had not been recorded.
    (3) No journal entry had been made on the retailer's books for several items returned to its suppliers.
    (4) An item purchased F.O.B. shipping point had not arrived at the date of the inventory count and had not been reflected in the perpetual records.

*17-12. Purchase cutoff procedures should be designed to test whether or not all inventory
    (1) purchased and received before year-end was recorded.
    (2) on the year-end balance sheet was carried at lower of cost or market.
    (3) on the year-end balance sheet was paid for by the company.
    (4) owned by the company is in the possession of the company.

*17-13. From which of the following evidence-gathering audit procedures would an auditor obtain most assurance concerning the existence of inventories?
    (1) Observation of physical inventory counts.
    (2) Written inventory representations from management.
    (3) Confirmation of inventories in a public warehouse.
    (4) Auditor's recomputation of inventory extensions.

*17-14. A CPA is engaged in the annual audit of a client for the year ended December 31, 19X4. The client took a complete physical inventory under the CPA's observation on December 15 and adjusted its inventory control account and detailed perpetual inventory records to agree with the physical inventory. The client considers a sale to be made in the period that goods are shipped. Listed below are four items taken from the CPA's sales cutoff worksheet. Which item does *not* require an adjusting entry on the client's books?

	Date (Month/Day)	
Shipped	Recorded as a Sale	Credited to Inventory Control
1. 12/10	12/19	12/12
2. 12/14	12/16	12/16
3. 12/31	1/2	12/31
4. 1/2	12/31	12/31

*17-15. The audit of year-end physical inventories should include steps to verify that the client's purchases and sales cutoffs were adequate. The audit steps should be designed to detect whether merchandise included in the physical count at year-end was not recorded as a
    (1) sale in the subsequent period.
    (2) purchase in the current period.
    (3) sale in the current period.
    (4) purchase return in the subsequent period.

---

*AICPA adapted.

*17-16. An auditor will usually trace the details of the test counts made during the observation of the physical inventory-taking to a final inventory schedule. This audit procedure is undertaken to provide evidence that items physically present and observed by the auditor at the time of the physical inventory count are
(1) owned by the client.
(2) not obsolete.
(3) physically present at the time of the preparation of the final inventory schedule.
(4) included in the final inventory schedule.

*17-17. After accounting for a sequence of inventory tags, an auditor traces a sample of the tags to the physical inventory listing to obtain evidence that all items
(1) included in the listing have been counted.
(2) represented by inventory tags are included in the listing.
(3) included in the listing are represented by inventory tags.
(4) represented by inventory tags are bona fide.

*17-18. In a manufacturing company, which one of the following audit procedures would give the *least* assurance about the valuation of inventory at the audit date?
(1) Testing the computation of standard overhead rates.
(2) Examining paid vendors' invoices.
(3) Reviewing direct labor rates.
(4) Obtaining confirmation of inventories pledged under loan agreements.

*17-19. Which of the following is *not* one of the independent auditor's objectives when auditing inventories?
(1) Verifying that inventory counted is owned by the client.
(2) Verifying that the client has used proper inventory pricing.
(3) Ascertaining the physical quantities of inventory on hand.
(4) Verifying that all inventory owned by the client is on hand at the time of the count.

Problems and Cases

*17-20. (Inventory Observation) Often, an important aspect of a CPA's audit of financial statements is the observation of the taking of the physical inventory.
REQUIRED
A. What are the general objectives or purposes of the CPA's observation of the taking of the physical inventory? (Do not discuss the procedures or techniques involved in making the observation.)
B. For what purposes does the CPA make and record test counts of inventory quantities during the observation of the taking of the physical inventory? Discuss.
C. A number of companies employ outside service companies that specialize in counting, pricing, extending, and footing inventories. These service companies usually furnish a certificate attesting to the value of the inventory.
   Assume that the service company took the inventory on the balance sheet date.
(1) How much reliance, if any, can the CPA place on the inventory certificate of outside specialists? Discuss.
(2) What effect, if any, would the inventory certificate of outside specialists have upon the type of report the CPA would render? Discuss.
(3) What reference, if any, would the CPA make to the certificate of outside specialists in the audit report?

---

*AICPA adapted.

*17-21.   (Inventory Count Instructions) In connection with his audit of the financial statements of Knutson Products Co., an assembler of home appliances, for the year ended May 31, 19X4, Ray Abel, CPA, is reviewing with Knutson's controller the plans for a physical inventory at the company warehouse on May 31. (Note: In answering the two parts of this question, do not discuss procedures for the physical inventory of work in process, inventory pricing, or other audit steps not directly related to the physical inventory taking.)

  1. Finished appliances, unassembled parts, and supplies are stored in the warehouse, which is attached to Knutson's assembly plant. The plant will operate during the count. On May 31, 19X4, the warehouse will deliver to the plant the estimated quantities of unassembled parts and supplies required for May 31 production, but there may be emergency requisitions on May 31. During the count, the warehouse will continue to receive parts and supplies and to ship finished appliances. However, appliances completed on May 31 will be held in the plant until after the physical inventory.

  2. Warehouse employees will join with accounting department employees in counting the inventory. The inventory takers will use a tag system.

  REQUIRED

  A. What procedures should the company establish to ensure that the inventory count includes all items that should be included and that nothing is counted twice?

  B. What instruction should the company give to the inventory takers?

*17-22.   (Inventory Problems) A processor of frozen foods carries an inventory of finished products consisting of 50 different types of items valued at approximately $2 million. About $750,000 of this value represents stock produced by the company and billed to customers prior to the audit date. This stock is being held for the customers at a monthly rental charge until they request shipment and is separated from the company's inventory. The company maintains separate perpetual ledgers at the plant office for both stock owned and stock being held for customers. The cost department also maintains a perpetual record of stock owned. The perpetual records reflect quantities only. The company does not take a complete physical inventory at any time during the year because the temperature in the cold storage facilities is too low to allow one to spend more than 15 minutes inside at a time. It is not considered practical to move items outside or to defreeze the cold storage facilities for the purpose of taking a physical inventory. Due to these circumstances, it is impractical to test count quantities to the extent of completely verifying specific items. The company considers as its inventory valuation at year-end the aggregate of the quantities reflected by the perpetual record of stock owned, maintained at the plant office, and priced at the lower of cost or market.

  REQUIRED

  A. What are the two principal problems facing the auditor in the audit of the inventory? Discuss briefly.

  B. Outline the audit steps that would enable you to render an unqualified opinion with respect to the inventory. (You may omit consideration of a verification on unit prices and clerical accuracy.)

17-23.   (Audit Procedures for Inventory) Curt Lettow, CPA, is reviewing the working papers of the predecessor auditor. He notes that in the audit of inventory, the following items were found:

  1. Client personnel incorrectly counted inventory.

  2. Goods out on consignment were not included in the inventory balance.

_____

*AICPA adapted.

3. Several items actually in physical inventory were not tagged.
4. The client had entered a purchase agreement and sustained a material loss. The predecessor auditor didn't recognize it.
5. Several boxes of widgets had been in inventory for the past ten years.
6. Inventory included items received on consignment from a vendor.
7. The client had misrepresented the existence of inventories held in a public warehouse.
8. Barrels of nails were half filled with sand. These were included in inventory.
9. Inventory was costed at lower of cost or market on an individual basis rather than at the aggregate lower of cost or market.
10. Inventory amounts were extended incorrectly in the inventory summary.
11. The inventory printout included some items that were listed twice.

REQUIRED
A. For each item listed, identify an audit procedure that should enable the auditor to detect the error.
B. For each procedure, identify the assertion addressed.

	Inventory	Accounts Payable	Cost of Goods Sold	Accounts Receivable	Sales
1. Merchandise costing $1,000 was mistakenly not counted on November 30.					
2. Merchandise costing $2,000 was mistakenly counted twice on November 30.					
3. An invoice for a November purchase of $3,000 was recorded in November.					
4. An invoice for a November purchase of $4,000 was recorded in December.					
5. An invoice for a November purchase of $5,000 was recorded in January.					

	Inventory	Accounts Payable	Cost of Goods Sold	Accounts Receivable	Sales
6. An invoice for a December purchase of $6,000 was recorded in January.					
7. Merchandise costing $7,000 was mistakenly not counted on November 30. The related invoice was recorded in December.					
8. Merchandise costing $8,000 was mistakenly not counted on November 30. The related invoice was recorded in January.					
9. Merchandise costing $9,000 was mistakenly counted twice on November 30. The related invoice was recorded twice — once in November and once in December.					
10. Inventory shipped 12/30/X4 was recorded as a January 19X5 sale for $10,000.					
11. Inventory shipped 11/28/X4 was recorded as a December 19X4 sale for $11,000.					

17-24. (Early Inventory Count) Tampa Industries took its physical inventory at May 31, 19X4, and compiled it to carry forward to its year-end, June 30, 19X4. All goods on hand were counted by the client.

The compiled inventory amounted to $639,000, but Tampa's records showed a balance of $713,000. At that date, the accountant credited the inventory account to adjust for the amount of the difference.

Jeff Henley, CPA, is performing the 19X4 audit of Tampa and has obtained the following information:

Receipts	Amount	Date Received	Invoice Date	Date Recorded
2975 Cases Canine Chow (KC)	$28,000	6/1	5/31	6/12
800 Cases Puppy Treats (PT)	17,000	5/31	5/23	6/5
75 Cases Dog Collars (DC)	6,000	6/1	5/28	5/31
120 Cases Flea Spray (FS)	7,500	5/23	5/16	5/25
50 Cases Dog Brushes (DB)	2,000	5/31	5/30	5/31
95 Cases Kennel Toys (KT)	3,000	5/27	5/20	6/1

The following information pertains to the inventory account from May 31 to June 30.

Balance at May 31 (after adjustment)	$639,000
Purchases—95 Cases Kennel Toys	3,000
100 Cases Doggie Biscuits (DDB)	5,000
800 Cases Puppy Treats	17,000
2975 Cases Canine Chow	28,000
100 Dog Beds (DBD)	5,000

Tampa's inventory account at June 30 had a balance of $697,000.

REQUIRED

A. What procedures should Henley use to test the balance carried forward from May 31?

B. List any adjustments to be made at June 30.

C. What is the actual difference between book and physical inventory at May 31?

D. Why should Henley test the shipping and receiving cutoff at May 31 and June 30?

17-25. (Purchase Cutoff) Linda Bridges, CPA, was engaged to perform the 19X4 audit of Purple Island Manufacturing Co. Mike Alsup, controller, requested that the physical inventory be taken on June 29, one day before the fiscal year-end.

The inventory count team properly counted all items physically in the warehouse. The count included all items represented by receiving reports up to 3972. Inventory represented by receiving report 3973 and succeeding reports was not included.

On June 30, Purple Island received inventory items represented by receiving report numbers 3973 through 3976. Bridges noted that only those items included in the physical count were included in the final inventory balance. She obtained the accounts payable schedule to perform cutoff tests. She was unable to reconcile the following items.

Information Obtained from Vendor's Invoice

Receiving Report Number	Amount of Vendor's Invoice	Date of Invoice	Date of Shipment	Shipping Term
3973	$4,533.72	6-30-X4	6-29-X4	Shipping Point
3974	6,713.97	7-01-X4	6-30-X4	Destination
3975	5,204.60	6-30-X4	6-24-X4	Shipping Point
3976	1,928.46	6-27-X4	6-30-X4	Shipping Point
3977	2,849.61	6-30-X4	6-30-X4	Shipping Point
3978	3,126.98	6-24-X4	6-13-X4	Destination
3979	7,041.71	7-06-X4	6-27-X4	Shipping Point

Invoice numbers 3975, 3976, and 3977 are presently included in accounts payable. The others are excluded.

Purple Island records inventory purchases by debiting purchases and crediting accounts payable.

REQUIRED
A. How are inventory and accounts payable cutoff related?
B. List any existing error in inventory or accounts payable for each receiving report. Prepare an adjusting entry to correct each error.
C. Which error would cause more concern to the auditor? Why?

17-26. (Linking Audit Objectives to Assertions for Inventory) The following list illustrates audit objectives for inventory.

1. Inventory reflected in the accounts represents a complete listing of products, materials, and supplies owned by the company and such assets are physically on hand, in transit, or stored at outside locations at the balance sheet date.
2. Inventory listings are accurately compiled, extended, footed, and summarized, and the totals are properly reflected in the accounts.
3. Inventory is valued in accordance with generally accepted accounting principles consistently applied, at the lower of cost or market.
4. Excess, slow-moving, obsolete, and defective inventory is reduced to net realizable value.
5. Inventory is properly classified in the balance sheet and disclosure is made of pledged or assigned inventory, major categories of inventory, and the methods used to value inventory.

REQUIRED
For each objective, identify the relevant client assertion(s).

*17-27. (Audit of Beginning Inventory) Giles Decker, CPA, is performing an audit of the financial statements of Allright Wholesale Sales, Inc., for the year ended December 31, 19X4. Allright has been in business for many years and has never had its financial statements audited. Decker has gained satisfaction with respect to the ending inventory and is considering alternative audit procedures to gain satisfaction with respect to management's representations concerning the beginning inventory, which was not observed. Allright sells only one product (bottled Brand X beer) and maintains perpetual inventory records. In addition, Allright takes physical inventory counts monthly. Decker has already confirmed purchases with the manufacturer and has decided to concentrate on evaluating the reliability of perpetual inventory records and performing analytical procedures to the extent that prior-year unaudited records will enable such procedures to be performed.

---

*AICPA adapted.

REQUIRED

What audit tests, including analytical procedures, should Decker apply in evaluating the reliability of perpetual inventory records and gaining satisfaction with respect to January 1, 19X4, inventory?

*17-28. (Audit of Payroll) In many companies, labor costs represent a substantial percentage of total dollars expended in each accounting period. One of the auditor's primary means of verifying payroll transactions is by a detailed payroll test.

You are making an annual audit of the Joplin Company, a medium-size manufacturing company. You have selected a number of hourly employees for a detailed payroll test. The following worksheet outline has been prepared.

Column Number	Column Heading
1.	Employee number
2.	Employee name
3.	Job classification
4.	Straight time hours worked
5.	Premium time hours worked
6.	Hourly rate
7.	Gross earnings
8.	FICA withheld
9.	FIT withheld
10.	Union dues withheld
11.	Hospitalization withheld
12.	Amount of check
13.	Check number
14.	Account number charged
15.	Description

REQUIRED

A. What factors should you consider in selecting a sample of employees to be included in a payroll test?

B. Using the column numbers above as a reference, state the principal way(s) that the information in each column would be verified.

C. In addition to the payroll test, the auditor employs a number of other audit procedures in the verification of payroll transactions. List additional procedures that may be employed.

Audit Judgment Case

17-29. Cal-Low Foods, Inc., produces low calorie–low sodium canned vegetables and dairy products. These products are packaged under private-label brands for eight national grocery chains. Cal-Low buys bulk vegetables and milk directly from growers and dairy farmers, processes them, and packages them in containers with individual grocery chain labels. The company currently produces 14 different canned vegetable products and 5 different dairy products: skim milk, American cheese, Swiss cheese, yogurt, and sour cream.

*AICPA adapted.

Monthly production quantities are established according to the contract specifications with the grocery chains. These contracts specify a minimum order quantity each month and allow the chains to increase the minimum order amount for a specific month by up to 30% if Cal-Low is notified by the 15th of the preceding month.

A grocery chain cannot decrease its minimum order amount without renegotiating its contract. In addition, the contracts specify that once the products are packaged with a private label they are considered sold. Cal-Low, however, agrees to store the packaged products for up to three weeks before shipment to help the grocery chains manage their inventory stock costs.

To reduce spoilage, most of the bulk foods are stored in refrigerated warehouses or frozen food lockers. Because Cal-Low produces both a standard grade and premium grade of canned vegetables for three of the grocery chains, it maintains an inventory of two different grades of each bulk vegetable.

Cal-Low's sales increased approximately 35% over last year, its first year of operation, because of heightened consumer concern about diet and health. To meet this demand, Cal-Low modified its bulk food acquisition during mid-year in two ways. First, each individual grocery chain began sending bulk vegetables to Cal-Low for processing. The quantities sent vary from 5 to 15% of the amounts needed to produce the minimum monthly orders. Second, Cal-Low has established buy and hold arrangements with about half of its suppliers. Under these arrangements, the supplier agrees to store bulk foods for Cal-Low for up to two months after Cal-Low has purchased them. In addition, because of the increased demand, Cal-Low cannot stop its shipping and receiving operations during the year-end inventory count.

This is Cal-Low's first audit and its fiscal year ends December 31. Its inventory costs are approximately 60% of all costs. The company purchases its bulk foods from 36 different producers in addition to the bulk food it receives from the grocery chains. Cal-Low maintains about a four-week supply of dairy products, but supplies of vegetables are usually greater, sometimes as much as eight months, because they are seasonal.

REQUIRED

1. For each of the five financial statement assertions for the inventory account, identify the major characteristics of Cal-Low's inventory that would influence your audit plan for inventory. Relate each characteristic to one or more specific assertions.

2. Prepare an inventory audit program that addresses each of the five assertions. That is, describe the audit procedures you would perform on Cal-Low's inventory and identify which assertion or assertions each procedure addresses.

Auditing Issues Case

17-30.   KELCO MANUFACTURING COMPANY

Kelco purchases large quantities of supplies and parts to be used for maintenance on the company's machinery and equipment. Shown below are Kelco's supplies and parts (asset) account for the year 19X7.

		Supplies and Parts			
Date	Reference	Amount	Date	Reference	Amount
Balance forward		$858,125			
12/25	RR#2012	21,002			
12/30	RR#2014	4,561			
12/31	RR#2015	3,429			
12/31	RR#2016	6,195			

You observed the physical inventory of supplies and parts in the company's warehouse on December 31, 19X7. When performing a cutoff test related to supplies and parts, you found that the last receiving report used was #2016. No adjustment has yet been made reconciling the physical count to the general ledger. Additionally, you obtained the following information:

1. Included in the physical inventory at December 31, 19X7, were supplies that had been purchased and received on receiving report #2013 but the company did not receive an invoice until 19X8. Cost of the supplies was $6,234.

2. On the evening of December 31, 19X7, there was a transfer truck parked at Kelco's loading dock containing the supplies recorded on receiving report #2016. The supplies were shipped by the vendor FOB destination. These were included in the physical count.

3. A shipment from a vendor containing supplies with a cost of $26,422 was en route on December 31, 19X7. The vendor had shipped the supplies FOB shipping point. The goods were received on January 3, 19X8, and receiving report #2017 was prepared upon receipt.

4. Included in the physical inventory were parts that had been rendered obsolete due to Kelco's purchase of new and more advanced machinery. The cost of the parts was determined to be $36,500.

REQUIRED

1. Prepare the adjusting entries that are required as of December 31, 19X7.

2. Assume Kelco already adjusted the general ledger account to agree with the physical count by making an adjusting entry to supplies and parts (asset) and supplies expense. The four items above are discovered subsequent to this adjusting entry. What adjusting entries should be made in this case for each of the four items?

Chapter *18*

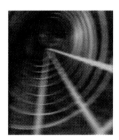

Understanding the Internal Control Structure, Assessing Control Risk, and Performing Substantive Tests: The Financing and Investing Cycle

Learning Objectives

- Explain the major activities in the financing and investing cycle.

- Describe the documents, accounting records, files, and flow of transactions in a typical financing and investing cycle accounting system.

- Explain how control risk is related to audit efficiency in determining substantive tests for accounts in the financing and investing cycle.

- Design and apply substantive audit procedures for the audit of stockholder equity and long-term debt.

- Design and apply substantive audit procedures for the audit of investments.

- Design and apply substantive audit procedures for the audit of property, plant, and equipment.

R obert Citron might have been a trailblazer. As treasurer of Orange County, California, he managed an $8 billion portfolio. The investment income it generated dwarfed the usual county revenue producer, the property tax. Because the state of California faces chronic budget shortfalls and was siphoning off all but $.06 of every Orange County tax dollar, it's a good thing he was able to post such enviable returns. As a result, Orange County is known for topflight schools and clean highways. Additionally, there were plans to revamp police, fire, and emergency systems to the tune of $82 million.

But those upgrades won't be happening—at least not anytime soon. Because of a total oversight, Citron's fund, which had been expected to produce $170 million in 1994, has now lost $2 billion. A supervisory board voted to liquidate the remainder of the investments and acknowledged that the county expects a $3.7 billion budget shortfall. The local bond rating has been slashed from AA to D, leaving two equally unappealing options: selling off depressed real estate or raising taxes.

Citron attempted to utilize innovative techniques to finance high-quality county operations without raising taxes. Instead, in the final analysis, he led the citizens of Orange County down a primrose path. But the failure was not entirely his. If the proper control and oversight systems had been in place, the magnitude of the disaster could have been headed off, or at least lessened considerably.

Source: Nanette Byrnes, "Orange County Is Looking Green Around the Gills," *Business Week*, January 2, 1995, p. 66.

The preceding five chapters discussed the internal control structure and substantive tests for three transaction cycles: the expenditure cycle for the purchase of goods and services, the conversion cycle in which those goods and services are converted into a finished product, and the revenue cycle in which the finished product is sold and cash is received. The fourth and final transaction cycle is the financing and investing cycle. This chapter discusses both the internal control structure and substantive tests for this cycle.

The *financing and investing cycle* encompasses generating capital resources and using these resources to invest in capital assets. Financing and investing cycle transactions can be classified into three major categories: (1) debt and equity transactions, (2) investment transactions, and (3) property, plant, and equipment transactions. Table 18–1 shows the primary activities in each category.

Understanding the Internal Control Structure for the Financing and Investing Cycle

Transactions in the financing and investing cycle are closely related to those in the revenue cycle and the expenditure cycle. The sale of debt and equity securities in-

Table 18-1	Financing and Investing Cycle Activities

Investment Transactions

- Purchasing and selling investment securities
- Receiving interest and dividends

Property, Plant, and Equipment Transactions

- Acquiring property, plant, and equipment
- Depreciating property, plant, and equipment
- Retiring property, plant, and equipment

Debt and Equity Transactions

- Issuing debt and equity instruments
- Paying interest and dividends
- Retiring debt instruments
- Acquiring, reissuing, and retiring equity instruments

volves the receipt of cash. Consequently, many of the internal control structure policies and procedures in the revenue cycle, discussed in Chapter 13, are relevant to these transactions. Investing in securities and purchasing property, plant, and equipment involve the payment of cash. Therefore, several of the internal control structure policies and procedures in the expenditure cycle, discussed in Chapter 15, are pertinent to these transactions. Because of these cycle relationships, this chapter discusses only additional elements of the control environment, accounting system, and control procedures related to financing and investing cycle transactions.

Control Environment, Risk Assessment, Communication, and Monitoring

As with the other transaction cycles, the control environment, risk assessment, communication, and monitoring components are broadly related to the financing and investing cycle. Some specific policies and procedures within these components, though, are more directly related to this cycle. For example, management's business planning and capital budgeting policies and procedures are relevant to acquiring capital; investing in capital assets; and purchasing property, plant, and equipment. In addition, management's identification and analysis of risks associated with new technology, rapid growth, new product lines, and corporate restructurings all may affect financing and investment cycle assertions.

Accounting System

The accounting records and procedures for financing and investing transactions are usually uncomplicated. As explained previously, part of the accounting system for these transactions is included in the revenue and expenditure cycle accounting systems. However, entities often establish additional accounting documents, records, procedures, and files specifically for these transactions. The following discussion briefly explains these special accounting system elements for each major transaction category in the financing and investing cycle.

Investment Transactions

Purchases and sales of investments typically require the board of directors' authorization. A record of the board authorization is made in the minutes. In some cases, the board may delegate authority for some or all investment activities to an entity officer such as the vice-president of finance or the treasurer. Entities often use written authorization forms to record the officer's approval. When investments are bought or sold, a *broker's advice* form is typically used. This form, prepared by the brokerage firm, specifies the details of the transaction and provides the basis for recording the cash payment or cash receipt. A broker's advice or cash remittance form also usually accompanies the receipt of interest or dividends. The payment and receipt of cash for investment transactions generally are processed as part of the expenditure cycle and revenue cycle, respectively.

The *security certificates* may be held by the entity or by an outside custodian. If the investment portfolio is large enough, the entity may maintain an *investment subsidiary ledger* on computer files or on hard copy. Table 18–2 shows the common accounts, documents, and files in an investment transaction accounting system.

Property, Plant, and Equipment Transactions

The acquisition of **property, plant, and equipment** is subject to many of the internal control structure policies and procedures for purchases discussed in Chapter 15. Similarly, a number of the internal control structure policies and procedures for sales, discussed in Chapter 13, apply to the disposition of these assets. Property, plant, and equipment transactions, however, often involve substantial amounts and

Table 18-2	Key Accounts, Documents, and Files for Investment Transactions*

Accounts

- Marketable Securities
- Investments in Stock
- Investments in Bonds
- Interest Revenue
- Dividend Revenue
- Gains (Losses) on Sales of Securities

Documents

Bond Certificate   An engraved document showing the number of bonds the investor owns.

Broker's Advice   A statement prepared by the securities broker setting forth the details of an investment transaction in bonds or stocks.

Stock Certificate   An engraved document showing the number of shares of stock the investor owns.

Journals and Ledgers

Investments Subsidiary Ledger A listing of investments and securities owned.

*The documents, journals and ledgers, and files may be prepared and maintained either manually or by computer.

affect operations for many years. Consequently, many entities frequently use additional accounting documents and procedures for these transactions.

Special requisition forms are often used to evaluate and justify the purchase of property, plant, and equipment. In many entities, these forms are part of the capital budgeting policies and procedures and may require several authorizations at top management levels. Once an acquisition is authorized, a purchase order or contract is prepared to acquire the asset.

The receiving procedures for property, plant, and equipment may also differ from those for other purchases. In some cases, special inspection procedures are necessary to ensure that the asset received meets the purchase order specifications or contract terms. For example, an engineer or architect may inspect a machine or building before it is accepted.

Entities ordinarily process cash payments for property, plant, and equipment through the expenditure cycle accounting system like other purchases. Vendor invoices, along with copies of the requisition form, purchase order, and receiving documents, are used to prepare a voucher. The voucher is approved and forwarded to the accounting department for payment and recording in the accounting records.

It is usually necessary, and always preferable, to establish subsidiary ledgers for property, plant, and equipment. These ledgers are generally established for land, buildings, leasehold improvements, equipment, and furniture and fixtures. They contain detailed information about each asset, including its description, identification number, acquisition date, location, cost, and depreciation method and amounts.

Dispositions of property, plant, and equipment frequently require the preparation of an *asset retirement order*, a form used to authorize and document the disposal of these assets. The form provides the basis for recording cash received from asset sales and for removing the asset from the accounting records.

Both large and small entities often use computerized fixed asset accounting systems. The computer updates subsidiary ledgers for acquisitions and disposals, and it automatically calculates and records such items as depreciation, investment credit, and property taxes. In addition, a number of control procedures are often integrated in the computer programs to check account codings and reconcile subsidiary and general ledgers.

Debt and Equity Transactions

Table 18–3 identifies the key accounts, documents, and files commonly used for debt and equity transactions. When an entity issues debt or equity securities, the issue must be authorized by the board of directors. This authorization is recorded in the board meeting minutes, and a formal contract specifies the terms of each issue. Bond or stock certificates are issued for cash, and a broker's advice or other cash remittance form is generally used to record the proceeds of the issue.

A variety of approaches are used to handle the issuance of debt and equity securities. In many entities, a bank or trust company may act as a registrar and transfer agent. The registrar helps ensure that bonds and stock are issued in accordance with statutory requirements and the authorization of the board of directors, and the transfer agent maintains detailed records of individual ownership of stock or bonds and of transfers among stock and bond owners. When a financial institution is not used for these services, the entity's internal legal counsel and secretary perform them. In these circumstances, the entity maintains stock and bond certificate books and stockholder and bondholder subsidiary ledgers in hard copy or on computer files.

Table 18–3 **Key Accounts, Documents, and Files for Debt and Equity Transactions***

Accounts

- Common Stock
- Preferred Stock
- Bonds Payable
- Paid-in-Capital
- Treasury Stock
- Premium (Discount) on Bonds Payable
- Dividends
- Dividends Payable
- Interest Expense

Documents

Bond Certificate   An engraved document showing the number of bonds a bondholder owns.

Bond Indenture (debt agreement)   A contract stating the terms of a bond issue between the issuing entity and the bondholder.

Broker's Advice   A statement prepared by the securities broker setting forth the details of a transaction involving sales of debt or equity securities.

Securities Contract   A formal written contract stipulating the terms of the issuance of securities.

Stock Certificate   An engraved document showing the number of shares of stock a corporate shareholder owns.

Journals and Ledgers

Stock Certificate Book   A record of all stock certificates that have been issued. It includes stubs indicating the number of shares issued and outstanding.

Shareholders' Ledger   A listing of shareholders and shares owned.

---

*The documents, journals and ledgers, and files may be prepared and maintained either manually or by computer.

Entities usually process interest and dividend payments through the expenditure cycle accounting system, although some may use special checks for these payments. In some cases, an entity may use an outside agent, such as a bank, to make these payments and to maintain interest and dividend records.

Control Activities

Although many of the control activities in both the revenue and expenditure cycles pertain to financing and investing cycle transactions, entities usually establish additional control activities that apply specifically to these transactions. Some of the most common control activities are discussed in the following sections.

Performance Reviews

The primary performance reviews for the financing and investing cycle concern the capital budgeting process. Management compares actual acquisitions of capital assets with the budget and follows up on any significant variances. In addition, management monitors the entity's investment plan, determining the overall outlay for investments and their redemption. Management may compare investment revenue of prior years with those of the current period, factoring in changes in investment strategy, to monitor the reasonableness of investment revenue. Managers may also review periodic reports from unit managers involved in capital asset acquisition and disposition and in investment purchases and sales.

Information Processing

A variety of control activities may be performed to check the authorization, accuracy, and completeness of conversion cycle transactions.

Authorization is one of the more significant control procedures for financing and investing transactions. Issuing debt or equity securities; purchasing or selling investments; and acquiring or disposing of property, plant, and equipment usually involve large amounts and significantly affect future periods. In addition, many securities are readily negotiable. As a result, entities generally require that these transactions be authorized at high management levels, such as by the board of directors or senior officers.

The various forms used to authorize and record financing and investing transactions should be designed to contain all of the information necessary to record properly a specific transaction. In addition, these forms are usually prenumbered and their numerical sequence is accounted for. For example, both investment authorization forms and property, plant, and equipment requisition forms should be prenumbered and should specify the data necessary to evaluate and record the transactions properly. In addition, stock and bond certificates should be serially numbered and recorded by number in a register.

A number of independent internal checks are applicable to financing and investing transactions. Supporting documents can be reviewed for proper authorization, consistent data, and proper account coding. Subsidiary ledgers can be periodically reconciled to a physical count or inspection of assets on hand. Independent personnel can account for the numerical sequence of unissued, issued, and canceled certificates.

Physical Controls

Unissued debt and equity security certificates and bond and stock certificates held as investments should be locked in a safe or safe deposit box or secured with an outside custodian. Property, plant, and equipment should bear identification tags and should be protected from unauthorized removal by secured facilities and clearly specified removal procedures. The subsidiary ledgers pertaining to these transaction classes should also be stored in secure areas.

Proper Segregation of Duties

Segregation of duties for financing and investing transactions is accomplished by assigning different departments or personnel the responsibility for authorizing these transactions, recording them, and maintaining custody of the related assets. Once authorized, general accounting department personnel usually enter these transactions in a journal and post them to the general ledger. Different personnel within that department should maintain the subsidiary ledgers. Responsibility for the custody of securities and property, plant, and equipment is normally assigned to independent entity personnel or to an outside custodian.

Assessing Control Risk for the Financing and Investing Cycle

For many entities, financing and investing transactions occur infrequently and involve large amounts. In such circumstances, it is usually inefficient to perform tests of controls. Instead, auditors often assess control risk at or near the maximum level and apply substantive tests to each transaction and related balance to obtain most of the evidence about the relevant assertions.

In some entities, however, the volume of some financing and investing transactions may be high. For example, a utility may frequently acquire and dispose of various types of equipment each year. A bank or insurance company may have many purchases and sales of investments during a year. In such entities, the auditor may direct tests of controls toward the specific, additional internal control structure policies and procedures (discussed previously) that pertain to these transactions. These tests of controls, together with the tests of controls for the revenue and expenditure cycle, may result in a relatively low assessed level of control risk for certain financing and investing cycle assertions.

The next section of this chapter discusses the key substantive tests for each of the three major categories of financing and investing cycle transactions. That section also explains how the assessed level of control risk might affect the application of those substantive tests.

Substantive Tests of Balances and Transactions: The Financing and Investing Cycle

Financing and investing cycle transactions affect several account balances. For most entities, the more significant of these accounts are usually investments; intangible assets; property, plant, and equipment; long-term debt; and stockholder equity.

Investments may be either long-term and classified as investments or short-term and classified as marketable securities. Management's intent distinguishes between long-term investments and marketable securities. If management intends to hold the securities for less than a year or the normal operating cycle, the securities are classified as current assets. Otherwise, the securities are classified as long-term investments.

Intangible assets are those assets that are used in operations but do not have physical substance. They include copyrights, patents, goodwill, and franchises.

Investments

For most entities, investments do not represent large dollar amounts and do not have a high degree of audit risk; thus the audit time spent on investments is usually limited. However, investments can be a very material asset for insurance companies, banks, and other financial institutions. In addition, investments in the form of securities are sometimes vulnerable to defalcation or theft. Although the auditor is concerned with all five audit assertions as described in Chapter 4, the existence and occurrence and the valuation assertions are probably the most important from the audit risk perspective.

The primary audit tests for investments are shown in Table 18–4. These include security counts, security confirmations, testing of valuation, and performance of analytical procedures.

| Table 18-4 | **Common Substantive Audit Tests for Investments** |

Common Audit Tests	Technique	Type of Test	Assertions
Perform security counts	Physical examination	Test of balances	Existence Rights and obligations
Confirm securities	Confirmation	Test of balances	Existence Rights and obligations
Test valuation	Vouching Confirmation	Test of balances	Valuation
Perform analytical procedures	Analytical	Analytical procedures	All

Security Counts

To determine that investments exist, auditors typically will physically inspect the securities. Generally, security counts should be made as of the balance sheet date because securities may be negotiable, and evidence that they exist on another date does not necessarily provide evidence that they also existed as of the balance sheet date. Of course, if control risk is low, the auditor may vary the timing of this audit test to a date other than the balance sheet date.

Security counts are often performed simultaneously with the count of cash and other negotiable instruments. In this case, the auditor gathers evidence as to all types of assets that are negotiable and liquid; in addition, the client cannot switch assets among these various accounts when the auditor is counting them. If counts cannot be made on the same day, frequently the auditor will place a seal over the boxes containing the securities so that the securities cannot be removed without the auditor's knowledge. This precaution also prevents the entity from transferring assets from one account to another.

Because of these considerations, the auditor should carefully perform a security count. The auditor should retain a listing of all securities and their locations; make sure that controls are in place during the count of securities, cash, and other negotiable instruments; and arrange for a client representative to be present during the actual count.

In performing a security count, the auditor should be alert and note such items as the description of the security, the ownership of the security, the certificate number, the number of shares of stock or the face value, and the name of the issuer. This information is generally recorded on a security count worksheet as shown in Figure 18-1. This worksheet provides evidence that the auditor has physically inspected each certificate and observed the appropriate information. Note that the working paper includes an acknowledgment by a client representative that the securities have all been returned intact to the entity. This acknowledgment prevents the client from claiming that securities were not returned. Carefully examining the security gives the auditor some evidence that securities are authentic and have not been forged.

Security Confirmations

Frequently, a client will have outsiders hold securities for safekeeping. In these situations, the auditor should confirm with the third party that these securities are being held in the client's name and obtain information on the number of shares, face value,

Figure 18-1 **Security Count Worksheet**

					No. of Shares or face value	

Plainsman Company
Long-Term Investments   M-2
Security Count
12-31-x4

	Initials	Date
Prepared By	LG	1/8/x5
Approved By	WA	1/14/x5

	Certificate Number			No. of Shares or face value
1	Box 591 at First National Bank			
2	x2 174	Alpha Company convertible deben-		$5000
3		tures, 5% dated 8/1/x3, due 8/1/x7		
4				
5	AC 1239	Beta Company, common stock no		$500
6		par value, dated 8-1-x4 ✓		
7				
8	BC 2341	Gamma Company, common stock ✓		$10000
9		1,000 shares, $10 par, dated 9-3-x4		
10				
11				
12				
13				
14	✓	Inspected certificate in the name of ABC Company		
15		with no endorsements		
16				
17		The above listed securities were counted in my presece		
18		and returned to me intact on 1-5-x5 at 9.00 A.M.		
19		David Atkins, President		
20		Michael Rogers, Treasurer		
21				
22		Note: I examined the bank entry seconds		
23		and noted the last entry to Box 591		
24		was on 10-3-x4. See confirmation		
25		letter from bank on J4		
26		T. Cooper		
27				
28				
29				
30				

and so on. As with all other confirmations, the auditor should maintain control over the confirmation from the time it is mailed until the time the response is received. This test provides evidence of existence and rights and obligations.

The Real World of Auditing

Investment Valuation

This matter involves Fleet's financial reporting, record keeping, and internal accounting controls in connection with the accounting treatment accorded to its marketable equity securities portfolio. The Commission (SEC) has determined that Fleet failed to write down the cost bases of certain of its marketable equity securities to their realizable values and recognize in its fiscal 1990 income statements the corresponding losses as required by generally accepted accounting principles (GAAP). As a result of the failure to comply with GAAP, the Commission has determined that Fleet's financial statements for the quarters ended June 30, 1990, September 30, 1990, and December 31, 1990 filed

with the Commission were materially inaccurate. The Commission has also determined that Fleet's internal accounting controls were insufficient to provide reasonable assurances that information pertinent to the proper accounting for certain of its marketable equity securities was adequately considered by responsible Fleet personnel. Therefore, Fleet failed to comply, in material respects, with Exchange Act Sections 13(a), 13(b), (2) (A) and (B) and Rules 12b–20, 13a–1 and 13a–13 thereunder.

Source: Securities and Exchange Commission Accounting and Auditing Enforcement Release No. 309, August 14, 1991.

Valuation Tests

Security counts and security confirmations provide evidence that investments exist and belong to the client (rights) but do not provide evidence that the securities are properly valued. The auditor should perform valuation tests to determine that the investment accounts are properly stated. These tests require the auditor to gather evidence of the cost of securities based upon his or her examination of documentation (for example, broker's advices and canceled checks). The auditor should also gather evidence as to the market value of the investment because, according to *FASB No. 12, Accounting for Certain Marketable Securities,* equity securities should be valued at the lower of cost or market. To obtain market values, the auditor can verify market quotations by referring to published security prices in newspapers and other publications. The auditor may also verify market value by direct confirmation with brokers or by appraisals.

When an entity owns at least 20% of the common voting stock of another entity, the investment should generally be accounted for by the equity method because the investing entity is presumed to be able to exercise significant influence. The auditor should determine that the equity method is properly used. If the client is not able to exercise significant influence, the auditor should gather evidence that no such significant influence exists and should account for the investment using the cost method.

The auditor should also be concerned that the underlying value of the investee's net assets exceeds the carrying value of the investments on the client's books. The auditor may determine this by examining the investee's audited financial statements.

Performing Analytical Procedures

Numerous analytical procedures exist for the examination of the investments account. For example, interest revenue may be calculated based upon a reconciliation of the principal balances in the investment account times the interest rate. Comparisons of specific accounts with balances in prior years or with budgets may also give evidence as to the fair presentation of investments in conformity with GAAP. For example, the auditor may compare investment revenue this year with investment revenue from prior years.

Effect of Control Risk on Substantive Tests for Investments

When investment portfolios are small and do not involve much activity, auditors usually assess control risk at or near the maximum level and obtain most of the evidential matter from substantive tests. However, for large portfolios, the auditor may perform tests of controls to support a lower assessed level of control risk. In such circumstances, the nature, timing, and extent of substantive tests for the assertions pertaining to investments should be related to the assessed level of control risk for those assertions. A low assessed level of control risk may allow the auditor to perform some substantive tests, such as confirmations, on less than the entire portfolio or at an interim date.

Intangible Assets

Legal documents exist for most intangibles. The auditor may examine these documents to determine that an intangible exists and is the right of the client. Valuation is generally based upon cost less amortization. The auditor can typically test cost by examining invoices and other documentation. The auditor should determine that the intangible assets are being properly amortized in conformity with generally accepted accounting principles, which require amortization over an intangible's useful life but not to exceed 40 years.

The existence and ownership of goodwill is somewhat more difficult to determine than the existence and ownership of other intangible assets. But because goodwill is only recorded when an arm's-length transaction occurs, evidence of goodwill is provided. For example, when a company purchases another company in an arm's-length transaction, reasonable evidence exists as to the market value of identifiable assets, with goodwill being the difference between the purchase price and the market value of identifiable assets. The auditor should also determine that goodwill is being appropriately amortized.

Property, Plant, and Equipment

According to GAAP, property, plant, and equipment represent long-lived tangible assets that are used in operations. This category includes land, buildings, equipment, capitalized lease property and equipment, and furniture and fixtures.

Property, plant, and equipment are initially recorded at cost. Additions, betterments and improvements, and extraordinary repairs should be capitalized when the expenditures either increase the useful life of the asset or improve its operation. Ordinary repairs and maintenance should be expensed as incurred. For plant and equipment, the matching principle requires a periodic and systematic charge to operations of the cost of plant and equipment through depreciation.

The property, plant, and equipment component often represents the largest element of total assets on the balance sheet. However, the volume of activity within these accounts is generally quite small. Most entities build new plants or purchase equipment much less frequently than they purchase inventory. Further, property, plant, and equipment is typically less vulnerable to fraud and misappropriation.

As with all material accounts in the financial statements, the auditor should gather sufficient evidence to be satisfied that property, plant, and equipment is fairly presented in conformity with GAAP. Thus, the auditor should reduce to an acceptably low level the risk of a material misstatement in property, plant, and equipment that could result from a violation of the five *SAS No. 31, Evidential Matter* (AU 326), assertions. In most engagements, the risk of a material misstatement in property, plant, and equipment is in the areas of existence, rights and obligations, and valuation.

Frequently the auditor prepares a lead schedule for property, plant, and equipment to summarize the activity in the major accounts for the year and the related allowance for accumulated depreciation accounts. This lead schedule allows the auditor to tie in the individual accounts per the ledger to the summary accounts that are often presented in the balance sheet. An example of a lead schedule for property, plant, and equipment is shown in Figure 18–2.

The most common audit tests for property, plant, and equipment are shown in Table 18–5. These include an analysis of additions and deletions, a search for unrecorded retirements, an analysis of repairs and maintenance, tests for depreciation, analytical procedures, a search for liens and mortgages, and an examination of lease agreements.

Analysis of Additions and Deletions

The auditor should determine that there is only a low level of risk that the ending balance for each class of property, plant, and equipment is materially misstated. Most of these accounts have few transactions during the year. Provided the prior-year balances have been audited, the beginning balance in each property, plant, and equipment account has already been supported. By supporting the additions and deletions to the general ledger account through the year, the auditor has by definition tested the ending balance. Because transactions in fixed assets typically are few, this supporting of individual transactions is the most common audit approach and is classified as a substantive test of transactions. Often auditors obtain support for transactions above a certain amount (e.g., $5,000) or examine a sample of additions to property, plant, and equipment.

Alternatively, the auditor could perform a substantive test of balances and analyze the ending balance rather than the changes in the accounts during the year. For example, if he or she wished to test the balances for property, plant, and equipment, the auditor would support each item included in the property ledger as of year-end. Except in first-year audits, this method is generally inefficient because it requires the auditor to test many more items than would be required through the substantive test of transactions of examining only additions and deletions.

In examining additions and retirements, the auditor is primarily trying to determine that the entity owns assets (existence and rights and obligations) that are properly stated at cost (valuation). The auditor generally supports additions through documentary evidence. The auditor may examine vouchers, invoices, contracts, and canceled checks to determine that property, plant, and equipment was purchased and recorded at the appropriate amounts. For retirements, the auditor should trace the original cost of the item and its accumulated depreciation to the detailed property records. Proceeds from salvage may be traced to the cash receipts journal and the bank deposit. If material, the auditor should recompute the gain or loss to determine that it is accounted for in conformity with GAAP.

Figure 18–2   **A Lead Schedule for Property, Plant, and Equipment**

Plainsman Co.   E-1
Property, Plant, and Equipment and Accumulated Depreciation
12/31/X4

Description	Balance 12-31-x3	Additions	Disposals	Balance 12-31-x4
Land	65000n	7000		72000 ✓
Buildings	427000n			427000 ✓
Equipment	69575n	10870 √	16935 √	63510 ✓
Fixtures	93575n	2000 √	4500 √	91075 ✓
	655150	19870	21435	653585
	T	T	T	TT

n   Traced to general ledger and prior year work papers
T   Column footed
TT Column footed and cross footed
√   Vouched additions – see E-3
√   Disposal received for proper treatment – see C-4
0   Tested depreciation provision – see C-5
✓   Traced to general ledger and trial balance

Search for Unrecorded Retirements

The analysis of additions and deletions to the property, plant, and equipment accounts is based on recorded transactions to support existence or occurrence. Of course, the auditor is also concerned that there may be significant unrecorded fixed asset transactions, especially retirements. This concern relates to the completeness assertion. The auditor might obtain evidence of unrecorded retirements by examining the cash receipts journal, sales documents, property tax records, and insurance records; by reviewing accounts related to credit or scrap sales (miscellaneous or other income); or by questioning personnel. The auditor should question management about property, plant, and equipment that is no longer productive and that has not been formally retired. If property, plant, and equipment is not used in operations, GAAP require that

Initials	Date
TC	1-10-x5
WA	1-12-x5

Depreciation Rate	Method	Accumulated Depreciation Balance x0	Provision	Disposal	Balance 12-31-x4
6%	S/L	166530	25620 0		192150 ✓
6.5%	S/L	27585	3200 0	10048 ✗	20737 ✓
4%	S/L	17530	2200 0	1072 ✗	18658 ✓
		211645 T	31020 T	11120 T	231545 TT

the items be classified either as investments or as other assets, rather than as fixed assets.

In searching for unrecorded retirements, the auditor may make a tour of the plant. If the tour is conducted early in the audit, that is, before examining property records, unrecorded retirements will generally be difficult to detect because the auditor will not be familiar with the client's property records. However, if the auditor tours the plant after having examined property records, he or she may discover items listed in the property ledger that are not located at the plant. Figure 18–3 is an example of a working paper for supporting equipment additions and retirements.

Table 18–5	Common Substantive Audit Tests for Property, Plant, and Equipment			

Common Audit Tests	Technique	Type of Test	Assertions
Analyze additions and deletions	Vouching	Test of transactions	Existence Valuation Rights and obligations
Search for unrecorded retirements	Vouching Inquiry	Test of transactions Observation and inquiries	Completeness
Analyze repairs and maintenance	Vouching	Test of transactions	Existence or occurrence Presentation and disclosure
Test and support depreciation	Reperformance	Test of balances	Valuation
Perform analytical procedures	Analytical	Analytical procedure	All
Search for liens and mortgages	Inquiries Inspection	Observation and inquiries Test of balances	Presentation and disclosure Rights and obligations
Examine lease agreements	Inspection	Test of balances	All

Analysis of Repairs and Maintenance

In most audit engagements, the auditor analyzes the repairs and maintenance expense account by vouching all charges over a certain minimum dollar amount to vendor invoices, work orders, purchase documents, and so on. This test serves two purposes: it supports repairs and maintenance expenses as having occurred during the year (existence) and it tests for proper classification of property, plant, and equipment (presentation and disclosure). This second objective is often the primary purpose of the test. By selecting large dollar amounts that have been charged to repairs and maintenance expense, the auditor is looking for items that have been expensed but that should have been capitalized.

Test and Support for Depreciation

The matching principle requires that an entity record periodic depreciation expense to match properly the cost of fixed assets against the revenues that those fixed assets generate. The auditor should test depreciation expense to determine that it is fairly stated and consistently applied. In addition, the auditor should determine that estimated useful lives and salvage values are reasonable. This can sometimes be difficult for certain equipment when technology changes rapidly, such as for computers.

To test the accuracy of the client's depreciation expense computations, the most common audit procedure is to examine the property ledger. By identifying the cost, salvage value, and depreciation method used for sample items in the property ledger, the auditor can recompute depreciation expense on a test basis. The auditor may foot

Figure 18–3 **Working Paper Supporting Equipment Additions and Retirements**

Plainsman Co.   B-3
Equipment Additions and Retirements
12/31/x4
Prepared By TC 1/8/x5   Approved By WA 1/10/x5

Additions

Voucher No.	Vendor	Amount	Description
(1) 0548	Technic Inc	3895 ✓	computer
(1) 0795	Samford Machinery	2000 ✓	motor
(3) 0799	Autos Inc.	4975	used van for delivery
		10870 T	

Retirements

Equipment No.	Description	Date Acquired	Date Retired	Cost	Accumulated Depreciation	Salvage Proceeds	Gain <Loss>	Federal Tax Status	ITC Recapture
M198	motor	1-3-x7	9-8-x4	1435	1073	50	<312>	L.T.	35
C150	computer	9-15-x3	7-17-x4	10000	4000	500	<5500>	L.T.	0
A585	delivery car	7-19-x1	5-21-x4	4000	3500	600	100	L.T.	0
S972	paint sprays	4-3-x1	2-9-x4	1000	1000	25	25	L.T.	0
G583	glass cutters	3-28-x0	11-11-x4	500	475	25	0	L.T.	0
				16935 T	10048 T	1200 T	<5687> T		35 T

T Column footed
✓ Examined vendor invoice, cancelled check and receiving report.
The expenditure is a proper capital charge.
(1) Replacement for item retired

the depreciation charges to see if total depreciation expense is accurate. Analytical procedures are an alternative way to test depreciation expense. For example, the auditor may recompute the depreciation expense booked by the client as a percentage of total depreciable fixed assets. If the percentage appears reasonable and consistent with prior years, the auditor may be satisfied that sufficient evidence has been obtained regarding depreciation expense. The auditor should also ascertain that the depreciation method did not change during the year and that fixed assets are not being depreciated beyond their salvage value.

By testing depreciation expense and retirements, the auditor gathers the evidence needed for accumulated depreciation. By testing the additions to accumulated depreciation (depreciation expense) and the reductions of accumulated depreciation (resulting primarily from retirements), the auditor also supports the ending balance in accumulated depreciation.

Analytical Procedures

Many analytical procedures relate to property, plant, and equipment. One procedure already mentioned is an analysis of depreciation expense as a percentage of fixed assets. Other analytical procedures include a comparison of expenditures with budget and a comparison of expenditures with expenses of prior years.

Search for Liens and Mortgages

The auditor should review liens and mortgages related to property, plant, and equipment because entities often pledge property, plant, and equipment as collateral to obtain mortgages and loans. Pledges as collateral must be disclosed in the financial statements according to generally accepted accounting principles. Thus, for the presentation and disclosure assertion, the auditor needs to gather evidence that mortgages and liens have been adequately disclosed. Typically, auditors gather evidence by making inquiries of management and examining documents. Auditors examine mortgage agreements, notes, bonds, loan agreements, confirmations, minutes of the board of directors, and other documents.

Examination of Lease Agreements

The auditor should examine lease agreements that have been transacted during the year by the client. According to GAAP, lease agreements may be classified either as capital leases or as operating leases. The auditor should read the lease agreement to determine that it has been properly accounted for in accordance with *FASB No. 13, Accounting for Leases*, and its subsequent amendments and interpretations. In examining lease agreements, the auditor is gathering evidence that fixed assets exist (capitalized fixed assets are from leases that should have been capitalized), that fixed assets are complete (capitalized leases that have not been capitalized do not exist), and that the leases have been properly valued. The auditor is also gathering evidence as to rights and obligations and presentation and disclosure.

Effect of Control Risk on Substantive Tests for Property, Plant, and Equipment

For many entities, property, plant, and equipment involves only a few assets of relatively high value. In such cases, the time required to perform tests of controls, even when the internal control structure is believed to be strong, may exceed the time required for substantive tests. Consequently, the auditor would usually assess control risk at or near the maximum level and use substantive tests to obtain evidence about the assertions for property, plant, and equipment. On the other hand, some entities have a high volume of property transactions. In these entities, it may be more efficient to perform tests of controls to support a moderate or low assessed level of control risk. The auditor may then be able to limit significantly the substantive tests necessary to obtain evidence about property, plant, and equipment assertions.

Long-Term Debt

Long-term debt includes notes payable, mortgages payable, and bonds payable that generally are due in more than a year or an operating cycle, whichever is longer. Frequently, long-term debts are collateralized by pledging assets as security. The issuance of long-term debt typically requires approval of the board of directors and involves contractual agreements. Although not many transactions involve long-term debt, those that do are generally material.

The more common substantive audit tests for long-term debt are shown in Table 18–6. These tests include obtaining confirmations, vouching additions and deletions, performing analytical procedures, and reviewing debt agreement provisions.

Obtaining Confirmation

Auditors generally obtain confirmations of long-term debt from lenders or trustees to gather evidence that such a debt exists and is an obligation of the entity. The confirmation also provides a method of discovering any unrecorded liabilities and, thus, provides evidence about completeness. Long-term debt owed to banks is generally confirmed as a part of the bank confirmation request discussed in Chapter 14. Other types of long-term debt that are owed to groups other than banks (such as mortgagees and bondholders) can be confirmed through those lenders or directly through

| Table 18–6 | Common Substantive Audit Tests for Long-Term Debt |

Common Audit Tests	Technique	Type of Test	Assertions
Obtain confirmations	Confirmation	Test of balances	Existence Rights and obligations Completeness
Vouch additions and deletions	Vouching	Test of transactions	Existence Rights and obligations
Perform analytical procedures	Analytical	Analytical procedures	All
Review debt agreement provisions	Inspection	Test of balances	Presentation and disclosure

a trustee. As with other confirmation procedures, the confirmation should be controlled by and returned directly to the auditor. By asking the lender to provide all details of long-term debt between the lender and the client, the auditor can obtain evidence as to whether these liabilities are properly recorded and disclosed by the client.

Vouching Additions and Deletions

Generally, only a few material long-term debt transactions occur during the year. Therefore, the auditor usually gathers evidence on each addition or deletion to long-term debt during the year. For additions to debt, the auditor should vouch the proceeds from the cash receipts records to deposits in the bank. Significant borrowings should also be supported by examining the debt instrument and tracing approval of the debt to the minutes of the board of directors. A review of the minutes should indicate any authorization for issuance of new long-term debt that has occurred during the year. For reductions of debt, the auditor may support the reduction by an examination of payments through the cash disbursements journal and canceled checks. For a debt paid in full, the auditor should also examine the canceled note.

Analytical Procedures

Numerous analytical procedures exist for testing long-term debt, including an analysis of the relationship between interest expense and total outstanding debt. When the expected interest expense is lower than the actual recorded interest expense, unrecorded long-term debt transactions may exist. Other analytical procedures include computations of ratios such as debt to equity and number of times interest is earned. Also, the auditor may wish to compare the long-term debt accounts with prior-year balances and with budget expectations. In addition to making a computation of interest expense, the auditor should be aware of accrued interest payable that should be recorded.

Review of Debt Agreements

Because long-term debt frequently has restrictive covenants, the auditor should review all debt agreements to determine that the client is in compliance with the covenants. The debt agreement should also indicate any pledging of the client's assets as collateral that may need to be disclosed in the financial statements.

If the auditor uncovers any violations of debt agreements, the violations should be investigated further and discussed with the client. In this situation the auditor would prefer that the client obtain a waiver from the lender so that the client does not have to meet the particular debt agreement in the specific circumstance. If the client does not obtain a waiver, the auditor generally would assume that the client has violated the debt agreement, the penalty provisions will be assessed, and the debt may need to be reclassified as short-term debt. Violations of debt agreements may also indicate going-concern problems for the client, with implications for the auditor's report. A review of debt agreements is important for the auditor to gather sufficient evidence as to presentation and disclosure. Examination of the actual notes, mortgages, and other long-term debt during the year also gives the auditor evidence as to the appropriate accounting treatment, including classification as long- or short-term and other disclosures. Figure 18–4 is an example of a long-term debt schedule.

Figure 18–4 **Long-Term Debt Schedule**

Plainsman Co.
Long-Term Debt Schedule
12/31/X4

D-1

Prepared
Approved

	Description	Balance 12-31-x3	Additions	Retirements	Balance 12-31-x4
	9% Note payable to bank, due $30,000 per year to 10-31-x6, secured by land and building	150000 π TB-2		30000 ✓	120000 c π TB-2

✓ Examined cancelled check
c Confirmed by bank
π Traced to prior-year working papers
π Traced to general ledger
✗ Examined cancelled checks for the January and October payments

Stockholder Equity

The primary stockholder equity accounts include common and preferred stock, contributed capital, and retained earnings. Although the frequency of transactions in stockholder equity is relatively small, the transactions that do occur are generally important. The primary areas of audit risk for stockholder equity typically are existence, valuation, and presentation and disclosure. The auditor should have in the permanent file the client's *articles of incorporation.* These articles provide evidence as to the classes of stocks the company is authorized to issue, the rights and preferences of each class of stock, the number of shares authorized, the par value, and any restrictions that may be included. Consequently, the articles of incorporation are important in examining the presentation and disclosure assertion.

Stock and Contributed Capital

In examining the stock and contributed capital accounts, the auditor's concern is that these accounts are fairly stated for the entity as a whole. The auditor focuses on the total stock issued and its contribution of capital. Because the entity, and not its

		Initials	Date	
	By	TC	1-20-x4	PBC
	By	WA	2-14-x5	

	5	6	7	8	9	10
			Interest Payable			
		Balance			*Balance*	
		12-31-x3	*Provision*	*Payments*	12-31-x4	
		2250 8	13050 ①	13500 ✓	1800 ② U	
		P	40		P	

Test of Accrued Interest
Note balance 120000
Interest rate .09
10800
Accrual period (11-1 to 12-31) x 2/12
1800
②

Test of Interest Expense
150000 x .09 x 10/12 = 11250
120000 x .09 x 2/12 = 11250
13050
①

shareholders, is the auditee, transfers of ownership among stockholders are not generally important. A sale of stock from one stockholder to another stockholder does not affect total ownership in the entity. Consequently, stock ownership by individual stockholders is not normally confirmed.

Because transactions are typically limited in the stock and capital accounts, the auditor usually examines all such transactions in the account. If the auditor has performed the audit engagement in the prior year and has examined all transactions during the current year, he or she has supported the ending balance. In analyzing transactions in these equity accounts during the year, the auditor generally examines the transactions by inspecting documentation. For example, when additional stock is sold, the proceeds should be recorded and can be traced to the cash receipts journal and deposit slips. Approval of the issuance of additional stock should be traced to the minutes of the board of directors or shareholders. These audit tests provide evidence of the assertions of existence, valuation, and presentation and disclosure. The auditor should be alert for the issuance of capital stock in nonmonetary transactions because this sometimes presents special problems with the valuation assertion. For example, the issuance of stock for equipment requires careful consideration by the auditor to determine that the transaction was properly recorded.

When an entity maintains its own stock records, the auditor should also examine the stock certificate book. The stock certificate book is a record of all stock certificates that have been issued and includes stubs that indicate the number of shares issued and outstanding. This book is similar to a check register in that it holds a series of unissued documents. When a stock certificate is issued, a stub remains to record the transaction. The auditor should examine the stock certificate book to determine that the stubs for the shares that have been issued have been properly completed, that any stock certificates that have been canceled have been reattached to the stubs, and that all unissued certificates are intact. In this way, the auditor can account for all certificate numbers by examining the stubs in the stock certificate book. By gathering evidence as to outstanding shares and multiplying this number by par value, the auditor has tested the stock account in the financial statements. Because changes in the stock account are usually infrequent, an auditor often uses a permanent or carryforward schedule to perform this test. An example of a carryforward stock certificate book schedule is shown in Figure 18–5.

If a client possesses treasury stock, this stock should be inspected and counted. Ideally the count should be performed as of the balance sheet date. If this is not possible, the auditor should reconcile the number of shares counted to the balance sheet date. Any changes in the number of shares of treasury stock that have occurred since the prior year should be properly supported. This would include tracing the transaction through the cash receipts or cash disbursements journal and determining that the purchases or sales of treasury stock have been accounted for properly.

In examining additions to stock accounts to test the existence and valuation assertions, the auditor should determine the cash proceeds and ensure that the appropriate amount has been entered into the stock account and the contributed capital account. Sometimes entities do not maintain stock certificate books and records. Rather, they use registrars and transfer agents to provide this service. Transfer agents receive and issue stock certificates and maintain a listing of shareholders for use in mailing annual reports and dividend checks. Registrars maintain a record of the number of shares issued and canceled and provide a check over the actions of the transfer agents.

Figure 18–5   Carryforward Stock Certificate Book Schedule

Plainsman Co.
Carryforward Stock Certificate Book Schedule
12-31-x4

Prepared By TC 1-18-x5
Approved By WA 2-2-x5

Certificate Number	Stockholder	Date Issued	Number of Shares	Date Retired	No. of New Certificates (if transfer)	Shares Outstanding Per Examination			
						19x3	19x4	19x5	19x6
44	K.R. Gordon	2-1-x3	1000			1000 n	1000 n		
45	L.A. Harris	2-20-x3	500			500 n	500 n		
46	J.L. Henkle	4-7-x4	700				700 n		
47	D.B. Mason	10-31-x4	500				500 n		
						100000	100000		
						+ 81 x	+ 81 x		
						100000 T	100000 T		

x Par value per articles of incorporation
n Examined stock book stub with federal tax stamp
√ Examined cancelled stock certificate attached to stub
T Column footed

Unused certificate remaining in
stockbook, per examination   48-100

F. Martin   T. Cooper
1-2-x4   1-20-x5

The auditor can confirm directly with the registrar the total shares authorized, issued, and outstanding at the balance sheet date. As with all other confirmations, this confirmation should be controlled by and returned directly to the auditor. The auditor should reconcile the confirmation reply with the stock accounts as shown in the general ledger.

Retained Earnings

Generally, the auditor examines all transactions in the retained earnings account. Assuming the auditor has performed the audit in prior years, he or she has already supported the beginning retained earnings balance. By examining all transactions in the retained earnings account during the year, the auditor gathers evidence of the ending balance of retained earnings. The two primary entries in retained earnings during the year are net income and dividends. Other entries may be made to retained earnings, including prior-period adjustments. If these other types of transactions occur, the auditor should also examine them. The net income figure is tested through the other phases of the audit, including the audit of revenues, expenses, and balance sheet accounts as previously discussed.

All dividends declared during the year should be tested, including tracing the dividend declaration to the proper authorization in the minutes of the board of directors. In examining the minutes, the auditor should note authorization, the dividend amount per share, the date of record, and the date of payment. The auditor should also support the entry by recalculating the dividend charge. These audit procedures provide evidence for the existence and valuation assertions. Further, the auditor should examine, usually on a test basis, the payment of dividends to individual shareholders. By obtaining the names of shareholders from the stock certificate book, the auditor can multiply the number of shares owned times the dividend payment as indicated in the minutes of the board to get the total dividend paid to each of the individuals. This amount can be traced to the cash disbursements journal and the canceled check can be examined. This audit test provides evidence that dividends did occur, that they are properly valued, and that presentation and disclosure are proper.

Sole Proprietorships and Partnerships

The preceding discussion assumed that the client is a corporation. Two other forms of business organizations exist: sole proprietorships and partnerships. If the auditor is examining the financial statements of a sole proprietorship or partnership, he or she must also test the capital section of these enterprises by gathering sufficient competent evidential matter. In general, the audit approach taken is to examine the individual transactions in the capital account. Once again, for a continuing auditor the beginning balance in the capital account of a sole proprietorship or partnership has already been supported. By examining the changes in the account during the year, the auditor has by definition supported the ending balance. Increases in the capital account for sole proprietors or partners should be traced to cash receipts. Decreases in the account should be a result of drawings and should be traced to cash disbursements.

For a partnership, the auditor should also examine the partnership agreement with particular emphasis on the distribution of net income as stated in the agreement, allowances for drawings, restrictions on drawings, and maintenance of capital at prescribed levels. In general, the same principles apply for the support of capital in any type of organization whether it is a sole proprietorship, partnership, or corporation. The basic thrust is for the auditor to examine the transactions that have occurred during the year. This includes examining additional capital investments, examining capital withdrawals whether in the form of drawings or dividends, and determining that net income is appropriately credited to the accounts. The auditor should also ascertain that the sole proprietorship or partnership does not intermingle business and personal transactions.

Operations

When expressing an opinion on the financial statements, the auditor is expressing an opinion not only on the balance sheet but also on the statement of cash flows and the income statement (that is, operations). The auditor's legal liability is for the fair presentation in conformity with GAAP of the financial statements taken as a whole. As a consequence, before forming an opinion on the financial statements, the auditor should gather sufficient competent evidential matter about the set of financial statements.

Limited Nature of Testing

During the audit of operations, the auditor gathers evidence to test the fair presentation of revenue and expense accounts in conformity with generally accepted accounting principles. Direct substantive audit tests of revenue and expense accounts for most audit engagements are usually limited. This results from a variety of reasons, including the relationships of (1) operations accounts to various balance sheet accounts, (2) internal control structure to tests of transactions, and (3) the income statement to the balance sheet.

Operations Accounts and Balance Sheet Accounts

Chapters 14, 15, 17, and 18 discussed the audit of various balances. Most of these accounts have been balance sheet accounts, including cash; accounts receivable; inventory; property, plant, and equipment; accounts payable; and long-term debt. However, in gathering evidence to test each of these accounts, the auditor also gathers evidence as to fair presentation of various income statement accounts. This is due to the nature of the double-entry bookkeeping system.

Accounts receivable are generated with a journal entry that debits accounts receivable and credits sales. Thus, when gathering evidence to test accounts receivable, the auditor is also gathering evidence that sales are fairly stated. Likewise, accounts payable frequently are generated with a credit to accounts payable and a concurrent debit to an asset or expense account. In gathering evidence to test accounts payable, the auditor is also gathering evidence on asset or expense accounts. Likewise, the audit of inventories has a direct effect on the determination of cost of goods sold. In addition, an overstatement or understatement in an income statement account must cause either another income statement, an asset, or a liability account to be misstated. If another income statement account is misstated, the net effect on net income is zero. The auditor's concern would be with whether the classification error is material. If an asset or liability account is misstated, the misstatement could be detected during the audit of the related asset or liability account.

Many audit tests on balance sheet accounts also include tests of income statement accounts. For example, when examining property, plant, and equipment, the auditor also typically performs a test for depreciation expense. Similarly, when testing long-term debt, the auditor also gathers evidence as to interest expense, and when testing investments, the auditor also gathers evidence as to investment income. Thus, even though many audit tests are classified as balance sheet tests, they also relate to income statement accounts.

Internal Control Structure and Tests of Transactions

Many audit tests that are classified as tests of transactions support income statement accounts. For example, the tests of transactions that were identified in the audit of sales in Chapter 14 support the revenue account of sales. Likewise, the tests of transactions regarding purchases in Chapter 15 support the fair presentation of cost of goods sold in the income statement.

Frequently, tests of transactions are performed as tests of controls. The auditor typically tests the effectiveness of the internal control structure policies and procedures to record properly revenue and expense accounts. The tests of controls may result in an assessed level of control risk for some revenue and expense assertions that may permit the auditor to limit substantive audit testing for those assertions.

Tests of controls often provide supporting evidence for operations where there are strong internal control structure policies and procedures over sales, cash receipts, purchases, and cash disbursements.

Income Statement and Balance Sheet

Some auditors believe that, once all balance sheet accounts are tested and the auditor has audited the balance sheet for both this year and last, the only other change in the balance sheet would be the result of operations (that is, net income). By adequately testing the balance sheet accounts in a continuing audit engagement, some auditors believe, net income is by definition supported because that is the only change in the accounts that has not been directly examined.

Although to some extent this is true, the auditor should remember that most of the balance sheet accounts have not been examined completely but rather have been examined only on a test basis. Thus no guarantee exists that each account is fairly stated, and the auditor really cannot make the inference that income statement accounts can be supported from an analysis of changes in the balance sheet during the year. For this reason, the auditor should generally perform some direct tests of revenue and expense accounts. These tests may include concurrent tests of transactions, tests of operation balances in connection with balance sheet accounts (for example, interest revenue with investments), or other substantive audit tests as identified in the following section.

Substantive Audit Tests

The auditor may apply many substantive audit tests to support revenues and expenses. Many of these have already been identified in the discussion of audits of related balance sheet accounts. These include testing interest revenue with investments; depreciation expense with property, plant, and equipment; and interest expense with long-term debt.

The most common substantive audit tests for operations accounts are analytical procedures. As noted in Chapter 11, the auditor may compute a variety of ratios, including the gross margin, profit margin on sales, net operating margin, ratio of certain expenses to revenues, return on total assets, and return on common stockholder equity.

The auditor can also perform tests for overall reasonableness. As discussed in Chapter 11, a test of reasonableness for revenue accounts is quite common if the appropriate data exist. For example, if examining an apartment complex, the auditor would know the number of apartments and the rental charge per month. If the auditor had some idea of the vacancy rate, he or she could estimate total revenues for the year and determine if recorded revenues appear reasonable.

Another common analytical procedure for operations is the comparison of revenue and expense accounts with those of prior years or with budgets. An example of such a working paper is shown in Figure 18–6. In performing this type of analysis, the auditor should be familiar with the behavior of the different revenue and expense accounts. For example, rental expense may be fixed and the auditor would not expect it to vary, regardless of the sales revenue level. On the other hand, other accounts could be variable (for example, sales commissions) and the auditor would expect them to vary in proportion to variation in revenues or production. In performing this type of analysis, the auditor should investigate further any unexpected variations or any nonvariations where a variation was expected. Generally these investigations include making an inquiry of the client and performing further audit tests as appropriate. For example, if the utilities expense increased dramatically and unexpectedly during the year, the auditor should make an inquiry of the client and consider further testing of the account. The client may respond that utilities expense increased dramatically because the client no longer generates its own electricity. The auditor could support this explanation by examining the accounts involved with the self-generation of electricity.

A common substantive audit test for operations other than analytical procedures is the review or analysis of certain revenue and expense accounts. For example, the auditor will typically review legal expenses to document which attorneys have been used by the client during the year. This identifies which attorneys to request an attorney's letter from, as discussed in the next chapter. Likewise, the auditor often analyzes officers' salary expenses, executive bonus expenses, various tax accounts, donations to charities, and so on. Many times this information is used in filing tax returns with the IRS and in filings with the Securities and Exchange Commission.

| Figure 18-6 | **Working Paper, Comparing Current- with Prior-Year Accounts** |

Plainsman Co.
Comparison of Revenues & Expenses with Prior Year
12/31/X4

R-2

	Initials	Date
Prepared By	RD	1/28/X5
Approved By	WA	2/11/X5

Account Title	Balance 12-31-X3	Balance 12-31-X4	Percentage Change	Explanation
Rental reserve	1800x	5400y	200%	adopted policy of leasing excess equipment, several of which were capital leases.
Interest income	0	800y	800%	Purchased CD during year.
Depreciation	36720x	31020y	<16%>	disposed of equipment and fixtures
Cost of Goods Sold	250000	300000y	20%	cost of materials increased during 19x4, due to shortages in market
Electricity expense	5000x	7500y	50%	rate hike granted Power company accompanied by an increase in production requiring extra shift

x Per prior-year audit
y Per working trial balance

Some account analyses have already been discussed in relation to the audit of various balance sheet accounts. For example, in examining property, plant, and equipment, the auditor typically also tests the repairs and maintenance account.

Statement of Cash Flows

The statement of cash flows presents an entity's gross amounts of cash receipts and cash payments classified according to operating, investing, and financing activities. For example, cash flows from operating activities include cash received from sales to customers and cash paid to suppliers and employees for goods and services, cash flows from investing activities include buying and selling the equity securities of another entity, and cash flows from financing activities include borrowing money and repaying the amounts borrowed.

The statement of cash flows is generated by analyzing changes in balance sheet amounts. If the auditor has audited the prior year's balance sheet and has obtained sufficient evidence that the current year's balance sheet is presented fairly in conformity with GAAP, the statement of cash flows generally has been supported. By performing auditing procedures on the balance sheet accounts, the auditor has obtained evidence that is used to support the statement of cash flows. For example, in auditing the investments account the auditor recognizes that the purchases and sales of investments will be shown in the statement of cash flows and plans the audit accordingly. The auditor should determine that the statement of cash flows has been prepared and presented in conformity with generally accepted accounting principles.

Income Taxes

Income tax expense, income taxes payable, and deferred income taxes often represent material accounts on the financial statements. For the income tax accounts, the primary areas of audit risk are in the assertions of completeness, valuation, and presentation and disclosure. To examine these accounts properly, the auditor should understand applicable federal and state income tax laws and regulations and authoritative pronouncements for the financial accounting of income taxes. This includes an understanding of timing differences, permanent differences, investment tax credits, and net operating loss carryforwards and carrybacks.

In most audit engagements, the auditor analyzes accrued income taxes payable for the year. This generally consists of a test of reasonableness for total income tax expense for the year and a verification of interim income tax payments during the year by reference to canceled checks and other documentation. Quite often the auditor verifies income tax expense when completing the income tax return because in many accounting firms the auditor not only performs the audit engagement but also prepares the income tax return for the client. These tests provide evidence to support the completeness, valuation, and presentation and disclosure assertions.

In addition to verifying income tax expense and income taxes payable, the auditor should also determine whether there are any deferred taxes as a result of timing differences and check the calculation of such taxes. Further, the auditor should make an inquiry as to the status of any prior-year returns that are being examined by revenue agents.

Significant Terms

Financing and investing cycle Activities related to capital funds acquisition through issuance of long-term debt and capital stock and the subsequent investment of these funds in producing assets.

Intangible assets Long-term assets lacking physical substance, which are used in operations, including trademarks, copyrights, patents, goodwill, and franchises.

Investments Assets acquired with the intention of holding them on a long- or short-term basis and that are auxiliary to central revenue-producing activities.

Long-term debt Present obligations, arising out of past actions or transactions, that are not payable within the operating cycle of the entity or within one year, whichever is longer.

Property, plant, and equipment Tangible assets, including land, building structures, and equipment, that are long-term and durable in nature, used in operations, and usually subject to depreciation.

Discussion Questions

18-1. What are five audit tests for property, plant, and equipment and what is the objective(s) of each?

18-2. Describe alternative methods of supporting the ending balance in property, plant, and equipment. Which is preferable?

18-3. What are the objectives of the analysis of the repairs and maintenance expense account?

18-4. What is the most important objective in the audit of investments? Why?

18-5. Describe audit procedures used to provide evidence as to the valuation of investments.

18-6. Because few transactions relate to long-term debt, why is this account of such concern to auditors?

18-7. Describe audit procedures designed to test additions to long-term debt. Describe those for retirements.

18-8. How do analytical procedures help indicate unrecorded long-term debt transactions?

18-9. How is the statement of cash flows generally supported?

18-10. What is the primary audit procedure used to examine stock and contributed capital accounts?

18-11. Which two entries are of concern to the auditor in testing retained earnings? How are these entries supported?

Objective Questions

*18-12. Where *no* independent stock transfer agents are employed and the corporation issues its own stocks and maintains stock records, canceled stock certificates should
  (1) be defaced to prevent reissuance and attached to their corresponding stubs.
  (2) *not* be defaced but be segregated from other stock certificates and retained in a canceled certificates file.
  (3) be destroyed to prevent fraudulent reissuance.
  (4) be defaced and sent to the secretary of state.

*18-13. Which of the following is an internal control structure weakness related to factory equipment?
  (1) A policy exists requiring all purchases of factory equipment to be made by the department in need of the equipment.
  (2) Checks issued in payment of purchases of equipment are *not* signed by the controller.
  (3) Factory equipment replacements are generally made when estimated useful lives, as indicated in depreciation schedules, have expired.
  (4) Proceeds from sales of fully depreciated equipment are credited to other income.

*18-14. The financial management of a company should take steps to see that company investment securities are protected. Which of the following is *not* a step designed to protect investment securities?
  (1) Custody of securities should be assigned to persons who have the accounting responsibility for securities.
  (2) Securities should be properly controlled physically to prevent unauthorized use.
  (3) Access to securities should be vested in more than one person.
  (4) Securities should be registered in the name of the owner.

*AICPA adapted.

*18-15. Which of the following is the *most* important internal control structure procedure over acquisitions of property, plant, and equipment?

   (1) Establishing a written company policy distinguishing between capital and revenue expenditures.

   (2) Using a budget to forecast and control acquisitions and retirements.

   (3) Analyzing monthly variances between authorized expenditures and actual costs.

   (4) Requiring acquisitions to be made by user departments.

*18-16. Which of the following audit procedures would be *least* likely to lead the auditor to find unrecorded fixed asset disposals?

   (1) Examination of insurance policies.

   (2) Review of repairs and maintenance expense.

   (3) Review of property tax files.

   (4) Scanning of invoices for fixed asset additions.

*18-17. The controller of Excello Manufacturing, Inc., wants to use ratio analysis to identify the possible existence of idle equipment or the possibility that equipment has been disposed of without having been written off. Which of the following ratios would best accomplish this objective?

   (1) Depreciation expense to book value of manufacturing equipment.

   (2) Accumulated depreciation to book value of manufacturing equipment.

   (3) Repairs and maintenance cost to direct labor costs.

   (4) Gross manufacturing equipment cost to units produced.

*18-18. Which of the following is the *best* evidence of real estate ownership at the balance sheet date?

   (1) Title insurance policy.

   (2) Original deed held in the client's safe.

   (3) Paid real estate tax bills.

   (4) Closing statement.

*18-19. In the audit of property, plant, and equipment, the auditor tries to determine all of the following *except* the

   (1) design of the internal control structure.

   (2) extent of property abandoned during the year.

   (3) adequacy of replacement funds.

   (4) reasonableness of depreciation expense.

*18-20. During the year under audit, a company has completed a private placement of a substantial amount of bonds. Which of the following is the *most* important step in the auditor's program for the examination of bonds payable?

   (1) Confirming the amount issued with the bond trustee.

   (2) Tracing the cash received from the issue to the accounting records.

   (3) Examining the bond records maintained by the transfer agent.

   (4) Recomputing the annual interest cost and the effective yield.

*18-21. An auditor compares 19X4 revenues and expenses with those of the prior year and investigates all changes exceeding 10%. By this procedure the auditor would be most likely to learn that

   (1) an increase in property tax rates has *not* been recognized in the client's accrual.

   (2) the 19X4 provision for uncollectible accounts is inadequate because of worsening economic conditions.

   (3) fourth-quarter payroll taxes were *not* paid.

   (4) the client changed its capitalization policy for small tools in 19X4.

---

*AICPA adapted.

*18-22. An auditor determines that a client has properly capitalized a leased asset (and corresponding lease liability) as representing, in substance, an installment purchase. As part of the auditor's procedures, the auditor should
  (1) substantiate the cost of the property to the lessor and determine that this is the cost recorded by the client.
  (2) evaluate the propriety of the interest rate used in discounting the future lease payments.
  (3) determine that the leased property is being amortized over the life of the lease.
  (4) evaluate whether the total amount of lease payments represents the fair market value of the property.

*18-23. During an audit, Sylvia Wicks, CPA, learns that the audit client was granted a three-month waiver of the repayment of principal on the installment loan with Blank Bank, without an extension of the maturity date. With respect to this loan, the audit program used by Wicks would be *least* likely to include a verification of the
  (1) interest expense for the year.
  (2) balloon payment.
  (3) total liability at year-end.
  (4) installment loan payments.

*18-24. Which of the following *best* describes the independent auditor's approach to obtaining satisfaction concerning depreciation expense in the income statement?
  (1) Verify the mathematical accuracy of the amounts charged to income as a result of depreciation expense.
  (2) Determine the method for computing depreciation expense and ascertain that it is in accordance with generally accepted accounting principles.
  (3) Reconcile the amount of depreciation expense to those amounts credited to accumulated depreciation accounts.
  (4) Establish the basis for depreciable assets and verify the depreciation expense.

18-25. When auditing an entity's statement of cash flows, an auditor uses which of the following as a primary source of audit evidence?
  (1) The guidance provided by the FASB standard on the statement of cash flows.
  (2) Analysis of significant ratios comparing the current year with the prior year.
  (3) Audit procedures applied to determine working capital at year-end.
  (4) Audit procedures applied to the balances and transactions related to the audit of the other financial statements.

*18-26. An auditor testing long-term investments would ordinarily use analytical procedures as the primary audit procedure to ascertain the reasonableness of the
  (1) valuation of marketable equity securities.
  (2) classification of gains and losses on the disposal of securities.
  (3) completeness of recorded investment income.
  (4) existence and ownership of investments.

*18-27. The auditor may conclude that depreciation charges are insufficient by noting
  (1) large amounts of fully depreciated assets.
  (2) continuous trade-ins of relatively new assets.
  (3) excessive recurring losses on assets retired.
  (4) insured values greatly in excess of book values.

*18-28. An auditor would use analytical procedures to test which of the following assertions for long-term investments?
  (1) Existence of unrealized gains or losses on the portfolio.
  (2) Completeness of recorded investment income.

---

*AICPA adapted.

(3) Classification between current and noncurrent portfolios.
(4) Valuation of marketable equity securities.

*18-29. Which of the following internal control structure policies or procedures would be most effective in maintaining proper custody of financing cycle assets?
(1) Access to securities in the safe deposit box being limited to only one officer.
(2) Personnel who post investment transactions to the general ledger are not permitted to update the investments subsidiary ledger.
(3) The purchase and sale of investments are executed only on the specific authorization of the board of directors.
(4) The recorded balances in the investment subsidiary ledger are periodically compared with the contents of the safe deposit box by independent personnel.

Problems and Cases

18-30. (Controls over Equipment) For each of the following situations, describe an equipment internal control feature that, if implemented, would prevent or detect the situation. Consider each situation independently.
A. Theft of a fixed asset at a remote plant location.
B. Computation of depreciation expense that exceeds the cost of the asset.
C. Loss on the destruction of property not properly insured.
D. Theft of property by an employee who reports that the property has been scrapped.
E. Acquisition of a fixed asset by a plant manager that seriously impairs the company's capital budgeting plans.
F. Acquisition of a fixed asset that provides no benefits to the company.
G. Inability to determine who is the manufacturer of a fixed asset that desperately needs maintenance and repairs.

*18-31. (Controls over Investments) The cashier of a bank, Tawanna Magouirk, is also treasurer of a local charity and is authorized to purchase $10,000 in U.S. bonds for the bank and a similar amount for the charity. She makes both purchases but misappropriates the bonds belonging to the charity. When an audit is made of the charity, the treasurer borrows the bonds from the bank and places them in the charity's safe-deposit box.
REQUIRED
Discuss the internal control structure policies and procedures you would recommend for the charity to prevent the occurrence of this manipulation.

*18-32. (Audit Program for Property, Plant, and Equipment) In connection with a recurring audit of the financial statements of the Louis Manufacturing Company for the year ended December 31, 19X4, you have been assigned the audit of the manufacturing equipment, manufacturing-equipment accumulated depreciation, and repairs to manufacturing-equipment accounts. Your review of Louis's policies and procedures has disclosed the following pertinent information:
1. The manufacturing equipment account includes the net invoice price plus related freight and installation costs for all of the equipment in Louis's manufacturing plant.
2. The manufacturing equipment and accumulated depreciation accounts are supported by a subsidiary ledger that shows the cost and accumulated depreciation for each piece of equipment.
3. An annual budget for capital expenditures of $1,000 or more is prepared by the budget committee and approved by the board of directors. Capital expenditures over $1,000 that are not included in this budget must be approved by the board of directors, and variations of 20% or more must be explained to the board. Approval by the supervisor of production is required for capital expenditures under $1,000.

*AICPA adapted.

4. Company employees handle installation, removal, repair, and rebuilding of the machinery. Work orders are prepared for these activities and are subject to the same budgetary control as other expenditures. Work orders are not required for external expenditures.

REQUIRED

A. Cite the major objectives of your audit of the manufacturing equipment, manufacturing-equipment accumulated depreciation, and repairs of manufacturing-equipment accounts. Do not include in this listing the auditing procedures designed to accomplish these objectives.

B. Prepare the portion of your audit program applicable to the audit of 19X4 additions to the manufacturing-equipment account.

*18-33. (First-Year Audit of Property, Plant, and Equipment) Hardware Manufacturing Company, a closely held corporation, has operated since 19X4 but has not had its financial statements audited. The company now plans to issue additional capital stock expected to be sold to outsiders and wishes to engage you to audit and render an opinion on the financial statements for the year ended December 31, 19X8.

The company has expanded from one plant to three and has frequently acquired, modified, and disposed of all types of equipment. Fixed assets have a net book value of 70% of total assets and consist of land and buildings, diversified machinery and equipment, and furniture and fixtures. Some property was acquired by donation from stockholders. Depreciation was recorded by several methods using various estimated lives.

REQUIRED

A. May you confine your audit solely to 19X8 transactions as requested by this prospective client, whose financial statements have not previously been audited? Why or why not?

B. Prepare an audit program for the January 1, 19X8, opening balances of land, buildings, equipment, and accumulated depreciation accounts for Hardware Manufacturing Company. You need not include tests of 19X8 transactions in your program.

18-34. (Using a Computer in Audit of Fixed Assets) The Jaguar Manufacturing Company is being audited by Young, Sells, and Peat, CPAs. The auditor in charge of fixed assets is concerned about the lack of a proper audit trail. A computer audit expert is summoned to the job and suggests that a generalized audit program be used in the verification of the accounts. The audit package does the following:

1. Foots the file and prints totals by category for all assets. Breakdowns are given for costs, new additions during the period, current depreciation and depreciation balance, and differences between book and tax depreciation.

2. Prepares listings of all additions over $10,000.

3. Recalculates all depreciation for both book and tax purposes.

The year-end master files for fixed assets can be obtained from the company for the past several years. The master file is separated into eleven categories:

1. Asset number.

2. Description.

3. Type.

4. Year acquired.

5. Original costs.

6. Accumulated depreciation (books).

7. Useful life.

8. Tax depreciation method.

9. Depreciation this year (books).

10. Depreciation this year (tax).

11. Accumulated depreciation (tax).

---

*AICPA adapted.

REQUIRED

A. List the reports and schedules that the auditor will need the computer program to generate.

B. Explain any additional procedures that might be necessary to satisfy the auditor that fixed assets are fairly stated.

*18-35. (Audit of Depreciation) In connection with the annual audit of Johnson Corp., a manufacturer of janitorial supplies, you have been assigned to audit the fixed assets. Johnson Corp. maintains a detailed property ledger for all fixed assets. You have prepared an audit program for the balances of property, plant, and equipment but have yet to prepare one for accumulated depreciation and depreciation expense.

REQUIRED

Prepare a separate comprehensive audit program for the accumulated depreciation and depreciation expense accounts.

18-36. (Audit of Leases) Joey Wheat, CPA, is performing the year-end audit of Grace Corporation. Grace leases much of its equipment and several buildings. Wheat has reviewed the following criteria for lease capitalization from *FASB Statement No. 13, Accounting for Leases:*

1. The lease transfers ownership of the property to the lessee by the end of the lease term.

2. The lease contains an option to purchase the property at a bargain.

3. The lease term is for 75% or more of the estimated economic life of the property.

4. The present value of the rentals and other minimum lease payments is equal to 90% or more of the fair value of the leased property less any related investment tax credit retained by the lessor.

REQUIRED

Explain how Wheat should audit the lease classifications based on the criteria above. Indicate the specific documentation he should examine and how he should satisfy himself as to fair value of rentals, estimated economic life, and so on.

*18-37. (Audit of Investments) As a result of highly profitable operations over a number of years, Eastern Manufacturing Corporation accumulated a substantial investment portfolio. In the audit of the financial statements for the year ended December 31, 19X4, the following information came to the attention of Bob Browne, the corporation's independent CPA:

1. The manufacturing operations of the corporation resulted in an operating loss for the year.

2. In 19X4, the corporation placed the securities making up the investment portfolio with a financial institution that will serve as custodian of the securities. Formerly, the securities were kept in the corporation's safe-deposit box in the local bank.

3. On December 22, 19X4, the corporation sold and then repurchased on the same day a number of securities that had appreciated greatly in value. Management stated that the purpose of the sale and repurchases was to establish a higher cost and book value for the securities and to avoid the reporting of a loss for the year.

REQUIRED

A. List the objectives of Browne's audit of the investment account.

B. Under what conditions would Browne accept a confirmation of the securities on hand from the custodian in lieu of inspecting and counting the securities himself?

C. What disclosure, if any, of the sale and repurchase of the securities would Browne recommend for the financial statements?

---

*AICPA adapted.

*18-38. (Audit of Investments) You have been engaged to audit the financial statements of the Elliott Company for the year ended December 31, 19X4. You performed a similar audit as of December 31, 19X3. A partial trial balance for the company as of December 31, 19X4, shows the following:

	Dr. (Cr.)
Dividends receivable	$ 1,750
Investments at cost: Bowen common stock	322,000
Investments at equity: Woods common stock	284,000
Dividend revenue	(3,750)
Equity in earnings of investments carried at equity	(40,000)

You have obtained the following data concerning these accounts:

1. The Bowen common stock was purchased on September 30, 19X4, for cash in the market where it is actively traded. It is used as security for the note payable and held by the bank. Elliott's investment in Bowen represents approximately 1% of the total outstanding shares of Bowen.
2. Elliott's investment in Woods represents 40% of the outstanding common stock that is actively traded. Woods is audited by another CPA and has a December 31 year-end.
3. Elliott neither purchased nor sold any stock investments during the year other than those noted above.

REQUIRED

For each of the above account balances, discuss the types of evidential matter you should obtain and the audit procedures you should perform during your audit.

*18-39. (Audit of Marketable Securities) You have been engaged by the Chicago Corporation to audit its financial statements for the year ended June 30, 19X4. On May 1, 19X4, Chicago Corporation had borrowed $500,000 from Lake National Bank to finance plant expansion. The long-term note agreement provided for the annual payment of principal and interest over five years. The existing plant was pledged as security for the loan.

Because of unexpected difficulties in acquiring the building site, the plant expansion had not begun by June 30, 19X4. To derive some revenue from borrowed funds, management had decided to invest in stock and bonds. On May 16, 19X4, the $500,000 had been invested in marketable securities.

REQUIRED

A. How could you verify the securities owned by Chicago at June 30?
B. In your audit of marketable securities, how would you
  (1) verify the dividend and interest revenue recorded?
  (2) determine market value?
  (3) establish the authority for securities purchased?

*18-40. (Audit of Long-Term Debt) A company has issued bonds for cash during the year under audit. To ascertain that this transaction was properly recorded, the auditor might perform some or all of the following procedures.

1. Request a statement from the bond trustee as to the amount of the bonds issued and outstanding.
2. Confirm the results of the issuance with the underwriter or investment banker.

---

*AICPA adapted.

3. Trace the cash received from the issuance to the accounting records.

4. Verify that the net cash received is credited to an account entitled "Bonds Payable."

REQUIRED

Discuss the audit objectives accomplished by each of the procedures above. Select the procedure you consider the best and state why you selected it.

*18-41. (Audit of Bond Covenant Agreements) The following covenants are extracted from the indenture of a bond issue. The indenture provides that failure to comply with its terms in any respect automatically advances the due date of the loan to the date of noncompliance (the regular due date is 20 years hence):

1. "The debtor company shall endeavor to maintain a working capital ratio of 2 to 1 at all times, and, in any fiscal year following a failure to maintain said ratio, the company shall restrict compensation of officers to a total of $100,000. Officers for this purpose shall include chairman of the board of directors, president, all vice-presidents, secretary, and treasurer."

2. "The debtor company shall keep all property that is security for this debt insured against loss by fire to the extent of 100% of its actual value. Policies of insurance comprising this protection shall be filed with the trustee."

3. "The debtor company shall pay all taxes legally assessed against property that is security for this debt within the time provided by law for payment without penalty, and shall deposit receipted tax bills or equally acceptable evidence of payment of same with the trustee."

4. "A sinking fund shall be deposited with the trustee by semiannual payments of $300,000, from which the trustee shall, in his discretion, purchase bonds of this issue."

REQUIRED

Indicate the audit procedures you would perform for each covenant. Comment on any disclosure requirements that you believe are necessary.

18-42. (Audit of Financing and Investing Cycle) Sam Cargo, CPA, is performing the 19X4 audit of Mims Corporation. While reviewing prior-year working papers, he notices that the auditor encountered the following:

1. Accrued interest revenue was computed incorrectly.

2. The fact was not disclosed that stock held in X Corporation had been pledged as collateral for a bank loan.

3. The schedule of marketable securities showed securities valued at $250,000. The general ledger account showed securities valued at $275,000. The $25,000 difference did not reconcile.

4. In March, an employee obtained securities belonging to Mims and sold them for his own personal gain. He replaced the securities in October.

5. In May, securities owned by the corporation were sold at a gain of $1,000. This $1,000 gain was incorrectly reported as net of tax.

6. On December 31, the market value of securities owned was $350,000. These securities were purchased five years earlier at $500,000.

7. The corporation owns 5,000 shares of stock that are held by an outside custodian. They are held in the name of Bill Cox, Mim's treasurer.

8. In April, the corporation purchased 10,000 shares of stock at $5 per share. The broker's fee was $300. The shares were recorded at cost and the $300 was expensed.

9. In February, Mims Corporation sold 100,000 shares of South Corporation, common stock. As a consequence, their investment of 25% dropped to 19%. They are still accounting for these shares on the equity basis.

REQUIRED

A. For each of the above, identify an audit procedure that Cargo may use to detect the error.

B. For each audit procedure, determine the audit objective met.

*18-43. (Audit of Expenses) State what documents or evidence the auditor would examine in the verification of each of the following:

A. Advertising expense, where advertising is placed through an agency.

B. Advertising expense, where advertising is placed directly in newspapers by the client.

C. Royalty expense.

D. Repair expense.

18-44. (Analytical Procedures for Income) You have performed the audit of Mount Olive Gifts Company for the past five years. Throughout these years, you have learned the following information regarding Mount Olive's operations.

1. Advertising accounts for about 5% of Mount Olive's expenses.

2. Salespeople receive a 10% commission on sales.

3. Fixed expenses of $500,000 consist of $400,000 for administrative salaries and $100,000 for depreciation.

4. Variable operating expenses are approximately 20% of sales.

5. Gross margin is approximately 45% of sales.

REQUIRED

If Mount Olive had revenue of $3 million, what would you expect net income to be under normal operations?

18-45. (Audit of Income Taxes) In connection with the audit of the financial statements of the UP Corporation, a CPA is reviewing the federal income taxes payable account.

REQUIRED

A. Discuss reasons why the CPA should review federal income tax returns for prior years and the reports of internal revenue agents.

B. What information will these reviews provide? (Do not discuss specific tax return items.)

18-46. (Audit of Stockholders' Equity) During 19X4, Whitefield Corporation had the following transactions:

1. On October 10, 5,000 shares of treasury stock were reacquired.

2. On May 30, employee stock options were issued.

3. On August 31, some employee stock options were exercised.

4. On February 2, a note payable was refinanced.

5. On July 2, common stock was issued to acquire Whitney Company.

6. On December 1, 2,000 shares of treasury stock were sold.

REQUIRED

Discuss the audit procedures the independent accountant should use to gather evidence of these transactions.

18-47. (Audit of Stock Options) Melissa Kay, CPA, is performing the year-end audit of Montgomery Corporation. Montgomery has a stock option plan and has included in a footnote to the financial statements a description of the plan; the number of options for shares authorized, granted, exercised, and expired; option prices; and the market prices of the stock on both the grant and exercise dates.

Kay knows that this information is not normally considered to be a part of the accounting records and has asked you about her responsibility for it.

REQUIRED

What is your response? Include any audit procedures you believe Kay should employ.

---

*AICPA adapted.

18-48. (Audit of Stock Accounts) Paul Roberts, CPA, is auditing the capital stock of Crusader Corporation and has noted the following:

1. In May, Crusader Corporation canceled 10,000 shares of treasury stock.
2. Crusader Corporation is considering future expansion. After locating a potential land site, 20,000 shares of stock were exchanged for the plot.
3. In October, 50 shares of $30 par common stock were exchanged for six $1,000 convertible bonds. The stock had a market value of $150.
4. In November, Crusader Corporation issued a 10% stock dividend.

REQUIRED

For Transactions **1–4** above, identify the audit procedures Roberts should use to gather evidence to support the accounting propriety of each.

18-49. (Balance Sheet Approach to an Audit) In your discussion with a member of the audit committee of an important client, you explain how your firm conducts a typical audit engagement. You state that your firm's audit philosophy is, where practicable, to perform tests of controls, perform analytical procedures, and perform direct tests of balance sheet accounts. At the end of your discussion, he says, "That sounds fine. I am impressed by your firm's credentials and your work. However, our financial statement users are more interested in net income and a continuous cash flow. I would rather have your staff emphasize the income statement."

REQUIRED

How would you respond in this situation?

Audit Judgment Case

18-50. Pineland Savings & Loan has been your audit client for the past ten years. Pineland has followed the traditional savings and loan operating philosophy of residential mortgage lending and investing in high-grade government securities. Although it has shown profits every year, lately the profits have been declining steadily.

To improve its income, last year Pineland began a new investment strategy. Management believes that residential office centers have enormous investment potential. These centers combine the concept of condominiums and office buildings by designating a specific number of lower-level floors for office space and retail stores, while the upper-level floors are residential quarters. The concept allows people who work in the offices to be very close to home and shopping.

Pineland's management has decided to provide financing for four of these centers; one each in the North, South, East, and West sides of Cityville. It has reached an agreement with Bull Contractors to build the centers. Under the agreement, Pineland will loan Bull 95% of the funds needed to acquire and develop the property for each center and construct the buildings. The loan origination fees will be included in the loan amount and the interest over the term of the loan will be added to the loan balance. Although Bull will have title to the centers they will be pledged to Pineland as collateral for the loan. In addition, the partners in Bull have personally guaranteed the loan. Bull is not required to make any payments on the loan until the projects are complete. Bull will either refinance the centers with another lender or sell them to third parties to obtain the funds to pay the loan. This arrangement gives Bull the financial resources to complete construction of the centers in three years.

Pineland has also begun to finance several leveraged corporate acquisitions. Under this investment strategy, the S&L buys high yield bonds of the combined companies and takes the assets of the company being acquired as collateral. Pineland management believes the increased yield on these bonds together with the returns from the residential office centers will improve its profitability substantially.

REQUIRED

A. Identify the specific factors the auditor should consider in assessing the risk associated with the two new investment strategies Pineland initiated.

B. For each of the investment strategies, state the major substantive audit procedures you would apply to the following financial statement accounts for the existence and valuation assertions.

- Investments in Residential Office Centers
- Investment Securities—Leveraged Corporate Acquisitions

Auditing Issues Case

18-51. KELCO MANUFACTURING COMPANY

In connection with the expansion program initiated by Kelco, the company's president Steve Cook implemented a comprehensive equipment replacement policy. Old and less

KELCO Manufacturing
Property, Plant, & Equipment & Accumulated Depreciation
12/31/X7

								Initials	Date
							Prepared By		
							Approved By		

COST	1/1/x7 BALANCE	ADDITIONS	DISPOSALS	12/31/x7 BALANCE
BUILDINGS	1250000	750000		2000000
EQUIPMENT	17500650	25792000	11252549	32040101
OFFICE EQUIPMENT	32490	21522	10025	43987
FURNITURE & FIXTURES	29282	4212		33494
	18812422	26567734	11262574	34117582
ACCUMULATED DEPRECIATION				
BUILDINGS	150000	65000		215000
EQUIPMENT	5250000	2477037	3938392	3788645
OFFICE EQUIPMENT	13924	6178		20102
FURNITURE & FIXTURES	8785	3139		11924
	5422709	2551354	3938392	4035671

efficient equipment was replaced with new high-tech manufacturing equipment. There were several additions and replacements of equipment during the year. The worksheet provided summarizes Property, Plant, and Equipment and Accumulated Depreciation for Kelco.

REQUIRED

1. There is significant audit risk associated with the balance of property, plant, and equipment. Describe at least three different audit tests that could be used to support the ending balances of property, plant, and equipment.
2. Discuss the advantages and disadvantages of each approach described above.

Chapter *19*

Completing the Engagement

Learning Objectives

- Discuss the importance of contingencies and related audit procedures.

- Explain the audit requirements regarding lawyers' letters.

- Describe the two types of events subsequent to the balance sheet date and the audit tests that should identify such events.

- Discuss the requirements for the client representation letter.

- Explain review procedures of the auditor.

- Describe the purpose and content of management letters and required communications with audit committees.

N o one phase of an audit engagement should be construed to be any more or less important than another. In this regard, the procedures to be followed in the completion of the engagement are as critical to the overall quality of the audit as the substantive tests performed during fieldwork.

An effective audit review process demonstrates the need for auditors at all levels of an engagement to have a thorough understanding of the client's industry and the nature of the transactions in which the client is engaging. Quality control aspects are often the main focus of the review process. Review notes often indicate the need to gather further information or undertake additional testing.

The scandal involving the audit of ESM Government Securities, Inc., from 1977 to 1982 demonstrates the need for a thorough review process and the need for auditors to understand the complex financial transactions related to specific industries, especially brokers and dealers in securities. In testimony from this case, partners assigned as second reviewers admitted that the firm only made cursory investigations during the review process, because its auditors lacked an understanding of the complex transactions involved. This breakdown in the review and quality control system of the audit firm clearly illustrates the importance of proper completion of an engagement. ■

Sources: R. J. Sack, and R. Tangreti, "ESM: Implications for the Profession," *Journal of Accountancy*, April 1987, pp. 94–101; M. Brannigan, "Auditor's Downfall Shows a Man Caught in Trap of His Own Making," *Wall Street Journal*, March 4, 1987, p. 33; and P. Roebuck, and K. T. Trotman, "A Field Study of the Review Process," *Abacus*, September 1992, pp. 200–210.

After the auditor has completed audit procedures in the specific audit areas discussed in the preceding chapters, he or she needs to perform certain generalized audit fieldwork procedures and wrap-up procedures to complete the engagement.

Completion of Audit Fieldwork

The generalized audit procedures that must be performed in the field to finish the audit include steps for examining contingencies, reviewing events that have occurred subsequent to the balance sheet date, and obtaining a client representation letter. The wrap-up procedures include reviewing working papers, drawing conclusions, securing client approval of adjusting entries and disclosures, drafting the management letter, and communicating certain information about audit scope and results to the audit committee.

Audit of Contingencies

FASB No. 5, Accounting for Contingencies, defines a *contingency* as "an existing condition, situation or circumstance involving uncertainty as to possible gain or loss to an enterprise that will ultimately be resolved when one or more future events occur or fail to occur." *FASB No. 5* also delineates the accounting and reporting requirements for ***loss contingencies***. Specifically, this standard of financial reporting requires that

any loss contingency that both is probable and can be reasonably estimated must be accrued. Contingencies that are probable but cannot be estimated and contingencies that are reasonably possible are not accrued but must be disclosed. Gain contingencies are not accrued until they are realized, although they may be disclosed.

Examples of loss contingencies include the following:

- Litigation
- Disagreement with the government regarding income taxes owed
- Collectibility of a receivable
- Guarantees of obligation of others

As part of the audit of the financial statements, the auditor should include audit procedures regarding loss contingencies to determine that all material loss contingencies have been properly accounted for and appropriately disclosed.

General Audit Procedures

By definition, a contingency is an uncertainty regarding the occurrence of a future event. The auditor's primary concern is the completeness assertion for contingencies, that is, determining if contingencies exist that have not been reported. This is often a difficult audit task because the auditor is attempting to discover an item that is unrecorded. Once having discovered a contingency, the auditor must evaluate the appropriate accounting and disclosure requirements for fair presentation in conformity with generally accepted accounting principles.

SAS No. 12, Inquiry of a Client's Lawyer Concerning Litigation, Claims, and Assessments (AU 337), identifies audit procedures that the auditor should consider with respect to loss contingencies. These procedures include the following:

- Inquiring of management regarding the possibility of loss contingencies and management policies for identifying, evaluating, and accounting for loss contingencies.
- Examining documents in the client's possession concerning litigation, claims, and assessments, including correspondence and invoices from lawyers.
- Reading minutes of meetings of stockholders, directors, and appropriate committees held during and subsequent to the period being audited.
- Reading contracts, loan agreements, leases, and correspondence from tax or other government agencies.
- Gathering information concerning guarantees from bank confirmations.
- Inspecting other documents for possible guarantees by the client.

These procedures represent some but not all of the many audit steps the auditor may consider in the examination of contingencies.

Lawyers' Letters

SAS No. 12 (AU 337.08) requires an auditor, as part of his or her gathering of evidence regarding fair presentation in conformity with *FASB No. 5*, to make certain inquiries of the client's lawyer about litigation loss contingencies. This written representation from the client's lawyer to the auditor is frequently referred to as a ***lawyer's letter*** or ***attorney's representation letter***. Ideally this letter informs the auditor of any litigation of which the lawyer is aware and any other relevant information that may require financial statement disclosure. The lawyer's letter should also give the auditor evidence, in the form of the lawyer's opinion, as to the expected outcome of any lawsuits and the likely amount of any liability.

Figure 19-1

Figure 19-1 **Flowchart of *SAS No. 12***

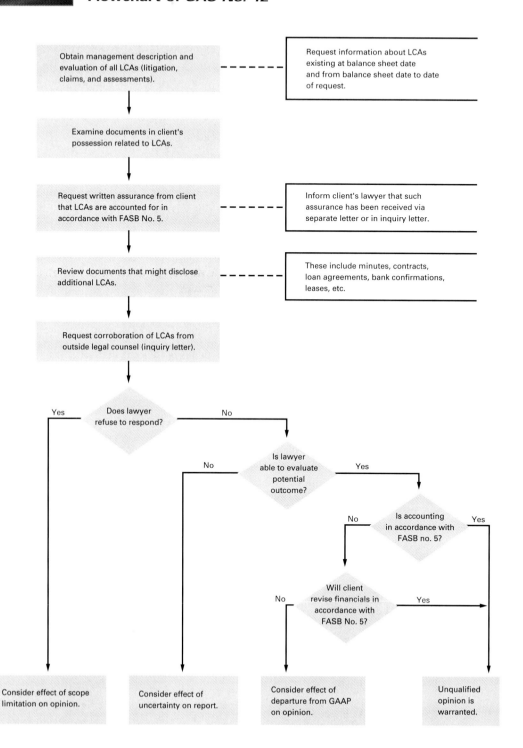

Potential Conflict   Although the auditor needs this type of information, lawyers may be reluctant to provide such information due to their client confidentiality requirements and the possibility of exposure to legal liability. Prior to the issuance of *SAS No. 12*, significant controversy existed between auditors and lawyers regarding the professional responsibilities of each group. *SAS No. 12*, along with an American Bar Association Statement of Policy, attempted to resolve this conflict between the auditor and the lawyer by establishing responsibilities for each profession (Figure 19–1).

Responsibilities   Responsibilities for contingencies and uncertainties exist for three parties: the lawyer, the client, and the auditor. Figure 19–2 illustrates the responsibilities of the parties and the chronological order of the steps involved.

In step 1 of Figure 19–2, the lawyer, as part of his or her professional responsibility, advises the client on litigation, claims, and assessments. After receiving this advice, the client discloses litigation, claims, and assessments to the CPA (step 2).

Figure 19–2   **Responsibilities of Lawyer, Client, and CPA for Litigation, Claims, and Assessments (LCAs)**

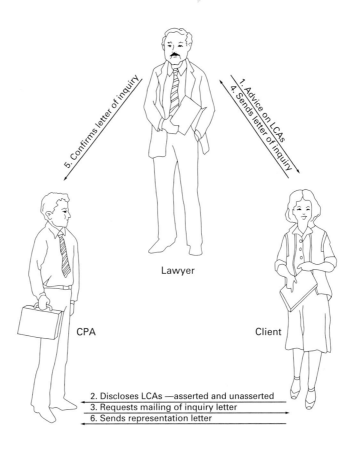

Lawyer

CPA

Client

5. Confirms letter of inquiry

1. Advice on LCAs
4. Sends letter of inquiry

2. Discloses LCAs —asserted and unasserted
3. Requests mailing of inquiry letter
6. Sends representation letter

In step 3, the CPA requests the client to send a letter of inquiry (see Figure 19–3) to the lawyers with whom the client has consulted concerning litigation, claims, and assessments. In this letter of inquiry (step 4), the client requests the lawyer to confirm three areas: (1) asserted claims, (2) unasserted claims that are probable of assertion and reasonably possible or probable of being unfavorable, and (3) the lawyer's advisory responsibility with respect to *FASB No. 5* pertaining to unasserted claims. The letter of inquiry may be either in long form, in which the client asks the attorney to comment on the completeness of information provided by the client, or in short form, in which the lawyer is requested to prepare the information rather than comment on the client's list. After receiving the letter of inquiry from the client, the lawyer confirms these items to the CPA in the lawyer's representation letter (step 5). Refusal by the client's lawyer to furnish the information requested in the client's letter of inquiry represents a limitation in the scope of the auditor's examination sufficient to preclude an unqualified opinion. Finally (step 6), the client sends a written representation letter to the CPA, as required by *SAS No. 19, Client Representations* (AU 333). The client representation letter is discussed later in this chapter.

The lawyer may confirm an *asserted* claim not disclosed by the client to the CPA. This is not considered a breach of lawyer-client confidentiality. However, in the case of an *unasserted* claim, no such disclosure option exists. The lawyer cannot unilaterally disclose an unasserted claim to the CPA but, rather, must request the client to disclose the unasserted claim to the CPA. If the client refuses, the lawyer may be forced to resign. In addition, management confirms in the representation letter that all claims (asserted and unasserted) that the lawyer has advised the client to disclose have been made known to the auditor.

Figure 19–3   **Client's Letter of Inquiry to Lawyer**

> **Cotton Trade Corporation**
> **2320 Madison Towers**
> **Chicago, Illinois 60602**
>
> **Mr. Bill Godwin, Attorney**   **January 14, 19X5**
> **Godwin and Godwin**
> **3043 Lansdowne Drive**
> **Seattle, Washington 98101**
>
> **Dear Mr. Godwin:**
>
> **Alsup and Caradine, CPAs, 2322 South Towers, Morrisville, New Jersey 08711, are making their usual audit of our financial statements. Please furnish our auditors with the information requested below involving matters as to which you have been engaged and to which you have devoted substantive attention on behalf of the Company in the form of legal consultation or representation. Your response should include matters that existed at December 31, 19X4, and for the period from that date to the date of your response.**

Figure 19-3 *continued*

Pending or Threatened Litigation
(excluding unasserted claims and assessments)

Please prepare a description of all material litigation, claims, and assessments (excluding unasserted claims and assessments). Materiality for purposes of this letter includes items involving amounts exceeding $25,000 individually or items involving lesser amounts that exceed $50,000 in the aggregate. The description of each case should include the following:

1. The nature of the litigation,
2. The progress of the case to date,
3. How management is responding or intends to respond to the litigation (e.g., to contest the case vigorously or to seek out-of-court settlement), and
4. An evaluation of the likelihood of an unfavorable outcome and an estimate, if one can be made, of the amount or range of potential loss.

Unasserted Claims and Assessments

We understand that whenever, in the course of performing legal services for us with respect to a matter recognized to involve an unasserted possible claim or assessment that may call for financial statement disclosure, if you have formed a professional conclusion that we should disclose or consider disclosure concerning such possible claim or assessment, as a matter of professional responsibility to us you will so advise us and will consult with us concerning the question of such disclosure and the applicable requirements of Statement of Financial Accounting Standards No. 5. Please specifically confirm to our auditors that our understanding is correct.

We have assured our auditors that you have not advised us of any unasserted claims or assessments that are probable of assertion and must be disclosed in accordance with Statement of Financial Accounting Standards No. 5.

Other Matters

Please identify the nature of and reasons for any limitation on your response. Also, please indicate the amount we (and our subsidiaries) were indebted to you for services and expenses on December 31, 19X4.

The scheduled completion of the audit is such that you should send your letter to Alsup and Caradine, CPAs, on or about February 25, 19X5.

Very truly yours,

Stan MacDonald

Stan MacDonald
Treasurer

Events Subsequent to the Balance Sheet Date

A financial statement presents a company's financial position as of a certain date (the balance sheet date). However, sometimes events or transactions occur after that date but before the auditor actually issues the audit report that may affect the financial statements. These events are referred to as *subsequent events*.

SAS No. 1, Subsequent Events (AU 560), identifies two types of subsequent events: those that provide additional evidence with respect to conditions that existed at the date of the balance sheet and affect the estimates inherent in the process of preparing financial statements (Type I), and those that provide evidence with respect to conditions that did not exist at the date of the balance sheet but arose subsequent to that date (Type II). Type II events should not result in an adjustment to the financial statements but may require disclosure in the statements.

Type I Subsequent Events

Certain events or transactions that occur after the balance sheet date provide additional evidence to the auditor about conditions that existed at the date of the balance sheet and affect estimates involved in the audit process. For example, the auditor may have difficulty determining whether or not a particular account receivable is collectible. The customer is in financial trouble and the auditor is undecided about the collectibility of the account. After the balance sheet date, this customer declares bankruptcy. Clearly this subsequent event gives further evidence to the auditor that the account is indeed uncollectible. Such events provide information that allows the auditor to adjust the financial statements.

Other examples of events that have a direct effect on financial statements include the following:

- Settlement of litigation for an amount different than that recorded
- Sale of investments at a price below the carrying value on the books
- Sale of obsolete or scrapped inventory at a price less than that recorded in the entity's records

The auditor should exercise care in determining that the event does in fact reflect a condition that existed at the balance sheet date. In the example involving the uncollectible account, the customer was in poor financial condition as of year-end. The event of filing for bankruptcy subsequent to year-end merely provided additional evidence of the poor financial condition of the customer. If, however, the customer had been in good financial condition at year-end but due to some unusual subsequent event filed for bankruptcy (for example, a flood or other natural catastrophe), the event would not reflect a condition that existed at the balance sheet date. Accordingly the auditor would not use that information to adjust the amounts in the financial statements. However, the event may need to be disclosed in the financial statements as a Type II subsequent event.

Type II Subsequent Events

Certain subsequent events provide evidence with respect to conditions that did *not* exist at the date of the balance sheet but arose subsequently. These events do not result in adjustment of financial statements but may be of such a nature that disclosure is necessary for fair presentation of the statements.

Examples of this second type of subsequent event include the following:

- Sale of a bond or capital stock issue
- Purchase of a business
- Litigation that arises subsequent to the balance sheet date
- Loss of plant or inventories as a result of fire or flood
- Loss of receivables resulting from conditions arising subsequent to the balance sheet date

Audit Procedures

By necessity, the auditor completes the audit subsequent to the balance sheet date. That period of time from the balance sheet date to the date of the audit report is referred to as the *subsequent period*. Many normal audit procedures performed during this time provide evidence of subsequent events.

For example, cutoff procedures that are applied as part of normal substantive audit tests typically use information subsequent to year-end. When performing a sales or purchases cutoff, the auditor obtains information regarding sales or purchases not only before year-end but also immediately following year-end. Likewise, in determining accounts receivable valuation, the auditor often looks at cash collections subsequent to the balance sheet date. Many situations occur where the auditor performs normal audit procedures that involve subsequent events.

However, in addition to these normal audit procedures, the auditor should perform other audit tests to ascertain whether or not subsequent events exist that require either adjustment or disclosure. *SAS No. 1* (AU 560.12) lists a variety of procedures, including the following:

Read Interim Financial Statements The auditor should read any available interim financial statements and compare them with the financial statements being reported upon. The auditor should particularly be concerned with any major changes reflected in those interim statements from year-end.

Management Inquiries The auditor should inquire of management as to whether any substantial contingent liabilities or commitments exist; whether there was any significant change in capital stock, long-term debt, or working capital to the date of the inquiry; whether there has been a change in the status of items that were accounted for in the financial statements on the basis of tentative or inconclusive data; and whether any unusual adjustments have been made during the period subsequent to the balance sheet date.

Read Available Minutes The auditor should read the available minutes of meetings of stockholders, directors, and appropriate committees. Important subsequent events such as lawsuits and the issuance of bonds are often discussed at these meetings.

Inquiries of Legal Counsel The auditor should make an inquiry of the client's legal counsel concerning litigation, claims, and assessments. This representation is obtained by receipt of the attorney's letter, as discussed previously.

Other Procedures   The auditor should make additional inquiries or perform other procedures that are necessary in the circumstances. For example, auditors frequently scan all journals and ledgers subsequent to year-end to identify unusual transactions.

Audit Personnel

The subsequent events review should be conducted by an auditor who is familiar with both the client and the particular audit engagement. To identify those items that require either disclosure or adjustment to the financial statements, the auditor must understand the client, its financial statements, and the audit procedures performed to date. This understanding is possible only if the auditor has a detailed knowledge of the client's business and the industry in which the client operates. The BarChris Construction Corporation case discussed in Chapter 3 indicates the importance of the performance of the subsequent events review by an auditor who has the requisite knowledge.

Client Representation Letter

Management representation letter

During an audit engagement, management makes many responses to inquiries by the auditor. These oral representations by client personnel are additional evidence regarding the fair presentation of the financial statements. Accordingly, these representations should be documented by the auditor. This is accomplished by the receipt of a ***client representation letter*** from management.

Critical

Purpose

The primary objective of the client representation letter is to document the oral responses that client personnel have provided in response to auditor inquiries. Not only does it provide additional evidence to the auditor, the letter also provides written documentation in case of a disagreement or a lawsuit between the auditor and the client. The second objective of the client representation letter is to emphasize to the client its responsibilities for the financial statements. The letter of representation should state that the financial statements are the representation of management and include other important representations that management has previously made orally. By requiring management to read these representations and then sign a written document, the auditor emphasizes to management the importance of these representations.

Scope Limitation Qualified

Requirements

SAS No. 19, Client Representations (AU 333), requires the auditor to obtain a written letter of representation from management. These written representations are a part of the auditor's evidential matter. According to *SAS No. 19* (AU 333.02), the client representation letter is not a substitute for other auditing procedures but nonetheless represents an essential component of audit evidence. Management's refusal to furnish a written letter of representation constitutes a limitation on the scope of the auditor's examination sufficient to preclude an unqualified opinion.

Items Included in the Letter

SAS No. 19 (AU 333.04) identifies a variety of items normally included in a client representation letter. For four of these items, *SAS No. 19* (AU 333.05) notes that no materiality limitations exist: that is, these representations should be in the letter regardless of materiality. These four items are

- management's acknowledgment of its responsibility for the fair presentation of the financial statements.

- availability of all financial records and related data.
- completeness and availability of all minutes of meetings of stockholders, directors, and committees of directors.
- irregularities involving management or employees.

SAS No. 19 (AU 333.06) also identifies a variety of other items that should be included in the client representation letter, provided these items are either individually or collectively material. For example, information regarding subsequent events, losses from sales commitments, losses from purchase commitments, gain and loss contingencies, and capital stock repurchase options or agreements should be included in the client representation letter. Although not required by *SAS No. 19*, other pronouncements effectively require the auditor to make some representations. For example, *SAS No. 12* (AU 337.09) requires the auditor to obtain a representation from management regarding unasserted claims.

Example

An example of a written representation letter from *SAS No. 19* (AU 333A.05) is shown in Figure 19–4. Auditors frequently modify the wording of this letter to make technical terms more understandable or to tailor it to the particular circumstances of the engagement. For example, many auditors modify the illustrative letter to include a representation that management acknowledges its responsibility for recording proposed audit adjusting entries.

Professional Judgment

Completing the Engagement

The auditor's primary means of corroborating the information concerning litigation, claims, and assessments furnished by management is the letter of inquiry to the client's lawyer. The auditor must properly exercise professional judgment in evaluating the responses or nonresponses to the inquiry, knowing that the lawyer is an advocate of the client and, therefore, is biased.

A lawyer is not required to breach the confidentiality obligation to the client when discussing litigation with the auditor. However, on the basis of the legal profession's code of ethics, the lawyer is prohibited from lying to the auditor. Once the auditor is satisfied that the lawyer's response is complete, he or she must determine whether an appropriate accrual has been made, or if disclosure is required of a loss contingency based on the likelihood of an unfavorable outcome and the effects, if any, on the auditor's report.

When a client's lawyer refuses to comment on a sensitive issue raised by the auditor, that refusal should be a warning signal to the auditor to scrutinize the issue in more depth. In the case of ESM Government Securities, Inc., as discussed in the opening vignette to this chapter, no documentation existed regarding the communication that took place between ESM's attorney, Steve Arky, and the Alexander Grant auditors. Proper documentation of the communication with the lawyer could have led the auditors to become aware of fraudulent transactions perpetrated by ESM. Even with lawyers, auditors are required to display a sense of professional skepticism in obtaining evidence.

Sources: R. J. Sack, and R. Tangreti, "ESM: Implications for the Profession," *Journal of Accountancy*, April 1987, pp. 94–101; M. Brannigan, "Auditor's Downfall Shows a Man Caught in Trap of His Own Making," *Wall Street Journal*, March 4, 1987, p. 33; and R. M. Temple, and J. M. Wolosky, "Evaluating Lawyers' Responses to Audit Inquiry Letters," *CPA Journal*, June 1994, pp. 60–61.

Figure 19-4

Client Representation Letter

Written record.

Powell and Hancock, Inc.
One Financial Center
Concord, New Hampshire 08114

Ms. Molly Lindsey, CPA   February 8, 19X5
3020 FTE Tower
Montgomery, Alabama 36101

Dear Ms. Lindsey:

In connection with your audit of the financial statements of Powell and Hancock as of December 31, 19X4, and for the year ending December 31, 19X4, for the purpose of expressing an opinion as to whether the financial statements present fairly the financial position, results of operations, and cash flows of Powell and Hancock in conformity with generally accepted accounting principles, we confirm, to the best of our knowledge and belief, the following representations made to you during your audit.

1. We are responsible for the fair presentation in the financial statements of financial position, results of operations, and cash flows in conformity with generally accepted accounting principles.

2. We have made available to you all (a) financial records and related data and (b) minutes of the meetings of stockholders, directors, and committees of directors, or summaries of actions of recent meetings for which minutes have not yet been prepared.

3. There have been no
   a. irregularities involving management or employees who have significant roles in the internal control structure.
   b. irregularities involving other employees that could have a material effect on the financial statements.
   c. communications from regulatory agencies concerning noncompliance with, or deficiencies in, financial reporting practices that could have a material effect on the financial statements.

4. We have no plans or intentions that may materially affect the carrying value or classification of assets and liabilities.

5. The following have been properly recorded or disclosed in the financial statements:
   a. Related party transactions and related amounts receivable or payable, including sales, purchases, loans, transfers, leasing arrangements, and guarantees.
   b. Capital stock repurchase options or agreements or capital stock reserved for options, warrants, conversions, or other requirements.

Figure 19-4 *continued*

    c. Arrangements with financial institutions involving compensating balances or other arrangements involving restrictions on cash balances and line-of-credit or similar arrangements.

    d. Agreements to repurchase assets previously sold.

6. There are no violations or possible violations of laws or regulations whose effects should be considered for disclosure in the financial statements or as a basis for recording a loss contingency. Nor are there other material liabilities or gain or loss contingencies that are required to be accrued or disclosed by Statement of Financial Accounting Standards No. 5.

7. There are no unasserted claims or assessments that our lawyer has advised us are probable of assertion and must be disclosed in accordance with Statement of Financial Accounting Standards No. 5.

8. All material transactions have been properly recorded in the accounting records underlying the financial statements.

9. Provision, when material, has been made to reduce excess or obsolete inventories to their estimated net realizable value.

10. The company has satisfactory title to all owned assets, and there are no liens or encumbrances on such assets nor has any asset been pledged.

11. Provision has been made for any material loss to be sustained in the fulfillment of, or from inability to fulfill, any sales commitments.

12. Provision has been made for any material loss sustained as a result of purchase commitments for inventory quantities in excess of normal requirements or at prices in excess of the prevailing market prices.

13. We have complied with all aspects of contractual agreements that would have a material effect on the financial statements in the event of noncompliance.

14. No events have occurred subsequent to the balance sheet date that would require adjustment to, or disclosure in, the financial statements.

James Hancock   *Eddie Powell*

James Hancock   Eddie Powell
Chief Financial Officer   Chief Executive Officer

Wrap-Up Procedures

Once having completed all substantive fieldwork audit procedures, the auditor is ready to wrap up the audit. However, several generalized procedures must still be performed before the report can be issued. These include reviewing the working papers, drawing conclusions, securing client approval of adjusting entries and disclosures, drafting the *SAS No. 60* letter, and communicating with the audit committee.

Working Paper Review

Partners get heavily involved

Thorough Review

Auditors at the supervisory level, including a partner of the firm, should perform a wrap-up review of working papers prepared by the audit staff. During this review, the auditor is required to use analytical procedures as noted in Chapter 11. In addition to this final or working paper review, many CPA firms require a second, or "cold," review. This second review typically is conducted by a partner in the firm who has not been involved in the audit. The second reviewer generally focuses on the quality of the audit work and the quality control standards of the firm. By having a cold review, the CPA firm attempts to reduce any bias towards the client or towards certain audit procedures.

The wrap-up review allows the auditor to evaluate the work of less-experienced personnel, indicates compliance with professional standards regarding supervision, and demonstrates the auditing firm's compliance with quality control standards.

Evaluating the Performance of Less-Experienced Personnel

Many audit procedures are performed by staff accountants who have little experience with a particular client or engagement. In these cases, even though he or she may have the necessary technical skills, the auditor may lack expertise with regard to the client or the engagement. The first standard of fieldwork requires that the work be adequately supervised. An audit senior or supervisor should review the audit work of inexperienced personnel to evaluate the judgments made during the performance of audit procedures and to document that the work has been adequately supervised.

Quality Control

The review process also allows the auditing firm to demonstrate its commitment to quality control standards. By assigning supervisory audit personnel the responsibility of reviewing audit working papers, the firm indicates that, although performance may vary among individuals, the review process by upper-level personnel will allow the firm to maintain high quality.

Reduction of Bias

The auditor performing a specific audit procedure sometimes becomes so involved in the mechanics of the particular procedure that he or she loses sight of its overall purpose. Likewise, the auditor may become so engrossed in performing the procedure that he or she forgets to document or communicate certain aspects or findings that result from applying those procedures. Thus, the third primary purpose of the review process is to counteract the bias that often is entered into the working papers by the auditor who is performing specific audit procedures.

When reviewing the working papers, the supervisory auditor looks for a variety of items. For example, the reviewing auditor should make sure the working paper is properly prepared, that is, that it is dated, headed correctly, and initialed. The supervisor should determine that calculations are accurate, that all balances agree with the working trial balance, and that all adjusting entries have been posted. One of the most important things the supervisory auditor does in the review process is to determine the purpose of the working paper: Does the working paper serve an important purpose? Does the working paper support the conclusions of the audit?

In reviewing working papers, the auditor must recognize that they are documentation of the evidence collected and conclusions drawn. They are the auditor's primary evidence that the audit has been conducted in accordance with generally accepted auditing standards and that the conclusions have been appropriately reached. As a consequence, the auditor must understand that working papers may become primary evidence in legal liability cases. Of course, the review process should never be designed merely to protect the auditor from legal liability exposure.

In the review process, the auditor should make sure that the working papers demonstrate that generally accepted auditing standards have been complied with, that the conclusions are appropriate, and that the items of evidence on each working paper support the overall conclusion that the statements are presented fairly in conformity with generally accepted accounting principles. Thus, a reviewer must make sure all numbers tie to the working trial balance and financial statements, there are no unanswered questions left in the working papers, the conclusions are stated clearly, and any material inconsistencies are further investigated so that all the evidence supports the auditor's overall conclusions.

Drawing Conclusions

The purpose of the audit is to gather evidence that will allow the auditor to issue an opinion that the financial statements are fairly presented in conformity with generally accepted accounting principles. At some point, then, the auditor must evaluate the evidence collected to make the determination regarding fairness. The auditor's basic question is "Given the evidence I have obtained, do I have reasonable assurance that the Financial Statements are fairly presented in conformity with GAAP?" The auditors have spent their time performing numerous audit procedures; while these procedures are crucial for the audit, the procedures themselves are not the final objective. Rather, all of the work the auditors have done should focus on the basic issue of whether in the auditor's opinion the financial statements are fairly presented. After performing the many detailed audit procedures (the trees), it is often difficult for the auditor to focus on the overall objective (the forest).

Client Approval of Adjusting Entries and Disclosures

The financial statements are the representations of management. Although the auditor may frequently prepare the necessary adjusting entries and draft the financial statements and related footnotes, management must nonetheless accept ultimate responsibility for the fairness of the statements. The auditor is responsible for the opinion on the financial statements, whereas management is responsible for the financial statements themselves.

During the course of the engagement, the auditor may determine that certain adjusting entries need to be made for the financial statements to be presented fairly in conformity with generally accepted accounting principles. The auditor may propose these adjusting entries; management must determine whether to accept them. Thus, the auditor should get management to approve any adjusting entries before they are recorded. Preferably, the auditor gives the client the list of adjusting entries, the client approves those adjusting entries, and the entries are then recorded by the client in the accounting records.

Likewise, notes drafted by the auditor for inclusion in the financial statements should also be approved by management. The notes, which are an integral part of the financial statements, are also management's representation.

During the course of the audit, the auditor may also propose several adjusting entries that, when materiality guidelines are applied, would be considered to have an

Figure 19-5 **Waived Adjusting Entries**

#	Accounts				Assets	Liabilities	Owner's Equity	Net Income		
							Effects on			
1	Salaries Expense	1000								
	Accrued Salaries		1000				1000	<1000>	<1000>	
2	Interest Expense	150								
	Accrued Interest		150				150	<150>	<150>	
3	Accounts Receivable	1100					1100		1100	1100
	Sales		1100				1100			
4	Repairs & Maintenance	300								
	Capital Improvements		300	<300>				<300>	<300>	
5	Advertising Expense	200								
	Accounts Payable		200				200	<200>	<200>	
	Total				800	1350	<550>	<550>		

Colby Industries — Proposed Adjusting Journal Entries. Prepared By JPC 2-12-X5

Net effect on financial statements immaterial. Above proposed AJEs waived. JPC immaterial effect on the financial statements. Immaterial adjustments are usually waived. However the auditor should prepare a working paper to document waived adjustments. Although individual adjusting entries may be immaterial, the sum of these waived adjusting entries could very well have a material effect on the financial statements. Figure 19–5 presents an example of a waived adjusting entry working paper.

SAS No. 60 Letter

SAS No. 60, Communication of Internal Control Structure Related Matters Noted in an Audit (AU 325), as discussed in Chapter 6, requires the auditor to communicate all discovered reportable conditions in the internal control structure to the client. In addition, auditors often include in the *SAS No. 60* letter other observations and suggestions regarding the entity's activities. For example, the auditor may recommend ways to improve cash flow or methods to maximize interest income. The auditor's experiences with a variety of entities and his or her understanding of the particular client give the auditor the necessary expertise to make recommendations beneficial to the client. Figure 19–6 shows an illustrative *SAS No. 60* letter. Table 19–1 summarizes the different types of letters used in auditing.

Figure 19–6   *SAS No. 60* **Letter**

To the Board of Directors of Macon Savings Bank:

In planning and performing our audit of the financial statements of the Macon Savings Bank for the year ended December 31, 19X4, we considered its internal control structure in order to determine our auditing procedures for the purpose of expressing our opinion on the financial statements and not to provide assurance on the internal control structure. However, we noted certain matters involving the internal control structure and its operation that we consider to be reportable conditions under standards established by the American Institute of Certified Public Accountants. Reportable conditions involve matters coming to our attention relating to significant deficiencies in the design or operation of the internal control structure that, in our judgment, could adversely affect the organization's ability to record, process, summarize, and report financial data consistent with the assertions of management in the financial statements.

CASH

Two of the bank accounts had not been reconciled for several months. One of the general ledger accounts contained substantial errors that resulted from misclassification of charges and that required adjustments to earnings at audit date. We also noted that some bank reconciliations had not been approved by an officer.

continued

Figure 19–6 *continued*

To prevent recurrences of this situation, we recommend that a time frame be established for the prompt reconciliation of each bank account at the end of each month. We also recommend that a control sheet be maintained for all bank statements from the time they come into the bank through the time the reconciliations and statements have been reviewed by an officer and placed in the file. The officer's approval should be clearly indicated on the reconciliation form.

MORTGAGE LOANS

Loan payments are often received by the bank which, for various reasons, cannot be entered by the tellers. These payments must necessarily be held until the account is further investigated and the payment subsequently entered. However, during our examination we noted a check that had been held for an unusually long period of time. Such a procedure not only results in a weakening of the internal control structure, but also reduces the bank's funds available for investment. We recommend that the bank maintain a memo control over all such payments. This control should include both the date payment was received and the date payment was entered. Further, this memo control should be reviewed periodically by appropriate supervisory personnel and any unusual time lags should be investigated.

The bank possesses several savings passbooks and certificates that have been pledged as additional collateral on mortgage loans. The bank maintains no formal register of this collateral. We recommend that the bank maintain a register of additional collateral pledged. We further recommend that all such collateral be placed under dual control. We also noted several savings accounts pledged for which there was no lockout or "Hold" status on the terminal. All pledged accounts should have a "Hold" status so that unauthorized withdrawals can be prevented.

HOME IMPROVEMENT LOANS

We noted three new home improvement loans that were neither noted nor approved in the minutes of the board of directors. The minutes of the board of directors should include approval of all loans.

GENERAL

We noted some journal voucher numbers that were used more than once. For journal voucher numbers to serve a useful purpose, it is imperative that numbers be used only once and in sequential order.

This report is intended solely for the information and use of the audit committee, management, and others within the organization.

Richard B. Hare

Richard B. Hare
Hare and Dozier, CPAs

Communication with Audit Committees

The continually increasing responsibility of audit committees to oversee the financial reporting process has created a need for improved auditor communication. *SAS No. 61, Communication with Audit Committees* (AU 380), makes the auditor responsible for ensuring that certain matters are communicated to those with designated responsibility for oversight of the financial reporting process. *SAS No. 61* requires additional audit-related communications beyond the requirements to communicate irregularities and illegal acts (as discussed in Chapter 3) and reportable conditions (as discussed in Chapter 6).

The communications required by *SAS No. 61* may be oral or written, but if they are communicated orally, the auditor should document them in the audit working papers. The communications specified are incidental to the audit and should be made on a timely basis, but not necessarily before the issuance of the auditor's report. Further, management may communicate some of the specified items to the audit committee, but the auditor should be satisfied that such communications have, in fact, occurred.

Information about irregularities and illegal acts as required by *SAS No. 53* and *SAS No. 54* and reportable conditions in the internal control structure as required by *SAS No. 60* must be communicated to the audit committee or those within the entity that have either formal or informal (e.g., the owner) oversight responsibilities for financial reporting. However, in addition *SAS No. 61* specifically requires additional

---

The Real World of Auditing

Auditor Communication with Audit Committees

Facts: An accounting firm was engaged to perform a year-end audit for a large commercial bank. During the audit year in question, the son of the bank president was employed by the bank as a securities broker and embezzled over $16 million. The accounting firm had uncovered multiple discrepancies in the trading accounts resulting from the embezzlement, but the firm failed to report these discrepancies to the audit committee. Instead, they reported the embezzlement to the bank president, who promised to settle the matter himself. He did not, however, act on the advice.

The embezzlement was later discovered by the bank's internal accounting department. The bank president and his son were dismissed, and the bank's board of directors and shareholders filed suit against the accounting firm for $20 million in damages.

Issues: The clients alleged that because the accounting firm knew of the relationship between the bank president and the embezzler, they were negligent in reporting the defalcation to the president. They also claimed that much of the damage could have been prevented if the irregularity had been reported to the appropriate level of management.

Resolution: This case was indefensible, and the accounting firm settled for the limiting of its professional liability policy, totalling $5 million.

Commentary: This was a case of absolute liability for the accounting firm, because it failed to report the irregularity to the appropriate level of management and to resolve the financial statement discrepancies.

Source: *Accountants Legal Liability Guide*, G. Spellmire, W. Baliga, D. Winiarski, Harcourt Brace Jovanovich, p. 3.38.

Table 19-1	Common Types of Letters Used in Auditing			
Type of Letter		Recipient	Sender	When Sent
Proposal letter		Client	Auditor	Before client engages an auditor
Engagement letter		Client	Auditor	Before audit begins but after the proposal is accepted
Lawyer's letter		Auditor	Lawyer	Near completion of fieldwork
Client representation letter		Auditor	Client	At completion of fieldwork
SAS No. 60 letter		Client	Auditor	At interim dates after completing parts of the audit or at earliest practicable date following completion of the audit

communications by the auditor (1) to the audit committee or any *formally* designated oversight group and (2) for all SEC engagements. These additional communications required by *SAS No. 61* include the following:

1. The auditor's responsibility in an audit and the nature of the assurance provided.
2. The auditor's responsibility for other information in documents containing audited financial statements. (This other information is discussed in Chapter 21.)
3. The initial selection of and changes in significant accounting policies or their application.
4. The process that management uses in formulating sensitive accounting estimates and the basis for the auditor's conclusions about the reasonableness of those estimates.
5. Any audit adjustments, whether recorded or not, that could have a significant effect on the financial reporting process.
6. Any disagreements with management, whether satisfactorily resolved or not, about matters that could be significant to the entity's financial statements or the auditor's report.

Required?	Chapter Reference	Authoritative Reference	Other Comments
Optional	Chapter 12	—	Letter by auditor describing his or her proposal.
Optional	Chapter 12	—	Optional letter by auditor outlining terms of the audit. Most auditors send engagement letters.
Yes	Chapter 19	*SAS No. 12* (AU 337)	Required if client has an attorney. Letter gives auditor evidence on litigations, claims, and assessments.
Yes	Chapter 19	*SAS No. 19* (AU 333)	Letter from client that documents important client representations.
Communication is required (preferably in writing)	Chapter 6	*SAS No. 60* (AU 325)	Reportable conditions observed by the auditor should be communicated, either in writing or orally. The auditor is not required to continue to communicate reportable conditions in subsequent audits.

7. The auditor's view on significant matters that were the subject of consultation with other accountants. (Second opinions are discussed in Chapter 21.)
8. The major issues discussed with management in connection with the initial or recurring retention of the auditor.
9. Any serious difficulties encountered with management in performing the audit (for example, did management set an unreasonable timetable for the audit?).

Significant Terms

Attorney's representation letter See Lawyer's letter.

Client representation letter A letter from management that documents management's oral responses to the auditor's inquiries about the fair presentation of the financial statements and management's responsibility for the financial statements.

Lawyer's letter   The written representation from the client's lawyer to the auditor that describes and evaluates pending or threatened litigation, claims, and assessments to which the lawyer has devoted significant attention. Also known as *attorney's representation letter*.

Loss contingency   Any condition involving uncertainty as to a possible loss by an enterprise that will ultimately be resolved when one or more future events occur or fail to occur.

SAS No. 60 **letter**   A letter from the auditor communicating reportable conditions in the internal control structure of the client.

Subsequent events   Events or transactions that have a potential effect on the financial statements and that occur after the balance sheet date but prior to the issuance of the auditor's report.

Subsequent period   The period of time from the balance sheet date to the date of the audit report.

Working paper review   Review by supervising auditors of the working papers prepared by the audit staff.

Discussion Questions

19-1.   What are the financial reporting requirements for loss contingencies?

19-2.   What is the auditor's primary concern regarding loss contingencies? Why?

19-3.   Discuss audit procedures described in *SAS No. 12, Inquiry of a Client's Lawyer Concerning Litigation, Claims, and Assessments,* for loss contingencies and state what objective each procedure might accomplish.

19-4.   What three parties are involved with the lawyer's letter? What are the responsibilities of each?

19-5.   What is the attorney's responsibility regarding disclosure of unasserted claims to the auditor?

19-6.   Define a *subsequent event.* Why are subsequent events important to the auditor?

19-7.   What are the two types of subsequent events? What is their effect on the financial statements? Give two examples of each type of subsequent event.

19-8.   Describe audit procedures that the auditor could perform to detect subsequent events.

19-9.   What qualifications should the auditor possess who is performing a subsequent events review? Why are these qualifications needed?

19-10.   What is the client representation letter and what is its purpose? Why does *SAS No. 19, Client Representations,* require a client representation letter?

19-11.   What effect would management's refusal to provide a written representation letter have on the audit?

19-12.   What six items are normally included in the management representation letter? Why are they included?

19-13.   How does materiality affect the inclusion of items in the client representation letter?

19-14.   How does the working paper review reduce bias in an audit? What other purposes does the review process serve?

19-15.   Describe the purpose of a second, or "cold," review.

19-16.   Why should the client have to approve all of the auditor's proposed adjusting entries?

19-17.   What are the purposes of *SAS No. 60* letter? Are *SAS No. 60* letters required?

19-18.   What are the auditor's responsibilities for communicating with a client's audit committee? Describe five items the auditor should communicate.

Objective Questions

*19-19. A CPA has received a lawyer's letter in which no significant disagreements with the client's assessments of contingent liabilities were noted. The resignation of the client's lawyer shortly after receipt of the letter should alert the auditor that
  (1) undisclosed unasserted claims may have arisen.
  (2) the lawyer was unable to form a conclusion with respect to the significance of litigation, claims, and assessments.
  (3) the auditor must begin a completely new examination of contingent liabilities.
  (4) an adverse opinion will be necessary.

19-20. The date of the client representation letter should coincide with which of the following?
  (1) The date of the auditor's report.
  (2) The balance sheet date.
  (3) The date of the latest subsequent event referred to in the notes to the financial statements.
  (4) The date of the engagement letter.

*19-21. The scope of an audit is **not** restricted when an attorney's response to an auditor as a result of a client's letter of audit inquiry limits the response to which of the following?
  (1) Matters to which the attorney has given substantive attention in the form of legal representation.
  (2) An evaluation of the likelihood of an unfavorable outcome of the matters disclosed by the entity.
  (3) The attorney's opinion of the entity's historical experience in recent similar litigation.
  (4) The probable outcome of asserted claims and pending or threatened litigation.

*19-22. Which of the following statements ordinarily is included among the written client representations obtained by the auditor?
  (1) Compensating balances and other arrangements involving restrictions on cash balances have been disclosed.
  (2) Management acknowledges responsibility for illegal actions committed by employees.
  (3) Sufficient evidential matter has been made available to permit the issuance of an unqualified opinion.
  (4) Management acknowledges that there are no material weaknesses in the internal control.

*19-23. An auditor performs interim work at various times throughout the year. The auditor's subsequent events work should be extended to the date of which of the following?
  (1) A postdated note.
  (2) The next scheduled interim visit.
  (3) The final billing for the audit services rendered.
  (4) The auditor's report.

*19-24. Auditors should request that an audit client send a letter of inquiry to those attorneys who have been consulted concerning litigation, claims, or assessments. The primary reason for this request is to provide which of the following?
  (1) Information concerning the progress of cases to date.
  (2) Corroborative evidential matter.
  (3) An estimate of the dollar amount of the probable loss.
  (4) An expert opinion as to whether a loss is possible, probable, or remote.

19-25. If the client refuses to furnish certain written representations that the auditor believes are essential, which of the following is appropriate?
  (1) The auditor can rely on oral evidence relating to the matter as a basis for an unqualified opinion.

---

*AICPA adapted.

    (2) The client's refusal does not constitute a scope limitation that may lead to a modification of the opinion.

    (3) This may have an effect on the auditor's ability to rely on other representations of the client.

    (4) The auditor should issue an adverse opinion because of the client's refusal.

*19-26. In an audit of contingent liabilities, which of the following procedures would be *least* effective?

    (1) Reviewing a bank confirmation letter.

    (2) Examining customer confirmation replies.

    (3) Examining invoices for professional services.

    (4) Reading the minutes of the board of directors.

*19-27. What is the primary source of information about litigation, claims, and assessments?

    (1) The client's lawyer.

    (2) The court records.

    (3) The client's management.

    (4) The independent auditor.

*19-28. Which of the following documentation is required for an audit in accordance with generally accepted auditing standards?

    (1) An internal control questionnaire.

    (2) A client engagement letter.

    (3) A planning memorandum or checklist.

    (4) A client representation letter.

*19-29. A charge in the subsequent period to a notes receivable account from the cash disbursements journal should alert the auditor to the possibility that which of the following has occurred?

    (1) A contingent asset has come into existence in the subsequent period.

    (2) A contingent liability has come into existence in the subsequent period.

    (3) A provision for contingencies is required.

    (4) A contingent liability has become a real liability and has been settled.

*19-30. A client has a calendar year-end. Listed below are four events that occurred after December 31. Which one of these subsequent events might result in adjustment of the December 31 financial statements?

    (1) Adoption of accelerated depreciation methods.

    (2) Write-off of a substantial portion of inventory as obsolete.

    (3) Collection of 90% of the accounts receivable existing at December 31.

    (4) Sale of a major subsidiary.

*19-31. The letter of audit inquiry addressed to the client's legal counsel will not ordinarily be

    (1) sent to a lawyer who was engaged by the audit client during the year and soon thereafter resigned the engagement.

    (2) a source of corroboration of the information originally obtained from management concerning litigation, claims, and assessments.

    (3) limited to references concerning only pending or threatened litigation with respect to which the lawyer has been engaged.

    (4) needed during the audit of clients whose securities are not registered with the SEC.

19-32. Which of the following auditing procedures is ordinarily performed last?

    (1) Reading the minutes of the board of directors meetings.

    (2) Confirming accounts payable.

    (3) Obtaining a client representation letter.

    (4) Tests of controls.

---

*AICPA adapted.

19-33. Which of the following reflects the conditions under which a loss contingency should affect net earnings?
(1) The loss is probable and the amount can be reasonably estimated.
(2) The loss is possible and the amount can be reasonably estimated.
(3) The loss is remote and the amount can be reasonably estimated.
(4) A loss contingency should never affect net earnings but should only be disclosed in notes.

19-34. The scope of the audit, including reference to the pronouncements of professional bodies to which the auditor adheres, is generally communicated to the client in the
I. auditor's report.
II. engagement letter.
III. representation letter.
   (1) I.
   (2) I and II.
   (3) I and III.
   (4) II and III.

*19-35. Which of the following procedures would an auditor ordinarily perform during the review of subsequent events?
(1) An analysis of related party transactions for the discovery of possible irregularities.
(2) A review of the cut-off bank statements for the period after the year-end.
(3) An inquiry of the client's legal counsel concerning litigation.
(4) An investigation of material weaknesses in internal accounting control previously communicated to the client.

Problems and Cases

19-36. (Contingencies) In an audit of the Marco Corporation as of December 31, 19X5, the following situations exist. No entries in respect thereto have been made in the accounting records.
1. The Marco Corporation has guaranteed the payment of interest on the ten-year, first-mortgage bonds of Newart Company, an affiliate. Outstanding bonds of the Newart Company amount to $150,000 with interest payable at 5% per annum, due June 1 and December 1 of each year. The bonds were issued by the Newart Company on December 1, 19X3, and all interest payments have been met by that company with the exception of the payment due December 1, 19X5. The Marco Corporation states that it will pay the defaulted interest to the bondholders on January 15, 19X6.
2. During the year 19X5, the Marco Corporation was named as a defendant in a suit for damages by the Dalton Company for breach of contract. An adverse decision to the Marco Corporation was rendered and the Dalton Company was awarded $40,000 damages. At the time of the audit, the case was under appeal to a higher court.
3. On December 23, 19X5, the Marco Corporation declared a common stock dividend of 1,000 shares, par $100 of its common stock, payable February 2, 19X6, to the common stockholders of record December 30, 19X5.
REQUIRED
A. Define *contingent liability*.
B. Describe the audit procedures you would use to learn about each of the situations above.
C. Describe the nature of the adjusting entries or disclosure, if any, you would make for each of these situations.

---

*AICPA adapted.

*19-37. (Audit Procedures for Litigation, Claims, and Assessments) Teresa Harper, CPA, has satisfactorily completed an audit of accounts payable and other liabilities and now plans to determine whether there are any loss contingencies arising from litigation, claims, or assessments.

REQUIRED

What audit procedures should Harper follow with respect to the existence of loss contingencies arising from litigation, claims, and assessments? Do *not* discuss reporting requirements.

19-38. (Review of a Lawyer's Letter) Foot, Tick, & Tie, CPAs, requested their client to send a letter asking its lawyer to provide a response directly to the auditor. The client responded by sending a letter similar to the one in Figure 19–3. The lawyer's response to the client's request is shown in Figure 19–7.

REQUIRED

A. What information in the lawyer's response letter is missing and which qualification in the response is unacceptable?

B. What action should the auditors take?

19-39. (Date of the Lawyer's Letter) Scott Johnson, CPA, is auditing Lakeview Corp. Johnson requests that Lakeview ask its lawyer, Stephanie Allen, to send a lawyer's letter to him dated February 15, 19X4, which is the anticipated date of completion of fieldwork. Lakeview responds that its understanding of *SAS No. 12, Inquiry of a Client's Lawyer Concerning Litigation, Claims, and Assessments,* indicates that specifying a date for the lawyer's response would violate the requirements of *SAS No. 12.* Lakeview further states that it sees no need for there to be a relationship between the auditor's report date and the lawyer's response.

REQUIRED

A. Should Lakeview's audit inquiry letter request Allen to specify the effective date on her response?

B. What is the relationship between the effective date of the lawyer's response and the date of the auditor's report?

19-40. (Responses in a Lawyer's Letter) The following represent responses from a lawyer to a client's letter of inquiry:

1. "We are of the opinion that this action will not result in any liability to the company."
2. "We believe that the plaintiff's case against the company is without merit."
3. "This action involves unique characteristics wherein authoritative legal precedents do not seem to exist. We believe that the plaintiff will have serious problems establishing the company's liability under the act; nevertheless, if the plaintiff is successful, the award may be substantial."
4. "We believe the company will be able to defend this action successfully."
5. "We believe the action can be settled for less than the damages claimed."
6. "We are unable to express an opinion as to the merits of the litigation at this time. The company believes there is absolutely no merit to the litigation."
7. "Based on the facts known to us, after a full investigation, it is our opinion that no liability will be established against the company in these suits."
8. "In our opinion, the company has a substantial chance of prevailing in this action."
9. "It is our opinion that the possible liability to the company in this proceeding is nominal in amount."
10. "It is our opinion that the company will be able to assert meritorious defenses to this action."

REQUIRED

For each of the above responses, indicate whether the response (1) clearly indicates that an unfavorable outcome is remote or (2) is unclear on the likelihood of the outcome.

---

*AICPA adapted.

Figure 19-7   **Lawyer's Letter to Auditors**

LAW OFFICES
PLAINTIFF & DEFENDANT
345 EAST 80th STREET
DALLAS, TEXAS 89521

Foot, Tick, & Tie, CPAs   February 3, 19X7
100 East Broad Street
Lubbock, TX 73215

Dear CPA:

We have been requested by Red Raider Incorporated to furnish you certain
information regarding pending or threatened litigation, claims, and
assessments which we had knowledge of as legal counsel for the company
as of December 31, 19X6, and as of this date.

The only action pending against this company or threatened against it of
which we are aware consists of an action filed pursuant to Section 301 of
the Labor Management Relations Act by a former employee. This matter
has been pending since December of 19X5 in the Federal District Court for
the Western District of Texas, Lubbock Division, and bears caption and
number as follows:

Jere Beasley, Jr., vs. Red Raider Incorporated Civil Action No. 733242.

At present, there is pending a Motion for Summary Judgment that will be
heard on March 19, 19X7. On the basis of the facts known to us and relevant
jurisprudence, we believe the complaint to be without merit.

There are no fees and costs currently due us from the company. This is due,
in part, to the fact that we anticipate billing this client at the conclusion of
the litigation referred to above unless it is of a more prolonged duration than
we expect.

Trusting that the foregoing will satisfy your requirements, I am

Very truly yours,

Peter M. Looser

Peter M. Looser

*19-41. (Subsequent Events Disclosure) Lancaster Electronics produces electronic components for sale to manufacturers of radios, television sets, and phonographic systems. In connection with his audit of Lancaster's financial statements for the year ended December 31, 19X4, Don Olds, CPA, completed the fieldwork two weeks ago. Olds is now evaluating the significance of the following items prior to preparing his auditor's report. Except as noted, none of these items has been disclosed in the financial statements or notes.

1. Recently Lancaster interrupted its policy of paying cash dividends quarterly to its stockholders. Dividends were paid regularly through 19X3, discontinued for all of 19X4 in order to finance equipment for the company's new plant, and resumed in the first quarter of 19X5. In the annual report, dividend policy is to be discussed in the president's letter to stockholders.

2. A ten-year loan agreement, which the company entered into three years ago, provides that dividend payments may not exceed net income earned after taxes subsequent to the date of the agreement. The balance of retained earnings at the date of the loan agreement was $298,000. From that date through December 31, 19X4, net income after taxes totaled $360,000 and cash dividends totaled $130,000. Based upon these data, the staff auditor assigned to this review concluded that no retained earnings restriction existed as of December 31, 19X4.

3. The company's new manufacturing plant building, which cost $600,000 and has an estimated life of 25 years, is leased from the Sixth National Bank at an annual rental of $100,000. The company is obligated to pay property taxes, insurance, and maintenance. At the conclusion of its ten-year noncancelable lease, the company has the option of purchasing the property for $1. In Lancaster's income statement, the rental payment is reported on a separate line.

4. A major electronics firm has introduced a line of products that will compete directly with Lancaster's primary line, now being produced in the specially designed new plant. Because of manufacturing innovations, the competitor's line will be of comparable quality but will be priced 50% below Lancaster's line. The competitor announced its new line during the week following completion of fieldwork. Olds read the announcement in the newspaper and discussed the situation by telephone with Lancaster executives. Lancaster will meet the lower prices, which are high enough to cover variable manufacturing and selling expenses but which will permit recovery of only a portion of fixed costs.

REQUIRED

For each of Items **1–4**, discuss the additional disclosure in the financial statements and notes required for the fair presentation of financial statements.

*19-42. (Subsequent Events) In connection with your audit of the financial statements of Olars Manufacturing Corporation for the year ended December 31, your post-balance sheet date-review disclosed the following items:

1. *January 3:* The state government approved a plan for the construction of an express highway. The plan will result in the appropriation of a portion of the land area owned by Olars Manufacturing Corporation. Construction will begin late next year. No estimate of the condemnation award is available.

2. *January 4:* The funds for a $25,000 loan to the corporation made by Pat Olars on July 15 were obtained by him from a loan on his personal life insurance policy. The loan was recorded in the account entitled "Loans from Officers." Olars' source of the funds was not disclosed in the company records. The corporation pays the premiums on the life insurance policy, and Dee Olars, wife of the president, is the owner and beneficiary of the policy.

*AICPA adapted.

3. *January 7:* The mineral content of a shipment of ore en route on December 31 was determined to be 72%. The shipment was recorded at year-end at an estimated content of 50% by a debit to Raw Material Inventory and a credit to Accounts Payable in the amount of $20,600. The final liability to the vendor is based on the actual mineral content of the shipment.
4. *January 15:* Culminating a series of personal disagreements between Pat Olars, the president, and his brother-in-law, the treasurer, the latter resigned, effective immediately, under an agreement whereby the corporation would purchase his 10% stock ownership at book value as of December 31. Payment is to be made in two equal amounts in cash on April 1 and October 1. In December the treasurer had obtained a divorce from his wife, who is Olars' sister.
5. *January 31:* As a result of reduced sales, production was curtailed in mid-January and some workers were laid off. On February 5, all the remaining workers went on strike. To date the strike is unsettled.
6. *February 10:* A contract was signed whereby Mammoth Enterprises purchased from Olars Manufacturing Corporation all of the latter's fixed assets (including rights to receive the proceeds of any property condemnation), inventories, and the right to conduct business under the name "Olars Manufacturing Division." The effective date of the transfer will be March 1. The sale price was $500,000 subject to adjustment following the taking of a physical inventory. Important factors contributing to the decision to enter into the contract were the policy of the board of directors of Mammoth to diversify the firm's activities and the report of a survey conducted by an independent market appraisal firm that revealed a declining market for Olars products.

REQUIRED

Assume that the above items came to your attention prior to completion of your audit work on February 15, and that you plan to render a standard audit report. For *each* of the above items:

A. Give the audit procedures, if any, that would have brought the item to your attention. Indicate other sources of information that may have revealed the item.
B. Discuss the disclosure that you would recommend for the item, listing all details that you would suggest should be disclosed. Indicate those items or details, if any, that should not be disclosed. Give your reasons for recommending or not recommending disclosure of the items or details.

*19-43. (Subsequent Events) The following unrelated events occurred after the balance sheet date but before the audit report was prepared:
1. The granting of a retroactive pay increase.
2. Determination by the federal government of additional income tax due for a prior year.
3. Filing of an antitrust suit by the federal government.
4. Declaration of a stock dividend.
5. Sale of a fixed asset at a substantial profit.

REQUIRED

A. Explain how each of the items might have come to the auditor's attention.
B. Discuss the auditor's responsibility to recognize each of these in connection with his or her report.

19-44. (Subsequent Events) In connection with his audit of the 19X4 financial statements of Smith Band Supply, Inc., Norman Godwin, CPA, observed the following material items. Fieldwork was completed on February 14, 19X5.
1. On January 15, 19X5, Botta, Inc., a major customer of Smith Band Supply, declared bankruptcy. Botta had been in financial difficulty for some time.

*AICPA adapted.

2. Cornet, Inc., a competitor of Smith Band Supply, filed a lawsuit against Smith on February 1, 19X5. Smith's attorney is of the opinion that the lawsuit is frivolous and the likelihood of an unfavorable ruling is remote.

3. Wittenburg Co. also filed suit on February 1, 19X5, against the company. Smith's lawyer believes an unfavorable ruling in this case is reasonably possible.

4. On January 22, 19X5, Kevin Wright Enterprises, a major customer of the company, filed for bankruptcy as a result of a devastating flood on January 10, for which Wright was uninsured.

5. On February 1, 19X5, a customer, Will Nance Supply Corp., declared bankruptcy as a result of an uninsured fire loss that occurred on December 14, 19X4.

6. On February 10, 19X5, Smith Band Supply settled a lawsuit out of court. The suit had originated in 19X2 and had been disclosed in prior years as a contingent liability.

7. On February 4, 19X5, Smith signed a contract to provide band uniforms to several Southeastern universities. This is the largest contract in the company's history.

REQUIRED

For each of these items, state whether Godwin should:

A. Propose an adjustment to the financial statements.

B. Propose note disclosure.

C. Take no action.

*19-45. (Client Representation Letter) In connection with your audit, you request that management furnish you with a letter or letters containing certain representations. For example, such representations might include the following: (1) the client has satisfactory title to all assets; (2) no contingent or unrecorded liabilities exist except as disclosed in the letter; (3) no shares of the company's stock are reserved for options, warrants, or other rights; and (4) the company is not obligated to repurchase any of its outstanding shares under any circumstances.

REQUIRED

A. Explain why you believe a letter of representation should be furnished to you.

B. In what way, if any, do client representations affect your audit procedures and responsibilities?

19-46. (Client Representation Letter) Kirby Williams, CPA, has drafted a client representation letter for the president and chief financial officer of his client, Lake Martin Marina, to sign. Included in the letter are the following items:

1. Management's acknowledgment of its responsibility for the fair presentation in the financial statements of financial position, results of operations, and changes in financial position in conformity with GAAP.

2. Reduction of excess or obsolete inventories to net realizable value.

3. Information concerning subsequent events.

REQUIRED

A. A management representation letter is required by *SAS No. 19, Client Representations.* Why is such a letter desirable for the above items?

B. Is the management representation letter audit evidence?

C. What other information should be included in the representation letter?

*19-47. (Client Representation Letter and Engagement Letter) The major written understandings between a CPA and a client, in connection with an audit of financial statements, are the engagement letter and the client representation letter. (You may want to review the discussion of engagement letters in Chapter 12 before answering this question.)

---

*AICPA adapted.

REQUIRED

A. **(1)** What are the objectives of the engagement letter?
    (2) Who should prepare and sign the engagement letter?
    (3) When should the engagement letter be sent?
    (4) Why should the engagement letter be renewed periodically?

B. **(1)** What are the objectives of the client representation letter?
    (2) Who should prepare and sign the client representation letter?
    (3) When should the client representation letter be obtained?
    (4) Why should the client representation letter be prepared for each examination?

19-48. (Review of Working Papers) Scotty Stanford, CPA, is a partner in the firm of Stanford, Benner, and Smoke, CPAs. Stanford's philosophy is that working papers should be reviewed during the engagement as sections of the audit are completed rather than solely at the completion of the engagement. However, Stanford still performs an overall review of the working papers at the conclusion of the audit. He believes that by reviewing the staff's working papers during the engagement, the staff receives better training and problems are identified earlier. Once Stanford completes his final review, the audit report and financial statements are typed. Stanford sees no need for another partner to review his work.

REQUIRED

A. Discuss Stanford's philosophy of reviewing working papers during the engagement as sections of the audit are completed.

B. Is the additional review at the conclusion of the audit beneficial?

C. Discuss Stanford's practice of not having a second partner review the working papers.

Audit Judgment Cases

19-49. (Subsequent Events) Alex Timmons, CPA, is nearing completion of fieldwork on the audit of Vickster Pharmaceuticals financial statements for the year ended December 31, 19X4. The morning the report was to be signed, Timmons read in *The Wall Street Journal* that the drug Accodren had been linked to many deaths of young children. Accodren is one of Vicksters most profitable products.

REQUIRED

What effect would this recent development have on the report on the financial statements of Vickster Pharmaceuticals?

19-50. (Attorney's Letter) Mary Schuler, CPA, received an attorney's representation letter which failed to disclose information related to one of the client's assessments of contingent liabilities. When questioned, the client seemed perplexed as to why the attorney omitted the disclosure. When the client called the attorney to get an explanation, the phone had been disconnected and the attorney was nowhere to be found.

REQUIRED

If Schuler is unable to get the attorney's assessment related to the omitted litigation, what effect will this have on the auditor's report?

Auditing Issues Case

19-51. ## KELCO MANUFACTURING COMPANY

You have just obtained from Kelco president, Steve Cook, management's description and all documents related to litigation, claims, and assessments (LCAs) of the company. After receiving in writing from Cook that all LCAs are accounted for in accordance with

FASB 5, you made inquiries of Kelco's legal counsel regarding LCAs. A portion of the attorney's representation letter is provided below:

ANDREWS, LINDSEY & SLINGERLAND
Attorneys-at-Law
171 Erudition Avenue
Pensacola, Florida 32583

March 26, 19X5

Re: Representation Letter
    Kelco Manufacturing Company

Dear CPA:

By letter dated February 28, 19X5, Steve Cook, President of Kelco Manufacturing Company, requested that we furnish you with certain information in connection with your examination of the accounts of Kelco as of December 31, 19X4.

Subject to the last paragraph of this letter, we advise you that as of December 31, 19X4, we were not engaged to give substantive attention to, or to represent, Kelco in connection with any material loss contingencies which existed as of December 31, 19X4, or of which we were advised from that date to March 26, 19X5, coming within the scope of clause (a) of paragraph 5 of the Statement of Policy referred to in the next to last paragraph of this letter, except as set forth below:

1. S. A. Rhodes, et al. v. Kelco Manufacturing Company, et al.: a complaint against Kelco for personal injury filed in the Circuit Court of Escambia County, Florida, seeking damages in the amount of Three Million Five Hundred Thousand Dollars ($3,500,000) and Punitive damages as the jury may assess. Discovery has just begun in this matter and we are not in a position at this time to evaluate potential liability or adequacy of insurance coverage. Kelco intends to vigorously defend this claim.

2. J. B. Bounds, et al. v. Kelco Manufacturing Company: On or about December 15, 19X4, Kelco received a letter from a Milton attorney, Jeff Thompson, asking Kelco to have their insurance carrier contact him regarding loss of business to Mr. J. B. Bounds' farming operations in Milton. Mr. Bounds claim is based on damage done on his property as a result of an accident involving one of Kelco's trucks that caught fire on his property. No suit has been filed at this time. We are not at this time able to evaluate potential liability but it appears that insurance coverage is adequate to indemnify any loss resulting from this claim. Kelco intends to vigorously defend this claim.

Pursuant to the ABA Statement of Policy referred to in the next to last paragraph of this letter, we are unable to respond to general inquiries about possible unasserted claims except those which our client has specifically identified and on which our client has specifically requested comment.

This response is limited by, and is made in accordance with, ABA Statement of Policy regarding Lawyer's Responses to Auditors' Requests for Information (December, 1975). Without limiting the generality of the foregoing, the limitations set forth in such Statement on the scope and use of this response (Paragraphs 2 and 7) are specifically incorporated herein by reference and any description of any "loss contingencies" is qualified in its entirety by Paragraph 5 of the Statement and the accompanying Commentary (which is an integral part of the Statement). With respect to matters recognized to involve unasserted possible claims or assessments that might be recognized by us in the course of performing legal services for Kelco Manufacturing Company, please be advised that as a matter of professional responsibility we do and would advise our client thereof. We do not undertake to determine the probability of assertion or whether disclosure is required by the Statement of Financial Accounting Standards No. 5 or any other disclosure standards, nor do we advise our clients in that regard.

This letter is solely for your information and to assist you in connection with your audit of and report with respect to, the financial condition of Kelco Manufacturing Company, and is not to be quoted or otherwise referred to in any financial statement of Kelco Manufacturing Company, or related documents, nor is it to be filed with or furnished to any governmental agency or any person without the prior written consent of this firm.

Signed,

Kate Lindsey

Kate Lindsey
Attorney-at-Law

The personal injury suit referred to in the attorney's representation letter is news to you. Cook provided you with no information related to the litigation. Upon inquiry of Cook his response is: "Oh, there is no chance of that guy winning that suit so I did not see any reason for disclosing that to you."

REQUIRED

1. How should you respond to Cook?
2. Assume that the financials require revision to be in accordance with *FASB No. 5*, and Cook refuses to do so. What effect will this have on the opinion to be rendered on the financial statements?

all litigation must be disclosed to the auditor

Part Five

Reporting Responsibilities

Chapters 20–22 include a presentation of the final product of an audit—the audit report—and describe (1) other types of reports an auditor can issue and (2) compilation and review reports.

Chapter 20 discusses the audit reporting options available to an auditor for a typical audit.

Chapter 21 describes other types of audit services and reports with which an auditor may be involved.

Chapter 22 explains the compilation and review reporting options available to an accountant when performing accounting and review services.

Chapter *20*

Reporting on Audited Financial Statements

Learning   Objectives

- List and explain the meaning of the four reporting standards.

- Identify the four sources of established accounting principles.

- List the basic elements of the auditor's standard report.

- Describe the types of opinions that are alternatives to the unqualified opinion.

- Explain the circumstances that require an auditor to modify both the opinion and wording in the standard report.

- Describe the type(s) of opinion(s) and related report wording appropriate for the three circumstances that require modification of both the opinion and wording in the standard report.

- Explain the six circumstances that require an auditor to modify only the wording of the standard report.

- Describe the auditor's reporting responsibility for comparative financial statements.

G enerally accepted auditing standards contain four reporting standards. These standards are used to produce an unqualified opinion of an entity's financial statements. The unqualified opinion is usually delivered as a standard report. Figure 20–1 on page 709 is an example of an auditor's standard report. The reason the report reads as a standardized letter is to reduce the likelihood of confusion among report readers and to easily identify areas where specific facts or information should be brought to the reader's attention.

Compare the annual reports of publicly held corporations such as Chrysler, Merck, and Ben & Jerry's, and near the end of each, you will see an independent auditor's report. The presentation and format of each annual report may differ significantly, but the language and comments of the auditor's report are standardized. This chapter will address elements of an auditor's standard report. The chapter also addresses and explains circumstances where any auditor would need to modify the wording in a standard report. ■

One of an auditor's primary roles is the *attest function*, in which the auditor adds credibility to an assertion by one party that is to be used by another party. The credibility added is in the form of an audit report that expresses assurance about the assertion.

Currently, independent auditors provide various levels of assurance about different types of assertions. The most common and highest level of assurance that an independent auditor can express is the audit report. The most common assertion upon which assurance is expressed is the financial statements. This chapter examines the auditor's reporting responsibility when expressing assurance based on an audit of financial statements.

Chapters 21 and 22 discuss reporting responsibilities for, respectively, assertions other than financial statements and levels of assurance based on attest services other than an audit. For example, CPAs express assurance on assertions other than financial statements, including internal control structures, specific accounts in financial statements, and compliance with laws and regulations. In addition, CPAs provide review services for financial statements, a level of assurance below that of an audit.

Reporting Standards

The auditor's report is the primary product of the audit process. Although audits may take hundreds or even thousands of hours to complete, the typical user of audited financial statements usually receives no more than an audit report consisting of three rather short paragraphs. This report, however, expresses the auditor's assurance about the credibility of an entity's financial statements. The type of report the auditor issues and its content and wording are directly influenced by the four reporting standards of generally accepted auditing standards. As presented earlier in Chapter 1, these four reporting standards are as follows:

1. The report shall state whether the financial statements are presented in accordance with generally accepted accounting principles.

2. The report shall identify those circumstances in which such principles have not been consistently observed in the current period in relation to the preceding period.
3. Informative disclosures in the financial statements are to be regarded as reasonably adequate unless otherwise stated in the report.
4. The report shall contain either an expression of opinion regarding the financial statements, taken as a whole, or an assertion to the effect that an opinion cannot be expressed. When an overall opinion cannot be expressed, the reasons therefor should be stated. In all cases where an auditor's name is associated with financial statements, the report should contain a clear-cut indication of the character of the auditor's work and the degree of responsibility the auditor is taking.

The First Reporting Standard

The auditor's report on audited financial statements must state whether the statements conform with ***generally accepted accounting principles (GAAP)***. GAAP provide a standard by which auditors judge the fairness of financial statement presentations. When the auditor states that the financial statements present fairly in conformity with GAAP, the auditor considers the following factors specified in *SAS No. 69, The Meaning of "Present Fairly in Conformity with Generally Accepted Accounting Principles" in the Independent Auditor's Report* (AU 411):

- The accounting principles selected and applied by management have general acceptance.
- The accounting principles are appropriate in the circumstances.
- The financial statements, including the related notes, are informative of matters that may affect their use.
- The information presented in the financial statements is classified and summarized in a reasonable manner, that is, it is neither too detailed nor too condensed.
- The financial statements reflect the underlying transactions and events in a manner that presents the financial statements within a range of acceptable limits.

General Acceptance

GAAP is a technical term that includes standards, rules, and procedures that define accepted accounting practice at a specific time. Because there is no single source for these principles, deciding which accounting principle is generally accepted can sometimes be difficult. Accounting principles are established as generally accepted through a hierarchy as discussed in Chapter 1. These sources of GAAP for commercial entities are listed in Table 20–1. *SAS No. 69* (AU 411) establishes two separate but parallel GAAP hierarchies: one for state and local government entities and one for nongovernmental (i.e., commercial) entities.

Appropriate Accounting Principles

Established accounting principles may permit alternative accounting treatments for the same transaction or event. In some situations, criteria may not exist for selecting among alternative accounting principles, and the auditor may conclude that more than one accounting principle is appropriate. However, the auditor should be aware that the substance of a transaction may differ materially from its form and that the principle selected should account for the substance of the transaction. Also, the auditor should understand that accounting principles continue to evolve as a result of experience and research and in response to changes in economic activities and changing user needs.

Table 20–1	Sources of Established Accounting Principles—Commercial Entities	
	Source	Examples
	A. Officially established by a body designated by the AICPA pursuant to Rule 203 of the Code of Professional Conduct (promulgated principle).	FASB Statements and interpretations, APB Opinions, and AICPA Accounting Research Bulletins. (Rules and releases of the SEC have similar authority for public companies.)
	B. Pronouncements of the FASB and the AICPA's Accounting Standards Executive Committee (cleared by the FASB) that *have been exposed* for public comment.	FASB Technical Bulletins, cleared AICPA Industry Audit and Accounting Guides, and AICPA Statements of Position.
	C. Pronouncements of the FASB and the AcSEC (cleared by the FASB) that *have not been broadly distributed* for public comment.	Consensus positions of the FASB Emerging Issues Task Force and cleared AcSEC Practice Bulletins.
	D. (1) Prevalent practice in a particular industry or (2) knowledgeable application of pronouncements in (B) or (C) above to specific circumstances.	AICPA accounting interpretations, "Qs and As" published by the FASB staff, and industry practices widely recognized and prevalent.
	E. Other nonauthoritative accounting literature.	FASB Concepts Statements, APB Statements, AICPA Issues Papers, International Accounting Standards Committee Statements, GASB Statements, interpretations and technical bulletins, pronouncements of other professional associations or regulatory agencies, AICPA *Technical Practice Aids*, and accounting textbooks, handbooks, and articles.

Adequate Disclosure

Although disclosure is discussed later in this chapter in more detail under the third reporting standard, the auditor should consider whether the financial statements, including related notes, disclose sufficient information to enable an informed reader to understand and interpret them. The auditor should also consider whether the classifications and summarizations in the financial statements are made in a degree of detail that is reasonable, that is, neither too condensed nor too detailed.

Acceptable Range of Approximation

Because the measurement and disclosure of financial statement elements often necessitate the use of estimates, approximations, and judgments, financial statements are not precise. However, the auditor must be satisfied that the amounts presented in the financial statements are within an acceptable range of approximation. The auditor uses materiality as a guideline in evaluating whether management's accounting estimates are within an acceptable range of approximation. If the range of approximation is significant enough to make a material difference in the judgment or conduct of financial statement users, the range is not acceptable.

The Second Reporting Standard

The *consistency standard* requires the auditor to give assurance that changes in accounting principles have not materially affected the financial statements or, if material changes in accounting principles have affected comparability, to ensure they are reported to financial statement users. Financial statement comparability can be affected by a number of different types of accounting principle changes as well as by other factors. These changes and their effects on the auditor's report are discussed in detail later in the chapter.

The Third Reporting Standard

The objective of the third reporting standard is to require that the auditor's report identify material deficiencies regarding disclosures in the financial statements. This reporting standard does not require a specific statement in the auditor's report, unless disclosure deficiencies exist.

The Fourth Reporting Standard

The purpose of the fourth standard of reporting is to ensure that the auditor's report communicates to financial statement users the degree to which they should rely on the financial statements. To achieve this objective, the fourth standard establishes several requirements concerning audit report content.

The first requirement is that the auditor must either express or disclaim an opinion on the financial statements taken as a whole. This requirement ensures that the audit report clearly states the degree of responsibility the auditor is taking for auditing the financial statements. The reference to financial statements "taken as a whole" means that the auditor's objective is to form an opinion as to whether the entity's financial statements meet the broad objectives embodied in the basic financial statements, such as presenting financial position, results of operations, and cash flows. The phrase "taken as a whole" applies equally to a complete set of financial statements and to an individual financial statement. However, the auditor is not expressing an opinion on individual items within the financial statements. In addition, "taken as a whole" includes not only the financial statements of the current period but also those of one or more prior periods presented for comparison with current-period statements. The phrase does not, however, prohibit the auditor from expressing different types of opinions on individual financial statements included in the set of financial statements.

Another requirement is that the auditor disclose in the audit report all substantive reasons for expressing other than an unqualified opinion. Thus, even though one particular circumstance might be sufficient to cause the auditor to qualify the opinion, if there are other substantive reasons that would also result in qualification, readers of the report must be informed of them as well.

The fourth standard also requires the auditor to report on any financial statement with which the auditor's name is associated and to state in the report the auditor's scope of involvement with the financial statements and the degree of responsibility the auditor is taking. As noted in *SAS No. 26, Association with Financial Statements* (AU 504), auditors are considered to be associated with financial statements when they consent to the use of their names in reports, documents, or written communications containing the statements or when they submit to the client or others financial statements that they have prepared or assisted in preparing. This association exists even if the accountant's name is not appended to the statements themselves.

Because an accountant can be associated with financial statements in capacities other than as an auditor, the report must inform the reader of the nature of the service the accountant has rendered. Reporting the nature of service helps define the degree of responsibility the accountant takes for auditing the financial statements.

In some situations, after delivering the report to the client, an auditor will discover facts that existed at the report date that would have affected the opinion had he or she been aware of them. The auditor is therefore associated with financial statements that he or she now knows are misleading. As discussed in Chapter 3, *SAS No. 1, Subsequent Discovery of Facts Existing at the Date of the Auditor's Report* (AU 561), requires the auditor in such a situation to notify the client and request that the client disclose these facts to the users of the financial statements. If the client refuses to notify users, the auditor should, after consultation with an attorney, notify users, including regulatory authorities having jurisdiction over the client, that reliance should not be placed on the auditor's report.

The Auditor's Standard Report

The auditor's usual objective is to express an unqualified opinion on an entity's financial statements. An ***unqualified opinion*** states that the financial statements present fairly in all material respects financial position, results of operations, and cash flows in conformity with generally accepted accounting principles. An auditor may give an unqualified opinion only when each of the following two conditions has been met:

1. The audit has been conducted in conformity with generally accepted auditing standards (GAAS).
2. The financial statements are in conformity with GAAP.

An unqualified opinion is most frequently expressed by issuing a standard report. The term ***standard report*** is used because it consists of three paragraphs containing standardized words and phrases having a specific meaning. Standard wording serves two purposes: it helps avoid confusion among report readers and it identifies readily situations in which the auditor has modified the standard report to bring specific circumstances to the reader's attention. A typical example of the auditor's standard report is shown in Figure 20–1.

Although the auditor's standard report is synonymous with an unqualified opinion, an important distinction exists between an audit report and an audit opinion. The ***audit report*** represents the entire communication about what was done and the conclusions reached. The ***audit opinion*** is only one part of the report—the conclusions reached. In certain circumstances, the auditor can modify the wording of the standard report but still express an unqualified opinion. Under other circumstances, the auditor will not be able to express an unqualified opinion, which, in turn, necessitates a modification of the wording of the standard report, including the opinion.

As discussed in Chapter 1, the standard report consists of an opening (introductory) paragraph, a scope paragraph, and an opinion paragraph. The ***opening para-***

Final

| Figure 20-1 | **Auditor's Standard Report** | # 1st Exam |

GAAS

> ① INDEPENDENT AUDITOR'S REPORT
>
> ② Stockholders and Board of Directors
> AU Company
>
> ③ We have audited the accompanying balance sheet of AU Company as of December 31, 19X5, and the related statements of income, retained earnings, and cash flows for the year then ended. These financial ⓐ statements are the responsibility of the Company's management. Our ⓑ responsibility is to express an opinion on these financial statements based on our audit.
>
> ④ We conducted our audit in accordance with generally accepted auditing standards. Those standards require that we plan and perform the audit to obtain reasonable assurance about whether the financial statements are free of material misstatement. An audit includes examining, on a test basis, evidence supporting the amounts and disclosures in the financial statements. An audit also includes assessing the accounting principles used and significant estimates made by management, as well as evaluating the overall financial statement presentation. We believe that our audit provides a reasonable basis for our opinion.
>
> ⑤ In our opinion, the financial statements referred to above present fairly, in all material respects, the financial position of AU Company as of December 31, 19X5, and the results of its operations and its cash flows for the year then ended in conformity with generally accepted accounting principles.
>
> ⑥ Able, Baker and Charlie, CPAs
> ⑦ February 15, 19X6

opinion paragraph GAAP

date of the audit Completion

Unqualified Opinion Report

responsibility as of the date

graph identifies the financial statements that were audited and states that the financial statements are the responsibility of the entity's management.

In the *scope paragraph* the auditor describes the nature of an audit and states explicitly that the audit provides a reasonable basis for the opinion on the financial statements.

In the **opinion paragraph**, the auditor communicates the results of the audit. This paragraph expresses an informed, expert *opinion* on the financial statements. It is not an absolute statement, because the auditor cannot guarantee that the financial statements are accurate. This paragraph satisfies the requirement in the first reporting standard concerning conformity with GAAP, the requirement in the third reporting standard regarding informative disclosure, and the requirement in the fourth reporting standard regarding expression of an opinion on the financial statements taken as a whole.

The report must have a title that includes the word "independent." The report is usually addressed to the groups or individuals that appointed the auditor. For corporate clients this may be the stockholders, board of directors, or audit committee. For unincorporated clients this may be the partners or proprietor, or the family unit in the case of personal financial statements.

The auditor's report is signed with the CPA firm name (manual or printed signature) because the firm assumes responsibility for the audit. The report is dated based on when the auditor has obtained sufficient competent evidential matter to meet the third standard of fieldwork, usually the date that fieldwork is completed.

In some instances, however, an auditor may discover a subsequent event requiring disclosure after the completion of fieldwork but before the report is issued (as discussed in Chapter 21). In this situation, the auditor may either extend the date of completion of fieldwork to the date of the subsequent event discovery or modify the dating of the report using *dual dating*, whereby the report is dated as of the original date of completion of fieldwork with another date referring to the subsequent event. An example of dual dating would be a report dated "February 15, 19X4, except for Note X dated February 27, 19X4."

Figure 20–2 summarizes the basic elements of the auditor's standard report as required by *SAS No. 58, Reports on Audited Financial Statements* (AU 508).

Figure 20–2	**Basic Elements of the Standard Audit Report**

1. *A title* that includes the word "independent."
2. *An address* to the entity whose financial statements were audited.
3. *An opening (or introductory) paragraph* that includes
   A. a statement that the financial statements identified in the report were audited.
   B. a statement that the financial statements are the responsibility of the entity's management, and that the auditor's responsibility is to express an opinion on the financial statements based on the audit.
4. *A scope paragraph* that includes
   A. a statement that the audit was conducted in accordance with GAAS.
   B. a statement that GAAS require the auditor to plan and perform the audit to obtain reasonable assurance about whether the financial statements are free of material misstatement.
   C. a statement that an audit includes
      (1) examining, on a test basis, evidence supporting the amounts and disclosures in the financial statements.
      (2) assessing the accounting principles used and significant estimates made by management.
      (3) evaluating the overall financial statement presentation.
   D. a statement that the auditor believes that the audit provides a reasonable basis for his or her opinion.
5. *An opinion paragraph* stating whether the financial statements present fairly, in all material respects, the financial position of the entity as of the balance sheet date, and the results of its operations and its cash flows for the period then ended in conformity with GAAP.
6. *The manual or printed signature* of the auditor's firm.
7. *Date of completion* of fieldwork.

[handwritten annotation: "What was done —"]

Types of Audit Opinions

As mentioned earlier, two conditions must be met before an auditor can issue an unqualified opinion. If one of these conditions is not met, the auditor will have to issue one of the following opinions.

- *Qualified Opinion* This type of opinion excludes a specific item from the auditor's opinion. Thus, the auditor expresses an opinion that the financial statements as a whole present fairly in conformity with generally accepted accounting principles, excluding the item or items specified in the report.
- *Adverse Opinion* This type of opinion states that the financial statements as a whole do *not* present fairly in conformity with generally accepted accounting principles. The auditor expresses this opinion when he or she believes that the financial statements taken as a whole are misleading.
- *Disclaimer of Opinion* This is not an opinion but rather a statement by the auditor that an opinion cannot be expressed. That is, the auditor has no opinion on the financial statements taken as a whole.

The specific circumstances encountered in the audit and its materiality generally determine the type of opinion necessary. To avoid obscuring the basic message, the audit report should give a brief explanation of the circumstance in a separate paragraph (preceding the opinion paragraph).

Modifications of the Standard Audit Report

Certain factors prevent the auditor from issuing a standard report:

- Circumstances may require a modification of both the wording of the standard report and the auditor's opinion on the financial statements.
- Circumstances may require a modification of the wording of the standard report but not a modification of the auditor's opinion.

Modification of Both Wording and Opinion

Three circumstances may prevent the auditor from expressing an unqualified opinion:

- *Scope Limitation* Circumstances may arise in the audit that prevent application of one or more audit procedures the auditor considers necessary.
- *GAAP Departure* A departure from generally accepted accounting principles, including adequate disclosures, may have a material effect on the financial statements.
- *Lack of Independence* As discussed in Chapters 1 and 2, if the auditor is not independent, he or she must disclaim an opinion on the financial statements. (If the entity is a nonpublic entity, a compilation report, as discussed in Chapter 22, is required.)

Each of these circumstances, when material, precludes the auditor from issuing an unqualified opinion and requires the auditor to modify the report wording not only to express a different type of opinion but also to describe the circumstance causing

			Table 20–2

Conditions That Preclude an Unqualified Opinion

Type of Report

Condition	Unqualified	Qualified	Disclaimer	Adverse
Limit on audit scope	If limitation is immaterial	If limitation is material	If limitation is very material	—
Departure from GAAP	If departure is immaterial	If departure is material	—	If departure is very material
Lack of independence (public company)	—	—	Only report that can be issued	—

the change in opinion. These circumstances are discussed in detail below, along with their effect on the type of opinion to be expressed and the modification of report wording. Table 20–2 summarizes the effects of each of these circumstances on the type of opinion submitted.

Scope Limitation

Circumstances sometimes make it impossible or impracticable to apply certain audit procedures the auditor believes necessary. Such restrictions on the scope of the audit may be imposed by the client, such as refusal to permit confirmation of accounts receivable or refusal to permit inquiry of outside legal counsel. *Scope limitations* may also arise because the client's records are not adequate to permit an audit of the financial statements or because of the timing of the auditor's work, such as when the auditor is appointed too late to observe physical inventory.

A scope limitation does not exist when the auditor is able to obtain satisfactory evidence by applying alternative procedures in place of those precluded by the restriction. In addition, when the auditor is asked to report on one basic financial statement and not on the others, a scope limitation does not exist as long as the auditor is able to apply all of the audit procedures considered necessary to express an opinion on that financial statement.

Effect on Opinion Because auditors cannot express an unqualified opinion unless they have been able to apply all of the audit procedures considered necessary, scope limitations require auditors either to express a qualified opinion or to disclaim an opinion. Note that an adverse opinion is inappropriate for scope limitations because such an opinion relates to a deficiency in the financial statements rather than to a deficiency in the scope of the audit.

Once the auditor has decided that an unqualified opinion is not appropriate, he or she must choose between a qualified opinion and a disclaimer of opinion. This choice is based on the importance of the omitted procedures to the auditor's ability to form an opinion on the financial statements taken as a whole. If the potential effects of the scope limitation are not so material as to preclude the auditor from forming an opinion on the financial statements taken as a whole, the auditor should issue a qualified opinion. Figure 20–3 illustrates a qualified opinion for a scope limitation.

If the potential effects of the scope limitation relate to many financial statement items, they may be so material as to preclude the auditor from forming an opinion on

Figure 20-3

Report with a Qualified "except for" Opinion Due to a Limitation on the Scope of the Engagement

(Opening Paragraph)

We have audited the accompanying balance sheet of AU Company as of December 31, 19X4, and the related statements of income, retained earnings, and cash flows for the year then ended. The financial statements are the responsibility of the Company's management. Our responsibility is to express an opinion on these financial statements based on our audit.

Opening paragraph is the same as in the standard report.

(Scope Paragraph)

Except as discussed in the following paragraph, we conducted our audit in accordance with generally accepted auditing standards. Those standards require that we plan and perform the audit to obtain reasonable assurance about whether the financial statements are free of material misstatement. An audit includes examining, on a test basis, evidence supporting the amounts and disclosures in the financial statements. An audit also includes assessing the accounting principles used and significant estimates made by management, as well as evaluating the overall financial statement presentation. We believe that our audit provides a reasonable basis for our opinion.

Wording of the scope paragraph is modified to include a restriction affecting the scope of the audit.

(Explanatory Paragraph)

We were unable to obtain audited financial statements supporting the Company's investment in a foreign affiliate stated at $2,500,000 at December 31, 19X4, or its equity in earnings of that affiliate of $300,000, which is included in net income for the year then ended as described in Note X to the financial statements; nor were we able to satisfy ourselves as to the carrying value of the investment in the foreign affiliate or the equity in its earnings by other auditing procedures.

Separate paragraph is added to explain the nature of the scope limitation.

(Opinion Paragraph)

In our opinion, *except for the effects of such adjustments, if any, as might have been determined to be necessary had we been able to examine evidence regarding the foreign affiliate investment and earnings,* the financial statements referred to above present fairly, in all material respects, the financial position of AU Company as of December 31, 19X4, and the results of its operations and its cash flows for the year then ended in conformity with generally accepted accounting principles.

Opinion is qualified "except for" any adjustments the auditor might have found necessary had he or she been able to examine the records supporting AU Company's investment in the foreign affiliate.

Figure 20-4	**Report with a Disclaimer of Opinion Due to a Limitation on the Scope of the Engagement**

(Opening Paragraph)

We were engaged to audit the accompanying balance sheet of AU Company as of December 31, 19X4, and the related statements of income, retained earnings, and cash flows for the year then ended. These financial statements are the responsibility of the Company's management.

[Scope paragraph of standard report is omitted to avoid overshadowing the disclaimer.]

Wording of the opening paragraph is modified to avoid stating "We have audited," and to delete statement of the auditor's responsibility to express an opinion.

(Explanatory Paragraph)

The Company did not make a count of its physical inventory stated in the accompanying financial statements at $349,000 as of December 31, 19X4. Further, evidence supporting the cost of property and equipment acquired prior to December 31, 19X4, is no longer available. The Company's records do not permit the application of other auditing procedures to inventories or property and equipment.

Separate paragraph is added to explain the nature of the scope limitations.

(Disclaimer Paragraph)

Since the Company did not take physical inventories and we were not able to apply other auditing procedures to satisfy ourselves as to inventory quantities and the cost of property and equipment, the scope of our work was not sufficient to enable us to express, and we do not express, an opinion on these financial statements.

The auditor disclaims an opinion on the financial statements because the significance of the scope limitation prevents the forming of an opinion.

the financial statements taken as a whole. Also, if the client imposes the scope limitation, the auditor usually does not express an opinion. Under these circumstances, a disclaimer of opinion is appropriate. Figure 20–4 illustrates a disclaimer of opinion for a scope limitation.

Effect on Report Wording   As Figure 20–3 illustrates, not only is the auditor's opinion changed when an "except for" scope limitation exists, the wording of the report is modified also. Report wording modification occurs in the following areas:

- The scope paragraph wording is changed to identify the scope limitation by adding the phrase "Except as discussed in the following paragraph" to the beginning of the first sentence in the paragraph.

■ A separate explanatory paragraph is added to the report to describe the scope limitation.

As Figure 20–4 shows, disclaiming an opinion because of a scope limitation requires modification of the opening paragraph to state "We were engaged to audit" instead of "We have audited," deletion of the scope paragraph to avoid overshadowing the disclaimer, and the addition of a paragraph explaining the reasons the audit did not comply with generally accepted auditing standards.

The opinion paragraph wording is changed either to express a qualified opinion (Figure 20–3) or to disclaim an opinion (Figure 20–4). In the qualified opinion, the phrase "except for" is used to qualify the auditor's opinion. The phrase refers to the potential effects on the financial statements and not to the scope limitation itself because the auditor's opinion relates to the financial statements. In the disclaimer, the auditor specifically states that an opinion cannot be expressed.

Departure from GAAP

When a departure from generally accepted accounting principles has a material effect on the financial statements, the auditor cannot express an unqualified opinion. Departures from GAAP include using inappropriate accounting principles, such as valuing property, plant, and equipment in a manufacturing company at current value rather than historical cost; improperly applying accounting methods, such as incorrect application of the LIFO costing method to inventory; and inadequate disclosure, such as failing to disclose the pledging of material amounts of inventory as collateral for a loan.

Effect on Opinion   When the financial statements contain a material departure from GAAP, the auditor should express either a qualified or an adverse opinion. A disclaimer of opinion is inappropriate because the auditor is in a position to express an opinion and cannot avoid disclosing a known departure from GAAP by denying an opinion on the financial statements.

The auditor's choice between a qualified or adverse opinion is based on the materiality of the departure from GAAP. Materiality is evaluated by considering (1) the dollar magnitude of the effects, (2) the significance of the item to the client, (3) the number of financial statement items affected, and (4) the effect of the departure on the financial statements taken as a whole.

If the departure from GAAP is not so material as to cause the financial statements taken as a whole to be misleading, the auditor will express a qualified opinion, as illustrated in Figure 20–5.

If the effects of the departure from GAAP are so material that they cause the financial statements as a whole to be misleading, the auditor will express an adverse opinion, as illustrated in Figure 20–6.

Consideration of Figures 20–5 and 20–6 helps clarify the effect of materiality on the auditor's decision to issue a qualified or adverse opinion. The qualified opinion in Figure 20–5 was issued because the client failed to capitalize leased assets that met the requirements for capitalization under generally accepted accounting principles. This departure caused both the property and the long-term debt accounts to be materially misstated. The misstatements in these accounts, however, when considered in relation to the financial statements as a whole, were not considered to be material enough to cause the statements taken as a whole to be misleading. Therefore, the auditor did not consider an adverse opinion appropriate.

(Opening Paragraph)

We have audited the accompanying balance sheet of AU Company as of December 31, 19X4, and the related statements of income, retained earnings, and cash flows for the year then ended. These financial statements are the responsibility of the Company's management. Our responsibility is to express an opinion on these financial statements based on our audit.

Opening paragraph is the same as in the standard report.

(Scope Paragraph)

We conducted our audit in accordance with generally accepted auditing standards. Those standards require that we plan and perform the audit to obtain reasonable assurance about whether the financial statements are free of material misstatement. An audit includes examining, on a test basis, evidence supporting the amounts and disclosures in the financial statements. An audit also includes assessing the accounting principles used and significant estimates made by management, as well as evaluating the overall financial statement presentation. We believe that our audit provides a reasonable basis for our opinion.

Scope paragraph is the same as in the standard report because no limitations have been placed on the scope of the audit.

(Explanatory Paragraph)

The Company has excluded, from property and debt in the accompanying balance sheets, certain lease obligations which, in our opinion, should be capitalized in order to conform with generally accepted accounting principles. If these lease obligations were capitalized, property would be increased by $5,500,000, long-term debt by $7,200,000, and retained earnings would be decreased by $1,700,000 as of December 31, 19X4. Additionally, net income would be decreased by $500,000 and earnings per share would be decreased by $.50 for the year then ended.

Separate paragraph has been added to explain the departure from generally accepted accounting principles and its effect on the financial statements.

(Opinion Paragraph)

In our opinion, *except for the effects of not capitalizing certain lease obligations, as discussed in the preceding paragraph*, the financial statements referred to above present fairly, in all material respects, the financial position of AU Company as of December 31, 19X4, and the results of its operations and its cash flows for the year then ended, in conformity with generally accepted accounting principles.

Opinion paragraph is qualified "except for" due to the departure from generally accepted accounting principles regarding lease capitalization.

The adverse opinion in Figure 20–6 was issued because property, plant, and equipment was stated at appraisal value rather than historical cost and because the client did not provide for deferred income taxes. These departures affected numerous accounts and, in the auditor's judgment, caused the financial statements taken as a whole to be misleading. Thus, the auditor considered an adverse opinion necessary.

Figure 20–6

Report with an Adverse Opinion Due to Departures from GAAP

(Opening Paragraph)

We have audited the accompanying balance sheet of AU Company as of December 31, 19X4, and the related statements of income, retained earnings, and cash flows for the year then ended. These financial statements are the responsibility of the Company's management. Our responsibility is to express an opinion on these financial statements based on our audit.

Opening paragraph is the same as in the standard report.

(Scope Paragraph)

We conducted our audit in accordance with generally accepted auditing standards. Those standards require that we plan and perform the audit to obtain reasonable assurance about whether the financial statements are free of material misstatement. An audit includes examining, on a test basis, evidence supporting the amounts and disclosures in the financial statements. An audit also includes assessing the accounting principles used and significant estimates made by management, as well as evaluating the overall financial statement presentation. We believe that our audit provides a reasonable basis for our opinion.

Scope paragraph is the same as in the standard report because no limitations have been placed on the scope of the audit.

(Explanatory Paragraph 1)

As discussed in Note X to the financial statements, the Company carries its property, plant, and equipment accounts at appraisal values, and provides depreciation on the basis of such values. Further, the Company does not provide for income taxes with respect to differences between financial income and taxable income arising because of the use, for income tax purposes, of the installment method of reporting gross profit from certain types of sales. Generally accepted accounting principles require that property, plant, and equipment be stated at an amount not in excess of cost, reduced by depreciation based on such amount, and that deferred income taxes be provided.

Separate paragraphs have been added to explain the departures from generally accepted accounting principles and their effects on the financial statements.

(continued)

Figure 20–6 *continued*

> *(Explanatory Paragraph 2)*
>
> **Because of the departures from generally accepted accounting principles identified above, as of December 31, 19X4, inventories have been increased $450,000 by inclusion in manufacturing overhead of depreciation in excess of that based on cost; property, plant, and equipment, less accumulated depreciation, is carried at $12,500,000 in excess of an amount based on the cost to the Company; and deferred income taxes of $2,500,000 have not been recorded; resulting in an increase of $2,950,000 in retained earnings and in appraisal surplus of $12,500,000. For the year ended December 31, 19X4, cost of goods sold has been increased $350,000 because of the effects of the depreciation accounting referred to above, and deferred income taxes of $1,000,000 have not been provided, resulting in an increase in net income of $650,000.**
>
> *(Opinion Paragraph)*
>
> In our opinion, **because of the effects of the matters discussed in the preceding paragraphs, the financial statements referred to above do not present fairly, in conformity with generally accepted accounting principles, the financial position of AU Company as of December 31, 19X4, or the results of its operations or its cash flows for the year then ended.**
>
> *Opinion expressed is adverse—the departures from generally accepted accounting principles are so material that the financial statements as a whole are misleading.*

Effect on Report Wording When a departure from GAAP exists, report wording is modified in the following areas:

- A separate explanatory paragraph is added to the report to disclose all of the significant reasons for the qualified or adverse opinion and to describe the departure(s) from GAAP and, if practicable, its effects on the financial statements.
- The opinion paragraph wording is changed to express either a qualified opinion or an adverse opinion. In the qualified opinion, the phrase "except for" is used to qualify the auditor's opinion. In the adverse opinion, the auditor states that, because of the effects of the departures from GAAP, the financial statements do not present fairly in conformity with GAAP.

The scope paragraph should not be modified for departure from GAAP circumstances because no scope limitation exists.

Figure 20-7	**Disclaimer of Opinion When Not Independent (Public Entity)**

> We are not independent with respect to AU Company, and the accompanying balance sheet as of December 31, 19X4, and the related statements of income, retained earnings, and cash flows for the year then ended were not audited by us and, accordingly, we do not express an opinion on them.
>
> *Reason for the lack of independence and any procedures performed should not be described.*

Lack of Independence

When an accountant is not independent, any procedure performed would not be in accordance with generally accepted auditing standards. Thus, *SAS No. 26* (AU 504.08–.10) requires the accountant who is not independent to issue a special disclaimer of opinion. Figure 20–7 illustrates the nonindependent disclaimer for financial statements of a public entity.

Modification of Wording Only

Circumstances may require modification of the wording of the standard report but not modification of the auditor's opinion on the financial statements. Six such situations exist:

- Part of the audit was performed by another independent auditor.
- A departure from a promulgated accounting principle is necessary to keep the financial statements from being misleading.
- A material uncertainty affects the financial statements.
- The auditor has substantial doubt about the entity's ability to continue as a going concern.
- A material change in accounting principles causes the financial statements to be inconsistent with those of the prior period.
- The auditor wishes to emphasize a matter regarding the financial statements but still express an unqualified opinion.

Part of Audit Performed by Another Independent Auditor

More than one audit firm may participate in an audit, particularly when the entity being audited is widespread geographically. For example, an entity may have its major operations in the Southeast audited by a local CPA firm while having its western subsidiary audited by a different auditor on the West Coast.

When involved in an audit in which part of the audit has been performed by other auditors, the auditor must first decide whether he or she can serve as *principal auditor* and report on the financial statements even though not having audited all of the subsidiaries, divisions, branches, or components that will be included in the financial statements. According to *SAS No. 1, Part of Audit Performed by Other Independent Auditors* (AU 543), in making this decision the auditor should consider

- the materiality of the portion of the financial statements audited in comparison with the portion audited by other auditors.
- knowledge of the overall financial statements.
- the importance of the components audited in relation to the entity as a whole.

The auditor must decide first if it is appropriate to serve as the principal auditor and then, if so, whether to assume responsibility for the work of the other auditor. The principal auditor is never required to assume responsibility for the other auditor's work. However, if the principal auditor does assume responsibility, he or she must be satisfied as to (1) the independence of the other auditor, (2) the professional reputation of the other auditor, and (3) the other auditor's work.

An assessment of the independence and professional reputation of the other auditor is normally accomplished through procedures, such as inquiries of the AICPA, colleagues, and members of the business community, and by obtaining a representation letter from the other auditor regarding his or her independence and familiarity with the entity's financial statements, accounting principles, and reporting requirements. To be satisfied about the other auditor's work, the principal auditor also considers whether to (1) visit the other auditor to discuss the audit procedures and results, (2) review the other auditor's audit programs, (3) review the other auditor's working papers, or (4) make supplemental tests of accounts examined by the other auditor. The principal auditor may also consider the other auditor's quality control policies and procedures in determining what procedures to apply.

If a principal auditor decides to accept responsibility for the other auditor's work, the standard report is issued without modification. In such a case, the report expresses an opinion on the financial statements as if the principal auditor had conducted the entire audit; no reference is made to the other auditors or their work in the audit report.

Generally, if the other auditor's opinion is qualified, the principal auditor's opinion will also be qualified, unless the qualification is not material to the financial statements on which the principal auditor is reporting. If the other auditor's qualification is not material to the principal auditor's opinion and the other auditor's report is not presented, the principal auditor will usually issue an unqualified opinion without any reference to the other auditor's report. If the other auditor's qualified report is presented, the principal auditor may decide to refer to the qualification and its disposition in an explanatory paragraph, though such reference is not mandatory.

If the principal auditor decides not to assume responsibility for the other auditor's work and is satisfied with the independence and reputation of the other auditor, the responsibility is shared. Sharing responsibility in no way raises questions about the quality of the other auditor's work, nor does it imply less assurance about the reliability of the financial statements. It means simply that the principal auditor is not in a position to assume responsibility for the other auditor's work as if the principal auditor had done the work.

Shared responsibility is communicated to audit report readers by a modification of the wording of the standard report. The opinion on the financial statements is not affected by the fact that more than one audit firm participated in the audit. Thus only the report wording—not the opinion—is modified.

The example of a shared responsibility report in Figure 20–8 illustrates the following modifications of wording in the opening, scope, and opinion paragraphs:

- *Opening Paragraph* The subsidiaries that the principal auditor has not audited are identified, preferably by name, and the magnitude of the portion of the financial statements audited by the other auditor is disclosed by indicating dollar amounts or percentages of appropriate criteria, such as assets or revenues. In addition, the principal auditor specifies that part of the audit was made by other auditors. (The other auditor need not be, and usually is not, identified. The other auditor's permission must be obtained, and his or her report also must be presented, if he or she is identified in the principal auditor's report.)

- *Scope Paragraph* The principal auditor indicates that he or she believes that his or her audit *and the report of the other auditors* provide a reasonable basis for the opinion on the consolidated financial statements.

- *Opinion Paragraph* The principal auditor indicates that the opinion is based in part on the other auditor's audit. The opinion itself is not modified simply because of shared responsibility.

Departure from a Promulgated Principle

As discussed in Chapter 2, Rule 203 of the AICPA Code of Professional Conduct precludes the auditor from expressing an unqualified opinion on financial statements that contain a material departure from a promulgated accounting principle. A promulgated accounting principle is one issued by the bodies designated by the AICPA to establish accounting principles, as discussed in Chapter 1. When such a departure exists, the auditor should modify the opinion just as for a departure from any other GAAP.

There is, however, an exception in Rule 203 that permits the auditor to issue an unqualified opinion, despite a departure from a promulgated accounting principle, when the auditor believes that, due to unusual circumstances, the departure is necessary to keep the financial statements from being misleading. When this rare situation exists, the auditor modifies the wording of the report by adding a separate explanatory paragraph, usually between the scope and opinion paragraphs. This paragraph describes the departure, the approximate effects, if practicable, and the reasons compliance with the principle would result in misleading financial statements. The opening, scope, and opinion paragraphs, however, are identical to those in the standard report. The opinion on the financial statements is unqualified.

Uncertainties[1]

Some matters affect the financial statements or required disclosures but have outcomes that cannot be reasonably estimated at the date of the auditor's report. These matters are termed ***uncertainties*** because it is not possible to determine whether the financial statements should be adjusted or in what amount.

According to *SAS No. 58* (AU 508), a matter involving an uncertainty is expected to be resolved at a future date, at which time sufficient evidence concerning its

---

[1]The Auditing Standards Board recently voted to eliminate the requirement to add a paragraph (after the opinion paragraph) for uncertainties in the auditor's report. The plan is to amend *SAS No. 58, Reports on Audited Financial Statements* and to issue a final standard by the end of 1995. Early application would be permitted. The amendment when effective would eliminate this section of the textbook.

| Figure 20-8 | Shared Responsibility Report |

(Opening Paragraph)

We have audited the consolidated balance sheet of AU Company as of December 31, 19X4, and the related consolidated statements of income, retained earnings, and cash flows for the year then ended. These financial statements are the responsibility of the Company's management. Our responsibility is to express an opinion on these financial statements based on our audit. *We did not audit the financial statements of B Company, a wholly-owned subsidiary, which statements reflect total assets of $20,000,000 as of December 31, 19X4, and total revenues of $45,000,000 for the year then ended. Those statements were audited by other auditors whose report has been furnished to us, and our opinion, insofar as it relates to the amounts included for B Company, is based solely on the report of the other auditors.*

Opening paragraph modified to communicate shared responsibility for the audit.

(Scope Paragraph)

We conducted our audit in accordance with generally accepted auditing standards. Those standards require that we plan and perform the audit to obtain reasonable assurance about whether the financial statements are free of material misstatement. An audit includes examining, on a test basis, evidence supporting the amounts and disclosures in the financial statements. An audit also includes assessing the accounting principles used and significant estimates made by management, as well as evaluating the overall financial statement presentation. We believe that our audit *and the report of the other auditors* provide a reasonable basis for our opinion.

Scope paragraph modified to indicate that the opinion is based, in part, on report of other auditors.

(Opinion Paragraph)

In our opinion, *based on our audit and the report of the other auditors,* the consolidated financial statements referred to above present fairly, in all material respects, the financial position of AU Company as of December 31, 19X4, and the results of its operations and its cash flows for the year then ended in conformity with generally accepted accounting principles.

Opinion paragraph modified to indicate shared responsibility for the audit opinion—note that the opinion is unqualified.

outcome would be expected to become available. The following are some common examples of uncertainties:

- Lawsuits against the client in which legal counsel is unable to form an opinion as to the outcome of the case, such as when the client is sued for patent infringement.

- Tax claims by tax authorities when precedents are not clear and potential liability cannot be determined, such as when the Internal Revenue Service claims the client owes additional taxes because a particular tax deduction is questionable.

- Recoverability of certain assets that depends on future operations or market conditions that cannot be evaluated with any degree of reliability, such as the ability to recover the investment in a plant designed to produce a product the demand for which may be substantially reduced by potential technological obsolescence.

Generally, matters whose outcomes depend on the client's actions and that relate to typical business operations are susceptible to reasonable estimation and, therefore, are estimates inherent in the accounting process, not uncertainties. For example, provisions for losses on uncollectible trade receivables and obsolete inventories, estimates of the useful lives of depreciable assets, and estimates of accruals for income taxes and product warranty obligations are not uncertainties because they normally can be estimated with reasonable accuracy.

When a material uncertainty exists, the auditor must decide whether he or she has gathered sufficient evidence to support management's assertions about the uncertainty and its presentation or disclosure in the financial statements. If the auditor has not obtained sufficient evidence, he or she should express a qualified opinion or should issue a disclaimer of opinion on the financial statements because of the scope limitation.

Similarly, if management has not properly disclosed the uncertainty, has used an inappropriate accounting principle, or has made an unreasonable estimate of a material uncertainty, the auditor should qualify the opinion or express an adverse opinion on the financial statements because of the GAAP departure.

If the auditor has obtained sufficient evidence about the uncertainty and management has accounted for and disclosed the uncertainty in accordance with generally accepted accounting principles, the auditor has to then consider whether to add an explanatory paragraph to the audit report because of the uncertainty. To make that determination, the auditor considers the likelihood of a material loss resulting from the resolution of the uncertainty.

Figure 20–9 illustrates the possible outcomes of the auditor's assessment of the uncertainty. If management believes and the auditor is satisfied that there is only a remote likelihood of material loss, the auditor would not add an explanatory paragraph to the audit report. However, if there is a probable chance of material loss and management is unable to make a reasonable estimate of the amount or range of loss, the auditor must add an explanatory paragraph to the audit report. In contrast, if a material loss is probable and can be reasonably estimated, management should provide for this in the financial statements and a standard, unqualified audit report would be issued.

| | Figure 20-9 | **Reporting on Uncertainties** |

	Probability of Material Loss		
	Remote	Reasonably Possible	Probable
Effect of Uncertainty on the Auditor's Report	The auditor will issue a standard unqualified opinion.	The auditor's decision to add an explanatory paragraph depends on the following: **1.** The magnitude of the loss (that is not recorded in the financial statements) relative to materiality. **2.** Whether the probability of unfavorable outcome is closer to remote or to probable.	The auditor will add an explanatory paragraph to the report when the amount of the loss cannot be reasonably estimated.

If the chance of a material loss is more than remote but less than probable (reasonably possible in Figure 20–9), the auditor's decision becomes more complex. In that situation, the auditor considers the following matters in deciding whether to add an explanatory paragraph to the audit report.

1. The magnitude by which the amount of reasonably possible loss (not recorded in the financial statements because it is not reasonably estimable) exceeds the auditor's judgment about materiality.
2. The likelihood of occurrence of a material loss (for example, whether that likelihood is closer to remote or to probable).

As the reasonably possible loss becomes larger or moves closer to probable, it becomes more likely that the auditor will add an explanatory paragraph to the audit report.

Figure 20–10 illustrates an auditor's report that contains an explanatory paragraph describing an uncertainty. *SAS No. 58* (AU 508) specifies that the explanatory paragraph must follow the opinion paragraph. Note, however, that no reference to the uncertainty should be made in the introductory, scope, or opinion paragraphs of the report.

Referring to Figure 20–10, if the uncertainty is subsequently resolved in 19X5 and recognized in the 19X5 financial statements of AU Company, the explanatory paragraph is simply dropped and no mention is made of it in the auditor's 19X5 report.

(Opening Paragraph)

We have audited the accompanying balance
sheet of AU Company as of December 31, 19X4,
and the related statements of income, retained
earnings, and cash flows for the year then
ended. These financial statements are the
responsibility of the Company's management.
Our responsibility is to express an opinion on
these financial statements based on our audit.

*Opening paragraph is
the same as in the
standard report.*

(Scope Paragraph)

We conducted our audit in accordance with
generally accepted auditing standards. Those
standards require that we plan and perform
the audit to obtain reasonable assurance about
whether the financial statements are free of
material misstatement. An audit includes
examining, on a test basis, evidence supporting
the amounts and disclosures in the financial
statements. An audit also includes assessing the
accounting principles used and significant
estimates made by management, as well as
evaluating the overall financial statement
presentation. We believe that our audit provides
a reasonable basis for our opinion.

*Scope paragraph is the
same as in the
standard report
because no limitations
have been placed on the
scope of the audit.*

(Opinion Paragraph)

In our opinion, the financial statements referred
to above present fairly, in all material respects,
the financial position of AU Company as of
December 31, 19X4, and the results of its
operations and its cash flows for the year then
ended in conformity with generally accepted
accounting principles.

*Opinion paragraph is
unqualified.*

(Uncertainty Paragraph)

*As discussed in Note X to the financial
statements, the Company is a defendant in a
lawsuit alleging infringement of certain patent
rights and claiming royalties and punitive
damages. The Company has filed a
counteraction, and preliminary hearings and
discovery proceedings on both actions are in
progress. The ultimate outcome of the litigation
cannot presently be determined. Accordingly, no
provision for any liability that may result upon
adjudication has been made in the
accompanying financial statements.*

*Explanatory
paragraph added to
highlight uncertainty.*

The Real World of Auditing

Rule 203 GAAP Departure ← *acceptable departure*

OAK INDUSTRIES, INC., DECEMBER 31, 1988

Report of Independent Public Accountants

To the Stockholders and Board of Directors of Oak Industries Inc.:

We have audited the consolidated balance sheets of Oak Industries Inc. and Subsidiaries (the "Company") as of December 31, 1988 and 1987, and the related consolidated statements of operations, stockholders' investment, and cash flows for each of the three years in the period ended December 31, 1988. These financial statements are the responsibility of the Company's management. Our responsibility is to express an opinion on these financial statements based on our audits.

We conducted our audits in accordance with generally accepted auditing standards. Those standards require that we plan and perform the audit to obtain reasonable assurance about whether the financial statements are free of material misstatement. An audit includes examining, on a test basis, evidence supporting the amounts and disclosures in the financial statements. An audit also includes assessing the accounting principles used and significant estimates made by management, as well as evaluating the overall financial statement presentation. We believe that our audits provide a reasonable basis for our opinion.

As described in Note 3, in May 1987, the Company exchanged shares of its common stock for $5,060,000 of its outstanding public debt. The fair value of the common stock issued exceeded the carrying amount of the debt by $466,000, which has been shown as an extraordinary loss in the 1987 statement of operations. Because a portion of the debt exchanged was convertible debt, a literal application of Statement of Financial Accounting Standards No. 84, "Induced Conversions of Convertible Debt," would have resulted in a further reduction in net income of $3,611,000, which would have been offset by a corresponding $3,611,000 credit to additional paid-in capital; accordingly, there would have been no net effect on stockholders' investment. In the opinion of Company management, with which we agree, a literal application of accounting literature would have resulted in misleading financial statements that do not properly portray the economic consequences of the exchange.

In our opinion, the consolidated financial statements referred to above present fairly, in all material respects, the financial position of Oak Industries Inc. and Subsidiaries as of December 31, 1988 and 1987, and the results of their operations and their cash flows for each of the three years in the period ended December 31, 1988, in conformity with generally accepted accounting principles.

COOPERS & LYBRAND
San Diego, California
February 10, 1989

Going Concern Matters

SAS No. 59, The Auditor's Consideration of an Entity's Ability to Continue as a Going Concern (AU 341), states that the auditor has a responsibility to evaluate whether there is substantial doubt about the entity's ability to continue as a ***going concern*** for a reasonable period of time. *Reasonable period of time* is defined as a period not to exceed one year beyond the date of the auditor's balance sheet.

The auditor must evaluate whether there is substantial doubt about going concern in the following manner:

1. The auditor considers whether the results of procedures performed in planning, gathering evidential matter, and completing the audit identify conditions and events that, when considered in the aggregate, indicate there could be substantial doubt about the entity's ability to continue as a going concern for a reasonable period of time. It may be necessary to obtain additional information about such conditions and events, as well as the appropriate evidential matter to support information that mitigates the auditor's doubt.
2. If the auditor believes there is substantial doubt about the entity's ability to continue as a going concern, he or she should (1) obtain information about management's plans that are intended to mitigate the effect of such conditions or events, and (2) assess the likelihood that such plans can be effectively implemented.
3. After evaluating management's plans, the auditor concludes whether he or she has substantial doubt about the entity's ability to continue as a going concern for a reasonable period of time. If substantial doubt remains, the auditor should (1) consider the adequacy of disclosure about the entity's possible inability to continue as a going concern for a reasonable period of time, and (2) include an explanatory paragraph (following the opinion paragraph) in the audit report to reflect that conclusion. If the auditor concludes that substantial doubt does not exist, he or she should consider the need for disclosure of the circumstances in the entity's financial statement.

Figure 20–11 illustrates an auditor's report that contains an explanatory paragraph describing an uncertainty about going concern. Note that the opening, scope, and opinion paragraphs are not changed, but an explanatory paragraph is added to the audit report to highlight the going concern problem. The explanatory paragraph must contain the phrases "going concern" and "substantial doubt" in order to clearly communicate the severity of the matter.

Lack of Consistency

The second standard of reporting (the consistency standard) concerns financial statement comparability. This standard requires the auditor to identify changes in accounting principles that have a material effect on the comparability of the financial statements.

Although a change in accounting principle is not the only accounting change that can affect financial statement comparability, it is the only accounting change that requires a report wording modification under the consistency standard. Thus, the factor that determines whether the auditor's report must be modified because of a lack of consistency is whether the accounting change involves a change in accounting principle (including a change in the method of applying a principle). Changes in accounting principle may take the following forms:

- Change from one GAAP to another GAAP, such as changing from the straight-line method to the declining balance method for depreciation of plant assets.
- Change in the reporting entity covered by the financial statements, such as when consolidated financial statements are presented in place of the statements of individual entities.
- Correction of an error in an accounting principle by changing from a principle that is not generally accepted to one that is, such as changing from an appraisal value basis for property, plant, and equipment to a historical cost basis.

Report with an Unqualified Opinion with Explanatory Paragraph Highlighting a Going Concern Matter

(Opening Paragraph)

We have audited the accompanying balance sheet of AU Company as of December 31, 19X4, and the related statements of income, retained earnings, and cash flows for the year then ended. These financial statements are the responsibility of the Company's management. Our responsibility is to express an opinion on these financial statements based on our audit.

Opening paragraph is the same as in the standard report.

(Scope Paragraph)

We conducted our audit in accordance with generally accepted auditing standards. Those standards require that we plan and perform the audit to obtain reasonable assurance about whether the financial statements are free of material misstatement. An audit includes examining, on a test basis, evidence supporting the amounts and disclosures in the financial statements. An audit also includes assessing the accounting principles used and significant estimates made by management, as well as evaluating the overall financial statement presentation. We believe that our audit provides a reasonable basis for our opinion.

Scope paragraph is the same as in the standard report because no limitations have been placed on the scope of the audit.

(Opinion Paragraph)

In our opinion, the financial statements referred to above present fairly, in all material respects, the financial position of AU Company as of December 31, 19X4, and the results of its operations and its cash flows for the year then ended in conformity with generally accepted accounting principles.

Opinion paragraph is unqualified.

(Going Concern Paragraph)

The accompanying financial statements have been prepared assuming that the Company will continue as a going concern. As discussed in Note X to the financial statements, the Company has suffered recurring losses from operations and has a net capital deficiency that raise substantial doubt about its ability to continue as a going concern. Management's plans in regard to these matters are also described in Note X. The financial statements do not include any adjustments that might result from the outcome of this uncertainty.

Explanatory paragraph added to highlight going concern problem.

- Changes in accounting principle that are inseparable from changes in accounting estimates. This type of change involves both a change in principle and a change in estimate, the effects of which cannot be separately identified, such as changing from capitalizing an expenditure to expensing it because future benefits have become doubtful.

Other accounting changes that may affect financial statement comparability but do not require modification of the auditor's report for a lack of consistency should be disclosed by management, when the changes are material, in the notes to the financial statements. If disclosure is omitted, the auditor's opinion would be qualified because of a departure from GAAP, not because of a lack of consistency. Accounting changes that affect financial statement comparability and require disclosure but do not require a consistency modification are as follows:

- Changes in accounting estimates, such as changing the estimated useful lives of depreciable assets.
- Correction of errors not involving accounting principles, such as correction of mathematical mistakes in determining inventory values.
- Changes of classification in the financial statements, such as changing the classification of an expenditure from general and administrative expense to selling expense in the income statement.
- Modifying or adopting an accounting principle for substantially different transactions or events.
- Changes in GAAP that have no material effect in the current year, but that are expected to have a material effect in future years.

When a change in an accounting principle has a material effect on the financial statements, the auditor should not modify the unqualified opinion on the financial statements. That is, the material change in accounting principle, if properly accounted for and disclosed in the financial statement, requires modification of the auditor's standard report, but not qualification or modification of the opinion paragraph.

When a lack of consistency exists, report wording generally is modified in the following ways:

- The opening, scope, and opinion paragraphs are not changed.
- An explanatory paragraph is added to the audit report, following the opinion paragraph, identifying the nature of the change and referring the reader to the note in the financial statements that discusses the change in detail.

Figure 20–12 illustrates an auditor's report that includes an explanatory paragraph necessitated by a material change in accounting principle.

Other Consistency Exceptions

Two other sets of circumstances relating to the consistency standard occur frequently enough in audit engagements to warrant brief discussion.

1. *First Audit of a Client* When an auditor has not audited the financial statements of a client for the preceding year, scope limitations may prevent the auditor from forming an opinion on the consistency of the current year with the prior year. The auditor's report should be modified for a scope limitation and the explanatory separate paragraph, which should precede the opinion paragraph, should indicate that an opinion on consistency could not be formed. The opinion is qualified "except for" or disclaimed.

Figure   20-12

Report with an Unqualified Opinion with Explanatory Paragraph Highlighting Lack of Consistency in the Application of Accounting Principles

(Opening Paragraph)

We have audited the accompanying balance sheet of AU Company as of December 31, 19X4, and the related statements of income, retained earnings, and cash flows for the year then ended. These financial statements are the responsibility of the Company's management. Our responsibility is to express an opinion on these financial statements based on our audit.

Opening paragraph is the same as in the standard report.

(Scope Paragraph)

We conducted our audit in accordance with generally accepted auditing standards. Those standards require that we plan and perform the audit to obtain reasonable assurance about whether the financial statements are free of material misstatement. An audit includes examining, on a test basis, evidence supporting the amounts and disclosures in the financial statements. An audit also includes assessing the accounting principles used and significant estimates made by management, as well as evaluating the overall financial statement presentation. We believe that our audit provides a reasonable basis for our opinion.

Scope paragraph is the same as in the standard report because no limitations have been placed on the scope of the audit.

(Opinion Paragraph)

In our opinion, the financial statements referred to above present fairly, in all material respects, the financial position of AU Company as of December 31, 19X4, and the results of its operations and its cash flows for the year then ended in conformity with generally accepted accounting principles.

Opinion expressed is unqualified.

(Consistency Paragraph)

As discussed in Note X to the financial statements, the Company changed its method of computing depreciation in 19X4.

Explanatory paragraph added to highlight change in accounting principle.

2. *Change in Accounting Principle Not in Conformity with GAAP* A change in accounting principle must meet three conditions specified in APB Opinion No. 20, *Accounting Changes,* to be in conformity with GAAP: (1) the new principle must be a GAAP, (2) the method of accounting for the change must conform with GAAP, and (3) the change must be justified. If one or more of these conditions are not met, the auditor's report on the year of change should be modified because of a departure from GAAP. In this situation, the paragraph explaining the GAAP departure should precede the opinion paragraph, and the opinion is qualified "except for" or adverse.

Emphasis of a Matter

Under certain circumstances the auditor may wish to emphasize a specific matter regarding the financial statements even though an unqualified opinion has been expressed. Examples of such matters include important events occurring after the balance sheet date or identification of the entity as a subsidiary of a larger enterprise.

These matters are not deficiencies in the financial statements. They represent matters, properly treated in the financial statements, that are, in the auditor's judgment, sufficiently important to be accentuated in the report. To emphasize matters in the report, the auditor includes a separate explanatory paragraph, usually between the scope and opinion paragraphs of the standard report, as shown in Figure 20–13.

Figure 20–13   **Report Emphasizing a Matter**

(Opening Paragraph)

We have audited the accompanying balance sheet of AU Company as of December 31, 19X4, and the related statements of income, retained earnings, and cash flows for the year then ended. These financial statements are the responsibility of the Company's management. Our responsibility is to express an opinion on these financial statements based on our audit.

Opening paragraph is the same as in the standard report.

(Scope Paragraph)

We conducted our audit in accordance with generally accepted auditing standards. Those standards require that we plan and perform the audit to obtain reasonable assurance about whether the financial statements are free of material misstatement. An audit includes examining, on a test basis, evidence supporting the amounts and disclosures in the financial statements. An audit also includes assessing the accounting principles used and significant estimates made by management, as well as evaluating the overall financial statement presentation. We believe that our audit provides a reasonable basis for our opinion.

Scope paragraph is the same as in the standard report because no limitations have been placed on the scope of the audit.

(Emphasis Paragraph)

As discussed in Note X to the financial statements, the Company has had numerous dealings with businesses controlled by, and people who are related to, the officers of the Company.

Separate paragraph has been added to emphasize related-party transmissions.

(Opinion Paragraph)

In our opinion, the financial statements referred to above present fairly, in all material respects, the financial position of AU Company as of December 31, 19X4, and the results of its operations and its cash flows for the year then ended in conformity with generally accepted accounting principles.

Opinion paragraph is the same as in the standard report because the auditor is simply emphasizing a matter, not citing a deficiency.

Comparative Financial Statements

When financial statements of one or more prior periods are presented on a comparative basis with those of the current period, the fourth reporting standard requires a report on those comparative statements. The type of report, its content, and who issues it depend on whether the current auditor is a continuing auditor or is following a predecessor auditor. In addition, the report is affected by (1) whether the opinion(s) on the prior-period statement(s) is the same as or different from the opinion on the current-period statements, (2) whether the opinion on the prior-period statements should be revised in light of new circumstances, and (3) whether the comparative statements are audited or unaudited. *SAS No. 58, Reports on Audited Financial Statements* (AU 508), provides guidance to the auditor on comparative financial statements.

Continuing Auditor

A *continuing auditor* is one who has audited the financial statements of the current period and of one or more consecutive periods immediately preceding the current period. Basically, the auditor must have audited the current period and at least the immediately preceding period to be a continuing auditor. Table 20–3 lists several situations and how the continuing auditor definition applies to them.

The reporting responsibilities for a continuing auditor differ from those for one who is not. A continuing auditor is responsible for updating the report on prior-period financial statements that have been audited and that are presented for comparative purposes. *Updating* requires the auditor to consider whether, based on information obtained in the audit of the current-period statements, the auditor should reexpress the same opinion on prior statements shown on the comparative statements or express a revised opinion on them.

Table 20–3 **Deciding Whether CPA Firm "X" Is a Continuing Auditor When 19X6 Is the Current Year and Comparative Statements Are Presented for 19X5 and 19X4**

Comparative Statements and Auditor Association	Is CPA Firm "X" a Continuing Auditor?
19X6—Audited by Firm "X" 19X5—Audited by Firm "X" 19X4—Audited by Firm "B"	YES
19X6—Audited by Firm "X" 19X5—Audited by Firm "X" 19X4—Audited by Firm "X"	YES
19X6—Audited by Firm "X" 19X5—Audited by Firm "B" 19X4—Audited by Firm "X"	NO—Firm "X" is a successor auditor.
19X6—Audited by Firm "B" 19X5—Audited by Firm "X" 19X4—Audited by Firm "X"	NO—Firm "X" is a predecessor auditor.

**Prior Opinion
Reexpressed**

After considering the information obtained during the current audit, an auditor may conclude that the opinion originally expressed on the comparative statements is still appropriate. Figure 20–14 illustrates an updated auditor's report when the opinion expressed in the previous period is reexpressed in the updated report. This report is essentially the standard report for a single period expressed in plural form because it both expresses an opinion on the current-period statements and repeats the opinion originally expressed on the prior-period statements. For example, in the opening paragraph, the term "balance sheets" is used, all of the years for which comparative financial statements are presented are indicated, and the term "based on our audits" is plural. In the scope paragraph, "We conducted our audits" in the first sentence and "We believe that our audits" in the last sentence are plural. In the opinion paragraph,

---

Figure 20–14   **Report on Comparative Financial Statements: Previous Opinion Reexpressed**

(Opening Paragraph)

We have audited the accompanying *balance sheets* of AU Company as of December 31, 19X5 and 19X4, and the related statements of income, retained earnings, and cash flows for the *years* then ended. These financial statements are the responsibility of the Company's management. Our responsibility is to express an opinion on these financial statements based on our *audits.*

Opening paragraph is modified to refer to "balance sheets," to cover two (or more) years presented, and to refer to "audits" as plural.

(Scope Paragraph)

We conducted our *audits* in accordance with generally accepted auditing standards. Those standards require that we plan and perform the audit to obtain reasonable assurance about whether the financial statements are free of material misstatement. An audit includes examining, on a test basis, evidence supporting the amounts and disclosures in the financial statements. An audit also includes assessing the accounting principles used and significant estimates made by management, as well as evaluating the overall financial statement presentation. We believe that our *audits provide* a reasonable basis for our opinion.

Except for the reference to "audits," the scope paragraph is the same as in the standard report.

(Opinion Paragraph)

In our opinion, the financial statements referred to above present fairly, in all material respects, the financial position of AU Company as of December 31, 19X5 and *19X4*, and the results of its operations and its cash flows *for the years* then ended in conformity with generally accepted accounting principles.

Opinion paragraph is modified to cover two (or more) years.

all of the years for which comparative statements are presented are referred to and the term "years" is plural. Because the report is updated, the report date for the comparative statements is, in effect, changed to the report date for the current-period statements—the date of the completion of the audit of the most recent financial statements.

In Figure 20–14, the opinion expressed on the prior-period statements (19X4) was the same type of opinion expressed on the current-period statements: both were unqualified opinions. In some audit engagements, the opinion expressed on the prior-period statements might not be the same type of opinion as that expressed on the current-period statements. For example, the opinion on the prior-period statements might have been qualified for a scope limitation, whereas the opinion on the current-period statements might be unqualified. When the opinion on the comparative statements differs from the opinion on the current statements, the auditor selects the appropriate report for the particular circumstance, just as if it were a single-period report, and combines the appropriate reports into a single report on both the prior-period and current financial statements.

Prior Opinion Revised

During the current engagement, the auditor might become aware of circumstances that would cause a change in the type of opinion previously expressed on the prior-period statements. For example, when departures from generally accepted accounting principles in prior-period statements are corrected in the current year by restating those statements, a qualified or adverse opinion on the prior-period statements is no longer appropriate.

Figure 20–15 illustrates an updated auditor's report when the auditor changes the opinion expressed on the prior-period statements because the client has restated those statements to conform with generally accepted accounting principles. The wording of an updated report that expresses a revised opinion on prior-period statements is modified by adding a separate explanatory paragraph preceding the opinion paragraph that discloses the following information:

- Date of the auditor's previous report.
- Type of opinion previously expressed.
- Circumstances that caused the revised opinion.
- That the updated opinion differs from the prior opinion.

Predecessor Auditor

When the current auditor is not a continuing auditor and the client presents comparative statements, two situations can exist: (1) the prior-period statements were reported on by a *predecessor auditor* or (2) the prior-period statements have not been reported on by any auditor.

If one or more prior periods included in the comparative statements have been audited by a predecessor auditor, either of the following reporting approaches may be taken:

- The current (successor) auditor may refer to the predecessor auditor's report in the report on the current-period financial statements.
- The predecessor auditor may reissue his or her report on the prior-period statements.

Figure 20-15

Report on Comparative Financial Statements: Opinion Revised to Reflect Restatement of Prior-Period Financial Statements to Conform to GAAP

(Opening Paragraph)

We have audited the accompanying balance sheets of AU Company as of December 31, 19X5 and 19X4, and the related statements of income, retained earnings, and cash flows for the years then ended. These financial statements are the responsibility of the Company's management. Our responsibility is to express an opinion on these financial statements based on our audits.

Opening paragraph is the same as in the standard comparative report.

(Scope Paragraph)

We conducted our audits in accordance with generally accepted auditing standards. Those standards require that we plan and perform the audit to obtain reasonable assurance about whether the financial statements are free of material misstatement. An audit includes examining, on a test basis, evidence supporting the amounts and disclosures in the financial statements. An audit also includes assessing the accounting principles used and significant estimates made by management, as well as evaluating the overall financial statement presentation. We believe that our audits provide a reasonable basis for our opinion.

Scope paragraph is the same as in the standard comparative report.

(Separate Paragraph)

In our report dated March 1, 19X5, we expressed an opinion that the 19X4 financial statements did not fairly present financial position, results of operations, and cash flows in conformity with generally accepted accounting principles because of two departures from such principles: (1) the Company carried its property, plant, and equipment at appraisal values, and provided for depreciation on the basis of such values, and (2) the Company did not provide for deferred income taxes with respect to differences between income for financial reporting purposes and taxable income. As described in Note X, the Company has changed its method of accounting for these items and restated its 19X4 financial statements to conform with generally accepted accounting principles. Accordingly, our present opinion on the 19X4 financial statements, as presented herein, is different from that expressed in our previous report.

Separate paragraph has been added that explains that the prior-year opinion has been updated.

(continued)

Figure 20–15   *continued*

> *(Opinion Paragraph)*
>
> **In our opinion, the financial statements referred to above present fairly, in all material respects, the financial position of AU Company as of December 31, 19X5 and 19X4, and the results of its operations and its cash flows for the years then ended in conformity with generally accepted accounting principles.**

Opinion paragraph is the same as in the standard comparative report because the financial statements for both years are now fairly presented in conformity with GAAP.

Reference to Predecessor Auditor's Report

Most frequently, the ***successor auditor*** refers to the predecessor auditor's report. In that circumstance, the successor auditor adds a sentence such as the following as the last sentence in the opening paragraph of the current-period report: "The financial statements of AU Company as of December 31, 19X4, were audited by other auditors whose report dated March 1, 19X5, expressed an unqualified opinion on those statements." This sentence contains three elements that must be included in the successor auditor's reference to the predecessor auditor's report: (1) the fact that the financial statements of prior periods were audited by another auditor (the other auditor should not be named), (2) the date of the predecessor auditor's report, and (3) the type of opinion expressed by the predecessor auditor, including the reasons for any explanatory paragraphs included in the predecessor auditor's report.

Predecessor Reissues Report

If a predecessor auditor is asked to reissue the report and agrees to accept that request, the predecessor auditor must perform the following procedures to determine if the original report is still appropriate:

■ Read the financial statements of the current period, primarily to determine whether they contain any information that might affect the report on the prior-period statements.

■ Compare the prior-period financial statements reported on with those that will be presented for comparative purposes, primarily to determine that the prior-period statements do not differ materially from their original presentation.

■ Obtain a representation letter from the successor auditor stating whether the successor's audit revealed any matters that might have a material effect on, or require disclosure in, the financial statements reported on by the predecessor auditor.

If the predecessor auditor decides that the opinion on the prior-period statements is still appropriate, the previous report should be reissued. The date of the reissued report should be the same as the date of the original report to avoid any implication that any records, transactions, or events after that date have been examined.

If, after performing the above procedures, the predecessor auditor believes transactions or events have occurred that may affect the previous opinion on the financial statements, he or she should perform whatever procedures are necessary to determine whether the opinion needs to be revised. If the predecessor auditor concludes that a revised report should be issued, the same reporting guidelines that apply to a continuing auditor's updated report also apply to the predecessor. However, the predecessor's updated report is normally dual dated rather than redated to the report date on the current financial statements.

Prior-Period Not Audited

In situations when the 19X4 financial statements were not audited by anyone, the auditor must report on both years presented as required by the fourth standard of reporting. For *public* companies,[2] the typical audit report is an audit report for 19X5 (standard three paragraphs for an unqualified opinion) followed by a paragraph for the 19X4 report which states:

> The accompanying balance sheet of AU Company as of December 31, 19X4, and the related statements of income, retained earnings, and cash flows for the year then ended were not audited by us and, accordingly, we do not express an opinion on them.

Significant Terms

Adverse opinion A type of opinion issued by an auditor that states that the financial statements do not present fairly the financial position, results of operations, and cash flows in conformity with generally accepted accounting principles.

Audit opinion That part of the audit report that presents the conclusions reached by the auditor.

Audit report The auditor's entire communication about what was done and what conclusions were reached in the audit.

Continuing auditor An auditor who has audited the financial statements of both the current period and one or more consecutive periods immediately preceding the current period.

Disclaimer of opinion A report by the auditor that states that an opinion cannot be expressed.

Generally accepted accounting principles (GAAP) A technical term that includes standards, rules, and procedures that define accepted accounting practices.

Going concern An entity able to continue for a period at least one year beyond the balance sheet date.

Opening paragraph The paragraph in the audit report that identifies the financial statements that were audited and states that the financial statements are the responsibility of the entity's management.

Opinion paragraph A paragraph in the audit report that expresses an informed, expert opinion on whether the financial statements are fairly presented in conformity with established criteria (usually GAAP).

---

[2]Reporting for nonpublic companies is discussed in Chapter 22.

Predecessor auditor An auditor who has audited the financial statements in the preceding period but is not the auditor for the current period.

Principal auditor The auditor who reports on the financial statements even though another auditor has audited some of the subsidiaries, divisions, branches, or components that will be included in the financial statements.

Qualified opinion A type of opinion issued by an auditor that states that the financial statements are presented fairly in conformity with generally accepted accounting principles, excluding specific items identified in the report.

Scope limitations Restrictions that prevent the auditor from applying one or more audit procedures the auditor considers necessary.

Scope paragraph The paragraph in the audit report in which the auditor states explicitly that the audit provides a reasonable basis for the opinion.

Standard report An audit report consisting of three standard paragraphs (opening, scope, and opinion) that expresses an unqualified opinion.

Successor auditor The auditor of the current-period financial statements who did not audit the preceding period's financial statements.

Uncertainty A matter whose outcome depends on future actions or events not under the direct control of the client but that may affect the financial statements.

Unqualified opinion A type of opinion issued by an auditor that states that the financial statements are presented fairly in conformity with generally accepted accounting principles.

Discussion Questions

20-1. What is meant by the auditor's attest function?

20-2. What are the four standards of reporting?

20-3. Describe the factors that a CPA considers to determine if financial statements are presented in conformity with generally accepted accounting principles.

20-4. How are accounting principles for commercial or nongovernmental entities established as generally accepted?

20-5. What is the purpose of the consistency standard under the second standard of reporting?

20-6. What is meant by the phrase "taken as a whole" when referring to financial statements under the fourth standard of reporting?

20-7. When is an auditor considered to be associated with the financial statements of a client?

20-8. Discuss the conditions that must be met before an auditor can give an unqualified opinion.

20-9. What is the difference between an auditor's report and an auditor's opinion?

20-10. What are the seven basic elements of the standard audit report?

20-11. What other types of opinions besides unqualified may an auditor issue? Explain what they mean.

20-12. What factors prevent an auditor from issuing a standard audit report?

20-13. Describe the circumstances that may prevent the auditor from expressing an unqualified opinion and tell what type of opinion may be expressed in each circumstance.

20-14. When would an auditor issue a qualified opinion and when would the auditor issue a disclaimer for a scope limitation?

20-15. How could an auditor issue an unqualified opinion when there is a scope limitation that is not client-imposed?

20-16. How does an auditor choose between a qualified or an adverse opinion when there is a departure from GAAP that has a material effect on the financial statements?

20-17. How should an auditor report on audited financial statements of a public company if he or she is not independent?

20-18. Under what situations may an auditor change the wording of the standard report but still issue an unqualified opinion?

20-19. What does a principal auditor consider before accepting responsibility for work done by another auditor?

20-20. When may an auditor issue an unqualified opinion when there is a departure from a promulgated accounting principle?

20-21. Under what conditions must the auditor add an explanatory paragraph to the audit report when there is a lack of consistency?

20-22. Under what conditions does the auditor's report not require the addition of an explanatory paragraph for a lack of consistency?

20-23. Explain the difference in uncertainties and estimates inherent in the accounting process.

20-24. What type of opinion may an auditor issue if he or she has substantial doubt about the ability of an entity to continue as a going concern? How should the audit report be modified, if it should?

20-25. What is the responsibility of a continuing auditor?

20-26. What must a predecessor auditor do before reissuing his or her previous report?

20-27. How would the successor auditor modify his or her audit report on the current period when the successor auditor plans to refer to the predecessor auditor's report?

Objective Questions

*20-28. The fourth reporting standard requires the auditor's report to contain either an expression of opinion regarding the financial statements taken as a whole, or an assertion to the effect that an opinion cannot be expressed. What is the fourth standard designed to prevent?
(1) The CPA from reporting on one basic financial statement and not on the others.
(2) The CPA from expressing different opinions on each of the basic financial statements.
(3) Misinterpretations regarding the degree of responsibility the auditor is assuming.
(4) Management from reducing its responsibility for the basic financial statements.

20-29. When restrictions that significantly limit the scope of the audit are imposed by the client, the auditor generally should issue which of the following opinions?
(1) "Except for."
(2) Disclaimer of opinion.
(3) Adverse.
(4) Unqualified with explanatory paragraph.

*20-30. The predecessor auditor, after properly communicating with the successor auditor, has reissued a report because the audit client desires comparative financial statements. The predecessor auditor's report should make
(1) no reference to the report or the work of the successor auditor.
(2) reference to the work of the successor auditor in the scope paragraph.
(3) reference to both the work and the report of the successor auditor in the opinion paragraph.
(4) reference to the report of the successor auditor in the scope paragraph.

*20-31. Which of the following will not result in qualification of the auditor's opinion due to a scope limitation?
(1) Restrictions imposed by the client.
(2) Reliance placed on the report of another auditor.
(3) Inability to obtain sufficient competent evidential matter.
(4) Inadequacy in the accounting records.

20-32. The auditor is obligated to add an explanatory paragraph to the standard audit report if which of the following is true?
(1) A material and probable uncertainty that cannot be estimated affects the financial statements.

---

*AICPA adapted.

      (2) Substantial doubt exists about the client's ability to continue as a going concern.

      (3) There has been a material change in accounting principles.

      (4) All of the above.

*20-33. It is *not* appropriate for the auditor's report to refer a reader to a financial statement note for details regarding which of the following?

      (1) A change in accounting principle.

      (2) A limitation in the scope of the audit.

      (3) An uncertainty.

      (4) A related-party transaction.

*20-34. When the client fails to include information that is necessary for the fair presentation of financial statements in the body of the statements or in the related notes, it is the responsibility of the auditor to present the information, if practicable, in the auditor's report and issue which of the following?

      (1) A qualified opinion or a disclaimer of opinion.

      (2) A qualified opinion or an adverse opinion.

      (3) An adverse opinion or a disclaimer of opinion.

      (4) A qualified opinion or an unqualified opinion.

20-35. Higgins Corporation is required to, but does not wish to, prepare and issue a statement of cash flows along with its other basic financial statements. In these circumstances, what should the independent auditor's report on the Higgins financial statements include?

      (1) An unqualified opinion with a statement of cash flows prepared by the auditor and included as part of the auditor's report.

      (2) A qualified opinion with an explanatory paragraph explaining that the company declined to present the required statement.

      (3) An adverse opinion stating that the financial statements, taken as a whole, are not fairly presented because of the omission of the required statement.

      (4) A disclaimer of opinion with a separate explanatory paragraph stating why the company declined to present the required statement.

20-36. When financial statements are prepared on the basis of a going concern and the auditor believes that the client may not continue as a going concern, what should the auditor issue?

      (1) A disclaimer of opinion.

      (2) An unqualified opinion with an explanatory paragraph.

      (3) An "except for" opinion.

      (4) An adverse opinion.

*20-37. An auditor may reasonably issue an "except for" qualified opinion for

	Inadequate Disclosure	Scope Limitation
(1)	Yes	Yes
(2)	Yes	No
(3)	No	Yes
(4)	No	No

20-38. Which of the following requires the addition of an explanatory paragraph to the auditor's report as to consistency?

      (1) Changing the salvage value of an asset.

      (2) Changing the presentation of prepaid insurance from inclusion in "other assets" to disclosure as a separate line item.

      (3) Division of the consolidated subsidiary into two subsidiaries that are both consolidated.

      (4) Changing from consolidating a subsidiary to carrying it on the equity basis.

---

*AICPA adapted.

*20-39. Management believes and the auditor is satisfied that the chance of a material loss resulting from the resolution of a lawsuit is more than remote but less than probable. Which of the following matters should the auditor consider in deciding whether to add an explanatory paragraph?

	Likelihood That the Loss Is Closer to Probable than Remote	Magnitude by which the Loss Exceeds the Auditor's Materiality
(1)	Yes	Yes
(2)	Yes	No
(3)	No	Yes
(4)	No	No

*20-40. A CPA's report on a client's balance sheet, income statement, and statement of cash flows was sent to the stockholders. The client now wishes to present only the balance sheet along with an appropriately modified auditor's report in a newspaper advertisement. The auditor may do which of the following?
   (1) Permit the publication as requested.
   (2) Permit only the publication of the originally issued auditor's report and accompanying financial statements.
   (3) Refuse to permit publication of a modified auditor's report.
   (4) Refuse to permit publication of any auditor's report in connection with a newspaper advertisement.

*20-41. When financial statements of a prior period are presented on a comparative basis with financial statements of the current period, for which of the following is the continuing auditor responsible?
   (1) Expressing dual-dated opinions.
   (2) Updating the report on the previous financial statements only if there has *not* been a change in the opinion.
   (3) Updating the report on the previous financial statements only if the previous report was qualified and the reasons for the qualification no longer exist.
   (4) Updating the report on the previous financial statements regardless of the opinion previously issued.

20-42. For financial reporting purposes, a change from a straight-line to an accelerated depreciation method was disclosed in a note to the financial statements and has an *immaterial* effect on the current financial statements. It is expected, however, that the change will have a significant effect on future periods. Which of the following should the auditor express?
   (1) An unqualified opinion followed by an explanatory paragraph.
   (2) An adverse opinion.
   (3) An unqualified opinion.
   (4) An "except for" opinion.

*20-43. An auditor includes a separate paragraph in an otherwise unqualified report to emphasize that the entity being reported upon had significant transactions with related parties. The inclusion of this separate paragraph
   (1) violates generally accepted auditing standards if this information is already disclosed in notes to the financial statements.
   (2) necessitates a revision of the opinion paragraph to include the phrase "with the foregoing explanation."
   (3) is appropriate and would *not* negate the unqualified opinion.
   (4) is considered an "except for" qualification of the report.

---

*AICPA adapted.

*20-44. When financial statements are presented that are *not* in conformity with generally accepted accounting principles an auditor may issue a(n)

	"Except for" Opinion	Disclaimer of an Opinion
(1)	Yes	No
(2)	Yes	Yes
(3)	No	Yes
(4)	No	No

*20-45. Unaudited financial statements for the prior year presented in comparative form with audited financial statements for the current year should be clearly marked to indicate their status and

    I. The report on the prior period should be reissued to accompany the current period report.

    II. The report on the current period should include as a separate paragraph a description of the responsibility assumed for the prior period's financial statements.

      (1) I only.

      (2) II only.

      (3) Both I and II.

      (4) Either I or II.

*20-46. Green Company uses the first-in, first-out method of costing for its international subsidiary's inventory and the last-in, first-out method of costing for its domestic inventory. The different costing methods would cause Green's auditor to issue a report with which of the following?

    (1) An explanatory paragraph as to consistency.

    (2) An "except for" qualified opinion.

    (3) An opinion modified as to consistency.

    (4) An unqualified opinion.

*20-47. An explanatory paragraph following the opinion paragraph of an auditor's report describes an uncertainty as follows:

> As discussed in Note X to the financial statements, the Company is a defendant in a lawsuit alleging infringement of certain patent rights and claiming damages. Discovery proceedings are in progress. The ultimate outcome of the litigation cannot presently be determined. Accordingly, no provision for any liability that may result upon adjudication has been made in the accompanying financial statements.

    What type of opinion should the auditor express under these circumstances?

    (1) Unqualified.

    (2) "Subject to" qualified.

    (3) "Except for" qualified.

    (4) Disclaimer.

Problems and Cases

*20-48. (Type of Opinion) For each of the following, state the appropriate type of audit report to issue (unqualified, qualified, disclaimer, or adverse).

    A. Subsequent to the close of Holly Corporation's fiscal year, a major debtor was declared bankrupt due to a series of events. The receivable is significantly material in relation to the financial statements, and recovery is doubtful. The debtor had confirmed the full amount due to Holly Corporation at the balance sheet date. Because the account

(handwritten margin notes: "qualified or adverse ... to if included", "operational unqual ... scope lim", "Disclaimer", "qualified")

was good at the balance sheet date, Holly Corporation refuses to disclose any information in relation to this subsequent event. The CPA believes that all accounts were stated fairly at the balance sheet date.

B. Kapock Corporation is a substantial user of electronic data-processing equipment and has employed an outside service bureau to process data in years past. During the current year, Kapock adopted the policy of leasing all hardware and expects to continue this arrangement in the future. This change in policy is adequately disclosed in footnotes to Kapock's financial statements, but uncertainty prohibits either Kapock or the CPA from assessing the impact of this change upon future operations.

C. The president of Lowe, Inc., would not allow the auditor to confirm the receivable balance from one of its major customers. The amount of the receivable is material in relation to Lowe's financial statements. The auditor was unable to determine the receivable balance by alternative procedures.

D. Sempier Corporation issued financial statements that purported to present its financial position and results of operations but omitted the related statement of cash flows.

*20-49. (Scope Limitation) You have audited Hagren Appliance Corporation's financial statements for several years and have always rendered an unqualified opinion. To reduce its current auditing cost, Hagren limited the scope of your audit of its financial statements for the year just ended to exclude accounts receivable and commissions payable. Hagren's officers stated that the type of auditor's opinion you would render was not important because your report would be used for internal management purposes only and would not be distributed externally. The materiality of the accounts not examined required you to disclaim an opinion on the fairness of the financial statements as a whole.

REQUIRED

A. Why does a CPA prefer that the scope of the auditing engagement not be limited? Discuss.

B. How would a client's assurance to a CPA that the auditor's report will be used only for internal purposes affect the scope of the CPA's audit and the kind of opinion rendered? Discuss.

*20-50. (Departure from GAAP) Sturdy Corporation owns and operates a large office building in a desirable section of New York City's financial center. For many years the management of Sturdy Corporation has modified the presentation of their financial statements by

1. reflecting a write-up to appraisal values in the building accounts, and

2. accounting for depreciation expense on the basis of such valuations.

Joan Wyley, a successor CPA, was asked to audit the financial statements of Sturdy Corporation for the year ended December 31, 19X8. After completing the audit Wyley concluded that, consistent with the prior year, an adverse opinion would have to be expressed because of the materiality of the apparent deviation from the historical-cost principle.

REQUIRED

A. Describe in detail the form of presentation of the separate explanatory paragraph (preceding the opinion paragraph) of the auditor's report on the financial statements of Sturdy Corporation for the year ended December 31, 19X8, clearly identifying the information contained in the paragraph to present the substantive reasons for issuing an adverse opinion. Do not discuss deferred taxes.

B. Write a draft of the opinion paragraph of the auditor's report on the financial statements of Sturdy Corporation for the year ended December 31, 19X8.

C. Would any modifications in the opening or scope paragraphs be required?

*20-51. (Use of Other Auditors) Meridian Corporation, an audit client of Tim Cantey, CPA, is a manufacturer of consumer products and has several wholly owned subsidiaries in foreign countries that are audited by other independent auditors in those countries. The financial

---

*AICPA adapted.

statements of all subsidiaries were properly consolidated in the financial statements of the parent company and the foreign auditor's reports were furnished to Cantey.

Cantey is now preparing the auditor's opinion on the consolidated balance sheet, statement of income, retained earnings, and cash flows for the year ended June 30, 19X4. These statements were prepared on a comparative basis with those of last year.

REQUIRED

A. How should Cantey evaluate and accept the independence and professional reputations of the foreign auditors?

B. Under what circumstances may Cantey assume responsibility for the work of another auditor to the same extent as if Cantey had performed the work alone?

C. Assume that both last year and this year Cantey was willing to use the reports of the other independent auditors in expressing an opinion on the consolidated financial statements but was unwilling to take full responsibility for performance of the work underlying their opinions. Assuming Cantey's audit of the parent company financial statements would allow him to render an unqualified opinion, prepare (1) the necessary disclosure to be contained in the opening paragraph and (2) the complete opinion paragraph of the auditor's report.

20-52. (Uncertainties) Buddy Whitlock, CPA, is auditing Purple Shirt Company (PSC), a closely held business, for the year ended December 31, 19X4. PSC is a defendant in a lawsuit that, if lost, would have a material effect on the financial statements. Barry Gunter is the attorney for PSC and has evaluated an unfavorable outcome as "reasonably possible." Neither PSC nor Gunter is able to estimate the amount or range of potential loss.

REQUIRED

A. What type of opinion should Whitlock issue?

B. If Gunter had concluded that an unfavorable outcome was "probable" and could be estimated, and PSC records the loss contingency, would Whitlock's audit report in **A** above change?

C. If Gunter had concluded that an unfavorable outcome was "probable" and could be estimated and Whitlock agreed, but PSC refused to record the loss contingency, what type of report should Whitlock issue? What factors should Whitlock use in assessing materiality?

D. If Gunter and PSC had concluded that an unfavorable outcome was remote and Whitlock agreed, what type of audit report should Whitlock issue?

*20-53. (Going-Concern Problems) You are the auditor of X Co., Ltd., a company that at December 31, 19X4, had working capital of $200,000, total assets of $2.5 million, and total liabilities of $2.2 million. During the three years ended December 31, 19X4, the company has sustained accumulated operating losses totaling $700,000. Management has been informed that current debenture holders will not renew a debenture of $500,000 maturing September 30, 19X5, and presently included in long-term liabilities. Although preliminary discussions have already been held with various commercial lenders, it presently appears uncertain as to whether or not X Co., Ltd., will be able to refinance its debt. As X Co., Ltd., has had liquidity problems from time to time, it may be unable to obtain adequate financing both to refinance its debenture and to provide additional working capital. In that case, it may not be able to continue its operations.

REQUIRED

A. What deviations (if any) may be necessary from a standard audit report?

B. Outline the minimum note disclosure that you consider adequate in the circumstances. What additional disclosure would be desirable?

*20-54. (GAAP and Consistency) You are engaged in the audit of the financial statements of Rapid, Inc., and its recently acquired subsidiary, Slow Corporation. In acquiring Slow

Corporation during 19X7, Rapid exchanged a large number of its shares of common stock for 90% of the outstanding common stock of Slow Corporation in a transaction that was accounted for as a pooling of interests. Rapid is now preparing its annual report to shareholders and proposes to include in the report combined financial statements for the year ended December 31, 19X7, with a note describing its exchange of stock for that of Slow Corporation.

Rapid also proposes to include in its report the financial statements of the preceding year as they appeared in Rapid's 19X6 annual report, along with a five-year financial summary from Rapid's prior annual reports, all of which have been accompanied by your unqualified auditor's opinion.

REQUIRED

A. Discuss the objectives or purposes of the standard of reporting that requires the auditor to state when GAAP have not been consistently observed over the past two periods.

B. Describe the treatment in the auditor's report of interperiod changes having a material effect on the financial statements arising from

(1) a change to alternative GAAP.

(2) changed conditions that necessitate accounting changes but do not involve changes in the accounting principles employed.

(3) changed conditions unrelated to accounting.

C. (1) Would the financial reporting treatment proposed by Rapid for the 19X7 annual report be on a consistent basis? Discuss.

(2) Describe the auditor's report that should accompany the financial statements as proposed by Rapid for inclusion in the annual report.

*20-55. (Consistency Qualification) Various types of accounting changes can affect the second reporting standard of GAAS. This standard reads: "The report shall identify those circumstances in which such principles have not been consistently observed in the current period in relation to the preceding period."

Assume that the following list describes changes that have a material effect on a client's financial statements for the current year.

1. A change from the completed-contract method to the percentage-of-completion method of accounting for long-term construction-type contracts.

2. A change in the estimated useful life of previously recorded fixed assets based on newly acquired information. *△ in estimate*

3. Correction of a mathematical error in inventory pricing made in a prior period.

4. A change from prime costing to full absorption costing for inventory valuation.

5. A change from presentation of statements of individual companies to presentation of consolidated statements. *restate as if they were at ijs*

6. A change from deferring and amortizing preproduction costs to recording such costs as an expense when incurred because future benefits of the costs have become doubtful. The new accounting method was adopted in recognition of the change in estimated future benefits. *△ in Principle*

7. A change to classify the employer share of FICA taxes as "Retirement Benefits" on the income statement instead of as "Other Taxes." *△ reclassify*

8. A change from the FIFO method of inventory pricing to the LIFO method of inventory pricing. *disclose effects*

REQUIRED

Identify the type of change described in each item above, state whether an explanatory paragraph is required in the auditor's report as it relates to the second standard of reporting, and state whether the prior-year financial statement should be restated when

prime costing
DM
DL
no OH cost

---

presented in comparative form with the current-year statements. Organize your answer as shown below.

Item No.	Type of Change	Should Explanatory Paragraph Be Added?	Should Prior-Year Statements Be Restated?

*20-56. (Emphasis of a Matter) Upon completion of all fieldwork on September 23, 19X4, Timothy Ross, CPA, rendered the following report to the directors of The Rancho Corporation.

> **To the Directors of The Rancho Corporation:**
>
> We have audited the accompanying balance sheet and the related statement of income and retained earnings of The Rancho Corporation as of July 31, 19X4. In accordance with your instructions, a complete audit was conducted.
>
> We conducted our audit in accordance with generally accepted accounting principles. Those standards require that we plan and perform the audit to obtain reasonable assurance about whether the financial statements are free of material misstatement. We believe that our audit provides a reasonable basis for our opinion.
>
> In many respects, this was an unusual year for The Rancho Corporation. The weakening of the economy in the early part of the year and the strike of plant employees in the summer of 19X4 led to a decline in sales and net income. We made several tests of sales records, and nothing came to our attention that would indicate that sales have not been properly recorded.
>
> In our opinion, with the explanation given above, and with the exception of some minor errors that are considered immaterial, the aforementioned financial statements present fairly the financial position of The Rancho Corporation at July 31, 19X4, and the results of its operations for the year then ended, in conformity with pronouncements of the Accounting Principles Board and the Financial Accounting Standards Board.
>
> Timothy Ross, CPA
>
> September 23, 19X4

REQUIRED
List and explain deficiencies and omissions in the auditor's report. The type of opinion (unqualified, qualified, adverse, or disclaimer) is of no consequence and need not be discussed. Organize your answer sheet by paragraph (opening, scope, explanatory, and opinion) of the auditor's report.

*20-57. (Comparative Financial Statements) J. Childs, CPA, has completed the audit of the financial statements of Straw Corporation as of and for the year ended December 31, 19X5. Childs also audited and reported on the Straw financial statements for the prior year. Childs drafted the following report for 19X5.

---

*AICPA adapted.

<u>Independent Auditor's Report</u>

March 15, 19X5

We have audited the accompanying balance sheet of Straw Corporation as of December 31, 19X5, and the related statements of income and retained earnings for the year then ended. These financial statements are the responsibility of the Company's management. Our responsibility is to express an opinion on these financial statements based on our audit.

We conducted our audit in accordance with generally accepted auditing standards. Those standards require that we plan and perform the audit to obtain reasonable assurance about whether the financial statements are free of material misstatement. An audit includes examining, on a test basis, evidence supporting the amounts and disclosures in the financial statements. An audit also includes assessing the accounting principles used and significant estimates made by management, as well as evaluating the overall financial statement presentation. We believe that our audit provides a reasonable basis for our opinion.

In our opinion, the financial statements referred to above present fairly, in all material respects, the financial position of Straw Corporation as of December 31, 19X5, and the results of its operations for the year then ended in conformity with generally accepted accounting principles.

J. Childs, CPA

Other information:
1. Straw is presenting comparative financial statements.
2. Straw does not wish to present a statement of cash flows for either year.
3. During 19X5, Straw changed its method of accounting for long-term construction contracts and properly reflected the effect of the change in the current-year financial statements and restated the prior-year statements. Childs is satisfied with Straw's justification for making the change. The change is discussed in Note 12 to the statements.
4. Childs was unable to perform normal accounts receivable confirmation procedures but used alternative procedures to satisfy himself as to the validity of the receivables.
5. Straw Corporation is the defendant in litigation, the outcome of which is highly uncertain. If the case is settled in favor of the plaintiff, Straw will be required to pay a substantial amount of cash, which might require the sale of certain fixed assets. The litigation and the possible effects have been properly disclosed in Note 11 to the financial statements.
6. Straw issued debentures on January 31, 19X5, in the amount of $10 million. The funds obtained from the issuance were used to finance the expansion of plant facilities. The debenture agreement restricts the payment of future cash dividends to earnings after December 31, 19X5. Straw declined to disclose the restriction in the notes to the financial statements. However, the debentures are properly accounted for and disclosed in Note 13 to the statements.

REQUIRED

Consider all facts given and rewrite the auditor's report in acceptable and complete format, incorporating any necessary departures from the standard report.

*20-58. (Comparative Financial Statements) For the year ended December 31, 19X7, Friday & Co., CPAs (Friday), audited the financial statements of Johnson Company and expressed an unqualified opinion on the balance sheet only. Friday did not observe the taking of the physical inventory as of December 31, 19X6, because that date was prior to their appointment as auditors. Friday was unable to satisfy themselves regarding inventory by means of other auditing procedures, so they did not express an opinion on the other basic financial statements that year.

For the year ended December 31, 19X8, Friday expressed an unqualified opinion on all the basic financial statements and satisfied themselves as to the consistent application of generally accepted accounting principles. The fieldwork was completed on March 11, 19X9; the partner-in-charge reviewed the working papers and signed the auditor's report on March 18, 19X9. The report on the comparative financial statements for 19X8 and 19X7 was delivered to Johnson on March 21, 19X9.

REQUIRED

Prepare Friday's auditor's report that was submitted to Johnson's board of directors on the 19X7 and 19X8 comparative financial statements.

20-59. (Audit Report Modification) The auditor's standard report consists of (1) an opening paragraph that differentiates management's responsibilities for the financial statements from the auditor's role in expressing an opinion on them based upon the audit, (2) a scope paragraph that explicitly acknowledges that an audit provides reasonable assurance within the context of materiality and briefly explains what an audit entails, and (3) an opinion paragraph. There are circumstances where the auditor's standard report is modified by adding one or more separate explanatory paragraphs, and/or modifying the wording of the opening paragraph, scope paragraph, or opinion paragraph.

For purposes of this question, assume the auditor is independent and has previously expressed an unqualified opinion on the prior year's financial statements. For the current year, only single year (not comparative) statements are presented. Also assume that the circumstances are material but do not warrant expression of either a disclaimer of opinion or an adverse opinion.

REQUIRED

Identify the circumstances necessitating modification of the auditor's standard report. For each circumstance indicate the type of opinion that would be appropriate and describe the report modification. Organize the answer as indicated in the following example:

Circumstance	Type of Opinion	Report Modification
1. The financial statements are materially affected by a departure from GAAP.	1. The auditor should express an "except for" qualified opinion.	1. The auditor should explain the basis and effects of the departure in an explanatory paragraph preceding the opinion paragraph and should modify the opinion paragraph.

---

*AICPA adapted.

20-60. (Audit Report Modification) Under the column captioned "Report Modification," match the number that represents the most appropriate modification for the circumstance described. Some answers may be used more than once.

Circumstance	Report Modification
A. Departure from GAAP, material but not pervasive	_____
B. Scope limitation, material but not pervasive	_____
C. Pervasive departure from GAAP	_____
D. Going concern matter	_____
E. Inconsistent application of GAAP	_____
F. Not independent and a public company	_____
G. Emphasis of a matter	_____
H. Work of another auditor is used as basis for opinion and the auditor decides to refer to the work of the other auditor	_____
I. Pervasive scope limitation	_____
J. Uncertainty	_____

Report Options

1. Add a separate explanatory paragraph preceding the opinion paragraph and modify the opinion paragraph to state, "do not present fairly in conformity with GAAP."
2. Indicate the division of responsibility for the audit in the introductory paragraph and refer to the other auditor's report in the opinion paragraph.
3. Delete the scope paragraph, add a separate paragraph, and modify the opinion paragraph to state, "We do not express an opinion."
4. Modify the scope paragraph, add a separate explanatory paragraph preceding the opinion paragraph, and add "except for" in the opinion paragraph.
5. Issue a one-paragraph report stating lack of independence, that the financial statements are unaudited, and that no opinion is expressed.
6. Add a separate paragraph following the opinion paragraph highlighting the matter, but issue an unqualified opinion.
7. Add a separate explanatory paragraph between the scope and opinion paragraphs.

Audit Judgment Case

*20-61. The following auditor's report was drafted by a staff accountant of Turner & Turner, CPAs, at the completion of the audit of the financial statements of Lyon Computers, Inc., for the year ended March 31, 19X9. It was submitted to the engagement partner who reviewed matters thoroughly and properly concluded that Lyon's disclosures concerning its ability to continue as a going concern for a reasonable period of time were adequate.

Independent Auditor's Report

To the Board of Directors of Lyon Computers, Inc.:

We have audited the accompanying balance sheet of Lyon Computers, Inc. as of March 31, 19X9, and the other related financial statements for the year then ended. Our responsibility is to express an opinion on these financial statements based on our audit.

*AICPA adapted.

We conducted our audit in accordance with standards that require that we plan and perform the audit to obtain reasonable assurance about whether the financial statements are in conformity with generally accepted accounting principles. An audit includes examining, on a test basis, evidence supporting the amounts and disclosures in the financial statements. An audit also includes assessing the accounting principles used and significant estimates made by management.

The accompanying financial statements have been prepared assuming that the Company will continue as a going concern. As discussed in Note X to the financial statements, the Company has suffered recurring losses from operations and has a net capital deficiency that raise substantial doubt about its ability to continue as a going concern. We believe that management's plans in regards to these matters, which are also described in Note X, will permit the Company to continue as a going concern beyond a reasonable period of time. The financial statements do not include any adjustments that might result from the outcome of this uncertainty.

In our opinion, subject to the effects on the financial statements of such adjustments, if any, as might have been required had the outcome of the uncertainty referred to in the preceding paragraph been known, the financial statements referred to above present fairly, in all material respects, the financial position of Lyon Computers, Inc., and the results of its operations and its cash flows in conformity with generally accepted accounting principles applied on a basis consistent with that of the preceding year.

Turner & Turner, CPAs
April 28, 19X9

REQUIRED

Identify the deficiencies contained in the auditor's report as drafted by the staff accountant. Group the deficiencies by paragraph. Do *not* redraft the report.

Auditing Issues Case

20-62.   KELCO MANUFACTURING COMPANY

You are about to prepare the December 31, 19X7 audit report. The following are items of concern:

1. The company changed from the FIFO to the LIFO method of accounting for inventory.
2. A guilty verdict in the lawsuit referred to in Chapter 19 would have a very material effect on the company's operations. The company's attorney has stated that it is reasonably possible that the company could lose the lawsuit.
3. Kelco loaned $3,000,000 to another company owned by Cook. The loan was made at below the prevailing market rate of interest and included very flexible repayment terms.

REQUIRED

Prepare the December 31, 19X7 audit report.

Chapter *21*

Other Reports

Learning   Objectives

- Identify and describe the six types of special reports.
- Explain the term *other comprehensive basis of accounting*.
- Describe the reporting options on internal control structure available to auditors.
- Describe the terms *other information, supplementary information*, and *accompanying information* and explain the auditor's responsibilities in each of these areas.
- Discuss the auditor's review of interim financial information and association with financial forecasts and projections.
- Discuss the auditor's reporting responsibilities for financial statements prepared for use in other countries and on the application of accounting principles.

For many years, financial statements prepared on the cash and tax bases of accounting have provided useful financial information to management, owners, creditors, and other financial statement users. . . . Because there is very little authoritative guidance that explicitly addresses cash- and tax-basis financial statements, practitioners frequently struggle with which (and to what extent) recognition, measurement, and disclosure rules apply to cash- and tax-basis statements. The recent proliferation of complex accounting rules issued by the FASB and the AICPA—particularly those related to disclosure of matters not measured in the financial statements—have exacerbated the practitioner's dilemma.

Views on which recognition, measurement, and disclosure rules apply to cash- and tax-basis statements are very divergent: On one end of the spectrum are practitioners who believe that all accounting standards should be stringently applied to all types of financial statements, regardless of the basis of accounting; on the other end of the spectrum are those who believe that authoritative accounting standards were developed solely for financial statements prepared in accordance with GAAP, and as a result, accounting standards do not apply to statements prepared on other comprehensive bases of accounting. ■

Source: Michael J. Ramos and Anita M. Lyons, *Preparing and Reporting on Cash- and Tax-Basis Financial Statements,* (New York: AICPA).

This chapter presents the audit reporting requirements for cash- and tax- bases financial statements along with discussion of other types of audit reports on specialized information. The preceding chapter discussed audit reports issued by the auditor after an audit of financial statements prepared in accordance with GAAP. However, auditing and attest standards also cover other situations in which the auditor issues other kinds of reports. These other types of reports include the following:

- Special reports
- Reports on internal control
- Involvement with other information
- Review of interim financial information
- Reports on financial forecasts and projections
- Reports on financial statements prepared for use in other countries
- Reports on the application of accounting principles

Special Reports

SAS No. 62, Special Reports (AU 623), identifies the following five types of *special reports*:

1. Reports on financial statements prepared on a comprehensive basis of accounting other than GAAP.
2. Reports on specified elements, accounts, or items of a financial statement.

3. Reports on compliance with aspects of contractual agreements or regulatory requirements related to audited financial statements.
4. Reports on financial presentations to comply with contractual agreements or regulatory provisions.
5. Reports on financial information presented in prescribed forms or schedules that require a prescribed form of auditor's report.

In addition, *SAS No. 75, Engagements to Apply Agreed-Upon Procedures to Specified Elements, Accounts, or Items of a Financial Statement* (AU 622), applies to an engagement in which the scope is limited to applying **agreed-upon procedures** to one or more specified elements, accounts, or items of a financial statement.[1] Table 21–1 presents in summary form the engagements, other than prescribed forms, discussed in *SAS No. 62* and *SAS No. 75*.

Other Comprehensive Bases of Accounting

Auditors frequently examine financial statements that are prepared on a basis of accounting that differs from GAAP. *SAS No. 62* (AU 623.02–.08) recognizes this and provides reporting guidance to the auditor when financial statements are prepared on an *"other comprehensive basis of accounting" (OCBOA)*. The auditor's report should provide reasonable assurance that the financial statements conform with OCBOA.

Types of OCBOA

According to *SAS No. 62* (AU 623.04), a measurement basis must meet one of four criteria to be classified as an OCBOA. The measurement must be

- a basis of accounting that the reporting entity uses to comply with the reporting provisions of a government regulatory agency to whose jurisdiction the entity is subject. For example, insurance companies use bases of accounting pursuant to the rules of state insurance commissions.
- a basis of accounting that the reporting entity uses or expects to use to file its federal income tax return for the period covered by the financial statements.
- the cash receipts and disbursements basis of accounting, and modifications of the cash basis having substantial support, such as recording depreciation on fixed assets or accruing income taxes.
- a definite set of criteria having substantial support that is applied to all material items appearing in the financial statements, such as the price level basis of accounting.

Reporting Requirements

When reporting on financial statements prepared in accordance with an OCBOA, the independent auditor should include an introductory paragraph, a scope paragraph, an explanatory paragraph describing the basis of accounting, and an opinion paragraph. The report should also include the word *independent* in its title.

Introductory and Scope Paragraphs The first two paragraphs should identify the financial statements audited and state whether the audit was conducted in accordance with GAAS. The introductory and scope paragraphs are equivalent to these same paragraphs in a report on financial statements that conform with GAAP.

[1]*SSAE No. 4, Agreed-Upon Procedure Engagements* (AT 500), was issued at the same time as *SAS No. 75*. The guidance in *SSAE No. 4* generally applies to engagements involving agreed-upon procedures when the information is not based on financial statement elements, accounts, or items. The significant difference between the two standards, other than their applicability, is that *SSAE No. 4* requires a written assertion as a condition of engagement performance.

Table 21-1	Summary of Special Reports		
Technical Requirements		Financial Statements on an Other Comprehensive Basis of Accounting (OCBOA) Other Than GAAP (*SAS No. 62*)	Opinions on Specified Elements, Accounts, or Items of a Financial Statement (*SAS No. 62*)
Engagements where applicable		Financial statements may be 1. income tax basis 2. cash or modified cash basis 3. regulatory agency basis of accounting 4. other criteria with substantial support (for example, price-level accounting)	Engagements may be 1. in conjunction with audit of financial statements 2. a separate engagement
Report form		1. Introductory paragraph 2. Scope paragraph 3. Explanatory paragraph stating basis of presentation, referencing note describing basis of presentation, and stating that basis of presentation is an OCBOA other than GAAP 4. Opinion paragraph 5. If the financial statements are prepared on a regulatory agency basis, a paragraph restricting distribution of the report	1. Introductory paragraph that identifies elements, accounts, or items audited 2. Scope paragraph 3. A paragraph that describes basis of presentation 4. Opinion paragraph 5. If prepared to comply with the requirements or financial reporting provisions of a contract or agreement that results in a presentation that is not GAAP or OCBOA (other than a regulatory agency basis), a paragraph restricting the distribution of the report
Auditing standards applicable		All standards apply.	All standards apply.

(handwritten margin note: reports are restricted*)*

Reports on Results of Applying Agreed-Upon Procedures (*SAS No. 75*)	Reports on Compliance with Contractual Agreements or Regulatory Requirements (*SAS No. 62*)	Financial Presentation to Comply with Contractual Agreements or Regulatory Provisions (*SAS No. 62*)

Acceptance of engagement is appropriate only if
1. parties involved agree to the procedures to be applied and take responsibility for the sufficiency of the procedures.
2. report distribution is restricted to specified parties.
	1. Bond indenture, loan agreement, or regulatory agencies may require compliance reports by CPA.
	2. Must be in conjunction with audit of financial statements.
		Financial statements prepared on a basis of accounting prescribed in a contract or agreement that results in
		  1. incomplete presentation otherwise prepared in conformity with GAAP or OCBOA (Type I).
		  2. presentation not in conformity with GAAP or OCBOA (Type II).

1. Indicate elements, accounts, or items to which the procedures were applied. 2. State that the procedures performed were those agreed to by the users. 3. State that the sufficiency of the procedures is the responsibility of the users. 4. List the procedures performed. 5. State findings. 6. Disclaim an opinion. 7. State that the report is intended solely for the specified users.	Negative assurance as separate paragraph of audit report or as separate report	1. Introductory paragraph 2. Scope paragraph 3. Paragraph explaining what the presentation is intended to present and referring to the note to the special-purpose financial statements that describes the basis of presentation and either a statement that the presentation is not intended to be a complete presentation (Type I) or a statement that the presentation is not intended to conform to GAAP (Type II) 4. Opinion paragraph 5. A paragraph restricting distribution of the report
Internal control and sufficient competent evidence standards do not apply. However, general and fieldwork standards are applicable.	All standards apply.	All standards apply.

Paragraph Describing the Basis of Accounting The report should also include a paragraph that states the basis of presentation of the financial statements on which the auditor is reporting and refers to the note to the financial statements that describes that basis. This paragraph should also state that the basis of presentation is a comprehensive basis of accounting other than GAAP.

Opinion Paragraph This paragraph should express the auditor's opinion (or disclaimer of opinion) on whether the financial statements are presented fairly, in all material respects, in conformity with the basis of accounting described. If the auditor concludes that the financial statements are not presented fairly on the basis of accounting described, all the substantive reasons for that conclusion should be disclosed in an additional explanatory paragraph.

In addition, if the financial statements are prepared in accordance with the requirements or financial reporting provisions of a governmental regulatory agency, a fifth paragraph should be included that restricts distribution of the report to those within the entity and the agency.

Titles of Statements

Terms such as "Balance Sheet," "Statement of Financial Position," "Statement of Income," "Statement of Operations," "Statement of Cash Flows," or similar unmodified titles are generally understood to apply only to financial statements intended to present financial position, results of operations, or cash flows in conformity with GAAP. Consequently, the auditor should consider whether the OCBOA financial statements being reported on are suitably titled. For example, a cash-basis financial statement might be titled "Statement of Assets and Liabilities Arising from Cash

The Real World of Auditing

Survey Reveals Broad Use of OCBOA Financials

In a recent national survey of member firms, PCPS (the AICPA's Private Companies Practice Section) received 2,175 responses on questions relating to Other Comprehensive Bases of Accounting (OCBOA).

Survey responses reveal that use of OCBOA among member firms is widespread with potential for even further application. Of the practitioners surveyed, 81% now use OCBOA for certain privately-held clients, while 36% say they have clients who could benefit from switching to OCBOA. "For small companies whose cash flow is parallel to their income and expense, OCBOA statements often make sense," said Jacob Cohen, chairman of the PCPS

task force on OCBOA. "OCBOA accurately reflects a company's financial transactions, yet it is less expensive and easier to interpret than GAAP. It's an important tool for reducing standards overload. Any firm that does not take advantage of OCBOA, where applicable, is missing the boat."

More than 50% of the OCBOA work reported in the survey is tax basis (50%), with cash basis accounting for 48%. Respondents issue OCBOA statements primarily for clients in industries such as professional services, healthcare, retail, real estate, construction, manufacturing and agriculture.

Source: PCPS Advocate, p. 6, September 1990, Vol. 11, No. 4 (American Institute of Certified Public Accountants).

Transactions," or "Statement of Increases or Decreases in Funds Arising from Cash Transactions." A financial statement prepared on a statutory or regulatory basis might be titled "Statement of Income—Statutory Basis." If the auditor believes that the financial statements are not suitably titled, the report should be qualified to disclose his or her reservations. A report on financial statements prepared on the entity's income tax basis is shown in Figure 21–1.

Opinions on Specified Elements, Accounts, or Items of a Financial Statement

Sometimes auditors are requested to issue a report on certain aspects of the financial statements. For example, a shopping mall that charges rent to its tenants based on a percentage of the tenants' sales may require a report by the auditor which states that the sales reported by the tenants are fairly presented in conformity with GAAP. Other examples include reports on royalties and profit participations.

Applicability of GAAS and Materiality

The auditor should plan and perform the audit and prepare the report with a view to the purpose of the engagement. With the exception of the first standard of reporting, the ten generally accepted auditing standards are applicable to any engagement to express an opinion on one or more specified elements, accounts, or items of a financial statement. However, because the first standard of reporting states that the auditor should indicate whether the financial statements are presented in conformity with GAAP, this standard is applicable only when the specified elements, accounts, or items are prepared in conformity with GAAP.

The audit of specified elements, accounts, or items may be undertaken as a separate engagement or in conjunction with an audit of financial statements. In such an engagement, the auditor expresses an opinion on each of the specified elements, accounts, or items encompassed by the report; therefore, the measurement of materiality must be related to each individual element, account, or item audited rather than to the aggregate thereof or to the financial statements taken as a whole. Consequently, the audit is usually more extensive than if the same information were being considered in conjunction with an audit of the financial statements taken as a whole.

Reporting

The auditor should not report on specified elements, accounts, or items included in financial statements for which an adverse opinion or disclaimer of opinion has been expressed if such reporting would be tantamount to expressing a piecemeal opinion on the financial statements (that is, if it would be an opinion as to a significant number of identified items in the financial statements). However, an auditor may express an opinion on one or more specified elements, accounts, or items of a financial statement provided that the matters he or she is reporting on and the related scope of the audit do not encompass so many elements, accounts, or items as to constitute a major portion of the financial statements. In this case, the report on the specified element, account, or item should be presented separately from the report on the financial statements of the entity.

An example of a report related to the amount of sales for the purpose of computing rental charges is shown in Figure 21–2.

Figure 21-1	Financial Statements Prepared on the Entity's Income Tax Basis

Independent Auditor's Report

Board of Directors
Spades Partnership

We have audited the accompanying statements of assets, liabilities, and capital—income tax basis of Spades Partnership as of December 31, 19X5 and 19X4, and the related statements of revenue and expenses—income tax basis and of changes in partners' capital accounts—income tax basis for the years then ended. These financial statements are the responsibility of the Partnership's management. Our responsibility is to express an opinion on these financial statements based on our audits.

The first paragraph identifies the financial statements audited. The auditor also emphasizes that the financial statements are management's responsibility.

We conducted our audits in accordance with generally accepted auditing standards. Those standards require that we plan and perform the audit to obtain reasonable assurance about whether the financial statements are free of material misstatement. An audit includes examining, on a test basis, evidence supporting the amounts and disclosures in the financial statements. An audit also includes assessing the accounting principles used and significant estimates made by management, as well as evaluating the overall financial statement presentation. We believe that our audits provide a reasonable basis for our opinion.

The scope paragraph states that the audit was conducted in accordance with generally accepted auditing standards.

As described in Note X, these financial statements were prepared on the accounting basis used for income tax purposes, which is a comprehensive basis of accounting other than generally accepted accounting principles.

The third paragraph refers to the note in the financial statements that states the basis of presentation upon which the statements were prepared.

In our opinion, the financial statements referred to above present fairly, in all material respects, the assets, liabilities, and capital of Spades Partnership as of December 31, 19X5 and 19X4, and its revenue and expenses and changes in partners' capital accounts for the years then ended, on the basis of accounting described in Note X.

The opinion paragraph expresses the auditor's opinion on whether the financial statements are presented fairly, in all material respects, in conformity with the basis described.

Powell and Co.
Certified Public Accountants

Figure 21-2   **Report Relating to Amount of Sales for the Purpose of Computing Rental**

Independent Auditor's Report

Board of Directors
Pawling Stores Corp.

We have audited the accompanying schedule of gross sales (as defined in the lease agreement dated March 4, 19X3, between ABC Company, as lessor, and Pawling Stores Corporation, as lessee) of Pawling Stores Corporation at its Main Street store, Brewster, New York, for the year ended December 31, 19X5. This schedule is the responsibility of the Pawling Stores Corp. management. Our responsibility is to express an opinion on this schedule based on our audit.

The first paragraph identifies the sales schedule, the lease agreement, and the parties to the agreement. The auditor also indicates that the schedule is management's responsibility.

We conducted our audit in accordance with generally accepted auditing standards. Those standards require that we plan and perform the audit to obtain reasonable assurance about whether the schedule of gross sales is free of material misstatement. An audit includes examining, on a test basis, evidence supporting the amounts and disclosures in the schedule of gross sales. An audit also includes assessing the accounting principles used and significant estimates made by management, as well as evaluating the overall schedule presentation. We believe that our audit provides a reasonable basis for our opinion.

The scope paragraph states that the audit was conducted in accordance with GAAS.

In our opinion, the schedule of gross sales referred to above presents fairly, in all material respects, the gross sales of Pawling Stores Corporation at its Main Street store, Brewster, New York, for the year ended December 31, 19X5, as defined in the lease agreement referred to in the first paragraph.

The opinion paragraph expresses the auditor's opinion on whether the schedule presents fairly, in all material respects, the gross sales as defined in the lease agreement.

This report is intended solely for the information and use of the board of directors and management of Pawling Stores Corp. and ABC Company and should not be used for any other purpose.

The final paragraph indicates that distribution of the report is limited to the parties identified.

Powell and Co.
Certified Public Accountants

Applying Agreed-Upon Procedures

An accountant may undertake an engagement to apply agreed-upon procedures to specified elements, accounts, or items of a financial statement. For example, an individual who is considering purchasing a business may request that the accountant reconcile the bank balances and confirm the accounts receivable of the business. The accountant is permitted to accept this type of engagement only if the parties involved have agreed to the procedures to be performed and if distribution of the report is limited to named parties involved.

An engagement to apply agreed-upon procedures does not constitute an audit conducted in accordance with GAAS. Only the three general standards and the first standard of fieldwork apply.

An example of an agreed-upon procedures report, issued in connection with claims of creditors in bankruptcy, is shown in Figure 21–3.

Figure 21–3   **Agreed-Upon Procedures Report**

Independent Auditor's Report on Applying Agreed-Upon Procedures

To the Trustee of XYZ Company:

We have performed the procedures described below, which were agreed to by the Trustee of XYZ Company, with respect to the claims of creditors of XYZ Company as of May 31, 19X2, as set forth in accompanying Schedule A. This engagement to apply agreed-upon procedures was performed in accordance with standards established by the American Institute of Certified Public Accountants. The sufficiency of these procedures is solely the responsibility of the trustee of XYZ Company. Consequently, we make no representation regarding the sufficiency of the procedures described below either for the purpose for which this report has been requested or for any other purpose.

Paragraph identifies parties that agreed to the procedures and states that the auditor is not responsible for the sufficiency of procedures performed.

The procedures and associated findings are as follows:

Paragraph sets forth the procedures performed and results obtained.

a. Compare the total of the trial balance of accounts payable at May 31, 19X2, prepared by XYZ Company, to the balance in the related general ledger account.

The total of the accounts payable trial balance agreed with the balance in the related general ledger account.

Figure 21-3 *continued*

b. Compare the amounts for claims received from creditors (as shown in claim documents provided by XYZ Company) to the respective amounts shown in the trial balance of accounts payable. Using the data included in the claims documents and in XYZ Company's accounts payable detail records, reconcile any differences found to the accounts payable trial balance.

All differences noted are presented in column 3 of Schedule A. Except for those amounts shown in column 4 of Schedule A, all such differences were reconciled.

c. Examine the documentation submitted by creditors in support of the amounts claimed and compare it to the following documentation in XYZ Company's files: invoices, receiving reports, and other evidence of receipt of goods or services.

No exceptions were found as a result of these comparisons.

These agreed-upon procedures do not constitute an audit, the objective of which is the expression of an opinion on the financial statements of XYZ Company or specified elements, accounts, or items thereof. Accordingly, we do not express such an opinion. Had we performed additional procedures, other matters might have come to our attention that would have been reported to you.

Paragraph indicates that an audit was not performed.

This report is intended solely for the use of the trustee of XYZ Company and should not be used by those who did not agree to the procedures.

Paragraph restricts use of the report.

Powell and Co.
Certified Public Accountants

Compliance Reports Related to Audited Financial Statements

Contractual agreements or regulatory agencies may require companies to furnish *compliance reports* by independent auditors. For example, loan agreements usually impose on borrowers a variety of covenants involving matters such as payments into sinking funds, payments of interest, maintenance of current ratios, restriction of dividends payments, and use of the proceeds of sales of property.

Under *SAS No. 62*, the auditor is allowed to give a negative assurance report on compliance with contractual agreements. A ***negative assurance report*** states that "nothing came to our attention that would indicate that these amounts (or items) are not fairly presented."

The auditor may give this assurance in a separate report or in one or more paragraphs of the auditor's report accompanying the financial statements. However, such assurance should not be given unless the auditor has audited the financial statements to which the contractual agreements or regulatory requirements relate and should not extend to covenants that relate to matters that have not been subjected to the procedures applied in the audit of the financial statements. The expression of negative assurance should specify that it is being given in connection with an audit of the financial statements. The auditor should ordinarily also state that the audit was not directed primarily toward obtaining knowledge regarding compliance. A separate report giving negative assurance should contain a paragraph stating that the financial statements have been audited, the date of the report thereon, and whether the audit was made in accordance with GAAS. A report on compliance with contractual provisions given in a separate report is shown in Figure 21–4.

Financial Presentations to Comply with Contractual Agreements or Regulatory Provisions

Auditors are sometimes requested to report on special-purpose financial statements prepared to comply with a contractual agreement or regulatory provisions. Generally, these types of reports are intended solely for the use of the parties to the agreement, regulatory bodies, or other specified parties. According to *SAS No. 62* (AU 623), these types of presentations fall into two categories:

1. Those that do not constitute a complete presentation of the entity's assets, liabilities, revenues and expenses (an incomplete presentation) but are otherwise prepared in conformity with GAAP or an OCBOA.
2. Those prepared on a basis of accounting prescribed in an agreement that result in presentations not in conformity with GAAP or an OCBOA.

Incomplete Presentations Otherwise Prepared in Conformity with GAAP or OCBOA

An auditor may be requested to report on a financial presentation to meet the special purposes of regulatory agencies or parties to an agreement. For example, the SEC may require a schedule of gross income and certain expenses of an entity's real estate operation in which income and expenses are measured in conformity with GAAP, but expenses are defined to exclude certain items such as interest, depreciation, and income taxes. Also, a buy–sell agreement may specify a schedule of gross assets and liabilities of the entity measured in conformity with GAAP but limited to the assets to be sold and liabilities to be transferred pursuant to the agreement. Such financial presentations are regarded as financial statements even though certain items may be excluded. The presentations differ from complete financial statements only to the extent necessary to meet the special purposes for which they are prepared. An example of a special report on such financial presentations is shown in Figure 21–5.

Figure 21-4	**Report on Compliance with Contractual Provisions Given in a Separate Report**

Independent Auditor's Report

Board of Directors
Luther Company

We have audited, in accordance with generally accepted auditing standards, the balance sheet of Luther Company as of December 31, 19X5 and 19X4, and the related statements of income, retained earnings, and cash flows for the years then ended, and have issued our report thereon dated February 16, 19X6.

The first paragraph identifies the financial statements audited and states that they were audited in accordance with GAAS.

In connection with our audits, nothing came to our attention that caused us to believe that the Company failed to comply with the terms, covenants, provisions, or conditions of sections 10 to 15, inclusive, of the Indenture dated July 21, 19X3, with ABC Bank insofar as they relate to accounting matters. It should be noted, however, that our audits were not directed primarily toward obtaining knowledge of such noncompliance.

The middle paragraph provides negative assurance about contract violations. The auditor notes that the audit was not directed toward obtaining such knowledge.

This report is intended solely for the information and use of the board of directors and management of Luther Company and ABC Bank and should not be used for any other purpose.

The last paragraph indicates that distribution of the report is limited to the parties to the contract.

Powell and Co.
Certified Public Accountants

Financial Statements Prepared on a Basis of Accounting Prescribed in an Agreement Not in Conformity with GAAP or an OCBOA

Sometimes auditors are asked to report on special-purpose financial statements prepared in conformity with a basis of accounting that departs from GAAP or an OCBOA. For example, an acquisition agreement may require the financial statements of the entity being acquired (or a segment of it) to be prepared in conformity with GAAP except for certain assets, such as receivables, inventories, and properties, for which a valuation basis is specified in the agreement.

These financial statements are not prepared in conformity with GAAP, nor can they be classified as OCBOA statements because they do not meet the requirement of being a measurement basis "having substantial support." In this situation, *SAS No. 62* (AU 623.27) allows the auditor to report on such financial presentations. An example of such a report is shown in Figure 21–6.

Figure 21–5 **Report on a Statement of Assets Sold and Liabilities Transferred to Comply with a Contractual Agreement**

Independent Auditor's Report

Board of Directors
Shovel Company

We have audited the accompanying statement of net assets sold of Shovel Company as of June 8, 19X4. This statement of net assets sold is the responsibility of Shovel Company's management. Our responsibility is to express an opinion on the statement of net assets sold based on our audit.

The first paragraph identifies the audited statement of net assets sold. The auditor emphasizes that the statement is management's responsibility.

We conducted our audit in accordance with generally accepted auditing standards. Those standards require that we plan and perform the audit to obtain reasonable assurance about whether the statement of net assets sold is free of material misstatement. An audit includes examining, on a test basis, evidence supporting the amounts and disclosures in the statements. An audit also includes assessing the accounting principles used and significant estimates made by management, as well as evaluating the overall presentation of the statement of net assets sold. We believe that our audit provides a reasonable basis for our opinion.

The second paragraph states that the audit was conducted in accordance with GAAS.

The accompanying statement was prepared to present the net assets of Shovel Company sold to XYZ Corporation pursuant to the purchase agreement described in Note X, and is not intended to be a complete presentation of Shovel Company's assets and liabilities.

The third paragraph identifies the note in the statement that describes the basis of presentation as defined in the purchase agreement.

In our opinion, the accompanying statement of net assets sold presents fairly, in all material respects, the net assets sold of Shovel Company as of June 8, 19X4, pursuant to the purchase agreement referred to in Note X, in conformity with generally accepted accounting principles.

The opinion paragraph states whether the statement is fairly presented in all material respects, pursuant to the agreement, in conformity with GAAP.

This report is intended solely for the information and use of the board of directors and management of Shovel Company and XYZ Corporation and should not be used for any other purpose.

This paragraph indicates that distribution of the report is limited to the parties identified.

Figure 21-6   **Reports on Financial Statements Prepared Pursuant to a Loan Agreement That Results in a Presentation Not in Conformity with GAAP or an OCBOA**

Independent Auditor's Report

Board of Directors
Five Points Company

We have audited the special-purpose statements of assets and liabilities of Five Points Company as of December 31, 19X5 and 19X4, and the related special-purpose statements of revenues and expenses and cash flows for the years then ended. These financial statements are the responsibility of the Company's management. Our responsibility is to express an opinion on these financial statements based on our audits.

The first paragraph identifies the financial statements audited. The auditor emphasizes that the financial statements are management's responsibility.

We conducted our audits in accordance with generally accepted auditing standards. Those standards require that we plan and perform the audit to obtain reasonable assurance about whether the financial statements are free of material misstatement. An audit includes examining, on a test basis, evidence supporting the amounts and disclosures in the financial statements. An audit also includes assessing the accounting principles used and significant estimates made by management, as well as evaluating the overall financial statement presentation. We believe that our audits provide a reasonable basis for our opinion.

The scope paragraph states that the audit was conducted in accordance with GAAS.

The accompanying special-purpose financial statements have been prepared for the purpose of complying with and on the basis of accounting practices specified in Section 4 of a loan agreement between DEF Bank and the Company dated October 10, 19X3, as discussed in Note X, and are not intended to be a presentation in conformity with generally accepted accounting principles.

The third paragraph refers to the note in the financial statements that identifies the loan agreement.

In our opinion, the accompanying special-purpose financial statements of Five Points Company as of and for the years ended December 31, 19X5 and 19X4, referred to above, are fairly presented, in all material respects, on the basis of accounting described in Note X.

The opinion paragraph expresses the auditor's opinion on whether the financial statements are presented fairly in conformity with the basis described in the note.

This report is intended solely for the information and use of the board of directors and management of Five Points Company and DEF Bank and should not be used for any other purpose.

The last paragraph indicates that distribution of the report is limited to the parties identified.

Prescribed Forms

Auditors are sometimes requested to complete *prescribed forms* or schedules designed by bodies with which they are to be filed. These forms sometimes also prescribe the wording of the auditor's report. For example, state licensing boards for construction contractors often require the auditor both to complete a prescribed form that presents financial information and to sign a prescribed auditor's report.

Sometimes, these prescribed report forms cannot be signed by the auditor because the report does not conform to the standards of reporting. For example, a report may include a statement that is not consistent with the auditor's responsibility. Sometimes the report can be made acceptable by inserting appropriate additional wording. In other situations, however, the auditor may have to reword the form completely or attach a separate report. In no circumstances should the auditor sign a report that violates professional reporting standards.

Reports on Internal Control Structure over Financial Reporting

Statements on Standards for Attestation Engagements (SSAE) *No. 2* (AT 400), *Reporting on an Entity's Internal Control Structure Over Financial Reporting,* allows the CPA to express an opinion on management's written assertion about the effectiveness of an entity's internal control structure (ICS) as of a specified date or for a specified period of time. The SSAE also allows the CPA to perform agreed-upon procedures on an entity's ICS. In such an engagement, the client and any other users of the CPA's report must agree to the procedures to be performed, and the CPA's report must be restricted to those users.

Engagement to Express an Opinion

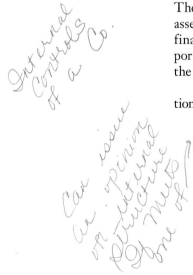

The examination of ICS for the purpose of expressing an opinion on management's assertion may be made separately from or in conjunction with an audit of an entity's financial statements. This type of report can be dated differently from the CPA's report on the financial statements and can be issued by a CPA who is not the auditor of the financial statements.

SSAE No. 2 allows a CPA to report on the ICS only if all of the following conditions are met:

- Management first evaluates the effectiveness of the entity's ICS using reasonable benchmarks or criteria for effective ICSs established by a recognized body. (See discussion of criteria that follows.)
- Management makes a written assertion about the effectiveness of the entity's ICS based on the criteria referred to in its assertion.
- Management is sufficiently knowledgeable about the entity's ICS to accept responsibility for its assertion about the effectiveness of the ICS.
- Sufficient evidential matter exists or could be developed to support management's evaluation.

Management may present its assertion in either a separate report that accompanies the CPA's report or in a representation letter. However, when management's assertion is only contained in the representation letter, the CPA's report is restricted to the use of the entity's management and board of directors.

A report expressing an unqualified opinion on management's assertion about an entity's ICS, when management's assertion is to accompany the CPA's report, is shown in Figure 21–7.

Figure 21–7

Report That Expresses an Opinion on Management's Assertion about the Effectiveness of Internal Control Structure over Financial Reporting

Board of Directors
Aerospace Company

We have examined management's assertion that Aerospace Company maintained an effective internal control structure over financial reporting as of December 31, 19X4, included in the accompanying management report.

The first paragraph identifies management's assertion about the effectiveness of the entity's ICS.

Our examination was made in accordance with standards established by the American Institute of Certified Public Accountants and, accordingly, included obtaining an understanding of the internal control structure over financial reporting, testing and evaluating the design and operating effectiveness of the internal control structure, and such other procedures as we considered necessary in the circumstances. We believe that our examination provides a reasonable basis for our opinion.

The scope paragraph includes a statement that the examination was made in accordance with standards established by the AICPA.

Because of inherent limitations in any internal control structure, errors or irregularities may occur and not be detected. Also, projections of any evaluation of the internal control structure over financial reporting to future periods are subject to the risk that the internal control structure may become inadequate because of changes in conditions, or that the degree of compliance with the policies or procedures may deteriorate.

The next paragraph discusses the inherent limitations of an ICS and discusses the risk of projecting an evaluation of the ICS to future periods.

In our opinion, management's assertion that Aerospace Company maintained an effective internal control structure over financial reporting as of December 31, 19X4, is fairly stated, in all material respects, based upon the criteria established in *Internal Control—Integrated Framework* issued by the Committee of Sponsoring Organizations of the Treadway Commission.

The opinion paragraph presents the CPA's opinion on whether management's assertion regarding the effectiveness of the entity's ICS is fairly stated, in all material respects, based on the COSO control criteria.

Criteria for an Effective Internal Control Structure

As mentioned in the preceding section, in order for management or the CPA to evaluate the effectiveness of an entity's ICS, benchmarks must be established against which the effectiveness can be judged. These benchmarks are referred to as control criteria.

The National Commission on Fraudulent Reporting (the Treadway Commission), in its 1987 report, recommended, among other things, that the accounting profession develop guidance on internal control to provide a common reference point for assessing the quality of internal controls. The Committee of Sponsoring Organizations of the Treadway Commission was formed to develop this guidance, and in September 1992, issued its report, *Internal Control—Integrated Framework* (the COSO Report). The report defines internal control and its components, provides tools for assessing internal controls, and addresses management reporting on an entity's ICS over financial reporting. The COSO Report is the most commonly used criteria for reporting on the effectiveness of ICSs.

Involvement with Other Information

Various Statements on Auditing Standards address information that is presented in addition to the basic financial statements. These include *SAS No. 8, Other Information in Documents Containing Audited Financial Statements* (AU 550); *SAS No. 52, Omnibus SAS-1987 (Required Supplementary Information)* (AU 558); and *SAS No. 29, Reporting on Information Accompanying the Basic Financial Statements in Auditor-Submitted Documents* (AU 551). The decision flowchart shown in Figure 21–8 provides an aid to understanding the particular SAS to use when these various types of additional information are encountered.

An understanding of the terms ***other information***, ***supplementary information***, and ***accompanying information*** is not critical to an auditor in deciding on the particular SAS to which to refer. What is critical to the decision is the answer to the following two questions:

1. Is the information included in an auditor-submitted document or in a client-prepared document?
2. Does the FASB or GASB (Governmental Accounting Standards Board) require that the information be presented?

The auditor has different reporting responsibilities for information appearing in an auditor-submitted document than for information appearing in a client-prepared document. In a ***client-prepared document***, such as an annual report to shareholders, it is reasonable to assume that the reader would expect that the auditor has audited only the information covered by the audit opinion and that the other information is being furnished solely by management. However, in a document bound in a CPA's own cover (that is, an ***auditor-submitted document***), the reader is most likely to assume that the CPA has audited and is taking some responsibility for all of the information in the document. Thus, the CPA should disclaim an opinion on accompanying information that is being furnished at the request of the client and that has not been covered by the audit.

Figure 21-8 **Flowchart of Decision Whether to Use *SAS No. 8, SAS No. 52,* or *SAS No. 29* for Additional Information. (The term *additional* information here includes *other, supplementary,* and *accompanying* information.)**

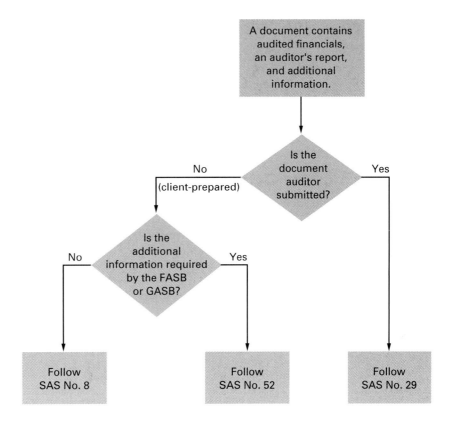

Client-Prepared Documents

Client-prepared documents are the responsibility of the client. For example, the annual report to shareholders is usually clearly discernible as the work of the client rather than the auditor. In such documents, the reader would generally expect the auditor's report to cover only the information identified in the audit report. Other information in the document usually can be clearly identified as furnished by management. For this reason, *SAS No. 8* (AU 550.04) provides that the auditor's responsibility for other information in a client-prepared document containing audited financial statements does not extend beyond the financial information identified in the audit report.

An auditor is not required to perform any audit procedures to substantiate the other information in a client-prepared document. However, *SAS No. 8* (AU 550.04) does require the auditor to read the other information and consider the manner in which it is presented to assess whether it is materially inconsistent with the financial statements. For example, in reading a president's letter in the annual report, the auditor should assess whether the president's comments about operating income are consistent with the income statement. If the auditor does not identify any material inconsistencies, no comment whatsoever is made about the other information. However, if the other information is not consistent with the financial statements, and the financial statements are correct, the auditor would consider taking one of the following steps:

- Requesting the client to revise the information to eliminate the inconsistency.
- Revising the audit report to include an explanatory paragraph describing the inconsistency.
- Withholding the audit report in the document.
- Withdrawing from the engagement.

The second potential course of action described above (revising the report) is known as *exception* reporting. That is, the auditor reports on the other information in a client-prepared document only if it is materially inconsistent with the financial statements. The following is an illustration of an explanatory paragraph when exception reporting is used:

> Attention is drawn to the fact that the presentation of the loss from disposal of a segment of the business in 19X4 included in the President's Letter on page X is different from the presentation of that loss in the statement of income referred to above, which is presented in accordance with generally accepted accounting principles.

The paragraph does not express or disclaim an opinion but merely draws the reader's attention to the fact that certain information outside the basic financial statements is inconsistent with the information in the financial statements.

While reading the other information to determine whether there is a material inconsistency, the auditor may become aware of other information that he or she believes is a material misstatement of fact even though it is not inconsistent with the financial statements. For example, the auditor may note that the president incorrectly states in the annual report that the client is the largest company in its industry. Even though this statement does not contradict the financial statements, the auditor may be aware that the statement is incorrect. *SAS No. 8* (AU 550.05) notes that the auditor may not have the expertise to evaluate the statement, that standards may not exist to assess the statement, and that valid differences of judgment or opinion may exist. However, if the auditor has a valid basis of concern, he or she should discuss the matter with the client, consider notifying the client in writing, and consider consulting legal counsel.

Auditor-Submitted Documents

Auditor-submitted documents are bound in the CPA firm's report cover and are sometimes printed on paper bearing the auditor's logo or watermark. The appearance of these documents often leads readers to assume that the auditor is taking some degree of responsibility for all the information in the document. As a result, *SAS No. 29* (AU 551.04) requires the auditor to report on all the information in an auditor-submitted document.

The auditor's report on additional information may be presented separately in the document or may be included as a separate paragraph of the auditor's report on the financial statements. Regardless of the method selected, the report must state that the audit was made for the purpose of forming an opinion on the financial statements taken as a whole, identify the additional information, and indicate that it is presented for purposes of additional analysis and is not a required part of the basic financial statements.

The auditor must either express an opinion on whether the additional information is fairly stated in all material respects to the financial statements as a whole or disclaim an opinion. Expressing an opinion is appropriate only when the information has been subjected to the auditing procedures applied to the financial statements. An auditor has no obligation to apply any auditing procedures to the additional information, and if the additional information in an auditor-submitted document has not been subjected to the auditing procedures applied to the basic financial statements, the auditor should disclaim an opinion on that information.

Supplementary Information Required by the FASB or GASB

The Financial Accounting Standards Board and the Governmental Accounting Standards Board require certain entities to present information supplementary to the financial statements. For example, FASB standards require information about oil and gas reserves and GASB standards require certain pension disclosures. Required supplementary information is not necessary for the fair presentation of financial statements in conformity with GAAP. However, the information is an essential part of the broader concept of financial reporting in general. For this reason, *SAS No. 52* (AU 558.06) requires an auditor to apply certain limited procedures to this information. These procedures are principally inquiries of management regarding methods of measuring and presenting the supplementary information.

The auditor's reporting responsibility on required supplementary information again depends on whether the information is contained in an auditor-submitted or a client-prepared document. When an auditor-submitted document contains required supplementary information, the auditor should disclaim an opinion on that information unless he or she has been specifically engaged to audit and express an opinion on the information. The disclaimer is required even though limited procedures must be applied to the information. The following is an illustration of a disclaimer:

> The supplementary oil and gas reserve information is not a required part of the basic financial statements of Tony Company for 19X4, but is supplementary information required by the Financial Accounting Standards Board. We have applied certain limited procedures that consisted principally of inquiries of management regarding the methods of measurement and presentation (or disclosure) of the supplementary information. However, we did not audit the information and we express no opinion on it.

In a client-prepared document, the exception reporting principle applies. *SAS No. 52* (AU 558.08) requires the auditor to report on the required supplementary information only if

- the required supplementary information is not presented, or
- the auditor concludes that the data are not prepared or presented in accordance with FASB or GASB requirements, or
- the auditor is unable to perform the limited procedures, or
- the auditor has unresolved doubts about the required supplementary information.

SAS No. 29 (AU 551.15) indicates that the auditor's report in an auditor-submitted document should also be expanded if any of the four exceptions above are encountered. When one of the above circumstances causes the auditor to report on the supplementary information in an auditor-submitted or a client-prepared document, the auditor's opinion on the financial statements would not be affected. This is because the required supplementary information is not considered by the FASB or GASB to be part of GAAP and, therefore, does not affect the financial statements.

Review of Interim Financial Information

Interim financial information includes current data during a fiscal year on financial position, results of operations, and cash flows. This information may be issued on a monthly or quarterly basis or at other intervals and can take the form of either complete financial statements, summarized financial statements, or summarized financial data, and may be presented alone or in a note to audited financial statements.

SAS No. 71, Interim Financial Information (AU 722), provides guidance to the independent accountant involved with interim financial information. According to *SAS No. 71*, the objective of a review of interim financial information is to provide the accountant with a reasonable basis for providing limited assurance that no material modifications should be made to the interim financial information to conform such information with GAAP. The accountant reaches this conclusion based on the performance of inquiry and analytical procedures. The accountant should first gain a sufficient understanding of the internal control structure before selecting the inquiry and analytical procedures that need to be performed. The procedures the accountant ordinarily applies include the following:

- Making inquiries concerning the internal control structure and any significant changes in that structure.
- Applying analytical procedures to the interim information.
- Reading the minutes of meetings of stockholders, the board of directors, and committees of the board of directors.
- Reading the interim financial information to consider whether the information conforms with GAAP.
- Obtaining reports of other accountants, if any, who have been engaged to review interim financial information of significant components of the entity, its subsidiaries, or other investees.

- Making inquiries of officers and other executives having responsibility for financial and accounting matters.
- Obtaining written representations from management.

A review report on interim financial information should include

- a title that includes the word *independent.*
- an identification of the interim financial information reviewed, and a statement that the information is the responsibility of management.
- a statement that the review was made in accordance with the standards for such reviews.
- a description of the procedures for a review of interim financial information.
- a statement that a review is significantly less in scope than an audit in accordance with GAAS and that, accordingly, no opinion is expressed.
- a statement as to whether the accountant is aware of any material modifications that should be made to the information to make it conform with GAAP.

In addition, each page of the interim financial information should be clearly marked "unaudited." Figure 21–9 is an example of a report on interim financial information.

[handwritten: Statement not an opinion]
[handwritten: Limited Assurance Report]

Prospective Financial Statements

[handwritten: Future oriented]

CPAs are increasingly involved with financial information that is future oriented. For example, a client may want a forecast of its earnings for the next year. Or a client may be considering whether to make an investment and therefore may want a projection of future cash flows. Information that is future oriented is termed *prospective financial information.*

In 1985 the Auditing Standards Board issued a Statement on Standards for Accountants' Services on Prospective Financial Information, *Financial Forecasts and Projections* (AT 200). The statement establishes standards for accountants providing different levels of service on prospective financial statements. Rule 202 of the Code of Professional Conduct requires accountants to comply with the statement when they are performing an engagement involving prospective financial information.

The statement establishes standards for the three types of services that can be provided on prospective financial statements *expected to be used by third parties:* compilation, application of agreed-upon procedures, and examination. The statement also prohibits the accountant from providing services on prospective financial statements for third-party use if the statements do not disclose the underlying assumptions or if projections (as defined below) appropriate only for limited use are to be distributed to *passive users*—that is, persons who are not negotiating directly with the user.

In addition, the Auditing Standards Division issued a companion pronouncement, *Guide for Prospective Financial Information.* This guide establishes preparation and presentation guidelines (analogous to GAAP) for prospective financial statements.

Financial Forecasts and Financial Projections

The attest statement (AT 200.06) defines ***financial forecasts*** as "prospective financial statements that present, to the best of the responsible party's knowledge and

Figure 21-9 **Accountant's Report on Review of Interim Financial Information for a Public Entity**

Independent Accountant's Report

Board of Directors
WEGP Company

We have reviewed [describe the information or statements reviewed] of WEGP Company and consolidated subsidiaries as of September 30, 19X4, and for the three-month and nine-month periods then ended. These financial statements are the responsibility of the company's management.

The first paragraph identifies the information or report reviewed.

We conducted our review in accordance with standards established by the American Institute of Certified Public Accountants. A review of interim financial information consists principally of applying analytical procedures to financial data and making inquiries of persons responsible for financial and accounting matters. It is substantially less in scope than an audit conducted in accordance with generally accepted auditing standards, the objective of which is the expression of an opinion regarding the financial statements taken as a whole. Accordingly, we do not express such an opinion.

The second paragraph explains that a review consists primarily of analytical procedures and inquiries and is substantially less in scope than an audit made in accordance with GAAS. Therefore, no opinion is given.

Based on our review, we are not aware of any material modification that should be made to the accompanying financial [information or statements] for them to be in conformity with generally accepted auditing standards.

Nothing was found that needs modification for the report to be in accordance with GAAP (negative assurance).

Powell and Co.
Certified Public Accountants

---

belief, an entity's expected financial position, results of operations, and changes in financial position." Financial forecasts are based on the responsible party's assumptions, reflecting conditions it expects to exist and the course of action it expects to take.

Alternatively, the statement (AT 200.06) defines ***financial projections*** as "prospective financial statements that present, to the best of the responsible party's knowledge and belief, given one or more hypothetical assumptions, an entity's expected financial position, results of operations, and changes in financial position."

A financial projection is sometimes prepared to present one or more hypothetical courses of action for evaluation, as in response to a question such as, "What would happen if...?" A financial projection is based on the responsible party's assumptions reflecting conditions it expects would exist and the course of action it expects would be taken, given one or more hypothetical assumptions.

In a *forecast*, all assumptions are expected to occur. In a *projection*, one or more (hypothetical) assumptions are not necessarily expected to occur (although they may if management chooses a certain course of action). For example, a company may project the construction of a new building without having made the decision to construct the building. All the other assumptions would be expected to occur if the hypothetical assumption occurs.

Prospective financial statements (forecasts or projections) may be presented as complete statements of financial position, results of operations, and cash flows, or may be presented in a summarized or condensed form. Certain items are required for a condensed presentation to qualify as a prospective financial statement, including revenues, gross profit or cost of sales, unusual or infrequent items, income taxes, discontinued operations or extraordinary items, income from continuing operations, net income, earnings per share, and significant changes in financial position.

Presentations that omit one or more of these minimum items are called *partial presentations*. Such presentations are not ordinarily appropriate for general use.

Levels of Service

As noted previously, the statement provides three levels of service on prospective financial statements expected to be used by third parties:

- *Compilation Engagement* A compilation engagement involves assembling prospective financial statements based on the responsible party's assumptions and considering whether the presentation appears to be presented in conformity with AICPA presentation guidelines and whether it is or is not obviously inappropriate. An example of a compilation report for forecasted financial statements is shown in Figure 21–10. (This is not an accounting and review services compilation, which is discussed in Chapter 22.)

- *Agreed-Upon Procedures Engagement* An agreed-upon procedures engagement is generally an engagement that involves (1) applying to prospective financial statements procedures that have been agreed to or established by specified users of the data (for example, a specific bank) and (2) issuing a report that enumerates the procedures performed, states the accountant's findings, and restricts report distribution to specified parties.

- *Examination* Examination is generally an audit that involves (1) evaluating the preparation, the support underlying the assumptions, and the presentation of the prospective financial statements for conformity with AICPA presentation guidelines and (2) issuing an examination report. The examination report expresses a positive opinion on whether the assumptions provide a reasonable basis for the prospective financial statements. Examples of a standard report on forecasted financial statements and projected financial statements are shown in Figures 21–11 and 21–12, respectively.

The logic underlying the examination procedures for prospective financial statements is basically the same as that underlying the audit of historical financial statements. However, the literature does contain some distinctive reporting requirements

---

Figure 21-10 **Compilation Report on Forecasted Financial Statements**

Board of Directors
XYZ Company

We have compiled the accompanying forecasted balance sheet, statements of income, retained earnings, and cash flows of XYZ Company as of December 31, 19X4, and for the year then ending, in accordance with standards established by the American Institute of Certified Public Accountants.

A compilation is limited to presenting in the form of a forecast information that is the representation of management and does not include evaluation of the support for the assumptions underlying the forecast. We have not examined the forecast and, accordingly, do not express an opinion or any other form of assurance on the accompanying statements or assumptions. Furthermore, there will usually be differences between the forecasted and actual results, because events and circumstances frequently do not occur as expected, and those differences may be material. We have no responsibility to update this report for events and circumstances occurring after the date of this report.

The first paragraph identifies the prospective financial statements presented by the responsible party and states that the accountant compiled the statements in accordance with standards established by the AICPA.

The second paragraph states that a compilation's limited scope does not enable the accountant to express an opinion on the prospective financial statement. In addition, it includes a caveat that the prospective results may not be achieved, as well as a statement that the accountant has no responsibility to update the report.

Powell and Co.
Certified Public Accountants

---

for examinations. If a prospective presentation fails to disclose one or more significant assumptions or if one or more significant assumptions do not have a reasonable basis, an adverse opinion is required. Similarly, if a scope limitation exists—that is, the inability to apply a necessary procedure because of circumstances or client restrictions—a disclaimer is required.

Reporting on Financial Statements Prepared for Use in Other Countries

Most U.S. companies prepare financial statements for use in the United States in conformity with GAAP accepted in the United States. However, some U.S. companies have valid reasons for presenting their financial statements in conformity with

Figure 21–11   **Accountant's Standard Report on an Examination of a Forecast**

Board of Directors
XYZ Company

We have examined the accompanying forecasted balance sheet, statements of income, retained earnings, and cash flows of XYZ Company as of December 31, 19X4, and for the year then ending. Our examination was made in accordance with standards for an examination of a forecast established by the American Institute of Certified Public Accountants and, accordingly, included such procedures as we considered necessary to evaluate both the assumptions used by management and the preparation and presentation of the forecast.

The first paragraph identifies the forecasted statements examined and explains that they were examined in accordance with guidelines established by the AICPA.

In our opinion, the accompanying forecast is presented in conformity with guidelines for presentation of a forecast established by the American Institute of Certified Public Accountants, and the underlying assumptions provide a reasonable basis for management's forecast. However, there will usually be differences between the forecasted and actual results, because events and circumstances frequently do not occur as expected, and those differences may be material. We have no responsibility to update this report for events and circumstances occurring after the date of this report.

The second paragraph expresses an opinion as to whether the forecast is presented in conformity with guidelines set up by the AICPA and whether the assumptions are reasonable.

Powell and Co.
Certified Public Accountants

accounting principles generally accepted in another country (non-U.S. GAAP). For example, a U.S. company may be a subsidiary of a foreign company or may wish to raise capital abroad.

SAS No. 51, *Reporting on Financial Statements Prepared for Use in Other Countries* (AU 534), provides guidance to the U.S. auditor who expresses an opinion on a U.S. entity's financial statements prepared in conformity with non-U.S. GAAP. The auditor should be familiar with the non-U.S. GAAP used in order to report on the financial statements and should consider consulting with accountants having expertise in such principles. The auditor should also understand and obtain management's written representations about the purpose and use of the non-U.S. GAAP financial

| Figure 21–12 | **Accountant's Standard Report on an Examination of a Projection** |

Board of Directors
The Five Points Company

We have examined the accompanying projected balance sheet, statements of income, retained earnings, and cash flows of The Five Points Company as of December 31, 19X4, and for the year then ending. Our examination was made in accordance with standards for examination of a projection established by the American Institute of Certified Public Accountants and, accordingly, included such procedures as we considered necessary to evaluate both assumptions used by management and the preparation and presentation of the projection.

The first paragraph identifies the projected statements examined and explains that they were examined in accordance with guidelines established by the AICPA.

The accompanying projection and this report were prepared for The Five Points Company for the purpose of negotiating a loan with DEF National Bank to expand The Five Points Company's plant and should not be used for any other purpose.

The second paragraph explains the purpose of the projection and indicates it should not be used for any other purpose.

In our opinion, the accompanying projection is presented in conformity with guidelines for presentation of a projection established by the American Institute of Certified Public Accountants, and the underlying assumptions provide a reasonable basis for management's projection assuming the granting of the requested loan for the purpose of expanding The Five Points Company's plant as described in the summary of significant assumptions. However, even if the loan is granted and the plant is expanded, there will usually be differences between the projected and actual results, because events and circumstances frequently do not occur as expected, and those differences may be material. We have no responsibility to update this report for events or circumstances occurring after the date of this report.

The final paragraph expresses an opinion on whether the projection is presented in conformity with the guidelines of the AICPA and whether the assumptions provide a reasonable basis for the projection.

Powell and Co.
Certified Public Accountants

statements. The auditor should comply with U.S. generally accepted auditing standards but might need to modify certain procedures for assertions embodied in the non-U.S. GAAP financial statements that differ from those in U.S. GAAP financial statements. (For example, some countries require inflation adjustments in financial statements, in which case the U.S. auditor would need to perform procedures to test the inflation restatement.)

According to *SAS No. 51* (AU 534.07), if the non-U.S. GAAP financial statements are prepared for use only outside the United States, the auditor may report using either (1) a U.S.-style report modified to present the accounting principles of another country (Figure 21–13) or, if appropriate, (2) the report form of another country. When the U.S. auditor uses the report form of another country, he or she should determine that the report would be used by non-U.S. auditors in similar circumstances and that the attestations contained in the report are appropriate. Non-U.S. GAAP financial statements are ordinarily not useful to U.S. users. Accordingly, if a company's financial statements are needed for use in both another country and the U.S., the auditor may report on two sets of financial statements, one prepared using non-U.S. GAAP and the other prepared using U.S. GAAP.

Reports on the Application of Accounting Principles

Accountants are sometimes engaged by entities, for which they are not the continuing auditor (that is, the entity is audited by another CPA), to provide consultations regarding a proposed or completed transaction. This type of consultation is often referred to as "opinion shopping" because some infer that the entity will shop around until it finds an accountant who will agree with its position and then hire that accountant as the auditor. There are public perceptions that opinion shopping is not in the public interest, because it may compromise the accountant's objectivity.

As a result of these concerns, the Auditing Standards Board issued *SAS No. 50, Reports on the Application of Accounting Principles* (AU 625). *SAS No. 50* applies to accountants who provide reports, written or oral, on the accounting treatments of proposed or completed specific transactions to persons or entities other than continuing clients. *SAS No. 50* does not discourage obtaining a second opinion, but it does provide for certain safeguards as discussed below.

Before providing advice, the accountant should consider the identity of the requestor, the circumstances and purpose of the request, and the use of the resulting report. *SAS No. 50* (AU 625.05) also requires the reporting accountant to exercise due professional care, have adequate technical training and proficiency, properly plan and supervise the engagement, and accumulate sufficient information to provide a reasonable basis for the professional judgment described in the report.

In forming a judgment the accountant should

- understand the form and substance of the transaction,
- review applicable accounting principles,
- consult with other professionals or experts, as appropriate, and
- perform research and consider precedents and analogies, as appropriate.

Figure 21–13 **Example of a Report on Non-U.S. GAAP Financial Statements**

Independent Auditor's Report

Board of Directors
Jetspace Institute Co.

We have audited the accompanying balance sheets of Jetspace Institute Co. as of December 31, 19X5 and 19X4, and the related statements of income, retained earnings, and cash flows for the years then ended which, as described in Note X, have been prepared on the basis of accounting principles generally accepted in the United Kingdom. These financial statements are the responsibility of the Company's management. Our responsibility is to express an opinion on these financial statements based on our audits.

The first paragraph identifies the statements audited and refers to the note to the statements that describes the basis upon which they are presented.

We conducted our audits in accordance with auditing standards generally accepted in the United States. U.S. standards require that we plan and perform the audit to obtain reasonable assurance about whether the financial statements are free of material misstatement. An audit includes examining, on a test basis, evidence supporting the amounts and disclosures in the financial statements. An audit also includes assessing the accounting principles used and significant estimates made by management, as well as evaluating the overall financial statement presentation. We believe that our audits provide a reasonable basis for our opinion.

The second paragraph states that the audit was conducted in accordance with U.S. GAAS.

In our opinion, the financial statements referred to above present fairly, in all material respects, the financial position of Jetspace Institute Co. as of December 31, 19X5 and 19X4, and the results of its operations and its cash flows for the years then ended in conformity with accounting principles generally accepted in the United Kingdom.

The final paragraph expresses an opinion as to whether the financial statements are presented fairly, in all material respects, in conformity with the basis described in the note.

Earle Fairly

Earle Fairly, CPA

Most important, the reporting accountant is required to consult with the entity's continuing auditor to ascertain all the relevant facts. The continuing auditor can often provide information not otherwise available to the reporting accountant, such as the form and substance of the transaction, how management has applied accounting principles to similar transactions, and whether the method of accounting recommended by the continuing auditor is disputed by management. Figure 21–14 illustrates an appropriate report on the application of GAAP.

Figure 21–14   **Example of a Report on the Application of GAAP**

To ABC Company

Introduction

We have been engaged to report on the appropriate application of generally accepted accounting principles to the specific transaction described below. This report is being issued to ABC Company for assistance in evaluating accounting principles for the described specific transaction. Our engagement has been conducted in accordance with standards established by the American Institute of Certified Public Accountants.

Description of Transaction

The facts, circumstances, and assumptions relevant to the specific transaction as provided to us by the management of the ABC Company are as follows:

ABC Company is the obligor on a long-term, taxable, publicly held debt obligation. The debt contains default provisions which may accelerate the term of the debt and demand immediate payment, but it is extremely remote that ABC Company will meet any of these provisions. Although the debt's indenture does not contain a specific defeasance provision, ABC Company would like to defease or satisfy the obligation without the debt necessarily being retired.

To effect this, ABC Company purchased a portfolio of noncallable U.S. government bonds, the cash flow from which can be actuarily demonstrated to satisfy all the future interest and principal payments due under the debt agreement. ABC Company delivered the bonds to a reputable trustee with irrevocable instructions to establish a trust, the sole purpose of which is to use the cash flow generated to satisfy all of the future interest and principal payments due under the debt agreement. The bonds are not subject to lien for any purpose other than in connection with this transaction.

(continued)

Figure 21-14 *continued*

Appropriate Accounting Principles

The above-described transaction effectively meets the criteria in paragraph 10 of the AICPA's Statement of Position on Accounting for Advance Refunding of Tax Exempt Debt; we believe that this will result in off-balance sheet treatment for ABC Company. Although this SOP relates only to tax-exempt debt, and not the corporate debt described above, it is presently the only guidance within the accounting profession regarding this type of transaction. The financial statements of ABC Company for the period in which the transaction occurs should include a general description of the transaction, including identification of the debt involved, along with disclosures required by paragraph 9 of FASB Statement 4. A general description of the transaction, including identification of the debt involved, should be disclosed in a note to the financial statements for each subsequent period until the debt and the bonds are retired.

Any gain or loss from the transaction should be determined in accordance with the provisions of paragraph 20 of APB Opinion 26 and should be classified in accordance with paragraph 8 of FASB Statement 4.

Concluding Comments

The ultimate responsibility for the decision on the appropriate application of generally accepted accounting principles for an actual transaction rests with the preparers of financial statements, who should consult with their continuing accountants. Our judgment on the appropriate application of generally accepted accounting principles for the described specific transactions is based solely on the facts provided to us as described above; should these facts and circumstances differ, our conclusion may change.

Powell and Co.
Certified Public Accountants

Significant Terms

Accompanying information Additional information beyond the basic financial statements (for example, a schedule of General, Selling, and Administrative Expenses) included in an auditor-submitted document.

Agreed-upon procedures An engagement in which the auditor agrees to perform specific audit procedures for restricted parties.

Auditor-submitted document A document bound in a CPA's own cover.

Client-prepared document A document such as an annual report prepared by the client.

Compliance reports Reports issued by auditors stating that the client is in compliance with aspects of contractual agreements or regulatory requirements.

Financial forecasts Prospective financial statements that present an entity's expected financial position, results of operations, and cash flows.

Financial projections Prospective financial statements that present, given one or more hypothetical assumptions, an entity's expected financial position, results of operations, and cash flows.

Interim financial information Current data during a client's fiscal year on financial position, results of operations, and cash flows, issued on a monthly or quarterly basis.

Negative assurance report A report stating that nothing came to the auditor's attention to indicate that the information is not fairly presented.

Other comprehensive basis of accounting (OCBOA) Financial measurement basis using either the cash, income tax, or regulatory basis, or another basis having substantial support.

Other information Additional information beyond the basic financial statements in a client-prepared document.

Prescribed forms Forms or schedules designed by bodies with which they are to be filed.

Report on internal control Report issued by the auditor based on an examination of internal control structure under standards in *SSAE No. 2, Reporting on an Entity's Internal Control Structure over Financial Reporting.*

Report on the application of GAAP An engagement in which an accountant is requested by an entity, for whom the accountant is not the continuing auditor, to provide a report regarding the proper accounting treatment of a proposed or completed transaction.

Special reports Audit reports under *SAS No. 62* in one of five areas: OCBOA financial statements, specified accounts or elements in a financial statement, compliance with aspects of contractual agreements, financial presentations to comply with contractual agreements or regulatory provisions, and prescribed forms.

Supplementary information Information presented in addition to the basic financial statements. However, this information is not necessary for fair presentation in conformity with GAAP.

Discussion Questions

21-1. What are the five types of special reports included in *SAS No. 62, Special Reports?*

21-2. According to *SAS No. 62*, what are the criteria for a measurement basis to be considered as another comprehensive basis of accounting?

21-3. What are the reporting requirements for an auditor who is reporting on financial statements prepared in accordance with an other comprehensive basis of accounting?

21-4. For OCBOA statements, why do auditing standards require that the titles of the financial statements not use terms such as "balance sheet" or "income statement"?

21-5. What are the reporting requirements when an auditor expresses an opinion on one or more specified elements, accounts, or items of a financial statement?

21-6. What is the purpose of an engagement concerning the application of agreed-upon procedures and when is it permissible to accept such an engagement?

21-7. When applying agreed-upon procedures, what items should the auditor include in the report?

21-8. What are the two types of special-purpose financial statements prepared to comply with a contractual agreement or regulatory provision on which an auditor can report?

21-9. Under what circumstances may an auditor sign a prescribed report form according to *SAS No. 62*?

21-10. What is a negative assurance report and how is it used? How does it differ from the standard audit report?

21-11. In accordance with SSAE, *Reporting on an Entity's Internal Control Structure Over Financial Reporting*, what two types of services may a CPA provide related to management's assertion about the effectiveness of an entity's internal control structure over financial reporting?

21-12. What conditions must be met for a CPA to examine and report on management's assertion about the effectiveness of an entity's internal control structure over financial reporting?

21-13. When a CPA is engaged to express an opinion on management's assertion about the effectiveness of an entity's internal control structure, where may management present its assertions? How does the location of management's assertion affect the CPA's report?

21-14. What is the COSO Report?

21-15. What is the difference in the auditor's responsibility for information included in auditor-submitted documents and in client-prepared documents?

21-16. What responsibilities does an auditor have for other information in a client-prepared document?

21-17. What is the auditor's responsibility when supplementary information required by the FASB or GASB is presented along with the financial statements?

21-18. In performing a review of interim financial information, what procedures should the accountant ordinarily apply?

21-19. What is included in a review report on interim financial information?

21-20. What is the difference between a financial forecast and a financial projection?

21-21. Discuss the levels of service a CPA can provide on prospective financial statements expected to be used by third parties.

21-22. Can a U.S. auditor provide an unqualified opinion on financial statements prepared in conformity with non-U.S. GAAP?

21-23. Why are users of financial statements concerned about opinion shopping?

Objective Questions

*21-24. Reports are considered special reports when issued in connection with
  (1) compliance with aspects of regulatory requirements related to audited financial statements.
  (2) pro forma financial presentations designed to demonstrate the effect of hypothetical transactions.
  (3) feasibility studies presented to illustrate an entity's result of operations.
  (4) interim financial information reviewed to determine whether material modifications should be made to conform with generally accepted accounting principles.

---

*AICPA adapted.

21-25. It is implicit in an auditor's unqualified opinion on management's assertion about the effectiveness of an entity's internal control structure over financial reporting that
(1) the entity has filed the proper documents with regard to the Foreign Corrupt Practices Act.
(2) the likelihood of management fraud is minimal.
(3) the financial records are sufficiently reliable to permit the preparation of the financial statements.
(4) the entity's internal control structure is functioning as designed by the audit committee.

21-26. All of the following are considered *special reports* except reports on financial statements
(1) in which the client has limited the scope of the audit.
(2) prepared in accordance with a tax basis of accounting.
(3) prepared in accordance with a cash basis of accounting.
(4) prepared for limited purposes, such as a report that relates only to certain aspects of financial statements.

21-27. Which of the following should be included when reporting on financial statements prepared on a comprehensive basis of accounting other than GAAP?
(1) A paragraph stating that the basis of presentation is a comprehensive basis of accounting other than GAAP.
(2) A paragraph that justifies the comprehensive basis of accounting being used.
(3) A paragraph that refers to authoritative pronouncements and explains the comprehensive basis of accounting being used.
(4) A paragraph stating that the financial statements have not been examined in accordance with GAAS.

*21-28. If the auditor believes that financial statements prepared on the entity's income tax basis are *not* suitably titled, he or she should
(1) issue a disclaimer of opinion.
(2) explain in the notes to the financial statements the terminology used.
(3) issue a compilation report.
(4) modify the auditor's report to disclose any reservations.

21-29. Which of the following is true when an auditor expresses an opinion on a specific item in a financial statement?
(1) Materiality must be related to the specified item rather than to the financial statements taken as a whole.
(2) No report can be issued unless the entire set of financial statements taken as a whole was audited.
(3) The attention received by the specified item is usually less than it would be if the financial statements taken as a whole were being audited.
(4) An auditor cannot express an opinion on a specific item in the financial statements if he or she has also been engaged to audit the entire set of financial statements, unless the auditor issued an unqualified opinion.

21-30. An auditor's primary concern when making a limited review of interim financial information consists of
(1) studying and evaluating documentation supporting the interim financial information.
(2) scanning and reviewing client-prepared internal financial statements.
(3) performing analytical procedures and making inquiries concerning significant accounting matters.
(4) confirming significant account balances at the interim date.

21-31. Which of the following would *not* be included in a report based on a limited review of interim financial statements?
   (1) A statement that the audit was performed in accordance with GAAS.
   (2) A description of procedures performed or a reference to the engagement letter that describes the procedures.
   (3) A statement that a limited review would not necessarily disclose all significant matters.
   (4) An identification of the information reviewed.

*21-32. Leslie Green, CPA, is requested to render an opinion on the application of accounting principles by an entity that is audited by another CPA. Green may
   (1) not accept such an engagement because to do so would be considered unethical.
   (2) not accept such an engagement because she would lack the necessary information on which to base an opinion without conducting an audit.
   (3) accept the engagement but should form an independent opinion without consulting with the continuing CPA.
   (4) accept the engagement but should consult with the continuing CPA to ascertain all available facts relevant to forming a professional judgment.

21-33. When an accountant examines a financial forecast that fails to disclose several significant assumptions used to prepare the forecast, the accountant should describe the assumptions in the accountant's report and issue a(an)
   (1) "except for" qualified opinion.
   (2) "subject to" qualified opinion.
   (3) unqualified opinion with a separate explanatory paragraph.
   (4) adverse opinion.

21-34. An accountant has been engaged to report on management's assertion about the effectiveness of an internal control structure without performing an audit of the financial statements. What restrictions, if any, should the accountant place on the use of this report if management's assertion accompanies the accountant's report?
   (1) This report should be restricted for use by management.
   (2) This report should be restricted for use by the audit committee.
   (3) This report should be restricted for use by a specified regulatory agency.
   (4) The accountant does **not** need to place any restrictions on the use of this report.

Problems and Cases

21-35. (OCBOA) Auditors often have to report on financial statements prepared on an other comprehensive basis of accounting.
   REQUIRED
   A. What changes should the auditor make in the standard audit report when the client uses the income tax basis of accounting?
   B. Is the modified standard report outlined in **A** above an unqualified or a qualified opinion? Why?
   C. If the client does not include a note that identifies the basis of accounting used to prepare the financial statements, can the auditor issue an unqualified opinion?

21-36. (OCBOA and GAAP Departures) Greg Taylor and Pound Lamb have formed T&L, a partnership to invest in real estate. In their partnership agreement, they specified that depreciation is not to be recognized on real property.
   REQUIRED
   A. Are such financial statements prepared in accordance with an OCBOA?
   B. What reporting alternative would the accountant for T&L have?

---

*AICPA adapted.

*21-37. (Reports on Specified Accounts) To obtain information necessary to make informed decisions, management often calls upon an independent auditor for assistance. This may involve a request that the independent auditor apply certain audit procedures to specific accounts of a company that is a candidate for acquisition and report upon the results.

At the completion of an engagement performed at the request of Uclean Corporation, the following report was prepared by an audit assistant and was submitted to the auditor for review:

> **To: Board of Directors of Uclean Corporation**
>
> We have applied certain agreed-upon procedures, as discussed below, to accounting records of Ajax Corporation, as of December 31, 19X4, solely to assist Uclean Corporation in connection with the proposed acquisition of Ajax Corporation.
>
> We conducted our audit in accordance with generally accepted auditing standards. These standards require that we plan and perform the audit to obtain reasonable assurance about whether the schedule of gross sales is free of material misstatement. An audit includes examining, on a test basis, evidence supporting the amounts and disclosures in the schedule of gross sales. An audit also includes assessing the accounting principles used and significant estimates made by management, as well as evaluating the overall schedule presentation. We believe that our audit provides a reasonable basis for our opinion.
>
> In our opinion, gross sales referred to above are fairly presented, in all material respects, as of December 31, 19X4, in conformity with generally accepted accounting principles. We therefore recommend that Uclean Corporation acquire Ajax Corporation pursuant to the proposed agreement.
>
> (Signature)

REQUIRED

Comment on the proposed report describing those assertions that are

A. incorrect or should otherwise be deleted.

B. missing and should be inserted.

21-38. (Prescribed Forms) A state's Medicaid reimbursement report contains the following statement, which must be signed by the CPA preparing the report: "I hereby certify that this agreement and the accompanying schedules are true and correct to the best of my knowledge and belief."

REQUIRED

A. Can the CPA sign this report? Why or why not?

B. What other reporting option would the CPA have?

---

*AICPA adapted.

21-39. (Compliance with Contractual Agreements) Bryan Johnson, CPA, is currently performing the December 31, 19X4, audit of Texas Microwaves, Inc. Texas Microwaves, Inc., has requested that Johnson review their loan agreement with First National Bank, dated October 10, 19X3, to determine their compliance and provide a report to the bank. Johnson reviews the loan agreement as a part of the audit. Nothing comes to his attention that would indicate noncompliance.

REQUIRED

A. Write a report, separate from the audit report on compliance with the loan agreement, for Johnson.

B. Write the audit report, including a reference to compliance with the loan agreement, for Johnson.

*21-40. (Accompanying Information) Auditors have certain responsibilities for information that accompanies the financial statements.

REQUIRED

A. What are the three conditions that must exist before *SAS No. 29, Reporting on Information Accompanying the Basic Financial Statements in Auditor-Submitted Documents,* applies?

B. Does *SAS No. 29* apply to accompanying information in audited financial statements of both *public* and *nonpublic* companies?

C. Is *SAS No. 52, Omnibus SAS-1987 (Required Supplementary Information),* ever applicable to a nonpublic entity that is not a state or local governmental entity? (Hint: This answer requires reading of *SAS No. 52.*)

D. When supplementary information required by the FASB or the GASB is presented outside the basic financial statements (for example, oil and gas reserve information) in an auditor-submitted document, is it *SAS No. 29* or *SAS No. 52* that applies?

*21-41. (Review of Interim Financial Information) Tony Godwin, CPA, who audited the financial statements of the GAG Corporation, a publicly held company, for the year ended December 31, 19X4, was asked to perform a review of the financial statements of GAG Corporation for the period ending March 31, 19X5. The engagement letter stated that a limited review does not provide a basis for the expression of an opinion.

REQUIRED

A. Explain why Godwin's review will not provide a basis for the expression of an opinion.

B. What review procedures should Godwin perform and what is the purpose of each procedure? Organize your response in two columns, headed "Procedure" and "Purpose of Procedure."

21-42. (Forecasts and Projections) Gina Brazil, CPA, has been requested by Art, Inc., to report on forecasted financial statements for next year. Art, Inc., plans to use this report to acquire additional capital from potential investors. However, Art, Inc., does not wish to disclose the underlying assumptions although both the company and Brazil believe that the assumptions are reasonable and appropriate.

REQUIRED

A. Brazil cannot accept this engagement as described. Why not?

B. Assuming that the issues identified in **A** are resolved as Brazil requested, what reporting options are available to her?

C. Assuming Art, Inc., would prefer the highest level of service, write the report for Brazil.

---

*AICPA adapted.

21-43. (Non-U.S. GAAP Financial Statements) Bob Farris, CPA, is performing the annual audit of Fashions, Inc., a U.S. company in which Le Brei Sportswear, a Swiss company, has recently acquired majority interest. Lewis Gayden, the president of Fashions, Inc., has notified Farris that the company plans to use Swiss GAAP for the current year. Gayden wants to know how this will affect Farris' report.

REQUIRED

A. Assuming the financial statements of Fashions, Inc., are only going to be used outside the United States, what are Farris' reporting options?

B. If the financial statements of Fashion, Inc., are to be used both in Switzerland and the United States, how should Farris respond?

21-44. (Opinion Shopping) Sandy Cook, CPA, has been requested to provide a report to Chalcedon Corporation regarding the appropriate accounting treatment of a complex sale/leaseback transaction. Chalcedon has informed Cook that the company understands that there could be friction between Cook and Chalcedon's continuing auditor. Thus Chalcedon has told Cook that an oral report would be sufficient.

REQUIRED

A. Can Cook accept this engagement?

B. If Cook is able to accept this engagement, what factors must she consider?

C. How should Cook reach a judgment on the sale/leaseback transaction?

Audit Judgment Case

21-45. Sprecher Brewery, a client of Best & Co., CPAs, obtains an annual audit of its GAAP-basis financial statements. This year, however, Sprecher also has requested an opinion on the fair presentation of its inventories and accounts receivable for purposes of complying with the covenants of a new $1,000,000 working capital loan. Michael Best, partner on the engagement, assigned Melinda Smythe to be the senior on the job.

In planning the engagement, Smythe has attempted to draft an engagement letter that includes an estimate of the cost of the engagement. However, she believes that *SAS No. 62, Special Reports*, describes various types of engagements Best & Co. could perform in this situation but is unclear about which is best:

(1) Audit of a specified element, account, or item of a financial statement

(2) Compliance with loan covenants based on an audit

(3) Audit of special-purpose financial statements presented to comply with a contractual agreement (that results in an incomplete presentation that is otherwise in conformity with GAAP).

Regardless of the engagement option chosen, Smythe believes the scope of the audit of the company's financial statements, which the firm has recently completed, is sufficient to enable Best & Co. to express an opinion on inventories and accounts receivable without performing additional audit work.

REQUIRED

A. Which reporting alternative is preferable in this situation and why? Do you agree with Smythe's assumptions about the scope of the engagements and, if not, why?

B. Draft the appropriate form of report.

Auditing Issues Case

21-46. **KELCO MANUFACTURING COMPANY**

Your firm has completed the audit of Kelco's financial statements. Steve Cook, Kelco's president, was pleased that you completed the audit in a timely manner. The audit report and financial statements were delivered to the company's bank last month. In order to maintain good relations with the company, you decide to call Cook to see what progress the company has made in obtaining the bank loan. Cook informs you that the bank has requested projected financial statements for the years ended December 31, 19X8 and 19X9, that take into account that the requested loan had been granted and makes assumptions that Cook believes are most likely to happen. The company accountant has completed those statements and Cook asks if your firm could provide him with a report attesting to the accuracy and reasonableness of the projected financial statements.

REQUIRED

1. Can your firm issue a report on projected financial statements?
2. Do you believe Cook wants a projection or a forecast? What is the difference?
3. Assuming you wish to issue a compilation report on Kelco's prospective financial statements, draft the report.

Chapter 22

Compilation and Review Engagements

Learning   Objectives

- Determine when Statements on Standards for Accounting and Review Services (SSARS) apply.

- Distinguish among compilation, review, and audit engagement objectives.

- List the essential differences in procedures between a compilation and a review engagement.

- Write a standard compilation or review report.

- Explain how GAAP deficiencies are handled in a compilation or review report.

- Determine if it is appropriate to change from an audit to a review or compilation engagement.

- Explain how to report on unaudited comparative financial statements of a nonpublic company.

- Determine when a prescribed-form compilation report is acceptable.

- Decide when it is appropriate for a successor accountant to communicate with a predecessor accountant in SSARS engagements.

Some practitioners believe that the requirements for a compilation engagement are limited to reading a client's financial statements and attaching a compilation report to them. Although a compilation report provides no assurance that the financial statements are in conformity with generally accepted accounting principles (GAAP), *SSARS No. 1, Compilation and Review of Financial Statements* (AICPA, *Professional Standards*, vol. 2, AR sec. 100), requires that the accountant perform certain procedures when compiling financial statements and go beyond those procedures if he or she has concerns about information supplied by a client. . . .

Although the standards for a compilation are modest compared with those for an audit or review, they require a CPA to approach the engagement armed with the knowledge and understanding required by *SSARS No. 1* and the professional competence and due care required by the General Standards of the AICPA *Code of Professional Conduct* (AICPA, *Professional Standards*, vol. 2, ET sec. 201). This preparation and expertise provide a CPA with a heightened awareness when reading the financial statements, and ultimately confer value on the accountant's compilation report. ■

Source: "Compilation and Review Alert—1994," (New York: AICPA, 1994), pp. 5–6.

In 1977, the AICPA formed the Accounting and Review Services Committee to develop pronouncements on the procedures and standards of reporting on unaudited financial statements or other unaudited financial information of nonpublic entities. For purposes of applying the pronouncements of the Accounting and Review Services Committee, a *nonpublic entity* is

> any entity other than (a) one whose securities trade in a public market either on a stock exchange (domestic or foreign) or in the over-the-counter market, including securities quoted only locally or regionally, (b) one that makes a filing with a regulatory agency in preparation for the sale of any class of its securities in a public market, or (c) a subsidiary, corporate joint venture, or other entity controlled by an entity covered by (a) or (b).

Statements on Auditing Standards (SAS) issued by the AICPA Auditing Standards Board continue to provide guidance to accountants who perform services in connection with audited financial statements of public or nonpublic entities, or with *unaudited* financial statements of public entities. An example of a service in connection with the unaudited financial statements of a public company is a review of the company's interim financial information (*SAS No. 71*).

Statements on Standards for Accounting and Review Services

Pronouncements of the Accounting and Review Services Committee are issued as **Statements on Standards for Accounting and Review Services (SSARS)**. The following statements have been issued:

- *SSARS No. 1 — Compilation and Review of Financial Statements* (December 1978).
- *SSARS No. 2 — Reporting on Comparative Financial Statements* (October 1979).
- *SSARS No. 3—Compilation Reports on Financial Statements Included in Certain Prescribed Forms* (December 1981).
- *SSARS No. 4—Communications between Predecessor and Successor Accountants* (December 1981).
- *SSARS No. 5—*(Superceded.)
- *SSARS No. 6—Reporting on Personal Financial Statements Included in Written Personal Financial Plans* (September 1986).
- *SSARS No. 7—Omnibus Statement on Standards for Accounting and Review Service* (November 1992).

Both compilation and review engagements must be performed in accordance with Rule 201 and Rule 202 of the rules of conduct of the AICPA Code of Professional Conduct. As discussed in Chapter 2, Rule 201—General Standards requires that the accountant

- undertake only those professional services that he or she can reasonably expect to complete with professional competence.
- exercise due professional care in the performance of professional services.
- adequately plan and supervise the performance of professional services.
- obtain sufficient relevant data to afford a reasonable basis for conclusions or recommendations in relation to any professional service performed.

In addition, SSARS are issued under Rule 202 of the rules of conduct of the AICPA Code of Professional Conduct. Rule 202—Compliance with Standards requires accountants to comply with the provisions of the SSARS pronouncements and to be prepared to justify departures from them.

SSARS No. 1 requires the accountant to issue a report whenever compiling financial statements (that is, when presenting the client's financial statements without expressing assurance on them) or reviewing financial statements (that is, when performing procedures to enable expression of limited or moderate assurance) of a nonpublic entity. It prohibits an accountant from submitting unaudited financial statements that the CPA has generated to clients or others unless he or she complies with the compilation or review standards.[1] In some circumstances, it may be necessary

---

[1]In September 1995, the Accountancy and Review Services Committee issued an exposure draft that would create a level of service below a compilation. The engagement would be an assembly service, and the accountant would not have to report on the financial statements. However, in order to be exempted from compilation requirements, the financial statements must be for the client's internal use only.

for an accountant to perform more than one service in connection with one set of financial statements. For example, an accountant who is engaged to review financial statements may first need to compile those statements. In that case, the accountant would need to issue a report only for the highest level of service rendered—the review.

SSARS No. 1, Compilation and Review of Financial Statements, provides guidance on the standards and procedures applicable to engagements to compile or review financial statements. *SSARS No. 1* does not establish standards or procedures for other accounting services such as preparing tax returns or providing bookkeeping services.

Compilation Engagements

The objective of a ***compilation engagement*** is to present data supplied by the client in financial statement format without expressing any assurance that no material modifications should be made for the financial statements to conform with GAAP or an other comprehensive basis of accounting (as discussed in Chapter 21). Accordingly, the accountant ordinarily is not required to make inquiries or perform procedures to verify, corroborate, or review the information supplied by the client. However, the accountant has a responsibility to (1) acquire knowledge about the accounting principles and practices of the industry in which the client operates to enable the accountant to compile financial statements that are in a form appropriate for an entity operating in that industry; (2) obtain a general understanding of the nature of the client's business transactions, the form of its accounting records, the stated qualifications of its accounting personnel, the accounting basis on which the financial statements are to be presented, and the form and content of the financial statements; and (3) read the compiled financial statements and consider whether they

---

The Real World of Auditing

Requirements to Perform Compilation and Review Engagements

With a movement afoot to relax or even drop the requirement that review and compilation services be performed only by persons who are CPAs or by licensed accounting professionals, *The CPA Journal* offered the following conclusion:

The compilation or review of financial statements seems easy when there are no problems. That logic simply does not hold up to close scrutiny. Compilation and review engagements, if performed in a manner that adds value to fi-

nancial statements, can only be performed by a skilled professional.

Although the scope of the compilation and review engagement differs significantly from the audit engagement, the required level of competence for the task, as well as the analytical and professional judgment skills necessary are not diminished.

Source: Larry P. Bailey and Marilyn A. Pendergast, "Compilations, Reviews and Audits: The Skills Required Relative to Public Confidence," *The CPA Journal*, August 1992, pp. 48–57.

Table 22-1	Checklist for a Compilation Engagement

Step No.	Action/Decision
1	Obtain an understanding with the client, preferably in writing, regarding the engagement. (For a new client, determine if communication with the predecessor accountant is desirable.)
2	Acquire the necessary knowledge of the client industry's accounting principles and practices.
3	Acquire a general understanding of the nature of the client's business transactions, the form of the accounting records, the stated qualifications of the accounting personnel, the accounting basis used, and the form and content of the financial statements. (It is not necessary to make inquiries or perform other procedures; however, if the accountant becomes aware that information supplied by the entity is incorrect, incomplete, or unsatisfactory, the accountant should obtain additional or revised information.)
4	Read the financial statements and determine if they are appropriate in form and free from obvious material error.
5	Consider whether all disclosures required by GAAP are provided. If they are not, go to step 6. If they are, go to step 7.
6	If the client has decided to prepare financial statements that omit substantially all of the disclosures required by GAAP, indicate this in a separate paragraph in the report. If most, but not all, disclosures are omitted, notes to the financial statements should be labeled "Selected Information—Substantially All Disclosures Required by Generally Accepted Accounting Principles Are Not Included."
7	Consider whether the financial statements contain departures from GAAP. If they do, go to step 8. If they do not, go to step 9.
8	Request the client to revise the financial statements. Failing that, consider modifying the report by adding a separate paragraph that describes the departure. If the effect of the departure has been determined by management or is known by the accountant, disclose the dollar effects in the report. (The report need not be modified for uncertainties, going concern matters, or inconsistencies if they are properly disclosed—see step 5.) Withdraw from the engagement if the departures are designed to mislead financial statement users.
9	Determine whether the firm is independent. If the firm is not, go to step 10. If the firm is, go to step 11.
10	If the firm is not independent, add a separate paragraph to the report stating "We are not independent with respect to XYZ Company."
11	Mark each page of the financial statements, including notes to the financial statements, "See Accountant's Compilation Report."
12	Date the report using the date the compilation was completed.
13	Issue the financial statements and related compilation report.

appear to be appropriate in form and free from obvious material errors. Table 22–1 summarizes the procedures to be performed when the accountant is retained to provide compiled financial statements of a nonpublic company.

Figure 22-1 **Standard Compilation Report**

> We have compiled the accompanying balance sheet of XYZ Company as of December 31, 19X4, and the related statements of income, retained earnings, and cash flows for the year then ended, in accordance with Statements on Standards for Accounting and Review Services issued by the American Institute of Certified Public Accountants.
>
> A compilation is limited to presenting in the form of financial statements information that is the representation of management (owners). We have not audited or reviewed the accompanying financial statements and, accordingly, do not express an opinion or any other form of assurance on them.

After completing a compilation of financial statements, the accountant should issue a report stating that

- a compilation has been performed in accordance with *Statements on Standards for Accounting and Review Services* issued by the American Institute of Certified Public Accountants.
- a compilation is limited to presenting in the form of financial statements information that is the representation of management.
- the financial statements have not been audited or reviewed and, accordingly, the accountant does not express an opinion or any other form of assurance on them.

The date of completion of the compilation should be used as the date of the accountant's report. Each page of the financial statements, including notes to the financial statements and any supplementary information, should include a reference such as "See Accountant's Compilation Report." Figure 22–1 illustrates the standard compilation report.

Departures from GAAP

If the financial statements include departures from GAAP, the compilation report should be modified to disclose the departures. The dollar effects of GAAP departures on the financial statements also should be disclosed in the report if they have been determined by management or are known as a result of the accountant's procedures. The accountant, however, is not required to determine the effects of a departure if management has not done so. In those cases, a statement that the effects of the departure have not been determined should be included in the report. Figure 22–2 illustrates a compilation report that discloses a measurement departure from GAAP.

Figure 22-2   **Compilation Report with GAAP Measurement Departure**

We have compiled the accompanying balance sheet of XYZ Company as of December 31, 19X4, and the related statements of income, retained earnings, and cash flows for the year then ended, in accordance with Statements on Standards for Accounting and Review Services issued by the American Institute of Certified Public Accountants.

A compilation is limited to presenting in the form of financial statements information that is the representation of management. We have not audited or reviewed the accompanying financial statements and, accordingly, do not express an opinion or any other form of assurance on them. However, we did become aware of a departure from generally accepted accounting principles that is described in the following paragraph.

As disclosed in Note X to the financial statements, generally accepted accounting principles require that certain lease obligations and the related assets be capitalized and included in the balance sheet. Management has informed us that such lease obligations and the related assets have been excluded from debt and property in the accompanying balance sheet and that the effects of this departure from generally accepted accounting principles on financial position, results of operations, and cash flows have not been determined.

If the financial statements omit substantially all of the disclosures required by GAAP, the compilation report should be modified to indicate clearly the omission by adding the following as the last paragraph of the standard compilation report:

Management has elected to omit substantially all of the disclosures required by generally accepted accounting principles. If the omitted disclosures were included in the financial statements, they might influence the user's conclusions about the company's financial position, results of operations, and cash flows. Accordingly, these financial statements are not designed for those who are not informed about such matters.

Lack of Independence

The accountant also may issue a compilation report when he or she is not independent provided that the following sentence is included as the last paragraph of the compilation report: "We are not independent with respect to XYZ Company."

Review Engagements

The objective of a ***review engagement*** is to obtain a reasonable basis, usually by making inquiries and performing analytical procedures, for expressing limited assurance that the financial statements are in conformity with GAAP or an other comprehensive basis of accounting. The objective of a review differs from that of a compilation, which does not express any assurance on the financial statements. A review also differs from an audit, which provides a reasonable basis for expressing an opinion on the financial statements by performing procedures such as assessing control risk and testing accounting records and by obtaining corroborating evidential matter through inspection, observation, and confirmation.

Though less comprehensive than an audit, a review engagement is more comprehensive than a compilation engagement and concentrates heavily on inquiry and analytical procedures, which must be described in the accountant's working papers. Ordinarily, those procedures include the following:

- Acquiring knowledge of the accounting principles and practices of the client's industry.

- Obtaining an understanding of the client's business, including a general understanding of the entity's organization, its operating characteristics, and the nature of its assets, liabilities, revenues, and expenses. This ordinarily involves obtaining a general knowledge of the client's production, distribution, and compensation methods; types of products and services; operating locations; and material transactions with related parties.

- Inquiring about accounting principles and practices and methods of applying them; procedures for recording, classifying, and summarizing transactions, and accumulating information for disclosure; actions taken at stockholders', board of directors', and similar meetings; whether the financial statements have been prepared in conformity with GAAP or another comprehensive basis of accounting consistently applied; changes in business activities or accounting principles and practices; events subsequent to the date of the financial statements that would have a material effect; and questionable matters arising in the course of making other inquiries or applying other procedures.

- Applying analytical procedures to identify relationships and individual items that appear unusual, such as comparison of the financial statements with comparable prior periods and with anticipated results, and study of the relationships within the financial statements that are expected to conform to predictable patterns.

- Obtaining a representation letter confirming the oral representations made by the client during the engagement. The representation letter is signed by the members of management who, the accountant believes, are responsible for and knowledgeable about the matters covered by the representation letter (for example, the chief executive officer and the chief financial officer).

- Reading the financial statements to consider whether they appear to conform with GAAP.

If, in performing the procedures listed above, the accountant becomes aware that information coming to his or her attention is incorrect, incomplete, or otherwise unsatisfactory, the accountant should apply additional procedures so that limited assurance can be expressed that there are no material modifications that should be made to the financial statements for them to conform with GAAP. The obligation to investigate questionable information conforms with the responsibility established by the *1136 Tenants' Corp.* case; that is, when suspicion is aroused, it should be pursued to a logical conclusion. In *1136 Tenants*, the courts held the accountant liable to his client, a cooperative apartment corporation, for damages of $174,000, plus interest of $63,000, less the accountant's counterclaim of $1,000, for negligence in failing to detect and report fraud by the building manager. The accountant's work consisted of maintaining ledgers and journals and preparing financial reports and federal and state income tax returns—for an annual fee of only $600. The accountant claimed that he was engaged solely to do "write-up" work, not an audit. The accountant did not have an engagement letter. The courts held that the accountant had been engaged to do an audit and that the procedures performed were incomplete, inadequate, and improperly applied. (As noted in step 3 of Table 22–1, the accountant also has a responsibility to investigate suspicious circumstances in a compilation engagement.) Table 22–2 presents a checklist for a review engagement that summarizes the procedures to be applied for that type of engagement.

After completing a review engagement, the financial statements should be accompanied by a report indicating that

- a review was performed in accordance with *Statements on Standards for Accounting and Review Services* issued by the American Institute of Certified Public Accountants.

- all information included in the financial statements is the representation of management.

- a review consists principally of inquiries of company personnel and analytical procedures applied to financial data.

- a review is substantially less in scope than an audit, the objective of which is the expression of an opinion on the financial statements taken as a whole and, accordingly, no such opinion is expressed.

- the accountant is not aware of any material modifications that should be made to the financial statements for them to conform with GAAP, other than those modifications, if any, indicated in the report.

The date of completion of the inquiry and analytical procedures should be used as the date of the accountant's review report. Each page of the financial statements, including notes to the financial statements, should include a reference such as "See Accountant's Review Report." Figure 22–3 illustrates the standard review report.

Departures from GAAP

If the financial statements include departures from GAAP, the review report should be modified to disclose the departures, including the effects of measurement departures if they have been determined by management or are known as a result of the accountant's procedures. In addition, unlike compiled financial statements, when the accountant engaged to review financial statements subsequently finds that a client declines to include substantially all required disclosures, the review report should identify the nature of the disclosures omitted from the statements. Figure 22–4 illustrates a review report that discloses departures from GAAP.

Table 22-2   **Checklist for a Review Engagement**

Step No.	Action/Decision
1	Obtain an understanding with the client, preferably in writing, regarding the engagement. (For a new client, determine if communication with the predecessor accountant is desirable.)
2	Determine whether the firm is independent. If the firm is, go to step 3. If the firm is not, do not issue a review report. (However, it may be possible to issue a compilation report—see Table 22–1.)
3	Acquire the necessary knowledge of the client industry's accounting principles and practices.
4	Acquire an understanding of the client's business, including (1) a general understanding of the entity's organization, (2) its operating characteristics, and (3) the nature of its assets, liabilities, revenues, and expenses.
5	Apply appropriate inquiry and analytical procedures to obtain a reasonable basis for expressing limited assurance that no material modifications should be made to the financial statements.
6	Read the financial statements to determine whether, based on the information presented, they appear to conform to GAAP. Obtain reports of other accountants for subsidiaries, investees, etc., if any. Indicate division of responsibility if reference is made to other accountants.
7	Perform additional procedures if information appears to be incorrect, incomplete, or otherwise unsatisfactory.
8	Describe in the working papers matters covered in steps 5 and 7. Also, describe unusual matters that were considered and how they were resolved.
9	Determine whether the inquiry and analytical procedures considered necessary to achieve limited assurance are incomplete or restricted in any way. If they are, go to step 10. If they are not, go to step 11.
10	Consider whether a compilation report should be issued rather than a review report. (A review that is incomplete or restricted is not an adequate basis for issuing a review report.)
11	Consider whether the financial statements contain departures from GAAP, including disclosure departures. If they do, go to step 12. If they do not, go to step 13.
12	Request that the client revise the financial statements. Failing that, consider modifying the review report by adding a separate paragraph or paragraphs. If the effect of the departure has been determined by management or is known by the accountant, disclose the dollar effects in the report. (However, the report need not be modified for uncertainties, going concern matters, or inconsistencies if they are properly disclosed.) Withdraw from the engagement if the departures are designed to mislead financial statement users.
13	Obtain a representation letter from the client.
14	Mark each page of the financial statements, including notes to the financial statements, "See Accountant's Review Report."
15	Date the report using the date the inquiry and analytical procedures were completed.
16	Issue the financial statements and the related review report.

[Handwritten margin notes: "Engagement letter" (near step 1); "Scope limitation or not Independent" (left margin)]

| Figure 22-3 | **Standard Review Report** |

We have reviewed the accompanying balance sheet of XYZ Company as of December 31, 19X4, and the related statements of income, retained earnings, and cash flows for the year then ended, in accordance with Statements on Standards for Accounting and Review Services issued by the American Institute of Certified Public Accountants. All information included in these financial statements is the representation of the management of XYZ Company.

A review consists principally of inquiries of company personnel and analytical procedures applied to financial data. It is substantially less in scope than an audit in accordance with generally accepted auditing standards, the objective of which is the expression of an opinion regarding the financial statements taken as a whole. Accordingly, we do not express such an opinion.

Based on our review, we are not aware of any material modifications that should be made to the accompanying financial statements in order for them to be in conformity with generally accepted accounting principles.

Circumstances That Preclude a Review Report

Two specific situations might arise that preclude the accountant from issuing a review report:

1. If an accountant is unable to perform the inquiry and analytical procedures considered necessary or if those procedures are restricted, the accountant should not issue a review report but may consider issuing a compilation report.
2. If an accountant is not independent, he or she is precluded from issuing a review report but, again, may consider issuing a compilation report.

Change from Audit Engagement[2]

If the accountant is engaged to audit the financial statements of a nonpublic entity and is later requested to change the engagement to a review or a compilation, several items should be considered before agreeing to the change. A request for a change from an audit to a review or a compilation engagement caused either by a change in circumstances affecting the need for an audit or by a misunderstanding of the nature of available services ordinarily is considered a reasonable basis for the change. However, a request that results from scope limitations might also prevent the accountant from issuing a review or compilation report. For example, if the client refuses to sign

---

[2]The guidance concerning a change in engagement from audit to review or compilation also applies to a change in engagement from review to compilation.

Figure 22-4 **Review Report with GAAP Measurement Departure**

We have reviewed the accompanying balance sheet of XYZ Company as of December 31, 19X4, and the related statements of income, retained earnings, and cash flows for the year then ended, in accordance with Statements on Standards for Accounting and Review Services issued by the American Institute of Certified Public Accountants. All information included in these financial statements is the representation of the management of XYZ Company.

A review consists principally of inquiries of company personnel and analytical procedures applied to financial data. It is substantially less in scope than an audit in accordance with generally accepted auditing standards, the objective of which is the expression of an opinion regarding the financial statements taken as a whole. Accordingly, we do not express such an opinion.

Based on our review, with the exception of the matter described in the following paragraph, we are not aware of any material modifications that should be made to the accompanying financial statements in order for them to be in conformity with generally accepted accounting principles.

As disclosed in Note X to the financial statements, generally accepted accounting principles require that inventory cost consist of material, labor, and overhead. Management has informed us that the inventory of finished goods and work-in-progress is stated in the accompanying financial statements at material and labor cost only, and that the effects of this departure from generally accepted accounting principles on financial position, results of operations, and cash flows have not been determined.

a representation letter, the accountant should withdraw from the engagement. In all cases, the accountant should exercise professional judgment in considering the propriety of accepting a change from an audit engagement to a review or compilation engagement. Some of the factors that the accountant should consider before agreeing to such a change are detailed in Table 22–3.

Comparison of Compilation, Review, and Audit

Because three types of services can be provided regarding the financial statements of nonpublic companies—compilation, review, and audit—the accountant must consider the service needed by each client and reach an understanding regarding the scope and limitations of the service to be provided. Table 22–4 presents nine characteristics common to compilation, review, and audit engagements, indicating the appropriate treatment for each type of engagement. Table 22–4 highlights the fact that the accountant's responsibilities for performing each type of engagement vary directly with the level of assurance expressed on the financial statements.

Table 22-3	**Checklist for Change in Engagement from Audit to Review or Compilation**

Step No.	Action/Decision
1	Consider (a) the reason given for the client's request, (b) the additional effort required to complete the audit, and (c) the estimated additional cost to complete the audit.
2	Determine whether the request for the change is caused by (a) a change in circumstances affecting the need for an audit, (b) a misunderstanding as to the nature of alternative services, or (c) restrictions caused by the client or by circumstances on the scope of the examination. If (a) or (b)—which provide a reasonable basis for requesting a change—go to step 3. If (c), go to step 4.
3	Consider issuing an appropriate compilation or review report. Make no mention in the report of the original engagement, the procedures performed, or the scope limitations. Go to step 5.
4	Evaluate the possibility that the information affected by the scope restriction may be incorrect, incomplete, or otherwise unsatisfactory. If the client prohibited you from corresponding with the company's legal counsel or refused to sign a client representation letter, do not issue a review or compilation report.
5	If the audit is substantially complete or the cost to complete is insignificant, consider the propriety of accepting a changed engagement.
6	If an audit engagement letter has been obtained, revise the understanding with the client regarding the nature of the services to be rendered.

Reporting on Comparative Financial Statements

SSARS No. 2, Reporting on Comparative Financial Statements, provides standards for reporting on ***comparative financial statements***—financial statements of two or more periods presented in columnar form. The appropriate form of report to be issued on the unaudited financial statements of nonpublic companies is determined by (1) the nature of the service rendered in each of the periods presented and (2) whether the same accountants (***continuing accountants***) or different accountants render services in each period. The effect of those factors on the accountant's report is discussed in the following sections.

Nature of Services Rendered

When a continuing accountant reports on the financial statements of two years—the most common situation—the following combinations of services are possible:

- The *same* service is performed in both years. (The financial statements of both years are either compiled or reviewed.)

Table 22–4	**Comparison of Compilation, Review, and Audit Engagements**		
	Compilation Engagement	Review Engagement	Audit Engagement
1. Level of assurance	No assurance as to GAAP.	Limited assurance as to GAAP.	Statements are fairly presented in accordance with GAAP.
2. Inquiry procedures	Inquiries not required unless information appears questionable.	Inquiry and analytical procedures required plus additional procedures if the information appears questionable.	Inquiry, analytical (*SAS No. 56, Analytical Procedures*), and other audit procedures.
3. GAAP disclosures omitted	Provides for an option in which substantially all disclosures required by GAAP may be omitted and need not be detailed in the report.	All disclosures required by GAAP must be included or report must be modified to identify the missing disclosures.	Inadequate disclosure requires qualified ("except for") or adverse opinion.
4. Known measurement departures from GAAP	Modified compilation report required.	Modified review report required.	Departure from GAAP requires qualified ("except for") or adverse opinion.
5. Accountant's independence	Accountant does not have to be independent, but compilation report has to indicate lack of independence.	Lack of independence precludes issuing review report.	Disclaimer required for a public company—*SAS No. 26, Association with Financial Statements;* nonpublic company compilation report may be issued.
6. Engagement letter	Recommended.	Recommended.	Not mentioned in SASs.
7. Representation letter	Not mentioned.	Must obtain.	Must obtain (*SAS No. 19, Client Representations*).

- A *higher* level of service is performed on the financial statements of the current period. (The financial statements of the current period are reviewed and those of the prior period are compiled.)
- A *lower* level of service is performed on the financial statements of the current period. (The financial statements of the current period are compiled and those of the prior period are audited or reviewed.)

Same or Higher Level of Service

When the continuing accountant performs the same or a higher level of service on the financial statements of the current period, an appropriate compilation or review report on the financial statements of the current period should be issued, and the prior-period compilation or review report should be updated. In issuing an *updated report* on prior-period financial statements, a continuing accountant considers the effect on the prior-period financial statement of information he or she becomes aware of during the current engagement. Based on that information, the report on the prior-period financial statements either reexpresses the previous conclusions or, depending on the circumstances, expresses different conclusions. An updated report should be dated as of the completion of the current engagement. Figure 22–5 illustrates an updated report on comparative financial statements. When the current-period financial statements have been audited and the prior-period financial statements have been compiled or reviewed, the guidance in statements on auditing standards is applicable.

Lower Level of Service

When the continuing accountant performs a lower level of service on the financial statements of the current period (for example, current period compiled; prior period reviewed or audited), there is no basis to update the prior-period report. Accordingly,

---

Figure 22–5

Report on Comparative Financial Statements: 19X5 Reviewed/19X4 Compiled

We have reviewed the accompanying balance sheet of XYZ Company as of December 31, 19X5, and the related statements of income, retained earnings, and cash flows for the year then ended, in accordance with Statements on Standards for Accounting and Review Services issued by the American Institute of Certified Public Accountants. All information included in these financial statements is the representation of the management of XYZ Company.

A review consists principally of inquiries of company personnel and analytical procedures applied to financial data. It is substantially less in scope than an audit in accordance with generally accepted auditing standards, the objective of which is the expression of an opinion regarding the financial statements taken as a whole. Accordingly, we do not express such an opinion.

Based on our review, we are not aware of any material modifications that should be made to the 19X5 financial statements in order for them to be in conformity with generally accepted accounting principles.

The accompanying 19X4 financial statements of XYZ Company were compiled by us. A compilation is limited to presenting in the form of financial statements information that is the representation of management. We have not audited or reviewed the 19X4 financial statements and, accordingly, do not express an opinion or any other form of assurance on them.

in those circumstances, the continuing accountant typically issues a compilation report on the financial statements of the current period that includes a description of the prior-period audit or review, the date of the original report, and a statement that the accountant has not performed any procedures in connection with that engagement after the date of the original report. In this situation, the report should be dated as of the completion of the current engagement.

Change of Accountants

When different accountants have performed services on financial statements included in a comparative presentation, the principal rule of thumb is that either the predecessor (old) or the successor (new) accountant must report on each of the financial statements presented. It is always possible, for example, for the **successor accountant** to compile or review and then report on prior-period financial statements that have been previously reported on by a **predecessor accountant**. In most cases, however, the successor accountant satisfies the requirement to report on all financial statements presented by referring to a predecessor's previous report. The reference should be made in a separate paragraph of the report on the current-period financial statements and should include (1) a statement that the prior-period financial statements were compiled or reviewed by other accountants, (2) the date of their report, (3) a description of the compilation disclaimer or review assurance included in the previous report, and (4) a description of any departures from GAAP or explanatory paragraphs included in the previous report. An example of the last paragraph of a successor accountant's report in this situation is as follows:

> The 19X4 financial statements of XYZ Company were compiled by other accountants whose report dated February 1, 19X5, stated that they did not express an opinion or any other form of assurance on those statements.

Prescribed Forms and Personal Financial Plans

SSARS No. 3, Compilation Reports on Financial Statements Included in Certain Prescribed Forms, provides for an alternative form of standard compilation report on financial statements in prescribed forms that call for departures from GAAP by either (1) specifying a measurement principle not in conformity with GAAP or (2) failing to request the disclosures required by GAAP. A **prescribed form** is any standard preprinted form designed or adopted by the body to which it is to be submitted, for example, forms used by banks, credit agencies, industry trade associations, or government and regulatory agencies. Neither *SSARS No. 1* nor *SSARS No. 3* applies to financial presentations included in tax returns, because such presentations are not considered to be financial statements.

The standards for performing a compilation and the accountant's reporting obligation as described in *SSARS No. 1* also apply to the compilation of financial statements included in prescribed forms. Under *SSARS No. 3*, however, an accountant may issue either a compilation report as described in *SSARS No. 1* or the *SSARS No. 3* compilation report, which is specifically designed for prescribed forms. The alternative compilation report in *SSARS No. 3* differs from the standard compilation report in *SSARS No. 1* in that GAAP measurement or disclosure departures required by the

Figure 22–6 **Compilation Report for a Prescribed Form**

> We have compiled the balance sheet of XYZ Company as of December 31, 19X4, included in the accompanying prescribed form in accordance with Statements on Standards for Accounting and Review Services issued by the American Institute of Certified Public Accountants.
>
> Our compilation was limited to presenting in the form prescribed by Third National Bank information that is the representation of management. We have not audited or reviewed the financial statement referred to above and, accordingly, do not express an opinion or any other form of assurance on it.
>
> This financial statement is presented in accordance with the requirements of Third National Bank, which differ from generally accepted accounting principles. Accordingly, this financial statement is not designed for those who are not informed about such differences.

prescribed form or related instructions need not be described in the report. However, departures from GAAP that are not permitted by the prescribed form and departures from the requirements of the form itself should be described in the compilation report in accordance with *SSARS No. 1*. An example of the standard compilation report for financial statements included in prescribed forms is presented in Figure 22–6.

SSARS No. 3 does not apply to review engagements. Accordingly, the provisions of *SSARS No. 1* have to be followed if a client requests a review of financial statements that are included in prescribed forms or if regulatory or other agencies require a review.

SSARS No. 6, *Reporting on Personal Financial Statements Included in a Written Personal Financial Plan*, is similar to *SSARS No. 3* in that it provides for an optional exemption from the *SSARS No. 1* standard compilation report. Frequently, CPAs are engaged to prepare personal financial plans for clients. Usually such plans contain financial statements and those financial statements omit disclosures required by GAAP and contain other GAAP departures. In those circumstances, a special form of report may be used in lieu of the standard compilation report, but only if the client agrees that the personal financial plan will not be used to obtain credit. The special report states that the financial statements have not been audited, reviewed, or compiled. Thus, the CPA is also not obligated to apply the *SSARS No. 1* performance standard.

Communications between Predecessor and Successor Accountants

Although a successor auditor is required to communicate with a predecessor auditor in connection with an audit of financial statements (as discussed in Chapter 13), such communications are not required in connection with the acceptance of a compilation or review engagement. However, *SSARS No. 4, Communications between Predecessor and Successor Accountants*, discusses the circumstances when communications between predecessor and successor accountants may be desirable and the types of inquiries a successor may decide to make. Furthermore, *SSARS No. 4* requires the successor accountant to request the client to communicate with the predecessor when the successor believes that the financial statements reported on by the predecessor are materially misstated.

Successor's Communications

A successor accountant may decide to communicate with a predecessor when (1) the information obtained about the prospective client and its management and principals is limited or appears to require special attention, (2) the change in accountants takes place substantially after the end of the accounting period for which financial statements are to be compiled or reviewed, or (3) there have been frequent changes in accountants. As noted in Chapter 2, the rules of conduct of the AICPA Code of Professional Conduct generally prohibit an accountant from disclosing confidential information about clients' affairs. Thus, a successor accountant should obtain the client's permission before communicating with a predecessor. A successor also should request the client to authorize a predecessor to respond fully to any inquiries.

A successor's inquiries may be either oral or written. Ordinarily, they would include questions about matters that might assist a successor accountant in deciding whether to accept the compilation or review engagement, such as information that might bear on management's integrity, disagreements about accounting principles or the need to perform certain procedures, management's cooperation in providing additional or revised information, and the predecessor accountant's understanding of the reason for the change in accountants. To facilitate the conduct of the engagement, a successor also sometimes reviews the predecessor's working papers or makes inquiries about problems encountered in prior periods.

Predecessor's Response

According to *SSARS No. 4*, if authorized by a former client, a predecessor must respond promptly and fully to a successor's inquiries. However, in unusual circumstances, such as litigation, a predecessor may limit the response, provided the limitation is indicated. In addition, although a predecessor ordinarily would allow a successor access to relevant working papers and would respond to a successor's inquiries about prior years, the predecessor may decide not to do so for valid business reasons, such as unpaid fees.

Significant Terms

Comparative financial statements Financial statements of two or more periods presented in columnar form.

Compilation engagement An engagement in which the accountant is retained to present data supplied by the client in financial statement format without expressing any assurance that the financial statements are in accordance with either generally accepted accounting principles or an other comprehensive basis of accounting.

Continuing accountant An accountant who has been engaged to audit, review, or compile and report on the financial statements of the current period and one or more consecutive periods immediately prior to the current period.

Predecessor accountant An accountant who has resigned or who has been notified that his or her services have been terminated.

Prescribed form A standard preprinted form designed or adopted by the body to which it is to be submitted (for example, forms used by banks, credit agencies, industry trade associations, or government and regulatory agencies).

Review engagement An engagement in which the accountant is retained to obtain a reasonable basis, usually by making inquiries and performing analytical procedures, for expressing limited assurance that the client's financial statements are in conformity with either generally accepted accounting principles or an other comprehensive basis of accounting.

Statements on Standards for Accounting and Review Services (SSARS) Pronouncements issued by the Accounting and Review Services Committee on the procedures and standards of reporting on unaudited financial statements of nonpublic entities.

Successor accountant An accountant who has been invited to make a proposal for an engagement to compile or review financial statements or who has accepted such an engagement.

Updated report A report issued by a continuing accountant that takes into consideration information on a previous report that the accountant becomes aware of during a current engagement.

Discussion Questions

22-1. What is a nonpublic entity according to the Accounting and Review Services Committee?
22-2. Do SASs or SSARSs apply to unaudited financial statements of public entities? Audited financial statements of public entities? Unaudited financial statements of nonpublic entities? Audited financial statements of nonpublic entities?
22-3. What is the objective of a compilation engagement?
22-4. What is the objective of a review engagement?
22-5. Does *SSARS No. 1* require that each page of financial statements be marked "unaudited"?
22-6. What elements should be included in the standard compilation report?
22-7. How are GAAP departures handled in a compilation or a review report?
22-8. Is it permissible to omit substantially all disclosures in a compilation engagement? A review engagement?
22-9. An accountant cannot issue a compilation report or a review report if he or she is not independent. Do you agree?
22-10. How does the objective of a review engagement differ from the objective of an audit engagement?
22-11. What are the primary differences between a review and a compilation engagement?
22-12. What is the accountant's responsibility in a compilation engagement if he or she becomes aware of incomplete information? In a review engagement?
22-13. When should the compilation report be dated? The review report?
22-14. What conditions preclude a review report?
22-15. Under what circumstances is it generally permissible to step down from an audit engagement to a review or compilation engagement or from a review engagement to a compilation engagement?

22-16. Are representation letters required in a compilation engagement? A review engagement? An audit engagement?

22-17. Does *SSARS No. 1* require that an engagement letter be obtained?

22-18. What important principle was set forth in the *1136 Tenants' Corp.* case?

22-19. Under what circumstances should a continuing accountant update his or her report on comparative financial statements?

22-20. If last year's financial statements were reviewed and this year's compiled, and you are a continuing accountant, how should you report on the comparative statements for this year?

22-21. Last year's financial statements were reported on by another accountant. The financial statements were incorrect. This year, as a successor accountant, you have corrected the client's financial statements for the prior year and plan to report on both years as being compiled by you. Is this acceptable?

22-22. Is a tax return a prescribed form? Is a tax return covered by *SSARS No. 1?*

22-23. *SSARS No. 3, Compilation Reports on Financial Statements Included in Certain Prescribed Forms,* provides for an alternative compilation report, if the prescribed form meets one of two conditions. What are the two conditions?

22-24. Should the accountant modify his or her report on a prescribed form if the financial statements included in the form contain GAAP departures?

22-25. Does the authoritative literature require a successor accountant to communicate with the predecessor accountant in a compilation engagement? A review engagement? An audit engagement?

22-26. Under what circumstances would a successor accountant usually decide that communicating with a predecessor accountant is worthwhile?

Objective Questions

22-27. Which of the following would not be included in a CPA's report based on a compilation of the financial statements of a nonpublic entity?
  (1) A statement that the compilation was performed in accordance with Statements on Standards for Accounting and Review Services issued by the American Institute of Certified Public Accountants.
  (2) A statement that a compilation is limited to presenting information that is the representation of management.
  (3) A statement describing the principal procedures performed.
  (4) A statement indicating that the financial statements were not audited or reviewed.

22-28. A CPA who is not independent may
  (1) accept a review engagement if the lack of independence is disclosed.
  (2) accept a compilation engagement if the lack of independence is disclosed.
  (3) accept a compilation engagement if the reason for the lack of independence is disclosed.
  (4) accept an audit engagement if both the lack of independence and the reason for the lack of independence are disclosed.

22-29. A CPA is required to comply with the provisions of Statements on Standards for Accounting and Review Services when

	Processing Financial Data for Clients of Other CPA Firms	Consulting on Accounting Matters
(1)	Yes	Yes
(2)	Yes	No
(3)	No	Yes
(4)	No	No

22-30. Which of the following procedures is *not* included in a review engagement of a nonpublic entity?
(1) Inquiries of management.
(2) Obtaining a general understanding of the client's business.
(3) Any procedures designed to identify relationships among data that appear to be unusual.
(4) Making an assessment of the internal control structure.

22-31. During a compilation of the financial statements of a nonpublic entity, the CPA finds that the financial statements contain a material departure from generally accepted accounting principles. If management refuses to correct the financial statements, what should the CPA do in response?
(1) Disclose the departure in a separate paragraph of the report.
(2) Issue an adverse opinion.
(3) Attach a footnote explaining the effects of the departure.
(4) Withdraw from the engagement.

22-32. What should the accountant do prior to commencing the compilation of financial statements of a nonpublic entity?
(1) Perform analytical procedures sufficient to determine whether fluctuations among account balances appear reasonable.
(2) Complete the preliminary assessment of the internal control structure.
(3) Verify that the financial information supplied by the entity agrees with the books of original entry.
(4) Acquire a knowledge of any specialized accounting principles and practices used in the entity's industry.

*22-33. In which of the following reports should an accountant *not* express negative or limited assurance?
(1) A standard review report on financial statements of a nonpublic entity.
(2) A standard compilation report on financial statements of a nonpublic entity.
(3) A standard comfort letter on financial information included in a registration statement of a public entity.
(4) A standard review report on interim financial statements of a public entity.

*22-34. An accountant has been asked to issue a review report on the balance sheet of a nonpublic company but not to report on the other basic financial statements. The accountant may *not* do so
(1) because compliance with this request would result in an incomplete review.
(2) because compliance with this request would result in a violation of the ethical standards of the profession.
(3) if the scope of the inquiry and analytical procedures has been restricted.
(4) if the review of the balance sheet discloses material departures from generally accepted accounting principles.

*22-35. Inquiry and analytical procedures ordinarily performed during a review of a nonpublic entity's financial statements include which of the following?
(1) Analytical procedures designed to identify significant deficiencies in internal control structure.
(2) Inquiries concerning actions taken at meetings of the stockholders and the board of directors.
(3) Analytical procedures designed to test the accounting records by obtaining corroborating evidential matter.
(4) Inquiries of knowledgeable outside parties such as the client's attorneys and bankers.

*AICPA adapted.

*22-36. Each page of a nonpublic entity's financial statements reviewed by an accountant should include which of the following references?
(1) See Accountant's Review Report.
(2) Reviewed, No Accountant's Assurance Expressed.
(3) See Accompanying Accountant's Footnotes.
(4) Reviewed, No Material Modifications Required.

*22-37. During a compilation of a nonpublic entity's financial statements, an accountant would be *least* likely to do which of the following?
(1) Omit substantially all of the disclosures required by generally accepted accounting principles.
(2) Issue a compilation report on one or more, but *not* all of the basic financial statements.
(3) Perform analytical procedures designed to identify relationships that appear to be unusual.
(4) Read the compiled financial statements and consider whether they appear to include adequate disclosure.

*22-38. When an accountant performs more than one level of service (for example, a compilation and a review, or a compilation and an audit) concerning the financial statements of a nonpublic entity, the accountant generally should issue the report that is appropriate for which of the following?
(1) The lowest level of service rendered.
(2) The highest level of service rendered.
(3) A compilation engagement.
(4) A review engagement.

22-39. An accountant may compile a nonpublic entity's financial statements that omit all of the disclosures required by GAAP only if the omission is
I. clearly indicated in the accountant's report.
II. not undertaken with the intention of misleading the financial statement users.
    (1) I only.
    (2) II only.
    (3) Both I and II.
    (4) Either I or II.

*22-40. Baker, CPA, was engaged to review the financial statements of Hall Company, a nonpublic entity. Evidence came to Baker's attention that indicated doubt as to Hall's ability to continue as a going concern. The principal conditions and events that caused the doubt have been fully disclosed in the notes to Hall's financial statements. Which of the following statements best describes Baker's reporting responsibility concerning this matter?
(1) Baker is **not** required to modify the accountant's review report.
(2) Baker is **not** permitted to modify the accountant's review report.
(3) Baker should issue an accountant's compilation report instead of a review report.
(4) Baker should express a qualified opinion in the accountant's review report.

Problems and Cases

22-41. (GAAP Departure) The Alba Nursing Home engaged Sheila Howe, CPA, to prepare, on the CPA's stationery and without audit, its financial statements for 19X4 and its 19X4 income tax return. From the accounting and other records, Howe learned the following information about the nursing home:
1. The Alba Nursing Home is a partnership that was formed early in 19X4. The Nursing Home occupies a large old mansion that stands on a sizable piece of ground beside a

---

*AICPA adapted.

busy highway. The property was purchased by the partnership from an estate that out-of-state heirs wanted to settle. The heirs were unfamiliar with the local real estate market and sold the property at the bargain price of $10,000 for the house and $5,000 for the land.

2. A few weeks after the purchase, the partnership employed a competent independent appraisal firm that appraised the house at $100,000 and the land at $50,000.
3. The property was then written up on the partnership books to its appraisal value, and the partners' capital accounts were credited with the amount of the write-up.
4. Additional funds were invested to convert the mansion to a nursing home, to purchase the necessary equipment and supplies, and to provide working capital.

REQUIRED

A. Assume that the CPA prepared the financial statements in accordance with the client's preference (reporting the house and land at appraisal values). In a compilation engagement, what is the CPA's responsibility, if any, to disclose the method of valuation of the assets? Discuss. Draft the report that the CPA should issue.
B. In this situation, how does the CPA's responsibility differ, if at all, from the responsibility she would have had if the engagement was
   (1) a review engagement?
   (2) an audit engagement?
C. If Alba Nursing Home, in addition to recording the assets at appraisal value, also changed the method of computing depreciation on its house from the double-declining balance method to the straight-line method in 19X5, how would
   (1) the compilation report be modified?
   (2) a review report be modified?
   (3) an audit report be modified?

*22-42. (Report Writing—Comparative Financial Statements) For the year ended December 31, 19X4, Novak & Co., CPAs, audited the financial statements of Tillis Ltd. and expressed an unqualified opinion dated February 27, 19X5.

For the year ended December 31, 19X5, Tillis Ltd. engaged Novak & Co. to review Tillis Ltd.'s financial statements, that is, to "look into the company's financial statements and determine whether there are any obvious modifications that should be made to the financial statements in order for them to be in conformity with generally accepted accounting principles."

Novak made the necessary inquiries, performed the necessary analytical procedures, and performed certain additional procedures that were deemed necessary to achieve the requisite limited assurance. Novak's work was completed on March 3, 19X6, and the financial statements appeared to be in conformity with GAAP that were consistently applied. The report was prepared on March 5, 19X6. It was delivered to Jones, the controller of Tillis Ltd., on March 9, 19X6.

REQUIRED

Prepare the properly addressed and dated report on the comparative financial statements of Tillis Ltd. for the years ended December 31, 19X4 and 19X5.

22-43. (Assurances in Compilations) The second paragraph of a compilation report states that the accountant has not audited or reviewed the accompanying financial statements and therefore does not express an opinion or any other form of assurance on them. Because of this statement, could you conclude that a compilation report provides absolutely no assurance about the financial statements or anything else? Also, do you think that financial statements that are accompanied by a CPA's compilation report provide more credibility or assurance than the same set of financial statements that a bookkeeper prepared but that are not accompanied by a compilation report? Discuss.

22-44. (Prescribed Forms) Rex Cruse, CPA, just completed the compilation of financial statements for Bristolite Corporation on a preprinted form supplied by Kerrville State Bank. The owner/manager of Bristolite plans to submit the preprinted form to Kerrville State Bank to support an application for an increase in the corporation's line of credit. The preprinted form indicates that fixed assets should be presented at an appraisal amount instead of at historical cost. Fixed assets represent a substantial percentage of Bristolite's total assets because Bristolite is a manufacturing firm.

REQUIRED

A. What reporting alternatives are available to Rex Cruse?

B. Present the reports required by the SSARS statements under each reporting alternative identified above.

22-45. (Computer-Prepared Financial Statements) R. Bob Smith, CPA, processes the input of Pawling Corporation (a nonpublic company) on a computer and produces monthly financial statements that do not include accounting adjustments for changes in inventories or taxes and do not include notes or a statement of cash flows. Adjustments are prepared and recorded annually.

REQUIRED

A. Should Smith attach a compilation report to Pawling Corporation's monthly computer-prepared financial statements?

B. Assuming that Smith can compile Pawling Corporation's monthly prepared statements, draft the compilation report that should be attached to the financial statements.

22-46. (Going-Concern Reporting) Outdoor Amusement Company, Inc., owns and operates five drive-in movie theaters. For several years, the company has experienced significant losses, negative cash flow, and adverse key financial ratios. The company engaged Roberta Freeman, CPA, to perform a review of its financial statements for the fiscal year ended March 31, 19X8. She notes that the company continues to experience significant losses for the current year and that it is in default on a major bank loan. Management indicates that the bank needs the reviewed statement to determine if refinancing is possible. Freeman concludes that there is doubt about the entity's ability to continue to exist. A trial balance of the company at March 31, 19X8, follows:

TRIAL BALANCE
OUTDOOR AMUSEMENT COMPANY, INC.
March 31, 19X8

Accounts receivable	$ 50,000
Land	500,000
Viewing screens	100,000
Concession buildings	25,000
Lighting and pavement	50,000
Drive-up speakers	50,000
TOTAL ASSETS	**$775,000**
Bank note payable	$700,000
Accounts payable	150,000
Wages payable	10,000
	860,000
Stockholders' equity	(85,000)
TOTAL LIABILITIES AND STOCKHOLDERS' EQUITY	**$775,000**

REQUIRED

A. How would the going-concern problems of Outdoor Amusement Company affect the accountant's review report on the financial statements?

B. How would the going-concern problems affect a compilation report when management elects to omit financial statement disclosures?

*22-47. (Review Report Deficiencies) The following report on the basic financial statements was drafted by a staff assistant at the completion of the review engagement of GLM Company, a continuing client, for the year ended September 30, 19X6. The 19X5 basic financial statements for the year ended September 30, 19X5, which were also reviewed, contained a departure from generally accepted accounting principles that was properly referred to in the 19X5 review report dated October 26, 19X5. The 19X5 financial statements have been restated.

To the Board of Directors of GLM Company:

We have reviewed the accompanying balance sheets of GLM Company as of September 30, 19X6 and 19X5, and the related statements of income and retained earnings for the years then ended, in accordance with generally accepted auditing standards. Our review included such tests of the accounting records as we considered necessary in the circumstances.

A review consists principally of inquiries of company personnel. It is substantially less in scope than an audit, but more in scope than a compilation. Accordingly, we express only limited assurance on the accompanying financial statements.

Based on our reviews, with the exception of the matter described in the following paragraph, we are not aware of any material modifications that should be made to the accompanying financial statements in order for them to be in conformity with generally accepted accounting principles applied on a consistent basis.

In its 19X5 financial statements the company stated its land at appraised values. However, as disclosed in note X, the company has restated its 19X5 financial statements to reflect land at cost.

November 2, 19X6

REQUIRED

Identify the deficiencies in the draft of the proposed report on the comparative financial statements. Group the deficiencies by paragraph. Do *not* redraft the report.

22-48. (SSARS Pronouncements) Indicate whether each of the following statements is true or false.

A. Automated bookkeeping or data-processing services performed by a CPA are subject to the standards and procedures set forth in SSARS.

B. When the accountant discovers an uncertainty during a review for which the outcome is not susceptible to a reasonable estimation, the review report should be modified.

C. A reviewed financial statement under *SSARS No. 1* can be issued without disclosures as long as the CPA's report includes the omitted disclosures.

D. *SSARS No. 3* provides the accountant with an alternative report for reviewed financial statements presented in a prescribed form.

E. Both compilation reports and review reports must indicate that the engagement was performed in accordance with standards established by the American Institute of Certified Public Accountants.

---

*AICPA adapted.

  F. *SSARS No. 1* requires the accountant's work papers to document in some manner all matters covered in the accountant's compilation procedures.

  G. When the current-year financial statement is compiled and the prior-year statement is reviewed by a continuing accountant, the accountant normally refers to the report on the prior-year statement.

22-49. (Cost of Various Engagements) Auditing Research Study No. 4, *The Market for Compilation, Review, and Audit Services,* presents research findings about the relative costs of audits, compilations, and reviews. According to the study, if the hours required for an audit are 100%, the cost of other services for a prospective client are as follows:

Service	Relative Cost
A compilation, without disclosures	22%
A compilation, with disclosures	32%
A review	49%

REQUIRED

  A. Identify the factors in a compilation without disclosures, a compilation with disclosures, and a review that cause those services to be less costly than an audit.

  B. Is it possible to accept a review engagement when all notes to the financial statements are to be omitted?

22-50. (Selecting Level of Service) The Newton Company has been a customer of Chase Lands Bank for several years. The bank is presently in the process of negotiating a new loan agreement. One of the factors being discussed is the level of outside accounting service to be performed. Past agreements have not required the performance of an audit. The bank is presently deciding on the level of accounting service to require: (1) a compilation or (2) a review.

REQUIRED

What factors do you think are most important to the Chase Lands Bank in deciding on the level of accounting service needed?

22-51. (Comparative Financial Statements) National Dimension, Inc. (NDI), a nonpublic company, has just retained Eileen Blum as its accountant. Blum investigated NDI before acceptance and, based on its reputation in the community, she decided that it would be a desirable client. NDI received an unmodified compilation report (standard wording) for the prior year. However, Blum notes that overhead (which is significant) was omitted from inventory in last year's report and that the predecessor's report failed to mention this departure from GAAP.

  Based upon guidance in *SSARS No. 4, Communications between Predecessor and Successor Accountants,* Blum notified NDI, and it notified the predecessor accountant. NDI had terminated the services of the prior accountant because of a personality conflict. When NDI calls the predecessor accountant to discuss the problem, the predecessor accountant tells NDI that he has "washed his hands" and "will not have anything else to do with" them. NDI, in the presence of Blum, tells the predecessor that last year's report was deficient, but the predecessor still refuses to take any action. Because of a loan agreement, NDI must present comparative financial statements. Furthermore, because of the size of the loan, First Bank & Trust wants reviewed current-year financial statements. The predecessor accountant will not reissue his report.

REQUIRED

  A. Is it permissible for Blum to correct and reissue the predecessor's report?

  B. How should Blum report on the comparative financial statements?

  C. Could Blum avoid the problem with the predecessor's report by stepping down to a compilation engagement from the review engagement?

*22-52. (Report Deficiencies) The following report was drafted by a staff assistant at the completion of the calendar year 19X5 review engagement of RLG Company, a continuing client. The 19X4 financial statements were compiled. On March 6, 19X6, the date of the completion of the review, the report was submitted to the partner with client responsibility. The financial statements for 19X4 and 19X5 are presented in comparative form.

To the Board of Directors of RLG Company

We have reviewed the accompanying financial statements of RLG Company for the year ended December 31, 19X5, in accordance with standards established by Statements on Standards for Auditing and Review Services.

A review consists principally of analytical procedures applied to financial data. It is substantially more in scope than a compilation, but less in scope than an audit in accordance with generally accepted auditing standards, the objective of which is the expression of an opinion regarding the financial statements taken as a whole.

Based on our compilation and review, we are not aware of any material modifications that should be made to the 19X4 and 19X5 financial statements in order for them to be consistent with the prior year's financial statements.

The accompanying 19X4 financial statements of RLG Company were compiled by us and, accordingly, we do not express an opinion on them.

March 6, 19X6

REQUIRED
Identify the deficiencies in the draft of the proposed report. Group the deficiencies by paragraph. Do *not* redraft the report.

22-53. Betty Montez, CPA, performs monthly services for her client Miller, Inc. Those services consist of the following:

- Coding entries in the cash receipts and cash disbursements journal to reflect the proper general ledger accounts, based on the client's description of the transaction.
- Preparing adjusting journal entries to record depreciation expense and the accrual and deferral of expenses.
- Performing a monthly bank reconciliation.

Montez enters the coded transactions on Miller's in-house computer and processes the data on software that produces the presentation shown in Figure 22–7.

REQUIRED
A. Is the presentation generated by Montez in Figure 22–7 a trial balance or a financial statement?
B. Does *SSARS No. 1* apply to your answer in **A** above?

---

*AICPA adapted.

Figure 22–7 **Miller, Inc.**

Account Number	Account Description	December 31, 19X4 Balance Sheet Debit	Credit	FYE Dec. 31, 19X4 Income Statement Debit	Credit
101	Cash—checking		10,302.98		
102	Cash—money market savings	17,004.40			
125	Accounts receivable—trade	49,550.36			
150	Inventory—resale	28,234.00			
160	Furniture and fixtures	10,931.12			
170	Accumulated depreciation		7,076.00		
180	Loans receivable	14,000.00			
190	Prepaid expenses	4,000.00			
200	Accounts payable		43,407.02		
210	Accrued expenses		1,227.00		
220	FICA W/H payable		4,838.98		
230	Federal income tax payable		1,184.00		
240	Non current notes payable		23,000.00		
250	Current notes payable		15,000.00		
300	Capital stock		36,000.00		
350	Retained earnings	17,333.85			
400	Sales				448,349.65
430	Interest income				127.98
500	Purchases			347,865.73	
510	Freight in			2,985.77	
610	Advertising			767.75	
615	Depreciation			3,566.76	
620	Insurance expense			2,197.88	
625	Salaries—officers			38,500.00	
630	Salaries—other			21,614.00	
635	Rent			7,200.00	
640	Interest expense			3,998.56	
645	Professional fees			4,785.00	
650	Travel			2,684.00	
655	Meals and entertainment			233.45	
660	Office expense			986.61	
665	Payroll taxes			7,672.82	
670	Utilities			1,409.18	
675	Telephone			2,992.37	
		141,053.73	142,035.98	449,459.88	448,477.63
	Net loss	982.25			982.25

C. How could the presentation be reformatted to make it clear that it is a trial balance?

D. Assume that Montez only submits the financial statement presentation to Miller, Inc. for client internal use. Does *SSARS No. 1* apply?

E. Could Montez avoid the applicability of *SSARS No. 1* by identifying the presentation in Figure 22–7 as "Tentative Draft"?

Audit Judgment Case

22-54. (Deficiencies in Compilation Engagement) Joe Faultfree's staff accountant has just presented the compiled financial statements to him for review.

REQUIRED

List the deficiencies in the compilation report and the financial statements. (Do not total the financial statements. Assume all totals are correct.)

Faultfree & Co.
Certified Public Accountants
Sage, Texas 78910

[handwritten: date missing (date comp. is completed)]

To the Board of Directors of
Lake Ridge, Incorporated

The accompanying financial statements of Lake Ridge, Incorporated have been compiled by us. All information included in these financial statements is the representation of the management of Lake Ridge, Incorporated.

Based on our compilation, with the exception of the matter described in the following paragraph, we are not aware of any material modifications that should be made to the accompanying financial statements in order for them to be in conformity with generally accepted accounting principles.

[handwritten: Should not issue any assurance — limited assurance]

Management has elected to omit some of the disclosures required by generally accepted accounting principles. If the omitted disclosures were included in the financial statements, they might influence the user's conclusions about the company's financial position. Accordingly, these financial statements are restricted to internal management use only.

[handwritten: restricted use.]

FAULTFREE & CO.
December 31, 19X5

[handwritten: does not identify the company — disclosure]

Lake Ridge, Incorporated
Balance Sheets
December 31, 19X5 and 19X4

Assets	19X5	19X4
Cash	$ (5,238)	$ 7,253
Accounts receivable	91,899	116,505
Inventory	171,583	144,727
Prepayments	9,050	3,097
Total Current Assets	267,294	271,582
Fixed assets		
Leasehold improvements	23,677	20,077
Equipment	55,414	53,321
	79,091	73,398
Accumulated depreciation	(45,235)	(35,235)
	33,856	38,163
	$301,150	$309,745

[handwritten: reclassify a/c overdraft? disclosure]

Liabilities and Stockholders' Equity	19X5	19X4
Accounts payable	$ 98,228	$140,382
Note payable	—	80,241
Loan payable to an officer	29,479	3,500
Total Current Liabilities	127,707	224,123
Long-term debt	55,322	71,137
Stockholders' equity		
Capital stock	890	890
Paid-in capital	52,837	52,837
Retained earnings	64,394	(39,242)
	118,121	14,485
	$301,150	$309,745

The accompanying notes should be read with these financial statements.

Lake Ridge, Incorporated
Statements of Income
For the Years Ended 19X4 and 19X5

	19X5	19X4
Sales	$732,423	$627,988
Cost of sales	415,322	425,909
Gross profit	317,101	202,079
Operating expenses		
Salary—officer	16,350	18,133
Salaries, wages and commissions	37,212	49,042
Payroll taxes	8,302	8,764
Shop expense	15,686	16,441
Truck and auto	13,885	8,080
Travel and selling	4,405	3,628
Advertising	7,167	7,518
Rent	10,180	7,272
Heat and light	5,702	3,464
Insurance	18,711	16,182
Telephone	8,334	7,020
Office supplies and expense	17,637	13,239
Depreciation	9,733	10,841
Legal and accounting	11,471	11,886
Interest	20,529	8,910
Entertainment	4,873	2,649

	19X5	19X4
Equipment maintenance	1,234	3,345
Taxes other than income	223	111
Bad debts	892	595
Miscellaneous	558	1,755
Total operating expense	213,084	198,875
Income before income taxes	104,017	3,204
Income taxes—state	381	304
Net income	$103,636	$ 2,900

The accompanying notes should be read with these financial statements.

Lake Ridge, Incorporated
Analysis of Sales By Territory
19X5

Territory	Amount
Southwest	$378,515
Southeast	156,202
Northwest	152,768
Northeast	44,938
Total sales	$732,423

Lake Ridge, Incorporated
Notes to Financial Statements
December 31, 19X5

NOTE 1—Accounting Policies

Fixed assets are being depreciated on a straight-line basis over estimated useful lives as follows:

Shop equipment	10 years
Leasehold improvements	3 years

NOTE 2—Federal Income Taxes

The company had no federal income tax liability or expense for 19X5 due to the utilization of a net operating loss carryforward.

Auditing Issues Case

22-55. **KELCO MANUFACTURING COMPANY**

Kelco president Cook has just informed you that his bank has requested financial statements for the quarter ended March 31, 19X8. The request is in response to Cook's request for a line of credit he would use to meet operating expenses. For the year ended December 31, 19X7, your firm expressed an unqualified opinion on the financial statements of Kelco Manufacturing Company. You made inquiry of the company's legal counsel as to the status of the major lawsuit referred to in Chapter 19. The attorney now believes that there is no possibility of a guilty verdict against the company.

Cook also informed you that the depreciation method applied to the company's equipment had changed. In prior years the company had used the straight line method, but due to the increased sales, the company decided to switch to the Double Declining Balance method. You completed the engagement on April 10, 19X8.

REQUIRED

Prepare the review report for the quarter ended March 31, 19X8.

Part Six

Internal, Operational, and Governmental Audits

Chapters 23 and 24 focus on audits other than financial audits.

Chapter 23 discusses governmental auditing.

Chapter 24 discusses internal and operational auditing.

Compliance Auditing

Learning Objectives

- Identify the auditor's responsibility for testing compliance with laws and regulations in the audit of a governmental entity's financial statements under GAAS.

- Describe the auditor's responsibilities in an audit in accordance with *Government Auditing Standards* that go beyond GAAS.

- Distinguish between the auditor's responsibilities for reporting on internal control structure in an audit in accordance with GAAS and in an audit in accordance with *Government Auditing Standards*.

- Identify governmental entities that must engage an auditor to perform an audit in accordance with the Single Audit Act of 1984.

- Describe responsibilities in an audit in accordance with the Single Audit Act of 1984 that go beyond *Government Auditing Standards*.

- Identify the differences in the types of reports on compliance with specific requirements and with general requirements applicable to major federal financial assistance programs.

- Contrast the auditor's responsibilities for testing compliance with laws and regulations applicable to major and to nonmajor federal financial assistance programs.

Three groups of standards affect the manner in which compliance audits are performed. The three groups are the Generally Accepted Auditing Standards, Government Auditing Standards, and the Single Audit Act of 1984. This chapter discusses these factors and the unique ramifications for clients required to have compliance audits.

In an era of federal- and state-government downsizing, groups receiving financial assistance are held increasingly accountable for how federal and state monies are spent, for example, by schools, social organizations, and universities receiving research grants. One particular example is the national government sales tax on gasoline purchases that is allocated to local and federal highway maintenance programs. The goal of a compliance audit is to see that such funds are spent in the manner in which taxpayers and congresspeople intend them to be spent. Frequently, all levels of government, from the federal government to state and local, require compliance auditing measures be met before approving or distributing multiyear disbursements of approved funds. This enables lenders to see that funds are being used as intended and to gauge levels of waste and monitor against fraud.

This chapter discusses the auditor's responsibilities in an audit in accordance with the Government Auditing Standards that go beyond GAAS. The chapter also explores government entities and responsibilities affected by the Single Audit Act of 1984. ∎

A governmental entity, like a for-profit business entity, obtains financial resources to carry out the programs and purposes for which it was created. Similar to management of a business entity, officials and employees responsible for a governmental entity are accountable for how that organization uses its financial resources.

Public officials, legislatures, and private citizens want to know if a governmental entity's financial resources are handled properly in accordance with its goals and purposes. Laws and regulations are created to prescribe how the funds are to be used and to ensure the accountability of those funds.

Certain laws and regulations require a governmental entity (and certain nonprofit and business organizations that receive governmental assistance) to engage an auditor to audit its financial statements and its compliance with laws and regulations to assure officials and the public that the entity properly uses governmental funds. This chapter discusses the auditor's responsibilities when engaged to perform such an audit.

Note: The authors are indebted to Mark S. Beasley, CPA, former technical manager, American Institute of Certified Public Accountants, New York, New York for assistance with this chapter.

Types of Audit Engagements for Governmental Entities

Officials who request an audit of a governmental entity's financial statements engage an auditor to perform an audit in accordance with one or more of the following:

- Generally Accepted Auditing Standards (GAAS)
- *Government Auditing Standards*
- Single Audit Act of 1984

SAS No. 74, Compliance Auditing in Audits of Governmental Entities and Recipients of Governmental Financial Assistance (AU 801), discusses the auditor's responsibilities when engaged to perform one of these audits.

Audits in Accordance with GAAS

As discussed in Chapter 3, *SAS No. 53, The Auditor's Responsibility to Detect and Report Errors and Irregularities* (AU 316), requires the auditor to design an audit that will provide reasonable assurance of detecting errors and irregularities that are material to the financial statements. Similarly, *SAS No. 53, Illegal Acts by Clients* (AU 317) (also discussed in Chapter 3), indicates that the auditor's responsibility to detect and report illegal acts having a direct and material effect on line item financial statement amounts is the same as that for errors and irregularities under *SAS No. 53* (AU 316). *Therefore, the auditor is obligated to design an audit that will provide reasonable assurance of detecting material misstatements resulting from **violations of laws and regulations** that have a direct and material effect on line item financial statement amounts. This responsibility exists in all audits and applies to governmental, nonprofit, and business entity audits.*

Laws Unique to Governmental Entities

Governmental entities obtain financial resources from various sources such as levying taxes, issuing bonds, and creating special assessments. Laws and regulations generally dictate the use of these funds. For example, a state may generate funds for maintaining its highways by levying a gasoline tax that is paid by the general public when purchasing gasoline. Generally, laws and regulations require that the funds received from the gasoline tax be used for the maintenance of the state's highways.

Governmental entities may also obtain financial assistance from other governmental entities in the form of grants, loans, loan guarantees, contracts, and other aid from various programs. Governmental entities that receive financial assistance from other governments include, for example, state or city governments, school districts, universities, and public housing authorities. The governmental entity providing the assistance generally identifies laws and regulations with which the recipient entity must comply to retain the financial assistance.

To comply with GAAS, the auditor must consider the types of laws and regulations applicable to a governmental entity that have a direct and material effect on line item amounts recorded in that entity's financial statements.

Audit Planning Considerations

Management is responsible for assuring that the governmental entity complies with the laws and regulations that apply to it. In planning the audit of a governmental entity's financial statements, the auditor should understand all laws and regulations that have a direct and material effect on line item financial statement amounts. To obtain this understanding, the auditor requests management to identify all laws and regulations that have a direct and material effect on the amounts in the governmental entity's financial statements. In addition, the auditor might consider knowledge obtained in prior years' audits; review any related grant or loan documents; or discuss such laws and regulations with the entity's chief financial officer, legal counsel, or program administrators.

The auditor uses this understanding of laws and regulations to assess the risk that possible violations may occur that would have a direct and material effect on line item financial statement amounts. Knowledge about whether management has designed and placed in operation internal control structure policies and procedures that monitor compliance with such laws and regulations also assists the auditor in evaluating the risk that possible violations of laws and regulations have occurred. Based on this assessment, the auditor designs audit procedures to provide reasonable assurance of detecting material misstatements in line item financial statements amounts resulting from violations of laws and regulations.

For example, the federal government provides funds through the Aid to Families with Dependent Children Program to help states provide financial assistance to needy dependent children and their parents or relatives with whom they reside. Regulations require recipient states to maintain an internal control structure procedure that reviews the determinations of recipient eligibility made by the state when disbursing those funds. When an entity receives aid from this federal program, the auditor must assess the risk that the federal funds are not applied properly towards eligible recipients. The auditor must have sufficient knowledge of the eligibility requirements to assess the risk that possible violations could have a material effect on the entity's financial statements. Using this assessment, the auditor should design audit procedures to test compliance with the applicable eligibility requirements for this federal financial assistance program.

Reporting Requirements

The auditor engaged to perform an audit of a governmental entity's financial statements in accordance with GAAS designs and performs audit procedures to obtain sufficient evidence to provide a basis for the report on the financial statements. Based

---

The Real World of Auditing

Continuing Professional Education Requirements for Governmental Audits

Government Auditing Standards requires auditors responsible for planning, directing, conducting, or reporting on government audits to complete 80 hours of continuing professional education (CPE) every two years, with at least 20 hours to be completed each year. Because state CPE requirements are frequently on a different time frame, this increases the amount of record keeping required.

Of these 80 hours, at least 24 should be in subjects directly related to the government environment and to government auditing. The 24-hour requirement applies to those planning, directing, reporting, and conducting *substantial portions of fieldwork* (that is, 20% or more of total chargeable hours are in governmental audits).

| **Figure 23–1** | **Compliance Auditing under GAAS** |

Procedures Performed

■ Testing of compliance with laws and regulations in accordance with the following:

SAS No. 53, *The Auditor's Responsibility to Detect and Report Errors and Irregularities*

SAS No. 54, *Illegal Acts by Clients*

SAS No. 74, *Compliance Auditing Considerations in Audits of Governmental Entities and Recipients of Governmental Financial Assistance (paragraphs .03–.07)*

Reports Issued

■ Opinion on financial statements

■ Report (oral or written) on internal control structure only when reportable conditions are noted

---

on the results of audit procedures, the auditor considers the effect of any detected violations of laws and regulations on the audit report.

Figure 23–1 summarizes the auditor's GAAS responsibilities for the audit of a governmental entity.

Audits in Accordance with *Government Auditing Standards*

An auditor may be engaged to perform an audit of a governmental entity's financial statements in accordance with *Government Auditing Standards, 1994 Revision* issued by the U.S. General Accounting Office (GAO). Furthermore, certain laws and regulations may require a governmental entity to engage an auditor to perform an audit in accordance with *Government Auditing Standards.*[1] In those circumstances, the auditor accepts other reporting responsibilities in addition to the report on the entity's financial statements. Therein lies the difference between an audit in accordance with *Government Auditing Standards* and an audit in accordance with GAAS: the auditor accepts reporting responsibilities, in addition to the report on the entity's financial statements, to

1. report on the entity's compliance with direct and material effect laws and regulations (including noncompliance with grants or contracts).
2. report on the entity's internal control structure in all audits.

Reporting on Compliance with Laws and Regulations

Government Auditing Standards includes the following requirements to report on compliance with laws and regulations:

The report on the financial statements should either (1) describe the scope of the auditors' testing of compliance with laws and regulations . . . and present the results of those tests or (2) refer to separate reports containing that information.[2]

---

[1]Not-for-profit organizations or business enterprises may also be required to engage an auditor to audit their financial statements in accordance with Government Auditing Standards.

[2]Comptroller General of the United States, *Government Auditing Standards, 1994 Revision*, page 52.

Testing Responsibilities

The auditor's report on compliance with laws and regulations required in audits in accordance with *Government Auditing Standards* is based on the results of audit procedures performed in connection with the audit of the governmental entity's financial statements. Thus, the auditor's testing of the governmental entity's compliance with laws and regulations that could have a direct and material effect on line item financial statement amounts to issue an opinion on the financial statements also provides the basis for issuing a report on the entity's compliance with those laws and regulations. In other words, *Government Auditing Standards* does not require the auditor to perform additional audit procedures beyond those procedures performed to issue an opinion on the entity's financial statements.

Reporting Responsibilities

To fulfill the *Government Auditing Standards* requirement for reporting on the entity's compliance with laws and regulations, the auditor usually issues a separate report that

- references both GAAS and governmental auditing standards and disclaims an opinion on compliance.
- disclaims an opinion on compliance.

Figure 23–2 contains an example of the auditor's report on compliance along with an identification of the required elements of that report. This example report is used when the auditor does not identify significant violations of laws and regulations or significant instances of noncompliance. If violations of laws and regulations or instances of noncompliance are detected, *Government Auditing Standards* requires the auditor to report all illegal acts (unless clearly inconsequential) and all material noncompliance.

Reporting on Internal Control Structure

Government Auditing Standards expands the auditor's responsibility to report on the internal control structure beyond that required by GAAS. As discussed in Chapter 6, in an audit in accordance with GAAS, *SAS No. 60, Communication of Internal Control Structure Related Matters Noted in an Audit* (AU 325), requires the auditor to communicate reportable conditions noted during the audit. *SAS No. 60* (AU 325) defines reportable conditions as

> matters coming to the auditor's attention that, in his judgment, should be communicated to the audit committee because they represent significant deficiencies in the design or operation of the internal control structure....

Expanded Reporting Responsibilities

Government Auditing Standards requires the auditor to issue a written report on a governmental entity's internal control structure in all audits. In contrast, GAAS requires an oral or written report *only when reportable conditions are noted during the audit*. Also, the elements of the written report required by *Government Auditing Standards* are more extensive than the elements required by *SAS No. 60* (AU 325)

| Figure 23–2 | **Sample Compliance Report Required by _Government Auditing Standards_** |

Mayor of City X
City X, Any State

Required Elements

We have audited the general-purpose financial statements of City X, Any State, as of and for the year ended June 30, 19X4, and have issued our report thereon dated August 15, 19X4.

Reference to the audited financial statements and audit report

We conducted our audit in accordance with generally accepted auditing standards and *Government Auditing Standards,* issued by the Comptroller General of the United States. Those standards require that we plan and perform the audit to obtain reasonable assurance about whether the financial statements are free of material misstatement.

Audit conducted in accordance with GAAS and Government Auditing Standards (GAS)
What GAAS and GAS *require*

Compliance with laws, regulations, contracts, and grants applicable to City X is the responsibility of City X's management. As part of obtaining reasonable assurance about whether the financial statements are free of material misstatement, we performed tests of City X's compliance with certain provisions of laws, regulations, contracts, and grants. However, the objective of our audit of the general-purpose financial statements was not to provide an opinion on overall compliance with such provisions. Accordingly, we do not express such an opinion.

Management is responsible for compliance.

Tests of compliance were performed as part of audit, not to provide an opinion on compliance — disclaimer on compliance.

The results of our tests disclosed no instances of noncompliance that are required to be reported herein under *Government Auditing Standards.*

No reportable instances of noncompliance

This report is intended for the information of the audit committee, management, and city council. However, this report is a matter of public record and its distribution is not limited.

Intended use of report

August 15, 19X4

when the auditor chooses to issue a written, versus oral, report about reportable conditions. The significant differences are as follows:

1. *Government Auditing Standards* requires an explicit statement that management is responsible for establishing and maintaining the internal control structure. Although management has the same responsibility when the auditor is engaged to perform an audit in accordance with GAAS, the *SAS No. 60* report does not require such a statement.

2. *Government Auditing Standards* requires the auditor to state whether he or she believes that any of the reportable conditions are material weaknesses and to identify any material weaknesses noted. A material weakness is

> a reportable condition in which the design or operation of the specific internal control structure elements does not reduce to a relatively low level the risk that errors or irregularities in amounts that would be material in relation to the financial statements being audited may occur and not be detected within a timely period by employees in the normal course of performing their assigned functions.

SAS No. 60 allows, but does not require, the auditor to identify material weaknesses separately in a report on internal controls.

3. *Government Auditing Standards* requires the auditor to indicate in the internal control structure report if any matters not considered significant enough to be reportable conditions were noted and reported to management.

Testing Responsibilities

Despite the differences in requirements for reporting on the internal control structure in accordance with GAAS and *Government Auditing Standards*, there is no difference in the nature, timing, and extent of audit procedures performed to issue those reports. In other words, the basis that the auditor uses for reporting on the internal control structure in a GAAS audit is the same as the basis the auditor uses for reporting on the internal control structure in an audit in accordance with *Government Auditing Standards*. That basis is obtained from audit procedures performed for the purpose of expressing an opinion on the financial statements.

An example of an auditor's report on a governmental entity's internal control structure required by *Government Auditing Standards* is presented in Figure 23–3 along with an identification of the required elements of the report.

Figure 23–4 summarizes the auditor's responsibilities for audits in accordance with GAAS and *Government Auditing Standards*.

Audit in Accordance with the Single Audit Act of 1984

The federal government provides billions of dollars each year in financial assistance to state and local governments. To ensure that these funds are used in accordance with applicable laws and regulations, auditors are engaged to perform audits of the recipient government's financial statements.

The United States Congress passed the **Single Audit Act of 1984** (the Single Audit Act) to establish audit requirements for state and local governments that receive $100,000 or more in federal financial assistance within a fiscal year. State or local governments that receive at least $25,000, but less than $100,000, of total federal financial assistance in a year, have the option of an audit performed in accordance with either the Single Audit Act or with federal laws and regulations governing individual programs in which the state or local government participates. State or local governments receiving less than $25,000 in total federal financial assistance are not required to have an audit.[3]

---

[3]Similar requirements set out in Office of Management and Budget (OMB) *Circular A-133, Audits of Institutions of Higher Education and Other Nonprofit Institutions,* apply to entities that receive federal awards that are not governed by OMB *Circular A-128.*

| Figure 23-3 | *Government Auditing Standards* Report on Internal Control Structure |

Mayor of City X
City X, Any State

Required Elements

We have audited the general-purpose financial statements of City X, Any State, as of and for the year ended June 30, 19X4, and have issued our report thereon dated August 15, 19X4.

Reference to the audited financial statements and audit report

We conducted our audit in accordance with generally accepted auditing standards and *Government Auditing Standards,* issued by the Comptroller General of the United States. Those standards require that we plan and perform the audit to obtain reasonable assurance about whether the financial statements are free of material misstatement.

Audit conducted in accordance with GAAS and Government Auditing Standards

The management of City X is responsible for establishing and maintaining an internal control structure. In fulfilling this responsibility, estimates and judgments by management are required to assess the expected benefits and related costs of internal control structure policies and procedures. The objectives of an internal control structure are to provide management with reasonable, but not absolute, assurance that assets are safeguarded against loss from unauthorized use or disposition, and that transactions are executed in accordance with management's authorization and recorded properly to permit the preparation of general-purpose financial statements in accordance with generally accepted accounting principles. Because of inherent limitations in any internal control structure, errors or irregularities may nevertheless occur and not be detected. Also, projection of any evaluation of the structure to future periods is subject to the risk that procedures may become inadequate because of changes in conditions or that the effectiveness of the design and operation of policies and procedures may deteriorate.

Management is responsible for the internal control structure.

Objectives of internal control structure

Inherent limitations in internal control structure

(continued)

Figure 23-3   *continued*

In planning and performing our audit of the general-purpose financial statements of City X for the year ended June 30, 19X4, we obtained an understanding of the internal control structure. With respect to the internal control structure, we obtained an understanding of the design of relevant policies and procedures and whether they have been placed in operation, and we assessed control risk in order to determine our auditing procedures for the purpose of expressing our opinion on the general-purpose financial statements and not to provide an opinion on the internal control structure. Accordingly, we do not express such an opinion.

Description of GAAS responsibility for obtaining an understanding of the internal control structure and assessing control risk

We noted certain matters involving the internal control structure and its operation that we consider to be reportable conditions under standards established by the American Institute of Certified Public Accountants. Reportable conditions involve matters coming to our attention relating to significant deficiencies in the design or operation of the internal control structure that, in our judgment, could adversely affect the entity's ability to record, process, summarize, and report financial data consistent with the assertions of management in the general-purpose financial statements.

Definition of reportable conditions

We noted the following reportable conditions:

■ Policies and procedures are not in place for reviewing reports filed for the Special Assessment Program to insure that City X files the required reports in a timely manner to maintain compliance with the reporting requirements of the program.

■ Evidence documenting management's approval of capital expenditures in excess of preauthorized limits is not obtained in accordance with management's policies and procedures.

■ Policies and procedures are not in place for restricting the use of City X vehicles for purposes other than City X business.

Description of reportable conditions noted

Figure 23–3   *continued*

A material weakness is a reportable condition in which the design or operation of one or more of the specific internal control structure elements does not reduce to a relatively low level the risk that errors or irregularities in amounts that would be material in relation to the general-purpose financial statements being audited may occur and not be detected within a timely period by employees in the normal course of performing their assigned functions.

Definition of material weakness

Our consideration would not necessarily disclose all matters in the internal control structure that might be reportable conditions and, accordingly, would not necessarily disclose all reportable conditions that are also considered to be material weaknesses as defined above. However, we believe none of the reportable conditions described above is a material weakness.

Identification of material weaknesses noted, if any

We also noted other matters involving the internal control structure and its operation that we have reported to the management of City X in a separate letter dated August 15, 19X4.

If applicable, other matters reported in a separate management letter

This report is intended for the information of the audit committee, management, and city council. However, this report is a matter of public record and its distribution is not limited.

Intended use of report

August 15, 19X4

Single Audit Act Responsibilities

The Single Audit Act extends the auditor's responsibility beyond GAAS and *Government Auditing Standards*. At a minimum, auditors engaged to audit a state or local government in accordance with the Single Audit Act perform an audit in accordance with *Government Auditing Standards*. That is, the auditor must

- report on the financial statements in accordance with GAAS.
- report on compliance with direct and material effect laws and regulations.
- report on the internal control structure.

These three requirements parallel the requirements of an audit in accordance with *Government Auditing Standards*.

Figure 23-4	**Compliance Auditing under GAAS and *Government Auditing Standards***

GAAS

Procedures Performed

- Testing of compliance with laws and regulations in accordance with the following:

  SAS No. 53, *The Auditor's Responsibility to Detect and Report Errors and Irregularities*

  SAS No. 54, *Illegal Acts by Clients*

  SAS No. 74, *Compliance Auditing Considerations in Audits of Governmental Entities and Recipients of Governmental Financial Assistance*

Reports Issued

- Opinion on financial statements
- Report (oral or written) on internal control structure only when reportable conditions are noted

Government Auditing Standards

Procedures Performed

- Same as GAAS

Reports Issued (if issued separately)

- Opinion on financial statements
- Written report on compliance with laws and regulations
- Written report on internal control structure

In addition, the Single Audit Act requires auditors to

1. report on a schedule of financial assistance that lists the federal assistance the entity receives.
2. report on compliance with laws and regulations applicable to each **major federal financial assistance program.** (Major programs are defined by the Single Audit Act.)
3. report on compliance with laws and regulations applicable to **nonmajor federal financial assistance programs** tested.
4. report on the schedule of findings and questioned costs.
5. report on the internal control structure policies and procedures relevant to federal financial assistance programs.

The remainder of this chapter describes the requirements of the Single Audit Act that extend beyond GAAS and *Government Auditing Standards*.

Report on a Schedule of Federal Financial Assistance

To help implement the Single Audit Act, the U.S. Office of Management and Budget (**OMB**) issued *Circular A-128, Audits of State and Local Governments* (**OMB Circular A-128**), which prescribes guidelines for complying with the Single Audit Act. The circular establishes that management is responsible for identifying all federal financial assistance programs as indicated below:

> In order to determine which major programs are to be tested for compliance, State and local governments shall identify in their accounts all Federal funds received and expended and the programs under which they were received. This shall include funds received directly from Federal agencies and through other State and local governments.

Management generally fulfills this responsibility by preparing a schedule of federal financial assistance identifying all federal financial assistance received within a fiscal year.

The Single Audit Act requires the auditor to report on management's schedule of federal financial assistance. To report on this schedule, the auditor assesses its appropriateness and completeness by considering evidence obtained while performing the audit of the financial statements. For example, audit procedures performed to evaluate the completeness of revenues recorded in the financial statements also provide evidence about the sources and types of revenues recorded. The auditor uses this evidence to corroborate the completeness of management's schedule. The auditor's report on the schedule

- acknowledges that the information in the schedule has been subjected to the auditing procedures applied in the audit of the entity's financial statements.
- includes the auditor's opinion about whether the information is presented fairly, in all material respects, in relation to the financial statements taken as a whole.

A sample schedule of federal financial assistance is presented in Figure 23–5.

Figure 23–5   **Illustrative Schedule for Federal Financial Assistance**

Schedule of Federal Financial Assistance
for the Year Ended June 30, 19X4

Federal Program	Program Amount	Cash as of July 1, 19X3	Receipts	Disbursements	Cash as of June 30, 19X4
A	$75,000,000	$2,500,000	$75,000,000	$68,000,000	$9,500,000
B	25,000,000	1,000,000	25,000,000	24,500,000	1,500,000
C	2,000,000	250,000	2,000,000	2,100,000	150,000

Table 23–1	Single Audit Act Schedule to Determine Major Federal Programs

Major federal programs are determined based on each federal program's expenditures in relation to the total of the entity's expenditures of all federal assistance programs received during the year:

(1) When Total Entity Expenditures of All Federal Funds Exceed	(2) To Be a Major Program, Expenditures for a Single Federal Program Must Exceed
A. $7 billion	$20 million
B. $6 billion, but are ≤ $7 billion	$19 million
C. $5 billion, but are ≤ $6 billion.	$16 million
D. $4 billion, but are ≤ $5 billion.	$13 million
E. $3 billion, but are ≤ $4 billion.	$10 million
F. $2 billion, but are ≤ $3 billion.	$7 million
G. $1 billion, but are ≤ $2 billion.	$4 million
H. $100 million, but are ≤ $1 billion.	$3 million
I. $100,000 but are ≤ $100 million	The larger of $300,000 or 3% of such total expenditures for all programs

Source: Adapted from the AICPA Audit and Accounting Guide, *Audits of State and Local Governmental Units*, 1994, p. 167. Used with permission of the AICPA.

Segregating Major and Nonmajor Federal Programs The Single Audit Act requires the auditor to test and report on the client's compliance with laws and regulations applicable to major and nonmajor programs. The Single Audit Act defines a major program in terms of the state and local government's expenditures of federal financial assistance under that program relative to its total expenditures of all federal financial assistance received. Table 23–1 presents the schedule contained in the Single Audit Act for identifying major federal financial assistance programs. Any federal program that does not meet the criteria outlined in Table 23–1 is, by definition, considered to be a nonmajor program.

Using the schedule in Table 23–1, management of a state and local government that receives the following federal financial assistance can identify its major and nonmajor federal financial assistance programs:

	Federal Fund Expenditures	Major or Nonmajor Program
Federal Program A	$ 75 million	Major
Federal Program B	25 million	Major
Federal Program C	2 million	Nonmajor
Total Federal Expenditures	$102 million	

In this example, the state or local government's total expenditures of all federal financial assistance exceed $100 million but are less than $1 billion. Therefore, as shown in column (1), line H of Table 23–1, both Federal Programs A and B are major programs because expenditures under each of these programs exceed $3 million. Because Federal Program C expenditures are less than $3 million, that program is classified as a nonmajor program.

Reports on Compliance— Major Programs

The Single Audit Act states that the auditor

> shall determine and report whether the government, department, agency, or establishment has complied with laws and regulations that may have a material effect upon each major federal assistance program.

To comply with the Single Audit Act requirement, the auditor should fulfill the following responsibilities:

Testing Responsibilities	Reporting Responsibilities
Perform auditing procedures designed to provide reasonable assurance of detecting material noncompliance with "specific requirements" applicable to major federal financial assistance programs.	Prepare report containing an opinion on compliance with those requirements or a statement that such opinion cannot be expressed.
Perform auditing procedures to test compliance with "general requirements" applicable to all federal financial assistance programs.	Prepare report containing a statement of positive assurance about items tested and negative assurance about those items not tested.

Audit Planning Considerations Because the Single Audit Act requires the auditor to issue a report on the entity's compliance with laws and regulations for each major program identified, the auditor must assess the effects of noncompliance noted in relation to the nature and size of the applicable major program under audit. Therefore, the auditor considers materiality differently from how it would be considered in an audit of the financial statements. For a GAAS audit, the auditor considers materiality in relation to the financial statements. When auditing an entity's compliance with laws and regulations applicable to each major federal program, the auditor considers materiality separately for each program. In other words, an amount material to a particular major program may not be material to another major program of a different size and nature.

Testing Compliance—Specific Requirements   The Single Audit Act requires the auditor to issue an opinion on compliance with *specific requirements* applicable to each major federal program. Specific requirements generally pertain to the following:

- *Types of services allowed*, which specify the types of goods or services entities may purchase with the federal program funds.
- *Eligibility*, which specify the characteristics of individuals or groups to whom entities may give federal program funds.

- *Matching, level of effort, or earmarking*, which specify amounts entities should contribute from their own funds toward projects paid for with federal program funds.
- *Reporting*, which specify reports entities must file.
- *Special tests and provisions*, which specify other provisions for which federal agencies have determined noncompliance could materially affect the program. For example, some federal agencies set a deadline for the expenditure of federal financial assistance.

The auditor must obtain an understanding of the specific requirements applicable to each major program. To assist the auditor, the OMB publishes the *Compliance Supplement for Single Audits of State and Local Governments* (**Compliance Supplement**), which contains compliance requirements applicable to many of the larger federal financial assistance programs and suggests procedures for testing compliance with these specific requirements. Table 23–2 contains an excerpt from the *Compliance Supplement* regarding the specific requirements related to allowability for the Aid to Families with Dependent Children Program.

For those programs not included in the *Compliance Supplement*, the auditor may identify the applicable specific requirements by

1. considering knowledge obtained in the prior-year audits.
2. discussing laws and regulations with the entity's management or legal counsel.
3. reviewing grant or loan agreements.
4. inquiring of federal, state, or local auditors or federal agency officials providing the assistance.

Designing Audit Procedures The auditor must obtain an understanding of the specific requirements for determining the nature, timing, and extent of audit procedures to perform to provide a basis for expressing an opinion on compliance for each major federal program. When designing audit procedures to test a client's compliance with specific requirements, the auditor must consider the nature of those requirements. For example, to test compliance with requirements applicable to the *allowability* of expenditures of federal program funds, the auditor designs audit procedures that provide a basis for evaluating how those federal program funds were used. These procedures should provide the auditor with a basis for determining if the funds were used for purposes that comply with the applicable allowability requirements of that program.

Evaluating Results of Audit Procedures The auditor should consider any noncompliance noted as a result of performing audit procedures and evaluate whether that noncompliance has a material effect on the applicable major federal financial assistance program. The auditor must consider the frequency of noncompliance identified and whether any instances of noncompliance identified result in questioned costs. **Questioned costs** typically relate to the following items:

- Unallowed Costs (costs not allowed under the requirements of the program)
- Undocumented Costs (costs charged to a program for which detailed documentation does not exist)
- Unapproved Costs (costs for which the program requires approval and the auditor cannot find evidence of approval)
- Unreasonable Costs (costs incurred that may not reflect the actions of a prudent person)

Table 23-2	**Specific Requirements—Allowability for the Aid to Families with Dependent Children Program**

Types of Services Allowed or Unallowed Compliance Requirement

Program funds are to be used to pay for

1. Direct Financial Assistance
   - Financial assistance for food, shelter, clothing and other items of daily living recognized as necessary for eligible participants by each program
2. Administration
   - Interviewing applicants, determining eligibility, and validating eligibility
   - Training state and local personnel who operate the program
   - Engaging personnel for program direction and management
3. Employment Experience
   - A Community Work Experience Program for AFDC recipients
   - A Work Supplementation Program for AFDC recipients
   - An Employment Search Program for AFDC applicants and recipients
4. Emergency Assistance
   - Assistance during one thirty-day period in twelve consecutive months to needy families in emergency or crisis situations to avoid destitution or to provide living arrangements, food, shelter, clothing, medical care, and transportation

Source: Adapted from Executive Office of the President, *Compliance Supplement for Single Audits of State and Local Governments (Revised April 1985)*, U.S. Office of Management and Budget, 1985.

An auditor may determine that a state or local government failed to file program progress reports in compliance with that federal program's specific reporting requirements. The auditor must report this violation as a finding of noncompliance; however, the violation would not necessarily result in questioned costs. In contrast, if the auditor determines that the governmental entity failed to document adequately its use of the federal program funds, the auditor would classify this finding of noncompliance and the related amount of undocumented expenditures as questioned costs.

In evaluating the effect of questioned costs on the opinion on compliance for each major program, the auditor considers the best estimate of *total costs* questioned for each major federal financial assistance program, not just the questioned costs specifically identified. Thus, when using audit sampling to test compliance, the auditor projects the amount of questioned costs identified in the sample to the items in the major federal financial assistance program from which the sample was selected.

Reporting on Compliance—Specific Requirements Figure 23–6 presents an example of a report on an entity's compliance with the specific requirements applicable to each major federal financial assistance program when the findings of noncompliance and questioned costs are not material to major programs.

| **Figure 23-6** | **Report on Major Program Compliance with Specific Requirements** |

Mayor of City ABC
City ABC, Any State

Required Elements

We have audited the general-purpose financial statements of City ABC, as of and for the year ended June 30, 19X4, and have issued our report thereon dated August 15, 19X4.

Reference to the audited financial statements and audit report

We also have audited City ABC's compliance with the requirements governing types of services allowed or unallowed; eligibility; matching, level of effort, or earmarking; reporting; claims for advances and reimbursements; and amounts claimed or used for matching that are applicable to each of its major federal financial assistance programs, which are identified in the accompanying schedule of federal financial assistance, for the year ended June 30, 19X4. The management of City ABC is responsible for City ABC's compliance with those requirements. Our responsibility is to express an opinion on compliance with those requirements based on our audit.

Audited compliance with specific requirements for each major program

Compliance is the responsibility of management. Auditor is responsible for expressing an opinion on compliance

We conducted our audit of compliance with those requirements in accordance with generally accepted auditing standards, *Government Auditing Standards,* issued by the Comptroller General of the United States, and *OMB Circular A-128, Audits of State and Local Governments.* Those standards and *OMB Circular A-128* require that we plan and perform the audit to obtain reasonable assurance about whether material noncompliance with the requirements referred to above occurred. An audit includes examining, on a test basis, evidence about City ABC's compliance with those requirements. We believe that our audit provides a reasonable basis for our opinion.

Audit conducted in accordance with GAAS, Government Auditing Standards, *and* OMB Circular A-128

Standards require auditor to plan and perform audit to obtain reasonable assurance about material noncompliance

The results of our audit procedures disclosed immaterial instances of noncompliance with the requirements referred to above, which are described in the accompanying schedule of findings and questioned costs. We considered these instances of noncompliance in forming our opinion on compliance, which is expressed in the following paragraph.

Reference to immaterial noncompliance and schedule of findings and questioned costs

Figure 23–6 *continued*

In our opinion, City ABC complied, in all material respects, with the requirements governing types of services allowed or unallowed; eligibility; matching, level of effort, or earmarking; reporting; claims for advances and reimbursements; and amounts claimed or used for matching that are applicable to each of its major federal financial assistance programs for the year ended June 30, 19X4.

Opinion on material compliance with specific requirements applicable to major federal programs

This report is intended for the information of the audit committee, management, and city council. However, this report is a matter of public record and its distribution is not limited.

Intended distribution of report

August 15, 19X4

When the auditor detects noncompliance with a specific requirement that he or she believes has a material effect on a major federal financial assistance program, he or she should express a qualified or adverse opinion on compliance for that program. Similarly, if the scope of the audit is restricted by the client or circumstances, the auditor may be precluded from obtaining sufficient evidence; thus, a qualified opinion or disclaimer of opinion may be needed. In such cases, the auditor should describe in the report the reason for the modified opinion or disclaimer.

Testing Compliance—General Requirements   The *Compliance Supplement*, in addition to containing specific requirements applicable to many of the larger federal financial assistance programs, also identifies nine *general requirements* that apply to all federal financial assistance programs. The general requirements are presented in Table 23–3.

Unlike the specific requirements that are applicable to a single federal financial assistance program, the same nine general requirements apply to all federal financial assistance programs. The *Compliance Supplement* notes that the general requirements

> involve significant national policy . . . for which failure to comply could have a material impact on an organization's financial statements [and] should be included as part of every audit of state, local, and Tribal governments that involves Federal financial assistance.

When performing the audit of a state or local government in accordance with the Single Audit Act, the auditor must test compliance with those general requirements applicable to the state or local government's federal financial assistance programs

Table 23–3	**General Compliance Requirements**

1. *Political activity* prohibits the use of federal funds for partisan political activity.

2. *Davis-Bacon Act* requires that laborers working on federally financed construction projects be paid a wage rate not less than the prevailing regional wage established by the Secretary of Labor.

3. *Civil rights* prohibits violation of anyone's civil rights in a program funded by the federal government.

4. *Cash management* requires recipients of federal financial assistance to minimize the time lapsed between receipt and disbursement of that assistance.

5. *Relocation assistance and real property acquisition* prescribes how real property should be acquired with federal financial assistance and how recipients must help relocate people displaced when that property is acquired.

6. *Federal financial reports* prescribes federal financial reports that must be filed.

7. *Allowable costs/cost principles* prescribes the direct and indirect costs allowable for federal reimbursement.

8. *Drug-free workplace* prescribes that grantees must certify that they provide a drug-free workplace.

9. *Administrative requirements* prescribes administrative requirements in addition to 4, 6, and 7 above.

and issue a report on that compliance. The auditor is required to issue a report on compliance with general requirements even if the government being audited has no major program.

Designing Audit Procedures The *Compliance Supplement* suggests audit procedures for testing compliance with the general requirements. Since the Single Audit Act was implemented, it has become generally accepted that the nature of those procedures outlined in the *Compliance Supplement* is adequate for testing compliance with the general requirements. The auditor exercises professional judgment to determine the extent of procedures necessary for testing compliance with the general requirements. Figure 23–7 contains an example of suggested audit procedures for testing compliance with general requirements related to political activity.

Reporting on Compliance—General Requirements The nature of the auditor's report on compliance with general requirements differs from that of the report on compliance with the specific requirements. The key distinction for reporting on the general and specific requirements is as follows:

- *Specific requirements* The auditor provides an opinion on the entity's compliance with the specific requirements.
- *General requirements* The auditor provides positive assurance about items tested for compliance and negative assurance for those items not tested.

Figure 23–8 presents an example of a report on the general requirements.

| **Figure 23–7** | **General Requirement—Political Activity with Suggested Audit Procedures** |

Political Activity Compliance Requirement Federal funds cannot be used for partisan political activity of any kind by any person or organization involved in the administration of federally-assisted programs.

Suggested Audit Procedures

- Test the expenditure and related records for indications of lobbying activities, publications, or other materials intended for influencing legislation or similar types of costs.

- Test the personnel and payroll records, and identify persons whose responsibilities or activities include political activity.

- Test whether the above costs, if any exist, are charged directly or indirectly to federally-assisted programs.

Source: Adapted from Executive Office of the President, *Compliance Supplement for Single Audits of State and Local Governments (Revised April 1985)*, U.S. Office of Management and Budget, 1985.

Reports on Compliance— Nonmajor Programs

When performing an audit of the financial statements, the auditor examines transactions to obtain sufficient evidence to support his or her opinion on the financial statements. Some of the transactions apply to nonmajor federal financial assistance programs. For example, the auditor may examine payroll transactions to test the assertions applicable to salary expense recorded in the financial statements. Certain of the payroll transactions selected may apply to expenditures of nonmajor federal financial assistance program funds. Nonmajor program transactions may also be selected as part of the auditor's evaluation of internal control structure policies and procedures over federal financial assistance programs.

Testing Compliance—Nonmajor Programs The Single Audit Act requires the auditor to test compliance for those transactions related to a nonmajor program that are selected as a part of the audit of the financial statements or as a part of the evaluation of internal control structure over federal financial assistance. The auditor should test compliance with the specific requirements that apply to those individual transactions.

In performing these procedures, the auditor generally does not address the general requirements or specific requirements that apply to the nonmajor program as a whole, such as matching and reporting requirements. Instead, the auditor typically tests compliance with those specific requirements that relate to allowability of program expenditures and eligibility of the individuals or groups to which the entity provides financial assistance. For example, if in the audit of the financial statements the auditor examined a payroll transaction that was charged to a nonmajor program, the auditor should determine that the individual's salary was correctly charged to the program. The auditor would not be required to determine whether the entity complied with the reporting requirements applicable to the nonmajor program.

Reporting Responsibilities Figure 23–9 contains an example of a report on compliance with requirements applicable to nonmajor federal financial assistance program transactions.

Figure 23–8

Sample Report on General Requirements Applicable to Major Programs

Mayor of City ABC
City ABC, Any State

Required Elements

We have audited the general-purpose financial statements of City ABC as of and for the year ended June 30, 19X4, and have issued our report thereon dated August 15, 19X4.

Reference to the audited financial statements and audit report

We applied procedures to test City ABC's compliance with the following requirements applicable to each of its federal financial assistance programs, which are identified in the schedule of federal financial assistance, for the year ended June 30, 19X4:

Identify general requirements tested

- Political activity
- Davis-Bacon Act
- Civil rights
- Cash management
- Relocation assistance and real property management
- Federal financial reports
- Allowable costs/cost principles
- Drug-free workplace
- Administrativo requirements

Our procedures were limited to the applicable procedures described in the Office of Management and Budget's *Compliance Supplement for Single Audits of State and Local Governments*. Our procedures were substantially less in scope than an audit, the objective of which is the expression of an opinion on City ABC's compliance with the requirements listed in the preceding paragraph. Accordingly, we do not express such an opinion.

Tests of compliance were limited to procedures described in Compliance Supplement and were not performed to provide an opinion on compliance.

With respect to the items tested, the results of those procedures disclosed no material instances of noncompliance with the requirements listed in the second paragraph of this report. With respect to items not tested, nothing came to our attention that caused us to believe that City ABC had not complied, in all material respects, with those requirements. However, the results of our procedures disclosed immaterial instances of noncompliance with those requirements, which are described in the accompanying schedule of findings and questioned costs.

Positive assurance on items tested

Negative assurance on items not tested

This report is intended for the information of the audit committee, management, and city council. However, this report is a matter of public record and its distribution is not limited.

Intended use of report

August 15, 19X4

| Figure 23-9 | **Sample Compliance Report on Nonmajor Program Transactions** |

Mayor of City ABC
City ABC, Any State

Required Elements

We have audited the general-purpose financial statements of City ABC, Any State, as of and for the year ended June 30, 19X4, and have issued our report thereon dated August 15, 19X4.

Reference to the audited financial statements and audit report

In connection with our audit of the general-purpose financial statements of City ABC and with our consideration of City ABC's internal control structure used to administer federal financial assistance programs, as required by the *Office of Management and Budget Circular A-128, Audits of State and Local Governments*, we selected certain transactions applicable to certain nonmajor federal financial assistance programs for the year ended June 30, 19X4. As required by *Circular A-128*, we performed auditing procedures to test compliance with the requirements governing types of services allowed or unallowed and eligibility that are applicable to those transactions. Our procedures were substantially less in scope than an audit, the objective of which is the expression of an opinion on City ABC's compliance with these requirements. Accordingly, we do not express such an opinion.

Reference to audit of financial statements and consideration of internal control structure over federal financial assistance programs

Procedures were not performed to provide an opinion on compliance.

With respect to the items tested, the results of those procedures disclosed no material instances of noncompliance with the requirements listed in the preceding paragraph. With respect to items not tested, nothing came to our attention that caused us to believe that City ABC had not complied, in all material respects, with those requirements. However, the results of our procedures disclosed immaterial instances of noncompliance with those requirements, which are described in the accompanying schedule of findings and questioned costs.

Positive assurance on items tested

Negative assurance on items not tested

This report is intended for the use of the audit committee, management, and the city council. However, this report is a matter of public record and its distribution is not limited.

Intended use of report

August 15, 19X4

Report on the Schedule of Findings and Questioned Costs

OMB Circular A-128 requires the auditor to report any instances of noncompliance found and any resulting questioned costs. When reporting questioned costs, the auditor must report only questioned costs specifically identified, not the best estimate of total questioned costs for the applicable major program. Figure 23–10 contains an example of the auditor's report of findings and questioned costs.

Reporting on Internal Controls Relevant to Federal Financial Assistance Programs

The Single Audit Act requires the auditor to determine and report whether the state or local government has internal control structure policies and procedures to provide reasonable assurance that it is managing federal financial assistance programs in compliance with applicable laws and regulations. To satisfy this requirement, the auditor should (1) obtain an understanding of the design of internal control structure policies and procedures relevant to the entity's compliance with specific requirements applicable to federal financial assistance programs and (2) determine whether

---

Figure 23–10   **Illustrative Schedule of Findings and Questioned Costs**

City ABC, Any State
Schedule of Findings and Questioned Costs
for the Year Ended June 30, 19X4

Program	Finding/Noncompliance	Questioned Costs
Public Housing Comprehensive Improvement Assistance Program		
1. Grant No. B-78-MC-14-00009	Of twenty-five vehicles examined, one vehicle equipped with special photographic equipment was purchased and used in sewer inspections. The vehicle was used to perform repair and engineering work in the Bancroft subdivision (which is an approved project). However, it was also used on a citywide basis. Furthermore, the Department of Housing and Urban Development (HUD) approval was not obtained prior to its acquisition.	$28,765
2. Grant No. B-80-MC-14-0009	Of thirty-six projects examined, monies were expended on two projects, Stanley Park and Syn Way, which were not approved by HUD because appropriate environmental review procedures were not followed. The city intends to repay HUD for these costs.	49,843
		$78,608

those policies and procedures have been placed in operation. *OMB Circular A-128* requires the auditor to "test whether these internal control systems are functioning in accordance with prescribed procedures."

Complying with the above requirement involves performing tests of controls to evaluate whether the design and operation of policies and procedures are effective in preventing or detecting material noncompliance with major federal financial assistance programs. The auditor should obtain a sufficient understanding of those policies and procedures to enable him or her to

1. identify the types of potential material noncompliance.
2. consider matters that affect the risk of material noncompliance.
3. design effective tests of compliance with requirements applicable to major federal financial assistance programs.

Though the Single Audit Act requires a report on internal control structure policies and procedures, it does not require the auditor to express an opinion on the internal control structure used in administering federal financial assistance programs.

Compliance Attestation under *SSAE No. 3*

Even in audits not covered by *SAS No. 74*, there has been a growing expectation among users that CPAs have a responsibility to detect noncompliance with laws and regulations that goes beyond *SAS No. 54, Illegal Acts by Clients* (AU 317). In nongovernmental audit engagements, CPAs should consider the expectations of management, the audit committee, and other users, along with any statutory provision that requires compliance attestation. If expectations or statutory provision exceed what is required under GAAS, the auditor should discuss with management the desirability of performing a compliance attestation engagement for specified laws or regulations, in addition to the audit of the financial statements.

In recognition of the need for compliance attestation, the Auditing Standards Board published *Statement on Standards for Attestation Engagements (SSAE) No. 3, Compliance Attestation* (AT 500) in December 1993. Under *SSAE No. 3*, the CPA reports on management's written assertion regarding compliance. Management must accept responsibility (evidenced through a representation letter) for compliance and must have made its own evaluation of compliance.

For assertions regarding an entity's compliance with specified requirements, CPAs may perform either agreed-upon procedures or audits, although audits are frequently less desirable and are used infrequently. The most visible application of *SSAE No. 3* today is the Federal Deposit Insurance Corporation Improvement Act of 1991. That act, among other things, requires the CPA to perform certain agreed-upon procedures on a bank's assertion about compliance with dividend restriction and insider loan laws and regulations.

Overview

The relationship between testing and reporting on compliance with laws and regulations in a Single Audit Act audit and an audit in accordance with GAAS and the *Government Auditing Standards* is summarized in Figure 23–11.

Figure 23–11

**Compliance Auditing Responsibilities under GAAS,
Government Auditing Standards, and Single Audit Act**

GAAS

Procedures Performed

- Testing of compliance with laws and regulations in accordance with the following:

  SAS No. 53, *The Auditor's Responsibility to Detect and Report Errors and Irregularities*

  SAS No. 54, *Illegal Acts by Clients*

  SAS No. 74, *Compliance Auditing Considerations in Audits of Governmental Entities and Recipients of Governmental Financial Assistance*

Reports Issued

- Opinion on financial statements
- Report (oral or written) on internal control structure only when reportable conditions are noted

Government Auditing Standards

Procedures Performed

- Same as GAAS

Reports Issued (if issued separately)

- Opinion on financial statements
- Written report on compliance with laws and regulations
- Written report on internal control structure

Single Audit Act of 1984

Procedures Performed

- Same as GAAS *plus*
- Testing of compliance with general and specific requirements applicable to federal financial assistance programs
- Obtaining an understanding of internal control structure policies and procedures relevant to compliance with specific requirements applicable to federal financial assistance programs

Reports Issued

- Same as *Government Auditing Standards* requirements *plus*
- Report on schedule of financial assistance received
- Opinion on compliance applicable to specific requirements of major federal programs
- Report on compliance applicable to general requirements
- Report on compliance applicable to nonmajor program transactions tested
- Report instances of noncompliance and questioned costs
- Report on internal control structure policies and procedures relevant to federal financial assistance

Significant Terms

Compliance supplement A publication issued by the U.S. Office of Management and Budget that contains general and specific program compliance requirements applicable to many of the larger federal financial assistance programs.

General requirements Compliance requirements involving significant national policy identified in the *Compliance Supplement* that apply to all federal financial assistance programs.

Government Auditing Standards A publication of the U.S. General Accounting Office titled *Government Auditing Standards* (1994 Revision), which contains standards for audits of governmental entities (frequently referred to as the "Yellow Book").

Major federal financial assistance program Defined by the Single Audit Act as any federal financial assistance program for which total expenditures of that program exceed specified amounts in relation to total expenditures of all federal financial assistance received during the year.

Noncompliance The failure to act in accordance with laws, regulations, or contractual terms pertaining to financial assistance received from a governmental agency.

Nonmajor federal financial assistance program Defined by the Single Audit Act as all federal financial assistance programs that do not meet the specified criteria to be considered a major program.

OMB The U.S. Office of Management and Budget.

OMB Circular A-128 A publication of the OMB, titled *Audits of State and Local Governments*, which provides guidelines for implementing the Single Audit Act of 1984.

Questioned costs Those costs incurred by the entity that may not comply with or may not be consistent with laws and regulations governing the allocability, allowability, or reasonableness of costs charged to federal financial assistance programs, and thus may not be reimbursable.

Single Audit Act of 1984 Legislation passed by the U.S. Congress that requires certain state and local governments receiving federal financial assistance to engage an auditor to perform a single coordinated audit of the applicable federal financial assistance program requirements.

Specific requirements Compliance requirements contained in the *Compliance Supplement* that are specific to a particular federal program. The requirements generally pertain to allowability, eligibility, matching, reporting, and other special tests and provisions.

Violations of laws and regulations *See* Noncompliance.

Discussion Questions

23-1. How does the auditor's responsibility differ under GAAS for a governmental entity and for a for-profit enterprise?

23-2. What is the auditor's responsibility for testing compliance with laws and regulations in an audit of a governmental entity's financial statements in accordance with GAAS?

23-3. What are the auditor's reporting responsibilities under GAAS for an audit of a governmental entity's financial statements?

23-4. What additional responsibilities does an auditor accept for an audit of a governmental entity's financial statements in accordance with *Government Auditing Standards* as compared to an audit in accordance with GAAS?

23-5. How does the auditor obtain a basis for reporting on an entity's compliance with laws and regulations in an audit in accordance with *Government Auditing Standards*?

23-6. What type of assurance does an auditor provide about a governmental entity's compliance with laws and regulations when reporting on compliance in accordance with *Government Auditing Standards*?

23-7. What two elements are required in a report on compliance in accordance with *Government Auditing Standards*?

23-8. What is the major difference between reporting on the internal control structure in an audit in accordance with *Government Auditing Standards* and reporting on the internal control structure in an audit in accordance with GAAS?

23-9. How can an auditor obtain a basis for reporting on the entity's internal control structure in an audit in accordance with *Government Auditing Standards*?

23-10. What three elements of a report on internal control structure under *Government Auditing Standards* are not required elements of a written report on internal control structure under GAAS?

23-11. What is the difference between the requirement for reporting material weaknesses in a GAAS audit and the same requirement in an audit in accordance with *Government Auditing Standards*?

23-12. When is the auditor of a state or local government required to perform an audit in accordance with the Single Audit Act?

23-13. What additional reporting responsibilities does an auditor have for an audit in accordance with the Single Audit Act beyond that required in an audit in accordance with *Government Auditing Standards*?

23-14. What is the auditor's responsibility for the schedule of federal financial assistance in an audit in accordance with the Single Audit Act?

23-15. How are major federal financial assistance programs identified?

23-16. How does the auditor's consideration of materiality in an audit of a governmental entity's financial statements differ from the consideration of materiality in an audit of compliance with applicable laws and regulations for major federal financial assistance programs?

23-17. Distinguish between the type of assurance an auditor provides about a state or local governmental entity's compliance with specific requirements and with general requirements.

23-18. What four types of requirements generally relate to a major federal financial assistance program's specific requirements?

23-19. What nine general requirements apply to all federal financial assistance programs?

23-20. Describe the four criteria for determining if a finding of noncompliance is a questioned cost.

23-21. What is the auditor's responsibility for reporting on internal control structure policies and procedures relevant to federal financial assistance programs?

23-22. How does an auditor select transactions to evaluate compliance with applicable laws and regulations related to nonmajor programs?

Objective Questions

23-23. When engaged to audit the financial statements of a governmental entity in accordance with GAAS, the auditor's responsibility for testing the entity's compliance with laws and regulations is

(1) restricted to maintaining an awareness of the possibility that violations of laws and regulations may have occurred.

(2) to design audit procedures to test compliance with laws and regulations in order to issue an opinion about the entity's compliance with laws and regulations.

(3) to design audit procedures that provide reasonable assurance that violations of laws and regulations having a direct and material effect on the financial statements are detected.

(4) to detect all violations of laws and regulations that could result in criminal prosecution.

23-24. *Government Auditing Standards* primarily differs from GAAS because *Government Auditing Standards* requires the auditor to do which of the following?

(1) Perform additional tests of compliance not required by GAAS.

(2) Perform additional tests of internal control structure policies and procedures not required by GAAS.

(3) Detect all violations of laws and regulations.

(4) Accept additional responsibilities for reporting on compliance with laws and regulations and internal control structure.

23-25. In an audit in accordance with *Government Auditing Standards*, the auditor's report about a governmental entity's compliance with laws and regulations is based on which type of audit procedures?

(1) Those performed to detect all instances of noncompliance.

(2) Those performed to issue an opinion on the financial statements.

(3) Those designed to provide a basis for issuing an opinion on compliance with laws and regulations.

(4) Those designed to provide absolute assurance of detecting material violations of laws and regulations.

23-26. In an audit in accordance with *Government Auditing Standards*, the auditor's report on the entity's internal control structure

(1) must be issued even when no reportable conditions are noted by the auditor.

(2) is the same as a written *SAS No. 60* report except that the auditor must identify all reportable conditions that he or she considers to be material weaknesses.

(3) must be issued when reportable conditions are noted; otherwise the auditor may provide an oral report about the entity's internal control structure.

(4) must contain the auditor's opinion about the entity's internal control structure.

23-27. In an audit in accordance with *Government Auditing Standards*, the auditor's report on the entity's internal control structure is based on which of the following?

(1) Audit procedures performed to issue an opinion on the entity's internal control structure.

(2) Audit procedures that are more extensive than the audit procedures that must be performed to provide the basis for a report on internal control structure required in an audit in accordance with GAAS.

(3) Audit procedures that are less extensive than those that must be performed to provide the basis for a report on internal control structure required in an audit in accordance with GAAS.

(4) Audit procedures performed in connection with the audit of the financial statements.

23-28. The auditor of a governmental entity has identified reportable conditions about the entity's internal control structure. *Government Auditing Standards* requires the auditor to do which of the following?

(1) Issue a written or oral report about the reportable conditions.

(2) Describe the reportable conditions in the report about the internal control structure with no consideration of whether those conditions are considered to be material weaknesses.

(3) Describe the reportable conditions in the report about the internal control structure along with a statement about whether those conditions are considered to be material weaknesses.

(4) Issue a written report that is required by GAAS (in accordance with *SAS No. 60, Communication of Internal Control Structure Related Matters Noted in an Audit*).

23-29. A local government received $450,000 during its fiscal year from three federal financial assistance programs. The local government's auditor would perform an audit in accordance with

(1) GAAS.

(2) *Government Auditing Standards.*

(3) the Single Audit Act of 1984.

(4) any of the above depending on whether a single federal financial assistance program provided more than $100,000 in assistance.

23-30. The Single Audit Act of 1984 requires the auditor to perform testing of compliance with laws and regulations

(1) that is the same as that required by GAAS.

(2) that is the same as that required by *Government Auditing Standards.*

(3) that is the same as that required by GAAS plus tests of compliance with the applicable specific and general requirements for federal financial assistance programs.

(4) that requires only testing compliance with specific requirements for federal financial assistance programs.

23-31. The Single Audit Act of 1984 requires the auditor to test compliance with laws and regulations applicable to nonmajor federal financial assistance programs

(1) in order to issue an opinion on compliance with laws and regulations applicable to nonmajor federal financial assistance programs.

(2) in order to determine that the entity complied with all general and specific requirements applicable to the nonmajor federal financial assistance program.

(3) in connection with the audit of the financial statements and not for purposes of issuing a report on compliance with laws and regulations applicable to nonmajor federal financial assistance programs.

(4) only for nonmajor program transactions examined in connection with the audit of the financial statements or the evaluation of internal control structure policies and procedures over federal financial assistance programs.

Problems and Cases

23-32. (Compliance Auditing under GAAS) The city of Rocky Mount engaged Beth Johnson, CPA, to audit the city's financial statements in accordance with GAAS for the fiscal year ended March 31, 19X4. During this period, the city received $50 million, which is material to the city's financial statements, in education funds from a state bond issuance. State regulations require that the bond proceeds be used to construct new schools.

REQUIRED

A. What is Johnson's responsibility for evaluating how the city used the education funds?

B. If Johnson determines that the education funds generated from the bond proceeds were used to build a city convention center, what reporting responsibilities does she have?

23-33. (Compliance Auditing under *Government Auditing Standards*) The Leighton Department of Welfare engages Macke Mauldin, CPA, to audit the department's financial statements in accordance with *Government Auditing Standards.* The department receives all of its funding from city tax collections. City tax laws determine how the department uses these funds.

REQUIRED

A. Describe how Mauldin's responsibilities for testing compliance with the tax laws applicable to the department's revenues differ from what his testing responsibilities would have been if he had been engaged to audit the financial statements in accordance with GAAS.

B. Describe the reports Mauldin is required to issue under *Government Auditing Standards.*

C. What type of assurance does Mauldin provide in his report about the department's compliance with the applicable tax laws?

23-34. (Reporting on Internal Control Structure under *Government Auditing Standards*) Anna Christian, senior accountant, has never performed an audit of a governmental entity's financial statements in accordance with *Government Auditing Standards.* Christian presented the following draft of the report on the entity's internal control structure to the engagement partner for review:

**Audit Committee and Management
Governmental Entity ABC**

In planning and performing our audit of the financial statements of Governmental Entity ABC for the year ended December 31, 19X4, we considered its internal control structure in order to determine our auditing procedures for the purpose of expressing our opinion on the financial statements and not to provide assurance on the internal control structure. However, we noted certain matters involving the internal control structure and its operation that we consider to be reportable conditions under standards established by the American Institute of Certified Public Accountants. Reportable conditions involve matters coming to our attention relating to significant deficiencies in the design or operation of the internal control structure that, in our judgment, could adversely affect the organization's ability to record, process, summarize, and report financial data consistent with the assertions of management in the financial statements.

We noted the following reportable conditions:

- Policies and procedures are not in place that require the documentation of management's approval of expenditures for repairs to Governmental Entity ABC's office equipment.

- Policies and procedures are not in place for management review to determine that all cash reconciliations are prepared on a timely basis.

This report is intended solely for the information and use of the audit committee and management, and others within the organization.

March 31, 19X4

CPA Signature

REQUIRED

A. Has Christian prepared the report required by *Government Auditing Standards*? If not, identify the significant differences in her report draft from the report on internal control structure required by *Government Auditing Standards*.

B. Describe how the auditor obtains a basis for reporting on internal control structure in accordance with *Government Auditing Standards*.

23-35. (Application of Single Audit Act) The city of Orlinda received and expended $400 million in federal financial assistance during the year ended June 30, 19X4, from the following programs:

	Federal Fund Expenditures for the Year Ended June 30, 19X4
Federal Program A	$375 million
Federal Program B	21 million
Federal Program C	2.5 million
Federal Program D	1.5 million
Total Federal Expenditures for City of Orlinda	$400 million

REQUIRED

A. Does the Single Audit Act of 1984 apply? If so, why?

B. Identify the major federal financial assistance programs.

C. Identify the additional reports required by the Single Audit Act of 1984 that are not required by *Government Auditing Standards.*

23-36. (Single Audit Act Testing Responsibilities) A governmental entity received $250 million in financial assistance from two federal financial assistance programs during the year ended December 31, 19X4. This assistance is material to the entity's financial statements. Kevin Cullen, CPA, is engaged to perform an audit of the entity's financial statements, and he determines that only one of the federal programs is a major federal financial assistance program.

REQUIRED

A. What is Cullen's *Government Auditing Standards* responsibility for testing compliance with laws and regulations for purposes of reporting on compliance?

B. What is Cullen's additional testing responsibility that must be performed to issue a report on compliance with the specific requirements applicable to the major federal financial assistance program?

C. What is Cullen's responsibility for testing compliance with requirements applicable to the nonmajor federal financial assistance program?

23-37. (Specific and General Requirements) Brenda Robbins, CPA, and Lynn Underwood, CPA, both participate in a continuing education program about the auditor's responsibility under the Single Audit Act of 1984. Robbins believes that an auditor engaged to perform an audit of a state or local government in accordance with the Single Audit Act of 1984 must issue an opinion on compliance with specific and general requirements applicable to major federal financial assistance programs. Underwood disagrees and believes that the auditor only has to issue an opinion on compliance with the specific requirements and negative assurance on compliance with the general requirements applicable to major federal financial assistance programs.

REQUIRED

A. What are specific requirements and what do they generally pertain to?

B. How do specific requirements differ from general requirements?

C. With which auditor do you agree?

Auditing Issues Case

23-38. KELCO MANUFACTURING COMPANY

You have just delivered the audit report for Kelco's financial statements for the year ended December 31, 19X7. During your meeting with the company president, Cook mentioned to you that he is on the city council of Seaside and is interested in your firm doing an audit. Upon further inquiry you discover that the organization receives financial assistance from the federal government. Cook informs you that the city expends federal funds in the amount of $7 million annually of which $195,750 is spent on a federal program for low income housing. After a lengthy discussion, you have determined that Seaside will probably require a compliance audit.

REQUIRED

A. Is the federal program for low income housing a major or nonmajor program? Distinguish between a Major and a Nonmajor program.

B. When performing a compliance audit for the low income housing program, what items should the auditor test?

C. What type of report should your firm issue related to the federally funded low income housing program?

Internal and Operational Auditing

O b j e c t i v e s

- Describe the role and purpose of internal auditing.
- State the requirements for professional certification for an internal auditor.
- Identify the responsibilities of the internal auditor.
- Identify and discuss the standards for the professional practice of internal auditing.
- Define operational auditing and identify its primary purposes.
- Describe the phases involved in performing an operational audit.

After a person makes the decision to become an auditor, he or she is faced with yet another decision—whether to become an internal or external auditor. The ramifications and responsibilities differ greatly between the two classifications. An internal auditor is not employed by a CPA firm, but, rather, by a company, government agency, or not-for-profit group. The internal auditor usually reports to senior managers or a company's board of directors, whereas an external auditor has a less-defined reporting structure consisting of the CPA firm for which he or she works and third parties (creditors and investors). Even the licensure requirements and names for internal and external auditors are different. The professional certification level for an internal auditor is as a certified internal auditor or CIA. The external auditor takes the certified public accountants' examination and, upon passing the examination and meeting the experience requirement, gains the CPA title.

This chapter explores some of the challenges internal auditors experience that do not directly affect external auditors, such as communicating results in-house, human relations and communications within their companies, and supervision. ■

Internal auditors are employed by a specific entity (for example, a corporation, government, or not-for-profit entity) to perform audits that the organization deems necessary. The Institute of Internal Auditors has defined *internal auditing* and its objective as

> an independent appraisal function established within an organization to examine and evaluate its activities as a service to the organization. The objective of internal auditing is to assist management and the board of directors in the effective discharge of their responsibilities.

Internal auditing is often referred to as "the eyes and ears of management." Internal auditors examine not only accounting and financial activities but other types of programs within the entity. Internal auditors often focus on compliance with policies and regulations and on improving operating efficiency. For example, they may evaluate an entity's compliance with federal laws regarding hiring practices or review the entity's cash management program for purposes of improving cash management. This broad description of internal auditing reflects the enormous potential services that internal auditing can provide to management and the board of directors.

Internal auditors differ in several ways from external auditors. Internal auditors are usually full-time employees of an entity; external auditors are not employees of the audited organization but have their own independent practice. Internal auditors often perform financial, compliance, and operational audits, whereas external auditors perform primarily audits of financial statements and examinations of internal control over financial reporting. In addition, internal auditors can affect the financial audit of an external auditor, as discussed in Chapter 6. For example, *SAS No. 55, Consideration of the Internal Control Structure in a Financial Statement Audit* (AU 319), states that one aspect of the control environment is "management's control methods

Table 24–1	**Comparison of Internal Auditors and External Auditors**	
	Internal Auditors	External Auditors
Employer	Companies, governmental units, and not-for-profit entities	CPA firms
Licensing	Certified Internal Auditors (CIAs)	Certified Public Accountants (CPAs)
Licensing required	No	Yes
Primary responsibility to	Senior management and board of directors	Third parties (investors and creditors)

for monitoring and following up on performance, including internal auditing." Thus, internal auditors may reduce the control risk of an entity.

Table 24–1 compares some of the characteristics of internal and external auditors.

The Foreign Corrupt Practices Act (discussed in more detail in Chapter 6) generated an increased emphasis on establishing and maintaining effective internal audit staffs. The act requires publicly held companies to devise and maintain systems of internal accounting controls to provide reasonable assurance that control objectives are being achieved. One method of gaining this assurance is to establish an internal audit department. Consequently, many companies covered by the Foreign Corrupt Practices Act have either established or increased the size and quality of their internal audit staffs. In addition, the 1987 report of the National Commission on Fraudulent Financial Reporting (the Treadway Commission) recommended that public companies establish qualified and independent internal audit staffs.

Internal auditing has evolved to meet the needs of entities and today is one of the fastest-growing segments of the accounting profession. As organizations have become more complex, internal auditors have responded by developing more specialized skills to meet the needs of those organizations. Many small and medium-size entities, and most large entities, today have internal audit staffs. Expansion in operations and in number of employees creates a demand for internal auditors who can provide assurances that financial, compliance, and operational controls are working properly and that the organization is achieving its objectives. The increasing importance of internal auditing is evidenced by the fact that the **Institute of Internal Auditors (IIA)**, the international professional organization of internal auditors, was founded in 1941 with only 25 members and now has more than 50,000 members in more than 100 different countries.

Objectives of Internal Auditing

As defined in the *Statement of Responsibilities of Internal Auditors* published by the IIA, "the objective of internal auditing is to assist members of the organization in the effective discharge of their responsibilities." To accomplish this objective, the internal audit staff is expected to furnish the organization with "analyses, appraisals, recommendations, counsel, and information concerning the activities reviewed." The IIA recognizes that the objective includes promoting effective controls at a reasonable cost.

The *Statement of Responsibilities of Internal Auditors* identifies the scope of internal auditing as encompassing "the examination and evaluation of the adequacy and effectiveness of the organization's system of internal control and the quality of performance in carrying out assigned responsibilities." The scope includes

- reviewing the reliability and integrity of financial and operating information and the means used to identify, measure, classify, and report such information;
- reviewing the systems established to insure compliance with those policies, plans, procedures, laws, and regulations that have a significant impact on operations and reports, and determining whether the organization is in compliance;
- reviewing the means of safeguarding assets and, as appropriate, verifying the existence of such assets;
- appraising the economy and efficiency with which resources are employed; and
- reviewing operations or programs to ascertain whether results are consistent with established objectives and goals and whether the operations or programs are being carried out as planned.

Professional Certification

Since December 1974, the IIA has offered the ***certified internal auditor*** examination. This is a two-day examination given semiannually in principal cities throughout the world. The examination consists of four parts: internal audit process, internal audit skills, management control and information technology, and the audit environment. Included in the examination (see Table 24–2) are such topics as professionalism and fraud detection, internal auditing administration, sampling, information technology, organizational behavior and management, economics, accounting, and finance.

The Real World of Auditing

SEC Charges Internal Auditor

For the first time in our memory, the SEC has charged an internal auditor with insider trading violations. The SEC has charged a supervisor of internal audit at Vista Chemical Co. in Houston, with making about $877,000 in illegal profits by buying Vista options and common stock before a buyout of the company was announced.

The supervisor used his position with Vista to obtain material nonpublic information about the merger plans, the SEC said. In addition to having conversations with Vista executives, the SEC charged, he gathered insight into the pending deal by reading the expense reports of Vista senior officers that reflected travel and other expenses during the negotiations. The SEC is suing for a return of the alleged profits plus three times the alleged illegal gains as a civil penalty.

Source: *Internal Auditing Alert Newsletter*, March 1991, p. 8. Published by Warren, Gorham & Lamant, Inc., Volume II, Number 2.

| **Table 24-2** | **Contents of the Certified Internal Auditor Examination** |

- **Part I—Internal Audit Process**
  Focuses on the theory and practice of internal auditing. Major areas include auditing; professionalism; and fraud detection, reporting, and investigating.
- **Part II—Internal Audit Skills**
  Includes specific skill emphasis on reasoning ability, communication skills, and dealing with auditees. Behavior skills, statistics, and mathematical skills are tested at the understanding and awareness levels.
- **Part III—Management Control and Information Technology**
  Deals with basic business disciplines essential to the practice of internal auditing. The major areas covered are organization and management, information technology, managerial accounting, and quantitative methods as a management tool.
- **Part IV—The Audit Environment**
  Examines traditional topic areas such as financial accounting and finance, economics, international developments relevant to the practice of internal auditing, government, taxes, and marketing.

To become certified, an internal auditor must not only pass the examination but generally must have at least two years of experience in auditing. The certification program also requires individuals to meet continuing professional education requirements. Worldwide, there are more than 20,000 certified internal auditors.

Code of Ethics

Consistent with other professional organizations, the IIA has established a code of ethics for its members. The IIA recognizes that the internal auditor has "an obligation to the profession, management, stockholders, and the general public to maintain high standards of professional conduct in the performance of his profession." The code of ethics consists of a preamble with 11 articles. The code is presented in Figure 24–1.

Standards of Internal Auditing

In 1978, the IIA issued *Standards for the Professional Practice of Internal Auditing*, the most authoritative statement about the nature and scope of internal auditing. Although this publication represented the first written auditing standards for internal auditors, the IIA has been active since its inception in 1941 in establishing responsibilities and developing the professional attributes of the internal auditing profession.

The purpose of the IIA standards is to

1. impart an understanding of internal auditing to others,
2. establish the basis for guidance and measurement of internal auditing performance, and
3. improve the practice of internal auditing.

IIA standards for the professional practice of internal auditing fall into five broad categories: independence, professional proficiency, scope of work, performance of audit work, and management of the internal auditing department. These standards are listed in Appendix A at the end of the chapter.

Figure 24–1   **IIA Code of Ethics**

THE INSTITUTE OF INTERNAL AUDITORS
CODE OF ETHICS

PURPOSE: A distinguishing mark of a profession is acceptance by its members of responsibility to the interests of those it serves. Members of The Institute of Internal Auditors (Members) and Certified Internal Auditors (CIAs) must maintain high standards of conduct in order to effectively discharge this responsibility. The Institute of Internal Auditors (Institute) adopts this *Code of Ethics* for Members and CIAs.

APPLICABILITY: This *Code of Ethics* is applicable to all Members and CIAs. Membership in The Institute and acceptance of the "Certified Internal Auditor" designation are voluntary actions. By acceptance, Members and CIAs assume an obligation of self-discipline above and beyond the requirements of laws and regulations.

The standards of conduct set forth in this *Code of Ethics* provide basic principles in the practice of internal auditing. Members and CIAs should realize that their individual judgment is required in the application of these principles.

CIAs shall use the "Certified Internal Auditor" designation with discretion and in a dignified manner, fully aware of what the designation denotes. The designation shall also be used in a manner consistent with all statutory requirements.

Members who are judged by the Board of Directors of The Institute to be in violation of the standards of conduct of the *Code of Ethics* shall be subject to forfeiture of their membership in The Institute. CIAs who are similarly judged also shall be subject to forfeiture of the "Certified Internal Auditor" designation.

STANDARDS OF CONDUCT

I. Members and CIAs shall exercise honesty, objectivity, and diligence in the performance of their duties and responsibilities.

II. Members and CIAs shall exhibit loyalty in all matters pertaining to the affairs of their organization or to whomever they may be rendering a service. However, Members and CIAs shall not knowingly be a party to any illegal or improper activity.

III. Members and CIAs shall not knowingly engage in acts or activities which are discreditable to the profession of internal auditing or to their organization.

IV. Members and CIAs shall refrain from entering into any activity which may be in conflict with the interest of their organization or which would prejudice their ability to carry out objectively their duties and responsibilities.

V. Members and CIAs shall not accept anything of value from an employee, client, customer, supplier, or business associate of their organization which would impair or be presumed to impair their professional judgment.

VI. Members and CIAs shall undertake only those services which they can reasonably expect to complete with professional competence.

VII. Members and CIAs shall adopt suitable means to comply with the *Standards for the Professional Practice of Internal Auditing.*

VIII. Members and CIAs shall be prudent in the use of information acquired in the course of their duties. They shall not use confidential information for any personal gain nor in any manner which would be contrary to law or detrimental to the welfare of their organization.

IX. Members and CIAs, when reporting on the results of their work, shall reveal all material facts known to them which, if not revealed, could either distort reports of operations under review or conceal unlawful practices.

X. Members and CIAs shall continually strive for improvement in their proficiency, and in the effectiveness and quality of their service.

XI. Members and CIAs, in the practice of their profession, shall be ever mindful of their obligation to maintain the high standards of competence, morality, and dignity promulgated by The Institute. Members shall abide by the *Bylaws* and uphold the objectives of The Institute.

Adopted by Board of Directors, July 1988.

Independence

Internal auditors place a high degree of importance on ***independence***. Independence allows the internal auditor to reach unbiased decisions necessary to properly serve the entity. Of course, because internal auditors are employed full time by the entities they audit, they do not have the perceived independence that external auditors have. Independence for the internal auditor is achieved through *organizational status* and *objectivity*. Therefore, this concept of independence is different from the independence the external auditor maintains under the AICPA Code of Professional Conduct.

Organizational Status

Organizational status aids in the maintenance of independence by the internal auditor. Often, the internal auditing department reports directly to the board of directors or its audit committee to ensure that the department or group it is auditing is not the one to which it reports. In some entities, the internal auditing department reports administratively to other departments in the entity but maintains its independence by communicating directly to the board of directors.

Objectivity

All auditors should be as objective as possible when performing an audit. The *Statement of Responsibilities of Internal Auditors* requires internal auditors to have an objective, independent mental attitude while performing an audit. Consequently, internal auditors should not subordinate their judgment on audit matters to that of others. Moreover, objectivity is presumed to be impaired when internal auditors audit any activity for which they have operating authority or responsibility. Internal audit staff assignments should be made so that potential and actual conflicts of interest are avoided.

Factors that may influence the independence of internal auditors include the following:

- Who sets the internal audit department's agenda
- Whether anyone can suppress the internal auditor's findings
- Whether the internal auditor has access to the audit committee of the board of directors without management's presence
- The frequency of meetings between the internal auditor and the audit committee of the board of directors
- Whether the internal auditor's recommendations are addressed on a timely basis
- Whether the internal audit department has a policy to rotate employees among various audit areas

Professional Proficiency

To discharge responsibilities properly, a professional person must have a high level of technical proficiency. According to the standards of the IIA, technical proficiency includes staffing; knowledge, skills, and disciplines; supervision; human relations and communications; continuing education; and due professional care.

Staffing

The internal auditing department should be staffed with people with the appropriate technical proficiency and educational backgrounds. The director of internal auditing determines what criteria should be used when evaluating education and experience and staffs the internal audit positions with personnel capable of performing their duties properly.

Knowledge, Skills, and Disciplines

The internal auditing department should collectively possess the knowledge and skills essential to practice internal auditing effectively, including an understanding of internal auditing standards. Each internal auditor should possess the technical proficiency to apply internal auditing procedures and techniques appropriately. *Technical proficiency* includes knowledge of the principles and techniques of auditing and a broad understanding of accounting, management principles, economics, law, taxation, finance, and computers.

Employees of the internal auditing department should preferably include personnel who have expertise in a wide array of disciplines, including accounting, finance, statistics, electronic data processing, and law. Quite clearly, each individual cannot be held responsible for having expertise in all of the various disciplines; however, each individual should have an appreciation of the fundamentals in these various areas sufficient to recognize the existence of problems or potential problems.

Supervision

Members of the internal audit staff should be properly supervised so that they may discharge their responsibilities adequately. Supervision represents a continuing process for an employee that should begin in the planning stage of the audit and end at its completion. The extent of supervision depends upon the person's level of expertise. Each internal audit supervisor has a responsibility to provide adequate instructions to staff and to determine that the work is being carried out properly.

Human Relations and Communications

To be effective, internal auditors must understand human relations and be able to interact satisfactorily with other people. Internal auditors should be skilled in both oral and written communications so that they can clearly convey audit objectives, evaluations, conclusions, and recommendations.

Continuing Education

Internal auditors should maintain their technical competence through continuing professional education. They should keep informed about improvements and current developments in internal auditing standards, procedures, and techniques. Certified internal auditors are required to complete a total of 80 hours of continuing professional education every two years. Those who do not meet the continuing education requirement may not advertise themselves as certified internal auditors.

Due Professional Care

The *Standards for the Professional Practice of Internal Auditing* require internal auditors to exercise due professional care in performing an engagement. The internal auditor is expected to perform an audit with the care and skill that any other reasonably prudent and competent internal auditor would exercise in similar circumstances. The concept implies reasonable care and competence, not infallibility or extraordinary performance.

In exercising due care, internal auditors should be alert to the following:

- Errors and omissions
- Inefficiency, waste, and ineffectiveness
- Conflicts of interest
- Conditions and activities where irregularities are most likely to occur
- Inadequate controls and needed compliance improvements.

Scope of Work

The standards for the scope of audit work give guidance to the internal auditor for the performance of financial auditing, compliance auditing, and operational auditing. The specific standards relate to the reliability and integrity of information; compliance with policies, plans, procedures, laws, and regulations; safeguarding of assets; efficient and economical use of resources; and accomplishment of established objectives and goals. These standards recognize that internal auditors perform a wide variety of audit functions.

Performance of Audit Work

Whereas the standards of the scope of audit work provide guidance as to what audit work should be performed, standards for the performance of audit work present guidance for overall audit structure, including the areas of planning the audit, examining and evaluating information, communicating results, and following up on the engagement.

Planning the Audit   The internal auditor should properly plan each audit. Planning should be documented and should include establishing audit objectives, obtaining background information, determining the resources necessary to perform the audit, communicating with all appropriate parties, identifying areas of audit interest, writing the audit program, identifying procedures to communicate results, and obtaining approval of the audit work plan.

Examining and Evaluating Information   The internal auditor should gather sufficient competent evidential matter to support the audit findings and be useful to the organization in meeting its goals. Auditors should document their findings through the audit working papers that record the information that the auditors obtain and any analyses that they make.

Communicating Results   The internal auditor's work is of little benefit to the entity if results are not properly communicated to the appropriate people. The internal auditor should submit a signed written report after the audit is completed. The standards for the professional practice of internal auditing encourage the internal auditor to discuss the conclusions and recommendations of the audit with the appropriate levels of management before issuing the final report. For example, when the internal auditor is auditing a branch location, he or she should discuss the conclusions and recommendations with the branch manager before issuing a final report to the home office. By meeting with the appropriate level of management, the internal auditor can gather further evidence of the validity of the findings, determine if any mitigating or unusual circumstances exist, and assess the effect of the findings.

Internal audit reports should be objective and clearly written. Reports should describe not only the scope and purpose of the audit but also the results of the audit. These reports should be both timely and constructive and may include recommendations for improvements. They may also acknowledge satisfactory performance and corrective action. An example of an actual internal audit report with an attachment of findings is shown in Figure 24–2.

Figure 24-2

Example of Internal Audit Report with an Attachment of Findings

Virginia E. Borden, Vice-president
Briarwood Division
PGD Corporation

Attached is an internal audit report on an activity within your division. The following data apply:

Location:	La Jolla, California
Type of Audit:	Wholly Owned Subsidiary Responsibility
Items Covered:	Cash, Accounts Receivable, Inventories, Property, Payroll, Sales, Purchasing, Accounts Payable, and Security
Period of Fieldwork:	3/11/X4–3/15/X4
Exit Conference:	
Date	3/15/X4
Attendees	Barry Prim
	Joe Christenberry
	Gladys Small
	Jim Neighbors
	John Benner

A response form is attached to the report for your use, if desired, in responding to this report.

Since the deficiencies found in this audit meet the criteria established in the Corporate Policy on Internal Auditing for formal reports, a summary of the deficiencies and a copy of your response to recommendations in this report will be distributed to corporate management and the Audit Review Committee. The attached detailed report will not be distributed unless specifically requested by an individual recipient.

We appreciate the assistance rendered to our auditors by your employees while completing this audit. One of our primary objectives is to assist you in maintaining the high standards established by the company for internal accounting controls.

INTERNAL AUDIT SECTION

Bob Welch

Bob Welch, Director

Following Up

Internal auditors should follow up on problems noted or recommendations made in the report. The internal auditor should determine either that any necessary corrective action noted in the audit report was taken or that management is aware of the risk associated with not taking corrective action.

| Figure 24-2 | *continued* |

ATTACHMENT
INTERNAL AUDIT REPORT

CASH

In our reconciliation of the combined petty cash/cash sales fund, we noted that customer checks had not been restrictively endorsed.* To discourage the possible misuse of company receipts, we recommend all checks be restrictively endorsed immediately upon receipt.

PAYROLL

A review of time cards during our week of fieldwork indicated supervisors were not always initialing manual time card entries. To document that all parties agree as to when work was started, ended, or resumed, we recommend supervisors be reminded of the need to initial all manual entries to time cards.

SALES

The signature of the customer or other receiver was not always being obtained on charge sales. The customer's signature is essential in order to document the completion of the sales transaction and to prove delivery of goods. We recommend the customer's signature be obtained on all charge sale invoices.

PURCHASING

Many purchase orders were prepared and approved after the receipt of goods. To ensure goods are for company use and are properly authorized prior to commitment of funds, we recommend purchase orders be prepared and approved at the time the order is placed.

ACCOUNTS PAYABLE

New vendors added to the accounts payable computer system were not being reviewed by anyone. To ensure no bogus suppliers are added, we recommend the controller or her designee review all new suppliers added to the accounts payable system for appropriateness.

Invoices were being matched to the purchase order by the same individual issuing the purchase order. To prevent possible misuse of purchase authority, we recommend invoices be matched by the accounts payable clerk.

*Similar exception noted in prior audits.

Management of the Internal Auditing Department

To work effectively, the internal audit function should be appropriately managed. The series of standards on the management of the internal auditing department establishes the responsibilities for the director of internal auditing. The director of internal auditing is responsible for determining that (1) the audit work performed achieves the general purposes and responsibilities as identified by management and the board of directors, (2) the resources of the internal auditing department are applied efficiently and effectively, and (3) the audit work conforms with the *Standards for the Professional Practice of Internal Auditing.*

The director of internal auditing also plans the responsibilities of the department. These responsibilities include establishing the goals of the internal auditing department and the work schedules, staffing schedules, financial budgets, and activity reports. The director of internal auditing is responsible for providing written policies and procedures to guide the audit staff and for establishing programs to select and develop the personnel of the internal auditing department.

The director of internal auditing often coordinates the efforts between the internal audit staff and external auditors. This cooperation ensures that the entity has adequate audit coverage and minimizes duplication of efforts. The responsibilities of the internal and external auditors were discussed in more detail in Chapter 6.

Finally, the director of internal auditing is responsible for establishing and maintaining a system of quality control. A quality control program should include the following elements: supervision, internal reviews, and external reviews. The work of internal auditors should be properly supervised to provide continuous assurance that it complies with internal auditing standards. The internal review should be performed periodically by qualified members of the staff to appraise the quality of audit work performed. Additionally, external reviews by qualified people who are independent of the organization are desirable. These reviews should, ideally, be performed at least once every three years to determine that the internal audit staff is in compliance with the *Standards for the Professional Practice of Internal Auditing.* These external reviews are similar to the peer reviews for CPA firms discussed in Chapter 1.

Interpretations of the Standards

To provide authoritative interpretations of the *Standards for the Professional Practice of Internal Auditing,* the IIA began issuing *Statements on Internal Auditing Standards* in 1983. The *Standards for the Professional Practice of Internal Auditing* represent broad guidelines for the internal auditor to follow. In practice, questions arise about applying the standards to specific internal auditing situations. The IIA answers such questions through *Statements on Internal Auditing Standards* issued by the Committee on Professional Standards and Responsibilities, a senior technical committee of the IIA. A listing of *Statements on Internal Auditing Standards* is shown in Table 24–3.

Operational Auditing

As defined in Chapter 1, ***operational auditing*** is a review of an entity's operating procedures and methods to determine their efficiency and effectiveness. At the conclusion of the operational audit, recommendations are typically made for improving procedures. Operational audits are sometimes referred to as *performance audits, management audits,* or *comprehensive audits.* Internationally, the term *value-for-money auditing* is the most frequently used term for operational auditing.

Table 24-3	Statements on Internal Auditing Standards

Statement No.	Title (date issued)
1	Control: Concepts and Responsibilities (1983)
2	Communicating Results (1983)
3	Deterrence, Detection, Investigation, and Reporting of Fraud (1985)
4	Quality Assurance (1986)
5	Internal Auditors' Relationships with Independent Outside Auditors (1987)
6	Audit Working Papers (1987)
7	Communication with the Board of Directors (1989)
8	Analytical Auditing Procedures (1991)
9	Risk Assessment (1991)
10	Evaluating the Accomplishment of the Established Objectives and Goals for Operations or Programs (1991)

Internal auditors often perform operational audits for their organizations. In performing an operational audit, the internal auditor typically examines the entity's policies and procedures to determine whether or not they (1) accomplish the goals of management (that is, their effectiveness) and (2) achieve these goals in the best possible and least wasteful manner (that is, their efficiency). As part of an operational audit, the internal auditor is concerned with how well the policies and procedures are being performed, whether they are meeting the objectives as established by management, and whether they can be improved. Governmental auditors, such as those employed by the GAO, also often perform operational audits. In addition, CPA firms perform operational audits as a part of their management consulting practice. These engagements are governed by *Statements on Standards for Consulting Services*, not SASs.

Although the primary purpose of operational auditing is to evaluate the effectiveness and efficiency of an organization, operational auditing often encompasses a third aspect: economy. The *evaluation of economy* is an examination of the cost and benefits of a policy or procedure. In the context of operational auditing, the evaluation of economy is a long-term consideration of whether the benefits of a policy or procedure outweigh its costs. A procedure may be effective and efficient, but over the long run it may be uneconomical. For example, an entity may have a policy of reimbursing employees for automobile expenses. The policy may be effective in that it allows employees to go to various locations as needed and it may be implemented in an efficient manner. However, in the long run, it may be more economical for the entity to buy or lease cars and allow employees to use them.

Purposes of Operational Audits

Operational audits usually are designed to meet one or more of the following objectives:

Assess Performance Any operational audit involves an assessment of the reviewed organization's performance. To assess performance is to compare an organization's activities with (1) objectives such as organizational policies, standards, and goals established by management or the engaging party, and (2) other appropriate measurement criteria.

Identify Opportunities for Improvement Increased effectiveness, efficiency, and economy are the broad categories under which most improvements are classified. The auditor may identify specific opportunities for improvement by interviewing individuals (whether within or outside the organization), observing operations, reviewing past and current reports, studying transactions, making comparisons with industry standards, exercising professional judgment based on experience, or using other appropriate means.

Develop Recommendations for Improvement or Further Action The nature and extent of recommendations developed in the course of operational audits vary considerably. In many cases, the auditor may be able to make specific recommendations. In other cases, further study, not within the scope of the engagement, may be required, and the auditor may simply cite reasons why further study of a specific area may be appropriate.[1]

Examples of operational audits are shown in Table 24–4.

Structure of the Operational Audit

The general structure of the typical operational audit is a five-phase process: familiarization, survey, program development, audit application, and reporting.

Familiarization

Before starting an operational audit, the auditor (or consultant) should become familiar with the activity or function being audited. To do this, the auditor reviews background information, objectives, organizational structure, and controls of the activity or function being examined and determines their relationship to the overall entity.

In addition, the auditor should clearly understand the purpose and scope of the engagement and the nature of the report to be issued. The auditor should also determine whether the individual or entity requesting the audit has the authority to do so.

This planning phase of the operational audit is similar to planning in a financial audit in that the auditor becomes familiar with the activity being audited and plans the staffing and audit approach. However, because operational audits are diverse, deciding specific objectives for an operational audit is often more difficult than deciding specific objectives for a financial audit.

Survey

During the survey phase of the operational audit, often referred to as a *preliminary survey*, the auditor should attempt to identify problem areas and those areas that are critical to the overall success of the activity or function. Usually a questionnaire is used to identify those aspects of the unit activity or function that should be addressed further.

---

[1]Special Committee on Operational and Management Auditing, American Institute of Certified Public Accountants, *Operational Audit Engagements*, AICPA, January 1982, page 3.

Table 24-4	**Examples of Operational Audits**

Taking Knocks Out Is Costly

During an audit of a cost-plus contract, the internal auditor determined that the coal mining contractor was purchasing premium, rather than regular, unleaded gasoline for the small mine vehicles. During the past year, the contractor had purchased 55,000 gallons of premium, unleaded gasoline at ten cents per gallon more than regular, unleaded gasoline. When asked why the premium was purchased, the contractor claimed premium gasoline reduced maintenance costs, but acknowledged that most of the small mine vehicles only had a useful life of three years.

The internal auditor wrote "$5,500" on a pad of paper and said, "This is how much more the use of premium gasoline cost this operation during the past year." Writing "9.15%" on the pad, the auditor said, "And this is how much money costs us today." The auditor did some quick calculations, wrote a six-digit figure on the pad, and said, "This is what it would cost us to borrow $5,500 every year over the 25 years of useful life of the mine."

The coal mining operator is now using regular, unleaded gasoline in the small mine vehicles.

See What the Others Are Doing

Credit card operations have several options that affect fee and interest income. Most obvious are the annual fees and the interest rates charged on unpaid balances. Little noticed, but still important, are the rates charged for cash advances.

The internal auditors, during an audit of the bank's credit card operation, obtained a sample of VISA and MasterCard applications from financial institutions in the area. A review of the applications disclosed a major source of revenue being lost by their bank. The other institutions charged a cash advance fee of 2% or more and immediate interest. The auditor's bank only charged a flat $2 fee and no interest if the next billed balance was paid in full.

The auditors informed management that a knowledgeable cardholder could secure cash advances up to the credit limit on the account, keep the money for as long as 59 days, and pay back in full for a charge of only $2. Without wanting to know how many of the bank's cardholders had done this or how much interest had been lost, management instituted higher fees immediately.

Freight In versus Freight Out

The internal auditors found that although the traffic department did an excellent job of negotiating outbound freight rates, no attempt was made to negotiate inbound freight rates. Inbound carrier selection was left to each supplier with the result that ton for ton, inbound freight charges were 40% higher than outbound charges.

The auditors recommended that the traffic department negotiate inbound freight rates with the suppliers just as they did for outbound freight. The recommendation was accepted and resulted in a savings of $233,200 during the first year.

Program Development

The auditor designs a work program, based on the audit objectives, that details the tests and analyses to be performed on those areas identified as critical as a result of the preliminary survey. In addition, the auditor schedules the work, assigns appropriate personnel to the engagement, determines the involvement of other personnel, and provides for the review of the working papers.

Audit Application

The audit application is the primary phase of the operational audit. The auditor performs the audit procedures identified in the work program to gather evidence, make analyses, draw conclusions, and develop recommendations. During fieldwork, the auditor should complete the specific audit steps and achieve the overall audit objectives of assessing effectiveness, efficiency, and economy. The types of audit evidence discussed in Chapter 5 and the evaluation of control structure discussed in Chapter 6 would also apply to the operational audit. As with a financial audit, the auditor must obtain sufficient competent evidential matter to afford a reasonable basis for the conclusions reached.

Reporting

The reporting phase is critical to the overall success of the operational audit. Generally, operational audit reports contain two major elements: (1) engagement objectives, scope, and approach, and (2) specific findings and recommendations. These reports often include an executive summary that highlights the contents and conclusions of the detailed report. Because these reports are generally not distributed to third parties, the wording of the report can be quite specific. An example of the introductory language of an operational audit report is shown in Figure 24–3.

Appendix A: Summary of General and Specific IIA Standards for the Professional Practice of Internal Auditing[2]

100 *INDEPENDENCE* Internal auditors should be independent of the activities they audit.

> **110** *Organizational Status* The organizational status of the internal auditing department should be sufficient to permit the accomplishment of its audit responsibilities.
> **120** *Objectivity* Internal auditors should be objective in performing audits.

200 *PROFESSIONAL PROFICIENCY* Internal audits should be performed with proficiency and due professional care.

> **The Internal Auditing Department**
> **210** *Staffing* The internal auditing department should provide assurance that the technical proficiency and educational background of internal auditors are appropriate for the audits to be performed.
> **220** *Knowledge, Skills, and Disciplines* The internal auditing department should possess or should obtain the knowledge, skills, and disciplines needed to carry out its audit responsibilities.
> **230** *Supervision* The internal auditing department should provide assurance that internal audits are properly supervised.

> **The Internal Auditor**
> **240** *Compliance with Standards of Conduct* Internal auditors should comply with professional standards of conduct.
> **250** *Knowledge, Skills, and Disciplines* Internal auditors should possess the knowledge, skills, and disciplines essential to the performance of internal audits.
> **260** *Human Relations and Communications* Internal auditors should be skilled in dealing with people and in communicating effectively.
> **270** *Continuing Education* Internal auditors should maintain their technical competence through continuing education.
> **280** *Due Professional Care* Internal auditors should exercise due professional care in performing internal audits.

---

[2]Source: *Summary of Standards for the Professional Practice of Internal Auditing,* Institute of Internal Auditors, 1987.

Figure 24-3   **Introductory Language for an Operational Audit Report**

To: Parent Corp. of Tennis Corp.
   353 E. 72nd St.
   New York, New York 10022

Re: W-One Corp.
   550 W. Magnolia Avenue
   Dallas, Texas 75215

In December 19X4 we concluded an operational audit of the Tennis Corp.

Objectives, Scope, and Approach

The general objectives of this engagement were as follows:

   —To document, analyze, and report on the status of current operations
   —To identify areas that require attention
   —To make recommendations for corrective action or improvements

Our operational audit encompassed the following units: Branch A, Branch B, and Branch C, and the entire home office operation. Our evaluations included both the financial and operational conditions of the units.

The operational audit involved interviews with management personnel and selected operations personnel in each of the units studied. We also evaluated selected documents, files, reports, systems, procedures, and policies as we considered appropriate. After analyzing the data, we developed recommendations for improvements. We then discussed our findings and recommendations with appropriate unit management personnel, and with you, prior to submitting this written report.

Findings and Recommendations

All significant findings are included in this report for your consideration. The recommendations in this report represent, in our judgment, those most likely to bring about beneficial improvements to the operations of the organization. The recommendations differ in such aspects as difficulty of implementation, urgency, visibility of benefits, required investment in facilities, and equipment or additional personnel. The varying nature of the recommendations, their implementation costs, and their potential impact on operations should be considered in reaching your decisions on courses of action.

[List of Findings and Recommendations]

Kirk Anders
Kirk Anders
Director of Internal Auditing

February 4, 19X5

300 *SCOPE OF WORK* The scope of the internal audit should encompass the examination and evaluation of the adequacy and effectiveness of the organization's system of internal control and the quality of performance in carrying out assigned responsibilities.

> **310** *Reliability and Integrity of Information* Internal auditors should review the reliability and integrity of financial and operating information and the means used to identify, measure, classify, and report such information.
> **320** *Compliance with Policies, Plans, Procedures, Laws, and Regulations* Internal auditors should review the systems established to ensure compliance with those policies, plans, procedures, laws, and regulations which could have a significant impact on operations and reports and should determine whether the organization is in compliance.
> **330** *Safeguarding of Assets* Internal auditors should review the means of safeguarding assets and, as appropriate, verify the existence of such assets.
> **340** *Economical and Efficient Use of Resources* Internal auditors should appraise the economy and efficiency with which resources are employed.
> **350** *Accomplishment of Established Objectives and Goals for Operations or Programs* Internal auditors should review operations or programs to ascertain whether results are consistent with established objectives and goals and whether the operations or programs are being carried out as planned.

400 *PERFORMANCE OF AUDIT WORK* Audit work should include planning the audit, examining and evaluating information, communicating results, and following up.

> **410** *Planning the Audit* Internal auditors should plan each audit.
> **420** *Examining and Evaluating Information* Internal auditors should collect, analyze, interpret, and document information to support audit results.
> **430** *Communicating Results* Internal auditors should report the results of their audit work.
> **440** *Following Up* Internal auditors should follow up to ascertain that appropriate action is taken on reported audit findings.

500 *MANAGEMENT OF THE INTERNAL AUDITING DEPARTMENT* The director of internal auditing should properly manage the internal auditing department.

> **510** *Purpose, Authority, and Responsibility* The director of internal auditing should have a statement of purpose, authority, and responsibility for the internal auditing department.
> **520** *Planning* The director of internal auditing should establish plans to carry out the responsibilities of the internal auditing department.
> **530** *Policies and Procedures* The director of internal auditing should provide written policies and procedures to guide the audit staff.
> **540** *Personnel Management and Development* The director of internal auditing should establish a program for selecting and developing the human resources of the internal auditing department.
> **550** *External Auditors* The director of internal auditing should coordinate internal and external audit efforts.
> **560** *Quality Assurance* The director of internal auditing should establish and maintain a quality assurance program to evaluate the operations of the internal auditing department.

Significant Terms

Certified Internal Auditor A professionally certified internal auditor who has met experience criteria and passed a two-day examination under the auspices of the Institute of Internal Auditors.

Institute of Internal Auditors (IIA) An international association dedicated to the continuing professional development of the individual internal auditor and the internal auditing profession.

Internal auditing An independent appraisal function established within an organization to examine and evaluate its activities as a service to the organization.

Operational audit A review of an entity's operating procedures and methods for the purpose of determining their efficiency and effectiveness.

Standards for the Professional Practice of Internal Auditing The most authoritative statement about the nature and scope of internal auditing.

Statement on Internal Auditing Standards Authoritative interpretations of the *Standards for the Professional Practice of Internal Auditing.*

Discussion Questions

24-1.   Define *internal auditing.*
24-2.   What is the basic objective of the internal auditor?
24-3.   What are the areas of responsibility for the internal auditor?
24-4.   Briefly describe the examination for certification in internal auditing.
24-5.   What are the five broad categories of *Standards for the Professional Practice of Internal Auditing*?
24-6.   Why is independence important for the internal auditor?
24-7.   How does organizational status affect the internal auditor's independence?
24-8.   What knowledge, skills, and disciplines are necessary for the internal auditor?
24-9.   What is the role of supervision in internal auditing?
24-10. Why are human relations important for the internal auditor?
24-11. Describe the concept of *due professional care* as it relates to the internal auditor.
24-12. What are the professional standards for the scope of work for internal auditing?
24-13. What are the professional standards for the performance of work for internal auditing?
24-14. What aspects of planning should the internal auditor consider?
24-15. Why is communication of results important to the internal auditor?
24-16. How should a report from an internal auditor be written?
24-17. Why is it important to follow up on problems and recommendations made in an internal auditing report?
24-18. What are the professional standards for the management of an internal auditing department?
24-19. What items is the director of internal auditing responsible for?
24-20. Define *operational auditing.*
24-21. What are the primary purposes of operational auditing? Which is a long-run consideration and why?
24-22. Discuss the phases involved in performing an operational audit.

Objective Questions

*24-23. Internal auditing can best be described as
   (1) an accounting function.
   (2) a compliance function.
   (3) an activity primarily to detect fraud.
   (4) a control structure function.
   (5) an activity that determines the fiscal integrity of financial statements.

---

*IIA adapted.

*24-24. A major responsibility of internal auditing is to
    (1) install sound accounting, financial, and operating controls at reasonable cost.
    (2) ascertain the extent of compliance with established policies, plans, and procedures.
    (3) account for the entity's assets and safeguard them from losses.
    (4) develop reliable management data.
    (5) All of the above.

*24-25. For which of the activities listed below could an internal auditor for ABC Life Insurance Company be held in violation of the code of ethics with respect to "conflict of interest"?
    (1) Designing an accounting system for a general agent of ABC Life Insurance Company.
    (2) Entering into a partnership engaged in land development.
    (3) Assisting members of a fraternal organization, of which the internal auditor is a member, in planning their life insurance coverage.
    (4) All of the above.
    (5) None of the above.

*24-26. The independence of the internal auditing department will most likely be assured if it reports to the
    (1) president.
    (2) controller.
    (3) treasurer.
    (4) audit committee of the board of directors.
    (5) vice-president of finance.

*24-27. The internal auditor's independence is most likely to be compromised when the internal audit department is responsible directly to the
    (1) vice-president of finance.
    (2) president.
    (3) controller.
    (4) executive vice-president.
    (5) audit committee of the board of directors.

*24-28. An internal audit staff should preferably include individuals
    (1) with an earned degree in accounting.
    (2) who have had previous experience with the organization.
    (3) with a business administration degree and an understanding of the tools of modern management.
    (4) with a specialized background, such as electronic data processing.
    (5) who collectively provide a reasonable balance of all the above backgrounds.

*24-29. The purpose of an opinion in an internal audit report would be to
    (1) describe the audit findings.
    (2) make audit recommendations.
    (3) present audit conclusions.
    (4) All of the above.

Problems and Cases

*24-30. (Role of Internal Auditing in an Entity) As the newly appointed director of internal auditing, you are concerned that the role of internal auditing in your organization has not been formally defined by executive management. You are considering formally defining in writing the role of the internal auditing department.
    REQUIRED
    A. What are the reasons for formally defining the role of internal auditing?
    B. What are major topics that should be included in describing the role of internal auditing?

---

*IIA adapted.

24-31. (Independence) Generally accepted auditing standards include a general standard relating to independence. Likewise, standards for the professional practice of internal auditing include a standard for independence.

REQUIRED
  A. Discuss the differences in meanings, if any, of the term *independence* as identified under generally accepted auditing standards and as identified under standards for the professional practice of internal auditing.
  B. Can internal auditors achieve the same degree of independence that CPAs or external auditors can achieve? Why or why not?

*24-32. (Role of Internal Auditing) Steve Ankenbrandt, president of Beeb Corp., has been discussing the company's internal operations with the presidents of several other multidivision companies. Ankenbrandt discovered that most of them have an internal audit staff. The activities of the staffs at other companies include financial audits, operational audits, and sometimes compliance audits.

REQUIRED
Describe the meaning of the following terms as they relate to the internal audit function:
  A. Financial auditing.
  B. Operational auditing.
  C. Compliance auditing.

**24-33. (Internal Audit Reports) The following is part of an interim audit report.

Subject: Controls over the billing of charges for parts-repair work.

Current procedures provide for using prenumbered sales order forms and recording sales orders for repairs in manually maintained logs. Those procedures also provide for creating manually serialized shipping documents and for the recording of such shipping documents in the sales order log. The recording of the shipping document numbers in the sales order log closes the sales order. This may give rise to a billing for the repair work. (Some work is done on a "no-charge" basis.)

Our examination of the sales order log disclosed a significant number of sales order numbers unmatched by shipping document numbers for the past two years. As a result, it is uncertain whether the repair work performed had been authorized for those orders. Specifically, we found that the sales order logs showed "no entry" for 71 (about 18%) sales order serial numbers spread randomly over a range of about 400 serial numbers covering a recent 12-month period. This indicated that billing personnel had not received sales orders for, or information about, the disposition of those serial numbers. Further investigation disclosed that 50 of the serial numbers showing "no entry" related to sales orders that had been voided or related to billings that had been closed at no charge. In addition, 16 other serial numbers related to sales orders that, in fact, were issued and were still open. However, we were unable to account for the remaining 15 serial numbers.

REQUIRED
The interim audit report contains errors made by the internal auditor. The errors involve numbers, computations, and logic. Identify three errors made by the internal auditor and state how you would correct each one.

---

*CMA adapted.
**IIA adapted.

*24-34. (Internal Audit Reports) The following sentences appear in the auditor's notes concerning an accounts payable activity. The sentences, which are in no logical order or grouping, are to be used in the audit report.

1. Generally, we are concerned with evaluating the system of control.
2. We did not seek to determine whether discounts were being taken.
3. The review of discounts was covered in a separate audit.
4. The accounts payable department is staffed by 15 employees.
5. Specifically, we set out to verify the sufficiency of the approvals and/or documentary support for the receipt of goods.
6. We found that written procedures were current and complete.
7. We were also concerned with the adequacy of distribution of charges to accounts.
8. We believe that the internal control structure is adequate.
9. The 15 accounts payable employees process 10,000 invoices each month.
10. Our test of 200 invoices requiring management approval showed that 35 were not approved.
11. In addition, the accounts payable employees process invoices for payment amounting to $30 million annually.
12. We believe the approval and support activities were not carried out satisfactorily.
13. Of 500 paid invoices we examined, 25% showed incorrect distribution to accounts.
14. We also believe that the function of distributing charges to accounts was not carried out satisfactorily.

REQUIRED

Construct a report outline, using the following section headings and putting the numbers of the sentences under the appropriate headings in a logical, consistent order.

A. Foreword.
B. Purpose.
C. Scope.
D. Opinions.
E. Statements of condition.

*24-35. (Role of Internal Auditing) The director of internal auditing for a marketing organization received the following memorandum from the controller:

> During the last audit of my department, the internal auditors on several occasions told the accountants and accounting clerks what they should do in carrying out their respective accounting tasks along with how and when they should do them. Some of my accounting supervisors were told that certain adjusting entries should be made to correct prior period errors and to adjust the carrying values of certain assets.
>
> I realize that the internal audit staff is very knowledgeable about accounting principles, accounting systems, and the activities within my department, since some of them previously worked in the department, and others are experienced accountants with various professional credentials. There is no question that the auditors' directions helped my department solve some of its problems and did, in fact, correct some significant deficiencies in the company's financial statements. Nevertheless, I strongly believe that the auditors were beyond their authority while performing this audit.

---

*IIA adapted.

REQUIRED

A. In terms of the *Statement of Responsibilities of Internal Auditors*, discuss the internal auditors' actions described above.

B. Identify three problems that may arise if the issue of authority is not resolved.

*24-36. (Internal versus External Auditing) Delta Machine Company is considering developing an internal audit department. A few years ago, the company began an expansion program that included the acquisition of new businesses, some of which are distant from the home office. Delta has used the acquired managements in most past acquisitions and expects to continue to do so. The corporate organization is decentralized, with the parent company (Delta Machine) setting the general policy. Divisions and subsidiary managements are quite autonomous; their performance is measured against budgets and return on investment targets established at the beginning of each year. The units of Delta manufacture and market their own products. The present companywide volume is $150,000,000.

Delta Machine has been audited by the CPA firm in which you are a manager. You have supervised the audit of Delta for the past three years. Delta has asked you to prepare a report on the activities that could be undertaken by an internal audit department.

REQUIRED

A. Prepare a report that describes

   (1) the different objectives of the external versus internal auditor.

   (2) the types of audits that an internal audit department might be expected to perform.

B. The company has indicated that you will be asked to head the internal audit department if it is established. Describe the change(s) in your audit philosophy and changes in your relationship to the firm management, if any, you believe should occur if you were to take this job.

Audit Judgment Case

24-37. Monica Lenard, CPA, and her former university classmate, Bob Burns, CPA, recently met at a university alumni function. They graduated ten years ago and both have been successful in their professional achievements. Monica is a partner in a large regional CPA firm and Bob is the director of the internal audit department for a major bank. As they discussed their relative responsibilities, a number of debatable points were made by one or the other. Here are those points.

(1) Independence applies to external auditors, not independent auditors.

(2) External auditors do not perform any compliance auditing work at all.

(3) External auditors are not concerned about operating efficiencies and are primarily concerned with making sure that the numbers add up.

(4) External auditors are required to notify external parties, such as regulators, when they find irregularities or illegal acts; internal auditors are not required to notify third parties about these matters.

(5) Internal auditors are obligated to coordinate with external auditors and Statements on Auditing Standards obligate external auditors to use the work of internal auditors if they are competent.

REQUIRED

Restate each of the points discussed above to more fairly reflect the professional responsibilities of the internal auditor and the external auditor.

---

*CMA adapted.

Auditing Issues Case

24-38. **KELCO MANUFACTURING COMPANY**

Kelco's president, Steve Cook, is very pleased with your firm's performance of the audit of his company's financial statements. The company was granted the loan it needed to further develop the company's oil prospects. The following is the dialogue of your conversation with Cook:

Cook:	I am very pleased with the audit services provided by your firm.
Your Response:	Mr. Cook, it has been a pleasure to work with your organization. Please let us know if we can be of service in any way.
Cook:	Well, that might be sooner than you think. Several things are bothering me. The investigation of the employees I suspected of stealing from the company confirmed that allegation. Also, I just do not think my company is being run in an efficient manner. The paperwork related to the accounting function is increasing tremendously. I think that the company needs to increase the size of its accounting department. What do you think?
Your Response:	Mr. Cook, it sounds as if you might need to create an internal auditing staff.

Cook has heard of internal auditors, but does not know how such a group could benefit his company.

REQUIRED

1. Explain to Cook the responsibilities of an internal audit staff.
2. Provide Cook with the benefits that could be provided by implementing such a staff within his organization.

Index

Index **885**

reports for use in foreign countries, 776–780
reports on internal control, 766–768
review of interim financial information, 772–774
special reports. *See* Special reports
supplementary information required by FASB/GASB, 771, 772
types of reports, 790
Output controls, 256
Outside documentation, 175

Paid voucher file, 523, 525
Parallel simulation, 277, 278
Partial presentations, 775
Partner, 17
Partnerships, 652
Password, 253
Payroll check register, 567, 568
Payroll summary, 567, 568
Payroll tax returns, 578, 590
Payroll transactions
    activities, 568, 570, 571
    completeness assertion, 573–578
    existence or occurrence assertion, 572, 573
    inventory, and, 617
    overview (chart), 574–577
    presentation and disclosure assertion, 578, 579
    rights and obligations assertion, 578
    valuation or allocation assertion, 578
Performance audits, 866
Performance reviews, 201
Periodic/discontinuous system, 245
Permanent file, 171
Perpetual inventory records, 566, 567, 586, 588
Personal financial plans, 807
Persuasiveness, 142
Pertinent control structure policies or procedures, 313
Petty cash funds, 482
Physical access control procedures, 254
Physical controls, 201, 202
Physical evidence, 153
Physical examination, 163
Pilot sample, 335, 360

Placed in operation, 205
Planned assessed level of control risk, 220
Planning the engagement, 405–440
    accounting estimates, 428
    analytical procedures, 386, 387, 420
    audit program design, 422–424
    auditability, 412, 414
    client acceptance, 409
    communication with predecessor auditors, 410–413
    engagement letters, 415–417
    fee arrangements, 412
    general planning, 418
    implementation stage, 422
    initial client contact, 407–409
    interim substantive testing, 425
    interim tests of controls, 424, 425
    knowledge of client's business, 418, 419
    knowledge of client's industry, 418
    management integrity, and, 410
    materiality, assessment of, 420
    overview, 407
    quality control considerations, 409, 410
    related parties, identification of, 419, 420
    risk factors, 420, 421
    risk of management misrepresentation, 421, 422
    specialists, use of, 426
    staffing, 426
    time budgets, 427, 428
    timing considerations, 424
Population, 307
Positive confirmation request, 155, 156, 499, 500
PPS sampling, 305, 354–360
Practice administration. *See* AICPA Code of Professional Conduct, CPA firms
Practice management software, 284
Precision, 345
Predecessor accountant, 806, 809
Predecessor auditor, 410, 429, 734, 738
Preliminary survey, 868
Prescribed form, 766, 806

Presentation and disclosure assertion, 128, 129
Price tests, 614, 615, 618
Principal auditor, 719
Principles of the Code of Professional Conduct, 51–53
Private Companies Practice Section (PCPS), 31
Privity of contract, 83
Probability-proportionate-to-size sampling (PPS), 305, 354–360
Probability sample, 308
Processing controls, 255, 256
Production order, 566, 567
Production transactions
    completeness assertion, 586, 587
    existence or occurrence assertion, 579, 586
    overview (chart), 580–585
    presentation and disclosure assertion, 589, 590
    rights and obligations assertion, 587
    valuation or allocation assertion, 587–589
Profession, 50
Professional ethics, 47–80. *See also* AICPA Code of Professional Conduct
    checklist, 49
    ethics, defined, 48
Professional Ethics Division, 69
Professional judgment
    auditing inventory, 610
    auditing, generally, 128
    completing the engagement, 679
    computers, and, 251
    ethical decisions, 64
    planning the engagement, 412
    revenue transactions, 446, 493
Professional organizations, 12, 13
Professional standards, 18, 19
    GAAS, 20
    general standards, 20, 21
    international standards, 32
    other standards, 31, 32
    standards of attestation, 25–28
    standards of fieldwork, 21–23
    standards of reporting, 23, 24, 704–708
Profit margin on sales, 384
Profitability ratios, 384